FINDING THE CONSTITUTION

Why Britain's System of Government Lost Its Way

Peter J. Stanbridge

Volume II: Parts VIII–XVII

IN MEMORIAM OF
PETER JAMES STANBRIDGE

The resolute and dedicated author of this work, an elegant and eloquent chronicler who passed away before its publication. He devoted thirty years to the crafting of this original and enlightening account of the evolution of our Constitution and its attendant political and judicial influences.

While the tenor of the latter chapters reveals the author's personally-held views, the main corpus delivers a unique perspective as it attempts to syncretise the ancient and modern systems of law and governance in the western world wherein Peter adduced evidence of a shared archaic constitution.

27 August 1930–18 October 2022

First published in Devon, UK, by Shakspeare Editorial 2023

ISBNs hbk Volume I: 978-1-9196360-8-5
Volume II: 978-1-7397590-1-8

ebk 978-1-9196360-9-2

Special thanks to:
Editor – David Alcock, davealcock76@yahoo.co.uk
Indexer – Michelle Brumby, www.simplythetext.co.uk
Typesetter and design – www.ShakspeareEditorial.org

Contents

Volume I

Preface xiii

Part I • Evidence of a Missing Constitution 1
Introduction 3
1 • Programme of Enquiry 8

Part II • The Indo-European Tradition of Government 13
2 • Institutions 15
3 • Scandinavia in the Migration Age (450–850) 23
4 • Programme of Enquiry 39

Part III • The Founding of the English Nation States 41
5 • The Early Settlements 43
6 • The Rise of Confederacies 141
7 • The Cultural Basis of English Society 203
8 • The Devastation and Unification of England 295

Part IV • The English Constitution of 927 349
9 • The Founding Nations (927) 351
10 • The Revolt of York 354

Part V • New Danish Invasions 361
11 • The Second Danish Invasion (975–1015) 363
12 • The Restoration of the House of Cerdic 384
13 • The Third Danish Invasion: The Normans (1066) 403

Part VI • Norman Feudalism and the Corruption of the Constitution .. 421
14 • The Continuity of English Law 423
15 • The Rule of Law is Partly Restored 476
16 • The King and His Councils 530
17 • The Centralisation of Justice 659
18 • Rising Prosperity and the Decline of Feudalism 703
19 • Confinement of the Great Council and Division of Parliament 779

Part VII • The Conflict Between King and Parliament 847
20 • The Rise of the House of Commons 849
21 • Radical Change in the Judicial Nature of Parliament 878
22 • The Legislative Process is Reversed 898

Volume II

Part VIII • The Reformation 957

23 • The Tudor Dynasty: Henry VII to Elizabeth I (1485–1603) 959
23.1. Restoration of the Power and Dignity of the Crown.................................. 959
23.2. The Restoration of the English Church 972
23.3. Whitehall, the Court of St James and the
Presumptuousness of Corporate Parliaments 1013

Part IX • Conflict Between King and Parliament.............................1091

24 • The Early Stuart Dynasty...1093
24.1. The Clash of Doctrines 1093
24.2. The Civil War (1643–49) 1157
24.3. The Commonwealth 1167
24.4. The Protectorate... 1173

25 • The Restoration Of The Stuarts: Charles II (1660) 1185
25.1. The Great Council Deprives the Privy Council of its Judicial Function 1192
25.2. The Extension of Parliaments 1195
25.3. Parliaments Become 'Sessions' and Electoral Periods Become 'Parliaments'1197
25.4. The Doctrine of the Supremacy of Parliament... 1198
25.5. The Commons Achieve Ascendancy Over the Lords 1200
25.6. The Shires (Local Government) Regain their Independence of the Crown 1207
25.7. The Privy Council is Usurped by its Cabinet Council 1211
25.8. The Stuarts Return to Catholicism 1215
25.9. Emergence of the Political Parties: Whigs and Tories............................... 1224
25.10. The Great Council Reasserts Control 1237

26 • The Glorious Revolution: The Defeat of Church Doctrine (1689) .1239
26.1. The Great Council and the House of Orange.. 1245
26.2. The Act of Settlement (1701) 1264
26.3. The Second Restoration of the Stuarts: Queen Anne 1271

Part X • The Empire and the Constitution 1275

27. The Birth Of Empire 1277
27.1. The Different Purposes of Colonies... 1282

28. The Constitutional Basis of Empire...1285
28.1. Empire According to Feudal Doctrine... 1285
28.2. Empire in Common Law 1288
28.3. Conflicts of Legal Tradition in America and South Africa........................ 1290

Part XI • The Legislature Appropriates the Executive..........................1317

29. The Intrusion of Parliament and Usurping of the Privy Council......1319
29.1. The Commons Controls the Privy Council 1320
29.2. The Executive Revolution: Parliament Usurps the Crown 1322
29.3. The Anglo-Scottish Union of 1707 1331

29.4. The Role of Government Shifts from the Lords to the Commons 1349
29.5. The End of the King's Influence in Parliament 1394

Part XII • The Legislature Appropriates the Executive (1832–1918)...1403

30. The Age of Liberalism **1405**

31. Parliamentary Developments **1409**
31.1. Electoral Reform 1409
31.2. The Doctrine that Royal Powers Delegated are not Returned 1417
31.3. Evicting the King from his Parliaments 1419
31.4. Relations Between the Lords and the Commons (1820–1902)................. 1436
31.5. Parliamentary Privilege and the Courts 1452

32. The Restoration of Shire Assemblies.. **1454**
32.1. Local Government: County, Borough, and District Councils (1888) 1454
32.2. The Doctrine of Constitutional Evolution... 1460

33. Final Separation of the Crown From the Monarchy......................... **1466**
33.1. The Civil List is Limited to the Royal Household.................................... 1466
33.2. Monarchy and the Formulation of Policy: The Victorian Age................. 1471
33.3. Organisation and Control of the Executive: The Trevelyan Report (1854) 1481

34. The Restoration of the Freeman.. **1494**
34.1. The Coronation Oath and the Church... 1494
34.2. The Sovereign's Private Secretary 1497
34.3. The Psychological Role of Monarchy... 1498

35. Judicial Changes.. **1505**
35.1. Reform of the Judicial Function of the Privy Council............................. 1505
35.2. Reform of the Crown Courts 1506
35.3. Reform of the Shire Courts 1512
35.4. The First Franco-German War (1870–71) 1514

36. The Commons Achieves a Monopoly of Power **1518**
36.1. The Parties Form an Oligarchy (1910–11) 1518
36.2. Ending of the Right of the Lords to Approve Legislation......................... 1519
36.3. The Legitimacy of Those Occupying the Peerage..................................... 1525
36.4. The Coronation Contract... 1530
36.5. The Menace of the Supremacy of Parliament... 1534

Part XIII • The Impact of Empire **1535**

37. Rebellion and Expansion in Africa (1900) **1537**
37.1. South Africa... 1537
37.2. Britain and Imperialism 1541
37.3. Rhodesia 1543

38. The First World War.. **1555**
38.1. Home Rule for Ireland (1914) 1555
38.2. The First World War (1914–18)... 1557
38.3. The Problem of the English Freeman and the Right to Vote 1566
38.4. Consequences of the War... 1568

39. The Inter-War Years (1918–45) 1570
39.1. The Spread of Socialism 1572
39.2. The Fragmentation of the First Estate.. 1576
39.3. The New Popularity of the Monarchy 1578
39.4. Government Moves from the Lords to the Commons 1581
39.5. The Dominions... 1589

40. The Second World War 1608
40.1. The Resurrection of Germany 1608

Part XIV • The Egalitarian Age and the Abuse of Power 1631

41. Equality and the Dissolution of Empire 1633
41.1. The Legal Status of the Crown 1635
41.2. Elizabeth II: The Monarchy Becomes the House of Windsor 1636
41.3. The Dissolution of the British Empire... 1640
41.4. The Rise of the Liberalist Movement and the
      Doctrine of Universal Equality 1659
41.5. Parliaments Progress from Representing to Ruling the People 1661

42. The Last Imperial Crisis 1680
42.1. Kenya... 1680
42.2. The Rhodesian Federation... 1680
42.3. Rhodesian Independence 1683
42.4. The Remnants of Empire 1688

43. Reaction to the Imperial Age 1691

Part XV • The Commons Appropriate the House of Lords 1693

44. Post-Imperial Government 1695
44.1. The Life and Death Instincts of Society...................................... 1695
44.2. Reform of the Civil and Criminal Courts (1971) 1695
44.4. Local Government – From Mega-Authorities to Joint Boards................... 1703
44.5. Appropriation of the Work of the Civil Service 1707
44.6. Judicial Review.. 1708
44.7. The Abuse of Democratic Process and Constitutional Principle:
      The Notion of Human Rights (1998)... 1716

45. European Integration 1719
45.1. Britain and the Common Market.. 1723
45.2. Britain and the European Union 1728

46. The Commons Usurp the House Of Lords (1999) 1730
46.1. Proposals for Basic Reform (1999) 1730
46.2. The Position of the Great Council in the Lords 1737
46.3. The Commons Becomes the Seat of Government (1992) 1738
46.4. Attempts to Introduce a Separation of Powers 1742
46.5. A Supreme Court of Appeal Displaces the House of Lords..................... 1748
46.6. The Supreme Court and the Constitution 1750

Part XVI • Parliament *Versus* the People 1753

47. Parliament *Versus* the People.......................................1755

47.1. Parliaments are Subject to Fixed Terms: The Benn Act (2011)................. 1755

47.2. The Parties and the Ship of State.. 1756

47.3. 'Brexit': Parliament Seeks to Impose its Will on the People (2016–19)..... 1757

47.4. Significance of the Brexit Crisis.. 1762

47.5. International 'Law'.. 1762

47.6. The Parliamentary Expenses Scandal 1763

47.7. Modern Parliaments and the Estates.. 1765

48. The Predicament Of Parliaments....................................1767

49. The Appointment of Ministers 1768

50. Conclusions 1770

Part XVII • The British Constitution in Common Law......................1773

51. The Legal Source of Political Power: The *Imperium* 1775

51.1. The Shire (County) Councils 1775

51.2. The Great Council 1777

51.3. The King... 1781

51.4. The King's Council 1785

51.5. Parliaments 1786

Bibliography 1790

Index..1794

PART VIII

•

THE REFORMATION

23 • THE TUDOR DYNASTY: HENRY VII TO ELIZABETH I (1485–1603)

W ITH THE DEATH of Richard III, the Plantagenet line of Anjou came to an end. The nearest surviving claimant was Edward, son of the duke of Clarence, and there were 'at least a dozen others with a better claim'[1] than the most obvious, Henry Tudor, earl of Richmond, whose legal entitlement was tenuous, if not spurious, but he had defeated and slain Richard in battle, and he enjoyed popular acceptance and, as was soon to be demonstrated, parliamentary approval. His mother, Margaret, was the surviving representative of the Beauforts of the house of Lancaster. Clearly ambitious, Henry Tudor had attempted, during the reign of Richard III, to invade England in conjunction with a rebellion by the duke of Buckingham, which had failed. In the summer of 1485 Henry had tried again, and at Market Bosworth, just west of Leicester, the King's army had been defeated and the King slain, leaving Henry Tudor to lay claim to the throne. A Parliament summoned to meet at Westminster in November was attended by a comparatively short list of bishops and lay lords, its first business being to declare Henry Tudor's right to the succession as Henry VII.

23.1. Restoration of the Power and Dignity of the Crown

In origin, the Tudors were a Welsh family, descended from a knight, Owain Tudur, or Owen Tudor, himself from a Welsh-speaking family of Anglesey, which claimed descent from the early Welsh princes. As a result of his marriage to Catherine de Valois, the widow of Henry V, he had become the earl of Richmond, only to be executed after the Lancastrian defeat at Mortimer's Cross, in 1461. His son, Edmund Tudor, had

1. M. Ashley, *British Kings and Queens* (London, 1999), 624–5.

inherited the title of Earl of Richmond and married Margaret Beaufort. It was their son, Henry, who now succeeded to the Crown.

His coronation as 'King Harry the VII' in 1485, approved by an Act of Parliament, marked the accession, therefore, of a Welsh dynasty, proclaimed as such on the field at Bosworth by the red dragon banner of the ancient Welsh hero, Cadwaladr.[2] Parliament also confirmed the right of his heirs to succeed him, but the weakness of his hereditary claim and his lack of standing were such that Parliament seems to have found it necessary to require him to increase the legitimacy of his succession by marrying Elizabeth of York, the daughter of Edward IV. Perhaps Edward's real ancestry had conveniently been forgotten by this time, or at least not divulged to the new Parliament, and at least the proposed marriage offered to bring the two houses of Lancaster and York together. Henry, while agreeing, refused to be made King merely in the right of his wife, and insisted that his reign be accounted to have started on the day of Bosworth, five months before the marriage. It was also necessary for Henry and his dynasty to enhance their claim to the throne by blackening the memory of Henry's predecessor and last legitimate ruler, Richard III. This they did, as already described, by misrepresenting him as a hunchback and a grasping schemer, who had even committed regicide, so that he was remembered by posterity with revulsion, as Richard 'Crookback'.

The loyal yeomen who had formed Henry's private bodyguard during his exile, and who had protected him on Bosworth Field, were formally constituted at his coronation as the royal bodyguard. As the Yeomen of the Guard, they were to continue in this role for the next 250 years, in place of a party of mounted knights. Their duties included the security of the royal palaces, including the royal bedchamber, and the tasting of the King's food in case of attempts on his life. From this last duty they acquired the popular name of 'beefeaters'. In more recent times they have continued to attend on the King on state and other ceremonial occasions.

The chief benefit brought by the accession of Henry Tudor was an end to the ruinous domestic conflict, and this was celebrated in the royal marriage and in the emblem of the new royal house, the 'Tudor rose', which combined, in a symbolic whole, the white rose of York and the red rose of Lancaster. With Henry there also came a new custom for naming

---

2. G. Williams, *The Land Remembers: A View of Wales*, 103–4.

dynasties – the third change in English history. In the early English period, it had been customary to follow the old Germanic practice of naming dynasties – and, indeed, any family – after the personal name of its acknowledged founder. Thus, the Cerdicing dynasty, which had ruled Wessex and England since the fifth century, had taken its title from its founder, Cerdic. From the Normans onward, feudal practice had been followed, whereby a dynasty had been named after its estate, or at least, by the estate of its founder, hence the Norman and Angevin dynasties. The adoption of surnames, from the thirteenth century onwards, had made available an alternative system, and with the decline of Church-Feudalism the importance of estates also declined. By ignoring his estate title of 'Richmond', which had been little more than an honour, and using his family name, Henry both asserted his Welsh ancestry and the importance of his family by establishing the 'Tudor' title.

The marriage of Henry VII and Elizabeth of York did not prevent the Yorkists from trying to regain power. To this end, they turned to the Scots for help, who responded by renewing their alliance with France in 1490. In spite of this, all attempts at insurrection and invasion were defeated, and with the execution in 1499 of Edward, Earl of Warwick and nephew of Richard III, the main threat from the House of York was brought to an end. Even so, the Tudor line, with its claim to the throne without any foundation in feudal law, would never be entirely free of dynastic worries.

Whether through temperament or the insecurity of his position, Henry VII resumed the despotic tradition of his Yorkist predecessors, Edward IV and Richard III. While usually remaining within the letter of the law, he often evaded the spirit of it by a variety of subtleties and stratagems. He expanded his authority ruthlessly in pursuit of the future security of both the government and his own dynasty, but in state policy his concern was for efficient and inexpensive government. To these ends, he reduced his dependence on Parliament for money by the more efficient management of the Crown estates. Penal statutes imposed a specific fine or forfeiture for a given offence, resulting in huge windfalls for treason from the various failed rebellions, led mainly by imposters. Although less spectacular in their benefits to the Crown, an increasing number of penal statutes were to become an important source of income for the Tudor dynasty. Henry revived the payment of feudal dues, and exploited to the full the various dues from his tenants-in-chief. On a convenient pretext, he collected a benevolence in 1491 from the now greatly weakened nobility – in spite of this practice having been made illegal by his predecessor – and through disinheritance and forfeitures he amassed more land than any of his predecessors. The ordinary revenue, with the exception of customs and the collection of the profits of justice, was transferred from the Exchequer to the Royal Household, where it was administered by the Treasurer of the Chamber, whose accounts were regularly scrutinised by the King. Revenue rights – in lands, fines, and wards – that had been neglected during the period of royal decline were identified and reasserted. The Duchy of Lancaster, which was now responsible for lands, provided the model for the introduction of new accounting methods and rapid auditing. One anomaly was the continued use of Roman numerals. The great advantage of this for managing the revenue was its convenience, its weakness being its dependence on the King's close attention and its lack of permanent organisation. Also, the exclusion of the Exchequer meant that there was no satisfactory record of outstanding items, and the King could not be sure that he was not being defrauded by his receivers. There was no difference, however, in the principle involved, in that it was the King's revenue, whether controlled by his Exchequer or by his Household. In so far as there was a difference, it was one of accountability.

23.1.1. The King's 'Majesty' is Asserted

Henry VII was one of the most efficient of the many businessmen who sat on the English throne, and the income from the Crown estates rose sevenfold between 1491 and 1504. Special agents, who extracted the benevolences and forced loans, also helped to reform the system of revenue collection. If a noble lived well, he was told that he could surely afford to make a gift to the King, and if he lived poorly, it was pointed out to him that he must be saving enough to do the same. By 1490 the royal accounts were balanced. Thus, Henry rejuvenated the monarchy, imparting a dynamism to the leadership of the nation that had too often been lacking. He and his successors in the Tudor line acknowledged the representative character of kingship, but also stressed its divine links, encouraging greater deference, employing new styles, and placing a greater distance between King and people. The King and his court became the centre of political and social life. In contrast to their French counterparts, they shone with a splendour that owed more to personality, physical appearance and propaganda, than it did to extravagance. Consequently, Henry and his Tudor successors attracted a lavish adulation from the people. Until now, the King had been addressed as 'His Grace' or even 'His Highness', but from the reign of Henry VII onwards the imported form of 'His Majesty' came increasingly into favour. To enable revenue to be collected more effectively and to maintain civil order, Henry built a more vigorous and effective civil service, which did much to create a strong and centralised government. In furtherance of this, the judicial role of the Privy Council was strengthened by the establishment of the Court of Star Chamber. So was established a semi-despotic tradition, based on King and Privy Council, that was to continue under his successors until the revolution of 1640. Yet Henry VII was not popular, and on his death in 1509 there was general rejoicing.

Meanwhile, the recent decimation of the feudal aristocracy on the battlefield, bitterly divided as it had been between its two houses; the removal of their military independence with the introduction of cannon; the expropriation of many of the great landed families; the resurgence of a prosperous middle class, and the imposition of centralised royal government with the advent of the Tudors; all contributed to the further decline of the feudal aristocracy. The shift in political influence from the nobility to the middle class continued, and this was helped by the new political stability, brought about by the Tudors through the Privy Council and the Court of Star Chamber. In 1536 there were complaints about the number of Councillors who were of humble birth, due to the King's preference for capable commoners who would serve him well and not be too independent. By 1553 the Privy Council comprised forty members, of whom four were bishops, fourteen were temporal peers, and twenty-two were commoners, who included the King's two secretaries. This marked an important change, reflecting the fact that the government of the realm was slipping out of the hands of the nobility.

Parliament continued to function normally under Henry, approving legislation and particularly the raising of taxes, but it no longer asserted itself. The nobles no longer wielded real power, and the middle class, which was represented by the House of Commons, took advantage of the new age of stability to turn its attention to more rewarding activities than politics. Also, there was a sharp decline in the frequency of Parliaments after 1497. Previously, between 1485 and 1497, Henry had summoned six Parliaments, but between 1497 and 1509, only one. Although the King enriched himself at the expense of the lords, the House of Commons was no less a part of the political and financial malaise. Two Speakers of the Commons, Empson and Dudley, were the King's extortionate tax-gatherers, and Henry's successor would court popularity in 1510 by having both executed.

The latter part of the fourteenth century and the first half of the fifteenth had been a period of economic stagnation, brought on by the Black Death, the Hundred Years' War and the first of the Wars of the Roses, causing a shortage of labour and heavy taxation, particularly on wool, in order to pay for the conflicts. Henry VII not only brought stability and relief from general taxation, but did his best to promote commerce, and it was towards commercial activity that the energy of the middle class was now directed, contributing to an upsurge in agriculture, industry and trade that had already become increasingly evident during the second half of the fifteenth century. The continued growth of sheep farming for wool, in order to supply the thriving English cloth-making industry, caused a transition from cornfields to pasture. Cloth-making became more mechanized and the range of fabrics increased, so that exports of cloth had recovered by 1500, and in 1553 some 40,000 pieces of cloth were exported in English ships. During the next fifty years, cloth exports more than trebled as prosperity grew on the Continent, where Antwerp had now become the commercial centre of Europe.

England was also the beneficiary of wider changes taking place across Western Europe. New developments in mineral processing, particularly in Germany, and the spreading use of the waterwheel as a source of power made bronze, brass and iron more readily available. At the same time, the growing use of cannon and small firearms caused the development of an armaments industry and a big increase in the demand for iron. In parts of England, such as the Weald of Kent and Sussex, water-power soon improved the mining of local iron and drove bellows that produced more iron of better quality in the blast furnaces that were now being built wherever good streams occurred within reach of the outcropping ore. Caxton had set up his printing press in Westminster in 1476 and this was now giving rise to a new field of manufacture, as well as a publishing industry. The boroughs and towns had been in decline, but this was more than offset by the new prosperity in the rural areas and villages. It was from the growing and newly self-confident middle class that the King increasingly drew his advisers and servants.

Maritime supremacy had already begun to shift from the Mediterranean countries to those bordering the Atlantic, and the sixteenth century was an age in which English adventurers, such as Cabot, Gilberht, Barlow, Amidas, Drake, and Raleigh, set out to exploit the opportunities of the Americas, or to circumvent the obstacle which they represented to the growing Oriental spice trade. It was because the Tudors had restored political stability, through the Privy Council and the Star Chamber, that the people – and more particularly the middle class – were encouraged to extend their activity still more widely into such areas as exploration, colonisation and piracy. In this way, their horizons were widened still further, leaving them happy to let the King remain in control of political issues.

An attempt was also made to integrate Ireland more closely with England. The Statute of Drogheda of 1494 was also known as Poynings' law, after Sir Edward Poynings, the Irish Lord Deputy. It stipulated that all laws recently enacted in the English Parliament should also apply in Ireland. It stated, moreover, that no Irish Parliament should be held without the consent of the King; and that no Bill should be brought forward in an Irish Parliament without his consent. Ireland had not been annexed to England in the way that Wales had been, and the Statute of Drogheda was a means of bringing Ireland more closely into line with England. The statute also implied that Ireland was not just a fiefdom, but an outright possession of the Crown.

Various claimants to the throne continued to cause trouble throughout the first half of Henry's reign, notably, Lambert Simnel and, in 1494, Perkin Warbeck. This made Henry nervous of his position, so that he was anxious to achieve recognition by other kings in Europe, including the Pope, who extended his full support in 1486. Anxious to avoid expensive wars, Henry endeavoured to establish an alliance with England's longstanding enemy, France, by first negotiating a political marriage with Scotland, while he was also pursuing another with Ferdinand and Isabella, the wealthy rulers of Aragon. An alliance was eventually made when Henry married their daughter, Catherine, in 1499. Four years later, Henry's own eldest daughter married James IV of Scotland. Meanwhile, an alliance was made with the German emperor in 1496, and his Welsh ancestry meant that he was highly regarded in Wales. Indeed, Welsh nobility were appointed to senior positions, including territory in the Welsh Marches, bringing to an end the English domination of Wales by the marcher lords. Meanwhile, an upsurge in trade and exploration caught the King's interest, which was further stimulated by Columbus's discovery in 1492 of the West Indies. This led Henry, in 1497, to finance a similar voyage by Giovanni Caboto, believed to be a Venetian sailor, who, as John Cabot, went on to discover Newfoundland. Sheen Palace, which had been badly damaged by fire in 1497, was lavishly rebuilt as Richmond Palace. On the other hand, the death of his eldest son, followed by that of his wife, caused Henry to become withdrawn. It was at Richmond Palace that Henry VII died in 1509, marking the end of a reign that some have seen as the birth of modern England, and leaving it with the rare benefit of good relations with Scotland and Wales. On the other hand, the close relations that he forged with Spain were destined to increase the difficulties faced by his successor.

He was succeeded by his second son, also named Henry. It had been expected that the King would be succeeded by his eldest son, Arthur, but Arthur had died seven years earlier, leaving Henry, who had been destined to go into the Church, and who had been given a correspondingly good classical education. Accommodating his father's wish to preserve the alliance with Spain, he now married Catherine of Aragon, the wife of his late brother, and both were crowned in Westminster Abbey only two weeks later, with Henry succeeding to the throne in his capacity as Henry VIII. It was under Henry VIII, who reigned from 1509 until 1547, that the power of the King reached its highest point since the reign of William the Conqueror. His position was all the stronger because he could claim to represent both branches of the Angevin succession – the Lancastrian, nominally, through his father, and the Yorkist through his mother, Elizabeth of York, daughter of Edward IV. He renewed the Spanish alliance, enabling England and Spain to form a common front against France. Faced with his new matrimonial status, Henry vacated the Tower of London in 1509 for more convenient accommodation. The detachment of his Yeomen of the Guard that was left to protect the Tower and guard the many distinguished prisoners who passed through its walls would later be designated in 1550 as a separate group, the Yeoman Warders of the Tower. They have continued to fulfil this duty to the present day, but from the outset of his reign, in 1509, Henry raised his own bodyguard, variously known as the 'King's Spears' and the 'Gentlemen Spears'. This was recruited from youths of noble birth, in contrast to the existing Yeomen of the Guard, and served as both cavalry and foot soldiers. In 1539 they would be reorganised as the 'Gentleman Pensioners', so called because they were paid. In their early years their Captain was often the Lord Chamberlain, and their title would be changed much later to that of the 'Gentlemen at Arms'.

Henry had little interest in the day-to-day affairs of government, and, satisfying himself that his ministers could be trusted, he devoted himself to foreign affairs. Left with little choice by his Spanish alliance through marriage, he supported his father-in-law, Ferdinand of Aragon, against the Moors in 1511. In the same year England joined Spain, Venice and the German Empire in the Holy League, which had originally been formed to protect Italy from foreign domination, and which now forced the withdrawal of Charles VIII of France, who had invaded Italy in pursuit of a claimed inheritance. The failure of this French expedition had three consequences for England:

1. It facilitated the spread of the Italian Renaissance to France, from where it spread to England.
2. It spurred Henry into a major reform and expansion of the Royal Navy in 1511. Indeed, this marked the true establishment of the Royal Navy, because most of his predecessors had relied on the requisitioning of ships when danger threatened, whereas warships were now specially built for the purpose, with two decks and gun-ports. These were an adaptation of ships' loading ports, and the arrangement allowed cannon to be ranged below deck and in greater numbers. Also, a technique for casting iron, rather than

bronze cannon was devised, making possible heavier, iron projectiles. A Papal embargo on trade with England caused embarrassment by depriving the latter of its source of alum, needed in the manufacture of gunpowder, but eventually an alternative source was found in Yorkshire that required a lengthy process of chemical extraction. Arguably, it marked the foundation of the English chemical industry.

3. In 1512, believing his position to be now strong enough, Henry stated his claim to the French throne.

Henry, being now set upon becoming a leading light in European affairs, embarked upon an expedition to France, against the advice of his Council that such a move would mean war with Scotland, as proved to be the case. Calais was still an English possession, and at nearby Guinegate, in Artois, Henry defeated the French in the Battle of the Spurs, so called because of the speed with which the French knights fled. He also took Tournai. A peace was then negotiated with France, in which it was agreed that Louis XII should marry Henry's sister, Mary, only for Louis to die a few months later. Mary then eloped with the duke of Suffolk, Charles Brandon, to be married in secret. It was only later, after paying a heavy fine, that the two were reconciled with the King. The constitutional significance of the event lay in the fact that their grand-daughter would be the ill-fated Lady Jane Grey.

The Scots, meanwhile, in accordance with their treaty obligations to France, invaded England in 1513. Henry had anticipated this, however, and the Scots suffered a crushing defeat at Flodden, in Northumberland, in which the Scottish king, James IV, lost his life. Peace with France and Scotland was concluded in the following year. Henry's ambitions found further expression in 1519, when, having been given some encouragement by the Holy Roman Emperor, Maximilian I, he put himself forward as a candidate to succeed him. In this he failed, but, determined to impress the new French king, Francis, in 1520 he arranged a meeting at Guisnes, near Calais, which was so lavishly prepared that it came to be known as the Field of the Cloth of Gold.

Henry added further to the splendid status of kingship that had been achieved by his father. The address of 'Your Majesty' was now accepted practice, and the Crown now appeared to be 'glorious and untouchable, yet accessible'. Yet, with all the pomp and ceremonial that attended his reign, Henry never cut himself off from his people,[1] and in this he achieved a fine balance between the two constitutional traditions, based on common law and Church-Feudalism.

23.1.2. Conduits (Symbols) of Royal Authority

The royal authority, or *imperium*, that was bestowed upon the newly crowned King by the Great Council, as its trustee, was not an abstract notion. It was understood as a magical force that was endowed in a physical form. Probably the oldest such form in Aryan society was the wand, rod or stick, represented, for example, by the staff of office, such as that used in Greek antiquity by Hermes, the divine messenger. Such a staff of office has been used by the King throughout English history, in the form of a sceptre. In the form of a 'black rod' of office, it has been bestowed upon the later Gentleman Usher, or as a baton or stick it has been granted to a military officer or, indeed, to any other minister or officer of the Crown. It is not a mere symbol of authority, but is infused with the royal power, or *imperium*, granted. Moreover, it is effective only in those hands for which it was intended. Such delegated royal authority is not transmitted by the word of the King, or even by a letter or other document, which is merely evidence of the intent of the delegation.

As we have noted elsewhere, the 'magical' power in such a rod or baton of office is automatically extinguished upon the death or deposition of the King who granted it, while the power in the sceptre returns automatically to the care of the Great Council. We have previously noted how the various staves of office held by a deposed King were broken up as useless by the officers of his successor.

The mace, originally a weapon of war and therefore a symbol of authority, also had its origin far back in Indo-European times, when it was usually made of rare stone, such as porphyry, which was carved, typically in the form of a horse's head, or bore magical inscriptions. The Royal Mace, as used in a Parliament, took the form of a heavy, gilded and embellished haft of gold, its head being also of decorated gilt, surmounted by a crown. It is an exaggerated and highly embellished

---

1. G. R. Elton, *The Tudor Constitution*, 12–14.

version of what must have been the original Royal Mace, because it is obviously too large, heavy and insubstantial to be used for its original purpose. Nevertheless, it is a mace. Consequently, what are often described as 'symbols' of royal authority are much more than that. They should be understood as instruments, agents or warrants of royal authority, that authority being contained within themselves, including the identity of the individual to whom it has been granted. The *imperium* is inactive in the hands of any other.

The sword, which became a later symbol of authority, was a development of the European Bronze Age, which followed the Indo-European dispersal. Although the sword was often used to represent royal authority, and achieved particular significance in Celtic society, it seems never to have superseded the more ancient authority of the mace.

23.1.3. The Renaissance

The sack of Rome by the Goths in 410 had seemingly destroyed much of what had survived of Roman literature and learning. Worse still, there had been a violent explosion across the Middle East and North Africa, from 632 onwards, spreading into Spain and the Balkans, of the newly converted Moslems of Arabia, for whom any culture or knowledge that was not recognised in their holy book, the *Koran*, was regarded as a threat to the teaching of its prophet, Mohammed, and his chosen Bedouin deity, Allah. His teaching had been strongly influenced by Judaism and Christianity, and had been moderate until he had been evicted from Mecca and forced to flee to Medina, which had caused him to take up banditry against those trading with Mecca, and to advocate extreme violence against all who resisted his teaching. As a result, not only had untold thousands been slain for opposing the armies and beliefs of his supporters, but all forms of art and literature that were deemed to pose a possible threat to Mohammedan teachings were destroyed. Whether the destruction of the great library in Alexandria had been by intent or accident is uncertain, but was more likely the former. Only Christians and Jews were tolerated, because their beliefs had done much to inspire Mohammed's own ideas. These and further conquests north of the Mediterranean had raised the possibility that Classical Greek and Roman knowledge and literature had largely been erased from western civilization. Being illiterate, he had left nothing, but memories of his teachings had later been collected by his followers and incorporated as the *Koran*.

The Moslem invasion of Western Europe had at least been halted and turned back at Tours, in France, in 1180. The re-capture of Toledo, in Spain, in 1085, had revealed it to be a centre of Moorish learning within the Moslem world, where Arabic translations of the learning of the Classical world had survived, enabling them gradually to be translated into Latin during the twelfth century. The threat to the Classical heritage was not over, however. The Ottoman Turks, who were Moslem converts, had captured Constantinople in 1453, driving numerous scholars into exile in northern Italy, particularly in Florence, taking with them shiploads of surviving Greek and Roman writings. The ensuing Turkish invasion of the Balkans was not stopped until it reached the gates of Vienna in 1529, after which there was a slow re-conquest of the Balkans that would not be completed until 1918, except for eastern Thrace.

The ensuing restoration of Classical learning in Europe, with the intellectual liberation that it brought from the stifling dogma of the Catholic Church, came to be known as the Renaissance. It did not all come at once. Classical Latin texts were rediscovered in the cathedral schools of Western Europe in the eighth and ninth centuries, and in the twelfth century the foundation of the early universities brought a light to the Greek philosophical works of Aristotle. Much Classical learning had been preserved in the intellectual and artistic centres of Western Central Asia, notably Bukhara and Samarkand. Nor was the newly rediscovered learning limited to that of the Greeks. Greek arithmetic and geometry were taken further by new ideas brought into the Middle East from India, most notably the Indian numbering system, including the use of nought, or zero, which was brought to Europe by the Arabs in a form adopted by them and described as 'Arabic' numerals. These replaced the awkward Roman system and contributed greatly to the further development of mathematics. The Babylonians had invented trigonometry, rediscovered by the Greeks, and the Arabs themselves made an important contribution in the form of algebra, where unknown numbers could be represented by symbols. In defiance of the strictures of the *Koran*, much of this material was preserved. The main Renaissance, inspired by an influx of Classical texts, occurred in northern Italy between 1378 and 1550, and the intellectual broadening afforded by this ancient Greek learning found expression in northern Italy in new forms of art, sculpture, architecture, literature and political thinking. The Renaissance spread from there to France, particularly following an expedition into Italy by Charles VIII in 1495, and from France it spread to Tudor England and other parts of Europe. The effect was a revival and florescence in arts and letters during the Tudor period, which affected art and architecture and even political thinking. Domestic architecture was at first reluctant to move away from the Gothic, but Italian influences crept into its decoration. The social and religious upheavals introduced by the Renaissance limited the construction of large buildings until after 1600, when they began to be commissioned by the Crown, rather than by the Church, employing independent architects, rather than craftsmen in their design. The effect ultimately was the replacement of the Gothic by the Classical style, imitating the rules that had governed Greek and Roman architecture, with simpler lines, a dome instead of a tower, a new emphasis on proportion, rather than uplift, and much more interior space and light, reflecting the new concern with clarity and logic, rather than the magic and mystery of the past.

23.2. The Restoration of the English Church

A long and smouldering issue that was destined to flare up during Henry's reign was a popular hatred of the Church, caused by its excessive wealth, clerical corruption, and a nationalistic resentment of the influence of the Popes. All clergy and even employees of the Church had immunity from criminal prosecutions, being subject to the ecclesiastical courts, which were often lax, and this right was regularly abused. Public hostility had come to the surface earlier, in the reins of Edward III and Richard II, through the influence of Wiclif and the Lollards, whose sentiments were still widely held, and Henry seems to have been attuned to the mood, because a statute of 1512 removed the benefit of clergy from many serious crimes. The issue was stirred up in 1515, when a London jury found that the bishop's officers had murdered a suspected heretic while he was in prison. The verdict was rejected by the bishop, and this precipitated a public outcry. The Church Convocation argued that no temporal court could try the Lord's anointed, and Parliament, vowing that the Church should protect no more murderers, declared that the Convocation had violated the Act of *Praemunire*, which protected royal authority from Papal interference in ecclesiastical matters. When Cardinal Wolsey, who was also Lord Chancellor, advised that the case be referred to Rome, the King replied that 'Kings of England have never had any superior but God alone'. It is thus already clear that, devout member of the Church though he was, Henry was independently and nationalistically minded. Two years later, Wolsey was appointed as Papal legate to England, a position that gave him greater authority even than the Archbishop of Canterbury.

The anti-clerical feeling that had been fanned a hundred years earlier, first by Wiclif in England, and then by Jan Hus in Bohemia, was now stirred again, this time in Germany by an Augustinian monk, Martin Luther, who in 1517 criticised the misuse of absolution and indulgences. By this time, northern Europe had become a sufficiently fertile ground for such independent religious thinking to take a secure hold, and it was Luther's act of defiance which finally set the Reformation of the Church into motion. His defiance grew rapidly into a revolt against the financial and intellectual corruption of the Church generally, giving rise to a permanent creed of Protestantism. Luther succeeded where Hus had failed, because he won the support of many of the German princes, who were willing and strong enough to stand up to the fulminations of the Church. Henry VIII, for once anxious to ingratiate himself with the Pope, Leo X, wrote a book[2] that criticised Luther, and for his efforts was rewarded in 1521 with a Papal grant of the title of *Fidei Defensor*, or 'Defender of the Faith'. It was a title that Henry retained by statute in 1544, and it has been used by all subsequent English Kings, even though most of them violated it, as Henry eventually did, by ruling in open opposition to the Church of Rome.

In 1519, Henry's mistress, Elizabeth Blount, bore him a son, who became Henry Fitzroy, Duke of Richmond. Meanwhile the Queen, Catherine, bore him six children, but only one of these, Mary, survived infancy, and by 1526, when the Queen turned forty, it was unlikely that he would have a legitimate heir. By 1527 he had become infatuated

---

2. *On the Seven Sacraments, Against Martin Luther, the Heresiarch, by the Illustrious Prince Henry VIII.*

with one, Anne Boleyn, giving rise to the prospect of a divorce. The Chancellor, Cardinal Wolsey, who had already distinguished himself as a negotiator, favoured the divorce option, and as the Pope owed Henry a favour, and had already sanctioned divorce for two kings of France, seemed unlikely to oppose it. The eventual ground for a divorce from Catherine was based on a Biblical reference in the *Book of Leviticus*, which castigated marriage to the former wife of a person's brother, in this case, Arthur, as being a form of incest. Consequently, it was argued, Henry's marriage to Catherine had been null and void from the outset, to which Catherine argued that her marriage to Arthur had never been consummated. Nevertheless, the fact that all her children had died, except Mary, seemed to point to a divine displeasure at the union with Henry. So confident was Wolsey of Papal approval that he persuaded the King to act, not through the English courts, but through Rome. Meanwhile, Anne Boleyn had been antagonised by Wolsey engineering the break-up of her previous marriage, so that she denied Henry her favours until, she said, she became his wife. It was a risky strategy to adopt, but it began to pay off by inflaming the King's passions further. Unfortunately for Wolsey's strategy, Pope Clement VII was, at the time when the petition was submitted in 1527, under siege in the Vatican from the troops of the German emperor, Charles V, who had not been paid and were busily sacking Rome. The ensuing prevarication by the Pope owed much also to the fact that Catherine was the aunt of the German emperor, and to have sanctioned the divorce would have implied that she had been living in sin for the last eighteen years. Not only was the Pope a virtual prisoner of the emperor, but he was looking to him to rescue Germany from Luther's influence and to protect the rule of his own family in Florence, the Medici.

Meanwhile, Anne Boleyn matched the King in education and intelligence, so that the relationship was soon intellectual, as well as physical. She was a supporter of the idea of Church reform, and undoubtedly did much to educate the King in this direction, for Henry, being a man of some intellect and anxious to learn, was a willing pupil. She introduced him to the writings of William Tyndale, who had committed heresy and a capital offence by translating the New Testament from Greek into English, but who was now asserting that the King, as ruler by divine right, according to Church doctrine, was properly the head of the Church and had the right to reform it. She also used her influence to turn the King against Wolsey, which was not difficult, in the light of his diplomatic failures. Meanwhile, from about 1520 onwards, Lutheran ideas had been entering England through the east coast seaports and spreading. Privately, Henry began to accept that there was much to be said for Luther and Wiclif, although in public he ordered the burning of books and pamphlets attacking the clergy. Tynedale, forced to flee into hiding abroad, and sought by three intelligence networks – those of the Crown, the Pope, and the German Empire – nevertheless managed to complete his translation of the New Testament in Cologne, and to publish it by devious means in 1526. He then moved to Antwerp, where he continued to work on a translation of the Old Testament, before being caught and burned at the stake in Belgium in 1536. His cause had been taken up by Anne Boleyn, who managed, too late, to win the King over. Such was Tyndale's influence, however, that some ninety per cent of the later King James Bible was a copy of Tyndale's translation. His achievement, however, went further. Believing, as he did, that all souls were equal, he helped to reinvigorate the movement to restore the political rights of ordinary men.

Under the combined influence of Luther's increasingly popular teaching and Henry's desire for pressure on the Pope, the Parliament approved various measures to prohibit clerical abuses. The Pope responded by threatening Henry with excommunication. Henry, enraged by the scruples of Cardinal Wolsey in pursuing his case, and goaded by Anne and others, and with the support of Sir Thomas More and most of the bishops, who suspected Wolsey of promoting Lutheranism, deprived him of the Chancellorship in October 1529. His office of Chancellor, and with it the holding of the Great Seal, were transferred to Sir Thomas More, and Wolsey's property was seized. In November of that year, frustrated by the prevarications of the Papacy, Henry summoned a Parliament that was destined to continue until 1536. It was to be remembered in history as the Reformation Parliament, because of the King's use of it to reform the Church. During its proceedings, the lords spiritual found themselves under great pressure from the Commons, supported by the lay lords, to relinquish the various entitlements of the Church. This they found themselves eventually forced to concede. Meanwhile, Wolsey, who was still Archbishop of York, had been accused of treason in 1530 and summoned to London. Knowing that he was probably on his way to the Tower, and perhaps aggravated by fright, he took ill and died on the way. That same year, twenty-two abbots signed a petition to the Pope in support of the royal divorce, and, at the suggestion of Thomas Cranmer, a cleric who supported Church reform, the King sent agents to English and European universities, seeking support for the illegality of his marriage. He also set up a commission to report on the need for an English Bible. After Parliament had been adjourned, the King, ably assisted by his new minister, Thomas Cromwell, found ways of putting the bishops under much greater and more direct pressure. Furious with the Church for having recognised Wolsey as Papal legate, Henry accused the whole clergy, assembled in Convocation at Westminster Abbey in January 1531, of having violated the Act of *Praemunire*, on the grounds that the whole clergy of England had supported Cardinal Wolsey's authority as Papal legate and, in effect, of asserting or maintaining Papal jurisdiction in England. Alarmed, and undoubtedly intimidated, as Henry had intended, the clergy eventually agreed to acknowledge the King as their 'especial protector, single and supreme lord, and, as far as the law of Christ allows, even Supreme Head, of the Church and clergy of England'.[3] Not all were cowed, however, with the bishop of Durham and others entering a strong protest against the King's new title.[4] The German Imperial ambassador recorded on 1 March 1531, that it was not until late on that day that the King first appeared in the Parliament since it had been reconvened, and had remained for the best part of two hours in the Lords' House, but did not go down to the Commons.[5] It therefore seems to have been not unusual for the King to visit the Lords, while engaged in their deliberations, as he is reported as doing on this occasion. Whether he ever visited the Commons is not clear.

Wolsey's protégé and the King's Secretary, Thomas Cromwell, meanwhile, was made a member of the Privy Council in the same

---

3. J. Gairdner (ed.), *Letters and Papers Illustrative of the Reigns of Richard III and Henry VII* (London, 1861), v. 71.
4. Wilkins, *Concilia*, iii. 744–5; R. W. Dixon, *History of the Church of England* (1884–1902), i. 61–7; J. E. Powell, and K. Wallis, *The House of Lords in the Middle Ages*, 565–7.
5. *Letters and Papers*, v. 60.

year. Being methodical and a little nervous as to his position, in these fraught circumstances, in advising the King what he could do by his own authority, and what he could do only with the authority of Parliament, Cromwell initiated a review of the royal prerogative.

The Parliament did not reassemble until January 1532, and was notable for the procedure followed in respect of a bill to prevent the further payment of annates to the Papacy. Up to this time, on the appointment of a new bishop or other incumbent, the first year's revenue of a see or benefice had been payable to the Pope. Such a payment was known as an annate, from Latin *annata*, or 'year's space', but the Pope was no longer recognised as head of the Church. Combining realism, avarice and antipathy towards the excessive wealth of the Church, the Act in Restraint of Annates of 1532 redirected all such payments to the benefit of the Crown. The imperial ambassador reported on February 28[6] that the King had thrice visited the Parliament to ensure that the bill would be passed, but that all the bishops and two abbots had opposed it, while the lords all consented except for the earl of Arundel. As the temporal lords, of whom there were about thirty present, were in the majority, the bill was passed. So far as is known, this was the first occasion on which the lords, both spiritual and temporal, decided an issue – its acceptance evidently having been regarded as valid – on the basis of a majority vote, in accordance with a ruling of 1515. It confirmed that, henceforth, all lords would be deemed to be lords temporal, in keeping with the feudal notion of their position. It was this principle that enabled Henry to overrule the Church in respect of the Papacy. Also passed by Parliament before the end of the session was an Act for the Submission of Clergy. This made the decisions of Convocation subject to the consent of the King. This and the Act in Restraint of Annates proved too much for the Chancellor, Sir Thomas More, who now resigned.

Soon afterwards, the King appointed the Speaker of the Commons, Sir Thomas Audley, who had taken an active part in drafting the anti-clerical legislation, as Keeper of the Great Seal. In February of 1533, Audley was made Chancellor. This left the position of Speaker in the Commons vacant, and a new Speaker – *parlamenteur aux estatz*, or 'negotiator to the Estates' – was accordingly elected. He was then presented to the King

---

6. *Letters and Papers*, v. 392, 413; J. E. Powell, and K. Wallis, *The House of Lords in the Middle Ages*, 568.

in Parliament[7] by deputies of the Commons, dressed in scarlet, and the King received him and responded by conferring a knighthood on the new Speaker.[8] This description confirms the earlier impression that the primary purpose of the Speaker was to represent, to the King, the views of the Commons. It was the Parliament of 1536 that took the final step in the process of separation from the Papacy, when it consented to a bill that extinguished the authority of the bishop of Rome.[9] By this time the crisis was past, finally ending the previous boycotting of Parliament by most of the bishops, heads of religious houses, and one of the archbishops. Cromwell received recognition by being created a peer, Lord Cromwell. There was probably no previous example of a person of such lowly origin as Cromwell, his father having been a blacksmith and innkeeper at Putney, attaining to a lay peerage, certainly not since the fourteenth century, and it generated great hostility. He had not even been made a knight until his elevation to the peerage, and this antagonism undoubtedly contributed to his fall, four years later.

The intellectual emancipation brought by the Reformation undoubtedly was the key that unlocked the religious domination of England by the Church.

23.2.1. The First Estate Leaves Parliament

During the 1514 session of Parliament, an Act[10] was passed, without the assent of any lord spiritual, withdrawing benefit of clergy – that is, their exemption from the jurisdiction of the ordinary courts – for certain crimes in respect of those in minor orders. In other words, lesser clergy were now answerable before the ordinary courts where they were accused of any of the offences listed. During a sermon in the following Parliament of 1515, the abbot of Winchcombe denounced the Act as contrary to the law of God, and declared those lords who had been party to it to be subject to the censure of the Church. At the lords' request, the King referred the matter to a number of leading theologians, and went on to ask the bishops to compel the abbot to recant. The latter refused, and one friar who rejected the abbot's view was charged before the Church

---

7. That is, in the Painted Chamber.
8. *Letters and Papers*, vi. 63.
9. *Statutes*, iii. 663–6.
10. *Statutes*, iii. 49.

Convocation. The friar appealed to the King, who referred the case to a council of lawyers, both lay and ecclesiastical. The judges ruled that the members of the Convocation were all subject to *praemunire*, that is, they were subject to penalties for 'suing in the court of another, in derogation of the regality of our lord the King'.[11] They further ruled that the King could hold a Parliament by himself with the temporal lords and commons, without the spiritual lords, who 'had no place there, except by reason of their temporal possessions'.[12]

Previously, the lords temporal and spiritual had been consulted separately in matters of common interest, on the implied ground, in common law, that they represented their respective Estates. The new view reverted from the common law principle that Parliaments represent all three Estates, to the feudal principle that the clergy attended only in their capacity as tenants-in-chief, and therefore as barons. On this interpretation, a Parliament could comprise only two Houses, and the notion of a third House, representing the clergy who had withdrawn from attending Parliament, had no constitutional basis.[13] This shift of interpretation from the idea that Parliaments comprised three Estates, to the feudal notion that they represented only two Estates, on the ground that the First Estate was not involved in the legislative process, was to have huge consequences in 1532, concerning payments to the Papacy.

23.2.1.1. The Garter Rolls

At some point not later than 1512, the Garter King of Arms began the practice of keeping a roll of the names of the lords, spiritual and temporal, who attended Parliament. Probably a new one was made for the beginning of each Parliament.[14] Those surviving rolls are of vellum, about nine inches wide and up to twenty feet in length, headed by the royal arms. There follow, in two columns, the lords spiritual and temporal, two by two. The lords spiritual are shown on the left, being to the right of the throne, and the lords temporal on the right, the exception being the Archbishop of York and his suffragan bishops, who normally sit on the King's left. Each is represented by a shield of arms with the name

---

11. *16 Richard II*, c. 5, in *Statutes*, ii. 84–6.
12. *Letters and Papers*, ii. i. 351–4.
13. J. E. Powell, and K. Wallis, *The House of Lords in the Middle Ages*, 554.
14. Ibid. 550–1.

above it. From 1539, the lay shields are surmounted by crests. These rolls evidently listed only those lords expected to be present at the beginning of the Parliament, although a few were inserted afterwards, their purpose being to provide a guide as to precedence in the marshalling and seating of the peers.

23.2.1.2. Parliamentary Procedure in the Sixteenth Century

The first parliament of Henry VIII was opened at Westminster on 21 January 1510, and a description of the opening session survives.[15] The lords, both spiritual and temporal, assembled for the occasion in the Queen's great chamber, after which they proceeded to the Abbey, the order of the procession being as follows:

- the esquires, knights and young lords
- the abbots attending the parliament
- the bishops, accompanied on every side by the officers of arms (the heralds)
- the dean and almoner Garter, wearing his coat of arms
- the Sword of State, borne by the lord Henry Stafford (the eight-year-old eldest son of the duke of Buckingham), accompanied on all sides by the serjeants of arms and four gentlemen ushers
- the King, his train borne by the Chamberlain of England, the Earl of Oxford, and supported in the middle by the Chamberlain of the Household, Lord Herbert
- all the lords temporal.

As the King approached the Abbey, he was met by the abbot and the chapter, and there 'took his sceptre and went under a canopy, as accustomed'. In the Abbey, all the lords proceeded to the choir, where the King sat on the throne, next to the altar. All the lords spiritual sat on the south side of the choir, on the King's left, while the temporal lords sat on the north side, the King's right. After the mass was finished, the King left, beneath the canopy and bearing the sceptre, pausing as he passed his father's hearse to pray for his soul. Although first mentioned in 1485, this parliamentary procession to hear mass at the Abbey was

---

15. British Museum, Add. MS., 5758, fols. 8–9. Repeated in J. E. Powell, and K. Wallis, *The House of Lords in the Middle Ages*, 543–4.

undoubtedly practiced from early times, and the roll shows that the peers wore much the same robes as they had a hundred years earlier, according to an illumination of 1399, and the same had been worn at coronations. Appropriately, the lords wore scarlet robes, with horizontal bands of white fur around them, just below the shoulder but above the elbow, according to their status. These might be partly obscured by a cloak. There was no differentiation between dukes and earls in 1399, but by 1512 an extra bar had been accorded to the dukes.[16]

Back in the parliament chamber, the throng was so tightly compressed that it was some time before the King could pass through and proceed to the royal seat, and the Chancellor, wearing the cap of maintenance on his head,[17] stood by the cloth of estate on the King's right hand and made 'a right noble proposition'. The Treasurer of England stood on the King's left side, while the Chamberlain of England stood a little before the King, on his left side. Meanwhile, the sword was held by the lord Henry Stafford. Garter stood near the Great Chamberlain, the Earl of Oxford. To the left of the throne sat the temporal lords, including the bishop of Durham, the Archbishop of York being abroad, while the bishops sat to the right, headed by the bishops of London and Winchester. The Lord Chamberlain stood on the carpet, next to the bishops and abbots. On the sacks in the centre were seated the Master of the Rolls, the Chief Justices, the other judges, clerks and officers. When the Chancellor had finished his proposition, and the other ceremonies had been accomplished, in accordance with custom, the King, nobly accompanied, returned to his chamber. The lords and others then left 'unto their dinners', while 'others took their leaves and so finished the day'.

A contemporary illustration of the opening of a parliament survives in respect of one held at Blackfriars, in London, in April 1523.[18] It was drawn by or for Thomas Wriothesley, the Garter King, and shows the King, crowned and seated on a canopied throne on a dais, reached by three steps, and holding the dove sceptre. His feet are resting on a cushion. The royal arms and garter are displayed above him. The purpose of the canopy over the King may go back to the days when parliaments were held in

---

16. J. E. Powell, and K. Wallis, *The House of Lords in the Middle Ages*, 477.
17. A velvet cap, trimmed with ermine, whose proper purpose was to ease the weight of a crown or helmet and keep it in place.
18. J. E. Powell, and K. Wallis, *The House of Lords in the Middle Ages*, plate XX, and 555–7.

the open air, the canopy being to protect the King from the sun and any shower of rain. On either side of the throne is a bench, on which are seated, on the King's right, the Archbishop of Canterbury and Cardinal Wolsey, Chancellor and Archbishop of York. Between Wolsey and the throne is a space, where, behind the back of the bench, is the Bishop of London, holding a scroll of his opening speech, which he is delivering on behalf of the Chancellor. The bench on the King's left is vacant, where the Archbishop of York would have sat, except that, as Chancellor, cardinal and legate, he had moved over to the King's right. The spaces immediately on either side of the throne would have been occupied by visiting heads of state. To the left of the King, between the far end of the bench and the wall of the chamber, appears to be an opening or passage, not directly visible to the King, which is crowded with people, the foremost of which are wearing chains of office. These may be the aldermen of London.

In front of the throne is a carpet, decorated with lilies, on which stand two earls, one to the right of the King holding his cap of maintenance. The other earl, to the King's left, holds the sword of state, already described, but viewed now as a symbol of the King's authority. To the King's left also stands the Chamberlain, the Earl of Oxford, with his white wand of office. On each side of the chamber is a row of benches, facing the centre. That to the left of the King – the 'temporal' side – is where the temporal lords sit, wearing hats, while a corresponding row of benches, to the King's right, is where the spiritual lords sit. Behind each row of benches is a gap, leaving room for a second row of benches against the wall. At the top end of the front temporal bench sits the duke of Norfolk, as the earl marshal, holding his baton. Only the dukes wear coronets, while the remaining peers wear hats. All wear Parliament robes. On the bench behind the dukes and earls, along the wall, sit eight barons, and on the cross bench at the far end of the chamber, facing the King, sit eight more barons.

To the right of the King, on the 'spiritual' side of the chamber, sit nine bishops on the front bench, while seventeen black abbots occupy the back bench. At its far end, the back bench continues part way across the chamber as a cross bench, behind the barons, on which sit a further six figures. All the bishops wear mitres. The end of the two cross-benches leave sufficient space, between them and the temporal front bench, to allow access to and from the far end of the chamber.

In the centre of the chamber are four woolsacks, in the form of an open square. The one nearest the King is occupied by two chief justices and the master of the rolls – the last not being present on this occasion. They are facing the centre of the chamber. The woolsacks on either side of the square are occupied by eight judges, four on each. On the fourth sack, facing towards the King, are four figures, bare-headed, who are probably 'serjeants of the law', two of whom may be the attorney and solicitor. Kneeling behind these are two bare-headed individuals with ink, quills and paper, being the clerk of the Crown and the clerk of the Parliaments. Extending across the chamber, behind the cross-benches, is the bar. This is shown as a rail, with a gap towards the 'temporal' end, leaving access to and from the sanctified area of the chamber. Outside the bar stands the Speaker of the Commons, accompanied by thirteen of his fellows, making this probably the occasion when the new Speaker, Sir Thomas More, was presented.

An illustration of a Parliament of Edward I, more than two centuries earlier, by the same artist, and evidently based on considerable knowledge, shows that there has been little change, apart from an absence of steps to the throne, and those seated with the King on the top bench were slightly different. On this occasion, the King is shown holding the Mace.[19] The freemen of London are not present. Neither drawing shows the Commons (apart from the delegation in 1553). This was probably because the Commons deliberated elsewhere, except when the full Parliament was assembled, in which case the members of the Commons would have stood outside the Bar, like the delegation shown. That they were not included in the earlier drawing was probably due to the lack of space available to the artist. There would probably have been little of interest for him to use in any case.

The lords' journals allow us to reconstruct the details of normal parliamentary procedure about this time. As in 1510, on the first day prior to the opening of a new parliament, the King and lords assembled in the White Hall, from where they proceeded to the Abbey for Mass. Upon their return, they reassembled in the Painted Chamber, with the

---

19. J. E. Powell, and K. Wallis, *The House of Lords in the Middle Ages*, plate XXI and Appendix B.

commons, for the opening. On those days when the Chancellor and other lords spiritual were absent in Convocation, the Treasurer adjourned the remainder of the parliament. Sometimes, the lords would impose a fine, typically of ten pounds, on those lords who did not attend. Bills submitted to parliament were read three times, being sometimes turned over to the law officers for amendment after the first or second reading. They were then sent down 'to the commons or lower house'. Petitions from the commons, submitted in the form of bills, might be referred back for amendment after the first or second reading, and, if necessary, more than once. The lords would sometimes refer a bill to a small committee of the members for the contents to be scrutinised more closely, as in the case of a bill in 1512 that was concerned with the punishment for murder.

Liaison between the lords and commons during deliberation was still conducted by means of a delegation or commission from the lords down to the commons, particularly where it was necessary to apprise the commons of details of which they had not been aware. However, a conference between lords and commons might be called to deal with outstanding bills. In 1515, for example, in order to deal with bills that had been passed by the commons but not by the lords before the parliament was prorogued, the Chancellor ordered that persons – presumably representatives – be summoned from each of the two houses to meet in the Star Chamber the following Monday, at eight o'clock, to confer and decide whether these should be admitted or dropped altogether.[20]

The closing sitting of a parliament was again held in the Painted Chamber. In the case of 1510, this was about five o'clock in the afternoon. The King was again seated on the throne, 'in the presence of the lords … wearing their parliamentary habits or robes, and also the whole people from the commons, or lower house'. The Speaker of the latter announced the grant of taxes that had been made to the King. The Chancellor then replied, after which the Clerk of the Crown read all the acts done for the public good in the present parliament, in order by their titles, and the reply to each, according to the royal pleasure, was endorsed thereon by the Clerk of Parliament proclaiming: *le Roy le veult, le Roy se advisera, soit fait come il est desire.*[21]

---

20. *Journals of the House of Lords*, i. 45.
21. *Ibid.*, i. 8–9.

We have previously noted that, at some point, the King sent one of his Serjeants-at-Arms to be present at the sessions of the House of Commons. During the absence from Parliament or either of its Houses while in session, it became the practice for the King to leave his Mace as a symbol of his presence, and it was a duty of the Serjeant-at-Arms on such occasions to bring the Mace and lay it on the table, from which moment the House was deemed to be in session, because the King was deemed to be present. The session was not over until the Serjeant had removed the Mace and returned it to safe keeping. As the sole reason for the assembly was to meet and consult with the King, or deliberate on his requests, its proceedings had no legal significance unless the King or his deputy was present and presiding, and this problem had been resolved by the presence of the King's Mace. This practice reflected the growing failure of the King to attend his Parliaments, which were crucial to his ability to implement legislative changes. It seems very likely that this arrangement had been agreed in the beginning, when the King had first recognised the proceedings of the Commons in the Chapter House as taking place 'within the Parliament'. The use of separate meeting places for the lords and commons had solved the problem of accommodating such a large gathering as a Parliament represented, and the symbolic use of the mace, in the charge of one of his Serjeants-at-Arms, had solved the technical problem of holding the Parliament together as a single assembly presided over by the King. Another duty of the Serjeant-at-Arms was evidently to maintain order in the Chamber and in its immediate vicinity, to enable the King's business to be conducted. To this end he carried the symbol of the King's presence, the Mace, into the Chamber at the beginning of each day's business, and removed it at the end for safe keeping. Following the appointment by the Commons of a Speaker at the beginning of each new Parliament, both the Speaker and the Serjeant would have needed to cooperate, so that, as the Speaker established his authority in the House, the King left it to him, on the advice of the members, to recommend whom he, the King, should appoint as the Serjeant's successor when occasion demanded. In this way, the members of the Commons quickly formed the erroneous idea that the purpose of the Serjeant-at-Arms was to represent the authority of the House, rather than that of the King, and that he was there to assist the Speaker. The purpose of the Speaker was, and continued to be, as the representative of the King's authority. The print of 1523, just described, shows the Mace being held by the Serjeant-at-Arms, who is standing at the Bar of the House, next to, and apparently announcing, a kneeling petitioner. It may at first seem surprising that the Serjeant should be carrying the Mace about with him in the course of what must have been a fairly routine duty, until it is realised that it is he who is the Mace's keeper, and that he must take the Mace with him as the symbol of the King's – and consequently his and Parliament's – authority in bringing the petitioner before Parliament.

On entering the chamber, it is said that members of the House of Commons bowed in the direction of the Speaker. It has been speculated that this was either out of respect for the Speaker, or for the missing altar, or that they were simply ducking to avoid knocking their hats off when passing beneath the screen.[22] However, there is an altogether more likely explanation. It is very likely that it had always been the practice for members of the Great Council and for those attending the Common Councils, or Parliaments, to bow in the direction of the King when joining or leaving the assembly. They had probably also stood whenever the King arrived or left. It was the courtesy of bowing to the King that was maintained by the Commons, because he was still there, in the form of the Mace and the royal coat of arms, presiding over its deliberations. When the King attended the full Parliament in person, those assembled undoubtedly did, as they still do, rise to their feet, and this must have been the case, as it still is, when the King arrives in or departs from the Commons chamber in his manifestation as the Mace. It is this same tradition that is followed in the Crown courts, when those present rise to their feet upon the entry or departure of the judge, not out of respect for the judge's person, but in honour of the King whom the judge represents.

It is only in Elizabeth's reign that evidence on parliamentary procedure becomes reasonably full, and it shows that the two Houses conducted their affairs according to sensible rules, and had probably been doing so for a long time. It is clear also that the Lords, 'always more "mature" and more businesslike, led the way'.[23]

In 1514, and probably earlier, it was the Speaker's usage to address the Lord Chancellor, who was the King's representative in Parliament, 'in the

22. J. Field, *The Story of Parliament*, 77.
23. G. R. Elton, *The Tudor Constitution*, 250.

name and on behalf of the Commons, to lay claim by humble petition to their ancient and undoubted rights and privileges, particularly that their persons and servants might be free from arrests and all molestations; that they may enjoy liberty of speech in all their debates; may have access to His Majesty's royal person whenever occasion shall require; and that all their proceedings may receive from His Majesty the most favourable construction.' To this, the Lord Chancellor responded that 'His Majesty most readily confirms all the rights and privileges which have even been granted to, or conferred upon, the commons by His Majesty or any of His royal predecessors'.[24] The rights and privileges enumerated by the Speaker referred only to the more important. The form of the address, as a humble petition, and the reference to privileges of the Commons, were a reflection of the feudal idea that all power had its source in the Crown. The reference to the ancient rights of the Commons, on the other hand, derived from the Aryan tradition of the supremacy of the assembly, which was endeavouring to reassert itself throughout the Middle Ages.

It appears that some Speakers took the rights of the House for granted and limited themselves at the beginning of every Parliament to craving the royal indulgence for their own particular difficulties in communicating the voice of the House to the King. If he did not cover himself in this way, the Speaker was perpetually exposed to the danger that the King, in his exasperation with the obstinacy or effrontery of the House, was liable to blame the messenger. In 1559, at the beginning of Elizabeth's reign, when the Speaker asked, not only that he might be pardoned for any unintended misrepresentation by him of the views of the House, or any unfortunate expression by him that might cause Her Majesty offence, but also that she grant certain liberties and privileges to the whole House, in particular:

1. that the House be granted access to the Queen's presence upon all urgent and necessary occasions;
2. that the members might have liberty and freedom of speech in the House;
3. that all members, with their servants and necessary attendants be exempted from all manner of arrests and suits during the Parliament, and during 'the usual space

---

24. Erskine May, *Parliamentary Practice*, 68, 69.

before the beginning and after the ending thereof, as
in former times hath always been accustomed'.

These the Queen conceded, conditional upon the second being used
in a manner consistent with the duties of the House, and provided it was
not used in a manner inconsistent with their reverence for, and obedience
to, their Sovereign. The third request was granted, so long as it was not
used for the purpose of defrauding creditors or the maintaining of injuries
and wrongs. We have seen that these liberties and privileges were not
new, although they had long been at risk. In common law, the sessions
of the Commons were always, and could only be, held in the Sovereign's
presence, so that the physical separation posed by the dismemberment
of Parliament or the Queen's temporary absences from it must always be
removed when either party requested it. As the constitutional purpose
of Parliament was the granting, or denial, of consent to the Sovereign's
wishes, freedom of speech was an implicit requirement. The right to attend
Parliament unhindered, also implicit in the law of the Constitution, is
evident in the earliest legal codes known to us. The ritual claiming of
these liberties and privileges – in reality, irrevocable constitutional rights
– was therefore not a begging of favours, but a process of reminder in
an age when the House of Commons was still unsure of itself as an
institution, and rulers could more easily exploit their position and invoke
feudal notions in justification.

This was a period during which the House of Commons developed
its self-consciousness as a corporate body and acquired a strong sense
of procedure and practice, particularly in matters of debate. It had to,
because, in the absence of the King or his Chancellor to manage the
proceedings, as the Constitution assumed, the Commons were left to
their own devices. They also had to find a solution to the much greater
procedural complexities of a dismembered Parliament imposed by Edward
III. In any case, in a better educated age, following the development of
schools and universities, the old *ad hoc* approach to proceedings was no
longer regarded as adequate. By about 1550, the House of Commons
had established that language must be decorous, that members must give
way to one another, that they must address the Speaker, and that in full
session – that is, other than in committee – no man could speak more

than once a day to any given bill. Meanwhile, the internal management of its affairs also became the right of the Commons. A statute of 1515 forbade any member of the House of Commons to absent himself prior to the conclusion of the Parliament without the licence of the Speaker and Commons. Effectively, this implied a delegation of the control of absence from the Crown to the Speaker. Absenteeism was always a problem, as members sought to reconcile their parliamentary duties and their individual professions and other private business, so that attendance was often thin, even on days of important business, much to Elizabeth's annoyance.[25]

It was the usual procedure for bills to be read three times in each House before a decision was taken, with the Speaker retaining an impartial stance. Very difficult bills could be read more times, and could be referred to committees, but some could be passed after only one or two readings.[26] The practice of introducing bills on parchment made amendment difficult, and after the reign of Henry VIII it became the rule that they should be on paper. Votes in the House of Lords were recorded individually, but the Commons reached its decisions by the time-honoured practice of acclamation. This was later replaced by voting on the basis of a simple majority.[27] The pressure during Elizabeth's reign was particularly great, partly because of the large number of bills, and partly because the Queen insisted on short sessions, leaving the majority of bills unconcluded. The proceedings of Parliament were held in secret, and discussion of them outside was a serious offence. The reasoning behind this was perhaps that the purpose of a Parliament was to meet the King's needs as ruler, and that discussion of its proceedings in the taverns could only cause mischief. It was based on a feudal view, overlooking the constitutional principle in common law that a Parliament was an assembly of all free men of the nation. The unruly and inappropriate behaviour of members of the House of Commons, who were in the habit of trying to address the chamber, several at a time, was criticised by the Speaker in 1589, when he reminded them that 'every member of this House is a judge of this court, being the highest court of all other courts, and the Great Council also of this realm, and so moveth them in regard

---

25. G. R. Elton, *The Tudor Constitution*, 253.
26. N. Pronay, and J. Taylor (eds.), *Parliamentary Texts of the Later Middle Ages*, 186.
27. J. E. Neale, *House of Commons*, 397.

thereof, that, as in all other courts, being each of them inferior to this high court'.[28] They should therefore behave accordingly.[29]

The Commons increased in size during the sixteenth century, from 296 to 462. This was due partly to the summoning by Henry VIII of members from the hitherto unrepresented shires and boroughs of Cheshire and Wales, but mainly it was due to the enfranchisement or restoration of boroughs, by the issue of letters patent, in response to pressure from the boroughs themselves. It was a time when the gentry had discovered a new interest in entering Parliament, and although a borough could only be represented in law by a resident, the seats of many had effectively been taken over by the rural gentry. Particularly in the reign of Edward IV, there had been an influx into Parliament of gentry and Crown officials into seats that should have been occupied by the burgesses, and this turned into a flood in the reign of Henry VIII. Thus, by the time of Elizabeth I, the House of Commons was composed largely of landed gentry. Most elections, whether for shires or boroughs, were not contested, and some boroughs did not trouble to return a member for a couple of centuries.[30] The boroughs were now poorly represented, but, on the other hand, the Commons acquired, 'men of social standing, independence, political training and experience, (who) could also fairly claim to speak for the political nation, a role which down to the Wars of the Roses had been more properly filled by the Lords'.[31] It is a period in the history of the Commons that is referred to as 'the invasion of the gentry', and it effectively converted the House from a body of local representatives into a stuttering political machine. There was frequent liaison between the two Houses by means of committees, in which the Lords lead the way, until about 1581, when the Commons reacted. It was resolved that the Commons' committee could not agree to anything with the Lords that had not been in their instructions from the House. Thereafter, conferences between the Houses became rare.

---

28. It is worth noting that the House of Lords was still regarded as the Great Council.
29. Parliamentary debate, 18 February 1589, D'Ewes, *The Journals of All the Parliaments During the Reign of Queen Elizabeth* (London, 1682). Quoted in G. R. Elton, *The Tudor Constitution*, 258.
30. J. P. Kenyon, *The Stuart Constitution 1603–1688* (Cambridge, 1986), 22.
31. G. R. Elton, *The Tudor Constitution*, 249.

23.2.1.3. Parliamentary Privileges

During the fourteenth and fifteenth centuries, those attending Parliaments asserted or gained various privileges, which have been defined as 'the immunities enjoyed by either house of parliament, or by individual members, as such'.[32] Before proceeding further we must remind ourselves, however, that a Parliament was nevertheless a temporary assembly, summoned into existence for a particular purpose. The so-called 'Houses' referred to the deliberations of various groups attending. The representatives of the Commons had endeavoured to establish their independence as a corporate body, with its own rights and privileges, in pursuit of a growing rivalry with the lords, whose influence had been severely weakened by the Wars of the Roses, and a growing ambition to wrest legislative and even executive powers from the King, although these ambitions on the part of the Commons had receded under the Tudors. Consequently, the Commons had projected their perception of their own House onto Parliament itself, having come to regard it is another corporate body, of which the Commons was such a major part that what were claimed to be the 'privileges of the Commons' were more often referred to as 'privileges of Parliament'. The point to be remembered, therefore, is that, in common law, there could be no such thing as a privilege of Parliament, and that what was so described was, in fact, a privilege to which those attending were entitled.

Although these privileges were submitted by the Commons to the Crown for confirmation, it would appear that they were nevertheless regarded as entitlements, whether royal approval were granted or not.[33] The Crown, where it clung to feudal doctrine, saw itself as granting privileges that it could, in theory, take away again, while the Commons, guided by an instinct for customary law, saw itself as seeking Crown recognition for privileges to which it was inherently entitled.

23.2.1.3.i. Privileges of Both Houses

A distinction should be made between the privileges of Parliament, which applied to both Houses, and the privileges of the House of Commons, to which we shall come later. There are two main privileges of Parliament in common law, freedom of speech and freedom from

---

32. *Shorter Oxford English Dictionary* (1992).
33. Erskine May, *Parliamentary Practice*, 69–71.

arrest. Freedom of speech in councils and assemblies had always been an underlying assumption in Aryan society, but attempts to muzzle it by overbearing rulers appear to have been a recurring problem since antiquity. The same problem manifested itself from time to time in Norman and Angevin England, usually because it was difficult to reconcile with the doctrine of the divine authority of kings. Nevertheless, freedom of speech in Parliament had always been accepted to some extent, for the simple reason that, as the King usually realised, it could not function usefully without it, so long as it was thought to be within the limits of propriety.[34] Undoubtedly, it had been very limited in Norman times, and had since varied from one reign to the next, and the problem was where the line between propriety and impropriety should be drawn.

In the reign of Edward III, for example, 'the commons did oftentimes … discuss and debate among themselves many things concerning the king's prerogative, and agreed upon petitions for laws to be made directly against his prerogative … yet they were never interrupted in their consultations, nor received check from the same'.[35] This may have had some bearing on the King's decision to clip the authority of the Great Council. Such freedom was not tolerated by his successor, Richard II. In 1397, when Sir Thomas Haxey[36] introduced a Bill for the reform of the Royal Household, an affronted Richard II ordered the lords, through the duke of Lancaster, to convey his displeasure to the commons at what he regarded as a grave invasion of his 'regality', and to ascertain from the Speaker the name of its author. Summoned to the royal presence, Haxey apologised and was forgiven. The Bill was then adjudged treasonable by the lords in parliament, with the King's assent, and Haxey was tried by the duke of Lancaster 'before the King and all the lords temporal and the commons of the realm in the White Chamber'. On admitting authorship, Haxey was then condemned to death by the Lords as a traitor. At the petition of the archbishop and all the leading clergy, however, that Haxey

---

34. This point was later made in 1523 by the Speaker, Sir Thomas More, when he pointed out at the opening of Parliament that, while due diligence had been taken in sending the most discreet persons up to Parliament, it was nevertheless often difficult in the heat of the moment for them not to express themselves in the chamber in 'boistrous [*sic*] and rude' language, instead of the 'painted polished speech' expected of them.

35. H. Elsynge, *The Ancient Method of Holding Parliaments*, 177.

36. Haxey was the keeper of the rolls in the Court of Common Pleas, but in parliament represented the abbot of Selby.

was a clerk under their jurisdiction, he was granted his life, and three months later was granted a full pardon. So far as is known, Haxey was not a member of the House of Commons, and may have been attending the parliament as a clerical proctor under the *praemunientes* clause.[37] It was because he had been charged with treason that he had been tried by the Lords, apparently in the presence of the commons, although it would seem that, by the Lords, was effectively meant the Great Council.

Such an interference with the freedom of debate was rare in the Middle Ages, and in 1399, following the accession of Richard's successor, Henry VI, the King and Lords approved a petition from Haxey for a reversal of the judgment against him, which he considered to be against the law and custom which had been before in Parliament. The Commons did not feel that this adequately stated the point, and later in the same year repeated the petition for the reversal of the judgment, for the sake of justice, as well as to save the liberties of the commons. By the assent of the King and Lords, it was agreed by the whole legislature that the condemnation of Haxey had been in derogation of the privileges of Parliament, and should be annulled and held to be of no force or effect. The incident was of importance because it established the principle that the King must not attempt to coerce Parliament by the arbitrary arrest or imprisonment of its members or agents. It is clear from the nature and tone of this incident that the Commons was trying to re-establish, with the support of the Lords, an ancient right which was well known to all, but which the King had tried to override. It was a principle that was fundamental to the very purpose of any folk-moot.

The Speaker of the Commons complained in 1400 that certain members of Parliament had been in the habit of acquainting the King with matters on the agenda of the Commons before the Commons had reached agreement on them, sometimes causing the King to become incensed. This had had the effect of inhibiting discussion. The Speaker asked the King to take no notice of such reports and to exert no royal pressure as a result of them. Henry acknowledged the right of the Commons to free debate, and promised not to listen to unauthorised accounts of their activities.

---

37. F. W. Maitland, *The Constitutional History of England*, 241.

Henry IV also proclaimed, in 1407, the right of the Lords and Commons to discuss any matters of national interest in the King's absence. In other words, it was not necessary for the King to be present in person. This was realistic, from his point of view, because it was impossible to be in two chambers at once, and inconvenient, in any case, to attend all such deliberations. From the point of view of the Lords and Commons, it enabled them to discuss these issues freely, without the risk of offending the King. The King's absence was no novelty. It was noted earlier that the King in Anglo-Saxon times was quite capable of going off on a hunting expedition and leaving his Council to deliberate in his absence, although it was not until 1407 that this practice of deliberating without the King seems to have received recognition as an entitlement. Even so, the principle that the King presided over the assembly, as he did over deliberations of the council, was never brought into question. This was emphasised in 1327, after Edward II had been imprisoned at Kenilworth Castle, and the Queen, Isabella, anxious to secure her son's succession, summoned a Parliament on 20 January and called upon it to depose the King. Parliament refused on the ground that it had no authority without the King's presence. Its motive is beside the point, and what is important from a constitutional point of view is that Parliament only exists in the presence of the King,[38] unless summoned by the Great Council.

The contradiction between the requirement that a Parliament was unlawful, otherwise, without the presence of the King, and the freedom of Parliament to deliberate in the King's absence was resolved by the King depositing the Royal Mace in the Commons as a symbol of his personal presence while he was away, thereby making its sessions lawful. In the Lords, likewise, the King was always present in the person of his Chancellor, but a symbol of the King's presence was placed in the centre of the chamber. Although the right to discuss the King's business without his presence in person was an extension of the principle of freedom of speech, in a sense it went beyond it. Thomas Young was imprisoned in 1451 for proposing in the House of Lords that the Duke of York be named as the heir presumptive. Progress in establishing a clear and unlimited privilege was not made until the reign of Henry VIII, who was

---

38. That Parliament can also be summoned by the Great Council has been noted elsewhere.

sufficiently self-confident to allow criticism in Parliament of his policies and even of his private life.

In 1512, a member of the House of Commons, William Strode, was prosecuted in the Stannary court in Devon. The semi-independent communities of the tin and lead miners of Cornwall and Devon had their own ancient customs and their own court privileges. The Stannaries, whose name derived from late Latin *stannum*, 'tin', were the districts comprising the tin mines and smelting works, and their jurisdiction belonged to the local Stannary courts, collectively known as the Court of the Lord Warden of the Stannaries, being courts of special jurisdiction, in derogation from the general jurisdiction of the courts of common law.[39] Strode had proposed certain Bills in Parliament to regulate the privilege of the tin miners, and as this affected matters which were the preserve of the Stannaries it was tantamount to a contempt of court. The court convicted, fined and imprisoned him for this reason. The House of Commons took the view that this had infringed the right of a member to speak freely within its precincts, and it led to an Act of Parliament which declared the proceeding against Strode to be void and, further, that all similar proceedings in future against members of Parliament were to be void and of no effect. This was not so much an assertion of freedom of speech as a formal recognition of the obvious point that, as part of the High Court of Parliament, the Commons and its doings were privileged against inferior courts of the realm.[40] The real problem, and it became acute in the reign of Elizabeth I, was the wish of some members to discuss matters that the Queen wished to keep out of Parliament. She did this by letting it be known indirectly that she favoured this or that, implying that members would do well not to cause her offence. This might have posed few difficulties but for the conflict that was created by members who wanted new policies, which the Crown opposed. The battleground chosen was the question of freedom of speech, and the leading challengers were two brothers, Paul and Peter Wentworth, who resented the Queen's pressurising of Parliament. They alleged that some members, implying the Privy Councillors, passed on to the Queen what transpired in the House, causing members to fear the consequences. Such inhibition had not existed in the time of Henry VIII. The Wentworths

---

39. Taswell-Langmead, *English Constitutional History*, 325, note 2.
40. And lawfully established by it.

went on to assert that free speech meant the liberty to discuss whatever the Commons deemed to be necessary for the good of the realm, and not just what was put before it by the Crown. Thus, Paul Wentworth contended in 1566 that a ban by the Queen on any discussion of the succession amounted to a breach of privilege. Ten years later, in 1576, Peter Wentworth took freedom of speech to its limit (until the House itself stopped him from continuing) by openly attacking the Queen for refusing certain laws intended for her own good against Popery, and, in so doing, setting herself against her nobility and people. He was imprisoned in that same year on the Commons' own authority. In 1587, he attempted, by a list of questions to be put to the House, which the Speaker prevented from being heard, to elaborate to the House his view that it could not properly discharge its function unless his interpretation of free speech were accepted.

Elizabeth had her own definition of the freedom of speech in Parliament, the best exposition of which was that given in a reply of the Lord Keeper of the Privy Seal to the Speaker's petition in 1593. Members were free to speak without hindrance on any Bill before them, he said, and Bills concerning matters of state, that is, those touching on the royal prerogative, could only be introduced by the Crown. In other words, issues which concerned the Queen in her person, such as her marriage or the succession, and in her office as supreme governor in things spiritual and temporal, notably, religion, foreign policy, the regulation of trade and the issue of letters patent, could not be raised in the House without her express permission. The royal pressure on Parliament of which Peter Wentworth and others complained was not so much improper influence as the inevitable pressure that Parliament was under during almost any session. The Sovereign had work to get through and issues to be resolved, and one like Elizabeth I, who had no time for fools, was frequently angry at, or contemptuous of, the 'idle brains' and mischief-making of certain members. Inevitably, therefore, the Commons often found itself under pressure or influence.

It has been said that freedom of speech was the only parliamentary liberty that hinged on political issues, that is, the relationship between the Crown and Commons, as opposed to constitutional and procedural issues.[41] In fact, this relationship was very much a constitutional issue, because it concerned the very purpose of the Commons, which, as the popular element in the national assembly, had the function of approving, or otherwise, the policies of the Crown. Once the nation in Parliament had been replaced by its representatives (whose representativeness must often have been in question), and once the pressure of modern government had caused a replacement of annual Parliaments that met for only a week or so, by fairly regular Parliaments, sitting for months on end, an entirely new situation was in the making. The representatives were no longer individuals from around the country, called upon to perform a public duty, but individuals discovering a vocation, forming factional alliances with each other, and, having tasted power, being anxious for more. In 1571 Strickland introduced some ecclesiastical bills and was called before the Queen's Council, and in 1576 Peter Wentworth made trenchant speeches about freedom of debate, causing the Commons itself to turn against him and commit him to the Tower. The same happened to him in 1588, the Commons acquiescing in the Queen's command that they shall avoid religious topics, which were particularly sensitive at the time. In 1593 she was more specific in the matter, and added the instruction that members were to vote only 'Aye' or 'No'. Apart from the right to deliberate on proposals before it, which included petitions, the role of a Parliament was, indeed, simply to approve or otherwise.

The privilege of freedom from arrest had been recognised from the earliest times, and it can be inferred from the common law principle known in Anglo-Saxon times as *mæthelfrith*, 'assembly peace', the preservation of peace in public assemblies, the violation of which had to be compensated twofold. It applied to all persons attending public assemblies, irrespective of their Estate, and in early Anglo-Saxon times it was enforced by particularly heavy penalties. The principle underlying this freedom in pre-Christian times had been that such assemblies enjoyed divine protection, for which purpose they were held on sanctified ground, where, by being made in the divine presence, agreements were sanctified. It was this sanction that ensured that laws would not be broken. It also provided the King and the courts with the added authority needed to enforce them. Those engaged in an assembly's task were accordingly

41. G. R. Elton, *The Tudor Constitution*, 268.

entitled to special protection, and the principle is first known to us through Kentish law, which stated that persons on their way to or from an assembly were protected by particularly heavy penalties from violence, obstruction or intimidation. It seems reasonable to assume, therefore, that the protection of a man's attention to parliamentary business was an important aspect of common law. The right was directed at molestation by individuals, because the offence was committed against the King's business, as well as against the individual attending to it.

Even after the Norman Conquest, people attending a General Council were protected by the earlier laws, particularly one enacted by King Æthelræd. This protection applied both to the attendance itself and to travel to and from. In respect of Parliaments, as the General or Common Councils were now called, it was generally claimed that this protection extended over a period of forty days before and after each session,[42] and it extended to the servants of those attending. This privilege in respect of the servant of a member of Parliament was declared by a statute of Henry IV of 1403. At the same time, Henry formally recognised the privilege of members of Parliament to be free from arrest on civil matters during a session of Parliament, and in going to, or returning from, one. In 1433, the privilege was to some extent confirmed in respect of both Houses in a general statute, which made anybody who assaulted a member attending a parliament liable to double damages.[43]

Inevitably, the privilege was occasionally ignored, and the Commons had no means of enforcing it in any case. This was brought out in the case of its own Speaker, who seems to have been especially vulnerable. In 1376 the Speaker of the Commons, Peter de la Mare, was thrown into prison for his conduct in the Good Parliament, and remained there until after the death of Edward III, when he was released by Richard II. Another Speaker, Thomas Thorpe, whose arrest and imprisonment was sanctioned by the Lords in 1453 for not paying a fine for trespass, committed while seizing property belonging to the Duke of York, who had been accused of debt. When the Commons complained to the King and Lords, the judges were consulted. The latter expressed the view that determination of its privileges was for Parliament itself, not the justices, and they took the opportunity to assert that no member of Parliament

---

42. Erskine May, *Parliamentary Practice*, 139.
43. 11 Hen. VI, c. 11. F. W. Maitland, *The Constitutional History of England*, 243.

should be arrested, except in cases of treason, felony, or contempt of Parliament. Despite this, the Lords held that Thorpe should remain in prison, and the Commons were forced to elect a new Speaker. Every Peer enjoyed a certain immunity from arrest in any case, because, as a baron of the realm, the person of a Peer was 'forever sacred and inviolable.'[44] This derived from the ancient principle that divine protection was accorded to those of noble birth, except in the conduct of war, just as it applied also to the clergy. In this way, the functional structure of society had been preserved since antiquity. This immunity did not protect a Peer from arrest by his fellow Peers, in the event of criminal charges.

A member of the Commons who had been arrested could only be released upon the issue of a writ, granted by Chancery upon the request of the Speaker. By contrast, a Peer needed only the intervention of the Lord Chancellor. In the sixteenth century it was taken to mean the right of every lord, knight and burgess, and his servants, to avoid arrest by any court other than that of Parliament itself, during the life of that Parliament.[45] The right was extended to a member's servants on the grounds that, without suitable attendance, he would be incapable of doing his duty. In the enforcing of this right, it was eventually felt that the Mace could be put to good use outside the chamber of the House of Commons, as well as serving its normal function inside. When George Ferrers, a burgess of Plymouth, was arrested in 1542 in a suit for debt while on his way to Parliament, the Commons decided to send the Serjeant-at-Arms to secure his release, it being considered that the Mace was enough evidence of the Serjeant's authority. The officers and others holding Ferrers refused to release him, however, without the usual writ and a brawl ensued, in which the Mace was brought into physical use and damaged, the crown being broken off. When the sheriffs of London arrived, they also refused the Serjeant's order, and he was forced to return to the Parliament House. The members of the Commons, who included among their number not a few Privy Counsellors, thereupon suspended their session and collectively repaired to the House of Lords, where the Speaker laid complaint before the Lord Chancellor, lords and judges there in session. The latter agreed that the action of the sheriffs amounted to a contempt of Parliament and left the question of punishment to the

44. W. Stubbs, *Constitutional History of England*, iii. 498.
45. G. R. Elton, *The Tudor Constitution*, 260.

Lower House. The Chancellor offered, there and then, to grant a writ, but the Commons refused, returning to their places and insisting that the authority of the Mace – which they now regarded, mistakenly, as the symbol of their own authority – be asserted. Meanwhile, the sheriffs had learned of the gravity of the situation, and when the Serjeant returned, they delivered their prisoner to him without demur. The Serjeant commanded them, however, to appear before the Speaker of the Lower House the next day, bringing with them all who had been involved in the arrest and holding of Ferrers, on a charge that they had wittingly procured the arrest of Ferrers in contempt of the privilege of the Parliament. When they appeared before the Speaker and members of the Commons the next morning, they were convicted and committed to prison. Ferrers, once released, could not again be arrested for the same offence, although Parliament subsequently enacted that the debt must stand.

The King, Henry VIII, now apprised of the circumstances and of the assertion by the Commons of its authority 'by warrant of the Mace', summoned the Lord Chancellor, the judges, the Speaker and the most senior members of the Commons. As reported by Holinshed,[46] the King commended the members of the Lower House for their wisdom in maintaining their privileges and declared that he, as the head of Parliament and attending it in person, was entitled to its privilege, not only for himself but also for 'all his servants attending there upon him'. It followed that not only Ferrers, but his servants attending him at the time, were equally covered by that privilege. The King went on to state and support the view of his justices that, when Parliament was sitting, both he, as its head, and its members were conjointly one authority, that is, the King in Parliament, and that any offence or injury committed against himself or any member of Parliament, while that Parliament was in existence, was committed against the King's person and against 'the whole Court of Parliament'. Moreover, the prerogative of Parliament was such that its privileges overrode the acts and processes of any other court. The King seems to have made no reference to the Mace, only to the need for the privilege of Parliament to be respected and enforced. In the circumstances, the judiciary and the King had little choice but to uphold, by implication, the authority of the Royal Mace and its officer in the

---

46. R. Holinshed, *Chronicles of England, Scotland and Ireland,* iii, 824–6.

manner in which they had been used, but without endorsing their use in such a situation in future. The inference appears to be clear enough, that the means which the Commons had used to enforce its privilege had no legal basis.

In a later instance, that of Smalley's Case in 1576, a Commons committee, perhaps because it suspected that Smalley's employer, Arthur Hall, was trying to use parliamentary privilege to evade a debt, reverted to the recognised procedure when it maintained that Smalley could only be freed from prison by a writ out of Chancery. In the face of Hall's obstinacy, however, the 'warrant of the Mace' was again resorted to in order to release Smalley. That the Mace was immediately accepted as authority enough on this occasion was then taken by the Commons as confirmation of its right to enforce its privilege by its own authority. The Upper House also enforced its privilege, when it discharged Lord Cromwell in 1572 of a writ of attachment obtained by a complainant. In violation of parliamentary privilege, the writ had ordered Cromwell to obey an injunction given in the Court of Chancery. In defining who were the servants of its members, the House of Commons, always more assertive in its claims, tended to be much more generous than the Lords.

The effect of these cases was to establish the right of each House to enforce the common privilege of Parliament claimed by its own members. The Commons went further, however, by concluding that it had the power of arrest and trial in such cases, using the authority of the Mace. That Parliament, as the highest court in the land, had the right in common law to try such offenders against its freedom and dignity was not in doubt,[47] nor was the right of each Estate to try its own – that is, only the House of Lords might try members of Parliament who belonged to the Second Estate, while only the House of Commons might try members from the Third Estate. On the other hand, there appears to be no evidence that Parliament enjoyed executive power, since it had already vested this in the King. Parliament was a purely consultative and judicial body. This was reflected in the established practice whereby Parliament, or its respective Houses, could bring about the arrest of an offender against its privilege by turning to the executive, represented by the Lord

---

47. Although we have no direct evidence, circumstantial evidence suggested, that Parliament had delegated its judicial function to the King in Council and retained only certain powers as a court of law.

Chancellor. If the offender were convicted by Parliament, again, it was the executive which had to carry out the sentence imposed by Parliament or its respective Houses. The assumption made by the Commons, that the Speaker could direct the Serjeant to arrest an offender, appears to rest on the question of whether the Serjeant, as an officer of the King, and therefore of the executive, believed that he had the King's authority to act outside the chamber of the Commons, which is doubtful, and this seems to be confirmed by the King's failure, in the Ferrers Case, to endorse the Serjeant's action. While the Ferrers and Smalley Cases undoubtedly set a precedent – and precedent has long been used by the courts as a means of establishing the common law – no precedent can override the common law of the Constitution. The members of the House of Commons have since felt entitled to arrest individuals considered to be in breach of privilege 'by sending their own Serjeant-at-Arms and claiming that his mace was sufficient authority',[48] but the Serjeant-at-Arms was the King's officer, entrusted with the King's Mace, and although he was expected to work with the Speaker of the House to the best of his ability, it would seem that successive Sergeants-at-Arms had forgotten that they were probably exceeding their authority in carrying out directions by the Speaker which they had not been authorised by the King to do. Even successive Kings probably did not know what powers the Serjeants in the Commons had originally been given and were not inclined to interfere. While the original arrangement seems to have been reasonably clear, therefore, and must still stand, as far as we know, over the passage of time it became confused in the minds of those concerned. Abuses of the right to freedom from arrest continued, causing the privilege again to be restricted, and it would not be until 1770 that an Act of George III would return the privilege to its ancient limits. This would state that freedom from arrest was guaranteed to members of Parliament only, not to their servants, and that the privilege was not to interfere with the administration of criminal justice.

A third common privilege claimed was the right to punish persons for contempt, whether committed by members or by others who had caused offence. Each House exercised this on its own behalf. Thus, in 1548, the Commons committed one of its members, John Storie, to the Tower, probably for having spoken disrespectfully of the Lord Protector, the duke

---

48. G. R. Elton, *The Tudor Constitution*, 261.

of Somerset. The member for Grantham, Arthur Hall, who published a book derogatory to the authority and power of the Commons, was in 1581 expelled by a unanimous vote, fined 500 marks, and sent to the Tower. Even less to the credit of the Commons was its treatment of one, Floyd, who was not a member, but had expressed his satisfaction with the success of the Catholic cause in Germany. The Commons in 1621 fined him £1000 and condemned him to stand in the pillory. The Lords resented this assumption of judicial power, causing the Commons to admit, after searching for precedents, that they had no jurisdiction, except where the privileges of their own House were infringed.[49] Not that this benefited Floyd, for the Lords condemned him to a more severe sentence.

As the Commons were not an executive body, it is difficult to see where they could have found the authority to punish outsiders, except on the grounds of contempt of court, but as it was Parliament in its judicial role that was the court of law, this was not a matter for the Commons. Disrespect to his Parliament was surely a matter for the King. It would seem, therefore, that it was only in respect of misbehaviour by its own members that the Commons could claim a jurisdiction, and even there, a serious breach of the peace of his Parliament, or anything offensive to the King himself, was a matter for his attention. Rules of behaviour and accepted punishments would seem to have been necessary to avoid arbitrary acts or troublesome judicial proceedings. There seems to be no evidence that such rules existed.

23.2.1.3.ii. Privileges of the Lords

Privileges that were specific to the Lords numbered four. The first and most important of these was the right of each Peer, as a hereditary counsellor to the Crown, to have audience with the King. Only in this way could the right to advise be implemented in full. The second privilege was the right of every Peer to be tried by his equals, that is, his fellow Peers. As we have noted, it was a privilege that traditionally extended to each of the Estates, but it was clearly asserted in the case of the Lords. The third privilege was that any Bills that affected the Peerage must originate in the Lords. The fourth was the right of every lord, originally by virtue of

---

49. F. W. Maitland, *The Constitutional History of England*, 244–5.

a royal licence that was seldom refused, to appoint another as his proxy. This right was destined to be abolished voluntarily in 1868.

The fourth privilege of the Lords – and this must have been in their capacity as the Great Council – related to the appointment and dismissal of the King's Ministers. In 1341, objections and allegations were raised in the Lords against certain office-holders of the Crown and the Commons demanded that ministers be appointed by the Parliament, and there be sworn to obey the law. This was another device to make ministers accountable to Parliament, and it was acceded to by Edward III, but later repudiated by him. It was seen how, in 1386, Parliament demanded that the juvenile and uncrowned Richard II remove from office certain ministers whom he had appointed without consulting the Great Council, and who had committed offences. It is to be noted, however, that this authority was exercised, not by Parliament, but by the Great Council. After the accession of Henry IV, in 1399, the principle was reasserted that the exercise of the royal authority should be limited and controlled by the King's Council, and that the King's Council itself should be controlled by Parliament. The obligation of the King's Council was, however, to the Great Council, of which it was effectively a standing committee. In 1404, the Commons attacked the organisation of the Royal Household and requested that the King appoint in Parliament the servants who were to compose the King's Council, and this was acceded to. This probably took place in the Great Council – the House of Lords – but we are now seeing the House of Commons endeavouring to usurp the authority of the upper House in this respect, made possible by the constitutional confusion that now prevailed. A body of regularly paid and sworn Councillors had already existed in the time of Richard II, and in 1406, in the reign of Henry IV, Parliament renewed this control by enacting further regulations, with the Commons referring to 'the great confidence which they had in the lords elected and ordained to be of the Continual Council', that is, the King's Council. The first clear case of impeachment of a minister and an employee of the Crown by the Commons occurred in 1376, when proceedings were begun against Lords Latimer and Neville and their agents. The usurpation by the Commons of the duty of the Great Council to ensure the proper governance of the people by the King was now almost complete.

23.2.1.3.iii. Privileges of the Commons

This brings us to those privileges and liberties particular to the House of Commons. The assertion of their privileges by the Commons has been described as aggressive, but, as Kenyon has suggested, it could alternatively be seen as excessively defensive, with a 'sinister' use of the rights and liberties of the people in general as justification for their own narrow, pedantic privileges.[50] While some of the privileges claimed by the Commons were undoubtedly necessary to the effective working of the Parliament itself, the House displayed a strong tendency to appropriate others for its own benefit. Thus, the Lord Chancellor rejected an attempt in 1585 to insulate members from any judicial process emanating from another court while Parliament was sitting. By the mid-sixteenth century, however, the Commons had acquired the right to decide whether a man was qualified for membership of the House. In 1553, for example, it agreed to the rejection of Alexander Nowell, on the grounds that, as a prebendary, he was already a member of the Convocation of the Church. In other words, he belonged to a different Estate, and so could not sit in the Commons. It should be kept in mind that the members of the House of Commons in the sixteenth century were not the ordinary freemen of England, but effectively an oligarchy of the more affluent landowning class.

Elections to Parliament were the responsibility of Chancery, which issued the writs, received the returns, and compiled the list of members. It also attended to any disputed or irregular election. As Elton has expressed it, however, 'the Commons crept into this business through their established claim to judge the qualifications of elected members'.[51] It marked the beginning of a long-term policy of the Commons to disentangle itself from the provisions of the Constitution. The House had already, in 1376, asserted its interest in the regulation of the election of its own members, during the reign of Edward III, and its concern had been acted upon by his successor, Henry IV. In 1581 the House appointed a permanent committee to deal with disputed election returns. In 1586, following what was alleged to be a rigged election in Norfolk, the Privy Council ordered the issue of a new writ. The matter was raised in the Commons, and in spite of an instruction from the Queen not to interfere, the Commons appointed a committee and decided in favour of

---

50. J. P. Kenyon, *The Stuart Constitution 1603–1688*, 25.
51. G. R. Elton, *The Tudor Constitution*, 264.

the original election. In its report, by a committee of the whole House, the Commons expressed the view that it was 'prejudicial to the privilege of the House to have (the matter) determined by other than such as were members thereof'. In effect, the members were asserting a prior right, over that of the Lord Chancellor, to hear and determine all matters affecting the validity of elections to the Commons. The question at issue was: who had the right to decide whether or not a member of the House had been properly elected, the King (through his Chancellor), who had summoned the members, or those summoned? It was a question that was inherent in the representative system, which had been imposed by the confederate basis of government. Both sides had an interest in effective consultation between King and people, which implied fair representation, but the elected members were concerned that, if the regulation of elections were left to the King, he would be able to manipulate them, in order to secure consent to proposals that might be unpopular. Against this, the existing members of the Commons might be inclined to ensure control by a faction. The two sides to this argument would become clear in the case of the Long Parliament of 1641, when the King was effectively deprived of his authority and the House of Commons rigged its own election in favour of the radical Puritans.

In common law, it may reasonably be assumed that the independent arbiter in the case of a disputed election was the Great Council, now sitting in its restricted capacity as the House of Lords. Fortunately, in the Norfolk case of 1586, the Chancellor and judges came independently to the same conclusion as the Commons, that is, that the original election be upheld, so that the issue did not come to a head. Disputed elections were one thing, but the right to call an election was another. The Chancellor refused in 1681 to issue a writ for a new election until the Commons had removed a member who had been convicted of felony, and so notified him of a vacancy.

The expansion of the powers of the House of Commons did not go unchallenged, even by its own members. Arthur Hall, in 1579–80, published two pamphlets in which he not only violated privilege by revealing proceedings in the Commons, but attacked its excessive claims to privilege and disproved its notions of ancient precedent, accusing it of being 'a new person in the Trinity'. The Commons reacted by fining, expelling and imprisoning him. Although the Queen subsequently remitted the fine and the imprisonment, Hall 'had only succeeded in presenting them with a splendid precedent for their powers to fine and imprison and in general to sit in judgement on a member for things done outside Parliament'.[52]

In addition to these privileges, certain lesser rights were claimed by the Commons, one of which was the right to elect a Speaker. Because Edward III had split Parliament, causing or allowing the commons to set themselves up as an independent corporate body without the King, they discovered the need for a foreman to manage their proceedings in the King's place. Such an appointment was now claimed to be a right. It had to be an approved right, otherwise the King would refuse to recognise him and the new House of Commons would be helplessly inarticulate. The first step was taken in this direction in 1376, when the still amorphous group of Commons appointed a 'foreman, or presiding officer. In the following year a newly elected foreman was presented to the Lord Chancellor by the Commons as their chosen 'parlour et procuratour', or 'speaker and agent', and it was in this year that the Parliament rolls contained the first mention of a 'speaker', which office, under that title, has since been continuous. It then became usual for the Crown to approve and confirm him as Speaker, whereupon it was regarded as the duty of the Speaker to claim, of the Crown, all the rights and privileges of the Commons, lest they be forgotten.

As indicated in the Speaker's representation, one privilege of the Commons was its right of access to the person of the King. By withdrawing to a separate chamber, even another building, for the purposes of deliberation, the Commons cut itself off from contact with the King. In order to complete its task, it might be necessary for the Commons to have word with the King, in which case, either the King would need to attend the deliberation, which was not very likely, because the Commons had chosen to withdraw from his Parliament, or the Commons would need to send a representative in the form of their Speaker. In practice, access to the King was now through the medium of the Speaker, taking the disintegration of Parliament a step further.

---

52. Ibid. 265.

A privilege of the Commons was said to be its right to confer with the Lords on all questions of importance that called for a joint response to the wishes of the King. The Lords took the view that it was the duty of the Commons to deliberate first, and then to report their views to the Lords, who would then be in a position to advise the King. The Commons, on the other hand, took the view that mutual discussion should take place between committees appointed by each House, and the first instance of this was in 1373. Next, the Commons pressed for the right to choose which lords they should negotiate with, and in 1402, the Commons won the agreement of Henry IV to its conferring with a select committee from the Lords on certain important matters. The King stipulated that this was granted as a favour, and not as a right. No doubt, the King was concerned lest the two Houses form an alliance against him. His approach to the issue was based on feudal doctrine, one implication of which was that the King granted such privileges only out of generosity. Indo-European tradition, on the other hand, saw no need for such a concession, because it brought king, lords, and commons together in common assembly anyway, in order that the king could request, the lords could advise, and the commons could decide. The right of conference between commons and lords was therefore implicit under that tradition.

Another privilege was closely related to the freedom of speech, in that it required the King to place the most favourable interpretation on proceedings in the Commons. In other words, he was not to take offence at anything reportedly said in the Commons, nor, indeed, to take note of anything that he might hear from the Commons, except from the mouth of the Speaker. In this way, members of the Commons were not prevented from criticising the Crown and serious conflict between the King and the House of Commons was to some extent avoided.

The Commons claimed the right to initiate money Bills. As noted above, this, like other privileges, was achieved in the reign of Henry IV, as the result of the confrontation in 1407 between the Commons and the King. The latter had believed that it was the proper procedure for such Bills to originate in the Lords, no doubt because it was the function of the Lords, as the Great Council, to advise the King of any need for taxation, including its purpose and the amount. He was disinclined to persist with this in the face of opposition from the Commons, whose function was to approve such Bills.

In order to judge the appropriateness of taxes sought by the Crown, a claim was laid to *the right to appropriate supply to specific purposes*. Once again, this must have been a responsibility of the Lords, but the Commons was perfectly entitled, in approving supply, to be assured as to how it was spent. The need for this right had grown out of the practice whereby some Kings requested a tax for one purpose, of which the Commons was likely to approve, and then spending it on something else. With the Great Council unable to direct the King, the latter had become very much a law unto himself. Kings were inclined to the view that the way in which the royal revenues were spent was their prerogative, which to a large extent it was, at a time when they had been elected to make such decisions, but they no longer represented, or were answerable to, the people, leaving the King with little reason not to divert his revenues to other purposes. It was often the case, therefore, that the King was irresponsible in the manner in which he spent money. Even feudal dogma was predicated, however, on the assumption that the King would exercise his power wisely, but under a religious system where transgressions and irresponsibilities could be forgiven through private confession and the giving of lands or moneys to the Church or to charity, the restraint on fiscal irresponsibility had little moral basis. Faced by the inability of the Great Council to supervise the system, the Commons was only too glad to appropriate the function to itself.

Closely related to this was the right of the Commons to audit the royal accounts. This was won in 1341, when Edward III agreed to a demand by the Lords and Commons that commissioners be appointed to audit the accounts of those who received money granted for the financing of the war. Although the right was afterwards repudiated by Edward, it was again granted in a more general form in 1379.

A further right, established in the reign of Henry IV, was to regulate the election of its own members. Members of the House of Commons were chosen under a writ directed to the sheriff. It was therefore a matter of vital importance to the Commons to regulate both the procedure of the sheriff and the qualification of the electors. From the outset, it would seem that the right to choose the representative knights was vested in the whole body of freemen and freeholders, and not limited to the lesser tenants-in-chief. Local elections for Parliament were still held in the shire assemblies, but these had suffered a severe decline, with most of their judicial functions appropriated by the Crown Assize courts and by the Quarter Sessions, presided over by the Justices of the Peace. Moreover, freeholders were no longer required to attend their monthly sessions in person, and manipulation of the elections by the sheriffs was widespread. In 1376, in order to prevent such malpractice, the Commons petitioned that the knights of the shire should be chosen by 'the better folk of the shires', but Edward III insisted that they be chosen by the common consent of the whole county, as had no doubt been the custom.[53]

This was declared in a statute of 1406, which stated that the election of knights from the shires for Parliament should be held by all those present in full shire assembly.[54] These, 'for the most part', comprised people who were later held to be of 'small substance and of no value', but the King was insistent on retaining customary practice, while the Commons were keen to limit voters to people of some standing. Until 1406, it had been the duty of the sheriff to report to Parliament the names of the elected members. However, following 'on the grievous complaint of the Commons of the undue election of the knights of shires for Parliament', in other words, rigged elections, the statute required that, after the election, the names of those chosen should 'be written in an indenture under the seals of them that did choose them'. This was then sent into Chancery. Shortly afterwards, in 1410, the justices of assize were given statutory power to enquire into the returns, and to fine sheriffs who returned persons who had not been duly elected. It was noted earlier that the responsibility for dealing with disputed elections resided with the Lord Chancellor.

It has been claimed by some writers that the practice of making money grants, or supply, dependent upon the redress of grievances by the Crown was also a privilege, but this was merely a tactic against which the King could do little. It was a simple process of bargaining which implied

---

53. H. Taylor, *The Origin and Growth of the English Constitution*, 526, 527.
54. It would seem that elections were held in the shire assembly, the ancient *scirgemōt*, because they were not a judicial process. The assembly did function as a judicial shire court, albeit with certain changes of participants and procedure. Failure to distinguish between the administrative and judicial aspects of its work means it is invariably referred to as a shire court.

equality between Commons and King. The principle of such bargaining can be seen as early as the charters of 1225, when Henry III made concessions to the three Estates in exchange for a grant of a fifteenth part of all their movable goods. This horse-trading with the Crown did not become established as a normal parliamentary practice, however, until the time of Henry IV, at the beginning of the fifteenth century. In terms of parliamentary procedure, therefore, it became accepted that, in response to a request by the King for a grant, the Commons would put forward, in a petition to the Crown, such grievances as required relief at the time. The success of this tactic gave the House of Commons a vested interest in the initiation of money bills, a right upon which it was now insistent. The tactic also had the effect of widening the scope of the Commons. Instead of being an assembly which approved, rejected, or approved with amendments, the King's initiatives, it was now an assembly which also proposed policies, a function that belonged properly to the Great Council, which was now barely able to exercise it. There is no reason to doubt that, in the assemblies that were the antecedents of the House of Commons, it was quite usual, and almost inevitable, for a variety of issues to be raised by the crowd, which the King had little choice but to respond to. In theory, such issues should already have been brought to the King's attention by the Great Council, but the Council could not be aware of all public issues, particularly those affecting particular interests and communities. It was limited, therefore, in what it could bring before the King to those matters that were of particular importance. The King might, in any case, have chosen to ignore them. Consequently, the assembly, and now the Commons, undoubtedly had an ancillary purpose in drawing attention to issues that had not been dealt with. Seen from this point of view, the raising of grievances was not a privilege but a normal function.

23.2.1.4. The Reformation Parliament of 1529–31

The failure of Cardinal Wolsey to obtain from the Pope an annulment of the marriage in 1529, between Henry VIII and Catherine of Aragon, left the King with no alternative but to achieve his aim through the use of his own authority and the support of the people. Wolsey was replaced as Chancellor in October of that year by Sir Thomas More, the first lay

Chancellor since 1381,[55] and the King confiscated York House, Wolsey's palace at Westminster.

A Parliament, which became known as the Reformation Parliament, because of Henry's intention to use it for the reform of the English Church, was summoned to meet at Blackfriars late in November 1529. During its proceedings, the lords spiritual found themselves under great pressure from the commons, supported by the lay lords, to relinquish various entitlements of the Church, which they found themselves eventually forced to concede. During the following year of 1530, after the Parliament had been adjourned, the King, ably assisted by his new minister, Thomas Cromwell, found ways of putting the bishops under much greater and more direct pressure, through a charge of *praemunire* – in effect, of asserting or maintaining Papal jurisdiction in England – on the grounds that the whole clergy of England had supported Cardinal Wolsey's authority as Papal legate. More than a year passed before the adjourned Parliament held its next session, this time at Westminster in January 1531. Meanwhile, a few days before the Parliament reassembled, the Convocation of Canterbury met in the Chapter House of Westminster Abbey. The charge of *praemunire* had not been pursued, but the Convocation struggled to win a restoration of royal favour by agreeing to a very substantial grant to the King. Even this did not appease Henry's anger, and further demands were piled upon the Convocation, including its recognition of the King as 'Protector and Supreme Head of the Anglican Church and Clergy'. After several days of negotiations, during which the clergy succeeded in having the words 'in so far as the law of Christ allows' added to the title, the archbishop, on February 11, put the question for their decision, adding that 'silence gives consent'. 'Then we are all silent', someone replied, and their consent was considered to be unanimous.[56] Eventually, the Convocation of York also made a grant to the King, but the bishop of Durham and others entered a strong protest against the King's new title.[57] The German Imperial ambassador recorded on 1 March 1531, that it was not until late on that day that the King first appeared in the Parliament since it had been reconvened, and had

---

55. *Letters and Papers*, iii. 2681.

56. Ibid. v. 71.

57. Wilkins, *Concilia*, iii. 744–5; R. W. Dixon, *History of the Church of England* (1884–1902), i. 61–7; J. E. Powell, and K. Wallis, *The House of Lords in the Middle Ages*, 565–7.

remained for the best part of two hours in the Lords' House, but did not go down to the Commons.[58] It seems to have been not unusual for the King to visit the Lords, therefore, as he is reported as doing on this occasion, while they were engaged in their deliberations. Whether he ever visited the Commons is not clear. However, the reference to the King not going down to the Commons implies that the latter were deliberating close at hand, probably in St Stephen's Chapel, because there must have been little likelihood that he would have walked all the way over to their former meeting place in the Abbey. Indeed, as we shall see, the move from the Abbey probably took place around 1530.

Henry VIII was forced, because of the unwillingness or inability of the Pope to annul his marriage to Catherine, and because of the opposition of the lords spiritual, to rely on the use of his own authority and the support of the people, in order to obtain his divorce. Cardinal Wolsey had been replaced as Chancellor in October 1529, by Sir Thomas More.

23.3. Whitehall, the Court of St James and the Presumptuousness of Corporate Parliaments

The removal of Cardinal Wolsey in 1529 seems to have led to a general re-location of activities at Westminster, beginning with the confiscation by the King of York House, which was Wolsey's palace at Westminster, and Hampton Court, in Middlesex. Before the year was out, the King moved his residence from the Palace of Westminster to York House, which, confusingly, he re-named 'White Hall', later Whitehall (not to be confused with the White Hall or White Chamber in the Palace of Westminster). This was followed, in turn, by a re-location of parliamentary proceedings at Westminster.

Henry was attracted to York House, because, being located a little to the north of the Palace of Westminster and, like it, adjacent to the Thames, it was agreeably situated close to the royal palace. Henry now appended to White Hall a convenient hunting estate immediately to the west. Much of this estate was to survive into modern times as a series of public parks, notably St James's Park, Hyde Park, Kensington Gardens

---

58. *Letters and Papers*, v. 60.

and Regent's Park. Just as Henry's palace at Westminster had become the venue for the holding of Parliaments and the Law Courts, so White Hall now became the main seat of royal authority, where the Privy Council met and the King's Ministers had their offices. It was not long before the abbreviated spelling, 'Whitehall', came into use. This geographical relationship, with Parliaments meeting in the Palace of Westminster and the executive housed at Whitehall, was destined to continue to the present day.

Meanwhile, with accommodation still so limited at Westminster, Henry began the construction nearby of a new palace in 1532. This was St James's Palace, a little to the north-west of White Hall, and this became his official residence. It has remained the official residence of all Monarchs to the present day, and it is to the Court of St James that foreign ambassadors are still accredited. As a result of this separation of royal and parliamentary accommodation, and in recognition of the grant of the permanent use of the Palace of Westminster for their deliberations, an emblem of the house of Tudor, the portcullis, was adopted by Parliaments as their insignia.[59] From now onwards, Parliaments invoked the authority of the Tudors as their own, appropriating to themselves a specious claim to a permanent, corporate status that was quite alien to the nature and purpose of a Parliament, which is merely a consultation for the purpose of providing advice. A Parliament existed only from the moment that it was summoned into being until it was dissolved. By affecting to assume a permanent, corporate identity, the 'members' of Parliament, as they now perceived themselves, gave notice that they no longer were a manifestation of the people, but appeared to be claiming, in effect, to be the successors to the Great Council. By so doing, they appeared to be giving vent to an ambition to becoming the central feature of the Constitution. It was a development that represented a growing affectation that offered to the people some benefits for the future but worrying implications of potential oligarchy.

At the beginning of 1533 the issue of the royal divorce became urgent, when it was discovered that the King's mistress, Anne Boleyn – who must have given way to Henry's demands – was pregnant. Faced with the option of a successor who would be illegitimate or himself open to a charge of bigamy, Henry married her secretly at White Hall

---

59. The portcullis insignia was acquired by the Tudors from their Beaufort ancestors, notably Margaret Beaufort, mother of Henry VII, and became the symbol of Tudor legitimacy.

on January 25. Now anxious to pursue the reform of the Church and its independence from Rome, but without compromising its position as the legitimate Church of England, which he saw as the basis of his authority, the King bribed and threatened the Pope into appointing Thomas Cranmer, Anne Boleyn's chaplain, as Archbishop of Canterbury, which he did on March 30. The Convocation of the clergy now declared that no Pope could grant dispensation for such a marriage as that between Henry and Catherine, and in so doing, the Convocation cancelled, in effect, the Church's approval of the marriage in the first place. Parliament thereupon abolished appeals to Rome by approving an Act that stated that England was competent to settle all cases in its own courts. For the first time since the Norman Conquest, the English judicial system had asserted its independence.

By now, a number of the universities that had been approached concerning the legitimacy of Henry's marriage to Catherine had advised in Henry's favour, and Cranmer accordingly pronounced the marriage null and void. The marriage was then formally annulled on May 23, and the Pope vainly responded by excommunicating Henry and annulling the divorce. Nevertheless, the King's divorce and re-marriage to Anne Boleyn were not popular in England, for Catherine was highly regarded, and when Anne was crowned at Westminster shortly afterwards, on 31 May 1533, the crowds who watched were quiet and sullen. In September of the same year, Anne gave birth to a daughter, Elizabeth, leaving Henry with two daughters but still no son.

Having thus committed himself, Henry in 1534 set about consolidating his control over the Church and severing its remaining ties with Rome. In an Act of the same year, Cromwell denied that canon law had any validity in England, thereby contradicting the earlier view of Sir Thomas More that canon law was the law of Christendom, to which, by implication, statute law was subordinate. Cromwell and the King had the benefit, however, of a growing Protestant reform movement that had the sympathy of Parliament. This led to various Acts that prohibited payments to, and the receipt of dispensations and licences from, Rome, culminating in the Act of Supremacy of 1534, which effectively marked the beginning of the English Reformation. This proclaimed that the King and 'his heirs and successors kings of this realm, shall be taken, accepted and reputed the only supreme head on earth of the Church of England', his rights as such being summarised in the preamble as being 'to have authority to reform and redress all errors, heresies and abuses of the same'.[60] The later institution of Queens regnant was therefore not included. As noted earlier, the Act was superfluous in its administrative sense, because the King's temporal authority over the Church had always been a royal prerogative in common law. Allegedly surrendered to the Pope by the Norman rulers, it was now restored to Henry by this and related Acts. In fact, it had been restored once before, in 1351, when, under the Statute of Provisors, Edward III had assumed the title of 'patron paramount' of the English Church, effectively displacing Papal authority. The basis of this prerogative undoubtedly lies in the priestly function of kingship, whose origin goes back to Indo-European times. It was now set out formally in another statute, which empowered the King to appoint bishops, a right that he had exercised as a matter of course during Anglo-Saxon times. A further Act for the Submission of the Clergy required all measures passed by the Convocation to be submitted to the King for approval, thereby reasserting, in effect, the constitutional position of the Convocation as a part of Parliament, representing, under the new arrangements since Edward III, the first House of Parliament. This gave the King effective power over both the clergy and ecclesiastical law, with the Court of Chancery now appointed as the final court of the Church.

In the same year, Parliament confirmed Henry's divorce and Elizabeth as his heir. Moreover, an Act of Succession, also passed in 1534, ordained in precise terms the future devolution of the Crown, and in so doing, departed from the previous practice of simply accepting the present King and his heirs in general. Declaring the Princess Mary illegitimate, it provided that any son born to Henry VIII and Queen Anne, or as the result of any other marriage contracted by the King thereafter, had priority as heir to the throne.

Henry had little difficulty in persuading Parliament and the people to break with Rome. Much as he was anxious to secure Papal recognition, Henry had shown a truculent attitude towards the Church even before his marital problems appeared. His central problem was to secure an heir to the throne, which successive wives had been unable to provide, and

---

60. 26 Henry VIII, c.1.

divorce was forbidden by Church doctrine. Important as it was to Henry, it was by no means unimportant to the country as a whole, which had endured enough from family and dynastic rivalries over the Crown. By himself becoming head of the Church of England, Henry ensured his own freedom to produce an heir. Being a formidable and not unpopular ruler, he was acceptable in this position, the more so because he left most of the effective religious headship of the Church to the Archbishop of Canterbury. Unfortunately, it was a solution that was destined to leave England rent over religious matters for several centuries to come, because, although the majority of the people either favoured or were willing to accept Protestantism, there remained a powerful minority who rejected it, and even the Protestants broke into factions.

23.3.1. Influence of Accommodation on the Development of Parliament

23.3.1.1. The Commons Move to St Stephen's Chapel
As the parliamentary session of January 1531 continued during most of the time that the Church Convocation was being held in the Chapter House, this raises the question of where the Commons were meeting. The removal of the King's residence in 1529 to the new palace of White Hall would have left more space available in the Palace of Westminster,[61] and the Commons must have been accommodated somewhere in the Palace in this year, if not a year or two earlier. The Chapter House had been inconvenient to the Commons, because it involved a considerable walk to and from the Parliament chamber, and also for informal discussions with the Lords in the White Hall.

Later evidence appears to support the view that they may have moved into St Stephen's Chapel. The Chapel had been designed to accommodate assemblies, and the new Protestantism had given rise to a more cavalier attitude towards sacred buildings. For the Commons to use the Chapel, the altar must have been removed. An expenditure recorded for the year 1549–50,[62] for 'sundry charges made and done in and upon the Parliament House at Westminster, sometime Saint Stephen's Chapel', has been assumed to be for the purpose of making the building ready for

---

61. J. E. Powell, and K. Wallis, *The House of Lords in the Middle Ages*, 566, footnote.
62. J. Field, *The Story of Parliament* (London, 2002), 76–7.

use by the Commons, but the statement in the accounts already shows a familiarity with the building as 'the Parliament House', and its designation as a Chapel seems already to be a memory. The work undertaken was probably not to convert it, but to provide for the better convenience of the Commons, well after they had begun to hold their meetings there. The alternative possibilities, that the Commons had returned to the Chapter House after 1531, or that the Commons had been using another chamber of the Palace during the intervening twenty or so years, are both inherently less likely. The only other likely accommodation in the Palace was the Queen's Chamber, which was probably too small and inconvenient of access. The Chapel, being close to the Parliament Chamber and to the Lords in the White Hall, allowed for greater speed in the conduct of business.

Henry VIII saw in the Commons a valuable ally against the Church, and in 1531 he needed to have the Convocation also close at hand, so that he could keep a close watch on its proceedings and interfere as necessary. The Chapter House was convenient for this, as well as being Church property, so that evicting the Commons and ordering them to use St Stephens – which was the King's chapel, to do with as he wished – would have been a logical solution. Consequently, the move to St Stephens probably took place around 1530.[63] St Stephens Chapel offered a more satisfactory place in which to meet, and it had the added advantage that it was adjacent to the White Chamber, where the Lords met. So much of English constitutional history was influenced by problems of accommodation. The Chapel became known as the 'Parliament House', where they were to remain for the next three hundred years. This was the third move by the Commons, having been transferred in their deliberations from the Painted Chamber to the Chapter House of the Abbey in 1352, then, some fifty years later, they had been moved to the Abbey Refectory, where they had met for well over a hundred years, until their move to St Stephen's Chapel. Once made, the transfer of the Commons to the Chapel probably became permanent, because Henry VIII saw the Commons as a valuable ally against the Church, and the Chapel, being close to Parliament and to the Lords in the White Hall,

---

63. Elton places the move in 1549, see *The Tudor Constitution*, 248.

allowed for greater speed in the conduct of business. They were to remain in St Stephen's Chapel for the next three hundred years.

A print of the House of Commons in session, made sometime after the move, shows the members seated around three sides of the elongated chamber, facing inwards, those on either side making use of the old Chapel stalls.[64] This left an elongated space in the centre, so that the majority of the members faced each other across the floor. On the fourth side was the Bar beyond which was the entrance to the chamber. The short return stalls on the fourth side provided some cross bench seating outside the Bar, due no doubt to the limited space. Behind the cross-benches was an original wooden screen, which separated the chamber from an ante-chapel, and supported a loft, from which services had previously been sung. The ante-chapel served as the Commons' lobby.

Towards the eastern end of the chamber was a dais, reached by a short flight of steps, upon which, on a small platform, was the Speaker's chair, from which he was afforded a view of the proceedings, including plaintiffs who appeared at the Bar of the House. Above the chair was the royal coat of arms. In front of the dais was a table, at which sat two clerks with their backs to the Speaker. On the table were books and papers used by the clerks, upon which was later placed the Royal Mace. It was convenient for the Speaker to be seated near the centre of the chamber, where he could best hear what was being said, although many members were seated behind him. The seating arrangement, whereby the majority of the members faced each other across the chamber, has been credited with inducing an adversarial attitude that helped to give rise to the later two-Party system. The print in question illustrates what appears to be a petitioner, kneeling at the Bar, and being introduced to the Speaker by a gentleman-at-arms, bearing the Mace.

A later illustration of 1653 shows that the dais had been removed, leaving the Speaker's chair on just its raised platform, but there appears to be a red stripe on the floor of the chamber, along the front of the benches on either side of the chamber, where the members' feet normally rested.[65] The stripe seems to have marked a limit, beyond which members were not allowed to stray into the centre of the chamber. Its purpose was probably to ensure that members did not obstruct the view from the

64. J. Field, *The Story of Parliament*, 73.
65. Ibid. 121.

Speaker's chair, or access each other to indulge in physical altercations. Meanwhile, the Bar, previously and properly a barrier, such as a rail, was now reduced to no more than a white line across the floor at the entrance to the chamber. This undoubtedly made it easier for members to enter and leave the chamber, but it detracted from its solemn significance. In the Lords, the Bar was retained as a bronze rail.

It was said to be the practice for members entering the chamber to bow their head. It has been suggested that this was either out of reverence for the former altar, or to avoid losing tall hats when passing through the screen.[66] A much more likely explanation is that the practice was out of deference to the presence of the King, represented by the Mace. The Chapel came to be known as the 'Parliament House', and here the Commons were to remain for the next three hundred years.

23.3.2. Extension of the Bar and Mace to the Commons

Mention was earlier made of an important procedural difficulty that had faced the commons when they retired to the Chapter House of the Abbey, in that their deliberations there were conducted outside Parliament, where they did not form a part of its proceedings. Also, they were not protected by the common law that had applied to all popular assemblies since antiquity. The ensuing advice of the Commons to the King would certainly have been included in the proceedings of Parliament, but not the discussion leading up to them.

Such was the hubris of the members of the Commons that they must have been keenly aware of this, and the move to St Stephen's Chapel – or St Stephen's Hall, as it had now become – was evidently seen as opening at least the possibility of extending the definition of the proceedings of Parliament in some way. By moving into the former Chapel, they were at least back within the Palace complex, separated from Parliament in the Painted Chamber only by the White Hall, where the Lords themselves deliberated. There is no evidence that the Lords were concerned by this problem. In any case, to the extent that they saw themselves as sitting as a Great Council, it was not an issue.

Only a few years after the Commons' move, the White Hall itself had become the Parliament Chamber, which it adjoined, and was reached

---

66. Ibid., 76–8.

from the Chapel by no more than a very short passage. This may have provided the Commons with the opportunity that it sought, to petition the King to recognise the Chapel as an extension of the Parliament chamber. To this end, two steps were taken, undoubtedly with the King's consent. One was to make the ground on which the Commons sat for the purpose of deliberation into an extension of the hallowed ground of Parliament itself, and this was only possible by treating the Chapel as an exclave of Parliament. That part of the floor of the former chapel on which the deliberations took place were hallowed and defined by a 'Bar', leaving the remaining part of the chamber, used for other purposes, outside the Bar. The walls of the Chapel formed a natural Bar on three sides, and the fourth side, beyond the rail or bar, adjoining the entrance, left sufficient space for visitors. It may be felt that there was a certain irony about the earlier deconsecration of the Chapel, before it could be used by the Commons, only to re-consecrate it for the purposes of a Parliament, but it was no function of the Christian deity to witness the agreements entered into, and laws passed by Parliaments. That was for a far older deity. In any case, Parliaments had no place in Church doctrine.

We shall find that the same principle applied for many centuries to the use of parish churches as places in which contracts and agreements were concluded, even though the reason was soon forgotten. Most of these early parish churches had the advantage of being located on ancient pre-Christian sacred sites, so that the church porch was used for the purpose in order not to offend the Christian deity. The human mind works on more than one level, and we find, over and over again, that the sub-conscious racial memory plays an important part in constitutional practice. It explains the importance that was clearly attached to the protection of the work of the House of Commons, by means of the Bar and sanctification.[67] The religious character of the work of Parliaments was certainly maintained, even if it was confused. Each session of the Commons began, and still does, with prayers, invoking divine guidance.

The problem of hallowed ground, on which to hold the proceedings of the House of Commons, was not the only detraction if the House was a part of the proceedings of Parliament. The other was the absence of the King, whose immediate or delegated presence was crucial to the

---

67. Ibid., 73.

lawfulness of the proceedings, if the aspirations of the Commons were to be met. It was the King, after all, who summoned Parliaments to seek their advice and consent. A solution was found in two ways. One was for the Speaker's chair to be emblazoned with the royal coat of arms, as shown in a contemporary illustration of the Commons in St Stephen's Chapel, previously noted, and the second was the sending by the King of an armed knight, holding the rank of Serjeant-at-Arms and bearing the Royal Mace – or a replica of it – to the Commons.[68] His intended function seems to have been twofold: to guard the Mace, which he is shown holding, and to ensure the respect due to it by maintaining order in its presence. The Serjeant-at-Arms was evidently placed on attachment to the Commons for the duration of each Parliament, usually several weeks of each year, as a reminder of the King's presence. Subsequently, a place was found for the Mace on the clerks' table, in the centre of the chamber, where it could rest in full view of those assembled while Parliament was in session. He was evidently regarded by the Speaker as being subject to his direction, like a servant, and rendering the position of the Serjeant-at-Arms as increasingly ambiguous.

The Serjeant-at-Arms remained in the King's employ, because neither the Commons nor the Parliament itself was other than transitory (as indeed was the King himself, although the Crown, as the executive arm of state, was a permanent institution). Parliament was not a corporate body, so that neither it nor the Commons was in a position to own property or employ people.[69] Each Parliament was unique, with a life-span usually of weeks, and in spite of the hospitality provided by the King, the Palace of Westminster belonged to the Crown. Nevertheless, the same individuals tended to be returned as representatives of the commons, time and again, creating an illusion of entitlement, and with it a growing sense of power that members enjoyed from their control over much of the King's revenue. This encouraged a perception among members of Parliament that they constituted an oligarchy at the centre of the Constitution, whose authority derived from their position, collectively, as the permanent representatives of the people.

---

68. A Serjeant-at-Arms could be in the service of any lord, not only the King, and was usually one of a number whose purpose was to arrest traitors and other offenders.

69. The Great Council, confined inside the House of Lords, was certainly a permanent institution, but this did not make the House itself permanent.

It is not surprising, therefore, that the Commons were soon taking advantage of their newfound dignity and the opportunities provided by the Serjeant-at-Arms and the Mace. It seems to have become the practice to use them to extract members who had been arrested and imprisoned for debt. This was famously illustrated in the Ferrers Case of 1543, which is more fully described above. Consequently, the practice was exploited to such an extent that, by the seventeenth century, the privilege of rescuing members arrested for debt had reached the point where it was almost impossible to get justice from any member of Parliament, and limits had to be set on what had become an intolerable nuisance.

It is plain that the negligence of the Tudors in leaving the members of their Parliaments to assert their own privileges extended also to the position of the Sergeant-at-Arms, whom the Commons began to regard as their own officer, with the Mace being perceived, not as the presence of the King, but as the authority and dignity of the Commons. It was a tendency that was destined to increase under the Stuarts.

23.3.2.1. Parliaments Move to the White Chamber (1536)

The Parliament of 1536 was opened, not in the Painted Chamber, where it had invariably been opened for at least two hundred years and probably longer, but in the larger White Hall or White Chamber. This had long been known as the Lords' House, and it continued to be used for their deliberations. The reason for the Parliament's change of venue seems to have been that it avoided the inconvenience and cost of preparing the Painted Chamber for the opening of each Parliament, and it was destined to continue thus until the nineteenth century. As a result of the change, the White Chamber became known as the 'Parliament Chamber', and it also would so remain until the nineteenth century. Meanwhile, the Lords retained their use of the White Hall for the purpose of deliberation when Parliament was not sitting.

23.3.2.2. The House of Lords in Tudor Times

The gradual disappearance from the House of Lords of those members of the Privy Council who were not of the greater baronage had the effect of promoting the concept of the Peerage in the House, and hence the perception of the Peerage as simply a privileged body. Not all members of the greater baronage were members of the Great Council, although they were entitled to attend both it and the House of Lords, which had now displaced it. It became the practice from the reign of Henry VIII onwards to extend the summons to all members of the greater baronage who sought it. In an effort to restrict attendance to those whom the King wanted as his councillors, private instructions to stay away were simply passed to those whose presence was not desired. Conversely, Peers who opposed the King apparently had no difficulty in obtaining a licence for their absence.[70] The Tudor period also witnessed the effective secularisation of the Lords. Under Henry VII there were forty-nine bishops and abbots in the House, and fifty-two under Henry VIII, but thirty-one abbots were removed with the dissolution of the monasteries between 1536 and 1539, and only five bishops were appointed in their place, so that by Elizabeth's reign there were only twenty-six lords spiritual. Meanwhile, the number of lay lords attending had been reduced by attainder, absenteeism and suspension to twenty-nine by the time of Henry VII, but by about 1530 their number had been increased again to between 50 and 60.

Because of the principle that the King should only raise a tax with the consent of the taxed, it had always followed that each group taxed itself, at a rate and on a basis acceptable to itself. This was inevitable, because the financial circumstances of each group – now reduced to the greater nobility, on the one hand, and the lesser nobility and commons on the other – had always differed quite considerably. The determination of taxes in the House of Lords was now the responsibility of a committee of the lords, appointed by the King and headed by the Lord Chancellor and the Lord Treasurer.

Journals of the proceedings of the lords were apparently kept by the clerk from 1497,[71] although the earliest surviving example is that for 1510, and the series, in so far as they have survived, is continuous only from 1554. The surviving journals were rebound in 1717, and an order was made in 1767 that they be printed, together with those rolls of parliament for the sessions for which the journals had been lost. Journals of the proceedings of the commons were kept from 1542. The lords' journals confirm that the normal seating arrangement of Parliament had always been based, so far as is known, on the principle that the clergy

70. G. R. Elton, *The Tudor Constitution*, 247, footnote.
71. *Journals of the House of Lords*, xiv. 537.

sat on the King's right, and the lay lords on his left. There were certain exceptions to this rule, however, in that:

- the Archbishop of York and his two bishops also sat on the King's left, above the laity
- the duke of Buckingham and the marquess of Dorset stood on the King's right, with the clergy, while holding the royal regalia

There was an exception to this on those occasions when the Archbishop of York was a cardinal, because this made him senior to the Archbishop of Canterbury. Thus, in the case of Kemp in 1449, and Wolsey in 1523, York sat on the King's right, above Canterbury, and his two northern bishops also followed him across to the 'spiritual' side of the chamber. Otherwise, it was not unusual for disputes to arise over precedence.

The King continued to preside over his Parliaments just as he had presided over the Great Council. In his absence the King was represented by his prime minister, the Lord Chancellor, who still appears to have sat, while the King was present, on the benches at the opposite end of the chamber. In the King's absence, he probably occupied the woolsack immediately in front of the throne. The remaining three woolsacks in the centre of the Chamber were occupied by those members of the King's Council who were not lords, notably the judges, the serjeants at law and the masters in Chancery. They had no voice in the House, but they played an important part as advisers and assistants, who often drafted bills. In 1539, the seating arrangement was fundamentally rearranged. An Act of Henry VIII of that year, which arranged the precedence in the order of sitting in the House, provided for the presence of leading Privy Councillors, such as the Lord Chancellor, Lord Treasurer, Lord Privy Seal, Lord President, and the Principal Secretary, as well as certain great officers of the Royal Household, if they were not of the greater baronage, just as the Constitution appeared to require, but in practice they did not avail themselves of the opportunity, with the exception of the Lord Chancellor. Many, in fact, sought election to the House of Commons.

Three of the four woolsacks in the centre of the Lords' Chamber were replaced in the reign of Elizabeth I by upholstered benches, with wool, no doubt, still being used for the upholstery. The exception was the woolsack immediately in front of the throne, which was now replaced by a wool-stuffed red hassock, still called 'the Woolsack', and this was now reserved for the exclusive use of the Lord Chancellor. Thus, 'the Woolsack' acquired a status of its own. It preserved the tradition of the use of woolsacks, but it could also serve as a reminder of the importance of wool to the Exchequer in the Middle Ages.

23.3.2.3. Tudor Parliaments

Good constitutional relations were helped by the practice of the Tudors of ensuring the election to Parliament of a good number of devoted Privy Councillors and royal officials. This ensured good liaison between the Crown and Parliament. The cooperation of Parliament was also assisted by the moderating influence of the Speaker, who, being chosen from among the senior members of the House, was himself made a Privy Counsellor, so that it had now become the practice for the Speaker to be nominated by the Privy Council. Many Speakers went on to prominent careers in the Government service. Henry VIII occasionally attended both Houses in person, and in 1536 he is recorded as himself presenting a Bill, although he was more inclined to have deputations wait upon him, so that he could influence members more directly.

The role of a Parliament was well understood in the Tudor period. As Sir Thomas Smith, author of *De Republica Anglorum*, or 'On the Commonwealth of the English', wrote in 1565, Parliament is 'the most high and absolute power of the realm', where consultation takes place 'to show what is good and necessary for the commonwealth': the barony for the nobility, and 'the knights, esquires, gentlemen and commons for the lower part of the commonwealth', with final decisions being made by the King. He went on to emphasise that every Englishman is intended to be there present, either in person or by procuration and attorneys ... and the consent of Parliament is taken to be every man's consent. Smith was not only commending the harmony of the Sovereign and people in Parliament, but making a clear statement of the constitutional principle that Parliament was the assembly of the whole people, not of the small group actually present in the Commons chamber, however representative they might be. This point was confirmed by Richard Hooker, writing about 1595, who stated that a Parliament 'consisteth of the King and of all that within the land are subject unto him; for they are all there present, either in person or by such as they voluntarily have derived their very personal right unto.'[72] That this principle underlying Parliament had survived the eight centuries or so, in such a decisive form, since it had last been possible in practice, seems to be further evidence that it had never lapsed – a Parliament, whether as a *Folcgemot* or as a General Council, had always remained open to any free man who chose to attend and be consulted.

By 'Parliament', both Smith and Hooker meant the Lords, as well as the Commons, for it was clearly accepted that, for an Act of Parliament to have validity, it must have the consent of both Houses. Thus, in 1489, the judiciary agreed unanimously that a certain act of attainder was no act, because, although it had the authority of the King and the Lords, 'nothing was said of the Commons'.[73] Hooker went further, referring to 'the Parliament of England, together with the Convocation annexed thereto'. By this he meant that, although the First Estate continued to meet separately in Convocation, it was still regarded as a part of Parliament, so that all three Estates were still included.[74] The religious aspect of Parliament's proceedings was also alluded to by Smith, when he stated 'that which is done by this consent is called firm, stable and sanctum (i.e. made sacred or inviolable), and is taken for law'. Its judicial function is also mentioned, in that Parliament 'defineth of doubtful rights whereof is no law already made', and, 'as the highest court, condemneth or absolveth them whom the (King) will put to that trial'.[75] Some remarks by contemporary commentators would be cheered by many modern authorities, in particular, a statement that the Lords were superfluous to Parliament: 'The King with his commonalty may keep the Parliament along, for the Commons have every one of them a greater voice in Parliament than hath a lord or bishop'.[76] It was an indication of how far the balance of power had shifted, and how well this was realised.

---

72. R. Hooker, *Works*, iii. 408–9.

73. A. F. Pollard, *The Reign of Henry VII from Contemporary Sources* (London, 1913), 19.

74. There were always two Convocations, one for each province of the Church, but Hooker viewed them as one, just as Parliaments in the Middle Ages were sometimes held in more than one place at the same time, for the sake of convenience.

75. *De Republica Anglorum*, 48–9.

76. *A Discourse upon the Statutes*, 113. Found also in the fourteenth century *Modus Tenendi Parliamentum*, for which see N. Pronay, and J. Taylor (eds.), *Parliamentary Texts of the Later Middle Ages*, chapters 1 and 2.

All contemporary illustrations[77] evidently depict the fully assembled Parliaments of Henry VIII, Elizabeth I, and James I, because the members of the House of Commons – only the front row of whom are usually visible – are gathered at the Bar of the Lords in Parliament. One of those at the Bar, in the case of the Elizabethan Parliament, is evidently the Serjeant-at-Arms of the Commons, as previously pointed out, because he is shown holding the Mace from that Chamber. The members of the Commons in the Elizabethan Parliament are shown as wearing swords, indicating that the prohibition in common law against the bringing of weapons to a Parliament was not being observed. In the Stuart Parliament of James I, some from the Commons are shown holding staves, others wearing swords, and others with neither. There is no evidence of weapons among the Lords.

In the King's absence during a Tudor Parliament, which was now usually the case, the Lord Chancellor assumed responsibility for the proper conduct of debates, applying the rules and traditions of the House of Lords and maintaining good behaviour. He was also an essential channel of communication, acting as the spokesman of the Lords in representing their views to the King, and in turn passing on the King's views to the Lords. Nevertheless, the Lords were jealous of their freedom to deliberate without being subject to the King's influence. The contradiction was resolved by the House regarding the Lord Chancellor's seat on the Woolsack as being outside the precincts of the House, so that the King's representative was precluded from taking any actual part in its debates. This only created another difficulty, however, because the Lord Chancellor was not only a high officer of the Crown but a Peer in his own right, and it was accepted that he could not be deprived of the freedom to speak in his personal capacity. This he could do only by stepping down from the Woolsack into the precincts of the House. In so doing, he temporarily discarded his office as Lord Chancellor and resumed the mantle of an ordinary peer for so long as he needed to make his contribution.

From 1522, the Lord Chancellor was assisted in his maintenance of order in the Lords by a Gentleman Usher, who was the King's personal attendant in the House. Previously, the usher's duties had been concerned

---

77. J. Field, *The Story of Parliament*, 83.

mainly with the requirements of the Order of the Garter, so that he had been formally known as the Gentleman Usher of the Order of the Garter, an office that had probably been created about the same time as the Order, around 1348. When Henry VIII redrafted the statutes of the Order in 1522, however, the Gentleman Usher was made an official of the Lords, where his main function was to maintain order and act as the King's personal attendant in the House. He was most readily identified by his staff of office, an ebony rod, surmounted by a golden lion, usually referred to as his 'black rod'. This gradually became incorporated into a new title, that of Gentleman Usher of the Black Rod. Nothing is known of the origin of the black rod itself, but the instrument was undoubtedly a form of sceptre, which, as we saw earlier, had a very long history in Aryan society as a symbol of sacred power, rather than physical authority. One duty of 'Black Rod', as he was apt to be known, was to summon the Commons to the Upper Chamber, that is, to form a full session of Parliament, in order to hear speeches from the throne or to receive notice of the royal enactment of Bills.[78]

An illustration, this time of a Parliament itself in session,[79] made during the reign of Elizabeth I, 1559–1603, shows members of the Commons assembled at the Bar, because the chamber was not large enough to accommodate the members of the Second Estate and the representatives of the Third. One figure, standing prominently at the Bar, is probably the Speaker addressing the Queen, while another is shown holding the Royal Mace of the Commons. It is likely that the scene shows the Speaker delivering the response of the Commons to the Queen's request to Parliament. Meanwhile, the Sovereign's own Mace appears to be held by a figure, probably the Chancellor, standing at the foot of the throne on the Queen's right.

23.3.2.4. The Constitution is Distorted by the Difficulties of Accommodation

The King's Chamber – also known as the Painted Chamber – which he made available, was evidently not satisfactory, perhaps because of its poor acoustic properties, and the Painted Chamber, the White Chamber, the Abbey Chapter House and the refectory at the Abbey were all used,

---

78. Improperly referred to as 'the royal assent', for which, see later.
79. J. Field, *The Story of Parliament*, 83.

at one time or another, for different purposes. In particular, the use of the Chapter House, and later St Stephen's Chapel, for deliberating by the commons, and the use of the White Chamber by the lords, with the Painted Chamber being used only for the opening and closing of Parliaments, led to a substantial and permanent disintegration of the parliamentary process. Eventually, the Painted Chamber was abandoned, and the formal opening and closing of Parliaments were transferred to the White Chamber, which was already used by the Lords. The Lords now found themselves holding their deliberations in the Parliament chamber again, while the Commons continued to be absent during most of the proceedings. It was an attempt to remove this anomaly that deemed St Stephen's Hall, where the Commons met, to be sanctified ground as an extension of Parliament, and caused the King to despatch his Mace to lend legitimacy to their proceedings.

The outcome was an articulated institution of three separate 'houses', meeting only occasionally as a Parliament, and, in case of the Clergy, not at all. The Church Synod overcame its loss of influence by insisting that its bishops in the House of Lords sit in their capacity as ecclesiastics, rather than as barons. The effect of this division into 'Houses' was to accentuate the separate identities of the Estates and promote rivalry. The House of Commons, having asserted its independence, displayed a growing ambition to displace the House of Lords as the chief influence on the control of royal policy. The House of Lords, meanwhile, was increasingly confused as to its own role and position. Thus, Parliaments were losing most of their coherence, reducing themselves to little more than ceremonial opening and closing sessions. This disintegration left the King more isolated. With the decline of the Great Council, and the loss of its legislative advice and constitutional supervision, the Crown was less constrained, but the initiative in legislative policy passed increasingly to the Commons.

It may be remembered that the practice of summoning elected representatives to attend Parliament, on the basis of separate constituencies based on the shires, had its origin in the confederate basis of the English Constitution. The full attendance of all free men still applied to the shire assembles, except that they had long ceased to exert a meaningful influence, and had been in decline for centuries.

23.3.2.5. Parliaments as Instruments of Change

The legislative performance of the Reformation Parliament, between 1529 and 1536, had a significant effect on Parliament's perception of itself. Until the 1530s, Kings had, constitutionally, called their Parliaments because they sought their 'advice' on the application of common law to particular issues.[80] The notion of elaborating common law to deal with new situations, in effect, creating new law, was still developing. Largely confined, hitherto, to approving new taxes, Parliaments were now being called upon to deliberate over, and consent to, Bills that were altering the whole nature of England and its relations with the outside world. This bred a new confidence that a Parliament's authority – and particularly that of the House of Commons – was unlimited, by comparison with which the scope of the royal prerogative was restricted. The whole emphasis of the perception of the Constitution was shifting: hitherto, government had been left to the King, with Parliament called upon to approve his more important proposals; now, Parliament had become an engine of radical change, albeit at the King's behest, leaving only mundane issues and details to the royal prerogative. That the new mood did not have a greater impact was due to the sheer political stature of the King himself, and his capacity to intimidate Parliament. Even so, Henry recognised his reliance on the Commons in this hour of need, and the fact that it had able men on its benches. Consequently, and for the first time, some of the King's Ministers were drawn from the Commons. The oft held idea that, from the time of the Reformation Parliament, this institution emerged as a new, legislative, rather than advisory, body, is mistaken, because all legislation involving Parliament was consent to proposals of the Crown, but there is no doubt that, from now onwards, Parliament was seen as a means of achieving change, rather than simply granting taxes. It was a reflection of changing needs, not of constitutional change.

The perceived expansion of parliamentary competence during the 1530s gave rise to a new, but muddled, concept of 'the King in Parliament', which was seen as superior in authority to that of the King alone. This perception of the enhanced status of Parliament was based on the idea of a change in its jurisdiction in regard to religion. Before 1529, limitations were believed to exist on the religious jurisdiction

---

80. G. R. Elton, *The Tudor Constitution*, 234.

of Parliament, exemplified by St German in his *Doctor and Student*, published around 1528.[81] This expressed the view that a statute of Parliament must be consonant with the law of reason and the law of God, and that by 'reason' was meant the law of nature. Any statute that was directed against the law of God would be void. As has been pointed out, 'If one thing was quite certain before the Reformation it was that statute could not touch matters spiritual because by the law of God these were reserved to the Church'.[82] A dictum arising from a case in 1506 alleged that 'no temporal act can ... make a temporal man have spiritual jurisdiction'.[83] This has been contrasted with the Acts of Parliament after 1529, which dealt habitually with 'the spiritual jurisdiction exercised by the King (a layman) as supreme head'.[84] The problem with this argument is that, constitutionally, as previously established, the King was not only a layman. He was also a priest.[85] St German rightly made the point that Parliament had no power to overrule the law of God. This was a recognition of the three functional Estates, where no Estate – in this case the Second and Third – could override the rights of another – in this case, the First, which held its own Convocations on spiritual matters. It was also a recognition of the Indo-European principle that human law must be consistent with *ius divinum*, the law of the gods, of which it was no more than a rendering. As Parliament's authority in common law extended to anything that the King might do in temporal matters, other than those that lay within the royal prerogative, the legislative development of the 1530s was notable only in the sense that Parliament was now being called upon to consent to legislation that went well beyond matters of taxation, hitherto the extent of the rights of the King in relation to the people.

Nevertheless, there was a perception at the time, not only that the scope of Parliament had been increased, but that there were many things which the King could do through Parliament that he could not do alone. In other words, it was a recognition that the royal prerogative was very limited in its scope. It was this that gave rise to the notion of the 'King in Parliament' as distinct from the King alone, and this in turn gave rise

81. C. St German, *Doctor and Student*, 27–73.
82. G. R. Elton, *The Tudor Constitution*, 237.
83. Quoted in C. H. McIlwain, *The High Court of Parliament and its Supremacy*, 277.
84. G. R. Elton, *The Tudor Constitution*.
85. The Church itself endowed the King at his coronation with divine authority, but only in temporal matters.

to a misleading doctrine of the sovereignty of Parliament. Thus, John Aylmer in 1559 would remark on 'the Parliament House, wherein you shall find these three estates: the King or Queen, which representeth the monarch; the noblemen which be the aristocracy; and the burgesses and knights the democracy ... If Parliament use their privileges the King can ordain nothing without them. If he do, it is his fault in usurping it and their folly in permitting it'.[86] It was this idea, quite correct in itself, that the King, with the assistance of Parliament, was superior to the King in person, which was accepted by the Tudors. It was a distinction that has persisted to the present day, its essence being that the royal prerogative is limited in its scope and that statute overrules edict. As we have seen, it was an unnecessary distinction, because the common law – *mos maiorum* – appears to subject all acts of the King, other than those of a more personal nature, to the consent or tolerance of a Parliament. But in the fifteenth and sixteenth centuries the influence of feudal thinking had left a degree of uncertainty as to the respective prerogatives of King and Parliament which the new concept of 'the King in Parliament' helped to resolve. The change in the nature of Parliament which took place about this time was not determined entirely by the demands of Henry VIII. Indeed, it was between the time of the accession of his predecessor, Henry VII, and the end of Cardinal Wolsey's rule that the system of master-records, known as the Roll of Parliament, was replaced by a Journal in the House of Lords and a clerk's book in the Commons. Legislation that had been approved was now defined in a printed sessional statute. By 1530, the King's Great Council, sitting in its uncomfortable role as the House of Lords, had reconciled itself to displaying the same courtesy towards the Commons as it had expected from them.

The break with Rome returned the Church, from being the Church of Rome in England, to which it had been confined since the Norman invasion of 1066, to its original role as the English Church, or Church of England. The Church before 1066 had acknowledged the Pope as its spiritual head, but for all administrative and even liturgical purposes it had been subject to the King, a relationship justified constitutionally, by his priestly function. The only real difference after 1534, compared with pre-1066, was that the Church no longer recognised even the spiritual

---

86. J. Aylmer, *An Harborowe for Faithful and True Subjects Against the Late Blown Blast Concerning the Government of Women.*

significance of the Pope. The change was also of great importance, in that it freed society intellectually. It was a shift that was reflected in the decision of the universities in 1535 to replace lectures in canon law with lectures in civil law.

Henry's break with Rome made his position vulnerable, for the Pope had excommunicated Henry in 1535 and affected to deprive him of his kingdom. This posed a serious risk of invasion by the Catholic countries, France and Spain, and Henry again set about improving England's defences. This was a task that demanded considerably more money than Henry had available, causing him to cast around for a major new source. Meanwhile, the King perceived an important threat to his new position as coming from the monasteries, whose allegiance to the King in matters temporal, and to the Pope in matters spiritual, had never really been in doubt. What was now in doubt was their willingness to accept the King in place of the Pope in spiritual matters. Increasingly, however, his eye fell on the huge wealth of the monasteries, so that their laxity and corruption now played into his hands. Perhaps more worrying in Henry's eyes was the strong link between the monasteries and the people. The monasteries were often hated for their corruption, but they were also a vital source of succour for those in need. In a superstitious age, they were seen as enjoying the literal protection of God, and Henry was unlikely ever to be accepted as head of the Church by the people if the monasteries rejected it. It was here that a brilliant solution offered itself. If the monasteries were dissolved, their lands and associated property would lawfully revert to the Crown. Not only would this rid the King of an important source of opposition to his new position as head of the Church, but, by appropriating their wealth and selling off their lands, buildings and other assets, he would realise more than enough money to meet his huge defence needs. Luckily, a breathing space was afforded by a war, which now broke out between France and Spain, over their conflicting ambitions in Italy and Spain's acquisition of Milan. Meanwhile, the practical effect in England of the dissolution of the monasteries would involve a massive transfer of wealth from the former monasteries to the construction of a defensive wall around southern England, in the form of a series of coastal fortresses of advanced design and the re-building of the fleet.

There were no real differences at first in dogma and theology between the independent Church of England and the Church of Rome. However, the Lord Chancellor, Thomas Cromwell, was also a religious reformer, and the King now appointed him to the new post of Vicar General. In this capacity he was the King's deputy in matters relating to the Church in England, and he put into effect a plan for the seizure of the Church's wealth. A commission for the inspection of all religious houses resulted, in 1536, in an 'Act whereby all religious houses of monks, canons and nuns which may not dispend manors, lands, tenements and hereditaments above the clear yearly value of £200 are given to the King's Highness, his heirs and successors, for ever.' In other words, it provided for the dissolution of the lesser monasteries and the transfer of their property to the Crown. Thus, the dissolution amounted to a transfer of property to the Crown by Parliament – whose approval was probably not needed, but was certainly desirable – in response to a petition. It was a procedure designed to make the acquisition legal and seemingly less outrageous. Once acquired by the Crown, the monasteries were then sold, mostly to wealthy landowners. By destroying these monasteries with no sign of divine wrath, Henry demonstrated to the people that his new position as Head of the Church in England had the approval of God. The same year saw the dissolution also of the Reformation Parliament, the first in history to continue for so long a period as seven years. In a fit of enthusiasm for the change taking place in the country, the Speaker of the Commons compared Henry VIII to the sun dispelling all noxious vapours and ripening all things good and necessary. Henry, however, was content to ascribe it all to the glory of God.

This happy state of affairs was just a burst of sunlight in the otherwise stormy year of 1536. At the beginning of the year Henry was wounded in the leg and suffered a heavy fall while jousting. It was an accident from which he never fully recovered, the injury and the misguided treatment keeping him a semi-invalid with a badly ulcerated leg. Over-indulgence over the years, expected of a successful ruler, caused excessive corpulence and poor health that, in total, badly affected his capacity to rule. Henry's attentions had also turned to another lady-in-waiting, Jane Seymour. The still loyal but saddened Catherine died in 1536, reducing the risk of invasion. The position of the Queen, Ann Boleyn, was now vulnerable, and various explanations have been suggested for her fall. She had been in conflict with Cromwell, may have been seen by him as a threat to his authority, and had antagonised many at court, but the charges of adultery that were brought against her were almost certainly spurious. In the same year of 1536, the King's marriage to Anne Boleyn was declared invalid, and shortly afterwards she was executed at the Tower. Parliament proclaimed her daughter, Elizabeth, to be illegitimate, a judgment that was confirmed by a second Act of Succession, and only a day later, and eleven days after the execution of the previous Queen, Henry and Jane Seymour were married.

These developments aroused considerable public opposition among that section of the population that was still loyal to the Catholic faith, but the religious issues provided an umbrella for a variety of other discontents. The rebellion began in Lincolnshire in 1536, where it soon petered out, but it was taken up much more strongly in Yorkshire, under Robert Aske. The antipathy was directed, not so much at the King, as at Cromwell, but by the end of the following year it was all over. The year of 1536 was significant also for Wales, when the King ended the chronic disorders of the Welsh Marches by incorporating all Wales into England. Several of the marcher lords who had been a particular problem were executed. Thus, a comprehensive political and administrative union of Wales with England was achieved, and would be completed by the granting, in 1541, of Welsh representation in English Parliaments. Nevertheless, the mountains of north and central Wales continued to shelter the Welsh language, and with it a strong sense of separate Welsh identity in the north and west until modern times.

Henry's alliance with Jane Seymour, meanwhile, seems to have been a happy marriage, and it was more fruitful, but Jane died in 1537 after the birth of her child, a son named Edward, leaving the King's grief to be at least tempered by the realisation that he had, at last, a male heir. The war between France and Spain, which had been occupying the attention of the Pope, meanwhile, was over by 1538, leaving him free to direct his attention elsewhere. Deciding that it was time to restore his authority in England, he ordered the excommunication of Henry to be put into force. It seemed to have no practical effect, but it added to the concern that

France or Spain, or both, would attempt a restoration of Catholicism in England through invasion.

With the smaller monasteries already dissolved, another Parliament in 1539 passed an Act for the Dissolution of the Greater Monasteries. Probably one sixth of all the land in England was thereby transferred into the King's possession, and this, in turn, was either given away or sold off to raise revenue, a very large part of which was used to build, along the south coast, the intended series of fortresses. Meanwhile, the new owners of the abbeys, mainly gentry and nobility, either adapted the buildings for residential use, as in the case of Lacock Abbey, or, in most cases, simply plundered the abbeys and priories for building materials, leaving them to fall into ruin, while the monks were pensioned off. The element of English society that probably gained most from the redistribution of monastic lands was the middle class, many of whom were wealthy merchants, who were thus able to establish themselves among the landed gentry. Overall, the dissolution brought about a considerable transfer of wealth and power from the Church to the middle class. Hitherto, imposing dwellings had been the castles and fortified manor houses of the nobility and wealthy gentry, designed as much for defence as for habitation, in which life had centred on the great hall, as it had done for a thousand years. One of the most obvious consequences of the disappearance of the monasteries, using the stone and lead so pillaged, was the construction of great country houses, which proliferated across the land, and which often dwarfed and outclassed the royal palaces.

The new trend, encouraged by the security and prosperity brought by the Tudors, was tempered by the influx of new ideas from the Renaissance. It was a tradition that was destined to last for three hundred years. It was symptomatic of the English Constitution that, apart from such exceptions as Henry VIII, the real power in the land was wielded by the leading nobility, the men who comprised the Great Council, or House of Lords, to whom the King turned for advice, but these were now supplemented by the landed gentry who controlled Parliament. The abbots and greater priors who had once formed a majority in the Great Council and the House of Lords, now ceased to sit, leaving only the archbishops and bishops in Parliament. One consequence of the Reformation and the dissolution of the monasteries, therefore, was that the Lords Temporal now formed a clear majority, and twenty years later, during the reign of Henry's younger daughter, Elizabeth, the number of lords sitting ranged between 78 and 91, of whom only twenty-six were Lords Spiritual, all of them bishops.

The destruction of the monastic tradition and its edifices in England coincided with a surge of Protestant feeling among the ordinary people. It found particular expression in antagonism towards what was regarded as idolatry, and this resulted in the destruction of images in and around churches and cathedrals, including Becket's shrine at Canterbury. This rejection of all forms of religious idolatry was reflected also in a shift in the nature of church music. Previously, music had been regarded as a form of prayer, but this was now seen as a form of idolatry, like dancing, in which the words were subsumed into the music. It was the spoken word that was now important, and music had to be adapted so that it was merely an accompaniment to the words. Medieval church music, with its chanting and complicated melodiousness, went into rapid decline, to be replaced eventually by the hymn.

The King attempted to stem this growing Protestant influence by the Act of Six Articles, of 1539, in which he set out the points of Catholic doctrine that were still to be followed. The break with Rome had also made it necessary to provide the English Church with new institutions and courts, and the enforcement of ecclesiastical law began with the issue, in each province and diocese, of temporary commissions for ecclesiastical causes. These were proper courts, composed of both clergy and laity, and their powers were very wide. They were not linked to each other or with the ordinary courts, and there was no provision for appeals. The most important of these 'commission courts', established by the King in his capacity as Supreme Governor of the Church of England, was that known as the Court of High Commission, whose jurisdiction was confined to the clergy of the Church. Later, Elizabeth I extended its scope, one of its main targets being the Popish priesthood. It came to be regarded as the court of appeal of the lower ecclesiastical courts, which routinely sat in judgment in cases of matrimonial and family law, usually involving laymen exclusively. As a result, the High Commission changed its jurisdiction from the clergy to almost any crime that could be brought within the purview of Christian morality, and it was able to impose almost any punishment short of mutilation or death.[87] A Court of Augmentations dealt with specific cases affecting the augmentation of the King's revenue from Church sources.

There was an element of contradiction, therefore, in Henry's religious policies. Even after the break with Rome, Henry had at first remained loyal to Catholicism, but his reading of Protestant texts had weakened his attachment. He acknowledged the growing tide of Protestantism by allowing certain reforms, most notable of which was his sponsorship of the English Bible, known as the 'Great Bible', which was published in 1539 and distributed to every church in the land. Nevertheless, in the Act for the Advancement of True Religion, four years later, the King forbade the labouring classes to read scripture. Thus, Henry felt his way in prescribing the new religious practices, choosing a compromise course between the Protestant radicals and the Catholic conservatives, as a result of which the newly emerging Church of England was the focus of a compromise religion that failed to satisfy either side.

A little over two years elapsed after the death of Jane Seymour before Henry married a fourth time, in 1540. Cromwell, under the mistaken assumption that the King's marriage intentions were political, and being anxious to nudge the King along the path of religious reform, scoured Europe in search of a wife of Protestant leanings and good family background. Henry's political isolation by the Papacy having left him exposed to possible invasion by the French or the Habsburgs, or both (the Habsburgs being the most powerful dynasty in Europe, whose various branches ruled both the German Empire and Spain),[88] a continental alliance, was therefore seen as advisable, preferably with Germany, but the only one of Protestant upbringing willing to take the bait was Anne, daughter of the Duke of Kleve, or Cleves, on the lower Rhine. Finding no way of meeting her without compromising both, Henry took Cromwell's advice and agreed, on the strength of a flattering miniature portrait and Cromwell's assurance that Anne was 'beautiful'. The choice was disastrous.

---

87. J. P. Kenyon, *The Stuart Constitution 1603–1688*, 158.

88. They were descended from the Count of Habsburg (*Habichts-burg*, hawk's-castle, in the north of what is now Switzerland), whose descendants rose through fortuitous marriages to become Holy Roman Emperors. One son of the Emperor, Maximilian I, was Philip the Fair, Duke of Burgundy, who in 1496 married Joanna the Mad, daughter of Ferdinand and Isabella of Spain, and thereby inherited the Spanish crown. Joanna's sister, Catherine of Aragon, had married Henry VIII of England, by whom she was divorced.

Of strict upbringing and naïve, Anne was determined to be a good wife, but Henry was horrified, and despite an effort to make the best of a bad business, the marriage seems not to have been consummated, and he divorced her six months later. Furious over the fiasco, and largely as a punishment for his disastrous counsel, the King took his revenge on Cromwell. Since 1459 and the anarchy under Henry VI, an Act of Attainder had sometimes been used without either a conviction in law or a manifest act of treason, and Henry VIII had resorted to this on several occasions as a means of disposing of enemies whose offence had fallen short of treason, or who would have defended themselves successfully in a trial.[89] A Bill of Attainder was now used against Cromwell, on the basis of a charge of treason, and he was executed in 1540. Anne, too ashamed to return home, remained in England for the rest of her life.

More serious attention was now turned to Ireland. Henry had hitherto been Lord of Ireland, but, following a revolt and its suppression, he arranged in 1541 for the Irish Parliament to elect him King of Ireland and head of the Irish Church. In the following year, Ireland was formally declared to be a kingdom. Thus, Henry VIII succeeded, in effect, to the position once occupied by the High Kings of Ireland, although his effective rule still did not extend over more than was bounded by the Irish Pale, that is, the eastern half of the island.[90] In 1547, English jurisdiction was established over the Irish Pale, which the Crown already controlled.

Meanwhile, the King's attentions had turned to another of the ladies of the court, Katherine Howard, a young girl who easily fell for handsome men. Despite her doubts about the King, whom she regarded as an old man, she was given every encouragement by her influential and ambitious, but strongly Catholic family, who included the Duke of Norfolk. Besotted by her, and barely a month after the annulment of his marriage to Anne of Cleves, Henry married her. Lacking in maturity and wisdom, the youthful Katherine Howard soon fell prey to other attractions, encouraged by the increasing indisposition of the King. The reformist faction, concerned at the Catholic influence to which the

---

89. G. R. Elton, *The Tudor Constitution*, 82.
90. A pale, originally a stake driven into the ground as part of a fence, had come also to signify a boundary. Often referred to simply as 'the Pale', it was nevertheless necessary to distinguish it from the English Pale, being the English territory in France that was still controlled from Calais.

King was now exposed, and anxious to see the resumption of the reform process, searched for, and soon found, evidence to discredit the Queen. Never one to be made a fool of, Henry ordered the arrest of her two lovers, and, following their execution, Katherine herself was beheaded in 1542. In the following year he took his sixth wife, Catherine Parr, a widow with strong reformist leanings, who, faced with the choice between Henry and the man whom she had been looking forward to marrying, had decided to give priority to her sense of religious mission. A good wife and step-mother to the King's three children – Mary, Elizabeth and Edward[91] – Catherine did her tactful best to encourage the King in the cause of reform. Through her influence, also, the King's previously rejected daughters, Mary and Elizabeth, were reinstated, being recognised by Parliament as heirs to the Crown in the event of the young Edward dying without issue.

It was now the turn of the Catholic faction to have its hostility aroused, and, through the Bishop of Winchester, Katherine Parr was accused of heresy. Forewarned, she succeeded in persuading the King that the charges were ill-founded, and that, while she had often discussed religious issues with him, this had been merely out of curiosity, and that she had never intended to influence him. By her quick-wittedness, she kept her head and would succeed in outliving him.

23.3.2.6. Royal Assent to Amended Bills is Delegated (1541)

Until 1541, it had been the practice for the King to attend Parliament when giving assent to a Bill. Indeed, it would hardly seem possible for any such contract between King and people to be agreed without the presence of both parties. The King's assent was necessary, not to the Bill itself, which, according to the law of procedure, the King had submitted in the first place, but because of the amendments which Parliament often insisted on making to his Bill before Parliament would consent to it. Only if a Bill had originated from a member within Parliament, as a private Bill, would the King's assent be necessary to the Bill itself, as distinct from its actual wording. This did not preclude the King from being represented, however, and a statute of that year gave authority for commissioners to act on the King's behalf in notifying Parliament of his assent.

---

91. Mary (b. 1516) was the King's daughter by Catherine of Aragon; Elizabeth (b.1533) was his daughter by Anne Boleyn; and Edward (b. 1537) was his son by Jane Seymour.

23.3.2.7. The Royal Seals

With the development of government and the judicial system, the King's decisions needed to be beyond question. That it was said that the King had verbally approved this or that measure was no longer sufficient, and even more so over succeeding generations, who had no memory of his assent. Enduring evidence of this was accordingly provided by the use of the King's seal, which could not be fraudulently duplicated because it was placed in the care of the King's most senior officer. The number of royal seals used on documents had increased by 1500 to three. In addition to the Great Seal of England, now in the possession of the Lord Chancellor, and the Privy Seal, which was held by the Lord Keeper of the Privy Seal – who was now referred to simply as the Lord Privy Seal – there was the King's Signet, now held by his Secretary.[92] They fulfilled a variety of functions. The Great Seal was also used to authenticate all original writs, that is, initiating actions at law, and certain other writs, such as writs of summons. It was also used by the Court of Star Chamber. The Chancery, which did the work associated with the use of the Great Seal, had long been the centre of government, but by the fifteenth century it had been the office of Privy Seal that had become the centre, because it collected administrative orders from all the King's officers and redistributed them to subordinate executive officers. This office in turn lost its primacy in the 1530s as individual officers were provided with courts and seals of their own.

The making of grants, in effect the disposal of royal patronage, required the applicant to submit his petition, which then received the royal approval, expressed by the King's signature. This practice had received formal recognition under a Council ordinance of 1444. The application was then passed to the Signet Office, which then forwarded it as a warrant bearing the royal Signet to the Privy Seal office. This in turn, by means of the Privy Seal, authorised the Chancery to affix the Great Seal, which alone carried legal force, so making possible the actual grant. Each office was entitled to fees from the applicant.

Seals now ceased to play a major or originating part in the process of government, and their place was taken by the Secretary. Until the reign of Henry VIII, the King's Secretary had functioned as a confidential servant

---

92. There were, in addition, the seals of the Exchequer and of the courts of common law, but these were simply smaller replicas of the Great Seal.

concerned with the King's correspondence, having charge of the royal Signet, and being familiar with diplomatic negotiations. Sometimes he had been a member of the Privy Council. His position was that of Principal Secretary, in order to distinguish him from the other secretaries of French and Latin, who were employed to write diplomatic correspondence in those languages. The first layman to hold the office was Thomas Cromwell, who made good use of his hold on the affairs of the realm and his freedom from routine duties, so that, by 1539, the importance of the office of Principle Secretary was second only to that of the high officers of state and of the Household. The position declined when Cromwell relinquished the office, but the Principal Secretary remained a key figure, and a warrant of 1540 divided the Secretaryship between two holders, of equal standing. This was partly because the volume of work had become too much for one, and partly because Henry's continued absence from London made it desirable to have one Secretary at Westminster and another at court. Later, they occasionally reverted to only one Principal Secretary, and by the end of Elizabeth's reign it was becoming usual to describe him as the Secretary of State.

In financial arrangements, Wolsey continued the 'Chamber system' introduced by Henry VII, whereby the revenue, other than customs, was managed in a semi-organised fashion by the Royal Household. Wolsey's successor in managing affairs, Cromwell, favoured a return to the old system whereby the revenues were handled by the Exchequer, rather than by the Household. The situation was greatly affected, however, by the new influx of revenue from the annexation of the monasteries, causing Cromwell to introduce wider reforms. These involved the creation of new departments, known as courts, for specific sections of revenue, the first being the Court of Augmentations in 1536. Over the next six years this was increased to six great courts or departments of state, without further affecting the Exchequer or the Duchy of Lancaster.[93] The complexity of the system was also its weakness, and after Cromwell's time these courts '

---

93. The two General Surveyors of Crown Lands, established by Wolsey, became a court in 1542 for the administration of the Crown lands collected by Henry VII and Wolsey. The Court of Augmentations, 1536, dealt with new Crown lands. The Court of First Fruits and Tenths, 1534, handled ecclesiastical revenue, the title being a reference to the payment of the 'first fruits' of all clerical dignities, benefices and promotions and the payment to the King and his heirs of a pension of a tenth part of the income from all possessions of the church. The Court of Wards and Liveries, 1540, collected all feudal dues.

were gradually amalgamated and absorbed into the Exchequer, until the Household was eliminated in favour of a return to the control of all revenue by the Exchequer. The Exchequer now established its own specialised sub-departments. Outside the Exchequer remained only the Duchy of Lancaster and the Court of Wards and Liveries, but their turnover was relatively small, and from 1554 onwards most of the Crown's resources were again administered by the Exchequer. In Elizabeth's reign the courts had to decide whether sums of money had been lawfully disbursed from the King's Exchequer. This led them to insist that neither the King's word, nor his signature were sufficient, and therefore no money should be issued without the King's own warrant, and that such a warrant must be sealed with the Great Seal or with the King's Privy Seal. Many laws were to develop from this, according to which the Great Seal was indispensable for some purposes, the Privy Seal for others, and the royal Signet for others, while for some purposes the King's word was sufficient.

23.3.2.8. The Constitutional Significance and Wider Implications of the Reformation

There is a natural temptation to regard the problems that Henry VIII had with his wives and with the Church as a reflection on his irascible temperament, which involved England as a whole in problems and consequences that it could well have been spared. In his later years he was an increasingly sick man, moody and intolerant, who did not hesitate to have anybody executed who crossed his path or caused him difficulties. The major issues of his reign represented a conjunction, however, of the problems of royal succession with a major tide in European history. Popular antipathy to the corruption and other excesses of the Church, and detestation of the Popes, had been widespread even before Wiclif's day, and although the Lollards had largely disappeared as a force, their views on Christianity and the Church had remained in the population, so that Luther's manifesto in Germany fell upon fertile ground. Henry's wives played an important part in history because they were the means by which the struggle between the Protestant reform movement and the conservative Catholic element in the Privy Council, and to a lesser extent in Parliament, was played out. It was the problem of the royal wives that made possible the break with Rome – a feat that only a ruler of Henry's personality and independence of mind could have brought about – and hence the restoration of a truly national Church that was constitutionally linked to the Crown.

Before the Norman invasion, the English Church had been largely independent of Rome, and the appointment of senior clerics had been the prerogative of the King whenever he had chosen to exercise it, while leaving spiritual matters to the Church. William I had ended this relationship, making the Church independent of temporal interference, but making it subject to direct control from Rome, so that, instead of being the English Church, it became the Church in England. Henry's own view was that his greatest achievement had been the establishment of the King as head of the Church and the banishment of the Pope from English affairs. In so doing, he unwittingly restored the English Church, but, by also allowing it to assume new, Protestant features, he had converted it into a distinct Church of England, without fully acknowledging any of the priestly characteristics of Indo-European kingship. Even so, the King once again stood at the apex, as the unifying force of the three Estates. Henry did much, also, to define the relationship of Crown, Parliament and Church, the three institutions which, represented respectively by Whitehall, the Palace of Westminster and Lambeth Palace, sat in close proximity to each other beside the Thames.

The Renaissance had helped to restore the more open and free thinking of pre-Christian times, releasing men from a circumscribed world of Christian guilt and condemnation, Heaven and Hell and the Feasts of the Saints, dominated by a clergy that, for the best part of a millennium, had been organised and had imposed itself with an almost Roman thoroughness. Through the access to the culture of early Greece and Rome that it had provided, the Renaissance had opened a vista indirectly to the Indo-European past, restoring the importance of the popular will and reintroducing the more open landscape of gods and goddesses, with whom men could converse. It also imparted a new rational and critical edge to thinking. Thus, the Reformation represented a rejection of the authoritarianism of the Orient, as embodied in and propagated by the Church, in favour of popular constitutionalism. In the process it largely demolished the idea of an absolute monarch, who received his authority from and was responsible only to God. No longer was the Church accepted as the only avenue of communication between man and God. With the idea of direct access between the individual and God, the Church was relegated to the roles of providing collective access, enlightenment and personal counselling.

This emancipation of religious thought from Church domination, and the reaction against the crass worldliness to which the Church had sunk, had turned Luther's challenge of 1517 into a religious revolt of central and northern Europe. The German Empire was not a centralised state like England and France, so there was greater scope for new movements to spread, and this is possibly the main reason why Luther succeeded, whereas Wiclif had failed. Also, there had been longer for the new degeneracy of the Church to become apparent. It was no accident that Protestantism tended to assert itself most strongly in those parts of Europe where Indo-European traditions had been strongest. In any case, the effect of Church imposts and solicitings in transferring much of the growing wealth of northern and central Europe across the Alps to Rome, in order to support its own extravagance, had generated resentment in those areas. The Protestant revolution failed in those states where a strong alliance was maintained between Church and rulers, enabling the Church to ride out the storm, as in France, the southern half of the German Empire, and the empires of Hungary and Poland. This was true also in Russia, but here the Orthodox Church, having been isolated from its roots for centuries by the Asiatic occupation of southern Russia, was closer to the people and closely identified with Russian nationalism. By contrast, the Roman Catholic Church and nationalism were at odds with each other. Europe outside Russia was a kaleidoscope of nations, which bore only a limited relationship to political boundaries, and here the Papacy could only maintain its authority by identifying itself with a dynastic system that the Church could influence directly. Under such a regime, nationalism presented itself as a threat to both the system of royal autocracy and the Church.

Coinciding with the reign of Henry VIII, the spread of the Renaissance from Italy to England had the effect of reinforcing Anglo-Saxon attitudes to government, while the ensuing Reformation gave a new lease of life to the free-thinking movement that had been inspired by the Lollards. Thus, the Act of Supremacy of 1534 amounted to a constitutional counter-revolution, restoring to the King his ancient Indo-European function as the religious head of the nation. This position had always been ambiguous, in that the Aryan king had occupied the highest priestly position without necessarily functioning as a priest. The same applied to Henry and his successors. He was now head of the Church without functioning as a priest, yet as King he still had a priestly function in common law. Henry's successors in the centuries following were to exercise this in a variety of ways, such as calling the nation to prayer in times of crisis and celebration, and initiating reviews of religious belief and ritual, such as the publication of new prayer books. Henry's own view of his position in the Church was, of course, a purely pragmatic one, but it is significant that neither he nor the English people saw anything incongruous about a King who assumed the position of religious head of the nation. It reflected a survival in the national psyche of an association of priesthood and kingship.

The Reformation in England had the effect of solving one problem while creating two. Through the monasteries and nunneries, the Church had provided a social insurance system that protected the poor from destitution and looked after them in sickness. This support was now gone, and eventually it would have to be replaced by the state itself. It also brought very largely to an end the construction of splendid churches and cathedrals. The second problem arose from the fact that, although the majority of the population were carried along willingly by the change in religious allegiance, a large and influential minority still adhered to the doctrines and rites of the Roman Church, and many of them secretly hoped for the restoration of the Pope as head of the English Church. This ideological division was to give rise to acute constitutional stresses in the years to come, so that the Reformation did not fully succeed in resolving the position of the King, leaving the contradiction over whether he was the appointee of the people or of God to persist for several centuries longer.

The Reformation should not be confused with liberalism. Thus, slavery was by now of minor importance, but it still existed, and the Vagrant Act of 1547 provided for two magistrates to adjudge any able-bodied vagrant as a slave, where anybody wanted him as such. The wretch was then to be branded with a 'V', and his condition of slavery was to last for two years. Only fifteen years later, a naval commander, John Hawkins, initiated English participation in the African slave trade by capturing a Portuguese slave ship bound for Brazil, and in 1564 the Crown happily lent him a ship for the purpose of transporting slaves in return for a share of the profits.

23.3.2.9. The Royal Prerogative and the Privy Council

The Tudors inherited an effective Privy Council, which numbered about fifteen or sixteen, but under Henry VII the number was increased rapidly to forty or fifty. Under Henry VIII it returned to about sixteen, and under Edward VI the size of the Council declined further to between twelve and sixteen. Under Mary the Council shot up again to about forty, in order to accommodate her supporters, while the Council of Elizabeth I was again reduced to between twelve and eighteen. In composition, the Council in the time of Henry VII consisted of between four and eight bishops, a 'fair representation' of the greater nobility, a number of inferior clergy, some knights and esquires, or gentry, and the law officers of the Crown, notably judges, the attorney general, solicitor general, and serjeants at law. The Council of Henry VIII included an increasing proportion of commons, and this marked an important change, leading in 1536 to a complaint that the Counsellors were of humble birth. By 'the nobility' had long been meant the 'greater' nobility, so that most of the so-called commoners who held office were in fact of the minor nobility, mostly knights. The word 'commons' was used to mean representatives of the communities, not 'commoners' in the sense of persons of base, or lowly ancestry. Thus, the commons included both high-born and low-born, that is, minor nobility – who were increasingly seen simply as persons of 'good' family – and commoners. As the King showed a preference for individuals who were capable, would serve him well, and would not be independent, so the control of government slipped out of the hands of the greater nobility. In the year of Mary's accession, 1553, the Council consisted of four bishops, fourteen temporal Peers and twenty-two commoners. Even under the later Anglo-Saxon Kings, the growing discrepancy between eldership of the people and membership of the *Witan* had been sufficiently in evidence for the King to include a number of thanes, and this was again recognised from the time of Henry VIII onwards by the inclusion of selected knights from the House of

Commons, whose status now corresponded fairly closely to the King's thanes of an earlier age. The knights in the Council tended to be chosen for their usefulness, because the Council was regarded by Henry as being as much an administrative instrument as an advisory body. This legislative/executive dichotomy was one from which the Council had always suffered: counselling the King on the one hand, and implementing his decisions on the other.

For the purposes of this executive role, some members of the Council held particular offices, the most important being the Lord Chancellor and the Lord Keeper of the Great Seal, who were of equal rank. They were followed by the Lord Treasurer, the Lord President of the Privy Council, the Lord Keeper of the Privy Seal, and the King's Secretary. The Secretary was one of the common members, and it is possible that the common laymen attended in their capacity as office-holders. The standing of the Secretary was steadily rising, and soon he exceeded the Keeper of the Privy Seal in importance. Usually, the Secretary was the chief minister of the Crown, and the volume of business became so heavy that, after 1539, there were usually two principal secretaries appointed. By the end of the period they had gained the title of 'Secretaries of State'. Because the members of the Privy Council were drawn from both the House of Lords and the House of Commons, contact between the three bodies was close, allowing the Privy Council to exert a real influence on both chambers of Parliament. The knights tended to be the natural leaders of the community, close enough to the people to be personally known to many of them and able to empathise with them. They were powerful and influential men in their own districts, well educated, and brought up to be used to authority and responsibility without abusing it. Moreover, they had a more strongly English ancestry than did the barons.

The functions of the Privy Council were to deliberate and advise, and, as consequently directed and delegated by the King, to administer or judge. Where this was impracticable, for example, in the case of judges in the courts of common law and in minor or urgent executive decisions, the King delegated his *imperium* through a stick or other instrument of office, the inference being that the officer advised the King on each matter, and that advice was accepted and responded to as an instruction. Thus, the principle that the people's *imperium* had been given to the King, not to his judge or minister, was preserved.[94] The proceedings of the Council were fairly informal and were held in one of the two rooms adjoining the Great Hall that were known as the Star Chamber, or *Camera Stellata*. The Council met regularly only during term-time, that is, in the periods when the law-courts were in session, and there were attempts to limit the hearing of suits to certain days, in order to leave time to attend to affairs of state.

Henry VII usually attended the Privy Council's meetings, and when he did he dominated its proceedings.[95] Sometimes the Council appointed committees, and these could be either standing committees or *ad hoc* committees to deal with particular problems. Apart from its judicial aspect, indeed, the committee system in the Privy Council became highly developed, dealing mainly with problems of legislation, administration, and taxation. In order to administer this, the King appointed a Lord President of the Council in 1497. Although head of the Council, the Lord President exercised no real power and the office became little more than an honorific title. In practice, the King presided, and if he was not present, this role was performed by the most senior officer attending, such as the Chancellor or Treasurer. Meanwhile, the matters receiving attention could range widely, such as the state of the coal industry in Newcastle, the prices charged by clothiers, assessing the damage done by the raids of the Scots, or arranging to ensure that a particular individual was elected to the next Parliament, or an alleged case of villeinage, that is, subjection to servitude. Effectively, it was now the Privy Council that governed the country, guided by the King, with Parliament being resorted to only as legislation was required. It was the only body that was now referred to simply as 'the Council', because the Great Council had, by the time of Henry VII, all but completed its transformation into a House of Lords.

The active existence of the Council was normally limited to the sixteen weeks of the law terms, because the King had to go on his travels, and most of his Councillors had interests to attend to in their own parts

---

94. It was the Great Council, now sitting in its capacity as the House of Lords, that was the custodian of the *imperium* bestowed upon the King, but it could not be used on its own authority, unless it took the grave step of deeming the King to have violated his regal contract with the people. For this it needed to be sure that it had popular support.
95. G. R. Elton, *The Tudor Constitution*, 89.

of the country.[96] Nevertheless, the work of government had to continue, for which Henry relied on a few select Councillors. There was also an inner group of Councillors who accompanied the King on his travels, and who were usually the holders of Household offices. This inner group comprised the most active and influential part of government, which the King preferred to retain in his own hands. These 'Councillors attendant upon the King' comprised what was better known as the 'Council Attendant'. They were mostly professional individuals who regarded their work as a full-time occupation. The resulting distinction between the Council in the Star Chamber and the 'Council attending upon his most royal person wheresoever he be'[97] was thus a distinction between the Council at different times of the year.[98]

Dealing with petitions had long been delegated to the Privy Council, and throughout its history the Council was inundated with petitions for relief, so that it repeatedly looked for machinery to deal with them. The Lord Chancellor, meanwhile, had become more specialised in his jurisdiction, with the result that the Court of Chancery left the hearing of more and more complaints for the attention of the Privy Council.[99] For the purpose of its judicial duties, most of which were in the nature of arbitration, the Privy Council normally held its hearings in the Star Chamber, for which reason the judicial sessions of the Council came to be referred to as the Court of Star Chamber.[100] Henry VII often himself attended Council sessions that dealt with judicial cases.

Although the Tudors inherited a strong kingship, they were not in full control of the country. Of immediate concern was the 'overmighty

---

96. Law terms, of which there were four in the course of the year: the Hilary Term (23 January–12 February); Easter Term (seventeen days after Easter Day until four days after Ascension Day); the Summer Term (six or seven days after Trinity Sunday until the Wednesday a fortnight after; and the Michaelmas Term (9 October–28 November). Much of the work of government was influenced by this calendar.

97. Statute of Liveries, 1504.

98. In this process of separation, we can see the beginning of a repeat of the historical process whereby the Royal Court, or *Curia Regis*, had become distinguished from the Great Council. It was an inevitable consequence of the fact that the great men of the realm could not leave their personal affairs for attendance at court for more than limited periods.

99. G. R. Elton, *The Tudor Constitution*, 163.

100. It will be remembered that, under the common law of the constitution, the jurisdiction of the Privy Council was limited to cases involving members of the Second Estate, which it dealt with on behalf of the Great Council. It had long ceased to recognize this limitation.

subject', the individual whose territorial and military power were sufficient to rival that of the king, at least in his own locality. In the period of political and social unrest that had preceded, accompanied, and now followed the Wars of the Roses, these magnates and their followers had been a particularly difficult problem. The 'overmighty subject', with his following of indentured, liveried and often armed retainers, identified by their lord's insignia, had been a product of Church-Feudalism. In addition to rewarding his retainers, their lord usually made use of his power and influence to support their cause in any law-suit, and this often resulted in judges and juries being in the pay, or at the mercy, of the lord and his henchmen. The effect had been the widespread decay of the judicial system. In addition to packing the shire courts and intimidating juries, the thugs who were drawn into these private armies often indulged in riotous assemblies and the committing of robberies and murders. Often, the indentures that bound these armies of followers were illegal in that their terms failed to specify that the retainer's first allegiance was to the King, or that the lord had simply failed to obtain a licence. Several Statutes of Liveries, of which that of 1504 was the most comprehensive, sought to regulate or ban the wearing of liveries and to make the retaining of them an offence, other than that of domestic servants. Officers of the Crown were given considerable powers to bring offenders to judgment, but the Act lapsed in 1509 and the problem continued to reappear. To deal with it, Parliament granted authority to the Court of Star Chamber to try and punish accused individuals. The misdemeanours listed in the statute were the 'giving of liveries or tokens' or retainers, by indenture by means of oaths, influencing a jury, aiding and abetting in litigation, exerting influence on sheriffs, for example, in the selection of juries; the acceptance by jurors of bribes, and participation in riots and unlawful assemblies. The statute also prescribed who was to sit on such cases, in particular, the Chancellor, the Treasurer, and the Keeper of the Privy Seal. Later, the Lord President of the Council was added. By asking Parliament for such authority, which previously had been exercised during the time of the last of the Lancastrians, it was undoubtedly felt by Henry Tudor, an upstart himself, that he needed to bolster his position before trying members of the nobility who were of more august ancestry than himself.

Although the particular tribunal set up by Parliament in 1487 functioned occasionally, it never achieved either prominence or permanence.

Meanwhile, the Privy Council continued its normal judicial sessions in the Star Chamber, exercising the King's power to remedy grievances, which had continued to come his way, brought either by private parties or, occasionally, by the Crown through the Attorney General.[101] It was highly regarded as a court. Thus, in the reign of Elizabeth I, so eminent and liberal-minded a justice as Sir Edward Coke described it as 'the most honourable court (our Parliament excepted) that is in the Christian world, both in respect of the judges of the Court and of their honourable proceeding according to their just jurisdiction and the ancient and just orders of the court'.[102] It was undoubtedly more efficient than the ordinary courts. By this time, the restricted tribunal set up under the statute of 1487, in respect of the giving of liveries or tokens, had served its intended purpose and ceased to function.

Particularly troublesome in the longer run were the innumerable ancient rights enjoyed by individuals and corporations, and even by large tracts of land, or 'liberties', where the King's writ was limited, or simply did not apply. Most of these rights had been made by royal grants during the Middle Ages, and some of the liberties were notorious refuges for criminals. Gradually, most of the liberties had reverted to the Crown, or been reduced by the application of the common law, while manorial jurisdictions had largely become defunct, as villeinage had almost disappeared and all freemen now could, and did, use the royal courts. Nevertheless, some areas of private jurisdiction remained. Henry VII undertook some reductions of these, for example, in a statute which incorporated the liberty of Tynedale into the shire of Northumberland. A more sweeping reform came during the reign of Henry VIII, when an Act of 1536 effectively removed the difference between the legal administration of liberties and that of the ordinary shires. All England was now uniform in respect of Crown jurisdiction and administration, with the exception of the palatinates of Lancashire and Durham.

---

101. Elton suggests (*The Tudor Constitution*, 163) that the Privy Council or Court of Star Chamber was not a true court at this stage, because it did not have the characteristics of regularity, known procedure, and public proceedings, features possessed even by the popular courts of antiquity. Even so, it was exercising a judicial function.
102. E. Coke, *The Fourth Part of the Institutes of the Laws of England*, 63–4, 65.

Henry did not participate actively in the work of the Privy Council, and under him the more active Councillors appear to have met more frequently and with more formality. It was the inner part of the Council – the Council Attendant – that now played a more prominent role, a process ended by the advent of Cardinal Wolsey as Lord Chancellor, who usurped its functions, so that it again became the large and intermittent body that it had been before. The distinction between the Council as a whole and an inner group was reinforced by Wolsey's successor, Cromwell, who by 1536 had achieved a relatively small Privy Council, composed of the office-holders. By 1540, the same councillors were, very largely, sitting alternately as a Privy Council, more or less the year round, their proceedings recorded in its Acts, and as a Court of Star Chamber, whose proceedings were recorded in its Books of Orders and Decrees. A quorum for the court was said to be eight, but often there seem to have been only three or four, and it seems to have been an occasional practice in the earlier years to fill out the membership of the court with outsiders, because of the difficulty of finding a sufficiently impressive 'presence' without doing so.[103] Indeed, according to Sir Thomas Smith, writing early in the reign of Elizabeth I, those sitting included 'other lords and barons which be not of the Privy Council and be in the town'. Such were councillors 'by birth' (*nati*), in that they were Peers of the realm. This was a reference to the right of all members of the House of Lords, as elders of the people, to counsel the King.

Mary I insisted on rewarding her loyal supporters with places on the Council, causing it to decline into ineffectiveness. Experience had shown that it was necessary to keep the size of the Council to below twenty, and Elizabeth I, aided by the natural attrition begun by Cromwell, returned to his principles and restricted it to the select 'inner' group of between twelve and eighteen sworn Councillors. Indeed, the tendency was for it to grow smaller, with thirteen in 1601, most of the work being done by a smaller group of four or five, notable among whom were the Lord Treasurer and the Secretary. Typically, the Council now excluded the judges and law officers, and Elizabeth appointed only one ecclesiastic.

The first clerk of the Council, William Paget, in his *Advice to the King's Council*, attempted in 1550 to preserve its procedures. These

---

103. G. R. Elton, *The Tudor Constitution*, 165.

distinguished between the Court and the Council Board, that is, the judicial work and the full Council in session. The Council's judicial proceedings were required to be attended by at least six members of the Council, and these were to be ratified by the rest of the Council.[104] The *Advice* specified the times of the Council's judicial sittings. Paget's rules probably represented 'a desired ideal rather than established practice, but they well illustrate the sort of organisation and routine that made the Tudor Privy Council such an effective instrument of government'.[105] It was the precursor of the Cabinet system that would begin to develop in the next century.

Since the time of Henry VII, it had been rare for the Sovereign to attend the Privy Council, and this emphasised further the disintegration of the Royal Court itself. Although, constitutionally, they were apt to be regarded as a single entity, a distinction must be made between the Royal Household; the Royal Court, which accompanied the Royal Household; the Privy Council; and the Royal Courts of Justice, which were administered by the King in Council. The separation of the Royal Court and the Privy Council was emphasised when Henry VIII moved out of his palace at Westminster and took up residence at White Hall, nearby. The Privy Council still went to the King's residence to hold meetings, but the days when the King's place of residence was the seat of government were now over. Hitherto, the Privy Council had used the Privy Seal, or relied on the signatures of its members to authenticate documents, but under Mary, in 1556, the Privy Council acquired its own seal, thereby restoring it as a distinct identity.

The resumption by the Privy Council of its judicial role under Henry VI, Edward IV and Henry VII had been intended to suppress the state of anarchy that had preceded and followed the Wars of the Roses. In this it was very effective, and the Tudors exploited the judicial power of the Council to the full, using it increasingly for the pursuit of their own interests. They recognised a duty to abide by, and apply, the common law and statute law, but this was often inconvenient to the King, who looked to the Court of Star Chamber to make up for the weakness of the independent

---

104. The six attending to include one of the secretaries of the Council and two of the following: the Lord Chancellor, the Lord Treasurer, the Lord Great Master, the Lord Privy Seal, the Lord Great Chamberlain, and the Lord Chamberlain.
105. G. R. Elton, *The Tudor Constitution*, 92.

judicial system. Meanwhile, the work of the Court of Star Chamber was improved by a clerical organisation, more regular proceedings and greater consistency, although a single register continued to be used for both the judicial and non-judicial sides of the Privy Council's work. The Court of Star Chamber was highly regarded and popular with litigants, because it handled cases quickly, was flexible, and was complete in its work, but the court made no attempt to extend its jurisdiction to common law. The Sovereign now rarely attended, leaving the conduct of judicial proceedings to the Lord Chancellor. All present made judgments on cases, but usually concurred with the pronouncements of the Chancellor and justices. In its role as the Court of Star Chamber, the Council not only applied the law, but also made it, not by legislation, but by interpretation. By this means it is of interest that, even now, the King, through his Council, did not make laws but 'discovered' them. As we have seen, this concept goes back to Aryan times, when law was seen as inherent in nature, as devised by the gods. The task of the Council, both Great and Privy, was accordingly to discover this law as it related to a particular problem, not to invent it. The Tudor age accordingly saw a marked increase in royal proclamations that emanated from these 'recognitions'. Although hitherto an efficient body, by the last quarter of the sixteenth century the Court of Star Chamber had lapsed into the inefficiency and dilatoriness that also affected the ordinary courts.

What was accepted under the Tudors as being within the royal prerogative was substantial, but not undefined. The distinction between the King in Parliament and the King in person, and the idea that the former stood above the latter was well recognised and was accepted by them.[106] In 1548, William Stanford, addressing himself chiefly to law students in his *Exposition of the King's Prerogative*, explained that the Crown's prerogative extended all honour, dignity and pre-eminence to the King's person and contained those rights enjoyed by the King which enabled him to discharge the task of governing. The number of prerogatives was infinite and therefore too tedious to recite, but, summarising what he evidently felt to be the more important, notably the inviolability of the King's person and possessions, and the freedom of the latter from toll and tax, he drew upon the *Prerogativa Regis* for a fuller exposition. This seems

---

106. Ibid. 13–14.

to have been written in the second half of the fourteenth century and was probably an administrative summary of the King's prerogatives. An important point that Stanford made, however, was that the authority for the prerogatives was not Parliament, but the common law.

Sir Thomas Smith, writing his *De Republica Anglorum* in 1565, was more specific on rights of a political nature, referring in particular to the making of war and peace, diplomacy, appointments to the Privy Council and to all the highest offices in the realm, whether administrative or judicial, temporal or spiritual, and absolute power on the field of war. The King could also absolve an individual from prosecution for an offence against the law, or pardon him if convicted. Thus, like Stanford, Smith believed that the royal prerogatives could be defined, and that they could be attributed to the common law. Henry VII and the lawyers regarded the rights arising from the King's feudal overlordship as the most important. Personal concerns and possessions, such as royal marriages and the Sovereign's government of the Church, were also within the prerogative, as Elizabeth made clear. Thus, in Tudor eyes, the prerogative was a department of the common law, which conferred upon the ruler certain necessary rights not available to the subject. In contrast to their successors, the Stuarts, the principle of *legibus solutus*, or 'exempt from the law', which the King wielded, really meant no more than a right to dispense with the law if equity demanded it. It was a principle that offered flexibility, but little more.

Legislation by the King, with or without the advice of his Council, took the form of legislative orders, ordinances, or proclamations. A proclamation was the publication of an ordinance, following its enactment by means of the King's signature in the exercise of the royal prerogative. Provision for ordinances had always existed, partly because Parliaments were summoned only at intervals, and partly because many of its Acts assumed, and some specifically provided, that the details and flexibility of the legislative programme should be left to royal proclamations. In 1531, the King raised with Sir Thomas Cromwell and the Lord Chancellor the question of his power to deal with a particularly important and urgent issue of the moment. In a conference with the leading justices, it was concluded that a search of existing statutes should first be made to see whether there was one that would serve the purpose, in which case a proclamation should be made based upon the statute in question. On this occasion an appropriate statute was indeed found, but Cromwell then raised the question of what could be done, in such circumstances, in the absence of such a law or statute. As reported in a letter written shortly afterwards, Cromwell reported the Lord Chief Justice as replying that 'the King's Highness, by the advice of his Council, might make proclamations and use all other policies at his pleasure ... and that the said proclamations and policies so devised by the King and his Council for any such purpose should be of as good effect as any law made by Parliament or otherwise'.[107] This should not be seen as conflicting with the common law rule, which had already been enunciated by Parliament in 1354, that no ordinance could overrule or conflict with a statute. Provided it did not do this, however, it had the same force in law as a statute.

23.3.2.10. The Act of Proclamations

The scope of the royal prerogative seems never to have been questioned previously, and the King, or Cromwell, seems not to have been satisfied by the advice of the Lord Chief Justice, because a Statute of Proclamations, sometimes known as the *Lex Regia* of England, was approved by Parliament in 1539. It seems likely that the real purpose of the original Bill was to deal with the obscure authority of the Crown's proclamations by making them enforceable in the ordinary courts. Ordinances, or prerogative laws, suffered from the disability that, because they were proclaimed by the King, with or without the advice of the Council, they could not be enforced in a court of common law. It had been left to the Privy Council, therefore, sitting as a court in Star Chamber, to enunciate and enforce the King's ordinances, but this had proved ineffective. The Act of Proclamations provided that: 'the King for the time being, with the advice of his honourable Council, ... or with the advice of the more part of them, may set forth at all times by authority of this act his proclamations, under such penalties and pains ...' as to his Council 'shall seem necessary and requisite; and that those same shall be obeyed, observed and kept as though they were made by act of Parliament'. The King's subjects should not be deprived of their inheritances, lawful possessions, offices, liberties, privileges, franchises,

---

107. Letter from Cromwell to the Duke of Norfolk, 15 July 1531, as reported in Merriman, *Cromwell's Letters*, i. 409–10.

goods or chattels. Nor should any offender be deprived of his life, unless he 'obstinately, willingly or contemptuously' departs out of the realm in order to evade trial, in which case 'he shall be adjudged as a traitor' and suffer death and forfeit his land and goods. No proclamation made by virtue of the Act should infringe any statute or common law, or any lawful or laudable custom of the realm. Offenders might be convicted and punished by the members of the Council, sitting with certain bishops and judges 'in the Star Chamber or elsewhere', on the basis of a 'confession or lawful witness and proofs' and thereupon 'pay such penalties, forfeitures of sums of money … and also such imprisonments' as specified in the proclamation. Offenders might also be brought to trial on the basis of any information given to the Council.

Thus, royal proclamations could only be issued with the concurrence of the Privy Council, and were subject to common and statutory law, but otherwise had the same force as an Act of Parliament. They could not be used to deprive individuals of their freedom, privileges or possessions, but no limit seems to have been set on the punishments that could be inflicted for offending against a proclamation, except that they must be specified in the proclamation in question, and they could not extend to a sentence of death. There was thus a fairly close correspondence between the Act of Proclamations and the common law of the Constitution, as we now understand it, the chief difference being that, in common law, any such proclamation that affected the interests of the people, or was of sufficient import, was subject to the approval of the next Parliament. Also, as with all legislation, it was subject to any advice that might be put forward by the Great Council, or House of Lords, for what it was now worth, that it was inconsistent with the Constitution or with the overall interests of the nation.

The Act went no further on the subject of enforcement, beyond stating that proclamations 'shall be obeyed, observed and kept as though they were made by act of Parliament'. It suggests that Parliament had opposed any specific provision for enforcement. Indeed, Parliament is known to have been opposed to the making of proclamations enforceable in the ordinary courts,[108] but it left the Act unworkable, and in 1547 it was repealed by Edward VI, still leaving the question of enforcement

---

108. G. R. Elton, *The Tudor Constitution*, 23.

unsettled, and causing the relation of proclamations to the law to relapse into obscurity. This only became darker and more irksome with the passage of time.[109] Dicey has suggested that the Act was repealed 'because of its inconsistency with the whole tenor of English law',[110] but it is more likely that Parliament was concerned about the dangers posed specifically to common law rights of life and property,[111] as well as a fear that the Act had placed too much power in the hands of the Sovereign. The repeal of the Act in 1547 made no difference to the actual issue of proclamations, because, even without it, Queen Elizabeth used them more freely than did her predecessors.

The central issue in the Middle Ages had been the King's attitude to the existing law and the question of the supremacy of statute over the King's will, and this had been settled by the various crises over the coronation oath. The problem in Tudor times was the attitude of the King to new statutes which he found displeasing. The Crown was therefore reduced to preventing the enactment of legislation unacceptable to itself. Henry VII did this largely by exercising a stringent control over parliamentary business, and sometimes went so far as to insert provisos after they had received the assent of the Lords and Commons. Fortunately, these were of an insignificant nature, and the practice was not continued by his successors.[112] Henry VIII took a more robust view of the legislative powers of the King in Council. Indeed, the statute of 1539, which has been called the *Lex Regia*, confirmed the power of the King to make proclamations, with the advice of his Council, which, on pain of a fine or unlimited imprisonment, had the force of statute. This Act was repealed in 1547, on the accession of Edward VI. In Maitland's view, the implication of this Act and its repeal is clear: they 'confirm the doctrine that the King is not supreme, the King and Parliament are supreme; statute is distinctly above ordinance or proclamation'.[113] During the reign of his successor, Mary, the judges, evidently with an eye to her temperament, delivered an opinion that: 'the King may make a proclamation *in terrorem populi*, to put them in fear of his displeasure, but not to impose any

109. D. Lindsay Keir, *The Constitutional History of Modern Britain, 1485–1937* (London, 1950), 116–17.
110. A. V. Dicey, *Introduction to the Study of the Law of the Constitution*, 49.
111. G. R. Elton, *The Tudor Constitution*, 23.
112. Ibid. 21.
113. F. W. Maitland, *The Constitutional History of England*, 253.

fine, forfeiture, or imprisonment: for no proclamation can make a new law, but only confirm and ratify an ancient one'. It cut little ice with the Crown. Elizabeth I freely issued proclamations, for example, banishing Anabaptists and Irishmen, and the export of corn, and in 1580 forbidding the erection of houses within three miles of London.

The only real weapon which the King possessed against unwelcome legislation was believed to be the right to dispense or release an individual from the effect of a law, whether common or statute, and the right to pardon an offender. It was used occasionally to ease the burden of a law on a particular subject, but Elizabeth I used it to make grants *non obstante*, or 'without obstruction', to allow individuals to enjoy monopolies in the interests of the Crown. This ability to exempt an individual from a law seems to have no basis in common law, and its origin must be sought in the feudal view of sovereignty.

There should be no basic conflict in principle between statute and royal will, because all statutes are the will of the King that has been consented to by a Parliament. In the latter case, the King may have been forced to make disagreeable concessions in order to secure the other features of his legislation. Otherwise, conflict can only arise if the King changes his mind and Parliament is unwilling to agree to the change, or if Parliament is unwilling to revoke or amend a disagreeable statute inherited from a predecessor. The problem arose after the Middle Ages because, as we have seen, Parliament had taken to initiating statutes itself and to using its power to block money grants as a means to blackmail the King into accepting them. For this development the King had himself partly to blame, because he had tried, from time to time, to impose feudal ideas as to the basis of his authority and he had ceased to consult the Great Council, in its guise as the House of Lords. The capacity of this latter body to provide satisfactory advice had, of course, long been in question, due to the intrusion of feudal doctrine and questions concerning the independence and suitability of Councillors, so that the Tudors were faced with a fairly general failure of the system.

Apart from the judicial functions of the Privy Council, conducted in the Star Chamber and its offshoot, the Court of Requests, there were certain quite separate courts established by the Crown, in particular, the Council of Wales and the Council of the North. To these, Henry VIII added other bodies, such as the Court of High Commission, the Court of Augmentations, and the Court of Wards and Liveries.

23.3.2.11. The Court of Requests

The Court of Star Chamber was not the only court operated by the Privy Council. Between 1539 and 1547 the Star Chamber, in accordance with the Act of Proclamations, also sat in company with the senior judiciary as a special tribunal to try offences against the King's ordinances. As a companion court to that of Star Chamber, there was also the Court of Requests. It had long been the practice for individual Privy Councillors to attend to requests to the King by poor petitioners for assistance with complaints, for example, that they had not obtained justice in the common law courts as a result of such practices as corruption, bribery, and the intimidation of jurymen. They also heard the appeals of tenants against their landlords, or of copyholders seeking to stay enclosures, or even of a widow asking for aid for herself and her son. These were primarily civil complaints, therefore, and the procedure was speedy and cheap. This practice was recognised by statute as a court in 1487. In 1493 Henry VII appointed a standing committee of eight to ten members of the Council to deal with them. It was this which came to be known as the Court of Requests, and it was really a minor court of equity. Originally, it travelled with the King and his Council, but from about 1516 onwards it held its sessions in the White Chamber at Westminster. For this reason, the Court of Requests was often referred to as 'the Council in the White Hall'. It was presided over by the Lord Privy Seal, and in order to minimise cost and inconvenience, the Court of Requests used the Privy Seal, instead of the Great Seal of Chancery. Cromwell, while engaged in reducing the size of the Privy Council, replaced the committee dealing with these requests in 1538–9 by appointing two Masters of Requests to preside over the court. Although, they now ceased to be members of the Privy Council, they were drawn from the lesser Councillors and so were still required to take a form of Councillor's oath. This, and other trappings retained by the Court of Requests, clearly continued to identify it with the Privy Council. Being a prerogative court, like Chancery and the Star Chamber, there was no jury, and, like them, its jurisdiction was challenged from about 1600 onwards by the courts of common law, who regarded the exercise by them of the King's equity as arbitrary and frequently cutting across their own function. From the outbreak of the Civil War, in 1642, onwards, the Court of Requests no longer sat.

The Court of Wards and Liveries was created by Henry VIII in 1541 to deal with the King's feudal dues arising from the old military tenures. Its sessions were held in the White Chamber, where the Court of Requests also sat.

23.3.3. The Borders and the Incorporation of Wales

Both in the Marches of Wales and on the Scottish border, there was recurrent lawlessness and incursions, and here the power of the Crown was at its weakest, calling for special arrangements. Even the country to the north of the Trent was remote from London. The Council of the North had its origin in a private council of Richard, Duke of Gloucester, who had administered the north on behalf of his brother, Edward IV. When he had succeeded to the throne as Richard III, he entrusted the council to his nephew. Under Henry VII it had lapsed by 1509, until Wolsey, concerned by the needs of defence against the Scots, established a new council under a new lieutenant. It exercised wide administrative and criminal jurisdiction, but it failed, except in Yorkshire, in the face of hostility from the northern magnates. Cromwell reorganised the Council of the North on a permanent basis under a Lord President. Established by royal commission, it became the instrument of government for the north, controlled from Westminster, where it was subordinate to the Privy Council, but not an extension of it. Thus, it had common law jurisdiction, which the Privy Council did not. From 1582 its sessions were always held at York, and it was to survive as a successful aspect of the administration of the realm until the Civil War.

Attention was turned also to Wales. All but four of the lordships of the Marches had been brought into royal possession by 1521, and all were subjected to increasing control by the Council of the Marches. The Council in the Marches of Wales had its origin under Edward IV, when it administered his lands there. It was revived by Henry VII for his son, the Prince of Wales, with competence over Wales as well as the Marches, but the Council was ineffectual until the 1530s, when Cromwell reorganised it as a formal body under a President, with both administrative and judicial authority, similar to the Council of the North. Under Henry VIII, the future of Wales was settled in a series of Acts of Union of 1535, 1536 and 1542. Under these, the lordships of the Marches were finally abolished, and the Council was given a new, statutory basis as the 'Council in the dominion and principality of Wales and the marches of the same'. The Principality now ceased to be in the direct possession of the Crown; the Welsh counties were reorganised; the same local administration was imposed as applied to the English shires; and a Court of Great Sessions was created, in addition to those of Quarter Sessions. As the highest administrative authority under the Privy Council, the Council of Wales and the Marches had a variety of functions, including that as the chief court of justice in its area. In effect, the whole of Wales was now incorporated into England, with English made the language of administration and justice, and provision made for Welsh representation in the Parliaments at Westminster. Prior to 1543, the authority of the Council had rested on the King's commission, but from that date it rested on statutory authority. Even more than its northern counterpart, the Council of Wales and the Marches functioned as a regional Star Chamber and Chancery, although, at the instance of parties, the Star Chamber proper withdrew cases from it and remitted cases to it. From Henry VIII onwards, the Council enjoyed a wide jurisdiction that was useful both to the Crown and to its subjects, and as the independence of the marcher lords was destroyed, so the Council of Wales lost its political function. The Council functioned reasonably well for another century, but it was troubled by graft, lack of funds, ineptitude, and longstanding opposition from the English border counties. It remained of administrative importance, although the civil and criminal aspects of its jurisdiction brought it increasingly into conflict with the more regular courts. Nevertheless, as the earliest of these regional experiments, it also survived longest, not being finally abolished until 1689.

A third such council, the Council of the West, was set up in 1539 in response to the restlessness of the Marquesses of Exeter and Cromwell's fondness for regional government. Modelled on the Council of the North, it covered Cornwall, Devon, Somerset and Dorset. It proved to be expensive and unnecessary, however, and it was abolished in 1540.

23.3.4. The Catholic Reaction

Henry VIII, 'Bluff King Hal', died at the Palace of Whitehall in January 1547, leaving three children, Mary, Elizabeth, and Edward. Edward's mother had been Jane Seymour, the third of Henry's wives, and he was only nine years of age when he succeeded to the Crown as King Edward VI. A Lord Protector of the Realm was appointed in the person of his cousin, the earl of Hertford, who was created Duke of Somerset. It was therefore Somerset who assumed the government, and the Protestant reformers took advantage of the King's minority to push through further changes. Somerset was inclined to exceed his authority, and fell victim to a rival faction led by the Earl of Warwick, who displaced Somerset as the young King's mentor. Somerset had led the reform movement, but Warwick was no less resolute a reformer, a policy to which the young Edward gave his eager blessing. His father had merely flirted with Protestant doctrine, but now a wholesale programme of conversion took place.

In 1548, the heresy laws were abolished, and in 1549 the first Act of Uniformity introduced Protestant doctrines into church services, imposed penalties for non-observance, and ordered the suppression of images and Latin primers. It also authorised the first English Book of Common Prayer, compiled by Cranmer. This, while Protestant, was only mildly so. Thus, religious practices were being prescribed by a secular authority. In the process of introducing his religious innovations, Henry had involved Parliament to a degree that was dangerous to his personal position as Supreme Head, because the religious affairs of the people were, in common law, the preserve of the clergy, in consultation with the King in his priestly aspect. They were therefore above manipulation by the other two Estates, as represented by Parliament. Nevertheless, King Edward's First Act of Uniformity in 1549 went a very long way towards subjecting the liturgy and ceremonial of the Church to the authority of Parliament.[114] This was probably inevitable in the circumstances, because the Church generally had been left behind in the new tide of religious thinking. The Second Act of Uniformity, in 1552, required every subject to attend church on Sundays and other days to be ordained holy days. It marked the beginning of the tradition that Sundays should be kept apart for religious purposes. At the same time, an Act was passed to subject ale-

---

114. G. R. Elton, *The Tudor Constitution*, 344.

houses to control by Justices of the Peace. Meanwhile, in 1551, Cranmer published the Forty-Two Articles, which provided a basis for Anglican Protestantism. Two years later, Thomas Cromwell became Chancellor, and everywhere a ruthless campaign of destruction and confiscation was pursued, in which images, statues, altars, roods, church bells and plate were smashed or plundered, and church walls were whitewashed and often emblazoned with Biblical inscriptions. Religious processions were banned, chantries were abolished and their lands were seized. At Oxford, there was a wholesale burning of the University's books. Edward's concerns were not confined to what he regarded as religious integrity, however, but extended to the founding of grammar schools and workhouses for the poor.

Whether Edward fully understood what was being done in his name is doubtful. His reign has been described as the most revolutionary in English history, for it transformed the religion of the country and, with it, its society and its politics.[115] It was during his short reign that the Church of England really acquired its separate identity, but it is clear that these reforms were by no means generally supported. Few had dared to object to the displacement of the Holy Catholic Church by the Church of England while Henry had been on the throne, but the minority of Edward VI and the new, blatantly Protestant, reforms resulted in the disaffection of the minority coming dangerously close to the surface. In 1549 it was necessary to put down a rebellion in Devon and Cornwall. Anxious to avoid revolution, particularly as the disaffected element in the upper classes was quite capable of leading one, the Government appealed to lower class Protestantism and to sentiment against the gentry.

The religious divide was not the only source of social and political friction. The continuing prosperity of the woollen industry made sheep-rearing more profitable than crops, and there was a widespread tendency for individuals with rights to the use of local common land to consolidate their title in the form of compact holdings, which they then enclosed by means of fences, walls, or dykes, depending on the nature of the country. It enabled them to manage their flocks better, but it also reduced the amount of common land available to their neighbours. There was a trend also to the consolidation of arable land by the exchange or purchase of

---

115. D. MacCulloch, *Tudor Church Militant: Edward VI and the Protestant Reformation.*

strips, but there is little evidence before 1500 that this also was being enclosed.[116] The movement in favour of the enclosure of land had been taking place since the fourteenth century, but the process accelerated, and the sixteenth century saw land enclosure taking place on an extensive scale, giving rise to considerable friction and social unrest, and even to widespread violence. Kett's Rebellion in Norfolk, in 1549, was motivated by economic hardship, and was directed particularly at the enclosure movement, the solution to which it saw in the abolition of the private ownership of land. The revolt had some brief success, before it was put down, and Kett hanged. Legislation was passed against enclosure, but it was only partly successful.

After only six years on the throne, Edward VI died in 1553 of consumption and congenital syphilis, inherited from his father, at the early age of sixteen. Both he and Northumberland were concerned lest the Protestant Reformation die with him, because his father, Henry VIII, had, by his second and third Acts of Succession of 1536 and 1544, acquired the right to bequeath his throne by will, either because there were no legitimate heirs at the time of the first Act, or because there were so few at the time of the second. The second Act had directed that, if Henry had no male heirs other than Edward, and if Edward should die without heirs, the Crown should go to Edward's sisters, Mary and Elizabeth, in that order, their legitimacy having now been restored. If all three lines failed to produce heirs, the Crown was to go to the heirs of his younger sister, Mary, Duchess of Suffolk, now represented by Lady Jane Grey. That Henry had given Mary's descendants precedence over those of his elder sister, Margaret, had probably been because Margaret had married James IV, King of the Scots, and Henry may have had an aversion to the idea of England being ruled by the Scottish dynasty, which was represented at the time by Mary, Queen of Scots. In the circumstances applying at the death of Edward VI, Henry's will bequeathed the Crown to Edward's elder sister, Mary, yet Mary, like her mother, Catherine of Aragon, was a devout Catholic. Shortly before his death, therefore, Edward had amended his father's will in favour of Jane Grey, who was an equally devoted Protestant.

---

116. J. Clapham, *A Concise Economic History of Britain*, 123–4.

23.3.5. The Problem of Female Succession

Neither Church-Feudalism nor common law provided for female succession. Consequently, as noted earlier, there is no feminine form of the word 'king'. The original meaning of the word 'queen' had simply been 'woman', but over the centuries it had come particularly to mean the wife of the King. A concession to the principle of kingship does appear to have existed in exceptional circumstances, where there was no generally accepted successor to the king, and where the widow of the late king shows exceptional ability in the management of royal affairs. Such, presumably, had been Seaxburh, the widow of the West Saxon king, Cenwealh, in 672; and subsequently Æthelflæd, widow of Æthelræd II, during 911–918, in her capacity as the 'Lady of the Mercians'. Both functioned, however, in the capacity of regent. Only a King with the commanding authority of Henry VIII, in the complete absence of an acceptable successor, would seriously have indicated a female successor in the royal line, in the capacity of Queen regnant. Even the legitimacy of Henry himself, like that of his father, had been questioned, but the succession in this case had been laid down by statute, that is, it had the support of Parliament, which could be held to override both common law and feudal provisions, particularly in the absence of an otherwise acceptable successor.

Lady Jane Grey was well-mannered and an accomplished scholar, great-granddaughter of Henry VIII and daughter of Henry Grey, Duke of Suffolk. Her claim to the succession was wide open to contention, because Edward's elder sister had a prior claim, both by right of inheritance and under the terms of the will of Henry VIII. Edward had tried to pre-empt the situation, but he had not ruled for long enough to establish his own authority sufficiently to do so. Nor did Lady Jane have any desire for the Crown. She had just been induced, against her inclinations, into marrying the son of the Duke of Northumberland, whose own ambitions were an added complication. Jane accepted the offer of the Crown against her better judgement, having been persuaded that her doing so would help the process of Protestant reform. She was obdurate, however, that her husband, Guilford Dudley, should not be proclaimed King.

The proclamation by the Council of Lady Jane Grey as Queen regnant antagonised the nobility and produced a popular outcry that the succession should not go to somebody who was not of the immediate royal line. The House of Tudor had been popular, and it was the feeling that only a true Tudor was acceptable. This was encouraged by Edward's half-sister, Mary, a Catholic, who, seeing her chance, raised an army in Norfolk to contest the Crown, which then marched on London. Faced by the mood of open revolt among the general public, Edward's army refused its support to Jane, who was now dependent on an army raised by her father-in-law, the duke of Northumberland. The latter was defeated, however, and Northumberland himself arrested, convicted of treason and executed. Mary returned from her temporary refuge in East Anglia, proclaiming her prior right to the succession as the eldest surviving daughter of Henry VIII and Catherine of Aragon, and carefully avoiding any reference to the religious question. It was enough to win over the citizens of London, and Mary was acclaimed as Queen regnant, although the qualification was overlooked. On 19 July 1553, only nine days after her accession and before she had been crowned, Jane and her husband were arrested by Mary and imprisoned in the Tower. Although the question of legitimacy was central to the succession of 1553 and to the demise of Jane Grey, it was the public reaction that had proved to be the decisive factor.

23.3.6. Mary and Elizabeth I (1553–1603)

Mary was crowned in October of the same year, and Parliament approved legislation that annulled the divorce of her father and Catherine of Aragon. This gave Mary a legitimate title to the succession, and at the same time made Edward VI illegitimate and a usurper. It also repealed the religious laws of Edward, bringing the country back to the state in which Henry had left it. There can be little doubt that Edward had been the lawful King on his accession, but it was Mary who had popular support when she usurped the succession from Jane. Mary was at first willing to be lenient towards Jane, whom she did not regard as a serious rival.

Meanwhile, the Church of Rome had embarked upon a counter-movement across Europe, known as the Counter-Reformation, bent on retrieving lost territory and lost souls, and to this end it pursued several strategies. The Society of Jesus, commonly known as the 'Jesuit Order', was founded in Spain in 1534 as a small 'army' of well organised and disciplined priests, charged with promoting a revival of Catholicism in Protestant Europe. Catholic rulers were urged by the Pope to embark on wars of restoration, causing the Habsburg ruler and last of the Holy Roman Emperors, Charles V, to launch a military campaign against the league of German Protestant states, between 1546 and 1547. Other rulers imposed Catholicism on their subjects and, in a series of bitter wars, revolts and repressions across central and North-Western Europe, the Catholic Church achieved some success in rolling back the Protestant tide. Even so, Protestantism retained its hold on northern Germany, Scandinavia, the north Netherlands, England, Wales and most of Scotland. The first Papal list of forbidden books was drawn up in 1559 and the reigning Queen of England, Elizabeth I, was declared by the Pope to be anathema, that is, excommunicated and consigned to eternal damnation. Meanwhile, the need for reform of the Catholic Church itself was finally acknowledged by the Papacy, and, at the Council of Trent, which opened in 1545, brought about changes both to the organisation and the doctrine of the Church. Whereas the wars of the Middle Ages had been motivated primarily by dynastic ambition, this was displaced in the wars of the sixteenth and seventeenth centuries by religious rivalry. It was a change in priorities that marked the beginning of the end of the feudal age across Europe.

As the daughter of Catherine of Aragon, Mary now asserted her Catholicism and her Spanish ancestry, together with her antipathy towards all that her father had stood for, by entering into a marriage treaty with Philip, King of Naples, who was destined to become Philip II of Spain two years later. Under the terms of this agreement, Philip was to have the title of 'King of England', but, on the insistence of Parliament, which opposed the marriage to Philip, was not to be crowned king. He was to have no hand in the government of the country; and he was not to succeed Mary in the event of her death. Despite his title, therefore, he was no more than the Queen's consort. Any child of Philip and Mary, however, was to inherit the Netherlands and Burgundy, as well as England. It was a very unpopular treaty, and Philip and the Spanish grandees were soon detested. In an attempt to forestall the impending marriage, there was a widespread insurrection in the south and west, led by Sir Thomas Wyatt. It was betrayed, however, and broke out precipitately at the beginning of 1554, so that it succeeded only in Kent. Lead by Wyatt, the rebels marched on London, crossing the Thames at Kingston. With Wyatt's force at the walls of London, Mary made an impassioned speech at the Guildhall, holding up her hand with the coronation ring upon it, invoking the ring as evidence of her obligation and loyalty to the English people. This display of spirit, aided by the loyalty of the Protestant nobility, and the capture of Wyatt, who had been trapped at Temple Bar, brought the insurrection to an end. Mary was now determined to root out all who opposed the Catholic Church, and when the imprisoned Jane, whose father, the duke of Suffolk, had been involved in the rebellion, now refused to renounce her Protestantism, she was executed for high treason. Mary's younger half-sister, Elizabeth, a Protestant, and suspected of complicity in the rebellion, probably with good cause, was sent to the Tower.

Queen Mary and Philip were married in the same year, and a reconciliation with the Pope made the latter once again head of the English Church, pronouncing a return to official Catholicism. The year was marked also by a second Act of Repeal, which removed all anti-Papal measures that had been passed since 1529, but only under stringent safeguards to protect the holders of former Church lands and to prevent the imposition of Church fees. The absolution of England from Papal censures came with a requirement, however, that all heretics be burned at the stake. The main Protestant areas were London, East Anglia, Sussex and Kent, and there ensued in the following year, 1555, such a fierce persecution of Protestants and heretics that the Queen became known to history as 'Bloody' Mary. The well-to-do were able to escape from the country, leaving the poor and the incapacitated to take the brunt of Mary's revenge. Apart from a few prominent clerics, including Archbishop Cranmer, most of the three hundred burned at the stake during her reign were ordinary men and women, including artisans, children, the elderly and the blind, and this left a legacy of bitterness. None were from the political class. Many were alienated from the Church of England, to form the festering basis of future dissident sects. The Spaniards pressed for Elizabeth's execution, but, luckily for her, the intervention of the Holy Roman Emperor ensured that her incarceration was a short one, and she was released. They also pressed for a dissolution of Parliament, which had agreed only grudgingly to the marriage terms. Mary herself complained that she spent days 'shouting at her Council'. Certain monasteries were restored. Too many people owned Church property that had been expropriated by Henry VIII to risk it by being outspoken, but the antipathy to Mary's religious leanings and the presence of the Spaniards was clearly evident.

Philip left England in 1556 to assume the crown of Spain, and in the following year paid a return visit, during which he persuaded Mary to enter the Franco-Spanish war in support of Spain. Parliament refused to give its support, as a result of which Calais, England's last possession in France and the pride of the realm for the last two hundred years, was lost in 1558. It was a loss that was treated as a national disaster and did much to destroy Mary's credibility as a ruler. Nevertheless, if Mary had lived longer or produced an heir, official English Protestantism might well have been extinguished, for there was little open opposition to her Catholic policies from the establishment. In the event, Mary and Philip had no offspring, and Philip, realising that he had no dynastic prospects in England, returned to the Continent. Like Edward, Mary had inherited her father's syphilis and suffered from deteriorating health. She was also depressed by the realisation that she would remain childless and without an heir; by the infidelity of Philip, who had lost all immediate interest in England; by the loss of Calais; by hostile Spanish policy in respect of English trade with its colonies; and by a belief that her reign had been a failure. In this last she was undoubtedly correct, because the persecutions had achieved little, beyond sowing more abundantly the seeds of hatred, from which the Church would never fully recover, and which would dominate political and constitutional attitudes for the next two hundred years. Mary now came to terms with the realisation that Elizabeth would be the heir, and she tried, unsuccessfully, to persuade her to retain her Catholic reforms.

Meanwhile, the will of Henry VIII, that Elizabeth should succeed Mary, was widely accepted, but religion had now become as important a consideration as legitimacy in deciding the succession. Elizabeth, as the daughter of another of Henry's wives, Anne Boleyn, was a moderate Protestant, and after the persecution under Bloody Mary there was deep-rooted opposition to another Catholic on the throne. On Mary's death in 1558, therefore, the throne passed to Elizabeth.

Even so, Elizabeth's position was by no means secure, because there were other powerful claimants to the throne. One was Mary, Queen of Scots, the great-granddaughter of Henry VII. She was also the Queen of France, for she had married Francis II, and French influence in Scotland was strong. Indeed, it was the French who encouraged Scottish Mary in her claim to England. Like 'Bloody' Mary, she was a Catholic, but her legal claim to the English succession rested on the fact that, in annulling the divorce of Henry VIII and Catherine of Aragon, Parliament had made Elizabeth illegitimate and therefore ineligible to succeed to the throne. There were others who were eligible, notably Catherine Seymour and Margaret Stanley, who also were great-granddaughters of Henry VII, but Mary, the Scottish queen, had the prior claim. For all this, Elizabeth's legitimacy had been restored by her father, who was known to favour his own descendants. Further complicating the issue was the possibility, if the Pope declared his opposition to Elizabeth, of war with both France and Scotland. There was also the risk of war with Spain, because Philip II believed that he had acquired a title to the English crown by his marriage treaty with Mary I, and he was unwilling to forgo it, even though the marriage treaty had precluded his retention of the title after her death. His proposal of marriage to Elizabeth was rejected. Fortunately, Philip had no wish to see England brought into alliance with France, and he was therefore reluctant to over-play his hand. For the time being, he intrigued against Elizabeth instead. Also, the growing dynastic and religious antagonism between England and Spain was heightened by an increasing colonial and trade rivalry in the Americas. From this political tangle over the succession, it can be seen just how far the feudal principle of kingship, as the proprietorship of an estate, had moved from the original Indo-European perception of supreme eldership of the people. Yet it was because the latter idea was still very strong, that the Council and Parliament had favoured Elizabeth.

She was fortunate in that, unlike her siblings, Elizabeth enjoyed good health and was athletic, and she was both intelligent and well educated, albeit with a vicious temper. Her position at first was under threat, not only from foreign powers, however, but also from the internal religious rivalry. There was a need to move with caution, and she was astute enough to do so. Both the court and the Privy Council – the Great Council, as an institution outside Parliament, now being treated as largely redundant – were split into factions, both extreme Protestant and Catholic. The House of Commons tended to take the former position, so that it was only the external threats from Spain and the Papacy that held Elizabeth's regime together. She retained the existing Privy Council, but added Sir William Cecil, the later Lord Burghley, as her Secretary of State. Under Cecil's guidance, counter-espionage now became an important arm of government, and with it went a considerable royal power in the disposal of conspirators. On Cecil's advice, a policy of 'tolerance' was embarked upon that was designed to weld the nation under a single religious faith, and Elizabeth steered a middle, if muddled, course between those of her former Protestant brother, Edward, and her former Catholic sister, Mary. The Catholic legislation of Mary was repealed, and a Bible was now to be available in every church. The Second Act of Supremacy, in 1559, once again abolished the Papal power in England and restored the first Act, which had been signed by Henry VIII. It also required all Church and state officials to take an oath of allegiance to the Queen as the 'Supreme Governor' of the Church in all spiritual, ecclesiastical, and temporal things or causes, in place of Henry's more decisive position of 'Supreme Head'. This second Act has since been interpreted as changing the title of the Sovereign from 'Supreme Head' to the more modest one of 'Supreme Governor', but this appears to be an error. Elizabeth's Act restored that of her father, including his title of Supreme Head, which his Act imposed upon his heirs and successors. That Elizabeth chose for herself the title of 'Supreme Governor', without her Act passing it on to her successors, can most credibly be explained by doubts as to whether a woman could be the Supreme Head of the Church in any case.

One consequence of the 'nationalisation' of the English Church by Henry VIII was a need for royal control and responsibility to be made effective. This was provided by Elizabeth I in the form of what came to be known, rather misleadingly, as the High Commission. Alongside the ordinary Church courts, permanent courts, comprising both clergy and laity, were set up in 1559, by means of commissions under letters patent, for the two provinces of Canterbury and York. That for Canterbury sat at London. Later in the same reign, other courts were established by commission for particular dioceses. These courts rarely interfered with diocesan affairs, being intended to deal with criminal matters affecting the Church, such as major cases of disobedience. In order to give effect to the Crown's supremacy throughout the realm, the Canterbury Commission was equipped with powers that extended beyond its provincial boundaries, to act as the High Commission for the whole. It thus formed the Court of High Commission, through which the royal supervision of the Church was operated.

The Act of Uniformity of the same year imposed a common religious service and required the use of the Prayer Book of Edward VI. Nevertheless, Elizabeth stifled the hopes of the evangelical reformers of Edward's reign when she re-established the Church as the independent Church of England under the Crown. This process was completed with the promulgation, in the Convocation of 1563, of the Thirty-Nine Articles of religion. These were based on, and replaced, the earlier and more strongly Protestant Articles that had been written by Cranmer. The Thirty-Nine Articles had no official standing, and were not even published at the time, but they represented 'the agreed views of a committee of leading theologians'.[117] They defined a compromise Church, largely Protestant in dogma, but retaining the traditional Catholic element of faith in the liturgy and preserving the unbroken line of bishops in the apostolic succession, so ensuring the continuity of the Church of England with its past. The new Prayer Book was a masterpiece of ambiguity wherever contentious issues were touched upon, so that the completely contradictory words of the mass book on the sacrament, and those of Zwingli, the Swiss Protestant reformer, were neatly brought together in the same sentence. There was also an authorisation of 'Popish' ritual and vestments. The danger of parliamentary interference in religion was realised in 1566, when the House of Commons tried to assert its part by promoting a Bill to confirm the Articles. Elizabeth stopped it, at the cost of losing several government Bills.[118] Nevertheless, whereas in law and political theory it is hard to avoid the conclusion that the supremacy of Henry VIII had been essentially personal, that of Elizabeth was essentially parliamentary.[119]

117. J. P. Kenyon, *The Stuart Constitution 1603–1688*, 131–2.
118. J. E. Neale, *Elizabeth and Her Parliaments*, i. 166.
119. G. R. Elton, *The Tudor Constitution*, 344.

In one sense the Church of England was a great achievement, retaining the sense of mystery, tradition and authority that appealed to so many adherents of the Church of Rome, while at the same time dispensing with what was regarded as superfluous symbolism and recognising the direct personal relationship between the individual and God. The function of the Church and the priesthood was therefore seen as being to assist the individual in this relationship, rather than acting as the channel of communication. As with all compromises, it only partly succeeded. To many 'Papists', only the Pope could be the direct link with the Apostles and so speak with divine authority on matters of belief. To many Protestants, the bishops represented an intrusion between God and man, not least in the retained celebration of the mass, which implied that the priest was a necessary intermediary between God and the individual. Furthermore, most of the surviving religious symbolism was pagan in origin, and therefore objectionable to the reformers. Because Elizabeth's Church was a compromise, it appealed to everybody and nobody, storing up dissentions which have continued to the present day. Of those adherents of Rome who refused to accept the new Church, most were to be found among the upper classes, from whom Protestantism had been thoroughly expunged at the beginning of the fifteenth century, during the repression of the Lollards. Eventually, Catholic sympathisers were destined to recover their self-confidence enough to become a source of agitation. On the other side were the large numbers of the Protestants who also dissented from the new compromise, because they regarded the Reformation of the Church as incomplete. Calling for its further 'purification' from the unscriptural and corrupt forms and ceremonies of the old Church, it was apparently they themselves who adopted the name of 'Puritans'. Many chose to dissent entirely from the Church. They came chiefly from the lower classes, where Wiclif's Protestantism had long and secretly survived. Consequently, 'Popery' and dissent were destined to retain associations of social class down to the present day, and large numbers of Protestants were eventually to break away under a series of sectarian leaders.

Thus, the Church of England emerged as an uneasy amalgam of High Church, which reflected strong Catholic sentiments, and Low Church, reflecting equally strong Protestant ideas. By and large, Church adherents of these two forms were either those who sought to avoid the persecution of religious extremists, or those for whom nationalist sentiment and devotion to the established social order were strong enough to react against the disintegrative effects of dissent. Nevertheless, actual Puritan influence at a political level was strongest among the mercantile classes in the towns and among the small country gentry, and during the reign of Elizabeth they began to return a majority to the House of Commons. For Elizabeth's Government, the survival of religious extremism, both Catholic and Puritan, represented an ongoing threat to the social order and an invitation to foreign intervention. It accordingly adopted a policy of 'non-tolerance' towards both extremes, and in order to cope with the hostility to Elizabeth's compromise, the laws of treason were widened, and Sir Thomas Walsingham, the Queen's private secretary, created a secret service that was the most efficient in Europe. The conflict with Rome prompted a Papal bull of 1570, which declared Elizabeth to be a usurper. This was countered by a law that prohibited the receipt or publication of bulls from Rome, and from now onwards, England found itself virtually in a state of religious siege, organised as much from within as from without.

The question of the Queen marrying and producing an heir did not at first arise, until it was realised at the beginning of her reign that she was carrying on an affair with Robert Dudley, the Earl of Leicester, brother of Guilford Dudley, who had been the husband of Lady Jane Grey. Robert Dudley was already married to Amy Robsart, though they saw little of each other. Known as 'the Gypsy', Dudley was a wholly unsuitable individual, and the affair gave rise to much concern. In 1560, his wife was murdered. It is most likely that this had been arranged secretly by Cecil, in order to compromise Dudley.[120] Elizabeth was shrewd enough to realise

---

120. History usually records that Amy Robsart died at Cumnor Hall after falling down a flight of stairs and breaking her neck. The recently discovered coroner's report (*The Virgin Queen's Fatal Affair: Revealed*, Channel 5, 18 November 2010), shows that she was killed by two blows to the head. It is also known that she had given all her staff time off, so that Cumnor Hall was empty. The likely explanation is that Cecil had sent her a message proposing that, as the Queen wished to pay her a secret visit, the likely implication being that it would be in connection with the philanderings of Amy's husband. With all witnesses removed, the assassin or assassins would have been able to enter and leave unobserved. The obvious suspect would have been Dudley, since Amy stood in the way of his hoped-for marriage to the Queen. Proceedings were not taken against him.

that her position would be compromised if she continued the affair, and promptly broke it off, yet there is little doubt that Dudley was the love of her life. It may have been this disappointment that played a part in her subsequent refusal to marry. It is even possible that she guessed that 'interests of the state' had been behind the incident, and that, although she henceforth devoted herself wholly to affairs of state, she avenged herself by refusing to marry anybody else. In any case, she was not one who would have allowed her position as Queen be compromised by any husband, hence the reputation that she earned as the 'virgin Queen'. It would spell the end of the Tudor dynasty.

Meanwhile, Francis II of France had died in 1560, and four years later his widow, Mary, Queen of Scots, had married her cousin, a lout by the name of Henry Stewart, Lord Darnley. It seems that the French at the Scottish court, unable to pronounce 'Stewart', converted it to 'Stuart', and this was the spelling that Mary retained.[121] In 1567 Darnley was murdered in confused circumstances that suggest that Mary's death had also been intended. She was widely detested, and a few months later was arrested and imprisoned, then forced to abdicate from the Scottish throne in favour of her son, James Darnley, who succeeded her as James VI. Escaping from captivity, Mary fled to England in 1568. Her presence here was doubly unwelcome, partly because, unless Elizabeth had children, Mary was a leading claimant to the English throne, and she was known still to have ambitions in that direction, and partly because she was a Catholic, which won her the secret support of the English Catholics. Accepting the advice of her Privy Council, Elizabeth had her placed under house arrest, well away from both Scotland and London. In spite of this, Mary's presence made her the cause for a northern rebellion by the Catholic earls in 1569. It also prompted fears of a Jesuit invasion and inspired a number of Catholic plots in the years that followed, in one of which Mary was implicated. She was now securely imprisoned in the Tower of London, where she posed the greatest problem of Elizabeth's reign. Although Mary was rejected by the great majority of the population, she was still a threat to the security of the realm and to the survival of the popular Protestant cause, yet the Queen could not bring herself to follow the wisest course and get rid of her. Elizabeth had herself been in the

---

121. G. F. Black, *The Surnames of Scotland* (New York, 1946).

same precarious situation, and Mary Stuart was almost her only surviving relative. Eventually, proof of Mary's complicity in one of the plots was produced, and for this she was executed in 1587.[122]

Meanwhile, the northern, mainly Protestant provinces of the Netherlands had succeeded in establishing their independence from Spain and coming together in the Union of Utrecht in 1579. They had been led by William the Silent, Count of Nassau and Prince of Orange, upon whom was now conferred the hereditary 'stadholdership'. Both the Netherlands and William's descendants were to play an important part in English history, but he himself was assassinated by a fanatical Catholic three years later. England reacted to Spanish and Catholic intrigue in 1585 by assisting the Dutch, who were again under threat from Spain, which had managed to retake Antwerp. On the high seas, English privateers, such as Drake and Hawkins, had begun as merchants, intending to trade African slaves for Spanish gold and silver in the West Indies, but had been driven off by the Spaniards with such violence and savagery against their crews, that they had embarked on a campaign of revenge and piracy against Spanish treasure ships. Elizabeth protested her innocence in the matter to the Spanish king, while investing money and even ships in their enterprises. The experience gained was put to good use by Hawkins, when he was appointed treasurer of the navy, because this led to a revolution in English naval design that was to stand the country in good stead. Not only were the new ships for the English navy lower and faster than those of traditional design, but they were able to carry three times the armament possible on Spanish galleons.

Repressive legislation against Popery was such that, if it had been applied effectively, Catholicism would have been eliminated in England, in the same way as Protestantism was eliminated in Italy, France, and southern Germany. That it was not was due to the use of amateur officials in local government, because Justices of the Peace were reluctant to enforce the law against their own neighbours, who often were relations by marriage. Even so, Catholicism was virtually eliminated from the

---

122. Although Elizabeth was persuaded to sign the death warrant, she added a note to the effect that the sentence was not to be carried out without her consent. Cecil took it upon himself to summon a meeting of the Council, which agreed to forward the note of execution to those holding Mary. In this way, Elizabeth's prevarication was overcome.

working class, but it survived among small numbers of the wealthier and more influential landed class.

The execution of Mary Stuart, together with increasing rivalry and conflict between England and Spain in the Caribbean and the war in the Netherlands, finally prompted King Philip of Spain to put an end to the Anglo-Dutch combination against him by preparing an invasion of England. He was delayed for a year, however, by Drake's attack on the Spanish fleet in Cadiz, which devastated both the fleet and its morale, but dithering by Elizabeth prevented the navy from carrying out its preferred strategy of keeping Spanish sea power bottled up, and in 1588, Philip finally despatched a great fleet under Medina Sidonia. Known as the Invincible Armada, its purpose was to pick up an army in Flanders for an invasion of England. The Spanish army in the Netherlands, under the Duke of Parma, was the most efficient in Europe, and altogether more formidable than anything that England had to oppose it, so that, once landed, the outcome would have been inevitable. Moreover, Elizabeth's continuing efforts to negotiate prevented the navy from making a pre-emptive strike, leaving it separated and on the defensive. Nevertheless, with fewer but more efficient ships, longer-range guns and better seamanship, the English fleet, under the immediate command of Drake, should have been able to conduct a very damaging running engagement with the Armada during its progress up the Channel to Calais. In practice, the English guns at first did little damage, and Sidonia did not run into serious trouble until his fleet reached Calais, where he hoped that the Spanish army in the Netherlands were ready to be picked up. Instead, the army had only just learned of the fleet's arrival, and needed at least a week to prepare. This left Sidonia in a perilous position, because there was no harbour at Calais, leaving him to lie offshore, exposed to the winds and the English. Drake decided to use a strong westerly wind and the tide to carry English fire-ships into the enemy lines, forcing the Armada to disperse in confusion. Now at the mercy of the westerly wind, the ships of the Armada were carried almost to destruction in the shallows and shoals off the coast of Zealand. Saved at the last moment by a shift in the wind to the south, they were then engaged off Gravelines by the English fleet, which caused devastation and carnage on many of the Spanish ships, although few were sunk. Although the English fleet was eventually forced to break off the engagement through lack of ammunition, leaving the outcome of the battle indecisive, the southerly wind continued to carry the Spanish ships northward, into the North Sea. Returning to Calais was now out of the question, as was a return down the English Channel, leaving no option but to head for home around the British Isles. Already short of supplies, this was a daunting prospect. Sidonia was well aware of the need to sail well clear of Ireland, for fear of being driven ashore by the westerly winds, which now reasserted themselves, but his navigation was thrown badly awry by a failure to take account of the current, which the Gulf Stream still maintains at these latitudes. Also, he ran into heavy storms. Inevitably, a large part of his fleet found itself driven onto the rocky shores of western Scotland and Ireland. Although 86 of the original 130 ships of the Armada returned home, the death toll from injury and starvation had been heavy, and the psychological impact on Spain was shattering. The weather had played the decisive part in the operation, but England was now acknowledged as the premier sea power in Europe, a position that was to dominate England's destiny for the next three hundred years.

In spite of her success against Spain, the later years of Elizabeth's reign were no less difficult. By 1598, all the great companions of her younger days – Leicester, Knollys, Hatton, Drake, Hawkins, Frobisher, Walsingham and Burghley – were dead, and a new generation had grown up which was becoming impatient. 'From the very success of her government the nation was outgrowing the rule of the (Privy) Council ... so that her last years passed in resisting much opposition in the Commons'.[123] Protestant feeling, which had defeated Spain, was now imposing a Puritan programme, which she hated. Even so, Elizabeth's relations with Parliament were generally good. Although the Tudor period saw the continued reassertion of the authority of the Crown, it was one in which comparative harmony was maintained between it and Parliament. The Crown showed a respect for Parliament and an understanding of its purpose, but ensured that it did not step beyond the proper field of its perceived authority. On its part, Parliament accepted its limits and revelled in the decisive leadership and fair-mindedness which, on the whole, it received. There was one other factor which bound the

123. K. Feiling, *A History of England*, 408.

Crown and Parliament together in a sense of common endeavour. This was nationalism, induced by the religious struggle, buttressed by the combined enmity of Spain, France, and Scotland, and stirred by successes and achievements on the high seas.

In spite of the warm relations between herself and the Commons, Elizabeth did not hesitate to put a Puritan member of the Commons, Peter Wentworth, in prison in 1576 for saying that she was curbing freedom of speech. She understood Parliament and knew how to manage it, without being repressive. In return, she commanded its loyalty and affection. The House of Commons was restrained in its attitude to the Crown without hesitating to speak out when it thought fit, and Elizabeth understood the need to accompany a rebuke with a word of conciliation. She coped with the problem of unwelcome statutes by simply vetoing them, and this she did freely throughout her reign. She also made use of another prerogative, to pardon those who offended against both common and statute law. To her Counsellors, however, she was an often-exasperating Sovereign who was ruled by whims and tantrums, and who could never be persuaded to think in other than the short term.

As the standing and influence of the House of Commons grew, so also there opened up an opportunity for individual members to exercise real influence by winning elevation to the Privy Council. Being a member of the House of Commons now offered a career opportunity, and, instead of being a duty, attendance became a privilege. The House attracted able young men from the upper middle class, and these now had the advantage of a broader and more thorough University education. A point had been reached where the Commons, as representers of the people, was overtaken by the Commons as political careerists.

23.3.6.1. The Court of Star Chamber

The Court of Star Chamber, had become so popular by the end of Elizabeth's reign that the Lord Keeper of the Great Seal and Master of the Rolls issued a series of orders in 1596, clarifying and expediting its procedure. There was a problem in that the judiciary in the Crown courts were largely dependent on fees for their income, and these were particularly lucrative in civil cases. The judiciary were appointed from leading barristers, as now, and these were in turn recruited mainly from the lower middle class of the lesser gentry. Their training at the Inns of Court was narrow and largely by rote. They were appointed by the Sovereign, by whom they could be dismissed at will, which, on the whole, 'was perhaps fortunate'.[124] Both judges and juries were difficult to deal with, and in the provinces the juries were subject to bribery and intimidation. They also persisted in their medieval role as witnesses to fact, and could even be interested parties. On the other hand, a jury could sometimes be cowed by a formidable judge. It is against this background that the popularity of the Court of Star Chamber can be seen, and it was only here that problem juries and delinquent sheriffs could be dealt with. The Star Chamber was popular with private individuals already engaged in civil litigation in the Courts of Chancery or Common Pleas, who were seeking to strengthen their case, or simply to harass their opponents by levelling ancillary criminal charges against them. Like the Common Law courts, the Star Chamber was administering the common law, although by a different procedure, which admitted written depositions as evidence, and permitted cross-examination of the accused under oath. Neither these differences nor the Court of Star Chamber itself prompted any objection from the common lawyers or from the judges of the common law courts, not least, perhaps, because it was presided over by the Lord Keeper, himself usually a common lawyer, or by the Lord Chancellor, assisted by the two Chief Justices.

One Irish event that was later to lead to important constitutional consequences was a rebellion of the northern Irish under Hugh O'Neill, the Earl of Tyrone, in 1594. Their success at Yellow Ford in 1598 caused the trouble to spread, causing the English position in Ireland to become precarious, until the uprising was largely suppressed in 1600. It was re-ignited by a Spanish expedition in the following year, until both the Spaniards and Tyrone's Irish army were decisively beaten at the end of 1601. The price exacted was the confiscation of the estates of the rebel lords, which would later be used as 'plantations' for Protestant settlement.

One of the great political problems of Elizabeth's reign was the question of her successor, and one that she never faced up to. Her near death from smallpox caused particular alarm over the matter. Although she admitted dalliance with various suitors and had a particularly enduring

---

124. J. P. Kenyon, *The Stuart Constitution 1603–1688*, 74, 75.

relationship with Robert Dudley, she never married. She refused to name a successor, but made it known that she considered James VI of Scotland, the son of her cousin, Mary, to be the lawful claimant to the Crown. Elizabeth's reign was considered to be 'glorious' by later generations, rather than by her own, chiefly because it was to stand out in contrast to England's experience under her successors, the Stuarts. Under Elizabeth, England had achieved unity in the face of the external threat, reached a religious compromise that was acceptable to most, and emerged as the dominant sea power, the precursor to the Age of Empire. By the end of her long reign in 1603, England was almost solidly Protestant, and a return to Rome was now out of the question.

23.3.6.2. The 'New Monarchy'

Under the House of York, the monarchy had been emancipated from the restraints of a powerful nobility. The effects reached their full realisation under the Tudors and were to continue under the Stuarts. One consequence was the destruction of the Catholic Church and the reversion to an English Church that owed its position to the King. Before the rise of the 'New Monarchy', the most common complaint had been the 'lack of governance', but this had been replaced by the danger of a despotism that was unrestricted by legal rules.[125] In the Middle Ages the subject might have few dealings with the Crown unless he happened to hold land directly from it, or to be a party to proceedings before the Royal Courts of Justice, but contact with it could no longer be avoided, as royal control spread through the social and economic affairs of the nation. These were brought under increasingly minute regulation, so that 'the intellectual convictions of each individual, the most intimate scruples of his conscience, became the subject-matter of royal inquisition and coercion.' This in turn required an overhaul of the institutions of government, the most notable beneficiary being the King's Council, which established new regional councils, and drew local officials under its control, most notably the sheriffs and the Justices of the Peace. New specialist staff came into being, who included the most able minds of the age.

Inevitably, the perception of the monarchy changed to one of unquestioned political sovereignty. This was both reinforced and justified

---

125. D. Lindsay Keir, *The Constitutional History of Modern Britain, 1485–1937*, 3

by reference to Roman jurisprudence, which was enjoying a revival on the Continent, and which had its effect on English legal and political thinking. With royal supremacy established over the Church, the King was left with a virtual monopoly of power. The Church had been subordinate to the Anglo-Saxon Kings, whose political power had been limited. The Norman and Angevin rulers had enjoyed political power, but had to share it with the Church, and their authority over the nobility had been tenuous. Now, the King ruled in an exalted and unrivalled position. Not surprisingly, this gave rise to a doctrine that all political power flowed from the King. It was the feudal doctrine of monarchy, but with the Church now in a subordinate position, and the outcome has been described as 'the last and greatest contribution to the development of the modern doctrine of sovereignty'.[126]

23.3.7. Local Government

23.3.7.1. The Lord Lieutenant of the County (1551)

Rather than restoring the sheriffs to their proper role, the muddle of English local government was perpetuated by a decision to create a new post. Following the uprisings of 1536–7, which had been motivated by a mixture of religious and political discontent, as well as unrest over the enclosures, Henry VIII appointed Lord Russell in 1539 as his temporary lieutenant in the West Country, and other such temporary appointments followed. During the reign of Edward VI, from 1551 onwards, in reaction to local disturbances, lieutenants were regularly sent to the shires, year by year, until, by the end of the century, the whole country was divided into regular districts, over which lords lieutenant presided, although it was not thought necessary to provide each shire with a lieutenant, holding office by letters patent. Thus, there was regularly appointed in each county or group of counties: 'His Majesty's lieutenant of and in the county of … ', his main task being to maintain order. To this end he had command of the shire militia, once known as the *fyrd*, on such occasions as it was deemed necessary to raise one. Effectively, he took over the functions of the feudal lords. He was also responsible for its training and equipment, and the appointment of the mustering masters.

---

126. Ibid. 4–5.

The Lieutenant was usually selected from the local landed nobility with close links with the Royal Court, hence the use of the designation 'Lord Lieutenant', although occasionally he might be a commoner. To assist him, he was usually empowered to appoint one or more deputies in each shire.[127] The Lieutenant, whose primary function was therefore military, was responsible for choosing contingents for service abroad. The system was used with great skill by Elizabeth I after 1559, when her lieutenants were expected to work with the help of the local Justices of the Peace and the gentry to maintain order.

In the original French, *lieutenant* meant simply a 'place holder', but it came to be used in English in the sense of 'deputy', and in this particular context the title of Lord Lieutenant meant a 'deputizing lord', or 'vice-regal lord'. Under the watchful eye of the Privy Council, he grew in importance to become the formal head of his shire. In this capacity, he was usually encumbered with additional duties, such as administering taxation and religious conformity. He was thus the link between the Crown and the shires, passing back information and advice, as well as taking instructions. To this extent he replaced the sheriff as the King's representative in the shire, although many of the sheriff's duties remained with the Justices of the Peace. The Lord Lieutenant could be appointed or displaced at will. His central function of responsibility for the military continued until 1871, when the Cardwell and Childers reforms of the army based the recruitment of infantry regiments on the counties.

23.3.7.2. The Hundred and Parish

The hundred remained as an entity for tax collection. This was undertaken by petty constables, appointed by, and assigned to the task by the assize justices. On the other hand, the hundred courts, like the shire courts and the seigniorial courts, had, since the time of Edward I, lost many of their functions to the royal courts. Thus, as the hundreds declined and the manors decayed, many of their functions were taken over by the parishes, which now emerged as the basic unit of local government. The county continued as a military district, whose militia was assembled by mustering masters. The responsibility for representing the King in each shire, or county, had been borne over the centuries by a

---

127. G. R. Elton, *The Tudor Constitution*, 463–4.

succession of officers: the alderman, the earl, and the sheriff, and latterly the Lord Lieutenant and the Justices of the Peace, of whom there were several in each county.

One consequence of the imposition of royal control over the Church was the appropriation for civil purposes of the local unit of ecclesiastical administration, which was the parish. The parish, so called from the earlier French *paroche*, ultimately from Greek *paroikia*, 'sojourning',[128] undoubtedly a reference to the presence of a priest, was originally an area or community served by a church and priest, to whom tithes and ecclesiastical dues were paid. These not only supported the priest and maintained the church, but were passed on in part to help support the Church hierarchy and to be used for charitable purposes.

The parish church was built and owned by the community, with an east-west alignment, so that the congregation addressed their prayers to the rising sun, a practice inherited by the Church from the ancient Indo-European tradition, but re-interpreted to mean the direction of the Holy Land. A church comprised two main parts. Its layout was based originally on the Roman basilica, itself derived from the Mithraic temple. At the eastern end of the church was the chancel: the inner sanctum and the domain of the parish clergy, which contained the altar and choir. Normally, it was separated from the rest of the church by a screen, or 'chancel', hence the name. The western end of the church was the nave, which belonged to the laity, who assembled there for religious services or to conduct community activities. The public entrance to the church was through a covered porch at the western end, and it was here that, for centuries, it was the practice to conclude contracts and agreements. This practice went back to well before Christian times, when such agreements were concluded in the presumed presence of the Old English deity, Tiw, whose name is preserved in Tuesday, and who was the ancient Indo-European Supreme Deity, whose original name may have been Ansura.[129] In many cases, the Christian church had originally been located on an ancient sacred site, in order to neutralise it, and this may explain why it was seen as being still appropriate to the divine witnessing of transactions,

---

128. *Shorter Oxford Dictionary*.
129. Better known today by his Indian title of Varuna. The Supreme Deity presided over agreements, both as Deiwos (English Woden) who ruled over the form of the agreement, and as Ansura (Tiw), who made it binding, that is to say, enforced it.

for which purpose the porch was probably used in order not to provoke the ire of the Christian deity, or the priest. Evidently, it was subconsciously believed that the ancient deity was still present and able to give divine sanction to the agreement. This same principle governed the holding of Parliaments.

Responsibility for the church lay with an elected churchwarden, who acted as the lay representative of the people of the parish in matters of church organisation, and who managed the various parochial offices and assisted the incumbent priest. There were sometimes two churchwardens. He or they were assisted by elected assistants, known as sidemen, or sidesmen. In 1555 the parish councils were made responsible for maintaining the local roads.

23.3.7.3. The Problem of Poverty

Although the monarchy had acquired immense wealth under Henry VII, and even more so under Henry VIII, following the dissolution of the monasteries, these assets had quickly been sold, and by the end of the sixteenth century a combination of war and inflation had, once more, put the royal finances under strain. Nevertheless, both Henry VIII and Elizabeth avoided excessive taxation. It was a time of prosperity, but there was also much poverty. The influx of captured gold and silver from America was causing inflation, as the value of currency, based on gold and silver, declined and other commodity prices rose. Wages did not keep pace, creating social disturbance and poverty. The enclosure of open field and common land was leaving an unemployed and landless class and promoting robbery. Poor relief had hitherto been left to the Church and charity, but the impoverishment of the Church by Henry VIII had forced Elizabeth to recognise it as a civil function. A number of Acts were passed to deal with social distress, such as the Beggars Act of 1536, which provided that local government should care for the poor by means of charitable alms and should put able-bodied vagabonds to work. The parish, with its financial and administrative arrangements, offered a more convenient administrative base than the hundred, and in 1538, the Vicar General, Cromwell, required the parishes to maintain records of births, marriages and deaths, in spite of much opposition from the public, who feared that the tactic was for the purpose of new taxation.

Officers, such as the overseers of the highways, appointed by the central government to the parish, rather than the hundred, probably because it was the parish that now had the administrative facilities, supervised the parishioners in essential construction and repair work. Yeomen, or common freeholders, were becoming of increasing importance as unpaid office-holders of the parish. Just as the gentry had risen to power in local government from the time of Edward III, so, after the Reformation, it was the yeomen who rose to power in local government as unpaid overseers and other minor officials.

In an attempt to deal with the central problem of widespread poverty, the Poor Law Act of 1598 appointed the churchwardens of every parish and certain householders as overseers of the poor. They were to be responsible to two Justices of the Peace and were authorised to provide workhouses for the impotent poor, help them with money or goods, set the poor to work, and collect taxes from the parishes, which became known as 'poor rates'. To these, other responsibilities were later added. It was a development of huge significance, because the state was now beginning to accept a direct responsibility for the individual problems of the people, which, until the reign of Henry VIII, had been born by the Church.

23.3.7.4. Justices of the Peace

The original function of the Justice of the Peace had been to enforce the law, but several local government functions had since been added. The Justices of the Peace had thereby assumed most of the duties of the sheriff, but the arrangement had failed to compensate for the decline in the latter's power and status. The power of the Justices of the Peace reached its highest point in the Tudor period. They were appointed by the Lord Chancellor and served under the Keeper of the Rolls in each county. Being men of substance, they continued to be unpaid. Recruited from the gentry and burdened with numerous responsibilities, prescribed under many statutes, they discharged their duties with ability. They were now both the central feature of local government and the trusted agents of the Crown. About twenty justices now served in each shire, and one of them had to be present at the courts of Quarter Sessions, for whose administrative functions he was responsible. They became responsible for a large number of judicial, policing and administrative tasks, such as the application of the Poor Laws and the appointing of Overseers of the Poor. The justices also supervised the building of roads, bridges, hospitals, sewers and prisons; they licensed inns and beggars, appointed surveyors and petty constables of the parish, made and enforced rules in times of plague, and enforced laws against Puritans and Roman Catholics. To this end, they were empowered in 1739 to levy local taxes, later unified as a single 'county rate', under the control of a County Treasurer. All local royal officials, except the Lords Lieutenant, were responsible to the Justices of the Peace, who were, in turn, responsible ultimately to the Privy Council.

Meanwhile, the standing of the sheriffs had declined still further, due to their corruption and rivalries and the transfer of power to the Justices of the Peace. There were obviously benefits to be had from the greater localisation of administration through the use of justices, not least that they were unpaid, more familiar with the problems of each district, and in closer contact with the parishes, but an important effect was the still further decline in the significance of the shire.

PART IX

•

CONFLICT BETWEEN KING
AND PARLIAMENT

THE SCOTTISH INTRUSION (1603–1689)

24 • THE EARLY STUART DYNASTY

24.1. The Clash of Doctrines

Elizabeth I left no heirs after her death in 1603. Her father, Henry VIII, had, by his second and third Acts of Succession of 1536 and 1544, acquired the right to bequeath his throne at his will, either because there were no 'legitimate' heirs at the time of the second Act, or because there were so few at the time of the third. The latter had directed that, if both Henry and his son, Edward, should die without heirs, the Crown should go to Mary and Elizabeth, in that order, their legitimacy having been accepted. If all three lines failed to produce heirs, as was now the case, the Crown was to go to the heirs of his younger sister, Mary, Duchess of Suffolk, who was now Lady Catherine Grey, sister of the late lamented Jane. Unfortunately, Lady Catherine Grey had ruined her chances in Elizabeth's eyes by an unacceptable and secret marriage, and she and her husband had accordingly been consigned to the Tower. Constitutionally, Elizabeth had no say in the choice of her successor, either in common law or under feudal rules, but there had long been confusion in such matters; the priority of Acts of Parliament was widely accepted. Although there were those in the Council who still favoured Lady Catherine Grey, it was the Queen's express wish that she be succeeded by the line of her father's elder sister, Margaret, Queen of Scots, which her father had expressly excluded from the succession. Margaret's descendants undoubtedly had a prior claim according to the accepted rules of the day, making the current claimant her great-grandson, James Stuart, who was already ruling as King James VI of Scotland. It was his mother, Mary, the deposed Queen of Scots, whom Elizabeth had executed, while his father had been the feckless Henry Stewart, Lord Darnley. It is not known which was the decisive factor in Elizabeth's choice of James over Lady Catherine. It is not at all unlikely, given her nature, that Elizabeth felt an antipathy to the idea of being succeeded by another woman, but it is also likely that she wished to make amends to James's mother, Mary, Queen of Scots. Either way, it was a decision that was in defiance of the will duly executed by Henry VIII, under the power of an Act of Parliament,[1] and it was to have profoundly unfortunate consequences for England.

Indeed, the advent of the Stuart dynasty was destined to bring the constitutional conflict between Indo-European and feudal ideas to a head. For half a millennium, these two traditions had been rivals in the traditions of English government, generating stresses and strains, but without meeting head on. Whenever their incompatibility had come to the surface, the Indo-European tradition had generally proved to be the stronger, but the feudal notion of kingship had again taken the offensive across much of Europe, chiefly as a reaction against the Reformation and its rejection of established authority. England had so far avoided the Counter-Reformation, but France was very much caught up in it, and the close ties between France and Scotland provided a channel which brought the wash of the Counter-Reformation, first to Scotland and then, with the Stuarts, to the corridors and chambers of Westminster and Whitehall. It was to bring to an end the harmony which had existed under the Tudors, between monarch, council, and assembly.

The Stewart, or Stuart, dynasty of Scotland was descended from one, Walter the Steward, the High Steward of Scotland, who had married Marjorie, daughter of Robert de Brus, or de Braose. Better known under its Anglicised spelling of Robert the Bruce, the name was derived from the family's ancestral home near Falaise in Normandy, which is now spelt 'Brieuse'. It was their son, Robert the Steward, who had become the Scottish king, Robert II, in 1371, who had been the true progenitor of the Steward, or Stewart, dynasty. Meanwhile, it was Mary, Queen of Scots, who had previously been married to the King of France, Francis II, who had changed the spelling of the family name from Stewart to Stuart, for the benefit of the French court. There was a rumour that James Stuart was illegitimate, in that he was not his mother's son.[2] If this was the case,

---

1. F. W. Maitland, *The Constitutional History of England*, 252–3.
2. According to the rumour, James had been switched at birth when Mary's own child was stillborn. The discovery, much later, of the remains of a newborn baby at Edinburgh Castle, where James was born, added some support to the suspicion, although nothing was proved. Some noticed a marked resemblance between James and John Erskine, Earl of Mar, who had been Regent of Scotland for a short while.

the Stuarts were a *parvenu* dynasty. Be that as it may, James had been reared by the Scots as a Protestant, much against his mother's will, so there was no religious obstacle to his claim to the Crown of England. In one sense it was a useful choice, because it neutralised the Scots as a source of constant trouble. On the other hand, there was an element of risk in the choice of James, on account of his Catholic family background. The common law of the Constitution required the Great Council to look, if necessary, among the greater English nobility in its search for a suitable successor to Elizabeth, but the choice of the Stuarts to establish a new dynasty was a consequence of feudal doctrine, which helps to explain why they were allowed to bring such a disastrous period to England's constitutional history.

Elizabeth's wish was acceded to a few days after her death in March 1603, and in May, as he arrived in London from Scotland, James Stuart was proclaimed King. The coronation followed, associating England and Scotland under the same House of Stuart. The arrangement has often been described as a dynastic union of England and Scotland, but it needs to be understood that no constitutional union was involved. There was not even a union of crowns: James simply wore two crowns, as King James VI of Scotland, and now also as King James I of England. James's own enthusiasm for a political union between the two countries was coolly received in London, and the matter was effectively shelved by being referred to a commission for investigation. Although James was proclaimed 'King of Great Britain, France, and Ireland' in October 1604, this was merely a title. England and Scotland remained different countries, although, out of deference to their sharing of the same individual as ruler, they extended certain preferences to each other, an option that was often exploited by the King. For example, Scots were allowed to serve in English armies and to settle in English colonies, and in 1621, King James granted the former French territory of Acadia, whose conquest had been made by the English on behalf of the English Empire, to a Scotsman, the Earl of Stirling, with an injunction that it was 'to be known as Nova Scotia, or New Scotland'. It would seem that, in his capacity as King of England, he was appropriating an English territory and, in his capacity as King of the Scots, granting it to a Scotsman, with the instruction that it was to be clearly labelled as Scottish. James, who viewed the world through feudal eyes, undoubtedly regarded both countries and their possessions as two estates under his common ownership, which he could dispose of as he thought fit, and sometimes the advice of the Privy Council was undoubtedly clouded by the same confusion.

For the first time, the royal coat of arms had no constitutional relevance to England. Hitherto, the political pretensions of England had been more or less determined by the titles claimed by the King. However, the arms of James I introduced the lion of Scotland to one quarter and the Irish harp to another. Until now, England's position in Ireland had not been deemed important enough to clutter the royal arms. The two remaining quarters in James's case each contained a sub-quartering of the arms of England (three lions) and of France (fleurs-de-lis), making it clear that, as King of England he retained his claim to France, but as King of Scotland he did not. It was thus a coat of arms that was appropriate to James himself and to the Stuart dynasty, but not to England, for which Scotland remained a foreign country.

24.1.1. Doctrinal Conflict

Throughout the Christian period, up to the Reformation, the two competing constitutional doctrines, Indo-European, or common law, and feudal, had succeeded in maintaining an unstable balance across much of Europe. The divine authority of kingship had been partly accepted, but the right of the people to resist its excessive use, and even to approve the ways in which it was used, had also persisted in varying degrees. This uneasy dualism was upset by the Reformation, and nowhere more so than in France. Here, the majority remained solidly Catholic, and therefore receptive to feudal ideas, but the new capitalist-artisan class and a significant proportion of the nobility turned to Protestantism. Persecution by the Catholics of the Protestants, or 'Huguenots', as they became known, caused both sides to take up arms, and the weak state of the French monarchy allowed the situation to get out of hand. It was not only a religious struggle, because the Huguenots recognised that only the control of government would secure their cause, and a political party was accordingly formed to bring about constitutional change.

The religious wars in France continued from 1562 until 1598, during which the very survival of France as a state was endangered, particularly by the growth of Huguenot provincialism. These disturbed times had the effect of focussing attention on the need for a strong monarchy, and this prompted an outright assertion of the principle of the divine origin of royal authority. No French writer expressed this more effectively than Jean Bodin, in his work *Six Livres de la République*, or 'Six Books of the Commonwealth', published in 1576. Bodin gave himself the ambitious task of doing for modern politics what Aristotle had done for the ancient world, but his main achievement was to bring the principle of the divine right of kings out of theology and, together with an analysis of sovereignty, to bring it squarely into constitutional theory.[3] Bodin argued that the presence of sovereign power distinguishes the state, or *république*, as Bodin called it, from all other groupings. From this, he drew the conclusion that citizenship was subjection to a sovereign, and sovereignty was the 'supreme power over citizens and subjects, unrestrained by law'. Sovereignty could not be restrained by law, because it was the source of law. The sovereign could not bind himself or his successors, and he could not be made legally accountable to his subjects. On the other hand, there is no doubt that Bodin regarded the sovereign as answerable to God and subject to natural law. The sovereign's control over common law derived from the fact that he sanctioned it to exist. In a monarchy, such as he regarded France and England, sovereignty resided in the king, and the function of the three Estates was therefore advisory only. Indeed, the Estates, like all other corporate bodies, could exist only by the sovereign's acceptance.

Bodin was not without flexibility in his view of governments. Thus, if a king was bound by an act of the Estates, as in the Holy Roman Empire, then sovereignty really resided in the assembly, and the government was an aristocracy. If the final power of decision resided with some sort of popular body, then the government was democratic. Bodin accordingly saw a clear-cut distinction between state and government. The state was that which possessed the sovereign power, while government was the mechanism through which that power was exercised.

Clearly, there were contradictions in Bodin's theory. For example, sovereignty was limited by natural law, and although there was no way of making a sovereign accountable for violating natural law, there was

---

3. See G. H. Sabine, *A History of Political Theory*, 340–52.

nevertheless an obligation upon him, for instance, to respect private property and to keep agreements. Despite his concern to ensure a strong, centralised monarchy, Bodin seems to have faced a struggle to reconcile feudal principles with an instinct for Aryan constitutionalism. Although Bodin's modernised version of the doctrine of divine right was native to France, it quickly spread to its ally, Scotland, where it was taken up by King James himself, several years before he assumed the throne of England. Scotland had long maintained close relations with France, each using the other as a foil against the common enemy, England, and much French influence had, as a result, found its way into Scottish law and outlook. In 1598, James re-stated Bodin's doctrine in his *Trew Law of Free Monarchies*. By free monarchies, he meant royal governments independent of coercion by others. 'The state of monarchy', James wrote, 'is the supremest thing on earth: for kings are not only God's lieutenants upon earth, and sit upon God's throne, but even by God himself they are called Gods'.[4] Conscious that such a notion could not be fitted into any legal or logical framework, James argued that the office of king was a 'mystery' into which neither lawyers nor philosophers might inquire. The legal element in monarchy was therefore legitimacy, as evidenced by lawful descent from the previous legitimate monarch. Drawing on dubious evidence in the case of Scotland, James argued that kings existed before there were estates of men, before parliaments were held or laws made, and that even the ownership of land existed only by the grant of the king. This was an allusion to the Aryan custom of royal trusteeship of the collectively owned land of the nation, but an institution that could easily be adapted to the clerical idea of God's earth. Consequently, kings were the makers of laws. Without the king, there could be no civil society, leaving the choice between submission to the king and complete anarchy. However, the issue was not one for reasonable justification, but the arbitrary and omnipotent will of God. The Canons of 1640, approved by the Convocations of Canterbury and York, stated that 'The most high and sacred Order of Kings is of Divine Right, being the ordinance of God himself, founded in the prime laws of nature, and clearly established by express texts both of the Old and New Testaments', that is, 'that kings should rule and command in their several dominions all persons of what

---

4. *The Political Works of James I*, ed. C. H. McIlwain, 307.

rank or estate soever, whether ecclesiastical or civil, and that they should restrain and punish with the temporal sword all stubborn and wicked doers'. For subjects to bear arms against their kings, even in defence, as 'St Paul tells them plainly they shall receive to themselves damnation'.

Consequently, James and his Stuart successors saw the royal prerogative very differently from the Tudors. In the eyes of the Stuarts, it comprised those rights bestowed by God, for which the King was answerable to God only. Hence, the prerogative was not part of the law, but stood over and above it. Whereas, to the Tudors, *legibus solutus*, or 'exempt from the law', had meant the right to dispense with the law if equity required it, to the Stuarts it meant freedom to disregard the law, because that was under the King. The accession of the Stuart dynasty was, in fact, in accord with the trend across Europe, which was towards benevolent absolutism, with assemblies such as Parliament being consigned to obscurity, but the English Civil War was to deprive the Crown of a standing army, and this rendered a similar evolution in England almost impossible.

The dilemma facing those who gave serious thought to constitutional problems during the reign of James I has been well expressed by Goldwin Smith: 'From the days of Jean Bodin to the days of John Austin, political theorists, jurists, and philosophers have sought to locate sovereignty. It must lie somewhere in every state. The first half of the seventeenth century confronted many critical questions: If the king's power was absolute how could there be any rights against him? If his prerogative was limited, who placed the limits upon it and who would determine the extent of those curbs? *Quis custodes custodiet?* Was the King's discretionary power derived from and limited by the law or not? Could it be abridged by an Act of Parliament? Were the common law courts to vacate jurisdiction in any cases where the royal prerogative was involved, in the areas that James I called "transcendent matters"? Indeed, could Parliament interfere with or control the royal prerogative in any legitimate way? Did the privileges and liberties claimed by Parliament belong to it by right or as the result of a royal act of grace? Questions such as these show the tragic dilemma of Englishmen in the years before the Civil War. The first solutions proposed by them were to be republicanism, egalitarian democracy, and ideas of government by the saints and other fantasies. The sword has never been a good political primer'.[5]

Important though the constitutional question was destined to be under the Stuart dynasty, it was the religious issue that would dominate the relationship between the Crown and Parliament. Under the Tudors, religious feelings had been displaced by nationalism, but the Stuarts lost little time in destroying nationalism – they were, after all, a Scottish, not an English family – leaving the way open for the return of religious conflict.

24.1.2. Parliament and the Issue of Royal Prerogative

James I regarded his Coronation Oath with great seriousness, so that he was always careful to work within the framework of the common law. Although he regarded himself as responsible to God, not to his subjects, James acknowledged that in all ordinary matters a King ought to give the same respect to the law of the land that he demanded of his subjects, but this was a voluntary submission which could not be enforced.[6] His rule was at first welcomed in establishment circles for the joviality of his court, after the dourness of the latter years of Elizabeth's reign, but he was a pedantic and rather inept individual, in contrast to the heartiness of the Tudors, and he was not popular. Also, he was a foreigner, whose Scottish accent, compounded by a speech disability, made him difficult to understand. Insecure from a childhood starved of affection and always fearful of assassination, he was given to a pomposity that did little to endear him to others.

During the closing years of Elizabeth's reign there had been a decline in Puritanism, and serious thought about radical reform of the structure and liturgy of the Church of England had been abandoned.[7] Nevertheless, there was widespread concern on minor matters, which Elizabeth had done little to resolve. Consequently, the first issue thrust at James upon his arrival in England was a Millenary Petition from the clergy, requesting a number of reforms. James responded by holding a conference at Hampton Court in 1604.

The new King was regarded with a certain amount of suspicion on both sides of the religious divide – by the Catholic minority, because he

5. G. A. Smith, *A Constitutional and Legal History of England*, 325.
6. G. H. Sabine, *A History of Political Theory*, 338.
7. J. P. Kenyon, *The Stuart Constitution* (Cambridge, 1986), 111.

was a Protestant, and by the Protestants, because of his Catholic ancestry and his obvious tolerance of, if not sympathy for, Catholicism. The Nonconformists in Scotland had antagonised him. He was personally committed both to a Scriptural basis for Christianity and to the principle of episcopacy, the survival of the bishops in the Church of England giving him cause for great satisfaction. It was his belief in the religious basis of monarchy that gave rise to his remark, 'No bishop, no King'. As a result of the Hampton Court conference and the subsequent work of the Church Convocation, which still met at the same time as the Parliament, minor changes were made to the Prayer Book, a new, Authorised, Version of the Bible was produced (1611), and new canons were issued for the discipline and governance of the Church. The King's call for tolerance towards Catholicism, and the prospect even of a formal accommodation, caused some alarm, and Parliament responded in 1604 by passing 'an Act for the due execution of the Statutes against Jesuits, Seminary Priests, Recusants, etc.'. A royal proclamation was issued in the same year, admonishing the King's subjects to conform themselves to the form of the church service, and requiring the clergy 'either to conform themselves to the Church of England and obey the same, or else dispose of themselves and their families some other ways as to them shall seem meet'. Rehabilitation of the clergy, long in a run-down and disorganised state, and many of them 'scandalous and unworthy', was achieved by Archbishop Whitgift and his successor through better selection and training.

The enforcement of conformity caused some opposition from both clergy and laity, and this was reflected in the House of Commons, which tried to bring in measures of its own. In this, it was hampered by its recognition that the 'supreme power, as well in the Church as in the Commonwealth' lay with the King. Some of those unable to come to terms with conformity fled to America. On the whole, James dealt tactfully with the reaction, which gradually died away, so that it has been said that 'James's finest achievement was the establishment of a religious *détente* which had entirely eluded Elizabeth'.[8] Even so, the House of Commons did not fully accept the King's position as Supreme Governor of the Church, taking the view that, as it had passed the original legislation establishing the Church in 1559, it was free to amend the terms of its establishment.

8. Ibid. 115.

24.1.2.1. Adoption of the Union Jack

For the sake of convenience, James was in 1604 proclaimed King of Great Britain, France and Ireland, and his armorial bearings differed from that of his English predecessors, as noted above, by adding the Scottish lion and the Irish harp to the English lions and French fleurs-de-lis. Apart from reflecting his English and Scottish titles, and perpetuating the now fatuous claim to France, these bearings gave a new status to the King's Irish inheritance. Such heraldic details may seem arcane, but they represent claims to legal title, often fully justified in law, whether enforceable or not, and are of constitutional as well as dynastic significance. James further used his prerogative in 1606 to achieve a symbolic union of the English and Scottish crowns by ordering a common flag, to be used for the two kingdoms when acting together, otherwise each would continue to use its own flag, that is, the red cross on white of St George, in the case of England, and St Andrew's white diagonal cross, or saltire, on blue in the case of Scotland. The common flag, or 'ensign armorial of the United Kingdom of Great Britain', combined the two. It was first intended for use on ships of the Royal Navy, where it was flown from the jack-staff, at the bow of the vessel, as distinct from the larger ensign, or naval standard, which was already flown. For this reason, it soon came to be known in popular parlance as the 'Union Jack'. The device could, and can, equally be referred to an ensign, flag, jack, banner or standard, but because it first achieved its full significance at sea, it was as the 'Union Jack' that it found popular acceptance for all purposes.[9] Even so, the new flag was not appreciated at first by the Scots, because St George's cross was superimposed on that of St Andrew, yet it reflected the political reality. For all its initial disfavour north of the border, the Union Jack was destined, following the actual later union of the two countries in 1707, to do probably more than any other piece of symbolism, apart from the monarchy itself, to unite the two nations in their future endeavours.

James's unfamiliarity with the English way of doing things also brought considerable conflict between himself and Parliament, whose control over his finances, and whose presumption in matters which he felt did

---

9. See particularly A. C. Fox-Davies, 'The Art of Heraldry', from A Complete Guide to Heraldry (1904). Also G. C. Rothery, The Concise Encyclopedia of Heraldry (London, 1994), 294–7. In later centuries, squadron ensigns were also flown, to be replaced by a single Royal Naval ensign, comprising the union on a flag of St George.

not really concern it, such as the affairs of the Church, caused him much irritation. Nevertheless, he did not question the nature of Parliament, even going so far as to remind members that the relationship was between the King and his people, and that members of the Commons represented the latter only in a figurative sense, implying that their opinions should not always be counted as reliable. He also emphasised that the purpose of the members of Parliament was 'to give him their advice', the function of consent receiving no mention.[10] James was no judge of men, and much resentment was generated by his appointment of court favourites. One in particular, George Villiers, later made the Duke of Buckingham, was a mediocrity who was allowed to wield considerable influence on policy, and who spent much of the Crown's money on extravagance. The Privy Council, no longer steered, disintegrated into dissension and weakness. He did not follow the Tudor practice of ensuring the election to the House of Commons of a good number of Privy Council members and royal officials, who were thus in a position to exert influence in both directions. This contributed to the Privy Council's loss of influence over the House, causing the close link between King and Parliament to be thereby broken at a time when it was badly needed. Greatly adding to his difficulties was his view of his own position, and under the Stuart dynasty the process of restoring the constitutional power of the King was to reach its ultimate development in an ideological sense. In a practical sense, however, it had already reached its high point under the Tudors. James followed the example of his Tudor predecessors and issued frequent proclamations, such as one forbidding the growth of London, despite advice from his judges that they were unlawful. These could only be enforced by the Privy Council, sitting in its judicial role as the Court of Star Chamber, which otherwise remained as popular and effective as ever.

James opened his relations with his first Parliament of early 1604 with a dispute over the right to determine the validity of elections, to which there was no clear outcome.[11] This was soon followed by another,

---

10. The King's speech at the opening of Parliament, 19 February 1624.
11. This hung on the Buckinghamshire Election Case of 1604, when Chancery attempted to bar the return of Sir Francis Godwin, who had been outlawed on a technicality, and to give the seat to Sir John Fortescue, a Privy Councillor. This was opposed by the Commons, which again alleged a right to arbitrate on election returns. In the end, a compromise was reached in which the election was quashed. It seems doubtful, in any case, whether James and his Ministers wanted Fortescue to take the seat.

over the right of Parliament to cite precedent as justifying its claim to privileges. In James's view, all parliamentary privileges were granted by the Crown, and so could be withdrawn at any time. Consequently, they could not be used against the Crown. The Commons responded with a statement in 1604, known as the Apology of the Commons, which stated that 'our privileges and liberties are our right and due inheritance', which 'cannot be withheld from us, denied, or impaired' without causing wrong to the whole realm. It complained that the King was receiving ill advice from private sources, and requested that he 'receive public information from your Commons in Parliament', which, apart from the higher nobility, represented the 'flower and power' of the kingdom. It went on to state that 'the voice of the people in things of their knowledge is said to be as the voice of God'. We have come across this phrase before, and it is consistent with the view of Aryan antiquity that it was through the people that the will of the gods expressed itself in the interpretation of the common law. Meanwhile, religious friction had continued unabated. An edict banishing Catholic priests led, in the following year, 1605, to a foiled Gunpowder Plot to blow up Parliament. There followed the passing of penal laws against Papists.

The size of the House of Commons continued to grow, from 467 in 1604 to 504 in 1640, as also did the number of contested elections, although these still remained a very small proportion of the total. Meanwhile, the greater nobility had become a select but relatively small group, a third of the old nobility having disappeared by the time of Queen Elizabeth's death, due to extinction or convictions for treason, and they had not been fully replaced by new creations. James I showed few scruples, permitting the Duke of Buckingham to sell Peerages to raise money or to reward his friends, so that the House of Lords increased from 55 temporal Peers – scarcely more than the members of the Great Council – at Elizabeth's death, to 126 by 1628. In order to save himself the trouble of having to be present in an institution which he regarded as having no legal significance, the King revised the ceremony of introduction. As the scandalised Garter King of Arms, Sir Edward Walker, lamented: 'The frequent promotions to titles of honour and dignity since King James came to the Crown of England took off from the respect due to nobility'.

24.1.2.2. Parliament and the Royal Finances

Inflation had been a problem, on and off, since the Black Death in the fourteenth century. Debasement of the coinage by Henry VIII had caused a new bout, until the coinage had been restored by Elizabeth I, but silver from the mines in Mexico and Peru had been flooding into Europe since about 1550, and was to continue to do so until about 1650. By increasing the supply of money, which was largely based on silver, without equally increasing the supply of goods and services, this had the effect of reducing the value of money. Thus, between the accession of Elizabeth and that of James I, the cost of living, according to a crude index, rose by 51 per cent.[12] This made it impossible for the King to live on his hereditary revenues, even in peace time, because these were largely fixed. Since the time of Edward III, the beginning of every reign had been marked by a grant to the new King of customs duties, a practice known as 'tunnage and poundage',[13] but this soon proved inadequate to James's needs, and he pressed Parliament for an additional yearly income.

Similar financial difficulties faced Parliament, and the House of Commons, being dominated by the landed class, who were reluctant to agree to new taxes, particularly as the Thirty Years' War at first caused an economic recession. The House, quickly possessed of a hostile mood, became more uncooperative as James's unpopularity in the country at large caused the people to elect individuals who were particularly ill-disposed towards him. As usual, the Commons exploited its power over taxation to 'screw' the King, who responded with numerous impositions and other schemes to raise money, such as resorting to the use of purveyance and ship money, without having to go through the process

---

12. Based on a composite figure for the prices of a dozen foodstuffs. See J. A. Clapham, *A Concise Economic History of Britain*, 186–7.

13. Tunnage and poundage: originally a reference to the charge per tun, or cask of wine, and the duty on all imports and exports, other than bullion and items paying tunnage, so that predominantly it applied to wool, assessed at the rate of so much per pound sterling. The term 'sterling' seems to have derived from Old English *steorling*, 'little star', a reference to silver pennies bearing a small star that were circulated in early Norman times. A pound weight of silver of a defined purity was equivalent to 240 starlings or sterlings, and these were accordingly used as a reliable measure of value for commercial purposes. One pound sterling was therefore a pound's weight of sterlings, numbering 240, that is, one pound of silver. It was the regulated purity of the silver used in the coins that gave the pound its importance as a measure of value.

of seeking parliamentary approval.[14] Mary and Elizabeth had already used such impositions and, in the closing years of her reign, Elizabeth had begun to exploit such fiscal rights as she had with great vigour, such as her distribution of monopolies, which had caused a parliamentary revolt in 1601. Its grievances had soon been revived after the accession of James, and in the Parliament of 1610, objections were raised to his use of these devices, most of which were either obsolete, such as feudal dues, or inappropriate, and so regarded as illegal. The Lord Treasurer, Salisbury, submitted a proposal for a rationalisation of taxation. This envisaged a regular income for the King in perpetuity, through a permanent land tax or an excise, in return for the King's surrender of his feudal rights of purveyance, wardship and marriage. This proposal for a 'Great Contract' found little favour with the King, who was reluctant to relinquish sources of income which had the advantage that they moved with inflation, in favour of a fixed sum which would only bring him back to the same problem. It also found little favour with the Commons, which was reluctant to agree to such a tax on its own class, and which was in any case unhappy about making the King financially independent of Parliament. Consequently, the proposal foundered, and the Commons therefore devoted itself to debating the King's power to levy impositions. This did nothing to solve the King's problem, until he forbade the Commons to continue. The Commons therefore embarked on a 'full examination' of the King's prerogative powers regarding taxation, and the King, weary of the haggling, dissolved Parliament in 1611.

24.1.2.3. Legislation by Royal Prerogative

Exasperation with the King's practice of making full use of the royal prerogative to legislate finally led the Privy Council in 1611 to consult the opinion of the Chief Justice, Coke, and three fellow judges on the legality of proclamations. The ensuing opinion found expression in the Case of Proclamations of that year. This concluded that a royal proclamation could not create an offence that was previously unknown to law, and that no prerogative existed except what the law allowed. The Statute of Proclamations of 1539 had confirmed the right of Henry VIII to ensure

---

14. Ship money could be levied on coastal towns in time of crisis for the purpose of ship-building. Purveyance allowed the Crown to buy victuals and commandeer transport at rock-bottom prices.

'the good order and governance of the country' by proclamation, and although this had been repealed by Edward VI, this repeal had been ignored, until the power was abused by James I. Now the judiciary had ruled against the King. The decision gave protection against the misrule of the Stuarts, but this rejection of the principle of administrative law, as it became known in France, created what would become a serious legislative problem. It meant that Acts of Parliament would have to fill the gap by their increasing complexity, as they found it necessary to anticipate every possible implication of the main principle behind each piece of legislation.

The Addled Parliament of April–June 1614, became known as such because it was locked in quarrelling with James over his impositions of customs duties without a parliamentary grant. That a Parliament composed overwhelmingly of landowners should be so preoccupied shows the existence of a powerful merchants' lobby, both inside and outside Parliament.[15] By this time, the King's financial position was desperate, but an appeal to Parliament to provide him with money fell on deaf ears. The Lords began to feel concern, and the Bishop of Lincoln, addressing them, referred to the 'Commons growing insolent', and alleged that it was 'more like a cockpit than a council'. Instead of discussing the King's financial needs, the Commons devoted itself to debating its grievances, so that it was dissolved without granting him a penny. It was the last Parliament to be called for seven years.

Hostility towards the Crown was now as important as the availability of money, and the King sank into a state of chronic indebtedness. Thus, in 1618 the Queen lay in state for ten weeks while the money was scraped together for her funeral, but when the Whitehall Banqueting House burned down in the following year, its reconstruction began within six months. The unsettled atmosphere was not helped by James's favouritism, mostly towards irresponsible and incompetent men like George Villiers, later Duke of Buckingham, who spent the King's money lavishly, and to whom the King granted monopolies. Selling monopolies to others was now one of the ways in which the King made money, but his successive failures in foreign affairs also counted against him, particularly as war-clouds gathered over relations with Spain.

---

15. J. P. Kenyon, *The Stuart Constitution*, 47.

24.1.2.4. The Mace and the Issue of the King-in-Parliament

James's conflict with Parliament soon began to affect parliamentary institutions, as is clear from an objection raised by the radical leader of the House, John Pym, who, in his extra-parliamentary life, was also an official in the revenue service, and who questioned the presence of the Mace in the House, complaining that he failed to see why either its presence or that of the Speaker was necessary to its proceedings. The close link between the Speaker and the Crown was well understood, and it is likely that Pym was aware of the tradition that the Mace represented the King's presidency over the proceedings of the Chamber. By this time, not only was there conflict between the Commons and the King, but there had arisen an issue as to whether the Speaker was the servant of the Commons or of the King. Pym's complaint, therefore, was probably an expression of anti-royal sentiment, rather than ignorance. The issue appears not to have been pursued, but the change of dynasty had marked a shift in attitude towards the nature of the Speakership and aroused hostility towards the presence of the Mace. Yet the Mace could not be removed without, at least symbolically, deposing the King, and so rendering the proceedings of the Commons null and void. It was undoubtedly in a reaction to this that members of the House of Commons invented a new interpretation of the significance of the Mace, notably, that it symbolised their own authority. In so doing, they further obscured the true nature of Parliament.

Questions over the King's right to impose taxes were aroused when the Earl of Salisbury became Lord Treasurer in 1608 and soon imposed duties on most imported commodities. The House of Commons called for an inquiry in February 1610, and the ensuing debate in June soon wandered from the immediate issue into a general discussion of the right to tax without consent. In a celebrated speech, James Whitelocke propounded the argument that taxation was vested in the Sovereign Authority, and this was neither the King nor Parliament alone, but the King-in-Parliament. This idea of the King-out-of-Parliament being subordinate to the King-in-Parliament, which was 'the most sovereign and supreme power above all and controllable by none', has influenced thinking to the present day, and shows that constitutional misconceptions were now gathering pace. Whitelocke was correct in his implication, whether intended or not, that the King alone had limited authority without Parliament, and that

Parliament was a powerless gathering without the King. Parliament was, by definition, therefore, the King-in-Parliament. Also, Whitelocke was mistaken in attributing absolute sovereignty to the King-in-Parliament, unless by this he meant Parliament as the assembled people, and not merely their representatives in the Chamber.

Elsewhere in western Europe the trend was towards enlightened despotism, as Church-Feudalism gained the upper hand and assemblies – the Estates-General in France, the Cortes in Spain, and the Diet of Brandenburg in Germany – disappeared. In Scotland and Ireland, the Parliaments were already the obedient tools of King and Council. For monarchy to triumph in this way, it needed a standing army and a paid bureaucracy in the provinces, and, if possible, a secure supply of money, although none had these, and it proved not to be vital. The Stuarts also had none of these, and James I saw clearly that the chief reason for his inability to impose royal authority was the absence of a standing army. There was not even a paid bureaucracy in the provinces that he could use to apply a personal rule, because the provinces were administered very largely by officials who were sufficiently affluent to provide their services free and were expected to meet most of their expenses out of their own pockets, or from the emoluments of their work. In contrast to most other countries, the expenses of the English Crown were closely scrutinised and controlled by the assembly, which, as representatives of the taxpayers, liked to do things as cheaply as possible. The solution, so far as James was concerned, was to fight a successful war, and from it inherit a standing army, with which he could assert his rightful authority. Consequently, he devoted much of his attention to foreign policy. His chief objective was a reconciliation with Catholic Spain, with which, as a Scottish ruler, he had no quarrel. Scotland's friendship with that country enabled him, in 1604, to bring an end to the war which had dominated so much of Elizabeth's reign. In 1611 he opened negotiations for the marriage of his son to a Spanish princess, and a few years later he had Sir Walter Raleigh executed as reparation to Spain for Raleigh's plundering of Spanish towns in South America. These efforts at reconciliation and alliance with Spain were intensely unpopular, but tolerated until the outbreak of the Thirty Years' War in 1618.

24.1.2.5. Committees of the Whole House: The Need for Secrecy

The functions of the Speaker in the Commons were much the same as those of the Lord Chancellor in the Lords. Although the Speaker was the agent of the Commons, he had to be acceptable to the King if he were to perform his functions effectively. For this reason, Speakers were frequently also royal servants and nominees of the King. In this role, the King was often, effectively, usurping the original purpose of the Speaker, which was to represent the views of the Commons. The Speaker was a useful channel of communication, but during an era of confrontation between King and Commons, his role could be a very difficult and even dangerous one. Under the Tudors and the Stuarts, the first loyalty of the Speaker was claimed by the Monarch, and often he acted as a royal informant. For this reason, under the Stuarts, the House of Commons adopted the practice of appointing a committee of the whole House to deal with matters of finance. Being only a committee of the House, it was not the House in official session, even though all the members of the House were appointed to it. Because the Commons was not now in session, neither the King, who, we concluded earlier, was embodied in the Mace, nor the Speaker, had a right to be present. Consequently, the Speaker vacated the Chair and the Mace was removed. This arrangement, which adds confirmation to the view that the Mace symbolised the King's presence, allowed members to speak freely without their words being reported back to the King, and became known as a Committee of Ways and Means, that is, ways and means of providing the money sought by the Crown. It was presided over by a Chairman appointed by the Committee, who came also to assume the role of deputy Speaker of the House. This device of 'going into committee' was destined to continue until 1968.

24.1.2.6. Culmination of the Counter-Reformation: The Thirty Years' War

The Thirty Years' War was the Catholic reaction to the rise of Protestantism in Europe, and amounted to a battle for supremacy between Lutherans and Catholics. The Counter-Reformation had been a half-hearted reform of the Church, such as the reform of the Franciscan order in 1526, but mainly it had been an attempt to expunge

Protestantism. This attempt had been marked by the creation of the Jesuits in 1534, the Roman Inquisition in 1542, and the Congregation for the Propagation of the Faith in 1622. It had also erupted in political strife between the Catholic League – established in 1609 by Maximilian II, Duke of Bavaria and German Emperor – and the Protestant Union, which had been created in the previous year by Frederick IV, Elector Palatine. So far, the Counter-Reformation had achieved little, but its provocation led to a Protestant revolt in Bohemia in 1618, when two newly-appointed Catholic governors were thrown out of a window of the palace in Prague, an event recorded in history as the Defenestration of Prague. The Protestant Union sent an army under Mansfeld and Turn to support the rebels, while the Catholic League responded by sending an Imperial army under Jägerndorf. The outcome was a victory for the Protestant forces, which then made an aborted attempt to seize Vienna. The confrontation deepened across the Empire, with the Bohemians declaring the new Catholic Emperor, Ferdinand, as deposed, and electing in his place the Elector Palatine, Frederick V, who happened to be the son-in-law of James I of England. Ferdinand responded by allying himself with the Catholic League and with Spain, whereupon Spain sent an army under Spinola to invade the County Palatine in the Rhineland.

England was inevitably drawn into the conflict, with James caught between the interests of his daughter and his wished-for *entente* with Spain, which was now regarded in England with revulsion. Unwillingly, he was driven in 1621 to give military assistance to his Protestant brother-in-law, while Spain and Catholicism were once more seen as the enemy by the country at large. James's efforts at mediation and intervention were futile. Frederick, whose brief tenure as Elector made him laughingly known as the 'winter king', lost his new crown at the battle of the White Mountain, near Prague, and fled into exile with his wife, leaving James looking foolish in the eyes of Europe. As its name suggests, the Thirty Years' War was destined to continue for the duration of, and well after, James's reign, convulsing much of the continent, but leaving England as a side-player. England's interest was chiefly confined, from now onwards, to the struggle in the Netherlands between the Dutch, who were bent on winning their independence, and the ruling power, Spain, which was detested for its efforts to suppress Protestantism.

24.1.2.7. Restoration of the Baronet

Meanwhile, an Irish rebellion led by O'Neill, Earl of Tyrone, which had been put down in 1601, had resulted in the confiscation of large estates in Northern Ireland. This opened the way for the Plantation of Ulster, from 1611 onwards, when the land was shared out to English and Scottish colonists. There had been several previous plantations in Ireland during the reign of Elizabeth, the purposes of which had been to establish Protestantism, in keeping with her Coronation Oath, and to ensure a more effective control over a country that was becoming a liability. These earlier attempts had either failed or been frustrated by O'Neill's forces.

As a means of raising money for the defence of settlers in Ulster, King James founded, by means of letters patent, the Order of Baronets, in 1611. This restored a much older title that had been introduced in the time of Richard II to denote barons who had ceased to receive a personal summons from the King, for whatever reason, effectively relegating them from the Peerage. To what extent, if at all, baronetcies had survived from that time is unknown. They had simply disappeared from the record, so that it is not known whether they had died out, or were simply not acknowledged. A baronet was required to be a gentleman of good birth, that is, his grandfather in the male line had borne a coat of arms. He was also required to have an estate yielding at least £1,000 per annum, which was undoubtedly necessary, because he was required to pay a stipend to thirty soldiers over three years. In rank, a baronet was between a baron and a knight, and was entitled to a knighthood, but he was not entitled to sit in the House of Lords. A baronet was thus descended from noble stock, but he was not himself a member of the greater nobility. The title was usually abbreviated to 'Bart' or 'Bt'. Shortly afterwards it was stipulated that baronets should have precedence immediately after the sons of viscounts or barons. Although its purpose was purely fiscal, and thus a form of corruption, the move did give recognition to an element in the lesser baronage. The original limit of 200 members was later rescinded. In 1619, the Order of Baronets of Ireland was established, followed in 1625 by Scotland and Nova Scotia. Only one woman was ever created a baronetess, and that was in 1635.[16]

---

16. Baronets would continue to be created until 1964.

In addition to his impositions, James I found a new source of income in the granting of benevolences and the issue of patents of monopoly on an unprecedented scale, particularly to his favourites. It was finally brought under control by Parliament, through the Monopolies Act of 1624, which confined the grant of monopolies to new inventions. Meanwhile, successive Lords Treasurer tried to maximize the income from Crown lands, while informers searched for encroachments, often committed generations back, on the royal forests or the Crown estates. In any litigation over property, the King, in his legal right as the lord of lands, had an overwhelming advantage, leaving a trail of legal and financial grievance. This common law right as lord of lands appears to be a reference to the ancient function of the King as custodian of all land in the realm.

24.1.3. Common Law, Statute Law, and the Prerogative

Provoked by the claims of James and his successors in the Stuart line into claiming constitutional supremacy, the House of Commons took advantage of the financial difficulties of the Crown to assert itself. The Stuarts reacted by regarding this as a challenge to their divine right. Whereas the Tudors had regarded the principle of *legibus solutus*, 'by the laws exempt', as meaning the right to dispense with the law if equity required it, to the Stuarts it meant a freedom to disregard the law, because the law was under the King.[17] As James I is reputed to have remarked in 1621: 'I will govern according to the common weal, but not according to the common will'. James was anxious to make his view of the monarchy clear, while at the same time reconciling it to the reality of its position, but his repeated 'digging' at his opponents did not fail to arouse animosity. In *The Trew Law of Free Monarchies*, published in 1598, he had asserted that kings were God's vice-managers on earth, that there were no limits to their power, and that the sole function of elected assemblies was to give advice. Indeed, he went further, declaring that 'the King makes daily statutes and ordinances … without any advice of Parliaments or Estates'. In a speech to Parliament in March 1610, James proclaimed that 'The state of monarchy is the supremest thing upon earth; for kings are not only God's lieutenants upon earth, and sit upon God's throne, but even by God

---

17. T. Smith, *De Republica Anglorum*, 58–62.

himself they are called gods'. However, while still retaining his special relationship with God, James went on to add that, in settled states, kings ought to abide by the law that their predecessors had helped to create. They were not bound to respect the rights and customs of their subjects, but, if they did not, they would find themselves answerable to God for what they did. Much as James believed that he was entitled to create such laws as he saw fit, without the advice of a Parliament of the people, he realised that he simply did not have the practical means available to be a despotic monarchy, such as a standing army, and he was therefore bound to accept his limitations with as much grace as possible. When the House of Commons complained in 1610 that he was abusing his right to issue proclamations by creating new crimes not hitherto recognised in law, and transferring existing crimes from one jurisdiction to another, the King consulted the two Chief Justices and accepted their decision against him. In the same year, he assuaged the annoyance of Parliament by suppressing a book that had reflected his own view of monarchy,[18] but not without including in his proclamation reference to 'all the deepest mysteries that belong to the persons or state of kings or princes, that are gods upon earth', pointedly adding that men 'spare not God himself'. Yet in some ways he was more moderate in his behaviour and more 'constitutional' than Queen Elizabeth had been.[19]

Opposition to the King's ideas came also from some of the judges and lawyers of the common law courts, led by the Chief Justice of the Court of Common Pleas, Sir Edward Coke. They took the stance that the royal prerogative power was subject to the common law, and that the rights of both King and Parliament were derived from, and defined by, precedent. It was the peculiar wisdom of the common law that determined the welfare of the people, something which the King could not do. Hence, the common law was greater than the Crown. This appears to be a reference to the Constitution, whose existence was implied, although no longer remembered as such. This element among the judiciary was usually determined to enforce these views, however, and there were several unpleasant scenes between Coke and the King.

Not all the courts took this line. The Court of Exchequer in 1606, in Bate's Case, upheld the King's long-exercised right to impose import duties

---

18. Dr John Cowell's law dictionary, *The Interpreter*.
19. F. D. Wormuth, *The Royal Prerogative, 1603–1649*, 93.

for the regulation of trade and the protection of local manufacturing, but it made a distinction between the King's 'ordinary' and 'absolute' prerogatives, the former being subject to the Court's ruling, the latter not. It held that impositions on foreign goods and all foreign relations were matters of state, and so belonged in the province of the King's 'absolute' power. Because the King must have revenues, he must and can take what he needs. As Chief Baron Fleming expressed it, the absolute power of the King was not being exercised for the benefit of any particular person, but for the general benefit of the people. The complainant, Bate, on the other hand, was concerned, not with the public good, but with his personal profit, which was not affected in any case, because he simply added the cost of the duty to the price of his wares. Moreover, the King had continually exercised this power, despite all Acts of Parliament against it. In other words, precedent had to be accepted.

A similar view was taken by the Court of Exchequer Chamber in respect of Calvin's Case, in 1608. In this, it was claimed on behalf of a Scottish minor, Robert Calvin, that a London freehold in the possession of two Englishmen in fact belonged to him. The defendants argued that Calvin was born in Scotland, and therefore was an alien. Under English law an alien could not own land in England, because land carried with it political duties which an alien could not perform. The plaintiff replied that Calvin had been born under the allegiance of James VI of Scotland after his accession to the English throne as James I; he therefore bore allegiance to the same king as the English, and so was not an alien. The defence responded that James VI and James I were separate kings holding separate offices. In their judgement of the case, Sir Edward Coke argued that whoever was born within the King's power or protection was not an alien, while Lord Chancellor Ellesmere took the view that to distinguish between James VI and James I amounted to a distinction between king and crown, which was dangerous and gave rise to too many absurdities. This judgement in favour of Calvin asserted, in effect, that allegiance belonged to the person of the king and not to the legal office.[20]

Another, different but related, and certainly significant, case of this period concerned an action for false arrest and imprisonment by a medical practitioner, Bonham. A monopoly of medical practice in London had

---

20. G. A. Smith, *A Constitutional and Legal History of England*, 306–8.

been granted by Henry VIII to the members of the College of Physicians, and this grant had been confirmed by Act of Parliament. Bonham, having been refused the right to practice, did so anyway, and was fined and imprisoned by the College. He responded by starting an action against it. Sir Edward Coke, now Chief Justice of the Court of King's Bench, citing precedents, ruled that, when an Act of Parliament is against common right and reason, or repugnant, or impossible to be performed, the common law will control it, and adjudge such an Act to be void. In effect, he was saying that there were principles of the fundamental common law which were superior to both King and Parliament.[21] Citing precedents from the Middle Ages, Coke held that the courts may hold a statute to be void, either because it conflicts with reason and common law, or because it intrudes on the royal prerogative. Coke's opinion was not subsequently maintained in English law, although it was accepted in a case of 1701,[22] and the belief that basic principles of common law could not be overridden by statute was common enough at the time. It has been pointed out that the cases in which judges actually announced that a statute could be invalid for infringing any other portion of the common law than that which guaranteed the integrity of the existing governmental structure are few.[23] This seems to be consistent with our earlier conclusion that, whether or not Parliament could override ordinary common law, it could not infringe *mos maiorum*, that is, the common law of the Constitution.

This issue brings us back to the point made earlier, that the Indo-European legal tradition sees law, whether common or statute, only as perceived divine law, or 'natural' law. Coke touched upon this, and although statute law has since overridden common law, or been given priority, on innumerable occasions, Coke's point was later to re-emerge in America as the basis of the principle of judicial review.

24.1.3.1. The Judicial Power of the King

The King's own judicial power came under question in 1607. At this time the judiciary of the common law courts were conducting an 'intermittent guerrilla campaign' against what they felt to be growing

---

21. Ibid. 308–9.
22. *City of London v Wood* (1701).
23. F. D. Wormuth, *The Royal Prerogative, 1603–1649*, 64.

competition[24] from the rival ecclesiastic courts and from the Court of Star Chamber, the Court of Chancery (against which they were accused of formulating a bastard equity of their own), the Council of the North and the Council of the Marches and Wales. The Archbishops controlled the Court of High Commission and had reinvigorated their consistory courts of appeal.[25] In his concern to preserve and expand the jurisdiction of the court of common law, Sir Edward Coke resorted with enthusiasm to the issuing by the King's Bench of writs of prohibition on matters of disputed jurisdiction. The ecclesiastical courts in particular were affected, Coke ruling that the ecclesiastical courts had no jurisdiction in cases where the common law courts provided a remedy, apparently on the ground that this represented unwarranted duplication. In 1607, the issue was contested in what became known as Fuller's Case. A Puritan lawyer, named Fuller, had insulted the Court of High Commission, for which he was sent to prison. Fuller appealed to the King's Bench for a writ of prohibition, known as a prohibition *del roy* – 'of the King' – alleging that the Court of High Commission had no power to imprison for contempt. The writ was issued and the case was referred to the Court of Exchequer Chamber, where the Archbishop, Bancroft, appealed directly to the King, requesting that he cancel the writ and stop the further issue of writs of prohibition by the King's Bench. He advised the King that, in the Church's view, in any case in which there was not express authority in law, the King himself might decide it; moreover, that the judges were but the delegates of the King, whose determinations he could himself rule upon. Coke, at the time Chief Justice of Common Pleas, then responded, claiming in his own later account that he had the unanimous support of all the judges of England and the barons of the Exchequer present. He declared that 'the King in his own person cannot adjudge any case ... but this ought to be determined and adjudged in some court of justice, according to the law and custom of England, and always judgments are given ... so that the Court gives the judgment'. Although the King might sit with his Lords as the supreme judge over all ordinary judges, and although he might sit in the Court of Star Chamber and the King's Bench, and although he was

---

24. J. P. Kenyon, *The Stuart Constitution*, 75–6.
25. The Court of Arches in London (for the Province of Canterbury), and the Court of Chancery in York.

always, in principle, present in any royal court in the judgement of law, the judgements were always those of the court.

Then, according to Coke, the King said that he thought the law was founded upon reason, and that he and others had reason as well as the judges. To this, Coke responded by saying that, while it was true 'that God had allowed His Majesty excellent science and great endowments of nature … His Majesty was not learned in the laws of his realm of England'. The causes which concerned the life and welfare of his subjects were 'not to be decided by natural reason (which the King claimed), but by the artificial reason and judgement of law, which law is an art which requires long study and experience before that a man can attain to the cognisance of it'. At this, the King was greatly offended, pointing out that this argument placed the King beneath the law, which amounted to treason. Coke replied by quoting Bracton's dictum that the King ought not to be under man, but under God and the law.[26] James eventually accepted the advice of the Court of Exchequer Chamber, to which the case had been referred, and with which Coke concurred, that the King's Bench should continue to issue writs of prohibition, but only with discrimination and sound sense.

This account was written later by Coke himself,[27] who was an intimidating man in his temper and character, so that the alleged unanimity of the judiciary on this occasion should be accepted with some reservation. Nevertheless, he was one of the foremost jurists of his generation, and his views, although 'highly controversial', were 'enormously influential'.[28] As Maitland has observed, although the King was constitutionally acknowledged to be 'the highest judge in the realm', he was not so in reality.[29] As we discovered, it was a function that he delegated to his justices, whose appropriate training he ensured. The Fuller Case was therefore a struggle over jurisdiction between the judicial function of the Privy Council, as exercised through the royal courts in respect of the Second Estate, or exercised through the Privy Council in the royal courts in respect of the Third Estate, and an ecclesiastical court that had been set up by the Privy Council. It was an issue that the Privy

---

26. *Quod rex non debet esse sub homine, sed sub Deo et lege.*
27. Coke, *Reports*, vi, 280–2 (part xii, 63–5).
28. J. P. Kenyon, *The Stuart Constitution*, 75.
29. F. W. Maitland, *The Constitutional History of England*, 269.

Council, as such, was perfectly capable of resolving, although in this case another of its royal courts, that of Exchequer Chamber, was chosen for the purpose. It was here that the issue was confused by the Archbishop, who, evidently believing that the King would favour the Church, tried to persuade him to make a personal ruling. The Chief Justice argued, in effect, that although the King was supreme judge, and in law presided over all his courts, he could not pass judgement in his personal capacity. He could only do so as the presiding judge in a court of law, in consultation with his fellow judges, whom he had appointed, in this case, the barons of the Exchequer. The judgement was not, therefore, that of the King personally, but of the court. The Chief Justice went further, claiming that, the state of the law and of the legal profession being what it now was, the King was no longer competent to sit as a judge in person. In constitutional law, he still presided over every national court which he had set up and to whose judges he had delegated his authority, but discretion and the interests of the plaintiffs were best served if he did not assert his judicial authority in person. There seems to have been no real conflict of principle on this occasion, bearing in mind that the King did not take the bait held out by the Archbishop, and that he evidently had no intention of personally asserting his judicial authority in any other way. What offended the King was that his judicial authority should appear to be questioned by his own justices. Meanwhile, the actual issue before the Court of Exchequer Chamber – the right of the King's Bench to issue writs of prohibition – was decided within it, if not specifically by it.

In the Case of Proclamations of 1610, the Court of King's Bench ruled that a royal proclamation was not a law. In the case at issue, a man who had built a house in a particular spot in defiance of a royal proclamation had not, therefore, committed an offence and so could not be brought to trial. Coke and his fellow judges, in their ruling in 1611, asserted that the law of England consisted of common law, statute law, and custom, and that a royal proclamation was none of these. The King had no prerogative but what the law of the land allowed him, and if an offence was not punishable in the Star Chamber, the prohibition of it by proclamation could not make it so. Coke's argument in this case was flimsy, yet its effect 'was virtually to destroy the legal grounds upon which the authority of proclamations had been deemed to rest'.[30] It was also in contradiction of earlier notable authorities. In the fifteenth century, Sir John Fortescue had argued that, outside the limitations of the law, the King was entitled to use his regal right to do as he wished, except that he could not make any imposition – by which he meant a tax – on his subjects.[31] Stanford and Smith had both asserted in the sixteenth century that royal proclamations had their basis in common law, by which they meant, not that royal regulations of themselves were common law, but that the right of the King to make them was founded in common law.[32] Any regulation creates an offence if it is not observed, but the ruling by Coke and his fellow judges implied that any laws proclaimed by the Crown were unenforceable. Such an interpretation rendered meaningless a feature of the Constitution that had always existed and had never previously been questioned in principle.

While the King had always been expected to refer all important decisions to Parliament for its consent, and while any of his decisions could be negated by Parliament, we have seen, nevertheless, that it had always been accepted that the King, on the advice of, or in consultation with, his Privy Council, must retain the right to make such decisions of an urgent or minor nature as were deemed necessary to the proper conduct of public affairs. It was a function that was recognised in both the feudal and Indo-European traditions. We have concluded, under the latter, that the prerogative was delegated by Parliament to the King in the first place as a part of the regal contract, and it was this that made its exercise subject to parliamentary supervision. The arbiter in the event of doubt was, of course, the Great Council. Coke evidently took a feudal view of the prerogative, namely, that it was an independent right and that it was therefore open to abuse, particularly in view of King James's own feudal perception of his position. Without realising it, therefore, Coke was taking a self-contradictory view of the King's position, and, in so doing, created a situation that implied, either, that Parliament had to be constantly on hand to approve every regulation, no matter how minor,

---

30. G. A. Smith, *A Constitutional and Legal History of England*, 311.
31. Fortescue, Sir John, *De Laudibus Legum Angliae*, trans. and ed. Chrimes, S. B., 1942.
32. T. Smith, *De Republica Anglorum*, ed. Alston (Cambridge, 1906). See also W. Stanford, *An Exposition of the King's Prerogative*.

or that all eventualities had somehow to be provided for within the broad framework of statute law.

This was a period in which rivalry between the common law courts, on the one hand, and the Chancery and prerogative courts, on the other, was never far from the surface. This was hardly surprising, given, for example, the spreading jurisdiction of the Court of High Commission into lay disputes, and in 1605 the judiciary insisted that only Parliament, the ultimate authority in common law, other than *mos maiorum*, could arbitrate between them and the High Commission. In reality, the chief motivation of the judges was less constitutional than financial, with 'every court striving to bring most moulture to their own mill', as King James put it.[33] A compromise was eventually secured between the Court of Common Pleas and the High Commission by the Lord Chancellor in 1611. Coke's particular target was the Court of Chancery, until matters finally came to a head with Peacham's Case in 1615, when, quite properly, he disputed the right of the King, in his capacity as supreme judge, to consult the judges individually before they tried a case.

Meanwhile, the long-running rivalry between the common law courts and Chancery over conflicting rulings was at last resolved in 1615, when the issue was submitted to James I. The King decided in favour of the Court of Chancery, and thenceforth equity was to prevail over common law.

In the following year Coke refused to postpone the hearing of a case[34] until the King had taken advice on the matter, and he was at once suspended. In this instance, Coke was being quite consistent, not in questioning the King's right, but in rebutting the actual practice of the King's involvement in judicial details, bearing in mind his earlier accusation of the King's inadequate training, and, from a constitutional point of view, his prior delegation to the judge in question. On the other hand, the King was the supreme judge in common law, even if it was no longer felt appropriate for him to exercise the function in person, and there is no doubt that James I took a keen intellectual interest in legal issues, so that his demand for briefing was no more objectionable in principle than the briefing that he expected from his Ministers. Even

---

33. Speech to Parliament, 21 March 1610.
34. The case was one of *commendam*, concerning the right of the Crown to confer an additional benefice on a bishop.

so, there was inevitably a suspicion that the King might try, thereby, to influence the rulings of his judges in cases involving the King's other functions.

It was over Coke's antagonism towards Chancery, however, not the issue in the Peacham Case, that finally persuaded the Lord Chancellor, Archbishop, and Attorney General to secure his dismissal in 1616.[35] He thereupon entered Parliament, but Sir Edward Coke's reputation as a great jurist was confirmed by the publication in 1624 of the first part of his *Institutes of the Laws of England*. In his Second and Third *Institutes* of 1642 and 1644, he insisted on the immemorial antiquity of parliaments, thereby implying – quite correctly – the primacy of that institution over kingship. His influence was destined to continue, both in legal thinking and in the motivation of Parliament.

Coke's finding has tended to be interpreted in a rather over-simplified manner as dispelling the King's claim to dispense justice in his own right. It will be seen that Coke did not question the constitutional principle that the King was the 'supreme judge over all other judges', nor that in principle the King was always present in any court in the judgement of law. In other words, Bancroft's view that judges were but delegates of the King was essentially correct. What he did maintain, however, was that the King could not sit in judgement other than in a properly constituted court; also, because the judgements made in a court were judgements of the court, the King could not overrule its judgements, as Bancroft had claimed, except, of course, on appeal on grounds of equity. The point that has always been lighted upon, namely, Coke's argument that legal judgements were not based upon reason, but upon the peculiar logic and conclusions of the law, with which the King was unfamiliar, and therefore the King was not competent to assert his right, was really a statement of common sense or elementary justice, and not of constitutional principle. It was seen earlier that it is in fact a function of the King, as the source of equity, to sit in judgement on the fairness and reasonableness of court judgements, a role delegated originally to the Court of Chancery, but this is a function of appeal. It must also be remembered that the courts in Coke's time viewed the King, James I, with suspicion, as influenced by

---

35. J. P. Kenyon, *The Stuart Constitution*, 76, footnote 10. See also L. A. Knafla, *Law and Politics*, 176–7.

feudal ideas and not bound, therefore, by the usual precepts of English, and hence Indo-European, justice.

The French notion of the divine right of kings, to which the Scottish House of Stuart subscribed, was imposing a severe strain on the English Constitution, in spite of James's caution, and central to it were the nature and scope of the royal prerogative. This had long been subject to question, particularly as feudal thinking had confused the issue, but King James's claims and his poor personal qualities as King had antagonised the House of Commons and brought matters to the fore. By the 1620s, both the King and his subjects realised that an imbalance existed, or was imminent, between the prerogatives of the Crown and the rights of the people, and this now led to a decade of tension. One of the chief defenders of the royal prerogative was the Lord Chancellor, Sir Francis Bacon, a famous essayist and writer on scientific method. The opportunity to demolish him came in the Parliament of the winter of 1621–2, when the Commons impeached him before the Lords on numerous charges of taking bribes from suitors at court. His conviction removed one of the King's chief pillars of support. It was the first occasion since the fourteenth century that the weapon of impeachment had been used by Parliament, and it heralded a new mood of taking action against royal officials and favourites who could not otherwise be reached.

24.1.3.2. The Great Protestation

Meanwhile, a new Parliament was called in 1621, but it fared little better than its predecessors. An earlier proposal for a marriage between James's son, Charles, and a Spanish princess was renewed at this time, but the Spanish terms included concessions to Catholicism which aroused much public hostility. The House of Commons insisted on detailed information on the proposal, and presented a petition against Popery. This petition drew an angry rebuke from the King, who stated that the House was not equipped to discuss foreign relations and must not insult the Spanish ambassador. They had ventured, he said, to 'argue and debate publicly of the matters far above their reach or capacity, tending to our high dishonour and breach of prerogative royal'. James went on to command that they should not, henceforth, presume 'to meddle with anything concerning our government or deep matters of state'. Tactlessly, he added that he felt himself to be 'very free and able to punish any man's misdemeanours in Parliament, as well during their sitting as after'. This was like a red rag to a bull, and after demanding and failing to receive a satisfactory explanation from the King, the Commons responded by recording what came to be known as the 'Great Protestation'. This claimed: 'That the liberties, franchises, and jurisdictions of Parliament are the ancient and undoubted birth right and inheritance of the subjects of England, and that the arduous and urgent affairs concerning the King, state, and defence of the realm … are proper subjects and matter of council and debate in Parliament'. Enraged, James, presiding over the Privy Council, personally tore the page containing the Great Protestation from the Journal of the Commons, then proceeded to dissolve Parliament, and imprison its leading members.

The King sent his son, Charles, and the Duke of Buckingham to Madrid in 1623 to negotiate the marriage treaty and to view the prospective bride. She disliked Charles, who was in any case told that he would have to become a Catholic. Badly treated, Charles and Buckingham returned to England in a very angry frame of mind, anxious to declare war, and the general public were delighted. James, faced with his son's opposition to the marriage, the royal family deeply divided on the issue, and the marriage provisions demanded by Spain for Catholics in England carrying worrying political implications, was persuaded by Buckingham to call his fourth Parliament, early in 1624, and even, in his speech from the throne, to seek its advice on foreign policy. In Parliament's eyes the Spanish terms were quite unacceptable, and although James was reluctant to abandon the chief objective of his foreign policy, he was eventually forced by an address from both Houses of Parliament to break off further negotiations.

Meanwhile, infuriated by the insult which he felt that he and England had suffered at the hands of the Spanish court, Buckingham formed an alliance with the Dutch in their struggle against Spain. Parliament refused, however, to approve any funds for the conflict, and the army and the navy were already so run down from lack of funding that an expedition to the Scheldt in the same year, 1624, resulted in appalling loss of life from lack of supplies and disease.

James I died in 1625. His reign had brought an end to the generally good relations between King and Parliament and opened a gulf between the Crown and the people. The religious gulf had also widened, with Puritan attacks on the bishops growing more violent and bitter. Meanwhile, parliamentary procedure had greatly improved during his reign, and the scope and importance of Committees of the House of Commons had been greatly increased. The Protestant revolution, reinforced by Coke's legal judgements and antipathy towards the King, had produced a House of Commons with a clear ideological perception of itself, reinforced by a newfound self-confidence and mood of individualism. James had tried to be firm but had failed miserably, and the House of Commons, scenting the commanding position of its power, had made itself insufferable. The Lords, horrified but helpless, could only look on. The Privy Council, which had been the keystone of government under the Tudors, had now declined into minor significance. James had never lost his desire to unite his two kingdoms, Scotland and England, but the English had no love of the Scots, and his various attempts had only met with a cool response.

24.1.4. Charles I and the Crisis Between King and Parliament

James was succeeded in 1625 by his surviving son, who reigned as Charles I of England, and at the same time inherited the Scottish Crown. Little more than a month after his father's death, Charles married Henriette Marie, better known as Henrietta Maria, the sister of Louis XIII of France.

Unlike his father, Charles never propounded a theory of kingship, and he seems never to have questioned the Constitution or the rule of common law, but he was more emotionally attached to the Church of England than his father. Conscientious in his position as the anointed of the Lord, he considered himself to be bound in honour to defend the prerogatives of the Crown, granted to him under the Constitution, and the right and duty to exercise them.[36] Relations got off to a bad start between Charles and Parliament, which met – the first of his reign – late in 1625. There were now many Puritans in the House of Commons, and they felt antipathy towards the Anglicanism of the King and downright

---

36. As we have seen elsewhere, this was not strictly the case. The royal prerogative was derived from the regal contract, of which the Coronation and the Coronation Oath were part, not from the constitution, even though the constitution clearly implied a regal contract.

hostility towards his Roman Catholic wife, Henrietta Maria. The new King did not help matters by his evident disdain of the Commons and the brevity of his address to it, so that even his secretaries could not explain his policy. This included support for a Huguenot revolt in La Rochelle and the *de facto* toleration of Catholics under the terms of the French marriage treaty. Although the Commons approved funding for the King to pursue the war against Spain, it was inadequate, and, mindful of the risk that he would dissolve Parliament as soon as he got his money for other purposes, it refused to vote new duties – tunnage and poundage - for the King for life, as was the custom, limiting them instead to just one year.[37] Even this failed to eventuate, because Charles dissolved Parliament before the Lords had approved the Bill.

The King sought to make his second Parliament, summoned early in 1626, more pliable than the first by appointing several of the leaders of the first Parliament as sheriffs, in order to be rid of them. In the event, the second Parliament, under the leadership of Sir John Eliot, proved to be even more intractable than the first. By order of the King, Lord Bristol, a particular enemy of Lord Buckingham, received no writ. As a result of intervention by the House of Lords – plainly acting in its stunted capacity as the Great Council – he received one, but was requested not to appear. He took his seat, nonetheless, and subsequently brought charges of corruption and maladministration against the Duke of Buckingham, who was then impeached in the House of Commons, where he was described by one of those bringing the charges, Sir John Eliot, a fiery Cornishman, as 'the canker in the King's treasure'. Charles, who regarded the wording of the charges as seditious, if not treasonable, announced his intention to proceed against those who, 'to express their rash and undutiful insolencies, shall wilfully break the circle of order, which without apparent danger to Church and state may not be broken'. As Charles saw it, it was incumbent upon him to defend the Constitution against trouble-makers, and those leading the attack, Eliot and Sir Dudley Digges, were arrested and imprisoned, even though Parliament was in session, and thus violating the sanctity of its proceedings. The business

---

37. An alternative view sees the granting of tunnage and poundage for only one year as the consequence of a decision by the Commons, apparently without malicious intent, to review the whole field of indirect taxation, although the review never took place. See J. P. Kenyon, *The Stuart Constitution*, 53.

of the House was thereupon suspended, including the grant of supplies, until the pair were released. Charles threatened, reminding his subjects that 'Parliaments are altogether in my power for their calling, sitting, and dissolution; and therefore, as I find the fruits of them to be good or evil they are to continue or not to be'. He was ignored, and Charles, in an attempt to save Buckingham from the impeachment, dissolved his second Parliament. There was certainly precedent for the King's imposition of tunnage and poundage without reference to Parliament, and, shortly afterwards, the Privy Council declared that tunnage and poundage had been enjoyed by the King since the reign of Henry VI, that it was an inseparable part of the King's revenue, and that it was independent of any parliamentary grant.

Meanwhile, the war with Spain widened into a war against France, due mainly to a personality clash between the Lord Chancellor, Buckingham, and Cardinal Richelieu. Through his ineptitude, Buckingham had already organised one disastrous expedition, to Cadiz in Spain in 1625, and in 1627 he led another, this time to France, to relieve the Huguenots in La Rochelle. It turned into a fiasco. This was the worst series of setbacks in memory, and it was widely felt as a national humiliation, blamed squarely on Charles's Government.

So financially desperate was the King by now, that he pawned the Crown jewels, mortgaged Crown lands, sold knighthoods, and attempted to obtain tunnage and poundage by royal ordinance. When nothing came of it, he attempted a forced loan in 1627, which amounted to taxation without parliamentary consent. Facing opposition, Charles imprisoned a number of men who refused to pay. They included five knights, led by Sir Thomas Darnel, who claimed arbitrary arrest and applied for a writ of *habeas corpus*, that is, a summons for their appearance in court, so that they could be charged with a specific offence, or otherwise released. It was granted and they were not charged, but the prison warden refused to release them, having received a warrant from two members of the Privy Council, ordering that the knights be held 'by special order of His Majesty'. The prisoners now invoked Chapter 39 of the *Magna Carta*, relating to arbitrary arrest. In the ensuing Darnel's Case, or the Case of the Five Knights, the Chief Justice rejected their application, citing an earlier precedent of 1591 and the needs of public policy: 'The precedents are all against you, every one of them,' he concluded, 'and what shall guide our judgements, since there is nothing alleged in this case but precedents? [We find] that if no cause of the commitment [to prison] be expressed it is to be presumed to be for matters of state, which we cannot take notice of'. So was left intact the presumed right of the King to imprison his subjects without showing cause.

The most strident form of the absolutist case was contained in Roger Manwaring's sermons on *Religion and Allegiance*, which he delivered before the King in 1627. According to Manwaring, the royal power was the highest of those ordained by God, placing the King even above the angels. 'No power in the world or in the hierarchy of the Church [could] lay restraint upon these supremes; therefore theirs [is] the strongest'. Even if the King flatly commanded against the law of God, according to Manwaring, his will could not be resisted. Those who patiently and meekly suffered of 'their sovereign's pleasure they should become glorious martyrs, whereas by resisting his will they should for ever endure the pain and stain of odious traitors and impious malefactors'. As for Parliament, such assemblies, while necessary for the ends for which they were first instituted, their purpose was not to give rights to kings. Rather, their purpose was to ensure the more equal imposition, and more easy exacting, of that to which kings had a right by natural and original law and justice. In short, the purpose of Parliament was to provide for the King's needs in as speedy and equitable way as possible. In Manwaring's sermon the oriental perception of kingship shines through quite clearly. Much as Charles must have enjoyed such a view of his position, however, he was too sensible a man to have taken it very seriously, and the assertions of individuals like Manwaring were generally ignored, as were those of radical philosophers, such as Hobbes.[38] Thomas Hobbes, writing about this time, concluded that men were basically selfish and ambitious, so that, in order to prevent society degenerating into a state of brutishness, they must agree to surrender their excess rights to a supreme sovereign, because, what benefits the state must also benefit the sovereign. Conversely, democracy would mean anarchy, and aristocracy merely multiplied the natural greed of the King. In reality, this was a patriarchal, rather than an absolutist age in England, and when Parliament protested at the content

---

38. Hobbes wrote a number of books, the most important, *The Leviathan*, in 1651.

of Manwaring's sermons, Charles agreed without argument to suppress them. The unsettled situation was reflected in a speech of Sir Thomas Wentworth, later Earl of Strafford, to the Council of the North in 1628, when he remarked that 'the joint individual wellbeing of sovereignty and subjection' had of late been the subject of 'distempered minds', which had 'endeavoured to divide the considerations of the two, as if their ends were distinct'.

Yet there was no basic disagreement between the two sides concerning the mutual inter-dependence of King and people. An excess of prerogative was oppression, while a pretended liberty on the part of the subject brought disorder and anarchy. One of the best expositions of how the Constitution was seen at this time was that by Pym, given during the impeachment of the Royalist cleric, Manwaring, in June 1628. The archaic style of Pym's reported speech[39] is not easily understood by modern ears, but is not difficult to paraphrase more simply. He said that three principles formed the foundation of the Constitution.

Firstly, the form of government in any state could not be altered without danger of ruination of the state. The purpose of government was to ensure the common good, and if this principle of mutual benefit were broken, the whole structure of society would dissolve into discord, with one part seeking to uphold the old form of government and the other part trying to introduce a new one, so that the one would devour the other. History was full of such calamities. Time brought a need for change, but every change was a further step towards dissolution. Only those things that were constant and uniform were eternal, and the most durable commonwealths had been those that had often reformed themselves according to their original institution and ordinance, thereby repairing the breaches that had been caused by time.

Secondly, 'the law of England, whereby the subject was exempted from taxes and loans not granted by the common consent of parliament', was not introduced by any statute, charter or royal sanction, but was the ancient and fundamental law of the Constitution. These first two principles had been evident 'in the government of the Saxons', and their vigour and force had outlived the Norman Conquest, imposing limits on the Conqueror himself. Possession of the Crown could be obtained

---

39. W. Cobbett (ed.), *State Trials and Proceedings* (London, 1809–26), 33 vols.

only by agreement, and in this the Conqueror had 'bound himself to observe these and other ancient laws and liberties of the kingdom', which he had confirmed by oath at his coronation. From him, the obligation had descended to his successors. They had often been broken, and just as often confirmed, by charters or Acts of Parliament, but the petitions by the King's subjects upon which these charters and Acts had been founded had been petitions as of right, which had demanded only ancient and due liberties. They had not been demands for new ones.

Thirdly, these liberties of the subject were not only beneficial for the people, but were honourable and profitable for the King, being necessary to his support and policies, a basic point in Hobbes's argument. This apparent paradox could be explained by the fact that, without these freedoms, there would be no industry, justice or enterprise, and therefore no means of meeting the King's needs. The only inexhaustible revenue to the Crown came from the hearts of the people and their bounty in Parliament.

From these remarks of Pym, it can be seen how well it was understood in the seventeenth century that the English Constitution had its origin in Anglo-Saxon times, and that its basic principles had survived the Norman Conquest. Pym leaves no doubt that he saw the basis of the Constitution being the principle of rule, by the people, for the people, which was provided for in a regal contract, and that the Constitution itself did not and should not change. It was often violated and even bent to suit changing needs and interests, but its basic principles must constantly be asserted, otherwise conflict and decline must follow. What comes through clearly in Pym's view, then widely held, was the unchanging and unchangeable nature of the Constitution. Both absolutists and democrats believed that the Constitution was an enduring arrangement, and that any attempt to change it in its essentials could only bring trouble. Charles himself in 1641 would warn Parliament of the danger of innovation or change, saying that reform was one thing, but the alteration of government was another. As Kenyon has pointed out, 'disagreement lay essentially in how to operate a constitution of whose nature few had any doubts'.[40]

Meanwhile, for many, the disaster at La Rochelle, which had now fallen to the French king and the Catholic cause, was the last straw in

---

40. J. P. Kenyon, *The Stuart Constitution*, 10.

relations between King and Parliament. The Parliament of 1628 was summoned in an atmosphere of debt, defeat, and disorder. Twenty-seven members had earlier been among those imprisoned for having refused to pay the King's forced loan. To Charles's desperate plea for money the Commons agreed that he should have it, but, apart from discussing it, made no headway. Instead, on the advice of Sir Edward Coke, they consigned their chief grievances to a Petition of Right.

24.1.4.1. The Petition of Right (1629)

The Petition of Right was Coke's response to the ruling in the Case of the Five Knights, which he intended as a set of general principles which would be a guide to the judges in future, when constrained by precedents or the lack of them. The Petition was read three times in each House. This document of 1628 cited various precedents and asked the King to cease actions 'not warrantable by the laws and practices of this realm'. Specifically, it requested that:

1. no man should be compelled to make any gift, loan, or benevolence or like charge without the consent of Parliament;
2. no one should be imprisoned unless on a specified charge;
3. soldiers and sailors should not be billeted in private houses;
4. martial law should not be imposed in time of peace, 'lest … Your Majesty's subjects be destroyed or put to death, contrary to the laws and statutes of this realm'.

Charles at first tried to prevaricate, but when pressed by both the Lords and Commons, he finally responded in words usually used in assenting to a private Bill: '*Soit droit fait come est desiré*', 'be it made right as is wished'. This did not give it any statutory basis and its legal standing is open to question, but it did represent a statement of constitutional principle, which was only put into statute law at a later date. For the time being it was a compromise, because its terms were in conflict with Charles's religious beliefs and he had not committed himself irrevocably. The Commons proceeded to consent to the raising of the King's money, but its mood of belligerence was unassuaged, and it proceeded to threaten Buckingham and to conduct a heated debate on the King's assertion that indirect taxation, such as tunnage and poundage, was not covered by the

Petition of Right. The King pointed out that his authority in this respect had been confirmed in the Bates Case of 1606. The Commons answered with a Remonstrance, or representation, that declared the levy of tunnage and poundage to be contrary to the Petition of Rights and an infraction of the liberties of the kingdom, and virtually invited the people to pay no tax by asking the King 'not to take it in ill part from those' of his 'loving subjects who shall refuse to make payment'. Next day, the King stepped in and prorogued Parliament. A group of London merchants, led by John Rolles, took the hint and refused to make payments, only for the Privy Council to order the confiscation of their goods, an action ratified by the Court of Exchequer, which ruled that the Petition of Right did not cover tunnage and poundage.

The House of Lords, which had been in general sympathy with the Commons since 1621, was alienated by the Remonstrance, and when the problem of the Duke of Buckingham was removed later, in 1628, with his killing by a disaffected lieutenant, there was general rejoicing in the land and a degree of reconciliation between the House of Lords and the King. The alienation from the Commons was not confined to the Lords. Sir Thomas Wentworth, a leading member of the Commons, deserted the popular party and became the King's chief adviser. The removal of Buckingham brought to an end the control of policy by a single faction, opening government to the manoeuvring of rival factions and royal favourites in the Privy Council. This inevitably brought the King himself to the fore in policy-making. One consequence was the rise of secret Catholics or sympathisers and a reversal in foreign policy to one that was pro-Spanish.

As a guide to the judiciary, meanwhile, the Petition of Right fell on deaf ears, because in the months and years ahead they showed that they were not prepared to abandon the principle of precedent in case law, in favour of vague statements of principle. When Parliament began its second session, early in 1629, the Commons found itself isolated, and isolated itself further, under the leadership of Sir John Eliot and Sir Dudley Digges, by returning immediately to the issue of indirect taxation. The loss of the Lords' support was probably influenced also by the fact that Eliot and others leading the attack were themselves leading merchants with a vested interest in the outcome. Customs officers who had enforced the collection of tunnage and poundage from Eliot, among others, were hauled before the Bar of the House. It was argued that the confiscation of members' goods, even between sessions, was a breach of parliamentary privilege. The strong Puritan element in the Commons also launched a bitter attack on the Government's ecclesiastical policy. In neither respect did the House of Commons obtain the support of the Lords. Unlike his father and, before him, Elizabeth, Charles, instead of playing off the two main parties in the Church, namely, the Puritans and those, the 'Laudists', led by the new Bishop of London, William Laud, now made the tactical mistake of coming down in favour of the Laudists. It was a conflict aggravated by bitterness over the failures of the Thirty Years' War against the Catholic powers of Spain and France, and particularly England's wretched inability to rescue the Huguenot citadel of La Rochelle. The consequences were a religious opposition to Charles's rule, and a renewed anxiety to eradicate Popery.

24.1.4.2. Division Within the Church of England

The Church of England had adhered to Calvinist orthodoxy, at least in its theology, since Elizabeth's accession in 1558, and this had been enshrined in her Thirty-Nine Articles of 1563, but there had emerged, by this time, a right-wing movement in the Church, whose most prominent spokesman was William Laud, and Laud was elevated to the See of St David's by a sympathetic Charles. This movement favoured the old Church ritual, vestments, ornaments and images, and marked the appearance of what came to be known as the 'High-Church' faction, leaving the Puritans as 'Low-Church'. The chief reason for the unpopularity of Laud's faction was the association of them with Catholicism, in particular, their views on ritual and their exaltation of bishops, claiming them once again to be fundamental to the Church, rather than a useful and acceptable addition. The popular suspicion of a Papist revival was increased by the favour shown to the High-Church faction by the King, who was himself linked in the public mind with Catholicism. Evidence that he was certainly moving towards it comes also from the sending of Court emissaries to Rome. There is no reason to believe that Charles ever considered turning to Rome, but there can be little doubt that he favoured a Church of

England that was much more Catholic in character, and that had close ties with Rome.

Meanwhile, the Calvinist movement itself was divided over the question of predestination, on which Calvin's own view has always been in some doubt. The orthodox position was that salvation was predestined by God to a minority of men, even though they were not free of sin, whereas the great majority of men inevitably faced Everlasting Fire. This assured salvation for the few was known as predestination. It had been disputed by Arminius of Leyden, who had died in 1609, and who had argued that, because Christ had died for all men, all could achieve salvation of their own free will (although even this was predestined by God). Laud's faction were often accused of supporting Arminius. Article 17 of the Thirty-Nine Articles of 1563 had temporised on the key question of predestination, but the available evidence shows, in fact, that Laud and his associates followed the ambiguous compromise already established in Article 17.[41] The King supported the orthodox view by securing the appointment of members of Laud's faction to leading positions in the Church during the parliamentary recess, with Laud himself becoming the Bishop of London, a development that has been described as the 'Laudian Revolution'. The Archbishop at this time, Abbot, was out of favour, so that whoever was the Bishop of London held a key position. After consulting with his bishops, the King had the Thirty-Nine Articles re-published. He also made it clear that he would not tolerate further debate on the issue by anybody but specialists. The controversy had a political, as well as a doctrinal aspect, because Laud's faction were generally supporters of the royal prerogative. Thus, when Parliament reassembled in 1629, many members of the Commons were dismayed at the promotion of Laud and others of his faction to many key positions in the Church during the recess, renewing fears of a return to Popery. The majority of the sees were now occupied by men who were allies of Laud, or who were willing to accept the King's authority unquestioningly. The Commons accordingly added to its review of the King's taxes an investigation into the state of the Church and the ecclesiastical policy of the Crown. It was difficult to contest the King's prerogative as Supreme Governor of the Church,

---

41. Letter to the Duke of Buckingham, 2 August 1625, from the Bishops of Rochester and Oxford, and Laud as then Bishop of St David's. See J. P. Kenyon, *The Stuart Constitution*, 136–8.

however, and the ensuing 'Resolutions on Religion' could go no further than calling upon him to confer senior Church appointments 'upon learned, pious and orthodox men', going on to remind the King that the doctrine and practice of the Church was properly defined in the Lambeth Articles of 1595.

Charles ordered a short adjournment to allow tempers to cool, but the House of Commons, determined to have its opinions recorded, voted against adjournment. When the Serjeant-at-Arms was sent to seize the Mace, the symbol of the King's presence in the House, without which its proceedings and resolutions had no constitutional authority, the Speaker, Finch, tried to comply with the royal order. He was immediately seized and held down in his chair by two of Eliot's younger supporters, so that he could not rise to pronounce an adjournment. The doors of the chamber were then locked. While the royal guards were called to break them open, the Commons voted on resolutions drafted by Eliot, that:

- whoever introduced innovations in religion, or supported Popery or Arminism (which was equated with Popery), should be considered enemies of the realm;
- whoever advised the collection of tunnage or poundage without parliamentary consent should also be considered enemies of the realm;
- whoever voluntarily paid tunnage and poundage thus levied should be considered a traitor to the liberties of the land.

The Commons then voted their own adjournment, the doors were unlocked and the royal messengers admitted.

This behaviour certainly went beyond what was acceptable to the moderates in the House, and the King, infuriated, accused the Commons of trying to usurp the authority of the Crown, scarcely betraying tact by asserting that 'princes are not bound to give account of their actions, but to God alone'. He had Eliot and eight other members of the Commons arrested and imprisoned, and a few days later, on 10 March 1629, Parliament was dissolved. A little over a fortnight later, the King announced that he had no intention of summoning another Parliament until the ringleaders had received 'condign punishment' and the people understood his 'intentions and actions' more clearly. Eliot later died in the Tower, being the only one of those arrested not to make submission to the King.

There followed, for the next eleven years, personal rule by Charles, advised by Bishop Laud and Sir Thomas Wentworth, who still ruled the north of England through the Council of the North. As history would confirm, the events of 1629 marked the climax in the struggle between the two ideologies of government: Oriental versus Indo-European; feudal versus common law. For a thousand years the two ideologies had managed to co-exist in an uneasy relationship, but the Stuarts had introduced the newly reinvigorated feudal doctrine of kingship from France, which had now led to what has been described as the greatest constitutional crisis in English history, and which would, 160 years later, destroy the French monarchy. It was a time of substantial emigration to the colonies in North America, mainly by Puritans who refused to live under an increasingly Popish King and Church. From 1629 until 1640 – the 'eleven years of tyranny' – Charles I ruled through the Privy Council. Yet the events of 1629 had not proved to be a victory for feudal doctrine, because Charles had not intended that they should. Regardless of his personal view of monarchy, he continued to observe the common law of the Constitution as he saw it, and ruled like an autocratic but elected King without a Parliament.

Tunnage and poundage continued to be levied by prerogative, with little evidence of opposition, although there was some murmuring when Charles invoked the defunct medieval imposition known as the Distraint of Knighthood, which the gentry now had to pay. He also raised revenue from fines by enforcing the old forest laws and made money from the sale of monopolies. The tax that generated the most opposition, although it was muted at first, was Ship Money. This was really the reimposition of an old levy which had required certain ports to provide ships in a time of emergency, but in 1634 the King imposed, by writ, a tax on land in coastal towns and counties. The reasons were North African piracy against English ships in the Mediterranean, the need to protect the North Sea fisheries, and the need to strengthen the King's fleet against the Dutch and the French, and in the following year the collection of Ship Money was extended to the inland shires and towns. All the money so raised was spent on ships, and Charles argued, plausibly enough, that the inland counties were just as much protected by them as coastal areas. The writs continued to be issued each year until 1639, and they marked the real beginning of the Royal Navy. Even by 1635, the Lord Treasurer had succeeded in balancing the royal budget, and the absence of a Parliament seems to have caused only limited criticism. This relative tranquillity owed much to the fact that the 1630s were a period of economic prosperity.

In foreign policy, Charles pursued his father's aim of recovering the Palatinate in southern Germany, first for Charles's brother-in-law, Frederick, and then for the latter's son, but he pursued it by means of tortuous diplomacy. He even had plans for an alliance with Spain to partition the Netherlands as the price of the Palatinate's restoration. For a time, Charles tried to secure an alliance with France, and it was in pursuit of his strategy that the King raised Ship Money to re-build the fleet and a small volunteer army was sent to Germany, neither to any avail. Charles was too weak to pursue an effective foreign policy, because he lacked the financial resources, and his prospective allies knew that, without the support of Parliament, he had little to offer in return for the favours that he sought.

Meanwhile, the later 1620s had seen the triumph of the Catholic Habsburg forces in Germany, culminating in the Edict of Restitution of 1629, which required the return to the Church of lands that had been taken from it since the Reformation. This had increased popular fears in England that the King was intending to do the same. The intervention on the Continent of a new champion of Protestantism, Gustav Adolf of Sweden, in the early 1630s, raised the hopes of militant Protestants in England, but with the entry of France on the side of the German Protestants and the Dutch Calvinists, it was clear that the religious conflict there had been replaced by a straightforward struggle for political self-interest. This was a period when France, under the guidance of Richelieu, was in the ascendant, while Spain was in decline, hastened by the costly war in the Netherlands and, after 1635, a war with France. Meanwhile, the Dutch had emerged as the leading commercial and colonial power, presenting England's Puritan merchant class with a conflict of interest: either they supported the Dutch as fellow Calvinists intent on survival, or they competed with the Dutch for trading dominance in the Far East.

Laud became Archbishop of Canterbury in 1633, and devoted his energy to imposing High-Church uniformity across the country, generating a bitter controversy between the Church and the Puritans. Censorship was employed, and severe punishments were meted out during the 1630s by the Court of Star Chamber. Ameliorating this was the abolition of torture in Britain in 1638. Moderates were increasingly alienated by Laud and by the King. In pursuit of his policy of achieving uniformity in England and Scotland, an attempt by Laud in 1637 to impose the Anglican episcopal system and liturgy on Scotland, including a modified version of the Book of Common Prayer, caused a riot in Edinburgh. In the following year, many Scots signed a Covenant for the defence of the reformed religion. Charles threatened to impose his will by force, and the Covenanters, as they became known, formed an army under Alexander Leslie, evicted the bishops, and held a general assembly in Glasgow, at which they abolished episcopacy and gave final form to the Scottish Kirk. When Charles moved against them in 1639, in what has come to be known as the Bishops' Wars, in an attempt to force the Scots to reinstate the bishops, the Covenanters captured Edinburgh Castle, Stirling and Dumbarton. They then met Charles's ragged army at Berwick. Charles, short of money to pay them, and the Scots, uncertain of how the English would react to invasion, decided in favour of a truce.

The collection of Ship Money at a time when there was no emergency was increasingly felt to be unjustified, and many refused to pay. In response to questions put by the King to the judges, the latter ruled that the King was indeed entitled to compel his subjects to contribute Ship Money in a national emergency, and it was for the King to decide when such an emergency existed. Of those who refused to pay, the Crown chose to sue John Hampden, a wealthy member of the gentry, who could be tried in the courts of common law, rather than two defaulting Peers, who could only be tried by their fellow Peers. In his trial before the Court of Exchequer Chamber, Hampden accepted that the King had the right to decide that an emergency existed, and therefore a right to impose the tax, but he argued that Ship Money had been raised on this occasion since 1634 and it was now 1637, so there had been plenty of time for the King to summon a Parliament to obtain its approval. This had not happened, therefore the tax had no legitimacy. The Crown argued that the King enjoyed absolute discretion in all matters relating to the defence and security of the realm. Other arguments were also submitted. The

case was heard before all twelve common law judges, who were divided
in their judgement, seven ruling in the Crown's favour and five ruling
against, so that the case was widely seen as a moral defeat for the King
and the standing of his government.[42]

It was in the following year, 1638, that things began to go wrong, but
it is not easy to identify the cause. The Hampden Case over questionable
taxation was a straw in the wind, but of more immediate importance
was the Scottish crisis and the King's ability to scrape together an army,
however ineffective, without recourse to a Parliament, and with the
evident intention of subduing the Scots. This caused considerable alarm,
because defeating the Scots would have put the High-Church faction
in total control. Laud's policies towards the Church, which had caused
the insurrection in Scotland, seem to have been a source of simmering
discontent. At the same time, the King's administrative machine was
incapable of waging a military campaign on land, any more than at sea,
and the system was now under intolerable strain. It was in the same year,
1639, that Wentworth was transferred from his responsibilities for the
north of England and appointed as Lord Lieutenant of Ireland, charged
particularly with watching the situation in Ulster. In the following year
he received the title of Earl of Strafford. It was on Strafford's advice that
Charles summoned another Parliament in April 1640, in the hope that it
would support him against the Scots. With it assembled the Convocation
of Canterbury. It became known as the Short Parliament, because, instead
of voting money to fight the Scots, it began to debate all its grievances
of the last eleven years.[43] Charles promptly dissolved it after only three
weeks, and once again imprisoned his leading opponents. In London
there were riots and attacks on Laud's palace, and new trouble broke out
in Scotland in the same year. The Scottish army occupied Newcastle and
Durham, and defeated an English force at Newburn. In the Treaty of
Ripon, Charles made peace with them, agreeing that the Scottish army
should remain in England and be paid by the King until the peace was
ratified by Parliament. It appears from this that the Scots were using their
position to force the King to summon a new Parliament, which they saw

---

42. G. E. Aylmer, *The Struggle for the Constitution* (London, 1963), 83–4.

43. It was a 'short' Parliament only in relation to the typical length of time for which
    Parliaments were now sitting. In common law they were usually expected to sit for only a
    day or two.

as an ally in their struggle, although whether they forced this upon the King under their own initiative, or the English Puritans had persuaded them to impose this condition, is open to speculation. Charles was now faced by actual or virtual revolt in both his kingdoms, and there can be little doubt that the Covenanters and Parliament each used the other in their common opposition to Popery and royal autocracy.

Because of the brevity of the Short Parliament, the Convocation of Canterbury took the unprecedented step of remaining in session after the dissolution, in order to approve a controversial series of new canons. These included a defence of the unpopular rites recently introduced into the Church, an explanation of the divine right of kings, and, as a measure against lurking Catholics, a requirement that all clergy take an oath not to introduce any Popish doctrine, other than that already established, nor to consent to the introduction of such by any member of the Church hierarchy. This last measure soon revealed the Bishop of Gloucester to be a secret convert to Catholicism, and this only seemed to confirm the popular suspicion of the creation by Laud of a Papist hierarchy, made worse by the King's blatant attempts to secure aid from Spain. It caused the anxiety and frustration of the preceding years finally to boil over.

24.1.4.3. The Long Parliament

In his desperation, Charles summoned a Great Council at York in October 1640, seeking its advice, but his Councillors – the Peers – told him that he had lost the support of the people, and that the only way in which he could buy off the Scots and pay his army was by summoning a Parliament and obtaining its consent to the necessary taxes. So far as is known, this was the last occasion on which the Great Council met and fully functioned as such, other than in its enforced confinement as a House of Lords. The Constitution has continued on its way as a rudderless and unballasted ship of state ever since.

Adding to the pressure on the King was a financial collapse, as the City of London failed in its efforts to raise further large loans.

Late in 1640, therefore, and with the greatest distaste, the King summoned a further Parliament, which became known as the Long Parliament, because it was destined to last for almost twenty years. The House of Commons, led by John Pym and John Hampden, was now in a strong position, and now dominated by the Puritans, who had taken most of the new borough seats that had been created, while conservative members had been turned away on the pretext that they were monopolists. Also, the mood of the Long Parliament was very different from that of the Short Parliament. The tone on each occasion was set by Pym. On the earlier occasion he had laboriously listed grievances, but in the Long Parliament he was much more brief and trenchant, hinting at a Catholic conspiracy to subvert the Government. The main cause of ill-feeling became evident in the acts of the new Parliament, one of which was to appoint a Committee on the State of the Kingdom, and another was to impeach Strafford for high treason and send him to the Tower, closely followed by Laud. The issue of taxation was dealt with by the Tunnage and Poundage Act, which gave the King the relevant customs duties and all the impositions that were being levied while Parliament met, but for two months only. Yet in spite of this sense of purpose, the Commons approached its task in a chaotic manner, with Bills often not originating in the committees appointed to consider what should be done. On fiscal and economic matters, the Commons had no policy at all, and a Bill to exclude the bishops from the House of Lords made little headway.

There followed Acts to abolish the Councils of the North and of the Marches of Wales, the Court of High Commission, and the judicial powers of the Privy Council itself, effectively the Court of Star Chamber.[44] In other words, it destroyed what had been the institutions of Tudor government, the purpose being to ensure that the King could never again rule without Parliament. However, it was not practicable to remove all the Privy Council's judicial functions, and its power remained to receive petitions from the Channel Islands, the Isle of Man, and Crown possessions overseas. The Long Parliament also declared invalid the canons for Church discipline, which Laud had seen through in the spring of 1640, because the Convocation of the Church had remained sitting after the dissolution of the Short Parliament, of which it was deemed to

---

44. It may be remembered that the right of the Privy Council to sit as a court of law, in respect only of accused individuals of the Second Estate, was exercised by it on behalf of the Great Council, whose right in the matter was founded in common law, and therefore not within the jurisdiction of a Parliament. However, the Privy Council had, for a long time, far exceeded its authority in common law.

be a part.[45] In order to pay off the Scottish and English armies, a special poll tax was granted, enabling peace to be arranged with Scotland.

Both Strafford and Laud were impeached, but no further proceedings were taken against Laud at this stage, and it was the impeachment of the Earl of Strafford in 1641 that dominated the first session of the House of Commons. To Pym and his supporters, the early arrest and trial of Strafford were necessary before Strafford could charge them with treasonable correspondence with the Scots, a belief that was probably not without foundation.[46] Opening the proceedings, Pym accused Strafford of 'the blackest treason to sow discord between King and people', which, had it succeeded, would have caused England to succumb to 'the ecclesiastical tyranny of the Pope' and 'the civil tyranny of an arbitrary, unlimited, confused government'. Strafford was further accused of 'arbitrary and tyrannical government' in the North and in Ireland, of deliberately provoking a war with the Scots in 1640, and of advising the King to dissolve the Short Parliament and rule arbitrarily. False evidence against Strafford and Laud was concocted, witnesses were intimidated, and any Irish witnesses who could testify on Strafford's behalf were locked away. Pym and his supporters took the view that such measures were justified, since it was felt that the critical point had been reached. The King had available to him armies in the North and in Ireland, and Pym claimed to have come by notes of a Privy Council meeting at which Strafford had advised the King that he was 'absolved from all rules of government' and that he was entitled to use the Irish army to subdue England, where the opposition had been claimed to be in conspiracy with the Scots.

However, probably none of the charges, even if they could be proved, amounted to treason, and the Lords were unwilling to accept the Commons' argument that the alleged actions of Strafford amounted to a kind of cumulative treason. Moreover, the Lords were concerned that, if this were allowed, no future Minister would be able to serve the King in safety. When it became clear that Strafford would never be found guilty of high treason by the judicial process of impeachment before the Lords, the Commons resorted to condemning him to death by an Act of Attainder. This was a means of convicting without trial, requiring no proof of guilt,

---

45. Under feudal rules it was not, of course, because the greater clergy sat only in their capacity
    as barons, and the lesser clergy only as members of the Third Estate.
46. G. E. Aylmer, *The Struggle for the Constitution*, 106.

and all that was required was an Act of Parliament that convicted and sentenced the accused. Extremists in Parliament forced moderates to stay away, and the Bill was approved in the Commons. Rumours of royal plots were spread, and panic and hatred erupted in the City. The Lords, alarmed by the rioting by London mobs, passed the Bill. With the ports closed off and armed mobs accompanying the presentation of the Bill, the King was thoroughly alarmed for the life of his wife and children. The Queen, Henrietta Maria, was widely rumoured to be at the centre of many Royalist plots, and was particularly hated, and it became clear to the King in Council that Strafford would have to be sacrificed if the situation were not to get totally out of hand. The Bill of Attainder was signed into law, and Strafford was sent to the Tower and executed. The trial of Archbishop Laud was delayed, probably because there had been dissension in Parliament over the use of attainder against Strafford, and because the Commons was divided over Church reform.

Meanwhile, Charles was forced to make concessions, agreeing to cancel all innovations in Church and state, and to deprive the bishops of their temporal authority, although he refused to exclude them from Parliament. The House of Commons had also been anxious to protect itself against an 'untimely adjourning, proroguing, or dissolving' of Parliament by the King, but Charles at first refused to sign the resulting Triennial Bill. This required that a Parliament be summoned not less than three years after the last sitting of the previous Parliament; that it be neither dissolved nor prorogued within at least fifty days; and that the Lord Chancellor of England, the Lord Keeper of the Great Seal, and the commissioners for the keeping of the Great Seal should, without any further warrant or direction from the present King or his successors, send out the necessary writs. In the event that this failed to summon a Parliament, as required by the Act, the Peers of the realm should assemble at Westminster, evidently in their half-remembered capacity as the Great Council, where any twelve or more of them should issue writs, under their own hands and seals, to the sheriffs for the necessary elections and summoning of a Parliament. If the peers fail to act, the sheriffs should themselves make the necessary arrangements. Moreover, no Parliament henceforth should be dissolved or prorogued within fifty days, except by the common consent of the Sovereign and both Houses. Charles objected that the Bill was a direct encroachment on his prerogative, but, faced by public demonstrations in London and Westminster and an implied threat to the Queen's person, he reluctantly signed it into existence as the Triennial Act of 1641. He also signed, unwillingly, a subsequent Bill stating that the present Parliament could not be prorogued or dissolved without its own consent. Both Acts were based on a deep distrust of the King, but they were justified in the Commons on the ground that, without them, it was becoming increasingly difficult to borrow money to pay off the Scots and disband the King's army.

Constitutionally, a Triennial Act was unlawful, because annual Parliaments were required in common law. By this time there was, however, a complication in that elections each year for new Parliaments were not practicable. Even so, the law might have been satisfied so long as at least one session of Parliament was held in each year.

In respect of the religious question, there were those who wanted no change to the Anglican Church, other than the removal of certain innovations introduced by Laud, while others, the Puritans, wanted to root out the episcopal system and remodel the Church on Presbyterian lines. Strong feelings were aroused. All that the House appears to have had in common was the belief in a Popish conspiracy. Parliament was prorogued in September of 1641, but each House left a committee to sit during the vacation.

24.1.5. The Constitutional Crisis (1642)

Charles weakened his own position further by travelling to Edinburgh, in an effort to shore up his position. There, he attempted to arrest the Presbyterian leaders, the Earl of Argyle and the Duke of Hamilton. At Westminster the Lords finally, in January 1642, passed the Bishops' Exclusion Bill, expelling them from the House, and after some hesitation Charles gave his assent in the following month. Meanwhile, in October 1641, news had been brought of an Irish Catholic rebellion in Ulster and the massacre of thousands of English and Scottish Protestant settlers. It had been sparked by the removal of Strafford and a fear of Puritan domination, and it quickly spread across Ireland. The success of the rebellion led to the establishment of a supreme council and a general assembly of Catholics at Kilkenny, which offered the King an army against

Parliament, in return for the redress of grievances. This left Parliament in a quandary. Charles had refused to disband his own Irish army, and Pym argued in the Commons that the King could not be trusted with the substantial army which was now needed to restore control in Ireland. In any case, events in Ireland resurrected the fear of a Popish plot, which rumour linked with Charles. It raised the whole question of control of the military by the Crown, which could use it against Parliament.

Determined to crush the rebels, Pym and the radicals wanted control of the army placed in the hands of Ministers, approved by the Commons, but it was argued that such a step would make Parliament superior to the King, which was precisely what the radicals favoured. A third group would agree only to a reduction in the royal power, so that King and Parliament would be equal. The Pym group, Puritan and anti-Royalist, declared that parliamentary government was the only practical solution, and the Commons approved an Instruction to the King that, if he did not comply with their request, they would take their own measures to suppress the rebellion. The Lords rejected it. Now at last the Committee on the State of the Kingdom published its report, known as the Grand Remonstrance. This laid the blame for England's troubles on the 'Jesuited Papists', the bishops and corrupt part of the clergy, and such members of the Privy Council and courtiers as had furthered the interests of foreign states for their own ends. It went on, among other things, to ask the King to curtail the power of the bishops, and proposed that the King should employ only Councillors and Ministers in whom Parliament had confidence, subject to their removal at Parliament's request, without a formal case being made out against them. It proposed to relegate the religious question to a general synod of selected clergy, assisted by some from other Protestant communities of Europe. After a fierce and bitter debate in the House of Commons, the Grand Remonstrance of 1641 was accepted by only a small majority, after which it was submitted to the King.

The longer-term importance of the Grand Remonstrance lay in its demand that the King's Ministers should be approved by and answerable to the Parliament. Of more immediate significance was the revelation that a considerable amount of support had now swung towards the King. Much of the manoeuvring at this time was conducted in an atmosphere of near hysteria and blind prejudice, both in Parliament and out, as rioting had resumed around Westminster and Whitehall. It seems very likely, as the King himself appeared to believe, that this violence had been organised by the radical element in the Commons. Pym took the view that the mob outside Parliament should not be disappointed, and anti-royalism in the Commons spread to a contempt for the House of Lords. It was argued that, as the Commons was a representative body, it could act independently of the Lords, who were no more than 'particular persons'. The radicals undoubtedly had the initiative, but their support had waned as fears grew of a breakdown in the social order. The House of Lords was itself divided, with the bishops supporting the King, but most of the temporal lords – effectively the Great Council – regarding them as the cause of much of the trouble. The bishops especially were deterred from attending by the rioters, leaving the temporal lords in control. When the bishops demanded that Parliament meet elsewhere, the Commons impeached them, and the rioters directed their attention towards the temporal lords for not expelling the bishops.

The abolition of the Court of Star Chamber in 1642 is difficult to account for, in view of its past popularity, and particularly as Parliament overlooked the moribund Court of Requests and the Court of Wards, which dealt with highly unpopular feudal rights. Wardship was later abolished by ordinance in 1646. The Act, which also abolished the courts of the Marches of Wales, the Council of the North, the Duchy of Lancaster, and the County Palatine of Chester, gave as its reasons for abolishing the Court of Star Chamber that it had exceeded the authority granted to it by statute, trying offences and inflicting punishments not prescribed in statute law, and that the court had been used to introduce an arbitrary power and government, including meddling in civil cases. This referred to its original establishment as a special court, with defined powers and membership, set up and entrusted to the Council by statute in 1487, whose purpose had been to deal with another exceptional situation. The terms of the statute had long ceased to apply, so that the court, which had come to be known as the Court of Star Chamber, had long ceased to have a legal basis, it having been resurrected by the King for other purposes. However, the most likely cause of Parliament's animosity towards the Star Chamber arose from the King's religious and economic policy in the 1630s, during which, in the absence of a Parliament at this time, the Crown had to resort increasingly to rule by proclamation, the enforcement of which, not being common law and so within the jurisdiction of the common law courts, had always been left to the Star Chamber. The removal of the Court of Star Chamber left a gap in the judicial system, however, because there was no longer a court of appeal in respect of, for example, allegations of judges intimidating juries. With the abolition of the Court of Star Chamber also went the power to enforce proclamations.

It has always been assumed that the Act deprived the Council wholly of its judicial function, but this cannot have been the case. The Privy Council continued to sift all petitions to the Crown, and to settle many disputes of a legal or quasi-legal nature, for example, disputes involving merchants on the high seas, the privilege of the Peerage, a dispute between the City of London and the University of Cambridge over the price of victuals, or receiving a petition from the East Riding of Yorkshire concerning flooding. The right of the Great Council in Parliament to delegate to the Privy Council its jurisdiction in respect of cases involving the Second Estate cannot have been affected, although it is doubtful whether the Commons would still have been aware of this. Meanwhile, the King seems to have made less use of the Council for advice and policy-making, preferring to appoint committees of Councillors for particular purposes, and not all members of these committees were necessarily Councillors, as in the case of a Council of War, which James had experimented with in 1621 and 1624.

Whether the King was emboldened, meanwhile, by the evidence of growing support in the Commons and elsewhere, or panicked by the loss of support from the House of Lords and the level of rioting, there is no consensus, but, at the beginning of January 1642, the King ordered the impeachment of leading figures from both Houses. They included Pym and Hampden, and they were charged with having subverted the fundamental laws and government and having treasonably invited the Scots into England during the recent troubles. This would have been a breach of parliamentary privilege, and the Commons refused to order the arrest of their five accused members. It was at this point that Charles made a serious tactical blunder. Acting on impulse, on a well-founded fear that Pym's party would impeach the Queen, Charles went himself, taking a posse of armed men with him, to St Stephen's Hall where the House of Commons was in session, with the object of personally arresting the five accused members. Warned of the King's approach, the five fled by boat down the Thames to London. When, a few minutes later, the King entered the chamber with his guards and demanded to know from the Speaker, Lenthall, where the five were, the Speaker is said to have replied that he had 'neither eyes to see nor tongue to speak in this place, but as this House shall direct me, whose servant I am'. In so responding, Lenthall was not making 'a revolutionary assertion of the power of the Commons to hold government to account', as has been suggested,[47] but merely covering himself by reminding the King of his limited role in the assembly.

The five fugitives were followed to London by the other members of the Commons, who met in the Guildhall. By a coincidence of fate, there had been an armed rebellion in the City in the previous month, when the populist Puritan party, which supported Parliament, had seized control from the King's allies among the wealthy aldermen. Here, the members of Parliament were secure against the King's officers, who otherwise would have been able to seize Pym, Hampden and the others of the five, and so perhaps broken the back of the opposition. Even so, the King's gross violation of parliamentary privilege,[48] as it was regarded, brought a reaction, not only from London, but also from the Great Council in the House of Lords and from the Inns of Court. This privilege, the freedom from violence and arrest, which was of great antiquity, was seen to have been violated in a particularly dramatic manner by the King's entry into the Commons in person, accompanied by armed men. Constitutionally, the King had every right to enter the Chamber, of course, but the entry of armed men to make arrests constituted a violation of the sanctity of the Chamber.

The Commons, emboldened by the turn of events, prepared an Exclusion Bill, designed to exclude bishops from the Lords. Meanwhile, the rebellion in Ireland continued, and in order to crush it, Parliament proposed to call out the militia. Again, the question arose of whether the King would use it against Parliament, and a Militia Bill was therefore

---

47. *The Economist*, 19 November 1994, 72.
48. And, indeed, the sanctity of Parliaments.

introduced, which gave Parliament the power to choose the Lieutenant in each county, who was responsible for its militia. This, in effect, took the power away from the King, depriving him of the only armed force available, and Charles, refusing to sign either Bill, then left for the more Royalist north, taking the Great Seal to York with him. There he was joined by a number of his supporters, who also realised that a violent confrontation was now inevitable. The Queen had fled to France a few days earlier. The Commons, not having access now to the Great Seal, replaced the Militia Bill by an 'Ordinance of the Houses'. In the Militia Ordinance of March 1642, the House of Commons purported to nominate and appoint Parliament's own Lieutenants in the counties. The Lords hesitated to approve it, but 'they associated themselves with the demand which lay behind it'. This could be seen as marking a radical departure from constitutional precedent, implying, as the Commons undoubtedly intended, that, if the Sovereign did not approve a Bill, Parliament could make it into law by ordinance. It was not approved by the House of Lords, however, which merely gave its moral support.[49] The situation was one in which the King was all but deposed, with the Great Council – the House of Lords – temporising. In these circumstances, the Militia Ordinance did not constitute law, but from now onwards men tended to regard themselves as free to choose sides and to decide for themselves what the law said.

Charles countered on 27 May with a royal proclamation that the people should disobey any ordinance of Parliament. Faced with an impasse, and confused by feudal doctrine, Parliament enunciated its own doctrine on 9 June, that the person of the King was distinguishable from the office of King, and the functions of that office could be exercised by Parliament, that is, the two Houses of Lords and Commons.[50] Parliament,

---

49. The common law of the constitution, as we now understand it, did provide for such a situation. In the event of a breakdown in relations between King and Parliament, the appropriate course would have been for the Great Council – now the House of Lords – to assess whether Parliament truly represented the popular will, and, if so, in its considered opinion, to advise the King accordingly. If the King failed to respond as the situation demanded, it was the duty of the Lords to depose him, subject to the will of Parliament, assuming that the Commons reflected the popular will, which was for the Lords to decide. This is what subsequently happened, except that Parliament did not stop there.

50. The conclusion was drawn earlier that, in the absence or incompetence of the King, common law attributed the royal functions to the Great Council, or House of Lords, not to Parliament.

in its assumed latter capacity as holder of the kingly office, ordained that the militia be controlled according to its ordinance, thereby overriding the royal proclamation of May 27, which was thereby deemed to have been issued by the King in his personal capacity, not by him through the office of King. It was a doctrine which Parliament would use to see itself through the ensuing civil war.

In June of 1642 a new document, the Nineteen Propositions, was submitted by Parliament to the King. These propositions were, among other things, that the King accept the Militia Ordinance until the matter could be settled by means of a Bill; that all fortified places be entrusted to officers appointed by Parliament; that the Church government and liturgy be reformed; that all appointments to the Privy Council and to Ministerial office be subject to the approval of both Houses of Parliament; that Parliament appoint guardians for the King's children; and that Parliament have the power to exclude from the Upper House all Peers created after that date. It thus proposed radical changes in constitutional relationships, yet, in the retrospective view of even one of the most radical men in the Parliament at the time, Sir Arthur Haslerigg, 'there was at this time no thought to alter government': all that members sought was 'our ancient liberties with our ancient government'.[51] It was a claim made in calmer retrospect, and was belied by the facts, but then, in any serious struggle, both sides are apt to adopt ever more extreme positions. Charles was in no doubt as to the radical nature of the Nineteen Propositions, and he rejected the whole document.

In his reply of June 18, the King, or his Councillors, set out his own, and probably their, view that England was not ruled as an absolute monarchy, nor as an aristocracy, nor as a democracy, but that laws were made jointly by the King, the Lords and the Commons, with government entrusted to the King, including command of the defence of the realm. The House of Commons, while an excellent convener of liberty, was never intended to share in government, nor to choose those who governed, but was solely entrusted with approving the levy of money and the impeaching of those who had violated the law for their own ends. The House of Lords, being entrusted with judicatory power, provided a screen and buffer between King and people, so preventing

---

51. T. Burton, *The Diary of Thomas Burton, Esq.* (7 February 1659), iii. 87.

any encroachment by the one on the other, and preserving the law which governed all three institutions of state. Since the power legally vested in both Houses was more than enough to prevent the exercise of tyranny, the proposed encroachment of one of the three institutions on the authority of another would undermine the whole system, concentrating all power in the House of Commons and reducing the country to a state of dissension and factionalism, which would eventually be dominated by a Jack Cade or a Wat Tyler. This summation is of great interest, in that it undoubtedly represented a widely held view of the Constitution at the time, and it enables us to see how far perceptions had shifted since the beginning of the Middle Ages. The idea that the three institutions of state were somehow in competition with each other, but were able to hold each other's ambitions in check, was an inevitable consequence of the notion of divine right, the decline and deformation of the Great Council into a House of Lords, and the replacement of the assembly of the people by an assembly of 'professional' representatives. The confused view of the House of Lords, on the part of the King or the Privy Council, nevertheless included a flicker of understanding when he, or it, made the point that it had, by its 'just judgements', a function 'to preserve that law which ought to be the rule of every one of the three'. It was a surviving recognition of the Great Council, in its enforced role, as the House of Lords, as the arbiter, or watchdog of the Constitution. What was now becoming a crucial issue, and one that has persisted to the present day, was the new principle that Parliament should decide who should be the King's Ministers. At the time, this idea was seen as a means of controlling an otherwise uncontrollable King. In fact, Charles's reply showed a 'more relaxed and liberal position' than he had formerly adopted,[52] and was remarkably prescient in its reference to 'a Jack Cade or a Wat Tyler', who was indeed to appear in the person of Oliver Cromwell.

The Commons had ceased to be interested in such arguments, however, and undoubtedly had expected their Nineteen Propositions to be rejected, because they had amounted to a transfer of executive authority from the King to Parliament. Controlled by minorities as it now was, because many of its members had crept away, Parliament must have devised the Nineteen Propositions as a means of provoking the King

---

52. J. P. Kenyon, *The Stuart Constitution*, 183, footnote 23.

into providing it with an excuse for a rupturing of the Constitution and resorting to decisive, unconstitutional action. It reacted to the King's rejection by appointing a Committee of Safety, declaring Charles to be an aggressor, and ordering the raising of an army, with the Earl of Essex in command. A month later, on 22 August, Charles raised his standard near Nottingham, ready for the civil war that was bound to follow. The response was lukewarm, but it was greatly helped by a declaration by Parliament, on 6 September, that the costs of the war must be borne by those who had been, or were to be, voted 'delinquents' by both Houses. Many of those with property now had a vested personal interest in ensuring a victory for the King. As each side manoeuvred for position, there ensued what can only be described as a propaganda war.

The main cause of this, the most serious constitutional breakdown in English history, was the religious conflict arising from the Reformation. More or less resolved, or at least stabilised, during the reign of Elizabeth I, this had been stirred up again by the arrival of the Stuarts, whose background and leanings were undoubtedly Catholic, in spite of their Protestant allegiance, bringing with them that other aspect of Catholicism, the doctrine of the divine right of kings. The Stuarts did their best to accommodate themselves to English constitutional principles, but the seventeenth century was a period when personal principles counted for a great deal. With the progress of the Catholic Counter-Reformation across Western Europe gathering pace, those in the Church of England who still had Catholic leanings were inclined to take advantage of it, while the Puritans, fearful of being over-run by the Counter-Reformation, were in no mood for compromise. Matters were made more volatile and given a political slant by the popular association of the King, perhaps mistakenly, with the Catholic revival movement, and the King aggravated matters by his doctrine of kingship and his lamentable lack of judgement. The effect was a constitutional confrontation between the Crown and Parliament, made possible by the rising power of the Commons. This, in turn, was made more acute by the progressive withdrawal of moderates from the House, embarrassed by the direction of events, and so leaving the House in the hands of the radical element. The latter, driven by Charles's obstinacy into making more and more extreme demands, reached the point where they lost patience and saw the only solution, effectively, as rule by Parliament alone, by which they meant the House of Commons. Charles at last saw this, and realised that constitutional process was at an end. If the Crown were to survive, he would have to fight for it. Even so, the great majority of those involved were almost certainly unwilling to become involved in a war over the issue. What brought matters to a head for Pym and the rest of the Puritan faction that now controlled the Commons was the Irish rebellion and the critical issue of who should control the army that was needed to suppress it, because if the King did, he would be able to crush the Puritan cause. To the King, relinquishing command of the army violated the very principle of kingship.

For the majority of the population, matters of principle mattered less than stability and a comfortable life, but for the time being they had been driven into acquiescence by the more aggressive factions on both sides. Until the moderates, with their more foggy outlook, regained control of the establishment, there could be little prospect of religious or constitutional compromise. Generally speaking, public sentiment in the south-east, from Lincolnshire to Hampshire, supported the Puritans, while public opinion in the north and west mainly supported the King. About a third of the country, from Yorkshire to Dorset, was either neutral or evenly divided. Those who were neutral were regarded by the Puritans as enemies, and driven into the Royalist camp. To some extent it was a conflict between town and country, with the later more inclined to support the King. There was also a social division, with the great majority of the nobility and probably a majority of the gentry siding with the King, whereas the merchant and yeoman classes were either neutral or favoured the Parliament. The feeling among the Puritans was that, if the King won, freedom of speech and conscience would be lost for ever, and the only way of winning was to deprive him of all his power. Such were the issues at stake that all methods were justified. Added to this was a growing element of hysteria and vindictiveness. There can be no doubt that the House of Commons had gone out of its way to provoke the King. It had even been willing to sacrifice the national interest in the pursuit of its vendetta with the Crown, helping, by its refusal to grant money, to bring about humiliating military defeats at the hands of the Spanish, the French, and the Scots. It was the single-minded view of the House of Commons that a resolution of the internal conflict came first, and that such external disasters could be used to bring further pressure on the King.

Yet this is all an explanation of what went wrong; not why. There is a stark explanation of why the Constitution broke down in 1642: the King simply misunderstood his position. He had been brought up in the Church Feudal tradition, whereas most members of the public, including those in the House of Commons, had not. He saw himself as the appointee and servant of God, not of the people, and he never understood why there existed this gulf between them and himself. While still in Edinburgh, in October 1641, he had announced that he was 'constant for the doctrine and discipline of the Church of England as it was established by Queen Elizabeth and my father, and resolved to live and die in the maintenance of it', and, on his return to London at the end of the year, ordered that religious services be conducted according to law. He had probably left it too late, but the issue was no longer straightforward. Parliament no longer really had a case, but it could reasonably be argued that, in common law, Charles had already forfeited his right to rule by his sustained efforts to govern in the face of public opinion. Yet deposing a King was usually a difficult and often messy process. In earlier times, when the King's councillors controlled most of the military forces of the nation and there was little disagreement about the Constitution, this had not been too difficult, but in the circumstances of Charles I it was complicated by several factors. The House of Lords was now a shadow of its former self, because its members no longer had access to large bands of fighting men, and their authority was disputed by a rampant House of Commons. The King himself and a significant element in the population accepted the Church's doctrine as to his divine right to rule, so that, even if they disagreed with his policies or his behaviour, they still felt impelled to support him.

For all the strife of Charles's reign, more beneficial changes had been occurring in other ways. In 1635, the King had made the royal postal service available to the public, and a service had been established between London and Edinburgh. The stage-coach revolution had begun in 1640, with the establishment of the first stage-coach lines and coaching houses at regular intervals across the country. The Lancashire cotton industry had its origin in 1641, when the first mills were opened in Manchester to process cotton imported from India. Less welcome developments were the introduction by Parliament of an income tax and a property tax in 1642.

24.1.5.1. The Increasing Disintegration of Parliament

Although the main causes of the rupture of 1642 were religious, it had serious consequences for the Constitution. As a result of the King's aggressive and undignified entry into the House of Commons on 4 January 1642, the members of the Commons had resolved to protect their right to free debate without interruption or intimidation. From that time onwards, the doors of the chamber were to be kept closed whenever the House was in session. Consequently, whenever the messenger of the Lords, the Gentleman Usher of the Black Rod, attempted to enter the Commons chamber to summon its members to join the King and the Lords in full Parliament, he found the doors closed against him. Only after the Usher had knocked with his staff three times was he admitted. This was to become a permanent tradition, asserting the alleged right of the Commons to deliberate without fear of royal intrusion. In so far as the Commons deliberated 'in Parliament', the King had every right of access for the purpose of such consultation that either side deemed to be necessary, and, of course, the House of Commons had claimed that its deliberations were conducted within the sanctified space of Parliament. Nevertheless, the Commons were not only the King's guests, to be treated accordingly, but they had a right to consult among themselves without interruption, except for the normal processes of Parliament, which Charles's intrusion was clearly not.

It was one more step in the destruction of Parliament as a coherent legislature, whose gradual disintegration had been, and continued to be, due to a series of developments:

1. the replacement of Parliaments of the people by assemblies of their representatives;
2. the destructive influence of the doctrine of divine right, which had encouraged a succession of rulers to behave in an arbitrary manner;
3. the policy of Edward III in by-passing the Great Council, resulting in the rupture of Parliament and the establishment of a House of Lords also as a separate authority in its own right;

4. the increasing burden of parliamentary work, extending sittings
    and giving rise to 'professional' representatives and their
    accretion into groups, bent on promoting particular interests;
5. the growing conflict between the Commons and the
    Crown, due largely to the King's view of himself, not as
    the representative of the people, but as the agent of God;
6. the increasing variety and complexity of issues before
    Parliament, calling for protracted deliberation, which
    furthered the consolidation of pressure groups in
    the Commons, based in ideological interests.

It was these developments that had eventually made the breakdown
of the constitutional process inevitable.

24.1.5.2. Jurisdiction in the Stuart Period

Royal, or prerogative, law, which had hitherto been accepted as a
necessary feature of government, had effectively been demolished under
the Stuarts, as a result of the rivalry between the Crown and Parliament.
Previously, the courts of common law had refused to hear cases brought
under prerogative law on the grounds that they were constituted to
enforce common law. This raises the question of why no courts were
established to enforce either prerogative law or statute law. In practice,
statute law came to be enforced by the courts of common law, who seem
to have had no jurisdiction in the matter. There is a possible explanation
for this. It is that statute law was originally viewed as the exposition, by the
King and people in Parliament, of hitherto unrevealed or misunderstood
customary law. Law could not be created, because all law already existed
as *ius divinum*, or divine law, and all that a statute did was to expound
the law as it was perceived. Invented law, as opposed to divine or natural
law, had no validity. Therefore, the King, through whom Parliament had
delegated most of its jurisdiction in respect of offences by the Third Estate,
to the specialised royal courts, was responsible in his capacity as supreme
judge for the trial of offences against the law, whether it was described as
'common' or 'statute' law. Since the late Middle Ages, the two had, for
some reason, been regarded as different kinds of law, but this had not
been reflected in the establishment of separate courts. This had left royal,

or prerogative law in an anomalous position since the abolition of the Court of Star Chamber. The Stuart Parliaments and judiciary preferred the King to refrain from proclaiming laws in the first place, even to the extent of denying that he had the right to do so.

24.2. The Civil War (1643–49)

That there was a conflict at all was due, not to a failure of the Constitution, but to a failure to observe it. The King had abused his position, out of ignorance and temperament; the House of Commons had behaved boorishly; and the House of Lords, in its capacity as the Great Council, had failed to deal with the crisis. There had been three reasons for this. One was that, although its sympathies generally lay with the Commons, it was not satisfied that the Lower House had the support of the people. Another was that it hesitated in the face of the widely held view that the King owed his position to God – which had incapacitated the Great Council itself – rather than the people. A third was that the House of Lords had lost much of its authority, leaving the House of Commons in the dominant position.

The emerging factions in the conflict were the Royalists and the Parliamentarians. The former saw the conflict as the 'Great Rebellion', while the latter saw it as a civil war. In fact, the division was by no means clear-cut. Even in the House of Commons, there were those who, having been intimidated, supported the King when it came to a showdown. The House of Lords, which had tried to be a moderating influence in the dispute, was very divided, with about half their number supporting the King, a quarter backing the Parliamentarians, and a quarter doing their best not to take sides, although, if the Scottish and Irish Peers are taken into account, the House was more or less evenly divided.[53] The bishops had already been excluded. Intimidation was one of the chief weapons used by the Puritans to win their case, because perhaps as many of the people supported the King as supported the Commons. The narrow-minded intolerance and arrogance of the Commons shocked and antagonised many people, just as did the King's bungling and high-handedness and

53. C. H. Firth, *The House of Lords During the Civil War* (London, 1910), 115.

the widespread fear of Papism. Many who supported the King detested the bishops. Many fought for the one side or the other out of simple obedience to the natural leaders in their own districts. Levies were untrained and lacked central organisation, and were unwilling to leave their own areas, so that much of the real fighting was done by the upper classes. It is one of the ironies of a Civil War, fought ostensibly between King and people, that the ordinary people played a comparatively minor part in the conflict. The armies employed were small and the war was relatively free from excesses.

The early part of the conflict was characterised by raids and indecisive engagements, such as the Battle of Edgehill, which took place two months after the King had first raised his standard. In these engagements, the Royalist cavalry, led by Prince Rupert, proved its superiority. Because it was in the cavalry that the strength of the King's forces lay, they became known popularly as the Cavaliers, from the Middle French *cavalier*, a horseman. They had the early advantage and relied on an early victory, because it was the Commons, supported by the moneyed men in London, who had the greater resources. Their chances of winning increased, the more drawn out the war became. The Parliamentary forces were commanded initially by the Earl of Essex, but the outcome would be decided very largely by the ability of one man, Oliver Cromwell, who had been one of the Puritan members of the House of Commons. Cromwell, referred to by Prince Rupert as 'Ironside', was given command of a 'Parliamentarian' army, raised in East Anglia and the east Midlands, comprising men who were both from Protestant sects and 'Independents', but whom Cromwell had selected for their religious dedication, irrespective of social standing or military experience. He converted his army into a highly disciplined and motivated force, which was also better equipped and promoted officers on merit, with the result that Cromwell's 'Ironsides' emerged as the best troops in the war. Just as it became customary to distinguish the two sides as Royalists and Parliamentarians, so it became the practice to refer to the opposing armies as the Cavaliers and Roundheads, the latter because it became fashionable among the Puritans to wear their hair close cut. This reflected the stern and uncompromising piety that existed among them, in contrast to the more relaxed and self-indulgent attitudes of the Cavaliers.

In order to rally Scotland to the support of Parliament, 25 peers and 288 members of the Commons signed the Solemn League and Covenant in September 1643. This was an attempt to make the religions of England, Ireland and Scotland as uniform as possible by reforming them 'according to the word of God, and the examples of the best reformed churches'. It extended to the Scots the hope of bringing England into the Presbyterian fold, while at the same time preserving the interests of the Protestant sects, and the hope was that it would induce the Scots to enter the fray. As a result, the Scots Covenanters invaded England and a Committee of Both Kingdoms was established to prosecute the war on the Parliamentary side. All clerics and civil and military officers were required to sign the Covenant. Charles, for his part, concluded a truce with the Irish Catholics in order to secure the assistance of Irish regiments. On the Parliamentary side, the war was dominated by the more extreme Protestants, and the conflict became more a Puritan rebellion than a revolt by the Commons.

On the whole, the war went well for the Royalists in 1643, but with no sign of a resolution. By the end of the year, Parliamentary forces held a corridor across the country, from Lancashire to Kent, including East Anglia, while the King's forces still held the areas to the north and west, with the exception of Hull and the west coast ports. The Long Parliament continued to sit at Westminster, devoting itself to trying to find a religious solution, for although the bishops had now been abolished and altars and stained-glass windows destroyed, no acceptable doctrine or order had yet emerged. Meanwhile, Charles summoned a rival – Royalist – Parliament at Oxford, his wartime capital, at the beginning of 1644. The key battle of the war was fought in July of that year, just west of York, on Marston Moor, where Cromwell and his Ironsides inflicted a decisive defeat on Prince Rupert's forces, thereby gaining control of northern England. In Scotland, meanwhile, there was a bitter division between the lowland Presbyterians, who fought as the Covenanters, and the Catholics of the Highlands and Isles, who, later in 1644, rose under the Duke of Montrose in support of the King. In successive engagements extending well into 1645, the Highland Royalists inflicted a series of defeats on the Covenanters.

One of the political factions among the soldiers were the Levellers, so called from their earlier practice, as an anti-enclosure movement, of levelling hedges and fences, and who now favoured an egalitarian society under a republic. There were also four main religious groups and groupings in England by this time: the Anglicans; the Presbyterians, who detested sectarianism and dreaded a Levelling revolution and army rule; the Protestant sects, such as the Baptists, Anabaptists, Seekers and Fifth Monarchy men. In addition, there were the Independents, who believed in the freedom of individual conscience. Among the population at large, and in the House of Commons, there can be no doubt, however, that the great majority supported the retention of the monarchy. There was also a dwindling number of Catholics, who wisely kept very much to themselves. Even on the Royalist side, religious coherence was lacking, while on the Parliament side the disunity was much worse. In consequence, strife between factions on the Parliamentary side, together with the blundering by its commanders in the west, came close to destroying the advantage gained at Marston Moor.

The beginning of 1645 saw the trial and execution of the Archbishop of Canterbury, William Laud, for treason, with little effort by the King to intervene on his behalf. The office of Archbishop was destined to remain vacant for fifteen years. Essex was replaced in 1645 by Sir Thomas Fairfax, but it was Cromwell who was now effectively in command of the campaign. Appointed lieutenant-general under Fairfax, Cromwell in 1644 reformed the Parliamentary army, whose nucleus was provided by the 'trained bands' – those relics of the feudal armies – along the lines of his own 'Ironsides', so that it emerged into history as the red-coated New Model Army. In June, the King, having unwisely divided his remaining army, was caught and decisively beaten by Fairfax and Cromwell in the Battle of Naseby, some ten miles to the north of Northampton. The King's captured papers revealed his plans to repeal anti-Catholic laws, introduce an Irish army, and hire foreign mercenaries.[54] While the reinstatement of Catholics might have been Charles's secret intention all along, it is equally possible that it was the price that he had to pay for Irish support. In September, the Scottish Covenanters under General Leslie finally inflicted a decisive defeat on Montrose's Catholic Highlanders, with the result that, from now onwards, Scottish involvement was on the Presbyterian side.

---

54. K. Feiling, *A History of England*, 481.

There followed a rather chaotic period, during which negotiations were conducted. The King surrendered to the Scots at Newark in May 1646, so bringing the first military phase of the conflict to an end. Playing for time, and pinning his hopes on a growing rift between the Presbyterians in Parliament and the Independents in the army, Charles rejected Parliament's proposals, known as the Newcastle Propositions, which called for a Presbyterian Church, Charles taking the Scottish Covenant, and Parliament controlling the militia for twenty years. In return for their back-pay, the Scots handed the King over to Parliament at the beginning of 1647, but the army and Parliament were now in open conflict. The problem with the army was that, having been selected from men notable for their religious commitment, it was mainly drawn from the lower classes and was highly politicised. It was also highly disciplined under Cromwell, but when it found itself encamped for months on end, unpaid, with Cromwell elsewhere, and realising that what they believed they had fought for was in danger of slipping away from them, they took on a radical character.

Parliament had shrunk to little more than a côterie. It had long exceeded its mandate of 1640, and half its members had fallen by the way or simply abandoned it. It might have strengthened its position if it had agreed to pay the soldiers and pass an Act of Oblivion, which would have indemnified them for crimes committed during the war, but it hesitated, believing that this would encourage the King to demand similar treatment for the Royalists. Instead, Parliament resolved on a showdown with the army by sending half to Ireland to deal with the rebellion and demobilising the rest without arrears of pay. The army reacted by electing representatives, who, together with a few radical officers, authorised the King to be seized and brought to the army headquarters at Newmarket, where he was held hostage. In order to preserve discipline, Fairfax agreed to the formation of an army General Council, which included himself and Cromwell, who, with other members of Parliament, had now abandoned it and joined with the army. Fairfax then approved a Declaration from himself and the army to Parliament, dated 14 June 1647, refusing to disband until the soldiers' demands were met. The Declaration demanded, among other things, the expulsion from both Houses of Parliament of 'delinquent' members; the passing of an Act of Oblivion that would protect the disbanded soldiers against any retribution; the imposition of a limit on the life of Parliaments and their protection against unwarranted adjournment or dissolution; and freedom for the people to petition it in respect of their grievances. Parliament did not respond, and when the House of Commons was ransacked by a mob, the army entered London and restored order.

As a new power in the land, the General Council tried to negotiate with the King, again without success. Even Cromwell was anxious to come to terms with Charles, his moderation being evident in an offer, drawn up by General Ireton, that he persuaded the army to make to the King in August 1647. This, known as 'The Heads of the Proposals', would have gone some way towards restoring the King and Constitution to their original position, subject to certain reforms to strengthen the position and representativeness of Parliament, with Parliamentary control of the army and the great offices of state for ten years. The army's proposals were also more lenient towards the Royalists than those which had been offered by Parliament, and demanded religious toleration. The 'Heads' also took note of popular grievances which had already been voiced by the Levellers in London. The King rejected them. There was now pressure from within the army for the ideas of the Levellers to be introduced, and at a meeting of the General Council, held in the church at Putney at the end of October 1647, the Levellers presented a document known as *The Agreement of the People*. This proposed a new constitution, comprising a single chamber legislature, elected on a broad franchise,[55] with full power in all matters, except that it should itself be bound by certain 'fundamental laws'. These included religious freedom for all Protestants and no military conscription. Constituencies were to be adjusted to ensure similar numbers of voters in each, showing that the basis of the Constitution had long been forgotten. There was no mention of either the King or the House of Lords, which, by implication, would be abolished. The document was debated by the Council, but there was concern as to whether it conflicted with the Council's own declarations, and whether it would lead to a better distribution of wealth, or simply to anarchy. In the end it was rejected by Fairfax, who, disowning the Levellers, demanded and received the obedience of the army, in return

---

55. It appeared, from ensuing discussions in the General Council, that the proposed franchise, being a controversial field in any case, excluded wage-earners, servants, and paupers.

for which he pledged to work to secure the interests of the soldiers and 'redress of the common grievances of the people'. The Commons also refused to sponsor the proposed constitution, and it seems that, the more that the Commons and the General Council came around to the idea of getting rid of the King, the more inclined they became to hold onto power themselves.

Early in November, the King escaped. While there is no evidence that Cromwell played any part in this, there is no doubt that it saved the situation, calling the army back to duty. It was an interruption from which, politically, the Levellers never recovered. Charles had fled to the Isle of Wight in the hope of restoring some independence to his position, only to be re-arrested and held there at Carisbrooke. At the end of the year he refused to sign four Bills presented to him by Parliament, which included a provision for Parliament to command the army for twenty years; for all Peers created by Charles to be excluded from the Lords; and for the two Houses to adjourn at their pleasure. Again, Charles was playing for time. On this occasion he was expecting help from the Scottish nobility, with whom he had made a secret treaty only a few days earlier. The Scots, horrified by the growing religious tolerance in England, and gratified by Charles's willingness to abolish episcopacy and to introduce Presbyterianism, agreed to restore him by force of arms. Charles himself once remarked that his only hope of regaining his kingdom was by getting the Presbyterians and the Independents to destroy one another, by drawing one or the other into an alliance with himself. When it became known that Charles had provoked another war, Parliament finally lost its patience. It responded, early in 1648, by renouncing its allegiance to the King and deciding to have no more communication with him. When the army, which had temporarily dispersed at the end of 1647, came together again at Windsor in May, feelings ran high.

It would be an oversimplification to say that this second phase of the conflict was now between Royalists and Parliamentarians, between Scotland and England, and between Presbyterians and Independents. Many faced conflicting loyalties, and many on the Royalist side supported the supremacy of Parliament, but dreaded the destruction of the Crown. A deep division now existed between the army and Parliament over the future of the monarchy. While a meeting of army officers at Windsor decided to bring the King to trial, on account of the blood that he had caused to be shed and the mischief that he had done, Parliament yet again attempted to open negotiations with him. A Scottish army entered England in August 1648, in support of the King, but it straggled southwards and was caught and totally defeated by Cromwell at Preston, ending all hope of Charles's return to the throne. Scotland itself was then occupied by Cromwell.

The King was now more popular than Parliament, and the army had to deal with several outbreaks of violence in Wales and the south. Parliament, trying yet again to reach an accommodation, opened negotiations with Charles for a 'personal treaty' at Newport, in the Isle of Wight, on the same basis as that of 1647. The army reacted by drawing closer to the programme proposed by the Levellers, who sought to appeal beyond Parliament to the people, but Fairfax insisted on preserving constitutional forms. In November a delegation of officers presented Parliament with a 'Remonstrance of the Army', demanding that the King and his supporters be brought to trial, with supreme power in the future being vested in a new Parliament, which could elect a new King if it wished. It was tantamount to the deposition of the King, but, being a very long document, Parliament deferred having it read to them, or debating it.

At the beginning of December, the army took the King into custody again. Troops moved into London and, overruling pleas that the Parliament be dispersed by force, the army's Council sent a contingent under Colonel Thomas Pride to conduct 'Pride's Purge'. This involved the eviction of the ninety-six Presbyterian members of Parliament who had voted for the Newport treaty, reducing the Long Parliament to what became known as the 'Rump' Parliament of fifty Independent members. With the Presbyterians out of the way, the 'Rump' House of Commons broke off negotiations with the King and decided to bring him to trial. Soon afterwards, the Independents, who were now in control of the army, undertook a purge of the Levellers. Most of their leaders were arrested, with Cromwell allegedly insisting before the Army Council that 'You must break these men or they will break you'.[56]

---

56. G. E. Aylmer, *The Struggle for the Constitution*, 137.

The swift pace of constitutional events was now accelerated further, when a proposal by the House of Commons, that a High Court of Justice be created to try the King, was rejected in the New Year of 1649 by the dozen Peers left in the House of Lords. The Commons reacted four days later by passing three resolutions: that God was the origin of all just power (almost a re-statement of customary law); that the Commons, by being chosen by and representing the people, had the supreme power; and that whatever was enacted or declared for law by the Commons, in Parliament assembled, had the force of law, irrespective of the concurrence of the King or the Lords. Two days later it passed a decisive 'Act' setting up a High Court of Justice of 135 persons to try the King. This declared that 'Charles Stuart, King of England … hath had a wicked design totally to subvert the ancient and fundamental laws and liberties of this nation and in their place to introduce an arbitrary and tyrannical government … he hath prosecuted it with fire and sword, levied and maintained a cruel war in the land against the Parliament and kingdom'. Charles was to be tried for these crimes and for treason against the people of England. The army had asserted its judicial supremacy by evicting the Presbyterian members of the Commons, but it had then acknowledged the House of Commons as the chief legal authority in the land by seeking its authority to try the King. It was a concession of political ground that the army never regained.

The deposition of the King was undoubtedly considered, but the nation was too divided on ideological grounds for that to be a durable solution, and after a trial on 30 January 1649, at which no defence witnesses were called, Charles was convicted and executed on the same day. Just before the execution, the House of Commons approved a Bill that declared the representatives of the people to be the source of all just power, and making it an offence to proclaim a new King. It did not receive the royal assent, and so had no legal standing. It affected to abolish both the Monarchy and the House of Lords, refuting both Church Feudal doctrine and overlooking the common law of the land, according to which 'the people' comprised all three Estates. Charles I was beheaded outside the Banqueting House of the Palace of Whitehall. Cromwell apparently took the view that it was a 'cruel necessity', in order to bring the deep divisions in the land to an end. That it was a highly unpopular act is beyond question. Only fifty-nine of the members of the court could be persuaded to sign the death certificate, and the execution had to be protected from the mob by a mass of soldiers, the mob being then dispersed by the cavalry.

The constitutional circumstances leading up to the trial and death of Charles I had been chaotic. Charles, as the appointee of God by right of descent, was not the King according to the requirements of common law. The House of Commons had become progressively less representative of public opinion as its members had melted away, pursuing its own course without any particular reference to public opinion. Under neither constitutional tradition, feudal or Indo-European, was there such an offence as treason against the people, or against the state, only against the King, as, indeed, against any man's lord.[57] Consequently, Charles could not have committed treason against himself. He had, however, violated the regal contract with the people, an offence of which he was probably quite unaware, and which he would not have acknowledged, even if he had. The Great Council in the House of Lords had long since lost its credibility, and its position was further complicated by the King's appointment to it, almost at the last moment, of hated Church leaders. The obvious solution, to depose the King, was not sustainable, because the country was bitterly divided over the issue. The King himself had lost all credibility, and was unaccommodating to the very end. Yet his execution was offensive to both constitutional traditions. How the function of the Earl of the Palace would have fitted into this situation is unknown. It was the first and only formal execution of an English King.

It has been argued in mitigation[58] that the trial broke new constitutional ground, in that Cooke, the Solicitor-General, was the first to adduce the concept of representative government, whereby the Commons could make law without the assent of either the King or the House of Lords, but this was special pleading. Because, he claimed, a King had never been tried before, the indictment by the Commons broke new ground, and was therefore 'a true Bill', demonstrating that the House of Commons could legislate on its own. The historical evidence demonstrates, however, that several English Kings had been tried and deposed, and neither the

---

57. Betrayal, which can be a crime against the state, is not quite the same thing as treason.
58. G. Robertson, *The Tyrannicide Brief* (London, 2006).

common law of the Constitution nor feudal doctrine provided that an assembly of the Third Estate could itself make law.

In February 1649, a Council of State was appointed by the Rump Parliament to act as the executive arm of government, its purpose being to direct domestic and foreign policy, and to ensure the security of the Government. It replaced the King's Privy Council, which had been abolished, leading the Council of State to be known, also, as Cromwell's 'Privy Council'. The new body consisted of forty members, of whom thirty-one were members of Parliament. The Council of State first met on February 17, under the chairmanship of Oliver Cromwell, with only fourteen members attending, but the first elected President of the Council, appointed on March 12, was John Bradshaw, who had presided over the court at the trial of the King. The members of the Council included the Duke of Suffolk and the Earl of Denbigh. On March 16, the Monarchy and the House of Lords were both abolished by the House of Commons, leaving constitutional power now vesting wholly in the 'Rump' of the Long Parliament. All reference to the King in legal documents was replaced by 'The Keepers of the Liberties of England', whoever they might be. Thus, England was now ruled by a self-perpetuating oligarchy.

24.3. The Commonwealth

On 19 May an Act was passed declaring England to be 'a Commonwealth or Free-State'. This brought protests from the Levellers over the lack of provision for a new Parliament, and their leader, Lilburne, submitted his *England's New Chains Discovered to Parliament*. There followed a series of mutinies in the army, inspired by the Levellers, which were put down by Fairfax, who then expelled the Levellers from the army. They were not the only frustrated element, for the army's General Council of officers continued to apply pressure for the reforms which it had been expecting. There were more urgent problems, however, and Cromwell now set off on a victorious campaign during 1649 and 1650 to put down the Irish rebellion.

Although the Rump Parliament still met with just fifty members, all belonging to the Independent faction, real power now resided with the army under Cromwell. It is clear that the legitimacy of the new regime was widely questioned, because a new Treasons Act was passed, making it a treasonable offence to question the 'supreme authority' of the Commons or to suggest that the Government was unlawful. What was supposed to be a free and democratic state soon acquired the character of a tyrannical oligarchy. Incest and adultery were made punishable by death, fornication by three months' imprisonment, and swearing by fines. The Blasphemy Act, which, among other things, by outlawing those who taught that the Elect were permitted to commit any sin, legalized, by implication, any less outrageous deviation by them. The people were generally hostile, Cromwell's moderation waned, and the leader of the Levellers, John Lilburne, was tried for treason in 1646–7 for criticising the Government as a tyranny and a usurpation. The trial was conducted by the House of Lords, exercising, in its role as the Great Council, the latter's powers of original jurisdiction. Although Lilburne appealed to the House of Commons, it gave him no support.

Meanwhile, the Royalist cause had been revived in Scotland and Ireland. Early in 1649, the Scots proclaimed the eldest son of Charles I, also called Charles, as their King, but the Irish, who had risen in his support, were put down by Cromwell, who landed and took the fortress at Drogheda. There, he had all the defenders who had not laid down their arms massacred, and Catholic landholders were dispossessed in favour of Protestant supporters of Parliament. The Irish Catholic clergy spread tales of the killing of innocent women and children at Drogheda, which Cromwell had expressly forbidden, and for which there is no evidence, yet it sufficed to create a legacy of bitterness, aggravated by the ensuing famine. Meanwhile, the youthful Charles landed in Scotland in June 1650, and took the covenant, against all his inclinations. He was then proclaimed as King of the Scots at Scone in the New Year of 1651. He then marched southwards to claim his English Crown. Cromwell replied by invading Scotland – Fairfax having refused to do so – and at Dunbar, at the beginning of September, defeated a Scottish army twice the size of his own. Leaving Cromwell in Scotland to capture Perth, Charles fell into Cromwell's trap by leading the Scottish army southwards into England, hoping for support from Wales. Overtaking it at last, at Worcester in September 1651, Cromwell totally defeated the Scots, and Charles was whisked in secret to Sussex, from where he fled back to France. Scotland, like Ireland, was soon under English rule, and Cromwell was effectively the guiding power in England.

This was the year in which the political philosopher, Thomas Hobbes, published his penetrating but cynical treatise, *The Leviathan*, with its proposition that all life was 'nasty, brutish, and short'. Drawing on the experience of his times, he saw men as driven by selfishness, their own ideas of good and bad, their desire for gain and glory, and their desire for power in order to ensure their own safety. Although peace and harmony could be achieved by following the 'laws of nature', man was too intemperate and short-sighted to follow these rules of his own volition; therefore, an all-powerful, sovereign authority was necessary to enforce them. In order to make this possible in an orderly manner, men must enter into a covenant with one another, in which they surrendered their excess rights as individuals. In the hope of individual gain at the expense of others, there were many who would disregard even the terms of this covenant, or social contract, hence the need for an absolute authority. Even so, the subject had a right to rebel if the acts of the sovereign conflicted with the purpose of his existence. There was an element of contradiction in Hobbes's argument, of which Hobbes himself was not unaware, and he accepted that men had to take a certain amount on trust. He went on to distinguish three types of sovereignty – monarchy, democracy, and aristocracy, of which he considered monarchy to be the most satisfactory option. The greed and self-interests of the monarch were simply multiplied in the case of an assembly or an aristocracy, while democracy, by Hobbes's very definition of human nature, could only bring anarchy.

Meanwhile, the Thirty Years' War – the Pope's Counter-Reformation against Protestantism – which had begun during the reign of James I and had been contributing so much to the anxiety and political tension in England, was reaching a conclusion. Although regarded as a single war, it had really been a succession of four periods of conflict, during which there had been changes in both the leading participants and their motives. The religious issue had remained fundamental, but the conflicts had increased in bitterness. The Catholic cause had been represented by Austria, at the head of the Imperial forces, and by Spain, which had been involved chiefly in the Netherlands. The leadership of the Protestant defence had shifted, first to the Danes, and then to the Swedes, but France had emerged as the dominant player during the final period. The turmoil was at last ended by the Treaties of Westphalia in 1648. Its broad outcomes were the restoration of Catholic control in central Europe, the independence of the Netherlands and Switzerland, the beginning of French hegemony in Europe, and the decline of Spain as a European power. England, although much affected by the outcome, had played little part in the struggle, having been too preoccupied with its domestic problems.

Parliament dealt with a shortage of money by often harsh and unsound financial measures, including heavy taxation, the sale of Royalist property, and a further sale of Church and Crown lands. There was much unemployment. Although the legitimacy of the Long Parliament had long expired in common law, not all its actions were without benefit. In November of 1650 the courts were directed to cease the use of Law French. In order to break the trading monopoly of the Dutch and to increase the number of English seamen, the Navigation Act of 1651 forbade the importation, into England or the colonies, of goods from Asia, Africa, Europe or the Americas, except in English or colonial vessels. Only where the goods were being imported into England or the colonies from Europe in the ships of the exporting country was an exemption made. The Navigation Act helped to establish the supremacy of the English merchant marine, but it also helped to provoke an Anglo-Dutch War in 1652, which erupted in the Battle of the Downs, in May of that year, when an English fleet defeated the Dutch. One of the achievements of the Commonwealth was the establishment by the Council of State of an Admiralty committee under Henry Vane, and below this an expert board of Navy Commissioners, which began the building of new warships, with better pay and victualling, so that the fleet, under Admiral Blake, began to emerge with a spirit similar to that of the New Model Army. The war against the Dutch was largely fought at sea, and, following another English naval victory off Portland and the decisive Battle of the Texel in the following year, peace was restored with the Dutch in 1654.

Meanwhile, trouble brewed between the army and the Rump Parliament. The latter, in an attempt to find a reconciliation with the Royalists, and faced by new demands from the army that it account in detail for all taxes collected in its name since 1642, hurriedly covered itself by passing an Act of Indemnity and Oblivion. It also negotiated for the return of confiscated Royalist estates, leading in 1652 to charges of bribery against parliamentary members. It also passed an Act of Settlement for Ireland. Most of its Acts, however, were repressive and arbitrary and many were ill-advised. A Perpetuation Bill was introduced in an attempt to make all existing members of Parliament members for life, but was dropped in exchange for the army's agreement, in November 1651, to its own reduction. Otherwise, the demands of the army were largely ignored, and it is remarkable that the army, which was apparently in a position to dictate its own terms, appeared to be so impotent.[59]

The unpopularity of the Commonwealth, or Free-State, administration was evident everywhere, and even the army opposed the war with Holland and was restive about the lack of reforms in the Church. An oath of 'engagement to the Commonwealth' was imposed on the entire adult male population, although how far this was carried out is unclear. Fairfax was by now distinctly unhappy with the situation, and became increasingly uncooperative. In 1650 he retired. Cromwell also was well aware of the public hostility, but realised that the Puritan revolution could only be brought to an end by the army summoning a new Parliament, except that the Rump Parliament stood in its way. He therefore did his best to resolve the frictions. When the leading members of Parliament tried to put through another Bill, early in 1653, concerning the future of the Parliament or its members – the contents of the Bill since being lost – Cromwell seems to have lost his temper. On 20 April 1653, with a force of musketeers, he cleared the chamber and locked its doors, declaring that it 'should give place to better men'. Pointing to the Mace which still lay in the chamber, Cromwell remonstrated: 'What shall we do with the bauble? Take it away!' Nobody seems to have been clear whether this was any more than a temporary interruption of Parliament, but there was no reaction from either the public or the judiciary. Indeed, the public's indifference or satisfaction can be imagined. In the event, it proved to be the dissolution of the Long Parliament – that is to say, what was left of it as the Rump Parliament.

This raised the question of a newly elected Parliament, for which the army had long been agitating. The problem was that a freely elected

---

59. G. E. Aylmer, *The Struggle for the Constitution*, 298.

Parliament would undoubtedly have ended Puritan rule and restored the monarchy, and with it the Stuarts. There was also an awkward constitutional issue: since the abolition of the Monarchy and the House of Lords, there had been nobody with the authority to summon or dissolve Parliaments. The Long Parliament had therefore been regarded as the supreme authority, but, with its disbanding, there had been created a constitutional vacuum. At a meeting of Cromwell and the army's Council in March of that year, Cromwell and his brother-in-law, General Desborough, pointed out that, if a new Parliament were summoned, the supreme power would not be the Parliament, but he or they who summoned it. They were evidently referring to the Monarchy and the Great Council (the Lords), but Cromwell understood that no Parliament would accept that any but itself was the supreme authority, because it represented the people. In spite of this, Cromwell and the officers acted as the supreme authority by summoning it. Finding themselves in such a cleft stick, Cromwell persuaded the army leaders to drop, for the time being, their demand for a new Parliament.

24.3.1. The Nominated Parliament

Cromwell now ruled in his capacity as the 'Lord General', commander-in-chief of the armed forces, a position that he was reconciled to by his sincere belief that he had been chosen by God for a high purpose, a belief that had apparently been confirmed by his victories in 1650 and 1651. A new assembly – the word 'Parliament' being carefully avoided – of 140 'saintly' members from England, with a few from Scotland and Ireland, was chosen by Cromwell and the Army Council. This group met in July 1653, promptly termed itself a 'Parliament', and moved into the Parliament House – the Painted Chamber – at Westminster. This assembly later became known, variously, as the Parliament of Saints, or the Little Parliament, because of the brevity of its existence, and as Barebone's Parliament, after one of its members, Praise-God Barbon. It is also referred to, more accurately, as the 'Nominated' Parliament. This may be the House of Commons that was depicted in a print of about this time, which had no royal arms above the Speaker's chair, although the Serjeant-at-Arms was still shown as bearing the Mace.[60] A new Council

---

60. Ibid. 152.

of State of ten members was appointed, and Cromwell became the Head of State.

The experiment was a failure. The new Parliament faced a formidable task of reform, particularly of the law and the functioning of the courts, but although the majority were moderate gentry of the sort from whom Parliaments had been drawn in the past, it was led by the minority of religious radicals, who were amateurs, with no grasp of the complexities involved, and its debates were interminable. The ideas considered were often more of a menace than the problems that they were intended to solve, alienating, in the process, the army's officers, the judiciary and the moderates in the Parliament itself. So concerned were the moderates by the end of 1653 that, on December 12, when most of the radicals were away at prayer, they carried a vote bringing the Parliament to an end and resigning their powers to Cromwell. As Cromwell remarked, 'I am more troubled now with the fool than with the knave'. As Cromwell had discovered, the sort of men who could carry a revolution through are rarely the sort of men who were competent to rule a country.

24.4. The Protectorate

Having already anticipated the situation, Cromwell had instructed General Lambert and the Army Council (Ireton having died in Ireland in 1651) to draw up a new, written constitution, called *The Instrument of Government*, which was published and came into effect on 16 December 1653. This, the first written constitution to be put into effect in any great state, tried to put into effect the Heads of the Proposals of 1647. However, it brought them much closer to the historic constitution, vesting 'supreme' legislative authority in a 'Lord Protector of the Commonwealth of England, Scotland and Ireland' and in 'the people assembled in Parliament'. Executive power was to vest in the Lord Protector, assisted by a Council of between thirteen and twenty-one members. On legal documents, the name and style of the Lord Protector was to replace all previous references to the Keepers of the Liberties of England. Parliaments were to be summoned every three years, and each must sit for at least five months. There was to be a single House, elected by constituencies that had been reformed along the lines of the earlier proposals, returning 400 members from England and Wales and thirty each from Scotland and Ireland. Cromwell's government already encompassed the British Isles, but, although still referred to as 'the three nations', they were now effectively united in a single Commonwealth, commonly referred to as 'the Protectorate'. On the same date as the publication of the *Instrument*, Cromwell, who was referred to in the document as the Captain-General, took the oath as the Lord Protector. Significantly, he used King Edward's Chair for the occasion, leaving no doubt as to his royal aspirations. By implication, he was appointed for life. It is often suggested that the post of Lord Protector was created in order to give Cromwell's authority constitutional form, but, while this is true, Cromwell and the army's leaders had come to realise that, by getting rid of the King, somebody had to take his place in the system of government if it were to work at all. He was provided with a fixed annual revenue to cover the costs of government and civil administration and a standing army of 30,000 men. He could not approve ordinances, or make war or peace, without the advice of his Council. The Protector and his Council could issue ordinances between sessions of Parliament, but only Parliament could grant supply and levy taxes. The Protector could only veto legislation that infringed the *Instrument of Government*. Religious freedom was granted to all except those who advocated 'popery or prelacy', or practiced 'blasphemy or licentiousness'. The franchise, hitherto based on a freehold of forty shillings, was now changed to personal property worth £200, presumably to keep out the Levellers and the democrats.

During the first six months of 1654 Cromwell used the powers available to him to promulgate a whole series of ordinances, mainly concerned with taxation and religious questions. By accepting and making full use of these powers, which were the equivalent of the royal prerogative, Cromwell and his followers were guilty of hypocrisy. Indeed, Cromwell's exercise of executive power went far beyond what Parliament would have tolerated from the Crown. The new Parliament, Cromwell's second, met in September 1654, and passed an Act empowering surveyors to assess the inhabitants of each parish, hire labour and carts and mend the highways, and this led to a rapid improvement in the roads and the ease of travel. Anglican clergy were forbidden to preach, the press was censored, and all artistic expression was subject to rigid rules. A formal Union of Scotland and Ireland with England and Wales was arranged, providing for freedom of trade and representation at Westminster. Peace was concluded with Holland. For all its failings, the Protectorate displayed an energy and efficiency quite unknown to the Stuart government, either before or afterwards. Like all revolutions, it also provided an opportunity for men of ability, who would otherwise have been unknown to history, to rise to senior positions in the state. This new display of ability was seen, for example, in Monck's Scottish government, in the Navy Commissioners, the new scientific Oxford, and such individuals as Thurloe, the Secretary of State, and Pepys, the future Secretary of the Navy.

One aspect of the settlement with Holland was to have relevance for England's later constitutional history. Maria, the eldest daughter of Charles I, had in 1641 married the Stadholder, or Governor, of the Dutch republic, William II. William had since died, and, because his son, Frederick, was still a child, the government of Holland was now controlled by the Estates-General. Nevertheless, this relationship between the Stuarts and the House of Orange made Cromwell uneasy. The Dutch agreed secretly to exclude all members of the House of Orange from the Stadholdership, but it was a commitment that was to hold for only a few years.

Meanwhile, the republican element saw the Protectorate as a return towards monarchy, yet the new Parliament proved to be much more independent than the Army Council had expected, or Cromwell would have wished. It also reflected the disordered political state of the country. Much of England was still Royalist, and the Puritans were irreconcilably divided. Parliament quarrelled with the Protector, insisting on debating the details of the *Instrument*, particularly provisions for a standing army, the Protector's veto, and his predetermined income. Whereas Cromwell and the army had tended to see the new Parliament as a product of the *Instrument*, the Parliament seems to have thought of itself as the inevitable product of the common law of the land, finding itself faced with a new set of restrictions for which it could see no constitutional justification. Within days of its assembling, Cromwell had purged it of nearly a hundred members who had questioned the legality of the *Instrument of Government* and the position of Cromwell himself. Even the diminished Parliament was far from pliable, however. It wanted control of the army and navy, objected to some of the powers of the Protector, and demanded that both the Council of State and the office of Lord Protector be subject to election, while the Puritan element was opposed to the liberalism of Cromwell's religious measures. Like its predecessor, Parliament wanted power and objected to rule by a military junta, while Cromwell, sympathetic though he was to government by consent, saw the divided nature of Parliament and feared that, entrusted with more power, it would simply reduce the country to anarchy and intolerance. Cromwell was learning, like James I and Charles I before him, that trying to govern the country in the face of a troublesome Parliament was extremely difficult.

Clearly, the Revolution had lost its way, and at the beginning of 1655, Cromwell dissolved the Parliament. This was followed by the first substantial Royalist insurrection in the West Country, in favour of the exiled Prince Charles, but it fizzled out. Cromwell continued with a programme of reducing the army and its rate of pay, in order to reduce the drain on the Exchequer, turning more to a strengthening of the militia. England and Wales were divided into ten military districts, each under a major-general, whose duty was to restore the militia, oversee the Justices of the Peace, suppress royalism, and enforce the anti-vice laws that had been passed by the Commonwealth. They were empowered to finance their work by a tax of 10 per cent on the estates of Royalists. This imposition of military rule was the most unpopular measure of all, because it became associated in the public mind with repressive Puritanism. Meanwhile, economic recession gripped the country, and the already heavy taxation was not enough to meet the Government's needs.

The Dutch conflict had scarcely drawn to an end before a new war broke out with Spain. Cromwell, a product of the Elizabethan Age, showed an interest in promoting the colonies, as well as a desire to pursue the struggle against Spanish influence. This gave rise, against Lambert's advice, to Cromwell's ambition for expansion in the Caribbean, known as the 'Western Design'. It took the form of an expedition, led by Admiral Penn and General Venables in 1655, to capture the West Indian island of Hispaniola. Quarrelling between Penn and Venables, and an undisciplined force of levies raised in the West Indies, led to an ignominious defeat in

Hispaniola, but a second attempt, this time against Jamaica, led to its capture in 1656. A graveyard of dysentery and yellow fever, it failed at first to attract settlers from New England, as had been hoped, and Spain responded to the incursion by declaring war.

24.4.1. Reaction by the Judiciary

By 1655, also, a mutiny among the judiciary was coming to a head, marked by resignations and courts that failed to convict, partly over attempted reforms of legal procedure, but mainly over their view that, while they had been willing to accept an illegal constitution for the sake of good government, they would not allow the executive to override it. It was pointed out that Cromwell's ordinances had never been confirmed by Parliament, and the validity of tax ordinances in particular was in doubt. The only solution was another Parliament. In September 1656, a new Parliament, Cromwell's third, was elected, with the major-generals encouraged to influence the voting as much as possible. About a hundred 'undesirable elements' were soon removed, and up to sixty others stayed away in protest. With the republicans now excluded, a monarchist sentiment now prevailed in the House, and there was a proposal in October that the Protectorate be made hereditary. Following the discovery of a plot to assassinate Cromwell, the Parliament approved, on 23 February 1657, a Remonstrance, later known as the Humble Petition and Advice. It recommended such a revision of the *Instrument* as to amount to a new constitution. It proposed that Cromwell become King, with the right to nominate his successor, because the office was 'known to the laws and to the people'. It is possible, therefore, that the movers of the Petition regarded a King as being at least subject to established rules, and therefore to the control of Parliament, whereas a Lord Protector was subject to nothing and nobody. This cynical view is hardly supported, however, by the fact that they also proposed the restoration of a second chamber, consisting of persons appointed for life by the 'King'. Because the document stumbled over the words 'lords' and 'upper', the second chamber was referred to simply as the 'Other House', a practice that became established over the years. Thus, the House of Commons has continued to refer to 'the Other House', perhaps because of a surviving resentment or jealousy of this notion of an 'upper' chamber and of the lords themselves. Meanwhile, the power of the Privy Council (by which name it was again referred to) was to be reduced, and the Protector was to be deprived of the power to exclude members from Parliament.

In responding to this proposal, prompted as it must have been by the years of near-anarchy and constitutional uncertainty, Cromwell found himself caught between the need for stability and the radical demands of the army. After several months of dithering, Cromwell eventually declined the Crown, probably due to pressure by the army, but otherwise accepted a compromise version of the Humble Petition, submitted by 'the knights, citizens and burgesses' assembled. This left him as Lord Protector, for which office he was presented with a golden sceptre. All that he now lacked was a crown, and on the coinage issued under his authority his image was displayed with one. He was accorded the right to nominate his successor, and between forty and seventy members from the existing House to the 'Other House'. Parliament reassembled in its new form in January 1658. Presbyterians and Republicans, who had earlier been excluded from the Commons, had now been re-admitted, and immediately began to plot with the Royalists and Levellers to overthrow Cromwell. In choosing members of the 'Other House', it removed from itself some of Cromwell's most able supporters. The republicans in the Commons, who tended to dominate its proceedings, violently attacked the 'Other House' and refused to accept it. This was unfortunate, because it is clear that Cromwell was coming round to the view that this relic of the House of Lords was the only one from which he could expect any sense. Early in February 1658, only sixteen days after Parliament had been reconvened, an angry Cromwell dissolved it, and during the last seven months of his life he ruled without a Parliament.

Cromwell died on 3 September 1658, and was buried in Westminster Abbey, with his effigy borne in the funeral procession wearing a crown and holding an orb and sceptre. It was the tragic and ironic gesture of the followers of a man who had set out to end the very notion of monarchy, with its 'baubles' and trappings, but, who, disillusioned by the consequences of their republicanism, had sought to restore the institution that their rebellion had replaced, and, in so doing, had come to see Cromwell himself as having inherited the very aura of kingship. The title of Lord Protector seemed no longer to be adequate. In the absence of a King, the whole Constitution seemed to have fallen apart. Popular disaffection was widespread, few were reconciled to the loss of the monarchy, and still fewer to the crime of regicide, which blighted those who now ruled the land. Yet those who shouted the loudest were the republicans. Cromwell, a man who had long suffered from manic depression, had believed, like most in his day, that everything was ordained by God. He had suffered from chronic indecision, on which occasions he had turned to prayer and the Bible for inspiration, and when he had finally made up his mind on an issue, it was usually in favour of the army, to which he had owed everything.

Oliver Cromwell was succeeded by his son, Richard, and the Privy Council now saw itself in a difficult position. The *Instrument of Government* had never been approved by a Parliament, and the Humble Petition had not been passed by a full Parliament, leaving a large question of legitimacy to hang over the Protectorate itself. Richard Cromwell accordingly accepted the Council's advice and summoned a new Parliament, based on the old franchise that had elected the original Long Parliament. This included a selection of Peers to the 'Other House', which was now referred to once again as the House of Lords. The new Parliament met in January 1659, but it was dominated from the outset by the republicans, who refused to recognise Richard Cromwell as the new Lord Protector. In April, Cromwell gave way to the army's general staff and dissolved it. The army then fell to quarrelling within itself, so that about all it could agree upon was its own autonomy and responsibility for its own system of promotion. In response to widespread pressure, Richard Cromwell then summoned the Rump of the former Long Parliament, in the hope of at last finding a legislature that would accept, and work within, the constitution of 1658. It was the first attempt to put the clock back and resurrect a degree of legitimacy, but it was also a response to a demand to restore the 'good old cause' and re-establish the Commonwealth. The reconstituted Rump Parliament assembled in May 1659, but it was soon clear that it had learned nothing and forgotten nothing. It persuaded Richard Cromwell to resign as Lord Protector, but it ignored the army's wish for new 'fundamentals'. It also favoured the idea of a single Church. In October, only five months after it had assembled, General Lambert responded to being cashiered by Parliament by marching on Westminster and expelling the Rump Parliament. In its place, he set up a military Committee of Safety, and another military dictatorship seemed imminent.

General Monck, a Royalist prisoner turned Parliamentarian, who had been responsible for the conquest of Scotland after the defeat of King Charles at Worcester, and who was still responsible for its administration, and who was a firm supporter of legal authority, was dismayed by Lambert's action. With an economic recession and the patience of the general public strained beyond endurance, Monck demanded a return to constitutional government, in whatever form. There had, in any case, been a reaction in the Army Council against military coups. The Rump Parliament was recalled on Boxing Day, 1659. Early in 1660, General Monck brought his army down from Scotland to London, where he assumed responsibility for public order as Captain-General, dispersing the English army to the provinces. As he might well have expected, he soon found himself in a confused and difficult situation, with the Rump Parliament imprisoning or dismissing its enemies, while he was caught between his own army, which had a loathing of monarchy, and rioting in the City against the soldiery, a flood of petitions for a free Parliament, and anger over the depressed state of the economy. Monck decided to leave responsibility to a 'free Parliament'. This he achieved by restoring, in February 1660, the old Long Parliament, including those still living members who had been expelled in Pride's Purge of 1648. So was restored the legitimate, if packed, Parliament that had existed prior to the overthrow of the Crown.

The Long Parliament finally dissolved itself in March and declared the holding of a general election for a new assembly. Prince Charles, now in the Netherlands, acting on suggestions conveyed in secrecy by General Monck, issued his Declaration of Breda on April 4, offering, subject to the approval of a freely elected Parliament, an amnesty to all, full payment of arrears to the army, a measure of liberty of conscience, and the confirmation of confiscated lands in the hands of their current holders. The pardon excluded, however, those named in Parliament, namely, those who had been involved in the trial of his father. Monck thereupon summoned a new Parliament, which met a few weeks later, on 25 April 1660, to consider the new Declaration. It became known to history as the Convention Parliament, and it included a House of Lords constituted as it had been before 1649. It came into being on a tide of Royalist sympathy, resolving to restore the monarchy with limited powers, and, finding Charles's terms acceptable, it sent him an invitation to return. It also took the opportunity to abolish feudal dues.

The English Civil War had its origin in a conflict of political doctrine between King and people, and it and its consequences were a model that was destined to be followed in France and Russia. In each case the civil war was followed by confusion that placed power in the hands of a political clique, which formed or gave rise to a dictatorship, that had been made possible by the abolition of the monarchy. The radicals who led the clique wished to transform society on an idealised egalitarian, and probably quite impractical, basis. The majority of the population, meanwhile, longed for a return to the stability of the old order, subject only to a few modest reforms. It was the radicals, with their determination and intolerance, who set the pace, yet all that was required was the acceptance by King and people of a common doctrine.

24.4.2. Three Institutions, Not Two

The aftermath of the Civil War demonstrated, as Hobbes and others had argued, that a Parliament without a King and House of Lords led only to anarchy. The country was rescued from this only by the emergence of a dictator, or of somebody able to assume the role of the King, and Cromwell became both. However, no group would accept the dictatorship option, and although the gap left by the abolition of the monarchy was partly filled by the strong and charismatic, if unpopular, figure of Cromwell, it reappeared after his death, because his son and successor had no claim to legitimacy. For all its acquired deficiencies and impotence, the only moderating factor during the turmoil of the Commonwealth and the Protectorate was the House of Lords, thereby confirming the ancient rule that political power must be divided between three institutions, not two. The war had not been between King and Parliament, because that would have been a constitutional impossibility. Parliament was the King and people in session. On the contrary, the war had been between the King and his supporters, on the one hand, and the Rump members of the House of Commons and their supporters on the other. It is doubtful whether the latter had the support of more than a minority of the population, and only a minority had been willing to fight for the King. Cromwell's regime had also alienated the people by killing the King. Charles had been very unpopular, even detested by many, but few had questioned his position as King, and his execution had brought revulsion against the regime and a general sense of national desolation. There was also a widespread sense of guilt that the atrocity of 1649 could not be blamed entirely on those who had carried it out. Cromwell had never been a popular man, and after the execution he, and all associated with him, had been widely hated. In Ireland, he had left a legacy of hatred of England and a religious gulf between Catholic and Protestant that was even deeper. The English hatred of dictatorship and military rule can be said to date from this time, and it is a sad comment on the popular association of Cromwell with democracy and parliamentary government. Cromwell and his followers failed to understand the importance of political tradition and symbolism, and after they had gone, almost everything that they had removed was enthusiastically restored. What could not be restored, however, was the wanton destruction of religious art and sculpture that had adorned the nation's churches and cathedrals.

24.4.3. The Republican Legacy

England had used the revolution to experiment with republicanism and military rule, yet in spite of the apparent opportunity for radical changes to the system of government, the country displayed no serious inclination to depart from the structure laid down in common law. For all its authoritarianism, the Commonwealth and Protectorate had been a period of fractiousness like no other, held together only by the personality of one man. With Cromwell's death, the whole structure had rapidly fallen to pieces, and it was with an immense feeling of relief that the people as a whole had at last been allowed to brush the army and the zealots aside and restore the monarchy. For all its past failings, the monarchy represented stability, legitimacy, and a political structure with which the people felt at ease. Meanwhile, the nation owed an eternal debt of gratitude to General Monck for his competence and integrity in rescuing it from the shambles to which the revolutionaries had reduced it, without trying, like most of them, to profit in any way from his position.

The reign of the Stuarts and the period of the Commonwealth illustrated starkly that the House of Commons was as big a problem as the monarchy. A body of professional politicians, ambitious and self-opinionated, without direction and responsibility, quickly became a menace, like the proverbial loose cannon. If they did not have the King or the Lords to quarrel with, they turned to quarrelling with each other. Without power and responsibility, they quickly became frustrated, bored and irresponsible. The constitutional role of the assembly was to question and consent, not to govern, a task for which it would have been totally unsuited. All the while it had been an assembly of the people, it had probably worked reasonably well, but, as an assembly of professional representatives it was volatile and liable to go in directions that were not always concerned with the will on the people.

The legacy of the Commonwealth and the Protectorate had not all been bad, however. It had settled the question of whether the King was an independent ruler, answerable only to God, or whether he was answerable to the other great institutions of state – the Great Council and Parliament – as in Anglo-Saxon times, except that the Great Council no longer exercised authority and was little understood, except as a problematic House of Lords. The Civil War had confirmed England's adherence to Protestantism and made it clear that a religious divide between the Crown and the people was constitutionally impossible. It also left an indelible impression that political revolution was abhorrent, that violence against the King's person was unspeakable, and that political conflict in the future must be resolved in accordance within the provisions of common law. It was a bitter lesson that other European countries had yet to learn. The execution of Charles I had sent shock waves across Europe, but it signalled the first dramatic break in the Church dogma of the divine authority of kings, and with it the whole structure of classical Church-Feudalism. That structure had already been breached decisively in England, but it was still firmly in place across most of Continental Europe, where it and monarchy were later destined to fall all the more heavily as a result.

The outcome of the English Civil War, in which the King was overthrown by the forces of Parliament, was perceived as a formal rejection of the feudal doctrine of monarchy and the establishment of a new principle, that of the supremacy of Parliament. Even after the return of the Monarchy under Charles II, Parliament continued to assert this principle. Not surprisingly, the outcome of the Civil War and the execution of Charles I marked the beginning of the rise of an ambitious House of Commons, even after the restoration of the Monarchy. Increasingly, the motive of the Commons would be to supplant the Monarchy by asserting control over the executive institutions of government. This it justified on the grounds that it alone represented the interests of the people.[61] Discovering that it could usurp the Monarchy and disregard the House of Lords, its progress from this time onwards would be marked by a growing conflict, defined not by party allegiance, but by the motivation of those members of the Commons who continued to regard it as their commission to represent the will and interests of the people, and of those who saw it as the means to political power. Constitutional forms would still be observed, but increasingly energies were directed towards increasing the role of the House of Commons. That members of the Commons felt able to pursue such a course may be attributed to the fact that the Monarchy was now shorn of its divine authority, while the Great Council, entangled in the House of Lords, had long been forgotten.

---

61. In common law all the great institutions represented the people: the King by his election and Coronation Oath; the Great Council as the representative of the component communities in the shires; and the Privy Council as the extension of the Great Council. That the House of Lords, as a part of Parliament, was not – unlike the House of Commons – elected, was simply due to the fact that all its members had retained the right of attendance, which the common people had not, on account of their number.

25 • THE RESTORATION OF THE STUARTS: CHARLES II (1660)

P ROCLAIMED AS KING on 8 May 1660, Charles II arrived in London three weeks later, on his thirtieth birthday, passing through Blackheath on the way, through the ranks of the army that had destroyed his father. On 28 May 1660, the Council of State, having, in effect, handed back to the restored Privy Council responsibility for the executive functions of the realm, was dissolved. On the same day, ten men found guilty of executing the former King were themselves executed, and the bodies of Cromwell and his fellow leaders were exhumed and hanged from the gallows at Tyburn. In a fatuous effort to erase in law the events of the last dozen years, Parliament declared that the reign of Charles II had begun legally in January 1649, following the execution of his father. So it was that, just as the Normans had pretended that nobody except Edward the Confessor had ruled England before them, so also the law of England under the restored Stuart dynasty pretended, in a fit of Church-Feudalism, that the Commonwealth and Protectorate had never existed. In spite of this, the new King in 1661 adopted Cromwell's New Model Army as his own, so that, for the first time, England had a professional army, which included infantry, cavalry and artillery.

The Stuart restoration in England left the Dutch Estates-General free in 1660 to rescind the agreement that it had made with Oliver Cromwell, to exclude the House of Orange from the Stadholdership. The restoration of the dynastic link between the Dutch Stadholdership and the English throne was to have future importance for the course of the English monarchy. In the circumstances, it is remarkable that Charles II was allowed to ascend the throne without any constitutional commitments or guarantees. People were tired and wished only to return to 'normality'. The Convention Parliament had said only that 'according to the ancient and fundamental laws of this kingdom the government is, and ought to be, by Kings, Lords, and Commons', and it had simply invited Charles 'to return and take up the government of the kingdom into his hands'. Apart from the stipulation of triennial Parliaments, the removal of the King's right to dissolve them at his own discretion, and the virtual abolition of the Privy Council as a court of law, nothing had changed since the beginning of the conflict. The Restoration Settlement was based on the Declaration of Breda and on the legislation of the Long Parliament that had been assented to by Charles I. All Acts passed by Parliament between 1642 and 1660 that had not received the royal assent were *ultra vires* and had no force in law. This left intact almost all the reforms carried through by the Long Parliament in 1641, the most important being the Triennial Act and the Act for the removal of the judicial functions of the Court of Star Chamber, other than appellate jurisdiction in respect of courts overseas. It also retained a power to arrest and examine suspected persons, but this was subject to an Act of 1641, which required a writ of *habeas corpus* in such cases. Other restrictions that had been imposed on the Crown before 1642 were still in place, such as the illegality of forced loans.

One important consequence of the abolition of the Court of Star Chamber was the freeing of Justices of the Peace and other local authorities from any kind of control, other than that which might be extended by the courts or Parliament. Also, the policy of curtailing the powers of the Crown severely limited the development of a system of administrative controls, particularly on the actions of the Civil Service.

Although the Restoration marked the defeat of the republican cause, it was implemented, not by the Cavaliers, but by converted revolutionaries. It marked the restoration of the rule of law, with the ending of arbitrary rule by prerogative, which had also included the taxes imposed by it, such as Ship Money and similar impositions. It also ended an era of written constitutions, whose provisions had either been discredited or deemed to be premature. The position of Charles II was basically different from that of his father, because the Crown had lost the means of asserting its will, and taxation, other than hereditary revenues and that approved by Parliament, never reappeared on any appreciable scale. It has been said that: 'far more than in 1640, Parliament itself was now accepted as a regular part of government',[1] in that those who attended the House of Commons were no longer willing simply to approve the policies of the

---

1. G. E. Aylmer, *The Struggle for the Constitution*, 171.

Crown. They were determined to tell the Crown what its policies should be, even though the right of Parliament in common law extended no further than the submission of petitions.

In this new atmosphere, in order for the King and his Ministers to manage the affairs of the realm in a reasonably effective manner, it was seen as essential for them to have some means of guiding the Lower House. This could best be achieved by patronage, particularly in the boroughs, which were more open to pressure than the shires, and by promoting a party in the Commons that would advance the King's policies. The franchise and the distribution of seats had been reformed by the Republic, but these changes had been abandoned in the elections for the last Protectorate Parliament, and were not now retained after the Restoration by the Chancellor, Lord Clarendon. The latter regarded the changes as desirable, but felt that they should be made 'more warrantably, and in a more auspicious time'. They thus remained an ideal. The legislation abolishing the Court of Star Chamber had not only removed a popular source of justice, but it meant that the Crown could no longer use the royal prerogative as the basis for public policy. This was a desirable reform, in so far as there existed statutory legislation deemed to provide for every emergency and unforeseen situation, and provided that Parliament could meet and approve legislation in time to deal with any circumstance, but the Protectorate had decided that these circumstances were not provided for. Consequently, it had been necessary to give to Cromwell a substantial prerogative, which he had put to good use. Otherwise, the monarchy had shown that the country could not manage without it. The Lord Chancellor, Sir Edward Hyde, Earl of Clarendon, in his speech at the opening of the new Parliament in May 1661, referred to the disastrous influence on events following the Civil War, 'when the common people of England would represent the Commons of England, and abject men, who could neither write nor read, would make laws for the government'. It was 'the grossest and most ridiculous pageant that that great imposter (Cromwell) ever exposed to public view, when he gave up the nation to be disposed of by a handful of poor mechanic persons, who, finding they knew not what to do with it, would (he was sure) give it back to him again, as they shortly did'. It was a view that was never seriously contested.[2]

---

2. J. P. Kenyon, *The Stuart Constitution*, 335.

The Convention Parliament continued until the end of 1660, when it was dissolved and a new assembly, known as the Cavalier Parliament, met in May 1661. Its composition was a reaction to sectarian disturbances at the beginning of the year, and it was so named because it was filled with young men, both Cavaliers and Anglicans, who particularly represented the landed gentry, earnestly believed in peace and order, and supported the Church and the King. The Presbyterians and other Puritan groups had all but been removed from the Commons, because the Puritan creed, that had been associated with Cromwell, was now hated by the majority of the population. Many of the Puritans, particularly among the nobility and the middle class – the very people with most influence in Parliament and local government – drifted into the Church of England. Because of its favourable sentiments, Charles did not dissolve the Cavalier Parliament for eighteen years. Meanwhile, its advent was followed by a flurry of much needed legislation. In reaction to the years of chaos, Parliament devoted itself to bringing order and conformity, and particularly to breaking the political strength of the non-Anglicans in local government and the administration. The Act of Indemnity and Oblivion, 1660, was a remarkable document, in that it was pervaded by a mood of reconciliation. All treasons and attainders since 1642 were rescinded by the Act. Lands expropriated were returned to the Crown and Church respectively, without compensation, leaving the many Puritans who had bought lands belonging to the Church badly affected. Former landed estates of the Royalists, by and large, were returned to them, and where they were not, their former owners were able to resume their estates by means of private Acts of Parliament.

One of the more important statutes passed by the previous Convention Parliament in 1660, and which was now confirmed by Charles II, had been the Act for the Abolition of Feudal Tenures. This now provided for the 'taking away of the court of wards and liveries, and tenures *in capite* and by knight's service, and purveyance, and for setting revenue upon His Majesty in lieu thereof'. Purveyance was the feudal right of the Crown to buy the needs of the Royal Household at a price fixed by the King's Purveyor, and of exacting the use of horses and vehicles for the King's journey. The most important source of feudal revenues, however, was wardship, whose abolition was particularly supported by the landed gentry, or lesser landholders. The intention of the Act was to replace the feudal benefits, received until now by the Crown, by a set revenue. The Act accordingly marked the formal conclusion of the system of feudal relationships, which had been established under the Normans, but had gradually been disintegrating since the Black Death of 1349. The fiscal consequences of the abolition of feudal tenures were considerable, but they were replaced by the revenue from:

1. Customs duties, granted to the King for life.
2. The so-called Hereditary Excise, levied on alcoholic beverages, coffee and tea, granted to the King and his successors in perpetuity.[3]
3. Additional excise on various commodities to make up the difference, granted for life.

Direct taxation was now to be reserved for wartime emergencies. In addition, there were a number of temporary taxes to pay off the army. The direct collection of customs and excise had to be abandoned in 1662 and contracted out to private cartels, as a result of which the revenue fell short of expectations. It had to be made up by special grant, or subsidy, and the imposition of a highly unpopular Hearth Tax on all but the poorest, which was abandoned in 1689. In addition to the above revenues, of course, the King had the rents from Crown lands. The effect of these changes was a shift in the tax burden, with the rich being taxed less and the poor relatively more heavily, although this was not the intention behind the changes. The main fiscal reform during the reign of Charles II, however, was prompted in 1665 by the Second Dutch War. Initiated by the Crown itself, the measure required that receipts should be subject to a separate system of account, thereby introducing the principle of strict accountability. It also required that those lending money to the Crown on the security of revenue from the land tax, which had been revived to help pay for the war, should be paid in rotation, according to the date of each loan.

Of the statutes that had been approved by Charles I, two were repealed, one being the Bishops' Exclusion Act of 1642, which allowed the bishops to be restored to their sees and to the House of Lords. The

---

3. The excise on coffee and tea had been introduced by Pym in 1643.

other to be repealed was the Triennial Act of 1641, in the mistaken belief that it might oblige the King to dissolve his present Parliament. The Act which replaced it in 1644 was a simple declaratory Act. This merely required the King to summon a Parliament every three years, with no minimum period for a session and no machinery to ensure that the triennial summoning was enforced. In fact, neither Act specified a maximum period for a Parliament, only that it be met by the King at least once every three years.

Socially, the Restoration brought a return to gaiety. Court life reappeared and glittered. Public office depended less on ability and was once again seen as a profitable source of benefits. Yet there was some continuity from the one regime to the other, from men at the top, like Monck, who became the Duke of Albemarle and head of a reformist Treasury Commission, to officials lower down, such as Samuel Pepys, whose *Diary* described the workings of central government during the 1660s, and whose attitude reflected both the old idea of service to the King and the new idea of public service to the state. Liberalising measures, such as the restoration of theatre, games and dancing, were counterbalanced by others that were repressive, and these came to be known as the Clarendon Code. This was because the measures were associated with the Lord Chancellor, Lord Clarendon, although he was opposed to many of them. It included the Corporation Act, 1661, which precluded from government, the magistracy or the management of borough corporations, those who failed to take the sacrament according to the Church of England. The Act of Uniformity, 1662, required all clergy to accept publicly, and use, the newly restored Book of Common Prayer, which had been adopted in the reign of Queen Elizabeth. No Presbyterian would accept it, and a fifth of the clergy were lost to the Church of England. The Act also required all clergy, academics, schoolmasters and tutors to make a declaration that they would not take up arms against the King or his officers, or endeavour to change the government of either the Church or the state, and that they would conform to the liturgy of the Church of England as currently established.

On the other hand, the Cavalier Parliament rejected pressure by the bishops to re-establish the Court of High Commission, which had originally been authorised by Elizabeth's Act of Supremacy, and which had formerly given so much judicial power to the bishops in cases deemed by them to be ecclesiastical. It also declined to authorise the canons of 1640, or any other canons promulgated without the approval of Parliament. Thus, Parliament assumed the right, henceforth, to control the discipline of the Church, arbitrate on the qualifications required of the clergy, and lay down the form of public worship. What had properly been the concern of the King and the First Estate was now appropriated to the Third Estate, which was hardly competent in the matter. The explanation for this intrusion of Parliament lies in the fragmentation of the original Church and the emergence in the population of a large section of dissenters. It was an admission, for the first time, that the Church of England no longer embraced all Protestants.

Those who refused to accept the Book of Common Prayer, or otherwise stayed outside the Anglican Church, were known as the 'Nonconformists', against whom a policy of persecution began in 1664. In an effort to control the practice of Nonconformist worship, the Conventicles Act, 1664, forbade religious conventicles – or meetings – of five or more persons, unless they were members of the same household. Under the Quaker Act of 1664, which forbade their meetings for worship, more than 5,000 Quakers were imprisoned. The clergy who had been evicted by the Act of Uniformity posed a particular problem, because they continued to preach at public gatherings. This was addressed by the Five-Mile Act of 1665, which prohibited all such clergy and other unlicensed preachers from coming within five miles of any city or borough, or the parish from which they had been evicted. The execution of these repressive measures was the responsibility of the Justices of the Peace, who were often only too glad to harass those who had once plagued them. Nevertheless, these measures did little to force dissenters – now to be found mainly among the lower classes – into the Church, and the enforcement of church attendance by the Elizabethan Acts, originally directed against Papists, proved to be ineffective.

Another statute at this time, which has had relevance down to the present day, was an Act Against Tumultuous Petitioning, in 1661. This was directed at 'tumults and disorders, upon pretence of preparing or presenting public petitions, or other addresses to His Majesty or the parliament'. The right of interested parties to petition the Crown has always existed, and has, indeed, been the basis of much of the modern legislative procedure, but in the last years of the reign of Charles I there had been, and there has continued to be, a tendency by interested parties to bring pressure upon the Crown by arranging for petitions to be accompanied by riots and disorders, nowadays more willingly tolerated and described as 'demonstrations'.

The Roman Catholicism that had been latent in the views of James I and Charles I was equally so in Charles II. In an unpopular move in 1662, which nevertheless accorded with his family's practice of marrying into Continental Catholic families, he married Catherine of Braganza, daughter of the King of Portugal. It was a worrying indication that Charles had inherited all the obstinacy, tactlessness and empathy with Catholicism of his predecessors.

25.1. The Great Council Deprives the Privy Council of its Judicial Function

English law had been characterised to some extent by a distinction between those cases involving a 'matter of state' and those affecting solely the interests of private litigants. With the removal of the judicial role of the Privy Council in 1641, this distinction was ended with the establishment of a monopoly of justice by the Great Council, in its capacity as House of Lords, as the superior court. Expressed in constitutional terms, the Great Council, not being subject to statute law, accepted the request of Parliament – in practice now, the House of Commons – that it cease to extend its judicial function to the Privy Council. It is doubtful whether the constitutional implications of this change were understood, even by the Upper House. Relations between Crown and subject were now left to be decided by the courts created by Parliament and, where appropriate, the House of Lords. English constitutional law, as it was perceived, was thus left to return to its basis in common law, that is, in favour of individual rights and property, as against the claims of the state to freedom of action in the pursuit of public policy.

25.1.1. Rule by the Propertied Classes

Nevertheless, the removal of the jurisdiction of the Privy Council meant a loss of efficiency in litigation in favour of the unwieldy, technical, and expensive process of the common law courts. The Privy Council had represented the public good, in which the common law courts were deficient. Also, common law was concerned only with the fulfilment of legal obligations, and not with the execution of policy. The effect was especially noticeable in the field of local government, which, released from central control, fell under the easy-going sway of common law judges, imposing a minimum performance on local officials consistent with the requirements of common law and statutory duties, and open only to the challenge of litigants bold and wealthy enough to undertake the risks of invoking their jurisdiction. Justices of the Peace and other local officials relapsed after 1660 into two centuries of virtual irresponsibility.[4] Both they and Parliament were drawn from the same social class. The place of government by the Crown was taken by the propertied classes in their own interest. parliamentary action was directed, not at administrative efficiency, but at the manipulation of tariffs. The main internal innovation of the restored Parliament was the Law of Settlement of 1662, which allowed parishes to deport newcomers within forty days of their arrival, unless they could find surety that they would never become a burden on the parish for poor relief. This allowed the propertied classes, upon whom the burden of poor-rates fell, to relieve themselves of possible future expense by sending poor persons back to their own parishes.

With the Parliaments, courts, and local administration now largely independent of royal authority, the King could no longer govern as his predecessors had done. Even in central government, he could only work in partnership with the leaders of the landed gentry, who were to dominate political life for the next two hundred years, annexing to themselves the chief offices under the Crown. As James II was to discover, they could bring to a standstill any government that tried to dispense with their co-operation.

25.1.2. The Scientific Revolution

The growing sense of orderliness and method made itself felt also in the beginnings of a scientific revolution during the Stuart dynasty. The

---

4. D. Lindsay Keir, *The Constitutional History of Modern Britain, 1485–1937*, 233–5.

Tudors had witnessed and contributed to the renaissance of Classical art and knowledge, freeing society from the intellectual *cul-de-sac* of Church teaching, and it was now that the first practical benefits of that release and rediscovery made themselves felt. It is likely that the religious and political conflict of the reign of Charles I, followed by the Civil War, did much to emancipate men's minds from the assumptions of the past and prompt an awakening of new ideas.

Since the Renaissance, natural philosophy had been dominated by the thinking of Aristotle, who had held that a complete understanding of the natural world could be achieved by reason, and who had illustrated this by his theory of elements. This stated that the natural world was composed of the four elements of earth, fire, air and water, and that each was attracted to its source. It was during the reign of James I that Sir Francis Bacon, essayist and Lord Chancellor from 1618 until 1621, rejected this approach, propounding instead the view that the advancement of knowledge depended, not on reason alone, but on verification through physical experiment, the assumption being that there was still much that we did not know about the physical world. It was on the basis of this 'scientific' method – from Latin *scientia*, 'knowledge' – that the great strides in understanding and technology were achieved in the following years. William Harvey in 1628 described the circulation of the blood. Jeremiah Horrocks predicted the transit of Venus across the sun in 1639. Robert Hooke published the results of his microscopic observations and was the first to describe the organic 'cell'. John Wallis in 1655 published a mathematical treatise on infinite series. Robert Boyle, between 1660 and 1662, developed his theory of atmospheric pressure, which he described as the 'spring of the air', and devised a pneumatic pump. Recognition by the King of the importance of this process of discovery was embodied in 1662 in the creation of the Royal Society, which became the major centre of scientific thinking in England. France followed four years later with its own *Académie Royale*. Isaac Newton developed the mathematical technique known as the calculus, and in his *Philosophiae Naturalis Principia Mathematica*, published in 1687, he propounded his laws of motion and the principle of universal gravitation, which described the mechanics by which all matter and objects interacted with each other.

The scientific revolution that was now taking place in England was only a part of a much wider European process, however, that was marked by other great figures, such as Kepler and Galileo in astronomy, Leibniz with the differential calculus, and Huygens in astronomy, the theory of centrifugal force, and the theory of light. The increasing contribution of England to scientific discovery can be illustrated by reference to a list of names quoted, some more than once, in a summary for the period.[5] Between 1450 and 1599, Continental Europe provided twenty-five references and England none. Between 1600 and 1700, Europe provided thirty-four references and England twenty-three, a contribution to the total of 40 per cent. The scientific revolution which thus unfolded marked a development in independent, objective thinking that had an inevitable effect on political attitudes. Political thinkers were no longer willing to consider just existing constitutional traditions, but were persuaded to undertake a fundamental reappraisal of political principles.

Another revolution occurred in communications. Henry VII had established a Master of the Posts in 1516, later to become the Postmaster General, while Charles I had opened his personal messenger service in 1635 to all who were willing to pay a fee for the privilege, thereby establishing the first public postal system. Messengers changed horses at certain inns, where delivered private letters were usually left for collection. Cromwell had granted a monopoly to the Office of Postage in 1654, and now Charles II established a General Post Office in 1660, improving both the revenue-earning capacity and the speed of the royal mail service by contracting it out. This improvement in efficiency was helped by the stamping of letters with the date and time of posting.

25.2. The Extension of Parliaments

By the sixteenth century, a specific terminology had come into use to define the parliamentary process. As in the past, when a new Parliament was summoned by the King, once it had assembled, it was 'opened' by him or his representative, with an explanation of why it had been summoned. Those present entered then into a deliberation on the King's request,

---

5. W. L. Langer, *An Encyclopedia of World History* (Boston, 1948), 454–7.

finally reporting to the King their advice in the matter. Afterwards, any other issues were considered, including petitions to the King.

25.2.1. Timing and Frequency of Parliaments

From the earliest times, it had been necessary for the timing of a popular assembly, to take account of other demands on the lives of the people, and this required it to be summoned, as far as possible, when the demands of stock-rearing, crop-growing and harvesting were at a minimum. Originally, the life of a Parliament appears to have been limited to a day or two, in addition to the time needed to travel to and from the place of assembly. England was a confederacy, and Parliaments consisted of elected representatives from each county. The travel involved made it necessary for them to be comparatively well-to-do individuals; of some standing in their own communities; able to afford the expense (unless that was met by the shire); able to defend themselves in the event of attack by thieves; and willing to accept the inconvenience of being away from home for such time as they might be needed.

Parliamentary business increased in the Middle Ages, and the practice of the King in referring petitions to Parliament also required it to sit for longer. Attendance had by now become an unwelcome burden. Developments during the Middle Ages must gradually have made travel easier, even so, many constituencies had come to be known as 'pocket' boroughs, because freemen were so few that they could readily be bribed by vested interests, such as the King himself, or the owner of the land. Consequently, membership of Parliament had become limited in many cases to those who were sponsored by the King (in what amounted to a conflict of interest) or a wealthy landowner with his own vested interest. Candidates tended to be those attracted by a convivial life, the politics of Parliament and, increasingly, the opportunities for advancement in power and influence offered by the emergence of political factions.

This affected the frequency of Parliaments, because elections cost money for those involved, causing elections to be deferred as much as possible. Aggravating this tendency, Kings faced with hostile Parliaments chose to defer summoning them. This problem was resolved to some extent by the passing of the Triennial Act of 1641, which required Parliaments to be separated by no more than three years, but this proved to be too short a period between elections. The electoral period was accordingly changed by the Septennial Act of 1715 to a maximum of seven years. This was more convenient for the holding of elections, but it could delay legislation for much too long.

25.3. Parliaments Become 'Sessions' and Electoral Periods Become 'Parliaments'

Parliaments were required to deal with an increasing amount of legislation, as well as guidance to the King on his response to petitions. Members also acquired a growing sense of their own importance, and with it, a greater preoccupation with issues other than those for which they had been summoned. Requiring Parliaments to sit for longer, in order to cope with the back-log of business, proved increasingly difficult to reconcile with the common law requirement of annual Parliaments. Members were expected to sit or make themselves available for much longer. Because Parliaments now continued beyond the year in which they were summoned, a parliamentary 'year' was referred to as a 'session', and it typically ran from after the end of the harvesting season, about November, until just before the beginning of the next. The session ended when it was 'prorogued' by the King, that is, he requested it (from the Latin *pro*, 'before', and *rogare*, 'to ask', with the meaning: 'to defer, or postpone'). In other words, the King wished to discontinue the business of the assembly without dissolving it, because he expected to re-convene it for another session, that is, extending the work of the Parliament into the following year. Thus, a Parliament might be required to continue through several annual sessions, until a new election made possible a new Parliament.

Meanwhile, each day of parliamentary business was reckoned to be a 'sitting', during which the members occupied the benches in the parliamentary chamber, unless or until members 'retired', according to their Estates, to deliberate on an issue put to them by the King, after which Parliament was 'reconvened' by the King or his representative, usually the Lord Chancellor. The sitting ended when it was 'adjourned', by a motion of adjournment, whether overnight, for a public holiday, or for some other purpose. Any interval in the work of a Parliament was referred to as a 'recess', typically overnight, but it might be for a public holiday, or until the opening of the next session.

The Triennial Act of 1641 also specified the minimum duration of a Parliament as being fifty days. So far as we know, common law did not specify the life of Parliaments, leaving their duration to the amount of work required by the King, with a limit set by the length of time that a free man could afford to be absent from his domestic and other responsibilities. What is clear, however, is that the law of the Constitution expected time to be left available for the holding of a new Parliament in the following year.

The maximum duration of a 'Parliament' was entirely at the discretion of the King, until eventually the Parliament Act of 1694 fixed it at no more than three years. The longer the Parliament, the less representative it became, increasing the possibility of political crises, so that the only direct contact with popular feeling was through the nature of petitions and other expressions of popular opinion. The modern facility of referendums was unknown, as well as impracticable, in the seventeenth century. The existing members of Parliament appear not usually to have seen this as a problem, however, because they began to see themselves, less as the expression of popular feeling, and more and more as fulfilling the role of the elected 'government' of the country.

A distinction in common law needs to be made, therefore, and has needed to be made since the late Middle Ages, between an annual National Assembly,[6] known as a 'Session', and a Parliament, which refers to an electoral period. This usually extends over several years. For constitutional and legal purposes in common law, therefore, it was and has continued to be the former that has been important.

25.4. The Doctrine of the Supremacy of Parliament

The Doctrine of the supremacy of Parliament arose out of the conflicting legislative rights claimed by the King and Parliament. According to Dicey, by 'Parliament' in this context is meant the King, the House of Lords, and the House of Commons, acting together, which may aptly be described as

---

6. As distinct from the shire assemblies, which were properly national assemblies, before they went into decline.

the 'King-in-Parliament'.[7] It possesses 'the right to make or unmake any law whatever; and, further, that no person or body is recognised by the law of England as having a right to override or set aside the legislation of Parliament'. For the purpose of clarification, Dicey defines a law as 'any rule which will be enforced by the Courts'. Thus, 'any Act of Parliament, or any part of an Act of Parliament, which makes a new law, or repeals or modifies an existing law, will be obeyed by the Courts'. Conversely, 'There is no person or body of persons who can, under the English constitution, make rules which override or derogate from an Act of Parliament, or which … will be enforced by the Courts in contravention of an Act of Parliament'. An exception exists in cases where 'Parliament either directly or indirectly sanctions subordinate legislation'. Dicey adds that legislative authority resided originally with the King in Council. There was also a system of royal legislation under the form of Ordinances and, at a later stage, Proclamations, which had much the force of law. To remove any doubts, an Act of 1539 empowered the Crown to legislate by means of proclamations, but this was repealed by Edward VI.

The problem with Dicey's definition is that it does not go far enough. It is the King, who is responsible for the executive function of government, and who requests the approval of a Parliament to new laws. Parliament comprises the Commons, the Lords and the Clergy, in so far as they choose to attend or be represented. Where proposed laws are approved by a Parliament on behalf of the people, the form in which they are approved is submitted to the King, who, subject to his assent, declares them to be Acts of Parliament. Alleged legal limitations on the sovereignty of Parliament, such as the law of morality or nature, or international law, have no basis, because the courts uniformly regard a law that is alleged to be a bad law as nevertheless a law, and therefore entitled to the obedience of the courts.[8] Another alleged limitation is that an Act of Parliament cannot overrule the principles of the common law,[9] but this doctrine has never received systematic judicial sanction and is now said to be obsolete.[10] A distinction needs to be made here, however,

---

7. A. V. Dicey, *Introduction to the Study of the Law of the Constitution* (London, 1923), 37 -82.
8. Ibid. 61.
9. W. E. Hearne, *The Government of England*, 2nd edn., 48–9; Maine, *Early History of Institutions*, 381–2.
10. A. V. Dicey, *Introduction to the Study of the Law of the Constitution*, 59, note.

between ordinary common law and *mos maiorum*, or the common law of the Constitution, which, as we have already noted, overrides statute law. Indeed, statute law, like Parliament itself, derives its authority from the common law of the Constitution. The problem is that, until now, *mos maiorum* has never been recorded, even in general terms.

25.5. The Commons Achieve Ascendancy Over the Lords

The harmony that had prevailed between the Monarchy and the House of Commons under the Tudor dynasty came to an end under the Stuarts, who looked to the House of Lords to give legal sanction to their actions. Indeed, the Lords were able for a time to act as mediators between the King and the Commons. Recognising the restored importance of the House of Lords in the government of the realm, James I had increased his influence there, and at the same time had augmented his depleted income by selling titles. In this way, the number of temporal Peers had doubled from fifty-five, at the end of the reign of Elizabeth, to one hundred and twenty-six in 1628, a little before the Civil War.[11] The membership of a fully representative Great Council would probably have been seventy-eight, and this inflation of the House of Lords had two effects: its prestige had been undermined, and it had tended to side with the King in his disputes with the Commons, diminishing the impartiality which it had always been expected to exercise.

The circumstances of the Great Council had probably been confused ever since it had been locked away as a House of Lords. Whether the normal replacement of members of the Council by their respective shires had continued after Edward III, or indeed after Edward the Confessor, is not known, because only those members of the House of Lords formally appointed by the King are recorded, and some of these, at least, were elevations to the greater nobility, whether or not as members of the Council. Membership of the Council, as distinct from membership only of the House, is not recorded, and there is no evidence that a formal distinction, or indeed a distinction of any kind, was made. Nevertheless,

---

11. J. P. Kenyon, *The Stuart Constitution*, 412.

the existence of the Great Council still appears to have been recognised in 1660, on the accession of Charles II, when the summoning of the Convention Parliament represented the return of legitimate government. Upon its reassembly, the Lord Chancellor, Clarendon, affirmed the new Government's faith in the House of Lords, both as a constitutional buffer between the Crown and the Commons and as a House of individual spokesmen for the established order in the provinces.[12] This remark appears to hark back to the function of the Councillors as the spokesmen of their respective shires. A further vestige of its purpose came to the surface with the apparent recognition at this time, not least by Clarendon, of the importance of the integrity of those elevated to the Upper Chamber. 'Your Lordships', Clarendon remarked in his address to the House of Lords on the Parliament's dissolution, 'will easily recover that estimation and reverence that is due to your high condition, by the exercise and practice of that virtue from which your honours first sprang', a sentiment that might equally have been addressed to the Roman Senate. Referring to the right of access of a member of the Lords to counsel the King, Clarendon went on to say that the people would judge the King himself in the light of their own example: 'They know very well that you are not only admitted to his presence but to his conversation, and even in a degree to his friendship, for you are his Great Council. By your example they will form their own manners, and by yours they will make a guess at the King's'. Even after allowance is made for Clarendon's personal views, it is evident that the House of Lords had emerged from the period of turmoil high in the public's esteem, an esteem that had not been sustained by the House of Commons. Whether Clarendon's reference to the Lords as 'the Great Council' reflected merely the survival of the name, or a recognition that the presence of the Great Council was the basis of the authority of the Upper House, is not clear. Too little is known about the House of Lords during this period, but the impression holds that, after 1660, no more Peerages were sold, elevation to the House was based on service, or the expectation of service, and no further 'grace-and-favour' or 'ornamental' Peerages were granted, 'except in the case of royal bastards and, occasionally, their mothers'.[13]

---

12. Clarendon's speech to both Houses, 29 December 1660.
13. J. P. Kenyon, *The Stuart Constitution*, 415.

It has been suggested that the outcome of the Civil War had fatally damaged the constitutional position of the House of Lords, because even the decision to offer the Crown to the future Charles II was made by the House of Commons, and without reference to the Lords. It has always been the prerogative of the people to choose the King, and the action of the Commons may be seen in this light, but only in the light of the advice of the Lords, whether or not it was rejected. Charles could have become King, in any case, only by the bestowal upon him of the *imperium* by the Great Council, now the House of Lords. The nature of the ceremony on this occasion was a clear indication of how the House of Commons now perceived itself.

The Lords (in this respect, the Second Estate) 'made a strenuous attempt' to continue the practice by which they taxed themselves separately, it having always been the practice that each Estate must approve its own contribution to the King's needs, and in the Poll Tax Act of 1660 they were allowed to nominate their own collector, with a committee of appeal consisting initially of eight Peers. On the other hand, the Assessment Act of 1660 went no further than to include the clause: 'Provided that nothing herein contained shall be drawn into example to the prejudice of the ancient rights belonging to the Peers of this realm'. The Lords never claimed a right to tax anybody but themselves, but the House of Commons now perceived itself as having the right, not only to agree to the level of its own taxation, but also to determine the taxation of the Lords. The Commons had brought into question the very basis of the Estate structure of society that had applied without question for millennia, and perhaps rightly so, in the light of the changing nature and needs of society, but the Estate system had provided a stability that society was not yet entirely ready to dispense with, as the Civil War itself had shown. Gradually, however, the right of the Second Estate to tax itself was no longer exercised, or the qualifying clause ceased to appear, so that by 1678 the separate right of the Lords had ceased to be acknowledged.

A similar struggle was waged over the right of the Second Estate to initiate and amend money Bills. The House of Commons (the Third Estate) had tried to assert a sole right to do so since the end of the fourteenth century, probably on the ground that the commons now supplied the greater part of the King's revenue, and had tenaciously blocked any attempt by the Lords to do so. The issue was resurrected in 1661, when the Lords introduced a minor Bill to raise money for road repairs at Westminster, but the Commons rejected both it and a similar measure in 1665. Undoubtedly, the Commons was determined to secure a monopoly of the right to initiate tax proposals. In a final attempt in 1677, the Lords introduced a Bill for the better payment of church rates, but the Commons simply ignored it. Over the issue of merely amending money Bills the Lords were at first more successful, amending the Poll Tax of 1660, for example, and deleting from the Post Office Act a clause that would have allowed members of Parliament to frank their own letters. When it came to the Lords amending a major finance Bill in 1671, however, a stalemate ensued, with each House alleging, and insisting upon, its respective right. Gradually the Commons ground down the Lords over successive Bills, with the last attempt being made in 1679. The House of Lords never accepted the principle that they had no right to amend a money Bill, denying it in 1740 and again in 1743, but they refrained from further testing it. It was an advantage that the Commons sometimes exploited by incorporating other Bills within money Bills, in order to make them immune from amendment, but the tactic was seen as highly controversial and did not always succeed. This expansion of its jurisdiction by the House of Commons into the financial jurisdiction of the Lords might have had some justification if its members had represented the commons in any meaningful sense, but the Lower House represented the more affluent yeoman farmers, who accounted for a very small part of the Third Estate, making it no less an oligarchy than the House of Lords itself – the Upper House being defined by family, and the Lower House by wealth.

The convention asserted by the Commons, but not accepted by the Lords, that all money bills should be initiated in the House of Commons, regardless of whom they affected, and that they should not be subject to amendment by the House of Lords, was to persist until the present day. The justification for this rule was that the Commons represented the greater part of the taxable capacity of the common people, to which the response of the Lords might well have been that their financial circumstances were quite different and needed to be managed in a different manner. In any case, it had always been accepted that neither

Estate should interfere in the affairs of the other. Whether this principle was supported in common law is unclear, but it is likely. Against this, the division of fiscal policy on the basis of Estate was slowly losing its relevance. That the Commons accepted that they had no leg to stand on was made evident in a debate on the 1671 Bill, when it was recorded that: 'Their Lordships had neither reason nor precedent offered by the Commons to back that resolution, but were told that this was a right so fundamentally settled in the Commons that they could not give reasons for it, for that would be a weakening of the Commons' right and privilege'.[14] In the struggle for constitutional power, the members of the Commons recognised that, while they could not remove the rights of the Lords altogether, sole control of the King's finances gave the Commons the key to political power, and to this end they showed far more tenacity than the Lords. There seem to be no grounds, however, for supposing that, in pursuing this course, the Commons were in any way reflecting the wishes of the people.

In judicial matters, meanwhile, the Lords had to assume much of the work formerly undertaken by the King in the Court of Star Chamber. As one lawyer remarked in 1663: 'The jurisdiction of the Star Chamber is now transformed into the House of Lords, but somewhat in a nobler way'.[15] This increase in the judicial function of the Great Council, in its guise as the House of Lords, in which it was responsible, constitutionally, only for cases involving members of the Second Estate, but which had been extended as the Court of Star Chamber, was not acceptable to the Commons. In the case of Skinner v The East India Company, Thomas Skinner, a merchant who had infringed the trade monopoly vested in the Company, and had his goods seized by the Company in Sumatra, petitioned the King in 1666. The Privy Council had tried to mediate, but failed, and in the following year the King had referred the matter to the House of Lords, because, although the judiciary had no such doubts, it was open to question whether the courts of common law had jurisdiction outside the realm, except in the case of crimes committed on the high seas. The Lords proceeded to assess damages against the Company, whose directors reacted by petitioning the House of Commons, querying the Lords' right to act at all in the case. They also pointed out that the damages

---

14. Conference, 20 April 1671, quoted by J. P. Kenyon, *The Stuart Constitution*, 424.
15. W. Holdsworth, *A History of English Law*, i. 367.

would fall on those members of Parliament who were also members of the Company, including its deputy governor, Sir Samuel Barnardiston, MP. In May 1668, the Commons voted that the Lords had exceeded their jurisdiction and were guilty of a grave breach of privilege. The Lords responded that the Company's petition against it was scandalous, and that the proceedings of the Commons had been a breach of the privileges of the Upper House. It ruled against the Company and assessed the amount of damages due. Barnardiston, who had refused to pay a fine imposed by the Lords, was imprisoned on the basis of what the Lords judged to be a contempt of court. When Parliament reassembled in October 1669, the Commons, taking offence at the detention of one of their number, at once passed another ringing resolution, defending its right to receive and judge petitions to the King (who had traditionally referred them to the Commons), without interference from any court, whereupon the King again prorogued Parliament until February 1670. When Parliament reassembled, the King prevailed on both Houses to abandon the case and expunge all reference to it from their journals.[16] The outcome was thus inconclusive, but the Lords made no further attempt to act as a court of first instance, except in cases of impeachment by the Commons. In effect, therefore, the Commons won again in its campaign for ascendancy over the House of Lords.

This left the jurisdiction of the Lords in respect of appeals. In the case of *Shirley v Fagg* in 1675, one Thomas Shirley appealed to the House of Lords against a ruling by Chancery in favour of a member of Parliament, Sir John Fagg. The Commons took this up as a breach of privilege, denying the Lords' right to hear appeals from Chancery, and arresting four barristers who were due to appear in a similar case. The Commons then imprisoned Fagg for answering Shirley's plea before the Lords, and dismissed the Commons' Serjeant-at-Arms when, at the request of Black Rod, he released the four barristers. It may be remembered that the Serjeant-at-Arms was provided by the King, and could be removed, therefore, only by the King, at the request of the Commons, but the *hubris* of the House had increased to such an extent that it had come to regard him as its own employee. Meanwhile, the Lords resolved to proceed no further with business until they received satisfaction.

---

16. J. P. Kenyon, *The Stuart Constitution*, 418–19, 422–3.

Parliament was prorogued from June to October 1675, for the case only to re-surface. The King therefore prorogued Parliament from November of that year until February 1677, during which the disputes were quietly dropped.[17] The appellate jurisdiction of the Lords was not again called in question, and it has survived to the present day.

The prerogative of grace-and-favour resided with the King, in his capacity as the supreme justice, and although he had delegated most of this function to the Lord Chancellor and the Court of Chancery after 1349, the latter had been in conflict with the common law courts ever since, until James I had decided in 1615 that the rulings of the Court of Chancery should have precedence. In spite of the work of the Court of Chancery, the King had maintained the primordial royal function as the ultimate source of justice, in that he was the arbiter in those cases where justice had not been found. More specifically, he heard appeals in cases apparently not provided for in common law, or where justice was simply not available. This was a residual function of the Crown, exercised either through the Court of Chancery or through the Privy Council. It was a function which, by its very nature, lay outside traditional justice, with its procedure of trial by jury, for the obvious reason that there was no established law by which it could operate. It had to resort to 'natural' justice, which the King was deemed to be better qualified to determine than were his representatives, the judges. In fact, Chancery had devised a set of rules to guide it, divined from the principles of natural justice, but the King in Council had been seen as more authoritative, and, because the Council was not hampered by irrelevant legal procedures, quick, effective and reliable. It would appear, therefore, that, as a royal function in common law, it could not be assumed by the Great Council (whether or not in its capacity as the House of Lords), nor, indeed, by any court that was not answerable to the King.

It is clear from these disputes within Parliament that the Civil War and its preceding squabble had undermined the whole perception of the common law of the Constitution, and that the House of Commons now took cognisance of the Constitution only where it suited. Both Charles II and James II resorted to the tactic of playing off one House against the other, as did Charles II when the Commons proposed to exclude his

---

17. Ibid. 419.

brother, James, from the succession. Nevertheless, the shift in the balance of legislative power was now unmistakable.

25.6. The Shires (Local Government) Regain their Independence of the Crown

The shires had been substantially depopulated by the Black Death of 1348–1350, but their affairs remained in the hands of the sheriffs, local landowners, parishes and town councils. By the late Middle Ages there had been a further extension of the boroughs, with towns and cities enjoying effective independence of the county, with their own sheriffs, Quarter Sessions, and other officials. Some cities, such as York, Bristol, Canterbury and Chester, included a substantial surround area, so that they were referred to as the 'Town and County of …', or the 'City and County of …', collectively known as the Counties Corporate. Others were created to deal with specific problems, such as Berwick-on-Tweed to deal with border problems, and Poole and Haverfordwest to deal with piracy.

The Civil War had a profound effect on local government. Previously, local government officers, such as sheriffs and Justices of the Peace, had been responsible to the Privy Council, and so were much subject to direction from above. The Act of 1641, which abolished the Court of Star Chamber, had the effect of preventing the King in Council from using the royal prerogative as the basis for public policy, because he no longer had the means of enforcing it in law. With the Privy Council stripped of most of its judicial, and hence executive, powers, it had to be left to the common law courts to decide issues on the basis of statute and common law. Local government was no longer answerable to the Crown for the exercise of its powers, and no longer subject to common standards. Legal questions concerning the relationships between government and governed were now decided by the courts alone. The result was the increased independence of local government. Justices of the Peace were free to act more on their own initiative and in their own interests. As a result, they because less responsible and less heedful of the public welfare.[18] As part of the general reaction against the Nonconformists that followed the return

---

18. G. A. Smith, *A Constitutional and Legal History of England*, 348.

of the Stuarts, the Justices of the Peace were often glad to harass the Puritans who had once plagued them.

25.6.1. The Withdrawal of the Third House of Parliament (1664)

The arrangement by which the clergy taxed themselves separately from the laity had continued since the Middle Ages. The Convocation of the Church of England had functioned as a third House of Parliament for the First Estate (and therefore, perhaps more correctly, as the first House of Parliament), although it had insisted on meeting separately from the other Houses and with separate assemblies for the provinces of Canterbury and York. It had never exercised its right of consent in secular matters, and had limited its involvement in the parliamentary process to negotiate taxes on the Church, including assessing their incidence. The earlier conclusion will be remembered that the King has no right to tax, other than his revenue entitlements in common law. He is entitled only to certain services due to him as lord, which in the Middle Ages were commuted to money payments and were no longer separately identified; also, he is entitled to the revenue from his private and Crown estates. All other taxes may only be raised by consent of the Estates.

One of the most important consequences of the religious conflict, during the reign of Charles I and the ensuing Civil War and the Restoration of the monarchy, was the imposition of parliamentary control over the Church. It took the form of a private verbal agreement in 1664 between the Chancellor, Lord Clarendon, and Archbishop Sheldon of Canterbury. Under this arrangement the clergy waived their right to consent to taxes on themselves, agreeing to leave this instead to the laity in Parliament (the other two Estates), in return for which the clergy were granted the right to vote in popular elections for members of the House of Commons. Whether the Archbishop had the right to conclude such an agreement need not concern us, but it was confirmed by an Act of Parliament in the following year, reciting the fact that the clergy had been assessed by the Commissioners named in the statute, without any objection being raised. A proviso was added, however, that 'nothing therein contained shall be drawn into example to the prejudice of the ancient rights belonging to the lords spiritual and temporal, or clergy of this realm'. In other words, the right of the clergy to tax themselves was not surrendered, and perhaps could not be in common law. It would seem that no Estate may, in common law, consent to taxes on behalf of another, except by the latter's consent, and such a consent – in effect, delegation – may be withdrawn, irrespective of any statute. Meanwhile, the agreement of 1664 marked the withdrawal of the Convocation of the Church of England from participation as a House of Parliament. It had always refused to function as one in any case, except in regard to tax.

There were probably several reasons for the agreement of 1664. The Church of England had accepted that it no longer fully represented the religious beliefs and practices of the community. Its position as the First Estate was therefore in question. The House of Commons was anxious to appropriate as much legislative power to itself as possible; and the Church, which had fluctuated in its desire to wield temporal power, had sufficient confidence in the Cavalier Parliament to surrender its involvement in matters of taxation.

25.6.2. The Summoning and Life of Parliaments

The seventeenth century was a period of wrangling between the Stuarts and their Parliaments which inevitably brought into question the frequency with which the latter should be summoned. The problem was not simply one of royal attitudes. Parliaments could be factionalised, quarrelsome and ineffective or worse, and could quickly cease to represent the changing mood of the people.

Although customary law requires annual Parliaments, and statutes of Edward III also required this, and more often if needed, Kings were often inclined to postpone them for as long as possible, and it was this that gave rise to the Triennial Act of 1664. The first two Parliaments of Charles I, who had no time for representative government, had been preoccupied with securing recognition of their privileges, and achieved nothing. The third Parliament sat, on and off, from March 1628 until March 1629, achieving only the Petition of Right, which provided that no man be compelled to make a gift, loan or similar imposition without the consent of a Parliament. There followed no Parliaments for almost eleven years, and the fourth, convened in April 1640, lasted less than a month, with still no supply, or financial grant, to the King. On September 24 of that year, Charles turned to the Great Council, which was summoned to a meeting at York. Here, the Council, in its last meeting outside the House of Lords, advised the King to summon another Parliament. Its advice also did much to end the King's obduracy. The ensuing Parliament, meeting in November 1640, was to become known as the Long Parliament, because it continued sitting until August 1642, on the eve of the Civil War, after which it became known as the Rump Parliament. Meanwhile, it secured the trial of Strafford, the exclusion of the bishops from the House of Lords, the abolition of the Court of Star Chamber, the Triennial Act, and an Act that ensured its own continued existence during its own good pleasure. It was finally dissolved by the Convention Parliament in 1660. The Triennial Act, of 1641, provided that a Parliament should be held every third year. If the Chancellor should fail to issue the necessary writs, the Great Council – or *Magnum Concilium*, as it was still recorded[19] – was to meet and issue writs (as we know, it had the right to summon a Parliament in any case, although this may have been forgotten). If not, its exercise, other than by statutory authority, would by now undoubtedly have fallen foul of the jealousy of the Commons.[20] In default of action by the Council – sitting as the House of Lords – the Act required the sheriffs and mayors to see to the election.[21] It was not until 1660 that the Long Parliament was finally dissolved by the Convention Parliament.

A constitutional doctrine was affirmed in 1678 by the House of Lords, after an examination of various precedents. This was to the effect that an impeachment by the Commons was not terminated by any prorogation or dissolution of Parliament. However, it would not be until a century later, in the trial of Warren Hastings, that the doctrine would become finally established.[22] It had been questioned whether, constitutionally, one Parliament could try a case that had been brought before another. They were, after all, different Parliaments, which might comprise different interests, elected with perhaps different concerns in mind. On the other hand, the House of Lords was not dependent on the summoning of Parliaments. As a permanent body, it did not automatically

19. F. W. Maitland, *The Constitutional History of England*, 293.
20. Among the Lithuanians, who had no king, it was the Council of Lords that summoned the *Seimas*, or Parliament.
21. The Triennial Act did not repeal the statutes of Edward III, which already required a Parliament each year.
22. T. Erskine May, *The Constitutional History of England*, ii. 93.

relinquish a case after the Parliament that brought it had been dissolved. Irrespective of the arguments actually adduced by the House of Lords at the time, therefore, it would seem that it was quite competent in common law to raise the case with a succeeding Parliament. Unless the House of Commons withdrew the charge, the House of Lords was bound to resume the trial, or, for that matter, continue it between Parliaments.

The reign of Charles II was not an easy one, and the next few years proved to be disastrous. A new conflict, the Second Anglo-Dutch War, was sparked in 1665 after the Dutch had seized a Swedish ship carrying ships' masts to England. The basic cause of enmity, however, was the colonial rivalry in America, where the English had taken possession of New Netherland and New Amsterdam, whose name they had changed to New York. In the same year there appeared the Great Plague in London, killing 70,000 people in the next few months and forcing Parliament to flee to the relative safety of Oxford. In 1666 the Great Fire of London raged for several days, destroying much of the City, including the splendid medieval cathedral of St Paul's. The Anglo-Dutch War, meanwhile, was proving indecisive, with naval victories on both sides, and the French and Danes joining the Dutch. The war reached a humiliating conclusion in 1667, when the Dutch fleet under De Ruyter sailed up the Medway estuary, burning Sheerness, sinking six English ships and towing away the English flag-ship, the Royal Charles. In the ensuing Treaty of Breda in the same year, a compromise was reached in respect of the American colonies, in which England retained New York, but lost Surinam in South America.

25.7. The Privy Council is Usurped by its Cabinet Council

Under the Tudors the membership of the Privy Council had been reduced to major office-holders and numbered less than twenty. James I had immediately increased the size of the Council to well over twenty. Under Charles I it rose to over forty. At the same time, it became less of an executive body and was more taken up with routine, such as dealing with petitions and disputes. Many councillors were appointed as a mark of favour, and rarely attended. In the twelve months which ended on 31

May 1630, those attending most frequently were the Lord Privy Seal, the Lord Keeper of the Great Seal, the two Secretaries of State, the Lord President of the Council, and the Bishop of Winchester. During this time, the Privy Council met on ninety-nine occasions, or once every three or four days, on average, of which the King attended only nine, and 'it is not always apparent what brought him'.[23]

Due mainly to the administrative ineptitudes of the Stuarts, the Privy Council became increasingly bloated, and its unwieldy size caused it to decline in importance. A particular problem was the difficulty of keeping its proceedings secret, and this led to the development of a system of temporary committees, to which the work of the Council was increasingly delegated. Confidential issues, such as the negotiations of 1621–4 over the Spanish marriage, were limited to the King and nine chosen Councillors. In 1621 and 1624, James I used a Council of War, which included several individuals who were not Councillors. These and many other important matters of the day did not appear on the Council registers, and so were probably managed by small *ad hoc* committees. Of particular importance was the establishment of a standing committee of the Privy Council, which outranked the temporary committees and soon came to dominate the Privy Council itself. It has been described as the work-a-day aspect of the Privy Council, but it did not acquire formal recognition until much later, in 1714, the year when Queen Anne was succeeded by George I. Meanwhile, it became much concerned with the colonies, Irish legislation, the Channel Islands, and similar matters.

25.7.1. Emergence of the Cabinet Council

The more important issues were handled by the King and a group of his more trusted councillors in a separate committee of the Privy Council, which, from the 'cabinet', or small private room in which their discussions were held, came to be known during the reign of Charles I as the 'Cabinet Council'. Although the earliest recorded mention of the Cabinet Council was in 1625, at the beginning of Charles's reign, references were already being made in 1611, in the time of James I, to 'Cabinet Counsellors'. The first reference to the Cabinet Council, as distinct from the Privy Council, does not appear, however, until 1644, still in the time of Charles I. Thus,

---

23. J. P. Kenyon, *The Stuart Constitution*, 429–33.

the Cabinet Council, or 'Cabinet', seems to have had its origin during the reign of James I, but it became fully established during the reign of his successor. It is evident that the Privy Council itself was scarcely being used in the reign of Charles I, whether as a policy-making or an advisory body, and the use of secret, undefined committees caused much suspicion in Parliament, which demanded, in the Nineteen Propositions, submitted in 1642, that the Privy Council be reduced in number to a maximum of twenty-five, and that it be made responsible for all policy decisions. As these two bodies, the Committee of the Privy Council and the Cabinet Council, became established, so the parent body, the Privy Council, became increasingly ossified and formal. However, there was no solidarity between the members of the Cabinet Council, because, although they could be identified with the same political faction, they were not members of a disciplined Party in the later sense of the word. Meanwhile, the chief problem with the Privy Council itself was the irregularity of its meetings.

The abolition of the Star Chamber had removed most of the judicial responsibilities of the Privy Council, and this had not only weakened it, but made regular meetings of the Council less necessary to the King. Although it still had the important function of advising the King on the exercise of his prerogatives, Charles did not regard himself as bound to consult it, or to follow its advice when he did, one reason being that he trusted very few. Suspicious by nature, he described the Privy Council as 'unfit for the secrecy and dispatch that are necessary in many great affairs'. Also, the Council was still large and unwieldy, consisting at this time of some fifty members. Consequently, the Council was not in regular session, and when the decisions reached by the Cabinet were laid before the Privy Council for ratification, it was not available. This left the administration of the royal authority effectively in the hands of a côterie of royal favourites, some of whom were those Privy Councillors who held high office, but who were responsible neither to the Privy Council nor to Parliament. The irritation which this arrangement caused eventually compelled Charles II to call upon Sir William Temple, in 1679, to devise a scheme for the reform of the system by which the Privy Council operated.

Temple concluded that it was necessary to bring into the Council a number of lords and commoners who wielded influence in both Houses of Parliament, but who were not felt to be hostile to the Government. In other words, Temple tried to do what the Tudors had done, that is, ensure the election of Privy Council members to the House of Commons, but the opposite way around: members of the Commons were to be brought into the Privy Council. These, together with the chosen lords and those appointed by the King, should comprise half the Privy Council, while officers of the Crown and the Royal Household should comprise the other half. He recommended that the size of the Council be reduced from fifty to thirty, comprising fifteen officers of state, ten lords, and five commoners. This Council should be re-vested with the powers that had been usurped by the Cabinet. As each Privy Council was appointed by the King, and so dissolved automatically on the King's death, Temple recommended that, in order to ensure greater continuity, a Privy Council should remain in office for six months after the King's demise. Temple's proposals were implemented, but within less than two years the new arrangement proved to be unworkable, and the Cabinet system was restored. Nevertheless, it was hated by Parliament, which saw this secret conclave, operating separately from the Privy Council, as unconstitutional and a threat to the proper and honest government of the country. The Act of Succession tried to suppress it by insisting that all decisions be taken by the Privy Council, but this proved impossible to enforce.

Charles II relied heavily on the Lord Chancellor, the Earl of Clarendon, who was the first to hold this office since the fall of his predecessor, the previous Lord Chancellor, Sir Francis Bacon in 1621, when he had been impeached for receiving payments from parties involved in suits. Since that time, the duties of the Lord Chancellor had been fulfilled by the lesser office of the Lord Keeper of the Great Seal. Under Charles II, the importance of the Cabinet Council and other committees of the Privy Council was greatly increased by the fall of the Earl of Clarendon in 1667. Clarendon was largely and unfairly blamed for the repressive legislation of the Cavalier Parliament, as well as the King's marriage to a Catholic, the naval defeats in the Dutch War, and even the Plague and the Great Fire of London. In the face of impeachment proceedings, he was forced to resign, and, after fleeing to France, he was convicted and sentenced to banishment for life. This changed the character of Charles's administration: instead of managing affairs by consulting with his

Chancellor, he turned to consultation with an inner circle of Ministers chosen by himself, that is, the Cabinet Council of James's reign, which now consisted of five Ministers, who were granted formal powers of summons and interrogation. This practice was more manageable and informal than the full Privy Council. There was much opposition to this, on the principle that decisions should be taken by the Privy Council, not by an obscure committee. After 1673, this committee acquired the nickname of the 'Cabal', probably after the initial letters of the names of its members: Lords Clifford, Ashley, Buckingham, Arlington, and Lauderdale, and because the description seemed apt.[24] Two of its members were Catholics, and it was widely suspected, correctly, that its aim was the rehabilitation of Catholicism.

By an Order in Council of 1668, standing committees of the Privy Council were created for foreign affairs, trade, the navy, and grievances. It was laid down that no matter was to be decided by the Council until it had been before the appropriate committee, and no matter was to be considered by a committee unless it had been referred to it by the Council. The most important of these committees was the Committee for Foreign Affairs, whose work often extended into other fields, such as advising the King on nominations for a new Speaker, or discussing the dismissal of two judges. Usurping the long-held role of the Lord Chancellor, the King's 'Chief Minister' at this time was the Earl of Danby, who was the Lord High Treasurer. The title of Chief Minister was still an informal one, and it is not clear whether this role was attached to any particular office during the seventeenth century.

25.8. The Stuarts Return to Catholicism

The King's duplicity had become evident following a Triple Alliance of 1668, between England, Holland and Sweden. This alliance had been intended to check the growing power of France under Louis XIV, when it was guided by the redoubtable Cardinal Mazarin. Ever since the Restoration, the right of the King to conduct foreign policy had been tacitly assumed, but ever since 1621, during the reign of Charles I,

---

24. From the French *cabale*, meaning a private intrigue of a sinister nature by a small group.

Parliament had been demanding that it be conducted in public view. Mazarin now sought to disrupt the Triple Alliance in 1670 by the Treaty of Dover with England, whose object was the acquisition from Spain of the provinces that comprise modern Belgium, for which he needed English naval support against Holland, which had its own claim to Spanish Flanders. The Treaty of Dover also included a private treaty, known to the Cabal, between King Charles and Louis of France, based on Mazarin's realisation, from contacts with the English Queen and fellow Catholic, Catherine, that he would be able to secure Charles's formal conversion to Catholicism and, he hoped, England's. In this secret treaty, Charles agreed to declare his conversion to Roman Catholicism, to be followed by his restoration of Catholicism in England, and to this end, Louis promised the support of an army in the event of a popular revolt. In accordance with the Treaty, both Charles and his younger brother, James, who was the Duke of York and Lord High Admiral, were secretly converted to Catholicism. James thereupon publicly announced his change of faith, but, to the French king's annoyance, Charles did not. James's declaration was of particular significance, because the King had no legitimate children, and in the event of his death James was destined to be his successor. The Cabal agreed to abandon the Triple Alliance, in return for annual subsidies from France and the ports of Sluys and Kadzand, on the island of Walcheren, at the mouth of the River Scheldt. In the event of success, England was also to gain Ostend, the island of Minorca, and territories in South America.

On the eve of his declaration of war against Holland, in April 1672, Charles, without reference to Parliament, issued a Declaration of Indulgence. This was part of his promise in the private Treaty of Dover, and in virtue of his 'supreme power' over the Church. The Declaration permitted freedom of worship and assumed the right to cancel all penal legislation against both Nonconformists and Catholics.[25] The inclusion of Roman Catholics caused a strong reaction throughout the country, and the Declaration was withdrawn in the face of opposition by Parliament, which asserted that statutes on ecclesiastical matters could not be suspended, except by statute. Shortly afterwards, with the onset of the highly unpopular Third Dutch War in the same year, the public aspect of

---

25. Charles had issued a previous Declaration of Indulgence in 1662, to dispense with the laws against dissenters, subject to Parliament's consent, which Parliament had refused to give.

the Treaty of Dover was put into effect. The French invaded Holland, only to be frustrated at first by the opening of the dykes and the flooding of large areas of the country, while England won an indecisive naval victory over the Dutch off Southwold. The French overran much of Holland, but, following the accession of Willem III as Stadholder in the same year, he was able to win the support of Brandenburg and the German emperor, enabling him to hold his own.

Meanwhile, Parliament responded to the King's religious manoeuvres by attempting to salvage something of the Clarendon Code, which it did by passing the Test Bill of 1673, which Charles was forced to sign. It required all holders of office under the Crown to take an oath and to accept the sacrament of the Church of England. The effect of this was to exclude all Catholics and Nonconformists from public office. In so doing, it forced the resignation of Prince James from his office of Lord High Admiral, and of the two Catholic members of the now hated 'Secret Committee', or Cabal, to which was attributed much of the blame for the King's unpopular foreign policies. The storm was a lesson that Charles never forgot and his brother, James, never learned. The procedure used in the passing of the Test Act was an illustration of the extent to which the rivalry between the Crown and Parliament, and the misconception by the Crown of its proper role, had long bedevilled the constitutional process. Instead of Parliament consenting to a Bill proposed by the Crown, the Crown was consenting to a Bill submitted by Parliament. This had long been the practice, of course, and it could be defended on the ground that petitions could originate in, or be sponsored by, Parliament, for adoption by the King, who then, if he approved of them, submitted them for Parliament's consent, after which the King was required to enact them. Nevertheless, examples like the Test Act, and the unresponsiveness of the Crown to the popular will, threatened the very principles upon which 'the constitution' was founded. The growing sense of confrontation was increased later in the year when the King's younger brother and heir apparent, James, maintained Stuart tradition by marrying a foreign Catholic, Maria d'Este of Modena. Maria, an Italian, and James's second wife, now adopted the Anglicised name of Mary, but the marriage, when added to James's own Catholicism, caused widespread public demonstrations, demanding that James be debarred from the succession.

Abandoning the war against the Dutch, England ended hostilities early in 1674 with the Treaty of Westminster. This opened the way for a new dynastic twist, with the marriage, in London in 1677, of Mary, the eldest daughter of the King's brother, James, to the Dutch Stadholder, William (Willem) III, Prince of Orange. William was a Protestant, as was Mary herself, and it may be remembered that William's mother had been Mary, daughter of Charles I of England, so that William of Orange was her cousin. The ties between the two houses were now quite strong, and these were to have implications for the future.

The religious issue in England came to the fore again in the form of the Popish Plot of 1678, when conflicting allegations were made that there was a widespread conspiracy to assassinate the King, install James on the throne, impose arbitrary rule and massacre leading Protestants. Plausibility was added by the murder of the magistrate before whom the deposition containing the allegations had been made, and with whom a written testament of the charges had been left. On the other hand, the leading accuser, Titus Oates, was a known liar with a disreputable past. In a society that was widely suspicious of Catholic intents, however, it was enough to cause a massive wave of anti-Catholic feeling, which resulted in the execution of several leading Catholics and the passing of the Papists' Disabling Act, which excluded Catholics from Parliament, with the exception of James as the heir apparent. James wisely fled to Brussels, and from there to Scotland, where he was far from being welcome. Parliament introduced an Exclusion Bill, which would have removed James from the succession, but Charles was adamantly opposed. It was the aristocratic leaders of the Exclusion faction who first acquired the label 'Whig',[26] there being as much concern to reduce the authority of the Monarchy as to eliminate the Catholic menace.[27] Charles himself was under no illusions about his younger brother, once remarking in half-serious jest that 'they will never kill me to make Jamie King!', but he had no children, and thwarted three attempts to have the Exclusion Bill passed.

---

26. Probably from the 'Whiggamore raid' on Edinburgh by West Highland Scots in 1648, a reference to the bewhigged 'demons' who ruled Scotland.
27. J. P. Kenyon, *The Stuart Constitution*, 376–7.

The Lord High Treasurer, the Earl of Danby, who usually enjoyed the informal title of 'Chief Minister', had made the King all but financially independent of Parliament. He had also been the chief architect of a Church monopoly of every branch of public life, and it was he who was next impeached by the House of Commons at the end of 1678 on a charge of treasonable correspondence with France. In fact, he had merely been acting on the orders of the King, pressing for a cash payment to him by Louis XIV. With Danby consigned to the Tower while the case pended, the King was forced to dismiss him from office. Charles promptly dissolved the Cavalier Parliament early in 1679, in an effort to save Danby, and sought to win popularity by also dissolving the Committee for Foreign Affairs, which had been at the centre of the storm. Then, in April, he dismissed the entire Privy Council. It was replaced by a new Council of thirty, of whom fifteen were Ministers, and of the remainder, ten were Peers and five were commoners. The Committee of Foreign Affairs was then replaced by a new Committee of Intelligence, whose responsibilities were not limited to foreign affairs. Meanwhile, a promise made by Charles to consult the Privy Council at all times was quietly forgotten, not least because he had been forced to appoint several members, including Ministers, whom he did not trust. As a result, important foreign policy matters were not being reported by the Committee of Intelligence to the Privy Council.

25.8.1. The Cabinet Crisis of 1679

It had been the practice of the King to submit all important affairs to the Cabal, or Cabinet, in the first instance, and the conclusions reached by the Cabal were then submitted to the full Privy Council for formal ratification. This had the effect of putting the whole administration of royal authority into the hands of a small group of favourites. They were effective more in their individual capacities than as a group. Nevertheless, they were closely identified in the eyes of Parliament and the public with all that was unpopular with the Crown's policies. The antipathy of Parliament towards the Cabinet became so intense, that in 1679 the King invited Sir William Temple to devise a suitable reform. Temple seems to have appreciated the need for a link between the Privy Council and Parliament, and proposed the abolition of the Cabinet and a reduction in size of the Privy Council from fifty to thirty, comprising fifteen officers of state, ten from the Lords, and five from the Commons. Meanwhile, members of the Privy Council were to remain in office for six months after a sovereign's death, in order to ensure continuity. In spite of its revised composition, the Council still proved to be inefficient, and within two years the executive power was again committed to a secret committee, Cabal or Cabinet, of the King's personal advisers, which was to continue until 1688.

Charles's capacity for sly manoeuvring was evident throughout his reign, and it is not clear why, in these circumstances, when he was not compelled by financial necessity, Charles decided to summon a new Parliament in March 1679. Perhaps he had hoped that it would be more moderate, but in May it attempted to pass an Exclusion Bill which would have removed James from the succession, for which reason it came to be known as the Exclusion Parliament. Charles blocked it by using his influence in the Lords, and kept the issue at bay by proroguing Parliament.

25.8.2. Extending *Habeas Corpus* to Acts of the King

It seems that the King had always enjoyed the right to assert his authority by seizing those charged with offending against it and passing judgement on those convicted. A distinction existed, therefore, between the duty of the King as guardian of the peace and as judge of offences against the law. In his judicial and executive capacities, he was himself subject to the law, represented by the Great Council in its capacity as guardian of the Constitution.

In practice, the King's sense of justice in respect of offences alleged against his peace, or against his own dignity, did not always accord with the requirements of the law, which held that an individual was innocent unless proved guilty. Royal negligence, or even vindictiveness, could leave an arrested person languishing in prison. Exceptions had been made over the years for certain offences, such as treason, or to guard against the accused absconding from justice, but the principle remained that no free man could be held in prison unless convicted and sentenced accordingly. It was in order to prevent the violation of this principle by local lords and other local authorities in the Middle Ages that the King, in upholding the rule of law, had been in the habit of issuing writs of *habeas corpus* in respect of individuals suspected of being held unjustly in local gaols. The reverse could also apply, however, as it did particularly under the Stuarts, and it had long been a matter of concern that the King could arrest and imprison in an arbitrary manner, because it was on behalf of the King that writs of *habeas corpus* were issued. In common law, the King had no authority to arrest, let alone imprison, except in accordance with the law, but this limitation did not apply under a feudal regime, where the King was the representative of God, and which the Stuarts regarded as the true basis of government.

The remedy for such infringements by the King applied in the same way. A person arrested and held in prison by the King or his officers without trial could submit a plea to the King, through his courts,[28] asking him to issue a writ of *habeas corpus* that required him to bring the complainant before a court, usually the Court of King's Bench. In order to bring the complainant to court, the King had to lay a formal charge against him. This meant that the King would have to prove it to the court, or otherwise release the accused. So it was that these writs, which had been necessary to the King to enable him to ensure the maintenance of his peace and the observance of the rule of law, could also be used against the King's own transgressions, because he also was beneath the law.

Consequently, writs of *habeas corpus* had become an effective weapon in the sixteenth century against the prerogative courts, such as the Star Chamber and High Commission. Under the Stuarts, the courts of common law had used the writs as a guarantee of the subject's right of free trial against the improper use of the prerogative. The Act of 1641, abolishing the Court of Star Chamber – which, in the absence of the Great Council, deprived a member of the Second Estate of the right of trial by his peers – had provided that any man imprisoned by order of King or Council could obtain a writ of *habeas corpus* from the Courts of King's Bench or Common Pleas. Upon the return of the writ, the sheriff, sheriff's gaoler, minister or other person to whom it was directed must certify the true cause of imprisonment. Nevertheless, several ways had since been found by the Crown of evading the *habeas corpus* device, particularly where political prisoners were involved. There were weaknesses in the wording of the provisions which could be used by the Crown to get

---

28. They were his courts in that he presided over them, but, as noted earlier, they were judicial extensions of Parliament, to which they were subject.

around them or to impose interminable delays, for example, by moving a prisoner from prison to prison, so requiring a new writ each time. A writer, James Harrington, was one of several individuals who had been removed from the Tower of London and placed where the writ did not run, such as Scotland, Ireland, the Channel Islands or the Scilly Isles.[29]

Various attempts were made to reform aspects of the procedure, but it was not until the first Exclusion Parliament of 1679, controlled by the Whigs under the earl of Shaftesbury, by which time the position of Charles II was under siege, that it became possible to pass the *Habeas Corpus Amendment Act of 1679*. This brought an end to these various practices and made it much more difficult to arrest a man on suspicion. Although there is a tendency for historians to side with the judiciary against the Crown, the tradition of impartiality had largely been abandoned during the reigns of James I and Charles I, and prominent judges like Scroggs, Jenner, Jeffreys and Keeling were 'atrocious bullies', accused, perhaps unfairly, of an inadequate knowledge of the law.[30] They should not be regarded too harshly, however. Charles I and, after the Restoration, Charles II, gave their high court judges patents *quamdiu se bene gesserint*, 'for as long as they conducted themselves well'. In 1667 the House of Commons passed a resolution that the fining and imprisoning of juries for giving a verdict against the judge's summing up was illegal, and this was upheld by the King's Bench three years later. After 1667, Charles reverted to patents *durante bene placito*, broadly, 'subject to the King's pleasure'. The judges were therefore under pressure to return acceptable verdicts, so that, in dubious cases, the less adequate the evidence, the easier it was for the judge. Also, the handling of partisan juries could now be left largely to the judge, because they were no longer disciplined by the Court of Star Chamber. In Bushel's Case, 1670, the King's Bench ruled that a judge could not punish a juryman for his verdict, unless there was evidence of corruption. However, the juryman was employed for his presumed familiarity with the circumstances, not for his impartiality, and the ruling did not change this.

In spite of the wide powers wielded by the Crown, they were not used in any systematic way before 1681, and the main concern of the day

---

29. The Scilly Isles were a Crown property, leased to the Godolphin family.
30. J. P. Kenyon, *The Stuart Constitution*, 391–2.

seems to have been 'the spectre of uncontrolled judicial discretion'.[31] In spite of their vulnerable position under the Crown, the judiciary displayed a great deal of independence. A Bill of 1674, which attempted to regulate judges' salaries and confirm their tenure, was defeated on the grounds that, if given absolute security, the judges would become a new power in the land, accountable to nobody.[32] The real pressure on the judges came from Parliament, rather than from the King. Thus, it was Parliament that secured the dismissal of four judges in April 1679, and it was only with difficulty that the King resisted pressure from Parliament to dismiss the Lord Chief Justice, Scroggs, in the following year.

Servants of the Crown were placed in an unenviable position by the incompatibility of the two constitutional traditions of common law and Church-Feudalism. Charles II, as an adherent of the latter, did not accept in principle that he was in any way bound by the law, other than in the interests of political discretion, and any servant who subscribed to the same philosophy, likewise, would be in no doubt that his only course was to obey the King. In 1679, the House of Lords, as the Great Council and arbiter on constitutional issues, ruled that an authorisation in the King's own hand was not a protection to his servant. The case of the Earl of Danby was of major importance, because it relied on the feudal principle that the King can do no wrong, and therefore he can authorise no wrong. Therefore, any servant of the Crown who committed wrong must have committed it without authority, thereby rendering himself liable. It was a device that could also be used against an errant ruler, as well as being a fundamental principle. It meant that, only when a servant of the Crown was acting within the law, or, in exceptional circumstances, in a manner perceived to be in the interests of the Crown, could he be said to be acting with the Crown's authority. Only when instructed by the Crown to commit an act that was at variance with the law did the royal servant face the dilemma of violating the law, or violating his fealty to the Crown. By commanding an illegal act, the King was acting outside the law, thereby violating his obligations under the regal contract and exposing himself to deposition.

---

31. William Petyt, member of Parliament, quoted in J. P. Kenyon, *The Stuart Constitution*, 394.

32. A. Grey (ed.), *Debates of the House of Commons from the Year 1667 to the Year 1694* (13 February 1674), ii. 415–20. See also J. P. Kenyon, *The Stuart Constitution*, 394.

Charles's practice of managing affairs through standing committees of the Privy Council would continue much the same as before under his successor, James II. According to a memoir by a French visitor, the Marquis de Torcy, written in 1687, the Privy Council was usually held once a week, in the King's presence. There was also the Cabal, or Cabinet Council, which was usually held every Sunday in the King's presence. Here, dispatches were read, and the answers to be sent deliberated upon. Those present were Prince George of Denmark, the Lord Chancellor, the Lord President, the Lord Privy Seal, the Secretary of State, the Commissioner of the Treasury and Chamberlain to the Queen (Lord Godolphin), the Lord Steward, and Lord Dartmouth. The last may have sat in his capacity as Master-General of the Ordinance and Admiral of the Fleet, or simply as one of the King's oldest personal friends.[33] However, the most important business was being transacted in the King's privy chamber with those Ministers that he had summoned, including the Lord President and the Jesuit Father Petre. The decisions taken here were then imparted by the King to the Privy Council 'for form's sake', several days before they were published. Foreign ambassadors often referred to a 'Catholic Council', whose composition is unknown. Meanwhile, such was the contempt, due to his own incompetence, in which James held the Privy Council, which now limited itself to routine business, that sometimes he simply sat with the clerks to issue Council Orders of a minor nature.[34]

25.9. Emergence of the Political Parties: Whigs and Tories

Undoubtedly, political factions had always existed in Parliament, and the simplest explanation of their basis might hold that, whereas some in Parliament are normally dissatisfied with society and wish to change it, others are sufficiently satisfied, and alarmed at what might take its place, as to be opposed to any change that is deemed to be unnecessary or of dubious effect. This is not an adequate explanation for the division of political outlooks, however, and it may be suspected that these conflicts are more adequately explained by inherited mental differences, because,

---

33. J. P. Kenyon, *The Stuart Constitution*, 442.
34. Ibid. 432.

once formed by maturity, they seem to be fixed for life. The psychologist, Sigmund Freud, described a division of the human mind into three functions: the *ego*, or conscious mind; the *super ego*, or conscience, and the *id*, or more primitive unconscious mind. Their respective influence on the inherited outlook and attitudes of individuals consequently ranges from the objective, where the influence of the *ego* is dominant, to the conscientious, where the influence of the *superego* is dominant, to the self-interested where the *id* is dominant. Accordingly, political attitudes are inherited at birth, and are slowly rationalised in the light of experience. There seems to be evidence, however, that the growing individual tends to progress from the dominance of the *id* in childhood, through the increased influence of the *superego* during adolescence, to the dominance of the *ego* in adulthood, except that, in many cases, this progression is not completed. The effect is a range of three outlooks in adult society, which is reflected in behaviour and in political attitudes and perceptions, and hence the Party system. Another influence is fortune in life. Some are bitterly resentful of their misfortunes, making them resentful of the prevailing social system, while others who have been fortunate in life are averse to anything that might pose a threat. Nevertheless, these influences of circumstance are normally overridden by the psychological make-up of the individual.

The origin of the political division that has survived down to the present day may be traced to the Long Parliament of 1640–1660, and more particularly to the division in the ranks of the reformers during 1641, between the High-Church followers of Laud, who defended the retention of bishops and the principle of the divine right of kings, and the radical, Low-Church element who called for the eradication of the bishops, 'root and branch', and who did not accept the notion that 'the King can do no wrong'. Since that time, at least, there has existed a basic distinction between the two factions, that is, as between those who display a consistent inclination to change society in directions that they believe to be for the better, and those whose basic concern is to preserve the stability and continuity of society from changes that could prove to be disastrous. The origin of political Parties may also be attributed to the increasing volume of legislation during the Middle Ages, resulting in a need for Parliaments to sit for longer than originally intended, allowing time for political factions in the Commons to form lasting alliances. This was because those who were conservative or radical on one issue tend to be conservative or radical on others. To be effective, a Party needs organisation and a recognised system of leadership, and these aspects gradually developed.

In the seventeenth century, the Party division was based, not on social class, because even the London mob, which turned out in support of the radicals, and demanded the execution of Strafford, had been engineered by, and to some extent was composed of, elements of the middle class.[35] In essence, we see in these factions a continuation of the struggle between Cavaliers and Roundheads, so that the political party division that was now to congeal can be traced back to before the Civil War. Many historians have looked to the origin of the political parties, rather, in the conflict over the Root and Branch Bill of 1641, following a brief period of unity among the reformers. At what point a faction became an organised 'party' is difficult to determine, but the distinction was essentially one of cohesiveness and acknowledged leadership. The real continuity of this division between conservatives and radicals becomes discernible in the House of Commons, which was eventually to develop into the organised 'Party' system that exists today. In its most basic sense, a political party is a group of people with similar concerns, aspirations and prejudices; a coalition of individuals with a similar axe to grind. The transition from simple and spontaneous factionalism to organised and self-perpetuating political parties appears to have occurred in the latter half of the seventeenth century in response to three rivalries: the religious issue of High Church versus Protestant; the issue of King versus Parliament; and the efforts of the House of Commons to neutralise the House of Lords.

Reference was made earlier to the problems faced by the Crown in managing affairs of state, while confronted by a House of Commons that was increasingly determined to take this function upon itself, and the consequent need for the Crown to protect its position by promoting a party in Parliament that would support its policies, in order for it to govern effectively. Those loyal to the Crown thus became the 'Court' faction in Parliament. They took the view that the King had yielded all

---

35. G. E. Aylmer, *The Struggle for the Constitution*, 110.

that could reasonably be asked of him, and that the welfare of the state required the preservation of what remained of the royal prerogative. The Parliamentarians, or Roundheads, were the heirs of the majority Puritan group in the Long Parliament, and were now perpetuated in the 'Country' faction. This faction believed that the King's concessions had been made only grudgingly, and that the only way to secure what had been won was to obtain further concessions that would ensure, irrevocably, that the Crown was subject to the dictates of Parliament at all times, a view that was inconsistent with the principles of the half-forgotten Constitution. Both factions were opposed to a revival of Catholicism and concerned at the evidence in the late 1670s of possible intrigue. Lord Shaftesbury, a leading adherent of the Country faction, warned of 'Popishly infected persons' in high places, and declared that 'Popery is breaking in on us like a flood!' To add substance, he claimed, with truth, that the King had received large sums from Louis XIV of France, and that the King had an army of 20,000 men. It was the reaction to the King's Catholic intrigues that lay behind the exposure of the Popish Plot of 1678, allegedly to assassinate Charles and establish Roman Catholicism in England. While the Court and Country parties were the dominant groups in Parliament, there were also those who did not identify with either, some of whom sought a compromise. These were the middle-men, like George Savile, Lord Halifax, leader of a moderate opposition group, who felt that they should 'trim' between the main factions, and so regarded themselves as 'Trimmers'.

The new Parliament of 1679 saw the virtual demise of the Court faction, in favour of the Country faction, which saw to it that the unfortunate Danby was sent to the Tower for five years. It also forced the King to send his brother, James, Duke of York, into exile. Bending before the storm, the new Privy Council appointed by the King contained members of the Country faction, including Lord Shaftesbury. Charles now felt himself to be under an inquisition, allegedly remarking that 'They have put a set of men about me, but they shall know nothing'. This attitude of confrontation did nothing to ease relations between King and Parliament. In the Exclusion Crisis that followed, it was the Country faction that made efforts to debar the King's legitimate heir and openly Catholic younger brother, James, from succeeding to the throne. Those who supported the Bill were accordingly known as Exclusionists, and the King again sought to head off the threat by proroguing, and later dissolving, Parliament. Lord Shaftesbury thereupon organised a nationwide petition that Parliament be called and that James be excluded from the succession. The Country faction, and the 'Exclusionists' or 'Petitioners' who promoted it, now acquired the nickname of 'Whiggamores', later abbreviated to 'Whigs'. The word was a reference to the Presbyterian insurgents from the west of Scotland, described as 'Whiggamores', who had marched on Edinburgh in 1648, an event known as the 'Whiggamore Raid'. The significance of the original word, *whiggamaire*, literally 'drive-mare', is obscure, but it acquired a contemptuous meaning. The Scottish Presbyterians had a long history of opposition to the Crown, hence their association with parliamentary politics.

The Anti-Exclusionists, who supported the claim of the King's brother, James, to the succession, although not necessarily James himself, belonged to the Court faction. From their abhorrence at the interference with the royal prerogative they became known as the Abhorrers, then acquired the more disparaging nickname of 'Tories', believed to come from the Irish word *toraighe*, or 'pursuer'. A *toraighe* was one of the dispossessed Irish of the early seventeenth century who became outlaws, or 'bog-trotters', and who subsisted by plundering and killing English settlers and soldiers. Later, the Anglicised form, 'tory', had come to refer to any Irish Papist or Royalist in arms, after the Irish Catholic army that had come to the aid of Charles I, hence the derisory application of the word to the English supporters of James. Thus, the Whigs and Tories, respectively, were dismissively described by their opponents as wild Scottish Presbyterians and Catholic Irish 'bog-trotters'. In the Tories one sees the cast of mind that was inclined to the feudal view of society, or, at least, to an ordered form of government in which the dignity and duties of kingship were respected. Upholders of the Church of England and the royal prerogative, they developed the idea of 'Non-Resistance', according to which rebellion against the legitimate ruler was never justified. It was a negative version of the principle of divine right. Opposed to Catholicism, they nevertheless never made it an issue. In the Whigs, on the other hand, one may discern an unconscious groping for a return to the Indo-European constitutional tradition, a quest in which they had been preceded by the barons of the thirteenth century and the knights and burghers of the fourteenth century. Their chief problem was that they did not understand the role of the King. The Whigs were especially hostile to Catholicism, drew much Nonconformist support, favoured further restrictions on the royal prerogative, and tended to display an antipathy to any form of authority. The more extreme were still republicans, and this exposed the Whigs to the accusation that they were trying to undermine the whole Restoration Settlement. On the other hand, they had built up the more efficient electoral machine, giving them control of the Commons. For the moment, however, it was the question of the succession that most divided the two factions. The Party system, as it now emerged, was not a disciplined organisation. Each party was essentially an alliance of like-minded members, drawn together as much by historical, family and local ties as by political ideas, who sought to combine their efforts and influence to attain their respective goals.

Between 1679 and 1681 the King summoned three Parliaments, the last at Oxford, well away from the London mobs, having dissolved each of the first two immediately when they revived the Exclusion Bill. Most of the Exclusionists wanted the succession to go to James's Protestant daughter, Mary, who had married the Dutch Stadholder, William of Orange. Gradually, the frenzy subsided, the Whigs became unpopular amid anxiety that they might cause another civil war, and grew divided among themselves over the issue. Some were now willing to accept James, provided his powers were limited by statute. Meanwhile, the Tories, languishing in opposition, became more united. In rejecting the Exclusion Bill yet again, and dissolving the Oxford Parliament, Charles offered to install Mary's husband, William of Orange, as a regent for James.

In the country at large, the early 1680s were a period of pro-Royalist, anti-Whig reaction. Charles II restored London from its drab years under the Commonwealth, bringing a return of the glittering London society and 'merrie England' of former times. The King led it to the full, establishing a race-course at Newmarket, patronising a restoration of the theatre, now centred on Drury Lane, instead of south of the Thames, as it had been in his father's reign, consorting with actresses, and establishing the Royal Hospital at Chelsea for army pensioners. He was also a patron of the sciences, supporting a scientific reformation with the building of the Royal Observatory at Greenwich, the appointment of the first Astronomer Royal, and the establishment of the Royal Society. Charles was, indeed, the man for the moment, because he arrived at a time of intellectual ferment. The Civil War had released pent-up attitudes and emotions, giving reign to wild and conflicting ideas about politics and society, only to be followed by the crushing failure of republican government under Cromwell, so that, when Charles II brought back stability and a relaxed approach to life, it acted as a new release of ideas, but this time as an escape from politics and religious fervour into organised, disciplined enquiry that found its outlet in science. Charles's reign marked a period of great scientific achievement, marked by men such as Hooke, Flamsteed, Newton, Halley and Wren. The redirected energy and curiosity also found an outlet in a new bout of colonisation, but one that was no longer driven by religious ideas.

From 1681 Charles ruled without Parliament, which was made possible for him by the subsidy that he was again receiving from Louis XIV. Some of the Whigs, including former officers of Cromwell's army, hatched a plot in 1683 to assassinate both the King and his brother, James, near Rye House, Hoddesdon, in Hertfordshire, on their way back from the races at Newmarket, the intention being to place Charles's eldest surviving illegitimate son, James, the Duke of Monmouth, on the throne. Monmouth was judged by many to be a legitimate contender on the grounds of a rumour that Charles had secretly married Monmouth's mother, Lucy Walter, while a young man in exile. Others, who were not convinced of this, would have been happy simply to make Monmouth legitimate by means of an Act of Parliament. The plot was thwarted when a fire caused the royal party to leave early, and the plot was later betrayed. Monmouth was banished to Holland.

25.9.1. The Alternation of Being 'In' or 'Out' of Office

Widespread support for the King grew, and this enabled him to move against the Whig leaders, some fleeing and others being condemned by packed juries, on the basis of minimal evidence, and executed. With the Whigs dispersed, members of the Court, or Tory, faction and those of like mind were appointed to offices under the Crown, or were simply able to take control of the institutions of state and local government. The period of Whig supremacy was thus replaced by one of Tory supremacy, the beginning of a pattern that has continued ever since, giving rise to a distinction and alternation between the 'Ins', or office-holders of the Crown, and the 'Outs': those who did not hold office. The shift in the popular mood and the eviction of the Whigs from positions of influence meant that the threat to James's eventual succession was averted, but the King was now dependent on the support of the Tories, who supported the Church of England, but who were no more inclined than the Whigs to accept a resurrection of Papism.

Neither republican nor Parliamentarian sentiment had died with the Restoration, and the type of political stress that had returned with the Stuarts even caused some to look back with nostalgia to the period of the Commonwealth. In his *Discourses*, written in 1680, Algernon Sidney, one of those implicated in the Rye House plot, saw the Commonwealth as an age of noble achievement for liberty, comparable to the great days of Greece and Rome. In a perceptive observation he held that 'Parliament and people have the power of making kings', and believed that the power of Parliament was delegated to the Crown, and so might be revoked in some unspecified way. In such sentiments we see, yet again, a surfacing of the Aryan instinct for common law government. Seeking to distance himself from doctrinal controversies, the King in 1681 delegated to a committee the task of proposing appointments to bishoprics and other benefices.

Charles's excesses had told on his health, however, so that in his later years he was a very sick man, incapable of effective rule, and in 1685 he died. Like his Stuart predecessors, Charles II had tried to steer the country back into the Catholic fold against its will, and all that he had learned from the Civil War had been greater discretion. Little had been achieved in resolving the constitutional conflict, because Charles had only limited success in hiding his belief in the absolutist, feudal view of his office, in contrast to the perception of a regal contract held by Parliament and people. No less of an anomaly were his religious beliefs, or sentiments, as religious head of a Protestant realm and its Church. In order to protect and further his own interests, Charles had made himself a willing lackey of France, which grated with the people. Through incompetence and indolence, rather than extravagance, he had wasted the country's financial resources, further limiting Parliament's willingness to approve taxes, and in so doing he had increased his dependence on the French. Throughout 1672, the Crown had been bankrupt. He had been shrewd and duplicitous – towards Parliament; towards the French; and towards the Dutch – but at least he had never been vindictive. The extent to which the public identified Charles with Catholicism had not been confined to England. The colonists in New England were strongly Protestant and, as a result, were increasingly alienated from the Stuarts and from the Crown. The English had to put up with it, but the colonists could see the width of the Atlantic between themselves and Charles II and, even more so, his openly Catholic successor. In the matter of the succession, meanwhile, Charles had thought only of family self-interest, and his brother's suitability or otherwise was seen by him as totally irrelevant. On the other hand, Charles II had done much to restore England, culturally and scientifically, after the wasted years of the Republic. By his own deftness, aided by a swing in public opinion in his favour, moreover, Charles had ousted the Whigs from power, and in so doing, brought stability after two decades of increasingly wild radicalism.

A particular danger of an organised Party system is the risk of a ruling Party being won over to an ill-considered philosophy or ideology, whose effects have not been properly thought through, because the Party system could easily impose it upon the country in a rash moment, leaving it very difficult to overturn.

25.9.2. James II: The Final Crisis

If Charles II had managed to resurrect the same constitutional problem that the Civil War had tried to resolve, his younger brother and successor, James II, was to succeed in going still further, by creating virtually the same crisis as that which had precipitated the War, only much more clumsily. If the English people had learned something from the traumatic events of the Civil War and its aftermath, the Stuarts had not.

When James ascended the two thrones of England and Scotland in 1685 – receiving both crowns, although they were treated as one for the purposes of the coronation – he did so as James II of England and James VII of Scotland. He was the first avowedly Catholic King of England since the Reformation, ruling a people who were overwhelmingly and devotedly Protestant. He was also a staunch believer in the divine right of kings, endeavouring to rule a people who believed in the supremacy of law and the primacy of Parliament. James behaved as the mood took him, had little patience with formalities, and had a tendency to take advice from a few intimates, although he tried to give it some familiar constitutional form.[36] The really important decisions were taken in complete privacy, leaving no surviving records. It was another recipe for disaster, but James had an advantage in that the English people had suffered more than their fill of revolution and republicanism. While the ideological relationship between King and people was not basically different from that existing in the reign of his brother, Charles II, he lacked his brother's astuteness and caution, so that a constitutional disaster seemed to be almost inevitable. However, James had one factor in his favour. It was the Court party, or Tories, who now controlled Parliament and the country generally, and the Tories believed in the need for strong kingship.

Not all the people were willing to accept the situation, however, and when Charles's allegedly illegitimate son, the Protestant Duke of Monmouth, returned from Holland and landed at Lyme Regis, in Dorset, to challenge for the Crown, he was strongly supported by the local population and by ordinary people in some other parts of the land. It was not enough to give him a realistic chance of success, however, because he did not have the support of the middle and upper classes, who were determined to give James a chance. Moreover, Monmouth's illegitimacy was a real obstacle. Proclaimed King at Taunton, Monmouth was defeated with ease at Sedgemoor in July 1685, a battle that was to be the last ever fought on English soil. Monmouth was executed in a bungled beheading on Tower Hill, and the uprising was followed by a wholesale judicial persecution of the West Country in the 'Bloody Assizes', by the now hated Judge Jeffries, with 320 sentenced to death and 840 to be sold into slavery. The opportunity was also taken to settle scores with suspect Whigs and others in London. A similar rising of Covenanters in the west of Scotland at the same time was also put down without difficulty. Judge Jeffries' brutality in dealing with Monmouth's supporters caused a wave of revulsion in the country, but was popular with the King, who appointed him Lord Chancellor (but quickly fell out with him).

---

36. J. P. Kenyon, *The Stuart Constitution*, 432.

Given an otherwise good start to his reign, and a new Parliament that was generous in its financial provisions, it was remarkable that James was able to turn the country against him so quickly. He used the opportunity of the Monmouth Rebellion to build up a large standing army, like his brother before him, well able to threaten Parliament from its encampment on Hounslow Heath. A new Court of Ecclesiastical Commission was set up, similar to the previously abolished Court of High Commission, which tried and suspended anti-Catholic and obstructive bishops. Catholic schools and chapels were opened in London. In order to find a way round the anti-Catholic restrictions of the Test Act, James had a test case prepared, after first packing the Court of King's Bench with judges known to be supportive of royal authority. The case of a Catholic army officer, Sir Edward Hales, convicted at Rochester Assizes of failing to take the oaths prescribed by the Test Act, was then pursued to the King's Bench in 1686. Here, the judges quashed the conviction, ruling that letters patent held by Hales from the King, dispensing with the oaths required by law, were valid. In its judgement the court ruled that:

1. the Kings of England were sovereign princes;
2. the laws of England were the King's laws;
3. it was therefore an inseparable prerogative of the King to dispense with laws in particular cases and for particular reasons;
4. the King himself was the sole judge of such circumstances and reasons; and
5. this was not a trust granted to the King by the people, but the remains of his sovereign power and prerogative, which could never be taken from him.

Here, at least, was a succinct statement of feudal philosophy, used to refute the ancient Indo-European tradition. It also left no doubt that James's next objective was to return the Church of England to the Papacy.

James had always taken the view that the Civil War and the subsequent difficulties faced by Charles II had been due to a royal failure to take a firm line, like a schoolmaster faced with unruly children, and he now felt strong enough to take it. With his legal position as an absolute ruler now confirmed by the hand-picked Court of Ecclesiastical Commission, and

Parliament prorogued and finally dissolved from 1685 onwards, James embarked on a policy of appointing Catholics to important positions around the country, from the Privy Council itself to the universities and the army. Fellows of Magdalen College, Oxford, who in 1687 refused to appoint a Catholic President proposed by the King, received a violent visit from him in person, accompanied by troops who forced their way in by the breaking open of doors, after which the Fellows were expelled from the College. Office-holders in local government, from the Lords Lieutenant and Justices of the Peace downwards, were evicted and replaced by Catholics and anybody else who seemed willing to collaborate with the King's designs. Because Catholics were often in short supply, individuals of often obscure social origin were drawn upon to fill vacated offices, and this posed a threat to the ruling classes, as well as to the Church.[37] In April of the same year, 1687, the King issued a Declaration of Liberty of Conscience, modelled on that produced, but quickly withdrawn, by his brother in 1672. It granted freedom of worship in England and Scotland to all denominations, including Catholics, and abolished all religious tests for office. Those benefitting most were the Catholics. A second Declaration of Liberty and Conscience, in April 1688, was ordered to be read in all churches. The Archbishop of Canterbury and six fellow bishops protested that the order was illegal, and petitioned the King not to insist on it being read. When their petition was printed and circulated, the King sent them to the Tower, asserting that their petition was a 'standard of rebellion', and prosecuting them for seditious libel.

Hostility to James was now widespread, accompanied by the growing fear of the army, which was now controlled by Catholics, and by concern over the future of Parliament itself. Yet James found himself in an increasingly futile situation, because there were too few Catholics to carry his policies through. The more open and forceful his policy of re-Catholicisation became, the more nervous the Catholics became of their position and the less support they gave him. A group of prominent individuals, both Whig and Tory, once again looked to the heir apparent in accordance with feudal doctrine and the Act of Settlement. This was the King's eldest daughter, Mary, a Protestant, who was married to the Dutch Stadholder and fellow Protestant, William of Nassau, Prince of

37. G. E. Aylmer, *The Struggle for the Constitution*, 211–12.

Orange. They also looked to William himself, who had Stuart ancestry and was highly regarded, and with whom they had long been in contact. One of the group, Edward Russell, was sent to the Netherlands to enquire as to William's intentions. Russell expressed the view to William that, for the sake of England, it was 'now or never'. At the time, James had Scottish regiments serving with the Dutch, and he was receiving money from the French to equip the English fleet. William's own preoccupation, meanwhile, was his involvement in the League of Augsburg, an alliance against the ambitions of Louis XIV of France. It was an alliance that had rallied support as Protestant Europe reacted to the revocation, by Louis, of the Edict of Nantes in 1685. This Edict, which had applied for nearly ninety years, had protected the Protestant minority in France, and by revoking it, Louis was seen as embarking on a new policy of Catholic restoration, of which Charles II had already been a beneficiary. William of Orange had a vested interest, therefore, in bringing England into the alliance, or at least keeping James II from forming a counter-alliance with the French. He replied in May of that same year, 1688, that, if invited by some of the 'most valued' men in the kingdom, he could come to their help in September. An important question was the attitude of the Scots to Mary of Orange as the successor to the throne. In response to enquiry, they set out to be difficult by indicating that they would choose a successor to the Crown of Scotland who was a Protestant, provided it was not the same person as succeeded to the Crown in England. In other words, they wished to dissolve the Anglo-Scottish union. In June, meanwhile, the Queen gave birth to a son, creating alarm at the realisation that, as he would undoubtedly be brought up as a Catholic, this opened up the prospect of a succession of Catholic rulers. Even Tories who had hitherto been loyal now began to turn against the King.

A case of seditious libel against the seven bishops came before the King's Bench in July, amid fierce public demonstrations. In the same month, James dissolved Parliament, so that, at this critical time, there was no Parliament in existence. The court case against the seven bishops raised a number of difficult questions, such as the privileges of the bishops as lords of Parliament, the proper place to present petitions, and the royal prerogative to suspend the requirements of the Test Act, and on these the judges were divided. Addressing the jury, Justice Powell remarked that he could see nothing seditious in what the bishops had done, and 'to make it a libel, it must be false, it must be malicious, and it must tend to sedition. As to the falsehood, I see nothing that is offered by the King's counsel, nor anything as to the malice … I can see no difference, nor know of one in law, between the King's power to dispense with laws ecclesiastical and his power to dispense with any other laws whatsoever. If this be at once allowed of, there will need no Parliament; all the legislature will be in the King'.[38] To great popular jubilation, the bishops were acquitted, and virtually all political factions were now united in a common antipathy to the King.

25.10. The Great Council Reasserts Control

On the same day as the verdict in the bishops' trial in 1688, and probably in the light of it, a formal invitation was dispatched to the King's son-in-law, William of Orange, signed by seven eminent persons, four of them Whigs and three Tories, so that the delegation represented both sides of Parliament. Reading the list, it is reasonable to regard six – the duke of Devonshire, the earl of Shrewsbury, the earl of Danby, Admiral Edward Russell, earl of Orford, and the bishop of London – as representing the Great Council in the House of Lords. A fifth, Lord Lumley, also represented the House of Lords, but probably was not a member of the Council. There were also three members of the House of Commons: Sir Thomas Osborne, Henry Compton, and Henry Sidney. It is a reasonable assumption, therefore, that the initiative was taken by the Great Council, which alone had the authority and sense of duty to take such a step, but that, in order to make the delegation representative of the people, the House of Commons was invited, and agreed, to contribute three of its members, while the House of Lords, other than the Council, provided one other. Between them, they represented both Houses of Parliament and both Parties, and later they were to be remembered as the 'Immortal Seven'. Significantly, the Council took this action without a Parliament, meaning that it acted in its formal capacity as the Great Council.

---

38. G. A. Smith, *A Constitutional and Legal History of England*, 365.

The invitation to William was that he come to England with an army, to save it from Catholic tyranny and to protect Mary's right to the succession. It was this invitation that would ignite the 'Glorious Revolution', but the factors that had precipitated it had been the birth of the King's son and the verdict of the court in the case of the seven bishops. Only the Council, in its capacity as custodian of the Constitution and of the *imperium* of the people, had the authority to undertake such an initiative, and eventually to decide, in the light of the wishes of the people, on the terms and conditions upon which William, or William and Mary, should rule. In alarm, James reinstated the Fellows of Magdalene College, but it was too late, and three months later, on 30 September 1688, when at last he saw his way clear, William issued a formal declaration of acceptance.

26 • THE GLORIOUS REVOLUTION: THE DEFEAT OF CHURCH DOCTRINE (1689)

WILLIAM III OF Nassau, Prince of Orange, Stadholder of the Dutch republic, was the son of William II. The old Frisian kings, of whom the best known to history was Radbod, had disappeared centuries earlier as conquests and dynastic alliances had brought this part of Frisia under the rule of foreign dynasties. The Germans had, by the Middle Ages, drawn a distinction between the *Hochland* and the *Niederland*, the upland country of central and southern Germany, and the coastal plain between it and the North Sea. This geographical distinction had long marked, also, a dialect difference between *Hochdeutsch* and *Niederdeutsch*, that is, High- and Low-German, of which the latter included Frisian, the dialect most closely related to English. It was probably by way of Friesland that the Jutes had arrived to found the first independent Germanic kingdom in Britain.[1]

The English were now much better acquainted, through trade and politics, with Holland, the lower-lying political centre of the region, south of the Zuider Zee, and with Flanders, by now known as the Spanish Netherlands, which lay still further south, beyond the Rhine delta. The region outside Spanish control had been entrusted by its successive German-speaking rulers to a *statthalter*, or 'place-holder', being the German word for a lieutenant-governor. The Dutch equivalent was *stadhouder*, rendered in English as a 'stadholder'. The Netherlands as a whole had been inherited by the Spanish branch of the Habsburg family and treated as part of the Spanish Empire, until the Protestant northern part had been freed under the leadership of William the Silent, the Stadholder at the time. In spite of the newfound independence of the Netherlands, William's status had remained that of Stadholder, although he was king of the Dutch in all but name. Holland was already dominated by its prosperous commercial class, which was too jealous of

---

1. To the Austrian Habsburgs, this low-lying region around the lower Rhine was part of the *Niederland*, Dutch *Nederland*, whose English form was 'Netherland', or 'Low Country'.

its independence to risk establishing a feudal type of monarchy, such as had become usual across most of Europe. William's ancestry, and now that of his great-grandson, William III, could be traced back to the Counts of Nassau, a German principality.[2] One branch of the family had come into the Dutch estates through marriage and imperial rewards for service. The Orange inheritance was quite separate. It related to the estate of Orange, in the Rhone valley, and had been a gift from a relative, although William I would have inherited it from him in any case.

Meanwhile, William III had some claim to the English throne in his own right, because his mother was Mary, the elder daughter of Charles I. In addition to being the grandson of Charles, he was married to Mary, the elder daughter of James II, who was second in line to the English throne after the infant son of James II. Both William and Mary were of interest to the Great Council and its supporters plotting against James: Mary, because of the relative strength of her claim to the succession, and William, because he had access to an army and other resources with which to overthrow the King, and because it was realised that he would probably be more effective than Mary as the *de facto* ruler. Apart from James's determination to return England to Catholicism, his deposition by the Glorious Revolution to which it gave rise can only be understood in the context of the wider European situation. Louis XIV of France had invested a great deal in the Catholic cause in England, and it is remarkable that he did not come to the assistance of his cousin, James, in order to forestall the Dutch involvement, but Louis was preoccupied at this moment with preparations for war against the German Empire, the objective of which was an extension of his influence eastward into Germany by way of the Palatinate. He was also giving close attention to a disputed succession to the bishopric of Cologne. Hardly less important was the fact that the last Habsburg king of Spain was now an invalid and almost an imbecile, with no direct heirs, and Louis held high hopes of appropriating parts of the Spanish Empire as soon as opportunity allowed. Louis could not afford another diversion, particularly if it led to an Anglo-Dutch alliance against him, whereas, by leaving William to his preparations, there was a good chance that Holland and England would neutralise each other in a mutual conflict. In any case, England was fairly

---

2. The title went back to Walram I, Count of Nassau, who died in 1198. His grandfather, Dudo, Count of Laurenburg, is the earliest of the family recorded.

solidly Protestant, and a French army sent to the aid of James II might well be caught up in a difficult campaign.

Meanwhile, William had his owns preoccupations. In particular, he was concerned by the ambitions of France, which included preparations for an invasion of the Netherlands, and he was busy putting together an alliance to meet them, known as the League of Augsburg. By becoming King of England, as he must have hoped, he would be able to add England to the alliance, otherwise, England might be led by James II into joining France against the League. This tense stand-off was suddenly eased in September, when Louis, convinced that the Dutch and English were about to neutralise each other, made a disastrous decision to move his main forces away from the frontier with the Spanish Netherlands, directing them instead into an offensive in the middle Rhineland. This left William free to go with an army to England to overthrow James, and on September 29 he sent a declaration to the Great Council, in its capacity as the House of Lords, accepting its offer and laying out his terms for a 'free and lawful Parliament'.

James was self-confident, and William could not be certain of his reception in England, so the latter made his preparations carefully, aided by English advice, and set sail with a large army. The Royal Navy posed a serious threat, but, due either to intrigue or negligence, it remained caught in the Thames estuary by an east wind, which also took William's invasion fleet to Tor Bay, in Devon. After a delay, due to bad weather, his landing at Brixham in November of the same year, 1688, sparked uprisings in various parts of England in his support. The King's army, sent to defeat him, disintegrated, particularly when its commander, Churchill, deserted to join William. Even the King's younger daughter, Princess Anne, abandoned her father and fled to York. The Queen and the baby, Prince James, were sent to France early in December, and the King, almost bereft of friends, with even the Catholic minority unwilling to help, because of its fear of reprisals, followed them a day later. In leaving, he endeavoured to sow as much confusion as possible by burning the writs for the new Parliament, issuing an order dissolving the army, and, in a fit of pique that characterised the man, dropping the Great Seal of England into the Thames. Caught at Sheerness, he was brought back to London. Meanwhile, on the day following the King's departure, the House of Lords asserted itself in its capacity as the Great Council by assuming the executive functions of state and acting as a provisional government. The Great Council, even in its enforced guise as the House of Lords, had always remained a government-in-waiting, in case normal constitutional government should fail, and the King's abandonment of his office, his disposal of the Great Seal, the invitation to William, and William's ensuing welcome by the people and senior officers of state had amounted to both an abdication and a deposition of the current ruler. A week later, William entered London, unopposed, and James succeeded at last in escaping to France, never to return. James may have feared his father's fate on the execution block, but there was little risk of that, and his flight to France, in which the Great Council and William probably connived, cleared the way for the election of a new King. Banishment had been the age-old solution in Scandinavian society for dealing with failed kings, and the departure of James II was in keeping with this tradition. Meanwhile, Louis allowed James, with a few supporters, to establish an ineffectual court-in-exile near Paris.

Following the arrival of William in London, the Great Council invited him, on 12 December, to assume office as a provisional government, in his capacity as Prince of Orange, so that his status would be that of a royal person. It also advised him to summon an Assembly of all who had served as members of the House of Commons in the Parliaments of Charles II, together with the Lord Mayor, aldermen and fifty councillors of the City of London. Clearly, the Council considered that James had crammed his Parliaments with the Court Party, whose loyalty to his beliefs rendered them unrepresentative of the people. Effectively, William had now been appointed Regent by the Council, and the subsequent gathering was as near as practicable (and as had been used several times in the past) to being a full assembly of the people. The Assembly met with William and the Lords on 26 December 1688, and, on its advice, William then summoned a new Parliament, which was opened on 22 January 1689. Because of an initial uncertainty whether a Parliament that had not been summoned by a reigning monarch had the full constitutional authority of a Parliament, it was referred to as a 'Convention' of the Estates of the realm, like that of 1660.[3] Constitutionally, as we have already seen, the Council had the authority to summon a Parliament at its own discretion.

Nobody seems to have been certain of William's intentions at this stage, and hopes and expectations were varied. One faction among the Whigs proposed that William should be made King, simply on the basis of a contract with Parliament, but this received no support from other groups who were steeped in feudal doctrine. The High-Church element still regarded James as King, and saw William and Mary as regents, until James's return could be negotiated on satisfactory terms, or until James's infant son, also James, was old enough. Another faction, led by the Earl of Danby and accepted by the moderate Tories, considered that Mary was already the Queen, because James had vacated the throne and also removed his son from the country, leaving Mary as his automatic successor. William should therefore be made Prince Consort. This argument was seen as hardly tenable, unless viewed in the light of a story, circulating at the time, and believed by many Whigs, that the infant James had not been born to the Queen at all, but had been smuggled into the palace in a warming-pan. According to this view, James had left no heir, although Danby and his group – which may or may not have represented the view of the Council – seem not to have taken the rumour seriously. Neither proposal was acceptable to William, who insisted on being at least co-equal with his wife, and even threatened, in desperation, to wash his hands of the whole business and go home again. Time was not on his side, because, as organiser of the League of Augsburg, which was about to go to war against France, he was urgently needed elsewhere.

Finally, a solution proposed by the moderate Whig faction was adopted, that the Prince and Princess of Orange, William and Mary, be declared King and Queen jointly and in their own right, and that the throne be offered to them by a Parliament, except that the administration should be the responsibility of William alone. It was further agreed that their election by a Parliament be conditional upon their acceptance of certain conditions. This was a return to the Whig view (and, of course, a requirement in common law), that relations between monarch and subjects were, and should be, contractual. Even the custom of joint rule by two monarchs was well established in English tradition, although

---

3. As we now know, the Great Council was fully entitled to summon a Parliament, but it clearly had forgotten what all its powers were.

it had not been used for centuries. A resolution was therefore passed that James II, 'having endeavoured to subvert the constitution of the kingdom by breaking the original contract between King and people, and having, by the advice of Jesuits and other wicked persons, violated the fundamental laws and withdrawn himself out of the kingdom, has abdicated the government and the throne is hereby vacant'. Here was a statement that asserted, not only the existence of the tacit 'regal contract' between King and people, but also the existence of 'the fundamental laws', referred to in these pages as the *mos maiorum*. The Lords objected to the use of the word 'abdicated' and to the declaration of the 'vacancy' of the throne, but eventually an agreement was reached. It was a clear restoration of Indo-European common law, but it evaded the proper conclusion that James had effectively been deposed, because he had 'violated the fundamental laws' and so 'broken the contract'. The argument that the throne was vacant because he had vacated it was superfluous, and evidently was included to satisfy those who still adhered to the feudal view of kingship. James's son was simply ignored, even though a minority in the country was still convinced that the infant Prince James was the only legitimate heir.

Some constitutional historians have regarded the events of 1688 as a revolution, not a legal succession,[4] on the grounds that there was no Parliament, because James had dissolved it, and the assembly that had hurriedly been summoned by the Prince of Orange upon his arrival, were the Peers and such members of the former Parliaments of Charles II as happened to be in London, together with the aldermen of London, and these did not constitute a lawful Parliament. However, by departing for France at short notice and dropping the Great Seal in the Thames, in an apparent rejection of his office, James had clearly signalled his abdication, and the Great Council had, by its constitutional right, which Edward III could not remove from it, deemed from the preceding events, quite reasonably, that the people rejected James as King. Moreover, on the basis of such evidence of the popular will as it could reasonably divine, the Council had offered the Crown to the Prince of Orange, as was its right, and this had been accepted. The Council had then followed such popular advice as it deemed to represent the will of the people by advising William

---

4. F. W. Maitland, *The Constitutional History of England*, 283–8.

to summon a 'convention' of the Estates (probably because this could be done fairly quickly, and thus limit the period of legal uncertainty, and because the bestowal of the Crown required the approval of all three Estates). The Convention concluded that James II had broken the original contract between himself and the people, and, having violated the 'fundamental laws' (that is, the law of the Constitution), he had withdrawn himself from the kingdom and thereby abdicated – on 11 December 1688, 'according to established legal reckoning' – when he had dropped the Great Seal into the Thames. On these grounds, William and Mary had been proclaimed King and Queen, upon which the Convention had declared itself to be the Parliament, passing important Acts, before it was dissolved early in 1690. A new Parliament, duly summoned by writs of William and Mary, then proceeded by statute to confirm their election as King and Queen, to rule jointly, and to confirm that the decisions of the Convention were true laws and statutes of the realm. Between James's abdication and the day, two months later, that William and Mary accepted the Crown, the Great Council clearly acted as a self-appointed regency council.

26.1. The Great Council and the House of Orange

At a 'Parliamentary Convention', undoubtedly summoned by the Great Council in its capacity as a Regency Council, held on 12 February 1689, after some hesitation by the House of Lords – that is, the Great Council as such – it was agreed that William and Mary be proclaimed King and Queen, with William solely responsible for the administration. They were made to understand that they would hold the Crown, not by right of inheritance, but by virtue of an Act of Parliament. The conditions to which they had agreed in turn were now presented to them as a Declaration of Rights, which they formally accepted, following which, they were proclaimed as joint Sovereigns on 13 February 1689. The Declaration listed most of the arbitrary acts of which the Stuarts had been guilty and declared them to be contrary to the laws of England. In order to remove any doubts, and following the precedent of 1660, the Parliamentary Convention thereupon passed its first statute on February 22, affirming that it was 'the Parliament of England', and always had been. In the same Act, it was proclaimed that 'their said Majesties at the request and by the advice of the Lords and Commons did accept the Crown and royal dignity of King and Queen of England, France and Ireland and the dominions and territories thereunto belonging'. The Act also settled the Crown on their heirs, and if there were none, the rights of succession were to pass to Mary's Protestant sister, the Princess Anne of Denmark, wife of Prince George of Denmark, and thence to Anne's children.

On 11 April 1689, King William III and Queen Mary II were crowned as joint sovereigns by the Bishop of London, on behalf of the Council, the Archbishop of Canterbury having declined to do so. By mutual agreement with the Scottish Parliament, they became King and Queen of Scotland at the same time, hence the fudging reference to the Kingdom of Great Britain in the Coronation Oath. Conveniently, under the numbering system of the Scottish succession, they happened to be also King William III and Queen Mary II of Scotland. William's acceptance of the English and Scottish crowns did not, however, affect his position and prior interest as Prince William III, Stadholder of the Netherlands.

Having thus restored the Constitution to working order, it seems that the Council, on the grounds of 'established practice', reverted to the position forced upon it by Edward III, that is, fulfilling its more limited duties as best it could, from inside Parliament, sitting as a House of Lords. The obvious question, in the light of the Council's reassertion of its constitutional authority, is why, once it had completed its task of securing a new King, it returned to the impassive and incongruous condition in the House of Lords to which Edward III had consigned it three centuries earlier. There may be several explanations: the confusion of its members over the doctrine of the divine right of kings; its awareness that, probably since the Norman invasion, its members no longer owed their position to the free men of their respective shires: only to their appointment by the King; and now, increasingly, to the growing assertiveness and jealousy of the House of Commons, whose respect for the law of the Constitution had steadily declined, and which undoubtedly saw the role of the Great Council as now belonging more appropriately to itself, except when Parliament fell victim to constitutional chaos, as had just been the case.

What is equally clear, however, is the reverence in which the Council was still held in times of crisis.

Finding Whitehall scarcely a tranquil place to reside, and perhaps too close to the suffocating presence of Parliament, William and Mary moved to the more rural setting of Kensington, nearly three miles further west, where they bought Nottingham House from the Earl of Nottingham in 1689, re-naming it Kensington Palace. William inherited a fiscal arrangement whereby the King was granted a revenue for life, which had given his predecessors a degree of independence, but a new rule of procedure was now imposed which made grants for no more than four years. When William objected, Parliament reacted obstinately by making supplies dependent on an annual grant. Such difficulties were frustrating and humiliating to William, but he had already invested so much precious time and effort in the enterprise, and he had so little of the former to spare, that he had little choice but to accept what Parliament was willing to concede. Another provocation in his eyes arose from the requirement, in the Bill of Rights, that Parliaments 'ought to be held frequently', bearing in mind the failure of the Triennial Act of 1664. The need for Parliaments was now governed by the annual requirement for legislation controlling the army to be renewed, but William was reluctant to give way over what he considered to be his prerogative to decide the frequency and duration of Parliaments. Another consequence of the Bill of Rights was that the size of the House of Commons could no longer be determined by the King alone, and in response to the need for better representation, the number of its elected members grew from 467 in 1603 to 558 in 1707.

So unsure were the constitutional lawyers of the time as to the legality of the Convention Parliament, because it had been summoned by 'the Lords', instead of by a reigning King, that the second Parliament of William and Mary, summoned in 1690, and the first to be regarded as regular, passed an Act of Recognition. This further ensured the legality of the legislation that had been passed by the Convention Parliament.

It has been said by Jennings[5] that: 'It was settled in 1689 that Parliament had supreme power and could control every aspect of national life'. To others, the Glorious Revolution established the basis of the

---

5. I. Jennings, *The Law and the Constitution* (Bickley, 1943), 84.

modern constitution. It would be more accurate to say that it resolved, finally, the great ideological struggle between the Church and common law perceptions of kingship. With the departure of James II had gone the last serious attempt to assert the idea of divinely appointed rulers. In its place was finally restored the ancient principle of the answerability of the King to his people. Even so, the separation of the two ideas was to take time, and some confusion has remained to the present day. The view expressed by Jennings is widely accepted, but it is constitutionally correct only with the *caveat* that a Parliament is the assembled people, not an assembly of delegates, who may, or may not, be representative, particularly as representativeness is liable to decline over time. This distinction was certainly not fully accepted in 1689.

The formal rejection of the feudal doctrine of kingship, implicit in the outcome of the Civil War and the terms of accession of William and Mary, meant that the notion that all land was vested in the King, not by the people on their behalf, but as the appointee of God, free to dispose of as he would, was no longer tenable. By default, all land had now reverted to its status in common law as folkland, held in communal ownership by the nation, but vested in the King as trustee, who could only dispose of it by popular consent. According to both constitutional doctrines, the King could only grant the use of it by lease, whether freehold lease or some other, less secure form of lease. As was noted earlier, all titles to land were titles to its use, not to the land itself. The real difference between the two ideologies lay in the fact that, under common law, the Crown could grant the use of land only with the consent of the people, whereas, according to feudal doctrine, the King could grant it (and repossess it) at his sole discretion, because nobody was in a position to dispute that God willed otherwise.

The events of 1689 marked not only the watershed between the dominance of feudal doctrine and the (at least partial) rule of common law, as it was still understood; they also marked a decisive shift in the balance of political power. During the Middle Ages the loose cannon in the English system of government had been the Crown; from now onwards, the loose cannon would be the House of Commons.

26.1.1. The Birth of Enabling Legislation to Limit the Prerogative

The Glorious Revolution of 1688 differed from that of 1640, in that the earlier revolt had been carried out by a Puritan minority who had then used it as a bold, radical and unpopular experiment, whereas that of 1688 had the support of the great majority and envisaged little real change, beyond the establishment, once and for all, of the supremacy of Parliament and the permanent incorporation of the effects of the Reformation. Because of the failure of the Stuarts to exercise the royal prerogative in accordance with what was acceptable to Parliament, the Crown was now severely limited by statute, removing flexibility and responsiveness from the process of government. In order to solve the problem which this created, Parliament found it necessary to approve comprehensive and cumbersome statutes, known as enabling legislation, designed to cope with every foreseeable situation, but at least removing the element of arbitrariness from the rule of law. Instead of the Crown responding to unusual situations by the quick drafting and implementation of ordinances, subject to possible later parliamentary amendment or even rejection, Parliament found that it could, and had to, anticipate situations through general statutes which prescribed the circumstances and extent to which the Crown might exercise its prerogative. A system of administration was thus created in which the Crown exercised its prerogative, apart from limited exceptions, only within the confines prescribed by statute. It is usual to say that these enabling statutes empowered the King to do such and such, but it was, and is, unnecessary to empower the King; rather, such statutes defined the conditions under which the King could and should exercise his prerogative. The monarchy did not again try to exploit its prerogative outside these new, statutory limits; nonetheless, it was to remain at the centre of affairs throughout the eighteenth century.

This clumsy and cumbersome system might have been avoided, together with the system of judicial intervention to which it would eventually give rise, had the Great Council resumed its proper responsibilities, together with the constitutional basis of its composition and the restoration of its required competence. The problem was that the Parties in the Commons had tasted power and were determined to retain it, entrenching a system of popular oligarchy.

These two great upheavals of the seventeenth century tend to be viewed as milestones in the struggle for liberty, but in reality the benefits accrued only to the propertied classes. As one anguished song of the time declared, 'Laws grind the poor and rich men make the law'. The absolute property rights of the landowners, founded in statute law, overrode the common law rights of the English peasantry, driving it off the land and into wage labour as the steady process of land enclosure continued, albeit at a quieter pace after the middle of the century.[6] Like the Restoration of 1660, the Settlement of 1689 restored central and local government to the Peers and the gentry, and to the ruling oligarchies in the towns.

26.1.2. The Coronation Oath

The old form of the Coronation Oath had required the King to uphold and keep the laws and customs of the people and to defend *leges quas vulgus elegerit*, 'the laws which the people shall choose'. This had been sworn by Edward II, and in similar terms by Henry VII. His successor, Henry VIII, had apparently insisted upon significant changes, and these are shown in his promise, as follows: to 'grant and hold the laws and approved customs of the realm lawful and not prejudicial to his crown or imperial duty, and to his power keep them and affirm them which the nobles and people have made and chosen with his consent'. This had marked a shift to the feudal view that the King enjoyed 'an indefeasible royal power which laws cannot restrain; the King will not bind himself to maintain laws prejudicial to his crown'.[7] It seems that this departure must have been dictated by Henry, with no evidence that the terms of his rule were disputed, and this would appear to have marked the high point of feudal intrusion into the conditions of monarchy, except that Henry proved to be more circumspect in practice than this high-handed attitude might have suggested.

A return to a more traditional basis for the regal contract was affected by Henry's successor, Edward VI, who swore to make new laws 'by consent of the people as had been accustomed'. The more usual form after Henry VIII, however, which seems to have been followed by Elizabeth I, James I, Charles I, Charles II and James II, involved a

---

6. C. Hill, *Liberty Against the Law*. Also, J. Clapham, *A Concise Economic History of Britain*, 194–200.

7. F. W. Maitland, *The Constitutional History of England*, 286–8.

promise by the new Sovereign to 'confirm to the people of England the laws and customs to them granted by the Kings of England, his lawful and religious predecessors: and namely the laws, customs and franchises granted to the clergy by the glorious King St Edward, his predecessor … and agreeing to the prerogative of the Kings thereof, and the ancient customs of the realm'. This referred only to existing laws, making no reference to the right of the people to choose their future laws. Indeed, the ancient formula, *leges quas vulgus elegerit*, had become the subject of a bitter controversy. The word *elegerit* could not refer to the future, it was claimed, because it was the task of the King to uphold the old laws which the people had chosen, not those which the people would choose. It was also pointed out that the oath effectively precluded the King from rejecting a Bill that had been passed by both Houses, so that the King had no part in the legislative process. Neither argument accorded with past experience, but in spite of this, *leges quas vulgus elegerit* was surely unacceptable because, it was argued, this meant that there were to be no laws except those chosen by the people. It was another example of the conflict of the two ideologies.

The accession of William and Mary marked a new self-confidence on the part of the House of Commons and a new start in the royal relationship. Parliament was at last in control, and the new dynasty was one that had been chosen by it and the English people, not imposed by a foreign conqueror and his descendants. The new Coronation Oath Act of 1689 tried to break with the past, objecting with suspicion that the oaths administered on previous occasions 'hath heretofore been framed in doubtful words and expressions, with relation to ancient laws and constitutions at this time unknown'. After all, perhaps there was a danger that the King might claim a right that stemmed from some obscure custom or law that Parliament had overlooked. The references in earlier coronation oaths to the legitimacy inherited from King Edward the Confessor and to ancient customs were accordingly jettisoned. Also dropped was any reference to the royal prerogative, and the kingdoms of England and Scotland were lumped together for the sake of convenience. The new oath simply required the future King and Queen to 'solemnly promise and swear to govern the people of this Kingdom of Great Britain and the dominions thereunto belonging according to the statutes in Parliament agreed on, and the respective laws and customs of the same'.

From this it can be seen that the Coronation Oath had passed, broadly speaking, through three phases.

1. The earliest, to our knowledge, had required the King to hold and keep the laws and customs of the people and to affirm *leges quas vulgus elegerit*, the laws which the people shall choose (Edward II), or, to make laws by consent of the people of the realm (Edward VI). It was the one most in keeping with the requirements of common law.

2. Under the weight of feudal doctrine, a compromise formula had then appeared which required the Sovereign merely to hold and keep the laws and customs of the people (Elizabeth I, Charles I). There was no longer a commitment in respect of future laws which would inhibit the right to rule.

3. Finally, the King was required to govern in accordance with the laws and customs of the people and the statutes of Parliament. In other words, future laws were now a matter for Parliament, rather than the people. While undoubtedly intended to be more specific, this change replaced the wishes of the people with those of Parliament, in other words, those of the ruling Party. It pointed to the triumph of the new political machine over democracy.

The reference in the oath to 'the Kingdom of Great Britain' was plainly a fudge. That no such kingdom existed can be seen in the Bill of Rights, which defined the position of the Crown generally and made no mention of Scotland. It seems to have been taken for granted that James II had abdicated the throne of Scotland at the same time as he fled from England, and that Scotland's affairs were still its own. Scotland was still very much under the control of the Presbyterians, who had no wish to have the Stuarts back, and in March 1689, a Scottish Convention Parliament ordered the proclamation of William and Mary as the joint sovereigns of Scotland. The reference to the Kingdom of Great Britain seems to have been a clumsy device to enable them to rule both England and Scotland, but it implied the unification of the two kingdoms, which no constitutional act had brought about. Nor had there been any intention of creating a union. This is quite clear from the reference later in the Oath to 'the Kingdoms of England and Ireland, the dominion of Wales, and the town of Berwick-on-Tweed, and the territories thereto belonging'. This part of the Oath referred to clerical matters, of course, hence the absence of any reference to Scotland, which lay outside the jurisdiction of the Church of England. Nevertheless, the continued existence of the kingdom of England implied that the separate kingdom of Scotland also still existed.

A further clumsiness appears in the exclusion of the Kingdom of Ireland from the rule of William and Mary, who took the Oath only as the rulers of 'Great Britain'. A possible explanation lies in the fact that the deposed and outcast James II had landed in Ireland with some followers a few weeks earlier, and been received in Dublin in his capacity as King with great enthusiasm. The Duke of Tyrconnel had raised a rebellion across Ireland in support of James, but the Protestants of Ulster had refused to accept him, declaring their allegiance to William and Mary. This forced James to lay siege to Londonderry. William and Mary regarded themselves as the rightful rulers of Ireland, and asserted their authority there in the following year.

Meanwhile, the Coronation Oath also required William and Mary, to the utmost of their power, to maintain 'the Protestant reformed religion established by law'. William was a Calvinist, closer to the Presbyterians than to the High-Church Anglicans, but he was a tolerant and practical man for whom principles of state counted for more than those of religion. For his first Ministry, William appointed both Tories and Whigs in an attempt to overcome the factionalism in English politics. In this he had little success, because the Whigs bitterly resented the Tories, associated as they unreasonably were with the hated Stuarts. It was an obligation of the King under common law to observe and protect the religion of the people, and for this to be possible there had to be an accepted state religion. The best that the King could do in an age that was riven by religious dispute was to tolerate the beliefs of the minority, so long as they did not conflict with the exercise of the accepted religion of the nation.

The Toleration Act, which followed shortly after the coronation, did not go this far, but it was a recognition that different religious faiths could co-exist by exempting, from the penalties imposed for not attending services of the Church of England, those dissenters who had taken the prescribed oaths of supremacy and allegiance. The High-Church element in the Church of England was willing to concede only a certain amount to the Puritans and, refusing to accept that anybody else could be King as long as James and his son remained alive, refused to take the oath of allegiance to William and Mary. Consequently, the Church was destined never again to embrace the entire Protestant community. The Toleration Act left the Catholics, Unitarians, Quakers and non-Christians without political and civic rights, although the penal laws against the Catholics were no longer enforced. The Unitarian Protestants were those who believed in a single God, and were thus seen as heretics, as opposed to the Trinitarian Protestants, who accepted the long-established view that God was three in one (the Father, the Son, and the Holy Ghost). A similar tolerance of minority beliefs was spreading elsewhere in Europe at this time, except in France, where Louis XIV was enforcing a greater religious uniformity. Indeed, throughout all the deliberations and processes that William's acceptance of the English crown had involved him in, it was France that remained his prior concern.

26.1.3. The Bill of Rights (1689)
Statutory effect was not given to the Declaration of Rights until well after the coronation, in a Bill whose terms had been settled well beforehand and which also settled the future succession to the Crown in accordance with feudal doctrine. Although the Bill of Rights was passed into law in December 1689, it has continued to be known as the 'Bill' of Rights. It stated that the Lords and Commons now assembled, in vindication and assertion of their ancient rights and liberties, declare that:

1. It is illegal to pretend to suspend laws or to execute them by royal authority without the consent of Parliament;
2. It is illegal to pretend to dispense with laws or to execute laws by royal authority;
3. The Commission that had established the late Court of Commissioners for Ecclesiastical Causes and all other commissions and courts of a like nature are illegal and pernicious;

4. It is illegal to levy money for, or to the use of, the Crown by pretence of Prerogative for longer, or for any other purpose, than has been consented to by Parliament;

5. It is the right of subjects to petition the King, and all commitments and prosecutions for such petitioning are illegal;

6. It is contrary to law to raise or keep a standing army within the kingdom in time of peace without the consent of Parliament;

7. Subjects who are Protestants may have arms for their defence suitable to their conditions and as allowed by law;

8. The election of members of Parliament ought to be free;

9. Freedom of speech and debates or proceedings in Parliament ought not to be impeached or questioned in any court or place outside Parliament;

10. Excessive bail ought not to be required, nor fines imposed, nor cruel and unusual punishments inflicted;

11. Jurors should be duly empanelled and returned, and in the case of trials for high treason the jurors ought to be freeholders;

12. All grants and promises of fines and forfeitures of particular persons before the conviction of offenders are illegal and void;

13. Parliaments should be held frequently, in order to redress all grievances and to amend, strengthen and preserve the laws.

After declaring that King James II had abdicated, the Bill went on to proclaim William and Mary, Prince and Princess of Orange, to be the 'King and Queen of England, France and Ireland and the dominions thereto belonging', and that, during their joint lives, the sole and full exercise of the royal power should vest in William, in the names of himself and Mary. This meant in effect that, when William was overseas, Mary would rule on his behalf. The Bill stated that the Crown had been accepted by their Majesties 'according to the resolution and desire of the said Lords and Commons contained in the said Declaration'. The significance of this was that they did not rule according to feudal doctrine, that is, by inalienable right, but in accordance with the will of the people, as expressed in Parliament; in other words, in accordance with customary law. The Bill observed also that: 'it hath been found by experience that it is inconsistent with the safety and welfare of this Protestant Kingdom to be governed by a Popish Prince or by any King or Queen marrying a Papist'. In regard to the succession, therefore, the Bill stated that:

1. The Crown should pass to the legitimate offspring of Mary, in default of which it should pass to the Princess Anne of Denmark or her offspring, in default of which again, to the offspring of William;

2. Those required to take oaths of allegiance should swear to reject the doctrine that rulers who had been excommunicated by the Pope could be deposed or murdered by their subjects, and that no foreign power or person should exercise any authority within the realm;

3. No person might succeed to the Crown who supported or held communion with the Church of Rome, or who married a Papist, and in any such case the people were absolved of their allegiance;

4. The succession should go only to a Protestant;

5. Each successor to the Crown should, at the time of taking the Coronation Oath, repeat a prescribed declaration refuting certain Catholic beliefs.

Another significant innovation was that the King was forbidden to raise or maintain a standing army in time of peace without the consent of Parliament. This was due to the practice of Charles II and James II of maintaining a standing army in such a manner as to pose a threat to it. Twice in the same century, the King had used military force in confrontations with Parliament, and, in order to ensure that Parliament could not again be intimidated, the Bill of Rights, 1689, declared that 'the raising or keeping of a standing army within the Kingdom in time of peace, unless it be with consent of Parliament, is against the law', while the Mutiny Act of the same year, which provided for pay and discipline, permitted the raising of an army and the exercise of martial law for a period of six months, until 10 November 1689, 'and no longer'. The Act also appropriated the royal prerogative to impose and maintain discipline, grant commissions to senior officers of the rank of colonel and above, call courts-martial, and punish officers and men in the event of mutiny or desertion. The choice of November 10 allowed time for the next Parliament to renew or modify the Mutiny Act. In the event, the import of the Act was renewed, and from that time onwards it was destined to be renewed, usually on an annual basis, in keeping with the provision in the Bill of Rights, thus enabling the army to remain in being. The Bill of Rights gave rise to the anomaly, therefore, that whereby the Crown was to retain a permanent Royal Navy and, in due course, to acquire a permanent Royal Air Force, the King's army existed only from year to year.

English kingship has always been subject to both noble lineage and suitability, even if the latter has usually been subordinated to the principle of automatic succession, but this was the first occasion on which religious adherence was formally specified by statute as being a factor in determining suitability. It was an inevitable consequence of the split in the Christian Church, brought about by the Reformation, because, under both doctrines – feudal and Aryan – kingship and religion were inseparable.

The advent of the House of Orange had cultural, as well as political and religious consequences. One effect was the opening of a window to new Continental influences. Great country houses were now built, for example, in a lavish Baroque style, with the Dutch connection celebrated in the construction of ornamental canals and other water features. There were some who still supported King James, for which reason they were known as 'Jacobites', after the Latin form of his name, *Jacobus*, and there were several Jacobite rebellions. The disaffected element were those who believed that James's right to the Crown was immutable. Those who openly rebelled were supported by the Scottish Highlanders, hostile powers (notably France), and various opportunists. James had already returned to secure most of Ireland in March 1689, and had the support of an Irish Catholic army and a French force in the siege of Protestant Londonderry, which was relieved after three months. Another Jacobite rising occurred in the Scottish Highlands, but this fizzled out in July, after the indecisive Battle of Killicrankie.

Meanwhile, William's Grand Alliance of those who had joined the League of Augsburg at last began to move into action with the opening of a war, in which England was now involved, from May 1689 onwards. Under the Stuarts, England had broadly been in alliance with France, the most formidable power in Western Europe, but under William, English policy was reversed by the throwing of its support behind France's enemies. It marked the beginning of a foreign policy based on opposition to any Continental state that was, or threatened to become, excessively powerful, and one criterion of this policy was the threat to which the Continental power exposed the Low Countries. The immediate cause of the War of the League of Augsburg was the French invasion and devastation of the Palatinate and its military successes along the Rhine, but the revocation in France of the Edict of Nantes, removing all protection from that country's Protestants, helped to galvanize other states. Sweden, Saxony, Bavaria and Spain, as well as the Netherlands and England, were brought into the alliance against France, yet, impressive as the alliance appeared to be, it performed poorly in practice. Although William had regarded England's support as an asset in the struggle, it also proved a liability, with James's Irish army and a French expeditionary force posing a threat in its rear. In 1690, leaving the conflict in Europe, William took an army across to Ireland and defeated James in the Battle of the Boyne, forcing James to flee back to France. This left the French and Irish holding out in Limerick, until the rebellion was finally brought to an end in the following year by the Treaty of Limerick, whose terms were not honoured by the mainly Protestant Irish Parliament. In Scotland, meanwhile, clan enmities and deception of the King by a senior officer, Sir John Dalrymple of Stair, who was determined to make an example of at least one of the clans, resulted in the unjustified Massacre of Glencoe, an incident that was exploited by William's enemies.

The main conflict in the Coalition's war against the French was now centred in the Netherlands, where William suffered a series of defeats, but survived to achieve some degree of success in 1695. At sea, the English and Dutch fleets put up a lacklustre performance until 1692, when the most critical point in the war from England's point of view, a threatened French invasion, was brought to nothing by the defeat and destruction of the French fleet off Cap del la Hogue.

26.1.4. Parliament is Treated as a Permanent Institution

A new version of the Triennial Bill was enacted in 1694, known as the Meeting of Parliament Act, which required a new Parliament to be summoned every three years, the original Act of 1641 having been repealed in 1664. The title is itself not without significance, because, rather than being, for example, the Summoning of Parliaments Act, the words used implied that 'Parliament' was a permanent institution that existed even during the three years between the dissolution of one and the summoning of another. It reflected a general attitude among Members of Parliaments that the institution had now achieved a dominant position in the Constitution, and its periodic, even fitful, existence was incompatible with its new, central importance in day-to-day government. This was a misapprehension, because Parliaments were, and always had been, the ultimate decision-makers, but this seems no longer to have satisfied those sitting in the House of Commons, who now saw themselves almost as the day-to-day decision-makers. Meanwhile, censorship of the press was discontinued. Over the three centuries that have since elapsed, the notion of a permanent Parliament, periodically renewed, has gained a wide but erroneous acceptance. Parliament existed in common law only when summoned into existence, which it must be, not less than once a year, until its business was done. Only the Upper House was permanent, and that was because it was a separate institution altogether.

At the end of 1694 Queen Mary died, leaving William to reign alone. In contrast to Mary, who had been greatly liked, William was never a popular King. He remained a Dutchman at heart, England being little more to him than a source of men and money for the war. He had no time for the factionalism of English politics and the vindictiveness and avarice of the Whigs, and little time for religious intolerance. While he managed to devote a great deal of time to the problems of England and of the British Isles, much of his reign was absorbed in trying to ensure the survival of his own country in its dogged war with the French.

26.1.5. Parliament on the Death of a King

The first triennial Parliament, William's third, met in the latter part of 1695, with the Whigs in control. Feudal doctrine, like common law, dictated the automatic dissolution of Parliament on the death of the King, because the King's writs expired with him. Without the King, therefore, Parliaments no longer served a purpose, unless they were reconvened by the Great Council, and the Council had scarcely functioned for almost three hundred years. In order to avoid a hiatus on the death of a Sovereign, however, in view of the possibility that the kingdom might be under threat at the time, an Act was passed in 1696 that required an existing Parliament to continue to meet and sit for six months after the King's death, unless prorogued and dissolved beforehand. This was pointless, however, because, without the King, no executive action could be proposed or carried out. In any case, the problem was largely solved by the prevailing rule of primogeniture and the Act of Settlement, which ensured the succession, but not without a hiatus, because the custom of instant succession had no constitutional basis. Temple had recommended in 1679 that, in the interest of continuity, the Privy Council should remain in office for six months after the King's death. The function of the Privy Council was to advise the King, and to implement his instructions where they fell within the royal prerogative, but the King's writ had no effect after his death.

To the extent that the House of Lords was the Great Council, it was unaffected by the death of the King, or, indeed, by any statutes of Parliament. This is just as well, because, upon the death of the King, and having a duty to ensure the continuity of government, it is usual for the Council to establish a regency, until such time as the successor is crowned. The Council is also entitled to summon a Parliament to deal with such urgent business as requires attention. In exceptional circumstances, therefore, such as a time of war, members of the dissolved Parliament might immediately be recalled by the Council to form a new Parliament. In this way, vital continuity is preserved.

The position of the King's (or Privy) Council on the death of the King is less clear. As a council appointed by the King to give him advice, it is specific to that King, and it becomes redundant on the King's death. It is for his successor to appoint a new one, although it has a permanent infrastructure, in the form of an office and trained clerks and others, which would undoubtedly remain in place until the new Council meets. It will be remembered that the most senior members of the Privy Council are drawn from the Great Council, and this helps to ensure continuity – although successive Privy Councils do not necessarily include the same members of the Great Council, since the choice is the right of the King's successor, bearing in mind that his preferred choice of Great Counsellors may choose to recuse themselves. It follows that Temple's provision was both inappropriate, because the Privy Council cannot advise a dead King, and unnecessary, because continuity is the responsibility of the Great Council.

26.1.6. The Civil List and the Banking Revolution

The reign of William and Mary was a time of financial evolution in England. The National Debt was created by the King in 1693, when he borrowed £1 million at 10 per cent interest, in order to pay for the war with France. It was in order to help finance the war that, in spite of the opposition of the goldsmiths, who had previously managed the Government's borrowing, the Chancellor of the Exchequer, Montagu, secured a charter in 1694 for the establishment of the country's first joint-stock bank, the Bank of England. Its purpose was to formalise the Crown's borrowing, conduct its monetary business, and arrange interest on its money. Apart from its royal charter, therefore, the Bank of England was a private venture by individuals willing to lend to it. This money, in turn, was loaned to the Crown, which, whenever it subsequently needed to borrow, it did so through the Bank. Depositors with the Bank were given a promissory note for the amount deposited, which could be redeemed on presentation of the note. In practice, the depositors sold the note to others when they needed their money, and these notes began to circulate as a form of currency. So was born the banknote, adding greatly to the availability of financial credit in the economy, so that the issuing of these notes became one of the Bank's major functions. The original loan and much of the subsequent borrowings of the Government were not repaid, except by further borrowings, leaving the Crown with an ongoing debt, known as the National Debt, the administration of which was in 1751 left to the Bank. These arrangements, while they left the Crown with a constant need to pay interest from its revenues, nevertheless provided it with a new and flexible means of meeting exceptional expenditure needs, exercised by the King's Ministers under the watchful eye of Parliament. The practice of financing government by simply creating credit had an important constitutional significance, in that it made regular meetings of the House of Commons imperative, because it alone could approve the necessary money Bills.[8] Only four years after the Bank was established,

---

8. Since the Middle Ages, the House of Commons had represented, in the Third Estate, the major source of the Crown's tax receipts.

the development of joint-stock companies received a major boost from the London Stock Exchange, which was set up in 1698. It was the world's first true exchange of this type, in which shares in companies could be bought and sold.

The King had hitherto enjoyed, for use at his own discretion, his hereditary revenues, comprising what remained of his original prerogative entitlements and 'tunnage and poundage', that is, the traditional customs and excise duties, this latter being granted for life. He also received the revenue from the Crown lands and the Duchy of Lancaster, although surplus revenue from the last was paid into the Privy Purse, which was used for the private needs of the King and his family. These moneys, together, covered the normal costs of government and the needs of the Royal Household. In addition, the King applied those taxes that had been raised by the consent of Parliament for the specific purposes intended. Whatever had remained of the King's annual income, after meeting the necessary expenses of government, had been at his absolute disposal, but there was also plenty of opportunity for abuse. There is no doubt that Charles II, for instance, had diverted to the Privy Purse large sums of money which had been appropriated by Parliament for the conduct of the war. Parliament was now resolved to prevent such abuses in the future, but it was also inspired by the methodical financial record-keeping of the Crown itself.

In 1698, under William and Mary, Parliament introduced a new arrangement whereby the King would receive £700,000 each year to cover the normal costs of government, such as the civil service, the judiciary, the royal palaces and parks, the costs of the Royal Household and family, and the King's personal expenses. This was termed the Civil Provision, and the items covered by it were referred to as the 'Civil List'. The £700,000 allocated was to be met from the King's traditional revenues – from the remaining prerogative rights, the hereditary customs and excise, and the Crown lands – and the receipts from a new 'tunnage and poundage' tax, granted for life. Any revenue that exceeded the £700,000 provided for was to be paid into an Aggregate Fund. This comprised those moneys that could only be spent by the consent of Parliament, and for the purpose consented to. It was an arrangement which left the King with little or no leeway, and William, understandably, felt that he was being penalised for the excesses of the Stuarts. Parliament was determined to increase its control over the Crown, however, to prevent it from again using revenues of state to pose a threat to itself, and William needed England's support for Holland too much to refuse to accept this restriction on his authority. This distinction, between revenues provided for what was now termed the Civil List, whose allocation was at the discretion of the King, and revenues raised and spent in accordance with parliamentary consent, usually for emergencies, such as war, had always existed, except that successive Kings had usually abused the latter, causing Parliament to examine how it was spent and insisting on it being spent in the manner approved. What was new was the ceiling placed on expenditures on the Civil List. It was intended to curb royal extravagance and political ventures, but it was based on the arbitrary assumption that the normal cost of government was fixed.

Some writers appear to have misunderstood the changes imposed on William III. Thus, it has been said that 'The constitutional effect of the Civil List Act was to provide Parliament with the leverage to limit royal discretion over government revenues, so that a distinction could for the first time be made between the revenues of the Sovereign and those of the state'.[9] Even in Anglo-Saxon times this distinction had been made – between what the Sovereign was entitled to and what he could only obtain with the approval of Parliament – and probably the greater part of the revenues of the Sovereign were devoted to purposes of state. In any case, as the head of state, what the Sovereign spent in connection with his office, even though difficult to define, was often a necessary expenditure of state.

The war with France ended, more or less in a draw, with the Treaty of Ryswick concluded between England, Holland, Spain, and France in 1697. The most important aspect of this treaty from England's point of view was that Louis XIV acknowledged the dynastic succession in England and promised not to give any further assistance to the Stuarts. Otherwise, the treaty marked a return to the *status quo*, with the return of all captured territory. Dutch troops were to garrison the chief fortresses in the Spanish Netherlands as a barrier between France and Holland.

---

9. V. Bogdanor, *The Monarchy and the Constitution*, 183–4.

26.1.7. Whitehall: Fire and Reconstruction

The year 1698 saw the destruction by fire of the Palace of Whitehall. Only the hall known as the Banqueting House survived, but the name of Whitehall continued to be applied to the site. Even the main thoroughfare, King Street, became known as Whitehall. Following its destruction, St James's Palace became the King's official residence. When the Banqueting House had previously been re-built in 1619, following its own earlier destruction by fire, its architect, Inigo Jones, had adopted the Italian Renaissance style, known as 'Palladian', in preference to the existing Tudor style of Whitehall. It had been deemed a success, and consequently, as the site of Whitehall was redeveloped for offices of the Crown, such as the Treasury, the Navy Office, the War Office and the Foreign Office, it was the Palladian example of the Banqueting House that was followed. The Banqueting House was used, meanwhile, apart from banquets, for the King to hold audiences with foreign ambassadors. It also became the venue for masques, a form of dramatic and musical entertainment that formed a central part of London's social whirl in the sixteenth and seventeenth centuries.

A Tory-dominated Parliament was returned at the end of 1698. By now, William had become increasingly unpopular because of grants of land that he made to his Dutch favourites, and there were so many disputes with him that William threatened to leave England for good.

26.2. The Act of Settlement (1701)

Queen Mary had died without issue, so that the heir to the throne after William's death would have been her sister, Anne, Princess of Denmark, but in 1700 the last of Anne's children died, creating a problem over the subsequent succession to the English Crown. In order to clarify the future succession, therefore, the last important component of the Glorious Revolution, the Act of Settlement, was passed in 1701. The Act stated that:

1. In default of the King, or of the Princess Anne of Denmark, producing any further children, in order to ensure the succession of the Crown in the Protestant line, William's

successor should be the Princess Sophia, Electress and Duchess Dowager of Hanover, and her issue, 'being Protestants'. Her husband was Ernest Augustus, Duke of Brunswick-Lüneburg and the first Elector of Hanover in Saxony. Sophia's claim lay in the fact that she was the daughter of Frederick V, the Elector Palatine[10] and King of Bohemia, and of Elizabeth, the latter being the daughter of James I. Sophia was thus the granddaughter of James I, but safely belonged to the German Protestant branch of the family. The succession of the House of Hanover to the English throne would therefore ensure that it was occupied by a legitimate descendant of the Stuarts, while excluding the Catholic line;

2. Any future successor to the Crown who became a Catholic, or reconciled to Catholicism, or who should marry a Papist, should be subject to such incapacities as the Bill of Rights provided;

3. All successors to the Crown should take the Coronation Oath prescribed in the Coronation Oath Act of 1689;

4. All successors to the Crown should join in communion with the Church of England;

5. In the event of a successor not being native to England, the latter should not be involved in any war for the defence of foreign countries without the consent of Parliament;

6. No successor should leave England, Scotland and Ireland without the consent of Parliament (this provision being later repealed in the reign of Queen Anne).

In other words, the succession should pass, after Anne's issue, to the Electress Sophia of Hanover, daughter of Elizabeth of Bohemia and granddaughter of James I, except that any future sovereign must be in communion with the Church of England.

The Act then turned its attention to matters of good government:

1. All matters relating to the good government of the kingdom that were properly cognisable in the Privy Council should

---

10. The Palatinate included much of south-west Germany and Hesse in central Germany. An Elector was a Prince who had the right to elect the German Emperor.

be transacted there and its resolutions signed by those
of the Council who advised and consented to them;

2.   No person born outside the realm, unless of English parents,
     should be eligible for the Privy Council, or Parliament, or
     any office of trust, or any grant of land or other title from the
     Crown (this was later repealed in the reign of Queen Victoria);

3.   No person occupying an office or place of profit under the
     King, civil or military, or in receipt of a pension from the
     Crown, should serve as a member of the House of Commons;

4.   Judges should hold office *quam diu se bene gesserint*. In
     other words, judges, who held their commissions from the
     King, were to hold office 'during good behaviour', instead
     of 'at the King's pleasure'. Also, they were to be removed
     or have their salary altered only upon an address from
     both Houses of Parliament. By this means, judges were
     now beholden to Parliament for their good conduct;

5.   The King's pardon under the Great Seal was not a bar to
     impeachment by Parliament. This ensured that any officer
     of the Crown instructed to carry out a royal order that was
     likely to conflict with the wishes of Parliament could not
     rely upon the King's protection. Thus, the Act confirmed the
     action earlier taken by Parliament in the Danby case of 1679;

6.   The laws of England, being the birth right of the people,
     the Crown should administer the Government according
     to them, and hereby ratify those already in force.

Item (4) was plainly at odds with the common law requirements
of the Constitution, because judges sat as representatives of the King in
his capacity as the Supreme Judge, and so was of no effect. This did not
detract from the second requirement of good behaviour. If the Great
Council had been functioning as required, it would undoubtedly have
insisted upon this requirement being consistent with the requirements of
the *mos maiorum*.

Apart from clarifying the succession and seeking to prevent the
abuses of the Stuarts, the Act of Settlement was clearly aimed at William
himself, whose prior responsibilities in his native Netherlands kept him

away for much of the time and drew England into a conflict in which she had no direct interest. The Act also attempted to destroy the secretive Cabinet system by fixing executive responsibility solely in the hands of the Privy Council. This meant, among other things, that future rulers must not evade the control of the Privy Council by transacting business through other channels. It also meant that Ministers were responsible for the acts of their Sovereigns, because their shared responsibility for decisions was evident in their signatures, as required by the Act. This section was repealed in 1706 because it was simply unworkable, and because, by that time, the fear of secret or confidential committees had receded. The real decisions were already being taken, not by the Privy Council, but by its offshoot, the Cabinet Council and, to a lesser extent, by the Committee of the Privy Council. Nonetheless, the Act did re-establish the point that all important Government decisions, by the King or by his Ministers, should be taken in the Privy Council itself, and that Ministers were accountable.

The Act of Settlement further specified that no foreign-born person, unless of English parents, could be a member of the Privy Council, or of either House of Parliament, or hold any public office, civil or military, or receive any grant from the Crown. It also re-stated the prohibition on any person who held an office or place of profit under the Crown, or who received a pension from the Crown, from serving as a member of the House of Commons. This clause, prohibiting persons holding office or places of profit under the Crown from being members of Parliament, was intended to prevent the King from exerting direct influence on the House of Commons, but this also proved to be unworkable, because it excluded Ministers from the Commons. The Place Act of 1707 accordingly amended the clause, so that elected members of the House of Commons could accept places of profit under the Crown, but could only continue as members of the House if they were re-elected. This was a device to allow members of Parliament to become Ministers of the Crown, so enabling Parliament to exert a direct influence on the Government itself. There was no intention of making Ministers responsible to Parliament, an idea that would not come until later. The provision ended any direct royal influence on the deliberations of the Commons, other than through Ministers who were themselves subsequently elected to the

Commons. This latter arrangement only compromised them, because they were now answerable as much to their constituents as to the King. The Act also precluded the satisfactory arrangement whereby the Tudors had maintained a close liaison with the House of Commons. Because Ministers now owed a dual loyalty, they were able to exploit it to wield a greater degree of independence. It was another step on the road to the isolation of the Crown from Parliament, and was, perhaps, due warning of the Commons' eventual ambition to rule the country on its own. The Commons had, after all, long since ceased to be an assembly of ordinary people: it was now a body of professional and ambitious politicians.

It hardly needs to be pointed out that this whole problem of liaison between the Crown and Parliament and the issue of the Crown manipulating Parliament, or Parliament manipulating the Crown, had arisen because of the disarticulation of Parliament. This had separated it from the Crown, and facilitated the replacement of the ordinary people in Parliament by increasingly well-organised Parties of professional policy-brokers. Members of Parliament were, of course, amateurs, in that they were not paid and no prior competence was demanded, but they were men of independent means to whom membership of Parliament offered an attractive career in the wielding of power. It has been pointed out by Jennings[11] that 'the constitution after the Act of Settlement could be described as a "mixed" or "balanced" constitution. The supremacy lay in Parliament, but national policy was determined by the king subject to certain controlling powers of Parliament'. This description reminds us of the point made by Polybius, when he attributed the success of Roman government to its 'mixed' nature, and Aristotle's point that only a 'mixed' constitution provided the balance that was essential to good and stable government. The point need hardly be made, however, that the Act of Settlement did not prescribe changes to the constitution, even though its drafters probably believed that it did. Rather, it was a significant step in bringing the practice of government more into line with the requirements of common law.

The Act of Settlement confirmed that the line of succession, subject to the Protestant requirement, should be according to the law of inheritance, which was based on the custom of primogeniture. The implication of

---

11. I. Jennings, *The Law and the Constitution*, 18.

this prescription was misunderstood. Establishment of this hereditary principle, it was commonly believed, 'brought to a close the interregnum between the death of one King and the election of his successor. Today there is no interregnum and the main legal significance of the coronation is the taking of the oath by the new Sovereign of his or her duties towards his or her subjects'.[12] It was widely taken to mean that, as we saw earlier, because the succession was now predetermined, no sooner was one King dead than his successor was automatically King. This convention was believed to be constitutionally valid, because 'immediately on the death of his or her predecessor the Sovereign is proclaimed by the Accession Council' which 'is afterwards approved at the first meeting of the new Sovereign's Privy Council'. Perfect continuity was thus achieved and the King never dies. Various authorities, struggling to reconcile the apparent contradictions, have been led to deduce from this that the Constitution had been changed and that 'The coronation therefore does not seem to be a legally necessary ceremony'.[13] Even under the Act of Settlement, however, there was usually a lapse of some hours, even days, between the royal demise and the convening of the Accession Council, and in any case 'There are two ceremonies which mark the accession of the new Sovereign', the first being the proclamation by the Accession Council, and the second being the Coronation, whose 'main significance … is the taking of the oath,'[14] whose terms are now fixed by statute. There was therefore no continuity, even under the Act of Settlement.

The Coronation was not only a taking of the Oath. It also comprised a procedure of recognition and an invitation to the assembled people to accept and give their allegiance to the proclaimed successor. Clearly, unless and until they did so, the previous acts of the Accession Council and the Privy Council counted for nought. Moreover, no person could be accepted as King until he had taken his oath of office, and was not formally invested in office until he had been crowned and presented with the Mace and other symbols of power. In practice, the Coronation procedure was not abolished by the Act of Settlement, or by any other Act, and it continued to be performed. Quite clearly, whether by the

---

12. A. W. Bradley, and K. D. Ewing, *Constitutional and Administrative Law* (London, 1997), 256–7.
13. F. W. Maitland, *The Constitutional History of England*, 343.
14. A. W. Bradley, and K. D. Ewing, *Constitutional and Administrative Law*, 256–7.

acceptance of the rule of primogeniture or by the Act of Settlement, the people committed themselves to no more than choosing their future Kings in accordance with certain agreed rules, which the Accession Council had to abide by. There are only two constitutional traditions known to us. Of these, the feudal doctrine states that the King is anointed by God, therefore, the office is bestowed during the Coronation ceremony. Indo-European customary law, or *mos maiorum*, on the other hand, appears to state that the King is elected by the people through the process of acclamation, and is installed in office on completion of a regal contract that is satisfactory to both sides. Moreover, because of its divine origin, no law can override *mos maiorum*. Therefore, according to both traditions, no claimant to the throne can be King until his coronation. The fact that the otherwise pointless coronation procedure was retained after the Act of Settlement is a clear confirmation that a continued adherence was still intended, in principle, to one or other of these constitutional traditions, however vaguely comprehended.

Nevertheless, 'In terms of common law doctrine, the sovereign never dies, but is immediately succeeded by his or her successor'.[15] By 'common law' is here meant a well-established tradition, not the common law of the Constitution, as defined, to which it is unknown. It is, nevertheless, the basis of the affirmation, dictum or formula on the demise of the Sovereign, that: 'The King is dead. Long live the King!' This idea is much older than the Act of Settlement, and undoubtedly derives from the French legal doctrine: *Le Roi est mort, vive le Roi!* which was slowly worked out during the Middle Ages. It insisted that the King's successor enters office at the moment of his predecessor's death, even though this conflicted with the requirement that the successor must first be inaugurated by separate legal and ecclesiastical rites.[16] Probably, it is an expression of the feudal notion that the King is appointed by God, who has already ordained who the previous King's successor shall be, ensuring his succession through the established rules of inheritance. Thus, the new King is predestined from the moment of death of the old one, even though he must be anointed and crowned. Citizenship of the United Kingdom depended on which legal tradition was invoked. In common law, a citizen of the new union was presumably anyone who could claim English, Welsh, or Scottish

15. V. Bogdanor, *The Monarchy and the Constitution*, 45.
16. P. E. Schramm, *A History of the English Coronation* (Oxford, 1937).

citizenship by right of inheritance, whereas, under feudal law, a citizen would have been anyone who was born in one or other of the three countries.

James II died in France in the latter part of 1701, and his son, James Edward, who came to be known as the Old Pretender, was proclaimed as King of Great Britain and Ireland by Louis XIV, despite his earlier promise not to interfere in the English succession. It had no practical effect whatever in England, beyond causing the attainder of James's estate and aggravating relations with the French.

26.3. The Second Restoration of the Stuarts: Queen Anne

William III died soon afterwards, in 1702, after falling from his horse. In the Netherlands he was succeeded by his cousin, Johann Wilhelm Friso, Duke of Saxe-Eisenach, while in England and Scotland he was succeeded by Princess Anne, daughter of James II and sister of the late Queen Mary. Her husband was Prince George of Denmark, Duke of Cumberland. As she now ruled England in her own right as the daughter of James II, her accession amounted to a second restoration of the House of Stuart, except that it was now in the Protestant line of descent. The accession of Queen Anne was not accompanied by any attempt to elevate her husband, Prince George, a good husband but a well-meaning nonentity, who was kept securely in the background. She was ill-equipped herself as a ruler, but she was cheerful and conscientious and relied heavily on the Lord High Treasurer, the Earl of Godolphin, as her Prime Minister.

Her accession was closely followed in the same year by the outbreak of a dynastic squabble known as the War of the Spanish Succession. The Spanish succession had been the chief preoccupation of all the Ministries of Europe since the Treaty of Ryswick, because the anticipated death of Charles II of Spain would mean the extinction of the Spanish House of Habsburg, and whoever inherited the Spanish throne would achieve a decisive advantage in the European balance of power. There were three claimants. One was the French king, Louis XIV, both through his mother, as Princess Anna of Spain, and through his wife, Princess

Maria Theresa of Spain.[17] The fact that both princesses had solemnly renounced their own claims was an embarrassment to Louis, which he endeavoured to overcome by inducing the *Parlement* of Paris to declare their renunciations null and void. The second claimant was the Emperor Leopold I, representing the German line of Habsburgs. His claim rested on the fact that he was the son of Princess Maria of Spain, and his wife was Princess Margaret Theresa of Spain.[18] The German Empire by this time existed in little more than name, the only effective power within it being Austria, but Leopold, as ruler of Austria, had increased his military strength by the conquest of Hungary and Bohemia. The third claimant was the Electoral Prince of Bavaria, his title being based on the fact that he was the great-grandson of Philip IV of Spain and grandson of the younger sister of Charles II.

The two great naval powers, England and Holland, were opposed to a dynastic union of either France and Spain, or Austria and Spain. In deference to these fears, the French king, Louis XIV, laid claim only on behalf of his grandson, Philip, Duke of Anjou. Leopold claimed only in the name of his second son, Charles. This was because his elder son would succeed him in Austria. In anticipation of the spoils, the powers – without the participation of Charles II of Spain and much to his provocation – had concluded two Treaties of Partition in 1698 and 1700, dividing up Spain and its possessions between the claimants. The sudden death of the Prince Elector of Bavaria in 1699 had narrowed the field to two, and shortly before his death in November of 1700, Charles II of Spain had switched his preference from the Austrian to the French contender, Philip of Anjou. Faced with a choice between the new will of Charles II and the terms of the Partition Treaty of 1700, by which it had been agreed that Charles of Austria should be the successor, Louis of France opted for the will. His grandson, Philip of Anjou, was accordingly proclaimed King Philip V of Spain.

From the standpoint of England and Holland, it was France that had posed the chief danger, rather than Austria. As the champion of Catholicism, France had pursued hostile policies towards Holland and

---

17. Anna was the elder daughter of Philip III of Spain, and Maria Theresa the daughter of Philip IV of Spain, half-sister of Charles II.
18. Maria was the younger daughter of Philip III of Spain, and Margaret Theresa was the daughter of Philip IV, and therefore sister of Charles II of Spain.

England, and had successively grabbed border states of the German Empire, including Burgundy and Alsace. So it was with Leopold of Austria that England and Holland formed a Grand Alliance in 1701. Its primary purpose was to exploit Spain's current weakness by evicting her from the Spanish Netherlands and from her possessions in Italy in favour of the Austrian side, in accordance with the terms of the Treaty of Partition. The main protagonist, however, proved to be France. The Spanish Netherlands, formerly Flanders, which approximated to modern Belgium and Artois, had for centuries been of critical importance to the two major rivals, England and France, as well as to Holland. Since the Middle Ages, when it had been represented by Flanders, it had decided for or against France. Louis had no intention of losing what he now regarded as rightfully belonging to his grandson and, by implication, to himself. He accordingly formed alliances with Savoy, Mantua, Bavaria and Cologne. Prussia and the other states of the Empire joined the Grand Alliance, founded by the League of Augsburg. The commanders at the head of the alliance were now Prince Eugene of Savoy, for the Empire; Churchill, now made the Duke of Marlborough, for England; and Heinsius for the Netherlands.

Eugene had successes in Italy, while Marlborough invaded the Spanish Netherlands and the Austrian Archduke, Charles, invaded Spain. Over the next few years Marlborough and Prince Eugene won victories at Blenheim in Bavaria, in 1704, in the Spanish Netherlands at Oudenarde, in 1708, and there again, in spite of appalling losses, at Malplaquet in 1709. Meanwhile Marlborough had won another victory at Ramillies, also in the Spanish Netherlands, in 1706, while Eugene finally evicted the French from Italy in the same year. The Grand Alliance then fell apart in 1711, following the death of the Austrian Emperor, Joseph, throwing the pattern of succession into confusion. In England the Whig-Tory Ministry had fallen in the previous year, mainly over the losses at Malplaquet. It was followed by a Tory Ministry that was concerned to reduce England's involvement in the war, and Marlborough was now removed from command. Fatally. this gave the initiative back to the French, who in 1712 proceeded to defeat the English under Albemarle at Denain, so recovering much of the Spanish Netherlands and setting the scene for the Treaty of Utrecht in 1713.

26.3.1. The Decline of the First and Second Estates

In common law, members of the three Estates hold their position by right of inheritance. Following the advent of the Christian Church, this ceased to be the case in respect of members of the First Estate, because membership of the clergy had been open to all, and advancement was in accordance with the rules of the Church and its monastic houses. Nevertheless, senior members of the Church continued to be accorded the privileges normally accredited to members of the First Estate, a status which they guarded jealously.

The Second Estate had been largely wiped out in the Battle of Hastings, and its survivors had mostly been dispossessed and relegated to insignificance. The Norman barons had not been accepted at first, but although many seem to have had comparatively insignificant origins, it is likely that all, or most, had their origin, either in the Danish Second Estate, which had led the invasion and establishment of Normandy, or in the Frankish nobility, who had imposed themselves on northern France. There is no particular reason, therefore, to regard the Norman barons who established themselves in England as being without an ancestry in the Second Estate, and this was ultimately accepted by the English. Nevertheless, membership of the Second Estate in common law was not restricted to those who belong by inheritance. As pointed out elsewhere, an outstanding individual of the Third Estate, particularly if he had won renown in battle, might be regarded as enjoying divine favour, and, in the light of the advice of the Council, such an individual might be elevated by the King to noble status. If his offspring during the succeeding three generations demonstrated their worthiness to follow in his footsteps, they and their family were usually accepted as belonging to the Second Estate by divine favour. By this means, the noble class was able to sustain itself.

During the Middle Ages, however, many individuals of the Third Estate were elevated to noble titles on the basis of royal favouritism, and particularly following the decimation of the Second Estate in the battle of Towton in 1461, there was an influx from the Third Estate of individuals who could hardly be regarded as having won divine favour. By the late Middle Ages, therefore, the Second Estate had declined, and few could lay a lawful claim to its privileges.

PART X

•

THE EMPIRE AND THE CONSTITUTION

27. THE BIRTH OF EMPIRE

WHAT IS MORE accurately described as the English Empire had its origin with the Statute of Wales of 1284. Ireland gradually followed, but the impetus to the establishment of an English Empire beyond the British Isles came from the Crusades to the Holy Land in the twelfth and thirteenth centuries, which were prompted by the Moslem occupation of Jerusalem. The expeditions were known as the *Croisées*, or Crusades, because they were 'marked with the Cross', and they were initiated at the behest of Pope Urban II, in 1095, with the object of recovering it from the pagans, who, exhorted by the prophet Mohammed, had conquered the Near East, North Africa and Spain. Led by the Franks, the Crusades ultimately failed, but they did introduce those involved, including the English, to the pleasures and benefits of Oriental spices, which were imported into the Middle East from southern India and beyond. In an age when it was difficult to preserve meat, spices served a useful purpose in hiding the taste, but they were soon in demand for their own sake for flavouring purposes. Brought back by the returning Crusaders to Western Europe, they were soon in demand there by the upper classes who could afford them. Controlled by the Arabs, the trade route from 'the Indies' lay by way of the Red Sea, thence overland to the Mediterranean. Here, the spice trade became a highly profitable monopoly in the hands of the Venetians. This eventually gave rise to speculative rumblings in the maritime countries of Western Europe, notably Portugal, Spain, France, the Netherlands and England, and in the fourteenth century the Portuguese began to look for a sea route around Africa to India, that was not controlled by the Venetians and Arabs. In 1488 they found it, and soon established a trading presence in the Indian Ocean. When the route by way of the Red Sea was closed in 1517 by the Ottoman conquest of the Near East, the Portuguese were left in full control of the European spice trade, which was now centred in Lisbon.

Meanwhile, a Genoese adventurer, Colombo, whose name was Latinised as Columbus, and who was already familiar with the Madeiras and Portuguese sailors, gained access to the Spanish court, and eventually persuaded the Queen, Isabella, that Spain could gain access to the Spice Islands, without a ruinous competition with the Portuguese, by finding a new sea route to the westwards. The idea of reaching Asia from this direction was not novel – Roger Bacon's *Opus Maius* of the late thirteenth century shows that the Greek idea that the Earth was a sphere was never entirely lost during the Middle Ages, and the translation of Ptolemy's *Geography* into Latin in 1410 had revived the idea – but this possibility was generally rejected. It seems likely, however, that the Portuguese were already aware of the existence of Brazil, and its potential as a source of iron, but believed it to be an island and had kept it secret. In 1492, Isabella finally agreed to finance an expedition, and in the same year Columbus reached land in the Bahamas, and subsequently Cuba, believing it to be a part of Asia. Although it was quite easy to establish a ship's latitude at this time, there was no way of establishing its longitude. A second expedition, to establish Spain's jurisdiction in the new lands, acquired Hispaniola and Jamaica.

Anxious to keep the Portuguese from exploiting this new, westward route, Spain induced Pope Alexander VI in the following year to proclaim a demarcation of their respective spheres of interest. This must have forced the Portuguese to disclose their knowledge of Brazil, because, when the Papal decision was formally ratified by Spain and Portugal in 1494, in the Treaty of Tordesillas, the demarcation between the two had been shifted from the mid-Atlantic westwards. This allowed Brazil to lie in the Portuguese sector, to the east of the Line of Demarcation, but it still allowed Spain to claim any new lands found to the west.

Meanwhile, news of Columbus's 'discovery' of a western sea route to the Indies ignited a wider interest. It was an Italian adventurer, Giuseppe Caboto, who launched England into the race by winning sponsorship from the merchant adventurers of Bristol, who had themselves been trying for some years to find Brazil, and who soon Anglicised his name to John Cabot. On the basis of money provided by the merchants of Bristol, Cabot obtained letters patent from the King, Henry VII, in 1496, and these authorised him to find and lay claim to new lands to the westward. In the following year he reached Cape Breton Island, and went on to explore the coast of a 'new found isle', which later became the name of Newfoundland. Cabot seems to have realised that the mainland extended too far north to offer an attractive route to the Indies, because, in 1498, he set off again from Bristol, intending to follow the coast southward as far as Brazil. It may have been Cabot who gave America its name, out of gratitude to Richard Ameryk, who seems to have been the dominant personality among the worthies of Bristol who had made his enterprise possible.[1] Rendered into a Latin form by the cartographers, the first recorded reference is to *Americi terra*, 'land of Americus', in 1507. The name has often been attributed to an Italian adventurer, Amerigo Vespucci, but, as has been pointed out elsewhere, the use of first names for new lands was normally reserved to royalty and saints, and if Vespucci had inspired it, the likely name for the continent would have been Vespucia. This makes it likely that it was the merchants of Bristol who first realised that what Columbus and Cabot had found was a new continent, and so gave to it its name of America. Also, Ameryk and his colleagues appear to have recognised that what had been found was blocking, not opening, their way to the Indies, and after Cabot's disappearance on his second voyage, having already wasted a great deal of their money, they showed no further interest. Appropriately, however, it was Bristol that would eventually give to English-speaking North America its form of speech.[2]

Although Spain did not find a way to the 'Spice Islands' – the East Indies – it indulged in exploration and conquest around the Caribbean early in the sixteenth century, spreading into Mexico and north-western South America, where it looted huge quantities of gold and silver from the 'Indians', particularly from the Incas. This was then shipped back to Spain, attracting the attention, first of the French, and then of English freebooters, such as Drake, Hawkins, Oxenham and Cavendish, who attacked the Spanish ships and ransacked the Spanish towns in and around the Caribbean. Driven by the hostility between England and Spain, and, on condition that she received a fair share of the proceeds, Queen Elizabeth had given covert support, in the form of letters of marque, to certain freebooters, such as Raleigh, Drake and Frobisher, to prey on Spanish ships between the Caribbean and Spain. Not only was the Queen involved, but also London merchants and the gentry at court.

---

1   A. E. Hudd, *Richard Amaryk and the Naming of America*, Proceedings of the Clifton Antiquarian Club (1909–1910), vii. 1.
2   Its rolled rs, common in the west of the British Isles, may have derived from a much older Iberian source that pre-dated Indo-European settlement in the British Isles.

The huge success of English piracy in the Atlantic and the Caribbean,[3] and with it the development of faster ships, led to the emergence of England as a sea power, which made possible the defeat of the Spanish Armada in 1587, and ensured the survival of the Protestant Church in England. The gold and silver that flowed into England, meanwhile, found its way into the economy, where it led to a significant increase in prosperity by expanding the money supply. It also helped in the financing of an English trading station in Virginia, in 1607, and of an East India Company in 1616. The enterprise in Virginia was based on the expectation of buying gold and silver from the Native Americans. This failed to materialise, but the discovery that tobacco grew well under local conditions not only saved the enterprise, but converted it into a thriving settlement for English immigrants, who exported the tobacco to England. The East India Company was intended as a commercial enterprise in pursuit of the spice trade, with the intention of establishing trading stations in the East Indies. It planned to do this, not by going west, but by taking the same route as the Portuguese, around the Cape of Good Hope. The Portuguese had since been displaced by the Dutch, and there followed a fierce and sometimes violent rivalry between the English and Dutch East India Companies. The Dutch succeeded in retaining their trading foothold in the East Indies, causing the English Company to divert its attention to establishing trading stations in India. It also used a European war to usurp the Dutch from their supply station at the Cape of Good Hope.

The new colonies in the Far East needed to be supplied and defended, not only against rival European nations, but often also against hostile or avaricious local rulers. This made it necessary for the East India Company to establish its own army. The chief threat, both in India and North America, now came from the French. England's increasing involvement in the West Indies and on the east coast of North America was further prompted by the discovery of other commercially viable commodities, a growing shortage of land in England itself, due to evictions and the enclosure of land for sheep farming, and the disaffection of non-conformist religious groups in England during a period of ideological

---

3   K. R. Andrews, *English Privateering Voyages to the West Indies* (Cambridge, 1959); *Elizabethan Privateering* (Cambridge, 1964); *Trade, Plunder and Settlement* (Cambridge, 1984); *Ships, Money and Politics* (Cambridge, 1991).

unrest. The economic attractions now included timber, furs and fishing in the north; tobacco, sugar-cane and cotton in the sub-tropical south; and good conditions for mixed farming in between. A serious obstacle to cultivation in the south on the scale needed to supply the profitable export market in England, however, was a severe shortage of labour. Not only were sub-tropical crops labour-intensive, but the heat in summer greatly deterred the recruitment of English labourers, and this imposed a severe limitation on the development of the southern colonies.

At the same time, England was involved in Continental wars that not only made it necessary to secure strategic naval bases in such defensible places as Minorca and Gibraltar, but European trading rivalries overseas and the long lines of communication made it necessary to secure more distant strategic bases, such as the Cape of Good Hope, to re-supply the ships. It was the Dutch, following the Portuguese to trade in the Spice Islands of Indonesia, who took advantage of the more reliable westerly winds of the southern Indian Ocean to reach their main commercial base in Java, who discovered Western Australia. Being semi-arid, it was of little interest to them, but the more attractive east coast became known in England from an exploratory voyage in the South Pacific by a ship of the Royal Navy, under Captain Cook, during 1768–1771. To this eastern side of the continent, he gave the name of New South Wales. It attracted little further attention until the high level of unemployment and crime in England in the late eighteenth and early nineteenth centuries, caused by the enclosure movement and the economic depression that followed the Napoleonic Wars, led to a crisis of overcrowding in the prison system. This prompted the idea of establishing cheaper penal settlements overseas, and several options were explored. It was concluded that the most satisfactory, in spite of its remoteness, was Australia, and in 1788 a fleet of supply and convict ships reached Botany Bay on the east coast. Several convict settlements were established, but it was soon realised that a population of free settlers was also desirable, in order to provide useful employment for the convicts when they were released.

Colonial affairs were retained within the domain of the royal prerogative until its collapse in 1642, with the outbreak of the Civil War. This opened the way for parliamentary intrusion. The North American colonies were hostile, because they were not represented in the English

Parliament, but the Long Parliament established a commission on colonial affairs in1643, put the rebellion down, and asserted its authority by passing legislation, such as the Navigation Act of 1651, that applied to all the American colonies. Even after the Restoration of the monarchy, the doctrine of parliamentary sovereignty over the colonies continued to be applied, in contravention of the requirements of common law, while Parliament at Westminster managed colonial affairs on the basis of feudal doctrines.

Meanwhile, new commercial opportunities beckoned, in Malaya, China and India. The Portuguese were being expelled from India by the French, until the English East India Company, having been brutally forced out of the East Indies by the Dutch, turned its own attention to India, where they gradually forced out the French, and fought to extend and protect their own trading interests. India was a congeries of independent or semi-independent states, with little in the way of infrastructure and often at war with each other and with the Company. The pursuit of trading opportunities required the establishment of fixed installations, such as harbours, warehouses, roads and even estates, in order to exploit on a large scale the local commodities that the Company sought. Nor could the Company develop its interests without exciting the hostility, or avarice, of some local rulers, making the negotiation of treaties and alliances, and even fighting local wars an essential aspect of its pursuit of commerce. The Native American states were themselves constantly fighting each other or the French, or indulging in political intrigue. A succession of conflicts and military successes enabled the Company to establish its rule over large areas, not because the Company had any ambitions in that direction, but simply because commercial success depended on access to supplies and markets and sheer commercial survival.

27.1. The Different Purposes of Colonies

As the English Empire grew, its various overseas territories were acquired for different reasons, or acquired different functions, allowing them to be categorised broadly as follows:

- *Commercial Enterprises* – the original purpose of the Empire, such as India, Malaya, Hong Kong, the African Gold Coast, Gambia and Nigeria.
- *Strategic Territories* – typically to protect the lines of Imperial communication, or to ensure access to more important prospects, or to forestall the ambitions of rival European powers. They included Minorca, Nova Scotia, Gibraltar, Kenya, and the Cape of Good Hope.
- *Protectorates* – usually capable of managing their own affairs, but liable to pose a future threat, or unable to defend themselves against Arab slave-raiding, or liable to attract the unwelcome ambition of rival powers. They included such territories as Barotseland, Nyasaland and Basutoland.
- *Settlement Colonies* – territories attractive to English settlement, such as Massachusetts, Georgia, New South Wales and Rhodesia.
- *Penal Colonies* – territories suitable for the establishment of prisons, such as New South Wales and Tasmania, to accommodate convicted criminals when prisons at home became too overcrowded and expensive to maintain.

Some territories, such as the Cape of Good Hope, Jamaica, Kenya, New South Wales, and Nova Scotia, were originally occupied for one purpose, but subsequently were used for another.

27.1.1. The Use of Slavery

There had been a flow of English slaves, abducted by the Barbary pirates to North Africa from coastal towns in south-west England, or from captured English ships in the Mediterranean. Their descendants are still in evidence in Algeria today. The Arabs had probably used sub-Saharan Africa as their source of black slaves for at least a thousand years, moving them northwards across the Sahara to North Africa, and from East and Central Africa by way of the Indian Ocean and the Red Sea to Arabia. The system had not caused a racial problem in Arabia because male slaves were castrated before they left Africa, adding to the appalling conditions under which they had been made to walk, in chains, over long distances to the coast. This made it necessary, however, for Arabia to import new supplies of slaves on a regular basis, hence the continuity of the trade. In West Africa particularly, local kings and chiefs had long run a profitable business by raiding neighbouring tribes for slaves, and then selling them to the Arabs, and when English traders tried to sell cloth and other industrial products in West Africa, and were offered payment in slaves, it did not take long for the traders to make the connection between this abundant source of cheap labour and the desperate shortage of labour, particularly for tobacco and cotton growing, in the southern colonies of America and in the West Indies. This new supply of cheap labour, transported across the Atlantic under appalling conditions, not only solved the labour problem in the southern colonies, but also enabled the settlements in Jamaica and other islands of the West Indies to flourish. Slavery had died out in England centuries earlier, and was now viewed with distaste, but it was not illegal. A trading pattern soon emerged, whereby cheap manufactured goods were exported to West Africa, in exchange for slaves, who were transported to the American colonies and the West Indies, enabling them in the seventeenth and eighteenth centuries to produce and export cotton, sugar and tobacco to England, in exchange for the more sophisticated industrial goods needed in the colonies. It was a mutually beneficial trading system, obnoxious though it was, that made possible the Industrial Revolution in England, which in turn gave rise to the Agricultural Revolution.

By the nineteenth century, however, the slave trade was giving rise to moral concerns in England and was made illegal throughout the Empire in 1807. The continuation of the trade, particularly by the Arabs, caused the Royal Navy to be employed in its suppression, mainly around Africa, until, aided by the further expansion of British rule in Africa, it was largely stamped out.

28. THE CONSTITUTIONAL BASIS OF EMPIRE

T HE ENGLISH EMPIRE was subject to **the rule of law**, but, as in England itself, the two rival legal traditions were followed by different interests, often with disastrous results. The common law of the Constitution inevitably applied, but the Crown applied and recognised only feudal doctrine.

28.1. Empire According to Feudal Doctrine

Feudal doctrine regarded overseas territories as estates of the Crown, much as the Crown regarded England itself, so that the 'empire' was seen as an accumulation of royal estates, acquired for varying reasons. Consequently, the 'Empire' had been bequeathed to the King by God, with England as the original 'family estate'. All individuals born on one of the King's estates were 'subjects' of the King, that is, they lived under his dominion and enjoyed his protection. Legally they belonged to the estate on which they were born, and were bound to it, regardless of the social Estate into which they had been born, and irrespective of any ethnic differences, because such differences were not recognised by God. The only exceptions were aliens, born outside the King's estates, who owed their allegiance, therefore, to the ruler of that estate. Citizenship, as defined by feudal doctrine, was based, therefore, on the principle of *ius soli*, the law of the ground, that is to say, on whose ground the individual was born. There was no provision under the feudal system for the individual to renounce his allegiance to the King, because ultimately this would be a rebellion against the will of God. The rebel's only hope of escaping retribution, unless he were powerful enough in his own right to defend himself against the King's just revenge, was by escaping from the King's jurisdiction by unlawfully absconding to a place where he was beyond the King's reach, or where he was assured of protection by another ruler.

The King could extend his sovereignty to a strange land, not otherwise claimed by a Christian ruler, it appears, if it was claimed by his representative, or person of some standing, leaving some identifying mark to prove it, such as a flag, to be followed by the publication of the King's formal claim and the permanent occupation on his behalf by his official representative, thereby incorporating it as a new estate under his title. This depended, of course, on his claim not being challenged by another sovereign ruler on the basis of a prior right. The territory of rulers not appointed by God – that is, infidel rulers outside the Christian world, whose claims were not, therefore, recognised by God – was not merely fair game, but in need of 'saving'. Thus, the Austrian Empire was won lawfully from the infidel Turks; the Russian Empire from the infidel Mongols; and the Spanish Empire from the pagan Native Americans. In the event of any dispute over sovereignty, the validity of the King's claim depended, in the last resort, on the means to enforce it. Thus, the claim *in situ*, by Drake, on behalf of Queen Elizabeth I, to the territory known as California, was of no effect, because the Queen failed to make a formal declaration of title, followed shortly afterwards by physical occupation on her behalf, the more so because the King of Spain had already given physical indication of an interest in the region. It is worth noting, also, that the King of England never laid claim to North America, unlike his French rival, who, in doing so, ignored the division of the Americas by the Pope between Spain and Portugal under the Treaty of Tordesillas.

There were normally four legal mechanisms, all within the royal prerogative, by means of which the King laid a provisional or inferred claim to overseas territories:

- The issue of *letters patent*, authorising an enterprise. The procedure was normally used to prescribe a form of government over the territory in question, such as that authorising the settlement and prescribing the government of the Narragansett Bay area, later known as Rhode Island, or to grant the jurisdiction of Newfoundland over Labrador in 1874.
- The grant of a *royal charter* to a private individual, group of private individuals, or joint-stock company, to embark upon a

commercial enterprise, usually in a specified territory. Notable examples were the Honourable East India Company in 1600, the London Company in 1606, the Hudson's Bay Company in 1670, and the British South Africa Company in 1889. While a charter ensured the Crown's recognition of and protection for the enterprise, and implied a right of the Crown at any time to withdraw its recognition, or to modify the conditions of the charter, it is by no means certain that it represented a claim by the Crown to territory acquired or used by the company. Thus, the territory within which the Hudson's Bay and East India Companies operated did not amount to a formal claim of royal sovereignty. Because the charter was incorporated in England, its provisions could be enforced in the English courts.

- The *direct enterprise of the Crown*, either military, as in the capture of Quebec in 1759, or civil with military support, as in the establishment of the penal colony at Botany Bay in 1787. A colony that fell under the direct rule of the Crown was known as a royal or Crown colony.

- The extension of *royal protection* to a foreign ruler, referred to as a 'protectorate'. This was usually granted in response to an appeal by the ruler, such as the King of Basutoland in 1843, or it could simply be imposed in order to serve a purpose, whether it was for the suppression of slavery by the Arabs in Nyasaland in 1889, or to preserve Britain's commercial interests, as in the case of Egypt in 1914.

In accordance with feudal doctrine, a grant of rights in a new territory that specified the limits of the territory and its apportionment or use, implied a claim by the King to that territory as a royal estate, within which indigenous rulers were fiefs of the King. This was because God only granted new lands to a King who had been appointed by Him as His agent in temporal matters.

The question of the legal basis of the occupation of Australia was not raised until the 1980s, when the country's Aboriginals, taking their cue from events elsewhere, laid claim to be the original owners of the land, implying a right to claim substantial compensation for dispossession.

Feudal doctrine was invoked, without being attributed, claiming that Australia had, at the time of British occupation, been *terra nullius*, that is, land belonging to nobody, because no jurisdiction, such as might have been claimed by an acknowledged ruler, could be identified. Consequently, no existing ruler or rulers in Australia had been recognised by the King. Even previous occupation, as signified by the presence of farms, buildings, fences or other features of an identifiable, ordered society had not been in evidence. As *terra nullius*, it had been land that the King was legally entitled to claim.

In summary, the Empire comprised several types of British possession. A permanent British settlement was properly a 'colony', as in the case of Virginia or New South Wales. There were also 'concessions', in which British commercial enterprises operated under treaty – amicable or otherwise – with local rulers, a prime example being Hong Kong. 'Protectorates' were established for reasons of Crown policy, whether it was to suppress Arab slavery, as in Nyasaland (later Malawi), or to forestall the inconvenient ambitions of rival powers, as in the examples of Barotseland and Bechuanaland. Other territories were secured for strategic reasons, either to protect British commerce or to provide bases for use in the event of war. They included Gibraltar, Aden and Singapore. Of these, the settled colonies were royal estates, according to feudal doctrine. In common law they were extensions of the English Constitution. The remaining types of British possession were, in both cases, managed by the Crown or by trading companies.

28.2. Empire in Common Law

In common law, derived from Indo-European customary law, the notion of citizenship is based on the principle of *ius sanguinis*, the 'law of the blood', that is, the principle of ancestry as the basis of the individual's position in society. A king's jurisdiction over his 'lieges' (as opposed to his 'subjects' in feudal doctrine) – that is, all who were participants with him in the regal contract – extended to them wherever they were, subject only to his ability to apply it.[1] This excluded places that were subject

---

1   Although the word 'liege' comes from the same word in French, from medieval Latin *letus*, *litus*, it was probably of Germanic origin and is to be seen in the Old English læt, who was

to the jurisdiction of another ruler, whose authority was recognised by the King. Within these limitations, the relationship between King and liegeman – who might be an itinerant trader or a settler – was the same as it would have been in England. Furthermore, where the King's liegemen in a distant land that was beyond the King's effective jurisdiction, formed a community with their own common assembly, they were entitled to call upon the King, either to send a suitable member of the King's family, or to propose an elder of their own community for election by them to rule on the King's behalf. This was not the procedure when the original Jutish, Saxon and Angle nations had crossed the North Sea, because the Jutish royal line had already become extinct; the Continental Saxons had formed a confederacy without a king; and the king of the Angles had accompanied them to Britain.

It seems to follow that the notion of 'empire', or 'political dominion', in common law applied properly only where the jurisdiction of the King was extended to territories inhabited by aliens, that is, people to whom he was not linked by *ius sanguinis*, and who were therefore not participants in the regal contract. Overseas colonies of free men who were the King's liegemen may be said to comprise, not an empire, but rather a 'commonwealth'. According to these definitions, England built an empire and a commonwealth, but during the years of their establishment, only the word 'empire' was used.

The exception to the close bond implied by the regal contract occurred in respect of the settlers in Massachusetts, whose arrival had been motivated largely by their hostile reaction, as Puritans, to the Stuart dynasty, with its Catholic leanings, and to the determination of the Church of England to maintain its episcopal tradition. It was not that the Puritans had been persecuted by the Stuarts, as they liked to believe, but rather that they had themselves been one of the most intolerant and aggressive factions in England that caused them to reject the regal contract. More difficult still was the relationship between the Crown and the French in Canada and the Dutch in the Cape Colony. While policy towards both was guided by feudal doctrine, concessions to the French were made by recognising their language, customs and right to self-rule; concessions that were undoubtedly forced upon the Crown by the threat

---

a free man whose status was next below that of a *ceorl*, and so not entitled to a freehold.

of defection to France. This was not a realistic threat in the case of the Cape Dutch, who eventually took a quite different course.

Under common law, new lands colonised automatically became the folklands of the colonists, and, because the colonists remained party to the regal contract, the land in question would have been regarded legally as vested in the King, as trustee.

An exception was India, where the English were not settlers, but employees of the East India Company, India being quite unsuited to settlement in any case, because of the climate and the absence of available and suitable land.

28.3. Conflicts of Legal Tradition in America and South Africa

After the Union of England and Scotland in 1707, England's Empire became officially the 'British' Empire, and the Scots, whose own attempt at founding an empire in Central America had failed disastrously, began to play a significant part in its affairs. The management of colonial affairs nevertheless remained in Westminster.

28.3.1. The American Revolution

England's commercial enterprises overseas were left very largely to pursue their own interests, but the Crown's application of feudal law to its relations with the colonists was bound to cause trouble, sooner or later, because the colonists regarded their circumstances very largely in the light of common law. As a result, there were three significant rebellions, two of them before the middle of the nineteenth century. The first, and most serious, was a joint rebellion by thirteen of the American colonies in 1775, and the second was by the Dutch inhabitants of the Cape of Good Hope in 1835.

At first, the interests of the Crown and the American colonies largely coincided and, with the exception of Massachusetts, which was established by the anti-royalist Puritans, loyalty to the Crown was generally strong, particularly in the face of the many Indian wars and the threat of French ambitions. In spite of a meddlesome Parliament, George III saw himself as God's temporal agent, with a responsibility to rule benignly, but leaving the settlers to manage their own local affairs in accordance with their respective written constitutions. This policy was basically accepted by Parliament, provided the interests of the colonists did not conflict with those of their own electors. The colonists, on the other hand, had their instinct for their rights in common law re-awakened by the vast spaciousness of North America and their comparative remoteness from Westminster, and this was given form by the political writers of the seventeenth century. Of particular influence was John Locke, who argued that government, and in particular the King, was responsible to the people, his power being limited by moral law. The realm was established by, and existed for, the well-being of the nation, which had the supreme power to alter the legislature when it acted contrary to the trust that reposed in it. Locke perceived natural law as a claim to innate, indefeasible rights inherent in each individual.[2] In spite of Locke's limitations as a thinker, the view of government that he propounded was largely in keeping with Indo-European customary law, and a clear rejection of feudal doctrine. The cracks in the political façade began to appear soon after the Seven Years War, following the removal of the French as a threat to the American colonies, particularly with the cession to the Crown by treaty, in 1763, of the St Lawrence valley and the whole of what was then known as Louisiana, a vast tract of North America lying to the east and north of the Mississippi, extending as far as the Appalachians. With the reliance of the colonies on the military protection of what was now Great Britain removed, the colonies exuded self-confidence, generated by their own prosperity and growing population. This made them impatient to extend their borders in search of new settlement opportunities, but the scope for this lay to the west, with all of Louisiana now open to those with the enterprise to seize it. This, however, the Crown expressly forbade, partly out of a sense of responsibility for the welfare of Native American tribes to the west, and partly to avoid the possibility of conflict with French settlers in Quebec, who still laid claim to the Great Lakes region and the whole of Louisiana, where many French settlements already existed. Contributing to the frustration in the colonies, Britain sought to reduce tensions with Quebec by defining its western border as the Illinois River. The effect was a growing frustration of the colonists with the Crown, which was now

2   G. H. Sabine, *A History of Political Theory*, 442–57.

seen as obstructive on a number of issues, where interests collided. The relationship was exacerbated, by about 1730, by the breakdown in the trading arrangements enshrined in the Navigation Act. This had given the colonies a protected market in Britain for their primary produce, while Britain enjoyed a protected market in the colonies for her manufactured goods. Upsetting this commercial relationship, the colonies were now developing manufacturing industries and exports of their own, which had free access to British markets, creating difficulties for British industrial towns, and raising demands for protection. Financial problems followed in the colonies, leading to the evasion of duties, prompting efforts by the Crown to enforce them, the more so as the war had left Britain with a huge public debt and financial responsibility for the administration of a huge new territory in North America. The growing animosity found an outlet particularly in criticism by the colonists of Britain's right to impose taxes, bearing in mind that the colonists were neither represented in the British Parliament nor even consulted on taxation in commercial matters. On the other hand, the colonies displayed a degree of irresponsibility in refusing to recognise the huge debt that the Crown had incurred while fighting the war and defending the colonies from the French.

The tensions had their epicentre in Massachusetts, whose inhabitants were mainly the descendants of the Pilgrim Fathers, Puritans from whom they had inherited a tradition of republicanism, fomented by Stuart misrule. It was Virginia, however, which took the initiative by inviting the colonies to a Continental Congress in 1774, with the object of reaching a better understanding with the Crown and Parliament. Twelve of the colonies accepted the invitation. The northernmost colonies and Georgia, in the south, failed to attend. The Crown was now anxious to make concessions, but Parliament, concerned for the interests of its own voters, was in no mood to compromise. Violence erupted in Massachusetts, bringing a confrontation with British troops, and a general insurrection soon followed. It was an insurrection that Britain failed to deal with effectively, due partly to French support for the colonists and a loss of interest by Parliament after the surrender of a British army at Yorktown. If the Crown had dealt with the complaints of the colonists in the light of common law, a satisfactory solution might well have been reached, granting to the colonies, which were by now well established, full powers to manage their own affairs, a mutually beneficial relationship with the Crown might well have been restored, but the adherence of the Crown to a feudal view of its position made the damage irreparable. This left under the aegis of the Crown only the French-speaking territory of Quebec, which distrusted the English-speaking colonies, and the northern British colonies of Nova Scotia, Newfoundland and Prince Edward Island. With their frustration and bitterness replaced by a sense of triumph, the thirteen rebel colonies, the regal contract already broken, declared their independence and formed a confederacy known as the United States of America. Many disaffected colonists refused to break the contract, however, and retained it in the only way now possible, by migrating northwards, amid much hostility, to settle north of Lakes Ontario and Erie, a region claimed by the Crown that was or became known as Ontario, and which the Crown now made available to them.[3] The Ontario colony became known as Upper Canada, while the French-speaking province of Quebec became Lower Canada.[4]

Much of the blame for the loss of England's colonies in North America has been unfairly directed at the King, George III, but although he was guided by feudal doctrine, he was a fair-minded man, and the affairs of the Crown were directed by Ministers drawn from the leading Party of the day, whose obligations were to the interests of their own constituents, rather than to the interests of the colonies. The real culprits in the breakdown of colonial relations were the Stuart dynasty, whose empathy with Roman Catholicism had not only alienated a large part of the English people, but also left many so divorced from the Crown that they had 'escaped' to North America, where they had, effectively, already broken their participation in the regal contract. It is possible that it was only the insecurity of initial settlement in a strange continent, and the threats posed, first by the Native Americans, and then by the French, that had prevented them from severing the link earlier. All it had needed was growing self-confidence and the removal of these external threats for the hated regal contract to be relinquished. Those colonies further south

---

3   North of the watershed, from where the rivers and streams drained to Hudson Bay, was claimed by the Hudson's Bay Company.

4   The name came from the local indigenous word for a village or settlement, which the French had assumed to refer to the entire region.

that had no serious dispute with the Crown evidently decided that the overriding interests of the thirteen lay in keeping together.

28.3.1.1. The American Constitution

Although the thirteen English colonies had broken the regal contract and no longer formed part of the Empire, it is instructive to see what permanent arrangement for co-operation and independent self-government was made by the alliance.

The former colonies now referred to themselves as 'states', a term related to the word 'estate' (French *état*). In its origin and nature, an American state – formerly colony – corresponded in its function to an English shire of a thousand years earlier, in that it encompassed the limits of a rudimentary nation. The early American colonies had varied greatly in size, however, because few had the space in which to grow to their natural limits, defined as the maximum extent beyond which its citizens were unable to attend a national assembly. A common reason was that the extent of the original colonies had been determined by letters patent and other legal grants and agreements drawn up in England, often before the colonists had left. Consequently, the legal boundaries of these colonies had been based on assumptions other than the needs of the eventual nation, into which the colonists would grow. Subsequent conflicts of interest were usually resolved within the limits of the original charters, which at least had the advantage that they caused agreements to be reached without recourse to fighting. Consequently, the early colonists rarely grew to their full potential as nations, and in some cases, such as Rhode Island, a small but independent colony was founded by a small group of the settlers inside a previous and legally defined territorial allocation. The resulting problems of population growth were prevented from finding a natural solution by the territorial expansion of the existing colony.

Another crucial influence was the invention of the technique of surveying, which could define a boundary quickly across even empty or barely settled territory, but only in the form of straight lines, running north-south, or east-west. Where colonies had been allowed to grow, more or less, to their natural extent, such as Georgia, the limits were set, not by settlement, but, all too often by straight lines, regardless of the topography. Only great rivers, lakes, mountain ranges and the sea usually interrupted these rectangular territories.

Colonies and subsequent states were much larger than an English shire, because the widespread use of horse transport enabled citizens to travel a much greater distance to attend a public assembly or a government office, which, ideally, were located in a central position. Because of the greater ease and speed of travel, the typical extent of a colony or state was therefore about 220 miles, or an average radius from the centre – that is, the maximum distance from a centrally situated popular assembly – of about 110 miles. This contrasted with about twenty-one miles for a typical English shire (or forty-two miles in extent). Later influences, such as the arrival of a railway or the development of a busy port, might upset this 'radius of convenience' by causing public institutions to be moved to the new centre of population.

The New England colonists were strongly opposed to the institution of hereditary kingship, as they were to any hereditary social class (unless it was based purely on wealth), but all favoured the retention of *de facto* common law principles, based on the belief that all colonists were free men. All decisions affecting the community should therefore be made by a popular assembly. Consequently, the Continental Congress of the Founding Fathers was succeeded by an elected assembly of representatives of the States. This assembly was accordingly to be known as the House of Representatives. It was equivalent, therefore, to an English Parliament before it sub-divided into two Houses. Each State was represented according to the number of its voters, so that some States inevitably were much more heavily represented than others, in accordance with the democratic principle. The absence of an upper chamber, comprising the political elite, was of some concern to the Founding Fathers, however, because they saw in such an institution a stabilising element. To what extent they saw the House of Lords in England having this effect is not clear, but, being well versed in the Classics, they noted a parallel in the Roman Senate. Most likely, their instinct for common law institutions made them dimly aware of the essential stabilising and guiding role of the largely forgotten Great Council. In order to fill this apparent void, the Founding Fathers provided for an upper chamber, to be known as the Senate, whose members would be elected by the people, like the

Representatives of the Lower House, but would sit for longer, only half being subject to re-election at a time. Because the United States was a confederacy of its member States, each was accorded two representatives (Senators), regardless of its population. This, it was hoped, would ensure greater continuity and greater experience, such as was to be expected in the House of Lords and the Roman Senate, or, more specifically, in the Old English *Witan*.

Opposition to the notion of a King as head of state left the problem of who was to be responsible for the executive function of government, and therefore the leader of the new Federation. The principle of elected kingship had long been forgotten. The answer was found in a President, with a Vice President, who would hold office for four years, with a maximum of two successive terms. He was the President, presumably, because he was deemed to preside over the Congress, in that he convened or adjourned either or both Houses. He also approved Bills passed by the two Houses and signed them into law. He did not preside over their proceedings. The initial means of selection for Presidential office was by means of a select group of individuals from the State legislatures, but this proved to be too complicated, and eventually, following the emergence of two political Parties, the Democrats and Republicans, each with a vested interest in the outcome, there emerged a system whereby each Party held a national convention of its members from the various States, who chose a candidate, decided on a platform of intended policies, and set up a Party organization for the duration of the period of office. The opposing candidates were subsequently presented to the general electorate. Other Parties were not precluded, but only the original two have succeeded in the eyes of the voters, partly because only the original two Parties amassed the financial resources to conduct an effective electoral campaign. The Articles of Confederation came into effect in 1781, and were ratified in 1788.

In this system we see, therefore, one very like that followed in England during the reigns of the early Stuarts, but with royalty and nobility excluded. Another important difference was that the system provided for a Supreme Court, with original jurisdiction in all cases involving ambassadors, other public ministers and consuls, and those in which a State was party, otherwise it enjoyed appellate jurisdiction in other cases coming before it, including cases involving questions of law or constitutionality. In effect, the leading judiciary presided over the system, instead of being subject to it, putting the court very much in the position, in constitutional matters, of the Great Council in England.

The choice of the American flag is also of constitutional interest. The attribution of the design to the arms of George Washington is questionable, because, being an unpretentious man, he is hardly likely to have agreed to it.[5] A more likely source, because it also used an arrangement of 'stars and stripes', was that of the Bristol entrepreneur Richard Ameryke, after whom Cabot is likely to have given America its name. The thirteen bars of the new flag were to represent the founding states of the union, and a blue 'Union' rectangle at the hoist was to contain a constellation of stars that was to represent all the states in the Union, including the new ones already being added, reflecting the imperialistic attitude to the continental interior, now that the French and the King stood in the way. As further states would be admitted to the Union, they would be represented in the rectangle, but not in the bars. Nevertheless, the fact that the new flag was very similar to Washington's own undoubtedly helped in its choice.

28.3.2. The Establishment of Canada

Lessons learned by the Crown from the loss of the thirteen American colonies were not lost as its policy towards the remaining North American colonies evolved. The Quebec Act of 1774 had, in any case, recognised the sensitive nature of governing an alien French population, including its claim to the Great Lakes and beyond. This was later compromised by the claim of the United States to the region lying south of the Great Lakes. It was further curtailed by the migration of loyalists from the south, following the Treaty of Paris. Many settled in what was now western Quebec, north of Lakes Ontario and Erie, west of the Ottawa River, where they were given land and assistance by the Crown. Meanwhile, an influx of disaffected American settlers into Nova Scotia caused it to be sub-divided in 1784, with its western part, across the Bay of Fundy, becoming the separate colony of New Brunswick.

Meanwhile, the Americans not only hated the loyalists who had settled further north, but they were resentful of the northern colonies for not joining them during the revolution, and they detested the continuing presence of the Crown in North America. Of more concern was the

5   G. C. Rothery, *The Concise Encyclopaedia of Heraldry* (London, 1994), 300–302.

development of American imperialism, as the new United States began its expansion westwards, and an American President, Jefferson, suggested that annexing Canada would be 'simply a matter of marching'. The opportunity came during the Napoleonic Wars, when Britain was heavily engaged in Spain and Portugal. The United States declared war against Britain in 1812, but an attempted conquest of Canada achieved little, and was followed by a corresponding invasion of the United States that culminated in the burning of Washington, until the antagonists restored peace in the Treaty of Ghent in 1814. Nevertheless, the fact that the future expansion of what would become known as Canada was not eventually blocked, westward of Ontario, by the rapidly expanding United States, and the fact that Canada eventually achieved its own outlet to the Pacific, was due largely to the existence of the Hudson's Bay Company. This had been incorporated in 1670, under the auspices of Prince Rupert, for the purpose of trading with the Native Americans, particularly in furs. For this purpose, it had been given a trading monopoly within the Hudson's Bay drainage basin, which had become known as Prince Rupert's Land. It covered a vast area, including the Saskatchewan River, which drained to the Bay by way of Lake Winnipeg, extended as far westwards as the Rocky Mountains, and included the Red River basin to the south.[6]

In 1783, the Northwest Company was established to operate between the territory of the Hudson's Bay Company and the Pacific. Its claim extended southwards as far as the border with Mexico, which at the time lay south of the forty-second parallel (which would later define the northern border of California). The territory of the Northwest Company came to be known as the Columbia region, after the river, and its advent led to the opening up of the west coast from 1807, with the activities of the company centred on the lower Columbia River, from which the new territory took its name. The attraction of Columbia at the time lay in a growing commerce in furs. In 1821, the Hudson's Bay Company effectively incorporated the Northwest Company, thereby extending its own operations to the Pacific.[7]

Meanwhile, ethnic agitation in Quebec was rewarded by the Canada Act of 1791. This divided Quebec into the two provinces of Upper Canada, which was mainly English-speaking, and French-speaking

---

6   This included large parts of what later became North Dakota and Minnesota.
7   Comprising what would later become British Columbia, Washington, and Oregon.

Lower Canada. They were separated by the Ottawa River, a tributary of the St Lawrence. Each was provided with a degree of autonomy, with an elected Assembly and a Legislative Council, which was presided over by a Governor. Legislation was subject to the right of veto by the Crown, provided it was exercised within two years of enactment.

Britain was much embroiled in the Napoleonic Wars, which extended from 1795 to 1815, after which it was preoccupied with a severe economic depression that lasted until 1820, causing it to be ill-prepared to deal with the rapidly expanding ambitions of the United States. In an attempt by both governments to avoid conflict, a treaty was agreed between them in 1818 that established a boundary west of the Great Lakes. This extended from the southern end of the Lake of the Woods, following the forty-ninth parallel as far as the Rocky Mountains. This involved the surrender of the southern part of the Red River basin, which was then incorporated into the new American states of Minnesota and North and South Dakota. West of the Rocky Mountains, the region known to Britain as Columbia, and to the United States as the Oregon Country, was to be left under joint occupation for ten years. The Pacific coast north of Columbia was claimed and, to a limited extent, settled by Russia. Meanwhile, the issue was finally decided by the relative weight of interest of the two powers in the region, Britain's interest being little more than the fur trade, because there were few settlers to take effective occupation. Mounting tension by the 1840's, caused by a growing flood of American settlement in the Willamette valley, south of the lower Columbia River, finally forced Great Britain to agree in 1846 to renounce its claim to southern Columbia – that is, the Oregon Country – in favour of a westward extension of the existing boundary along the forty-ninth parallel to the Pacific. The exception was the retention by Britain of Vancouver Island. In the tract of territory so relinquished, the American states of Oregon, Washington and Idaho would eventually be established.

In 1837, meanwhile, there was rebellion in both Upper and Lower Canada, resulting from constitutional conflicts between the respective, popularly elected Assemblies, on the one hand, and their Governors and appointed Legislative Councils, on the other, over vested interests. In the following year, Lord Durham was appointed Governor-in-Chief of all the British North American colonies. Although he was forced by the Crown to resign a few months later, over his lenient treatment of the rebels (an echo of why the American colonies had been lost in the first place), he had been in office long enough at least to assess the situation. The outcome in 1839 was his *Report on the Affairs of British North America*, known as the Durham Report. This recommended a union of the two Canadas and the granting to them of responsible government. This caught the attention of the House of Lords, and led to its proposals being implemented by the British Parliament in 1840, as the Union Act. This provided for a common Governor, Legislative Council and Assembly, in which Upper and Lower Canada were equally represented. The issue of responsible government was evaded for a decade, however, until a further crisis in 1849, over the costs of the rebellion, brought about its implementation.

Meanwhile, tension between the United States and British North America continued unabated, fuelled, not only by the continuing animosity of the Americans, and particularly of Irish immigrants to America,[8] but also because its rapid westward expansion generated a mood of imperialism that encouraged ambitions towards the whole of North America. In 1867, the purchase by the United States from Russia of Alaska appeared to threaten Canada's security still further. The problem of defending the colonies from their southern neighbour was not the only one. The territorial divisions between the two colonies also hampered communications, particularly between Upper Canada and the Atlantic coast. Both problems could be reduced by political unification, yet a full union was deemed to be impracticable, because of the conflicting interests of language, culture and religion, as well as the problem of democratic representation over such a vast area.

The British North America Act of 1867 accordingly brought together Upper and Lower Canada, New Brunswick and Nova Scotia, to form a confederation of the four colonies as four provinces in a new and independent Dominion of Canada. The description of Canada – and, indeed, all its sister colonies around the world as they matured into full independence – as a 'dominion' is another example of possible legal confusion. A dominion is a 'sovereign authority' or 'sovereignty',[9] or a territory subject to the jurisdiction of a king, or, in this case, Queen Victoria. This is its meaning in common law and, by the same definition,

---

8   These gave rise to the Fenian raids on Canada, beginning in 1866.
9   *Shorter Oxford Dictionary* (1973).

Great Britain was itself a 'dominion', just as Canada could also be described as a kingdom. Under feudal doctrine, however, 'dominion' had a narrower meaning as 'the domain of a feudal lord'. It is doubtful whether the Crown itself, given its long history of legal confusion, was ever quite clear. It is likely, however, that the description of Canada as a 'dominion' was chosen because it had an absent Sovereign, in contrast to the United Kingdom, where the Sovereign was resident.

Prince Rupert's Land was bought from the Hudson's Bay Company by the Canadian Government in 1870, and British Columbia was then able to join the Dominion in 1871. This extended Canada to the Pacific. The particular problem faced by the new Canada was that, because the climate limited settlement largely to the south, in a strip several thousand miles long, but rarely more than a few hundred miles wide (and often a fraction of that), containing little but forest, the natural trading links of the east, mid-west and British Columbia, respectively, lay with their corresponding parts of the United States, to the south.[10] It was in an effort to hold Canada together, both politically and economically, as well as to promote settlement in the west, that the Canadian Pacific Railway Company was chartered in 1881 to build a transcontinental line. The southern part of Prince Rupert's Land was then divided into several new provinces, as Manitoba, Saskatchewan and Alberta, in addition to British Columbia. Meanwhile, settlement increased in the west, between Manitoba and the Rocky Mountains, attracted by the fertile open plains, or 'prairies'.

To an even greater extent than the United States, Canada was an artificial creation, effectively a string of emergent nations extending across the continent, from Newfoundland and Nova Scotia, in the east, to British Columbia in the west, forced to form a single confederacy by the common threat from the south and held together by a common allegiance to the Crown. The Canadian Provinces, or 'nations', were similar in size to their neighbours south of the border, and apparently for the same reason of the early availability of horse transport, except that they extended into a huge area of what was still forested 'wasteland' in

---

10   The United States also had a potential problem of at least three possible confederacies centred in the north-east, the Mississippi basin and the West Coast. A break-up was delayed by massive westward migration, which prevented strong regional identities from forming, and by the early arrival of the railway and the telegraph, which did much to hold the new country together.

the north. The exceptions were Nova Scotia, New Brunswick and Prince Edward Island, whose smaller size was due to the fact that they bordered the sea.

Canada was an offshoot of the thirteen 'American' colonies further south, but the two differed constitutionally in two respects, apart from the fact that the former incorporated the French colony of Quebec. The first was that Canada remained party to the regal contract, whereas the United States rejected it. The second was that the *de facto* head of the executive in Canada would eventually be its Prime Minister, but not its head *de lege*, because this continued to be the King. By contrast, both the head of the Executive in the United States and the head of state was the President.

28.3.2.1. Newfoundland

Isolated from the interior, except by sea, and facing out onto the North Atlantic, Newfoundland was never a part of anywhere else. Its lack of political clout allowed Britain to cede fishing rights to the Americans on the coasts of Newfoundland and Labrador in 1818, but responsible government was granted to it as the Dominion of Newfoundland in 1855. Limited resources and a lack of accountability kept Newfoundland struggling with debt during much of its independent existence. American fishing rights were restricted after 1906, and in 1927 the interior of Labrador, as far as the watershed, was incorporated as a part of Newfoundland. The persistence of financial mismanagement, corruption and government debt, however, caused the Crown in 1933 to revoke Newfoundland's Dominion status, in favour of temporary government by a Royal Commission. It was not until 1948 that the future of Newfoundland was finally decided by referendum, albeit by a small margin, and in the following year the colony finally gave up its ambition of independence by joining Canada as its tenth province.

28.3.3. South Africa

England had no commercial or settler interest in the Cape of Good Hope, only a strategic interest in Cape Town, but it was drawn further and further in by its growing dispute with the existing Dutch settlers, and this was largely of its own making. It was only much later that the attractions of commerce and settlement made themselves evident.

South Africa was strategically placed on the sea route to southern Asia and Australia. It appeared to offer little inducement to settlement, until the Dutch East India Company established a re-victualling station at the Cape of Good Hope, where its ships, after sailing all the way down the west side of Africa, were at last able to turn east. Settlers were introduced to supply the ships with fruit and vegetables, giving rise to the small town and port of Kaapstad, or Cape Town. To the north of the colony extended the semi-arid and desert regions of Namaqualand and the Kalahari, while to north-east and east extended the semi-arid Karroo and the coastal mountains, where the interior plateau reached the sea.

Of the indigenous inhabitants, the Hottentots and, in the interior, the Bushmen, or San, were particularly hostile and an unsuitable source of labour. This caused the Dutch to import Indonesian slaves from the East Indies. The shortage of Dutch women eventually caused the appearance of a population of mixed race, or 'Coloureds'. As the Indonesians were Moslems, they referred to the Hottentots as 'kaffirs', or infidels. Meanwhile, the Dutch settlers had multiplied and spread eastwards, along the Cape coast, and north-eastwards into the Karroo, many adapting to the dry conditions by becoming cattle farmers. Under the Treaty of Paris of 1814, Great Britain annexed the Cape for its own strategic use.

28.3.3.1. The 1820 Settlers

The Crown imposed English as the official language, and replaced the Dutch institutions of central and local government with corresponding English ones. The Dutch were antagonistic to these changes, and, in order to increase the British character of the Colony, some 2,000 British settlers were imported into the eastern Cape in 1820. Known as the 1820 Settlers, these formed the first British colony in South Africa, establishing important settlements at Port Elizabeth, East London, King William's Town and Queenstown. Unfortunately, they arrived just in time to meet the first of the warlike Bantu, from the northern interior, an Early Iron Age people who were more advanced that the Hottentots, who had already established themselves in the Eastern Cape and were now spreading along the south coast, westwards. The English settlers were unprepared for this and suffered accordingly, having to rely on the local Dutch kommandos, or mounted volunteers, for their defence, in a series of bitter conflicts, known as the Kaffir Wars, until British troops eventually arrived. A border between the Cape Colony and the Bantu was eventually established on the Great Kei River, but it had to be defended as more Bantu arrived from the north. Meanwhile, the northern extent of the Cape Colony, which was administered by a Governor and Council, was ill-defined.

28.3.3.2. Racial Discrimination and Humanism

Inevitably, the Crown took a feudal view of its position in the Cape Colony, imposing whatever laws it deemed to be appropriate and in its own best interests, as well as those of the Dutch, the underlying policy being to Anglicise the Colony. The Dutch, as estranged cousins of the English, as well as being Calvinists, saw their position in the light of common law and the requirements of the Biblical Old Testament. They defended these and their own language with particular intensity, feeling that their very identity was under threat. Unfortunately for mutual relations, a wave of social liberalism was sweeping Britain at the time, and when slavery was abolished throughout the Empire in 1833, and was imposed in the Cape Colony in the following year, it had crippling implications for the Dutch community, particularly the farmers, who relied heavily on black slave labour. The abolition of slavery might have been accommodated, given time, but what could not be accommodated by the Dutch farming community was what it saw as the relentless imposition upon it of conformist laws that were destructive of Dutch culture, and, worst of all, the imposition of political and social equality between themselves and the relatively primitive and despised non-white population. In a situation that was analogous to the eve of the American Civil War, twenty-seven years later, and just as bitter, this was regarded by many as the final straw.[11]

28.3.3.3. The Great Trek

With little prospect of achieving a successful revolution, a large part of the Dutch farming population – the *boere*, or 'farmers' – decided in favour of leaving the Cape Colony altogether, and establishing a free and

11   E. Walker, *A History of Southern Africa* (London, 1957), 59–105; 176.

independent Dutch republic on the African Plateau, about two hundred miles to the north-east, which exploration had shown to be well over 3,000 feet above sea-level and better watered. Accordingly, thousands of Dutch farmers, with their families and livestock, left the Cape Colony in 1835 and headed north-eastwards, between the dry Karroo to the west and the mountains of the Drakensberg to the east, crossing the upper Orange River (which flowed westward), and eventually reaching the open *veld*, or grass-covered uplands of the Plateau. They travelled in independent groups, or 'treks', using horses and covered ox-wagons. At first, their progress was unopposed, because the previous inhabitants of the Plateau had recently been devastated by the ravages of a Bantu people known as the Zulus, whose homeland lay to the north-east, between the plateau and the Indian Ocean. It has been estimated that the Zulus had slain the best part of two million Bantu of other tribes,[12] leaving much of the 'highveld' wide open to the Dutch. About two hundred and fifty miles north-east of the Orange River, the Plateau was crossed, again from east to west (because the plateau tipped in that direction), by the Vaal River, before it turned south to join the Orange. The Great Trek, as it became known, was a phenomenon that almost exactly paralleled the great American migrations to the West. Isolated in the interior, the *Voortrekkers*, as they came to be known, gradually forged for themselves a new identity, in which they were no longer Dutch, but 'Africans', or *Afrikaners*, as distinct from the indigenous 'Kaffirs', or Bantu. Long isolated, even before the Great Trek, they spoke a degraded rural form of the 'High Dutch' that was still spoken in the Western Cape, referring to it as *Afrikaans*, or 'African'.

The *Voortrekkers* were, by and large, an uneducated people, beyond a knowledge of the Bible, with little or no knowledge or experience, except at a local level. The Dutch were close cousins of the English, largely separated from each other for the best part of one and a half millennia, and it is of interest, therefore, to look at the constitutions that they now devised in their isolation, to see whether they had any correspondence with the common law of government in England. Establishing themselves between the Orange River and the Vaal, two groups, led by Maritz and Potgieter, were the first to establish a crude constitution at Thaba Nchu,

---

12	G. M. Theal, *History and Ethnography of Africa, South of the Zambezi, Before 1795*, i. 396. See also E. Walker, *A History of Southern Africa*, 176.

so named after the mission station where it was drawn up, and known as the republic of Transorangia. Following the arrival of another trek, led by Retief, a year later, in 1837, while Maritz and Potgieter set off on a campaign against the Matabele, Retief, having had some education, supervised the drawing up, at Vet River, of a revised constitution. This was still known as the Thaba Nchu constitution, and it had as its basis[13] *Het Volk*, the People, comprising the four hundred men of his own trek, who, when summoned, formed a popular assembly. This elected a Parliament, known as the *Volksraad*, or 'People's Council'. Initially, this comprised six representatives, meeting under a President (whose function might be said to correspond to that of the King). Its purpose was to legislate and administer such laws as might be agreed by a general assembly of the people (Volk). When the *Volksraad* sat in its judicial capacity, however, it did so, not under the President, but under the *Landdrost*, or magistrate. Later, the *Volksraad* was increased from six to twenty-four elected members. Military matters were managed, not by the President, however, but by a Governor and Lieutenant-General, advised by an elected Council of Policy. This may have been the *Volksraad* sitting in a wartime capacity.[14]

The enlarged *Volksraad* was elected by the men of each 'field cornetcy', a field cornet being a mounted officer who carried a flag in battle. A field cornetcy formed either a district or a number of families, which must have corresponded roughly to an English hundred. The word 'cornet' comes from Latin *cornu*, a 'horn', which was once used to lead in war, in much the same way as the English hundredman must have originally led his hundred in battle. As a territory, a cornetcy would have been more extensive than the English hundred, because of the use of horses for travel and ox-wagons for transport.

There being no First or Second Estate, lost in Holland well before they had even moved to the Cape, the function of a Great Council was provided, in effect, by the Nine Articles of association. This was the source of legal guidance in constitutional matters, there being no group of individuals with the education, experience, authority and legal background necessary to form a Great Council. If the system had a serious weakness, it was that it lacked an effective civil service. As in all Indo-European societies, moreover, it excluded the local native population,

13　E. Walker, *A History of Southern Africa*, 204.
14　Ibid. 204.

which was left to govern itself, in accordance with its own traditions. The only real difference, therefore, between the English Constitution in common law and the constitution devised by the *Voortrekkers*, was their division of the civil and military functions of the 'king'.

In 1837, other groups of the *Voortrekkers*, led by Retief, proceeded further north, crossing the Vaal. This area was already occupied by a break-away group of the Zulus, known as the Matabele, who, under the leadership of Mzilikazi, fiercely attacked the intruders, who, at night, formed their wagons into a defensive circle, known as a *laager*. Men, women and children caught on the open *veld* were killed, except for those carried off into captivity. Meanwhile, reinforced by another trek from the Cape, disagreement among the leaders at first delayed further action. Retief left for the Natal coast, the only access to the outside world, in the hope of negotiation with the British. Meanwhile, a group of one hundred and thirty-five men, led by Potgieter and Uys, fought a running battle with the Matabele, lasting nine days, along the Marico River, inflicting a decisive defeat, and causing Mzilikazi to lead his survivors away to the north, beyond the distant Limpopo River. The *Voortrekkers*, now left in possession of the southern Transvaal, over the next few years gradually extended their territory northwards from the Vaal to the Limpopo, and in 1852 the Transvaal was proclaimed as the South African Republic. Three years later, its seat of government was established in the south, at Pretoria, where the road to the north passed the eastern end of the Magaliesberg.

Meanwhile, a third group of the *Voortrekkers*, led by Uys, formally broke with Retief, with the intention of descending the escarpment of the Drakensberg into Natal and founding a third Dutch republic. Retief, seeing Natal as the only access to the sea and the outside world, and having himself descended into Natal with a small group, intent on negotiating with the British, achieved little. Turning his attention to negotiating with the Zulus, Retief established good relations with the Zulu chief, Dingaan, by retrieving cattle, guns and horses stolen from him by a rival chief. Returning with a party of about seventy companions and thirty 'Coloured' servants with the cattle, but not the guns and horses, Dingaan made to them a grant of all the land between the Tugela and Umzimvubu Rivers, but, alarmed by the progress of events, immediately followed this with treachery, by massacring Retief and his party. He then launched attacks on those groups of the *Voortrekkers* who had already established themselves in parts of Natal, wiping out one of their *laagers*, while others stood firm, then descending on the British settlement on the coast, at Port Natal and annihilating it. News of the disaster brought up many more of the Dutch from the Eastern Cape and, under the leadership of Pretorius, a strong force entered Zululand, late in 1838, and inflicted a decisive defeat on the Zulus in the battle of Blood River. Occupying the ruins of the Zulu capital, he found not only the remains of Retief and his party, but also the deed of cession of Natal in Retief's wallet. The fleeing Dingaan was killed by the neighbouring Swazis, whom he had only just attacked in a failed attempt to restore the morale of his own *impis*, or regiments. The victory by no means ended Zulu power, but it made possible the establishment of a third Dutch republic, of Natalia, with its capital at Pietermaritzburg.

28.3.3.4. *The Reaction of the Crown*

The reaction of the Crown to the departure of the Dutch cattle farmers from the eastern Cape Colony on the 'Great Trek', meanwhile, was one of dismay and outrage. As already noted, according to feudal doctrine, a Crown colony, much like England itself, was regarded as a feudal royal estate, whose inhabitants, provided they were born there, were bound to it in service to the King, in accordance with the legal principle: *nemo potest exuere partriam*, literally, 'nobody sets aside the sovereignty of the native land'; that is, the *Voortrekkers* could not leave the Cape Colony without royal permission. Consequently, they had committed a treasonable offence. Large areas of the Colony were, after all, now depopulated and unproductive, and it was the Dutch who had provided the 'kommandos', who alone had been effective against the Bantu in the Eastern Cape. The only way in which the defectors could escape from their liability to British justice was by submitting to the jurisdiction of another sovereign authority, recognised by the King, and the only option here was the current ruling Queen of Portugal, which had an alliance with Britain. The Portuguese had previously laid a nominal claim, recognised by Britain, to all Africa north of the twenty-sixth parallel of south latitude, which crossed the Plateau about one hundred and forty miles north of the Vaal. This allowed the Crown to lay a nominal legal claim of its own to the area south of this, which effectively included all or part of the three Republics, even though the Crown, like the Portuguese, had no means of enforcing it. British subjects south of the parallel were nevertheless now liable, according to feudal doctrine, to the jurisdiction of the Cape courts for crimes committed outside the Colony, provided the accused and relevant witnesses could be returned to it, in order to face justice. To give effect to this, native chiefs north of the Colony were subsidised, among other things, to enforce the Cape laws by capturing and returning alleged offenders, although this was something that they were hardly likely to do. In the meantime, the only retribution that was available to the Crown was to isolate the rebels in the interior, by depriving them of all contact with the outside world. In particular, this meant denying them access to the east coast, and the infliction of retribution in accordance with the Punishment Act, as opportunity arose.

28.3.3.5. Natal

In pursuit of this, a second British colony was established in Natal in 1843. This had its origin in British traders from Cape Town, led by Francis Farewell, who in 1823 had prospected the trading possibilities of Natal. Farewell and a few companions had then negotiated with the Zulu chief at the time, Shaka, and in 1824 obtained possession of a large tract of land south of the Tugela River that included a bay on the coast, referred to as the 'port or harbour of Natal'. The homeland of the Zulus was in Zululand, immediately to the north of Natal, over which they claimed sovereignty. Ten years later, a petition from merchants in Cape Town, asking for the creation of a British colony in Natal, was rejected by the Cape government on the ground of cost. In 1835, the settlers themselves laid out a town at the site of Port Natal and named it Durban, after the then governor of the Cape Colony.

Three years later, the *Voortrekkers* arrived from the interior, taking possession of Natal and evicting the British settlers before establishing it as the Republic of Natalia, with a seat of government at Pietermaritzburg. This was not far inland from Port Natal, raising the real possibility that it would provide the *Voortrekker* republics with their outlet to sea, threatening the policy of containment and isolation of the truants. Accordingly, after an initial defeat of the British force by the *Voortrekkers*,

Britain reoccupied Port Natal in 1843 and formally annexed the whole of Natal, including the Republic of Natalia. Although the *Voortrekkers* were now consulted, in a gesture of goodwill, as to the new form of government, the conditions demanded by the Crown were seen as intolerable, causing the majority of the *Voortrekkers* to return to the Highveld in the interior and the disintegration of the republic. Natal now came under the administration of the Governor of the Cape Colony, of which it was regarded as a district, and British immigration followed, perhaps much of it from the Cape Colony. The Zulus, meanwhile, were provided with a large reservation in the north of Natal, thereby establishing the principle of native reserves, not unlike the reservations in North America. Later, in 1898, British diplomacy again responded to an attempt by the *Voortrekkers* in the Transvaal to establish an outlet to the sea, further north, at Delagoa Bay, north of Zululand, by persuading the Portuguese to establish control of Delagoa Bay and its hinterland, making it a Portuguese colony. In a supreme example of British vindictiveness, this effectively denied the *Voortrekkers* of all further hope of access to the Indian Ocean.

The Crown, meanwhile, being determined to bring the rebels in Transorangia back under its authority, mounted an expedition from the Cape Colony in 1848, occupying the territory, proclaiming British rule, and re-naming it the Orange River Sovereignty. Lacking the resources to administer it, however, and fearing that the new South African Republic, north of the Vaal, might take action, Britain arranged the Sand River Convention between the parties in 1852. This effectively recognised the independence of the South African Republic, while the latter agreed not to intervene south of the Vaal. Here, under the terms of the Convention of Bloemfontein, agreed two years later, the Crown, finding itself lacking the resources to sustain the arrangement, withdrew its jurisdiction from the Orange River Sovereignty altogether, leaving it as an autonomous state under the watchful eye of a British Resident, whereupon it celebrated by changing its name to the Orange Free State. The feudal principles that guided British policy remained unchanged, however, as the new British Resident made clear, when he urged the British Government to extend British rule 'over all Her Majesty's subjects to the north'.

28.3.4. Australia Cites Feudal Doctrine

The highly profitable spice trade with the East Indies had been pioneered by the Portuguese, after they had discovered the Cape route to the East. This had enabled them to by-pass the old trade route through the Red Sea, which was controlled by the Arabs and the Venetians, who had made substantial profits from the trade. England's own empire in the east, the gateway to which was the Cape, was built by the Honourable East India Company, which had been founded in 1600 with the intention of securing a share in the spice trade. The Dutch followed hard on the heels of the English, and in the fierce competition that followed, were able to seize control of the trade with the Spice Islands, better known as the Moluccas, located in the East Indies. This forced the East India Company to re-direct its trading activities to India, where it found itself in competition with the French, the Portuguese having been reduced by now to a fairly minor presence.

Our concern is with 'colonies', not with trading 'concessions', where royal jurisdiction did not usually extend. The significance of the East Indies arises, therefore, from the discovery by the Dutch traders that the quickest way to the Indies was not north-eastwards across the Indian Ocean, but eastward from the Cape, following the prevailing westerly winds – known as the 'roaring forties'. At the appropriate longitude, they then turned northward, to Java. Inevitably, some ships overshot, revealing Australia, but the west coast of the continent revealed a mostly arid interior, causing the Dutch to regard Australia as a hazard, rather than an attraction, after a number of their ships were wrecked on its coast. In fact, the continent had long been known to the natives of Indonesia, and even to the Chinese, but they had not been attracted by it. Even the Portuguese had found it, but they had been wrecked on the south coast, so that news of the discovery may never have reached Portugal. Although *Terra Australis* was of no commercial interest to them, it was of interest to Dutch explorers, and after sailing round the 'Southern Land' and Tasmania, off the south coast, they went on to discover New Zealand, further east. A British naval officer, Cook, despatched in 1768 to investigate the South Pacific, explored the coast of New Zealand and went on to report favourably on the eastern side of Australia, which he named New South Wales. The Crown saw little of interest in such remote places, however, until a crime wave in England, caused mainly by widespread dispossession caused by the enclosure movement, filled the prisons to overflowing. The option then presented itself of establishing penal colonies overseas. Existing British colonies rejected the idea, and this left New South Wales as a possibility, because its remoteness was an asset, as well as a problem. This removed the possibility of ex-convicts returning to England to add to the crisis. Accordingly, the first convict settlement was established at Botany Bay, in New South Wales, in 1788, and the town and port of Sydney was developed a short distance away. Other convict settlements followed, including one on the island of Tasmania, off the south coast, and another, to forestall French ambitions, in Western Australia. It was then realised that a settled free population would provide employment for both convicts and ex-convicts, without which they tended to become lawless bush-rangers. Such were the attractions of New South Wales for farming, particularly after it was discovered that sheep produced a high-quality wool that could be exported profitably to England, that it was not long before free settlers greatly outnumbered the convicts. The convict settlements left a legacy of bitterness among the ex-convicts and their descendants at having been relegated to Australia in the first place, and then not repatriated after the convicts had served their sentences. It was a lasting consequence of the callousness of the English penal system at the time.

At the time of the first settlement of Australia, the continent was already inhabited by an Early Stone Age people, referred to as the 'Aborigines', and the ensuing friction had led to them being decimated over large areas. Consequently, it was only in the north that they survived in significant numbers. It was a widespread expectation that they would eventually become extinct, solving the social problem, but in the meantime, unsuccessful efforts were made to enable them to adapt to a civilized society. As in the Cape Colony, the eighteenth century had brought an upsurge in humanitarian ideals in England, which led to political chaos in the Cape, but the remoteness of Australia provided it with some protection. A lack of empathy with the new ideas meant that the issue of Aboriginal welfare and dispossession did not come to a head until 1992. This gave rise to the view that the Aboriginals had been unjustly deprived of their lands, and, if so, it ought to be decided what compensation or restitution would be appropriate. As the main defence, it was argued that, at the time of settlement, Australia was, according to feudal law, *terra nullius*, or 'no-man's land', because there were no recognisable rulers and no evidence of prior occupation, such as might have been evident from the prior existence of permanent dwellings and cultivation. The land was therefore freely available. According to this doctrine, either the land was the demonstrable estate of a ruler, which could be proved by title, or it was virgin land which God had not yet granted to anybody. This doctrine had been applied by the Crown throughout the colonial Empire. At the same time, the Aboriginals fell outside the scope of English common law, and therefore were subject to the principle of *force majeure*. This principle of taking possession of Australia at the expense of their predecessors had been followed by the Aboriginals themselves, according to the evidence of archaeology and ancient traditions, as one wave after another of Aboriginals had landed in Australia in antiquity and forcefully taken possession from their predecessors. It was not inappropriate, therefore, that English common law applied only to the settlers. The Aboriginal issue was not, therefore, a matter of law, but one of public policy.

Administratively, the island of Tasmania was in 1825 the first part of Australia to be granted the status of a separate colony, and in 1831 Western Australia also was established as a self-governing colony, centred on the Swan River in the south-west. In 1841 a fourth separate colony of South Australia was established on the east side of the Gulf of St Vincent. Ten years later, the southernmost part of south-eastern Australia was also established as the separate colony of Victoria. This was centred on Port Philip Bay, which gave access to the wide and fertile Latrobe Valley, extending to the east and west, and partly isolated from the north of the colony by the south-western extremity of the Great Dividing Range.

This range extended up the east side of Australia, separating the well-watered coastal plain from the dry interior. Well up the east coast, a fifth colony, Queensland, was established in 1859, centred on the Brisbane River. Thus, each of these colonies originated on the coast, from where settlement gradually spread out into the wilderness. Although much of the interior of Australia was largely uninhabited, rural roads were soon infested with lawless individuals, mostly escaped or ex-convicts, and the administrative area of each colony needed to be defined for purposes of jurisdiction. To this end, the Crown drew boundaries, typically about halfway between each centre of settlement and colonial government. It may have been no coincidence that the settled centres of each of the four mainland colonies – Sydney in New South Wales, Brisbane in Queensland, Melbourne in Victoria, and Adelaide in South Australia – were almost equidistant from each other, typically 400–440 miles, which may have been determined by sailing times along the coast, because overland travel was still hazardous. The exception was Western Australia, which was separated from the other colonies by a large desert. The government of each colony was initially provided by the Crown, which accompanied or even preceded any significant settlement. Constitutionally, Australia had the easiest history of all Britain's colonies. Prompted by electoral reform in Britain, an elected majority was admitted to each Legislative Council in 1842. Australia benefitted also from the reform of government in Canada, with the Australian Colonies Government Act of 1850 granting each colony the right to amend their own constitutions and fix their own tariffs, subject to Crown approval.

Gold was found in Victoria in 1851, causing an influx of workers and adventurers from overseas, including many Chinese, who became the centre of so much social trouble, both cultural and racial, that immigration by them was restricted four years later. Meanwhile, the administration by New South Wales of what had come to be known as the Northern Territory was rendered impracticable by the establishment of Queensland. This responsibility was accordingly transferred to South Australia in 1863, but, because of its isolation, the Northern Territory was at the same time provided with its own basic form of administration. The last convicts arrived in Australia in 1867, and a few years later an overland telegraph was extended from Adelaide to Darwin, on the north coast. Following agitation for the continent to be politically united, following the example of the United States, the six colonies were brought together in a common federation in 1901, to be known as the Commonwealth of Australia. This was largely modelled on the American example, but retained the features of responsible government that had been inherited from England.

A particular problem attaching to federation and, indeed, the original delineation of the states, was that it overlooked geography. The biggest natural region in Australia that had great economic potential was the Murray-Darling basin. This was the drainage area of the Murray-Darling River system, which was now divided between three states, yet it was subject to alternate floods and droughts that called for a common system of management. The obvious solution was a common administrative body to manage irrigation and river flows and, perhaps, establish a series of desalination plants along the east coast, which might also be in different states, from which water could be pumped over the Dividing Range into the basin, as required. Unfortunately, it soon became evident that the interests of the states were conflicting, yet there was no constitutional provision for such issues to be resolved.

28.3.5. The Conflict Between Feudal and Customary Law

One of the problems of Empire was the recurring conflict between customary law, which the overseas settlers usually drew upon when they endeavoured to assert what they saw as their rights, and Church-Feudal principles, which guided the Crown and were so called because they were introduced by the Church. Customary law was based on hereditary rights which, obviously, could not be extended to outsiders.

The American Founding Fathers drew upon customary law, hence the often-perceived conflict between their assertion of democratic principles in their dealings with the Crown and their contentment with the principle of slavery, which was to confuse a later age. While common law recognised slavery, however, it also endowed the slave with certain rights, including the right to earn his freedom, or have it granted by his owner. In antiquity, slavery usually became relevant as a result of war, in which case it appears usually to have been a temporary imposition, or it was as a solution to the social conflict between Indo-European and alien societies. A more enduring solution was usually the separation of the two societies, as in Australia and the former American colonies, on the basis of recognised reservations. Both practices were forms of cultural and social self-preservation.

PART XI

•

THE LEGISLATURE
APPROPRIATES THE EXECUTIVE

29. THE INTRUSION OF PARLIAMENT AND USURPING OF THE PRIVY COUNCIL

PRIOR TO THE Reform Bill of 1830, the strength of the two Parties in the Commons is unknown, nor did they account for all those in the House. Many members paid more attention to the various other groups, cliques and compacts within the House. The distinction between the early Whigs and Tories was not so much between two organised groups, as between two different casts of mind, whose fairly consistent and predictable reactions to issues gave them each a sense of common cause, and rallied them around certain leaders. In this broad sense the two parties had probably always existed, because men have always been broadly divisible into those anxious for change and those anxious to avoid it. It was only from the time of the Stuarts onward that some degree of organisation and continuity can be discerned. The party caucus, or separate meeting to rally like minds, is probably as old as the two alignments themselves, and in the seventeenth century the party was an informal clique, led by its more influential members, the appointment of a leader being achieved through consensus. The word 'caucus' originated with the American political Parties in the eighteenth century, and would not be adopted in Britain until the nineteenth century, when it would come to refer to the group that guided Party policy and appointed the Party leader. However, the caucus by another name had come into existence long before this.

One consequence of the removal from the King of his right to exercise the royal prerogative for any but the most minor purposes was that it was now almost impossible for the King to rule, except with statutory powers provided by Parliament. Hitherto, he had needed Parliament's consent to important laws that directly affected the interests of the people, such as the raising of revenue, but otherwise he had been fairly free to manage the day-to-day affairs of the country as he thought fit. Unfortunately, the Stuarts had ignored the wishes and interests of the people, and this had brought about the revolution of 1689, resulting in the severe curtailment of the royal prerogative.

Since 1066, the King had not been elected by, nor had he been answerable to, the people, and although the Great Council had usually carried out its duties in a responsible manner, it had largely ceased to represent the member nations of the kingdom. Since Edward III the situation had deteriorated further, with the Great Council forced to exercise its functions with great difficulty from inside Parliament, before largely ceasing to function altogether. As a result, there had been no supervision of the processes of government. Meanwhile, the accidental basis of the royal succession, determined by birth alone, and the substantial indifference of the Monarchy to the popular will, particularly by the Stuarts, had led to a succession of constitutional crises. The success of the Glorious Revolution in 1689, and the virtual removal from the Crown of the power to govern, had left a constitutional vacuum, into which the leader of the majority Party in the Commons was only too ready to step, and the only limit on the powers of the majority Party was the right of the House of Lords to veto legislation that it regarded as contentious.

Thus, a situation had been created that allowed Parliament to manipulate the King in the conduct of his duties, and this removed the distinction between the executive and legislative functions of government. The intended purpose of Parliament was to represent the wishes and welfare of the people, not to become involved in the functions of government, for which members of Parliament were not equipped, and which might require their involvement in issues that were not related to the public interest. Supervision of the activities of the Crown, to ensure that they did not exceed the provisions of the law, was properly the function of the Great Council.

29.1. The Commons Controls the Privy Council

Meanwhile, under the Tudors, the King's Ministers had been elected to the Commons, so that they could influence its deliberations and report back to the King. William III was appalled, however, by the factional fighting and intrigue in English politics that had developed under the

Stuarts, and refused to recognise the factions at all. In an attempt to bring order to the situation, he picked men from both Parties in about equal numbers to form the Ministry, in which capacity they sat also as members of the Committee of the Privy Council. In order to deliberate undisturbed on policy issues, however, they also sat as a Cabinet Council, which effectively was a sub-committee of the Privy Council. It was through the Privy Council, however, that they advised the King.

In so doing, William restored the direct link between the Privy Council and the Commons that had been established by the Tudors and lost under the Stuarts, except that the arrangement was now fundamentally different. It had the effect of transferring the political initiative from the Crown to the Commons, because it was now the members of the House – and hence of the political parties – who were able to control the Privy Council and the making of policy. It marked the first step by Parliament from advising the Crown to appropriating it. It was a step for which, not only was it unfitted, but which interfered with its intended function of representing the wishes and interests of the people.

For some years William acted without a Prime Minister, adopting a neutral stance, but the mixing of appointees from both Parties proved to be impractical, because they could rarely agree. The Tories were opposed to England's involvement in the War of the Spanish Succession and adopted a policy of obstruction. The King, submitting to the advice of the Earl of Sunderland, agreed to abandon his position of constitutional neutrality and commit all the great ministerial offices to the Whigs, who happened to be the dominant Party in the House of Commons at the time. The Whig Ministry quickly learned to make it a rule to stand behind each other collectively, when attacked by their political opponents in Parliament, and this practice quickly led to them being known as the Whig 'Junto', from a Spanish word, *junta*, meaning an administrative council or committee. For a time, therefore, the Whigs formed an oligarchy.

In 1699, following the summoning of William's fourth Parliament, it was realised that the Tories were now in the majority in the House of Commons. A situation of political anarchy developed, between the conflicting aims of the Whig Government and the wishes of the Tory Parliament. It was during this period of conflict between the Ministry and Parliament that the Act of Settlement was passed, and with it an unsuccessful attempt to end the Cabinet system. It was during the subsequent reign of Queen Anne, following the death of William, who had to manage with an unsympathetic Whig Ministry on the one hand, and a supportive Tory-dominated Parliament on the other, that the idea of a 'loyal opposition' first found expression. The first recorded use of the term 'opposition' in connection with Parliament occurred in 1704, soon after her accession.

29.2. The Executive Revolution: Parliament Usurps the Crown

29.2.1. A Change of Party Becomes a Change of Government

After disposing of James II, treating William III as little better than a puppet – he found the Commons to be unmanageable – whose only interest in Britain was in the use of the Royal Navy against the French, then bending the malleable Queen Anne, followed by George I – who could not even speak English, and was more often in Hanover than in England – the Parties in Parliament had enjoyed a 'dream run' in exercising power, and felt, not only that they could direct the government of the country as they chose, but that, as representatives of the people, they had every right to do so.

Indeed, a state of near anarchy continued until the dissolution of the first Parliament of Queen Anne in 1705. Anne did her best to uphold the function of the Crown by always presiding at Cabinet Councils, and she tried to prevent factional control by appointing mixed Ministries where she could. Her second Parliament in 1707 was also the first Parliament of Great Britain, following the Union with Scotland, when the presence of the Scottish members ensured a majority for the Whigs in the Commons. When Anne was finally forced to yield control of the Ministry again to the Whigs in 1708, by admitting the Earl of Sunderland to office, she did so with great reluctance. In so doing, she returned harmony to the system, but she realised that, by giving control of affairs exclusively to either Party, she would no longer have any control or influence. Leaving one faction in complete control removed any means of ensuring moderation in Government policy.

The problem caused by incompetent Kings, and the impossible situation caused by the principle of automatic succession, which Parliament had assumed could only be resolved by itself assuming power, overlooked the provision in the coronation procedure for election of the King by the people. Also overlooked was the well-established practice of deposing unsatisfactory rulers. The Monarchy may have argued that it held office by divine right, but it is clear that Parliament no longer accepted this.

29.2.1.1. The Civil Service Becomes the Tool of Parliament

Her fourth Parliament, in 1710, saw a clear majority for the Tories, and her relief was reflected in the willingness with which she acceded to a complete change in the Ministry to match the new colour of the House of Commons. Anne changed her Ministry because it suited her, not because it suited the Tories, but it was the first clear-cut and peaceful transfer of political power under the Party system following a general election, and it set a precedent, because the Parties in the Commons were not slow to latch onto this practice as a means of securing power. Consequently, the Parliament of 1710 was claimed by them as establishing two new conventions, namely:

1. That the Sovereign appoints a new Ministry for each Parliament.
2. That the composition of the Ministry is determined by the majority Party in the House of Commons.

From here it was but a short step to the idea that the majority Party in the House of Commons formed the Government.

In this way, the Sovereign was being forced aside to make way for the dominant Party leader. William III had been the last Sovereign to veto a major Bill, and Anne was now the last to reject any Bill passed by both Houses. No Bill has been vetoed by the Crown since the reign of Queen Anne, except in the case of a colonial legislature. This reluctance to veto domestic Bills did not reflect any intention by the Crown to relinquish its right to do so, even though the Whigs objected to it on principle. So far as both Kings and Parliament were concerned – certainly in the view of the Tory Party – the Sovereign has remained fully entitled to refuse to enact any Bill to which he or she is opposed, except that an important precedent had undoubtedly been set.

The English system of government had, for centuries, provided for a *de facto* division of function, to ensure that each aspect – legislative, executive and judicial – was properly attended to. The new system represented a complete breakdown of that principle, with the same individuals now controlling both the legislative and the executive functions of government, converting it into an alternating oligarchy. The only redeeming feature of the new system was its retention of periodic general elections, whose function was now changed from choosing the most satisfactory representative for each constituency, to deciding which Party should enjoy political power, undermining the function of the local Member of Parliament. Whether politicians were competent to govern the country depended very largely on chance. The common law requirement of the Sovereign to choose his or her Ministers, in consultation with the Great Council, had long broken down, because the Great Council had long ceased to advise in the matter, and had long since probably lost the competence to do so. Nor was it in any position to insist on the resignation or dismissal of a Minister who was not seen to be competent, or to have the confidence of either Parliament or the people. Even the King had ceased to be elected, so that he was not fully competent to appoint Ministers.

The effect fell particularly on the Civil Service. It would not be until the next century that reform of the Civil Service, prompted by the disaster of the Crimean War, and inspired by the reform of the Indian Civil Service, converted it into a first-class administrative system. Unfortunately, it had already suffered a major loss. Under the Crown, it was subject to Ministers capable, in principle, if not yet in fact,[1] of being appointed according to their experience and perceived ability, and holding office for as long as was deemed appropriate, but, under the control of Parliament, it became subject to Ministers who usually had no known competence for the role, and whose only quality was their loyalty to the leader of the majority Party in Parliament. The fact that they usually held office for only one or

---

1   In practice, they had hitherto been appointed according to the social seniority of their families, or according to the sometimes-disastrous whim of the King.

two years, ensuring that they remained unsuitable, perpetuated the scope for friction between Ministry and Minister.

In practice, it would be found that Parties in office behaved in a fairly restrained manner, but the revolution did much to give rise to the fallacious doctrine of the Supremacy of Parliament.

29.2.2. The Commons Encroach Upon the Lords

Shortly afterwards, in 1712, a Tory majority in the House of Lords was achieved by the agreement of Queen Anne to a request from the Commons to create a dozen Tory Peers. It was the first example of manipulating the membership of the Upper House for the benefit of a political Party in the Commons. It was noted earlier that it had always been accepted that neither House (or Estate) could, or would, interfere in the membership or procedures of the other, undoubtedly because to do so would be a violation of common law. The established practice, whereby the Sovereign elevated members of the Third Estate to the ranks of the Second, had long been necessary, since the decimation of the latter at Hastings, and by the introduction by the Normans of the legal principle of primogeniture. This had resulted in a steady attrition of noble families, as they failed to produce surviving sons. The extinction of the Second Estate had been avoided by the practice of the King of elevating individuals, on the basis of his own judgement and inclination, many of them quite unworthy of the honour. Consequently, the Second Estate, as defined in common law, had effectively disappeared after the reign of Edward the Confessor, and an unelected Norman Second Estate had gradually disappeared, either because its members had been unable to meet the requirements of the new law of inheritance, or because they had been decimated by war, particularly at Towton.

Common law did not recognise individuals elevated by the King to the Second Estate, other than by their exceptional courage or achievement, nor, necessarily, did it recognise their progeny, even of those elevated by right. It was noted earlier that a family was defined in common law as extending over four generations, and this principle allowed the family of an individual elevated to the Estate to be accepted by it after four, relatively flawless, generations. By this mechanism, the Second Estate was able to renew itself. It may have been remembered by the Lower

House, however, that the *raison d'être* of the House of Lords was the Great Council, whose particular qualities were experience, wisdom, and grasp of the law of the Constitution, which the Commons evidently felt were readily available among the leading members of its ruling Party.

The view was now taken by the House of Commons that it was itself capable of judging suitable candidates from its own ranks, and, taking into account that there was no formal limitation on the size of the of the Upper House, it now became a practice for the ruling Party to seek to control the House of Lords by this means, in order to ensure that its Bills would not be opposed. That Queen Anne acceded to the request was undoubtedly influenced by the unabashed opportunism in the practice displayed by many of her predecessors.

29.2.3. The Privy Council is Usurped by its Cabinet Committee

Under Queen Anne, meanwhile, the Cabinet Council met in her presence at least once a week to decide major policy questions. Her Ministers soon found that they stood a better chance of persuading her if they discussed the issues in advance and took a united stand, and this may have helped to promote the idea of Cabinet unanimity. The Whig Ministry under William III had already learned the wisdom of standing together when criticised by their opponents in Parliament. Anne's concerns proved to be well founded, when, to her discomfort and distaste, on yielding to a demand by the triumphant Whigs that they replace the Tories in her Cabinet, it became evident that the chief casualty was the Sovereign herself. Finding that she no longer had any choice in the membership of her Cabinet, her sovereignty became, as she expressed it, 'no more than a name'. Presiding over a Tory Ministry whose outlook was similar to her own posed no great difficulty, but, faced by a Whig Cabinet, which now formed a common cause against her, she found that she had little influence over the decisions made. It was a distinction of Queen Anne's reign that she was the last Sovereign, up to the present day, to refuse assent to a Bill that had been passed by Parliament. This was in respect of the Militia Bill of 1708, although her refusal appears to have had the approval of her Ministers, and no objection seems to have been raised in Parliament, which did not question the Sovereign's right to reject a Bill against its wishes.[2] Ministers had always enjoyed a particular place in the Privy Council because of the executive authority wielded by them, but it was this conversion of the Ministers in the Privy Council into a united Party faction that gave added strength to the concept of Cabinet Government. This was a significant development, because of the greater influence of the Privy Council in Parliament. In one sense it represented a return to Tudor times, when corruption had ensured that members of the Privy Council had also been elected to the Commons, establishing a direct link between the two and making a close cooperation possible. Now, it was the leaders of the Commons who sat in in the Privy Council, depriving the latter of its independence. The executive function of government was now controlled by the legislative function, ensuring that the government of the realm was controlled by an elected oligarchy.

The King's right to veto Bills had become an issue because of three constitutional failures:

1. For well over 600 years, the Sovereign had not represented the people, and so had no constitutional right to propose or reject Bills.
2. Since the reign of Henry VI, Parliament had, by submitting petitions drafted as Bills, and insisting upon their acceptance, effectively appropriated from the King much of his executive function to initiate legislation on the basis of administrative need. This removed the distinction between the executive and legislative functions of government.
3. The legislative function of the King had now been displaced by the leader of the largest Party in the Commons, who was likely to introduce Bills to which the King was opposed.

This raised the question: who was now responsible for government? The correct answer was, of course, the King, through his Privy Council and the Civil Service. The proper function of the leader of the largest Party in Parliament was to represent the interests of the people. This principle had now collapsed.

---

2   For example, in the Irish crisis of 1912–14, the Unionists advised George V to withhold his assent from a Bill giving home rule to Ireland, but the Liberal Prime Minister, Asquith, advised the King against.

Thus, we see the gradual emergence in the seventeenth century, as a power in its own right, of that inner circle of the Privy Council, known as its Cabinet Committee, which achieved a form very similar to that existing today. This created a constitutional problem, in that the function of the Privy Council was now being usurped by its own sub-committee – the Cabinet – in deciding matters of state, simply because successive Kings, and now Queen Anne, were administratively inept – partly because they had succeeded to the Crown by hereditary right alone, instead of displaying prior ability to the Great Council and to the people to justify their election, and partly because they allowed the Parties to take control. It is a problem that has continued to the present day. The adoption of a Cabinet of half-a-dozen had been the inevitable consequence of the King finding the Privy Council, with its inflated fifty members, too large and ill-chosen for effective policy-making. The new arrangement was disliked, both by Parliament and by the Privy Council, because it usurped the Council by reducing it to a largely passive role. On the other hand, Parliament disliked the original Cabinet system because it concentrated power in a small côterie of individuals over whom it had no control. Under Queen Anne, the Cabinet system was answerable to nobody except herself, but she no longer had any control over it. Hence there were efforts to do away with the Cabinet. These were unsuccessful because, short of a substantial reduction in the size of the Privy Council, it was found to be a better way of dealing with Government business. In short, the inflated Privy Council of fifty was too large to be an effective policy-making body, while a Cabinet of five was too small to accommodate the leading officers of state, judges and others, necessary to the proper working of the executive arm of government.

We have already seen how even the needs of the early Medieval state had imposed impossible demands on the Privy Council, so that, in particular, it had to redirect most of the judicial functions that had been imposed upon it by Parliament, by way of the King, onto several committees, which became royal courts of law. Political administration was subject to the same pressure. The danger was always that the Privy Council would simply disintegrate into a plethora of autonomous committees, and in so doing lose its capacity to control, coordinate and give reliable advice. To some extent this was already happening. As its committees – including the Cabinet Committee – dealt with the more specialised or difficult areas of government, and became more autonomous in the process, they left the Privy Council with the more routine and formal advisory and agency functions, depriving it of any real ability and influence, leaving it to ossify, while its more important agency and advisory functions were left to its committees.

By the time of George I, meetings of the Cabinet Council were regarded as meetings of the Privy Council, because the Cabinet consisted of the leading officers of the Crown, who formed the inner circle of the Privy Council. It was a prime example of the process of fudge and muddle that characterised so much English, and now British, government. It would later be described as the 'evolution' of government, but, because it had been such a critical aspect of the rise of the House of Commons, it acquired the more discrete description of 'evolution' through the establishment of new 'conventions'. Undoubtedly, the practice of establishing new conventions had always been a feature of government, but not to the extent of violating the law of the Constitution.

Members of the Cabinet Council retained their respective seals of office, with which they could authorise an Order in Council for whatever business the King had in mind.[3] This left the parent body, the Privy Council, which alone occupied a constitutional position in the process of government, with little more than routine work to deal with. As a committee unknown to the Constitution, decisions of the Cabinet were of no legal effect, but this limitation was overcome by the assumption that a decision of the Cabinet amounted to a decision of the Privy Council.

29.2.3.1. Dividing Offices of State

Meanwhile, a practice had appeared of dividing certain important Cabinet offices, known as putting them into 'commission'. The practice was first adopted on the accession of William III in 1689, when the office of Lord High Admiral was replaced by Lords Commissioners, that is to say, by a First, Second and more Lords of the Admiralty, in that order of seniority. It may have been hoped that this would spread the burden of responsibility, or that a committee, so composed, would be capable of more reliable decision-making than was possible by a single individual. A more significant reason for the change may have been to

3   F. W. Maitland, *The Constitutional History of England*, 394–5.

make it more difficult for the King to influence the Admiralty, bearing in mind the hopes of William III to use the Royal Navy in the Continental conflict. Except for a couple of restorations of the office of Lord High Admiral, the arrangement whereby his duties were committed to a board or commission has been perpetuated to the present day.

Until the seventeenth century, the Exchequer assessed the King's debts, collected his revenues, and authorised expenditure, while the Treasury stored the King's money. Both the Exchequer and the Treasury were presided over by the Lord High Treasurer. During the seventeenth century, the Treasury acquired an increasingly independent existence as it became responsible for newer and more important revenues. Meanwhile, the Exchequer declined in importance. Under Cromwell's Protectorate, from 1653, the Treasury was placed under a Treasury Board of Commissioners, becoming a full department of state that appointed its own staff and largely superseded, but did not wholly replace, the Exchequer in its management of the public finances. Although a Lord High Treasurer was again appointed in 1661 by Charles II, the Treasury was again placed in the charge of a Board of Commissioners from 1667 onwards. The office of Lord High Treasurer was not abolished, but it was entrusted to the Commissioners acting in his capacity. The Treasury now controlled Customs, Excise, and other forms of tax revenue. Meanwhile, the essence of modern budgetary systems was determined by a series of measures introduced during 1689 and 1690. These gave rise to a new system that required estimates and accounts for supplies, which were divided according to their specific purposes, which were known as 'appropriations'.

A further change came in 1714, at the beginning of the reign of George I, when the Treasury Board was replaced by at least six Lords Commissioners of the Treasury. Their titles were numbered according to seniority, beginning with the First Lord Commissioner. The Third, Fourth, Fifth and Sixth became known as the 'junior' Lords Commissioners. The original office of Lord High Treasurer has thus remained 'in commission' ever since. Although the declining importance of the Exchequer was destined to lead to its eventual abolition over a century later, in 1833, the Chancellor of the Exchequer had been appointed as one of the members of the Treasury Board, and subsequently as one of the Lords Commissioners of the Treasury. This enabled the Chancellor's office to survive.

29.3. The Anglo-Scottish Union of 1707

After William and Mary, there was much friction between England and Scotland over the succession. There was also friction over trade and over the war with France. There was a move on the part of the Catholic element in Scotland to have James's son and natural heir, James the Pretender, installed on the Scottish throne, and this may have been decisive in persuading Westminster that, until the two kingdoms were permanently united, Scotland would continue to be an endless source of trouble, not least in providing a base for Stuart ambitions. Following its disastrous Darien adventure in 1698, which had squandered all its resources, Scotland now had only two options open to it. One was to remain independent and backward, and the other was to enter into a new economic partnership with England under a common crown. It was not an easy choice, because, if independence meant perpetuating Scottish poverty, union undoubtedly meant a state of subordination to England. Meanwhile, the English ruling class became alarmed at the Scottish hostility that was directed at it. Finally deciding that there was only one solution to the Scottish problem, it now did its best to make the choice as stark as possible for the Scots. The English Alien Act of 1705 classified the Scots as 'aliens' for trade and other purposes. For its part, the Scottish establishment recognised that if their traders were to be largely isolated from their only important market, Scotland would be economically ruined, unless a permanent agreement could be reached. Unfortunately, this reality was largely lost on the Scottish lower classes, who held England to blame for most of their problems.

Ratification had a hard passage through the Scottish Parliament. It was strongly opposed by the lower and middle classes and by the Presbyterian Kirk. If there was intense hostility towards England in Edinburgh, there was downright hatred in Glasgow. Union was also opposed by the Jacobites, who saw themselves as losing their last chance of restoring the Stuarts to the throne. On the other hand, union was supported by the Scottish nobility, who could see the ruination of Scotland as the only alternative. Being a much poorer country, with a sixth of England's population and paying only a fortieth of England's taxation, it was in a weak position. The burgesses were won over by a few more tax concessions, and the Scottish Kirk at last recognised that it was not the English establishment, but the Jacobites, who were its real enemy. Even so, there is little doubt that a fully democratic Scottish Parliament would have rejected the treaty.

The outcome was the Treaty of Union between Scotland and England of 1706. It was ratified in an Act of Union, formally described as 'an Act for the Union of the Two Kingdoms of England and Scotland', passed by the Scottish and English Parliaments in 1706.[4] It came into effect on 1 May 1707. The Treaty and ensuing Act of Union declared that the two kingdoms should be forever united in a single United Kingdom of Great Britain, under Queen Anne and, in default of any issue that she might still have, such successors as those 'upon whom the Crown of England is settled'. The United Kingdom was to be represented by a single Parliament of Great Britain. The Act left no doubt, however, that this Parliament would simply be the English Parliament, sitting at Westminster, in which representation was to be extended to representatives of the Scots, both in the House of Lords and in the House of Commons. The Scots were to retain their own courts and existing system of law, subject to appeal to the House of Lords. Provision was also made for the retention of the Presbyterian establishment in Scotland and the safeguarding of the position of the Church of England. Although existing Scottish law and the Scottish judicial system were to continue to be observed, they were to be subject to any new statutes enacted in respect of the United Kingdom as a whole. Commercially, Scotland was to have the benefit of free trade with England and its colonies. There were other provisions, notably, common tariffs and taxation, the retention of the feudal jurisdictions in the Highlands, and compensation for the heavier English debt. Although declared to be an equal union, it was anything but, and it could hardly have been expected to be otherwise, because, in terms of wealth and population, Scotland was dwarfed by its southern neighbour. Unsurprisingly, there was no mention of the Great Council. This would not have been affected in any case, because its members would still have

4   6 Anne, c. 11.

been elected by the English shires. Its advice and powers would still have applied, in principle, to the English part of the common Constitution.

The dual monarchy that had existed since James I, during which Charles I, Charles II and James II had each received a separate Scottish coronation, was to be regarded from now onwards as a single 'British' monarchy. Nevertheless, Queen Anne was not required to undergo a new coronation as Queen of Great Britain, and she continued to wear the English crown, as did her successors. The Scottish crown and sceptre, becoming redundant, were simply left in Scotland. The armorial bearings of Queen Anne remained essentially that of her predecessors, except that the arms of England and Scotland were now joined as one. Most of England's rulers, from Edward II onwards, had been crowned while seated on King Edward's Chair, which had been made to incorporate the Scottish coronation stone. Consisting of Old Red Sandstone, possibly Scottish in origin, it was said that, after their defeat of the Picts, the Scots had brought the Stone to Scone, where the Medieval Scottish kings were crowned. The incorporation of the Stone in the English coronations had long been taken to signify that any English King, so crowned, was also King of the Scots, and this interpretation seems to have continued with, and since, the accession of James I. The King was to remain head of the Church of England, by which agency he continued to be crowned. The only Scottish element in the coronation of the head of state, from this time onward, was the Moderator of the General Assembly of the Church of Scotland, who joined with the Archbishop of Canterbury in presenting a Bible to the new King.

An amending Act in the same year[5] provided that there should be a single Privy Council for Great Britain, specifying that 'such Privy Council shall have the same powers and authorities as the Privy Council of England . . . at the time of the Union and none other'. In effect, the Scottish Privy Council ceased to exist and the English Privy Council, with additions to its membership as the Queen might appoint, continued to advise her. Meanwhile, the Great Seal of England was to remain in use until a different Great Seal of the United Kingdom could be devised on the order of the Queen's successor. In all matters, other than the sealing of writs to elect and summon Parliament, and the sealing of foreign treaties and public acts and orders which concerned the whole United

5   Ibid., c. 40.

Kingdom, the Great Seal of England was to remain in use for all matters relating to England, while a Seal to be appointed by the Queen was to be used in Scotland for all other matters pertaining to Scotland. This latter was to replace the Great Seal of Scotland, which was discarded, perhaps because it would have implied the continuance of an equal state. Thus, except in respect of common legislation, the state of England continued unimpaired, through the use of its Great Seal, while Scotland now had the standing of a dependent state, for which the Queen used a Seal which she had made for the purpose. In effect, she ruled Scotland by virtue of her position as Queen of England, in the same way as she ruled Wales and Ireland, except that Scotland retained a greater degree of autonomy. What emerges from all this is that, whatever might be read into the wording of the Act of Union, and whatever may have been understood by the Scottish negotiators, it did not replace the English Constitution with a new British Constitution, and no such replacement was intended, beyond a change of jurisdiction. The English Constitution continued, with adaptations to meet the needs of the Scots. It could hardly have been otherwise. The economic and political disparity between the two countries was not lost on the Scots, for whom an equal union could never have been a realistic expectation. This was evident in the new flag of the Union, on which, to the annoyance of the Scots, the cross of St George was superimposed over that of St Andrew.

Whereas the new Union marked a dramatic change of circumstances for Scotland, in England the new Union was hardly noticed, and when, in 1867, over 160 years later, Walter Bagehot entitled his famous treatise on the government of the United Kingdom, *The English Constitution*, he was merely expressing both the popular perception south of the border and the constitutional reality. The process of Anglo-Scottish unification was, indeed, much the same as that followed by the House of Wessex in its gradual unification of the English kingdoms. The Crown was granted ever wider *imperium*, matched by its expanding jurisdiction and answerability to the people. This is of fundamental importance to the interpretation of the common law Constitution, because it supports the impression that it has continued to apply down to the present day, with its institutions intact.

Nevertheless, the real beneficiaries of the Union were the Scots. In fiscal and representational terms, they were favoured, enjoying a disproportionate voice in Parliament and receiving what amounted to subsidies in the allocation of expenditure, and this bias was to give rise in later years to what became known as the 'West Lothian Question'. For the first time, effective administration and communication facilities were extended to the Highlands, not only to impose the effective jurisdiction of the Crown on a lawless region, but also to enable the spread of prosperity. The Union did indeed, bring prosperity to Scotland, and the old conflicts came to an end, causing the Scots to blossom as inventers, thinkers, writers and explorers, such as Adam Smith, James Watt, David Hume, James Boswell, Robert Burns, Sir Walter Scott, Lord Macaulay, Thomas Carlyle, Robert Louis Stevenson, and David Livingstone. Like the Irish, they now also rode the great ship of Empire that England had launched. With the much bigger market and sources of capital that the Union placed at their disposal, the Scots were to play an important part in the Industrial Revolution that was soon to follow. New markets became available overseas, and new lands were opened for settlement. Influential posts became available across the globe, and Scotland's military tradition was felt on almost every continent. These new opportunities should not obscure the tragedy of the Highland Clearances, which was not unlike the enclosure movement in England, but it was made inevitable by the Scottish insistence on the retention, in the Treaty, of the feudal system that had long operated in the Highlands.

29.3.1. Government and Parliament Continue After the Death of the King (1707)

One of the functions of the Great Council was to ensure the continuity of constitutional government when the King was absent, or indisposed, or, if following his death, until such time as his successor was crowned. It did this by appointing a Regent, or a Regency Council. Since it had ceased to be appointed, and been incarcerated in Parliament and, therefore, ceased to function in any meaningful way, the Great Council had left a large gap in the Constitution, which the political Parties in Parliament, oblivious of the reason, endeavoured to fill by introducing new practices.

Prior to the Regency Act of 1707, during the reign of Queen Anne, an existing Parliament was automatically dissolved upon the death of the King, because the royal summons had lapsed and the Parliament no longer had a legal existence, and therefore could serve no practical purpose. Likewise, the commissions of all officers of the Crown, including Ministers, expired automatically upon the King's death, until the wishes of his successor were known. Their warrants died with the King. Constitutionally, these gaps would have been provided for by the Great Council, which, because the *imperium* had automatically been returned to it on the King's death, took the King's place and had the authority to reinstate all commissions. With no effective Great Council to maintain this continuity, it had been assumed that the commissions of all royal officers, civil and military, had lapsed until his successor took his place. Even this was not a problem in theory, because of the Medieval English doctrine of immediate succession, and the Act of Settlement had removed the uncertainty surrounding it, but an interregnum or sorts was inevitable in practice. Not all successions occurred immediately, and the hiatus left by the death of the Sovereign could leave the realm directionless and vulnerable.

Now that the parliamentary Parties wielded the powers of the Crown, however, they no longer accepted that they should be retired from office until the successor to the Crown saw fit to summon them. Accordingly, the Act of 1707 required an existing Parliament to continue for a period of six months after the King's demise, unless earlier prorogued or dissolved by the successor to the Crown. If, however, the demise of the Sovereign occurred while Parliament was adjourned or prorogued, it was immediately to 'meet, convene and sit' for the next six months, unless prorogued or dissolved sooner. Where there was no Parliament in being at the time of the royal demise, the last preceding Parliament was to reassemble and so continue sitting for six months, with the same conditions applying. The Act also required the Sovereign's Privy Council to continue in office, even though there was no King or regent to advise, and to act for a period of six months after the King's death, unless sooner determined by the successor to the throne. Likewise, all holders of Great Office were to remain in office for a period of six months, unless they were sooner removed and discharged by the royal successor. The Great

Seal was to continue in use, even though there was no King or regent to use it, until such time as the successor to the Crown ordered a new Seal to be made.

The fact that it was now necessary to look to the Continent, in order to find a Protestant successor in the royal line, meant that there was liable to be a delay of weeks, if not months, before a successor could occupy the throne. Further provision was therefore made in the Regency Act that, in the event that the successor to the Crown should be away from the country at the time of his or his predecessor's demise, the administration of the Government, in the name of the successor, was to be carried on by the following seven officers: the Archbishop of Canterbury, the Lord Chamberlain or the Lord Keeper of the Great Seal, the Lord High Treasurer, the Lord President of the Council, the Lord Privy Seal, the Lord High Admiral, and the Lord Chief Justice of the Queen's Bench, together with such number of other subjects of the realm as the successor should decide. Collectively, they were to form the Lords Justices of Great Britain. The Lords Justices were to exercise, in the name of the royal successor, all the latter's powers, as if he or she were present, until such time as the latter should arrive or otherwise determine their authority. Decisions were to be made by a majority, and in any case not less than five, of the Lords Justices.

These provisions can have been of no legal effect, because they were already provided for in the Constitution. Unfortunately, neither the Crown nor Parliament appear to have any memory of this, or, if it was remembered, Parliament may have taken the view that the new provisions were needed in order to take account of the new executive role of the House of Commons in the process of government. They were incorporated in the Act of 1707.

29.3.2. The Doctrine of the Separation of Powers

The idea that a constitution contains three elements was first stated by Aristotle, who, as a Greek, may well have been referring to a distant memory of Indo-European tradition, remarking that these elements 'are, first, the deliberative, which discusses everything of common importance; second, the officials; and third, the judicial element'. These could also be described as the legislative, executive, and judicial functions. He went on to point out that the difference between constitutions corresponds to the differences between each of these elements, and if they are well arranged, the constitution itself is bound to be well arranged.[6] In the first part of the eighteenth century, Bolingbroke expressed the view that it was the 'division of power' between King and Parliament and 'the balance of the parts' that ensured 'the safety of the whole'.[7] About the same time, it was Montesquieu who opined also that there could be no liberty if the legislative and executive powers were combined in the same entity – as had now effectively become the case in Great Britain – nor if the role of justice were not separated from the legislative and the executive roles. Blackstone, while he accepted Montesquieu's doctrine, did not believe that there should be total separation, as this could lead, for example, to the legislature dominating the executive.

In spite of its defects, the comparative success of the British system of government and the fact that the people of Great Britain enjoyed a greater freedom than those of most other countries, had not gone unnoticed elsewhere. It was even commented upon in Britain itself. The English philosopher and political thinker, John Locke, prompted by the Revolution of 1688, noted the new supremacy of Parliament and the independence of the judiciary, which he termed the 'executive', because the courts applied the law. From this, he was the first to draw the conclusion that, 'in all well moderated monarchies and well-framed governments', legislation and the execution of the laws were in distinct hands.[8] Locke died in 1704. Other English writers extolled the 'balanced' or 'mixed' nature of the Constitution. A more fundamental conclusion was drawn by the French writer, Montesquieu, who visited England in 1732 and noted that it enjoyed far more liberty than most other countries. In his subsequent *L'Esprit des Lois*, or 'The Spirit of Law', written in 1748, he drew the conclusion that the English people owed their freedom to the separation of powers in the English system of government.[9] Like Aristotle, he distinguished three kinds of power, the legislative, executive, and judicial, and suggested that by ensuring that each was controlled by different people, tyranny would be avoided, since no one person or group

6   Aristotle, *Politics*, Bk iv, xiv, 1297b35.
7   H. S. Bolingbroke, *Remarks on the History of England* (1748), 80–83.
8   J. Locke, *Two Treatises of Government* (1690), vol. II, ch. XII.
9   Montesquieu, *L'Esprit des Lois* (1748), bk XI, ch. VI.

would be in a position to promote and protect their own interests. 'Again, there is no liberty', he wrote, 'if the judiciary power be not separated from the legislative and executive. Were it joined with the legislative, the life and liberty of the subject would be exposed to arbitrary control; for the judge would then be the legislator. Were it joined to the executive power, the judge might behave with violence and oppression'.

As Montesquieu was well aware, such a complete division of powers did not exist in Britain, even if, in practice, it did to a limited degree. He concluded that Parliament enacted legislation, for example, but did not control the executive. The King and his Ministers controlled the executive but could not enact legislation. Yet Ministers were members of, led, and were to some extent guided, by Parliament, and the King's consent was necessary to all legislation. Parliament could not control the judiciary, yet the House of Lords was also a court of law. Montesquieu was led to his logical conclusion that, if a partial division of powers produced such a degree of freedom, a more complete division must ensure even greater freedom. In reaching this doctrine, however, Montesquieu was not so unrealistic as to suppose that total separation of powers was either possible or necessary. So long as the whole power of one function was not exercised by the same hands as possessed the whole power of another function, the fundamental principles of a free constitution would not be subverted.[10]

The doctrine of the separation of powers exerted a considerable influence on British constitutional thinking, and it was Blackstone who, in his *Commentaries on the Laws of England*, published in 1765–9, summarised the Constitution as comprising 'the supreme legislative power or parliament, and the supreme executive power, which is the king'.11 In practice, the doctrine had little effect on the further development of Britain's system of government, yet Montesquieu's interpretation of the British Constitution was destined to have a widespread influence, affecting particularly the future constitutional course of the American colonies.

If the relevance of the doctrine to the British system of government, as it was now being practiced, was limited, and becoming less so with the increasing absorption of the executive function by the legislature, its

---

10 Madison, *The Federalist*, No. XLVII.
11 Sir William Blackstone (1723–1780), Professor of English Law at Oxford, whose lectures were published as *Commentaries on the Laws of England*, 4 vols (1765–1769). See Book I, chap. IX. See also F. W. Maitland, *The Constitutional History of England*, 415.

relevance to the common law Constitution was quite different. Here, Parliament (elected by the people) had a legislative function and a judicial function (in respect of the Third Estate); the King (who was elected by the people) had an executive function and a judicial function (as the dispenser of equity); and the Great Council (which was elected by the people) had a judicial function (in respect of the Second Estate); also an executive function (in supervising the executive actions of the King), and a legislative function (in supervising the legislative actions of the King). It also had a consultative function, which it could enforce through its other functions. There was a wide discrepancy, therefore, between the two traditions.

29.3.3. The Hanoverian Dynasty

Anne died in 1714, after a comparatively short reign. As none of her children had survived her, the next in line was the Princess Sophia, Electress and Duchess Dowager of Hanover. Sophia's claim derived from the fact that she was the daughter of Queen Elizabeth of Bohemia, who had been the eldest daughter of James I of England. Sophia was the wife of Ernest Augustus, Duke of Brunswick-Lüneburg and Elector of Hanover. Unfortunately, Sophia had died just six weeks before Queen Anne, leaving the succession to pass to Sophia's eldest son, Prince Georg Ludwig, who had succeeded his father as Duke of Brunswick and Lüneburg and Elector of Hanover in 1698. The title of Elector referred to his position, granted to his father, as one of the nine rulers of Central Europe who formed the College of Electors of the confederacy known as the Holy Roman Empire, and which elected the German Emperors.[12] George's claim to the English throne was by marriage alone, therefore, and it is very unlikely that he would have pursued it, but for the invitation extended in accordance with the requirements of the Act of Settlement. He was now fifty-four years of age, and it is doubtful whether he had any wish to accept, but it certainly enhanced his own position and that of his son, and he must have felt that he had little option but to do so.

The feudal practice, whereby dynasties were named after their estates, held in their own right, had been abandoned in England since the Tudors, because they had no family estate of their own, leaving them with no option but to use their family name. The Stewarts, or Stuarts,

12   Hanover had become an electorate only in 1692.

had been of equally insignificant origin, despite becoming Kings of the Scots, and also, having no family estate, had only their name to draw upon to proclaim their identity. Consequently, it was not until the advent of the House of Brunswick-Lüneburg, usually referred to more simply as the House of Hanover, that dynasties returned to the English throne in all their feudal splendour. King George I of Great Britain and Ireland, as he now became, was the son of Ernest Augustus, Elector of Hanover, and could trace his direct descent through such antecedents as Henry the Lion of Saxony, Henry the Proud of Saxony and Bavaria, and Welf (Guelph), Duke of Bavaria, to Azzo II, Margrave of Este,[13] between Padua and Ferrara, in northern Italy, who had died in 1097.[14] Because Welf had been the head of that branch of the family to which George belonged, it had been known as the Welfing line.[15] Three of George's predecessors, including his father, had been reigning sovereigns. Feudal practice attached more importance to land than to family, however, so that, as explained earlier, a notable individual was styled according to the name of his estate, not his ancestry. The problem with this tradition was that a man's estate could change from generation to generation, and in the case of George I of England he was also duke of Brunswick, duke of Lüneburg and duke of Hanover. His British subjects regarded him as the last, making him the founder, in Britain, of the Hanoverian dynasty.

The dukedom of Hanover, which covered a large part of Lower Saxony, was a region rather smaller, and certainly less wealthy than England, hence the tendency in Britain to deride George's family as 'minor princelings', an attitude promoted by the peeved Tories, who had opposed the invitation to George, and who were encouraged, no doubt, by the family's lack of social refinement. The restoration of the historic link between this part of Germany and the Saxon English might have been expected to be welcomed by the latter, but the connection had long been forgotten. To make matters worse, the political complexities of the German Confederation, and the fact that few people in England even knew where Hanover was, meant that George was not at first taken very seriously by the English or the

---

13 *Markgraf* – the earl or count responsible for a frontier province.
14 J. Louda, and M. Maclagan, *Lines of Succession: Heraldry of the Royal Families of Europe* (London, 1999), Tables 99 and 100.
15 Rendered in the Italian branch as the 'Guelphs'. Their opponents, supporters of the Hohenstaufen cause, were the Waiblings, based on the fortress of Waiblingen, in Bavaria. Their name was rendered in Italian as the 'Ghibellines'.

Scots. George regarded his kingship of Great Britain as an additional duty to his primary one as duke and Elector of Hanover, and this added to the difficulty by causing resentment. More importantly, the language problem and a preoccupation with their Hanoverian responsibilities were to render it a weak dynasty at first, and this was to have profound consequences for the British system of government.

George's wife, Sophia Dorothea, had been imprisoned by him for life for her amorous derelictions, and George was often in the company of his half-sister, Sophia Charlotte, who had become excessively corpulent, so that when they were seen together they were referred to as the 'Elephant and Castle', a name immortalised by an inn in Newington, in South London. George's one public mistress, however, was Ehrengard Melusine von Schulenburg, whom he may subsequently have married in secret, because the Emperor, Charles VI, created her Princess von Eberstein. Robert Walpole regarded her 'as much queen of England as anyone ever was', and in 1719 she was given the title of Duchess of Kendal. The standing of the Monarchy had been seriously undermined, however, by public antagonism towards the succession of foreigners on the throne – first William of Orange and now George of Hanover – if not by James I, compounded by the diminution of the Monarchy by the growing power of the House of Commons. To make matters worse, George was shy and preferred to stay out of the limelight, and this was increased by his inability to speak English.

George, who was crowned as King of Great Britain and Ireland in 1714, had already led an active life, having seen service in the Dutch and Turkish wars. During the War of the Spanish Succession, he had commanded the Imperial Army on the upper Rhine between 1707 and 1709, and had formed a good relationship with John Churchill, the future Duke of Marlborough. Resourceful and ambitious, he was also vindictive, used to getting his own way, and boorish, as shown by his treatment of his wife, Sophia. On the other hand, it was his love of music that caused him to bring his director of music, the composer, Friedrich Händel, over to England from Hanover. On one of the few great public occasions during his reign, George moved from London in 1715 to Hampton Court by boat on the Thames, to the accompaniment of an orchestra playing the 'Water Music', which Händel had been commissioned to write for the occasion.

The advent of the new dynasty meant a radical rearrangement of the royal coat of arms. German coats of arms were far more complicated than their British counterparts, due to inter-marriage between the many more independent states, so that the Welfing contribution had to be greatly simplified. One quarter of the arms represented the union of England and Scotland by being subdivided between the English lions and the Scottish lion. Two further quarters were occupied by the Irish harp and the fleurs-de-lis of France, respectively. The fourth quarter, representing the House of Hanover, was subdivided into the two lions of Brunswick (similar to those of England), the blue lion and red harts of Lüneburg, and the white horse rampant, on a red background, of Westphalia. Superimposed on the quarter was a smaller shield, bearing the crown of Charlemagne, representing George's position as the Arch-Treasurer of the Holy Roman Empire. The most interesting feature of the new royal arms from an English point of view was the arms of Westphalia – the red horse rampant on a white background. This derived from the fact that both George and his wife, Sophia of Brunswick-Zelle, who was his niece, had inherited, on both their respective heraldic arms, this ancient emblem, or blazon, which had been adopted by Westphalia. The white horse on a red background was the same emblem as that adopted by the English county of Kent, said to be traceable to the flag of its founders, Hengest and Horsa, who had effectively founded England (as distinct from Britain) over 1,200 years earlier. This ancient emblem, undoubtedly of religious significance and in widespread use as a charm in northern Germany until recent times, was a reminder of the close historic ties between Saxony and England. It would remain on the British royal coat of arms, un-remarked, until the time of George V.

29.3.4. The King and Parliament

George was made to understand that he held the Crown, not by right of succession, but in accordance with a provision in the Act of Settlement. Like William III, he was therefore a protégé of Parliament. This raised a constitutional question, however. Feudal doctrine recognised only succession by right of inheritance, which was the reason for George's accession in his capacity as the husband of Sophia. Common law recognised succession only by right of popular election. It must be supposed, therefore, that the people had, through the Act of Settlement, elected in advance the claimants specified by it. Much as it stretched credulity, therefore, in common law, George was King by right of popular election, not by the will of Parliament. George was King therefore by right of inheritance and by right of popular election.

For his part, George had reason to feel bitterness towards the Tories, whom he blamed for having, at the end of the War of the Spanish Succession, returned to France most of the territory that the allies had won. Compounding George's resentment, the Tories had shown favour towards his rival, James Stuart, the Pretender to the British throne. As the Tories had feared, in the formation of his first government he favoured the Whigs, contriving to have them returned with a large majority in Parliament, led by Townsend, Stanhope and Walpole. In return for the King's support, the Whigs duly impeached the Tory leaders responsible for surrendering British honour and interests in the Treaty of Utrecht. Otherwise, as the King had no grasp of English, and his interests lay in Hanover, the Whig Government enjoyed considerable freedom. The Tories, still mildly nostalgic for the direct line of descent, had even intrigued with the Pretender, James, being half inclined to the view that it would be better to be in power under the Catholic Stuarts than out of power under Protestant George. Even after his accession, and perhaps partly because he was unpopular, the fear of a return of the Jacobites was far from over. In 1715 there was a Jacobite rising in Scotland, led by the Earl of Mar, which saw the arrival, and quick departure again, of the Pretender, James, as the rebellion collapsed in the following year.

Partly because of the Jacobite scare, Parliament in 1716 replaced the Triennial Act by the Septennial Act, prolonging its own life to seven years and making this the full legal term for future Parliaments. This kept the Tories out of office, and with them the risk of collusion with the Jacobites, but it also ensured that members of Parliament enjoyed a more comfortable period of office. The longer life now given to Cabinets enabled Ministers to acquire some degree of professional experience. This was important, because ministerial office in the past had gone to men who, as members of the Second Estate, had been brought up from childhood to the prospect of high office, learning much about statecraft from the circles in which they moved, so that even incompetents were not without some training. The background of Ministers drawn from the Commons at this time was often that of yeoman farmers, used to a degree of responsibility and management ability, but this would not last as the electorate expanded. It seems clear that, while these Acts were the product of mutually acceptable practice, they could be nothing more. Common law required annual Parliaments, which would have been incapable of providing competent Ministers from the ranks of the House of Commons.

The financial arrangements agreed with George I were similar to those that had applied to Queen Anne, with certain sources of revenue – mainly the old prerogative rights, in addition to the Crown Lands, the hereditary excise, and certain excise and customs duties granted for the duration of his reign – provided for the civil government of the realm, the support of the royal household and the honour and dignity of the Crown; except that, in addition, the Sovereign was to receive a further sum of £120,000 for the service of his household and family and his necessary expenses and occasions. This was to come from certain taxes, which collectively comprised the Aggregate Fund. By this means it was intended that the King should continue to have the total of £700,000 at his disposal that had originally been agreed with Charles II.

Although both Queen Anne and George I were subject to the limits of the Civil Provision, both incurred expenditures on the personal items in the Civil List that were well in excess. These debts were met by Parliament, but were charged against the Civil List itself. The revenues available to the King were, nevertheless, sufficient to enable influence, and often corrupt influence, to be exerted on Ministers and on Parliament. The King might no longer have the financial resources to act independently of Parliament, but the eighteenth century saw him still in a strong enough position to manipulate the functioning of government. In this, the Crown merely reflected the political ethos of the age. Prior to the Middle Ages, the possession of land had reflected political power, but since the Middle Ages it had been the possession of land that had conferred political power. In the mid-eighteenth century the return of the members of the House of Commons, numbering nearly two hundred, was largely determined by the bribery, blackmail, and other pressures and corrupt practices of about seventy-five interrelated families. These included both Peers and commoners, but in almost all cases they were considerable landowners.[16] Men hungry with ambition or greed were always open to such influence. Seats could usually be bought for £7,000 or £8,000, and when elections were contested, they were often bitter and costly, but after the Septennial Act of 1716, increasing the life of Parliaments from three to seven years, contestants were willing to spend even more. Also, the polls were kept open for fifteen days, making the cost of electioneering even higher. Members of Parliament were not paid, so that, in order to recoup such high costs, the indirect perks of membership had to be high. It was a vicious circle, and adherence to political parties was largely irrelevant to the election process.[17] Constitutionally, the country was in an awkward transitional phase, in that the King no longer had the power to rule, as he had previously been expected to, and the system of rule by political Parties had not properly developed, leaving the King with a function but no means of carrying it out, except by manipulation. As George III once remarked: 'Certainly the times are not so virtuous that persons will labour for the public without reward'.[18] Corruption was motivated not so much by licentiousness as by a sense of hard realism in a materialistic age.

Until 1714, the Treasury had variously been administered by the older office of Lord High Treasurer or, latterly and more usually, a Treasury Board of Commissioners. In 1714 the department was placed under a new body, the Lords Commissioners of the Treasury, who exercised this function jointly. When the most senior, or First Lord Commissioner of the Treasury, sat in the House of Lords, the principal Government financial spokesman in the Commons was the Chancellor of the Exchequer, but when the First Lord of the Treasury was a member of the House of Commons – where use of the full title was a licence, because he was not a lord – he also occupied the office of Chancellor of the Exchequer. It may be remembered that the Chancellor's office had originated as the Chancellor of the Court of Exchequer, an essentially judicial office, which was subordinate to that of the former Lord High Treasurer, and so, presumably, subordinate also to the First Lord of the Treasury. Subsequently, the Chancellor of the Exchequer became the

---

16   G. Smith, *A Constitutional and Legal History of England*, 394.

17   L. Namier, *Monarchy and the Party System*, the Romanes Lecture (1952).

18   H. Butterfield, *George III, Lord North, and the People, 1779–1780*, 195, note (1949), quoting from a letter to the Secretary of the Treasury, John Robinson.

Second Lord of the Treasury, who was responsible chiefly for the raising of the public revenue and the control of its expenditure.

29.3.5. The Office of Prime Minister

So far as we know, the King had always appointed a chief, first, or prime, Minister, although the earliest reliable evidence comes from the Normans, when he fulfilled the role particularly as deputy, during the King's absences. Originally, he may have used a member of the royal family, but this would have been liable to give rise to unwarranted ambitions, and the use of a leading member of the Second Estate had become more usual. This practice should be traceable back to Anglo-Saxon times, when it is recorded that, in the reign of Edward the Confessor, the Great Seal, with which the King authenticated his writs, had been entrusted to the Lord High Chancellor – the title used to distinguish him from lesser chancellors, such as the Chancellor of the Exchequer. In the early Norman period, the position of chief Minister was occupied by the Chief Justiciar, or Chief Justice, a position jointly held in 1067 by Odo of Bayeux and William FitzOsbern, during the absences of William I, when they effectively acted as a regency. During the centuries that followed, the King often left much of the day-to-day running of the country to his chief Minister. In 1272, the Lord High Chancellor inherited from the Chief Justice the role of first Minister. The position was one of *primus inter pares*, or 'first among equals', in that the first Minister had enjoyed seniority over the other Ministers of the Crown without holding any formal office as such, and without having any formal authority over them. He stood in for the King in all the royal duties except those relating to the Church,[19] but as the early appointees were usually bishops, they, at least, were able to attend also to Church matters. The Lord High Chancellor was thus the head of both the King's executive and judicial functions, as well as being the King's representative in Parliament, a combined role which, as 'Chancellor of England', he was to hold with distinction for centuries.

George I had much difficulty in reconciling himself to a parliamentary system that required him to seek approval for most of his actions, particularly in matters of foreign policy, which included the protection of Hanover's interests, which were outside Britain's jurisdiction. He was also

---

19   This exception undoubtedly referred to the priestly function of the King, which no member of the Second or Third Estates could occupy.

severely hampered by his ignorance of English, preferring to communicate in French, so that he had to rely on his son, George Augustus, now Prince of Wales, to help translate during meetings of the Privy Council and the Cabinet. This became still more of a problem after 1717, following a rift with his son that had arisen from the King's imprisonment of his mother. This forced the King to leave the management of Cabinet meetings, a task that he deputed, not to the Lord Chancellor, as precedence required, but to an ordinary Minister. Failure of the King to attend his Councils had been nothing new. Henry VIII had attended very few. The division of Parliament into separate Houses and the rising power of the political Parties in the House of Commons had made it increasingly necessary for the Sovereign to deal with the leader of the dominant Party of the day, who was now as likely to sit in the Commons as in the Lords. Queen Anne had conceded control of the Ministry to the dominant Party in the Commons, a practice which, it insisted, George I should follow as a matter of convention. Conventions had become such a vital factor in the emergence of the new system of government that it may have been seen as desirable for it to be established as a part of the process of government itself.

In 1717, Sir Robert Walpole, who had been appointed by Queen Anne as a member of the Privy Council on behalf of her husband,[20] had held various important offices under the Crown, including that of Treasurer. He had also become the intermediary between the Government and the Whig leaders in Parliament, where he was a prominent member, and he had been an advisor and close friend of Caroline of Ansbach, the wife of the Prince of Wales. He was the Paymaster General at the time, and already, effectively, the King's chief Minister, in preference to the Lord Chancellor, who had held the position for centuries. Walpole also won the King's confidence by brokering a reconciliation with his son and political rival, the Prince of Wales. In 1721, he was appointed as the First Lord of the Treasury, the most senior of the successors in commission of the Lord High Treasurer, and it is usually from this date that he has been credited with the role of looking after domestic affairs as the King's first, or 'prime' Minister, although Walpole himself rejected the description. The King regarded foreign affairs as remaining in his own hands. It was certainly in error that he inherited the title of First Lord, because he was not a member of the Second Estate, but a commoner, albeit the

20   Prince George of Denmark, who had occupied the position of Lord High Admiral.

inheritor of ten manors in East Anglia. The problem of an alternative title must have exercised minds at the time, and it was a problem that inevitably arose where offices, previously regarded as appropriate only to members of the Second Estate, were increasingly passed on to individuals of the Third Estate. First Lord of the Treasury was now being treated as an established title, not as an attribution. The duties of the Lord Chancellor, meanwhile, were now limited to those of head of the judiciary and the representative of the King in Parliament. In other words, the Chancellor still represented the King in respect of the judicial and legislative functions of the Crown.

With Walpole representing him, the George I gradually withdrew from attending Cabinet meetings. The King was probably unfamiliar with the long-established convention that it was a duty of the Lord Chancellor to act as his chief Minister, and it may be supposed that Walpole's fellow Ministers used the King's confidence in Walpole to break the convention in order to transfer the office from the House of Lords to the House of Commons, a move that would bring the judiciary under the control of the ruling Party. This was to be of profound constitutional significance, because it meant that the Commons now had effective control of the Cabinet.

29.4. The Role of Government Shifts from the Lords to the Commons

As Walpole was the leader of the dominant Party in Parliament, he exercised a considerable control there also. Because he, and increasingly his successors, were members of the House of Commons, his self-interest and loyalty were likely to lie as much there as with the King. Walpole may not have perceived his new position in this light, but it must have been very evident to others, and it confirmed a major constitutional shift. For millennia, in keeping with the principles of common law, decisions on behalf of the Crown had been made by members of the Second Estate, of which the King was part. With Walpole, and increasingly with his successors, decisions of the Crown were being made by, or under the guidance of, the Third Estate. Whereas the Lord Chancellor still represented the King in his legislative and judicial capacities, the Prime Minister, in the person of Walpole, now represented the King in his executive capacity. Walpole's authority was limited, however, by the fact that he had no control over the appointment of his fellow Ministers, a right which continued to be exercised by the King. By contrast, some of his predecessors in the House of Lords had enjoyed so much authority that, effectively, they had been able to appoint their own. Despite his designation, the position of Prime Minister was only a role, not an office of state, and it was in order to ensure that he had the necessary authority and influence with his colleagues, that it would remain the practice for Prime Ministers to occupy the office of First Lord of the Treasury. This was doubly convenient, because, as First Lord, he was in control of Government funds, and this gave him considerable power to assert his position.

For the best part of the next two hundred years, the function would variously be given to members of either Estate – Lords or Commons – before it would come to be regarded as being in the right of the leader of the majority Party in the Lower House. During this time, the King's chief Minister would come to be known invariably as his 'Prime' Minister, but, like all the King's officers, he retained this position at the King's pleasure. As it was later described by Lord Morley in 1889, 'the Prime Minister is the keystone of the Cabinet arch. Although in Cabinet all its members stand on an equal footing, speak with an equal voice, and, on the rare occasions when a division is taken, are counted on the fraternal principle of one man, one vote, yet the head of the Cabinet is *primus inter pares*, and occupies a position which, so long as it lasts, is one of exceptional and peculiar authority'.[21] It was the Duke of Wellington who saw the value of a Prime Minister appointed, not from the House of Lords, but from the House of Commons, expressing the view in 1839 that: 'I have long entertained the opinion that the Prime Minister of this country, under existing circumstances, ought to have a seat in the other House of Parliament, and that he would have great advantage in carrying on the business of the Sovereign by being there'.[22] It is not clear whether he envisaged the Prime Minister being appointed from among the members of the Commons, or simply being given the benefit of a seat there, as well as in the House of Lords, as needs demanded; nor is it clear whether, by

---

21   Cited in S. L. Gwynn, *The Life of Walpole* (1932).
22   Parliamentary Debates, 3rd Ser., Vol. 47, Col. 1016, cited in I. Jennings, *Cabinet Government*, 21.

the 'existing circumstances' he was referring to the Chartist troubles of the time, or whether he was taking a longer term view. At all events, there was a reluctance to adopt this idea, in spite of the success of William Pitt the Younger in 1783–1801. Between the time of Wellington's proposition and 1902, after which the position was continually filled from the Commons, six Prime Ministers were appointed from the House of Lords. As Bagehot observed in 1867, 'a principal advantage of the House of Lords . . . consists in its thus acting as a reservoir of Cabinet Ministers . . . it would undoubtedly be difficult to find, without the lords, a sufficient supply of chief Ministers'. The improvement in general educational standards after Bagehot's day certainly improved the prospective calibre of candidates from the Commons, but the general point was to remain true, that the calibre of regular members of the House of Lords in matters of state consistently remained above that displayed in the Commons.

29.4.1. The Doctrine of the Social Contract
The Renaissance, the Reformation, the Civil War, the rise of the universities and the development of education all contributed to an emancipation of English thinking from the religious conformity of the Middle Ages. The often-autocratic rule of Popes and Kings was subjected to scrutiny and speculation. If society was not divinely ordered, as Church doctrine insisted, then what did order it?

Three political philosophers in particular devoted their attention to it. Thomas Hobbes wrote *The Leviathan* in 1651; John Locke his *Essays Concerning Human Understanding* in 1690; and, in France, Jean-Jacques Rousseau his *Discourses* in 1750 and 1755, and his *Du Contrat Social* in 1762. They were therefore writing between the time of the Commonwealth and the early reign of George III. Between them they drew attention to the brutishness of human existence without social organisation and the motivation of men to come together, therefore, and form a social contract, as Rousseau described it, whereby they agreed to give up some of their freedom in order to achieve the benefits of cooperation under a common system of government, an idea that mirrored the common law principle of the upward delegation of the *imperium* of the people. Whereas Hobbes thought that an individualised existence must be 'solitary, poor, nasty, brutish, and short', Rousseau could at first see nothing but good, not so much in the 'noble savage' as in the ordinary, bewildered citizen. Nevertheless, all could see a rational basis for social cooperation.

Rousseau at first took an opposite view from Hobbes that was a precursor to Socialism, arguing that men were born free, equal and virtuous, but had been put in chains and made wicked by the perverse institutions of society. Men had natural rights, and these could only be recovered by a revolution through which the 'general will' of the people could be made supreme. It was an optimistic view of human nature that would be picked up a hundred years later by Karl Marx. Hobbes and Locke regarded individual freedom as the primary requirement, with social cooperation as a necessary means to protecting it, but Rousseau's later thinking reacted against this idea of a society based on individual selfishness. For inspiration, he turned to Plato, who had taught that it was the community that was the chief moralising agency. As a result, Rousseau's writing shifted from 'defiant individualism' in his earlier work to equally 'defiant collectivism' in his later *Social Contract*.[23] The value of any social group, according to Rousseau, consisted in the happiness or self-satisfaction that it produced for its members, and especially in the protection of their inherent right to own and enjoy property. A community had no value in itself, but it protected values, because it rested on universal unselfishness, which was a product of the 'general will'. It followed that law flowed as a consequence of this. Law was not the primary consideration behind the social contract, as claimed by the individualist thinkers, Hobbes and Locke. As Rousseau saw it: 'The body politic, therefore, is also a moral being possessed of a will; and this general will, which tends always to the preservation and welfare of the whole and of every part, and is the source of the laws, constitutes for all the members of the state, in their relations to one another and to it, the rule of what is just or unjust'. Thus Rousseau, whose thinking was at best 'cloudy' and often contradictory, so that it never produced a coherent system, nevertheless went beyond the utilitarian view of society, as deduced by Hobbes and Locke, and saw society as an entity in itself. Through the benefit of the social contract, brutes become civilised by virtue of citizenship. By invoking classical Greek thinking, Rousseau initiated an era of political philosophy which was to reach its culmination, at the beginning of the nineteenth century, in the writings of Georg Hegel, with

23   C. Vaughan, *Political Writings of Jean Jacques Rousseau* (Cambridge, 1915).

his concept of the *volksgeist*, or soul of the nation. It was a line of thinking which saw the moral and political soul lying in the people, which spread its influence to the individual, rather than, as Hobbes and Locke had seen it, residing in the individual, who protected himself by entering into a soulless contract with his neighbours.

Such musings were lacking in any scientific basis, but they expressed the growing wish of society in Northwestern Europe to break the shackles of the feudal tradition and to re-discover a political arrangement of which all seemed to be dimly aware. Rousseau even went so far as to speak of an 'inalienable right' of the individual to equality before the law, implying some moral force outside any legal system devised by society, and as such a reassertion of *ius divinum*. It was also a reassertion of the status of the free man, that starting point of all Aryan society. Rousseau's early perception of a 'general will' triumphing over the existing institutions of society also seems to reflect an almost sub-conscious recognition of a need for one political tradition to overthrow another, which had enveloped it like a canker. It was the 'general will' that bound people together and gave them a sense of common purpose, and the social contract was not so much an agreement between the individuals composing society, as Rousseau had thought – with no institution, apparently, to express it – as the contract by which society expressed its will through the elected King. With the exception of Rousseau's original nostalgia for the 'noble savage', Hobbes, Locke, Rousseau and similar thinkers were not looking back to some idyllic past, but rather, looking to a future of enlightened government based on principles which, they instinctively felt, should be in place. In this, they shared political instincts that had much in common with those of the barons who had forced King John to sign the *Magna Carta*, or the followers of Jack Cade, or the Puritans under Cromwell. Dimly, they were all aware of a constitutional tradition that had been violated, and of a system of law which stood outside the enactments of successive authoritarian Kings. Nowhere did these resurrected ideas have greater impact than in the American colonies, where their motivation had lain behind much of the original settlement, and where guidance was being sought during their period of constitutional crisis.

The notion of the social contract appears to look back, either to the common enterprise, whereby a group of free men, who formed a common nation or a confederacy of nations, agreed to delegate their *imperium* to appointed officers, or chose to enter into a regal contract with an elected ruler. They were two contracts that, together, formed the basis of an ordered society beyond the bounds of direct kinship. These philosophers expressed the re-emergence in the eighteenth century of the Indo-European political tradition after more than eight centuries of Church-Feudalism.

29.4.2. The Seven Years War: Britain Diverts Her Military Efforts to the Empire

George I liked to spend the summer and autumn in Hanover, and it was while on his way there, in June 1727, that he died. He was therefore the first King to be buried abroad since Richard I, in this case in Hanover, and it was probably as he would have wished.

His only son, George Augustus, born and brought up in Hanover before his father had succeeded to the British throne, had already distinguished himself at the Battle of Oudenarde in 1708. He had nevertheless learned to speak English, although with a German accent, and his hostility towards his father over the treatment of his mother later caused him to identify more closely with Great Britain than he did with Hanover. His attempt to assert his authority on succeeding to the throne in 1727 by immediately replacing Walpole with Sir Spencer Compton, the Earl of Wilmington, came to naught when Compton was unable to form an administration. Walpole was returned to office. In his turn, Walpole accommodated the King by obtaining for him a larger share of the Civil List. With the country under the strong political control of Walpole, who continued to enjoy the backing of the new King's wife, Queen Caroline, who also carried much influence with her husband, the King did little to interfere. Like his father, however, George II was very much a soldier, and Walpole had great difficulty in keeping him out of Continental wars that were of little benefit to Great Britain. After the death of the Queen in 1737, Walpole's star began to wane. His extensive use of patronage, his pro-French policy, and his attempt to impose an excise on wine and tobacco, made him unpopular, and early in 1742 he was forced to resign. He was replaced as Prime Minister by the Secretary of State, Lord Carteret, who in turn was replaced in the following year by

Henry Pelham, who, appointed First Lord of the Treasury, now became, by default, the King's Prime Minister.

International events were dominated at this time by the War of the Austrian Succession. This had been precipitated by the death in 1740 of the Austrian Emperor, Charles VI, leaving the succession to his young daughter, Maria Theresa, who was married to Francis, Duke of Lorraine. This was hardly acceptable to other aspirants, while those with territorial claims against Austria regarded this moment of weakness as an excellent opportunity. Charles Albert, the Elector of Bavaria, King Philip V of Spain, and Augustus III of Saxony were all claimants to the Austrian throne, and France, as always, had a vested interest in the outcome. Prussia, under Frederick II, who was to become Frederick 'the Great', immediately occupied Silesia in furtherance of an existing claim. In the following year, 1741, an alliance against Austria was concluded between Bavaria, Spain and France, later joined by Saxony and Prussia. It was the involvement of France that was of concern to Great Britain, mainly because of France's designs on the Austrian Netherlands, but George II, being anxious to protect Hanover, proclaimed its neutrality.

There followed a successful invasion of Bohemia by the alliance, and in 1742 Charles Albert of Bavaria was elected Emperor. Meanwhile, the Austrians had been forced to retreat into Hungary, where Maria Theresa won the full support of the Hungarians by promising the nobility freedom from taxation. Carteret now prevailed upon George II to form an alliance between Hanover and Austria, to be financed by Britain. He also induced Maria Theresa to cede Silesia, thereby securing the withdrawal of her most dangerous enemy, Prussia, from the alliance. The Austrians now proceeded to drive the alliance out of both Bohemia and Bavaria, turning the new Emperor into a fugitive. Meanwhile, a combined Hanoverian, British and Hessian army under George II, leading in his capacity as Elector of Hanover – Britain and France being not officially at war – marched across Germany with the intention of cutting off the French retreat from Bohemia. It failed in this, but it inflicted a defeat on the French and Bavarians at Dettingen in June 1743. If nothing else, this ended the French army's reputation for invincibility, and it was the last occasion on which a British (or English) King commanded an army in battle. Carteret now prepared the ground for a coalition against France itself, planning a territorial compromise between Maria Theresa and the new Emperor, Charles VII. These intentions were frustrated by Prussia, which, worried by the success of the Austrian alliance and the vulnerability of Silesia, re-joined its former alliance with France against Austria. In the ensuing conquest of Bohemia in the following year of 1744, the Prussians found themselves deserted by the French, who left them exposed and forced to withdraw. Carteret, meanwhile, accused of high-handedness and of favouring Hanover at Britain's expense, had been forced to resign. A break in the Continental impasse occurred in 1745, when the Emperor died, because his son had no wish to contest the succession. It led to a treaty in the same year, between Bavaria and Austria, that enabled Maria Theresa's husband to be elected as Emperor Francis I.

France, meanwhile, avenged its defeat at Dettingen by scoring a victory against the British army under the command of the King's second son, the inept Duke of Cumberland, at Fontenoy in May 1745, thus opening the way for France's conquest of the Austrian Netherlands. At the same time, France decided to hobble Britain by again lending her support to the Stuart cause. The pretender, Prince James, had given up his ambition to claim the British Crown, leaving the Jacobites to turn to supporting his son, Charles Edward, who was accordingly referred to by his enemies as the Young Pretender, to distinguish him from his father, James, the Old Pretender. Backing for the Pretender came mainly from the Catholic north-west of Scotland, where, because of his allegedly good looks, he was known as 'Bonnie Prince Charlie'. Encouraged by his new French support, he arrived in Scotland in July 1745 and, much against his father's wishes, immediately inspired a second Jacobite rebellion. As further encouragement, he had been promised the help of a French army, provided he received support in England. Although the Jacobites were strong only in the Highlands, the rebellion coincided with the absence of the British army on the Continent, leaving Britain largely undefended. George II, like his father, regarded Hanover as his primary responsibility, and was often over there, as on this occasion, leading the army in its defence. This made it difficult for his Ministers in London to deal promptly with the Jacobite crisis. The state of British unpreparedness, the incompetence of Pelham's Whig government, and the blundering of General Cope allowed Charles a series of military successes, most notably at Prestonpans, which enabled him to enter England and advance south as far as Derby. By now it was clear, however, that the English uprising on which Charles had naïvely counted would not materialise. At Derby, with no sign of the French and the impending return of the main British army, Charles's followers lost their nerve and refused to go any further. This gave enough time for two British armies, under Wade and Cumberland, to assemble and move in upon them. Disillusioned and short of food, many of the Highlanders had already returned home. With his forces now starving, Charles retired northwards into Scotland, pursued by Cumberland. In desperation, Charles foolishly accepted combat with Cumberland's far superior forces on the plain of Culloden, north of Inverness, and was routed. His followers were then mercilessly hunted down, and Charles was lucky to escape back to France. So ended the last attempt of the Stuarts to regain the Crown. It was not only a political relief to Britain, allowing troops to be diverted elsewhere in the Imperial interest, but a relief to the Lowland Scots, who, delighted by the outcome at Culloden, were finally reconciled to the House of Hanover and freed to devote their energies to commerce and industry. The effect was a resumption of the rapid economic and intellectual development of the Lowlands, and of Scotland's participation in the further development of the Empire.

The reign of George II saw an outpouring of patriotism that was expressed most enduringly in music. No doubt it owed much to the success of the Empire in North America and India, but it must have owed something also to the new industrial achievements, the personal success of the King at Dettingen, and the final resolution of the Stuart problem. The composer Thomas Arne wrote *Rule Britannia* in 1740, and in 1745 the future national anthem, *God Save the King*, a long-established song, the origins of whose music and words are both unknown, received its first public performance. Meanwhile, the war on the Continent had rumbled on, indecisively, with the conflict between Britain and France having shifted its main theatre of operations away from Europe, to India and North America, where the competition was at its most keen. Nevertheless, the French conquest of the Austrian Netherlands had left Hanover dangerously exposed, and this caused Britain and Hanover to conclude a treaty with Prussia. With this, the Treaty of Aachen of 1748, the war ended, confirming the Austrian succession of Francis and Maria Theresa; France's final abandonment of the Stuarts; and insurance for the future of Hanover. Even so, it left many issues in Europe unresolved, and for Great Britain, the treaty left her unable to avenge her defeat at Fontenoy.

Even before the end of the War of the Austrian Succession, there had been taking place a complete realignment of the powers, commonly known as the Diplomatic Revolution. Austria had hoped to improve her chances of regaining Silesia from the Prussians by concluding an alliance with Russia. France, alarmed by the growing strength of Prussia and the Anglo-Prussian alliance, formed its own alliance with Austria. Meanwhile, Spain had remained in alliance with France. Prussia now saw herself as surrounded and under dire threat from the alliance of Russia, Austria, Saxony and France, and, realising that neither Russia nor France was ready for war, decided to strike first, in what was to come to be known as the Seven Years' War. The most dangerous member of the alliance at this time was Austria, and the only way into Austria lay through Saxony. Nevertheless, it was Great Britain, where Pelham had been succeeded as Prime Minister in 1754 by the Duke of Newcastle, who broke the peace by giving formal recognition to the fighting between herself and France in North America, formally declaring war on France in May of 1756. It was the first step to the Seven Years' War, although it was not fully set in motion until August, when the Prussians invaded Saxony.

Thus, Great Britain, Hanover and Prussia were now arranged against France, Austria, Saxony, Russia and Spain. Events in Europe at first went badly for Britain, with the loss of the Mediterranean island of Minorca to Spain and the defeat of a British army by the French at Hastenbeck in 1757, closely followed by the surrender of the British army at Kloster-Zeven, as a result of which Hanover was lost. Because of the loss of Minorca, Newcastle had been forced in 1756 to resign as First Lord of the Treasury – and Prime Minister – in favour of the Duke of Devonshire, with William Pitt, known to history as Pitt the Elder, appointed as Secretary of State. Devonshire proved inadequate, and in the following year the Duke of Newcastle resumed his former position as First Lord of the Treasury and Prime Minister. Pitt had, by now, taken over the direction of the war. He had previously opposed British involvement in the European theatre during the War of the Austrian Succession, because he regarded it as serving mainly Hanover's interests. Instead, he advocated a concentration on the overseas conflict with France, in order to secure Britain's trading interests. In Pitt's view, Britain's proper field of concern was not Continental Europe, but overseas, where its trading interests lay, and it was these that were the true source of Britain's wealth and power. This meant investing in the Royal Navy, rather than the army, a view that brought him into conflict with the King, who, as a born soldier, was devoted to the army and to the Continental rivalries.

This change of direction under Pitt had won him popularity, but his disagreement with the King greatly hampered his advancement to high office. Even so, it was a serious military situation that Pitt had to deal with at the beginning of the war and it was his obvious grasp of strategic issues that had given him his chance. Pitt was bound to accept some involvement on the Continent on Prussia's side, not only because of the King's insistence, but Britain simply could not afford to see France triumphant in Europe. From this time onwards, however, Britain's participation in the Seven Years' War was limited to financing Prussia's war effort and giving some military assistance in Germany, while concentrating her main effort overseas against the French. Indeed, thenceforth more generally, Great Britain's foreign policy tended to be guided by her imperial interests, limiting her Continental involvement to the constructing of alliances and subsidising her allies against any Continental country deemed to pose a threat to Britain herself or to her overseas interests.

For Frederick the Great, of Prussia, the conflict seemed to hang in the balance, losing as many of the main battles of the war as he won. The highlight of Britain's limited contribution came at the Battle of Minden, on the River Weser, in August 1759, when British and Hanoverian troops under the command of Ferdinand, Duke of Brunswick, defeated the French, making possible the liberation of Hanover. Late in the same year, a French invasion fleet was destroyed by the Royal Navy in Quiberon Bay, in Brittany. This left the way open for Pitt to concentrate on driving the French out of North America, a policy that was crowned by success when Quebec was captured by General Wolfe in 1759. In India, meanwhile, under Clive's leadership, the East India Company at last became the master of Bengal.

29.4.3. The Militia Act and the Lords Lieutenant (1757)

Prior to the process of English unification, it had been a requirement of all free men in common law that they render military service to the King in the defence of the nation (originally the shire). It was an obligation that had not ceased with confederation as a common kingdom, although the evidence points to the probability that the liability for service was no longer restricted to the defence of the shire, but was extended to the defence of England. The responsibility for the *fyrd* in the shire passed to the sheriff, and, with the onset of the Middle Ages, its use had largely been displaced by the employment of professional and volunteer armies, able to operate abroad, unhampered by agricultural and other domestic commitments.

Nevertheless, the *fyrd* – or, as it was now referred to, the 'militia' – while still having its basis in the shires, had remained a valuable resource. Under Henry VIII, the sheriffs handed over their military responsibilities to the King, who, in place of the sheriffs, made temporary appointments more directly under his control. What had long been lacking had been the proper organisation and equipment of the militias, and the Militia Act of 1757 reinforced existing practice by providing for the appointment, by the King, of Lieutenants for the various counties, ridings and such other places indicated 'in that part of Great Britain called England, the Dominion of Wales and the town of Berwick upon Tweed'. Their purpose was to take full command of their respective militias. There was also to be a Deputy Lieutenant in each county, and adjutants and sergeants were to be appointed from the regular army. The number of private men actually to be raised under the Act was to be specified, both in total and for each county, with the Privy Council being entitled to vary the number in each county. Chief Constables were to furnish lists of men between eighteen and fifty years of age, with actual service for each three years being decided by lot.

In the event of invasion, or the imminent danger thereof, or in case of rebellion, it was in the right of the King to order his Lieutenants to assemble the militia, subject to the notification of Parliament, if sitting, or to a declaration in Council, followed by a Proclamation. In the event that Parliament was not sitting, a proclamation was to be issued for it to assemble or be summoned. Because almost all holders of the Lieutenancies were Peers of the Realm, they were referred to as 'Lords Lieutenant'.

29.4.4. The Right to Legislate is Appropriated by the Commons

It was under the administration of Walpole, from 1721 to 1742, that the Cabinet system and the Party system took the form that they were to follow until 1832. The increasing pressure of political responsibilities was to lead successive Prime Ministers to delegate most of their Treasury duties to the other Commissioners of the Treasury, particularly the Second Lord, leaving the Prime Minister with virtually no ministerial powers or duties. Following the abolition of the Exchequer itself, the Treasury became a ministerial department under the Chancellor of the Exchequer, and although the Lords Commissioners of the Treasury retained certain powers, they became little more than formal in nature, while the Chancellor of the Exchequer achieved considerable influence through his direct control of the Treasury from the middle of the nineteenth century onwards. The remaining five Lords of the Treasury, being Party appointees with now little to do, became Government Whips, responsible for Party discipline. More recently, the number of Lords Commissioners of the Treasury has varied, according to needs.

Thus, the function of the Lord High Treasurer was taken over by the Lords Commissioners, originally five, but variable in number. Because of the burden of duties attached to the Prime Minister as First Lord, it was the remaining Lords who were required to share them. In practice, it was the Second Lord Commissioner who assumed the role of Chancellor of the Exchequer, and with it the duties of the defunct office of Lord High Treasurer. Walpole in fact held both offices, as First Lord and Prime Minister, and as Second Lord and Chancellor of the Exchequer. More usually, however, it would be the Second Lord Commissioner who would hold the office of Chancellor of the Exchequer. The remaining Lords Commissioners took over such duties as were assigned to them by the Prime Minister, their number being variable, according to needs.

To summarise, the Lord High Treasurer had been replaced by (usually) five Lords Commissioners of the Treasury. Of these, the First Lord became the Prime Minister; the Second Lord became the Chancellor of the Exchequer (under whom now came the Treasury), and the remaining Lords Commissioners usually became the Party Whips. Meanwhile, the Chancellor of the Exchequer (the Exchequer having been abolished) assumed responsibility for the Treasury.

It was under these conditions and Walpole's strong leadership, both under George I and his successor, George II, that three principles were established:

1. That the inner circle, or standing committee of the Privy Council, meeting as the Cabinet, should be composed of Ministers bound by a common political programme, in effect, the majority Party in the Commons.

2. That the Ministry should retain office no longer than it could control a majority in the House.

3. That the King should not veto any Bill that was approved by the two Houses of Parliament.

So firmly were these conventions established in the eyes of the House of Commons that they were able to withstand the efforts of George III and George IV to dispose of them. It was under George III that the handling of affairs in the American colonies gave rise to such widespread dissatisfaction by 1782, both in Parliament and in the country at large, that in March of that year, the House of Commons passed a series of motions hostile to Lord North, who was the Prime Minister and Chancellor of the Exchequer, and had headed a Tory Ministry since 1770. These motions culminated in one that proclaimed: 'that the House can no longer repose confidence in the present Ministers'. It was lost by a narrow margin, but when the motion threatened to be renewed, with the possibility that it would this time succeed, Lord North tendered his resignation. This came to be regarded as a precedent, establishing a convention that a Minister who lost a motion of confidence in the House of Commons must resign. It ensured that Ministers were beholden, not to the King, but to the House. It underscored the principle that King and Parliament must work in harmony if the country were to enjoy effective government. These changes also meant that the King no longer had responsibility for legislation, which had now passed to the dominant group in the House of Commons.

Like the establishment of the principle of legal precedent, the changes in constitutional practice achieved since the Revolution of 1688 were through tacit acceptance only, the practice known as convention. Thus, various conventions were accepted, of which the law (and hence the courts) knew nothing, and still know nothing, because they had no constitutional basis. They marked a progression in a gradual *de facto* transfer of power that made the Crown directly answerable, through the House of Commons, to the people (as was already the case in common law, except that answerability was through Parliament, not the Commons). According to Church-Feudalism, the King was answerable only to God. This transfer of power to the Commons was achieved by means of the following:

- By the emergence of the Cabinet Council, concentrating power in the hands of the dominant Party in the House of Commons (by-passing the Privy Council because of its excessive size and unwieldy nature).
- The emergence of central direction by the office of Prime Minister, who controlled the dominant Party in the Commons, although it was only later that he established a degree of legal recognition through mention in statutes.
- The establishment of a requirement that the King should appoint as Ministers those of whom the House of Commons approved (in order to ensure that the dominant Party controlled the Ministry).
- An insistence that the King should dismiss Ministers of whom the House of Commons did not approve (to ensure their answerability to the dominant Party).
- The establishment of a principle of collective responsibility of Ministers (to ensure coherent government and its adherence to the policies of the Party).
- The establishment of an obligation on the part of a Minister to resign if he received an adverse vote in the House of Commons (to ensure that he managed his Ministry in an effective and responsible manner, and to ensure that he was answerable to the dominant Party for his policies).

These became established practices in the functioning of government. In effect, they marked a seizure of political power by the House of Commons, and specifically by its biggest Party, or coalition of Parties. It resulted in the intrusion of the leading Party into the executive field of government, through control of the Civil Service, for which it was ill-suited, because there was no requirement that members of the House of Commons should have any training or experience in management and public administration, let alone affairs of state, with which most members of the House of Lords had at least some familiarity, because they moved in those circles. The constitutional purpose of Parliament was to approve Bills submitted by the Executive and advise on policy, in view of the familiarity of the Commons with the needs and mood of the people.

The proceedings of the Cabinet were secret, and remain so to this day, by virtue of the fact that every Minister was a Privy Councillor who had therefore taken the oath of secrecy first demanded by Edward I. For a long time, the proceedings of the Cabinet were not even recorded, and this was undoubtedly because the Cabinet Council was an informal gathering, with no legal authority. Only decisions reached by the Privy Council were of constitutional significance. In the early days, also, Ministers undoubtedly felt that they could remember what they had decided, and it was only later, when embarrassing contradictions occurred, that it was considered necessary to record what had been agreed.

This unrecorded code of tacit understandings, outside the law, out of which the later ministerial system evolved, supplemented the various statutes of a constitutional nature which had been completed by the end of the Revolution of 1688. By now, the prerogatives of the Crown, the privileges of Parliament and the rights of the subject were variously defined, rightly or wrongly, by the *Magna Carta*, the Bill of Rights, and the Act of Settlement. Down to 1688, the Constitution, as it was at that time understood, consisted of dimly remembered customary law and feudal doctrine, supplemented, amplified, and sometimes overridden by statute. After this date, the changing pattern of political power and practice was being accommodated by the new practices, which came to be known conventions, because they had no standing in law.

29.4.4.1. Royal Proclamations are Reduced to Orders in Council

New laws, promulgated by the King through the royal prerogative, in consultation with his Privy Council, whether they were statutes or regulations, were still referred to, up to the end of the eighteenth century, as Royal Proclamations. The Royal Proclamations issued in 1807, were referred to, however, as Orders in Council. These Orders were issued in response to Napoleon's Berlin Decrees of the previous year, imposing an embargo on trade between Great Britain and Continental Europe, and they imposed a counter-blockade on the Continental ports under French control. No reason seems to have been given for the change in title, but undoubtedly it was driven by a desire on the part of the Parties in the Privy Council to obscure the fact that such measures had legal standing only because they were issued under the prerogative of the King, in his constitutional capacity as head of the executive function of government. It was a symptom of the appropriation of the Executive by the Legislature.

It is unclear, in fact, whether the term 'Order in Council' was an innovation. It may have been that the King, in consultation with his Councillors, had always drawn up such a law as an order 'in Council', that is, as the outcome of a Privy Council session, but it was then issued as a Royal Proclamation. The practice of distinguishing the Proclamation from the Order may simply have been discontinued. This may have been due to carelessness, or it may have been deliberate, as already suggested, but the latter explanation is supported by the fact that, from this time onwards, Royal Proclamations were always referred to as 'Orders in Council'. Constitutionally, the Privy Council was an advisory body that had no powers of its own, other than those judicial powers that had been delegated to it by the Great Council, a mechanism that had long since been forgotten.

This diminution, almost to the point of removal, of the constitutional function of the King was thus an important aspect of the quiet revolution that was now taking place under the hand of the elected representatives of the landed gentry. It was made all the more possible by the fact that the new House of Hanover owed its existence as much to the Parties in the House of Commons as to the Great Council in the House of Lords. Furthermore, it was very unsure of its own constitutional rights.

The thinking of the Parties in Parliament was undoubtedly guided by a distant memory of the rights of the people, but it was also steeped in feudal doctrine, as a result of which they perceived the Kings of the past as war-leaders who had seized power and embraced feudal doctrine, in order to justify and maintain, in perpetuity, their unlimited and unquestionable authority, which they had often exploited to the full. Any means was justified, therefore, of bringing the Monarchy under control and subordinating it, once again, to the authority of the people in Parliament.

29.4.4.2. The Industrial Revolution

The Hanoverian dynasty presided over the Industrial Revolution in Britain, which resulted from a unique combination of events and circumstances. Its essential precondition was the Renaissance, leading to the Age of Enlightenment, which was Western Europe's own contribution to intellectual progress, and which promoted the principle of objectivity, taking the form of scientific curiosity and a growing inventiveness. A contributory condition was the rise of Protestantism, with its work ethic and its exhortation to individual attainment; also the growing Empire, which made available a range of plentiful materials. The central feature of the Industrial Revolution was the development of the textile industry. The manufacturing of local wool developed along the rivers of south-west Yorkshire, where the millstone grit of the Pennines provided both an abundance of soft water for processing and the power to drive the numerous water-mills. Meanwhile, cotton manufacturing developed on the opposite side of the Pennines, in Lancashire after 1641, based on cotton imported from India, by way of Liverpool.

The growth in demand led to the invention of processing machinery, and steam engines followed to drive it. This permitted the cheaper, large-scale production of textiles, which soon sought export markets in Western Europe and the colonies. This, in turn, was made possible only by the invention of metallurgical processes that led to the large-scale production of relatively cheap iron and steel. This required an abundant supply of coal, which, coincidentally, was abundantly available in a series of large coalfields in the North and Midlands. The ever-deeper mining of these benefitted from the earlier needs of the Cornish tin-mining industry, which had required a means of keeping the mines drained of seeping water, a solution to which was found in the invention of the steam engine in 1712, which was capable of pumping water out of the mines. Meanwhile, the large-scale manufacture of woollen goods, through its demand for labour and wool, completed the land clearances necessary for the raising of sheep, which in turn made available the extra labour needed by the new industries. Meanwhile, a new supply of high-quality wool became available from the new farming industry in Australia.

On the far side of the Pennines, the further development of the cotton industry was dependent on a new and abundant source of cotton, as well as the soft water and a humid climate. The new supply came from the cultivation of cotton on a large scale in the American colonies, itself made possible only by the arrival of an abundant supply of cheap, slave labour from West Africa. This had been made possible by the Arabs, who had been buying slaves for centuries, the supply of which came from local tribal wars, largely motivated by the profits accruing to African chiefs. As was noted earlier, the purchase of the required slaves was financed by the export of textiles and small industrial goods from England to West Africa. The dependence of the American colonies on slave labour continued until the progress of the Industrial Revolution made possible the invention of the cotton 'gin'. Thus, it was the Empire that played an important part in the development of the Industrial Revolution.

The new industries required a means of transporting bulk goods cheaply, and this led to the construction of a network of canals after 1770, much of the labour for which was available from Ireland. The overall effect was an economic boom that began in 1786. A need for the transport of people and higher-value goods also appeared, and this was met by the adaptation of the steam engine in 1814 to run on rails, a technique previously invented, using trollies on wooden rails, to clear spoil from the mines of Northeastern England. The quality of roads was greatly improved by the use of tar. Meanwhile, the rapidly growing import of wool from Australia and cotton from America demanded larger ships, which could now be constructed of iron and steel and propelled by the new steam engines. A newly urbanised industrial population could only be supported, however, by a huge increase in agricultural production, and this was made possible by the devising of new cultivation methods and the invention of agricultural machinery. Meanwhile, the new industrial towns and cities, and particularly London, provided ready markets for the new output from the farming industry. The rapid development of the new industrial towns, and the exploitation of labour caused by intense commercial competition, resulted in cramped and unhygienic accommodation. This gave rise to widespread ill-health and political unrest.

The new sense of Empire, commercial supremacy and national self-confidence was reflected noticeably in a change of the architectural style adopted for the many great country houses that began to appear. The rich pretentiousness of the Baroque style gave way to the even more pretentious and assertive Roman style, known as 'Palladian'. It now seemed appropriate that, with an Empire far greater in extent than that of the Romans, and with the prosperity to support it, great private and public buildings should imitate the august example of Rome itself, however inappropriate they might be to an English setting. Not unsurprisingly, the new fashion was set by the first member of the minor gentry in the House of Commons to become Prime Minister, Sir Robert Walpole.

The overall effect was financial inflation, which also affected the landowners, who were often unable to meet their rising costs, because the rents paid by their tenants were often fixed by custom or copyhold. The old landed nobility found the basis of its wealth and influence eroded, while a new class of rich industrialists and traders sought upper class respectability, buying landed estates or marrying into the landed nobility, who needed the money that such alliances brought. In this way, the *nouveaux riches* were able to buy their way into the aristocracy and overflowed into the House of Lords. The effect was a new era of political and constitutional turbulence, the weathering of which the Hanoverian dynasty was ill-equipped to endure.

The more important consequences of the Industrial Revolution included a redistribution and rapid growth of the population, much of which would become urbanised in great cities; also the emergence of Great Britain as the leading world power; an eventual and rapid rise in living standards, and the restoration of freeman status to the great majority of the population. All this would have a significant implication for the nature of government itself.

29.4.4.3. George III

George II died in 1760 and, his own son Frederic having died several years earlier, the succession passed to his grandson, George III. His mother was Augusta, daughter of the Duke of Saxe-Gotha, but he was the first of the line to have been born and brought up in England, and throughout his life he never visited Hanover. It was rumoured, and it was probably true, that George had, several years earlier, secretly married Hannah Lightfoot, the daughter of a shoemaker from Wapping, by whom he had allegedly produced three children. With any evidence carefully hidden, and being still only twenty-two years of age and officially fancy-free, he was now drawn to Lady Sarah Lennox, but was advised that he should marry a German princess. So it was that in 1761 Charlotte of Mecklenburg-Strelitz became Queen. All the Hanoverians married German princesses, which did not help to assimilate the dynasty into English society, and it undoubtedly contributed to the prejudice against them that has re-surfaced from time to time down to the present day, yet it was no novelty. Almost all the Norman and French rulers of England had married French women, and their assimilation had been far more protracted. All but one of the Stuarts had married foreigners. It was a political practice followed by royal families all over Europe, usually under the influence of feudal doctrine, but in George's case to maintain the ancestral link, and with it his family's acceptability, in Hanover, which was important to him. In the following year, upon the birth of a son at St James's Palace, the King bought Buckingham House, formerly the London home of the Duke of Buckingham. This stood a little over half a mile west of Whitehall, and its chief attraction was its forty-five acres of gardens. It was a residence – sometimes referred to familiarly, to this day, as 'Buck' House – that later came to symbolise the Monarchy.

As a King, George displayed some of his grandfather's obstinacy and his father's lack of sound judgement. He was also too trusting, but he was good-hearted, keen to do what was right, capable of being flexible and conciliatory, and deeply religious. There is little doubt that his mother – by whom he was dominated, having lost his father at an early age – was to contribute to some of his more unfortunate decisions. Unlike his two predecessors, George III took a direct interest in the affairs of Great Britain and its colonies, and attempted to restore the role and authority of the King in the management of the realm that, by default, had been lost by his two predecessors. To give support to this, he appointed his former tutor and close friend, the Earl of Bute, to the Ministry. At first, the King was unable to exercise any real authority, because the Whigs were in power, and the first ten years of his reign were difficult ones. Following his accession in 1760, the King stopped Britain's subsidies to Prussia, leaving the latter in dire distress in its conduct of the Seven Years' War. Its position was only saved by the death of the Russian empress, Elizabeth, at the beginning of 1762, because her successor, Peter III, was a great admirer of Frederick. The consequence was a peace treaty between Russia and Prussia. Six months later, Peter was deposed and succeeded by his wife, Catherine II, but Russia remained out of the war, and this left Prussia in a much stronger position. With the support of the Prime Minister, the Earl of Bute, George III now negotiated an end to the war with France, and under the Treaty of Hubertusburg in 1763, concluded between the main Continental powers, a general conclusion was reached to the Seven Years' War, leaving Prussia as the dominant power in Europe. The Treaty of Paris, concluded in the same month between Great Britain, France and Spain, confirmed Britain as the leading colonial power, with France shorn of most of her colonies and forced to cede Louisiana west of the Mississippi to Spain, and Florida and the Gulf coast westward as far as the mouth of the Mississippi ceded by Spain to Great Britain, in exchange for Cuba. Meanwhile, the growing wealth of Great Britain, as a result of her overseas trade and the Industrial Revolution at home, had played an important part in financing the war efforts of her allies, so that she acquired the reputation of being the 'Paymaster of Europe'. Although France had played a leading role in the European struggle, her efforts to assert a role as Europe's leading power had achieved little. Great Britain had generally played a minor part in the Wars of the Spanish and Austrian Successions and the Seven Years War, and although they had been of little direct relevance to her own interests, they had nevertheless played a crucial role in enabling her to establish herself as the world's greatest imperial power and ruler of the seas. In each war, she had, arguably, been the main beneficiary.

At home, the old threats and issues that had defined the Parties – the Jacobites and the identity of the Church – no longer hung over the country, so that the Tories were all but irrelevant, while the Whigs had been in power for so long that their principles had become more or less universally accepted, leaving the Party to dissolve into groups. The only Whig Prime Minister with whom the King had got on well was the Earl of Bute, who, being of Scottish descent, was a staunch Royalist. He had taught the young King that he should exercise the powers that had been given to him, unlike his predecessors, but in doing so, George found that he had to come to terms with Party politics. In his efforts to control Parliament the King relied on the use of patronage and bribery, funded out of royal revenue. The resulting 'placemen', organised by Bute's secretary as the 'King's friends', formed a group in Parliament who were sometimes enough to tip the balance, or were at least able to divide the King's opponents. The biggest problem faced by the King was finding a satisfactory Prime Minister, one whom he could get along with, who was also competent, and who was capable of commanding parliamentary support. Bute had proved to be unpopular, so that he had been forced to resign in 1763, to be followed by a succession of equally disappointing Prime Ministers. So had emerged a situation in which the King believed that he could not rule, except through a Prime Minister, who in turn had to juggle his obligations to the King while at the same time retaining the confidence of a workable majority in Parliament. Parliament was itself divided into shifting and inconsistent factions within the Whig majority. Although George III is prone to criticism for his use of patronage, he was merely doing what had been accepted practice by his predecessors and, wherever opportunity has allowed, by most Prime Ministers down to the present day. It was the only way which the King could find of fulfilling the responsibilities that had been placed upon him. Although he was an intelligent and cultured man, he was often stubborn, exercised his patronage in a blatant manner, and lacked the political flair that was demanded by events.

Ever since the restoration of Parliament in the thirteenth century, the Commons had been filled with members of the landed gentry and well-to-do city burgesses, who alone had retained their freeman status. The choice of representatives had been based on the belief that only men of some standing in society, as reflected in their assets, were responsible or knowledgeable enough to be entrusted with representing the interests of their community and guiding the ship of state. It appeared that this verdict had been fully justified by England's prosperity since the Middle Ages, her high standing among the powers of Europe, and the great success of her overseas ventures. Not everybody in the House of Commons now accepted this view, however, because some – who must have preserved some instinct for the common law – believed that the right to elect them belonged to all responsible men. With the other great divisive issues now out of the way, it is not surprising that the issue of fair representation in the House of Commons increasingly came to the fore.

An attempt at reform of the system of representation had been made by Cromwell, whose achievements had not outlived him. Representation depended, however, not only on the right to vote, but also on the choice made by the voters being respected by the Crown, and this issue was central to the case of John Wilkes. In an age of locally manipulated elections, royal patronage of candidates was not the only corruption of the electoral process, but Wilkes, a member of the House of Commons, chose to target the King. He therefore subjected the King to insulting and abusive remarks, which were published in a newspaper and which, in previous generations, would have led to his execution for treason. In the event, he was arrested and expelled from the Commons at the beginning of 1764. Wilkes was re-elected by Middlesex to the next Parliament in 1768, but was expelled by a majority vote of the 'King's friends' in the Commons. This was not the end of the story, however, because Wilkes was thrice elected and thrice rejected, and on the last election his opponent, who had received a small minority of the votes, was declared elected. This was a victory for the King, but it stirred up so much animosity towards him that, when Wilkes was eventually returned as the member for Middlesex, the principle of the freedom of election to the House finally became established, regardless of opposition to the candidate by the House or by the Crown. In 1782 a motion was carried in the Commons to expunge from the record the resolution rejecting him as 'subversive of the rights of electors'.

29.4.4.4. The Royal Finances

The accession of George III saw yet another significant change in the matter of the royal finances. Under his father, the allowance for the Civil

List had been increased to £800,000 a year, but Parliament had remained jealous of the fact that it had no control over expenditure from it. The new King had accordingly been persuaded to surrender to the Aggregate Fund – which consisted of such revenues and the expenditures from them as were controlled by Parliament – and for the duration of his life, those revenues that traditionally accrued to the King.[24] These included the not inconsiderable income from the Crown Estate. In exchange, he was to receive, from the Aggregate Fund, the amount of £800,000 a year that had been allocated to his predecessor. Thus, George III was no worse off in the amount available to meet both his state and his personal commitments, but Parliament now had control over all the traditional revenues of the Crown, leaving the King entirely dependent, financially, upon Parliament.

The Crown Lands, the revenues from which had been vast after the Norman conquest, had been considerably reduced by alienation, only to be expanded again in the fifteenth century as the estates of nobles were appropriated. The Crown Lands had then been reduced again by the Tudors and, even more so, by the early Stuarts, who had also sold off a large part of the Duchy of Lancaster. From the reign of George III onwards, therefore, it became the practice of sovereigns to surrender, for life, the revenue from the Crown Lands, whose original purpose had been the personal support of the King and his family. The King had, however, retained certain other titles, and in his capacities as the Duke of Cornwall and Duke of Lancaster he still enjoyed significant revenues outside the control of Parliament. He also had the benefit of the revenue from the Kingdom of Hanover, which, in principle at least, was related to his duties there.

In spite of his supplements, the King consistently spent in excess of his allowance, and in 1769 he was forced to apply to Parliament to discharge the accumulated debt. It came at an unfortunate time when the King was unpopular, not least over the persecution of Wilkes. An enquiry into the causes of the debt was demanded, amid suggestions that it was incurred in the corrupting of members of Parliament, and Edmund Burke, a prominent politician and writer, published a critical pamphlet on 'The Causes of the Present Discontents'. The apparent royal

---

24   That is, his hereditary revenues, comprising what remained of his original prerogative entitlements and 'tunnage and poundage', the customs and excise duties granted for life.

extravagance continued, and a further request from the King followed in 1777 for relief of debt and an increase in the annual amount for the Civil List. Eventually, a new Ministry under the Marquess of Rockingham, which was dedicated to financial reform, secured in 1782 the consent of a disgruntled Parliament, which was already faced with the cost of a war in the American colonies. Burke's Economical Reform Act of the same year provided for closer parliamentary supervision of the Civil List, and in so doing 'destroyed the conception of the Civil List as an independent financial provision for the Crown'.[25] Examination of the King's expenditures revealed, however, that most were related, not to the comfort and dignity of the Sovereign, but to civil service and judicial salaries, annuities to members of the royal family, and pensions for public services. Clearly, the King's financial difficulties reflected an increase in the costs of government, as well as personal extravagance, but it provided Parliament with an excuse to extend its control still further over the functions of the Crown. Consequently, during George's reign, the Civil List was gradually reduced by removing from it most of the regular costs of government. From a practical point of view, these changes in the financial provisions for the Crown were undoubtedly to the good, but they raised two issues:

1. The need for Parliament to be satisfied that the demands made on the people were reasonable in the circumstances.
2. The need for the Crown to manage its affairs in an efficient manner.

In common law, the executive function was the responsibility of the King – whether directly or through his Ministers – in consultation with his Privy Council. He was responsible also for the collection and disbursement of all public revenue and expenditure, subject to the advice of a Parliament. To what extent the King had a right in common law, either in his official capacity or as a private individual, to the benefit of Crown Estates, the Duchies, and other sources of personal royal income, is another question. The sources of royal income may be distinguished as follows:

---

25   E. A. Reitan, 'The Civil List in Eighteenth Century British Politics', *The Historical Journal*, 9, 3 (1966), 318–337.

- The Aggregate Fund, whose revenues were
  raised and disbursed on the King's behalf by his
  Ministers (in practice, now, all public revenue and
  expenditure), subject to parliamentary consent.[26]
- Monies from the Aggregate Fund that were provided for
  the Civil List, which were disbursed by officers of the Royal
  Household on the King's behalf, and at his discretion.
- Monies from the royal estates that were managed on the
  King's behalf, and at his discretion, by officers of the estates.

The House of Commons was now viewing matters in a very different light. After all, money was the basis of political power, and Parliament no longer saw itself simply as an advisory body with a power of veto. Edmund Burke, an Irish member of the Whig Party in the Commons, wrote a pamphlet in 1770, entitled: *Thoughts on the Cause of the Present Discontents*, in which he argued that George III was upsetting the balance between the Crown and Parliament by seeking to rule without due acknowledgement of the Party-political system, which Burke evidently regarded as now being a part of the Constitution. There was also an element of self-interest in the Commons' own point of view. As members of Parliament had increasingly, by being appointed as Ministers, taken over many of the powers and duties of the Crown, so Parliament had increasingly attracted ambitious Members who saw even greater opportunities for themselves by edging the King further out of his executive role. Whether, however, members of Parliament were best suited to the holding of high executive office, and whether it was desirable that such offices should be held by people who had been elected to look after the interests of the people by reviewing the King's Bills, were crucial questions that had now arisen and were not being answered. That they had arisen at all was due largely to the absence of the Great Council.

Of the minor, yet significant, innovations around this time, one was the establishment in 1771 of the practice of publishing speeches made in the House of Commons. This was in spite of the protests of its members, who may have seen themselves as being held to account for

---

26   It needs to be remembered that the hereditary or traditional revenues of the King had only been surrendered to the Aggregate Fund during his lifetime. Entitlement to them was seen as a royal prerogative, and his successor could not be bound by his surrender agreement.

their remarks. From 1774 onwards, the verbatim reports of proceedings in both Houses of Parliament were printed on their behalf by one, Luke Hansard. Meanwhile, the growth of the Civil Service had placed growing pressure on its accommodation in Whitehall. This led to a decision that the site occupied by Somerset House should be used for this purpose. Somerset House was a little-used royal palace in the Strand, overlooking the Thames, which had been owned by the Crown since 1549, following the execution of its previous owner, the Duke of Somerset, and in 1775 the original building was accordingly demolished and replaced by a new Somerset House for use as offices for the Inland Revenue.

The domestic and foreign responsibilities of the two Principal Secretaries of State had been divided, on a geographical basis, following the accession of William and Mary in 1689, with one assuming responsibility for the South while the other became responsible for the North. In 1782 their portfolios were changed to Home and Foreign Affairs, respectively. So occurred one of the great divisions of ministerial responsibility, and hence of the orientation of the civil service, with the rise of a 'Home Office' and 'Foreign Office'.

A new fiscal reform by William Pitt the Younger, in 1787, consolidated the revenues from the customs and excise duties into a single fund and secured public liabilities upon it. From this time onwards, the national revenue from all sources was paid into this 'Consolidated' Fund, held in the Exchequer account at the Bank of England. It permitted a more efficient allocation of resources, and finally removed the distinction between what the King was accountable to Parliament for, and what he was not. The Bank of England had been set up as a joint stock company, its purpose being mainly to provide loans to meet the needs of the Crown, but it now became the Government's banker for all purposes. Payments from the Consolidated Fund were to be approved by statute, but of an ongoing nature, so that they did not require to be voted annually. Among the expenditures met from the Consolidated Fund was, and continues to be, the Civil List. Another was the judiciary. However, the biggest item chargeable to the Fund each year was the payment of interest on Government borrowings, known as the national debt. The Consolidated Fund was not the only means of financing the needs of government, another being through Supply, which had its origin in the Middle

Ages. Supply services involved expenditure that could only be incurred if authorised by an Appropriation Act. It was assessed and voted by Parliament each year. The essential difference was, therefore, and remains, that the one form of expenditure was subject to parliamentary scrutiny and review each year, whereas the other was not.

While the fiscal system ensured that all taxation and expenditure, other than that remaining to the royal prerogative, was subject to parliamentary approval, the Crown ensured that it retained a firm grip over Parliament by means of a standing order of the House of Commons, dating from 1713, in the reign of George I. This prevented the House from considering new taxes or expenditures, except on the recommendation of the Crown, as signified by a Minister. This was in keeping with common law procedure, according to which Parliament approved acts of government and was entitled to submit petitions, but did not itself attempt to govern. This was a restriction in principle, but not in practice, however, because the Crown was now effectively controlled by the Commons.

29.4.4.5. The American Rebellion

Attention was distracted in 1775 by an uprising in the American colonies. It affected the thirteen colonies lying to the south of Nova Scotia, and Lord North's Ministry was accused of ineptitude, heavy-handedness and contradictions in policy, for which the King faced much of the blame. In putting the rebellion down, the King was able to make use of his German connection to Britain's benefit by drawing his forces as much from Hanover and the adjoining German states as from Great Britain itself. At first, the army won a succession of victories, leading to an expectation that the rebellion would soon be over, but the obduracy of the rebels, who declared the independence of the colonies in 1776, together with the opportunistic support which they received from France, as well as several military and political blunders on the part of the Crown, combined to bring about a reversal of fortunes. Ever ready to grasp an opportunity, France declared war against Britain in 1778, and Spain soon followed. In 1780 Britain declared war on the Dutch, who also had been giving support to the colonists.

Although the King was not to blame for the circumstances leading to the revolt, Lord North complied with his determination to suppress it, in spite of growing and vociferous opposition from the Whigs in Parliament. Instead of the rebellion being suppressed, however, ineffective command in the field led to a stalemate. In 1778, Lord North offered terms to the colonists, but with France now involved it was already too late. To make matters worse, from this time onwards, there was mounting popular disillusion with the war. Also, the issue of the American colonies was having to compete with mounting domestic pressure for electoral reform, particularly against the influence of the King in Parliament through his 'placemen'. In 1780, the Commons carried a resolution by George Dunning 'that the influence of the Crown has increased, is increasing, and ought to be diminished'. It was not that Dunning or anybody else believed it to be either necessary or desirable to remove the influence of the Crown, but rather that the King's 'fund of influence' was so great that 'nobody else could compete'. It is remarkable that moves for political reform in the late eighteenth century were taking place in Great Britain and the American colonies simultaneously. That the colonies were influenced by the reformist mood in Britain is beyond question, but there can also be little doubt that developments in America had the effect of stimulating the mood for electoral reform in Britain itself.

That the Tories were able to survive the election of a new Parliament in 1780 was due more than anything to the Gordon Riots of that year. These were caused by a reaction to the Roman Catholic Relief Act of 1778, to which the King had already found difficulty in giving his consent, because it conflicted with his Coronation Oath – an oath to which the Parties had long failed to attach any importance, probably because it implied that the King still occupied a constitutional position that the Parties no longer saw as relevant. There had already been much violence in Scotland against the concessions to the Catholics, and when, in June 1780, Lord George Gordon, as head of the Protestant Association, led a procession to Parliament to present a petition for the repeal of the Act, a mob of thousands besieged Parliament. Later in the day it went on a rampage. The magistrates failed to act, and the rioting was only ended when the King took the initiative by bringing in the army and militia. Martial law was declared and the cavalry charged along Downing Street. The ensuing election was a reaction against the riots, with a public vote of approval of King and Government. Nevertheless, the effect was short-lived.

The surrender of Lord Cornwallis at Yorktown in 1781, besieged by a rebel army on the landward side and a French fleet off the coast, was disastrous for the King and for North's Ministry. The King considered abdicating, and Lord North resigned six months after the fiasco. Yorktown was not decisive to the outcome of the war in a military sense, but in the face of pressure at home for an end to the conflict with the colonists, Yorktown brought an end to the political will to continue, and no further serious attempt was made to pursue the war. Meanwhile, France diverted its attention to the British colonies in the West Indies, intending to follow up its success by using its naval supremacy to evict Britain from the region. The sugar industry in the West Indies was of much greater economic value to Britain than its North American colonies had been, because the revenue from sugar replenished the Treasury and was a major source of Britain's commercial prosperity. The main French fleet, heading for Jamaica in 1782, was met and destroyed by the British West Indies fleet under Admiral Rodney, in a decisive action off Les Saintes, a group of islands off Dominica. This forestalled a Franco-Spanish attack on Jamaica and not only finally secured British control of the Caribbean, but restored British naval supremacy. It came too late, however, to save the Government of Lord North, who, faced by an increasingly hostile Parliament, and anxious to end the American War as soon as possible, was opposed by the King and tendered his resignation in the same year. The King called upon Lord Rockingham to form a new Ministry, but Rockingham declined without guarantees of American independence and economic reform, and these were given. Rockingham died a few months later, but his successor, the Earl of Shelburne, continued his mandate to negotiate a peace. The ministerial changes that accompanied Shelburne's assumption of office included the appointment of William Pitt the Younger as Chancellor of the Exchequer. In the Preliminary Treaty of Paris of 1782, the independence of those American colonies involved in the uprising, which had now confederated as the United States of America, was recognised.

The effect of the loss of the American colonies was moral and psychological, rather than material, because the West Indies were commercially far more valuable to Britain. Even so, the American colonies and India tended to be seen as the jewels in the Empire and the loss of the former came as a severe blow, particularly to George III, who felt it keenly for the rest of his life. The loss of the colonies was blamed on the King, whose influence also suffered a sharp decline with the resignation of the compliant Lord North. Nevertheless, it cleared the air and imparted a new humility in the King, whose popularity tended to rise from this time onwards. The immediate lesson learned from the loss of the colonies was that it had been due to the excessive political privileges that had been granted to them in the first place. This was a remarkable attitude, given that it was held by Ministries that were headed by politicians from a Parliament that had, for centuries, campaigned against the feudal views and standards of the Monarchy.

Shelburne was forced to resign, in his turn, in the face of a vote of censure over his peace negotiations. In the main Treaty of Paris of 1783, reached between all the main contestants, the independence of the thirteen American colonies, which had now established themselves as the United States of America, was formally recognised, and Britain agreed to pay a war indemnity of £10 million. She also ceded a number of territories to France, the largest being Senegal, while Florida and Minorca were returned to Spain, in exchange for Gibraltar and the Bahamas. The Americans' demand for the whole of Canada, and France's for a complete restoration in India, were both resisted. The Dutch, meanwhile, were isolated and not only gained nothing, but were forced to concede Britain's right to trade in the East Indies.

Among the notable changes in the Empire during the reign of George III was the growing practice of slavery, which had been of little importance in England since the twelfth century. It was still recognised by the courts, and many of those convicted over the Monmouth Rebellion, following the Battle of Sedgemoor of 1685, had been sentenced to be sold into slavery. The slave trade between West Africa and the American colonies had flourished since the mid-sixteenth century, and had been supported by Charles II and James II, who followed the Spanish example by drawing up laws to enforce and spread hereditary slavery, stacking the courts to ensure favourable rulings. It was a policy that co-existed readily enough with the doctrine of Church-Feudalism, in that it applied the principle that the common inhabitants born on an estate were tied to it, and owed their labour and other services to their lord, in exchange for the continued right of abode and a basic livelihood. Nevertheless, the doctrine did not approve of slavery as such. By contrast, the Stuarts took no exception to the moral principle of slavery, particularly as it under-pinned the vital revenues of the Crown that had their origin in the tobacco and sugar plantations. In 1564 the Crown had lent a ship to the privateer, John Hawkins, in order to derive some direct profit from the traffic. Much of the prosperity, which was ultimately paid for by English consumers of sugar and cotton goods, and by the slaves themselves through their wretched conditions of employment, had accrued to the merchants of Bristol and Liverpool. Yet slavery had not been confined to the southern American colonies. Slaves from West Africa had also been introduced by the Dutch into New Amsterdam, later New York, which still depended upon them for labour.

In a judgment in respect of the case of a fugitive Negro slave, James Somersett, in 1772, however, the Lord Chief Justice, the Earl of Mansfield, concluded that slavery was not 'allowed or approved by the law of England'. It was a judgment that was open to question, because English statute law had never forbidden it; nor did common law. Nevertheless, the Mansfield judgment reflected the growing influence of the Quakers and other humanitarian reformers, who were motivated chiefly by their opposition to the Atlantic slave trade, but also by the often cruel and callous treatment within Britain itself of workers and their families, and nowhere more so than in respect of child workers. On the other hand, there was strong opposition to the abolition of the slave trade, particularly from interests involved in the West Indies. For this there were two main reasons. One was the fear of sugar and other producers that abolition of the slave trade would be followed by the abolition of slavery itself, as a result of which they would lose their labour-forces, or they would no longer have any control over them. This would greatly increase the price of the affected commodities. The other reason, undoubtedly, was that British colonists in the West Indies were now vastly outnumbered by their slave populations, causing them to fear for their own safety and for their very survival as communities if the slaves were set free and then given civic rights. An Order in Council of 1805 prohibited the slave trade with the former Dutch colonies. This was a concession that many producers in the West Indies were willing to make, because, recognising that abolition was now becoming inevitable, they sought first to incapacitate their French and Dutch competitors. In 1807, slavery within Great Britain was formally abolished, and in 1833 it was abolished throughout the Empire, although it persisted in various forms for decades afterwards.

29.4.4.6. Attempts at Political Reform

There followed a period of instability at Westminster, with the Whigs again in the ascendancy under Charles Fox, which led to a brief coalition under the ineffectual Duke of Portland. With the war over, it was possible to deal with other problems that had long been neglected. Irish demands were met, notably by the repeal of the Act of 1719, which had enshrined the sovereignty of the British Parliament and the appellate jurisdiction of the House of Lords; also, that part of Poynings' Act which had made Ireland subject to the Privy Council. Other reforms reduced the scope for political graft and electoral influence, but Bills moved by Pitt the Younger for parliamentary reform were thrown out. This period of Cabinet weakness induced a scramble – by Burke to secure office for his Irish kinsmen, and by the Whigs to have party men in every important place. There was also a Bill that would have usurped the chartered rights of the East India Company and opened the way for Party control over Indian affairs. Supported by the City, the King used his influence to persuade the Lords to reject the Bill, and Pitt was asked to form a Ministry. Only twenty-four years of age, Pitt was discounted by his enemies as a 'schoolboy', but, with little initial support, he out-manoeuvred them and formed a Ministry that was to survive for the next seventeen years. The King was well disposed towards Pitt, although Pitt usually had his own way. Moreover, he managed without the use of court patronage.

The greatest achievements of the younger Pitt were the restoration of the country's finances after the war and his reforms of government in India and Canada. With the East India Act of 1785, Pitt imposed parliamentary control over the East India Company, whose policies and administration in the sub-continent had been severely criticised. Constitutionally, Parliament's interest in the Company, as in the American colonies, was limited to the use of such tax revenue for their benefit or control, as in the use of soldiers and ships, but such limitations were not recognised by the Parties in Parliament, whose ambitions extended to the furthest reaches of the Crown's authority. Meanwhile, the attempts of Pitt to reform the system of parliamentary representation in 1782 and 1783 had been defeated. In 1785 he tried again, proposing a modest amount of reform, but again without success. It was argued that the existing system had produced good government, and changes to the system of election not only threatened this, but would upset the balance of the Constitution that had been established by the Glorious Revolution of 1688. The emergence of a Cabinet system that was controlled by the dominant political Party in the House of Commons had resulted in a further transfer of power away from the King to the landed gentry, who, through the development of their own patronage, now controlled the nomination of members to the House of Commons. Of the 658 members returned to the Commons in 1816, 487 were the nominees of Government and 267 were the nominees of private patrons. Of the last, 144 were members of the House of Lords.[27] Added to this was a new system of bribery and purchase. Members who had secured their seats by corrupt means expected, in return, to be bribed by Government with places and pensions, and ultimately with gifts of money from the Treasury itself. The development of this degree of corruption was largely a consequence of the development of the Party system, because each Party had a vested interest in securing control of nominations. During their largely unfettered periods in power, moreover, they had the means by which to secure it. It was a trend which George III had himself been willing to exploit.

At issue was not only the scope of the parliamentary franchise, but also the appropriateness of many existing constituencies. The Industrial Revolution had begun during the eighteenth century, and it was during George's reign that James Watt perfected the steam engine, and the Luddite riots, against the loss of jobs to the increasing mechanisation of production, broke out in 1811. The rapid changes in population density brought a heavy concentration in some shires and boroughs, and a depletion in others, so that representation in Parliament was now very uneven. The effect was to leave thinly inhabited rural areas with far more influence than the industrial towns and cities. Some boroughs had virtually ceased to exist through emigration, as in the case of Old Sarum. Dunwich, in Norfolk, was now at the bottom of the sea, due to coastal

27   Oldfield, *Representative History*, vi. 285.

erosion, but it still returned two burgesses to Parliament. Many boroughs were 'owned' by particular individuals or cliques, who were in a position to decide who should represent them in Parliament. Alternatively, a seat could be bought. Vested interests in the existing electoral arrangement were too great, and a major upheaval would be required to overcome them. It was pointed out, on the other hand, that the existence of these nomination, or 'rotten', boroughs, so called because they had decayed, was an asset to Parliament. They provided a means by which men of particular ability could be advanced by their patrons, without being dependent on the fickleness and narrow outlook of the electors. A notable example of parliamentary advancement through the rotten boroughs had been William Pitt the Elder, but in spite of its benefit to his father, it was William Pitt the Younger who, when denouncing the rotten borough, insisted that 'if it does not drop, it must be amputated'. A second argument for the retention of the rotten borough was that a vote in Parliament was a personal asset, and therefore an item of property, which could not simply be taken away. Moreover, it was related to property qualifications, and to alter the system was seen to be an attack on legitimate rights.

The pressure for reform encountered a major setback in 1789 with a revolution in France. The immediate cause of the upheaval was the virtual bankruptcy of the French Government, due to the cost of successive wars, particularly – and ironically – the financial and material support that it had given to the American colonists in their war of independence. This had helped to inflate prices in France, a development made worse by food shortages due to crop failure. The need for a big increase in taxation accordingly provoked strong opposition, and the French king found it politic to summon the long-defunct Estates General, or Parliament, something that English Kings had never ceased to do. Unfortunately, this provided a release for pent up frustration in a population that had been influenced by American ideas on equality and democracy and stirred further by the very notion of revolution. The Third Estate in France had promptly insisted that it alone represented 'the people', and was therefore the Parliament, but it was hardly representative of the lower classes. The mood had been enough to spark trouble, and the liberalism and indecisiveness of the government of Louis XVI had allowed the situation to get out of hand, as mobs rampaged in Paris and the provinces. Both in Parliament and in his *Reflections on the Revolution in France*, Edmund Burke in 1790 decried the Revolution and the political theories of liberalism, yet there was widespread popular support for the revolution in Britain at first, and the American writer, Thomas Paine, responded to the likes of Burke with his book, *The Rights of Man*, which achieved a ready sale with its defence of the aims and achievements of the Revolution. Nevertheless, there was growing concern in official quarters in London and other capital cities as the radicals increasingly took control in France. The flight and recapture of the French king only aggravated the situation. The French public had long directed its frustrations particularly at the Queen, the Austrian Marie Antoinette. It had been difficult to direct hostility at the king, who was a mild and quite enlightened man, so that it had been directed particularly at the queen, because of her earlier extravagances and because she was an Austrian. When the Austrian government, following the arrest of the French king and queen, threatened a reprisal against France if they were harmed, it applied a flame to an emotional tinder-box, in a country in which paranoia had taken control, and the radicals increasingly felt themselves to be out of their depth. Whereas previously there had been some hope of retaining at least a figurehead monarchy, this was now swept aside, amid calls for the execution of Louis and even the queen. At a more pragmatic level, it was argued that, all the while they remained alive, France's enemies had a strong motive to invade and suppress the revolution, which now descended out of control into a blind carnage of the upper classes – mainly descendants of the Frankish and Visigothic nobility – that displayed a different temperament from that of the basic stratum of French society. For an explanation of the excesses of the revolution, compared with the greater emotional stability of France's eastern neighbours, one may, perhaps, look to the pre-Celtic[28] inhabitants of France, who had survived the glacial period in the warmer south-west. This appears to account for the social, temperamental and intellectual differences that distinguish French society from that of its Germanic neighbours to the east. As the French nobility and its sympathisers were executed in their thousands, the French Second Estate was largely swept away.

Austria and Prussia, alarmed at the threat posed to themselves by the example of a successful revolution, formed an alliance in February 1792, while trying to avoid provocation. It was the moderate radicals in France,

---

28   The Celtic stratum having been effectively destroyed during Caesar's conquest of Gaul.

the Girondists, however, who actively sought a war, chiefly as a means of protecting themselves from the extremists, and in April, in support of a failed revolution in the Austrian Netherlands, they took the lead in declaring war against Austria. After initial reverses, which further fanned the flames of revolutionary excitement in France, the French defeated the Austrians at Jemappes and occupied the Austrian Netherlands. Emboldened by success, and now enthused into carrying the Revolution across Europe, the Convention in Paris issued a proclamation, offering French assistance to all peoples wishing to overthrow their governments, and opened the Scheldt and the Meuse to navigation, in defiance of various treaties. At the beginning of 1793, Louis XVI was executed in pursuit of the domestic 'terror'.

Great Britain reacted by demanding that France withdraw from the Netherlands, at which France excitedly declared war on both Britain and the Dutch Republic and attempted to exploit a revolt in Ireland, which temperamentally had its own roots in Iberia. An organisation known as the Society of United Irishmen had been formed in 1791 to unite Catholics and Protestants in forcing a reform of the Irish Parliament. Stimulated by the example of French republicanism, this quickly turned into a revolutionary means of achieving Ireland's complete separation from Britain. Appeals to the French for assistance in the planned uprising were responded to by the French, who sent two large expeditions to help the Irish, the first of which was scattered by a storm in 1796, while the second had to be abandoned. The rebellion by the United Irishmen nevertheless broke out in 1798, and its outcome was their defeat at Vinegar Hill in that same year, and the crushing of the movement. In England itself there had been widespread unrest since 1795. Pitt had already, in response to the war with France, introduced several repressive measures against revolutionary agitation, including the Traitorous Correspondence Act of 1793 and the suspension of the right of *habeas corpus* in 1794, to be renewed annually. The King's popularity declined, and there were two assassination attempts on him, although the sanity of both assailants was in question. There was a duel between the Foreign Secretary, Lord Castlereagh, and the War Secretary, Canning, over a failed expedition to capture Antwerp in 1809, and there was a scandal over the behaviour of the King's daughter-in-law, Caroline of Brunswick, who had to be sent on a grand tour of Europe. Most of the public hostility was aimed, however, not at the King, but at the Government, and in 1812 the Prime Minister, Spencer Perceval, was assassinated. Offsetting these darker developments, national morale was raised by the victories of Nelson and Wellington. The middle classes and the nobility both prospered from the war, leaving the lower classes feeling neglected.

The first phase of the Continental war ended in 1797, leaving France in possession of the left bank of the Rhine and in control of northern Italy. A new coalition against France was mounted in 1798, but ended in failure. The small, neglected, ill-trained and ill-equipped British army, made up in numbers by contingents from other nationalities, was defeated and decimated in the Netherlands. In France, at the end of 1799, Napoleon Bonaparte, a Corsican upstart but brilliant general and administrator, became First Consul, with dictatorial powers. He followed this with victories against Austria. A respite came with the Treaties of Lunéville in 1801 and Amiens in 1802, through which Napoleon hoped to consolidate his gains and bring peace.[29] His hopes in this direction were ended in 1805 with the formation of a Third Coalition against him, comprising Britain, Austria and Russia. French plans to invade Britain were dashed in October of that year, when the combined French and Spanish invasion fleets were defeated off Trafalgar. This established Britain as the dominant naval power for the remainder of the nineteenth century and ended Napoleon's invasion hopes. Six weeks later, Austria was decisively beaten in the battle of Austerlitz, causing it to sue for peace, which was concluded in the Treaty of Pressburg at the end of December 1805. Napoleon now proceeded to establish the Confederation of the Rhine, of June 1806, incorporating all the German states east of the Rhine, with the exception of Austria, Prussia, Brunswick and Hesse. In so doing, he brought an end to the Holy Roman Empire. Meanwhile, with Austria already severely affected by the Treaty of Lunéville, the Holy Roman Emperor, Francis II, had assumed the more realistic title of Francis I, Emperor of Austria, in 1804, upon which he now laid down the German Imperial crown for good.

Having kept out of the last coalition, Prussia now felt threatened by the Confederation of the Rhine and France's apparently permanent

---

29   Under the Treaty of Lunéville, Louisiana, which France had lost to Spain under the Treaty of Paris in 1763, was returned to France.

position in Germany. She accordingly entered the field, but was routed by the French at Jena, and again at Auerstädt, in October of 1806. Napoleon was now free to enter Berlin and, in the Berlin Decree of November of that year, proclaimed a blockade of Great Britain, thereby inaugurating the 'Continental System' that closed Continental ports to British trade. It was only partly effective. Prussia and Russia remained at war with France, but the Prussians were driven back after the battle of Eylau, and in June 1807, Russia suffered a serious defeat in the battle of Friedland. Unwilling to continue, Prussia and Russia agreed terms with France a few weeks later, in the Treaty of Tilsit. Meanwhile, Portugal had refused to comply with the ban on trade with Britain, and in order to make Britain's commercial isolation more effective, the French invaded Spain early in 1808. Britain responded by sending an expeditionary force to Portugal, under the command of Wellesley. In order to relieve the ensuing pressure on her position in Portugal, Britain persuaded Austria to embark on a new war in Germany, but in the battle of Wagram in July 1809, the Austrians were defeated and had to surrender extensive territory, under the terms of the following Treaty of Schönbrunn. In Spain, Wellesley, helped by Spanish forces, eventually inflicted a decisive defeat on the French at Salamanca in July 1812. Although the Peninsula War was a side issue, it was important in tying down French forces and, by giving new encouragement to Britain's allies, keeping the opposition to Napoleon alive. Meanwhile, friction between Russia and France, and the rivalry between Napoleon and Tsar Alexander for pre-eminence in Europe, resulted in the invasion of Russia by a French 'Grand Army' in June 1812. The Russians withdrew, adopting a 'scorched earth' policy that left nothing for the French. An indecisive but costly battle at Borodino allowed the French to enter Moscow in September, only to find that it had been burned by the Russians, like everything else in Napoleon's path, making the city untenable for the winter. Finding Alexander unwilling to make terms, in mid-October Napoleon led a retreat from Moscow. Appalling losses were suffered along the way, from starvation, attacks, the contested re-crossing of the Berezina, and the onset of winter, causing Prussia now to join with Russia. An indecisive series of battles followed in Germany, and in August 1813, Austria joined Russia and Prussia, all three receiving war subsidies from Great Britain. The withdrawal of French forces from Spain to meet the new threat at last ended the stalemate in the Peninsula, allowing Wellesley – now the Duke of Wellington – finally to defeat the French at Vittoria in June and to advance into France. In Germany, meanwhile, the allies were defeated at Dresden in August, yet in October, in the 'Battle of the Nations', fought near Leipzig, Napoleon suffered a crippling defeat. Retreating into France, he put up an able defence, but at the end of March 1814, the victorious allies entered Paris, forcing Napoleon to abdicate.

At the Congress of Vienna, which began in October of that year, the victors agreed on a rearrangement of Europe. The key figures in the negotiations were the Austrian Chancellor, Metternich, and Lord Castlereagh. The latter had previously kept the alliance together, and now he devoted himself to restoring the balance of power in Europe. As far as possible, he endeavoured to return it to its condition before the French Revolution, and also to ensure the security of the sea and land routes to India.

Before the Congress had finished its work, however, Napoleon returned secretly to France, from his banishment to the Italian island of Elba, in March 1815, and was restored to power in Paris. Austria, Britain, Prussia, and Russia quickly concluded a new alliance, with the Duke of Wellington placed in command. Raising an army, Napoleon led it into Belgium, where he met a hurriedly assembled army of British, German and Dutch troops at Waterloo. The French wore themselves down in repeated assaults on the British lines, but might eventually have succeeded, if it had not been for the arrival, towards evening, of a Prussian army under Blücher. The exhausted French army was routed, and Napoleon abdicated a second time, being captured at Rochfort by the British Admiral Hotham. He was again banished, this time to St Helena, in the South Atlantic. The Congress now completed its work, having agreed on numerous adjustments of boundaries, the dissolution of Napoleon's Rhineland Confederation, and its replacement by a German Confederation. This included Hanover, which now became a kingdom, enlarged by the incorporation of East Friesland and several other areas, thereby making George III of Great Britain also the King of Hanover, with a vote in the new German Diet. During the Seven Years and Napoleonic Wars, Hanover had suffered a great deal, on account of its English connection, but it had also shared fully in the intellectual life of eighteenth-century England, one benefit of which had been the founding of the University of Göttingen in 1736. The ensuing Second Peace of Paris of November 1815, among other things, returned France to its frontiers of 1790. The son of the late French king, the juvenile Louis XVII, having died in captivity, it was the brother of Louis XVI who returned to France to become Louis XVIII.

Although the successes of the French army during the war had owed something to the patriotic fervour which had swept through it after the Revolution, and later to the military genius of Napoleon, it owed much also to the reforms introduced in 1793 by Carnot, a member of the Committee of Public Safety. These had had the effect of creating a vast 'citizen' army, made more efficient by the principle of promotion on the basis of ability, rather than noble seniority, or, as in the British army, by purchase of the King's commission. This had a constitutional aspect of equal relevance to England. Prior to the Middle Ages, all freemen had been committed to military service as the need arose, normally for a limited period each year, in order that crops might be sown and harvests collected. Apart from this vital requirement, the whole nation could be mobilised, although in practice only parts were normally mobilised at a time, as the field of conflict and tactical needs demanded. This had changed in the Middle Ages, as the obligation to military service was commuted to a money payment, so that kings, who now fought mainly over dynastic estates, had to rely on specially raised armies. The French reforms of Carnot largely restored the old principle that all freemen were liable to military service. With the vastly greater populations that now existed in each state, this represented a military capability on a huge scale. Britain, meanwhile, having long associated the army with the constitutional ambitions of the Stuarts, and having accordingly brought it under parliamentary control, had diminished its effectiveness so completely that it was of little use for Continental wars. If it had not been for the Royal Navy, which had not been victimised by Parliament, Britain would undoubtedly have fallen under French rule.

Luckily, some lessons were learned and the army was restored to some degree of effectiveness in time to defeat Napoleon at Waterloo. Nevertheless, the Napoleonic Wars inaugurated a new era, in which the small, usually mercenary, army gave way to a restoration of the principle of universal military service, or at least a liability to it, and this paved the way for the nature of the wars that were destined to follow.

For all concerned, the French Revolution and the ensuing Napoleonic Wars had been a stern warning against the dangers of radicalism. The fear of its consequences during the 1790s had the effect on Britain of causing it to freeze all further attempts at electoral reform for the next thirty years. Rule by the middle classes had, after all, made Britain into a first-class power and the most prosperous country in Europe. It had also built a still considerable Empire and established a commercial dominance that extended around the world. If rule by the mob could have the horrifying consequence experienced in France, then any significant extension of the franchise was liable to have a disastrous result for the country as a whole. It should therefore, it was concluded, be resisted at all costs.

It was in response to this new insecurity that the definition of high treason was amended by the Treasonable and Seditious Practices Act of 1795. Since the time of Edward III, it had been defined, in so far as the King's person was concerned, as the encompassing of his death. It was now extended to include the actual or contemplated use of force, in order to make the King change his measures or counsels. It was also widened to include the intimidation of either or both Houses of Parliament, in which case the convicted person was to 'be deemed, declared and adjudged a traitor', to be punished 'as in cases of high treason'. Whereas one can betray a person, such as the King, or even a group of persons to whom one owes loyalty, however, one cannot betray an institution, such as a House of Parliament.

29.4.5. The Union of Great Britain and Ireland (1801)

An Irish uprising in 1798 was regarded in Westminster as a salutary warning that Ireland was a vulnerable back door, particularly to French ambitions, and that the only way of closing it, and at the same time resolving the Irish problem, was by a constitutional settlement along the lines of the union of England and Scotland. The Act for the Union with Ireland, in 1801, provided for the kingdoms of Great Britain and Ireland to be combined under the name of the 'United Kingdom of Great Britain and Ireland'. It also provided that there should be one Parliament of the United Kingdom, to which Ireland was to send four lords spiritual, sitting by rotation of sessions, and twenty-eight lords temporal, elected for life by the Irish peerage, to sit in the House of Lords; and one hundred commoners, to sit in the House Commons. In order to accommodate the extra members, the House of Lords, which had hitherto been accommodated in the Parliament Chamber, or Painted Chamber, was forced to find somewhere more spacious. It was therefore moved in 1801 into the Court of Requests, or White Hall, which adjoined it. Although, as in the case of the union between England and Scotland, no mention was made of the Parliament being in Westminster, it was evidently taken for granted as being the common Parliament, with the result that the Irish Parliament was dissolved, like the former Scottish Parliament.

The Isle of Man and the Channel Islands were accounted for by virtue of the facts that the King was also the King of Mann and, in his former capacity as Duke of Normandy, otherwise since renounced, he still retained the fiefdom of the Channel Islands. He had enjoyed the suzerainty of the Isle of Man since 1333, but the title had fallen to royal appointees, and it had not been until 1765 that the King of England, by this time King of Great Britain, had resumed his constitutional position as the King of Mann, in his capacity as the King of England. Both the Isle of Man and the Channel Islands accordingly remained outside the United Kingdom, largely self-governing under the Crown. The churches of England and Ireland were to be united into one Protestant episcopal church, to be known as the United Church of England and Ireland. Pitt proposed to make some concessions to the Roman Catholics, but the King was persuaded (and correctly) that this would involve a breach of his Coronation Oath. Pitt thereupon resigned, so ending eighteen years in office. He was replaced by Henry Addington.

One effect of the Union with Scotland in 1707 had been the unification of the Orders of Baronets of England and Scotland, to become the Baronets of Great Britain. This precedent set in chain a further revision in 1800, when the title of the Order was changed by the Union with Ireland to become the Order of Baronets of the United Kingdom.

The durability of the new union was by no means assured. England was by far the dominant partner, both economically and politically. Wales and Ireland had been incorporated as a result of conquest by the Normans, and the Isle of Man had come under the suzerainty of Edward

III in 1333. The Channel Islands had come under the Crown by feudal inheritance. Only Scotland had been incorporated by mutual agreement, and even then almost certainly against the will of the majority of Scots. Only the coincidence of royal marriage had produced, in James IV of Scotland, a chief claimant to both the Scottish and English crowns, and this link had been strengthened by their common economic and religious interests. Britain and Ireland, on the other hand, were deeply divided by religious antagonism, and were separated by the Irish Sea, making the union between the two inherently difficult to maintain, because acceptance of Irish Catholicism was a contravention of the Coronation Oath, and hence of the policy of the Crown, as Pitt had found to his cost. In support of the King's opposition to any consideration of emancipation for the Catholics, he could point to the anti-Catholic Gordon Riots of 1780, in addition to his constitutional obligation. The Government of the United Kingdom was legally obliged to promote Protestantism in Ireland by whatever reasonable means available, but it was an obligation upon which it wisely defaulted. If the King had defaulted from his oath of office, or allowed his Ministers to do so, by acceding to the Catholic Emancipation Bill in respect of England he would have been morally obliged to abdicate. It could be argued, however, that the King would not have defaulted by accepting the Bill in respect of Ireland, because this part of the Coronation Oath applied to George III as King of England, not to him in his capacities as King of Scotland and King of Ireland. It was noted earlier that the union of the English and Scottish crowns, upon which arrangement the union with Ireland was based, was probably not, either in common law or in terms of actual arrangements, founded on a newly created common monarchy, any more than it had created a new 'British' Parliament. George III was the King of England, King of the Scots, and King of Ireland, but his Coronation Oath related only to the first. His title as King of Great Britain and Ireland was a legal fiction.[30]

The occasion of 1801 saw the approval by the Privy Council of a new version of the Union Jack, designed to reflect the new union with Ireland. It was achieved by incorporating the diagonal red cross of St Patrick, which was joined with the existing white-on-blue cross of St Andrew, in a style known as 'counter-changing', so that each colour was uppermost

---

30   The same principle would be followed in respect of the future Dominions of the British Commonwealth.

in two quarters. The central join therefore resembled a swastika, although this effect was hidden by the superimposed cross of St George with a white border. It was published, not by the Crown, but by a commercial printer, with the result that conflict immediately erupted between the War Office and the Admiralty, each of whom produced different versions. The army version was, and still is, more square. Nevertheless, the issue of whether the Union Jack was strictly a naval flag, or could be flown also on land, was to continue until 1908, when, in reply to a parliamentary question, the Earl of Crewe, probably finding himself with no alternative, was to confirm that 'The Union Jack should be regarded as the national flag and it undoubtedly may be flown on land by all His Majesty's subjects'. Nevertheless, the history of the Union Jack was very like that of the British system of government. It was not, and to this day is not, recognised in law, and has no official shape or colour. Meanwhile, the Napoleonic Wars had finally laid to rest all further pretension to the throne of France, and about this same time, George III altered the royal coat of arms, removing the French *fleur-de-lis* for the first time since Edward III and giving the arms of Hanover a more central place.

29.5. The End of the King's Influence in Parliament

Just as it was a violation of the principles of the Constitution for Members of Parliament to meddle directly in the affairs of the Executive, so also was it a violation for the King to meddle in the deliberations of Parliament, not least by exerting inappropriate influence over individual members. That the Executive had been mismanaged by the King for centuries is beyond doubt, but it was the role of the Great Council to deal with such matters, albeit in consultation with Parliament. Executive duties required, in any case, training and abilities that few members of Parliament possessed.

George III was a man of wide interests and intellect, with a fascination for agriculture and botany which gave rise to his nickname of 'Farmer George'. His long, and otherwise outstanding, reign was complicated by bouts of madness, whose symptoms included periods of incoherent speech, rapid changes of mood, and even total delirium. The problem may have been aggravated by arsenic, recently identified in his remains and ultimately lethal, which had presumably been introduced as part of his medication. Although the King was not very popular during the latter part of his reign, when the illness became more persistent, there is no doubt that the people felt sympathy, to such an extent that he was referred to as the 'Father of the People'. The existence and function of the Great Council having been lost to public memory, regency provisions in the event of the absence or incapacity of the King had never since been clearly established, but had taken the form of either a regency council or a regent, usually referred to as a 'Protector'. Some rulers had made specific provision for regencies in the event of their death before their successor came of age. During the temporary insanity of George III in 1788, a Regency Bill – which was, of course, *ulta vires*, because it conflicted with the constitutional function of the Great Council – was submitted, and this became the subject of a squabble between Pitt, the Prime Minister, and Fox, the leader of the Whigs, but it could not be enacted because of the King's condition. Eventually, a legal fiction was resorted to by which the royal assent was assumed to have been given. It is not clear whether the earlier role of the House of Lords and the Privy Council in taking the initiative in providing for such situations had been forgotten, but it seems likely that the House of Commons was no longer in the mood to leave such matters to other institutions. Dealing with all such situations by statute ensured that the House of Commons remained in control.

In the event, the Bill proved to be unnecessary because the King recovered. When the same problem arose in 1811, with a formal declaration of the King's insanity, a Regency Act was passed which designated his son, George Augustus, Prince of Wales, as the 'Prince Regent'. Clearly, if the King was 'insane' he was in no position to sign the Bill, so that the 'Act' was a fabrication and no 'Prince Regent' was legally appointed. The constitutional procedure, as we have seen before, would have been for the King's insanity to be declared and provided for by the Great Council. Since the fettering and decline of that Council, this task had fallen to its standing committee, the Privy Council, for noting by the House of Commons, upon which it was for the House of Lords (representing the Great Council) to make a decision on the regency and, in this case, appoint the Prince of Wales to that position. From this time onwards, George III lived at Windsor, blind, neglected and half forgotten.

It is all the more unfortunate that the 'Regency' coincided with a difficult period in the country's history. The end of the conflict with France in 1815 resulted in a long and severe economic depression as a result of market dislocation and the discharge of men from the army and the Royal Navy. The key issues were unemployment and hostility to the Corn Law of 1815, whose purpose was to sustain the price of grain to farmers and landlords by prohibiting cheaper imports, unless the domestic price reached the 'famine' level of eighty shillings a quarter, which was still unaffordable to many of the poor. Each issue aggravated the other, causing an outbreak of political radicalism and a return of the public pressure for electoral reform, it being assumed that this would, in some way, make possible an easing of economic conditions. With the French Revolution still fresh in the minds of the authorities, however, there was little inclination to treat the restlessness with much sympathy, and when violence erupted at Spa Fields in London, in 1816, and at St Peter's Field in Manchester, in 1819, the latter was put down by a cavalry charge that caused the death of several people, an event that became known as the 'Peterloo Massacre'. Spa Fields and Peterloo resulted in repressive legislation against seditious meetings and seditious libel, the temporary suspension of *habeas corpus*, a ban on training in the use of arms, and the authorisation of magistrates to search for, and seize, weapons considered a danger to public peace. Radical journalists were curtailed by a stamp duty on newspapers, but tension was heightened in 1820 by the discovery of the Cato Street conspiracy to assassinate the entire Cabinet by the use of explosives.

In spite of the severe difficulties faced by the ordinary population, the period of the Regency was socially and intellectually dazzling. The Prince Regent, spoiled by his father, profligate and a womaniser, and little interested in his official duties, lived at the centre of a social whirl, the subject of adoration by London society, helped by his good looks and sharp mind. He was able to get his many debts paid for by the King or Parliament. It was the period of the social dandy, Beau Brummel, and such writers and poets as Sheridan, Byron, Southey, Keats, Shelley and Wordsworth. It was a time when the running of the country depended heavily on successive Prime Ministers – the Duke of Portland, Spencer Perceval, and the Earl of Liverpool.

Few of Britain's Kings have had their names besmirched so effectively as George III, and much of this hostile propaganda was spread by the Whigs. The antipathy of George towards the Whigs, the conflict between the Whigs and the King's 'placemen' in the Commons, and bitterness over the loss of the American colonies, all contributed to this legacy of ill-feeling. Against this, it is to the King's credit that, out of the political soup of the day, he eventually picked out, elevated, and steadfastly supported, in William Pitt, one of the most able men ever to hold the position of chief Minister, and, moreover, to accept his important reforms, even though they had the effect of destroying the King's own control over Parliament. Although the King's popularity was at a low level during the Wilkes affair, causing an expression of republican sentiment, and suffered further with the loss of the American colonies, a sharp swing in sentiment was brought about by the French Revolution and the ensuing Napoleonic Wars. Even George's bouts of madness did not dim the new popular affection for the Monarchy, and it was ironic that his final and most devastating bout of madness, together with the onset of his blindness, coincided with the high point of George's popularity.

The King died early in 1820, after an exceptionally long reign. He was succeeded by his son, the Prince Regent, as George IV, who also inherited the crown of Hanover. George entered his reign with a political bombshell by demanding that his Ministers institute a divorce proceeding against the Queen, the former Princess Caroline of Brunswick. The marriage had been arranged by his father twenty-five years earlier, as part of Parliament's condition for meeting the young man's debts, no doubt in the hope that a wife would have a stabilising influence, but the choice had been disastrous, and the marriage had broken down shortly afterwards. Caroline had now returned from the extended grand tour imposed upon her, in order to claim her rightful position as Queen. The King's reputation for debauchery while still Prince of Wales had left him unpopular in the country at large, and public sympathy for Caroline, who was considered to have been badly treated, was such that she was met on her return with scenes of public rejoicing. A Bill to effect the divorce and deprive the Queen of her title was introduced into the Lords, where it was narrowly passed, but had to be dropped, in the face of the overwhelming public support for her and the Bill's almost certain defeat in the Commons. An important consequence of this fiasco and the continuing separation was that there would be no surviving legitimate children of the marriage. To the King's disinterest in affairs of state and his lack of responsibility was added a serious decline in his health, caused by personal excess, and this rendered him almost incapable of fulfilling his office, even if he had possessed the will to do so. Undoubtedly, his over-eating reflected a severe medical condition, but it caused him to be lampooned in the popular press and contributed further to the decline in the standing and constitutional importance of the Monarchy. It played into the hands of the politicians, who had by now, by default, largely usurped the King's authority.

This decline in the constitutional role of the King had been precipitated by James II, greatly increased by the inability of George I to communicate with his Ministers, and now accelerated by the extravagance and incompetence of George IV, both as King and in his previous role as Prince Regent. It had been an almost inevitable outcome, sooner or later, of the blind acceptance of the principle of succession by the ordinary rule of inheritance, but it had also owed as much to the ambitions of Party leaders and their followers in the House of Commons, who saw in the King an open door to their own advancement. An unintended achievement of George IV was the creation of a Scottish national identity, other than that imposed by geography. A few weeks after his coronation in 1821, the King went on a royal progress through the United Kingdom, visiting Ireland and Scotland. The latter was at the urging of Sir Walter Scott, who, anxious to use the occasion to establish a common Scottish identity, persuaded the authorities there to greet the King lavishly in Edinburgh with a display of men and women in Highland dress. Tartans, kilts, sporrans, bagpipes and other features put together for the occasion were not widely used or even known in the Highlands themselves, and totally alien to Edinburgh, which had always remained basically English, but the event was a huge success, and Scott's hard work and imagination succeeded in establishing the idea of a common Scottish culture and identity, both within Scotland itself and in the eyes of the outside world.

The reign of George IV was marked by a swing in sentiment towards free trade. Great Britain's emergence as the pioneer of the Industrial Revolution, deriving its increasing prosperity from exports of manufactured goods, offset by a growing dependence on imported food and raw materials, had been hindered by the mercantilist policies that had been inherited from the Middle Ages, which had sought to protect trade. Great Britain now led the world in technology and industrial production and had no effective competitor, so that self-interest now dictated a need, not for the protection of domestic industries, but the promotion of free trade. The cost of living and social stability were much affected by the cost of imports, which was increased by import duties, while exports were affected by protectionist policies elsewhere. Economic liberalism went well with the new political liberalism that had flowed from the English and French philosophers, which had been further inspired by the American and French Revolutions. David Ricardo's *Principles of Political Economy*, produced in 1817, was an important statement of *laissez faire*, or free enterprise economics, and established economic theory as a subject quite distinct from politics. A liberal faction emerged among the ruling Tory Party, however, generating friction with the conservative element. At first, the difficulties were smoothed over by the conciliatory management of Lord Liverpool, who was Prime Minister from 1812 to 1827, and subsequently Lord Canning was able to cope for a time by means of a coalition of liberal Tories and moderate Whigs. The sympathies of the Duke of Wellington, however, who was Prime Minister from 1828 to 1830, lay with the conservative wing of the Tories, and the liberals in his Ministry became increasingly alienated and resigned from office. As a compromise, the Corn Laws were amended in 1828, allowing the import of foreign grain, with duties fixed according to a sliding scale that varied inversely with the current price of British corn.

The religious issue returned in 1828, when the leader of the Catholic Emancipation Movement in Ireland was elected to Parliament by the voters of Clare. Under the provisions of the Test Act, no Catholic or Nonconformist could hold public office, and this created an impasse. Both Wellington and the Home Secretary, Sir Robert Peel, were bitterly opposed to Catholics in office, but they also feared that civil war in Ireland would follow if the restrictions on Catholics were not removed. The Test Act was repealed in the same year, and, against vigorous opposition from the right-wing Tories, Wellington forced the Catholic Emancipation Bill through Parliament in 1829. In Wellington's view, the terms of the

Act were sufficient to get around the difficulty posed by the Coronation Oath, which Pitt had found insuperable. It granted Catholics the right of suffrage and the right to sit in Parliament and to hold public office, with the exception of the offices of the Lord High Chancellor, the Lord Keeper or Lord Commissioner of the Great Seal of Great Britain or Ireland, and Lord Lieutenant and other governorships of Ireland. In return, an oath was required of those elected or appointed, denying that the Pope had any power to interfere in the domestic affairs of the realm, repudiating any intentions against the established Church, and recognising the Protestant succession to the Crown. Meanwhile, the reign of George IV marked the beginning of the end of the Order of Baronets. He rescinded the right of the eldest son of a baronet to be knighted, although the custom persisted until Victoria's reign, and the further creation of baronetcies was not destined to end until 1964.

During the fifty years from the Ministry of William Pitt the Younger, in 1783, to the accession of William IV, in 1831, the royal system of creating and maintaining majorities in the House of Commons was steadily decreased and eventually brought to an end. The main reason was that the supply of funds available for patronage was gradually reduced. Parliament had no control over expenditure in the eighteenth century, nor was there a clear distinction between the public revenue and the private income of the Crown, so that available funds could be used for almost any purpose, without the Government being accountable. The House of Commons resolved in 1780, however, 'that it is competent to this House to examine into and to correct abuses in the expenditure of the Civil List revenues, as well as in every other branch of the public revenue, whenever it shall seem expedient to the wisdom of the House to do so'. Such proposals for reform were the responsibility of the King's Ministers, in default of which they were, if it had been functioning, the duty of the Great Council. In the event, Burke's Place Act of 1782 prohibited officers of the Crown who were engaged in the management of the royal finances from giving their votes at elections to Parliament. It also classified all expenditures under the Civil List into six types, required a separate departmental budget for each, a separate royal official to authorise all expenditures from each, and that the accounts of all departments be audited. The Place Act also took a further axe to sinecures, abolishing 134 offices in the Royal Household and the Treasury. Pitt had already abolished 765 unnecessary revenue offices several years earlier. A commission of public accounts was appointed in 1785 to examine the whole financial system, and in the same year five commissions were appointed to audit all public accounts. Even the hereditary revenues of the Crown were slowly brought under control, and only the Privy Purse remained at the full disposal of the King. Even a Keeper of the Privy Purse was appointed to replace the former domestic financial officers. Expenditures from the Privy Purse included the maintenance of the King's private estates, the interior maintenance of the royal palaces, and the salaries of the royal officers and servants. The Keeper of the Privy Purse was also responsible for administering the revenues of the Duchy of Lancaster and, in the event of the minority of the Duke of Cornwall or the vacancy of the honour, those of the Duchy of Cornwall. This did not affect the actual Privy Purse. This had once been used to meet the King's immediate requirements, usually while travelling, and it was still produced at a King's coronation, when it would contain a hundred silver coins, to be distributed along the way as 'largesse'.

Long before the Reform Bill of 1832, therefore, the King and his Ministers had relinquished the use of public funds for political purposes. Moreover, the Bribery Act of 1809 made the use of bribery by the Crown in the counties and boroughs almost impossible. The promise of Peerages in return for the delivery of seats in the Commons was rejected as wrong in 1812, and by 1820 the granting of honours for political purposes was greatly reduced. Many of these changes occurred under the Prime Ministership of William Pitt. There were many other legislative changes and administrative reforms of a similar nature during this period, and royal influence in Parliament was not the only factor. The heavy cost of the Napoleonic Wars and other conflicts imposed cuts on all unnecessary expenditures and made the proper accounting for all moneys essential. Even so, this is unlikely to have been achieved without the ability and perspicacity of Pitt. These changes were also accompanied by a shift in public attitudes in favour of integrity and accountability in public life. As the King gradually lost his control over Parliament and policy, it shifted to his Ministers, who now began to assert their direct authority over the

Civil Service. At the same time, the House of Commons itself remained corrupt, and the shadow of reform now began to move in its direction.

PART XII

•

THE LEGISLATURE APPROPRIATES THE EXECUTIVE (1832–1918)

30. THE AGE OF LIBERALISM

THE CHURCH HAD a strong influence during the Middle Ages, with its doctrine that the King was the appointee of God, and that he represented God in temporal matters. One consequence of this doctrine had been the overriding of common law in constitutional matters, although the influence of common law never disappeared entirely. A reaction to feudal doctrine had then come from the Renaissance of Greek Classical thinking, which, apart from bringing the Middle Ages to an end, had two main, inter-related consequences. One was a doctrinal revolution within the Church that had led to the Reformation of the sixteenth century, during which a part of Northern Europe had broken free of the Papacy in Rome. The second had been the Enlightenment, or the Age of Reason, which, if not opposed to religion, had at least promoted agnosticism, and emphasised the ideals of duty and social order. It had found support in a new perception of the universe, as described by Isaac Newton and Copernicus. The scientific revolution of the seventeenth century, which had been a consequence of the Enlightenment, continued into the eighteenth century, leading to great strides in the understanding of the natural world. The dominant thinker of the Enlightenment, which reached its height in the eighteenth century, was Immanuel Kant in Prussia. Whereas it had led, in France, to the development of political philosophy and materialism, in the hands of such men as Voltaire and Diderot, in Germany it had taken a more cultural form, under the influence of such writers as Goethe and Schiller, and particularly in a new appreciation of nature. In England it had been dominated by the philosopher, Locke, while in Scotland it had produced an interest in political economy, at the hands particularly of Hume and Adam Smith. Each of these national directions had, or was to have, important consequences for history.

Meanwhile, however, the Age of Enlightenment had sown the seeds of its own demise, and after the death of Kant in 1804, it came to an end. The new political philosophy in France had led to the French Revolution, with all its excesses, promoting a new period of political repression. Meanwhile, the intolerable conditions that accompanied the Industrial Revolution in Britain left the Government eventually with no choice but to intervene with a whole series of regulations, while Darwin's theory of the origin of species, published in 1859, had the effect of undermining the stable universe that Newton had postulated.

The social thinking of the ruling class in the last quarter of the eighteenth century and the first quarter of the nineteenth was dominated by several influences. The banker, David Ricardo, in his *Principles of Political Economy and Taxation*, argued in 1718 in favour of complete economic freedom, which would cause rents, interest, profits and wages to find their true, equilibrium level. Adam Smith's *Inquiry into the Nature and Causes of the Wealth of Nations*, published in 1776, advocated the cause of economic liberalism, arguing that prosperity came from allowing resources to be directed to where they yielded the highest return. Jeremy Bentham, in 1789, proposed a comprehensive system of rational legislation, and set forth a philosophy that advocated those policies that brought 'the maximum benefit for the greatest number of people', a utilitarian argument later pursued, in 1825, by James Mill. Meanwhile, the anti-revolutionary teaching of Edmund Burke, whose *Reflections on the Revolution in France*, published in 1790, criticised political liberalism for its consequences, while Malthus, in his *Essay on Population*, published in 1798, caused further despondency by raising the prospect of an ever-growing population that would drive down wages to mere subsistence. At a more immediate level, the social situation was hugely aggravated, particularly in Lancashire, by large numbers of Irish immigrants, who drove down wages and, in so doing, delayed the introduction of labour-saving machinery. On the other hand, the Irish provided much of the abundant cheap labour for the canal construction boom of the latter half of the eighteenth century. Such was the poverty that women and children were willing to take employment under appalling conditions, creating a legacy of bitterness towards immigration and free markets. The Evangelical wing of the Church and the social reformers, such as Wilberforce, promoted the worthiness and salvation of the individual. Nevertheless, the most important influence came from the new political economists, whose *laissez faire*, or 'let be', thinking was guided by the growing dependence of Great Britain on international trade, which it now dominated, and which brought the prosperity that often goes with specialisation – making it the 'workshop of the world'. Unfortunately, the population was growing nearly as fast as the prosperity, so that the working class was slow to realise any benefit.

Liberalism was not merely a liberation from artificial controls, with dire consequences for the working class; it also had a humane aspect, with a growing belief in the need for intervention against these dire consequences. There were two groups of interventionists. The first recognised the benefits of liberalism, yet believed that it could not be left to run itself, and that humanitarian concerns made it necessary for Governments to impose statutory limits and requirements to ensure that the weak were not exploited by the strong, and that certain basic standards were imposed in the interests of all. The second interventionist group held that liberalism was fundamentally flawed, because it did not require the individual to accept responsibility for the effects of their actions on others. The solution to this, it claimed, required society to be organised on a different basis, whereby the means of production would be owned by society as a whole, rather than by individuals. Such a Utopian system came to be known as 'socialism', whose emergence during these years will be returned to in due course.

Meanwhile, the liberalising ideal had been extended to restrictive practices by workers. The Acts of Walpole and the Pelhams forbade workmen to combine in trade unions for the purpose of raising wages by restricting the availability of labour, while the Combination Act of 1799 made trade unionism illegal. The Act was given added impetus by the fear of revolution caused by the upheaval in France. Competition caused working hours in mining and industry to be excessive, and young children were employed in the textile mills, as well as women. The wretched conditions of employment and the crowded accommodation began to prompt a movement for change. In response to disturbances, the Combination Act was repealed by the Trade Union Act of 1825, which made it an offence to use violence or intimidation in order to bring about changes in employment conditions, although it permitted unions to meet for the purpose of negotiating better conditions. These were only partly relieved by the Factory Act of 1833. In spite of this, trade unionism took a major step forward in 1830 with the formation of the National Association for the Protection of Labour, representing a federation of about 150 unions, and this was further stimulated by general disappointment with the results of the Reform Act of 1832. Political agitation was then provoked by the case of six Dorchester labourers in 1834, who received the harsh sentence of transportation to the colonies after organising a trade union of agricultural workers in Dorset. The problem in the case of the 'Tolpuddle Martyrs' was not their creation of a trade union, but their use of secret oaths and ritual in the pursuit of their aims, cutting a raw nerve in view of the violence and even murderous crime that had characterised the methods of some of the early trade unions.[1] The immediate effect of the case was disastrous for the union movement, which effectively collapsed, but the memory of the Tolpuddle Martyrs would provide a rallying cause for the socialist labour movement later in the century.

The Age of Liberalism reached its climax in 1841 with the establishment of free trade, but it was already under attack. In the same year, the report of a Royal Commission appointed to investigate the coal-mining industry, shocked all England with its revelations of brutality, exhaustingly long hours of work and absence of safety-devices, the employment of women and children, and the wretched moral and sanitary conditions under which employees lived and worked. The evils of a liberal industrial society were also subject to attack in various novels published soon afterwards.[2] Yet as early as the 1830s, Parliament had gone against liberal ideas with hesitant attempts to legislate on hours and conditions of work. In this it was motivated, partly, by humanitarian sentiments, and partly by the more effective organisation of trade unions. The pressure for the regulation of employment increased greatly after 1867, following the first enfranchisement of a considerable body of ordinary workers. By about 1870, the influence on legislation of the liberal view – that the competitive system should be left to regulate itself – was overtaken by that of working-class voters, who believed that the system must be regulated, as a matter of principle, in the interests of social welfare.[3]

1   K. Feiling, *A History of England*, 837.

2   For example: Disraeli's *Sybil* in 1845; Gaskell's *Mary Barton* in 1848; and Kingsley's *Alton Locke* in 1850.

3   A. V. Dicey, *Law and Opinion in England During the Nineteenth Century*, Lecture VII (1905).

31. PARLIAMENTARY DEVELOPMENTS

31.1. Electoral Reform

The need for electoral reform arose from the absence of the Constitution and the growing social problems in the new industrial towns and cities, compounded by the failure of the Government to alleviate them. There was widespread unrest in favour of an extension of the franchise to ordinary working men, and this evoked a general sympathy among the middle class, but there was opposition among the landowners, who controlled the House of Commons, due mainly to a fear of the possible consequences of allowing control to pass to a revolutionary movement, in the light of what had happened in France. In any case, involvement in the personal problems of the people had never been regarded as a proper function of the Crown. Representation in Parliament had always been seen as the particular right of free men, it not being appreciated that most of those who now worked in industry and mining had once been free men themselves, who had lost their rights in earlier times, through no fault of their own. All the while that freemanship was defined in terms of the possession of a freeholding – a requirement that had been demanded by the Normans, until it had effectively been amended in 1430, by Henry VI, to the holding of free land or tenement to the value of forty shillings a year, after the deduction of all charges – the problem would remain.

A further problem of representation had arisen since the Middle Ages, which may be summarised as follows:

1. England is a confederacy of the shires, which are represented equally in the English Parliaments.
2. In the Middle Ages the emergence of a number of prosperous towns led to the granting to them of additional representation. This should have been in the shire assemblies, but new delegations of judicial and executive power to the King by

the shires, whether made directly or through the English Parliaments, greatly reduced the value of representation in the shire assemblies in favour of representation in the English Parliaments, which was granted. This violated the principle of equal representation of the shires, because some shires had more or bigger towns than others.

3. This problem was accentuated in the eighteenth and nineteenth centuries as a result of land clearances by owners anxious to convert their land to sheep farming, causing the eviction of tenants, most of whom could only find employment in the new industrial towns. These tended to be concentrated in certain shires. This migration not only broke the link of shire identity for many families, but resulted in the depopulation of many shires and a huge increase in population in certain others. Meanwhile, the lack of government response to the social problems in the increasingly congested industrial towns led to a growing demand by these towns for direct representation in Parliament, which alone could influence action by the Crown. When these towns were at last granted a direct representation in Parliament, based on population size, this so upset the parity between the shires that no attempt was made to maintain it. Indeed, the reason for parity had already been forgotten by 1213. In any case, the shire assemblies were now long defunct, except for judicial purposes, and these had long been appropriated by the Crown.

4. The extra representation granted to the new industrial towns and cities, on the basis of their population, introduced a huge disparity in the principle of equal representation of the shires, as well as ignoring the shires in drawing up the electoral boundaries.

As a representative assembly of the shires, the House of Commons had lost its relevance. Even as a representative assembly of free men, the House had little relevance. The boroughs represented in Parliament, of which there were 203, had widely differing constitutions and practices. Their methods of election varied, nearly all adult men being voters in some cases, while others applied qualifications, such as financial status, period of residence, or, in the case of 'close' boroughs, voting was limited to freemen of the borough or even to members of the governing body. Some were referred to as 'rotten' boroughs, because their representatives were elected by only a handful of people. Old Sarum and Dunwich had disappeared altogether, the first having been abandoned, and left with only seven voters, and the second was now at the bottom of the sea, yet it still returned a member to Parliament. There was corrupt control of elections in certain towns, and in some, referred to as 'pocket' boroughs, single families or individual patrons had gained the absolute right to return candidates. Such a borough was therefore 'in their pocket'. Nearly half of the seats in the House of Commons were controlled by patrons, including the King himself, and only a third of the members of the House were freely chosen. The qualification for electing the representatives of the counties was still the possession of a forty shillings a year freehold. Of the 558 seats in the Commons, 405 were accounted for by the English boroughs, and eighty by the English counties.

There was a double problem, therefore, in that only a fraction of the total number of free men, as determined by ancestral right, enjoyed representation, and some constituencies represented almost nobody, or represented the interests of individuals for whom they had never been intended. They were problems that the new industrial economy had at last thrown into perspective, with the emergence of industrial towns and cities, inhabited by landless men and their families who had nobody to turn to for the alleviation of their problems. Some of these new towns even extended across shire boundaries, pulling their interests in different directions, as in the case of Birmingham, which had now spread from Staffordshire into Warwickshire. Adding to the social problems of the new 'working' class, the abolition of the monasteries had long since removed the system of social security. Even if the monasteries had still existed, they would have been poorly located in relation to the new towns, and probably quite inadequate to serve their needs.

Even without representation, it should have been possible for Parliament to appreciate the problems that the Industrial Revolution had created, and to have made the necessary provisions, but Parliament was filled with men whose condition of life, typically as well-to-do farmers, was quite different, leaving them with a very limited understanding of what was required. Meanwhile, the American and French Revolutions had resurrected the common law principle of the political rights of all free men, causing the ruling class in England to believe that, if the agitators were not kept under control, the discontent would erupt into another revolution. Nevertheless, there were reformers in Parliament, and it was they who presented the Reform Bill of 1831. Inevitably, it faced strong opposition from those two thirds of the members of the Commons whose election had become the object of criticism, causing it to be withdrawn on amendment in the Committee stage. So central had the Bill become to Whig sentiment, however, and so strong the feeling on the issue, that Lord Grey secured a dissolution of Parliament. Following a second, bitterly fought election campaign on the issue of 'The Bill, the whole Bill, and nothing but the Bill', strongly supported by public opinion, the Whigs were returned with an increased majority. The second Reform Bill was passed by the Commons with a large majority, but it was rejected by the House of Lords, many of whom, as large landowners, had a vested interest themselves in the existing electoral arrangements. Nevertheless, their opposition was not entirely due to self-interest. Like many in the Commons, they believed, correctly, that the country had prospered under the system of equal regional representation, based on the shires, and that to give undue representation to the industrial towns, merely because they contained more people, would be likely to upset what had been a stable system. Representation had been based on communities, not on numbers of people. Moreover, if the composition of Parliament were based, not on independent and responsible men of substance and experience, but on the number of mill-workers, wagoners, miners, potters, weavers, metal-smiths, unskilled labourers and the general run of society in each district, the implications could, it was believed, be horrendous.

Public opinion now erupted in violence, and Bristol was in the hands of the mob for two days. Parliament was prorogued while yet another Bill was prepared. Early in 1832, the third Reform Bill passed the Commons with a still greater majority, but the Lords insisted upon amendments that were unacceptable. With the country seemingly on the verge of civil war, Grey advised the King to create new Peers as the only way out of the impasse. The King, quite properly, refused to elevate men to the

Peerage for purely political ends, and the Cabinet resigned. Wellington found himself unable to form a new Ministry, and Grey was recalled. Recognising the gravity of the situation, the King now promised him the new Peers that he sought, but only if they were needed. Rather than abuse his prerogative in this way, it is possible that it was at the suggestion of the King that Wellington, without the knowledge of the Cabinet, circulated a letter among Tory Peers, warning them of the consequences if the Bill were not passed, and calling upon them to desist from further opposition. If the duke's letter had indeed been inspired by the King, the latter would, no doubt, have felt that this would be a lesser abuse of his authority than what Grey had been asking. As a result, whether out of respect for the Duke of Wellington or their concern at the prospect of an influx of radical Peers, enough of the recalcitrant Tory Peers withdrew during the final vote to allow the Reform Bill to receive the approval of the House of Lords in June 1832.

That the problem posed by the additional representational needs of the emerging towns and boroughs had long been recognised, is shown by the extra seats that had wrongly been granted to them during the Middle Ages. The problem had been caused by the centralisation of political power. A clear distinction must be made, however, between:

a. the equal representation of the shires, whose delegations had made the common English kingdom possible in the first place, and which had been set in 1213 at four 'discrete' men from each shire, possibly in keeping with a much older requirement, and further specified in 1227 as knights;

b. the restoration of all free men and their direct representation in the shires; and

c. the need for the direct representation of the interests of the growing towns in the common Parliaments of England, due to the failure of the existing representatives and the defunct state of the shire assemblies, which alone could now provide for their growing economic and social needs.

The problems of the new towns and cities called for common solutions, for which, it seemed, only the common English Parliaments, through the Crown, were now able to provide. The reality by this time was that the confederate requirements of the Constitution had long been forgotten, but, even if they hadn't, common policies had long been called for. It was a situation that the Great Council alone would have had the competence to resolve.

In the event, the Reform Act of 1832 was passed, being 'an Act to amend the representation of the people in England and Wales', effectively, that is, of the Third Estate. To this end, and, like previous such reforms, oblivious to the equal constitutional rights of the shires, it divided twenty-six of them into two, each of which was represented by two members, while eight shires received an additional representative.[1] Yorkshire, hitherto represented by four members, received two more, so that, appropriately in this case, the three ridings each returned two members.[2] At the same time, of the previous 203 boroughs, the smallest fifty-six lost their representation, while thirty that were a little larger had their representation reduced from two to only one each. Two more each had their representation reduced from four to two. Offsetting these reductions, twenty-two large towns, hitherto unrepresented, were granted two representatives each, while another nineteen (with a further two in Wales) were each awarded one representative.[3] The overall effect of the changes was that the number of English representatives was reduced by seventeen, and the number in Wales increased by four. The representatives of the counties were increased from ninety-four to 159, while thirteen extra members were reallocated to Scotland and Ireland. Within the boroughs, meanwhile, all householders paying £10 annual rental – a substantial sum – were granted a vote, and the franchise within the counties was widened. For freeholders, the forty shilling qualification which had been imposed in 1430, thereby disqualifying the great majority of common law freemen, was retained, but long-term leaseholders for sixty years or more, and copyholders paying £10 annual rent, were now also given the vote. A copyholder was a tenant of part of a manor, held at the will of its lord according to the custom of the manor, and so held by copy of the manorial court-roll. Those short-term leaseholders and tenants-at-will who paid £50 annual rent or more were also given the right to vote. Effectively, about half the middle class were

1   Three Welsh counties also received an additional representative.
2   Lincolnshire's three shires do not appear to be the result of ancient ethnic divisions.
3   The boundaries of these new divisions were defined in a separate Act.

now enfranchised, but none of the working class.[4] One effect was that the number of boroughs controlled by members of the Peerage was reduced. On the other hand, it soon became evident that, as more votes had been created, more votes were available to be sold.[5] The effect of the Act was to increase the size of the electorate in England from an estimated 400,000 to about 650,000, or by more than 60 per cent, but this was out of a population of around twenty-four million, so that only about one in ten of adult males was entitled to be represented. Scotland and Ireland were the subject of separate bills, which remodelled the franchise along similar lines to those in England. All members of the nobility retained their right to sit in the House of Lords, purely because, unlike the Commons, their chamber could still accommodate them.

Although it was not fully recognised for what it was at the time, the Act of 1832 re-established the principle of the sovereignty of the people. Just as the Revolution of 1688 had transferred the executive function from the King to the House of Commons, so the Reform Act of 1832 shifted the control of the Commons away from the landed gentry and the burghers to the industrial and commercial middle class, most of whom were the product of 'upward migration'. Voting was still open, and therefore exposed to unfair influence. Apart from the changes themselves, some commentators have suggested that the most significant feature of the episode was the evidence that, provided there was a sufficient sense of crisis, the House of Commons was capable of reforming itself. This overlooked the fact that reform was properly the duty of the King (on the advice of the Council), because it was he who issued the summons and was, effectively, the host. Attendance in the Commons was still based on the representation of communities.

The Reform Act of 1832 was followed three years later by the Municipal Corporations Act, which, with the exception of London, imposed a standard form of organisation on all the boroughs. Hitherto, the 'freemen', that is, the members of the ruling body, had often been very few, but under the new structure, every individual who occupied a building in the borough, for which he paid poor rates, and who resided

---

4   Defined in the *Shorter Oxford English Dictionary* as: 'The grade or grades of society comprising those who are employed to work for wages in manual or industrial occupations'.
5   T. Erskine May, *The Constitutional History of England Since the Accession of George the Third, 1760–1860* (New York, 1895), 253.

within seven miles of the borough, was entitled to be enrolled as a burgess. It was the burgesses who now constituted the borough, although it did not necessarily follow that they were parliamentary electors. A uniform system of local government was provided for the boroughs, based on a mayor, aldermen and councillors.

The pressure for a widening of the franchise was scarcely met by the Reform Act of 1832. On the contrary, the Act was seen by the agitators as just an important milestone on the journey to the ultimate objective of universal adult male suffrage, as in France and America, in effect, the full civil restoration of the idea of the English freeman, without regard to a property qualification. In 1836 a Workingmen's Association in London set forth its program in a petition to Parliament, which became known as the 'People's Charter'. It demanded manhood suffrage, voting by ballot, abolition of the property qualification for members of Parliament, the payment of members, equal electoral districts, and annual Parliaments. Supporters of the charter, known as the Chartists, toured the country and soon gained enthusiastic support from the public, so that, in 1839, a National Convention of Chartists was held in London. Parliament felt that it had already made more than enough concessions, and the charter was rejected in the same year. This led to serious riots in Birmingham and in Newport, in South Wales, the latter being suppressed quite savagely. A Second National Convention of Chartists was held in 1842, and a second petition to Parliament was rejected. By now, extremists had taken over the movement, bent more on revolution than reform. A huge Third National Convention, the last, was held in 1848 and the charter was again presented, but it had the misfortune to coincide with an alarming insurrection in Paris, the overthrow of the French king, Louis Philippe, and the declaration of a new French republic. The charter was again rejected. With this, and amid the consternation generated by a wave of disturbances across Europe, set off by the upheaval in France, public support dwindled, Chartism collapsed, and with it, for the time being, agitation for reform. Nevertheless, the concern for more franchise reform did not die in Parliament itself, and several unsuccessful attempts were made during the 1850s by the Whig leader, Lord John Russell, and the Liberal leader, Gladstone. Russell's efforts led nowhere, and Gladstone's faced opposition from within his own party, led by Robert Lowe. Lowe said that he did not trust the moral and intellectual competence of the working classes, and maintained that the proposal to extend the franchise to them would lead to the end of true democracy. Gladstone was imbued, however, with a belief in the inevitability of the cause, insisting that one could not fight against the future, whatever that meant, and that time was therefore on the side of the reformers. There were thus reformers and opponents to reform in both Parties.

31.2. The Doctrine that Royal Powers Delegated are not Returned

Various indulgences by the King in favour of the Parties in Parliament, such as the practice of appointing the leader of the majority Party in Parliament to the office of Prime Minister, and then accepting his advice as to the choice of his fellow Ministers, or the acceptance by the King of the advice of his Prime Minister on policy matters, or the suspension of the King's right to veto bills approved by Parliament, represented major concessions or delegations. By definition, the words delegation and concession imply a temporary arrangement, and therefore a right to retrieve. Having gained such advantages from the Crown, however, the Parties refused to recognise this right, alleging that it had established a new convention, namely, that royal powers, once delegated, could not be returned. This convention was used as a device by which the powers of a presumed absolute monarch could be appropriated in the interests of the people. It enshrined a new principle, inspired by Bagehot's view that England had no constitution. All it had, it appears, was a system of government that was subject to change in the light of changing circumstances, which had displaced a system where kings had enjoyed a right to rule and to exercise absolute power. Royal power had gradually slipped away, in the face of the Enlightenment and royal incompetence, to be replaced by an emergent parliamentary system, based upon the notion that the rights and interests of the people took precedence over those of the Crown. The mechanism for this transition had been the appropriation, as a result of delegation, of the King's legislative and executive powers to Ministers appointed, not at the King's discretion, but from the leaders of the dominant Party in Parliament. It was the view of the Parties that these delegations had not been at the discretion of the King, but had been inevitable in the light of the realisation that political power resided, not with the King, but with Parliament, in its capacity as the representative of the people. They had, therefore, been lawful restorations to the people in Parliament, not delegations, and as such could not be returned to the King. Bagehot's views did not go this far, but they were important because they said what the Parties in the House of Commons wished to hear. In reality, as we now know, the King's delusions of absolute power were simply that, instilled by the vested interests of the Church. English kings had never enjoyed absolute power lawfully, because they were subject to the requirements of the common law. This stated that the King enjoyed such powers as were bestowed by the Council on behalf of the people, their exercise being subject to the requirements of the law for as long as he continued to be King.

The convention that powers delegated by the King could not be returned was, therefore, illogical, but was based upon the assumption that the King had not been entitled to them in the first place, although, as we now know, he was entitled to exercise those powers that had been bestowed upon him by the Council, on behalf of the people, at the time of his coronation.

The problem was that Parliament had only a hazy instinct for what the common law said. In any case, Parliament was not the people, and the people were themselves confused after nearly 800 years of foreign and clerical domination. Membership of Parliament had, for many sitting on its benches, become a career, and it is not surprising that some, particularly among the beneficiaries of electoral reform, saw opportunities in this situation for personal advancement. Compounding the situation, few had any idea whether the King was merely the most recent of a long line of successful opportunists, or whether he had a meaningful constitutional function in common law, other than formally appointing Ministers. Never had the system of government been more in need of guidance by the Great Council, of whose existence the Parties were almost certainly unaware, and, being on the verge of achieving complete control of government, would probably have refused to recognise in any case. There being no constitution, the right to wield power depended entirely on who had control of the levers of government. If the Commons had been aware of the true significance of the House of Lords, its future would undoubtedly have come under dire threat.

31.3. Evicting the King from his Parliaments

Because of the problems accumulating in the absence of the Great Council, it had been a requirement since 1696 that the automatic dissolution of a Parliament after the death of the King should be delayed by six months.[6] For the same reason, it had already become the practice of the Privy Council, since 1679, to remain in existence for six months. The Succession to the Crown Act of 1707 had then provided that, if the Sovereign died while Parliament was prorogued or adjourned, it must reassemble at once without a summons, a seeming impossibility, because its commission had automatically lapsed. Even statutes were subject to the requirements of the Constitution. Its proposed reassembling without being summoned was presumably to recognise the successor to the throne and to deal with any issues arising in the meantime, for which, having no powers, other than to advise the King, it was obviously unsuited in any case.

It is also worth remembering that, after it had been dissolved, a Parliament ceased to exist. It had been summoned into being for a purpose, after which it was dissolved, either at the King's instruction or as the automatic consequence of his death, after which no Parliament existed in any form until such time as a new Parliament was summoned into existence. Career politicians took a very different view of their position and prospects, however, and were anxious to secure their own permanence. This led to the Representation of the People Act of 1867, which proclaimed that, in recognition of the 'great inconvenience' that might arise of limiting the life of any Parliament that might be sitting at the time of the King's death, any such Parliament should continue sitting for the duration of its intended life, unless dissolved sooner by the Crown. What possible purpose it could serve by continuing to sit is unclear, other than to approve the royal successor on behalf of the people – naming or proposing him being the function of the House of Lords – and the 'great

6   Regency Act, 1707.

inconvenience' was not identified, because Parliament had no executive function. The King's Ministers, with their commissions no longer in effect, would have been redundant. The Constitution provided for this, of course, by the Council immediately confirming their appointments, until such time as the King's successor saw fit, in the light of the Council's advice, to decide on their commissions, until a new Parliament had been summoned.

It is difficult not to interpret the above provision in the Act, however, as part of a policy of separating Parliament from the King and making it into an independent and permanent body. Perhaps it was intended that this provision would also make Parliament available, in its new capacity as an executive body, to deal with any other issues arising during the interregnum. What is clear from this is, that Parliament now regarded itself as an enduring institution, until the next general election in five or seven years, or whatever interval it chose to make. It was a new arrangement that would come naturally to political Parties that saw themselves as permanent institutions. It was an illusion, however, that would soon give rise to a serious constitutional problem. It probably marked another development. Hitherto, political Parties had usually seen themselves as promoting policies that were known to have electoral support. They now seem to have regarded themselves as free to embark on policies, in addition to those concerned with urgent and unforeseen measures, without electoral approval. Within a century, this would be giving rise to constitutional crises. These developments help to explain another provision (52) in the Act, which modified the prohibition on any member of Parliament from holding an office of profit under the Crown. The new provision allowed a person who had held office under the Crown, and who had subsequently been elected to Parliament, to accept any other such office or offices. It thereby provided a way around the requirement that a member of Parliament who became the holder of such an office, was forced to relinquish his seat, because he could now resume it by the simple expedient of obtaining re-election.

The Demise of the Crown Act of 1901 went further, by providing that the holding of any office under the Crown should not be affected by the death of the King, nor any fresh appointment to the Crown rendered necessary. Its formal purpose was to provide for continuity of office, but, as we have just seen, this was already provided for under the common law Constitution, and was therefore *ultra vires*. Its intention, once again, could be seen as making Parliament independent of the King.

31.3.1. Full *versus* Representative Parliaments

It is necessary at this point to re-state the difference between a full and a representative Parliament. A 'full Parliament' was an assembly of all free men, known in the shire as a *scirgemot*, or 'shire-moot', with the members of the three estates undoubtedly sitting separately. A Parliament of England, on the other hand, representing a confederacy of the shires, could only be a representative Parliament. The Reform Act of 1832 had the beneficial effect of recognising many – but by no means all – free men who had for centuries been regarded as unfree, on the ground that they had lost their freeholds. The shire assemblies had, since 927, increasingly delegated most of their powers to the Parliaments of all England, in which also there now sat Welsh, Scottish and Northern Irish representatives, making them Parliaments of the United Kingdom. As was noted earlier, the shire assemblies were now defunct, that is, until an attempt to restore them was made by the Municipal Corporations Act.

31.3.2. The Whigs and Tories Become the Liberal and Conservative Parties

By the time of the first Cabinet of Lord Melbourne, which replaced Earl Grey's Ministry in 1834, the labels 'Liberal' and 'Conservative' were beginning to replace the older ones of Whig and Tory, although the mildly derisive term 'Tory' never entirely ceased to be used. At first, the term 'Liberal' was applied to the more radical Whigs, and it did not finally become accepted by the Party until 1868, so that Melbourne still headed a Whig Cabinet. The label 'Conservative' was generally adopted by the Tories after the Reform Act. The consolidation of the two political groupings, or 'parties', in the House of Commons and their development into disciplined organisations arose from the growing tendency of voters, particularly after the expansion of the electorate and its spread into the cities, to be guided by the respective stances and policies of the Parties, rather than by the personality of the individual candidates. The candidates had been well known to small electorates, but enfranchisement had so increased the size of the electorates that personal acquaintance was no longer possible. Voting was influenced instead by the desire for either change or stability. Representation in Parliament became more and more impersonal, lending importance to a new Party 'system' that was characterised by its organisation and discipline. An important milestone about this time was the appointment by each Party of a 'whipper-in', a term borrowed from the sport of fox-hunting with hounds, an important pastime with many members of the Commons, whose duty it was to ensure that the members of the Party were present whenever there was an important division in the House, so that they could vote on a measure in support of Party policy. From his function of 'whipping up' the members during critical stages in the parliamentary process, this official soon came to be referred to as a Party 'Whip'. The Parties were no longer groups of like-minded individuals, but disciplined bodies.

This two-Party system has been a recurring feature ever since, and a feature of politics that seems to have been in evidence from earliest times. It appears to be explained by recent research, which has shown that a disposition to conservatism or radicalism is inborn in the individual at birth, and is probably inherited. It follows that, as the individual matures, he must look for evidence to justify his natural disposition. It may well be an evolutionary trait that seeks to retain social stability, on the one hand, while promoting innovation – for good or ill – on the other. The implication is that affairs of state are decided, less by objective judgement, and more according to the balance of radically inclined and conservatively inclined individuals called upon to make it. It would lead to a system based on strife for dominance by competing groups driven by radicalism or conservatism, and as the ultimate choice for the coming Parliament is made by the electorate, policy must tend to move in first one direction and then the other, as the consequences of the ratio of inherently radically and conservatively inclined individuals. This would infuse vitality into Government decision-making, but must also give rise to wastefulness and questionable decision-making. The Party system of government institutionalised this pattern.

31.3.3. The New Palace of Westminster

Disaster struck in 1834, when the Palace of Westminster was destroyed by fire. This rather haphazard agglomeration of greater and lesser buildings had first come into being in the eleventh century, and been steadily added to over the intervening years. It had been vacated by the King in 1532, when Henry VIII had moved into his new Palaces of Whitehall and St James, since when the Palace of Westminster had been used mainly for his Parliaments, although officially it had remained a royal residence. Indeed, it continued to be the practice for a King elect to spend his last night before his coronation in the Palace at Westminster, perhaps to assert his right to it as a royal residence and to remind those attending Parliaments that they would continue to owe their use of the palace to his hospitality,[7] in spite of the fact that the King had a duty to provide suitable accommodation for them, because they had been summoned by him for his convenience, as well as because they attended as a matter of right. Since 1801, the Lords had been meeting in the Court of Requests, while the Commons had, for several centuries, been meeting in the more imposing St Stephen's Chapel, which had come to be referred to, also, as the Parliament Chamber. The only building to survive the destruction of 1834 was the Palace's central feature, the Great Hall.

A new and grander Palace of Westminster was obviously called for, designed to meet, not the domestic needs of the King, so much as the particular needs of his Parliaments, now that he had moved to his new Palaces. Because the surviving buildings at Westminster were mainly Gothic in style, and because the fashion of the period was one of Gothic revival – in subconscious reaction to the revolutionary and social turmoil of the age – those submitting competitive entries for the design of the new structure were required to employ either a Gothic or an Elizabethan style. The winning entry, by Charles Barry, favoured the former, because it would harmonise better with the adjoining Westminster Abbey. The early nineteenth century was a time of Empire and growing national self-confidence and pride in its leading institutions, and no expense was spared on the embellishment of the new building complex. Consequently, it was not completed until 1867.

---

7   Today, the royal bed occupies an honoured place in the Speaker's apartment, perhaps as a reminder to the Speaker that he also enjoyed the King's hospitality.

The new Parliament building was to be situated within the Palace grounds, on the site of the previous buildings. That Parliaments would continue to enjoy accommodation provided by the King was inevitable, because a Parliament was a consultation, arranged and required by him, for his own guidance. Nevertheless, by the nineteenth century, a Parliament had come to be regarded by the leading political Parties as a permanent institution, like themselves, although the luxurious interior of the new chambers, aligned from north to south, that were provided for the deliberation of the Commons and Lords, respectively, reflected the majesty of the King himself. Provision was made for the Lords to deliberate in the southern Chamber, which could be extended to act as a Parliament Chamber by including the Throne, which occupied an exclusive area at its southern end. No provision was made, however, for attendance in the Parliament Chamber by the Commons, who were required, during a full Parliament, to stand at the Bar at the northern end of the chamber, reflecting the constitutional confusion that existed by this time. The exclusion of the Commons from the hallowed ground of the Parliament Chamber on such occasions was surely an oversight that precluded them from making any contribution, beyond replying, like witnesses, to questions from the Throne.

Meanwhile, the traditional colours of the two Orders were displayed in the upholstered leather seating in the two Chambers: red for the Lords and green for the Commons, demonstrating their respective social and functional identities that had survived over the millennia.

Barry's design of the Parliament building, complemented by the outstanding embellishments by Augustus Pugin, particularly of the interior, was a triumph. Of particular significance was the splendid decoration and lustre of the chamber used by Parliament and the Lords. This is unlikely to have been intended just for Parliament, because the decoration of the House of Commons was much more restrained, in spite of the presence there also of the King, in the form of the Royal Mace, and although the hereditary nobility were always held in deep respect, this hardly accounts for the celebration and importance attached to the Upper House. It seems possible that the exceptional splendour of the Upper Chamber was a subconscious tribute also to the eminence and constitutional primacy of the Great Council, whose constitutional significance outranked even that of the King.

The new Palace of Westminster was completed in 1870, some thirty-six years after the fire, and it has continued in use to the present day. All that was retained of the original complex was the Medieval Great Hall, better known as Westminster Hall. The scattered jumble of solid Norman and more decorative Tudor styles of the original Palace were thus replaced by a much more coherent structure in the Gothic Perpendicular style, complementing that of the nearby Westminster Abbey, which, like the Great Hall, had not been affected by the fire. It was not the most practical style for its purpose, but it epitomised the period during which the English Constitution had begun to re-emerge from the ideological muddle of the late Middle Ages. For the first time, also, the two Houses of Parliament had separate accommodation that had been specially designed for them, enshrining in stone the constitutional misconceptions of the age. Each Chamber had a lobby, or entrance hall, the two lobbies being separated by a Central Lobby, which was intended mainly for public use, to facilitate meetings between members of Parliament and their constituents. According to the new scheme, the King's entrance to Parliament was under the Victoria Tower, leading to the Robing Room, thence through a Royal Gallery to a rear entrance to the Chamber of the House of Lords. Access to the two Chambers by their respective members was by way of the Peers' and Members' Lobbies, respectively.

Barry had taken the view that the building should, in truly democratic fashion, be accessible to the general public, so that they could meet individual members of Parliament in the Central Lobby, or even proceed to a Strangers' Gallery in the Chamber of the House of Commons, where they could watch and listen to the proceedings. Like the King, the Peers, Members and general public all had their own separate access to the building. On the floor of the Commons chamber were two parallel red lines on the floor, one in front of each of the two sets of inward-facing benches, and it is likely that these were a carry-over from a practice that had been followed in St Stephen's Chapel. Their purpose was said to keep the Members seated on opposite sides of the House two sword-lengths apart, in case tempers flew.

31.3.3.1. Adaptation to Common Law Needs

It was noted earlier that the House of Lords probably came into being to accommodate the members of the Great Council, after it had been suppressed by Edward I. The common law Constitution requires the Council to function, for which purpose new accommodation would need to be provided outside Parliament, because the existing Lords' Chamber would be unable to provide, or have ready access to the necessary legal and other facilities needed by the Council. Meanwhile, the chamber of the Commons would need then to accommodate both Houses. This, in turn, would require a reduction in the number of existing Members, and the influx of hereditary lords would require them to be limited by a process of election, on much the same basis as the commons. The incoming lords would have the right to dedicated seating in red, rather than green, leather. In view of the limited space in the Commons chamber, the old Lords' chamber, with the Throne, might then continue to serve as the Parliament chamber.

31.3.3.2. Representation of the King in Parliament

Just as the King may delegate his judicial and executive functions, so also he may delegate his parliamentary duties to the most senior officers of state, except that, just as he indicated his presence in courts of law by the display of the royal coat of arms in their proceedings, and in all functions of the executive by the display of the Crown, so also he indicated his presence during the proceedings of Parliament, in both Houses, by the display of the royal Sceptre. No decisions of Parliament were valid, in spite of the presence of his appointed representative, without the presence of the Sceptre, which was the responsibility of a properly appointed officer, to whose care it was entrusted when Parliament was not sitting.

31.3.4. Socialism and the Romantic Movement

The shock of the Industrial Revolution led in the nineteenth century to three reactions: a cultural reaction against the visual and physical ugliness of the new Industrial Age; a practical reaction that led to the trade union movement as a means of forcing better conditions of employment; and a political reaction that resulted in legislation to improve the living conditions of the new working class. The cultural reaction was expressed in the Romantic Movement, which sought a return to traditional art and architecture, a eulogising of rural landscapes and a rustic way of life. The architectural revival found expression particularly in a return to the Gothic style of the Middle Ages, notably for public buildings, which drew inspiration from nature, reaching its high point in the new Parliament building at the royal palace of Westminster. There was also an impulse to personal self-improvement through self-education, promoted, for example, by the Workers' Educational Association. The Romantic Movement was not limited to Great Britain, and it was accompanied by the rise of socialist ideals, hard on the heels of nationalism, which had spread across Europe after the spark had been ignited by the French Revolution.

Socialism was to a large extent a resurrection of the egalitarianism of the Lollards, and of the even earlier ideal of free men with rights, inherited from the Aryan past. The socialist movement took three somewhat divergent paths. Democratic Socialism, as represented in Britain by the new Labour Party, favoured the collective ownership, by the state, of social services and the means of production. Communism had its basis in a social theory, propounded by Marx and Engels, that was expressed in their *Communist Manifesto* of 1848. This was further developed by Marx in his book, *Das Kapital*, which was an exposition of 'scientific' socialism, on the basis of an elaborate analysis of economic and social history, through which he arrived at the idea of 'capitalism'. According to Marx, the Industrial Revolution was used by those with access to money to multiply their wealth by exploiting their industrial employees. This concentration of 'capital' – or the accumulated savings of society – in the hands of a socially privileged and exploitative minority, according to Marx, also used the resulting profit to gain control of the levers of government. Society, according to Marx, could be divided into two classes: the capitalists and the 'workers', and the latter could only achieve a truly egalitarian and internationally-based 'socialist' society through violent revolution. Communism had its only real success in Russia, where it degenerated into a dictatorial and oppressive oligarchy that ultimately collapsed. The third path was taken by National Socialism, which rejected the internationalism of the other movements, in favour of retaining the ideal of the nation. With its origin in Germany, to which it particularly related, and led by Adolf Hitler, its future was compromised when Hitler embarked on a war of conquest in Eastern Europe, which quickly spread to Western Europe. Unlike the other two socialist movements, it made no attempt to espouse egalitarianism, and promoted national identity by 'removing' minorities. Even its socialism was compromised by an alliance with the industrialists for financial reasons. Only democratic socialism was able to survive, and then by compromising with the existing structure and traditions of society.

Fascism, which flourished briefly in Italy, under Mussolini, spreading to Spain under General Franco, was authoritarian, like Communism under Stalin, and nationalistic, like National Socialism under Hitler. Like its German counterpart, it had benefitted from the ineffectualness of the post-war democratic system, to promote a strong national identity based on the example of Imperial Rome. It adopted a form of representative government based, not on the representation of communities, but on the representation of established trades and professions. It was led by Mussolini, in the dictatorial capacity of Duce, or 'Leader'. Whereas National Socialism resonated, to a very limited extent, with other North European countries with a common Germanic ancestry, the appeal of fascism was limited to a few Mediterranean countries, and those with an inherited Mediterranean tradition, mostly in South America.

31.3.5. The Lords and Commons Represent Opposed Interests

Up to the nineteenth century, the Lords and Commons had represented the upper and middle classes, respectively; that is, the Second Estate and the more affluent stratum of the Third Estate. While they were in conflict over many issues, they also had much in common, including an interest in maintaining social stability and promoting Great Britain's commercial and political interests abroad. By the end of the century, as a result of the widening of the franchise, the Lords and Commons had come to represent interests that were diametrically opposed.

After the failure of Chartism in the mid-nineteenth century, working-class political activity declined, but the adverse effects of liberalism on conditions of employment had led to a growth of trade unions and public concerns. In a lecture at Oxford in 1880, on 'Liberal Legislation and

Freedom of Contract',[8] Thomas Hill Green criticised the prevailing view of liberalism – that it had its basis in the freedom of pursuit and contract – on the ground that, although the chief objective of citizenship was the preservation of freedom, it did not consist merely of the restraint of authority. Rather, its purpose was to make the common good available to all. Freedom of contract was a means to this end, but only if the contracting parties were not in a grossly unequal bargaining position, as was usually the case under conditions of large-scale production. Indeed, this view had been taken by the law itself, for example, in respect of contracts that resulted effectively in a form of slavery. Consequently, where freedom of contract was exercised between unequal parties, it was right that there should be interference by Parliament to ensure that there was an increase in the ability of the individual to contribute to the common good. In other words, a liberal government should legislate in a case where the law could remove an obstacle to the highest moral development of its citizens. That is, *laissez faire* liberalism should be modified by social legislation where this was in the interest of society.

Green's modified view of liberalism,[9] while far removed from Marx's idea of socialism, was nevertheless not far removed from the ideas of the Fabian Society. This was founded in 1884 by a group of middle-class intellectuals, whose purpose was to conduct research into social and political questions, using the results to promote the common good by gradual and democratic means.[10] This should be achieved by a liberal form of socialism, whereby the Crown would appropriate the basic industries and use their profits for the public benefit.

The impact of the growing influence of the working class in general elections was at first muted by its dependence on representation by middle-class parliamentarians, but an avenue to political advancement had been opened, and well-funded organisations like the trade unions were soon able to put up their own leaders for parliamentary election. Also, the doctrine began to seep through to a part of the electorate, namely, that they had a moral entitlement to appropriate the wealth of

---

8   *Works*, iii. 365.

9   Green's political thinking was more fully set out in his *Lectures on the Principles of Political Obligation*, edited from notes after his death by R. L. Nettleship.

10   For this reason, the Society was named after Fabianus Maximus, who, in the Second Punic War, foiled Hannibal by avoiding direct engagements, the implication being that socialist success would be achieved, not by an attempt at revolution, but by more gradual means.

the rich and re-distribute it to the poor. Alarmed by this shift of attitude within the Commons, the members of the House of Lords saw themselves increasingly threatened as a social class. It had the effect of making the House increasingly defensive and conservative, and this reduced the Party divisions within it.

It is a principle in ordinary common law, expressed in Clause 52 of the *Magna Carta*, that a man's property may not be taken from him, except as restitution for debt, or in compensation for an offence committed, or as may be necessary to meet the agreed needs of the Crown. This principle had been enshrined in the American Constitution, as Amendment V in the Bill of Rights. However, whereas the principle had been supported by all remaining free men in the Middle Ages, it was now in danger of being trampled by the resentment and avarice of the mob, which felt, in some obscure way, that their former assets had somehow been progressively taken away from them, as Marx had alleged. In large measure they were correct. The problem was not only the huge disparity in personal wealth in English society, but also the feeling among many ordinary men that they no longer had any status in society.

In 1893, the Independent Labour Party, or I.L.P., was founded, under the leadership of Keir Hardie, a Scottish coalminer who had become a trade union organiser. Its purpose was to promote the socialist aims of the labour unions, independently of the Liberal Party, and in 1900 it took the lead in setting up a Labour Representative Committee, which was supported by the Trades Union Congress, the Fabian Society, and the Marxist-inclined Social Democratic Federation. Its purpose was to sponsor parliamentary candidates in the general election. After the election of 1906, when cooperation from the Liberal Party enabled the Committee to win twenty-nine seats, the latter changed its name to the 'Labour Party'. Its purpose was to improve the lot of the workers, but from the outset it was very much under the influence of the Fabian Society, which led it to adopt a policy of 'common ownership of the means of production'. Its ultimate goal, therefore, was the transformation of Great Britain into a fully socialist society, in which the community as a whole would own and control the means of production, distribution, and exchange, and would share the benefits equally. It was a very theoretical approach, because it begged more questions than it answered, but it held a great appeal for many voters.

31.3.6. Population as the New Basis of Representation

Meanwhile, the advent of a new Conservative Ministry in 1866, under Lord Derby, coincided with a rapid spread in the demands of ordinary workers for reform of the suffrage. Only one man in six was yet represented in Parliament, and the new working class was virtually excluded. The dominant figure in the new Ministry was Disraeli, the Leader of the House of Commons. A limited reform Bill, introduced by Gladstone earlier in the year and defeated, had given rise to violent demonstrations, and this persuaded the adroit Disraeli that the Conservatives would be wise to make electoral capital by taking the initiative. Already, the Tories were associated in the popular mind with opposition to reform, and if it was to come, it was better for them to catch the tide. Disraeli not only introduced a new reform Bill, but was eventually persuaded, by the practical realities of defining the payment of rents and rates, to extend radically the scope of the proposed reform.

Thus, it was the second Reform Act, the Representation of the People Act of 1867, which did not apply to Scotland or Ireland, that greatly extended the suffrage in the boroughs to all adult males who were householders or tenants for not less than twelve months, who paid a rate for the relief of the poor, or who were lodgers of one year's residence who paid an annual rent of £10 or more. In the counties, the franchise was extended to all owners of land with an annual value of £5, and to all tenants who paid £12 annually in rent. There was also a small redistribution of representation from the smaller boroughs in favour of the larger industrial cities and towns. New boroughs were created and the representation of the counties was increased. The Act had the effect of doubling the size of the electorate, from about a million to two million. Thus, Disraeli had 'dished the Whigs' and done what the Lord Derby had earlier described as 'taking a leap in the dark'. The leader of the Liberals, Robert Lowe, reacted with sarcasm by observing that: 'We must now at least educate our master'. The following Scottish Reform Act of 1868 was generally founded on the same principles as the English Act, and gave seven extra seats to the Scots. An Irish Bill in the same year extended the borough franchise.

These reforms extended the franchise in Britain to the 'respectable' artisans and other small householders, who formed a large part of the working class. It did not include the rural labourers and those not living in separate abodes. Effectively, it restored the right to attend Parliaments to the remainder of what would, in the prevailing circumstances, have constituted the freeman class – where defined as those men of good standing who held a tangible stake in society, such as a freeholding. An alternative definition of a free man is one who has inherited this status. If this is the correct definition, it cannot be lost through misfortune. Unfortunately, the evidence for it can. According to this definition, it can only be surmised that the majority of men at this time had unwittingly inherited an entitlement to free status, in which case the process of reform still had some way to go.

The Act of 1867 had other significant effects. It finally allowed the organisation of political Parties to reach out into the constituencies, entrenching them in the electoral system, and elevating the position of Party leaders to make them the key figures determining Government policy. This, in turn, enforced a collective approach to Cabinet government, and 'the period of collectivism which began about 1870 . . . as soon as the franchise was extended to the skilled workers in the towns . . . added enormously to the functions of government'.[11] Party leaders were now beholden to those who bore the brunt of the new social conditions, and were forced to lead the Crown into new fields of responsibility for the general populace, such as education, the control of conditions of employment, social insurance, pensions, and housing. There have been various attempts to describe the British class structure of the nineteenth century, that was to persist into the late twentieth century, but it cannot be defined according to incomes, and the following, in generally descending order, is probably as good as any:

1. The old *nobility*, defined by long-held hereditary titles.
2. The gentility, or *upper middle class*, usually belonging to, or descended from, the hereditary knighthood, or long-established freeholders, who, like the old nobility, endeavoured to send their sons to the better public schools, and thence to

11   W. I. Jennings, *The Law and the Constitution* (Bickley, 1943), 87, including footnote 1.

Oxford or Cambridge, and for whom the armed services or the Church offered the most desirable and worthy careers.

3. The *lower middle class*, typically members of the professions, and mostly of upper working-class origin.

4. The *nouveaux riches*, usually successful leaders in commerce and industry, and mostly of upper working-class origin.

5. The *upper working class*, usually the skilled, who endeavoured to adhere to certain standards of dress and behaviour, took basic education seriously, and were normally practising adherents of Protestant churches. This was the second most numerous group.

6. The *lower working class*, the most numerous group, who were typically unskilled or semi-skilled.

The Reform Act of 1867 had the effect of extending the franchise to probably most of the upper working class (5) and some of the lower (6).

The issue of electoral reform came to the fore, once again, in the early 1880s. Expenditure of £2.5 million had been incurred by the political Parties in the general election of 1880, much of it on bribes, and in order to rectify what was felt to be an undesirable practice, and perhaps to save the Parties from expense, the Corrupt and Illegal Practices Act was promulgated in 1883. This endeavoured to restrict expenditures by all Parties in a general election to £800,000, and limited the amount that might be spent by any candidate for election purposes. At the same time, the penalties for corrupt practices were greatly increased.

The third Reform Bill, which was also introduced by Gladstone's ministry and passed onto the statute book as the Representation of the People Act of 1884, applied to the United Kingdom as a whole, and extended the voting right of householders in the boroughs and towns to the counties, thereby largely standardising the franchise and achieving virtual manhood suffrage. Its chief effect was to extend the vote to the agricultural labourers. The right to vote was now granted effectively to every male over twenty-one years of age who occupied any land or tenement of a yearly value of £10 or more. Only those living with families and those of no fixed abode were excluded. The Act added to the franchise a further two million voters, nearly twice the number added in

1867, and nearly four times that added in 1832. The franchise, and with it freemen status, was thus extended to nearly all adult male residents. It also increased the number of representatives in the House of Commons to 670, making the new Chamber, designed by Barry only fifty years earlier, already too small. Effectively, it restored the role of the popular assembly to what it had been in early Anglo-Saxon times, namely, to a common assembly of all free men, except that attendance was now replaced by formal representation. Expressed in another way, it might be said that all men entitled to the hereditary status of freeman in common law had now been restored. They were no longer entitled to freeholdings, because there was probably no longer the land available, even if the landowners had been reduced to holdings more in keeping with their rights in common law. The problem had now disappeared, because most free men were now earning a livelihood by other means. Classical Church-Feudalism had been unravelling for a long time, from the introduction of Judicial Circuits in the time of Henry II to the abolition of Military Tenure in 1660, but the last traces would not be removed until the Law of Property Acts of 1922–25. What was most important, however, was the restoration of the personal right to be heard in the assembly, and it represented the final overthrow, at the popular level, of the ideology of Church-Feudalism.

Although the Act of 1884 had the effect of enfranchising much of the working class, the latter made no attempt to seek power by itself. It was now reconciled to the social order, and lacked the education to participate, so that it was far from clear what changes it hoped to see brought about. The old ruling classes remained in control of Government until the beginning of the twentieth century, by which time there had been a spread of socialist ideas and the formation of an active socialist movement. This would provide an ideological sense of direction, however unsatisfactory, to men who were otherwise largely uneducated.

Whereas the Act of 1884 had changed the size of the electorate, the Redistribution of Seats Act, 1885, brought about a new and radical change in the distribution of representation, made necessary to some extent by the limited size of the Chamber of the House of Commons. Under the Act, all boroughs with fewer than 15,000 inhabitants ceased to have separate representation. Considerable changes were made to county and borough boundaries for electoral purposes, resulting in a more equitable representation in the Commons on a *per capita* basis, but finally obliterating the constitutional importance of the shires. These, the historic or political counties, which were the foundation of the Constitution, could not legally be abolished, or their boundaries amended, but they finally ceased to be the basis of representation in the House of Commons. For the first time, the unit of representation was largely the individual, rather than the community. One reason for this was that the county had largely ceased to be a community since the population upheaval of the Industrial Revolution, while other communities now claimed a greater significance. Numerical equality, based on 'one vote, one value', became the guiding principle. From this time onwards, a distinction existed between the traditional, or 'political' counties, and the new electoral districts, which in many cases continued to make use of the county names, even though they did not coincide. The new system tried to reconcile, on the one hand, the perceived need for each member of Parliament to represent the same number of electors, in the interests of fairness, and at the same time to acknowledge that people comprised very different interest-groups, according to community or occupation.

Nevertheless, geography, as represented by the old shires, was still very important. Workers in Bristol and workers on Tyneside did not necessarily have the same outlook and interests, or face the same problems. The new constituency system had now been manipulated so that each, as far as possible, represented the same interest-group, according to geographical identity, and, at the same time, roughly the same number of voters. As other countries adopted the democratic process, it was the usual practice for them to solve this problem by treating the whole country as a single constituency. This solved the problem of *per capita* representation, but ignored the very real interests of different communities that, in England, were the foundation of the common law system and the federal basis of the Constitution.

Ireland, meanwhile, had long ceased to be regarded as a royal fiefdom, and much the same increases in popular representation were extended to the Irish as to the English, Welsh and Scots. Nevertheless, Ireland remained as a distinct and insoluble problem. The Catholic majority, guided by Irish nationalism, were continuing to demand home rule under a separate Parliament, and some were demanding independence, but they were fiercely opposed by the Protestant minority, whose ties were with Britain. The Protestants were represented by the 'Unionists' and the Conservative Party in the north. In the south also, the landed class was mostly Protestant, and many of those who sat in the House of Lords owned Irish estates. Keen also to resolve this problem, Gladstone introduced two Irish Home Rule Bills, the first in 1886 and the second in 1893. Both were defeated, the first by the Conservatives and the second by the House of Lords.

31.3.6.1. *Civic Rights in Common and Statute Law*

By extending the franchise and freeman status to nearly all adult male residents in England, the Act of 1884 undoubtedly included many Irish residents and other immigrants who had no such entitlement in common law. Constitutionally, therefore, in respect of England at least, the Act had the effect of restoring the common law rights of the native inhabitants, whose claim to free status rested, not in statute law, as represented by the Act, which was thus legally irrelevant, but in their rights according to common law. Immigrants and others whose ancestors had never enjoyed the rights of English freemen, on the other hand, now exercised the right in accordance with statute law. There accordingly emerged in 1884, if not earlier, a distinction between civic rights in common law and civic rights according to statute law.

31.4. Relations Between the Lords and the Commons (1820–1902)

Relations between the two Houses during the reign of the Tudors had been fairly good, because the overriding authority of the Monarchy had not been in question, but, under the inept rule of the Stuarts, the rivalry had been resumed. As feudal rules had broken down and Protestantism had shifted the focus to the rights of the individual, Parliaments began to be seen again for what they properly were: assemblies of the people, particularly after the electoral reforms. Viewed in this light, both the House of Lords and the King were increasingly seen as relics of feudal society. Adding fuel to the implications of this reassessment, the leaders of the Parties in the House of Commons, sensing their own rise to prominence in the workings of government, were increasingly seized with political ambition.

What was not appreciated – because the volume of legislation being presented to Parliament was now such as to keep it sitting for much of the year, so that the distinction between one Parliament and the next had become blurred, giving rise to a sense of its own permanence – was the constitutional reality that Parliaments were temporary institutions with a life, according to the law of the Constitution, of significantly less than a year, whereas the House of Lords, by virtue of its origin and nature, was a permanent institution with far-reaching powers, most of which had long been forgotten.

The nature of the House of Lords, as an independent part of the legislature, was first seriously threatened by the Reform Bill of 1832, when the King was forced by the Whig Prime Minister, Earl Grey, into agreeing to create eighty new Peerages in order to ensure its passage. Faced by this threat, the Lords gave way, so that a mass creation of Peers for political ends was avoided. It was evidently this incident that the Lord John Russell had in mind when he remarked in 1839 that, when such an impasse had to be, and could be, resolved by such corrupt means, it was clear that there was something fundamentally wrong, either with the legislation at the heart of the controversy, or with the constitution or its interpretation. To create new Peers in order to force a particular policy through Parliament would have been a flagrant abuse of the royal prerogative.

The French Revolution had already sown uncertainty in 1789, and in the period immediately after 1832 the older Peers felt that society was in dissolution, and that it was incumbent upon them to make a last stand. In support of their position, they emphasised the independence of the Lords as a separate House of the legislature. The younger Peers, especially the Liberals, such as Durham and Macaulay, felt that this attitude could no longer be sustained. Luckily, the situation was saved by an alliance of Peel and Wellington. The authority of the Duke of Wellington in the House of Lords was considerable, while Peel promoted a conception of the Conservative Party in the Commons that was distinct from that of the old Tory Party, which still persisted in the Lords. The Tories in the Lords were guided through the first half of the nineteenth century by a series of particularly able Conservative leaders, without obstructing either the reform of local government or the repeal of the Corn Laws. Even the Reform Bill of 1867 was safely weathered, because it had been initiated by a Conservative administration under the Earl of Derby. Liberal-minded Peers, in ignorance of the true constitutional nature and purpose of the House, had endeavoured to define a new and more acceptable role for the Lords. In 1846, Lord Derby argued that 'the function of this House is to interpose a salutary obstacle to rash and inconsiderate legislation: it is to protect the people from their own imprudences. It has never been the course of this House to resist a continued and deliberately formed opinion. To the expression of such opinion your lordships have always bowed and always will bow'.

31.4.1. The Acceptability of Life Peerages

It had been accepted that appeals from the lower courts could be heard by any three Peers, and it could be argued that any three fair-minded men were capable of deciding whether a judgment by a court was reasonable or not. The attitude of the leading judiciary since Stuart times, that only highly trained judges were competent to decide what was a reasonable judgment, may have owed as much to self-interest as to sound argument, but it had been the practice of the Peers since 1844 to leave the judicial work of the House to such of its members as were legally qualified, for which reason these members were known as the Law Lords. However, a serious problem emerged by 1856, caused by a shortage in the quorum of Law Lords. It was felt that this could only be met by appointing leading members of the judiciary to the House. The Liberal Prime Minister at the time, Viscount Palmerston, was a democrat by nature, and evidently averse to the creation of heritable baronages for judges. He advised the Queen, therefore, to fill the gap by making two eminent judges Peers for life, but the Committee of Privileges of the House of Lords refused to accept the idea and advised that the Crown should act by statute, which, obviously, the Lords could then reject. In the same year, a life Peerage was granted by the Queen to a retired judge, in the capacity of Lord Wensleydale, but he was not admitted to the House of Lords. The advice of the Lords to the Crown in 1856 was that a patent which gave no more than a Peerage for life would not entitle the grantee to be summoned to Parliament, that is, to sit in the Lords, because a Peerage created by patent must be inheritable. The point was that each House represented an Estate, and membership of an Estate was hereditary, a requirement that affected membership and representation in the House of Commons just as much as it did the Lords. In spite of this, a Bill was introduced in 1859, again by Palmerston, to enable life Peers to be created, not more than four at a time, and not exceeding a total of twenty-eight. This was rejected by the House of Lords on the ground that it violated the basic principle,[12] as well as threatening a new influx of upstarts with money but no breeding, and this caused a new strain in relations between the two Houses. It also raised the fundamental principle that neither House had the right to interfere in the affairs of the other, as well as the common law principle of *quod omnes tangit*, that 'What concerns all should be approved by all'. In this context, by 'all' was meant all Estates, except that the First had long rejected involvement in temporal matters.

Under the law of the Constitution, Parliaments comprised all three Estates, meeting by right in common assembly, but with the undoubted further right to deliberate separately and to advise the King accordingly. Since the breaching of the requirements of the Constitution in 1338–9, following the crisis between Edward III and the Great Council, the Council had insisted on transferring its meetings to Parliament,[13] to be held during the deliberations of the Second Estate. Probably because of the practicalities of this, and the need to preserve the dignity and discreteness of its meetings, it had evidently demanded the right to hold these separately. Edward had evidently agreed to make a chamber available for the purpose. All other members of the Second Estate, evidently, had thereupon decided to transfer their own deliberations to this chamber, in order to maintain the unity of the Estate in its advice to the King. Evidently, the Council had agreed to the presence of other members of the Estate when it deliberated on Council matters. In this way, deliberations

---

12   In effect, that the Lords, like the Commons, were an hereditary Estate.

13   This was undoubtedly because much of the advice rendered by the Council to the King concerned matters which the King submitted, or had intended to submit, for the attention of Parliament, advice that may particularly have irked the King and led to the rupture in the first place. The King could not, however, legally thwart the rights, let alone terminate the existence, of the Council.

of the Council and those of the Estate as a whole were conducted in this chamber. Not to be outdone, the Commons had obtained the right to withdraw to a chamber of their own. The Council members occupied their position by right of election in their respective shires, a practice that must have ended with the Norman conquest and the decimation of the English Second Estate at Hastings. It can only be supposed that the replacement of Counsellors over the intervening years had been at the discretion of the King. This would greatly have undermined the constitutional position of the Council, and may have accounted for its subordination by Edward III.

The extension to the royal succession by the Normans of the law of private inheritance, based upon the principle of primogeniture in the male line, a practice that may have been instigated by the Church,[14] had replaced the English law of inheritance. This appears to have been based on the principle of agnatic seniority in the male line, that is, inheritance by the nearest male relative, such as a brother or son – in effect, an individual with the same male ancestor – subject, in the case of a chief or king, to confirmation by election. The new principle had the inevitable effect, given that there were always some individuals who had no surviving sons, of causing more and more houses, royal as well as noble, to become extinct. Even by the Middle Ages, the point had been reached when the King, in order to avoid being left without a Second Estate to give him support, had presumed the right to elevate individuals from the Third Estate. Members of the Second Estate normally acquired their status by the right of inheritance, or by the facility whereby outstanding individuals of the Third Estate, who were evidently favoured by the gods, had been recognised as such by common agreement between the King and the Second Estate, to be elevated by the Sovereign accordingly, examples being Marlborough and Wellington. As a result of the adoption of the law of primogeniture, this practice acquired a new importance as a means of maintaining the Estate. Common law had always provided for a few outstanding individuals of the Third Estate to be so elevated, not by the King, but by a consensus of the Second Estate – in practice, probably by the King on the advice of the Great Council. Many of the

---

14   This would have brought the law of succession more into line with the Church's doctrine that the King was God's representative in temporal matters. By so restricting the law of succession, it was easier to identify God's appointed.

individuals who had been elevated by the King at his own discretion had been royal favourites who would never have been acceptable in more normal circumstances.

In 1873, the appellate jurisdiction of the House of Lords was abolished by Gladstone's Liberal Government, only for it to be restored in 1876 by the Appellate Jurisdiction Act of Disraeli's new Conservative Government. This permitted the creation for life of two Lords of Appeal in Ordinary, with the possibility of two more. These were to hold the rank of Baron, being the lowest of the five ranks of Peerage, and as the Act provided for both men and women, the title of the latter was to be the new one of 'Baroness'. On this occasion, several 'life Peers', both men and women, were appointed, but they could only sit in the House for as long as they held their judicial appointments, which effectively meant for life. The Appellate Jurisdiction Act brought the House of Lords into line with the Privy Council, which in 1833 had been provided with a specialised and suitably qualified Judicial Committee, designed to exercise the Council's own judicial functions. Thus, a solution was found to the problem of reconciling, on the one hand, the judicial functions of the King and Parliament and, on the other, the perceived need for appeals to be guided by judicially qualified individuals. A further Act in 1887 permitted all retired Lords of Appeal to sit for life as members of the House of Lords. Like the hereditary Peers, the new life Peers were entitled to the prefix of 'Right Honourable'. Ephemeral Peerages were not new. Leading clergy had for centuries been granted Peerages for the duration of their tenure of office, which was normally for life, and since the Reformation this had not even been justified on the grounds that they were landlords. Effectively, the Lords Spiritual held honorary Peerages in recognition of their wisdom as counsellors to the King, which could not be passed on by inheritance, and the admission of judicial Peers followed in the same tradition. Even so, the admission of judicial Peers was concluded in the face of opposition by the Lords, who objected on the same grounds, that nobility was not an office, but a state of being that could be inherited.

31.4.1.1. Life Peerages Granted to the Council, Not the Lords

Elders of the nobility who had attended meetings of the *Witan* in Anglo-Saxon times would undoubtedly have taken the same view as the hereditary lords in the nineteenth century, that the leading clergy and others who regularly attended meetings of the *Witan* did so, not as members of the Second Estate, but as advisers to the Council, usually (and informally) appointed for life. In this capacity they can only have been appointed by the Council, not by the King, not only because the King is appointed by the Council (although the King often, or usually, presided over the Council), but because the King is advised on the law, as well as other matters, by the Council, and has a limited existence, which the Council does not. The designation in the nineteenth century of 'life Peer' belonged in the same category, despite the mistaken belief that they were created in statute law as 'Peers'. The life Peers appointed from the nineteenth century onwards were only honorary Peers, appointed for life in an advisory capacity, not to the House of Lords, but to the Great Council. Moreover, they were not so appointed by the relevant statute, which would have been *extra vires* in the circumstances, but by the members of the Council. Consequently, it was in their capacity as advisers to the Council that the life Peers sat, inappropriately, in the Upper House. They were not entitled to vote in either institution, although it seems that they often did so in practice.

31.4.1.2. The Right of the Commons to Interfere in the Affairs of the Lords

No less significant was the fact that the Appellate Jurisdiction Act of 1876 presumed that the Commons had a right to involve itself in matters concerning membership of the House of Lords. It had always been recognised that, in keeping with common law, neither House had a right to interfere in the procedures or membership of the other. It was an aspect of the principle of *quod omnes tangit*, or 'what concerns all should be approved by all'. Equally, the Second Estate had no right to interfere in the affairs of the Third, but the political Parties in the Commons had outgrown their station, and the struggle over the question of life Peerages turned the question of the House of Lords itself into a political issue after 1856. This had been bound to come in any case, because democratic ideas permeated the lower classes, as a result of the French and American Revolutions and the views being expounded by political philosophers. The claim, by the House of Lords, of an equal right to consent to legislation came to be seen as conflicting with those ideas. Nevertheless, neither Party was willing to attempt to reform the House of Lords, because the Conservatives feared a reduction in their strength as a result, and the Liberal Party feared an increase in the efficiency and acceptability of the Upper House.

A second period in the relations between the two Houses during the nineteenth century began around 1860. The Lords rejected a Bill in that year, introduced by Gladstone, who was then Chancellor of the Exchequer, supported by Lord John Russell and the Liberal Government, to abolish the excise duty on paper. This provoked Palmerston, who was Prime Minister at the time – and who, as a mere viscount, sat in the Commons – to move a string of resolutions against the Upper House. By the time of the 1867 electoral Reform Bill, which effectively restored popular sovereignty, the claim of the House of Lords to be an independent part of the legislature was increasingly regarded as difficult to maintain. The anomaly could have been resolved simply enough by the members of the Great Council reverting to their proper constitutional position as an independent body outside Parliament, thereby removing the artificial separation of Parliament into Houses and leaving the lords in general to sit alongside the commons in Parliament, but this was long forgotten.[15]

Instead, a new interpretation of the function of the House of Lords was regarded as necessary, adding to the muddle. Fortunately, previous politicians had already indicated a way. Thus, Lord John Russell had said in 1839 that it was the duty of the House of Lords to exercise a wide discretion, but the formulation of a new theory was largely the work of the Marquess of Salisbury, whose various Ministries extended from 1885 to 1902. According to Salisbury's view, it was the function of the House of Lords to revise the legislation approved by the Commons. If the Lords believed that a measure did not have the support of the country, it should reject it, causing it to be referred to the electorate. If a general election

---

15　This might raise speculation that, comprising leading members of the Second Estate, the restoration of the Great Council could have entrenched the interests of the Estate, except that members of the Council were properly the leading and most respected men of their respective shires, and as such, capable of being replaced by the communities represented.

should endorse the measure, the Lords must give way. At first sight, this theory seemed plausible, within the perceptions of the day, because it provided for both popular sovereignty and the revision of Bills, but in practice the House of Lords was seen by Liberal and Labour Ministries as containing a permanent Conservative majority, because of the social class from which its members were drawn. It was a class, moreover, that was increasingly under attack, on the grounds that it occupied an unfairly privileged position. One constitutional commentator, Ivor Jennings, pointed out that Lord Salisbury's theory made the assumption that the House of Lords was a better judge of opinion in the country than the politicians who depended upon that opinion for their election. Indeed, the principal danger of conflict between the Houses in the nineteenth century arose, he believed, from the hereditary basis of the House of Lords and the increasingly representative, and egalitarian-minded basis of the House of Commons.

For their part, the gradual removal of the landed aristocracy from its contact with the people, as the latter moved into the industrial towns, had increasingly divorced the Second Estate from the lives of the ordinary people, who saw in the landed aristocracy little of relevance to themselves. The old relationship, based on landholdings, was gone. As poorer men, whose background was in the mines and mills, became entitled to make their voices heard in the Commons, resentment and jealousy became an important element in the constitutional struggle. In fact, the landed nobility had themselves come under economic siege, as the farming sector declined in the face of free trade, bringing greater competition from the colonies, particularly in wheat and wool. A few, such as the Duke of Bridgwater, revived their fortunes by becoming industrialists, but others were forced to shore up their position by marrying the sons and daughters of successful industrialists and traders, who were only too glad of the opportunity to improve their social status. This has usually been seen as beneficial to the landed nobility, restoring fortunes and infusing new blood and broadening their outlook, but social 'contamination' on this scale brought into question the very principle of noble birth and lineage. Democrats and rationalists, both within the Commons and out, such as Mill and Bagehot, resented the 'unrepresentativeness' of the Lords, and accused them of being out of touch with the country, making them less and less amenable to the wishes of the Commons.

Meanwhile, the whole perception of the Peerage was changing, as the two Parties jostled for control of the Upper House, and as successful industrialists lined up to be elevated to the baronage. The Commons in general, and the Liberals in particular, sensed that they had a vested interest in removing the landed nobility and replacing them with their own appointees, who, as life Peers, would extend the control of the Commons over the Lords, and, as holders merely of an honorary title, would not be able to pass on their seats in the Lords to offspring who might well grow up with a disposition towards the Conservative Party. The King had used his presumed power of elevation to the Peerage as a political tool, and now the Parties sought to control this mechanism for their own benefit. At the same time, however, the Parties needed money to win elections, and the new rich were willing to pay handsomely for the dignity of a seat in the Upper House. This, and the onslaught on the position of the Whig families by the Younger Pitt, increased the size of the House of Lords much faster than its numbers were being reduced by the natural extinction of inherited titles. At the time of the Restoration in 1660 there had been 139 Peers. By 1714, as a result of the union with Scotland, among other matters, the number had grown to 168, and they had still totalled only 174 at the time of the accession of George III, in 1760. By 1820, however, as a result of the union with Ireland and the surrender of royal control over patronage, in the face of intrusion into the process by the political Parties, a total of 128 new titles had been created, accelerating the decay of the House of Lords. Meanwhile, the reform of representation in the Commons had the effect of increasing the sense of class division between the two Parties in the House, as the interests of the working class were increasingly pitted against those of the middle class.

At the same time, Party divisions in the House of Lords were being erased. In the past, the nature of the House of Lords had been determined by which branch of the ruling oligarchy in the Commons was in power, Whigs or Tories, but from 1832, as the Whig Party in the Commons became more liberal, their fellow Whigs in the Lords reacted by becoming more conservative. The effect was one of constitutional polarisation. In the eighteenth century, moderate Whig and Conservative factions were to be found in both Houses, providing for a fair degree of common ground, but the nineteenth century saw an influx of more radical members into the Commons, forcing the Lords into a more defensive position. This tendency was particularly noticeable after 1867, and it reached its first crisis over the Irish Home Rule Bill.

Inter-House rivalry became acute again in 1884, over the question of the redistribution of parliamentary seats. The situation became extremely tense, because Gladstone denied that the House of Lords could force a dissolution, and summoned an autumn session to reintroduce the Bill. The debates were accompanied by agitation to end or amend the House of Lords, with the slogan of 'the House of Lords versus the People'. John Bright, a prominent agitator for free trade, proposed as an alternative to the absolute veto of the Lords that it should have only a suspensory veto. The main opposition to the Bill had arisen, not over the effects that it would have in Britain, to which Parliament was now fully resigned, but over its effect in Ireland, where, it was pointed out, the new provisions would lead to a Nationalist majority. The opposition came particularly from the Lords, leading to a demand by the radicals in the Commons to 'mend or end' the Upper House's veto. In the end, the joint efforts of Gladstone and the Queen enabled the measure to go through, subject to conceding a demand by the Conservatives that there should be only single-member constituencies.

The radical extension of its electoral basis in 1884 appears to have given the House of Commons a new sense of its own importance, and a new identity that would eventually lead to a new constitutional crisis. Previously, it had represented the landed class of the Third Estate, which had shared, to some extent, a common interest with the Second Estate in containing the landless and uneducated majority in the Third. Following the influx into the House of Commons of the landless majority, the House lost its sense of common interest with the Second Estate, inheriting instead the antipathy and resentment which the lower classes had held towards the upper classes since Norman times, followed by the exploitation of the Middle Ages. The Monarchy had already been subordinated to the House of Commons, and there now emerged agitation for the overthrow of the House of Lords. Hitherto, the political scene had comprised four components: the monarchy, the nobility in the House of Lords, the middle class in the House of Commons, and the restless but voiceless working class. To some extent, Lords and Commons had been forced to form a common front, first, against the wilfulness of the Monarchy, and subsequently against the demands of the new working class. Now, the Monarchy had been all but neutralised and the working class had joined the middle class in the Commons. The scene had been set for a final showdown between the Commons and the Lords. Having already triumphed over the Crown, the House of Commons could now set its sights on removing the last obstacle to the complete appropriation of legislative and executive power.

In 1893, only ninety-one Peers voted for a Liberal measure, and eighteen years later it would have been necessary for the more socialist-oriented Liberal Party to create 500 Peers in order to pass the Parliament Bill. The problem was not just an influx into the Commons of new members who represented the interests of the poorer classes; it was aggravated by the spread of socialist philosophy, which rejected social distinctions based on inherited wealth and status. By the end of the nineteenth century, therefore, the House of Lords found itself increasingly in opposition to a large part of public opinion, which demanded the taxation of wealth, which was seen as the plundering of the members of the Upper House. Adding to the tension in 1893 was an Irish Home Rule Bill. This ignored the objections of Ulster and enjoyed only lukewarm support in the Liberal Party itself. It was heavily defeated in the Lords, but on this occasion the action of the Upper House had the support of the electorate, and its rejection of the Bill was greeted with general relief. Faced by this, Gladstone's colleagues in the Cabinet dissuaded him from taking the issue to the country. In his last speech in the Commons, Gladstone again attacked the House of Lords, saying that their rights represented a state of things that could not continue. Nevertheless, the Irish Home Rule Bill was also a pointer to the future in another sense, because it demonstrated that, on some issues, the House of Lords reflected public opinion better than did the Parties, which were becoming more ideologically driven, and increasingly inclined to pursue policies of their own without reference to the people.

Although the pressure for the creation of life Peers had come originally from the shortage of those with a judicial training, it opened up a new avenue of thinking among the Liberals. This was that life Peerages offered a means to ridding the House of Lords of its hereditary Peers, who, in keeping with the principle of male primogeniture, would gradually become extinct in any case, unless new ones were created.

Legislative deadlock was reached, meanwhile, if the two Houses were unable to agree on a Bill, and this was by no means uncommon. Usually it forced the Commons to modify its proposals in order to get them accepted, but on basic issues this was not enough. The Lords were sometimes willing to bend on major issues, but only in the face of public violence. In other cases, the proposed measures were simply abandoned for the time being. This problem could be a very serious one where the ordinary raising of revenue and commitment of expenditure were concerned, the more so because the Commons themselves had long since established, as a means of controlling the King, a rule that Parliament had to approve expenditure on an annual basis. Since the fifteenth century it had been accepted, although there seems to have been no constitutional basis for this, that only the Commons could initiate money Bills, but it had not affected the right of the Lords to veto them. It was a problem that always came to the fore during periods of Liberal Ministry, when radical fiscal ideas were usually proposed, and this enraged Gladstone. The Earl of Rosebery succeeded Gladstone, and during the remainder of the Liberal Ministry followed a policy of deliberately provoking the opposition of the House of Lords, with the idea of arousing the passions of the electorate. Thus, the Local Government Act passed three times between the Houses, and there was a great deal of trouble over Asquith's Employers' Liability Bill. Unfortunately for the Government, the public did not share its indignation against the Upper House. It is significant that hostility towards the House of Lords usually came, not from the electorate, but from the political Parties in the Commons.

By the beginning of the twentieth century, the Peerage had grown to about 570, with one of the outstanding contributors to this inflation having been Gladstone himself, who used it for corrupt purposes. The size of the House of Lords had itself become a problem, even without the addition of life Peers. The Lords had thus undergone a change of character, from one of close cooperation by aristocratic families, small in size, powerful in wealth and social prestige, and, on the whole, taking its responsibilities for the welfare of the country seriously, to a much larger, more heterogeneous body, that was more divided in its interests and attitudes.

An increasingly important factor in politics was the spreading circulation of weekly and daily newspapers during the latter half of the nineteenth century. Although newspapers had first appeared in England in the seventeenth century, and although they influenced public attitudes during the Crimean War of 1854–56, it was not until the tax on them had been abolished in 1855, and the rotary press had been introduced in 1857, that 'the press' began to achieve a mass circulation and to carry the influence of its journalists and editors into every household. Through its rapid circulation of news and the manipulation of political attitudes through the manner in which information was selected and presented, the press became, in turn, a key factor in the manipulation of Government policy and Party election manifestos. Indeed, such was the influence of the press upon public thinking that cynics eventually referred to it, along with other and later news media, as the 'Fourth Estate'.

The nineteenth century saw the House of Commons reach a position of supremacy in the system of government. As a result of periodic elections, it now chose the Government, maintained it in office, and brought about its downfall. It controlled the executive and was the intermediary between the executive and the electorate. Generally, it was held in high standing. From this point onwards, however, the Party machines took its place, subordinating Parliament and the Crown to Party leaders capable of attracting, entertaining and manipulating the masses. The industrialisation and urbanisation of society insulated people from the natural world and stimulated the emergence of new political ideologies, provoking their opponents into counter-philosophies. Fed by ideologies, the Party system grew even stronger, using the institutions of government, in turn, to establish ideologies, and promoting the notion of the Constitution as something that was malleable in its own convenience.

31.4.1.3. The Rise of Imperialism

Disraeli formed a brief Ministry in 1868, and a more lasting one from 1874. It was on his own initiative in 1875 that he negotiated and bought for Britain a controlling interest in the Suez Canal, an action subsequently ratified by Parliament, and one that provided Great Britain with secure access to India and the Far East by the shortest possible sea-route. In its turn, control of the Suez Canal promoted a new strategic interest in the Mediterranean and the Red Sea, and the securing of their control at either end. Fortunately, these strategic positions had already been secured, in a haphazard manner, by the acquisition of Gibraltar, Malta and Aden, which became bases for the Royal Navy.

Imperialism has been defined as the principle or spirit of empire, including the advocacy or spirit of imperial interest.[16] It could also be defined as the acquisition of colonies for their own sake. It had its origin in the rise of European nationalism and a resulting rivalry between nations for aggrandisement, regardless of whether the colonies in question offered real benefits, or an attractive opportunity for the re-settlement of surplus population. The purchase of the Suez Canal was a reaction to the rise of imperialism, rather than imperialism itself, but Disraeli saw mutual benefit in a closer association of the Monarchy and Empire, and this was achieved through the Royal Titles Bill of 1876, which declared the Queen to be the 'Empress of India', in keeping with a long tradition of Indian emperors, who had themselves usually been outsiders. Queen Victoria, Empress of India, was seen as a new Britannia, providing the focus and sense of purpose which was now demanded by the Imperial Age. It was a role for which she was well fitted by her sentiments and by her sense of what was politically appropriate.

The anti-Liberal bias of the Queen became most marked after the Liberals opposed the Imperial title, yet, although Victoria was becoming increasingly partisan in Party politics, her popularity was undimmed. It reached its heights in the Jubilee years of 1877 and 1897, during which time she was fortunate in having a Conservative Ministry under the shrewd and able guidance of Lord Salisbury. Popular once more, Queen Victoria finally withdrew from an active and constant role in politics, and after her the Monarchy was to become a focus of tradition and ceremonial. It still exercised some prerogatives, and its theoretical powers were still regarded as considerable, but, through lack of use, a convention came to be recognised by Parliament that they would not be exercised. Yet they were not seen as irrelevant. On the contrary, many saw them as a safeguard against unconstitutional action by the Government or by Parliament.

16   *Shorter Oxford English Dictionary*, Oxford University Press, 1973.

Meanwhile, the new title did much to imbue the nation with a sense of imperial pride, and this new awareness became a political necessity as Great Britain found herself caught up in the new Age of Imperialism, when rival European powers entered into a scramble for colonies for the sake of self-aggrandisement. Arguably, Britain's own began with Cecil Rhodes, who saw a territorial link, between the Cape Colony and the British condominium in Egypt, as an end in itself, by acquiring a new scope for British settlement and a Cape to Cairo railway, as well as protecting the interests of the Cape. Rhodes's philosophy was based on a belief that the interests of the world would best be served if its affairs were led and managed by the British, by which he particularly meant the English, with what he saw as the ideals promoted by the English public school system of fair play, self-discipline, justice and integrity, and a respect for the rule of law. Otherwise, comparatively little of the British Empire could be attributed to simple imperialism, beyond the protection of existing interests and, as the world's leading naval power, the mopping up of a large number of scattered and often uninhabited islands, again, probably, as a precaution against any future threat to trade. The British Government itself played little part in the expansionism of the comparatively short Imperial Age, which, for all its ramifications, was driven very largely by self-motivated idealists, leading relative handfuls of motivated, enterprising and often courageous men, bent as much on exploration as on territorial expansion. Indeed, the Foreign Office often found itself dragged unwillingly into acknowledging first one new colony, then another, protesting bitterly at the cost of its administration. A feature of the Imperial Age was the idealism and the hardship faced by the men and women who were driven by it, particularly in Africa, where it was accentuated by the competition from rival powers. Imperialism was an overflow of nationalism, generated across Europe by the rise of the nation state, in place of the great dynastic alliances and rivalries of the Middle Ages, during which the sense of identity of the community and of the ordinary individual had been very largely suppressed. In a very real sense, British imperialism represented, like the American expansion towards the Pacific and the Dutch migration northwards from the Cape Colony, a resumption of the great expansionary migrations of their Indo-European ancestors from the Volga steppes.

31.5. Parliamentary Privilege and the Courts

Cases involving possible breach of parliamentary privilege had long been a potential source of friction between Parliament and the courts, because, unless Parliament was willing to devote itself to hearing such cases, it was necessary for the courts to do so, and this meant that they needed to know the extent of their jurisdiction to decide on the existence and extent of parliamentary privileges. This, Parliament had never been willing to do, being jealous of its right to interpret its own privileges, which had long been established as part of the *lex et consuetudo parliamenti*, or 'law and custom of Parliament'. As such, it enjoyed the status of law, an odd situation, because it was for the King to decide such matters, no doubt after due consultation.

This issue was brought to the fore in 1840, in the case of *Stockdale v Hansard*, when the House of Commons claimed to be the absolute and sole judge of its own privileges. The court resolutely maintained the right to determine the nature and limit of parliamentary privilege, should it be necessary to decide these questions in adjudicating upon the rights of individuals outside the House.[17] For this to be possible, the court concluded that if Parliament were to extend its existing privileges beyond the established law and custom of Parliament, it should do so, not by a mere resolution of the House, but by statute. This was done in 1868, for example, when Parliament used the Administration of Justice Act to end its own jurisdiction to determine disputed elections, conferring it instead on the courts. Otherwise, the courts could only make their own interpretation of parliamentary privilege.

The issue was resurrected in the Bradlaugh affair of the 1880s. Bradlaugh, an atheist elected to Parliament on successive occasions, having failed to take the oath as required by statute, eventually sought an injunction against the Serjeant-at-Arms, to restrain him from carrying out a resolution of the House that he be excluded. The court held that, this being an internal matter of the House of Commons, the court had no power to interfere. As Lord Coleridge remarked, 'If injustice has been done, it is injustice for which the courts of law afford no remedy'.[18] It was

---

17   A. W. Bradley, and K. D. Ewing, *Constitutional and Administrative Law* (London and New York, 1997), 243–4.

18   *Bradlaugh v Gossett*, 1884.

emphasised that the House was entitled to interpret the relevant Act as it wished, for example, by passing a resolution that Bradlaugh was entitled to make an affirmation instead of the requisite oath, for the purpose of determining a right to be exercised in the House. However, this did not protect Bradlaugh against an action for penalties taken against him in respect of rights that he might exercise outside, and independently of the House.

32. THE RESTORATION OF SHIRE ASSEMBLIES

T HE LOCAL GOVERNMENT Act, 1888, finally restored the shire assemblies, which had declined into insignificance during the Early Middle Ages, as a result of both the delegation of powers to the Crown and, more importantly, the appropriation of powers and functions by the Crown without due process in law. In this way, the very assemblies upon which the English confederal system of government during the Early Middle Ages had largely, or wholly, been established, ceased to exist, throwing legal doubt on the whole system of government based at Westminster.

Unintentionally, the Act of 1888 had the effect of restoring the foundations of the constitutional structure. Representation of the shires in Parliament had not, arguably, been affected, because Parliaments had continued to function, although it had long ceased to be recognised. Representation of the towns and cities, that is, representation on the basis of population, had long been thrown into disarray by the pattern and extent of urban growth since the Industrial Revolution, and in many cases the shires themselves had been changed quite arbitrarily, for the sake of central government convenience, further violating constitutional requirements.

32.1. Local Government: County, Borough, and District Councils (1888)

The free trade and other *laissez faire* policies of the eighteenth and nineteenth centuries that accompanied the industrialisation of the economy, and the massive drift of population into the cities, gave rise to much distress among the working classes. The growth of cities and large-scale production methods also had undesirable consequences for all classes, such as the accumulation of human and industrial waste, a high rate of industrial accidents, the use of children, excessive working hours, and a high incidence of disease, leading to popular agitation for the introduction of humanitarian policies. Not all the changes that followed made life easier, and the new measures that were called for led to a revolution in the structure and character of local government. The Poor Law Amendment Act of 1834 limited the payment of charitable doles to sick and aged paupers, but it established workhouses, where the able-bodied poor were put to useful employment. It ended the system whereby low wages were supplemented by the dole, which had the unintended effect of perpetuating low wages. The Act placed the control of poor relief in the hands of three Poor Law Commissioners, later succeeded by the Poor Law Board and, still later, in 1871, by the Local Government Board.

The Industrial and Agricultural Revolutions and the sprawling cities to which they gave rise had rendered inadequate the existing arrangement for maintaining the King's peace. This had long relied on paid watchmen in the larger towns and unpaid town and village constables, acting under the Justices of the Peace. In order to remove the widespread corruption and administrative abuse that existed in most municipal governments, which were elected by those still classed as freemen, the Municipal Corporations Act was passed in 1835. It abolished the charters of a number of small boroughs and introduced a uniform system in all other boroughs and urban districts. The new Municipal Councils were to be elected by male ratepayers and freemen on a rotation system, so that one-third of councillors retired each year. Each council was to elect a Mayor each year, and Aldermen every six years, and was required to appoint a Town Clerk and other officials. It was empowered to pass such by-laws as seemed necessary 'for the good rule and governance of the borough'. A new Act in 1840 extended the right to vote in Council elections to all persons paying a rent of £10 a year, and required boroughs to appoint police forces, which were to be subject to control by Watch Committees.

In the counties, meanwhile, the Justices of the Peace had already been empowered in 1839 to maintain police forces, a provision that was made compulsory seventeen years later. A member of the new police forces, although now paid, was still classed as a Constable, and the county forces were referred to Constabularies. Local criminal justice had long been entrusted to the Justices of the Peace, sitting in Quarter Sessions, while civil justice had been the responsibility of local Courts of Requests, which had come into being in the Middle Ages to hear cases not exceeding forty shillings. The latter were now replaced by the County Courts Act of 1846, which established a local system of County Courts, with civil jurisdiction, serving fifty-nine circuits. The Justices of the Peace were to preside at the new County Courts, in addition to the Quarter Sessions. At first, the County Courts were intended to deal only with small civil actions involving sums of money under £20, but later legislation allowed the County Courts to hear cases involving much larger amounts, so that they came to form the most important body of inferior tribunals. In principle and to a limited extent, therefore, the new County Courts restored the ancient tradition of shire assemblies sitting in their judicial capacity. In Scotland the corresponding tribunals were the Sheriff Courts.

None of this addressed the chronic health problems that had been caused by the Industrial Revolution, and these needed a comprehensive system of local authorities to deal with them. The Public Health Act of 1875 accordingly provided for the establishment of Urban, Rural and Port Sanitary Districts, which were to cover every part of England and to be responsible for such tasks as the provision of sewers and drains, the speedy interment of bodies, and the provision of hospitals for infectious diseases. The Urban Sanitary Districts were to include municipal boroughs, but whereas the boroughs were both general purpose and health authorities, the Urban Sanitary Districts were to be concerned only with health matters. The duties of the Rural Sanitary Districts were to be administered by the Poor Law guardians. Under the pressure of other needs, however, it soon became necessary for these new authorities to become responsible for a wide range of other local administrative functions, in addition to health. So it was that, in 1894, the functions of the system were broadened. The Urban Sanitary Districts became general purpose Urban Districts, under elected Councils, while the Rural Sanitary Districts became general purpose Rural Districts, administered by Boards of Guardians.

The whole basis of English local government, meanwhile, was changed in 1888 by the Local Government Act. This transferred the administrative authority of the Justices of the Peace and Quarter Sessions to the elected County Councils and to those boroughs with a population in excess of 50,000. Because these boroughs now had the same powers as a County, they were referred to as County Boroughs. The new County Councils not only had functions of their own, but were also given a general supervisory responsibility for the smaller authorities in their areas. In evidence presented to the Royal Sanitary Commission, on whose recommendations the Act was based, it was held that the existing small local government units, being in most cases composed of traditional communities, should retain the interest of electors in their affairs, but that the new administrative area, the county, even if it were elective, would not incite any real communal spirit – undoubtedly, in part, because many of them no longer coincided with the original shires. The county would therefore provide a buffer, possessing more local knowledge than Parliament, but subject to less local prejudice than the existing bodies. The county could be used, therefore, to administer unpopular Government measures and to absorb the shock of local displeasure.

Unfortunately, the identities of the shires often had, and continued to be, ruthlessly erased by the growth in population and the failure to retain the identity of shire borders, and this was reflected in parliamentary representation. The purpose of a parliamentary election is to allow the citizens in each constituency to provide a respected member of their community to represent their interests. According to the common law of the Constitution, the constituencies in England comprise its member nations, as represented by the historic shires. This had long ceased to be the case in practice, and there were several reasons for this. One was that, as a result of the growth in population, many communities had spread across shire borders, and so lost their shire identities. The classic example was London, which extended beyond its original location in Middlesex, across four shire boundaries, which were allowed to become erased in the process.

This was a dire commentary on the extent to which the political importance of the shires, the basis of the Constitution, had declined, along with the regional cultural differences of which they were once a part. In many cases, the ethnic basis of the shires had almost disappeared. This decline had been greatly hastened by the loss, since the Middle Ages, of the shire assemblies, in both their civil and judicial roles. Even the sheriff had been reduced to a minor figure. Consequently, in principle, the County Councils and County Courts inherited the administrative and judicial roles of the ancient shire assemblies, except that the shire boundaries were greatly distorted and they were impositions of the Crown, except that, neither the Crown nor Parliament had any power to change them.

To enable the County Councils to carry out their duties, which included the provision of a local police force, the central Government provided them with annual grants, in addition to the local property tax, colloquially known as the 'rates', and other revenues which they were empowered to raise. This policy, of funding the Councils partly by means of Government grants, ensured that the Crown could, in those areas where it chose, dictate to the Councils what their policies should be. Meanwhile, the responsibilities and importance of the County Councils increased steadily, not least because the size of the counties enabled them to provide certain services, such as education and police, much more efficiently than the smaller District Councils – which could be seen as a partial resurrection of the former hundreds – whose importance was destined to decline as a result. At the same time, the transfer of the Courts of Quarter Sessions to the boroughs and to the counties, made a borough equivalent to a county for judicial, as well as administrative, purposes. Thus, the earlier administrative structure, based on the parishes, Justices of the Peace, boroughs, and municipalities, was replaced by a new one, based on the parishes, Urban and Rural Sanitary Districts, boroughs and municipalities, all under the layer of County Councils and County Boroughs. The Justices of the Peace, who had lost their administrative role, now sat in both the Courts of Quarter Sessions and the County Courts. The process was destined to go much further as the population grew, so that the people felt almost completely divorced from the shires in which it lived.

It is now possible to trace the long history of the means by which the Crown asserted its administrative control locally, as well as nationally. At first, the King's agents had been the *Ealdormen*, then the Shire Reeves (or Sheriffs), then the Justices of the Peace and the Lords Lieutenant, and now, to provide for the restoration of democratic government, the elected but financially dependent County Councils.

Meanwhile, the parish continued to operate as the lowest tier of local government. It was still responsible for the roads in its area, until taken over by the District Councils. The Parish Councils Act of 1894 required them to be appointed by election. The Justices of the Peace, who had been the most important local government authorities until the mid-nineteenth century, now declined in importance, as their administrative functions were taken over by elected authorities. The County and County Borough Councils replaced the Justices of the Peace as the link and buffer between central and local government. The sheriffs, who had largely been supplanted by the Justices of the Peace and the Lords Lieutenant, now preceded them into administrative insignificance in the face of the new structure. Only in their judicial role did the Justices of the Peace continue to perform a necessary service. The Local Government Board, which was responsible mainly for Poor Law relief, also had various powers to make or approve changes in the area and status of local authorities, usually made necessary by the spread of urban development or the need for adjacent authorities to combine their resources. Proposals for change often involved rivalry, as happened sometimes between County Councils and County Boroughs. General legislation was sometimes required, such as the Local Government Act of 1929, in order to effect numerous adjustments at the same time, and it soon became clear that the Local Government Board was inadequate for its task. In 1919 it became the Ministry of Health.

These provisions excluded London, which had always been treated separately for local government purposes. There were several reasons for this, some being historical. For example, London appeared earlier than anywhere else as a prominent centre; it had for centuries been favoured by the King as his permanent seat; and it had represented the strongly entrenched interests of the merchants of London, particularly in the City. The sheer size of London had usually daunted local government reformers, who felt unable to apply the same solutions as were adopted elsewhere. Consequently, reforms in London tended to come later than in other areas, by which time ideas had changed and the nature of the reform was different. From 1855 onwards, greater London was administered by a Metropolitan Board of Works, but this was soon felt to be inadequate. The Act of 1888 treated the area covered by the Board as a separate county, placing it under a London County Council. This was achieved by appropriating large parts of Middlesex, Essex, Kent and Surrey, and London's status as the largest town in Essex (Middlesex having been appropriated by it at an early date) finally disappeared. A subsequent Local Government Act of 1899 subdivided the Council's jurisdiction into twenty-eight Metropolitan Boroughs, it being hoped that, in this way, local responsibility would be combined with an overall coherence of administration.

The philosophy underlying local government differed radically, as between the feudal and Aryan traditions. The former derived all temporal authority from the Crown, which in turn derived it from God. Local government was therefore the gift of the Crown, and this had been the presupposition of all local government legislation since the Middle Ages. Indo-European tradition took the opposite view, asserting that English democracy had its basis in local government, from which, by a process of upward delegation, the Crown and Parliament had come into being. The system of English local government, based on the hundred, the *gé* or lathe, and ultimately the shire, had since been circumvented, their functions appropriated, and left to die, as they were replaced by new structures imposed by a Crown and Parliament that had no power to do so.

32.2. The Doctrine of Constitutional Evolution

Liberal thinking, meanwhile, extended to constitutional issues. Successive writers extolled the virtues of a legislature that no longer represented the interests of a particular class, but society in general. At the same time, one of their number, John Stuart Mill, expressed his concern at the prospect of the tyranny of the majority, which placed the ignorance of the lower classes above the knowledge possessed by their superiors. It was a journalist, Walter Bagehot, however, who first looked critically at the constitutional process, showing a greater interest in the actual processes of government, which he found to be at variance with the requirements of what was then deemed to be the Constitution, as described by legal authorities.

Noting the decline of the Monarchy and the House of Lords, and the electoral reform of 1832, whose effects were still making themselves felt, Bagehot, in his *The English Constitution*, published in 1867, rejected all previous interpretations, such as the notion of a joint sovereignty of the three powers – the Monarchy, the aristocracy, and the commons – or the idea of a division of powers between the legislature, the executive, and the judiciary. Because the system of government had been undergoing constant change, he regarded an historical approach as useless, because it dealt only with the past, and was therefore irrelevant to the way in which things were done in the present. He concluded that England had a 'living' constitution, which was in constant change, and which could only be understood by dividing its institutions into two classes – the 'dignified' parts, 'which excite and preserve the reverence of the population', and the 'efficient' parts, 'by which it, in fact, works and rules'. To practical men, the dignified parts were unnecessary, because they were of no practical benefit, but it was these dignified parts of Government that drew the people and so gave it motive force, which the efficient parts could then employ to govern. Each institution had both dignified and efficient features, but in Bagehot's view the Monarchy and the House of Lords were essentially the dignified parts of the constitution, while the Cabinet and the House of Commons were its efficient parts. The 'efficient secret' of the English Constitution might be described as 'the close union, the near complete fusion, of the executive and legislative powers', a view that was almost the opposite of that reached earlier by Montesquieu. The connecting link was the Cabinet, which Bagehot saw as 'a committee of the legislative body selected to be the executive body'. Thus, Bagehot saw the constitution as functioning in the same way as a religion, in which the purpose of the Church was to rule the people according to its own lights, but, in order to keep them docile and obedient, it was necessary to ply them with theatrical displays, which engendered awe and subservience to the elected 'priesthood' sitting in the House of Commons. His was an unedifying portrait, therefore, of an imposed system that represented itself as democratic, but which had perfected the art of manipulating the electors.

Much of Bagehot's view of Government was based on his observation that the lower and middle orders of society were 'narrow-minded, unintelligent, incurious', and his conclusion that 'The masses of Englishmen are not fit for an elective government'. The Commons led, and the nation would follow, but there were limits beyond which the nation would not go, and the Commons must therefore lead only where it thought the nation would follow. In its turn, the Commons chose and dismissed its statesmen. The Prime Minister was expected to lead, while the Commons guided, but he could only lead where he believed the Commons would follow, and if he failed to lead, the Commons, like a spoiled child, would become unmanageable.

To Bagehot, the constitutional role of the King had been reduced to a purely nominal one, largely limited to appointing Prime Ministers and signing documents, because his original powers had withered away and become redundant through lack of use. Even so, Monarchy served the necessary purpose, firstly, of concentrating the attention of the masses on one person who does interesting things, appealing to the popular incapacity for reason, and so making strong government possible. A republic, on the other hand, distracted the masses with the activities of the many, all doing uninteresting things. Monarchy was strong, because it appealed to human feelings, whereas republics were weak, because they appealed to the understanding.

Bagehot saw the Monarchy as reinforcing government by invoking religion. Charles I had been the 'Lord's anointed', because kingship had been a divine institution. After the Revolution, William III had ruled by vote of Parliament, with 'no consecrated loyalty to build upon'. By the time of Queen Anne, however, there had been a change of feeling, and 'the old sacred sentiment began to cohere about her', so that she had been regarded as again ruling by 'God's grace'. In their turn, George I and George II, because they had been elected for purely statesmanlike reasons as non-Catholics, degrading the Monarchy from 'its solitary pinnacle of majestic reverence' and reducing it to 'one only among many expedient institutions', had the effect of depriving the Crown of any sentiment of religious loyalty. With George III the common feeling had returned, and the English had been 'ready to take the new young prince as the beginning of a sacred line of sovereigns'.

Thirdly, the Monarch was also the head and focus of society, receiving foreign ministers and rulers, giving the finest parties, leading 'the pageant of life, and representing the Government in the eyes of the people'. Fourthly, the Sovereign had come to be regarded as the head of morality, the virtues of George III and Queen Victoria having 'sunk deep into the popular heart'. This was a consequence of the new constitutional monarchy, whose occupations were 'grave, formal, important, but never exciting'. Finally, the institution of royalty provided a 'disguise', which distracted the people and gave an impression of continuity, behind which the real rulers of the nation could change without the people being aware of it.

The practical importance of the Monarchy, according to Bagehot, lay in its role in appointing the Government, while being outside the power of the political Parties to control, and in exerting control over particular Ministers and a certain degree of control over the Cabinet. Bagehot insisted that the Queen's first Minister 'is bound to take care' that the Queen 'knows everything which there is to know as to the passing politics of the nation. She has, by rigid usage, a right to complain if she does not know of every great act of her Ministry, not only before it is done, but while there is yet time to consider it – while it is still possible that it may not be done. To state the matter shortly, the Sovereign has, under a constitutional monarchy such as ours, three rights – the right to be consulted, the right to encourage, the right to warn'.[1] The right to be consulted flowed automatically, it seemed, from the fact that the Queen's Ministers were exercising their powers in her name.

Bagehot's treatise, essentially a work of journalism, rather than of learning, was out of date almost immediately, being overtaken by the second Reform Act, which ended the form of parliamentary government which Bagehot had described. It was overshadowed, in any case, by more scholarly works, such as John Stuart Mill's *Representative Government*, published a few years earlier, and the masterly works of such as Anson and Jennings, yet it was to influence attitudes down to the present day, because it fitted the perceptions that politicians held of themselves, for which reason it was still promoted as the best introduction to the subject that was available. One reason was the very journalistic quality of the work. Another was Bagehot's conclusion that the constitution was not fixed, but continually evolving to meet new interests and needs, and that the seat of power lay with the Cabinet and the House of Commons, for which reason

---

1   W. Bagehot, *The English Constitution*, 112–13.

it proved popular with elected politicians, who endeavoured to enshrine it in constitutional law. The weakness of Bagehot's thinking was that he simply described what he observed, with little in the way of insight. He criticised Mill's work as a 'paper description' of the constitution, rather than a description of the 'living reality'. To Bagehot, it was the external appearance of the body of the creature that mattered, not the skeleton from which it hung, because he did not really believe that one had ever existed. Until comparatively recently, he believed, the constitution had been only partly formed. Consequently, no definable structure had ever existed, so that he saw no reason to question what he found. He accepted the practices that he observed because they were there, in the same way as he accepted the changes that were taking place because they were the 'living reality'. His notion of the three 'rights' of the Sovereign – to advise, to encourage, and to warn – was meaningless, however, except in the context of the Sovereign's delegation, but not relinquishment, so that it did not, and could not, entirely absolve the King of all responsibility for the use or misuse of his powers by his Ministers. The basic defect of Bagehot's argument, indeed, was his assumption that in earlier times the constitution had been only partly formed. It was like an embryo, which had begun as nothing more than a heroic chieftain, and had slowly developed into the form in which Bagehot found it, largely formed but presumably still far from complete. It was not surprising, therefore, that it was a 'living thing', and that to view it from the perspective of the past was pointless.

Bagehot's work had more influence on English political thinking than almost any other, because it seemed to explain the reality of government. It also brought an air of legitimacy to many new practices, and offered an alternative to the many who felt that previously accepted constitutional principles were at odds with the new radicalism. It also implied a deeply rooted objection to revolution. It gave rise to a new theory: that of English constitutional evolution, as it tried to adapt to changing political ideas. Like other constitutional writers, Bagehot's work would probably have slipped gradually from view, except that it told the political Parties exactly what they wished to hear. Having usurped the Crown, and their ambitions by no means fully satisfied, they must have been well aware that they stood to be accused of insurrection, yet here was an argument that fully justified their actions and paved the way for more. Far from being relegated to the growing genre of historical commentary, Bagehot's book became the Bible of the political Party system, relegating the past and opening the way to the future of Party Government. There was nothing inherently wrong in this, except that it made no attempt to accommodate the common law of the land, of which Bagehot appeared to know little and to care even less.

33. FINAL SEPARATION OF THE CROWN FROM THE MONARCHY

33.1. The Civil List is Limited to the Royal Household

George IV died in June of 1830. His only legitimate offspring, Charlotte, had died in 1817, leaving none of the four elder sons of George III with an heir to the throne in the next generation. This realisation had already sent the fourth eldest, Edward Augustus, Duke of Kent, hurrying to marry Mary Louise Victoria, daughter of the Duke of Saxe-Coburg Saalfeld and sister of Prince Leopold, husband of the ill-fated Charlotte. She had always been known as Victoria, and between them, in 1819, Edward and Victoria had produced a daughter, also named Victoria, who thus became the heir to an ageing dynasty.

Meanwhile, George IV was succeeded by his younger brother, William IV, who was already nearly sixty-five years of age. His wife was Adelaide, daughter of the Duke of Saxe-Meiningen, who had produced no children. William had never expected to succeed to the throne, and had enjoyed a not undistinguished career in the Royal Navy, for which reason he was nicknamed the 'Sailor King'. In these circumstances, William saw himself as essentially a caretaker monarch, holding the throne for his niece, Victoria, and determined to survive long enough to prevent her mother, now Duchess of Kent, from becoming regent. Because he saw himself as little more than a caretaker, William IV insisted on a much-reduced coronation ceremony that dispensed with several of the procedures, notably, the Challenge by the Sovereign's champion, the Elevation of the King, whose purpose was to allow him to be recognised by the people, and, finally, the Coronation Banquet. At his age, perhaps, William felt that being raised up above the congregation might be too unnerving an experience, or, more simply, that it celebrated a personal attainment that, as a stand-in, he did not deserve. In later coronations, only the Banquet would be restored. The elevation of the new King had been a requirement of any elected ruler since antiquity, so that the people could recognise him, and history records various alternatives, such as standing on a large rock or, in the case of the West Saxon kings, being raised onto the 'king-stone'.[1] The essential requirement was, and still is, however, for the King elect to stand briefly in a position from which he may clearly be seen and acclaimed by the people, for which purpose the congregation in Westminster Cathedral might be said to be adequate.

An accession to the Crown required the summoning of a new Parliament, and in the ensuing general election the reform of the House of Commons emerged as the campaign issue. The Whigs, who adopted reform as their main programme, were returned with a majority, but William, exercising his prerogative to choose his Prime Ministers, retained the Duke of Wellington and his Tory Ministry in office. As a weak ruler in what he regarded as a weak position, William had agreed, upon his accession in 1831, to surrender the various remaining revenues of a public nature, such as the Civil Provision for Ireland, the hereditary revenues of Scotland, the droits, or rights, of the Crown and Admiralty,[2] and the West India duties. In return for these, he was to be granted an increase in provision for the Civil List.[3] At the same time, the Civil List was to be relieved of all remaining charges relating to actual government, such as judicial salaries and the salaries and pensions of diplomats and members of the Civil Service. The remaining expenditures that were still attributable to the Civil List were to be categorised, so that a specific annual sum could be appropriated to each category. Even these expenditures were to be referred for investigation by a Select Committee of the House of Commons. This separation of the fiscal needs of government from the personal needs of the King and his family was consistent, on the one hand, with the increasing delegation of the King's executive responsibilities to his Ministers and, on the other hand, with the increasing answerability of Ministers to their supporters in Parliament. Undoubtedly, both Parliament and the King's Ministers regarded this as

1   Still on display in Kingston-upon-Thames. The 'Stone of Scone' was used by the Scottish kings.

2   Droits: rights or perquisites. The droits of the Court of Admiralty included proceeds arising from the seizure of enemy ships, wrecks, etc.

3   Report on Civil Government Charges, 1831.

completing the transfer, to the Ministry, of the King's executive powers and responsibilities for the government of the Realm, which was now answerable, not to the King, but to Parliament.

At this point it is pertinent to look at the common law of the Constitution, according to which, it appears that the right to impose and collect taxes, as well as their disbursement, belonged to the King, in his capacity as head of the executive function of government, subject to the advice of his Ministers and the advice and approval of Parliament. The appointment of Ministers was itself subject to the advice of the Council, which undoubtedly took the views of Parliament into consideration. For the King to reject the advice of the Council was a matter for concern, because, if the Council took the view that the King was ruling in an irresponsible manner, particularly if it had the support of Parliament, it could demand (and if necessary, enforce) the King's abdication. In the light of this, the Civil List was effectively a list of the budgeted revenues and expenditures of the Crown, including the needs of the King in his civil duties and the needs of the Royal Household. Income from, and expenditure upon, the royal estates were independent of the Civil List.

Following the resignation of Wellington in 1830, in favour of a Whig Ministry, the settlement of the question of the Civil List was passed into the hands of Earl Grey. In its enquiries, however, the Select Committee did not think that scrutiny of the details of the King's domestic household was consistent with the respect due to His Majesty, although it nevertheless recommended the reduction in salary of several officers of state. To this, the King protested that 'If the people, according to the new Bill, are really to govern the House of Commons, and the House of Commons is to decide upon the amount of salary I am to give to my servants, then the prerogatives of the Crown will in reality pass to the people, and the Monarchy cannot exist'. His Ministers gave way, and persuaded the House of Commons to restore the Civil List to the amount originally proposed, but in future it was to be used purely for 'the dignity and state of the Crown and the personal comfort of their Majesties', that is, the Royal Household.[4]

This process of paring down the Civil List was regarded as being of major constitutional significance. From 1830 onwards, the King's

---

4   T. Erskine May, *The Constitutional History of England Since the Accession of George the Third, 1760–1860*, i. 245–7. Also, Roebuck's *History of the Whig Ministry*, ii. 159.

personal expenditure was finally separated from general government expenditure, a principle that was to be followed down to the present day. From now onwards, the amount to be spent on matters of state should be decided, not by the King, but by Parliament. It effectively marked the end of the King's role as head of the executive function of government. His legislative function as the primary source of Bills presented to Parliament had been compromised long ago (due to the King's own failure and obduracy) by the practice of Parliament of blocking the King and appropriating petitions to itself and presenting them as Bills. The constitutional failure of the Monarchy that had brought about the loss of its legislative function had also now brought about the loss of its executive function. The most obvious cause of this gradual constitutional collapse had been the acceptance, since the onset of the Middle Ages, of the feudal doctrine of Monarchy, itself a prescription for unsuitable successions and inappropriate royal policies, which could not be removed, and the licentious royal behaviour that had resulted. The unsuitability for office even of Britain's more recent kings had been evident in their corrupt political patronage, profligacy, promotion of self-interest, and the loss of the American colonies, which was blamed on George III. Furthermore, because of the principle that the King, as God's anointed, could do no wrong, liability for mistakes of the Crown had lain, not with the King, who was the legal and often actual author of its policies, but upon the King's Ministers, putting them into an invidious position. Since the development of the practice of appointing leading members of the House of Commons to Ministerial office, an incompatibility had become evident between their position as servants of the Crown and their duty as representatives of the people. There was a further difficulty in that expenditures by the Crown on the needs of Government did not necessarily require Acts of Parliament, yet Parliament believed that it had an interest in how all the revenues levied on the people were used.

Against this, the common law that had governed kingship, before the adoption of the doctrines of the Church, also did not have a particularly good record. The chief reason was, perhaps, that in those early days the power of the King had severely limited the ability of the Council to impose upon him the rule of law.

In spite of the intention of Parliament to separate the Monarchy from the Crown, the royal authority continued to be important in the administration of the nation's affairs. The accession of a new King was always followed by the summoning of a new Parliament, the mandate of the old one having expired with his predecessor who had summoned it, and this required a general election. Since the Government was composed of the King's officials, it was natural that the new monarch should have the right to make his own choice, subject to the approval of the House of Lords (the Great Council), which must sensibly have taken the sentiments of the House of Commons into consideration. Sovereigns at this time did not hesitate to let their political sympathies be known, and Governments could be changed at the King's wish. Although his Ministers were left with a large measure of freedom to initiate policy, in practice, a strong negative control over their actions was maintained, allowing a contradiction to emerge between the wishes of the King and the wishes and interests of his Government.

This situation could not be changed until a new principle could be introduced into the system. It was a principle that had lain semi-dormant for centuries, but it was not difficult to invoke, nor was it difficult for it to win a wide acceptance. Nevertheless, it needed a stimulus to give it a new credibility, and that stimulus was provided by the French Revolution, which expressed the Indo-European principle that all free men, being subject to the acts of Government, had a right to be heard in the formulation of its policies. Put more forcibly, the sovereign power – the *imperium* – resided, ultimately, not with the King but with the people.

33.1.1. The End of the Link with Hanover (1837)

In spite of his limited circumstances, and perhaps because of them, William IV lived beyond his means, and his debts had to be met from his family's German income. He died in 1837, and, having no legitimate children of his own, the Crown passed to his niece, Victoria. In Hanover, meanwhile, Salic law did not provide for female succession while there was a male descendant of the Welf family, so the succession passed instead to Victoria's uncle, Ernest Augustus, Duke of Cumberland. William IV was the last British King, therefore, who was also the King of Hanover. Neither country had really benefitted from the link, and both regarded the division of responsibilities as a liability, because the two countries had few common interests, other than history. The link had made a German army available to England during the American Revolution, but it had also served to keep the King distracted in varying degrees from his duties in either country, and this already had had a detrimental effect on the royal prerogative. On the other hand, the severing of the link would leave Victoria unable to claim the revenues from Hanover which had provided her predecessors with such a valuable supplement to the royal income, and this helps to explain the personal financial stringency that would mark her reign.

33.2. Monarchy and the Formulation of Policy: The Victorian Age

Victoria was aged eighteen at the time of her accession. She was the daughter of William's younger brother, Edward, Duke of Kent, who died when she was still young, while her mother, also Victoria, was the daughter of the Duke of Saxe-Coburg-Saalfeld. Upon her accession, she moved from Kensington Palace into Buckingham Palace. This was the former Buckingham House, which George IV had decided to have extensively re-built. Fortunately, the reconstruction had just been completed, and Buckingham Palace was to remain the official London residence of the Sovereign until the present day.

At the general election, made necessary by Victoria's accession, the Whigs declared that they had the Queen's favour and were accordingly returned with a majority, so conforming to the long-established pattern whereby the voters were guided by the royal will. The Queen was young, her ideas were unformed, and she had no political experience. Her mother, who had quarrelled with her late father, expected to dominate the scene, but, throughout her early life, Victoria turned regularly for advice to her wise uncle, King Leopold of the Belgians, and his own German adviser, Baron von Stockmar, who instructed him in the duty of a monarch to act constitutionally. The danger from this source came from the fact that their understanding of the royal position was based upon Continental examples, which gave them ideas as to the rights of the Monarchy in England that were scarcely acceptable to the House of Commons. Nevertheless, von Stockmar's advice was generally moderate and valuable, for instance, in bringing about a reduction of expenditure by the Royal Household. Indeed, the tradition of careful management by the Monarchy of its own affairs dates from this time. During her early years on the throne, Victoria was also much under the influence of her Hanoverian governess, Baroness Lehzen, with whom the Prime Minister, the Lord Melbourne, found himself frequently in competition. Lord Melbourne, as an eminent Whig politician, was available to assume the position of the Queen's Private Secretary, and so was able to guide her political actions, which he did in the direction of what became known as 'constitutionalism', that is, adherence to constitutional principles as recognised by the House of Commons. The chief problem was that Melbourne's dominance produced a danger of Whig control of the Government, so that, in 1840, the Queen wrote to King Leopold that 'the Whigs are the only safe and loyal people'.

Although self-willed and liable, on occasion, to rebuke her Ministers, Victoria made no serious attempt to undermine their position. It was still she, as Queen, who chose her Prime Ministers, but always with an eye to practical politics. Thus, following the suspension of the Jamaican constitution in 1839 by a small margin in Parliament, Lord Melbourne felt that his position had been seriously shaken, and resigned.[5] The young Queen was now faced with the prospect of replacing what she regarded as her political friends with what she regarded as her enemies. She therefore sent, rather unwillingly, for the Conservative leader, the Duke of Wellington, who advised her to send for Sir Robert Peel, for whom she conceived a personal dislike which she did not attempt to conceal. In what is known as the Bedchamber Question, Peel refused to form a Ministry unless the ladies of the Queen's bedchamber, who all came from Whig families, were changed in favour of Tory ladies. Undoubtedly, Peel was entitled to request such a change, since Peel felt that the attachment of the Queen to the Whig cause was so public that some mark of royal confidence was necessary before his Government should take office. Peel would, after all, have been placed at a disadvantage if the private confidences of the Queen were shared with the wives of his

---

5   Following the abolition of slavery in Jamaica, a wave of disorder and economic dislocation had swept the island.

political enemies. The Queen reacted with indignation, and turned again to Melbourne, who agreed to form another Ministry. The issue would have been more serious but for the fact that Peel's Party was in a minority. There was a threatened recurrence of the incident two years later, with the beginning of Peel's Ministry in 1841, but on this occasion the matter was solved by merely changing the Mistress of the Robes.

In 1840, meanwhile, Queen Victoria married Prince Albert of Saxe-Coburg and Gotha. He was the second son of Ernest Augustus, Duke of Cumberland, who was the fifth son of George III. Because Victoria was unable, in Salic law, to inherit the crown of Hanover, it went to Ernest Augustus in 1837, who succeeded his brother, William IV, as well as becoming Duke of Saxe-Coburg and Gotha. Ernest's son, Albert, was therefore Victoria's first cousin. Consequently, the monarchy was strongly German in connection and very unpopular, and Victoria's demand that Albert be given the title of 'King Consort' was whittled down to 'Prince Consort', and even that was not granted until seventeen years later, which left Victoria feeling very bitter towards the British Establishment. Albert's Civil List, or annual allowance voted by Parliament for Household expenditure, was similarly reduced. He replaced Melbourne as the Queen's Private Secretary, declaring, on Stockmar's advice, that he was her Permanent Minister. Even so, Victoria was determined to fulfil the royal function alone, and Albert was not admitted for some time to the Queen's audiences with her Ministers. It was only when the Queen fell pregnant and her preoccupation was directed elsewhere that Albert was able to stand in for her. For all the hindrances placed upon him, Albert proved to have a shrewd political instinct and set a high standard of personal integrity, so that the Queen's Ministers, realising that he had an excellent grasp of the issues with which he was expected to deal, encouraged the Queen in future to have Albert present at her audiences. Victoria was deeply devoted to him, and from this time onwards his advice replaced that of Baroness Lehzen, who had been responsible for the Queen's private correspondence.

The numerous marriage alliances of the Saxe-Coburg family, meanwhile, included the royal houses of France, Belgium and Portugal, so that Albert in particular had close contacts, giving rise to royal policies that often clashed with those of the Cabinet. However, Victoria's courage in facing two failed attempts on her life, the decent behaviour and moderate expenditures of her court, and the example of happy domesticity set by her increasingly numerous offspring, brought about a slow recovery of respect for the Crown. Albert himself was a well-informed individual, open to art and learning, and with a punctilious sense of duty, so that, increasingly, he became joint ruler of the nation in fact, if not in name. Albert's father and brother had been notorious womanisers, and the separation of his parents had greatly contributed to his own unhappy childhood. This, and his studious nature, had left him with a strong sense of moral values, which he not only impressed upon Victoria, but, through her, upon the Government and, gradually, upon the nation. Indeed, it was Albert who gave the Victorian age its reputation for morality, bringing to an end, at the same time, the reputation of the Monarchy for licentious behaviour and instilling into it the principle that it must set an example.

The view that the Government was, literally as well as in principle, 'Her Majesty's Government' survived until 1846, when the question arose as to the distribution of loyalties of her Prime Minister. Sir Robert Peel, as Prime Minister, was supported by a Conservative Party composed of landowners pledged to preserve the Corn Laws, which maintained the price of corn and so protected the English farmer at the expense of the newly urbanised working classes. The Government had been elected on this very question in 1841, following lavish expenditure by the landowning interests. Nevertheless, the issue was forced by a bad harvest in 1845 and the Irish potato famine, and in 1846 Peel secured a repeal of the Corn Laws. He did not feel himself bound by the Party programme or responsible to the Party, but bound only by his own word and by his conception of his duty to the Queen. The alternative to repeal was starvation by a wide section of the public, and since the Duke of Wellington, the leader of his Party in the House of Lords, had the influence to persuade that body to repeal the Corn Laws, Peel stayed in office and was able to pass the Bill with the support of the Whigs.

Political Parties were still at a relatively early stage of their evolution, held back by the nature of the electorate and by the way in which elections were conducted. Election campaigns were so expensive that local constituency compromises were easily reached and more than half the seats were uncontested. Electors voted on the basis of their own communities' interests, rather than on national issues as decided by Party leaders. Thus, voters' interests were fairly fixed, and many members of the House of Commons knew that they held their seats only from the support of their own constituents. Consequently, the Whig and Conservative Party leaders had little control over their members. Not only did this leave the Queen with a certain degree of choice in whom she invited to form a Ministry, but she often had no alternative but to wield some discretion in the matter.

Although the need for Cabinet solidarity had long been recognised, it was not enforced, probably because there was no real means of doing so. Under the Whig Ministry of Lord John Russell, from 1846, the indiscrete and boisterously nationalistic foreign policy of Palmerston, the Foreign Secretary, as well as his tendency to ignore royal suggestions and advice, which may have owed something to his Irish origin, dissatisfied Victoria for a long time. Palmerston occasionally sent off despatches without sending them to the Queen, complaining that she kept them too long. While Victoria was aware of Palmerston's good qualities, she never showed respect for his character or intellect, and for his part, Palmerston resented the hints of Prince Albert. Relations were so bad that, in 1850, the Queen and Prince Albert complained to the Prime Minister, Lord John Russell, that they had had no communications with Palmerston for a year.

Matters came to a head in 1850 over the Don Pacifico affair, when a British naval squadron placed a blockade on all Greek vessels using the port of Piraeus, and forced a settlement on the Greek Government over claims against it by a Moorish Jew of Gibraltar, who had claimed thereby to be a British subject. Palmerston survived a hostile House of Commons by invoking the Roman Imperial concept of *civis Romanus sum*, 'I am a Roman citizen', so equating British patriotism with the higher role of the British Empire to protect its citizens, however lowly. For the Queen, however, this was one excess too many, and, assisted by Prince Albert and Baron von Stockmar, she drew up a memorandum in 1851, demanding that she be kept informed and that, once she had approved a measure, it not be altered arbitrarily. Palmerston promised to mend his ways, but a few months later, without waiting to consult the Cabinet, Palmerston gave to the French ambassador his approval of a *coup d'état* in France by Louis Napoleon, which overthrew the French Second Republic. The Cabinet, adopting the Queen's attitude, passed no judgement on the coup and instructed the British ambassador in Paris to adopt a neutral stance, and to carry on as though nothing had happened. It is worth noting that Palmerston was well aware, during this period, that Normanby, the ambassador in Paris, was conniving against him through his wife, Lady Normanby, who was a friend of the Queen, and through his brother, Colonel Phipps, who was secretary to Prince Albert. From Palmerston's point of view, therefore, the affair was a backstairs intrigue. Nevertheless, the embarrassment caused by Palmerston's action provided the Queen with the excuse that she needed to force his dismissal. In a breach of etiquette, the Prime Minister read in the House a memorandum from the Queen on the duties of Lord Palmerston, as follows: 'The Queen requires, first, that Lord Palmerston will distinctly state what he proposes in a given case, in order that the Queen may know as distinctly to what she is giving her royal sanction. Secondly, having once given her sanction to such a measure that it be not arbitrarily altered or modified by the Minister. Such an act she must consider as failing in sincerity towards the Crown, and justly to be visited by the exercise of her constitutional right of dismissing that Minister. She expects to be kept informed of what passes between him and Foreign Ministers before important decisions are taken based upon that intercourse; to receive the foreign despatches in good time; and to have the draughts for her approval sent to her in sufficient time to make herself acquainted with their contents before they must be sent off'. The Queen's dismissal of Palmerston a few days later was not entirely due to his unconstitutional actions. It was politically desirable to Lord John Russell, and was certainly not regretted by his colleagues in the Cabinet.

The implicit attempts of the Queen to control foreign policy generated a measure of resentment in the Cabinet, nonetheless. Lord Clarendon, desired by the Queen as Palmerston's successor, declined office, and Lord Granville evaded a request for a general statement of the principles of action governing foreign affairs. Commenting on the situation, Clarendon remarked that the Queen and Prince Albert laboured under the curious misapprehension that the Foreign Office was their peculiar department and that they had a right to control, if not direct, the foreign policy of England. Fortunately, a crisis was averted by the tact of Ministers, but the difficulties arose basically because the Queen was being more conscientious than Parliament had grown used to. Indeed, the Queen was often more sensible about military operations, for example, than her Ministers, deploring the despatch of inadequate forces and doubtful generals to the Crimea and India, and pleading, without success, for a display of mercy after the Indian mutiny had been suppressed. In order to exercise her right of consultation, Queen Victoria always insisted on ample information. All lists of appointments, drafts of despatches, and outlines of proposed legislation were sent to her. Every night, a report was made to her by the Prime Minister. After every Cabinet meeting an additional report was also made. Palmerston and Gladstone submitted reports on the Cabinet in a form which did not reveal differences of opinion, whereas Disraeli informed the Queen of the various shades of opinion within the Cabinet. All despatches were generally submitted to the Queen and not altered afterwards. The first Liberal Government, comprising the Whigs and the Peelites, was formed under Palmerston in 1855.

The Queen acknowledged that her Ministers must do what they thought best and that the responsibility for what they did rested upon them, but whatever they thought best had her full and effectual support. Nevertheless, she reserved the right, and indeed had the duty, as necessary, to point out to them that what they proposed to do was, for one reason or another, bad, and that – for this reason and that – a course which they did not propose would be better. For example, Queen Victoria and her advisers were the first to realise the seriousness of the Indian Mutiny of 1857, and it was largely due to her insistence that sufficient reinforcements were available to save the situation. The Queen also exerted her influence to dampen down the anti-Indian hysteria created by the Indian atrocities, and to moderate the retribution that was exacted. A further instance of the value of royal advice was the intervention of Prince Albert in the Trent affair of 1861, when his tactful rewording of the Government's response to the boarding of a British ship by the United States Federal navy, and its forcible removal of two Confederate envoys, might well have averted British involvement in the American Civil War.[6] On the other hand, royal

---

6   Confederate states commissioners were removed from the British steamer, *Trent*, by a
     Federal steamer, *San Jacinto*, provoking a sharp protest from Great Britain and a risk of war.

intervention was not always helpful. Royal sympathies tended to take a legitimist view of foreign revolts, for example, over the Italian struggle for independence from Austria, while popular and Ministerial sympathy lay with the Italians. The Queen in 1877 threatened to abdicate over the Government's failure to give assistance to the Turks in the Russo-Turkish War. The attitude of the Queen may have been known to the Turkish Government and may have led them to discount the refusal of Ministers to assist them, so prolonging the conflict.

The Queen's influence was also evident in domestic policy. Thus, in 1867, the Tory Party took up the question of parliamentary reform at the instance of the Queen, and it was due to her influence that the opposition of various members of the Cabinet to certain clauses was eventually overcome. Disraeli was forced, on the insistence of the Queen, to adopt, as official Conservative policy, support for a Bill, introduced in 1874 by the Archbishop of Canterbury, to suppress ritualism in the Church of England. Again, in 1884, it was the Queen's intervention in the constitutional dispute between the House of Lords and House of Commons, concerning the redistribution to accompany the third Reform Bill, which resulted in a compromise. Whatever the merits or otherwise of royal influence on the actions of Ministers, as a Sovereign's reign increases in length, so he or she acquires knowledge and experience which few Ministers can equal. Indeed, a Sovereign endowed with intelligence and application has more experience of constitutional custom and practice, and more experience of affairs at the end of ten years than is possessed by the average Minister. It is the responsibility of the Minister, as a representative of the popular will, nevertheless to assess the sagacity of that advice, particularly in relation to the interests of his electors.

The Duke of York, the future George V, was set by his tutor to read Bagehot's *The English Constitution*, and to write a condensed version of the chapter on the Monarchy. The same view of the Monarchy, notably the notion of the three 'rights' – to advise, encourage, and warn – was to be taught to his successors, and at least the form of them is probably still being followed today.

33.2.1. The Doctrine of Ministerial Responsibility

In view of the shift in power from the King to the House of Commons, on the ground that the Commons represented the people, whereas the King did not (the principle of elected kingship having long been forgotten), it was increasingly believed that, in one important respect, the position of the King's Ministers should be altered. As holders of the King's commission, they were his agents in the management of affairs of state, and therefore responsible to him for their actions. This did not fit well with a House of Commons which now saw itself (as represented by its majority Party) as the elected Government, from whose members the King's Ministers were now drawn, and who saw themselves as answerable, not to the King, but to the Party, and through the Party to the electorate. It was a constitutional muddle, but one with which Parliament was quite happy, so long as the King did not try to influence his Ministers. This reorientation took time, however, and Queen Victoria still saw her Ministers as answerable to her as well as to the Party.

The rejection of the idea that the King's Ministers were his agents and representatives, which was obviously incompatible with the position of Ministers as elected members of Parliament, gave rise to various new propositions:

1. That Ministers were the representatives of their Party with a mandate from the electorate.

2. That Ministers could hardly be expected to impose their Party's wishes on those of the Crown, while leaving the King to take the blame for any mistakes that were made.

3. That it would be necessary in future for the King to choose his Ministers, not, firstly, because they were acceptable to him and, secondly, because they could control the House of Commons, but entirely because they could control the Commons, and that control would depend to an increasing degree upon their influence with the electorate.

4. That the resignations of Governments should depend, not on their ability to satisfy the wishes of the King, but on their failure to carry out their mandates from the electorate.

There was now confusion between the right and duty of the King to initiate policy in the public interest, in the light of advice that he received, as had previously been the case, and the right of his Ministers to initiate policy in the light of their Party's presumed mandate from the people. However, these changed perceptions would only form during Victoria's reign.

As head of the executive function of government, the King bore responsibility in common law for the proposing and enforcing of legislation, and, within the sphere of his prerogative, for the formulation and execution of day-to-day policy. It was a constitutional requirement in common law that he exercise this *imperium* with the advice of the Great Council – now a withered entity in the House of Lords, no longer known to the system of government that had been developing – and of the Privy Council; also, that legislation by statute be with the consent of Parliament, and that the exercise of the royal prerogative be within limits acceptable to both the Council and Parliament. The complexity of the modern world made it impracticable, in any case, for the King to exercise his executive function in person, requiring its delegation to his Ministers, whom he appointed for their demonstrated wisdom and ability in affairs of state. This, however, gave rise to a conundrum. As head of the executive, the Sovereign still bore the responsibility for any actions carried out in his name, yet feudal doctrine held that the Sovereign could do no wrong. This paradox was resolved in Victoria's reign by the doctrine of Ministerial responsibility, which was expressed in 1859 by the Prime Minister, Viscount Palmerston, as follows: 'The maxim of the British constitution is that the Sovereign can do no wrong, but that does not mean that no wrong can be done by Royal authority; it means that if wrong be done, the public servant who advised the act, and not the Sovereign, must be held answerable for the wrong-doing'.[7] This was, of course, at variance with the requirements of common law, according to which the King was responsible for his actions, and of those acting on his behalf, for which he could be deposed, yet this did not absolve his Ministers.

What Parliament was now proposing to do, on the grounds of royal ineptitude and the promotion of democratic government, was to appropriate to itself the role of the executive function of government,

7   A. C. Benson, and R. B. B. Esher (eds.), *The Letters of Queen Victoria* (London, 1908), iii. 449.

while retaining the legislative function for which it was appointed. The case was hardly in question, because, since the onset of the Middle Ages, Kings had been chosen on the basis of Church doctrine, not in accordance with the will of the people or their perceived competence but on a haphazard basis that only God was deemed to understand. Rather than rectify what had clearly gone wrong with the rules of succession, the Parties assumed that they were the obvious alternative. There was a clear fault in this view. The function of Parliament was, on behalf of the people, to approve the actions of the executive, not assume executive responsibilities for which they had no training and probably no aptitude. At worst, Parliament's policy could be interpreted as a gradual seizure of power for the pursuit of Party and personal interests.

33.3. Organisation and Control of the Executive: The Trevelyan Report (1854)

This was a period that reflected the sense of confusion that followed the establishment of the supremacy of the House of Commons over the Crown – not the supremacy of Parliament, because the King was part of, and central to, the workings of Parliament. The Commons had now appropriated most of the legislative and executive powers of the Crown, which it then re-delegated to those of its members whom it appointed, and to whom the King was now expected to grant his authority. Constitutionally, such bodies as the Poor Law Commission were established to exercise powers vested in them, not by the relevant Minister in the name of the King, who exercised this right with the approval of Parliament, but by the relevant Minister with the authority of the Commons. The House quickly learned the importance of making these bodies accountable to a designated Minister. Because Parliament had no executive powers, the new system worked only because a Minister was still appointed by the King, but on the advice of the appropriate representative of the Commons, and exercised his royal authority in the light of the advice that he received from the Commons. Also, the Commons were still dependent for its policies on a Bill that received the approval of the House of Lords and the assent of the King, although the

King's assent was now expected as a formality, as also was his proclamation of it as an Act of Parliament. Consequently, the procedure was little changed, except that the King's role was now reduced to what has been described as a 'post-box'.

In its pursuit of these innovations, the Commons was forgetting that it had been summoned into being expressly to represent the will and interests of the people, not to rule in place of the King. Equally, the King, in attributing his office to God, was oblivious of the requirement in common law, that his office was held by him at the will and sufferance of the people, to whom he was answerable. Totally forgotten, also, was that relations between King and Parliament, and the performance of each – bearing in mind that Parliament was merely a legislative body – were subject to the overview of the Great Council, in its capacity as the protector of the nation and ultimate authority on the common law of the constitution.

During the period of reform after 1832, new agencies were created to administer statutory schemes, such as the Poor Law and the Colonial Service, which were beyond the capacity of Ministers to supervise, except in general terms. Parliamentary dissatisfaction with these and other boards followed, and the confusion was resolved by ensuring that, in future, administration was conducted through a Minister and his department, in whom the powers were vested, and who sat in Parliament and so could be regarded as answerable. Thus, the Poor Law Commission in 1847 was replaced by a Ministry, and after the Northcote-Trevelyan report of 1854, there developed a principle of Ministerial responsibility to which the Civil Service deferred by assuming a position of anonymity. That is to say, the relevant section of the Civil Service did not involve itself other than in its capacity as agents of the Minister. The requirement for Ministers to be members of Parliament was, of course, to ensure that Ministerial offices were held by chosen members of Parliament and were answerable directly to Parliament. This answerability was achieved by requiring Ministers to be available in Parliament for the purpose of questioning.

Another formative influence on the executive was the Crimean War of 1854–6, fought over the Russian occupation of the Danubian Principalities. The conflict was essentially between Turkey and Russia, but Britain and France entered an alliance with the Turks, because of their concern that Russia was manoeuvring to occupy the Straits and so gain naval and political access to the Mediterranean. In the prevailing mood of national self-confidence that flowed from industrial strength and world influence, given an additional edge by the Anglo-Russian rivalry in Central Asia, it was not difficult to stir up a degree of popular enthusiasm for intervention on Turkey's behalf. As a music-hall song of the day expressed it:

> *'We don't want to fight, but by jingo if we do,*
> *We've got the ships, we've got the men, and got the money too.'*

The word 'jingo', originally a piece of conjuror's gibberish to announce the appearance of something unexpected, thus came to be applied to those who favoured intervention in the war, and were accordingly described as 'jingoists'. Later, it was used to denote anybody who displayed a bellicose form of nationalism. Russia, meanwhile, having now withdrawn from the Principalities, a strategy was adopted to invade the Crimea, with the object of depriving Russia of Sevastopol, which was its chief naval base in the Black Sea. The campaign went badly, with the allies unable to take the town, amid much evidence of administrative and military incompetence. The bad news from the Crimea, added to revelations by the Sevastopol Committee, directed public criticism to the administration of the various War departments, and through them to the departments of civil government. The attention of the House of Commons, itself culpable through its neglect of the armed forces, was drawn by various speakers to 'the manner in which merit and efficiency have been sacrificed in public appointments to party and family influences'.[8] The Civil Service was described by the Permanent Secretary to the Treasury as overstaffed in numbers, inactive, and incompetent.

The outcome was a report on the Civil Service by Sir Charles Trevelyan and Sir Stafford Northcote. The thinking in this had its origin in the earlier reform of the Indian Civil Service, following the exposure of the scale of corruption and scandal during the rule of the East India Company and the mixture of distaste and jealousy which it had aroused. The acceptance of bribes and gifts in the Indian service

---

8   W. C. Costin, and J. Steven Watson, *The Law and Working of the Constitution: Documents 1660–1914*, 465–7.

had been forbidden in 1765, and from 1813 recruits had been required to complete a period of study on India, and to produce a certificate of good conduct. Nevertheless, criticisms of the Indian Civil Service had continued, and a Parliamentary Committee under Lord Macaulay had been formed in 1835 to advise on further reforms, which had led to India having the first modern, professional civil service. Northcote and Trevelyan drew on the conclusions of the Macaulay Committee, and in their report, published in 1854, recommended the abolition of the system of direct appointment by the Crown to senior posts, known as patronage, and proposed the introduction of recruitment by open competition. This was achieved by an Order in Council of 1855. Civil Service Commissioners were appointed to oversee the new method of recruitment, and the system of direct royal appointment was phased out. An Order in Council of 1870 provided that all candidates for ordinary posts should also, at the discretion of departmental heads, sit an open competitive examination. Almost all the chief departments quickly adopted the new Order, the only notable exception being the Foreign Office. Although the system of royal appointments at the discretion of the Crown was discontinued, nevertheless, all senior appointments to the Civil, as well as the Military Services, remained royal appointments in common law, although now on the basis of the requirements laid down. For the first time, the administration of the country was in the hands of an able and largely incorruptible Civil Service, independently based on ability, and this was undoubtedly one of the outstanding features of British government in the nineteenth century. In this, it owed much to the experience of the Empire.

It was never in question that the Sovereign – now Queen Victoria – had the right and the duty to rule, or to appoint those who acted on her behalf. The impossibility of ruling effectively without the cooperation of the House of Commons, however, had made it essential to appoint Ministers who commanded its support. The first to be chosen must, therefore, be the Prime Minister, who must, under the new arrangement, be the most effective leader in the majority Party. This needed to be demonstrated before he was appointed, and it was accordingly the practice for the Sovereign to entrust the prospective Prime Minister with the task of forming an administration. This placed the onus on the Prime

Minister designate to submit to the Sovereign the names of individuals for Ministerial appointment. His ability to form a credible administration was then accepted as proof of his influence within his Party, and that he was able to find the support of colleagues in whom he had confidence. If his administration were to be effective, it must also have a consensus of sorts on policy matters, and the personalities concerned must be capable of working with each other. It was then for the Sovereign to accept or reject the names put forward. Victoria did, indeed, feel that the choice was ultimately hers to make. After all, every Minister exercised her powers on her behalf, not the Prime Minister's. Her personal animosities and occasional spitefulness aside, Victoria believed that, as Queen, she had an ultimate duty to protect the interests of the country and its constitution; the Prime Minister – Party vested interests aside – felt that he was answerable to the electorate for the policies of the Government.

For some time, the office of Lord High Treasurer had been filled by five Lords Commissioners. They comprised the First Lord, the Chancellor of the Exchequer as Second Lord, and three junior Lords. Legally, they had, for the most part, equal powers, and during the eighteenth century they had met as a board, and this practice of holding formal meetings for the transaction of business was continued until 1856, when they were discontinued.[9] Control fell more and more into the hands of the Chancellor of the Exchequer, with the junior Lords relegated very much to a subordinate status. The First Lord of the Treasury, meanwhile, was left with very little official work, and was usually appointed to the role of Prime Minister. Meanwhile, Acts of Parliament began to refer to 'the Treasury', and an Act of 1849 declared this to mean that the requisite Bill should be signed by two of the Commissioners. The importance of this signing function was clear from the fact that, when Parliament had granted a supply to the Sovereign, no money might leave the Exchequer without a warrant under the royal sign manual, countersigned by two Lords of the Treasury, and no money voted by Parliament might be spent until the King had signed a warrant which had been countersigned by the Lords of the Treasury.

Apart from the importance of Treasury signing powers, no less significant was the huge number of documents typically requiring the King's signature. During the incapacity of George III in 1811, in order

9   W. R. Anson, *The Law and Custom of the Constitution*, ii. 172.

to enable Ministers to obtain money, Parliament had passed a resolution authorising and commanding the issue of money, to which the King had been in no condition to give his consent. It is doubtful, therefore, whether the resolution and subsequent release of money had been legal.[10] When George IV found it difficult to write, an Act of Parliament in 1830 authorised the use of a stamp, to be affixed in his presence.

By and large, the Queen acceded to the Prime Minister's advice in respect of the appointment of her other Ministers, but there was ample room for conflict. Thus, after 1851, the Queen vigorously opposed the appointment of Palmerston as Foreign Secretary. In 1886, the Prime Minister's nominee for the War Office was unsuccessful. On taking office in 1895, Chamberlain had to explain away his republican views, and the career of Dilke was cut short by the Queen's objection to his divorce. Up to this time, however, political Parties were poorly organised and often had no definite leaders, and sometimes a number of rival leaders. In 1859, for example, Russell and Palmerston were rivals for leadership of the Whig Party, and the Queen therefore sent for Lord Granville as an alternative to both of them. It was only when Granville proved unable to form a Government, because Russell refused to serve under him, that the Queen finally sent for Palmerston. Such divisions left a considerable onus on the Queen in deciding whom to call upon.

In 1871, the Queen lost control of the army. At the same time, the Lords Lieutenant were deprived of their control of the county militias (the *fyrd* of earlier times). Parliament had long exercised an indirect control over the army through the system of annual appropriations, but actual control of the armed forces belonged constitutionally to the Crown, and Victoria always felt that the armed forces fell under her personal control. As a result, the position of the army was equivocal, its actual control being vested in the Commander-in-Chief, appointed from the Horse Guards, normally a royal nominee or a member of the royal family. A second system of control was based on the War Office, but the Queen now had little say in the appointment of the Secretary of State for War, who was linked with the Government of the day. Consequently, the two authorities – the Commander-in-Chief and the Secretary of State – were almost independent of each other, and the limits of their conflicting powers were ill-defined. The harsh lessons of the Crimean War showed that this,

10   F. W. Maitland, *The Constitutional History of England*, 408–9.

among other aspects of military management, was no longer tenable, and Cardwell, at this time the Secretary of State for War under Gladstone's ministry, set about a comprehensive reform of the British army. In what are known as the Cardwell reforms, the Army Regulation Act of 1871 abolished the system of purchasing commissions and the right to hold commissions on any other basis than regular promotion according to ability. In pursuit of this principle, and in order to remove the previous confusion, the Act placed the army wholly under the control of the War Office. It also changed the terms of service, thereby establishing a trained reserve. The reform of the army was ongoing during the latter part of the century, and in 1899, as a result of experience of the use of camouflage in India, the red coats of the army were replaced by 'khaki' field uniforms, the word having been taken from the Urdu for 'dust-coloured'. While the reforms brought a great improvement in military efficiency, the complete appropriation of the army resulted in a growing estrangement between the Queen and Gladstone.

33.3.1. Relations Between Queen Victoria and Her Ministers

Bagehot's prescription of the royal right to advise was exercised publicly over Gladstone's policy in Egypt in 1884–5, which exposed, as never before, the demerits of government by Parliament. The British fleet had bombarded Alexandria in 1882, in response to a nationalist uprising in which many Europeans had been killed, and which posed a threat to the Suez Canal, as well as to all Christian communities. It was followed by a British restoration of the corrupt and incompetent Khedive in the following year. Meanwhile, the Sudan, through which the Nile flowed and which was 'a model of misery, a market for slave caravans, a hive of Arab fighting-men and petty tyrants', and which was under the nominal rule of Egypt, had seen the emergence in 1881 of a fanatical *Mahdi*, or 'Messiah', in revolt against the Egyptians. In 1883 the rebels exterminated an Egyptian army led by a British commander, Hicks. A public clamour at home to save the Egyptians in the Sudan forced the Government to appoint a legendary but impulsive commander, General Gordon, to organise the evacuation of the garrison and refugees from the territory, appointing him Governor-General of the Sudan for the purpose. Gladstone was opposed to further involvement in the Sudan, regarding the *Mahdi*'s followers, who, over the next two decades, were to be responsible for obliterating three-quarters of the population, as a people 'rightly struggling to be free'.[11] The Queen disapproved of her Ministers' decision to evacuate the Sudan, but, when Gordon then pointed out that an evacuation would involve fighting, for which he needed reinforcements, and requested the employment of Zebehr Pasha for the purpose, this was refused. This was due to the opposition of the House of Commons to the use of Zebehr Pasha, who had been a great slave-trader, although, ironically, the evacuation of the Sudan would have abandoned it to slavery. It is possible that Gordon failed to withdraw from Khartoum more in the hope of forcing the Government to provide him with enough forces to defeat the *Mahdi*, in order to avoid relinquishing the Sudan, than because he was unwilling to risk exposing his force to annihilation by leaving the defensive protection of Khartoum. Whatever Gordon's motives, by March 1884, he was surrounded there by the *Mahdi*'s overwhelming numbers. Gordon now requested that forces at Suakin, on the east coast of the Sudan, be used to open up an escape corridor, but a group of her Ministers, led by Gladstone, feeling themselves to be drawn into the situation against their will, and blaming Gordon, who had antagonised them by referring to 'smashing the *Mahdi*', and describing the abandonment of the garrisons as an 'indelible disgrace', refused, Gladstone asserting that Gordon was in no danger. Public attention at this time was still focussed on a new, third Reform Bill. The British agent in Egypt, Sir Evelyn Baring, now warned that it was necessary to send a relief force, for which General Sir Garnet Wolseley was already available in Egypt, but Ministers, furious at the turn of events, chose to let General Gordon stew where he was. The Queen disapproved of the delay, and wrote to Gordon's sister, expressing this view. She also suggested to General Wolseley that he resign his commission in order to bring pressure to bear on the Ministers. The Queen was also in touch with the Liberal leaders, Hartington and Goschen, in an effort to force Gladstone's hand, and Baring reproached the Government for being 'deaf to humanity and honour', but it was not until August that an ultimatum from Hartington compelled Gladstone's faction to make a decision. Consequently, it was not until October that Wolseley's force set out, but it took until

11   K. Feiling, *A History of England*, 988.

January to fight its way to Khartoum, by which time it was too late. There was an upsurge of national indignation and a motion of censure in the Commons, which Gladstone barely won, and the Queen sent open telegrams criticising the 'frightful' delay and referring to 'the stain left upon England'. Although the Queen's disapproval of Gladstone's policies and prevarications over the issue was probably right, and undoubtedly had popular support, this public expression by the Sovereign had come to be regarded as quite unconstitutional, because it confused the issue of accountability. It was fortunate that, in Gladstone, the Queen was at least dealing with a Minister who had the greatest respect for the Monarchy. If the common law of the constitution had been applied, it is more than likely that the Great Council would have seen a need to exert its influence in the issue.

It may be said that the general election of 1880 was the first in which the electorate chose the Prime Minister. Disraeli's second Ministry had run from 1874, and the country was in the grip of economic depression and unrest. Gladstone, a man much dedicated to humanitarian principles and the interests of minorities abroad, gained considerable support from speeches in Midlothian, in which he denounced the Government for both its domestic policies and its imperialism. Largely on the former account, the Liberals won the election, but the Queen refused to accept Gladstone as her Prime Minister. The only other Liberal leaders, Hartington in the Commons and Granville in the Lords, did not enjoy the support of the Liberals as a whole, nor of the electorate, and Gladstone refused any position other than that of Prime Minister. The Queen eventually had to give way.

A more difficult problem arose in 1885, after Gladstone had resigned over an amendment to his budget, and been succeeded by a Conservative Ministry of caretakers under Lord Salisbury. In the ensuing general election, the Conservative Party was defeated, but the election was remarkable in that, while the Liberals as a whole won a clear majority, severe divisions appeared in the Party over the question of Home Rule for Ireland. The pattern in the Commons was confused further by the substantial Party of Irish Nationalists under the leadership of Parnell, who antagonised many by his abusiveness. Gladstone, formerly opposed to Home Rule, now secretly favoured it. With the Liberal Party divided and demoralised, not least by Gladstone's furtiveness, the Government was defeated, with elements of the Liberals uniting with the Conservatives over the issue to form the Unionist Party. Thus, the issue of Home Rule shattered the old grouping of Parties. The Queen declared that, in view of the peculiar views of Gladstone, she did not want him as her Prime Minister. Her inclination, and the advice of Lord Salisbury, was towards the formation of a moderate coalition, and she therefore sent for Goschen.

The Queen's Secretary saw Goschen, who advised him to see Gladstone, pointing out the danger of delay if the public should associate this with the Queen's dislike for Gladstone. On this occasion, the Queen was not trying to secure a Party with popular support, but was trying to defeat Gladstone and so prevent home rule for Ireland. There is no doubt that Gladstone controlled the greater body of popular support in the new Parliament, but, equally, this support did not extend to the question of home rule. Indeed, Gladstone was invited subsequently to form a Ministry early in 1886, which then introduced his Home Rule Bill, but this was then defeated in the House of Commons. Parliament was thereupon dissolved, and in the election that followed Gladstone was defeated on the critical home rule issue. It seemed that the Queen's interpretation of the popular will had been correct, and, indeed, there is no doubt that it was accepted that the Queen had the right to judge that the Party leader did not represent the people. After the great struggle between Disraeli and Gladstone, however, the extension of the franchise and the development of Party machines, which centred popular attention on Party leaders, the need for the Sovereign to exercise judgement regarding the choice of Prime Ministers began to decline. At the same time, the Queen's right and duty to act over issues of popular support exposed the Prime Minister to a far greater political risk. Meanwhile, it increasingly came to be regarded that the Sovereign should abide by the advice of the Prime Minister in the matter of the choice of her other Ministers.

The Queen took advice on constitutional questions from other politicians and lawyers who were not in office, as well as from her Prime Minister, and she sometimes gave advice where she saw a need, but such was the state of flux in constitutional perceptions that there is no doubt that Victoria's reign saw a shift. Actions by her that, at the beginning of her reign, were accepted as being within her entitlement were, by the end of her reign, becoming regarded as unconstitutional. Her correspondence with Lord Melbourne, both in and out of office, was followed by discourse with Disraeli, both in and out of office. By the time of the latter, such freedom of contact was regarded as unacceptable, particularly as Disraeli did not treat it with the discretion that it deserved.

33.3.2. Parliament Cannot Separate the King from the Crown

While the policy of transferring the executive powers of the King to Parliament, and with them the responsibility for the Ministry, was seen by Parliament as a practical solution to the need for Ministers to be answerable directly to Parliament, this could not be reconciled constitutionally, either with feudal doctrine or with the requirements of common law. According to the former, the King was answerable to God alone, and so could not surrender his rights. Parliament was evidently thinking in terms of common law, in so far as it was still understood, which was very little. If we assume that William IV had been elected by the people, as the coronation procedure provided, even though he was deemed to have received his right to rule from God, through the Archbishop of Canterbury, it was within his right, nevertheless, to delegate all or part of his executive powers to his Ministers, to rule on his behalf, but they remained answerable to him and, through him, to the people assembled in Parliament. Parliament was a legislative body, with no executive function. Consequently, Ministers could not derive their powers from Parliament, even though they might be answerable to it, through the King. Parliament tried to get around this by propounding the doctrine of Ministerial responsibility. In origin, however, this referred only to those acts that exceeded the royal prerogative. Ministers could have no constitutional powers of their own. Consequently, if Ministers ceased to derive their powers from the King, they could obtain them from no other source. Nor could they be appointed by anybody but the King, whose servants or agents they were.

It followed that it was constitutionally impossible to separate the Crown, or its Ministers, from the King, who alone could appoint them. All that Parliament could do was to require that Ministers be answerable to it through the King, rather than the King being answerable in person.

This principle was already recognised in the right of Parliament to impeach the King's Ministers, but not the King himself.[12] The King was personally answerable to Parliament now only for his domestic expenses, where they exceeded the provision made. Even the nature of the revenues was liable to be understood. They were the King's revenues, raised by him, either in accordance with his rights in common law, or in accordance with the consent of the people, whose interests were represented by Parliament.

While Parliament appeared to have placed itself in full control of public expenditure, in addition to the right to approve new taxes, it had no executive power to levy them. Only the King had the executive authority, through his Minister, to collect the public revenue. Equally, whilst the direction and extent of public expenditure were now subject to parliamentary approval, only the King, through his Ministers, had the executive power to spend it.

It is evident that Parliament was confused as to the nature of the royal authority, and this brings us back to the executive right of the King to rule. In common law, the people exercised their right, through Parliament, or by means of a referendum, to elect the new King, in this case George IV, but the *imperium* was held by the Great Council, in its capacity as the custodian of the people, which, in its turn, bestowed it upon each new ruler. However, the men of the shires appear to have been unable to elect new members to fill vacancies in the Council since the eleventh century, and since the fourteenth century it had been able to function only as the House of Lords. Unless it is to be accepted that there had been no legitimate ruler since the Early Middle Ages, and therefore no statute law since that time, it must follow that successive Kings had continued to receive their *imperium* from the Council in its capacity as – in effect – the greater baronage in the House of Lords; furthermore, that vacancies in the Council had continued to be filled by appointment by senior members of the House of Lords and, once crowned, the King. The consent of the free men of the shires in question can only have been presumed. It had been a thoroughly unsatisfactory arrangement, but, without it, all legitimacy of government must have ceased in the Early Middle Ages.

---

12   Except where the gravity of the King's transgression was such as to merit his deposition; but for this the authority of the Great Council was also needed.

33.3.3. The 'Crown' Accepts New Responsibilities

The constitutional effects of the decline of rural England and the growth of large towns was not limited to electoral issues. They created a demand for the government to accept a whole new range of responsibilities, which it was reluctant to do, not only because they required additional expenditures, and therefore heavier taxes, but also because it had never been conceived that it was a function of the King to manage the lives of the people, beyond enforcing the law. The people were no longer self-reliant, however. They had been driven off the land, which had always provided the means of subsistence, and their communities had been broken up. They were now the victims of a different world in which they also faced new problems, with over-crowded housing, pollution, industrial and mining injuries, malnutrition, the rapid spread of diseases in congested areas, and a high incidence of crime as well as an ever-present risk of unemployment and destitution.

The stresses of the new, urban society and the development of new technology offered a fertile ground for thinkers who could suggest new explanations for this harrowing, yet stimulating, tide in human affairs. The Church had nothing to offer, except the prospect of retribution for sin and the prospect, for others, of a better life after death. During the eighteenth and nineteenth centuries, therefore, new hypotheses about society and its welfare sprang up, while for those who retained their religious convictions, it was not difficult to place the blame on a wealthy, self-serving Church that had lost its way. Mutual self-help was one solution, and accusing the upper classes of avarice was another. The new deficit in human welfare could only be met by the Government, but it was an entirely new range of responsibilities that the Government accepted with some reluctance.

34. THE RESTORATION
OF THE FREEMAN

34.1. The Coronation Oath and the Church

Although the religious conflict within the country had apparently been removed by the Glorious Revolution, the position of the Crown in relation to the Church was again coming under attack from certain quarters. It was argued by the Catholics in Ireland and the Nonconformists in Wales that it was unjust that the Church of England and Ireland should be singled out for privileged treatment, bearing in mind that it represented only a minority in those two countries. Nationalism was particularly strong in Ireland, and in 1869 the Irish Church Bill sought to dissolve the union between the two Churches and to disestablish the Church of Ireland. The Queen saw this, however, as a direct challenge to her Coronation Oath, which had pledged her to 'maintain the Protestant reformed religion established by law' and to 'maintain and preserve inviolately the settlement of the Church of England and Ireland and the doctrine, worship, discipline and government thereof as by law established, within the Kingdoms of England and Ireland'. The Bill proposed, however, to break up the Church and renounce the settlement of its Irish part, and was therefore one which the Queen could not have signed and enacted without terminating her constitutional right to rule. The only courses open to her were to reject the Bill or to abdicate, of which she did neither.

It may be argued that she acted in accordance with the feudal principle that the Sovereign's position was unchallengeable; that she could not be bound by any previous undertakings that she might have given; and that she could do as she saw fit. Such an argument could not have been acceptable to Parliament, which, by the Glorious Revolution, had specifically renounced the feudal view of kingship. That the Queen now so violated her oath of office, in order to accommodate the wishes of Gladstone's Liberal Ministry and of Parliament, marked a return to the unconstitutional government that was already evident in Pitt's day. Gladstone undoubtedly took the view that, because of the devolution of royal powers, such decisions were now the responsibility of the Queen's Ministers. Nevertheless, the Queen, and therefore her Ministers, were still bound by her Coronation Oath, which had been required of her by the people. It may be argued that the resulting Irish Church Act was in accordance with the will of the people, but the will of the people had already specified what the Queen might and might not do for the duration of her reign. Part of the purpose of the Coronation Oath was to ensure the longer-term consistency of government. It might be held that an offending part of the Coronation Oath could be amended, provided it was agreed by the Sovereign and endorsed in a general election held specifically for the purpose, or in a freely held referendum, followed by a service of dedication of the new Oath in the same cathedral as the coronation had been held, but no such amendment was considered. The Queen violated her oath by approving the Bill, rendering her liable, under the common law of the Constitution, to be deposed.

Pressure in the latter part of the nineteenth century for the disestablishment of the Church in England followed the widening of the franchise and the removal of restrictions on the entry into Parliament of those who did not belong to the Church, itself possibly a contravention by the Queen of her Oath by summoning them.[1] To some of these, the Church of England represented the preserve of the landed gentry and a source of privilege. Welsh members of Parliament, who were adherents of the Free Churches, agitated for the disestablishment of the Church of Wales, to which Queen Victoria objected at last on the ground that this would be the first step towards the disestablishment and disendowment of the Church of England. Indeed, Gladstone, still the Prime Minister in 1885, claimed in a speech in Midlothian that 'the severance of the Church of England from the State' was a question to which 'the foundations of discussion had already been laid'.[2] The general election of 1906, which marked a return of the Liberals to government, was the first to produce a House of Commons which was not predominantly Anglican, and ten

---

1   Probably not, however, because common law assumes the existence of only one religious belief, and accordingly makes no distinctions on religious grounds.

2   Cited in Earl of Selborne, *A Defence of the Church of England against Dis-establishment*, xi.

years later Lloyd George became the first non-Anglican Prime Minister. It posed the question, not only of whether the Queen could appoint as her Prime Minister someone who was not an adherent of the established Church without violating her oath of office, but also how a Parliament and Government dominated by non-Anglicans could legislate for an established Church of which they were not members, and in such a way as neither the Church nor the Sovereign, as its head, might find acceptable. Parliament had no jurisdiction, in any case, over the Church in spiritual matters without the approval of the First Estate, represented by the general Synod of the Church of England. Relations between Church and State hinged on the Sovereign in her spiritual capacity, and this also was beyond the competence of Parliament. The Sovereign was enthroned in accordance with the religious beliefs of the nation, however nominal they might now be, and her authority to rule derived in part from that source, in the sense that the *imperium* had been bestowed upon her at the coronation. In common law, monarchy was difficult to reconcile with a secular state. The problem was the acceptance by the population of a common religious belief, but its fragmentation into various sects, for which common law made no provision. Nevertheless, only the established Church enjoyed a widespread common acceptance as the channel for religious belief for the benefit of the people as a whole. It also had the advantage of continuity, and continuity was important in constitutional matters.

In spite of these difficulties, no attempt was made after Victoria's death to change the terms of the royal oath, so as to provide for exceptions in Ireland and Wales, until the accession of George V, when the reference in the Coronation Oath was changed from the 'Church in England and Ireland' to the 'Church of England'. During his reign, the Church in Wales, which was an extension of the Church of England, was disestablished in 1914, but the King had already sworn to 'maintain and preserve inviolately the settlement of the Church of England', by which his Ministers and Parliaments were equally bound. Consequently, the reform involved, once again, an unwarranted presumption that a constitutional commitment could be overridden by statute. One is left with the impression that, while the House of Commons was tenacious about its own supposed constitutional rights, it paid scant attention to constitutional requirements that did not affect it, unless they stood in its way. Not least, the Irish Church Act and the Bill to disestablish its Welsh counterpart came at a time of growing dismissal of the constitutional importance of the Monarchy, yet this was at a time when it was as important as it had ever been.

34.2. The Sovereign's Private Secretary

Until 1805, the Home Secretary had been responsible for the King's official correspondence and had been his constitutional adviser, as well as being responsible for the work of the Home Office. This had not been a satisfactory arrangement, but there had been opposition to the appointment of a Private Secretary to the King, for fear that he would come between the King and his Ministers, so restricting Ministerial influence at a time when a conflict of interest was still believed to exist between the King, on the one hand, and his Ministers and Parliament on the other. The first Private Secretary to the Sovereign, Sir Herbert Taylor, was appointed in 1805, owing to the blindness of George III, which was preventing him from dealing with his correspondence. As Taylor was known to be a Tory, this arrangement met with the approval of Pitt, who was the Prime Minister at the time. Even so, the alarm of the House of Commons was expressed in a debate in 1812, when it was argued that it was unconstitutional to allow a Private Secretary access to Cabinet secrets, or for the King to communicate with his Prime Minister through a third person.[3] In response, it was explained that the office was intended only to meet a temporary situation, and that a Sovereign in full possession of his faculties would not require such assistance. However, the Prince Regent – later George IV – had appointed his own Private Secretary in 1812. Meanwhile, upon succeeding to the throne in his turn, William IV reappointed Sir Herbert Taylor as his Private Secretary. Taylor seems to have fostered in the King's mind a new view of his obligation towards his Ministers, in particular, that the King should not go against them over the Reform Bill, even though Taylor himself disliked it. He did his best to help Ministers in getting it passed in 1832, by writing to Tory Peers on the King's behalf, asking them to be absent for the critical

3   V. Bogdanor, *The Monarchy and the Constitution*, 197–214.

division, in order that the Bill could go through. Even this did not stop the criticism that the Private Secretary was 'an irresponsible advisor, who exerted undue influence over the Sovereign by intruding his own views at the expense of those of his Ministers'.[4]

Queen Victoria found herself unable to manage without a Private Secretary, and eventually her husband, Prince Albert, effectively assumed the role. After his death, she used General Grey for the purpose, but it was not until 1867 that the post became officially recognised. It was then remunerated from the Civil List, not, as it had been under George IV and William IV, from the Privy Purse, from which the Sovereign's domestic expenses were paid. Undoubtedly, this arrangement was intended to ensure that the post was obligated as much towards Parliament as towards the Queen. Although, from this time onwards, Private Secretaries understood their role as being to assist the Sovereign in his or her relations with Ministers of all Parties; nevertheless, for some time they did not hesitate to proclaim their Party affiliations.

34.3. The Psychological Role of Monarchy

The Monarchy has tended to set the tone of British society. Under the Regency, and indeed under the Hanoverians generally, London society bubbled and was intellectually stimulated. There was some resentment at the dour regime imposed by Victoria, but she and her husband opened up a new era of moral integrity and dedication to the national interest. Fashionability and a degree of social levity returned under the influence of her son, Edward, whose philanderings troubled the national conscience less in 1890 than the revelation of his involvement in the illegal game of baccarat. Albert and Victoria had produced a large family, with four girls and four boys, and between them they projected a well justified image of happy domesticity. This contrasted with most previous reigns, when royal consorts and children had largely been hidden from the public eye. This picture of the central role of the family, aided by the Queen's sound political instincts and Albert's discretion, did much to account for the great popularity of the Monarchy at this time.

---

4   Ibid. 199.

The death in 1861 of her beloved Albert, the Prince Consort, not only removed one of the most able and influential men of the age, and an invaluable basis of support for Victoria, but so distressed her that, although she kept in touch with public affairs through her Prime Minister, she withdrew altogether from public life into the seclusion of Osborne House, on the Isle of Wight, and Balmoral. Far from disappearing from the public ken, however, this caused her to become very unpopular. It was felt that she was not earning the grants made to her from public funds, but this mercenary explanation is hardly enough to account for the growing depth of public hostility. Because Victoria had enjoyed great personal popularity, the resentment that her years of seclusion caused can be interpreted in only one way: the function of monarchy was not only constitutional; it was also psychological. Victoria's reclusiveness in no way interfered with the constitutional process, but it did deprive the people of a very important psychological support. The Monarchy served as the focus of national identity and as the colourful binding element in the sense of social coherence, and it provided, certainly in the case of Victoria, a figure to look up to, even if one did not always approve of it. In short, it was the Monarchy that in large measure gave the people their sense of nationhood and their sense of being a single society. By contrast, politicians were always divisive. This aspect of the Sovereign's role is of key importance, and one that is often overlooked. Never was the importance of this function more apparent than during the years of Queen Victoria's withdrawal from public life, during which the people felt not only deprived, but spurned. Indeed, resentment towards the Queen verged on a widespread republicanism; yet, in a perverse sense, Victoria's unpopularity was a measure of her popularity and constitutional importance. The critical period of the Monarchy came to an end unexpectedly in 1871, when the heir to the throne, Victoria and Albert's second child, 'Bertie', contracted typhoid fever, like his father, and was not expected to live. His seemingly miraculous recovery so overjoyed the Queen that the spell was broken, and at a formal thanksgiving service, Victoria not only appeared in public again for the first time since the Prince Consort's death, but she did so in robes trimmed with ermine. The popularity of the Queen and of the Monarchy were suddenly transformed, and she never again withdrew from public life.

Meanwhile, the marriage in 1858 of Victoria's eldest child, Victoria, to Frederick, the future King of Prussia and German Emperor, caused the Queen some anguish, because it meant that she, a mere Queen, would be outranked by her Empress daughter. Great Britain was by now the leading economic and imperial power in the world, but any prospect of her being re-designated as Empress of Great Britain, no matter how appropriate, was ruled out of the question by a popular antipathy to imperial titles since the time of Napoleon. In one of his most clever moves, Disraeli, the Conservative Prime Minister of the day, found a solution to this problem which not only preserved the right of the British monarchy to deal with that of Germany on equal terms, but had the effect of focussing public attention on the Empire, which had been expanding at a phenomenal rate. Under the Royal Titles Bill of 1876, the Queen was granted the title of 'Empress of India'. The Queen was flattered and it caused great enthusiasm in India, but it was opposed by the Liberals, who were antagonised by any elevation of the Crown, seeing it as un-English, and arguing that the title had disreputable associations with the fallen French Emperor, Napoleon III, and the tragic Emperor Maximilian of Mexico. However, the proposal neatly avoided applying Napoleonic affectations to Britain itself, and it soon won popular approval. The opposition of the Liberals was muted by a promise that the title would not be used in Great Britain, and Victoria was proclaimed Empress in Delhi in the following year. It is probably the only example in history where a ruler was an emperor by virtue of being a king. Indeed, George V would be proclaimed in Delhi in 1910 as 'King Emperor'.

In spite of its demotion by Parliament to a nominal role, the ritual of Monarchy underwent a notable development in the reign of Queen Victoria and her successors. Her assumption of the dignity of Empress of India drew attention to the paucity of formal ceremonial in Britain, compared with other states that were ruled by emperors, notably Austria, Russia and Germany. Britain was no longer a second-rate power on the fringe of Europe. Quite apart from the question of simple dynastic rivalry, it was becoming realised that the indigenous inhabitants of much of the Empire expected the pomp and ceremonial of authority to be proportional to the status of the ruler. Constitutional monarchy was a subtle concept that was not understood in much of Empire, and it was confusing to be presented with a ruler who did not display evidence of her position. After all, prominence and self-confidence were the essence of good and effective leadership, and a leader who tried to hide himself or herself was hardly one to inspire trust, or to exhibit the sort of power and authority in which people were likely to place much confidence. Even within Great Britain, this question of the display of royal authority and occasion, if only as the personification of power, involved issues that went deep into the popular psyche, because the people identified with it. At the very least, it was now felt that an Empress should be treated as such, with formal parades and processions to mark the royal progress on state occasions, including the lying in state of the dead monarch and the coronation of their successor. Much of this ritual in other countries had been taken from the example of Rome, which in turn owed much to Oriental practices, but they seem also to have included less flamboyant Indo-European traditions which had long been neglected.

The popularity of the Monarchy reached its height in the Golden Jubilee of 1887, which brilliantly drew attention to the Queen's role as the symbol of Imperial unity, and yet again in the spectacle of the Diamond Jubilee of 1897. These celebrations, particularly the latter, marked a key point in British history. The British Empire had almost reached its greatest extent and it was firmly centred on London. The Industrial Revolution had made Britain into the world's leading economic power, transforming the country and giving it an almost unlimited self-confidence. It was a mood that found expression in the observation of Cecil Rhodes that to be born an Englishman was to win first prize in the lottery of life. When Victoria was born, Britain had been a predominantly rural country; now, it was overwhelmingly urban. Yet this rapid transformation had brought widespread poverty and deprivation in the form of urban slums and a harsh and bleak industrial existence. What the country needed was a colourful and uplifting element, bringing brightness and diversion into public life, to lift people out of the drudgery of daily existence, and one, moreover, which they could feel a part of, and this was provided by a marked increase in state pageantry. Nor was the ceremonial based on artificial colour and display, but gave visible effect to centuries of constitutional tradition and practice.

Until Victoria's reign, and more particularly since the Middle Ages, the Monarchy had set only a limited store on public display. It has been said that the Hanoverians had been too busy entertaining themselves to be troubled with entertaining the masses, but Victoria's reign had hitherto been marked by informality and a total lack of ostentation, largely at the insistence of Albert and Victoria themselves, but also because the House of Commons made little financial provision for such matters, having long been concerned to minimise the importance of the Monarchy. Foreign competition and the national exuberance of the period opened up a new perspective. The establishment itself had become inept, and the Queen's coronation had been marked by such informality and sloppiness as to cause public disapproval. Due in no small part to the perceptiveness of Disraeli and Gladstone, the latter part of Victoria's reign marked a complete reversal. The pomp and pageantry of the two Jubilees and, to some extent, a restoration of the Medieval splendour of the Crown, provided the tonic which the country needed, and it was accentuated by the very large and extremely popular Imperial component, in the form of military and other contingents from all over the Empire. The centre-piece of this national celebration was the Monarchy itself. Indeed, through the marriages of her various children, the Queen was now regarded as the grandmother of Europe, for her grandchildren included the future Emperor of Germany, Wilhelm II, and Alice, the Tsarina of Russia. There was hardly a royal family in Europe that did not have a matrimonial link with Victoria, and most were present at her Diamond Jubilee. The royal pageantry, so restored, was destined to continue to mark state occasions during the following century.

34.3.1. The Dynasty of Saxe-Coburg and Gotha

Victoria was destined to rule for over sixty years, and, despite the loss of most of the American colonies, two of the features most associated with her reign were the accelerated growth of the British Empire, until it became the greatest in history, and the popular enthusiasm which accompanied it. Under her reign, indeed, the destiny of the British people reached its zenith, with the Monarchy emerging in a blaze of glory under the Imperial Crown. Yet the cost was high, as the Empire became littered with the isolated graves of men who had died 'for Queen and Empire'. Still more were unmarked, their occupants having died lonely deaths as the victims of malaria, blackwater fever, sleeping sickness, dysentery, typhoid fever and snakebite, not to mention wild animals, such as lion, leopard and African buffalo. Yet the Imperial glow and the glitter, and the sheer majesty of the Crown, hid the stark reality that the constitutional standing of the Monarchy was already seriously undermined; that the star of the constitution was in rapid decline as it was pushed aside. After the exuberance of the Imperial Age, the nation's morale could only go into decline.

With Victoria, the Hanoverian dynasty reached its end, and she was succeeded in 1901 by her eldest son, Edward, whose father had been Albert, the Prince Consort. Edward VII was, therefore, the founder of a new dynasty, that of Saxe-Coburg and Gotha. If the House of Hanover had been descended from Azzo II of Este, the House of Saxe-Coburg and Gotha traced its lineage back to Dietrich, Count of Hassegau, who had died about 982. His descendant, Thimo, had built the castle at Wettin, on the River Saale in Thuringia, from which the dynasty had thereafter derived its ancestral name. Each branch of the family had then superimposed upon the name of Wettin the names of the estates which they, in turn, had inherited, in accordance with the feudal custom followed on the Continent. In the case of Albert's branch of the family, this was Saxe-Coburg and Gotha. This proliferation was a consequence of the Salian Frankish custom of dividing an inheritance between the sons, without which most would have disappeared from history, as had happened in England.

King Edward was already sixty years of age at the time of his accession, and had been little involved in state affairs. Just as his mother had been more and more excluded from the practical workings of politics in her later years, so also was Edward VII, as a result of which he was inexperienced in matters of state. The process of exclusion from active government was furthered, in any case, by the fact that he displayed little interest. Consequently, Edward's position in relation to his Ministers was not as sound, or his influence as great, as his mother's had been. Victoria had set a dangerous precedent, however, in her dislike of constitutional formalities and ceremony, even delegating the opening of Parliament. Various of her predecessors in the Middle Ages had, similarly, left the opening of Parliaments to their Chancellors, but at least they had been present themselves, and had presided over the proceedings. Victoria's slackness had been offset by her huge popularity, but it had ceased to remind the people and the politicians of constitutional realities, which some had been inclined to forget. Edward VII rectified this. Being fond of ceremonial occasions and a stickler for the formalities of state, he insisted on his coronation being restored to its earlier splendour, and resumed the practice whereby the King opened his Parliaments in person. He also insisted on a prior view of despatches, and did not consult his Prime Ministers as to their successors when he felt that the choice of the succession was obvious.

35. JUDICIAL CHANGES

35.1. Reform of the Judicial Function of the Privy Council

Hard on the heels of the Reform Act came a further reorganisation of the Privy Council, with the object of imbuing it with the professionalism that had come to be expected of the courts of law. In spite of assumptions to the contrary, the Privy Council was not, constitutionally, a court of law. Its proper function was that of advisory body to the King in day-to-day matters, including the dispensation of his equity. Nevertheless, since the incapacitation and apparent demise of the Great Council, it had been called upon to perform some of the latter's judicial duties, notably in respect of offences by members of the Second Estate and those offences against the Crown defined as high treason.

These duties were now extended by the Judicial Committee of the Privy Council Act of 1833, which provided that all appeals to the King-in-Council should be heard and reported upon by a Committee of the Council. To be known as the Judicial Committee of the Privy Council, this was to comprise certain Counsellors who were deemed to be legally competent, notably: the President of the Council; the Lord High Chancellor; the Lord Keeper, or First Lord Commissioner, of the Great Seal; the Lord Chief Justice, or Judge of the Court of King's Bench; the Master of the Rolls; the Vice Chancellor of England; the Lord Chief Justice, or Judge of the Court of Common Pleas; the Lord Chief Baron, or Baron of the Court of Exchequer; the Judge of the Prerogative Court of the Lord Archbishop of Canterbury; the Judge of the High Court of Admiralty; the Chief Judge of the Court in Bankruptcy; and all members of the Council who had previously held any of the offices just mentioned. In addition, the King was entitled to appoint, at his discretion, two further members of the Council. The Committee was to hear all appeals 'lain to the Crown in Council', including appeals from Admiralty Courts abroad, and any other courts in His Majesty's dominions abroad that had, up until that time, enjoyed a right of appeal to the courts in England. It was also required to hear such additional matters as were referred to it by the Crown.

The Judicial Committee was to sit as a separate committee of the Privy Council, but it had no authority to make decisions. It was the Privy Council itself, not its Judicial Committee, that was to continue to be the tribunal. The purpose of the Act was not to undermine the judicial position of the Council, nor to compromise its wider functions, but to ensure that the judicial work of the Council was conducted in a professional manner. To this end, the Judicial Committee was required to submit its advice to the King-in-Council, who then, at his own discretion, made an Order that could draw upon that advice in making its judicial decision. Inevitably, sloppy interpretation of these arrangements has since caused the Judicial Committee to be treated as a separate body that independently makes the Council's judicial decisions, but this is a misconception. The Judicial Committee has no judicial authority.

35.2. Reform of the Crown Courts

The criminal code had long been falling out of step with changing circumstances. Many offences once considered serious and subject to severe penalties were now seen as comparatively minor, and this was particularly true of the game laws. Not surprisingly, poaching had always been a serious problem for landowners, who had been in a position to make the laws and penalties so harsh that juries, as often as not, refused to convict. Indeed, the colonisation of Australia, and hence of New Zealand, can be traced directly to the unsatisfactory legal situation, as social distress filled the prisons to overflowing. Meanwhile, the failure of juries to convict had the effect of encouraging crime still further.

While English law was generally deemed to be satisfactory, there had nevertheless been growing criticism of the legal machinery. It was felt that there was a multiplicity of costly courts, with competing jurisdictions. The modern rules of equity had been fixed fairly firmly by Lord Nottingham in the seventeenth century and by Lord Hardwicke in the eighteenth. By the nineteenth century, the judges in Chancery were following precedents as strictly as those in the courts of common law. The effect was two sets of tribunals in England, empowered to deal with the same matters, but in many cases compelled to proceed on entirely different principles. Chancery, the court of equity, often intervened in cases heard in the common law courts in order to prevent suitors from claiming rights that were valid in common law but deemed to be unjust by Chancery. Equity had itself become a system of law, rather than a check on defects in the application of common law, once vested in the judgement of the King. As a result of this confusion, it was not always clear whether a case should be pursued in common law or in equity, and sometimes a suitor who had already fought an expensive case through one court discovered that he should have taken it to another.[1]

Reform came with the appointment of Sir Robert Peel as Home Secretary in 1822. Peel consulted, among others, Jeremy Bentham, the most prominent of the Utilitarians, whose ideal of 'the greatest happiness for the greatest number' was reflected in a view of law that it was an instrument of social welfare whose purpose, as with most institutions, was to achieve happiness for the many, rather than the few, and whose 'utility' could be assessed on this basis. Over the next few years, Peel secured the removal of numerous harsh penalties, ended the use of Government spies among the workers, and the prosecution of radical agitators and the press. There followed a steady decrease in crime. Meanwhile, in order to curb crime in the growing district of London, in 1829 he established the Metropolitan Police for the London area, other than the City. This was to be under the direct control of the Home Secretary, and over the next quarter of a century the idea of establishing police forces was adopted throughout the country.

Many problems were resolved by the Judicature Act of 1873, which, with supplementary Acts, consolidated into one Supreme Court of Judicature the three courts of common law – Exchequer Pleas, Common Pleas, and King's Bench – together with the Court of Chancery, the Courts for Probate, Admiralty and Matrimonial Causes, and certain

---

1   G. Smith, *A Constitutional and Legal History of England*, 459.

minor courts.[2] The newly created Supreme Court of Judicature was not in itself a court of law, but was to comprise two principle divisions: a High Court of Justice and a Court of Appeal. The High Court included the jurisdictions of the Queen's Bench, Chancery, and the Probate, Divorce and Admiralty Divisions. The Act had provided for five divisions, but the Common Pleas Division and the Exchequer Division were merged in 1880 into the Queen's Bench Division, leaving the three just listed. Appeals from all three – the High Court, the Court of Appeal, and the Queen's Bench – were to the Court of Appeal, from which, in turn, appeals lay to the House of Lords.

Meanwhile, below the High Court were the local courts of criminal jurisdiction, known as the Magistrates' Courts, and the County Courts, which were concerned with civil cases. The Judicature Acts thus removed the competing jurisdictions and various anomalies that had grown up or been imposed over the years, and made for a simpler process. It was also less expensive. It was generally believed that the three courts that comprised the High Court – the Queen's Bench, Chancery, and the Probate, Divorce and Admiralty Divisions – had been established by the prerogative of the Crown, while the Court of Appeal was created with the consent of Parliament, but, as we learned earlier, constitutionally, all except the Court of Appeal had been established originally as a standing committee of Parliament and placed under the jurisdiction of the King. The Court of Appeal exercised the King's right of equity.

Meanwhile, the Court of Chancery had now ceased to be a court of equity, and became a court of complete jurisdiction.[3] In keeping with the principle contained in the Act of Settlement of 1701, no judge of the Supreme Court of Judicature could be removed, except as the result of a

2   The Court of Common Pleas at Lancaster, the Court of Pleas at Durham, and the ancient courts erected by the Commissioners of Gaol Delivery (in respect of the inmates of specified gaols), the Commissioners of Oyer and Terminer ('Hear' and 'Settle', normally royal justices with authority to deal with criminal cases), and Commissioners of Assize.

3   The Central Criminal Court, set up in 1834, was a 'local' court, to serve as a permanent assize for the greater London area. Its sessions were held in the keep, or 'old bailey', of Newgate Prison in the City of London (hence 'Old Bailey'). It also came to exercise jurisdiction over crimes committed on British-registered ships on the high seas. English common law applies only to crimes committed on land, as deemed to be in an identifiable county. A legal fiction therefore has it that all crimes committed on British ships occurred in the parish of St Mary le Bow, Cheapside, Middlesex, therefore within the Old Bailey's jurisdiction. Also heard there were offences against the Official Secrets Act, the Corrupt Practices Act, and the Treachery Act. In these respects, the Court was not a local court.

direct and formal address to the Crown by both Houses of Parliament. The salaries of the judges were determined by Parliament, and they were precluded from becoming members of Parliament, or taking part in political activities. In these ways, it was hoped that the courts could function without political interference.

The first major step in eliminating the distinction between lawyers in common law and practitioners of civil law had been taken in 1857, when the secular courts took over the jurisdiction that had hitherto been held by the ecclesiastical courts in matters of probate and matrimonial causes. This process was virtually completed when the Judicature Act absorbed Admiralty, Probate and Divorce as a Division of the High Court. The Act provided that the judges of any one division might serve in another, and that common law and equity were to be administered concurrently in all divisions – further confusing the distinction between the judicial function belonging to Parliament and the right of equity enjoyed by the King. The Act also provided that, where there was variance or conflict between the rules of equity and the rules of the common law with reference to the same matter, the rules of equity should prevail. In this way, the Act reconciled common law and equity by the simple expedient of giving precedence to equity. This accorded with the intent of the common law of the constitution, which gave the King, as the source of equity, the right to overrule a court of common law, where a complaint had been raised and the King believed that the court had wrongly interpreted the law in the case in question. Meanwhile, Chancery now ceased to be a court of equity, becoming, instead, a court of complete jurisdiction. By so delegating the King's right of equity to the courts of law, the Act gave to the courts an enormous power of discretion.

This discretion was not inconsistent with the original principle underlying ordinary common law, which endeavours to reconcile itself with the divine law inherent in nature. It is because common law often fails to meet this standard, whatever that may be, that resort to equity is sometimes necessary. It may be questioned, however, whether the presumed insight of the King can be passed on to the ordinary judiciary. Of course, not even the King's equity is infallible. As we have seen, equity and common law were not separate concepts, the difference between them being that common law is the accepted interpretation of the people.

The practical effect of the Judicature Act was to speed up the judicial process by removing the need for appeals on the grounds of equity.

Parliament appears to have been within its rights, under Aryan tradition, in insisting that the salaries paid by the King to his judges be subject to its consent, and in insisting that the King dismiss his judges only with the consent of Parliament, in the manner prescribed; furthermore, that the King dismiss judges where it is the express wish of Parliament. Neither requirement seems to have directly affected the King's right in common law to delegate his judicial role to appointed judges, or to set the standards of judicial practice.

The Court of Appeal, which sat in lieu of the King, took over the jurisdiction of a number of existing courts,[4] including certain of the functions of the Privy Council. It was created mainly to hear appeals from the High Court. With equity now being dispensed in the lower courts, the function of the Court of Appeal was not to apply equity to judgments in law, but to hear complaints, always on questions of law and usually on questions of fact.[5] Reflecting the increasingly complicated state of the judicial system, it was concerned only with civil appeals. After 1875, the Court of Appeal took over jurisdiction from several other appeal courts, such as the Court of Exchequer Chamber and the Court of Appeal in Chancery. It also took over certain of the functions of the Judicial Committee of the Privy Council. The Court of Appeal was provided with several *ex officio* judges, headed by the Lord Chancellor – who seldom acted – and five 'working judges', known as the Lords Justices of Appeal. It did not review the facts of a case, accepting them as already decided by the lower court. It took no evidence, had no jury, and accepted the facts as provided, being concerned only to determine questions of law. As with the lower courts, however, it could review a judgment in a case where, it was alleged, the presiding judge had failed to direct the jury correctly, or where the evidence presented to the jury made necessary a verdict other than that given. There was no appeal to the Court in criminal cases, although a person summarily convicted in Petty Sessions, despite his or her plea of innocence, would have had the case heard again at Quarter

4   Notably, the Court of Exchequer Chamber, the Court of Appeal in Chancery, the Court of Appeal in Lancaster, and the Court of the Lord Warden of the Stannaries (which operated several courts of mines in Cornwall and Devon.

5   The processes of appealing had already been widely amended by the Common Law Procedure Acts between 1852 and 1860.

Sessions. A further avenue for criminal appeal was not opened until the creation of a Court of Criminal Appeal in 1907.

An appeal from the Court of Appeal lay to the House of Lords. The hearing of appeals, in effect, the dispensing of equity, is, as we have already seen, a particular right and attribute of the King, delegated like his other judicial functions. This appellate role would, in fact, have been to the Great Council, which properly was a court of law in respect of the Second Estate, not to the House of Lords itself, although the distinction had long been forgotten. In keeping with the mood for judicial reform, the House of Lords (i.e. the Great Council) had refined its own approach to its task. Hitherto, it had used its ordinary sittings for the conduct of its judicial business, but it had become clear that ordinary Peers did not possess the legal knowledge required. Accordingly, the Appellate Jurisdiction Act of 1816 had provided for the appointment of twelve Peers, to be styled the Lords of Appeal in Ordinary, to improve the legal expertise of the House. Those so appointed, being not of the Peerage, and requiring to be elevated accordingly, were expected to have held high judicial office for a minimum of two years. This did not affect the right of the other Peers to continue to exercise their judicial role, because the judicial work of the House was carried out during its ordinary sittings, it being the rule that an appeal could be heard by any three Peers, irrespective of whether they had legal qualifications. The presence from this date, however, of senior judges elevated for the purpose, did ensure that the House carried out this function in a more professional manner.

Even this was seen as unsatisfactory, and in the O'Connell case of 1844, the point was made by the Lord Chancellor by ignoring the presence of lay Peers. From this time onwards, it became an accepted convention that no lay Peer should take part in appellate work. It meant, in effect, that appeals had to be heard during a restricted session, in other words, by a judicial committee of the Lords. On the other hand, it soon became clear that the Lords of Appeal in Ordinary were now hardly sufficient for the task by themselves. In 1873, the Liberal Government under Gladstone abolished the appellate jurisdiction of the House of Lords, only for it to be restored by Disraeli's Government, which provided for the shortage of legal expertise by passing the Appellate Jurisdiction Act of 1876. This enabled the appointment by the Crown, questionably on the advice of the Prime Minister, of two Peerages for life, to enable them to take part in the judicial business of the House. They were required to have held high judicial office for at least two years, or to have been practising barristers for at least fifteen years. Designated as Lords of Appeal in Ordinary,[6] they were entitled to sit and vote in the Upper House. Others were added later. The Act also underwrote the existing convention by requiring that appeals should not be heard by the Lords unless at least three of the following were present: the Lord Chancellor, Lords of Appeal in Ordinary, and such other Peers as held, or had previously held, high judicial office. Appeals were usually heard by five Law Lords, but seven might sit in exceptional circumstances. As was noted earlier, constitutionally, the Lords of Appeal in Ordinary were appointed as advisers to the Great Council, not to the House of Lords.

In spite of entrusting its appellate duties to what had become a Judicial Committee, the House of Lords as a whole could not absolve itself of responsibility for judgments made on its behalf. Accordingly, the statute of 1876 acknowledged this by requiring the Judicial Committee to submit its recommendation to the full Chamber of the House. Consequently, the judgements were still those of the House of Lords – that is to say, of the Great Council, not of its Committee.

35.3. Reform of the Shire Courts

The shire, or county courts as the Normans had called them, had all but lapsed by the eighteenth century, as a result of the intrusion of royal assizes, coroners, and the transfer of judicial responsibilities to new entities, including the Justices of the Peace, but they were revived in 1846 by the County Courts Act to deal with small civil actions. Basically, a shire or county court was an autochthonous local assembly, or shire-moot, sitting in its judicial capacity, and presided over by the elected shire reeve, in which justice was also dispensed, and which the King had also used since the Middle Ages from which to dispense royal justice. Local justice had withered as the King had appropriated more and more of its jurisdiction – or, rather, as the shires had been persuaded

---

6   In 1856, for the first time, a retired judge had been granted a Peerage for life, but without the right to sit or vote in the House of Lords.

to delegate more and more. Even the appointment of the shire reeve had been assumed by the King. Nevertheless, the shire assembly had continued in existence, used, for example, in the election of members of Parliament, although even this function had been appropriated to the new electoral constituencies. The assembly had continued to be used by the King for judicial purposes, although few freemen now attended, except as juries and as observers of proceedings.

According to *mos maiorum*, the common law of the constitution, it was from the shires that the King derived his authority. Consequently, he could not appropriate the functions of the shire assemblies, whether administrative or judicial, other than by their delegation. The County Courts Act should be seen, therefore, as a rearrangement of the judicial function of the shire assemblies by the King, using powers delegated by them for the purpose, in order to ensure uniformity.[7] Except in their judicial aspect, however, the shire assemblies effectively ceased to function.

The jurisdiction of the shire or county court after 1846 was held by appointed, paid magistrates, in place of the sheriff. Why the sheriffs were bypassed in this manner is not known, except that a sheriff does not appear to have been a judicial officer and he had acquired a bad reputation under the Normans. The jurisdiction of the county court was confined at first to the settlement of small financial claims, especially the recovery of small debts within the county, but this was soon expanded to the administration of common law, with equity being added after 1868. Although the jurisdiction of the county court could in some areas be almost unlimited, it was precluded from actions that involved difficult legal problems, such as libel. As judges on the county court circuits, the Chancellor – using the delegated powers implied – appointed selected barristers.

One consequence of the County Courts Act was that the Medieval courts baron were virtually superseded. Their Medieval companions, the

---

7   It is possible to assume that these delegations by the shire assemblies, being judicial in nature, had been to Parliament, for re-delegation for use by the King, but, as the functioning of these county courts were also an administrative problem, there seems to be no reason to doubt that the delegation in these cases was to the King. Obviously, a considerable supposition is involved at this late date, when most judicial and executive actions involved the enabling of documents, but the alternative is to suppose that the county courts and county, county borough and district councils had, and continue to have, no legal foundation. These delegations may have been made implicitly at a much earlier date, but not used until now. In any case, no significant objections to these developments appear to have been raised in the counties.

courts leet, fell into virtual disuse after 1848, as a result of the Summary Jurisdiction Act, relating to powers granted to courts to make certain rulings without recourse to a jury.

35.4. The First Franco-German War (1870–71)

This conflict, better known as the Franco-Prussian War, did not greatly affect Great Britain, but it was the first symptom of a new rivalry that would eventually engulf Britain in a succession of profound upheavals that would eventually shatter Britain's place in the world. These upheavals had their origin in the long-cherished political ambitions, on the one hand, of France to follow the example of Charlemagne and annex the Rhineland and become the dominant power in Continental Europe, and, on the other hand, the rise of a united Germany. They were objectives that were incompatible with each other. France's ambitions had hitherto been held in check by competing alliances, in which England had sometimes played a significant part. As a military power, France was very effective, but only under a monarchy. Austria had been in decline, while Prussia, which had emerged as an important military power under the leadership of Frederick the Great, now found a new ambition, inspired by its chancellor, Bismarck, to unite the German-speaking states of Northern Europe under the Prussian crown, which by this time embraced most of northern Germany, from Westphalia to East Prussia and Silesia. The sense of a common German identity had emerged since the French Revolution, and Prussia's initiative had found a new edge with the beginning of the Industrial Revolution in Continental Europe, at the centre of which lay the great coalfield of the Ruhr valley, adjoining the lower Rhine, which had become the centre of a major iron and steel industry. Similar industrial regions were developing in Lorraine and the valley of the Meuse, all of which had military, as well as economic implications, but the most important was the Ruhr, which lay in Prussian Westphalia. These political and economic developments added urgency to the protection of France's ambitions, to which end she conspired to prevent further German unification.

This Franco-German rivalry had its roots in the Migration Age, when Germanic groups from southern Scandinavia had spread across much of Continental Europe. A particularly successful confederacy, which emerged around 200, was that of the Franks[8] on the east bank of the Rhine, which at that time formed the frontier of the Roman Empire. By about 350, a group of the Franks had crossed the Rhine and settled for a while, mainly in Brabant, in northern Belgium, where they served as *foederati* in the Roman army. For convenience, we may refer to them as the West Franks, although for a time they were known to the Romans as the Salian Franks.[9] The main body of the Franks – the East Franks[10] – remained east of the middle Rhine, although later they spread across it into the Moselle valley.

Around 400, the West Franks gained prominence under the Meroving dynasty, spreading across northern Gaul as Roman authority crumbled. Under Clovis, from 486 onwards, the West and East Franks were temporarily reunited, forming an empire across much of Gaul and western and southern Germany. Clovis established his royal seat near Paris, so that, for the first time, the West and East Franks, including much of Germany, found themselves subject to a king whose seat of government lay well to the west of the Rhine. Under his successors, the empire was extended into northern Italy, before going into decline. It was re-vitalised, between 768 and 814, by Charlemagne, who established his seat of government more centrally, at Aachen, also west of the Rhine, and so expanded the Frankish empire – from the Baltic to central Italy – that the Pope, seizing an opportunity to establish some influence over it, crowned Charlemagne as 'emperor'.

Subsequently, the borderland between the West and East Franks was confused, running approximately through Lorraine, before the two halves again fell apart, to form the kingdom of Francia, or Frankenland, in former Gaul in the west and the fractured German states to the east.

---

8   The name is probably a reference to their boldness and courage. See L. Musset, *The Germanic Invasions: The Making of Europe, AD 400–600* (London, 1975), 68.

9   Latin *Salii*, possibly from Latin *salire*, 'to leap', a reference to the fact that they had leapt the Rhine frontier into the Roman Empire.

10 Modern historians refer to them as the Ripuarian Franks, from Latin *riparius*, 'frequenting river-banks', a reference to their location on the banks of the Rhine, between the Moselle and the Mause. However, the name is unrecorded at this time. See L. Musset, *The Germanic Invasions: The Making of Europe, AD 400–600* (London, 1975), 69.

By now, the East Franks had ceased to exist as an effective alliance, and had assumed their local German identities.[11] That the West Franks held together under a single, if fractious, dynasty, was probably due to their more vulnerable position. They increasingly dominated a much larger native Gallic population that had been partly Romanised, and that regarded the Franks with resentment and disdain. The West Franks, who had settled within the Roman Empire, had enjoyed close contact with the Romans, and this common Roman association seems to have been used by the Franks as the basis of cultural unity in France. Thus, the West Franks dominated Gaul as a military aristocracy, but at the expense of their own identity, adopting Latin speech and largely absorbing the Gallo-Roman culture, which was otherwise allowed to continue almost undisturbed. One effect of this adoption of a Romanised culture by the West Franks was for them, with the full encouragement of the Church, to assume the mantle of Imperial Rome and fulfil its destiny. Thus, the 'French', as they increasingly became, were able to harness their own fighting qualities as Franks to the post-Roman cause. In this, they were often to find themselves let down, however, by much of the native Gallo-Roman population, whose Gallic element had been largely destroyed by the Romans under Caesar. The residual population had inhabited the region since before the Ice Age, making it significantly different from the inhabitants of northern and Central Europe. Since the ambition of the Roman Empire had been to extend its control and influence across Continental Europe, east of the Rhine, so it now fell to the French, imbued with their new-found sense of cultural identity and destiny, to turn that ideal into a reality. It was an attitude that influenced French policy throughout the Middle Ages and well into the twentieth century.

The Germans in the east, with whom the East Franks had now merged, and who resented French affectations, established a confederacy of their own. Under the Saxon king, Otto the Great, who was crowned at Aachen, the Germans invaded Italy, where Otto assumed the Italian crown and took control of the Papacy. His successor, Heinrich II, impressed by the Roman tradition, had himself crowned 'emperor' in Rome in 1014. A century later, Frederick I, 'Barbarossa', of the Hohenstaufen dynasty of

---

11   Collectively, the German-speaking population of this part of Europe referred to themselves simply as the 'people' – *deut*, the same word as Old English *theod*. Their speech was *deutsch*, or Anglo-Saxon *theodisc* ('thedish'), a word long since disappeared from English.

Swabia, had adopted for the German confederacy and its appendages the style of 'Holy Roman Empire', thereby combining the status of both the Church and Rome. The Holy Roman Empire was for long an obstacle to France's ambitions, but Napoleon had brought this to an end in 1806. In so doing he had opened up Central Europe to French hegemony. France was now faced with the prospect of a new and altogether more effective German Empire, unified by Bismarck, and based, not on a romantic title bestowed by the Pope, but one founded on nationalism and new industrial success, and guided by the military tradition of Prussia. A united Germany would block France's ambitions and be capable of exerting a greater influence in central and eastern Europe than France could ever hope to. Prophetically, perhaps, Charlemagne had been a German, not a Gaul.

The cause of the war of 1870 was France's refusal to acknowledge the process of German unification under Prussia, and its determination to humiliate Prussia. For his part, Bismarck welcomed an opportunity to settle the issue. Of the interested bystanders, Russia kept its neutrality, and Britain was interested only in preserving the independence of Belgium. Belgium, the former Austrian Netherlands, had rebelled against Dutch rule in 1830, and, under the aegis of Lord Palmerston, who was concerned at a possible spread of French influence, had established itself in the same year as an independent state. Austria shared the concerns of the French at the expansion of Prussia, but retained its neutrality for the time being. It was in this context that France declared war on Prussia in 1870, only to suffer a crushing defeat. Early in the following year, following the fall of Paris, France ceded Alsace and part of Lorraine, and reverted to being a republic by overthrowing Napoleon III. In the Hall of Mirrors at Versailles, Bismarck rubbed in his victory by proclaiming Wilhelm I as the Emperor of Germany, having been induced by the general wish among the German states that Wilhelm should be installed in this capacity, rather than in the capacity of King of Prussia.

36. THE COMMONS ACHIEVES A MONOPOLY OF POWER

36.1. The Parties Form an Oligarchy (1910–11)

The Labour Party was an amalgamation of the socialist movement, the radical wing of the Liberal Party and the trade unions, dedicated to the ideals of an egalitarian society in which the means of production and distribution were owned by the people. It retained the principal of parliamentary government. It was this defection of the radical Liberals that played a key part in the admission of the trade union movement into Parliament, because it was the Liberals and Conservatives who, together, had largely monopolised political power in the House of Commons. This 'duopoly' appears to have been because voters preferred a simple choice between two adaptable Parties – one progressive and the other cautious or conservative – and therefore strong enough to ensure effective government, rather than an array of political options that appeared to offer confusion and indecisiveness. The chief exception to a two-Party system was the representation of nationalist movements – usually the Irish. Socialism was inherently republican, and it was therefore revolutionary, without espousing violence. The shock of this defection of the radical element to the Labour Party had the effect, eventually, not only of relegating the rump of the Liberal Party eventually to a minor role in Parliament, but of causing it to shift its policy, from one of promoting *laissez faire* to one of moderate intervention in the affairs of society and the removal of all distinctions based on inherited rights.

In such an intensifying political environment, both the House of Lords and the Monarchy now found themselves increasingly being brushed aside, and each left to fulfil a largely formal role. Constitutionally, Parliament was the people, and the people comprised all three Estates, now reduced to two and in the process of being reduced to one,[1] summoned each year,

---

1   The third, the Church, or First Estate, having withdrawn from the affairs of Parliament,

having long since been divided by a political eruption into two Houses. The Lower House had now divided itself into two (or sometimes three) permanent and well-organised political Parties, each with its own agenda, but with the dedication of the radical element, among other things, to the seizing of executive power from the Crown.[2] The Parties had, in turn, transformed the House of Commons from a place of consultation into a permanent institution of state.

36.2. Ending of the Right of the Lords to Approve Legislation

Since the establishment of the Labour Party, bolstered by a transfer of the increasingly radical element in the Liberal Party, the latter had undergone a shift in outlook, largely abandoning its ideal of *laissez faire* in favour of a more radical and interventionist policy, designed to overcome the social problems created by the Industrial Revolution and the Enclosure Movement.[3] In keeping with its egalitarian sentiments, it now took a highly critical view of the House of Lords. The Liberal politician, Lord Rosebery, had, indeed, called for a future Liberal Government to challenge the power of the House of Lords.

There was a Conservative Ministry between 1895 and 1905, which had little difficulty with the House of Lords, but this was followed by a Liberal Government under Campbell-Bannerman, with a substantial majority in the Commons, making it likely that it would embark upon a policy of more drastic legislation to curtail the rights and privileges of the Upper House. Campbell-Bannerman's view of the Lords was that they

except in respect of taxation involving itself.

2   The earliest evidence of this was (1) the gradual appropriation from the Crown of the right to deal with petitions, followed by (2) the insistence on the right of Parliament to submit Bills to the King, and in a ready-drafted form the King could not amend. Both developments had been the result of royal incompetence, and they had (3) entirely reversed the function of Parliaments, from consenting to the legislative requirements of the Crown (to enable the King to fulfil his constitutional duty), to obtaining the consent of the King to legislation submitted from the floor of Parliament. The incompetence of the King undoubtedly owed much to the unconstitutional method of his selection.

3   This distinction into right and left outlooks and policies had its origin in Continental, and particularly French, practice, where parliamentary assemblies sat, not on either side of the chamber, as in England, but in a semi-circle facing the convenor, in which the radicals occupied the seats on his left, while the conservatives congregated on his right.

were distinguished by 'purely ornamental ancient privileges', and that they should be deprived of all legislative power. Such were the attitudes in the Commons at this time, however, that it is difficult not to suspect that the motivation of the Party was not merely to remove privilege, but also to dispose of a constitutional rival. To help deal with the social problems of the day, the new Government passed the Trades Disputes Act and the Workmen's Compensation Act, both of 1906. Meanwhile, Edward VII viewed the approaching crisis with a great deal of alarm, and tried to postpone or forestall it. On the one hand, he tried to prevent a rejection by the Lords of an Education Bill and the Licensing Bill in 1908, and on the other, he expressed his disapproval of a speech at Billingsgate by the fiery and radical Chancellor of the Exchequer, Lloyd George, which attacked the Upper House. The King also removed threatening observations on the House of Lords from the Royal Speech from the Throne in 1908. Nevertheless, a state of confrontation had arisen in which the Liberal Government of 1906–11 was said to 'plough the sands', because the Lords rejected so many of its Bills.[4] Campbell-Bannerman was succeeded in 1908 by Lord Asquith, and attention turned towards the issue of the House of Lords, the Government taking the view that the House of Commons had the power to make constitutional changes, including the right to interfere in the affairs of the Upper House. Nor did it see a need to consult the people in the matter. Parliament had already proclaimed its supremacy, the House of Commons taking the convenient view that, by Parliament, was meant itself, because, it believed, it was elected by the common people to do whatever it deemed appropriate. The common law requirement that the three Estates must be consulted equally was now under attack, as also was the constitutional prohibition on the interference of one Estate in the lawful affairs of another.[5]

The crisis was finally reached with the 'People's Budget' of 1909, when the Chancellor of the Exchequer, Lloyd George, who had taken office in the previous year, sought to meet the cost of naval expenditure and the Party's welfare reforms. This sought to shift the main tax burden away from the producers of wealth to its possessors by imposing a tax

---

4   I. Jennings, *The Law and the Constitution* (Bickley, 1943), 167. See also Spender and Asquith, *Life of Lord Oxford and Asquith*, i. xiv.

5   The First Estate having withdrawn from involvement in parliamentary affairs, except in respect of taxation that affected itself.

on the value of land, increasing death duties, and imposing a super-tax on incomes over £3,000, together with levies on unearned income and rates on monopolies, such as liquor licences. This was seen by some, particularly the more successful industrialists and merchants and the richer among the landed classes, represented mainly in the House of Lords, as discriminatory and iniquitous, and as marking the tide of a socialist revolution. The King, foreseeing the danger that the Lords might reject it, asked the Prime Minister, Asquith, if it would be constitutional for him to see the leaders of the Lords. Asquith replied that it would be, but he refused to agree to the King making an offer to the Lords that, if they passed the Budget, he would dissolve Parliament. In the event, the Budget proposals were rejected by the Lords, precipitating a crisis and prompting Lloyd George to explode: 'should 500 men, ordinary men, chosen accidentally from among the unemployed, override the judgement of millions of people who are engaged in the industry which makes the wealth of this country?' This was, of course, a gross exaggeration, and the terms of the Budget had not been an electoral issue. Many Peers had not approved of extensions to the franchise in the first place, and now they saw the birds of folly coming home to roost. The enfranchisement of the working class had brought a whole sheaf of social reforms for their benefit, through expenditure on education, working men's compensation, old age pensions, and national insurance, and now it was the Peers in particular who were being called upon to pay for it. Indeed, it probably was an innovation, that one Estate should be called upon to pay for the benefits granted to another, but then the whole basis of society had shifted once again.[6] Asquith argued that the Lords were in breach of the Constitution, because, by tradition, only the Commons introduced money Bills, and the Lords had previously refrained from initiating or amending them. It followed, he argued, that it was unconstitutional for the Lords now to do either.

Asquith now resorted to the unethical course of advising the King to abuse his own authority by creating sufficient Liberal Peers to enable the Bill to pass through the Lords. The King objected that the creation of new Peers on such a scale would reduce the Upper House to ridicule. While the King was credited with the right to establish Peerages, ostensibly as

6   From the support of the extended family, to the support of the monasteries, to the support
      of the Poor Law, which no longer provided what was needed.

a reward for loyalty or achievement, it had never been suggested that an individual should be ennobled for the sake of his vote. Setting this consideration aside, in the face of a still greater issue, the King suggested to the Prime Minister that he should consult the electorate on such a step. Clearly, the King regarded popular opinion as the decisive factor in deciding such an issue. The King then enquired whether it was possible to create life Peers only, and so avoid the permanent effects of so large a creation. Finally, he enquired whether he was entitled to send summonses only to those Peers favourably disposed to the Budget, and not to those known to be opposed. Asquith responded by asking for a dissolution of Parliament.

The general election of January 1910, was fought, not on the question of reform of the House of Lords, but on the Budget. The election saw the Liberals returned, but with a markedly decreased majority, which could only just be regarded as an endorsement of the Budget, let alone a mandate to reform the Lords. The Irish Nationalists, for whom the Budget and the rights of the House of Lords were irrelevant, now agreed to support the Budget, but only on condition that the Government agreed to its demands on Home Rule. With this assurance given, the Budget was again passed by the Commons, and the House of Lords accepted it without Asquith needing to request his additional Peers. In giving their reasons for supporting the Budget, the Lords stated that the electorate had clearly shown its desire for it.

King Edward VII died on 7 May 1910, and was succeeded by his second son, George, who now reigned as George V. He took his duties seriously, possessed considerable insight and sound judgement, and had a rigid respect for what he understood to be the Constitution. Nevertheless, when faced by a crisis, he was willing to put pragmatism before principle. Whereas Victoria had been all too ready to give way to her feelings, fortunately without any serious ill-effect, the sagacity of George V was to prove of real benefit to the Governments that served under him. He had a more relaxed approach to his duties than his father, and this was reflected in his abandonment of the practice of viewing despatches before they were sent, being content to receive them at the same time as they were submitted to the Cabinet.

Meanwhile, the confrontation over so important and urgent a measure as the Budget, and now, also, the Government's new commitment to Irish Home Rule, had, in his eye, brought to a head the issue of the right of the House of Lords to veto Bills approved by the Commons.[7] In the light of the new political ferment, the Parties did not regard the Lords as having the right to deny the will of the people, which, as their representatives, the Parties deemed to be paramount. It was essentially a Party-political issue, because the electorate had given no clear indication of its support for a conflict with the Lords. The Party leaders were anxious to avoid having to ask the new King to use his prerogative powers so soon, but it proved impossible to find an agreement to postpone the issue. The King tried in vain to bring about a settlement, and promised to create the necessary new Peers, if the result of a dissolution of Parliament should prove favourable. In the pervading climate, and in the absence of a constitution, the King was only too well aware that a refusal to create Peers would endanger the Monarchy itself. He therefore stipulated, firstly, that the House of Lords be given an opportunity to pass the measure, and, secondly, that his promise to create new Peers should not be published before an election.

Accordingly, late in 1910, ignoring the principle in common law that neither Estate should interfere in the membership and proceedings of the other, Asquith introduced a Parliament Bill 'for the regulating of relations between the Houses of Parliament'. This provided that:

- The Lords could not delay, by more than one calendar month, any measure certified by the Speaker of the House of Commons as a Money Bill. Thereafter, it could be submitted directly for the royal assent.
- Any other public Bill, passed by the Commons and not approved by the Lords in three successive sessions, whether of the same Parliament or not, could be presented for the royal assent and become law, provided at least two

---

7   Constitutionally, the issue was the right of the Lords to differ from the Commons in their advice to the King. In such an event, it was incumbent upon the two Estates to reach agreement before submitting their advice. The King was, after all, seeking the advice of the people as a whole on such an issue of common concern, not this or that Estate, unless the issue was of primary concern only to one, which was not the case here. The segregation of Parliament into separate Houses, made necessary by the refusal of the then King to accept the advice of his Great Council, had created a system that was inevitably confrontational.

years had elapsed between the Second Reading of the Bill
and its final, un-amended passing by the Commons.
- Excluded from these provisions was any Bill to extend the
maximum duration of Parliament beyond five years.
- The life of each Parliament was to be limited
to five years, instead of seven.

The result was scenes in both Houses, with opponents of the Bill
accusing the Liberals of trying to 'revise at ten days' notice the constitution
of eight hundred years'. The King arranged secret conferences between
the Liberal and Conservative leaders, but, when the Lords rejected the
Bill, Asquith went to the country again in November 1910, claiming an
apparently irreconcilable divergence of opinion. The Liberals lost their
majority, with themselves and the Conservatives each being returned
with 272 seats. Whether those who returned forty-two Labour seats were
interested in the issue, or simply supported the creation of a socialist
society, it is impossible to know, but the sympathies of the new Labour
members were certainly with the Liberals, giving the latter a majority on
the issue. Everything hung, therefore, on whether the various nationalist
groups, who had little interest in the outcome, but had won eighty-four
seats, were willing to honour their agreement with the Liberals over
Home Rule. Ignoring the vote of the Irish members, who had no direct
interest in the issue, the electorate had voted 2,467,219 in favour of the
reform, while 2,275,400 had opposed it, representing a majority of 8 per
cent. When this was translated into seats in the House, at 314 to 272,
the effective majority in the House was 15 per cent. The Commons again
passed the Bill and the Lords neutralised it with amendments. Asquith
then announced that the King had agreed to create some five hundred
Liberal Peers, in order to force the Bill through the Upper House, and
the Commons was adjourned in uproar. Faced with the threat of being
inundated by new Peers, and thereby reduced to impotence, let alone
ridicule, the House of Lords finally gave way. The majority of the Lords
boycotted the occasion in protest, with the result that, out of a total of
about 900 members, only 245 voted, approving the Bill by 131 to 114.
The Act was promulgated in August 1911. Thus, the historic right of
the Lords, as the Second Estate, to be consulted on the same basis as the

Commons, representing the Third Estate, had now been removed, except, of course, that *mos maiorum*, or the common law of the Constitution, cannot be overridden by statute law.

This episode has been covered in some detail because it was the first occasion in modern times on which the House of Commons affected to change the Constitution. The election of 10 January 1910, had been fought on the acceptability of the Budget, which, since the Lords were essentially required to pay for it, should have seen the Liberals returned with a substantial majority, but they were not, undoubtedly because the electorate were concerned over the intention of the Liberal Government to change the constitution, and more particularly by hobbling the House of Lords. As the Government had clearly expected, its feud with the Lords was not popular. In the event, the King had not abused his position by creating new Peers for Party ends, and the Upper House had agreed not to exercise its right of veto in future. The Commons interpreted this as an amendment of the system of government, which it probably was in practice, but it could not detract from the right of the Great Council to veto proposals of the Crown that it judged to be *ultra vires*, or to advise the Crown on important issues of policy.

That the House of Lords continued to command the respect, and indeed, the awe, of the people, there can be no doubt, because it would still be tangible half a century later. Whether this respect was a tribute to the continued sagacity and standing of its members, or to a subconscious awareness of the continued presence of the Great Council, even in its compromised form, it is impossible to say.

36.3. The Legitimacy of Those Occupying the Peerage

The action of the Commons in threatening to remove the rights of the Lords raises the question, also, of whether the Lords themselves occupied their seats lawfully. The common law assumes the existence of three hereditary Estates, or Orders of society, and requires each to be consulted on changes to the law. It could be said that the Estate structure ended with the advent of the Christian Church after 600. This terminated the hereditary nature of the First Estate, and the Norman invasion of England in 1066 had ended it in respect, also, of the Second Estate, imposing, in its place, members of the Norman, French and Breton Second Estates. Most of the members of the English Second Estate had, in any case, been slain or dispossessed. Subsequently, the imposition of the law of primogeniture seems to have ensured that the few survivors of the English Second Estate eventually became extinct.

In spite of this, the Estate structure, and with it the *Witenagemōt*, or Great Council, were taken over by the Normans and continued to function and, in due course, to be recognised by the people. What may be regarded as their lawful restoration came a few centuries later, when their respective members were again able to claim English ancestry, as their Norman and French predecessors died out as a result of the operation of the law of primogeniture. What was still missing, however, was their shire connections and their legitimacy, because many were undoubtedly mediocrities unworthy of the honour. Thus, while the House of Commons sought to violate the Constitution by ending the right of the Second Estate to consent to Bills, it seems likely that the Great Council was itself composed very largely of unsuitable individuals, owing their position to royal favour, and therefore devoid of any right to membership of either the Second Estate or the Council. We have already noted that there was no such institution, in law, as the House of Lords, having been a compromise arrangement arrived at as a result of the schism between Edward III and the Great Council.

It also needs to be understood that:

1. members of both Estates attended, or were represented in, Parliaments as a result of their hereditary right as free men;
2. whereas members of the Third Estate – the common people – had long since grown in number to the extent that Parliaments were unable to accommodate them, requiring, instead, a system of representation, members of the Second Estate were so few in number, being expected to take the brunt of the carnage in times of war, that their allotted seats in Parliament had continued to be adequate;

3. the existence of the two Houses of Parliament, in addition to Parliament itself, was an anomaly imposed, following an abuse of the Constitution by Edward III.

36.3.1. The Privy Council is Subject to a *Coup d'État*

The accession of George V in 1910 followed the accepted procedure, with a meeting of the Accession Council – which was probably an offshoot of, or substitute for, the long-forgotten Great Council – to approve the necessary Proclamation. Afterwards, the Privy Council was re-convened, so that it might satisfy itself as to the good intentions and commitment of the successor to the Throne, and to hear an appropriate declaration from him. This required him to swear to uphold the rule of law and constitutional government. The duty of hearing the declaration and, if satisfied, recommending him to the people in Parliament, properly belonged to the long-forgotten Great Council. In its absence, the most senior members of the Second Estate in the Privy Council – itself a standing committee of the Great Council – effectively acted on its behalf. In so doing, they were acting as custodians of the *imperium*. These were duties that members of the Third Estate in the Privy Council could not perform, because they could not have been members of the Great Council.

Following the approval and election by Parliament of the successor to the Throne, and the bestowing upon him of the *imperium*, following his coronation and endowment with the Sceptre, the function of the old Privy Council was ended, upon which it resigned. This allowed the new King to appoint his own Privy Council, with or without the same members. The procedure had conveniently become confused, however, in that the previous Privy Council presumed its right to continue as the new Privy Council. This had the effect of ensuring the continuation of the ruling Party in Ministerial office, depriving the new King of his right to appoint his own Ministers. The establishment of a new convention could have ensured this, but it would have brought the change into the open, and Ministers may have preferred to avoid this. Such continuity was achieved by the members of the old Privy Council individually declaring their allegiance to the new Sovereign. In effect, therefore, his advisers were imposed upon him, which was almost certainly contrary to customary law.

From 1910, however, even this requirement was dispensed with. By what authority Asquith made this change is unclear, but, by implication, the Privy Council was no longer recognised as being the King's Privy Council. Effectively, it was now treated, not as a Privy Council, but as an independent body, comprising the previous Ministers of the Crown, who, as a result, were no longer bound by the Coronation Oath. Effectively, therefore, in 1910 and 1911, the Parties in the House of Commons had achieved a final *coup d'état*, depriving the King of his last constitutional function. Although the King was still required to approve new legislation by appending his signature or seal, it was clear that he was no longer expected to exercise any discretion, even of a most formal nature. The Privy Council, no longer deriving its *imperium* directly from the Great Council, nor subject to its guidance, was effectively reduced to a formal administrative and procedural office, except for its retention of a very limited judicial function for which it was not intended in any case. There can be no doubt, therefore, that Asquith abused his office and gave George V illegal advice, which was of no legal effect.

36.3.2. The Crown in Crisis

The institution of the Crown was now in a state of crisis, because there was no longer any correspondence between its purpose, as expressed in the rite of coronation, and the reality in which it now found itself. The Parties explained the new situation by separating the 'King' from the 'Crown', according to which the Crown was now defined as the executive functions of the former. This had already been largely the case for centuries, because it was quite usual for the King to delegate much of his executive responsibilities to Ministers appointed for the purpose. These had usually been drawn from men of the Second Estate, most of whom were used to responsibility and had a wide experience in affairs of state. The chief problem had been the chaotic basis on which kings were chosen, since they depended on the lottery of royal birth. Unsuitable royal sons had for centuries been a recipe for executive incompetence. While the common law of the Constitution accepted the principle of succession within the Second Estate and especially royal succession, it interposed a requirement of popular election, in the light of advice from the Great Council. This procedure had long been superseded under Church-Feudalism, whose choice of Ministers had been based more on royal favourites who were usually quite unsuitable. The absence of the Great Council had allowed the situation to deteriorate. The replacement of the Stuart dynasty by that of the early Hanoverians had represented a distinct improvement in the competence of the Crown, but their lack of English and distraction by affairs in their native Hanover had allowed the Parties to gain a degree of control over government and raised the ambitions of Party members, until the present situation had been reached, whereby the ruling Party in Parliament had completely displaced the King in the management of affairs of state. The Parties in the Commons had also been fortunate around this time in producing men of real ability, such as Pitt, Peel and Disraeli, allowing the Commons to become entrenched in the Ministry. Meanwhile, the growing delegation of executive functions by the King, which the Parties tenaciously held onto, had left the King with little but his non-executive functions. It was a process that owed much to the effective absence of the Great Council, which would not have allowed the Constitution to be overridden in this way, just as it would not have allowed the Monarchy to make such a mess of its responsibilities. Like any rudderless ship, the system of Government had given way to confusion that some institution or group was bound to exploit. The Parties hailed the changes as a huge benefit to ordinary men and women of the Third Estate, but they had yet to run their course.

There were three problems with this new state of affairs: it left the King with no discretion, which properly was guided by the advice of the Great Council; elected members of Parliament rarely had the necessary experience of executive Government that fitted them for Ministerial responsibilities; and their appointment left them with a conflict of interest – were they in office to approve policy, or to make it? The difference between the two roles decided whether they should, or should not, be members of Parliament.

The nature of kingship and its duties are defined in the coronation rite. This needs to be understood, both in filling the office and enabling it to fit it properly into the wider requirements of the Constitution.

36.4. The Coronation Contract

A coronation, as practised since the reign of Edgar, involves two rites: the election of a new King and his installation. Because all the nations of the confederacy are involved, both rites, unavoidably, require the election of delegates, in the same way as the holding of a Parliament, and for this reason, both events are held at the same time. For the Church, this is no problem, because it does not require an election of the successor to the Crown, because it specifies him as the eldest son of the late King, and if there is no son, then in accordance with the law of primogeniture, regardless of suitability. Edgar also insisted on the retention of the Coronation Oath, while the Church insisted on both rites being held in a House of God – since 1066 in Westminster Abbey – not a sacred site, and the coronation itself being conducted, not by a representative of the Great Council, which held the *imperium*, but by the Archbishop of Canterbury, on behalf of the Church, to the accompaniment of the liturgy. In spite of this corruption of the rite, it is of interest that so much from pre-Christian antiquity has survived.

The constitutional rights and duties of the King, as laid down in the proceedings, bore little relationship to the new realities of kingship. As we know, the form of the rite[8] followed since the beginning of the Middle Ages, and later recorded in the *Liber Regalis*, with two important revisions in the seventeenth century, was a combination of that prescribed by the Church, and that previously required in common law. Following a procession of the participants to the Abbey, the coronation rite, which was organised by the Earl Marshal on behalf of the Great Council, the King elect, wearing a crimson robe, which proclaimed him as a nobleman of the Second Estate (from which kings were chosen in common law), received the homage of his fellow lords of the Second Estate, followed by the 'recognition', involving his presentation by the Archbishop (originally perhaps by the leader of the Council) to the assembled people, who were asked whether they were willing to do him homage and service. If so, this was followed by his election by the acclamation of the people,[9] whereafter

---

8   Based on the procedure followed at the installation of Elizabeth II in 1953.

9   The Church regarded this as a foregone conclusion, and therefore unnecessary, because the succession was determined by the law of inheritance, whereas, in common law, the Great Council found and offered a suitable and popular candidate.

he took his seat on the Throne. He then took the Coronation Oath, the wording of which was prescribed by common law, amended by statute, subject to the approval normally of the Great Council, although it had not functioned effectively since Edward III. The Oath used was based on a statute of 1688, since when it has been changed a number of times by various constitutional statutes. Undoubtedly, any such changes must be subject to the consent of the reigning Monarch and the people, including those in the British Dominions to whom they will also apply. The essence of the Oath, however, is a promise to govern the peoples of England, Scotland, Wales, Northern Ireland, Canada, Australia, and New Zealand, and those other members of the Commonwealth that accept the rule of the Crown, including the King's 'possessions and other territories to any of them belonging or pertaining, according to their respective laws and customs'.

A religious service ensued, conducted by the Archbishop of Canterbury, during which the Archbishop anointed the King elect with oil,[10] in accordance with Church tradition. He was then divested of his crimson robe, before taking his seat in King Edward's Chair, where four knights held over him a golden canopy. Arguably, this symbolised the Sun, and represented the blessing of the Supreme Deity. The Archbishop then vested the King elect with holy oil (an Oriental custom) and placed the Crown on his head (in common law, this function should undoubtedly be performed by the leader of the Great Council), while pronouncing the words of a solemn benediction. The King elect was now regarded as the King, and he was then arrayed in white alb, over which he now wore a golden tunic with a girdle that was so like the vestments of a bishop that he was judged by some to be both layman and priest (which in common law he now undoubtedly is, the white and gold undoubtedly symbolizing, respectively, the light from the sky and the divine Sun). His hands were then touched by the golden spurs of chivalry (properly, they would have been placed on his feet), representing his duty to lead in war. He was then presented with the Sword of State, with which the Archbishop bad him to punish evil-doers and protect the law-abiding, in contrast to the significance of the rite in common law, where it may have represented the temporal power of the King to preserve the peace, enforce what was right, and defend the people from their enemies. He was also

10   An Oriental custom.

girded with the Jewelled Sword and presented with gold bracelets to symbolise sovereignty and wisdom. He was then required to stand before the altar and commit himself to God, replacing, perhaps, a much older pre-Christian rite.

The King elect was now invested with the Royal Robe and Stoll and presented with the Orb, of which the latter symbolised the universal dominion of the Cross. In customary law, the Cross represented the Supreme Deity in his aspect as the Sun. The new King was also vested with the Ring, representing his union with the people, perhaps in both traditions. He now received the Sceptre, adorned with a cross, which, according to the Church, represented power and justice, but which, in customary law, endowed the King elect with the *imperium*, or his right to rule, the cross representing divine authority as represented by the Sun Goddess. In his left hand he now received the Rod with the Dove, symbolising his investment with the power of equity and mercy, which he enjoyed according to both traditions of kingship. Lastly, he was vested with the Crown of England, said to be the Crown of Edward the Confessor (St Edward's Crown), to the accompaniment of trumpets. The inclusion of King Edward's Crown (the Church rendering him as St Edward) was a specifically Norman rite, endowing them and their successors with the right to rule over England. The King then takes Communion and presents the Church with gifts. In the final part of the coronation, known as the Recess, the King dons the royal robe of purple velvet and the Imperial State Crown, to denote his dominion across the seas.

To general celebration, the new King was then seated upon the Throne, where he received the fealty of the archbishops and bishops and the homage of the lay Peers of the Second Estate. Bearing the Sceptre and Orb, and wearing the Imperial Crown, he then proceeded among the people to what, in an earlier age, was the Coronation Banquet, but which was no longer held.

As a constitutional process, it could not be changed by statute, beyond the details of its execution, including the requirements of the Coronation Oath. It is quite clear, therefore, that the executive authority vested in the popularly elected King. In early times, this was a straightforward arrangement, in which his duties were largely confined to the enforcement of the law and leading the people in time of war. From an early date, however, he found it necessary to appoint 'ministers' to undertake specific duties, and these were drawn from men of experience and ability, usually earls from the Second Estate, or thanes from the Third Estate, with whose competence he was already familiar. In all that he did, however, he was subject to the advice of the leading men of the land, sitting in the Great Council, who were themselves appointed by the people, and who were able, not only to render advice and undertake important executive duties, but also to enforce his abdication if he flouted the law or raised the opposition of the people in Parliament. This left one big problem: the lack, until society became more advanced, of an executive and judicial infrastructure that had the capacity to enforce the law. As society became more complex, so the King delegated more and more to his Ministers, as, indeed, the Council should have insisted, including their suitability for their task. The King was dependent upon the support of the Council (which had played an important part in securing his election, and could use its influence to unseat him). Its advice to the King, if couched in appropriate terms, he was expected to follow, the ultimate arbiter, in practice, being Parliament. The Council itself was answerable to those who had appointed it, and who were capable of removing unsatisfactory members. It may be added that the value of political Parties lay in their ability to mobilise and lead public opinion.

The system had been rendered ineffectual by the Church, which, by restricting the regal succession to the accident of birth (effectively, the King's son) and denying abdication, permitted many incompetents, self-seekers and even tyrants to assume the Crown, leaving the people often unprovided for and unprotected.

This leaves us in no doubt that the *imperium* was, and still is, vested in the King, as head of state, chosen by the people and subject to his Coronation Oath. In principle, he acts through his Ministers, with the advice and guidance of his Great Council, subject to the consent of his Parliaments, which are themselves guided by the Party system. This takes its cue from general elections and popular opinion, expressed, where needed on crucial issues, by general elections and referendums. In this way, the threat of oligarchy and misrule can be avoided. The reality by now, however, was that the legislative and executive head of state was now the Prime Minister, at the head of the executive Ministers of the Crown, meeting as the Cabinet Committee that was now separate from the Privy Council, able to rely on the proclaimed principle of the Supremacy of Parliament to act in an autocratic manner. There was nothing to preclude a Party in office from assuming the character of an oligarchy, and deferring general elections indefinitely. Nevertheless, there were now inherent conflicts in the system that were capable of paralysing it, and that would become apparent in the years to come.

36.5. The Menace of the Supremacy of Parliament

The Doctrine of the Supremacy of Parliament, however ill-founded, now opens the door to a permanent oligarchy. Any group of unprincipled individuals, who managed to secure control of a political Party and offered a sufficiently attractive manifesto (which it is not bound to honour) at a general election to be returned with an overall majority, could then use a political or economic crisis, real or engineered, to justify passing legislation deferring the next general election on an indefinite basis. This would be sufficient to establish indefinite rule by what had now become a permanent oligarchy. It could ensure its perpetuation by a further Act that provided for retiring members of Parliament to be replaced by nominees of the Crown.

In common law, the Sovereign could simply dismiss such a Parliament, but, by convention, the Sovereign no longer enjoys such a power. If the Commons worried lest the House of Lords re-discovered the Great Council and allowed it to re-establish itself, preferably by inviting the shires to elect new members in order to restore its full credibility, the oligarchy in the Commons could simply forestall such a possibility by abolishing the House of Lords. Oligarchy is the worst form of government, because it is permanent and irremovable.

In short, all that now separates the United Kingdom from a potential dictatorship is for the wrong people to win a general election.

PART XIII

•

THE IMPACT OF EMPIRE

37. REBELLION AND EXPANSION IN AFRICA (1900)

BY THE NINETEENTH century, the willingness of the Crown to assume new colonial burdens was soon exhausted by the increasing acquisition of new territories, which cost the Treasury money and imposed new liabilities upon the army and the Royal Navy. They also brought a great increase in diplomatic problems. The further Britain's interests extended, moreover, the greater the need to protect their commercial and strategic supply lines, which now extended around the world. Our concern is not, however, with the financial, economic and political consequences of Empire, but rather with the legal implications for its British inhabitants.

37.1. South Africa

The main region of Imperial concern at this time was South Africa, where the discovery in 1867 of diamonds near the Orange River, above its junction with the Vaal, brought an important new factor into the politics of the region. A considerable new industry developed between the Orange and Vaal rivers, centred upon Kimberley.[1] This was located in the west of the Orange River Sovereignty, and it brought an influx of British miners and speculators. The diamond diggings did not give rise to a new colony, because the boundary of the Cape Colony was simply extended northwards to include the main part of them. The diamond industry may also have spurred an ambition in the Crown to bring the Cape, Natal, and the two Afrikaner republics into a federation under British control, because the Cape Colony, with the support of the Crown, was now strong enough to project its power to the Vaal, and probably beyond. In furtherance of this ambition in 1877, it annexed the

---

1   The site was the farm 'Vooruitzigt', which Lord Kimberley declared unpronounceable, causing the site eventually to be re-named after him.

South African Republic, in violation of the Sand River Convention. In consequence, the Republic reverted to its previous name as the Transvaal.

A Zulu rebellion in Natal now diverted Britain's attention, prompting the *Afrikaners* in the Transvaal also to rebel, winning victories at Laing's Nek and Majuba in 1880. Under the ensuing Treaty of Pretoria, the independence of the South African Republic was again recognised, but under British suzerainty. In the same year, as a portent of the future, a virtual monopoly of the diamond industry was achieved by two business rivals, Barney Barnato and Cecil Rhodes. Meanwhile, the renewed confidence of the *Afrikaners*, following their victories, as is shown by a letter, written in 1881 by Paul Kruger, the future President of the South African Republic, to President Brand of the Orange Free State, in which he proclaimed that 'it shall be from the Zambezi to Simon's Bay,[2] Africa for the Afrikander'.[3]

37.1.1. The Witwatersrand

He spoke too soon, for, only six years later, in 1886, rich gold reefs were discovered on the Witwatersrand, or 'White Waters Ridge', in the southern Transvaal. This led to a great influx of mainly British and Australian prospectors, followed by many more immigrants, mainly British, who were attracted by the industrial and commercial opportunities to which the developing mining complex was giving rise. Earlier gold discoveries in the area had been concealed and closed down by the government in Pretoria, due to a fear that the ensuing gold rush would swamp the young republic and its Dutch culture, but the new discovery could not be hidden. The town of Johannesburg was founded on the Rand in the same year, followed by a string of other mining towns along the Rand, to the west and east of it, for about forty miles. By 1890, there were 450 mining companies operating.

Because of the seeming political irreconcilability between the *Afrikaans*-speaking Republic and the English-speaking Rand, the latter became effectively a third British colony in South Africa, to the extent that, by 1895, the mining population was on the verge of a revolution against the government in Pretoria, demanding civil rights that the government would not and could not concede, without the country's

---

2   Just south of Cape Town, better known as False Bay.
3   *Cambridge History of the British Empire*, viii. 509.

Dutch identity and culture being swamped. A misjudgement by the leader of a Rhodesian attempt, led by Jameson, to give military support to the expected revolt, known to history as the Jameson Raid, ended in disaster, due to prior intelligence having been passed to Pretoria. This crisis was soon overtaken by another, much bigger crisis, but the British settlement on the Rand was of sufficient importance in population and wealth, by this time, to play a crucial political and economic role in South Africa's future.

Tensions with Britain continued, with the latter effectively imposing a customs union in 1889 on the Orange Free State and the Cape Colony. This provoked a defensive alliance between the Free State and the South African Republic. Suspicions over Britain's ambition to achieve a federation of the Afrikaner republics with the Cape Colony, inevitably under Britain's ultimate control, erupted in 1899 in open conflict, known as the South African War; but also as the Boer War.[4] It was a bitter conflict, in which Britain had no real answer to the Afrikaner tactic of using highly mobile, mounted commandos that lived off the land. The solution eventually adopted by the new British commander, Kitchener, was a scorched earth policy to destroy the sources of supply to the commandos. To this end, farms and livestock were destroyed over a vast area and the Afrikaner women, children and the elderly were herded into 'concentration camps', of which there were eventually forty-five. Originally intended to accommodate refugees, under Kitchener, these were used as a political and tactical policy, evidently with the intent, not only of cutting off supplies to the commandos, but of decimating the Afrikaner population, through starvation and disease, a brutal policy that was unintentionally aided by attacks by the commandos on British sources of supply. Between 1900 and 1902, 48,000 died in the camps, due in part to deliberate neglect, and at the end of the conflict, of the 28,000 prisoners of war, 25,630 were deported to various places overseas.[5] The Afrikaner cause was openly supported by Germany, creating an *entente* between the two that would have its consequences over the next forty-

---

4   From the Dutch *boer*, meaning 'farmer'.
5   Half a century later, Great Britain was particularly loud in its condemnation of German concentration camps, used to eliminate the Jews, despite the fact that Britain was in no way involved. There is a temptation in this to see an expression of guilt.

three years. The war ended with the capitulation of the two Afrikaner republics, formalised in the Treaty of Vereeniging of 1902.

Thus, the rebellious descendants of the *Voortrekkers* were finally forced back under the rule of the Crown, in keeping with the requirements of feudal doctrine, with savage punishment meted out in the process, as the two former Dutch republics were now administered directly as Crown Colonies. The Governor of the Cape, Milner, was transferred to the Transvaal to undertake the formidable task of reconstruction. Overcoming local opposition in the Cape and Natal, quite apart from the helpless opposition of the former two Afrikaner republics, he endeavoured to bring all the colonies under central control. In this, he was frustrated by the British Government, which did not believe that there was a sufficient local support for such a development, added to which, the Premiers of Australia and Canada were loudly indignant.[6] Nevertheless, Milner introduced unitary policies, including the extension of the Cape legal system to the former republics and the establishment of an Intercolonial Advisory Council, reinforced by an administration based on efficiency and integrity. It included a common Native policy. Meanwhile, a growing public mood in favour of some form of integration was reflected in the decision of the Afrikaner Bond, a fiercely pan-Afrikaner, anti-imperialist movement, to increase its appeal to the English-speaking section of the Cape population. With economic recovery, political interest in the north made a slow revival. In Pretoria, Smuts and Botha formed a close relationship, to become the political leaders in the Transvaal, and welcomed the change in London towards a more liberal administration under Campbell-Bannerman's Liberal Party. This caused Smuts to go to London to bargain for self-government, as a result of which he became inspired, like Rhodes, to work with Botha towards a united South Africa, this time within the Empire. Meanwhile, the *Afrikaners* in the former republics began to re-discover their connections, through language, with the Cape Dutch, leading to a celebration of *Afrikaans* as a language in its own right. Nevertheless, this growing reconciliation with the Cape Dutch left the great majority of the *Afrikaners* in the former republics as resentful, hostile and uninvolved as ever, leaving the way open for the small but growing liberal element to seize the initiative.

---

6   F. Troup, *South Africa: An Historical Introduction* (London, 1972), 191.

Milner was replaced by Lord Selborne in 1905, but Milner's administration promoted the idea of unitary government as the only way to resolve the many other problems, such as those relating to railway tariffs, customs and labour policy. Early in 1908 an intercolonial conference to prevent a break-up of the Customs Union led to a proposal by Smuts for a national convention to discuss union. The Convention met late in 1908, and devised a scheme whereby the existing four colonies would become provinces, each under an elected council, with an executive committee and an administrator, appointed by the government. To satisfy colonial rivalries, Pretoria would be the administrative centre, Cape Town the seat of the legislature, and Bloemfontein the seat of the judiciary. Both Dutch (*Afrikaans*) and English were to be recognised, in principle at least, as official languages, as well as the general use of Roman-Dutch law. Meanwhile, the Cape African and Coloured voters would lose their right to sit in Parliament. The proposed Constitution could be amended only by a two-thirds majority in both the common Assembly and Senate. Although there was opposition, both in Westminster and the Cape, to the limitations on the participation of the non-White population, the British Government was convinced that, if Black interests were insisted upon at this stage, it would disrupt the proposed Union and alienate the moderates. Fearing pressure from Australia and Canada against the practice of imperial intervention in the concerns of a self-governing colony, the South Africa Act of 1908 implemented the constitution thus proposed, but with an assurance by the Crown to the adjoining Black Protectorates – Swaziland, Basutoland, and Bechuanaland – that they would not be transferred to the Union without consultation. In all this, the sullen Afrikaner population showed little interest and played little part.

As in Canada, the relationship of the English-speaking population[7] to the King continued to be defined by the regal contract.

37.2. Britain and Imperialism

The Imperial Age affected Britain profoundly. Already, in the reign of George II, the sense of British expansion and primacy across the world

---

7   More specifically, those whose descent through the male line is indicated by the inheritance of an English surname.

had given rise to a national sense of pride and achievement that was expressed memorably in a song by Thomas Arne, whose refrain: 'Rule, Britannia! Britannia rules the waves!' attributed Great Britain's position in the world, first and foremost, to the Royal Navy. Yet it would have achieved little without the contingents of the British army in distant places, and the enterprise, courage and self-belief of thousands of British men and women, not a few of whom paid the ultimate, and often grisly price, commemorated in lonely and long-forgotten graves. Romantic stories, songs and poems related to every corner of the Empire, each of which imparted its own flavour, from the harsh wilderness of Canada to the hot plains of Australia and the dry and rugged mountains of South Africa. It was the exotic culture and wealth of Indian civilization that particularly caught the public's imagination, giving rise to stories and ballads, from the loyalty of 'Gunga Din' to 'The Road to Mandalay'. Nobody promoted the East, and Britain's position in it, more vividly than Rudyard Kipling, but epic tales of explorers were coming out of Africa, with references to the vastness of its interior, inhabited by primitive tribes who indulged in witchcraft, to mighty rivers, such as the Congo and the Zambezi, as well as stories about lions and elephants, gold, Arab slave-traders, and the ruins of lost civilizations. In what seemed like the middle of nowhere, Livingstone discovered the unsurpassed splendour of the Victoria Falls, while romantic novels by Rider Haggard gave a legendary quality to 'King Solomon's Mines', based on the discovery of the Zimbabwe ruins. In quite different contexts, Olive Schreiner related *The Story of an African Farm*, Paterson recounted the ballad of 'The Man from Snowy River', and Robert Service celebrated 'The Law of the Yukon'. All this, and far more, stimulated the imaginations of people in Britain, gave them a romantic view of their country's achievements, and stirred in them the spirit of adventure that imparted optimism and pride. For the restless, the adventurous, the enterprising and the self-reliant, as well as the 'black sheep' of 'society' families, the colonies beckoned, and at the core of it all, as Rhodes had once said, was the belief that 'to be born an Englishman is to win the first prize in the lottery of life'. The crusade of the humanitarian movement to stamp out slavery affected the prosperity of the West Indies, but elsewhere it even added to the Imperial dream by giving a new, humanitarian mission to the Royal Navy, which also had the unintended effect of extending the authority and responsibility of the Crown into new areas, including the Shire Valley and Nyasaland.

Nowhere was Imperial pride felt more strongly than in the perceived majesty of the Constitution, particularly in the august nature and wisdom of the House of Lords, while the House of Commons represented the beacon of democratic government. It was the Crown that was the focus of the Empire, however, and with the addition of the title of 'Empress of India', and the dispersion of her family among the royal houses of Europe, Queen Victoria emerged at the pinnacle of international society.

37.3. Rhodesia

By the late nineteenth century, the future of that huge tract of Southern Africa lying north of the Limpopo River was becoming of increasing interest. The Germans had an interest in South-West Africa and East Africa, while the Portuguese had established colonies on the west coast, in Angola, and on the east coast, in Mozambique, so that both had interests in the African Plateau in between. Indeed, the Portuguese had long laid a nominal claim to the interior, but had been unable to assert it. Meanwhile, the South African Republic had its own interest in the region to the north of the Limpopo. The British Government was concerned that these interests posed a potential threat to its own in South Africa. However, it was Cecil Rhodes who was the first to take a practical interest in the region, seeing it as a means towards completing a territorial link between the Cape with Egypt.

For Great Britain, the establishment of Rhodesia marked the high noon of the Imperial Age. Nevertheless, Cecil Rhodes was fortunate in that the maturing of his ambitions for Africa coincided with the Prime Ministership of Lord Salisbury, who was one of the few British Ministers who had an empathy with the overseas settlers. British politicians were already losing interest in Imperial ventures, and liberal-minded Church missionary societies were becoming active throughout the Empire. Despite its eventual success, however, Rhodesia would be doomed from the start by the fact that its indigenous inhabitants were destined, not to dwindle or die out, as in North America or Australia, but, as in South Africa, to respond to White rule by proliferating. As with South Africa also, Rhodesia's interests would particularly be affected, and adversely so, by the conflict between common law and the Church-Feudal tradition in its constitutional relationships with Great Britain. Both traditions expected those seeking permanently to depart from the royal realm to settle overseas to obtain the King's consent, as at least a courtesy in common law, and rather more than that under feudal arrangements, because the royal estate might be unable to spare them, as had been the case in the Cape Colony, or unwilling to do so, as in the case of absconding criminals. Some of the self-sown colonies in North America had been established by people who were such a problem in England that the King had undoubtedly been glad to see them go, whereas the obtaining of a royal charter was not only a formal royal approval to leave, but also a royal blessing on a venture that might stand the emigrants in good stead.

Because of its constitutional significance, and the fact that the history and nature of Rhodesia are no longer well known, compared with that of the surviving British Dominions, some particular attention is merited.

The native inhabitants of the region occupying that segment of the Great African Plateau, about five hundred miles across, between the Limpopo and Zambezi Rivers, were collectively known as the Mashona. Their territory had earlier been reduced by at least a third by the arrival, from the Transvaal, of the Matabele, led by their king, Mzilikazi, who had defeated and subjugated the Mashona, taking occupation of the south-western part of the region, where, significantly, Mzilikazi had named his capital Bulawayo, meaning 'Place of Slaughter',[8] which told its own story. The remainder of the region was known to Europeans as Mashonaland, which extended eastward to a mountain range – the Eastern Highlands – which separated the plateau from the coastal plain of Mozambique, which had long been occupied by the Portuguese.

The Matabele imposed an annual 'tax' on the Mashona. This was collected each year by Matabele *impis*, or raiding parties, which simply burned and pillaged, abducting the cattle, young women and boys, of whom the last were destined to be trained as warriors. Everything else was destroyed or killed, including the older men and women, forcing the Mashona to live on inaccessible rock outcrops, or 'kopjes'.

---

8   The spelling of place and other names is that used in official records at the time.

By 1890, Cecil Rhodes had acquired control of a large share of the gold mining industry and a virtual monopoly of the diamond industry in South Africa. In spite of his commercial acumen and success, however, Rhodes was an idealist, who lived frugally and had little interest in money, except as a means to a political end, which to him meant the spreading of British civilization, a sentiment that attracted support from many of his colleagues. To this end, he sought to extend British jurisdiction and settlement from the Cape to Egypt, which had fallen under British control in 1883, intending to consolidate it by building a railway from the Cape to Cairo, through territory yet to be occupied by British settlers. More than anybody else at the time, it was Rhodes who epitomised the spirit and self-confidence of the Imperial Age, which coincided closely with the long reign of Queen Victoria.

As a first step towards realising this dream, Rhodes aimed to bypass the two Afrikaner republics and establish British settlement to the north of the Limpopo, on the highveld between that river and the Zambezi, ignoring the prior claim to this whole region by the Portuguese, who had never succeeded in asserting it. The only effective ruler in the region was the Matabele king, Lobengula, who by this time had succeeded his father, Mzilikazi. In 1888, Charles Rudd, a representative of Rhodes, was finally able to secure from Lobengula, in spite of the hostility to it of most of his *indunas*, or headmen, and at the cost of considerable gifts, including rifles, an agreement that came to be known as the Rudd Concession. This granted exclusive mining rights, including the right to establish farms to provide food for the miners, in both Matabeleland and Mashonaland, as far north as the Zambezi, over which Lobengula claimed sovereignty. In granting the Concession, however, Lobengula was motivated, reluctantly, not by the gifts, but by his recognition that, just as the Matabele themselves had been unstoppable in their northwards march from the Transvaal, so now, were the Europeans. There is no doubt that the Matabele understood what they were signing, because it was fully explained to them by the Rev, Charles Helm, a member of the London Missionary Society, whose integrity was not in doubt.[9] The hostility of the headmen of the Matabele to the concession represented trouble for the future, however, and Lobengula later tried to backtrack on the agreement. Rhodes and his supporters, on the other hand, faced a torrid

9   L. Gann, *A History of Southern Rhodesia* (New York, 1969).

time in achieving approval for the Concession in London. Nevertheless, Rhodes founded the British South Africa Company and obtained a royal charter for it in 1890. The favourable attitude of the Government towards the grant of a royal charter was based on the concern of the Government to keep the African interior out of the hands of foreign powers and avoid the risks that this would involve, and Rhodes alone was in a position to meet the cost of this. The purpose of the royal charter seems to have been threefold: to give the enterprise the legal standing that would allow it to raise the necessary money on the London capital market; to obtain recognition and support for the enterprise by the Crown; and to give the Company a standing in its dealings with other powers, particularly when concluding or acting upon treaties. From the point of view of the Crown, the charter, whose terms were suitably wide, provided a means of keeping the interior out of foreign – particularly German[10] – hands, having too little funds itself for the purpose, and no means of controlling the activities of British frontiersmen in the region. The area granted to the Company, for an initial period of twenty-five years,[11] including all necessary administrative powers, was vaguely defined as extending north of the Limpopo and west of Portuguese Mozambique. There was no mention of a northern limit to the Company's jurisdiction, in spite of the wish of the Colonial Office that it be defined as the Zambezi. On the other hand, the request by Rhodes that it include Bechuanaland, to the south-west, was left unresolved for the time being, perhaps in deference to the sensibilities of the humanitarian movement.[12]

1890 was a momentous year for Rhodes, because it saw him become the Premier of the Cape Colony, and it marked the launching by him of his British South Africa Company (BSAC), to be established in northern Mashonaland. To this end, and in view of the high risk of attack by the Matabele, the Company planned the operation as if it were a military undertaking. The several hundred carefully chosen prospectors, farmers, tradesmen and future administrators, as well as African wagon-drivers, were formed, trained and equipped as a military 'Pioneer Column',

---

10   Germany had developing interests in South-West Africa and Tanganyika in East Africa, and undoubtedly had an ambition to connect and settle the two.

11   The Concession had been granted, to the concessionaires, not to the Crown, which was not in a position, therefore, to dictate the terms of its occupation. The grant by the Crown can only have related, therefore, to that area not already covered by the Concession.

12   There being active Church mission stations already in the region.

escorted by the first contingent of nearly five hundred mounted men of the BSAC's Police, who were also to garrison forts constructed along the way.[13] A telegraph line was also to be erected. The only way into northern Mashonaland, however, was by means of the Hunters' Road, a well-established track that passed through Matabeland and Bulawayo, where hunters and prospectors would stop and seek the permission of Lobengula before proceeding further. In view of the tense situation, however, this was out of the question. The solution was provided by twenty-three-year-old Frank Johnson, who had impressed Rhodes (himself only thirty-six) with his experience in this part of Africa and his grasp of what was required, including the feasibility of the route to be taken. This was to be a wagon road through the virgin bush of the uninhabited lowveld, well to the east of Matabeleland. Rhodes was a good judge of men, and the operation was to be organised and led by Johnson, under contract.

The operation went without incident, apart from a delay while a way was found of getting the wagons up a thousand-foot escarpment. This took the Column onto the grassy upland. Just four weeks later, the site of the fifth and final fort, Fort Salisbury, was established, on 12 September 1890, at the completion of the four-hundred-mile trek. The site was located near the main watershed of Mashonaland, at an altitude of just over 5,000 feet. Here, after a trek of 400 miles, the Column disbanded with a final parade, at which the Union Jack was flown (the Company flag having been 'mislaid') and a proclamation was read annexing to 'the British Empire' the territory defined in the Concession. This was, of course, a violation of what Lobengula had intended, but then he could neither read nor write, and later did not know what he had signed. Colquhoun, the Administrator appointed by the Company, now took control, and it was the Company's flag that would be flown over his office as the new township of Salisbury took shape.[14]

Thus, the Crown was not involved in the founding, planning, execution or subsequent government of the new colony, which would eventually be named by the Company as 'Rhodesia', after the man himself, but it was

---

13   Professional military advice, obtained by Rhodes from General Sir Frederick Carrington, was that such an operation would require 2,500 professional soldiers and cost at least a million pounds, which, according to Johnson, was absurd, adding that, with 250 men, he 'would walk through the country'. Various other frontiersmen took a similar view. T. Bulpin, *To the Banks of the Zambezi* (Johannesburg, 1965), 263.

14   Now known as Harare.

well aware of its purpose and the benefit of its establishment for Britain, without any charge to the public purse. During the preparations, contact was maintained with the British High Commissioner in Cape Town.

As soon as the Column was dismissed, many of its members set off to prospect for gold, while others negotiated with local chiefs for the purchase of land for farms. There followed a steady flow of settlers from the south by wagon, boosting the tiny settlement, including the first group of *Afrikaners*, comprising the Moodie Trek, which settled in the Eastern Highlands. North of the Zambezi, the Company had previously concluded agreements with the Barotse chiefs in the west; with King Leopold, in respect of the Belgian Congo border to the north; and with local native chiefs in the north-east and east, in respect of the whole region between the Zambezi, Lake Nyasa to the east, and Lake Mweru, just the north, of which extended Lake Tanganyika, 500 miles north of the Zambezi. In 1893, an outpost and settlement were established near the southern end of Lake Tanganyika, and in 1896, an Administrator for the region north of the Zambezi was appointed by the Company. Such was the physical separation imposed, however, by the great rift valley of the Zambezi – a hot, dry region, infested with tsetse fly, largely uninhabited, and much of it forming a deep and largely inaccessible gorge, that was difficult to cross – that north and south were administered independently of each other.

Meanwhile, that part of the colony south of the Valley, about the size of France, where most settlement was taking place, faced formidable problems. Gold occurrences proved to be small and scattered; there was the ever-present risk of its line of communication to the south being cut by the Matabele; and in spite of the prevailing healthy climate, the region was subject to a range of tropical diseases that posed a risk to man and beast, including malaria, redwater and blackwater fevers, sleeping sickness, bilharzia and rinderpest, which would take years to bring under control. Fortunately, the early lawlessness that appeared in other parts of the Empire was not a feature of the Rhodesian frontier. The Company's police force, whose name was changed to the British South Africa Police, gradually acquired a reputation for competence, moderation and integrity, and administrative corruption was rare. Purely 'native' criminal cases were at first left to the African community.[15]

15   L. Gann, *A History of Southern Rhodesia* (New York, 1969).

37.3.1. The Right of Native Kings

Meanwhile, the strained relations between the Company and the Matabele were bound to come to a head, and in 1893 the treaty was broken by a Matabele *impi*, which entered Mashonaland near Fort Victoria, in the south, and attacked some Mashona villages. There is no doubt that the Company's interpretation of the Concession far exceeded Lobengula's intention, but when it also became clear that Lobengula still regarded Mashonaland as his fiefdom, and did not recognise the border, it was evident that the matter must be resolved, a view shared by Sir Henry Loch, the British High Commissioner in Cape Town. Loch was the nominal head of the Cape government, of which Rhodes was Prime Minister, but he also represented the interests of the Crown in South Africa generally, and he had control of an ill-disciplined Imperial force, the Bechuanaland Border Police. The Company responded by forming two mounted columns of the BSAP and settlers, which converged on Bulawayo. In spite of being outnumbered by about 18,000 to 1,100, the columns had the benefit of three advantages. One was mobility, another the well-tried defence offered by the wagon *laager*, and the third the use of the Maxim gun, this being the first occasion in history when this early machine-gun was effectively used in warfare. Although the Matabele had excellent rifles, their shooting was erratic, and they followed traditional tactics, with mass attacks that were disastrous in the circumstances. Inflicting two defeats on the Matabele, the columns advanced on Bulawayo. Meanwhile, the Colonial Office ordered that negotiations with Lobengula were to be conducted by the High Commissioner, which would undoubtedly have resulted in Matabeleland becoming a Crown Protectorate. This was undoubtedly motivated, in part, by Colonial Office resentment of the independence of the Company, but it was probably motivated also by the consideration that Lobengula was regarded as the 'king' of the Matabele. In accordance with feudal doctrine, despite the fact that Lobengula was not a Christian ruler, his status justified his territory being treated as a Protectorate, not a Colony. This would have precluded British settlement in Matabeleland. Rhodes was strongly opposed to the idea, and in the event it was the Company's columns, not the Bechuanaland Border Police, that entered Bulawayo, which Lobengula had already destroyed and abandoned. There was little sympathy for the Matabele, who were now experiencing, in a much-ameliorated form, what they had long inflicted upon others. Matabeleland was thereupon annexed by the Company, and in order to make its future status clear, a European settlement was immediately established on the site of Bulawayo, which would eventually become the colony's second largest city. Lobengula fled, but died a few months later, with no successor being appointed.[16]

Further south, meanwhile, Rhodes, in his capacity as Prime Minister of the Cape Colony, arranged for the annexation, by it, of Bechuanaland, lying between the Cape Colony and Rhodesia, as a protectorate. In so doing, he established territorial continuity, as well as a route for the Cape railway to be extended to the north, by-passing the hostile Afrikaner republics, whose own ambitions north of the Limpopo had been thwarted.

Meanwhile, it had long been the policy of the Crown, in keeping with feudal law, to resolve the 'treason' committed by the *Voortrekkers* in leaving the Cape Colony without permission – the idea of punishment having now been dropped – by bringing them back under its jurisdiction. This made the Crown favourable to the idea of preventing their further 'escape' northwards, beyond the Limpopo. Rhodes, however, had been pursuing the prospect of British occupation north of the Limpopo for a very different reason. Unlike the Crown, he had no vendetta against the *Afrikaners*, with many of whom he had always been on the friendliest of terms, but he regarded the bringing of the two republics into his scheme as essential for the extension of the Empire northwards. The detour through Bechuanaland was unsatisfactory, and he undoubtedly recognised the *Afrikaners* as cousins of the English. To this end, he sought to use the discontent of the British settlers on the Witwatersrand, who were seeking civic rights, as a means to bringing the South African Republic under the Crown's jurisdiction. As already noted, the settlers were known in 1896 to be planning a revolt against the government in Pretoria, and

16 A tragic figure at the end, believed to have taken poison. The campaign of conquest also ended tragically, when a small force, inadequate for the task, was sent from Bulawayo to try to locate Lobengula. Near the Shangani River, exhausted and in appalling conditions of recurring rain-storms, and unaware of the considerable Matabele army that was still with the king, a mounted patrol of thirty-seven men, under Major Alan Wilson, was sent ahead, only to find itself surrounded. According to reports, it fought until it had used up its ammunition, whereupon the few survivors stood and sang the national anthem, while being shot, speared and clubbed to death. The Shangani Patrol episode had much the same significance for the founding of the new nation as the Gallipoli Campaign had for the Australians. See R. Blake, *A History of Rhodesia* (New York, 1978), 108–11.

he arranged for a volunteer force of the BSA Police, under Jameson, who had succeeded Colquhoun as Administrator, to be brought down from Rhodesia to the Bechuanaland border with the Transvaal, in order to give military support to the rebellion. There is reason to believe that Chamberlain, the Colonial Secretary, was party to the plot.[17] In the event, the rebellion failed to take place, and although Rhodes ordered Jameson, at the last moment, to cancel his incursion, Jameson, an impetuous man, embarked upon it in any case. Unfortunately, the Republic's government had been well aware of what was afoot, and had taken appropriate steps, with the result that the 'Jameson Raid' became a military and diplomatic disaster. Rhodes was blamed, leaving him with little choice but to resign as Prime Minister of the Cape.

In Rhodesia, meanwhile, triggered by the depletion of the BSA Police, two rebellions broke out in the same year, that nearly destroyed the colony. The Matabele Rebellion was caused by a lack of effective administration in the region, brought to a head by a double affliction of drought and rinderpest, which destroyed the crops and decimated the cattle. Inevitably, the disaster was associated by the Matabele with the arrival of the Europeans, but it also owed much to incitement by a leading priest and former slave of the Matabele, Mkwati, who was credited with magical powers and who stirred up a fanatical zeal. The small number of White settlers in outlying parts of Matabeleland were hideously butchered, and the acting Administrator (Jameson being absent) succeeded in collecting together enough local volunteers and survivors to establish the Bulawayo Field Force, which proceeded to win two victories over the rebels. It was then joined by a column from Salisbury, organised by Rhodes, who happened to be in Mashonaland at the time.[18] Also due to arrive was an Imperial force from Bechuanaland, that had been despatched by the British High Commissioner in the Cape. Meanwhile, following a third defeat by the Field Force, the Matabele retreated into the almost impenetrable rocky fastness of the Matopo Hills, about ten miles to the south of Bulawayo.

---

17   R. Blake, *A History of Rhodesia,* 130–1, 139.

18   Rhodes's resignation from the BSA Company (and from the Cape Government), which had been tendered to the board in London, following the Jameson disaster, was eagerly sought by the Colonial Secretary, who had good reason to get Rhodes out of the way, but the Company had delayed. Cabling its doubts to Rhodes, the latter had replied, 'Let resignation wait – we fight Matabele tomorrow'. R. Blake, *A History of Rhodesia*, 133.

It was at this juncture that the Mashona also rose, unexpectedly, massacring the depleted White population, which was scattered over a huge area of Mashonaland, in isolated mines, farms and stores. This revolt had its origin in numerous grievances, but also, like the Matabele Rebellion, it owed much to the incitement of a spirit medium, given further impetus by a small group of escaping Matabele. A hasty *laager* was formed at Fort Salisbury, and every effort was made to rescue survivors from the outlying communities, in many cases involving considerable heroism. The small relief force sent to the Alice Mine near the Mazoe River, was later commemorated with a Victoria Cross.[19] Nevertheless, because of its fragmented nature, the Mashona rebellion took many months finally to put down. Defeat of the Matabele in the Matopo Hills promised to be particularly slow and costly, an expense that the Company could ill-afford. In the event, Rhodes initiated peace talks. With three European companions and a Tembu scout, and at great personal risk, he rode into the rugged hills for several miles and held a conference, or *indaba*, with the Matabele chiefs, watched by the thousands of Matabele warriors in the surrounding hills. Rhodes, who got on well with Africans and had a good understanding of the African mind, listened to their grievances over four days. Most proved to be of a fairly minor nature, and he promised to attend to them all, as indeed, he subsequently did. It was a courageous act that made a deep impression on the Matabele, as would later become apparent.

In 1897, the Crown recognised the Company's territory north of the Zambezi as 'Northern Rhodesia'. That south of the Zambezi accordingly became known in the following year as 'Southern Rhodesia'. The former included the land of the Barotse, an indigenous people who inhabited the marshy region of the upper Zambezi in the west, ruled by a king, Lewanika, who had sought British protection from the Portuguese in neighbouring Angola. Because the Crown recognised Lewanika as a king, Barotseland was granted the status of a self-governing Protectorate. In this capacity, Barotseland was incorporated into Northern Rhodesia. This policy of recognising Native kingdoms as Protectorates had previously been followed by the Crown in respect of Swaziland, east of the Transvaal, and in respect of Basutoland, in the Drakensberg, between Orangia and Natal. It would later be followed in respect of the Baganda in East Africa,

19   Ibid., 123–43.

whose kingdom would be preserved as the protectorate of Uganda.[20] The autonomy of the Barotse king was formalised in 1899, when the Crown secured the agreement of the Rhodesian Government for Barotseland to come under the aegis of an Administrator, who, together with judges and magistrates, were to be nominated and employed by the Company, but appointed by the High Commissioner for South Africa.[21]

37.3.2. Government in Southern Rhodesia

The BSAC provided for a Legislative Council in Southern Rhodesia, which was first elected in 1899. Settlement in Northern Rhodesia had not yet reached the point at which this was feasible. Whereas Roman-Dutch law applied south of the Zambezi, the Colonial Office, undoubtedly with an eye to appropriating it in the future, had insisted that English common law should apply north of the river. The Colonial Office had never been reconciled to the independence of the Company, and it seems increasingly to have nursed an ambition to detach and appropriate Northern Rhodesia. This coincided with the growing humanitarian movement in Britain and the spread of socialism, causing the interests of the indigenous inhabitants of the Empire to become uppermost in the minds of the intellectual elite, who looked to philosophy, rather than history, for guidance. For these, the moral validity of the Empire itself was coming under scrutiny, and it was a trend that the Marxists were not slow to exploit. For Rhodesia, born at the very zenith of the Imperial Age, when the spirit of the open steppes had once again found an outlet, from Montana to New South Wales, such a moralising view of the world and history was incomprehensible. The ideological conflict was already on a collision course, and of all the new nations established by the Empire, none would feel the effect of the impending collision more harshly.

Rhodes died in 1902, and was buried at his chosen site in the Matopo Hills, on the summit of a granite *kopje* which he had once described as

---

20   That the policy was not applied in the case of the Matabele kingdom was due to the fact
      that authority was exercised in the region by the BSA Company, not by the Crown.

21   That it had failed to do so in the case of the Matabele kingdom may have been due to
      some uncertainty as to whether Lobengula could be regarded as a king, rather than a chief,
      but more so to the fact that the Rhodesian Government, which had asserted prior claim
      to the kingdom, had no wish for its own citizens to be deprived of the right to settle there.
      There are good grounds for believing, in any case, that Lobengula took his own life and
      that no attempt was ever made to appoint a successor, implying the end of the dynasty. See
      R. Blake, *A History of Rhodesia*, 111–12.

'the View of the World'. During the event, which it had been assumed by the representatives of the Southern Rhodesia Government and the BSA Company would be of interest only to the White population, those attending were astonished by the arrival of thousands of Matabele, who proceeded, from a respectful distance, to honour the dead man with the royal salute of *Bayete!* which the Matabele had never used before, except in honour of their own kings. It is unlikely that any other European in the history of Africa had ever received such a spontaneous honour from its native inhabitants. Later in the same year, large copper deposits were discovered in Northern Rhodesia that would eventually give rise to the Rhodesian Copper Belt, one of the world's biggest mining complexes. Fortunately, a bridge over the Zambezi at the Victoria Falls, completed in 1905, not only permitted a road and rail connection between south and north, but went on to provide rail access to the developing mines. Meanwhile, the hoped-for gold bonanza that had attracted many settlers to Southern Rhodesia had failed to materialise, beyond a scatter of small mines, and it was not until about 1910 onwards that the farming industry really began to find salvation in the cultivation and export of tobacco. Meanwhile, in 1907, the Company had granted the settlers a majority of the seats in the Legislative Assembly, and Charles Coghlan, who was destined to become Southern Rhodesia's first Prime Minister, was elected to the Assembly in the following year.

38. THE FIRST WORLD WAR

38.1. Home Rule for Ireland (1914)

Ireland had always been a problem for England, because it had no real interest there. It had been inherited from the Normans and their Angevin successors, which had led to English settlement in the east, within the 'Pale'. Meanwhile, as the English had gradually regained control of their own country from the Angevin dynasty, the subsequent Reformation introduced a division between a newly Protestant England and a still Catholic Ireland. This had led to organised attempts to establish Protestant settlement in the north of Ireland, and this had generated a new antagonism. The native Irish, who had inherited a volatile temperament, probably from an ancestry that went back to immigration from the Iberian Peninsula in Neolithic times, had subsequently absorbed a Celtic culture, and later still Roman Catholicism, leaving them tenaciously opposed to any intrusion, let alone partition.

Previous attempts to pass Home Rule Bills for Ireland had been thwarted, first by the 'Unionist' Conservatives and then by the House of Lords. Nevertheless, the Liberal Party had committed itself to Home Rule, as the result of a cynical deal struck with the Irish Nationalists, in order to secure the passage of the quite unrelated People's Budget of 1909. Accordingly, a new Bill was initiated in 1912, which provided for both an Irish Parliament and continued representation in Westminster. Opposition to the Bill came particularly from the Ulster Protestants, who were of English and Scottish origin and, anxious to preserve their British identity, refused to be absorbed by a Roman Catholic Ireland. Twice the Bill was passed by the Commons in 1913, and twice rejected by the Lords. Meanwhile, opposition to the Bill in Northern Ireland itself grew steadily more shrill and organised, with the raising of a force of Ulster Volunteers. A third passage of the Bill through the Commons in May

1914, ensured its adoption as a statute under the new legislative rules that had been imposed upon the House of Lords, but by now the opposition in Northern Ireland had reached its peak. With the Home Rule Bill having not yet received the royal assent, Asquith introduced an amending Bill as a compromise, in an attempt to avert civil war in Ireland. This would have allowed Ulster to opt out of the new arrangement for six years. The Lords insisted on there being no time limit for Ulster, and the opposition of the Nationalists to the amending Bill, allowing an Ulster opt-out, became intense. The crisis was now overtaken by the Great War, the clouds of which had been gathering for several years, and the storm finally broke in August 1914. The Home Rule Bill, without the Ulster provision, received the royal assent in September, but a simultaneous Act, designed to avert domestic upheaval at such a momentous time, declared that it was not to come into effect until after the war. Meanwhile, the Government pledged that an amending Bill dealing with Ulster would be introduced.

Great Britain's preoccupation with the war had unfortunate repercussions in Ireland. The Nationalists had no interest in the war, beyond hoping for Britain's defeat, and the frustration caused by the suspension of the Home Rule Act for the duration left a volatile brew, which Germany did not fail to exploit. Not surprisingly, there was a rebellion in Southern Ireland in 1916 – the Easter Rising – fomented by an Irish nationalist leader, Sir Roger Casement, who had earlier fled to Germany, and who had now returned, to be landed on the Irish coast from a German submarine. The insurrection was suppressed after a week of fighting, and Casement and other Irish leaders were executed, implying that, in the circumstances of the war, the rising had been viewed as high treason, and this left a legacy of increased bitterness. Not to be thwarted, the Irish republican movement, *Sinn Fein*, held a convention in Dublin in 1917, at which they drew up a constitution for an independent Irish Republic, electing De Valera as its President.

In Nonconformist Wales, meanwhile, the constitutional standing of the Anglican Church had long been seen as an affront, and the Welsh Disestablishment Bill of 1914 provided at last for the disestablishment there of the Church of England. Welsh bishops were no longer to sit in the House of Lords, and the Church in the four Welsh dioceses would thus be free to manage its own affairs. It would relieve the bishops in Wales of much local hostility, but the measure contradicted the Coronation Oath of George V, and so was of no legal effect in common law. It was statute law, however, that weighed with the courts and with the Parties. The Bill now followed an almost identical course to that of the Irish Home Rule Bill, being rejected in the Lords and finally by-passing the Lords, but being deferred from coming into operation until after the war.

38.2. The First World War (1914–18)

The relevance of the First World War was to be its profound effect on Britain's constitutional arrangements. The rise of nationalism across Europe in the wake of the Napoleonic Wars gave rise to a conflict of national, rather than dynastic, interests in the late nineteenth century. These were held in place by a complex system of alliances and counter-alliances, at the centre of which sat the German chancellor, Bismarck, whose overriding concerns were to head off the growing Socialist movement in Prussia, led by the Communists; the unification of the German-speaking states under the Prussian crown; and the resulting threat posed by an increasingly outclassed France, which saw German unification as a threat to its influence in Europe and its ambition to annex the Rhineland. More immediately, France was driven by a determination to avenge its defeat and humiliation in 1871. For this, however, it felt the need of an ally, and Great Britain was the obvious candidate. Britain, meanwhile, remained largely outside this frenetic system of alliances, preferring to sit in a state of 'splendid isolation'.

The system of alliances and the adroitness of Bismarck maintained the peace in Europe until Bismarck was dismissed in 1890, following the accession of the young Wilhelm II as Emperor of Germany, who was unhappy about Bismarck's close relations with Russia, and anxious for better relations with Austria and Great Britain. Wilhelm was a young man, intelligent, idealistic, and sympathetic to the working class, but impulsive and obstinate, and he soon felt a desire to manage affairs for himself, rather than rule in the shadow of Bismarck. As a result, the system of stabilising alliances quickly began to unravel. The conflicts that followed have usually been lumped together by historians as a single war, partly because events were, to a considerable extent, interrelated through the web of alliances and counter-alliances, but this disguises the reality that what followed were two wars – between Russia and Austria, and between France and Germany – over quite separate issues: Russia's desire for influence in the Balkans, in the one case, and France's desire for revenge and territorial gain on the other. Great Britain gave its support to France because of its concern that Wilhelm's naval policy, made possible by Germany's industrial rise, posed a growing threat to its own naval supremacy. Neither Austria nor Germany stood to gain from such a war, but Germany now found itself under threat from France in the west, now supported by Britain, and from Russia in the east. The latter was because of Germany's long-standing alliance with Austria, blocking Russia's ambition to control the Dardanelles. Germany now faced the nightmare prospect of having to fight two wars at once. It was Germany, therefore, that was the link between the two wars. Bismarck could have coped with the problem; Wilhelm could not.

A side effect of these two pending conflicts was a third, an Anglo-Ottoman war, which, in spite of Britain's forthcoming defeat at Gallipoli, in pursuit of the Franco-German war, was to arise from Britain's wish to use the opportunity to remove the Ottoman threat to its interests in the Suez Canal and the Persian oilfields.

38.2.1. The Austro-Russian War

By the late nineteenth century, Russia was beginning to industrialise and had acquired ambitions to become a naval power. She had access to the Baltic and the Atlantic through St Petersburg, but not in winter, and she had no outlet from the Black Sea to the Mediterranean, because Ottoman Turkey, at the instance of Britain and France, denied it access through the Bosporus and the Dardanelles, known as 'the Straits'. Russia's desire to seize the Straits, through overland access through the southern Balkans, caused Turkey to form a military alliance with Germany. Meanwhile, Russia's concern that a Dual Alliance between Germany and Austria in 1879 was aimed at itself had been offset by Bismarck, who had maintained close relations with Russia. This had not been sustained by the German Emperor, however, leaving Russia to suspect that Germany's purpose was to keep her out of the Balkans. This now caused Russia to see Germany as a threat. In 1908, Austria had annexed Bosnia and Herzegovina, on the western side of the Balkan Peninsula, and this had caused outrage in Russia, which had seen it as an intrusion into her own area of special interest, which had close cultural ties with Russia through the Pan-Slav movement and the Orthodox Church.

By 1913 the Balkans were in turmoil, with Serbia and northern Bulgaria at war with the Ottoman Turks, and the Greeks in rebellion against Turkish rule. In June of 1914, the successor to the Austrian throne, the Archduke Franz Ferdinand, while on a visit to Serbia, was assassinated in Sarajevo by an agent of a Serbian revolutionary group, almost certainly with the complicity of the Serbian government. Austria, inclined to declare war against Serbia, held back at first, when it realised the possible implications, but Russia, hoping for a general war that would free her to invade the Balkans, and assured of French support, mobilised. This caused Austria to respond, in the expectation of German support. Russia had no quarrel with Germany, only the fear that Austria would invoke its treaty with Germany. Now anticipating the worst, the German general staff favoured a pre-emptive war to defeat France, before proceeding to dismember the Russian Empire.[1] Although Germany was becoming a major industrial power, and Russia was only in the early stages of industrialisation, it had much bigger coal and iron ore resources than Germany, as well as a bigger population, causing Germany to be concerned at the prospect of a future industrial colossus on its eastern border. There was not even a buffer state between them, because Poland at the time was a part of the Russian Empire.

Austria now declared war on Serbia, and Turkey declared war against Russia. The main theatre of the resulting conflict, however, was between the Russians and the Germans and Austrians on the North European Plain, between the Baltic and the Carpathians, particularly in Poland and Galicia.[2] Germany's hope of a quick victory over France in 1914 was not realised, leaving Germany fighting two wars. By 1917, however, Russia was close to collapse, and Germany sought to weaken Russia further by transporting a group of Russian Communist revolutionaries, led by Lenin, who had been hiding in Switzerland, to cross Germany in

---

1   F. Fischer, *Griff nach der Weltmacht*.
2   The region between Poland and the Carpathians.

order to foment a revolution in St Petersburg. The ploy was successful, and the Tsar abdicated in March 1917. In November the Communists seized power, and in December sued for peace, and, in keeping with the plan of the German general staff, the Germans and Austrians occupied the Ukraine. Here, Germany set up an independent government. This occupation was soon terminated by the ending of the war, but it was an event that was to have greater significance for the future. In view of the growing crisis in the west, however, peace was formally concluded in March 1918, and the armies were withdrawn. The Austrian Empire was now on the verge of collapse, as desertions from the army increased and the various nations forming the Empire rose in rebellion or simply asserted their independence.

Meanwhile, an Anglo-French landing at Salonika, in Greece, brought about the surrender of Bulgaria at the end of September, separating the Turks from their Austrian and German allies. This compounded Turkey's problems, because her empire was already wilting under the pressure of the Anglo-Ottoman War.

38.2.2. The Franco-German War

Apart from the tension with France, there was also tension between Germany and Great Britain, arising from a telegram (the 'Kruger telegram') that had been sent by Wilhelm II in 1896. This had congratulated President Kruger of the South African Republic, following its defeat of the Jameson Raid, which Wilhelm had assumed to be the work of the British Government. Britain had responded by threatening that, if Germany intervened in the South African conflict, the Royal Navy would impose a blockade on the German coast. In anticipation of this, Britain had developed plans for such a blockade, and Germany was induced to look to its defences by constructing a fleet of its own that it planned to be two-thirds of the size of the Royal Navy. This conflicted with Britain's defence policy, which was to ensure that the Royal Navy was at least the size of the world's next two largest navies. The outcome was a naval arms race from 1898 onwards. It was probably by 1914 that Germany, realising that a war with France probably meant a war also with Great Britain, switched to building a fleet of submarines that could be used to blockade Britain in the event of a conflict. An Anglo-German war was unlikely, in itself, because neither country was in a position to invade the other.

By the turn of the century, meanwhile, Britain and France had resolved most of their colonial rivalries, particularly over Egypt and Morocco, and this was confirmed in an Anglo-French reconciliation in 1904, which became known as the *Entente Cordiale*. Germany may have suspected that this also contained a secret military agreement aimed at itself. France inflamed relations with Germany by involving Britain in its negotiations with Morocco, a country on which France had designs but was of particular interest to Germany, because it provided a much-needed naval staging post in the Atlantic. Anticipating the worst, German strategy was to inflict a quick defeat on France and Britain, before transferring its main forces to the east, to deal with the expected Russian attack, which was expected to take much longer to mobilise. Consequently, the war, when it came, was essentially a Franco-German conflict, because France was the prime mover. That Britain so readily joined the conflict may be attributed to anxiety over the growing power of Germany, in parallel with Germany's own anxiety at the growing power of Russia.

The Franco-German War, which could have been so easily avoided, but was motivated mainly by France's desire to avenge itself for its humiliating defeat in 1871 (which, with Great Britain as an ally, it was now in a position to do), was now precipitated by the effect on Russia of the assassination of the Austrian archduke in Sarajevo, in June 1914. Germany, now under threat in the east and west, enquired of France what its attitude would be in the event of a Balkan war. To this, France gave a non-committal reply, and promptly began to mobilise. In a final effort, Germany approached Britain, offering not to attack France if Britain could guarantee France's neutrality. Three hours later, receiving no reply, and anticipating having to fight on two fronts, Germany declared war on Russia, who was expected to need six weeks to mobilise. Germany's strategy against France, meanwhile, was to launch an outflanking attack through Belgium, catching the main French forces – which were preparing to invade Germany through Lorraine – in the rear. Maintaining its momentum, the German army was to occupy Paris. Its invasion of Belgium would have allowed the latter to invoke a guarantee that Great Britain had given to Belgium in 1830. Germany hoped that Britain would no longer feel bound by it, or alternatively, that Britain could be persuaded to stay out of the war by Germany offering to respect Belgium's integrity, in exchange for Belgium's permission to send troops across its territory. However, Britain not only regarded itself as committed diplomatically to the preservation of Belgium's neutrality, but she regarded the existence of an independent Belgium as an insurance policy against the domination of the Channel coast by a major, and potentially hostile, power. The German request was rejected, and only three days after the commencement of hostilities with Russia, Germany, accepting the inevitable, sought to take the initiative by declaring war on France, at which Britain declared war on Germany. On the following day, 4 August 1914, Germany launched its pre-emptive attack.

What followed was to be the most disastrous war in modern European history, with profound and enduring consequences, not least for Great Britain. Nevertheless, apart from the initial misgivings, a European war was generally popular. Italy had long been looking for an opportunity to acquire territory from Austria, and Britain was glad of a chance to put an end to Germany's rivalry. Nevertheless, the Serbian crisis would probably have remained a Balkan conflict, but for France, which was now able to use it to her advantage by drawing upon her alliances with Russia and Britain. We are probably entitled, therefore, to define this, usually described as 'the Great War', as being essentially the Second Franco-German War, into which Britain was willingly drawn.

Largely unprepared for the war, however, Britain sent an Expeditionary Force to take over the section of front line around Mons, between the Belgians and the French. By the end of August 1914, the French were in retreat from Lorraine, and the British were defeated at Mons. By the end of the year, the French had retreated almost to Paris, leaving a great westward bulge in the front line. Nevertheless, the French held onto the fortress of Verdun in the south, while the British held Ypres in the north, as well as the nearby Channel ports. Supply difficulties now forced the Germans to shorten the line by withdrawing from the Marne to the Aisne, and their inability to make further progress was due to a transfer of forces to the east, where the Russians had launched an offensive earlier that the Germans had expected.

Although the 'Western' front extended from the Channel coast to Switzerland, the southern half was hilly and wooded, making operations difficult, so that the military effort on both sides was largely concentrated along a corridor 200 miles wide, into which millions of men were concentrated. Here, the tactics of earlier wars were no longer feasible. The machine-gun inflicted massive losses on exposed men, and barbed wire offered a good defence, exposing the attackers to even heavier losses. The French had invented artillery that was not thrown out of alignment by its recoil, which was now absorbed by cylinders of oil, making possible accurate and rapid artillery fire. The only protection from machine-guns and artillery bombardment were trenches. These were at first intended as temporary shelters, but advancing infantry, even supported by heavy concentrations of artillery fire, proved ineffective against machine-gun fire from opposing trenches, protected by barbed wire. The result was a more static form of warfare, the outcome of which depended upon the respective rates of mutual attrition. The availability of rail transport made possible a steady stream of supplies, and the invention of tinned food allowed the men to be kept in the trenches throughout the winter. The near-impossibility of controlling and directing operations on this scale was soon overcome by another invention, the telephone. The only trouble with the telephone was that it could not be used once the troops had moved forward in attack, and this loss of contact at critical times helped to ensure that most attacks ended in chaos, reinforcing the static nature of the conflict and adding to the appalling loss of life. The introduction of the use of gas added further to the misery of those on the front line.

Germany attempted to break the stalemate by imposing their submarine blockade of Great Britain, but this involved the sinking of American ships, and the most important effect of the blockade was to bring the United States to the brink of war with Germany. Meanwhile, Germany gambled on the hope that Britain could be starved into withdrawing before the United States could play an effective part in the war. By 1916 the manpower losses were so great that Britain was forced to follow the example of other countries by introducing compulsory general conscription. Meanwhile, state-sponsored propaganda had been born on both sides, often of the crudest kind, in an effort to maintain morale. The United States declared war on Germany in April 1917, and the German high command was now intent on getting Russia out of the conflict by promoting a revolution. To this end, as previously mentioned, Germany let loose the exiled Russian Communists, to cause a distraction that would get Russia out of the Austro-Russian War. The success of this ploy allowed the transfer of much of the German army in the east to the Western Front, where, for the first time, it was numerically stronger that the combined British and French. This permitted a final attempt to defeat Britain and France before the Americans could train and arrive in large enough numbers to affect the course of the war, and before starvation in Germany and lack of supplies, due to the British naval blockade, made Germany incapable of pursuing it. The outcome of the war was now finely balanced. The final, and greatest, German offensive in the spring and summer of 1918, concentrated on the weakest part of the Allied line, where the French and British armies joined, the British army having taken over the whole of the line from the Channel to the Somme. In spite of advancing up to forty miles down the Somme and Oise valleys, and in July crossing the Marne at one point, the German offensive ground to a halt, held by the British before Ypres and on the Somme, and by the French and the newly arriving Americans further south. Both sides had suffered very heavy losses, but the Germans were near to exhaustion, and with the Allies now building ships faster than the Germans could sink them, and the arrival of the main American forces pending, it was clear that Germany could no longer win the war. The German commander, Ludendorf, tried to negotiate with the American President, Wilson, in the mistaken belief that he would offer better conditions than the French and British, but Wilson demanded democratic government in Germany, and an end to the monarchy, which it blamed for the war. Ludendorff now gave way to the politicians, who formed a coalition, in which the Socialists were the dominant party. Pétain, who was now the French commander-in-chief, demanded both heavy reparations from Germany that would incapacitate it, and the permanent occupation by France of Alsace-Lorraine and the west bank of the Rhine.[3]

At the end of September 1918, the German Socialist coalition, to which the Emperor now transferred control, immediately appealed for

---

3   The commander of the American forces, Pershing, also argued for a complete German defeat, rather than an armistice, otherwise Germany in twenty years would simply try to settle accounts.

an armistice on the basis of the American terms, known as the Fourteen Points. On 9 November, the leader of the Socialist majority in the coalition proclaimed Germany a republic, and on 11 November a German armistice commission, composed of politicians, met Marshall Foch at Compiègne. The terms offered by Foch were so harsh that the Germans had the greatest difficulty in accepting them, but concluded that they had no choice. They would probably not have been accepted by the men in the field, and the resulting resentment would have consequences for the future, but Germany had collapsed internally. The terms of the armistice were designed to reduce Germany to helplessness, so that she would have no choice but to accept whatever peace terms were subsequently imposed. These were decided between the Allies at Versailles, early in the following year, and included the transfer of Alsace-Lorraine to France and the granting to Poland of a broad corridor to the Baltic that would leave East Prussia isolated. Other penalties and compensations were designed to cripple Germany for decades to come. The retribution was imposed chiefly by France, with America withdrawing early from the conference, unable to be party to the severity of Germany's punishment, but having at least achieved its aim of establishing a League of Nations to deal with international disputes in the future. The German army had been under the impression that all that had been agreed to was an armistice, and its disbanded members now blamed the Socialists for the disaster. This and the penury to which the population was now subjected provided fertile ground for a bitter reaction.

38.2.3. The Anglo-Ottoman War

Britain, France and Russia now found themselves to be allies, and at the outbreak of the Austro-Russian War, the Ottoman Turks were allied to Germany. This had the effect of closing the Straits, between the Mediterranean and the Black Sea, to their use by the allies. When Britain endeavoured to capture the Straits in 1915, in the hope of opening up a new front against Germany, the enterprise failed disastrously. Otherwise, Britain's objectives in 1915 were to protect, from Ottoman occupation, the Suez Canal and the pipeline from its oilfields in Persia, whose outlet in the Persian Gulf was at Basra, at the mouth of the Tigris, which lay within the Ottoman Empire. Consequently, Britain had occupied Basra at the end of 1914.

In two campaigns, conducted over the next four years, based in Egypt and the Persian Gulf, the collapse of the Ottoman Empire was achieved. This had been aided by an Arab revolt, which Britain had promoted, and gradually conquered the Ottoman Empire south of the thirty-seventh parallel north, which included future Syria and Iraq.[4] Meanwhile, an agreement between Britain and France provided for an independent Arab state, or federation of states, to be mainly within the British sphere of influence, while the French sphere – even though France had played little or no part in the conflict – was to include the coastal strip of Syria, Cilicia to the north, and southern Kurdistan to the east. The fall of the Ottoman dynasty followed.

All three wars were formally ended in 1918, with France taking possession of the Lebanon and being granted Syria by Britain, in spite of Arab opposition. Britain, whose only interest in the region was to ensure that no other major power could threaten the Suez Canal or her oil supply in Persia, was prevailed upon by Jewish interests to declare Palestine to be a future home for 'the Jewish people', a policy that would have major consequences for the future. Meanwhile, Arabia was recognised as independent, under King Hussein of the Hejaz.

38.3. The Problem of the English Freeman and the Right to Vote

As the war approached its end in 1918, and with it the forthcoming election, the heavy price paid by the millions of ordinary men in the service of their country forced the ruling class to recognise, not without some discomfort, that there were still several million who had volunteered or been summoned, for military service in what was, in effect, a revival of the *fyrd* in respect of all the English shires, supported by the Welsh,

---

4   The Turks were reduced to their homeland in central Anatolia (once the homeland of the Hittites), where they established a new seat of government at Ankara. Here the government was usurped by the army, under the Westernising leadership of Kemal Atatürk, who established a new and much smaller empire by evicting the Greeks from western Anatolia and the Armenians and Kurds from eastern Anatolia. Britain did not intervene, because the new empire did not pose a threat to the Middle Eastern oilfields.

Scots and Irish, without having any influence on how their lives were governed. Women workers in the munitions factories, and hospitals had also made a vital and direct contribution to the war effort, enabling the country to achieve total mobilisation for the first time in its history. Even before the war, women campaigners for the right to vote had been active. Indeed, the idea of extending the franchise to women had originally been proposed at the time of the debate on the Second Reform Bill, by John Stuart Mill, a member of Parliament and political economist. It had not been until 1903, however, that this had been taken up by the Women's Social and Political Union, which had been founded by Mrs Emmeline Pankhurst and had embarked on a campaign for the extension of the franchise to women. Known as the Suffragette Movement, it had been suspended in 1914 as wartime patriotism diverted attention.

With a post-war general election now in the offing, the Prime Minister of the day, Asquith, calculated that a widening of the male franchise to men, and the enfranchising of women with the same property qualifications as had already been applied to men, would enhance the Liberal vote – in other words, it was an issue of Party benefit, not law or social benefit. Consequently, the Fourth Reform Act – the Representation of the People Act 1918 – extended the franchise to all men over twenty-one years of age who occupied a residence or business premises with an annual value of £10, or who held a university degree. It also extended the vote to women over thirty years of age, provided they occupied a property with an annual value of £5, or their husbands met that qualification, or if they held a university degree. The Act increased the number of voters by about eight million, of whom six million were now women. The extension of the vote to women endowed them only with a statutory right, because in common law only free men, as the heads of their respective families, had a right to attend or be represented in popular assemblies.

The enfranchisement of women had no immediate effect on British politics, perhaps because women tended to vote the same way as their menfolk. It would not be until the spread of women's education and the emancipation of women, nearly half a century later, from their restrictive role as mothers and housewives, that women would come to exert a significant influence in elections.

38.4. Consequences of the War

The humiliation and hardship imposed upon Germany after the war, through political upheaval, hyper-inflation, unemployment and shortages, as a direct result of the massive reparations demanded by France, compounded by Franco-Belgian occupation of the Rhineland, gave rise to an upsurge in xenophobia during the 1930s, the brunt of which would be borne by the Jews and Gypsies, the former and the Communists, with whom they were closely identified in the minds of many, being blamed for much of Germany's woes. The consequences for the French would follow two decades later. Meanwhile, the appropriation of large areas of Germany's territory by its neighbours after 1918 would have a destabilising effect, not least because the abolition of the monarchy, on American insistence, left Germany bereft of a stable leadership. The appropriation of Germany's empire by the Allies added to the general bitterness.

38.4.1. The Undermining of the Estates

Hitherto, the benefits of Empire to Great Britain had been mainly commercial, but the war of 1914–18 had brought a voluntary flood of military assistance to Britain from the Dominions, as well as considerable assistance from the Colonies. The Canadians, Australians, South Africans and New Zealanders had played a significant role on the Western Front, and the South Africans and Rhodesians had kept a German army bottled up in East Africa. The Australians and New Zealanders had also played an heroic part in the fateful attempt to occupy the Straits. An effect of the War had witnessed a change in the relationship between Great Britain and the Dominions, from one of benign patronage to one of virtual equality, with a reversal of the role of the former as guide and protector of Dominions and colonies to one of dependency upon them, not only for support in a time of crisis, but also as a valuable export market.

At home, during previous wars, the nobles of the Second Estate had led in battle, normally mounted, as had usually been the case for more than four thousand years, wherever they had fought in open country, since when, the men of the Third Estate had provided support on foot, holding the line whenever the fighting limited the scope for the use of cavalry. The advent of the machine-gun and barbed wire in the constricted space of the Western Front had left little opportunity for mounted men, and both Estates had been reduced to the trenches, fighting alongside each other, with little to distinguish the two. No longer able to shine in battle, the nobility of the Second Estate had lost, very largely, their unique social and military status in the eyes of ordinary free men, and at the same time had been forced to appreciate, and to rely upon, the fighting and personal qualities of the latter. Nevertheless, in keeping with its military tradition, its losses were still relatively much greater than they were for the Third Estate, and even these were now horrific. After 1918, the Estates drifted apart again, but the mystique that had distinguished the Estates no longer held, and the Socialist movement was able to exploit the battered social barrier. Meanwhile, the bitter disillusionment caused by the wanton carnage bred a cynicism towards the significance of life that undermined the authority of the Church, and with it the standing of the First Estate, itself already under attack from increasing scientific revelations. The post-war years accordingly witnessed an acceleration in the disintegration of the Estate structure of English society, and with it the institutional structure of the British system of government.

The Representation of the People Act of 1918 extended the right to be represented in Parliament to all women over thirty who were local government electors, or the wives of such electors. In 1928, this was extended to all women, on the same basis as men. In the light of this 'universal' franchise, the eligibility to vote was limited only to a minimum voting age of twenty-one years, and freedom from any legal incapacity, such as insanity, imprisonment, or being a Peer of the Realm. Finally, an elector must be registered as a resident of a parliamentary constituency. Meanwhile, the continuation of the right of Irish citizens to vote, and to enter and leave Britain at will, seems to have reflected on a refusal to acknowledge, in keeping with feudal principles, that Ireland was now a foreign country.

39. THE INTER-WAR YEARS (1918–45)

T HE GREAT WAR of 1914–18 was a watershed in both British and European history. To all the leading European participants, the effects were disastrous. Some ten million men were killed, with the heaviest losses suffered, in declining order, by Germany, Russia, France and Austria. Even so, Great Britain lost about 950,000 men killed, with over two million wounded. Most of the participating states were bankrupted, and only Great Britain retained its monarchy, the chief reason being that it had, once again, become beholden to the people. The Austro-Hungarian Empire disintegrated; Russia was in revolutionary chaos; and Turkey subsequently restored its self-respect by retrieving all that part of its former empire that had lain within Anatolia[1] and underwent a Westernising revolution that ended the moribund sultanate. Meanwhile, the political malaise that had afflicted France's Third Republic returned, only more deeply. Only the United States emerged stronger than when it had entered the war.

In Britain, the disastrous personal and economic consequences of the war had prepared the ground for a social revolution by the working class, which felt that the system owed it some recognition for the huge sacrifices that it had made. The more radically minded suspected that the basic purpose of the war had been to preserve the privileged position of the upper classes by keeping the lower classes where they had always been. The pre-war world, dominated by Great Britain, France and Germany, was now replaced by one that was increasingly under the influence of the United States, and under threat by Communist Russia. Meanwhile, the German colonies, logically and in accordance with accepted practice, now fell as prizes of war to appropriation by France and Great Britain, but, in an act of remarkable hypocrisy, the United States, which owed its own existence to the British Empire, and which had itself seized much of North America and half of the islands in the Pacific, objected on

---

1   The Turks inhabited only central Anatolia, centred upon Ankara. Western Anatolia was essentially Greek, while eastern Anatolia was inhabited by the Armenians and the Kurds, most of whom were evicted or massacred.

the grounds that this would be morally wrong, and that the German colonies should be vested in a new League of Nations, to be allocated under mandate only to France and Britain for the purpose of leading their inhabitants to independence.

Within Britain, the consequence of the war was a social and political revolution. This arose out of the very nature of the conflict. In earlier wars, the fighting had been done mainly by the ruling military class, the Second Estate, supported by ordinary men of the Third Estate who had served either by virtue of their feudal obligation, or as volunteers. The Great, or Second Franco-German War had proved to be well beyond the capacity of this arrangement, and it had been necessary for Parliament to approve the conscription of ordinary men in their millions, in a restoration of the liability, in effect, of all free men for service in the *fyrd*. From now onwards, the upper class – the political establishment – realised that it was no longer they who defended the country from its enemies, although they might lead in its defence. On the contrary, they now owed a debt of gratitude to ordinary men. In recognition of the service now demanded of them, Parliament in February 1918, while the war was still at its height, approved the extension of the vote to most men over twenty-one years of age who did not already possess it. In so doing, Parliament effectively completed the recognition of all free men who had been deprived of their status for centuries. Hardly less important had been the manner in which the war had been fought. Hitherto, the military class had led from the front, forming a separate group on the battlefield, usually enjoying privileged conditions (which they normally had to pay for themselves) and accommodation. On the Western Front they had lived in the trenches alongside their men, whom they had learned to understand better and to respect. Conversely, the ordinary soldiers in the trenches had, in most cases, rubbed shoulders with the officer class for the first time, and realised that, by and large, they were ordinary men like themselves. The lesson was not forgotten after the war, and it was soon translated into a substantial breakdown in the social class divide. Thus, the war effectively marked the final re-emergence of the ordinary freeman. His voice was once again heard in the popular assembly, although now it was only possible through the ballot-box. In return, he was once again liable for military service whenever the King called upon him to provide it.

Meanwhile, religious issues were no longer seen as important, being displaced by social and economic preoccupations, leaving pressure for the disestablishment of the Church of England to be largely forgotten. There was an increasing need for greater independence on the part of the Church, partly because it was recognised that a growing proportion of members of Parliament were no longer adherents, and hardly competent to decide on Church matters. Also, Parliament could no longer afford the time to give attention to Church matters. An attempt was made, therefore, to distance Church and Government by means of the Church of England Assembly (Powers) Act of 1919, commonly known as the Enabling Act, which replaced the Church of England Assembly by a General Synod, and gave it powers to legislate on Church matters. Church statutes, known as 'Measures', had to be laid before both Houses of Parliament (that is, the other two Estates), which could accept or reject, but not amend them. Once accepted by Parliament, Church Measures must be submitted for the royal assent. The Synod could also enact regulations, known as Canons. These had no statutory authority, binding the clergy but not the laity, and they were submitted directly to the Crown for the Royal Licence to promulgate them. Thus, the twentieth century saw the partial restoration of the First Estate in its legislative role. The presence of Church elders in the House of Lords ensured the continued interlocking of the three Estates.

39.1. The Spread of Socialism

The War of 1914–18 had the effect of releasing pressures that had been building during the nineteenth century, but it added new pressures of its own. The horrors caused by killing on an industrial-scale caused Romanticism to give way to a new movement, Realism, which reflected a fear of the ruthless bleakness of the industrial world with an obsession with all that was bare, empty, pitiless or grotesque. Even so, there was continuity with the Romantic Age, in that it continued to see the world through the eyes and mind of the individual. The destabilising and disillusioning effect of the Great War gave socialism its opportunity. In the midst of the conflict, German intelligence had arranged for Russia's Communist revolutionaries, led by Lenin, who had found sanctuary in Switzerland, to be transferred back to Russia, whose army and government were in a state of near collapse. Exploiting this, the Communists had partially achieved a revolution in 1917 which, as the Germans had hoped, had forced Russia to withdraw from the war, allowing Germany to fight on one front (in the West), instead of two. Inspired by events in Russia, the Communists had attempted a revolution in Germany.

In Great Britain, where communism had little appeal, the Labour Party formed its first moderate socialist Government under Ramsay MacDonald at the beginning of 1924, although it did not have an overall majority and had to form a coalition with the Liberals. In the face of a severe economic depression, which began in 1929 and lasted through most of the 1930s, the Labour Party was returned to office between 1929 and 1935, again under Ramsay MacDonald, but it was again unable to implement its radical policies, because of its dependence on Liberal support. In particular, the Government was divided over the question of financial support for the unemployed, and whether the economic situation could or should be rectified by state intervention.

Meanwhile, the search for collective security during the post-war years resulted in the creation of the League of Nations and the World Court, but there was no means of making them effective. There was also an unwillingness on the part of the non-European powers – particularly the United States, the Dominions and Japan – to assume responsibility for anything outside their respective spheres of interest. Within continental Europe, France endeavoured to assert her position of leadership, while Germany sought to evade or revise the crippling terms imposed upon her in 1919. Even so, the years from 1924 to 1930 were generally characterised by prosperity and diplomatic fulfilment. The Locarno Treaties were signed in 1925, guaranteeing the new, post-war borders and providing for arbitration over international disputes. A new Bank for International Settlements was established in Basel in 1929, representing all the principle central banks. In 1930 the evacuation of the Rhineland by Allied troops was completed.

There followed a new period of instability between 1930 and 1939, during which the system of security treaties was subjected to repudiation and revision, due chiefly to a resurgent Germany, which had borne the brunt of the new system. It was also a period of international financial crisis that first became evident in a stock market crash in New York in 1929, followed by a prolonged economic depression. Sterling, long the medium of international exchange, had been underwritten by convertibility into gold, but in 1931, Britain, faced with a crushing national debt inherited from the war, was forced to abandon this, in order to allow the currency to devalue to a more realistic level, in the face of a serious trade deficit. This set off a round of defensive devaluations by other countries. Trade declined and unemployment grew throughout the Western world. In both Germany and Italy, much of the blame for the economic crisis of the immediate post-war years, was laid against their democratically elected governments, which were seen as weak and ineffectual, because they were riven by Party rivalries. In Italy, the low esteem in which governments were held was made worse by the high level of official corruption. Among many in the working classes, the highly disciplined Communists appeared to offer better government and a greater concern for their interests, and its spread caused alarm, even among the more moderate Italian Socialist Parties. At this point, an alternative was offered by Benito Mussolini. Unaligned with any Party, Mussolini emphasised the importance of the Italian state and the legacy of Imperial Rome. With himself as *il duce*, 'the leader', he offered something more solid and familiar than the revolutionary internationalism of the Marxists. In 1919 he founded the first *Fascio di Combattimento*, later followed by others. The *fascio* was a reference to the symbolic bundle of sticks, the *fasces*, once carried by the *lictor* who attended a magistrate in Imperial Rome, and Mussolini used it as the new symbol of the Italian state, causing his followers to be referred to as 'Fascists'. The Communists saw the Fascists as the most serious threat to themselves, and, while the clear majority of the Italian electorate in 1921 continued to support the Liberal and Democrat Parties, a violent struggle was taking place between the two marginal groups. The Fascists later proved to be the better led and organised, and a widespread fear of the Communists among the middle classes and small owners of property led to a growing support for Mussolini.

In furtherance of the cause, a Communist International, or 'Comintern', was founded in 1919 to direct the revolutionary activities of Communist Parties around the world. Meanwhile, the Russian economy had almost completely collapsed by 1921. The following year saw the bringing together of Russia, the Ukraine, White Russia and Transcaucasia as a federation under the title of the Union of Soviet Socialist Republics, a *soviet* being a 'workers' assembly'. The expectation that the establishment of one Communist state would lead to worldwide revolution, causing a collapse of the whole Western 'capitalist' system, failed to materialise, however, and a new dogma, that of the possibility of 'communism in one country', took its place. Lenin died in 1924, and in the resulting power struggle between Stalin and the left-wing faction, under Trotsky, Stalin emerged as the victor. Aware that his own life was now at stake, Trotsky fled into hiding in Mexico, where he was eventually found and shot. Stalin introduced a series of five-year plans that concentrated on re-starting the country's process of industrialisation. A shortage of grain, due largely to the government's own pricing policies, persuaded it to embark on the consolidation of agriculture into collective and state farms, but opposition from the peasantry, particularly in the more prosperous Ukraine, resulted in a policy of deliberate starvation of and deportation to Siberian labour camps, resulting in the death of millions.

The great majority of the British public regarded communist Russia with as much revulsion and fear as they had the French Revolution, and no single act perpetrated by the Revolution was greeted with more abhorrence than the murder in 1918 of the Tsar, Nicholas II, and his family at Yekaterinburg. The Labour Party quickly realised the folly of its identification with Soviet Russia and the dread with which socialism was now widely regarded, yet the attraction of a system based on social equality and social security remained. Bismark had attempted to head off the threat of socialism in Germany by introducing a system of social security, but the Conservative Party in Britain had showed no inclination to follow suit. Fear of, and hostility towards, the rising tide of socialism, particularly of communism, had generated an antagonism within the Conservative Party towards any policy associated with socialism, irrespective of its merits, and for this short-sighted attitude it would eventually pay the price. Meanwhile, one important lesson of the Russian

Revolution was ignored in Britain. Communist Russia was officially now a parliamentary democracy, but with only one political Party. Great Britain was a parliamentary democracy with three political Parties, but it required only one of these, while in office, to pass a Bill banning the others, which the King must sign, according to the new convention. In this way, a similar oligarchy could easily have established itself in Britain. Politically and constitutionally, Britain was walking a tightrope.

39.2. The Fragmentation of the First Estate

The rise of Protestantism had relegated the adherents of Rome to a minority outside the Church of England, but it had also caused a conflict within the Church. The outcome had been a division between the dominant 'High Church', which retained the episcopal tradition; 'Low Church', which had dispensed with all forms of decoration and other forms of 'distraction'; as well as a Catholic form of 'High Church' that retained many earlier practices, such as the use of incense. In spite of the retention of diverse forms of service within the Church of England, there had been an outflow of adherents, particularly among the lower classes, in favour of various 'Nonconformist' churches, such as the Methodist, Wesleyan and Baptist. This fragmentation had been due not only to doctrinal differences. The Industrial Revolution and the drift of population from the country into the towns and cities had created a clerical vacuum there, as the provision of pastoral care in the new towns had been unable to keep pace, leaving an opportunity which the Nonconformist churches had helped to fill. Meanwhile, the constitutional standing of the Church of England had all but disappeared, except for the retention of royal patronage. The General Synod had long refused to sit with the other two Estates in Parliament, or to participate in secular matters, even in the matter of its own taxation, and it had lost the right to legislate on Church matters.

The General Synod met at least twice in each year, having long been divided into the two Provinces of Canterbury and York, which were administered by their respective Convocations. There were also the three common Houses of Bishops, Clergy and Laity, the members of the last being elected by the various local deanery synods. At a local level, within each diocese, and below the various deanery synods, were the parish councils. In 1855, the Convocation of Canterbury considered a report and address to the Sovereign which sought Victoria's consent to it sitting in future as an 'acting' body, by reviving its power to enact its own legislation, subject to royal approval, as opposed to remaining purely a deliberative body. The same consent, some argued, should be extended to the Convocation of York. In particular, it was felt that there was a need for the Convocation to legislate on measures needed for enforcing discipline among the clergy; the extension of the Church; the modification of its services; the reform of the representation of the clergy in the Provincial Synod of Canterbury, and the amendment of representation of the clergy in the Lower House of Convocation. The Archbishop and others opposed the move, on the ground that it would not have the support of the laity or of the Church generally, which believed that the Convocation was improperly constituted, and this could bring the very survival of the Convocation into question. The Solicitor-General had previously advised that the Convocation would have to go to Parliament for such powers as it sought, but he had since changed his mind, and now advised that 'the sanction of Her Majesty was quite sufficient for the purpose. If Convocation sent up an address for licence to act, and it was refused, it would be an unconstitutional course, and entirely without precedent'. The address was then referred to the Lower House of the Convocation. In order to strengthen the position of the Church, a national Church Assembly was created in 1919, yet, apart from the conduct of spiritual business and the routine administration of its affairs, the Church was largely confined to the promotion of educational and humanitarian activities. Even the influential missionary societies of the nineteenth century were largely the product of the Methodist and Evangelical movements.

In spite of the standing and apparent independence of the Convocations of the Church, with the right to sit as a separate House of Parliament, the House of Commons was unwilling to concede its authority in this direction any more than in any other, even in doctrinal matters. This was obviously a violation of the equality of the Estates in Parliament. In 1927 and 1928, the Commons even defeated attempts to secure a revision of the Book of Common Prayer. The reason why the Commons ignored the constitutional standing of the First Estate was probably because the Commons, having appropriated the powers of the King, had assumed that the role of the King in spiritual matters had also passed to itself, even though they were obviously outside the competence of Parliament. The scope of parliamentary influence – both lords and commons – was limited to the temporal aspects of the Church, and even these were still available to the Church in the event that it chose to resume its parliamentary rights. Nevertheless, by its internal conflicts of doctrine, with their dramatic popular implications, the Church of England had played into the hands of the political Parties. Having long refused to be involved in parliamentary issues, except through its representation in the House of Lords, which hung solely upon its feudal claim as a landlord, the Church itself had long been a target of the Commons. More importantly, it had lost the support of a large section of the population, which was now more Protestant than the Church in its leanings.

39.3. The New Popularity of the Monarchy

The years immediately preceding and during the Great War, including the greater part of the ensuing inter-war years, belonged to the reign of King George V, who had succeeded his father in 1910. George's elder brother, Prince Albert, had been expected to succeed to the throne, and George, a retiring and insecure young man, had gratefully embarked on a successful career in the Royal Navy. This had provided him with a sense of identity and direction, for he had loved the sense of order, discipline and tradition which the Navy had provided. When Albert had died, unexpectedly, in 1892, George's naval career had ended, throwing him into public life, for which he was quite unprepared. During the year following his brother's death, he had married Mary, daughter of the Duke of Teck, who had been betrothed to his brother. In spite of this, it proved to be a very happy marriage, and this was to be of crucial importance. George's father, Edward VII, had been a philanderer, who had led the life of a playboy, and had more than once appeared in court as a witness in cases involving scandal. He had also been a socialite and leader in the fashions of the day, in which he had followed the royal traditions that had preceded Queen Victoria. George V set a new tone, however, more in keeping with that of his grandmother, Queen Victoria, in that it was based on family life and moderation, and this was to make him the first King since Charles I not to be tainted by sexual scandal.

During the first crisis of his reign, the conflict between the Liberal Government and the House of Lords over the latter's constitutional right to be consulted on legislation (and by implication, to veto it), the King had displayed tact and a willingness to accept the democratic principle over the interests of the Peers. In so doing, he moved away from the tradition whereby the Monarchy aligned itself with the nobility, both socially and politically, towards an engagement with the commonalty. The next royal crisis had arisen out of the War with Germany, and the popular reaction against all things German, which had made the royal family, with its strong German connections, including its name, particularly vulnerable. The association of German Gotha bombers that attacked London with the name of the dynasty of Saxe-Coburg and Gotha, had been particularly awkward, and the King had been willing to align the dynasty clearly with Britain in the war effort by changing its name to Windsor. This sense of royal vulnerability was continued after the war with the rise of socialism, which rejected the notion of inherited social standing, which pointed to a demise of monarchy – and with it the King's extended family – from much of Europe as a result of the war. The King's realisation, that the survival of the British Monarchy depended on its relationship with the common people even caused him to sacrifice his cousin, the Tsar Nicholas, to the mercies of the Bolsheviks. It also caused him to be the first British ruler to show a direct interest in the welfare of the ordinary working people, undertaking public tours to visit mines and factories, and even football matches. He also used the new gadgetry of radio to initiate a practice of Christmas broadcasts to the nation. In his dealings with the new Labour Government of Ramsay MacDonald, in 1924, he not only received his new Ministers as constitutional protocol required, but dealt with them in a friendly, welcoming manner that put their initial hostility at rest. This helped to ensure that a conflict between this and future Labour Governments and the Monarchy was averted, establishing the King's position as being above Party politics.

The example of George V would be followed by his successors, but the true significance of his reign lay in his recognition that the Monarchy owed its position, not to God, but to the people, as, indeed, common law dictated. William III had already brought an end to the waxing and waning doctrine of the King as the temporal representative of God, to whom alone he was responsible, and acknowledged that he was answerable to the people, but it was left to George V to accept the ancient principle that the King owes his position to the people.

The post-war years in Great Britain were much less unstable than they were on the Continent, yet they were trying years of economic dislocation and social and political readjustment. As the political Parties in the House of Commons consolidated their power over the Crown and the House of Lords, the practical role of the King became increasingly limited. In order to describe this new situation, the expression 'constitutional' monarchy came into vogue. What this meant in legal terms was simply that the feudal perception of kingship had finally been rejected, and the King was now expected to function within the rules prescribed by common law. To the Parties, however, it meant that the King was subject to the evolving conventions that the Parties themselves established. In practice, therefore, by 'constitutional' monarchy was meant the function of a figurehead that also acted as a constitutional 'letter-box', through which legislation and appointments of state were directed and formally confirmed. This new perception of the constitution had gained uncritical acceptance as an established and irreversible system. Once conventions were established, it was asserted, there could be no going back, yet, constitutionally, a convention was no more than a convenient elaboration of constitutional law, not a substitute for it, and tenable for only so long as it served its purpose within the law.

It was suggested by Sir Ivor Jennings that constitutional conventions 'keep it in touch with the growth of ideas', and that 'the effects of a constitution must change with the changing circumstances of national life'.[2] The old conflict between common law and feudal principles had never been fully understood, and so had never been satisfactorily resolved, so that the conventions appeared to be the only bulwark against the divine authority of the King. As an exponent of this new concept of 'constitutional monarchy', Jennings recognised the dilemma that it posed. 'On the one hand', he wrote, 'it is easy to exaggerate the influence of the monarchy by adopting a legalistic attitude and emphasising the

2   I. Jennings, *The Law and the Constitution* (Bickley, 194), 80–1.

part played by the Crown in the theory of constitutional law. On the other hand, it is easy to minimise the royal function by stressing the great trilogy of Cabinet, Parliament and People'.[3]

Applying the new idea of constitutional monarchy, Jennings reiterated the point made by Bagehot, only more strongly, by suggesting that the King now had only one function of prime importance, and that was to appoint the Prime Minister. As the Prime Minister must be able to command the support of the House of Commons, he must be the leader of the majority Party. When he was first called upon to form a Government, in 1924, the leader of the Labour Party was easily identified, because the Party insisted on the right of its members to choose their leader, which they did annually. The Conservative Party did not follow this practice, the leader of the Party when in office taking this position by virtue of being Prime Minister. The leadership of the Party was thus uncertain until after the King had made his choice, although in making this choice, the King was certainly guided by his estimation of who was most likely to wield influence. In opposition, the Party once again became leaderless. As Jennings pointed out, this left the King with a choice of Prime Minister only when the Conservative Party had a majority in the Commons, or when no Party had an overall majority. It was not until 1964 that the parliamentary members of the Conservative Party decided to elect their leader, instead of leaving him to the King's judgement. To these instances of royal discretion must be added occasions when the system of government ceased to function smoothly. The existence of three Parties in the Commons – the Conservative, Labour and Liberal – sometimes meant that the Ministry in office was not the only one that could command a majority. Such occasions were a rarity, but when they occurred, they could leave the King with a difficult choice.

39.4. Government Moves from the Lords to the Commons

Most, and often all, Ministerial positions had originally been filled from the Lords, although even in Anglo-Saxon times it had been quite usual to give important positions to the King's thanes, who were chosen on merit.

3   Ibid. 103.

In the Middle Ages it had been a royal practice to elevate certain members of the commonalty to the Peerage, in order that they could be appointed to Ministerial office. The elevation of individuals from the Third Estate to the Peerage had been necessary, from time to time since the onset of the Middle Ages, in order to keep the Peerage from dying out. However, the rise of the Party system in the House of Commons exerted increasing pressure on the Crown to recognise the importance of public opinion and the fact that most of the King's revenue was contributed by the commonalty. This led to a gradual transfer of Ministerial appointments during the eighteenth and nineteenth centuries, from the Lords to the leading Party in the Commons.

This transition increasingly deprived the Crown of its main source of educated and experienced Ministers who were familiar with affairs of state, almost from childhood, who had usually been brought up imbued with a tradition of public service, and who had already, in many cases, held responsible positions in civil and military life long before they became entitled by inheritance to sit in the House of Lords. Even members of the Commons who achieved Ministerial positions were, in the early days, typically members of the landed gentry, with experience in the management of their own estates, who had often held, and continued to hold, responsible positions in the professions or local affairs, such as justices of the peace. By the second half of the nineteenth century, however, the House of Commons was increasingly filled by men with a limited grasp or experience of affairs of state, or of the holding of responsible positions that required a capacity for sound and objective judgement. Not a few held positions in the trade union movement, but although these involved some organising ability and a close involvement in social problems, they required a devotion to a single-minded cause, rather than the detached objectivity demanded in the framing of public policy. Some were motivated by a sense of public service, but others were driven mainly by ambition. The first deciding issue with which they were faced by selecting committees was whether they supported the private or state ownership of public services. These committees were often driven by a desire to choose young people with bright ideas, particularly those who would appeal to young voters, which was hardly a recipe for mature policy-making. Not infrequently, selection committees were guided by the political fad of the day. The overall effect during the late nineteenth, and more especially during the twentieth century, was a rise in poorly considered policy-making and a decline in the competence of public administration, under governments that were more sympathetic to the needs of the people, but less able. Unfortunately, this coincided with an era in which Government involvement in the day-to-day affairs of the country was far greater than it had ever been before.

In 1923, the Conservative Prime Minister, Bonar Law, resigned from the office through ill-health and gave the King no advice as to his successor. The choice facing the King lay between Lord Curzon and Stanley Baldwin. Of the two men, Curzon was probably unsuitable for his person and for the objections being raised to a Prime Minister in the House of Lords, where he would be less accountable to the Parties in the Commons. It was in the Commons, also, that the Parliamentary Opposition chiefly existed, and it was there that it had to be confronted. On the other hand, Baldwin's experience of the Cabinet was limited to eight months. Although there had already been seventeen Prime Ministers appointed from the Commons, the ensuing choice of Baldwin was of constitutional, as well as personal, significance, for it marked the transference, for reasons of practical politics, rather than suitability, of the office of Prime Minister from the House of Lords to the House of Commons. In so doing, it hastened the demise of the Upper House as a major institution of State.

A more difficult situation arose not long afterwards, when Baldwin was defeated in the Commons, precipitating a new election in 1923–24. This resulted in the Conservative Party winning 258 seats, the Labour Party 191 seats, and the Liberal Party 158. The Labour and the Liberal factions at once combined to vote Baldwin out of office. Although, together, they formed a majority, there was nevertheless a risk that the Liberals might withdraw their support, leaving Labour in the minority. The King had to decide who to send for to replace Baldwin, the Labour Party leader, Sir Ramsay MacDonald, or the Conservative leader, Asquith, or neither. If the King should send for Ramsay MacDonald and the Liberals deserted him, the country would be faced with a new election, when one had only just been held. On the other hand, the King would be creating an ineffective minority Government if he sent for the Conservative leader. This was a time of economic difficulties and social unrest, with a widespread fear of socialist revolution spreading from Russia, making it essential to have an effective Government. In January of 1924, therefore, the King appointed Ramsay MacDonald, and with him the first Labour Government. As social unrest continued, the Liberals soon withdrew their support and MacDonald found it impossible to carry on. The King accordingly decided that there should be a second election in October of the same year, as he considered that the danger of denying the Labour Party the right of an appeal to the country outweighed the burden imposed on the public of another election. Due partly to the publication of the Zinoviev letter, by which the Third Communist International allegedly called upon the British people to rise in revolution, the Conservatives were elected with a large majority, and Baldwin returned to office.

The discretionary role of the King was taxed yet again in 1931, during an economic crisis and widespread unrest. The Labour Party, now in office for a second term, had only a small majority over the Conservatives, and either Party, given the support of the Liberals, could have defeated the other. Faced by the economic situation, a mood of cooperation emerged between the Government and Opposition, with drastic proposals for reducing expenditure being placed both before the Cabinet and before the leaders of the Opposition. The Cabinet was divided over the proposals, some considering them too harsh on the unemployed, but the Opposition was determined that the schemes should be implemented, and rejected suggestions by the Labour Government for a compromise solution. Ramsay MacDonald considered the condition of the country to be so serious that the split in the Government must be ended at all costs. He resigned, and the King, worried at the possibility of a Labour Party in opposition at so difficult a time, immediately gave him a commission to form a coalition Government with the Opposition leaders. In the event, the proposal for a coalition received a majority support in the House of Commons, and a further majority from the electorate two months later.

Among later constitutional writers, Harold Laski argued that MacDonald should not have been asked to form a new Government, because he represented nobody. He had been appointed by Labour, and having forfeited Labour support by resigning, it was improper for him to accept a commission. In Laski's view, the King should have sent for one of the Opposition leaders, and should have consulted other Labour leaders.[4] Jennings argued that the King did not act in an unconstitutional manner. Laski's view implied that only Party caucuses should, in effect, appoint the Prime Minister, yet caucuses were not publicly elected bodies and had no constitutional standing. To accede to the idea that Prime Ministers should be appointed according to the decisions of Party caucuses would represent a transfer of power from the Cabinet to a Party committee. The King's primary duty was to find someone who could command the support of a majority in the Commons, irrespective of Party allegiances, and the ultimate test of the propriety of the choice must be the vote of the whole House, not of one Party.

Meanwhile, the long history of franchise reform was finally brought to a conclusion in 1928, with the Equal Franchise Act, designed to extend the vote to women on the same terms as men. All individuals over twenty-one years of age who met short residence requirements and were not legally disqualified by such disabilities as lunacy, or by criminal offences, were now entitled to vote in Parliamentary and Local Government elections. This measure introduced a further five million women and three million men to the voters' roll.

The worldwide economic depression that took hold unexpectedly in 1929 had begun with a stock market crash, and grew steadily worse as the world's governments tried to relieve the effects by increasing tariffs and supporting prices. In 1931 the financial system itself collapsed, necessitating the abandonment by Great Britain of the gold standard, according to which the value of the pound sterling was determined by the price of the metal. The move was followed by most other countries, but, in spite of the chaotic effect on exchange rates, a gradual worldwide economic recovery began to make itself evident.

39.4.1. Independence for Southern Ireland (Éire)

The general election of 1918 saw the Coalition Government of Liberals and Conservatives returned to office, but it also brought a great victory for the nationalist *Sinn Fein* candidates in Ireland, where the accumulated frustration had at last been unleashed. Instead of taking up their seats at Westminster, they organised their own Parliament in Ireland, the *Dáil*

---

4   For this and a number of other points in this chapter, the writer is particularly indebted to notes from lectures in 1948 and 1949 by R. B. Dorling, Glyn Grammar School, Epsom.

Éireann, and declared Irish independence. The *Dail* was suppressed, resulting in a campaign of terrorism against all who were identified with British authority, British and Irish alike. It led to an open and vicious war between the *Sinn Fein* activists and specially recruited British forces, who came to be known as the 'Black and Tans', from the parallel between their khaki uniforms and black belts and the 'Black and Tans' Hunt in Munster.

The end of the Great War brought a need, in any case, to reactivate the Irish legislation passed in 1914, and this was achieved in the Government of Ireland Act of 1920, which provided for Northern and Southern Ireland each to have its own Parliament, the first being in respect of six of the nine counties of the province of Ulster that were mainly Protestant. This now constituted 'Northern Ireland', while the remaining provinces, henceforth, were to be known as 'Southern Ireland'. Each was to retain seats at Westminster. The representatives elected to the Southern Irish Parliament, overwhelmingly from *Sinn Fein*, again promptly boycotted it, because they rejected Britain's right to make such arrangements on their behalf. Instead, they declared themselves to be the *Dáil Éireann*, or 'Irish Parliament', effectively ignoring the Southern Irish constitution that had been established under the Act. In an effort to break this impasse, two conferences took place between the Irish leaders and representatives of the Crown, as a result of which an agreement was reached whereby the Government at Westminster in 1921 granted Dominion status to Southern Ireland, which was to be re-named the Irish Free State. This was then endorsed by the Irish *Dáil* in 1922. Previously, the Irish leaders had rejected the offer of Dominion status, undoubtedly on the ground that the Irish were not British, but the more level-headed realised that Britain would only proceed along what it saw as 'constitutional' lines. Meanwhile, Northern Ireland retained the constitutional arrangement of the 1920 Act, which had specified which powers were to be retained by the Parliament in Westminster, leaving all remaining powers to the Parliament of Northern Ireland.

Revolutionary sentiment among the more extreme Irish Nationalists remained strong, however, refusing, on principle, to recognise the settlement between the Irish Free State and the United Kingdom, in spite of the overwhelming popular support for the new Government displayed in the Irish election of 1922. It was an illustration, perhaps, of the two very different Irish temperaments – the indigenous Irish and the more recent Irish, representing the early Viking and Medieval English settlers – that even this was not accepted by the nationalists. The minority faction, led by De Valera, which was both anti-British and republican, embarked on a new campaign of assassination and arson against those who implemented the settlement. Those assassinated included the Prime Minister of the Irish Free State, Michael Collins. The reaction of the British Government, driven by frustration and its dedication to feudal doctrine, was to embark on a rigorous repression of the Republicans. Later in the same year, the *Dáil* proclaimed a new Irish Free State, together with a constitution that was similar to that at Westminster. Under this arrangement, the King was accepted as the head of state, and was represented in the Irish Free State by a Governor-General, but with an elected Senate as its upper House.

The new arrangements for Southern Ireland failed to bring peace to the region. The elected Republican members refused to take their seats in the *Dáil*, and the Irish Minister of Justice was assassinated in 1927, after which the Republicans reversed their decision. The next Irish general election of 1932 saw an upsurge of support for the more moderate Republicans, who, with the help of the Labour Party deputies, succeeded in forming a Republican Government under the radical leader, De Valera, whom they elected as their President. A further election in 1933 yielded a small overall Republican majority in the Southern Irish *Dáil*, putting the radicals in power for the first time. The bleak relations between Great Britain and the Irish Free State, meanwhile, were made worse by a tariff war from 1932 to 1936, which was disastrous for the Irish farming industry. It underlined the reality that Anglo-Irish relations were based as much on mutual economic interests as on political realities, but it did nothing to change Irish attitudes. A resolution of the trade dispute only seemed to bring attention back to the constitutional issue, and later, in 1936, a new republican constitution was adopted that simply ignored the British connection, declaring the Free State to be a 'sovereign, independent and democratic state' under a President. Under the influence of De Valera, the oath of loyalty to the King was abolished in 1937, the signature of the Governor-General was no longer required on legislation, and appeals to the Privy Council were discontinued. At the same time, the official name of the country was changed to Éire, the

Irish name of Ireland. This referred, however, to Ireland as a whole, and was asserted to be so by the nationalists, leaving Southern Ireland – the Irish Free State – as exactly that. Douglas Hyde, a Protestant, was elected as Southern Ireland's first President a year later, in 1938, thus completing the transformation of Southern Ireland into a republic. The fact that Hyde was a Protestant was taken as a gesture towards the predominantly Protestant Northern Ireland, and efforts had been made over the years to try to find a reconciliation between the north and south, but elections held in the north in 1938 resulted in an overwhelming victory for the Unionists. It was now clear that, for the foreseeable future, at least, any hope of re-unification was out of the question.

By the end of the 1930s, therefore, a constitutional stand-off existed between Great Britain and the Irish Free State, with the former still seeing the relationship in the context of feudal doctrine, according to which Southern Ireland was still referred to as an estate of the Crown, to which certain privileges had been granted, while the Free State saw itself as an independent republic, under continuing threat from its powerful neighbour. Lingering hopes of a reconciliation between Southern Ireland and the Protestants of Ulster delayed the final break between Great Britain and the Irish Free State, which in 1937 became the semi-independent state of Éire, but the war only served to deepen the division between the south and north. Mainly out of spite, Éire had flirted as closely with Germany as it dare, whereas the Protestant majority in Northern Ireland had been wholly committed to the war, the bond having been strengthened by the Battle of the Atlantic, during which Northern Ireland's strategic importance and its ship-building capacity had played a crucial role against the German submarine menace. The election of a Labour Government in Britain at the end of the war, and with it the emergence of a new attitude towards the Empire, meant that the contribution of Northern Ireland was quickly forgotten in London. Religious differences were seen merely as an exacerbating factor in the political division between the native Irish, who laid an historic claim to all of Ireland, and the descendants of the Anglo-Scottish 'plantations' in Ulster, whose loyalty lay with their 'protector', the King.[5]

---

5   The native Irish – the Catholics – argued that the Protestants were occupying Ulster illegally, to which the Protestants responded that the Catholics had forfeited the land as a punishment for rebellion against the King.

By 1949, the patience of the Government of Southern Ireland over the issue of Northern Ireland was exhausted, and a Republic of Ireland was formally proclaimed. Britain, which had chosen to regard Southern Ireland as an independent British Dominion, now saw no alternative, but to pass the Ireland Bill, recognising the new republic, but reaffirming Northern Ireland as an integral part of the United Kingdom. By consenting to the Bill, the King, George VI, renounced, in effect, the regal contract with the members of the Protestant minority in Southern Ireland, who had long accepted the fact. In spite of the severance of the political tie between the Irish Free State and Great Britain, the latter still clung to feudal doctrine in respect of the relationship. Thus, it continued to insist that, in spite of the reality of Irish independence, Southern Ireland continued to be regarded legally as an estate of the Crown.

39.5. The Dominions

39.5.1. Changing Relationships

39.5.1.1. Canada

In 1982, Canada sought to establish its legal independence beyond question, including its right to amend its constitution without reference to the Imperial Government. It therefore reached agreement with the latter for the 'patriation' of the British North America Act of 1867, that is, the original document. This was accompanied by the passage of a Bill in the Canadian Parliament, in the same year, which effectively re-named the British North America Act as the Constitution Act. Although there have been a number of ensuing Constitution Acts in Canada, the Act of 1982 has continued to be used as the basis for defining the division of powers between the Provinces and the Federal Government.

39.5.1.2. Australia

By the mid-nineteenth century, the United Kingdom was encouraging the Australian states to come together, but there was little public interest, because the smaller states feared domination by the larger, and the American Civil War only added to the disinclination. Growing

French and German activity in the Pacific had led, however, to the formation of a Federal Council of Australasia in 1889, and in 1891 the Premier of New South Wales, Henry Parkes, led pressure for the creation of a Convention that drew up a federal system of government. Lack of public support and a failure to resolve certain issues, such as policy on tariffs, caused the momentum to lapse, however. A new and similar set of proposals, but with an added provision for responsible government, led to them being submitted to electors in the various Colonies, all of which, except Western Australia, ratified them. The resulting Bill was then submitted to the Imperial Parliament, according to which the Colonies would become States, and Australia as a whole would become a federal 'Commonwealth'. Subject to the inclusion of a provision, sought by the Chief Justices of the various Colonies, that the right of appeal from the High Court to the Privy Council, concerning limitations on the powers of the new federal government, or of the States, could not be curtailed by the British Parliament – which did not represent Australians in any case – a new Commonwealth of Australia Constitution Act was passed in 1900.

Although this achieved federation, Australia as a whole was still a self-governing British colony, a status that was resolved by the Statute of Westminster, 1931. This freed the Dominions from Imperial restrictions and removed nearly all the remaining authority of the British Parliament to legislate for them. The Statute was formally adopted by Australia – as the Statute of Australia Adoption Act, 1942 – whose effect was backdated to 1939. Even this did not remove the paramountcy of Imperial law in the Australian states, however, an oversight that was eventually removed by the Australia Act, 1986. At the request of each state, this was passed also by the Australian Parliament, which took the opportunity to remove the last avenues of appeal from the Australian courts to the Privy Council. In keeping with the procedure followed previously in respect of Canada, and at the request of the Australian Government, the original copy of the Australia Act was formally patriated to Australia in 1990.

39.5.1.3. New Zealand

Meanwhile, New Zealand had followed a different course. An important development in the competitive relationship between European settlers and the indigenous Maori people was the Treaty of Waitangi, in

1840, by which some five hundred chiefs ceded sovereignty to Britain, in return for a guarantee of their lands and other possessions.[6] This did not end the fighting, but it established a legal principle. Otherwise, the New Zealand constitution took the form of a series of legal documents and judicial decisions. The Constitution Act, passed by the British Parliament in 1846, gave authority to the government in New Zealand, but, due to disturbances, the Crown subsequently back-pedalled, repealing the Act and replacing it with the New Zealand Constitution Act of 1852. This had the Governor appointed by the Colonial Secretary, instead of the New Zealand House of Representatives. Subsequent changes related particularly to the distribution of provinces. The Constitution Act of 1986 referred to the three branches of Government as the Executive Council (or Cabinet); the legislature, comprising the House of Representatives and the Sovereign in Parliament; and the judiciary. No constitutional role seems to have been recorded for the Sovereign as such. As had been the case in respect of Canada and Australia, constitutional rights were being granted by the Imperial Government in accordance with the tenets of feudal doctrine, without the King, rather than according to customary law.

Meanwhile, the pace of industrialisation of most of the Dominions during the Second World War, out of necessity, because of the disruption of trade, had the effect of turning the system of Imperial Preference from a mutual trading benefit into a source of friction. Many of the goods that the Dominions had formerly imported from the United Kingdom were now being manufactured by the Dominions themselves. Also, the balance of power had been shifting. The mother country had already found it necessary to turn to them for assistance in the South African War, and she had good reason to be grateful for their assistance during the war of 1914–18. Great Britain had come to realise that she now needed the Dominions more than they needed her, and that the time had come to treat them as economic, as well as political equals. Only in Southern Ireland and South Africa had there been a widespread refusal to support the war effort: the Catholic nationalists in the one case, and the embittered *Afrikaners* in the other, with many in each group openly expressing their hope of a German victory. Nevertheless, many from the Afrikaner population joined with the English-speaking volunteers in serving the Crown on the battlefront.

---

6   The Maori were indigenous to the extent that they were a Polynesian people who had settled in New Zealand – mainly North Island – several centuries earlier.

In Canada, many French Canadians who had been motivated to serve appear to have been so more out of loyalty to France than to the Crown.

For Great Britain, the shattering experience of the First World War and the acceptance of the principle of mandates – or temporary custodianship – over the former German colonies – marked an important turning point in her perception of the Imperial purpose, although the way forward had already been foreshadowed by the acceptance of the principle of Dominion status. The biggest problem now faced by the Crown was reconciling, on the one hand, the common law entitlement of all beneficiaries of the regal contract – in this case, British settlers overseas – to the enjoyment of their rights as free men, including the right to self-government, and, on the other hand, its feudal duty to protect the common welfare of all the inhabitants, equally, of the King's overseas estates. It may be remembered that, while the cornerstone of the feudal system had been the recognition of differences of social rank and territorial claims, it was blind to differences of race and culture, and knew nothing of the regal contract. Britain's recognition of humanitarian ideals had the effect of giving new importance to these feudal principles that had guided the Crown since the Middle Ages, posing a new conflict with the principles of common law. There was a further problem, in that Great Britain had realised that the Empire had outlived its purpose, which had been to expand and protect Britain's trading interests in a previously lawless, often hostile, parochial and economically backward world, which had now, as a result of the influence of Empire, become economically integrated, productive and increasingly subject to the rule of law, without the need of Imperial government.

39.5.2. Southern Rhodesia

The constitutional link in customary law between the Rhodesian settlers and the Crown was destined to be particularly difficult, because of the huge natural and political obstacles – isolation, disease, formidable native hostility, and the problem of finding an economic base. Civilization was a thousand miles away, and while the post-war years found most of the five British Dominions prospering, Rhodesia was still struggling. The supposed gold reef that had attracted so many settlers to Southern Rhodesia in the beginning had proved to be illusory. Although the gold certainly existed, it was in small, scattered deposits, and where mining had taken place, it was on a relatively small scale. Meanwhile, the growing and curing of tobacco was still in its infancy. The conquest of the many lethal or debilitating tropical diseases that afflicted men and animals was making progress, but depended upon containment and research, some of which was taking place in Rhodesia itself, and measures to control them were beginning at last to achieve a measure of success. The BSAC had yet to find a commercial basis for its own success, and its legal requirement to meet the costs of the new colony's administration was, in addition to the costs imposed by the Matabele and Mashona rebellions, still draining the Company financially, forcing it to make repeated appeals to its disillusioned investors on the London Stock Exchange.

In 1907 the nominated members in the Legislative Council were reduced to five, giving the elected members from the settlers a majority, but leaving the Administrator with a veto. The dominant figure now emerging in the Council was Charles Cohglan, who was destined to become the country's first Prime Minister.

The key to paying off the Company's mounting debt was seen as being the sale of the remaining unalienated land in Southern Rhodesia, and in 1914 the elected members of the Legislative Council had reaffirmed an earlier vote of 1908, asking for an immediate settlement of the land question, asserting that the Company owned the unalienated land only in its capacity as the government of the territory, and not in its capacity as a commercial enterprise. The Crown, which had long failed to make up its own mind in the matter, had then referred the ownership of unalienated land to the judicial advice of the Privy Council. This was bound to add years of further delay, but in the meantime the Crown issued a second, Supplementary Charter, providing that, at any time after 29 October 1914 – when the Charter of the Company was due to expire – it could be extended for a further ten years. Moreover, if a majority of the Rhodesian Legislative Council should pass a resolution in favour of responsible government, and could show that the country could afford to pay for it, the Crown might comply. By now, the Great War was overtaking the issue, and the colony continued under Company rule. The prospect of re-uniting the two Rhodesias administratively, in order to save expense, was considered in 1914, but the idea was rejected. The savings would be small, and geography, and the size of the Black population to the north of the Zambezi, which contributed little to the economy and posed a political liability, were too daunting for its elected members. With the settlers unwilling, and probably unable, to assume the Company's administrative debts, the Company was determined to retain its ownership of minerals and unalienated lands as its only real assets. Without these, however, any elected government would be financially hamstrung.

In its eventual and questionable judgment in 1918, the Judicial Committee of the Privy Council[7] ruled that the Company had conquered the territory on behalf of the Crown, as a result of which the Natives had lost their title to the land; that the Crown had sanctioned the system of White settlement and Native reserves, and assumed the right itself to dispose of all land not in private ownership. It further ruled that the Crown had, through Orders in Council, put the Company in as its Administrator; that the Crown had sanctioned the system of White settlement and native reserves; retained the right to dispose of all land not in private ownership, and, furthermore, that the Charter did not provide the Company with a commercial right to the unalienated land. However, the Company had incurred costs in securing the unalienated land, and once the Crown put an end to the Company's administrative role, it would be entitled to claim reimbursement, either from public funds, or from the sale of the land. In other words, the new Southern Rhodesia Government would not be able to use the unalienated land for its own benefit until the Crown's debt had been cleared. The judgment raised difficult questions, not least the right of the Crown to the unalienated land, title to which belonged to the Company, also the overriding of the interests of the shareholders. The best that could be said was that the verdict was less a legal judgment than a clumsy attempt at a political solution. The Privy Council's ruling was followed by the appointment of a commission to assess the amount that the Company would be entitled to claim from the Crown in respect of its administrative deficits.

The Council's ruling completely misrepresented the Company's position. The Crown (under Queen Victoria) had merely recognised the Company's intentions and given its approval, in the form of the Charter, which had been crucial to the raising of money on the London Stock Exchange. The Privy Council's perception of the relationship was based,

7   L. Gann, *A History of Southern Rhodesia* (New York, 1969), 231–50.

however, on feudal doctrine. If we view the relationship in the light of common law, Rhodesia was not a royal estate, but the product of a private enterprise, represented by a group formed as a Company, whose objectives had received the royal approval. It was a process that had clearly followed the traditional pattern upon which England itself had been occupied and settled, except that the Company's commission to rule the new territory had been limited to twenty-five years, after which it would be free to function purely in its commercial capacity, leaving the function of government to the settlers. Because of the intervention of the War of 1914–18, this obligation of the Company had been extended, and when the time came, the settlers demanded to assume the full government of the territory. This, the Company was only too willing to concede, except that it was unable to repay its debt to the Crown, which was a necessary prerequisite to its new function as a commercial enterprise. The Company, unable to repay, pointed out that it would now be the liability of the forthcoming, elected Southern Rhodesia Government, whose interests at this point were represented by the Legislative Council. The settlers refused to accept the liability, because the prospective tax revenues would be quite inadequate. In fact, the debt could readily have been repaid from the sale of some of the territory's assets, such as the unalienated lands and the railways, but these belonged to the Company only in its governing capacity, and not in its capacity as a private company.

The Crown had regarded Southern Rhodesia hitherto as a protectorate, but it now proposed that it should become a Crown colony, which would make it easier to raise money on the capital markets, such as the stock exchange. This status, however, would make the British Government responsible for native policy, which was unacceptable to Rhodesia, which had its own Native Department, from which Britain had far more to learn than to contribute. Also, Southern Rhodesia had no need of protection from its neighbours; indeed, in relation to the size of its population, it had contributed more men to the Great War than any other dominion or colony. Indeed, Rhodesians had volunteered in such numbers that legislation had been passed, preventing those in key occupations from going away to fight. It had been the women, the under-aged and the elderly, who had kept the farms and the rest of the country functioning for four years. This readiness to enlist must be attributed, partly to the

Victorian legacy of imperial service and self-belief, and partly to the country's tradition of military service that had been basic to Southern Rhodesia's own establishment and survival. Meanwhile, such was the Company's accumulating deficit in respect of the cost of administering the country, that it could see little prospect that responsible government by the settlers, which undoubtedly would inherit the debt, would succeed in paying its way. The settlers themselves, while demanding greater self-government, refused to accept responsibility for the debt, however, blaming it on the Company's own extravagance.

In 1919, the pro-British and liberally minded General Smuts was elected as the Prime Minister of South Africa. Smuts was keen to amalgamate Southern Rhodesia with South Africa, in order to increase the liberal vote against the political conservatism of the Afrikaner majority,[8] and the BSAC, supported by an important element in Rhodesian mining and commerce, looked towards this as a solution to Southern Rhodesia's financial problems. The Rhodesian farming population, on the other hand, tended to be against the idea, as also did the small Indian and Coloured communities, and in this they received the support of Sir Charles Coghlan, the leading member of the Southern Rhodesia Legislature.

The country's finances were in a satisfactory state by 1922, but such was the accumulating deficit faced by the Company, in respect of the costs of administration, that it could see little prospect that responsible government, which undoubtedly would inherit the debt, would succeed in paying its way. Meanwhile, the settlers refused to accept responsibility for the debt. In November of that year, a referendum was held on whether to join the Union of South Africa or assume the status, offered by Britain, of a Crown colony. The outcome was a clear majority against union with South Africa, and with it, Rhodes's hope of a united Southern Africa. The outcome also shifted the regional division between South and Central Africa southwards, from the Zambezi to the Limpopo. It is pertinent to add that, in spite of the welcome that had been offered by Smuts, a large section of South Africa's Afrikaner population were hostile to Southern Rhodesia. The region north of the Limpopo had long been regarded by them as the direction of their own future destiny, but its appropriation by Cecil Rhodes

---

8   At the time, the Afrikaner electorate was bigger than the English-speaking electorate, and of the existing four Provinces, two were predominantly English-speaking and liberally inclined, while the other two were predominantly Afrikaans-speaking.

and the British government had been seen, not only as depriving them of this, but also as completing their encirclement, with a view to forcing them back under British control. Many *Afrikaners* did settle in Rhodesia, but this did nothing to assuage the bitterness that many felt.

Meanwhile, the BSAC reacted to the referendum result by submitting to the Crown a Petition of Right, claiming payment for its administrative deficit, based on Britain's offer of Crown colony status. The Crown consented to settle the Company's claim, while appropriating all the unalienated land and public structures in both Rhodesias, apart from the mineral rights, which the Company was allowed to keep. The newly elected, Southern Rhodesia Government was to receive the unalienated land and the public works, but agreed to make a substantial payment to the Crown, equal to more than half of what the latter had paid to the Company. This prompted the complaint that the settlers were the only British community in Imperial history that had been required to pay for the privilege of self-government.[9]

A British review of Southern Rhodesia's future constitutional position – known as the Buxton Report of 1923 – favoured self-government on a similar basis to that enjoyed by Natal, with a constitutional Governor, who represented the King, replacing the Administrator, with effective power vested in a Cabinet that was responsible to an elected legislature. In the same year, Southern Rhodesia was annexed by the British Government as a Crown Colony. Indeed, the requirements of Dominion status were probably met, and failure to achieve this would soon prove to be disastrous for the Colony, because the winds of liberalism were already beginning to blow through the corridors of Westminster. Effectively, Southern Rhodesia had now been annexed, its administration now headed by a Governor, who represented the King.[10] It retained full internal autonomy, subject to restrictions against discriminatory racial legislation, except with the sanction of the Crown. The existing Native Department remained largely unscathed, and the existing Legislative Assembly was elected on much the same non-racial, but property-weighted basis as in the Cape. The Land Apportionment Act, separating Black and White interests, was not challenged.

9   L. Gann, *A History of Southern Rhodesia* (New York, 1969), 248.
10   Britain's constitutional thinking insisted that the Governor did not represent the King but the Crown, meaning the ruling Party leaders who had long since appropriated the royal position (as opposed to advising it).

North of the Zambezi, with effect from 1924, the Colonial Office at last succeeded in gaining control, from the Company, of all Rhodesia north of the Zambezi. This included both the White-settled North-Western Province, lying between the Zambezi and the Belgian Congo, and the overwhelmingly Black Northern and Eastern Provinces. Northern Rhodesia now lost its independence of the King's British Government, becoming formally a British Protectorate, within which the British inhabitants were granted a degree of self-government, leaving the indigenous inhabitants to be administered by the Colonial Office. Meanwhile, relieved of its responsibility for the costs of government in both territories, the BSAC now became a wholly commercial enterprise.

It could probably be said that the main purpose of the Charter, granted in 1890, had been to grant royal recognition to the venture, defining its scope of operations for the benefit of investors and for the purpose of authorising its dealings for the benefit of neighbouring and other affected governments. To this end, it prescribed the form of government of the venture and its purpose as a commercial undertaking. Queen Victoria's British Government had no involvement in the issue, except in so far as it affected Britain's own interests. These were that no other power should take possession of the territory north of the Limpopo, and any expenses that might be incurred. Such expense as the British Government was put to, notably military assistance, had, in fact, been refunded by the Company. Once the colony had become established and capable of self-government, the implied intention was that the Company should relinquish administrative control, on such terms as might be agreed between the Company and the elected government of the territory, providing thereby that the Company should thenceforth become a purely commercial enterprise. In the light of events, the colony divided into three – Southern Rhodesia and North-Western Rhodesia, separated by the Zambezi. This would leave the North-Eastern Province, which would be a matter for consideration between the interest parties when the time came.

39.5.3. The Imperial Conference of 1923: Divergences of Interest

At the Imperial Conference in London in 1923, meanwhile, the right of the Dominions to conduct their own foreign relations was recognised. From now onwards they were separate international identities. Constitutionally it might be said that the King functioned separately as the head of each Dominion, conducting relations with other heads of state through his respective representatives in respect of each Dominion. In order to avoid conflict and ensure the greater effectiveness of their association, common policies were followed on issues of common interest, based on mutual agreement.

Southern Rhodesia's peculiar position was subsequently recognised in a convention that she enjoyed the right to conduct her own external affairs in respect of those relations that were of immediate interest to her, as a result of which, she appointed her own High Commissioners to Great Britain and South Africa, and her own diplomatic representatives in the neighbouring Portuguese colony of Mozambique. It was difficult for Rhodesia to manage its affairs further, because it still lacked the resources to do so.

It was not long before Britain discovered that her own freedom of action in foreign affairs could be limited by this policy of mutual agreement with and between the Dominions. The Geneva Protocol of 1924, for the peaceful settlement of international disputes by compulsory arbitration, which had been submitted by the British Prime Minister, Ramsay MacDonald, had eventually to be rejected, owing to the opposition of the Dominions. They considered that the risks in such a scheme were too unequal, and, as the Canadian representative, Raoul Durand, pointed out in respect of his own country: 'We live in a fireproof house, far from inflammable materials'. Much the same could be said of the other Dominions, who were more concerned, in any case, to rid themselves of outside interference, than to submit to new forms. As was now being discovered, the Dominions could have very different interests from Great Britain and, indeed, from each other.

39.5.4. The Dominions Office: Sovereign Independence for the Dominions

A separate Dominions Office was set up in 1925, although both the Dominions and the colonies were represented in the British Cabinet by the Secretary of State for the Colonies. In 1930, the new importance of the Dominions and the very different nature of the issues affecting relations with them was recognised, and a separate Secretary of State for the Dominions was created, so completing the dual structure. The process of separating the Empire into two groupings was taken a stage further by the fourth Statute of Westminster of 1931, which gave legal force to the various conventions regulating relations between the Parliament of the United Kingdom and the legislatures of the Dominions, notably by granting sovereign independent status under the Crown to the Dominions of Newfoundland, Canada, South Africa, Australia, and New Zealand. Under this arrangement, five new monarchies were, in effect, created, George V becoming King of each of these Dominions separately, as well as being King of Great Britain and Northern Ireland. This grant excluded Southern Rhodesia, whose Prime Minister, Sir Godfrey Huggins, did not feel that it was yet in a strong enough financial position to meet the external costs of full independence. The Preamble to the Statute of Westminster of 1931 declared that it would be in accord with the established constitutional position of the members of the Commonwealth, in relation to one another, that any alteration in the law or the succession to the throne or the royal style and titles should require the consent of the Parliaments of all the Dominions.

Such an arrangement was only workable in practice if it were assumed that King George V wore six crowns, or, as previously suggested, wore the same crown in respect of six different realms. This was because the interests of the various Dominions and the United Kingdom differed from each other, and it would have been impossible for the King, as a common head of state, to fulfil several conflicting roles at once. Constitutionally, the King's Ministers in his various Dominions were simply implementing his wishes, although in reality it was the Ministers who were making the decisions on his behalf. He could hardly be enacting racially discriminatory legislation in South Africa and criticising it in Canada. The only solution was a presumed division of the crown, so that he was a different head of state in each of his realms, in respect of the interests of which he received separate advice. The existence of several independent monarchies, but not crowns, was finally recognised, in effect, in the abdication crisis of 1936, when the Dominion Governments were invited by Baldwin to tender advice to the King separately, and the South African Government decided to provide for its own royal abdication. Henceforth, he ruled in separate realms but wore the same crown, making him at once the King of Canada, King of New Zealand, and so forth.

Apart from the Irish Free State, only one Dominion failed, and that was Newfoundland, which in 1933 was faced with bankruptcy. By force of circumstance, Newfoundland reverted to the status of a Crown colony in that year, when, on the basis of the report of a Royal Commission, approved by the Newfoundland Parliament, the government of Newfoundland was surrendered to a temporary commission, nominated by the British Treasury. Great Britain assumed responsibility for the colony's finances until such time as it again became self-supporting.

By 1925, the diplomatic unity of the Commonwealth had already disappeared. Instead of acting as a group, the Dominions had taken to pursuing their diplomatic interests separately. Thus, even in 1923, Canada had made a separate treaty with the United States, and none of the Dominions was represented in the Locarno Treaties of 1925, which concerned only Great Britain and other European countries. Indeed, by 1926 the Commonwealth, as the group had come to be known, was close to breaking up. Southern Ireland was effectively an independent state which the Crown refused to recognise, except as a Dominion, because feudal doctrine did not accept that an overseas estate of the King could achieve independence, except by rebellion, and that treason demanded severe punishment, as in South Africa. Southern Ireland, Éire, endeavoured to compromise by asserting that the authority of the Crown arose simply from an arbitrary association of the state with the Commonwealth. It also stated its refusal to be involved in any British wars. South Africa, with its large and still bitter Afrikaner population, occasionally displayed similar sentiments and showed signs of following a similar course to Ireland. In Canada, a constitutional crisis erupted over the refusal of the Governor-General to grant a dissolution to Mackenzie King. These worrying developments in Ireland, South Africa and Canada, driven largely by considerations of common law, led to another Imperial Conference in 1926.

39.5.5. The Imperial Conference of 1926: Legislative Independence

The Conference achieved a definition of Dominion status. This declared that Great Britain and the Dominions were 'autonomous Communities within the British Empire, equal in status, in no way subordinate one to another in any aspect of their domestic or external affairs, though united by a common allegiance to the Crown and freely associated as members of the British Commonwealth of Nations'.[11] Otherwise, the Conference displayed an unwillingness on the part of the Dominions to agree to any arrangement for reaching rapid common decisions on foreign policy, still less any federal type of arrangement between them, if only because all held different views and they were dispersed around the world, with limited interests in common. The situation was temporarily dealt with by a declaration drawn up by Lord Balfour at the time. The Balfour Declaration of 1926 contained two essential points: it recognised the autonomy of the Dominions in both their domestic and their foreign and inter-imperial relations; and it recognised that, within the Commonwealth, Great Britain had special functions which must give her a special position. The tendency after the Conference was for the first part of the Declaration to be remembered and for the latter part to be ignored.

The Conference also agreed that the legal obstacles to autonomy must be removed, and this was achieved in the Statute of Westminster of 1929. By this Statute, the convention that no Imperial legislation should be applicable to a Dominion without its request became established in law. Other provisions of the Statute abolished the extra-territorial limit on Dominion laws, and also the repugnancy test for Dominion legislation, which had allowed the Crown to nullify any legislation that it found to be unacceptable. It was also provided that all Dominion legislation should be enforceable in its own respective courts, so that the Dominions could now legislate on the prerogative of the Crown and on their own constitution. However, Canada, Australia and New Zealand requested that the Statute should impose a limit on their own powers to alter their constitutions. Except for this last provision, the relationship between the Dominions, and between the Dominions and Great Britain, was based at last on customary law, and all that linked them now was their common adherence to the regal contract. Meanwhile, the common avenue of

---

11   Imperial Conference, 1926: Summary of Proceedings (Cmd. 2768), 14.

judicial appeal to the Privy Council remained unaffected. In consequence of the 1929 Statute and the general unwillingness to establish separate institutions, there was created a cumbersome machinery for the purpose of Imperial consultation, which functioned during the 1930s. It took place at various levels. In particular, there was Dominion representation on the Committee for Imperial Defence, and in order to deal with commercial issues, an Imperial Economic Conference was held in Ottawa in 1932.

Only two Dominions availed themselves to the full of their new freedoms, notably the Irish Free State and the Union of South Africa. The majority of the electorate in each case had been forced into the Empire against their will, and so faced the greatest pressures of accommodation. In each case, also, the antagonism was accentuated by an ethnic difference. Ireland repudiated the 1921 treaty with Britain, the constitution of 1921, the right of appeal to the Privy Council, and the oath of allegiance. There had never been and could never be a regal contract with the native Irish, whose relationship with England, and hence with Great Britain, had been based on conquest. Later, in 1937, Ireland introduced a new constitution of its own making, and so went its own way, although it remained within the Commonwealth. South Africa, in its Status of the Union Act of 1943, declared itself 'a sovereign independent state' in every respect, and went on to make changes in the franchise and changes in Native representation and in the official language. It abolished the royal prerogative of disallowance, and limited the discretion of the Governor-General in assenting to legislation.

It has been argued that, because Parliament in the United Kingdom is supreme, it cannot surrender its supremacy in legislative matters. It can revoke or amend any Act, and hence any concession that it has ever made. Therefore, this must apply equally to powers surrendered to the Dominions. In practice, Parliament would have been unable to enforce any such measure, as the example of South Africa showed only too clearly. All constitutional rules, like statutes, are ultimately subject to their enforceability. In any case, in matters of the royal prerogative, it was a long-established convention, contrary to feudal doctrine that, what the King gave, he did not take away. It was an extension of the deep-seated habit of mind that the courts had introduced, that what had become established could not be changed. This unchangeability was a feature of common law, but that had evolved over centuries, and more probably millennia, and must be distinguished from established practice, which can never be irreversible.

39.5.5.1. Governors and Governors-General

The implications of the Statute of Westminster, 1929, were certainly questioned. Although it referred to the King as the symbol of the free association of members of the British Commonwealth of Nations, it was increasingly accepted that he was separately the head of state in each case, and that he held separate offices as King of Canada, King of Australia, and so forth. The fact that the Kings of each of the Dominions, one of which, constitutionally, was Great Britain itself, were the same individual, possessed of their collective *imperiums*, represented by the same Crown and the same Sceptre, much like England and Scotland under James I, posed no constitutional difficulty in itself, but it did pose practical ones. Because he could not be in London, Ottawa, Canberra, Wellington, Pretoria, and Salisbury at the same time, he was represented in each of the Dominions by a Governor, and endeavoured to compensate for his personal absence by periodic state visits to each, usually associated with a constitutional function, such as the opening of a Parliament. The introduction of the office of Governor-General was necessary in Canada and Australia, because each of these was a federation of Provinces or States, in each of which the King was already represented by a Governor, and it was necessary in both cases for the Governors to be co-ordinated and represented at a federal level by a common Governor-General. The latter was not constitutionally senior to the Governors, each of whom was responsible directly to the King in any case, but it was widely, and mistakenly, perceived that a Governor-General was senior to a Governor, implying that some Dominions were senior to others, which was not the case. In order to avoid this, it was agreed that each Dominion should have a Governor-General, even though the qualification was meaningless in respect of South Africa and New Zealand, which were not federations. Only in Southern Rhodesia was the King still represented by a Governor, because it had not yet been recognised as independent *de lege*, in addition to being, for all practical purposes, independent *de facto*. In practice, however, the Governors-General would be pushed aside, constitutionally, like the King in the United Kingdom, in order to leave consultations between Britain and the Dominions to be undertaken directly between their Prime Ministers.

It was realised, however, that the position of the Crown as the symbol of unity was weakened by the fact that the King might be called upon to act on irreconcilable advice from the various Dominions. This became evident on what is referred to as the abdication of Edward VIII in 1936, when the tendency to regard the King as separate personalities was given formal significance by the suggestion of Baldwin that the Dominions tender advice to the King separately. Canada responded by requesting an Imperial statute to recognise the abdication in law, which then had to be enacted, and to which Canada then assented. This Act was superfluous, because an abdication is a unilateral constitutional act, and only if the authority of the King is withdrawn by Parliament, depriving him of the *Imperium*, is statutory authority required. Meanwhile, Australia and New Zealand merely assented to the abdication, which was equally superfluous, although either legal acknowledgement of an abdication or the recognition of the new King is undoubtedly required in each case. South Africa did neither, since she regarded it as within her competence to provide for a separate abdication. Southern Ireland simply accepted the abdication and recognised George VI. Already, the King was effectively seen as holding separate offices concurrently, as King of Canada, King of South Africa, King of Great Britain and Northern Ireland, and so on. By implication, Edward VIII had relinquished his crown in respect of each of his Dominions individually, albeit in a single act.

39.5.6. The Imperial Conference of 1937: The British Commonwealth of Nations

In order to remove the connotation of 'empire', which the Dominions in their newly independent status found increasingly distasteful, and in order to make them appear more as gatherings of equals, the Imperial Conferences acquired, in 1937, the new name of 'Commonwealth Prime Ministers' Conferences'. Out of deference to history, these Conferences were held in London, with the position of the British Prime Minister being merely that of *primus inter pares*. The group as a whole now assumed a formal identity as 'the British Commonwealth of Nations', with each establishing formal diplomatic contact with the other through a High Commissioner, which avoided the more formal and alien implications of 'ambassador'. British Prime Ministers increasingly consulted with their opposite numbers in the Dominions on matters of common concern, such as trade and defence, but it was in the regular Commonwealth Prime Ministers' Conferences, attended by Great Britain, Canada, Australia, New Zealand, South Africa and Southern Rhodesia that the group achieved its most effective role as a political force. The effective status of Southern Rhodesia as a Dominion dates from the recognition by the Crown, in 1933, of the title of its Premier as that of Prime Minister, its economy having at last found its feet. While the order of seniority of the Dominions was that just listed, it was not long before the Prime Minister of Southern Rhodesia, Sir Godfrey Huggins, who had been in office the longest, was recognised as the Commonwealth's 'elder statesman'.

The only Dominion to fail, and therefore to drop out of the Imperial Conferences, was Newfoundland, whose financially incompetent and corrupt government had caused it to default in 1933. At its own wish, Newfoundland had reverted in that year to the status of a Crown colony, as a Royal Commission recommended the setting up of an interim commission to manage the colony's affairs. This was appointed by the British Treasury and was subject to its supervision. The arrangement was successful, and in 1948 a referendum among the Newfoundlanders decided, by a narrow majority, to join Canada as its tenth Province. As one of the oldest and geographically most isolated and independently-minded of the original colonies, the decision was a difficult one, but Newfoundland's natural resources were very limited.

The Commonwealth arrangement was a popular one, giving the Dominions a role in world affairs that they would not otherwise have enjoyed, and at the same time increasing Britain's negotiating position in international diplomacy. The Commonwealth had proved itself to be at its most effective in time of war, all the Dominions except the Irish Free State having gone to Britain's aid in 1914, and about to go to her aid again in 1939. Three bonds enabled the Commonwealth to function well. One was the constitutional link, represented chiefly by the sharing of a common head of state, towards whom, on the whole, a genuine sense of allegiance was felt. The second was the inheritance of a common history and traditions. The third was the widespread sense of common ancestry, represented by the inclusion of the majority of its inhabitants in the regal contract.

40. THE SECOND WORLD WAR

40.1. The Resurrection of Germany

The armistice of 1918 was preceded and followed by an increasing political and economic collapse in Germany, which the Communists did their best to exploit. The situation was made far worse by the Allies, who both demanded and took huge reparations in the form of money, equipment and goods. At the same time, the forced abdication of the Emperor, Wilhelm II, and the abolition of the monarchy had left the country leaderless and devoid of any political focus or sense of identity. Representatives of the governments of the German states met in Berlin to agree on the election of a new national assembly, which met at Weimar at the beginning of 1919 to adopt a new republican constitution. This led to unstable coalitions and a largely ineffectual system of government. Furthermore, its willingness to cooperate with the Allies in meeting the demands imposed at Versailles brought it into widespread contempt. Meanwhile, with its economy either dismantled or producing for the Allies, unemployment and starvation soon became widespread, with revolts all over the country, led by the Socialists in Bavaria, the Communists in Berlin, Munich, the Ruhr and elsewhere, and by the Monarchists in Berlin. Meanwhile, the French and Belgians organised a rebellion in the Rhineland, which France was hoping to annex. The Communists viewed the situation as ripe for a seizure of power. The democratic Socialists had much electoral success, but didn't know how to use it. The nationalists bitterly opposed the Versailles Treaty and longed to see a restoration of Germany to its former position as a leading European power. The Monarchists made no headway with a people disillusioned by the failed ambitions of Wilhelm II, upon whom the war was largely blamed. There was also a strongly anti-Jewish reaction, particularly among the nationalists, who resented the prominent part that the Jews played in the Communist and Socialist movements, blaming them for Germany's collapse in 1918.[1]

National Socialism emerged in the 1920s as a merging of three streams of discontent: Socialism, which saw the collapse of the old order in 1918 as opening the way for a new, egalitarian society; nationalism, which saw the defeat of 1918 and the appropriation of large parts of Germany by its neighbours as a national humiliation, for which it saw the Jews as a primary cause; and Romanticism, which sought a revival of pagan German culture from the depredations of the industrial age. This merging found expression in the insignificant National Socialist Party, the *Nationalsozialistische Deutsche Arbeiterpartei* or NSDAP, which would have come to nothing, but for the fact that it attracted the attention of one of the vast army of unemployed ex-servicemen, Adolf Hitler, who saw in it the means to his own self-realisation. His energy and self-conviction soon brought him the leadership of the Party, and it was leadership that Germany desperately needed. The democratic system, known to history as the Weimar Republic, which the Allies had imposed on Germany, proved to be little more than a system of ineffectual, bickering Parties, at a time of massive national debt, unemployment, and scarcity. There was also widespread anxiety that the Communists would soon take control of the country.

As Party leader, or *Führer*, Hitler looked to the example of the newly risen Italian demagogue, Mussolini. Whereas Fascism promoted the central importance of the state, National Socialism promoted the ethnic identity and welfare of the German people. This excluded the Jews, who were also widely blamed for most of Germany's troubles, particularly as a result of their prominence in the Communist and Socialist movements. Hitler's own antipathy towards them may also have owed much to his probable Jewish ancestry, said to have been the result of an affair, voluntary or otherwise, between his grandmother, Maria Schicklgruber, as a girl in service in Graz as a cook to a Jewish family, named Frankenberger, and the son of her employer.[2] As a result, it was said, she had a son, Alois, who was to become the father of Adolf. The disgrace was covered up, but the

---

1   Sources used for the war of 1939–45 and the events leading up to it, supplemented by the writer's own recollections, are too numerous to record, but a good basic source, although biased, is still W. Shirer, *The Rise and Fall of the Third Reich* (London, 1960).

2   W. Maser, *Hitler*, (1973), 1–21; J. C. Fest, *Hitler* (London, 1974), 14–17. The grounds are quite strong, but the name of the father is not recorded, leaving no factual evidence.

rumour seems to have been well known locally, and it is likely that Hitler learned of it when still a schoolboy, only for the issue to become one of increasing sensitivity during the era of German nationalism. Another formative influence on the National Socialist, or 'Nazi', Party, was the militant wing of the Communists, which made use of well-organised gang violence, in order to break up its meetings. The response of the 'Nazis' was to form their own militant group, the *Sturm Abteilung*, or 'storm-troopers', who launched the Party onto a violent path. In the event, it was this ability to deal with the Communists that gave the Party, on the one hand, a reputation for uncompromising effectiveness in a chaotic age, but also antagonised many Germans who saw it as a potential dictatorship. Crucially, it was Hitler's own charismatic and uncompromising character that made him stand out by the beginning of the 1930s.

In 1933, the 'Nazi' Party came to power legally, but only by resorting to highly questionable practices. Hitler became Chancellor of Germany and soon acquired dictatorial powers, and when the German President, Hindenburg, died in the following year, Hitler effectively took his place. He now embarked on a series of policies: to end the restrictions and obligations imposed upon Germany by the Allies after the last war; to restore the German economy; and to remove from German society 'decadent' cultural and genetic influences, including habitual criminals, 'mental defectives', and non-ethnic Germans, the most numerous of whom were the Jews. These groups were to be transferred to concentration camps while a Jewish national homeland was found for them, well outside Europe. None of the countries approached, however, were willing to accept them, and Palestine was rejected as an option because of the hostility of the Arabs. Meanwhile, conditions in the camps were appalling.

Nevertheless, as Hitler's economic policies began to take shape, he drew widespread admiration from other countries, which were themselves, by now, mired in a deep, worldwide economic depression, accompanied by large-scale unemployment. Germany, now prospering and engaged in a technological re-birth, was now attracting widespread international admiration that was only gradually being eclipsed by a growing condemnation of the treatment of its minorities.

40.1.1. The 'Abdication' Crisis

George V died in 1936 and was due to be succeeded by his eldest son, Edward. Unlike his father, against whose strict upbringing he rebelled, he was thoroughly 'modern' in outlook and behaviour, given to informality and a genuine concern for the welfare of the poor and the unemployed, which made him hugely popular. His insecure behaviour and attitudes had been a matter of great concern to his father, however, and he now caused concern to Lang, the Archbishop of Canterbury, who was a firm believer in the need to uphold the dignity and pageantry of the Monarchy. Compounding the problem, Edward decided to marry a divorced American woman, Mrs Wallis Warfield Simpson, who was in the process of obtaining a second divorce, which had not yet become final. The situation was one of the utmost concern to the Prime Minister, Baldwin's Ministry, as well as to the Dominion Governments. Nobody was more concerned than the Archbishop of Canterbury, Lang, because the Church of England did not sanction divorce, and approved the ethical standards that had characterised the Victorian, and much of the post-Victorian, era, which had been adhered to strictly by George V. This made divorce objectionable in the eyes of most people. For the future King, destined to be the head of the Church, this posed almost insuperable difficulties. A royal wedding, involving a woman who, in the eyes of the Church, was already married; the coronation of a King who had all but disbarred himself as head of the Church; and a prospective Queen who was, in any case, a commoner, unlikely to win the respect of the people, put the Archbishop in an almost impossible situation. Any child of such a marriage would, in the eyes of the Church, be illegitimate. Even a morganatic marriage, that is, one where the bride retains her former lower station, their issue having no claim to succeed to the possessions or title of the father, was opposed. Baldwin dithered, and, unwilling to force a constitutional crisis, was inclined to accept Edward's demands, but the Archbishop was not. In this, he was fortified by his recognition, in Edward's younger brother, Albert, a happily married man whom he deemed much better suited to the throne. Lang accordingly resorted to intrigue to help sway the Prime Minister. Thus, it was suggested, through a senior member of the clergy, that Edward had sought hypnotherapy to cure him of a drink problem; furthermore, it was suggested that the hypnotherapy had diverted Edward's obsession from alcohol to Mrs Simpson. The Archbishop warned the Prime Minister that this could lead to violent disagreements between the future King and his Ministers. Whether Baldwin was persuaded by this is unlikely, but it soon became known to Edward that both the Prime Minister and the Archbishop were opposed to his marriage. This may have brought a secret relief to Edward, because he probably knew how unsuited he was to the discipline demanded of the role. He may even have seen the marriage as a way out. In a broadcast to the nation on 5 December 1936, nine days after Mrs Simpson's decree *nisi* was granted, Edward announced that he could not rule as King without Mrs Simpson as his wife, and accordingly renounced his claim to the throne. The events of 1936 are described as the 'Abdication' Crisis, but they are more properly described as the 'Succession Crisis', because, as was indicated earlier, an uncrowned King, or King-Elect in common law, is not in a position to abdicate the throne.

Even so, Edward had been, and remained, popular, not least because of his obvious sympathies with the plight of the millions of unemployed. A remark made by him during a visit to the coal mines of South Wales in November of 1936, that 'something must be done', for the first time brought the Monarchy into close contact with the ordinary people, while at the same time bringing irritation at the apparent involvement of the future King in politics. Despite his popularity, public opinion played a large part in Edward's renunciation. As was noted by a *Daily Telegraph* columnist long after the event: 'Historians should note that in a letter from Alison Macleod about the abdication of Edward VIII, she pointed out that it was not the nobs who pushed him off the throne, but the masses. "We began to hear, *Stand by the King!* Then came the weekend, and MPs went home to their constituencies. They heard there what I also heard in buses and trams . . . they disapproved of divorce. Indeed . . . on the Thursday, finding his party in disarray about the King, Baldwin urged Tory MPs to cancel their weekend engagements, go to pubs and working men's clubs, listen and meet again on Monday. They went. They met. There was no more argument. The King went".'[3] Edward's intention of marrying Mrs Simpson was perfectly legal and consistent with the Act of Settlement, the only conflict being over his obligations to the Church of England, which was already trying to devise ways around the difficulty.

3   *The Weekly Telegraph*, 18 December 1996.

However, it was not the law that prevailed, but the most ancient and powerful of all constitutional traditions: that the King rules only by the will of the people.

Although convention has always regarded Edward as a King, with the gratuitous title of Edward VIII, he was never crowned, and constitutionally functioned merely in the role of Regent for less than a year. As noted earlier, the tradition that the successor to the crown is regarded as King from the moment of death of his predecessor owes its origin to the delayed coronation of Edward I and the feudal presumption of divine intent. It has no basis in the common law of the constitution. Furthermore, as pointed out earlier, in connection with the Act of Settlement, the retention of the coronation procedure after 1701, even though it had ostensibly been rendered superfluous by the Act, confirms that the Monarchy was still regarded subconsciously as subject to the requirements of *ius maiorum*. As to Edward's choice of wife, feudal doctrine does not recognise divorce, nor did the Church of England. Customary law does not attribute a constitutional function to the Queen, in any case, except as the lawful mother of the King's children. There are plenty of examples in Aryan society of kings marrying widows. The sanctity of marriage was nevertheless an important feature of Aryan culture, and this was crucial to the crisis over the succession. In keeping with their priestly function, Kings are expected to be flawless.

Following consultation with the Dominions, and at the request of Canada, Edward's renunciation was given statutory effect by His Majesty's Declaration of Abdication Act of 1936. Prior to this, Edward's intention had merely been communicated by the Prime Minister informally to the Dominion Governments. Even if Edward had legally been King, as Parliament evidently believed him to be, there would have been no constitutional need for his abdication to be confirmed by statute. A King did not require the consent of Parliament in order to abdicate: all that was needed was a proclamation by the King in Council. The regal contract, which did not yet exist in Edward's case, was voluntary and could be repudiated by either side, but good manners dictated that reasonable grounds should be given formally for repudiation, either that the contract had been irrevocably breached by the other party, or that one side or the other felt unable to honour it. To breach the contract otherwise was clearly dishonourable and deserving of retribution. Edward was not yet King, and the question did not arise, but he clearly owed an explanation to the people for the renunciation of his claim. The public might have been less hostile if they had seen Edward as a less promising King, but he had been popular, and his decision had brought a bitter end to their expectations.

The Abdication Act of 1936 did contain two important provisions, however. One, which required the consent of the Dominions, barred any future claim to the throne by Edward or his descendants. The other abolished a requirement of the Royal Marriages Act of 1772 that all descendants of George II, other than the Sovereign and the issue of princesses who married into foreign families, obtain the permission of the King before contracting a marriage. This requirement had been designed to forestall a potentially embarrassing marriage to a Catholic, but this fear had largely evaporated. Edward vacated the succession in December 1936, and was succeeded by his younger brother, who was crowned as King George VI in May 1937. His prospects as King were wholly unpromising. Repressed by his overbearing and demanding father, who regarded him as unsuitable to wear the Crown, George VI was a shy, retiring man with a bad stammer. However, he had previously married Elizabeth Bowes-Lyon, daughter of the Earl of Strathmore and Kinghorne, which was doubly fortunate, in that it revived the Scottish connection with the Monarchy and, a strong person herself, she gave him the support and self-confidence that he desperately needed. She was also politically shrewd, which was to bring its reward in the next generation. In his relations with his Ministers, the indications are that George VI received a copy of the Cabinet minutes, the daily printed despatches, and probably followed parliamentary debates through the official records. In his appreciation of these documents, he had the assistance of an expert staff.

At the request of the new King, that some permanent statutory provision be made for the infancy, incapacity or absence abroad of the Sovereign, the Regency Act of 1937 was promulgated – again, a superfluous measure, because this was already a constitutional function of the Great Council. The Act sought to provide that, in the event of the minority or permanent incapacity of the Sovereign, the next person in line to the throne who had reached the age of twenty-one be appointed as Regent, and that the Regent should carry out all royal functions, except assent to any Bill altering the order of succession to the throne, or certain provisions of the Acts of Union with Scotland. In the event of the temporary absence or incapacity of the Sovereign, the alleged Act provided for the establishment of a Council of State. There had been difficulties over the previous Council of State at the time of the illness of George V, in 1928, when the Irish Free State, as a member of the Commonwealth, had objected to the inclusion of members of the British Government. The Irish Government had maintained that this gave the impression that the British Government could act as intermediary between the Sovereign and other nations of the Commonwealth. As a result, only royal personages had signed documents relating to the Irish Free State, and the Imperial Conference of 1930 had agreed that only members of the royal family should be eligible to be Counsellors of State. Consequently, the Act of 1937 provided that a Council of State was to consist of the spouse of the Sovereign and the four persons next in line of succession to the throne who had reached twenty-one years of age. Any two present would constitute a quorum.[4]

40.1.2. The Second World War (1939–45)

Several international crises were developing during the 1930s that were to have a profound influence on political, and even constitutional, thinking. Although they were distinct conflicts, in the sense of being in respect of different issues, they prompted or impinged upon each other, to the extent that historians lump together as the Second World War, as they do in respect of the previous conflagration. This lumping together, on the grounds of their interaction with each other, does as much to confuse the situation as to clarify it. The three conflicts were the Russo-German War, the Anglo-German War, and the Japanese Imperial War, and they were interrelated mainly in that the one led to the other. Their causes, however, were quite different.

All were precipitated by Hitler's ambition to find compensation for Germany's loss of its territory and significance in 1918, which he saw as necessary to Germany's future well-being. Whereas Great Britain and France had continued to benefit from their empires, because of the raw materials and other important commodities that they provided, as well

4   V. Bogdanor, *The Monarchy and the Constitution*, 47.

as the reserves of military manpower, strategic positioning and scope for the settlement of surplus population that they offered, Germany had been, in Hitler's view, unfairly deprived of such assets. Hitler therefore looked to the Ukraine and Caucasus for compensation, since they offered *lebensraum*, or living space, for its population, as well as important raw materials, such as grain, coal, iron ore and oil. This would require the defeat of the Soviet Union, which, however, would itself be of great benefit to the whole Western world, because it was the source of the Communist threat. If nothing else, the removal of this threat would win international gratitude, which would ameliorate any alarm that Germany's eastward expansion might cause. Germany's intentions needed to be kept secret, however, so as not to arouse a Russian response.

In order to invade Russia, Germany needed to secure access to the Russian border, and on a sufficiently wide front, without causing consternation in Moscow. This in itself was an attractive prospect, because it would allow the retrieval of much of Germany's territory, taken from her at the end of the last war.

Hitler's first needs, however, were to regain control of the Rhineland from the occupying French and Belgian forces, followed by the completion of the unification of the German people that had been initiated by Bismarck. This would involve the unification of Germany with Austria; also the German-settled Sudetenland, a strip along the border with Czechoslovakia. Luckily, France was not only incapacitated by an economic depression, like Germany, but it was on the verge of civil war between the Communists and the nationalists. This allowed Germany to retrieve its industrial heartland without effective opposition. Meanwhile, the time taken to achieve all this would allow Germany to re-build her military strength for the main conflict. The economic and military revival of Germany, together with the *Anschluss* with Austria and the crisis over the Sudetenland, aroused the concern of Great Britain and France that Poland would be next. They took the mistaken view that Hitler's objective was to establish German hegemony over Central Europe, to which they were unshakeably opposed. At two conferences held in Munich, Hitler, being convinced that neither would go to war over the issue, particularly as neither had vested, or even strategic interests in Poland, willingly signed a guarantee of Poland's integrity. The British

Prime Minister, Neville Chamberlain, was left in no doubt, however, as to Hitler's intentions, but avoided causing a new crisis, while attending to Britain's rearmament – all too late, as it turned out.

40.1.2.1. The Russo-German War (1941–45)

Hitler realised that he must move while he had the advantage, and the occupation of the Sudetenland was quickly followed by the occupation of all Czechoslovakia. This gave him a commanding position for an invasion of Poland – which would retrieve German territory on the North European Plain, around Poznan, and provide Hitler with his corridor to the east. It would also provide much-needed access to the Romanian oilfields. Hitler's concern now, was not Britain and France, who had no economic or strategic interest in the outcome, but Russia. He accordingly sought to forestall Russian alarm by entering into a secret pact with Stalin, the Russian leader, to partition Poland between them. To this overture, Stalin agreed, and at the beginning of September 1939, both countries invaded Poland, Germany from the west and Russia from the east, partitioning Poland between them. At the same time, Britain and France unexpectedly declared war on Germany.

The timetable for Germany's invasion of Russia was now delayed, when Germany's ally, Italy, led by Mussolini, who had already conquered Albania, complicated matters by embarking on an invasion of Greece, only to be defeated and to appeal to Hitler for help. Hitler's loyalty to his ally may have been coloured by a concern that Britain and France might see the Balkans as an opportunity. Whatever the reason, Hitler postponed his invasion of Russia by a crucial six weeks of the remaining North European summer by invading the Balkans in June 1941, heading off a British invasion of Greece.

When Germany then invaded Russia, Stalin was taken completely by surprise (although his intelligence system was not). Having previously given vent to his paranoia by eliminating much of the Russian officer class, Russia suffered a rapid defeat, after which Stalin wisely left the conduct of the war to his new generals. Hitler did not. The loss of the six weeks found the German invasion slowed down by the autumn rains, so that, instead of taking Moscow before the winter, the invasion was stalled on the edge of both it and Leningrad (St Petersburg), leaving the German army dangerously exposed, as well as ill-equipped, for the coming winter. Road and rail communications with the rear were limited and subject to attack. Meanwhile, Russia's ability to fight a sustained war was achieved by a super-human transfer of its war industries to the east, from Russia to Siberia. There followed a series of Russian winter advances and German summer advances, until Hitler decided on a redirection of effort in 1942, towards the Caucasus oilfields. The northern flank of this advance was exposed to the industrial city of Stalingrad, located on the west bank of the Volga, and Hitler expended every effort to take the city, without success, until the German army involved found itself surrounded during the ensuing winter, and eventually forced to surrender.

The spring of 1943 marked a decisive turn in the war, with a crucial victory for the Russians in a tank battle at Kursk, in the northern Ukraine. The German army, seriously weakened by a commitment of forces to the war in Western Europe, and deprived of supplies by the bombing of Germany in pursuit of that war, now found itself unable to hold the line against the Russians. A slow, hard-fought retreat followed, westward into Poland by 1945, followed by the fall of Berlin and the suicide of Hitler in May of that year.

40.1.2.2. The Anglo-German War

The British Prime Minister, Neville Chamberlain, assumed that Hitler's ambitions related to Central Europe, but played for time by creating a climate of goodwill, which put Hitler off-guard. France had already re-armed, with outdated equipment and tactics, like Britain. Following the German invasion of Poland, Britain and France declared war on Germany at the beginning of September 1939. Hitler, taken by surprise, and having no ambitions in Western Europe, had made no real preparations in that direction. After a lull that lasted well into 1940, while Germany prepared to attack, Britain, characteristically, was in no position to take the initiative, and France was unwilling to act on its own. Apart from a precautionary invasion of Norway – and with it Denmark – by Germany, in order to ensure the protection of its iron ore supplies, the war did not really begin until 1941, when Germany launched an invasion of Belgium, directed at outflanking France's Maginot Line. Using entirely new tactics, known as a *blitzkrieg*, based on the use of fast-moving tanks and motorised infantry, bombing from the air, supplemented by commando operations against strong-points, both the French and British armies were forced into rapid retreat. A swift German advance continued to the coast near Boulogne, leaving the British Expeditionary Force with no option but to retreat to the coast at Dunkirk, a few miles east of Calais, in the hope of rescue by sea. Meanwhile, further demoralised by Britain's apparent exit from the war, the shattered French army continued its retreat across France.

That the British army (and a part of the French army) in Flanders avoided immediate destruction or surrender was due to Hitler, who, having no quarrel with Britain, and concerned only to punish France for its treatment of Germany after 1918, was anxious to reach agreeable terms without humiliating Britain. While Hitler waited, expecting peace negotiations by Britain, the shambles of the Allied army at Dunkirk began to be rescued by an armada of small boats and naval vessels. Finally, under great pressure from his commanders and with no sign of negotiation from Britain, Hitler allowed operations to resume, beginning with the annihilation of what remained of the British and French armies cornered at Dunkirk. Under the ensuing peace treaty, France was to be divided, with the north and west remaining under German occupation, and a sympathetic French government, based in Vichy, in central France, retaining control of the centre and south of the country.

Without France, Britain had no prospect of winning the war, and her only sensible option was to negotiate as honourable an exit from it as possible, with Hitler still willing to offer good terms, although less generous than those offered at Dunkirk. He was, after all, anxious to devote his full attention to the impending Russo-German War. Churchill was now Prime Minister, however, and his continued determination to defeat Hitler defied all apparent logic. During the lull that followed the Dunkirk disaster, Hitler even sent his deputy, Hess, on a risky secret mission, in the hope of by-passing Churchill and dealing with the peace faction in the Conservative Party. Hitler's terms apparently involved an agreement, under which Germany would withdraw from Western Europe, except for the return to Germany, by France, of Alsace-Lorraine. Churchill, determined to pursue the war, refused to allow Germany's terms to be published or presented to Parliament, and imprisoned Hess as a criminal.

Hitler's terms were believed to include a German withdrawal from Western Europe, except for the retrieval of Alsace-Lorraine. Churchill's attitude, apart from his own love of a 'good war', seems to have been that Hitler should not be allowed to achieve a dominant position in Europe, to which end he held to a pious hope that the United States could again be drawn into the conflict, as it was in 1917, which seemed very unlikely. Britain's position was now dire, with a German invasion pending.

Against all expectations, however, Britain frustrated Germany's planned invasion by gaining aerial supremacy, and Hitler turned his main attention to his forthcoming campaign in Russia, leaving it to the German submarine fleet to isolate Britain from its sources of supply. This would have succeeded, but for American cooperation through the supply of new ships and the successful development of anti-submarine warfare. A breakthrough for Britain occurred with the attack by Japan on the American Pacific fleet, upon which Hitler unaccountably declared war on America.[5] There existed a German-Japanese defence treaty, but the nature of the Japanese attack had not activated its terms. The United States and Britain, now allies, agreed to give priority to the war in Europe, and there followed an Anglo-American invasion of Italy, by way of North Africa, Churchill having proposed this initiative because he did not have faith in untried American troops being used in a frontal assault on German-occupied northern France, which was now heavily defended.

It was June of 1944, therefore, before an Anglo-American invasion of France was finally launched across the English Channel into Normandy. Overcoming fierce resistance, the Allies were able to take, first Paris and then Brussels. Overwhelmed by the Anglo-American advance, and in spite of a doomed German counter-offensive in Ardennes, the German army failed to repel the Allies, who succeeded in crossing the Rhine in March 1945. German opposition now became increasingly sporadic, as Germany used its remaining strength in a desperate bid to hold Berlin against the Russians, who were by now fighting their way into the city, as the two wars now approached a common end. The Americans reached the middle Elbe early in April, but remained there, leaving it to the Russians to take Berlin. As they fought their way into the city at the beginning of May, Hitler committed suicide, after handing over command to Admiral

---

5   Hitler, based on experience during the previous war, did not rate America's ability to fight a war highly.

Dönitz, who surrendered to the British commander, Montgomery, a few days later.

The formal end of the Anglo-German War was declared by Churchill and the American President, Truman, on 8 May 1945, and the end of the Russo-German War, by Stalin, a day later. Germany was now divided into three occupation zones: British, American, French and Russian. That the French were accorded its own zone was due to Churchill, in an attempt to salvage a little of France's self-respect, but equally likely because France had accused him of betrayal by withdrawing from France.

40.1.2.3. The Japanese Imperial War (1931–45)

Japan's imperial expansion had its origin with the growth of military self-confidence, resulting from its decisive victory over Russia in 1905, causing it to embark on the conquest and annexation of Korea in 1910. As an industrialising country, the world economic crisis of 1929 raised the problem of Japan's lack of economic self-sufficiency and the limited size of its domestic market for its manufactured goods. Japan accordingly looked to the example of the British Empire, which had provided it with a guaranteed market for British industries, a guaranteed source of food and raw materials, as well as space for the settlement of Britain's surplus population. However, it was the Mukden 'incident' in Manchuria in 1931, when a Japanese officer was killed by the Chinese, that provided the justification for more positive action, leading to the occupation of Manchuria. Japan was divided at the time, between its experiment with parliamentary government, which had no control over the military, and the growing ambitions of the latter, inspired by Japan's long military tradition. In 1937, the army undertook an invasion of China, taking control over much of the eastern and central parts of the country.

Japan's imperial prospects widened considerably after 1940, when the conquest of the Netherlands and France by Germany opened an opportunity for Japan to seize their colonies in South-East Asia, only to prompt a warning against further designs by the United States. In December 1941, Japan delivered what was expected to be a knock-out blow against the American Pacific fleet at Honolulu, in Hawaii. At the same time, Japan launched a successful conquest of the American Philippines, French Indo-China, the Dutch East Indies and British Malaya, effectively neutralising Britain also. March of 1942 saw the Japanese invade and occupy another British colony, Burma.

Meanwhile, America recovered from its defeat at Pearl Harbor with remarkable speed, and its concern to keep the Japanese from occupying Australia resulted in a Japanese naval defeat in the battle of the Coral Sea, early in May 1942, when a Japanese fleet was defeated. This was followed a few weeks later by what was probably the crucial battle of the war, when a Japanese invasion fleet was defeated by the Americans off the island of Midway, in June 1942. This ended Japan's hopes of defeating the United States and securing control of the Pacific, and by mid-1943, the re-conquest by the Americans of the Pacific islands had begun. Japan's position in South-East Asia, which depended almost entirely on supplies by sea, was now under American attack. In a final throw of the dice, a Japanese attempt to invade India was defeated in a battle just inside India, on the Imphal Plain, around Kohima.

Kohima marked the turning point in Japan's ambitions on the Asian mainland, and it was followed by a gradual re-conquest of Burma. Meanwhile, the Americans re-took the Philippines, and by 1945 the American advance in the Pacific had brought Japan within the range of American aircraft. Two American atomic bombs, dropped on the Japanese cities of Hiroshima and Nagasaki, finally caused the Japanese Emperor to order an end to the war. The terms of Japan's surrender were signed in Tokyo Bay aboard an American warship,[6] and included the withdrawal of Japan from the Asian mainland, which included China. Effectively, the conflict ended on 2 September 1945, nearly four months after the end of the other two conflicts in Europe.

40.1.2.4. Political Consequences

In a speech during the closing months of the conflict, Germany's propaganda minister, Goebbels, had warned that a division of occupation of post-war Europe between the Allies would result in Russia imposing its authority and Communist system on the countries under its control, and that this would result in the erection, as he put it, of an 'Iron Curtain' across Europe. Goebbels' prediction proved to be all too true. The countries of Eastern Europe had socialist dictatorships imposed upon them, held together and co-ordinated as a single political and military

6   In fact, on the US ship *Missouri*, in Tokyo Bay.

bloc. This promoted an outflow of population anxious to escape, which in turn led to the imposition of a tightly controlled border across Europe, defined by barbed wire, observation posts and minefields, with a high wall running across Berlin. This 'Iron Curtain' extended from Lübeck, on the Baltic coast, to the Adriatic at Trieste, except that Austria was soon freed from partition by a treaty that guaranteed its neutrality. Only Greece avoided the trap because of a British military intervention against a Communist insurgency.

Under the post-war settlement, Poland lost much of its territory in the east, through annexation by Russia, and was compensated with a similar area in the west that caused Germany to lose all its territory east of the Oder and Neisse River. Thus, Poland as a whole was shifted almost bodily westwards, while retaining its historic homeland on the upper and middle Vistula. This caused a huge shunting of population westward, adding to the movement of a huge number of people who had been displaced by the war, or were seeking political asylum in Western countries.

Churchill's decision to pursue the war cost Western Europe four years of German occupation, but undoubtedly saved Russia (and Communism) from defeat by diverting Germany's resources. It also ensured that a nationalistic German empire would not emerge across Central and Eastern Europe, as far as the Caucasus. His decision also led to the subjection of the British colonies in South-East Asia to Japanese occupation, resulting in the rise of post-war anti-colonial sentiment in the region and the disintegration of the British Empire. Meanwhile, Britain, effectively bankrupted by the wars, was enabled to continue only by American loans and the lease of strategic naval bases. The Dominions, on the other hand, had been forced by shortages to industrialise, so that they, like the United States and Russia, emerged much stronger from the war, leaving Great Britain no longer at the apex of the world order, with an old and inefficient industrial economy, burdened with debt, and no longer able to compete with other industrial countries. By contrast, the other countries of Western Europe had the benefit of aid through the American Marshall Plan, which enabled them to re-build and modernise their industrial economies. The United States itself reverted to a mood of partial isolationism. A significant consequence of the war, also, was that English displaced French as the medium of international communication.

Greatly strengthened and revitalised by the war, Russia embarked on a renewed policy of world Communist domination, posing a direct threat to Western Europe and supporting Communist insurrections around the world. The United States was slow and unwilling to recognise the new reality. Britain, meanwhile, now itself ruled by a socialist government, responded to the spreading nationalism in India and the colonies and India by formally granting independence to them, beginning with India. Meanwhile, it required Churchill, who was widely respected in America, to open its eyes to the new threat posed by Russia. The effect was an armed confrontation, known as the 'Cold War'.

40.1.2.5. Moral Consequences

Few issues at the end of the war absorbed the attention of the West – and not least Great Britain – more than the fate of the Jews in German-occupied Europe, as a result of a policy of 'ethnic cleansing'. The sparse surviving evidence suggests that the original intention had been to find a national homeland for them outside Europe, but none of the countries approached, mostly in the Southern Hemisphere, had been willing to take them, and Palestine had been rejected as unsuitable because of the hostility of the Arabs. Hitler himself had taken little or no interest in the fate of the Jews, who faced a great deal of brutality. After the fall of France, Madagascar was evidently seen as a dumping ground for Europe's Jews, but this proved to be impracticable while Britain remained in the war. Meanwhile, the policy of eradication had been extended to other European countries that fell under German occupation. Faced with a choice between releasing the Jews or eliminating them by shooting or gassing, the latter policy was adopted. Towards the end of the war, with the programme still far from completed, the movement of surviving inmates to camps further west, away from the advancing Russians and public exposure, greatly added to the overcrowding. This led to an outbreak of typhus in the camps. The breakdown of the transport system, in the face of constant air attack, resulted also in the starvation of the survivors, leading to the final breakdown of any form of administration. This was the situation that greeted the arrival of Allied forces, leading to an outcry in Western countries. An attempt by the Allies to assess the number who had died in the camps was complicated by international

Jewish organisations, which endeavoured to use the situation for purposes of compensation, to help finance a new Jewish homeland in Palestine. The original estimate of twelve million deaths, having been rejected as a statistical impossibility, caused the estimate to be reduced to six million, which was accepted.

Germany was not the only country guilty of inhumane policies. Since its revolution, Russia had followed a practice of shooting or incarcerating 'trouble-makers' and members of the upper classes in *gulags*, or concentration camps, located in remote areas of the Soviet Union – usually the Arctic or remote regions of Siberia, where conditions were such as to make survival all but impossible. To these unfortunates were added German prisoners of war. However, it was the fate of the Jews at the hands of the Germans that caused by far the greater repugnance in Britain. This was understandable, with Russia being an ally and much further away, but the promotion of a sense of guilt in Britain long after the war, as if Britain itself had been partially responsible, may have been a device for moulding popular acceptance of new and radical liberal policies at home. A stretched parallel was drawn between the German atrocities against the Jews and Britain's administration of its non-White colonies.

As early as 1941, Roosevelt and Churchill had issued a declaration of their peace aims, grandly entitled the 'Atlantic Charter'. Apart from disclaiming any territorial ambitions after the war, this had proclaimed the right of nations to choose their form of government; the restoration of self-government to those countries that had been forcibly deprived of their sovereignty; the right to equality of economic opportunity for all nations, including their access to raw materials; free traverse of the high seas; the promotion of friendly collaboration between peoples; fair labour standards; social security; freedom from fear and want; the abandonment of the use of force to settle disputes; and the disarmament of aggressor nations. This combination of liberal and socialist idealism, which owed much to the sentiments of President Roosevelt, was to set the tone for the post-war years in Western Europe.

Such ideas were gradually to enmesh Great Britain in an idea that she had herself originated, and were to have a profound effect, both on the British legal system and on the way in which the British constitution was itself regarded. The Bill of Rights of 1689 had provided the model for the

American Bill of Rights of 1789, which in turn provided the inspiration for some of the sentiments of the Atlantic Charter. Their application was taken over by the United Nations Organization, the new successor to the League of Nations, which in 1948 adopted a Universal Declaration of Human Rights. If the Bill of Rights had inspired the concept of such a Declaration, the actual content of the latter was influenced more by the late eighteenth century writings of Thomas Paine. In his *The Rights of Man*, Paine had supported the idea of 'natural rights', as distinct from 'civil rights', and had tried to re-state and assert the principles of English common law. Consequently, American influence pervaded the Universal Declaration of 1948, which proclaimed, in typically ringing American phraseology, that: 'It is essential, if man is not to be compelled to have recourse, as a last resort, to rebellion against tyranny and oppression, that human rights should be protected by the rule of law'. The Declaration was therefore one of principle, yet it was very largely a re-assertion of the Indo-European political tradition, with the important difference that it applied to all human societies. Also, it applied back-to-front, so to speak, in the sense that the Declaration was not intended as the basis, in accordance with which law was to be made, but was intended as law itself, and as such was alien to the Indo-European tradition. This was based upon the uncircumscribed freedom of the individual, except where its exercise broke a law. The new system assumed that the individual had no freedom, except where specified. Some governments did not subscribe to the Declaration, the most notable being those of the Communist bloc in Eastern Europe, South Africa and Saudi Arabia, which saw it as creating problems for themselves. In the same year, and with the fate of the Jews in Europe clearly in mind, the United Nations adopted a Convention on the Prevention and Punishment of a new crime, that of Genocide, a word that properly means the 'annihilation of a race', except that the Convention applied it to any ethnic group. A new principle also was the popular 'right to protest', implying the use of violence, which was quite different from the right in common law to petition the King. The new system was also based upon an abhorrence of all racial, religious and cultural discrimination, such as the Russians had applied against the Ukrainians and the Crimean Tartars, and the Germans against the Jews and Gypsies. The right to petition implied a constructive process, whereas a 'protest' could be taken to include mindless violence, as often would prove to be the case.

A year later, in 1949, a consultative Council of Europe was established, committed to the support of freedom and the rule of law. The Council comprised the foreign ministers of the states of Western Europe, including Great Britain, and it was based symbolically in the once German, but now French, border city of Strasbourg. One of the achievements of this Council was the establishment, in the same year, of a European Convention on Human Rights, based on the United Nations declaration, but couched more in the French legal tradition. These rights were intended as a guide, since they were not enforceable in law unless a country chose to adopt them. Great Britain would not do so for another fifty years, because they clashed with the principle upon which the English legal system had been built.

This upwelling of egalitarian righteousness found a ready response in Britain's new, more militant, Liberal Socialist Establishment, which found its first target in the outcome of the South African elections of May 1948. Here, the coalition government of the United and Labour Parties, led by General Smuts, was defeated by a conservative coalition, representing a reawakening and participation of the Afrikaner voters, represented by the National and Afrikaner Parties, led by Dr D. F. Malan. Smuts had been popular in Britain because of his support and wise counsel during the war, and because he had pursued a fairly liberal racial policy at home. Malan, by contrast, drew his support from much of the Afrikaner population, which had felt a strong empathy with the policies of Hitler's Germany, not in respect so much of the Jews, but of the indigenous black Bantu, or 'Africans', and the Cape 'Coloureds'. Nor had Germany's support for them during the South African War been forgotten, a war that had left a legacy of bitterness that had underlain the refusal of most of the Afrikaner population to support Britain during the Second World War, or to become involved, until now, in the constitutional system that Britain had imposed on South Africa. Within Britain, public opinion as a whole was largely non-committal on the issue, seeing some merit on both sides, but an uncomprehending resentment of this alienation on the part of the new Liberal Socialist Establishment added an edge to its antagonism towards the new South African government, particularly because it was committed to the restoration of a much stricter policy of racial segregation.

40.1.2.6. New International Organisations

The United States had an entirely different perspective on the world. Occupying, with its northern neighbour, Canada, an area as big as a continent, with only one significant culture and that little more than two centuries old, the complexities of Europe and its history were largely beyond the comprehension of most Americans. Understandably, after being drawn into two European wars, the American reaction was to regard Europe as being incapable of managing its own affairs, the only solution to which was the creation of international organisations that would impose a semblance of order. Great Britain accordingly found itself enmeshed increasingly in a plethora of treaties and international organisations.

The League of Nations, based in Geneva since 1919, was replaced in 1945 by a United Nations Organization, to be based in New York, where the Americans could keep a closer eye on it. Of further concern was the economic depression of the inter-war years, which had contributed to the rise of the National Socialists in Germany, and which had already, in 1929, led to Britain and America taking the lead in establishing a Bank for International Settlements, located in Basel. This was followed after 1945 by the creation of an International Monetary Fund, whose purpose was to stabilise the world's currencies, and an International Bank for Reconstruction and Development, better known as the World Bank.

Political stability against a possible German resurgence, was provided by the Brussels Treaty of 1948, between Great Britain, France and the Benelux countries, comprising Belgium, the Netherlands, and Luxemburg. This was both a military alliance and a basis for cooperation in economic and social matters, but it was soon realised that the real threat facing the Brussels Treaty came, not from Germany, but from Russia, which dominated its own alliance of Communist-ruled states in Eastern Europe, known as the Warsaw Pact. In the year following the Brussels Treaty, a defensive military alliance was accordingly formed in the west, known as the North Atlantic Treaty Organisation, or NATO, which included Great Britain, West Germany, Italy, the United States, Canada and the Benelux countries.

40.1.3. The Constitution of the United Kingdom After 1949

It is now possible to define what had become of the Constitution of the United Kingdom, also known as Great Britain and Northern Ireland. It comprised, as its basis, the English Constitution, whose House of Commons at Westminster now included representatives of the Third Estates of Wales, Scotland and Northern Ireland. Certain members of the Second Estates of those countries had been granted seats in the House of Lords.

PART XIV

•

THE EGALITARIAN AGE AND
THE ABUSE OF POWER

41. EQUALITY AND THE DISSOLUTION OF EMPIRE

THE EFFECT OF the Second World was like that of a gunshot amid the lofty snow-covered peaks of the Imperial Age, setting off a whole series of political avalanches. The ensuing fifty years would witness equally dramatic developments in the nature of British government. The Monarchy had, since the Norman dynasty, been widely seen as founded on feudal doctrine and had ruled largely in accordance with its precepts, but it had now been reduced by the House of Commons to little more than a legislative 'post box'. With the House of Lords crippled as a legislative body since 1910, the majority Party in the House of Commons had found itself in control of both the legislative and the executive functions of state. Whether this had been the unintended effect of a simple desire to incapacitate a self-serving and incompetent Stuart Monarchy, or had been driven by the ambitions of political Parties, must be left to individual judgement, but by dispossessing the King as head of the executive, the majority Party in Parliament had found itself in control of the Ministry, and therefore of the Crown, a function for which it was ill-equipped and, with few exceptions, ill-suited. It was also incompatible with its proper constitutional duty to represent the interests and wishes of the people. The leaders of the House of Commons also faced a dilemma, because they were unable to do both without a conflict of interest. Although many would still be drawn to serve in the House of Commons as the representatives of the people, as was their lawful purpose, there must have been not a few who were now being drawn to a parliamentary career chiefly by an ambition to attain executive power as Ministers of the Crown. These were incompatible functions, which had placed the House of Commons in a contradictory situation, with significant consequences for the people. One constitutional problem had been resolved, only to create another that had more worrying implications that time would confirm.

The political landscape that lay ahead of Great Britain immediately after the Second World War was hinted at by the alleged remark of one British soldier among the thousands being visited by Churchill, just before the invasion of France in 1944. Churchill was accompanied by Ernest Bevin, the Minister of Labour in the coalition government, who was a leading member of the Labour Party and a former trade union official. Bevin was recognised by some of the men, prompting the soldier in question to call out: 'Hey, Ernie, when we've finished doing this job for you, will you put us back on the dole?' It was a sardonic reference to the crucial importance of the working class in the pursuit of the war, in an age of massed armies, in contrast to its relegation between the two world wars to little more than an economic convenience, in that it was in great demand when there was a high level of economic activity, but dispensable and unemployed, with little to live on, when the demand was low. Capital also suffered from this dependence on economic demand, but whereas capital was inanimate, labour was not, and labour was keenly aware of the hardship that came with unemployment, which the socialist movement had taught it to associate with a private enterprise economy.

The general election of July 1945, was followed by the return of a Labour Government – for the first time with a clear majority – and the beginning of an Establishment revolution that would have constitutional consequences for the remainder of the century, as well as causing profound social and economic changes. The Establishment prior to 1945 had remained largely identified with the upper and upper middle classes, represented by the well-educated, conservative or traditionally liberal in outlook, with a strong sense of duty, patriotism and stoicism, but oriented more to the political interests of Great Britain than to the social interests of its people. It was the experiences and newfound self-confidence of the working and lower middle classes, resulting from experience in the war, that introduced the socialist ideological revolution, driven to bringing about the ideal of economic equality and social security 'from the cradle to the grave'. In order to ensure that the economic benefits of society were allocated, either equally or according to need, there followed a policy of appropriation by the state of the basic means of production. This covered all the more important basic industries and services, from coal mines and railways to road transport and medical services, which were placed under the control of statutory bodies created for the purpose. The reforms went much further, with the nationalisation of the Bank of England and the establishment, with the National Parks Act, of a policy of preserving areas of outstanding natural beauty. A new system of town and country planning ensured, among other things, the establishment of protected 'green belts' around London and other major cities, to prevent the further blight of urban sprawl, while retaining the access of urban-dwellers to the healing benefits of open countryside. The greatest achievements of this period, in the eyes of the general public, however, were the provision of free medical treatment under the aegis of a new National Health Service, and the introduction of National Insurance, which provided for a degree of financial security for all.

41.1. The Legal Status of the Crown

The feudal principle that the Crown could not be sued, because the King was above the law, had remained unchanged for nine hundred years, until 1947, when the legal standing of the Monarchy was profoundly affected by the Crown Proceedings Act. This related to claims against the Crown, not against the Monarchy itself, the two having already been separated by Parliament, when it appropriated the legislative and executive functions of the Crown. Hitherto, the question of the legal liability of the Crown had been governed by two principles:

1. That the 'the King can do no wrong', therefore, he cannot be held liable for any action, committed by him, or on his behalf, that would be unlawful if committed by an individual.
2. That the King cannot sue himself in his own courts.

The difficulty resulting from these principles arose from the increase in state regulation, and with it the extension of the foregoing royal privileges to a wide range of central Government activities. Not only were actions of the Crown being decided and taken by numerous officers, often at a relatively junior level, but more and more private individuals were being exposed to them, and more and more frequently, without the benefit of legal protection from their abuse. The Act accordingly made the Crown liable in areas of both tort and contract. It provided that civil proceedings against the Crown must be instituted against the relevant Government Department, or, if no Government Department had clear responsibility, the proceedings must be brought against the Attorney General or, in Scotland, against the Advocate General for Scotland. This was much later affected by a ruling of the House of Lords in 1994, when it decided that an injunction could be granted in an action against a Minister of the Crown personally.[1] The ruling also decided that applications for judicial review were not proceedings against the Crown, but against a Minister or other officer of the Crown. Thus, with certain exceptions, the Crown, in the person of its officers, was placed in the same legal position, both in tort and contract, as a private individual. In other words, the King may and must sue himself in respect of those functions that he has delegated. Instead of intervening administratively *in situ*ations where his officers are accused of being in breach of the law, the King must hear the accusations in his own courts and pass judgement accordingly, although in practice he will delegate this responsibility to one of his justices.

The situation in common law appears to be only slightly different. If the King contravenes the law, he cannot sue himself in his own courts, which, as we have already seen, are extensions of Parliament in its judicial capacity. The King is subject, however, to the judgement of a Parliament, sitting in its judicial capacity, where summoned for the purpose by the Great Council, which exercises justice in respect of the Second Estate, to which the King belongs, exposing him to possible deposition by the Council on the advice of Parliament. In the event of an offence by one of the King's officers, by abusing or misusing the powers vested in him, where they have not been explicitly so directed by the King, it would appear that the officer is liable for trial before one of the King's courts on the same basis as any other individual.

41.2. Elizabeth II: The Monarchy Becomes the House of Windsor

The popularity of the British Monarchy was at its height at the end of the war. The esteem in which it was held owed much to the fact that

---

1   *M v Home Office* (1994).

the King and Queen had remained in London throughout the Blitz, and displayed a genuine compassion for its citizens during their ordeal. Buckingham Palace itself had been bombed, and the King and Queen had toured the heavily bombed areas of the East End of London shortly after the disasters, talking to survivors. A particular impression had been made by the Queen, whose kindness, strength of character and obvious tenacity made her, in the eyes of many, one of the foundations upon which the morale of the people had rested. Hardly less important had been the great sympathy and affection in which the King was held, and the strong loyalty that he had commanded, on account of his obvious sincerity and courage, not least in his lifelong struggle against shyness and an inhibiting stammer. That he could cope with the burdens of Kingship at all was due largely to the encouragement of the Queen, whose own popularity and political wisdom also imparted a glow to the Monarchy. It was widely appreciated that she never attempted to upstage her husband. The consequence had been that, during the reign of George VI, the British Monarchy reached the highest point in its modern history, not only in its popularity, but in the deep sense of devotion that it stirred in the people.

George VI died in 1952, leaving two daughters. His elder brother, Edward, had produced no children, leaving the sole contender for the succession as the King's elder daughter, Elizabeth. She had recently married Prince Philip of the Hellenes, the son of Prince Andrew of Greece and Denmark. His grandfather had been King George I of the Hellenes, but the ancestry of the family went back to the Danish royal house of Oldenburg. The ancestry of that house, in its turn, went back to Egilmar, Count of Oldenburg, near the mouth of the River Weser in Lower Saxony, who had died in 1108. During the intervening centuries, the descent had been through the Dukes of Holstein-Sonderburg. Several of the Duke of Edinburgh's direct ancestors had been kings of Denmark, so that, in spite of an inclination among some at the time of the coronation to ridicule his supposedly 'obscure' ancestry, Philip's lineage was one of the oldest in Europe. On the distaff side, Prince Philip's mother was Princess Alice of Battenberg, the daughter of Louis of Battenberg, Marquess of Milford Haven. Louis was, in turn, the son of Alexander, Prince of Hesse, a small German state east of the middle Rhine. Alice's mother had been Victoria, daughter of Louis IV, the Grand Duke of Hesse. The name of Battenberg had been adopted by Philip from Alice's grandmother, Julia, Princess of Battenberg,[2] who was a former Polish countess. It was through the female line, also, that Prince Philip was able to trace a connection with the British Royal House. This lay through his great-grandmother, also Alice, who had been a daughter of Queen Victoria. During the Great War, the family of Prince Philip's mother had been forced, by widespread anti-German feeling in Britain, to Anglicise their dynastic title in 1917 from Battenberg to Mountbatten.

According to feudal rules, the succession should have gone to Philip, and his family certainly had expectations in that direction, but succession by the King's eldest daughter had precedents in England, and public opinion favoured Elizabeth. Nor did Philip's German connections help him after two wars with Germany. His other connection, the Greek monarchy, was considered minor, and not well-established. In the event, the succession went to Elizabeth. Still a young woman of twenty-five, she had her father's sincerity and sense of dedication and her mother's grasp of political events. Prince Philip, on the other hand, found himself with no formal position and not even a personal identity. This was because members of the European Second Estate had never possessed or needed a surname, because they were, and had been since the onset of the feudal age, identified by their respective estates, and these were liable to change with each generation. Philip, not being in the direct line of the Greek succession, had no estate of his own. As a serving officer in the Royal Navy, Philip had, prior to the marriage, renounced such claim as he had to the Greek throne, there being a number of prior claimants in any case,[3] and had become naturalised as a British subject. In so doing, he had followed his mother's example by taking the surname of Mountbatten. As the future Queen's husband, he had then been elevated, at the time of the marriage, to the title of Duke of Edinburgh, thereby reasserting the Scottish connection of the dynasty.

Both feudal doctrine and common law were based on the principle of patrilineal succession, and so would have required a male relative of the late King to be the successor, but English practice had been modified since the Middle Ages to allow, in the absence of a male claimant, for

2   The name of Battenberg, in Hesse, formerly belonging to the counts of that district, had been resurrected for her benefit. The marriage was morganatic.
3   The Greek monarchy was deposed in 1974.

the succession to pass to the eldest daughter of the late King. On this occasion, the caretaker Government, headed by Sir Winston Churchill as Prime Minister, with the support of Parliament and the Dominion Governments, decided in favour, therefore, of retaining the existing Windsor line, in spite of the fact that this would entail a Queen regnant. In so doing, they followed the many precedents already set by Mary I, Elizabeth, Mary II, Anne, and Victoria, and the general public appeared to support the decision.

The marriage nevertheless meant that Elizabeth took her husband's adopted family name of Mountbatten, to which Elizabeth's grandmother, Queen Mary, took exception, letting it be known to the Prime Minister's Private Secretary that she favoured the perpetuation of the adopted family name of Windsor,[4] a suggestion with which the Prime Minister, Churchill, was in full agreement. British statute law already provided for family names to be changed, and the manipulation of the name of the dynasty was seen as entirely a matter for the new Queen, in consultation with the Prime Minister. This nonchalance towards pedigree contrasted with the rigorous importance attached to family names among the Continental aristocracy, which had continued to adhere to the Salian law of inheritance, based on the principle of *ius sanguinis*, or parallel versions of it. This divergence of the law of inheritance in England may be traced to the apparent rejection by the Normans of Salian law, in favour of the Church-Feudal principle of primogeniture, which had already caused a great deal of dynastic trouble, particularly in causing in the frequent extinction of English lineages, and the consequent need for the King to elevate commoners in order to sustain the Second Estate, on which he relied. Although this practice had maintained the noble order, it had for centuries undermined the importance of ancestry, and indeed the very meaning of ancestry, making it acceptable for the name of the British dynasty itself to be changed. In this case, therefore, the royal descent was deemed to be through Elizabeth, thereby ensuring the continued use of the Windsor name by Elizabeth and her successors. It also precluded Prince Philip from becoming King.

Elizabeth was accordingly crowned in February 1952, as Queen Elizabeth II. Upon her accession, she proclaimed that she and her descendants were to retain her maiden name of Windsor, thereby, like

4   Adopted by the royal family during the First World War, in place of Saxe-Coburg and Gotha.

her predecessor, Elizabeth I, invoking the ancient, pre-Indo-European matrilineal tradition that seems to have applied across large parts of Europe in the Stone Age. Perhaps out of recognition of her husband's disappointment, and the fact that they had been born before their mother became Queen, this declaration did not apply to their two existing children, Charles and Anne. In the event, they chose to reconcile the two sides by using the combination, Mountbatten-Windsor.[5] Elizabeth had been groomed for the Crown by her grandmother, Queen Mary, from whom she had imbibed the tradition of selfless royal duty, combined with a capacity for dignity, while from her mother she inherited a genuine interest in, and concern for, the ordinary people. These were qualities that helped to carry the Monarchy through a new era of political and social turbulence.

41.3. The Dissolution of the British Empire

In 1918–22, the German historian, Oswald Spengler, had published his monolithic *Decline of the West*, in which he had studied all the great civilizations of the past and concluded that all were cyclical in nature.[6] The rise of a civilization, he concluded, was marked by its dedication to an obsessive idea or purpose, and was characterised by physical energy and religious, racial, or other intolerance, an emphasis on discipline, and a eulogising of simplicity and hardship. When a civilization reached its peak, it was characterised by a flowering of the arts and philosophy, while its ensuing decline was marked by luxury, indulgence, cosmopolitanism and moral corruption. Spengler concluded that Western European civilization, which had spread across the world, had reached its zenith around 1890, and was already in decline by the war of 1914–18, which he saw as an inevitable part of the process. He did not see a civilization as necessarily disappearing after its decline, however. The plant might remain, but it no longer flowered or grew, and it was susceptible to every disease. Spengler's work had largely been ignored, not only because of its size and turgid nature, but because few at the time believed its conclusions. Even in 1922, it had not been apparent to many that Western civilization was

---

5   Princess Anne used the surname 'Mountbatten-Windsor' in her 1973 marriage certificate.
6   O. Spengler, *The Decline of the West* (New York, 1932).

in decline, particularly in the light of the technological revolution that was still occurring. It was the Second World War that, Spengler would surely have believed, finally achieved the downfall of Western Europe as one of the great civilizations.

Great Britain had emerged from the war impoverished and effectively bankrupt, having sold her overseas investments and borrowed heavily from the United States to finance the effort. There was widespread bitterness that America did not write off the loan, or at least ameliorate its terms, because its own economy had enjoyed a huge benefit from the war. In many ways, Britain was economically now worse off than defeated West Germany. Whereas the United States contributed substantially, through the Marshall Plan, to the reconstruction of West German industry, enabling it to emerge with new and efficient factories, British industry was left by the war in a run-down and uncompetitive state. Apart from putting Japan back in its place, like a 'Jack-in-the-Box', America followed two policies: first, to make Europe 'grow up' and behave in a responsible manner, and second, hypocritically for a country that owed its existence to the British Empire, and had since acquired for itself one of the biggest empires in history, from the Appalachians to the Philippines, to settle old accounts by easing Britain, the Mother Country, off its imperial pedestal. To this end, America began by opposing the attempt by Britain and its European neighbours to retrieve their colonies in South-East Asia.

The war had left a widespread unease towards ethnic discrimination, and the advent of socialist governments in Western Europe, faced with rising Asian nationalism, triggered the beginning of a collapse of Europe's empires. The military successes of the Japanese in South-East Asia, reaching as far as the eastern border of India, had stirred Asian nationalism and shown that the European colonial powers could easily be defeated. Egged on by Japan, existing Indian nationalism was rampant by 1945, and the colonial powers had the utmost difficulty in reasserting their authority in South-East Asia. France, whose national humiliation in 1940 demanded that she re-assert herself abroad, only entangled herself in futile wars in Indo-China and Algeria. The new British Labour Government in 1945, led by Clement Attlee, made no attempt to restore permanent British rule in South-East Asia, confining itself to negotiating a dignified exit with a grant of independence, even giving military assistance against a

Communist incursion that was already engulfing China. Only Hong Kong was effectively restored, and willingly, to British rule. India was granted independence in 1947. One of the benefits of British rule in India had been that it had united a politically splintered sub-continent and forced the various religious and ethnic groups to live together, and its removal lifted the lid on a cauldron of rivalries and deep-seated hostilities, all of which were overshadowed by the long-repressed antagonism between the two main religious groups, the Hindus and Moslems. The latter insisted on forming a separate state, which they named Pakistan, or 'Peace State', and this led to a panic as all those millions caught on the wrong side of the new frontier tried to cross to safety on the right side, many being massacred along the way.

Meanwhile, the granting of independence to India and Pakistan had required the description of the jurisdictions of the new Queen regnant to be amended, and this was achieved by the Imperial Titles Act, 1953. This declared the Sovereign to be: 'Elizabeth II by the Grace of God of the United Kingdom of Great Britain and Northern Ireland and of Her other Realms and Territories, Head of the Commonwealth, Defender of the Faith'. Gone was the reference to her as 'Empress of India'. It is significant that these were described in the Act, not as jurisdictions, as they undoubtedly had been, whether in common law or according to feudal doctrine, but merely as 'titles', reflecting the new view of her position that was taken by the Parties in Parliament.

Conscious of its own hypocrisy, the United States granted independence to the Philippines and other American overseas colonies able to stand on their own feet. Meanwhile, Arab nationalism had been growing in the Middle East since the overthrow of the Ottoman Empire, only to clash in Palestine with the consequences of the Balfour Declaration of 1917, which had promised a Jewish national homeland there, without consulting its Arab inhabitants. The British mandate now found itself struggling to limit the influx of Jews, following the end of the war in 1945, and trying to keep the immigrant Jews and the Arabs apart. This caused the Jews to launch a terrorist campaign against the British occupation force, causing Britain to abandon its mandate. During the 1960s, by contrast, Britain's withdrawal from its colonies and protectorates elsewhere proceeded in a relatively dignified manner.

Meanwhile, the newly independent Pakistan and India, both of which became republics, were offered by the Labour Government, and accepted, an invitation to become members of the Commonwealth. There is no reason to doubt that the Government was fully aware of the implications and may well have been motivated by them. From the Labour Government's point of view, the purpose of converting the Commonwealth from a closely functioning alliance of independent British states into a multi-racial and multicultural association seems to have been twofold: first, to maintain Britain's sense of Britain's importance in a world that was now overshadowed by the United States and Russia, and, secondly, to provide a common meeting-place where British Ministers could now mix on humbler terms with the non-white rulers of the Indian sub-continent. India and Pakistan were followed into this new relationship, over the next twenty years or so, by a stream of former colonies and protectorates, the effect of which was to complete the transformation of the former Commonwealth. What had previously been the 'British Commonwealth of Nations', an association of countries sharing a common British ancestry and political traditions, including a continued allegiance to the Queen as their common Head of State, based on the continuation of the regal contract, was now transformed into a simple association of states, under the name of the 'Commonwealth of Nations', linked only by their previous connection with the British Empire. The Queen agreed to continue in the capacity of mere figurehead of the new association.

The previous Commonwealth Prime Ministers' Conferences, held every four years, were replaced by Commonwealth Heads of Government Meetings, a mouthful abbreviated to CHOGMs, so called because many of its members were now republics, whose executive heads were their Presidents. This created a problem, because British Commonwealth Prime Ministers were not heads of government. It was resolved by implying that these were conferences, not between 'heads of government', but between '*de facto* executive heads' of government. The purpose of these meetings was still to discuss issues in which they found a common interest, but the chief common interest proved to be racial, and took the form of haranguing South Africa and Southern Rhodesia over their racial policies, and Britain over its failure to bully South Africa into acquiescing in Black rule, and forcing Britain to impose Black rule on Southern Rhodesia. In neither of these was Britain in any position to do anything, beyond exerting political pressure. South Africa and Southern Rhodesia had remained as members of the new Commonwealth, by virtue of their membership of its predecessor, but both found their membership increasingly untenable. Both countries enjoyed considerable sympathy and support from a section of the British public, and the idea of expelling either from the Commonwealth was not popular with the other members of the former British Commonwealth. Nevertheless, in the face of the hostility shown by its new members, the last Commonwealth meeting that was attended by the South African and Southern Rhodesian Prime Ministers – Dr Verwoerd and Sir Roy Welensky – was that held in 1960.

A few months later, in 1961, South Africa withdrew from the Commonwealth and declared itself a republic. The dissolution of the Central African Federation at the end of 1963 was used by Britain as an opportunity to terminate Rhodesia's participation, presumably on the ground that the Queen had withdrawn its *de facto* status as a Dominion, although no record of this has been found. Certainly, no purpose was served by Rhodesia (as it was now formally known) continuing to attend. The meaninglessness of the new Commonwealth became evident when Mozambique was admitted, despite the fact that it had no connection with the former Empire, beyond its former close diplomatic relationship with Rhodesia and South Africa.

Whereas the former British Commonwealth of Nations, comprising the Dominions of Canada, Australia, South Africa, New Zealand and Southern Rhodesia, had enjoyed a constitutional relationship with Great Britain, through their common recognition of the Queen as their respective heads of state, there was no longer any formal channel through which this relationship could be conducted, because the new Commonwealth had no constitutional significance. Britain's decision to join the European Union finally broke the historic link.

Under the Conservative Government elected in 1951, Britain had fully intended to maintain its military and political presence in the Middle East, which was still its chief source of oil, and in the Indian Ocean and South-East Asia, where it was still involved, for example, in helping the newly independent Federation of Malaysia to suppress a

Communist uprising and to defeat an invasion of it by Indonesia. Egypt's nationalisation of the Suez Canal in 1956 posed a direct threat to Britain's ability to operate in southern Asia, as well as being an unacceptable seizure of property. It led Great Britain and France to form a military alliance which attempted to re-take the Canal. This aroused the strong opposition of the United States, which had its own interest in the region, as well as an antagonism towards any further assertion of political and strategic interest by Great Britain, which it regarded as imperialism, and threats were made to impose financial sanctions against Britain. As Britain was massively in financial debt to the United States, as a result of the War, and was itself in the midst of its post-war economic crisis, the Prime Minister, Anthony Eden, who was in poor health, cancelled the operation and resigned, to the great consternation of the French. The political humiliation of the Suez Crisis caused Britain never again to maintain a significant presence east of Suez, leaving a void in the Middle East to be filled by other powers. France fared no better. Humiliated by a successful Communist rebellion in Indo-China, it was then forced to abandon Algeria in 1962, where a vicious war of independence had been raging for several years.

41.3.1. Consequences

Of much greater importance, in terms of its eventual consequences, was an aggressive new movement that seems to have been a modified form of socialism that had turned its back on the state control of industry, combined with an aggressive form of liberalism that seems to have owed much to the old anti-slavery movement. This now dedicated itself to promoting the interests of what it perceived to be society's – and the world's – underdogs, by establishing a new egalitarian and anti-imperialist world. The mainspring of this new 'liberalist' movement seems to have been the reaction that it had generated to the excesses of National Socialist Germany's attempt to eradicate the Jews, which it saw, by a remarkable stretch of the imagination, as related to Britain's Imperial Age and its subject black inhabitants. By association, the British people bore an implied responsibility for the persecution of the Jews that called for national contrition. In this way, reality was contorted to justify the admission of large numbers of non-white immigrants from the former

Empire, presumably in an act of contrition. At the same time, a memorial to the Jews, in recognition of the implied contribution of the British people to the persecution of the Jews took the form, among other things, of a proposed memorial to them in the grounds of Parliament itself. It was a manipulation of history to justify an unpopular policy to facilitate large-scale immigration.

According to common law, however, the immigration of 'aliens' was not a matter for the Crown. Just as Scotland was the territory of the Scots, and Wales was the territory of the Welsh, so also was England the territory of the English, being an aspect of common law that neither the Crown nor any Party in Parliament had the right to violate without the consent of those whose interests might be affected.

The liberalist movement set about achieving this by penetrating the institutions of government and journalism for the purposes of promoting the welfare of those who were disadvantaged in society and eradicating, not nationalism and racialism themselves, but specifically White nationalism and racialism. The new liberalist movement accordingly turned a blind eye to these sentiments in other races, such as those which gave rise to the violent policies of the Afro-Asian Bloc and the (White) Communist states in Africa, no matter how strident or violent they became. As a long-term solution, however, it promoted a policy of non-White immigration into Britain, particularly from the former colonies, thereby creating a multi-racial society that would, it believed, lose both its nationalism and its racialism, as the races became accustomed to living together. That this was a naïve and risky policy was obvious enough to some, if not too many, but it quickly became evident that those implementing it believed that racialism did not exist in Britain, and was only acquired, like a form of disease, from imperial contagion.

The dissolution of the British Empire had important domestic consequences. It ended, for example, the original reason for the Union of England and Scotland, at least from Scotland's point of view. Scotland had entered the Union in order, chiefly, to gain access to the English Empire and all its trading and other benefits, having failed miserably to found an empire of its own. With the Empire now gone, the outlet for Scottish nationalism had gone with it.

41.3.2. Citizenship

Citizenship is a statement of identity, taking one of two forms. In common law it is defined as *ius sanguinis*, or 'law of the blood', that is, the law of descent, usually through the male line, which determines the society to which the individual belongs.

The definition of citizenship that has been applied in England since the Norman Conquest of 1066, however, is the feudal one, which is based on the principle of *ius soli*, or the 'law of the ground', usually rendered as the 'law of the soil'. This states, in effect, that a man's identity, and therefore his allegiance, depends upon his place of birth, regardless of the status or location of his parents. He is deemed to belong to the estate of the feudal lord on whose land he is born, consequently, all men born within the King's dominions, or 'estates', owe their allegiance to him as his subjects, and are consequently entitled to his protection. It follows from this that an individual may not leave his lord's estate without his permission, otherwise the lord risks losing the benefit of his labour. It was the use of this doctrine for political ends that seems to have prompted an Article of the *Magna Carta*, which reasserted a principle of common law by stating that 'it shall be lawful for any man to leave and return to our kingdom unharmed and without fear . . . except in time of war'.[7] By contrast, feudal doctrine made no distinction on the basis of geography, race, religion, language or culture, because the law relating to the King's estate or estates was the same, whatever its location. From a citizenship point of view, therefore, the principle of *ius soli* applied to the whole British Empire, whose inhabitants, provided they were born within it, were automatically British subjects. The same principle is to be seen in the estates of the Habsburg dynasty in the fifteenth century, which embraced such far-flung possessions as Austria, Spain, the Netherlands, Sicily, Milan and Tunis.

The difference between the two legal traditions may be illustrated by the example of a man who lives with his wife whilst in another country. If a child is born to them whilst they are there, it inherits, in common law, the nationality of its father, whereas, under feudal law, it inherits the nationality of the country in which it is born. Both legal traditions regard women as dependants of their father, or of their husband, if married. Common law accords greater rights to women than does feudal

7　　Article 42.

law, but in recent times the rights of women have been greatly increased by statute law.

Since the Middle Ages, the arbitrary age of twenty-one years has been taken as the minimum age of maturity, and hence of suitability for citizenship. However, the minimum voting age was reduced to eighteen years by the Representation of the People Act of 1983. The chief argument put forward in support of this was that it was the minimum age for military service, and if such a teenager was old enough to die for his country, so it was said, he must also be old enough to vote in a parliamentary election. This is a false argument, however, because the second requires maturity, whereas the first does not. It was subsequently proposed that the minimum age should be reduced to sixteen years, as a means of promoting a greater interest among young adolescents – that is, in effect, immature individuals – in public affairs. This pressure was undoubtedly motivated by one of the Parties, which sought to exploit the widely held belief that the young are attracted to radical ideas, thereby giving an electoral advantage over its rivals. Adolescents from puberty do indeed go through a stage of rebelliousness associated with an instinctive need to assert identity as individuals, in contrast to their previously dependent state of childhood. In a political context, however, this rebelliousness often takes the form of ill-considered radicalism, which can be exploited to political advantage.

Such opportunism, sacrificing electoral responsibility for political gain, is not in the public interest. On the contrary, modern society has delayed maturity. In previous centuries, juveniles usually reached maturity by their mid to late 'teens, by which time they needed to find employment, followed by marriage and the raising of families. This need to be self-supporting, and to accept responsibility for a family, demanded a degree of maturity, as a result of which, adulthood by the age of twenty-one was the accepted norm. By the late twentieth century, juveniles were being retained in education for much longer, particularly where they continued to universities, causing employment, marriage and the establishment of families to be delayed until nearer thirty, and often later. It follows that the age of maturity, and hence entitlement to citizenship, has significantly increased, not fallen, and to ignore this is to promote electoral irresponsibility.

41.3.3. Immigration in Common and Statute Law

Since the tenth century, when England was united as a confederacy under the West Saxon royal house of the *Cerdicings*, the protection of the borders against intrusion by 'aliens' had been the duty of the King, in his executive capacity as the representative of the nation's interests. In practice, for several centuries, he delegated to certain local earls the responsibility for controlling the Welsh and Scottish 'marches' (so called from the Old English *mearc*, or 'boundary').

What appears to be the common law of entry is covered in the *Magna Carta*, which states, effectively, that:

1. It is lawful for any man to leave and return to the kingdom, except in time of war, with the exception of convicted criminals and those from a country with which the kingdom is at war (Clause 42). This appears to refer to the right of any English freeman.
2. All merchants may enter or leave the kingdom, and may stay or travel within it for the purpose of trade, with the exception of those from a country with which the kingdom is at war, where that country denies this right (Clause 41).

By granting entry, the King deems the intentions of those admitted, such as foreign traders and emissaries, to be beneficial to the public interest. An illustration of the requirement that the King protect the public interest is illustrated, for example, in the poem *Beowulf*, where a coastguard in the service of the Danish king, stationed on a cliff-top, rides down to challenge an arriving party of Geats, led by Beowulf, and demands to know their business. Being satisfied, he allows them to pass.[8] The principle is again demonstrated in the account of three ships' companies of Norse Vikings, who landed at Portland, sometime between 786 and 802, who were accosted by the Reeve of Dorchester, who had ridden down to ask their business, and who discovered too late that their business was anything but peaceful or in the national interest.[9] Persons normally refused entry included those who had been judicially exiled.

Like all royal prerogatives, however, the King's right to admit or refuse entry must undoubtedly be subject to the constitutional principle

---

8   *Beowulf*, 229–300.
9   F. Stenton, *Anglo-Saxon England* (Oxford, 1947), 237.

in common law – all too often ignored – that any act of the Crown that affects the interests of the people is subject to their consent. In particular, the land belongs to the people and cannot be alienated to foreigners without their consent. Although the temporary admission of foreigners – for example, for purposes of trade, diplomacy or travel – is a matter for the royal prerogative, the permanent admission of foreigners affects the permanent interests of the people, and not only because it will probably result in the foreigner acquisition of land and other assets, to the detriment of the interests of local inhabitants. Feudal doctrine is significantly different, however, in that foreign entry is wholly subject to the royal prerogative, because the land is deemed to belong to the King.

The entry of foreigners into Britain has always been a vexed issue, leading to rootless groups, such as Jews and Gypsies, being debarred from entry on various occasions, or evicted, as in 1290, 1530, and 1547, as a result of public opposition that has sometimes erupted in riots. The immigration of Flemings and French Huguenots, in response to trouble in their respective homelands, also gave rise to local disturbances, but these were over trade competition, and they were offset, in practice, by their introduction of valuable skills, such as in weaving. From the 1880s, another influx of Jews led eventually to the institution of certain controls on immigration through the Aliens Act of 1905.

Movement within the British Empire was not restricted, because it was largely confined to British traders, settlers, administrators and military and naval personnel, with the exception of agreed transfers of indentured labour, for example, from India to South Africa, and from Polynesia to Australia, to work on the sugar estates. Movement into the Empire from outside, however, was not controlled, perhaps because it was seen as a benefit, rather than a problem. Thus, such inflows as did occur, particularly those from China and New Caledonia to Australia, to work on the mines and sugar estates, or the shipment of slave labour from West Africa to the American colonies, was regarded as beneficial. Such migrants could also be expelled, as, indeed, were most of those entering Australia.

By the early part of the twentieth century, it was officially recognised that Britain was overpopulated, and it became Government policy to encourage emigration to the colonies. In 1905, for example, the Colonial

Office was considering a plan to resettle Britain's surplus population in various parts of the Empire, along similar lines to that of the 1820 Settlers in the Eastern Cape. By 1911, the population of Great Britain had reached forty-five million, and the logic of the Government's position would seem to have dictated that there should be no significant immigration from any source, other than by returning British settlers and their offspring from the Dominions and colonies, who did so by statutory right as British subjects, and in their common law right as members of the nation. The motivation behind the Government's policy of restricting foreign immigration was not merely the availability of jobs, but also a need to maintain the quality of life. The greater the population per square mile, and the greater the density of housing, the greater the problem of public health, the greater the traffic on the roads, the greater the imports needed to sustain them, the greater the cost of providing fuel and water for human and industrial consumption; also, it reduced the amount of land available for food production and the availability of natural environment that was necessary to ensure the health of the nation. It was the increasing desperation of city-dwellers to find natural surroundings and unimpeded sunlight that drove the nature movement of walkers, cyclists and others during the early part of the century.

All individuals born within the United Kingdom and Empire before 1914 were deemed, in keeping with Church-Feudal doctrine, to be British subjects of the Crown, and as such entitled to a right – and, indeed, duty, of return. This was formalised in British legislation of 1914, which confirmed their freedom of movement within the Empire, including the United Kingdom. As such, it was a simple statement of Church-Feudal doctrine, effectively, that all born within the King's estates (Great Britain and the colonies) owed common allegiance to the King as his subjects, and therefore enjoyed freedom of movement between them. Obviously, the legislation was at variance with common law, which extended freedom of movement within the Empire only to free men and women in their capacity as participants in the regal contract. This right did not extend to the Empire's other inhabitants, whose right of movement was determined by such laws as the respective Dominions, Colonies and Protectorates might enact. The legal situation, as represented by the legislation of 1914, had posed few problems, because most movement within the Empire (and hence into and out of the United Kingdom) had been overwhelmingly by White British traders, officials, settlers and military personnel. In 1946, the Canadian Parliament passed the 'Canadian Citizenship Act', which established a separate Canadian citizenship, prompting a Commonwealth conference, held in London in 1947. This concluded that each Dominion was free to legislate in respect of its own citizenship, while retaining the principle of a common citizenship within the Commonwealth, defined as that of 'British subject'.

By the end of the twentieth century a reaction had set in against the very notion of Empire, and against the former British Empire in particular, which was dismissed as 'colonialism'. It may have reflected a profound sense of national loss among the older population, but among many of the younger generation it took the form of a violent rejection of all aspects of the Empire, including monuments to its most outstanding figures.

The cultural destruction wreaked by the anti-imperial tide inevitably extended to the demolition of visible and intellectual reminders of the Imperial Age, such as the Commonwealth Library in London, which was sold off, and the British Empire Museum in Bristol, which was closed and its exhibits dispersed. A new generation of university students, whose forefathers had built the Empire, but about which they now knew very little, drew a sense of purpose and self-righteousness from offence at the sight of memorials to leading figures and heroes of the Imperial Age by inflicting as much damage to them as possible. The most vulnerable were those relating to slavery, from which Britain benefitted enormously, through the trade in cotton and sugar, which did much to promote the Industrial Revolution and the benefits that it eventually brought to the world at large. Nothing could morally have justified such slavery, particularly on the scale required, but it now presented itself as a convenient target for the self-righteous. Nor was there any interest in penalising other beneficiaries of the trade, notably the Arabs, who had benefitted from it for centuries, or the African chiefs in West Africa for their profits in promoting the trade. Similar cultural vandalism had accompanied the French and Russian Revolutions and the rise of National Socialist Germany, and was equally mindless.

Meanwhile, Britain's enthusiasm for the new, multi-racial Commonwealth had quickly palled, and relations with the former British

Commonwealth were neglected by successive liberalist governments, both Labour and Conservative, leaving Britain without a sense of direction. At the same time, membership of the projected European Union was wholly consistent with liberalist ideals, with membership of the European Common Market perceived as the first step in the new alignment. Close political relations with the United States had been a partial solution, but the relationship was too one-sided, as Britain discovered during the Suez Crisis, and was largely confined to joint ventures, such as the Iraq Wars of 1991 and 2003.

A significant feature of liberalist philosophy, in keeping with its Liberal origin, was the promotion of free trade, the most notable consequence of which was a massive transfer of capital and technology from the West to China, which emerged as a profitable market, but also as a major power with newly acquired worldwide ambitions.

When Great Britain granted independence to India and the various colonies, with the prospect of more to come, and following a Commonwealth Conference, the British Nationality Act was introduced in 1948. This created a new class of 'citizens of the United Kingdom and Colonies', who, combined with the citizens of the Dominions, were divided into 'British subjects' and 'Commonwealth citizens' (more or less in keeping with the requirements of common law). All, however, retained the same right of entry to, and residence within, the United Kingdom, which, with the exception of British subjects, the dissolution of the Empire should have ended. Dissolution of the Empire had an unexpected consequence, however. Far from appreciating their new-found independence, many citizens of the former colonies reacted against their own (indigenous) governments, which they saw as corrupt and presiding over a diminishing quality of life and prospects. Enterprising individuals in Britain made the most of the situation by acquiring old ships and offering cheap passages from the Caribbean to Britain. So popular did this prove to be, that West Indians took the opportunity in their thousands. Gradually, the source of the influx shifted to such regions as Pakistan, India and East Africa. The chief practical justification from Britain's point of view was that the immigrants provided a seemingly limitless supply of cheap labour, initially for the benefit of the textile industries, which had become uncompetitive, and subsequently for a growing labour shortage that threatened to drive up wages and, of course, reduce productivity. The driving force behind immigration, however, was the attraction of the higher standard of living and government in Britain.

The losers from this mass immigration were the British working class, because what the immigrants were seeking were unskilled and semi-skilled jobs and working-class housing, particularly as successive governments made little attempt to provide the additional infrastructure that the immigration demanded. Inevitably, the working class saw itself as under threat, and began to react accordingly, a reaction made the more intense by their perception of the immigrants and their cultures as being 'alien'. As the socialist policy of nationalisation increasingly began to fail, due to problems of mismanagement, under-investment, and permitted exploitation by the trade unions, leading to the abandonment of the policy in commerce and industry, so there was an ideological drift back to liberalism, but one that emphasised the idea of universal equality, which underlay the immigration programme. The role of immigration appears to have been to demonstrate and enforce the ideological benefits of a plural society. Thus, for many years, the justification for the immigration programme was given simply as 'diversity', without any explanation of why this was beneficial. The Conservative Party, feeling that it was being left behind in this new ideological age, strove to adapt, and for many years, the Parties observed an undeclared agreement not to allow the immigration question to become an issue in general elections.

Antipathy towards the immigrants from the working class, the tensions aroused particularly by efforts of the immigrants to find accommodation, and the consequences for the British communities affected was dealt with brutally by the introduction of repressive legislation. For the Establishment it was an uncomfortable awakening when, on the one hand, it had bitterly attacked other countries that had racial problems, and, on the other, it had held up British people as an example of tolerance and absence of racial 'prejudice', only to discover that the same tensions were emerging in Britain. The problem was due, partly, to a prejudiced outlook on the part of the Establishment itself, which had no doubts about its own assessment of the situation, and partly to an unwillingness to accept the huge cost of investment in infrastructure that such a policy required. Disillusionment and resentment would affect much of the immigrant population itself, and would occasionally erupt in dramatic violence.

The middle class, to which the Establishment itself belonged, was largely unaffected by the immigration policy, and may even have benefitted to some extent from the availability of cheap labour, caused, not by a reduction in wages, the minimum of which was fixed by law, but by the plentiful supply of semi-skilled and unskilled labour that the influx caused. The semi-skilled and unskilled working class reacted to the economic, social and psychological pressure by withdrawing into itself, suffering a decline, or at best, stagnation, in its living standard, with unemployment never far away. The liberal establishment reacted to the emerging situation by, among other things, displaying a certain alienation from its own British identity and showing hostility towards it.

As the source of immigration shifted from such areas as the West Indies and Africa to southern Asia, which had a relatively advanced culture of its own, a new effect would appear in the form of different cultural and religious beliefs. These took forms that were at first shocking to British people. Religious fanaticism grew, aggravated by local antipathy and the policy of a particular foreign government, for which money was no object, and which pursued its own policy of religious promotion, perhaps in the hope of changing the character of Western society. This dangerous trend introduced its own form of violence, which took the form, not of mindless rioting, as hitherto, but of planned terrorism. Immigration from these sources, on the other hand, also brought able professional workers, particularly in the medical field, such that Britain became in danger of failing to train its own.

There followed a series of further immigration Acts, not to prevent the influx, but to manage it in a way that did not discriminate on a racial basis. In so doing, they excluded those British people overseas who were still party to the regal contract, but separated from Britain by two generations or more. This declared that Canadians, Australians and others with ancestral roots and relatives in the home country were now *personae non grata*, and it led to a reaction by the former Dominions, which had, until now, retained an open door to all from Britain and the former Empire who were 'British subjects', but who were now re-classified as 'aliens'. British immigration policy caused a profound sense of betrayal throughout the former British Commonwealth, breaking one of the critical bonds that had held it together. While the policy of the Labour Party was driven by ideological beliefs, it was beginning to receive support from new economic thinking, which saw a rapidly growing population and an influx of new skills as a recipe for economic growth, based on an expanding domestic market and an increasing labour supply.

Meanwhile, the Conservative Party had been undergoing its own painful revolution in outlook, because a new generation was growing up in Britain that had no memory of the days of Empire and was strongly influenced by the new socialist ideals. The loss of Empire and, with it, of Britain's central place in the world, had inevitably left a deep scar in the national psyche, to which the country could only come to terms by rejecting the old ideals of enterprise and conquest, and embracing a new morality of contrition and egalitarianism, which involved either blotting out the past, or crudely misrepresenting it. The Conservative Party decided that, if it were to compete with Labour, it must embrace the new attitudes that were becoming such a feature, not only of Britain, but of the post-imperial world generally, in response to Europe's decline and the new primacy of the United States, which had itself long become a cosmopolitan society. Accordingly, the Party had turned to sponsoring only those members who subscribed to the new multi-racial and multi-cultural ideals. The Party, now led by Macmillan, accordingly passed the Commonwealth Immigrants Act of 1962, which limited itself to making a distinction between those citizens from the Commonwealth who had 'familial' and ancestral links with the United Kingdom and those who did not. It ameliorated the revolution, but only slightly.

41.3.4. Post-War Immigration and the Abuse of Power

Migration from and to the United Kingdom up to about 1950 was largely confined to British traders, government officials employed in the colonies, British emigrants to the colonies, and contingents of the armed forces being transported to and from different parts of the Empire. As most were British subjects, foreign immigration was minimal. From the 1950s onwards, however, the spread of cheap radio-sets and, later, access to television, brought the outside world much closer, and with it a universal awareness of the higher standard of living enjoyed by the United

Kingdom and other parts of the Western world. All that was lacking was the means of getting there.

The first impetus to large-scale immigration to Britain from the former colonies came from post-war industrialisation, particularly in the Indian sub-continent, where import duties could now be imposed on British goods, such as textiles. Cheaper imports and reduced exports caused a decline in British textile industries, which the Government sought to offset by allowing the import of thousands of non-European workers, particularly from Pakistan. The policy was a failure, but the Asian immigrants were allowed to remain. Meanwhile, successive Governments were perplexed how to deal with the situation, which had arisen because immigrants from the former colonies and other territories of the Crown were, in keeping with feudal law, classified as British subjects. Legislation had simply not kept pace with the fundamental changes that had followed the war, and this was to pose a serious threat to social stability in Britain.

In 1948, a group of enterprising individuals were offered cheap fares from Jamaica to London on board an old ship, the 'Empire Windrush', which at the time was preparing to sail from Kingston with spare capacity. As a result, the ship arrived in Britain with well over a thousand prospective West Indian immigrants, precipitating a political crisis. Whether successive Governments had simply ignored or discounted the risks posed by admitting a racial problem, or had been too embarrassed by the post-war sentiments already described, to risk being accused of passing racially motivated legislation, is unclear. The Labour Government of the time, headed by Clement Attlee, in spite of its egalitarian and internationalist sentiments, was deeply concerned at the development, as was the succeeding government under Churchill after 1951. Partly by coincidence, but also reflecting the stirring of new, post-war, sentiments, a new British Nationality Act, 1948, creating a new status of 'Citizen of the United Kingdom and Colonies', came into effect at the beginning of 1949. Its purpose appears to have been to adopt the more egalitarian notion of 'citizen', in place of the feudal designation of 'subject'. Even so, it still retained the feudal principle of common identity of subjects within the Queen's dominions. Like its predecessor, it also ignored the racial issue because one had not previously existed. The Government was now caught between the threat of domestic instability, arising from this new 'alien' influx, undoubtedly opposed by the majority of the working class, and the strong objection in liberal circles to any form of discrimination on racial grounds.

Sentiments typical of the later 'liberalist' movements were already beginning to stir by this time, in keeping with the rise of the Labour Party, which had not previously taken a clear stance on the issue, being primarily concerned with establishing public ownership of the means of production and public services, and the abuse of political and humanitarian rights by Russia and Germany.

Immigration from the former Empire was largely uncontrolled, with the result that it included many groups who jarred with many British perceptions and standards, generating friction on the part of the host population and resentment and frustration on the part of the immigrants, giving rise to outbreaks of mob violence. Later, religious friction prompted street attacks and attacks on public transport, resulting in loss of life among the native British population. The friction and violence was both racial and religious in character. The Government responded, not by curtailing immigration or repatriating offenders, but by imposing repressive legislation, in the form of the Race Relations Act of 1965. This penalised all forms of racial discrimination, but in practice it was directed mainly at the native British working class, which was bearing the brunt of these changes, not the least of which was the movement of immigrants into working-class residential areas, causing a widespread displacement of population, much as had happened in the northern United States, following the abolition of slavery in the south. New legislation in Britain curtailed freedom of association and freedom of speech, changes that struck at the heart of English common law.

No general election or referendum had authorised the post-war immigration policy, or the repressive legislation that was resorted to in order to accommodate it. Indeed, the Parties colluded with each other at general elections in order to prevent the issue from being raised.

41.3.5. The Missing Requirement: Identity

The consequences for Britain of the doctrine of universal equality were undoubtedly of great benefit to previously neglected issues, which had often been discriminated against, such as homosexuality, and groups with infirmities and 'under-privileged' backgrounds. On the other hand, it was hostile to another basic human need, namely, a sense of identity, or belonging, which it regarded as destructive, particularly in the form of nationalism.

The fundamental defect of the doctrine of universal equality was that it ignored a fundamental human need, namely, a sense of identity. Indeed, the egalitarian doctrine was itself largely a reaction against what had been regarded as the excessive expression of identity, whether, national, racial, religious or communal, which it blamed for most previous wars and forms of persecution, as well as the Empire, although this was a relatively minor explanation. The building of the Empire had owed most to the opportunities for trade, land for the settlement of surplus British population, and the call of gold, supplemented by the need for administrators to govern it. The reality was probably that the need for identity was far stronger than the need for equality.

41.4. The Rise of the Liberalist Movement and the Doctrine of Universal Equality

The state ownership of basic industries, introduced by the Labour Government after 1945, was not a success, because of poor financial management, as the Government failed to understand the importance of ploughing profits back into the system to meet the demands of competition and the depreciation of equipment, and because of industrial exploitation by the trade unions, on whom the Labour Party was financially dependent. The effect was the growing atrophy of the means of production, which was crucial in a country that depended for its livelihood on exports in a very competitive environment. Unwilling to admit to failure, succeeding Labour Governments endeavoured to support the economy and limit unemployment by subsidising failing industries, particularly coal-mining, but this did nothing to deal with the causes of the problem.

The effect was Britain's relative economic decline as the 'sick man of Europe', which was only halted by the de-nationalisation of its basic industries and the advent in 1979 of a Conservative Government under

Britain's first female Prime Minister, Margaret Thatcher. Thatcher's first major focus was on British military assertion in the Falkland Islands, in the South Atlantic in 1982. These islands had been invaded and annexed by Argentina in April of that year, following favourable signs from the Foreign Office, which at that time was sympathetic to the divestment of what remained of the British Empire. Thatcher was horrified, but was persuaded that a re-conquest was militarily possible. Embarking upon it in May of the same year, the re-conquest was completed in June, in the face of the overwhelming problems of distance and lack of military preparedness. Her second major impact followed the closure of many uneconomic coal mines in 1984 and the laying off of 20,000 miners, leading to a strike and violent confrontations with the police. Thatcher's sustained response finally broke the power of the trade unions and allowed a major industry that was no longer viable to be gradually closed down. It involved a huge social cost, however, that few political leaders would have been prepared to face, by creating large pockets of permanent unemployment, due to the absence of alternative employment in the mining areas. Having served longer than any other Prime Minister in the twentieth century, she was forced to resign in 1990 by a revolt within her own Party, caused partly by a highly unpopular poll tax and dissatisfaction among her fellow Ministers. She was replaced by John Major in 1990.

It may have been the advent of the Major Government that marked the rise of the liberalist cause as a distinct movement in Britain, although its influence was not limited to the Conservative Party, nor specifically related to the Liberal Party, but was now pervading the Establishment. It undoubtedly owed much to a reaction against the authoritarian regimes in Germany and Russia, and particularly to the persecution of the Jews in Germany from the 1930s. Adding to it was the post-war break-up of the Empire, giving rise to a new age of anti-imperialism. Inevitably, the emphasis of the liberalist movement was on egalitarianism, social as well as political. It had no Party structure and no recognised leadership, and was probably what Hegel would have described as a *volksgeist*, without formal organisation or membership, but clearly recognisable to participants and opponents alike, that gathered momentum and swept through the political establishment, bent upon the promotion of egalitarian policies throughout society.

An important consequence of this outlook was the immigration into Britain of non-White races, particularly from the former Colonies, and an antagonism towards everything and everyone associated with the former British Empire. In pursuit of this, the movement had no qualms about being physically destructive, such as achieving the closure and dispersal of the British Empire Library and the British Empire Museum, extending later to attacks on imperial monuments. Associated with this desecration was the promotion of a new doctrine of internationalism and a rejection of all recognition of social, racial and religious differences. Nor was the movement confined to Great Britain, gradually spreading through the Western world. One feature of it was the restoration of free trade, which had the benefit of promoting a greater efficiency in the use of resources. This set in progress a mass movement of capital and technology to China, which appeared to offer an almost unlimited future market for Western goods, but which also gave rise to a new and threatening Communist world power.

Nevertheless, the liberalist movement also brought benefits to many minority groups that were the victims of social prejudice, such as homosexuals, or were too few and expensive to provide for, such as the aged or disabled. The new society would be international, cosmopolitan, liberal, and to all intents and purposes, sexless and secular. For some, the fate of the Jews in wartime Germany was used as a powerful argument in favour of the liberalist trend, whose ultimate purpose seemed to be the destruction of almost all sense of identity. Like any *volksgeist*, it was a reaction against a past that had found a new idea. It was not limited to Great Britain, although it was particularly strong there, but spread through those Western countries that had built empires and been directly involved in the Second World War.

41.5. Parliaments Progress from Representing to Ruling the People

41.5.1. Parliaments Abuse Their Function

Having usurped the Crown and reduced the House of Lords to a legislative 'bus-stop', it was perhaps inevitable that the House of Commons should step into the constitutional vacuum that it had created. It did so by extending its role of representing the people to becoming the government of the people. During the second half of the twentieth century, the political Parties in the Commons were finding it difficult to reconcile their acquired control of the legislative and executive functions of state with their constitutional duty to represent the interests of the people. The Party system in Parliament was popular with the people, because it gave them a feeling that they had some control over their lives, because they were able to decide, to some extent, through general elections and the policies offered by the contending Parties, the way in which they were governed. The problem with the Party system, however, was that it lent itself to 'rule by faction', in that it was ideological factions that increasingly comprised the Parties. The policy decisions of Governments were dictated primarily by the ideological interests of the Party, rather than by practical issues, better described as 'common sense'. The effect was that Governments were inclined to introduce radical policies that could only be restrained by the election of a new Government, by which time much of the damage that ideological policies had caused could not be reversed.

With the dissolution of the Empire, nowhere did this conflict become more apparent than in matters of migration and citizenship. Seeking to head off the worst of the mounting social problems, an amending Act of 1968 limited the right of entry of those who had no parental or grandparental links with the United Kingdom. While this limited the inflow to those who already had family connections, the perceived need for non-discrimination violated the common law right of return by excluding those British people overseas who were still party to the regal contract, but separated from Britain by two generations or more. This declared that millions of Canadians, Australians and others with ancestral roots and relatives in the home country were now relegated to the category of *persona non grata*. The bitterness felt by the old Dominions over their new treatment by the motherland was given little attention by the latter.

In none of these changes was the British public consulted, in spite of the fact that the majority were directly or indirectly affected by them. The British Immigration Act of 1971, which came into operation in 1973, the same year as the United Kingdom joined the European Economic

Community (EEC), made further changes. The most significant was to exclude 'non-patrials', that is, those 'citizens of the United Kingdom and colonies' who were not born in the United Kingdom. One effect was to preclude an anticipated influx of Indians who were being evicted from East Africa, but whom India refused to admit. This led to condemnation by the Commission on Human Rights, a recently established body in Britain, on the ground that their exclusion from Britain represented a degrading treatment contrary to Article 3 of the European Convention on Human Rights, which Britain had subscribed to. The Act was also criticised on the ground that the new category of 'patrial' made it racially motivated in favour of those from the original 'White' Dominions.

Evidently, the House of Commons had been converted to the feudal view, held by many of England's Medieval Kings, but which Parliament had excoriated since the Middle Ages, that the Crown was entitled to adopt any policy that it chose. Nor was Parliament obliged any longer, it appeared, to seek or defer to the wishes or interests of the people. Statutes defining British citizenship, or controlling immigration, were not referred to the electorate, and for a number of years there was an informal consensus between the Parties that the issue of immigration should not appear during general elections. That Britain was suffering from a major, but unacknowledged, constitutional breakdown was beyond question. The implied explanation was that basic ideological issues must take priority, an explanation that not long ago had been used in respect of Germany. Russia had no tradition of parliamentary government, or constitutional monarchy, so that a comparison had no relevance.

The Race Relations Act of 1965 outlawed discrimination in public places on the grounds of colour, race, or ethnic or national origins. It also made it an offence to incite racial hatred. This was evidently not enough, because an ensuing Act of 1968 extended these offences to cover employment and housing. That racial problems persisted is obvious from the further Act of 1976, which established a Commission of Racial Equality, whose purposes were to promote racial equality; encourage greater integration and better relations between the races; eradicate discrimination and harassment, and promote equality in all public services. The reaction to the Act was far from encouraging, Lord Justice Denning comparing the use by the Commission of its investigative power to 'the days of the Inquisition', while the House of Lords was forced to declare that the Commission had no power to launch investigations into employers' affairs where there had been no allegation of discrimination.

With popular opposition by now either suppressed or reduced to apathy, the ethnic problem was now being overtaken by concerns over a much wider range of perceived inequalities identified by the new concept of 'human rights', and in 2004, the Commission was merged with a new Equality Human Rights Commission, whose purpose was to monitor human rights and protect equality in respect of age, disability, gender, race, religion and other factors.

Nor was abuse of constitutional principles limited to immigration. In August 1961, Great Britain applied for, and was granted, membership of the European Economic Community, later re-named the European Community, a free trade area that had been established in accordance with the Treaty of Rome, of 1957, which now embraced much of Western Europe, but to which Britain had not been party. One of its requirements was the free migration of workers and their families and dependents between the member states. In common law, the Crown had no authority to commit Britain to such a treaty without popular consent, particularly as it gave to the Community considerable powers to legislate, but ten years later, in 1972, the issue was finally submitted to a popular referendum, which endorsed membership. The problem now was that the intent of the Community was to progress to a full constitutional union of member states, a prospect that was clearly outside the terms of the referendum.

41.5.2. The Decline of Parliamentary Standards

A further significant change in the nature of Parliaments took place during the second half of the twentieth century. Hitherto, Members of Parliament had usually been individuals with an existing and well-established career, typically in the professions or commerce, or who came from established families with a tradition of public service. They were meant to be men of integrity, whose background had given them a fairly broad and balanced perspective in life, as well as a grasp of public affairs. Once they had entered Parliament, they had usually divided their time between their private occupations and their engagements with public policy. They were expected to take a balanced and responsible view of their public duties, and their chief deficiency was their lack of insight into the lives and problems of the working classes. Because they owed little to the state themselves, they had tended to the view that the individual was responsible for his own life, and that governments should meddle as little as possible.

In order to accommodate the personal commitments of Members, sittings of the House of Commons were deferred until the afternoons, and the lost time was made up in the evenings. Members were also satisfied with modest remuneration for the time that they devoted to parliamentary affairs. Those appointed to the Ministry were, as a rule, already used to responsibility, and although Ministerial office normally required their close attention, such men were normally content to leave the day-to-day running of the country to the professional Civil Service. Appointments to the higher levels of the Civil Service were, in any case, subject to exacting academic standards, ensuring that the Service was well able to cope with responsibility and the making of sound decisions in other than Party policy matters. All that Ministers were expected to provide was guidance to Departmental heads on the nature and direction of Government policy.

The second half of the century witnessed important changes, as Members of Parliament were drawn less from individuals with a successful, or at least an assured, occupation, who were willing to provide the time for public service as parliamentary representatives, to individuals who had no assured occupation, but were drawn to public life more in the pursuit of a political cause, following the advent of a Labour Government in 1945. Such individuals tended to be younger, often with a career to fall back on, such as employment in the trade union movement. Increased parliamentary salaries were designed to provide, not only full financial support to Members, but an element of compensation for the very high risk of unemployment in the event of the Member losing his seat in a General Election. Such individuals had a much better appreciation of the country's social and economic problems, but a more limited background overall and only a superficial grasp of the wider issues. They also had a more limited understanding of the system of government and, in many cases, a reformist outlook that left them with less respect for the political system than their predecessors. Their chief contribution lay in a willingness to deal with social issues that previous Parliaments had preferred to neglect. Consequently, Members of Parliament now tended to be younger than their predecessors, and more driven by political ideals. Because of their different circumstances and social background, many saw Parliament as a career, rather than as a form of public service. This would encourage not a few Members to exploit the financial benefits available. This would eventually undermine the high public respect in which the House of Commons had previously been held, eventually making it necessary to impose restrictions on the behaviour of Members.

Political pressure to make parliamentary careers more readily available to women also brought a need to change the hours of parliamentary sittings, to bring them more into line with the normal working hours of the general public. This had the effect of making it almost impossible for a Member to continue any normal career that he might have followed outside Parliament, which may have helped to maintain a sense of perspective. The shift in the composition of the Commons and its greater involvement in social affairs reinforced its growing tendency to such long sittings that Parliament was increasingly regarded as a permanent institution, rather than as an annual consultation. These changes contributed to a different attitude towards the holding of parliamentary office, in which the concept of service as representatives of the people was replaced by the notion of a promising career in the Ministry, offset by the recurrent risk inherent in general elections.

41.5.3. The Ministerial Spoils System

For membership of Parliament to be seen as a promising career, in contrast to its original function as a public duty, inevitably implied a real prospect of reward, which, under these new circumstances, meant a career as a Minister of the Crown. This was a duty that the Parties in the Commons had wrested from the House of Lords, not on the grounds of greater competence, because the Lords undoubtedly had the advantage of greater experience of affairs of state and greater responsibilities in life, typically as extensive landowners, patrons of the arts, or bearers of the tradition of military service – but on the grounds of a better understanding of the needs of the people.

The leaders of ruling Parties were now in a very different situation, devoted to managing the executive functions of government and anxious to increase discipline within the Party, in order to carry them into effect. The whole orientation of Party leaders was towards the implementation of Party policies, whether or not they were sought by the electorate, and to this end Party discipline had become of greater importance. Party whips were a helpful tool to this end, but more important was the ability of the Prime Minister to enlist the support of influential Members with offers of Ministerial appointment. Obviously, the more Ministerial posts that there were to distribute, the greater the control that the Prime Minister could exert and the greater the loyalty of Party members was likely to be. This led to an increasing multiplication of Ministerial offices, achieved by sub-dividing existing portfolios and creating new ones, so that many new Ministries were of limited importance. Also, Ministers were increasingly inclined to add to their sense of importance by involving themselves beyond issues of Government policy by obtruding into areas that properly belonged to trained and experienced civil servants. The situation led to a further abuse of the system, with the creation of Ministries as inducements to outspoken members of the parliamentary Party, in an effort to keep them quiet. The result was often trivial portfolios, as in October of 2018, when it was reported that a Minister for Suicide Prevention had been appointed.

As the situation grew more and more out of hand, it resulted in a tier structure that distinguished between those Ministries of sufficient importance to attend Cabinet meetings and those that could safely be excluded. In spite of this, the Ministry continued to grow in size, as also did Cabinet meetings. Traditionally, Cabinet membership had been about a dozen, with eighteen considered the maximum for effective decision-taking. Now, Cabinet meetings had grown to monstrous numbers who could hardly be squeezed around a huge table. As a result, Cabinet discussions took on the character more of parish meetings, and because general agreement was more difficult to reach and the majority present found little opportunity to speak and were consequently ignored, the power of the Prime Minister in the decision-making process increased correspondingly. Instead of being *primus inter pares*, or 'first among equals', the Prime Minister acquired a more authoritarian, almost presidential, function in the direction of affairs, steadily usurping still further, not only the function of the King as the head of government, but increasingly the Cabinet itself.

Meanwhile, the Ministry tended increasingly to obtrude its right of decision-making downwards, reducing the responsibility of the upper ranks of the Civil Service. This undoubtedly had a detrimental effect, both on the Civil Service and on Ministerial decisions. Inexperienced Ministers either imposed their own ill-informed opinions on their advisers, or simply forwarded Civil Service views to Cabinet decision-making, without reconciling them properly with Government objectives. The general effect seems to have been a downgrading of the importance and responsibility of the Civil Service, and with it the general competence of Government decision-making. Where there was conflict, senior civil servants were publicly accused of interfering in Government policy-making. This reduction of the importance of the Civil Service made it possible to lower the standards of admission, which suited the Government's policy of making the Civil Service more representative of the ordinary people, and less 'élitist', probably at the cost of a further decline in the competence of Government decision-making. As few Ministers now had any executive training in other fields, and often little aptitude for such high office, the standard of Government decision-making undoubtedly suffered further. Ministers rarely held a portfolio for more than a couple of years, and often for less, whether because they were unequal to the task and did not have time to learn, or because of their impatience to be moved to more senior positions, or because their Ministerial careers were simply interrupted by general elections. Such short tenures of office were rarely sufficient to enable Ministers to become competent in any portfolio, let alone more generally in the management of affairs of state. On the other hand, incompetent Ministers could be an advantage to their departments, leaving senior civil servants with greater freedom to manage policy. It was not the normal function of a Minister, in any case, to involve himself in the internal working of his department, which was the duty of the Civil Service Commission; his function was to ensure that the policy of the department was, at least, not inconsistent with overall Government policy, or, if circumstances appeared to call for it, to persuade his fellow Ministers that overall policy should be amended.

The overall effect, however, was probably a tendency to decline in both the standard of Government policy-making and its implementation.

Meanwhile, the respect which earlier members of the Commons had held for what they regarded as 'the Constitution' had long been in decline, and after about 1950 it declined more rapidly. This owed much to the increasingly rapid disintegration of the system of government, as respected institutions, such as the Monarchy and the House of Lords, were thrust aside, and socialist philosophy, introduced by newer and younger Members of Parliament, made its presence felt. Most at risk were venerable offices of state that had their origin in the Middle Ages or earlier, and which had long been regarded as the keystones of the parliamentary system. Now they were regarded as 'outmoded'. Some Prime Ministers, but perhaps most notably Blair, saw it as part of their mission to 'modernize' the system of government, to make it more like that of the United States. Meanwhile, acknowledged authorities on the 'constitution', such as Dicey, Anson, Maitland, Erskine May, and even the more adaptable Jennings, who had previously been read and observed with reverence, were now set aside as 'outdated', and left to gather dust on library shelves. The chief reason for this was probably their failure to acknowledge the basic shifts in political power that had continued at a fast pace. The 'constitution', whose purpose had been to define the process of decision-making and to preserve political stability, and which had previously been treated with respect and even awe, witnessed, in the second half of the twentieth century, a gradual shedding of this respect, as institutions came increasingly to be regarded as dispensable where they obstructed the growing monopoly of legislative and executive power enjoyed by the Parties in the Commons. All that remained largely untouched was the judicial function of government, and this now had little left to protect it.

A symptom of these changes was the growing appropriation of power by the office of Prime Minister. The executive agents of government are the King's Ministers, appointed by him for the purpose, to which end he is advised by his Prime Minister, who is chosen on the basis of his influence in Parliament. At the end of April 2019, the then Prime Minister, Theresa May, believed that she had reason to call for the resignation of the current Minister of Defence over a serious breach of confidence. When he vehemently denied this and refused to offer his resignation, she simply issued a statement from her official residence at 10 Downing Street, personally dismissing him from office in a notable usurpation of power. A Minister is appointed by Sovereign, at this time Queen Elizabeth II, and it follows that only the Queen had the right to dismiss her Ministers. Where a Minister resigns, the function of the Prime Minister is to present the letter of resignation to the Queen for acceptance, and where it is necessary to dismiss a Minister, the duty of the Prime Minister is limited to advising the Queen accordingly. If that advice is accepted, the Sovereign hands a letter of dismissal to her Prime Minister for the notification of the Minister in question. This delegation is appropriate, because it limits the demands on the Queen and helps to ensure that the Prime Minister is involved in all matters pertaining to the Ministry. Whether Mrs May's action was already a well-established procedure, or whether she took it on her own initiative, makes no difference. Ministers of the Crown are not employed by the Prime Minister, and the above practice was symptomatic of the gradual process of concentrating all political power in the hands of the Parties in the House of Commons, a process that was only possible, like earlier abuses by the Monarchy itself, because the 'regulator' of constitutional practice had been prevented from functioning since the reign of Edward III.

41.5.4. The Judicial and Legislative Functions of the Lords

The constitutional powers commonly attributed to the House of Lords have been legislative, judicial and advisory, as might be expected of a body that, since the reign of Edward III, has combined the legislative role of the Second Estate in Parliament on the one hand, and the supervisory, advisory and judicial roles of the Great Council on the other. Although the judicial role of the Upper House, in its aspect as the seat of the Council, was limited to members of the Second Estate, it had also, since the fourteenth century, accepted responsibility for appeals from the Third Estate, because the Commons had rejected the duty. This had made the House of Lords the court of appeal for both Estates. The arrangement had continued until the establishment of the Courts of Appeal, in 1875, which had usurped the role of the Great Council by leaving the House with jurisdiction only in respect of appeals, from both Estates, on points of law. Meanwhile, the common law right of the individual to be tried by his peers was maintained by providing that the trial of members of the Second Estate was presided over by the Lord High Steward. This office had not been permanently filled since the fifteenth century, making it necessary for a Lord High Steward to be appointed for each trial, as well as for the purpose of coronations. The last trial of a Peer by his fellows was that of Lord de Clifford, who was tried for manslaughter in 1935. The advisory function of the House had ceased to be exercised since the reign of Queen Victoria, who discouraged it. Nevertheless, its right to advise the Sovereign still exists.

It may be remembered that the right of the Lords to be consulted, equally with the Commons, in respect of Bills presented to Parliament, arose from the principle of *quod omnes tangit*, or 'what concerns all should be approved by all', it having been accepted that each Estate should be consulted where its interests were affected, and that they should be consulted jointly where the interests of both Estates were affected. In practice, both Houses had been allowed to demur from, and effectively veto, any Bill. This practice of consulting both Estates had come under criticism, following the decline of feudal tenure and the transition from an agricultural to an industrial society, because the Upper House now represented only a small section of the population. This had followed the restoration of freemanship to most of the commonalty, which had greatly increased the size of the Third Estate. At the same time, the Third Estate had become highly diversified, with some descending into acute poverty, while others acquired wealth, education and influence, causing the Estate system to lose much of its functional significance. In the nineteenth and early twentieth centuries, the House of Commons increased its importance by extending its representation to include much of the 'Lesser Baronage', leaving only the 'Greater Baronage' to be represented by the House of Lords.

It had been the practice of the Lords, since 1844, to leave the judicial work of the House to such of its members who happened to be legally qualified, for which reason the latter became known as the 'Law Lords'. This confined most of the Peers to their legislative function. In order to prevent the judicial work of the House from interrupting its legislative role, it was agreed in 1948 that, as a temporary measure, because it could have no constitutional authority, the hearing of appeals should be left to an Appellate Committee of the House, which could meet separately, even when the House was not sitting. The main objection to this arrangement was that the Law Lords were precluded, through pressure of work, from much of the legislative proceedings of the House. The practice became permanent, however, and the growing pressure of work on the Appellate Committee itself sometimes became such as to require it to function as two Committees. Accordingly, the work of the House of Lords was increasingly divided between those who addressed themselves to its legislative role, and those who, as Law Lords, devoted most of their time to the Appellate Committee. Thus, like the Royal Courts of Law, which had always functioned outside – although still, constitutionally, as a part of – Parliament, so also did the Appellate Committee, which functioned outside of the House of Lords, while remaining a part of it.

41.5.5. Rivalry Between the Houses

Relations between the Second and Third Estates had been irreparably damaged by the Normans, who had usurped the former. This alienation had been aggravated further by the ensuing feudal system, which had persisted through most of the Middle Ages. The immediate cause of rivalry between the Houses of Parliament for legislative supremacy had its origin in the rise of a political class in the House of Commons who comprised two rival Parties. Representing the interests of voters and meeting the requirements of the King could be a tedious occupation, whereas the prospect of gaining control of the apparatus of government was altogether more inviting. The power of the King had been broken by 1689, diverting the ambitions of the Commons towards its remaining rival, the House of Lords, whose right of veto over legislation was regarded by many in the Commons as morally untenable, because it was now those represented by the Commons who contributed much the greater part of the national revenue. The Lords nevertheless asserted their historic right, like the Commons, to veto Bills that were seen to affect their interests adversely. The Constitution afforded equal rights to the Estates, and it was this, really, that was now in dispute, because the costs of the State, once met chiefly by the Lords, were now being met by the Commons, and with the change in contribution, there was also a shift in the sense of entitlement. It may also be that the Commons resented the historic right of the Lords, both individually and collectively, to have access to, and to advise the King. No real progress by the Commons in asserting their supremacy over the Lords was possible, however, until the Parties had gained control of the Crown.

The first attack on the Lords had come in 1911, when the Upper House had been forced, as the result of an unconstitutional threat by the King, to renounce its right to veto Bills. Furthermore, in respect of a money Bill, or a Bill certified by the Speaker of the Commons as a money Bill, which effectively meant most Bills, the House of Lords was restricted by the ensuing Act merely to delay such a Bill, and for not more than two sessions of Parliament. We now know that this restriction was irrelevant and of no effect, because the proper function of the House, in its true capacity as the Great Council, had the constitutional duty to advise the King where Bills were contrary to law, and thereby veto them. Moreover, if the Council deemed any Bill to be contrary to the national good, it was entitled to advise the King accordingly. In either case the King was bound either to withdraw the Bill or to amend it. Indeed, the Great Council, in its guise as the House of Lords, had no place in Parliament. Its restoration as the oldest and only permanent part of the Constitution would, indeed, have the effect of causing all members of the Second Estate to return to their proper seats in Parliament, alongside the Commons, with each sitting as an Estate, not as a House, and each Estate being required to approve Bills submitted by the King.[10] Prior to the submission of a Bill to Parliament, however, it would have been submitted to the Great Council, for its advice that it did not conflict with the common law of the constitution, and for any other observations that the Council chose to make. These would be reported to Parliament.

Meanwhile, the attack by the Commons against the Upper House widened with the election of Labour Governments, to the mounting of a direct challenge to the principle of hereditary titles as a qualification for the making of parliamentary decisions. The Parties also promoted the idea that it was the number of free men and women affected that was important. This overlooked the reality that members of the Upper House were, on the whole, better educated and more experienced in

10   Under current and long-established practice, Parliament assembled only at its Opening and prior to its Dissolution.

affairs of state than members of the Commons, having, since childhood, lived with them whilst being imbued with the tradition of public service. It is self-evident, moreover, that the members of the Upper House had much more to lose from adverse decisions by Parliament. For their part, the members of the Commons had far more to gain from decisions of Parliament. Jennings has argued that the members of the Upper House were 'responsible to nobody but themselves',[11] a grudging view based upon the fact that all members of the Second Estate, being fewer in numbers, enjoyed the right to attend a Parliament. Members of the Third Estate also enjoyed the right to attend, but, because of their number, attendance had to be restricted to their elected representatives. It might be added, however, that most ordinary freemen had little interest in attending, so long as their interests were represented. Indeed, lack of attendance had been a real problem since before the Middle Ages.

By the mid-twentieth century, the basic question being raised by the Labour and Liberal Parties was one of principle, whether the Second Estate served a necessary purpose that justified its privileged position in Parliament. The purpose of Parliament was simply to ensure that each Estate was consulted. The problem was that consultation was now perceived as being on a *per capita* basis, whereas constitutionally it was based on the respective needs of the Estates. It was the great disparity in numbers that implied privilege, because, constitutionally, the Estates were treated equally.

The majority of the general public, perhaps reflecting their instinct for common law, seem to have been much less concerned with the egalitarian aspect than with the constitutional, as was noted in respect of the crisis of 1909–10. The deep respect in which the House of Lords had been held and the sense of its crucial importance to their own interests, constitutionally, in their own minds, elevated it above the political Parties, imparting a distinctive aura of authority and majesty to the Upper House that was unmistakable. This helps to explain why the Upper House was a Party, rather than a popular, issue.

41.5.5.1. The Right of Trial by One's Peers

The right of the individual, in common law, to be tried by his peers, was recorded in the *Magna Carta*, but was abolished by the Labour

---

11   W. I. Jennings, *The British Constitution*, 89.

Government in 1948. The arbitrary reason given for the removal of this right in common law was that the trial by Peers of members of the Peerage amounted to a form of judicial privilege, in that it violated the notion of universal equality for the sake of individual justice. Judicial privilege arises only if the standard of evidence in one court is different from that in another, or if judgments for the same offence in one court are different from those in another. The purpose of the right to be tried by one's peers is to ensure that the standard of evidence is not affected by social or other group considerations. It is usual today for an accused to have the right to reject members of a randomly selected jury whom he might believe to be biased against him, and it might be said that this affords much the same protection to the accused as he would have received in a trial by his peers, provided that the choice of jurors available to the accused is such as to enable him to choose a jury from his own Estate if he wishes.

41.5.5.2. The Establishment of a Supreme Court

The function of the House of Lords as a court of appeal – undoubtedly derived from the former constitutional function of the Great Council as the court of law for the trial of members of the Second Estate – but forced, since the fourteenth century, due to the dereliction of the House of Commons, to assume responsibility also for appeals from convicted individuals of the Third Estate, was ended by the Constitutional Reform Act of 2005. This Act transferred the appellant jurisdiction of the House of Lords to a new Supreme Court, which came into existence in 2007. The inspiration for this appears to have been, in part at least, the admiration of the Prime Minister of the day, Tony Blair, for the American system of government and his dislike of constitutional traditions. Unlike the House of Lords, the jurisdiction of the new court excluded Scotland. It also lacked the ancient judicial authority of the Upper House, with its august standing in the public mind. This became clear in 2019, when the new court allowed itself to become embroiled in a constitutional (and contentiously political) issue concerning parliamentary procedure, in which its judgment was severely criticised.

41.5.6. The Commons 'Manages' the Lords Through the Creation of Life Peerages

On a petition by Lady Rhondda, in 1922, there was an attempt to use the Sex Disqualification Removal Act to introduce women members into the House of Lords, but the Committee of Privileges of the House reported adversely on the proposal. It was evidently accepted in Anglo-Saxon times that a high-born woman of royal stock, such as the wife or daughter of the King, or any outstanding high-born woman, such as the Abbess Hild, could be admitted as a royal counsellor. There seems to be no evidence, however, that this practice was recognised in common law.

Meanwhile, there had been a problem of finding enough Peers who were legally qualified, and this had been met by raiding the judiciary. Doing this without creating hereditary Peerages, had been met in 1856 and 1878 by the introduction of judicial 'life' Peers. *De facto* life Peerages were not new. The admission of leading clergy in Anglo-Saxon times had been justified by their ability to give learned advice to the King, and in the Middle Ages their admission had been justified on the ground that, as the holders of Church lands, they were tenants-in-chief of the Crown. Since the clergy were expected to be celibate, and so had no legal offspring, they were effectively life Peers. Roman Catholicism in the Church had ended in the reign of Henry VIII, but Church reforms had since permitted the clergy to marry. The House had got around the problem of their sons inheriting seats by deeming their sons, who did not inherit their father's office in the Church in any case, not to possess the right of inheritance of such seats in the Lords. The Lords Spiritual had always, therefore, been life Peers.

There accordingly followed the Life Peerage Act of 1958, introduced by the Conservative Government of Harold Macmillan, and giving statutory recognition to the new status of 'Life Peer'. It provided for the creation by the Queen, on the advice of the Prime Minister, of men and women as Peers with the rank of 'baron' or the new title of 'baroness'. This was in addition to the existing judicial life Peers. One attraction of life Peerages, in the eyes of the political Parties, was that it removed the voting unpredictability of their descendants – sons whose political sentiments were not infrequently the opposite of those of their fathers.

The Life Peerage Act of 1958 was contrary to the common law of the Constitution by affecting to elevate to the Peerage, not by election by the Peers and appointment by the King,[12] but by statutory right. However, because the Normans had rejected Salian law in favour of Church-Feudal doctrine, it had been necessary over the centuries for the King to replenish the Second Estate by the arbitrary elevation of members of the Third Estate. Such elevations had always been permissible in common law where the achievement of an individual of the Third Estate had been such as to indicate divine favour. In practice, since the Middle Ages, the King had presumed the right to appoint whomsoever he pleased, resulting in many spurious members of the Lords. It was noted earlier that the direct descendants, over three generations, of a man who had been elevated legitimately, were deemed to have inherited his noble status provided they were perceived as having sustained his noble character. It is not clear whether the elevation of a woman to the Council was permissible in exceptional cases, as suggested by the example of the Abbess Hild.

41.5.6.1. The Right to Renounce a Title

The tradition of public service that, in the nineteenth and twentieth centuries, pervaded the families represented in the House of Lords, resulted in the sons of some Peers doing a political apprenticeship in the House of Commons, before inheriting their seat in the Lords. When the King ceased to recruit his Ministers from the Upper House, a seat in the House of Lords became fatal to any member of the hereditary nobility who had Ministerial ambitions. Thus, Clement Attlee, as Prime Minister, had no option but to reject a request in 1950 by Mr Quintin Hogg, who had just succeeded to the title of Lord Hailsham, that he be allowed to continue to sit in the House of Commons. Likewise, the House of Lords rejected, in 1955, a request by Viscount Stansgate, that he be allowed to renounce his title in order to pursue his career in the Commons. Nor was it only a personal problem. Prospective Party Leaders and Prime Ministers were being lost as they succeeded to family titles. On the death of Viscount Stansgate in 1960, his son, an elected member of the House of Commons, Antony Wedgewood-Benn, succeeded to the title, but his

---

12   As would have been the case in the original war-band, where addition to the Council would have been extended to a new leader of noble ancestry and a significant addition of warriors to the enterprise, or in the case of a warrior of outstanding reputation.

admission to the Commons in his capacity as Antony Wedgewood-Benn was refused in 1961, on the ground that his election as Mr Wedgewood-Benn did not remove the fact that he was Viscount Stansgate. The High Court confirmed this in the same year by ruling that, as Lord Stansgate, his election victory was invalid because he was ineligible, and that his defeated opponent was therefore the new Member.

This issue, of lords wishing to stand as commoners, was due to the switch of Ministerial recruitment from the Upper to the Lower House. This change had been based, not on the perceived ability and integrity of candidates, but on the need of the King to secure the support of the House of Commons, if for no other reason than for its consent to levy the necessary taxes on which the continuation of government depended. The Party system had developed out of the ability of a majority group, provided it were disciplined, to control Parliament and so dictate policies to the King. In order to ensure the harmony of the system, the King had been left with no alternative but to appoint the leaders of the majority Party to his Ministry, leaving him also with no option but to grant them considerable latitude. It was a deformation of the Constitution that had been brought about by the need to keep Parliament sitting for much of the year. Because the same members attended for up to five years, they had to do so as paid professionals, because they were no longer self-supporting and because of the impracticability of holding a general election each year. It was this rigidity of modern Parliaments that had permitted the rise of permanent and disciplined groups able to control them, their ability to discipline their members sufficiently to retain power being made possible by the preference of the electors, not for relatively unknown candidates, but for well-known candidates with predictable interests. The outcome had been the enforced appointment by the King of Ministers, not on the basis of their demonstrated ability for the office, but their leadership of a particular group in the House of Commons.

The problem of Lord Stansgate was overcome by the Peerage Act of 1963, which allowed a Peer to disclaim his title, without prejudice to the right of his successor upon his death. It provided that, where a member of the House of Commons succeeded to a title, he was allowed one month in which to disclaim it, otherwise he must resign from the House.[13] In the same year, Lord Home disclaimed his title and reverted

13   Under the common law of the Constitution there are no 'Houses of Parliament', of course,

to being Sir Alec Douglas-Home, Leader of the Conservative Party and, subsequently, Prime Minister. Lord Hailsham, with a similar expectation, took the same step, and Lord Stansgate did likewise. The motivation of Stansgate was also driven by his socialist principles, which caused him to prefer to be known in public life simply as 'Tony' Benn.

---

and in principle the Act simply allowed Stansgate to sit and vote with the Commons instead of the Lords.

42. THE LAST IMPERIAL CRISIS

42.1. Kenya

The demise of the British colony in Kenya, in East Africa, preceded the Rhodesian crisis. This colony had been established in 1902, following the imposition of a protectorate by the Crown in 1895, the chief motive for which may have been to forestall German ambitions in East Africa. British settlers had here taken up land that had previously been granted by the British Government to a syndicate established for the purpose in a fertile region of the Central Highlands that held great promise. The Kenya settlers had therefore been subject, from the outset, to the control of the British Government, and although they had been allowed limited rights, once the territory had been established as a Crown Colony, Kenya had been regarded in terms of feudal doctrine, as usual as a royal estate. This had precluded the settlers from claiming separate rights of self-government, except to a very limited degree, and when, early in the 1960s, in the face of emergent and militant African nationalism, Britain decided to relinquish its claim to the Colony, the settlers were unable to assert a separate right to self-determination, because feudal doctrine did not recognise them as a separate community within Kenya. Also, the settlement of Kenya came too late, as the Empire was on the point of toppling. The Kenya settlers were accordingly deprived of, but compensated for, the loss of their lands.

42.2. The Rhodesian Federation

In the South African general election of 1948, the Afrikaner electorate finally participated, and for the first time since the establishment of the Union. The result was the election of a National Party government, under the Prime Ministership of Dr D. F. Malan, whose chief objectives were to free South Africa of its imposed English-speaking and liberal native policies, and to facilitate recognition of *Afrikaans* as an official language, like English. In practice, it went further than this, removing the previous policy of Anglicising South Africa and promoting *Afrikaans* as the official language, consistent with the country's Afrikaner majority in the population. Previous policies had generated a great deal of bitterness, and it was now seen as 'pay-back' time. Also imposed was a stricter policy of racial segregation.

In Britain, the Labour Government of Clement Attlee was replaced in 1951 by a Conservative Government under Churchill, which took the view that the two Rhodesias should be reinforced as a more liberal counterweight to the new South Africa by combining them in a federation. Southern Rhodesia agreed to the scheme on the understanding that Salisbury would be the site of the new federal capital. It also stood to gain from the wealth that was now flowing from the Northern Rhodesian Copperbelt. The British population of Northern Rhodesia greeted the project with delight, because of the new security that such a federation offered, as well as an opportunity to escape from what they saw as the pro-Black policies of the Colonial Office, which retained responsibility for the administration of the African areas north of the Zambezi. As a condition of federation, the British Government insisted on the inclusion of Nyasaland, which was overwhelmingly Black and had always been a financial burden on the British tax-payer. The three territories were established, as the clumsily named Federation of Rhodesia and Nyasaland, in 1953.

Economically, the Federation proved to be an outstanding success, the wealth from the copper mines funding huge improvements in the infrastructure of all three territories, and foreign capital and British immigrants flowed in, turning Salisbury into what was, by the more modest standards of the day, one of the world's first skyscraper cities, like a small version of Johannesburg. Southern Rhodesia itself already had the second biggest and most advanced economy in Africa, with rapid industrialisation that, like other Commonwealth countries, had owed much to the shortages of the recent war. Indeed, the 1960s were Southern Rhodesia's 'golden age', with an increasingly diversified economy, substantial British immigration, and Black education and social services that were the best in Africa. In soil and wildlife conservation, the country was a world leader.

The good times were not to last, however. The end of the copper boom and a worldwide economic recession curtailed, but did not end the prosperity, as Rhodesian industries continued to expand, and mining and farming diversified. Immigration and the birth-rate caused the White population to grow almost as rapidly as the Black. A far more serious cloud on the horizon was the growing post-war nationalism and racialism of the indigenous inhabitants of the Empire, particularly in Africa and southern Asia, causing Britain and France, under the added pressure of American anti-imperial policy, to grant independence to their Colonies. In 1960, there was Black rioting in both South Africa and Rhodesia, and at the end of June the Belgian Congo was suddenly granted independence, resulting in horrific social chaos and massacres of its White population, causing a flood of Belgian refugees southwards through the Federation, on their way to South Africa. Similar horrors erupted in the adjoining Portuguese colony of Angola, where, among other things, Europeans were fed through a saw-mill. In the same year, at a Commonwealth Heads of Government Conference in London, both the South African Prime Minister, Verwoerd, and the Rhodesian Federal Prime Minister, Welensky,[1] found their presence made untenable by the hostility of the leaders of the new Afro-Asian bloc. Early in the following year, South Africa withdrew from the Commonwealth, and at the end of May proclaimed itself a republic. For English-speaking South Africans, this meant the automatic termination of their regal contract.

As independence advanced southwards in Africa, borne on an emotional tide, so also, Black nationalist movements grew in the Federation and South Africa, with London providing a liberal-minded haven for activists on the run. In Northern Rhodesia and Nyasaland, the nationalist movements had enjoyed the tacit support of the British Colonial Service, which had bitterly resented Southern Rhodesia's growing influence in the region. In particular, the Service was acutely aware of the conflict of interest between its own dedication to the eventual independence of the region under majority African rule, and what it saw as the establishment

1   Welensky attended on the basis of Southern Rhodesia's *de facto* status as an independent British Dominion.

of the permanent dominance of Central Africa by a Southern Rhodesia under White rule.

Alarmed at the overall political situation, and the embarrassment that it was causing to Britain's own international position, particularly in relation to the new Commonwealth, now brought to a head by nationalist mob violence in Nyasaland, which eventually had to be put down by the Southern Rhodesian army,[2] Great Britain – now under the Conservative Premiership of Harold Macmillan – withdrew the two northern territories from the Federation in 1963, thereby terminating it. Adding a deliberate insult, in Southern Rhodesia's eyes, Britain granted immediate independence to both Northern Rhodesia and Nyasaland, under the new names of Zambia and Malawi, while reversing the legal status of Southern Rhodesia, which was entitled to resume its previous status as a *de facto* independent Dominion under the Crown, to that of a British Crown Colony, until such time as it also agreed to Black majority rule. While this may have been possible according to statute law, it was not possible in common law, and caused a strong reaction of bitterness and sense of betrayal on Rhodesia's part, which now saw itself as a disposable pawn in Britain's efforts to restore its own influence in the new Commonwealth.

Meanwhile, South Africa, no longer a participant in the regal contract, made preparations for conflict with the rest of the world by developing an armaments industry and establishing itself as the world's fourth nuclear power. Relations between itself and Rhodesia remained cool, however, because South Africa's Afrikaner majority was still inclined to regard Rhodesia as part of the former British strategy of encirclement.

42.3. Rhodesian Independence

According to a persistent rumour circulating in Rhodesian Government circles since the Second World War, Churchill, who was then the British Prime Minister, had in 1940 personally offered independent Dominion status to the Southern Rhodesian Prime Minister, Sir Godfrey Huggins, in recognition of his country's exceptional military commitment to the war effort, in relation to its resources, as well as its offer of aircrew training

---

2   The Nyasaland Police having ceased to be effective.

facilities. Huggins is said to have declined the offer, on the ground that Southern Rhodesia 'had no need of it'. As Huggins had pointed out, it would have involved the country in substantial costs, which it could ill-afford, to provide for the additional international diplomatic representation around the world. It already conducted its own *de facto* diplomatic relations with its neighbours, South Africa and Portuguese Mozambique, which was all that was required for the time being. The Rhodesian economy had grown substantially since then. The country had inherited the high standards of Queen Victoria's reign, and Huggins had been a product of the English public schools, like Churchill, with a profound belief in the integrity of English gentlemen who ruled in the Westminster corridors of power. But 1940 had belonged to a different world, and, if the rumour was well founded, as it probably was, Rhodesia was now to pay heavily for its nonchalance.

Rhodesia's reaction to the granting of independence to its two northern neighbours was to demand Britain's recognition of its own. With the return of a British Labour Government in 1964, however, led by Harold Wilson, an avowed antagonist of Empire, and particularly of Rhodesia and South Africa, Rhodesia regarded its new position as morally and practically intolerable. Its political status was unique, in that it had founded and governed itself from the outset, developing its economy through its own efforts, with little more than the formal approval of Queen Victoria and her successors, with whom its relationship had been founded by the status of its settlers as participants, by inherited right, in the regal contract. In two world wars, it had contributed military service and other facilities out of all proportion to the size of its settler population. Since its founding, therefore, it had fallen outside the legal jurisdiction of the Sovereign's British Government. Such financial benefit as Rhodesia had received from the Crown, notably in the settlement of the Company's administrative debts in 1923, had been more than repaid by the transfer of ownership of Northern Rhodesia and the acquisition by Britain of ownership of unalienated lands in Southern Rhodesia. The Colonial Office had long sought to include Rhodesia in its colonial administrative system, hence its insistence that Southern Rhodesia accept the status of 'Crown Colony', yet nothing in the settlement of 1923, even an agreement in respect of Rhodesia's treatment of Natives, had involved any actual transfer of government, making the settlement essentially a treaty between equals under the Crown, which was represented at this time by King George V. Effectively, therefore, Rhodesia had always been, and remained, in common law, an independent British dominion under the Crown.

The dissolution of the Federation, meanwhile, had marked the drawing up of battle-lines between the newly independent Black states to the north of the Zambezi, which had established themselves, by treaty, as the Organization of African Unity (OAU), whose chief purpose at this time was the eradication from Africa of all remaining forms of colonial rule, which it deemed to include the rule of European minority governments. It was the policy of the OAU to further this by promoting incursions into Southern Africa by groups of armed 'freedom fighters', who were regarded by their opponents as mere 'terrorists', not least because of their barbarous treatment of women and children. Continuing attempts by the Rhodesian Government to secure Britain's recognition of its independence, which greatly affected Rhodesia's international position – for example, in its ability to raise foreign loans, or enter into formal treaties – made no progress in the face of the British Government's condition that Rhodesia must first grant universal adult suffrage, tantamount in Rhodesia's view to the political and economic suicide of its White population. The British Government took the view that it had a 'duty of care' towards Rhodesia's native inhabitants, based on its view that the country was a British colony, in accordance with feudal doctrine, but this was, of course, at variance with common law.

Adding gunpowder to the cocktail, Russia now perceived an opportunity to further the downfall of South Africa and Rhodesia (which now jettisoned 'Southern' from its name), Russia's objective being, it was widely believed, to achieve control of South Africa and use its industrial base for the subversion of South America, and later Central America, in what would amount to an outflanking of the 'capitalist' Western world. To this end, and avoiding a confrontation with the United States, Russia now promoted, indoctrinated and armed terrorist 'freedom' movements in the Portuguese colonies, most notably in Angola, on the west coast, and Mozambique on the east coast, of Southern Africa. These would provide Russia with access to South Africa. Meanwhile, the United States, the standard-bearer for democratic independence movements, now became alarmed at the opportunity that the situation offered to Communist expansion, and, perceiving a need to remove the main source of regional tension, adopted a policy of reducing South Africa by promoting liberal subversion from within. To this end it seems to have courted South Africa's ambassador to the United States, a converted liberal named 'Pik' Botha. Under successive Prime Ministers, the South African cabinet was infiltrated by liberals who were not even members of the governing Nationalist Party.

Meanwhile, with no progress being made, or in prospect, the Rhodesian Government finally, in November of 1965, issued a formal and unilateral declaration of Rhodesia's independence, popularly known as 'UDI', while at the same time reaffirming its loyalty to the Queen.[3] Taking advice from her British Prime Minister, however, the Queen saw her position in terms of feudal doctrine, and in keeping with this, in an address delivered at a meeting of the Commonwealth Parliamentary Union in Jamaica, early in the following year, she gave her full support to that advice. By so doing, she renounced her regal contract with the Rhodesian people. The fact that the Rhodesian Prime Minister had declared his country's continuing loyalty to the Queen, indicated quite clearly that the spat was between the Queen's two governments, and did not involve the Queen. This carried no weight in British legal thinking, because Rhodesia's position as a Dominion had not yet been through the statutory process of establishment. The point has already been made that the status of British territories overseas is not subject to Parliament, in which they are not represented, except in respect of any monetary benefits paid by the British taxpayer, to whom Rhodesia was not in debt. Indeed, Rhodesia's status in relation to the Sovereign was not the concern of the British Government, beyond the offering of advice where it believed its own interest was affected. The assumption of Dominion status, already clearly implied during the inter-war years, with the tacit recognition of all parties, could not now be changed by the Queen's British Government. Her Rhodesian Government had already made it clear that its loyalty to Queen Elizabeth was not in question, and she was bound to follow its advice in the matter, not the advice of her British Prime Minister. Unlike the American colonies and South Africa before her, therefore, Rhodesia

3   UDI, short for Unilateral Declaration of Independence.

had asserted its independence from British Government interference, but not its regal contract with the Queen. It was the Queen who had severed this, causing Rhodesia to fall outside the scope of this book.

In the eyes of the British Government, which saw the crisis in terms of feudal doctrine, Rhodesia had committed treason against the Crown and was regarded, therefore, like the American colonies and the *Afrikaners* of South Africa, as guilty of a criminal act. The British Prime Minister at the time, Wilson, was advised by Britain's military commanders that the use of force might involve Britain in another bitter conflict, like the earlier South African war, and that on this occasion the sympathies of the British armed forces lay with the Rhodesians. Wilson was accordingly persuaded to limit Britain's punitive response to the imposition of economic sanctions.

What the Western liberal establishment failed, or chose, not to recognise in reality, was that what it was demanding in Southern Africa was not just an extension of the franchise, but a complete displacement of one society by another. In South Africa, which had a relatively much larger White population, the extension of the franchise would result in the displacement of White society by Black society, and with it all political power and all but a very small proportion of South African employment. In Rhodesia, it resulted, as many had anticipated, in the complete obliteration of White society. One of South Africa's Prime Ministers, Hendrik Verwoerd, had foreseen what was coming and attempted to solve the problem on both sides by his *apartheid* policy, which was based on social and political separation, but equal economic and political opportunity for both races. This was not radical enough to suit either the Black nationalists or South Africa's critics, and he was assassinated before he could fully implement the policy.

The demise of South Africa and Rhodesia was all but fatal for the British Commonwealth of Nations. Hitherto, the two African members had held it together by completing the bond across the world, between Canada and Australasia. Britain's decision to merge with the European Union was all but disastrous for what remained of the British community of nations. Britain's later decision to back out of the EU helped to sustain what remained of the British Commonwealth, but the damage was done, and its members now looked largely to their individual futures.

Meanwhile, its successor, the new Commonwealth of mainly non-White states, now deprived of its *raison d'être* – the destruction of White Southern Africa – gradually faded away.

42.4. The Remnants of Empire

Following the relinquishment of most of its Empire, Britain found itself left with a number of minor territories, most of which had been acquired for their strategic importance. Their role had greatly diminished as the Empire was dissolved. While some had been unoccupied and unclaimed, and some had been the object of British settlement, they were usually too small to support their own independence, and in some cases, such as Gibraltar and Cyprus, their strategic importance had not entirely been lost with the end of Empire. Meanwhile, the Government had, in 1966, combined the Colonial Office with the Commonwealth Relations Office, which now functioned as the Commonwealth Office. This rearrangement was pursued further in 1968, with the amalgamation of the latter with the Foreign Office, to produce the Foreign and Commonwealth Office (FCO). This undoubtedly saved administrative expense, but the effect was all but disastrous for the remaining British territories, because the Foreign Office never had much interest in the Empire, and now even less with what was left over. Worse still, it had little aptitude for colonial administration, which it saw as a distraction from its proper role of conducting relations with foreign powers. Not only had it little interest in these waifs and strays of the Imperial Age, but it was still gripped by the 'anti-Empire' mentality of the 1960s and 70s, and quickly discovered that its new colonial liabilities were a serious complication of its diplomatic interests, particularly in respect of its relations with such countries as Spain, China and Argentina.

At best, these remaining territories suffered from neglect, and at worst, the FCO did its best to manipulate affairs in such a way as to get rid of them. Its negligence was helped by the attitude of the British Establishment of the day, which also regarded the Empire as an embarrassment to be forgotten, in keeping with liberalist sentiment, whereas the new multi-racial Commonwealth was regarded as an achievement to be celebrated. One consequence was a long-running crisis over the future of Gibraltar, which was seen as getting in the way of relations with Spain. Another was the status of British Somaliland, which had been off-loaded onto Somalia, the former Italian Somaliland, whose incompetence and religious fanaticism had quickly persuaded the former British colony to assert its independence under the name of Somaliland, which the Foreign Office refused to recognise. Shunned by the rest of the world, in consequence, Somaliland struggled, drawing upon what was left of its British heritage, not only to survive, but to set it apart as a contrast to the poverty and chaos of Somalia.

This irresponsibility of the Foreign Office was nowhere more evident than in its relations with the Falkland Islands and their British inhabitants, who could rightly claim the Queen's protection under the regal contract. Anxious to offload them, surreptitiously, to an ambitious Argentina, albeit three hundred miles away, the delays and intrigues resulting from a negligent British Government caused the Argentinians to lose patience and mount a military invasion of the Falklands and South Georgia in 1982. Luckily for their inhabitants and Britain's own longer-term interests, the Prime Minister at the time was Margaret Thatcher, the only Prime Minister since Churchill – and possibly Sir Anthony Eden – who still valued Britain's imperial legacy. By a further stroke of good fortune, Britain had not quite finished disposing of its capacity for long range military operations, in consequence of which, and using Ascension Island in the South Atlantic as a staging base, a brief but costly military campaign saw the re-conquest of the Falklands and South Georgia, and the return of their British inhabitants to the protection of the Crown. That the achievement was rammed home to make it politically, as well as militarily, decisive was due to Thatcher's decision to sink the Argentine cruiser, *Belgrano*, with great loss of life. It posed no significant threat, but its loss had a further salutary effect on Argentine ambitions. The critical importance of Ascension Island to the re-capture of the Falklands was an example of the contingent strategic value of such apparently 'useless' islands and other minor territories around the world, another being the Chagos Islands in the Indian Ocean, whose value was quickly perceived by the Americans, who were granted a lease. It was a reminder also that Britain still had an Empire, however small. It was, indeed, these scattered remnants of Empire, rather than the troublesome new Commonwealth, that allowed Great Britain to continue to assert itself as a world power.

These relics of Empire, now known as the British Overseas Territories, fourteen in all, and mostly small islands, were scattered around the globe. They were either unable to support the requirements of independence, and therefore were glad to remain under British protection, being allowed such self-government as was practicable, or they were uninhabited and at risk of occupation by unfriendly powers, who might well make use of them for aggressive purposes. The exception was the British military base on Cyprus, at Akrotiri and Dhekelia, a Crown territory agreed with Cyprus at the time of its independence. The inhabitants of these British Overseas Territories were, in some cases, British settlers within the regal contract, the largest of these being the Falkland Islands in the South Atlantic. Fortunately, the unsuitability of the Foreign and Commonwealth Office as guardian of Britain's remaining territories was eventually recognised, causing the responsibility for them to be transferred to a new, and still unsuitable department, because of its lack of focus, that of the Minister of State for the Commonwealth and the United Nations.

The British Overseas Territories did not include the previous Crown Dependencies, that is, the Channel Islands and the Isle of Man and the British Antarctic Territory.

43. REACTION TO THE IMPERIAL AGE

ALL GREAT MOVEMENTS in history are followed, inevitably, by an opposite reaction, which, in the case of the Imperial Age, gained momentum with the beginning of the new millennium. It began with the onset of official amnesia, during which the celebration of imperial achievements and even the preserving of official records of an age that had extended over five hundred years and given rise to the modern industrial and scientific world were either relegated to official amnesia or overlooked in lecture theatres. As new generations appeared that had no personal recollection of it, and were only too glad of an opportunity to teach their elders, the reaction progressed further, with an effort physically to destroy all commemoration of imperial events. This was made easier by locating imperial events that could be seen as discreditable and giving them a new significance. Amongst some, the reaction took a physical form, with the desecration of monuments and tarnishing of reputations that had been honoured for a century and more.

The end of the Imperial Age inevitably gave rise to an ideological reaction against it several decades later, particularly amongst members of the up-and-coming generation. The importance of the Imperial Age to Western Civilization can hardly be over-stated, however. Inevitable in itself, following the introduction of new commodities from the East, in response to the Crusades, it had led to the establishment of exploration and trading contacts, which precipitated the growth of European empires that swept aside many local cultures and opened them to Western influence, not least in the spread of Western languages, ideas and technology. The spread of Black slavery to America, seen as the biggest black-spot of imperialism, nevertheless, through the ensuing development of trade in cotton, in particular, was one of the biggest factors in the development of the Industrial Age and the ensuing Agricultural Revolution, accompanied by the Scientific Revolution, which gave Britain world leadership and the gradual spread of worldwide prosperity. Without the Imperial Age, it is probably safe to conclude that Western Europe is unlikely to have remained much as it was in the fifteenth century. Travel outside Europe would have continued to be difficult and risky, and would have needed an acquaintance with a number of languages. Many – sometimes abhorrent – cultural and religious practices around the world would have continued, with localised warfare and hostility to outsiders. Sub-tropical and tropical diseases would have continued to make travel hazardous. Our concern, however, is with the constitutional history of England and Great Britain, and of the latter's overseas Empire, as it has developed in the context of wider history. Sober judgement would return in due course, but it had long been a feature of modern history that the moral digestion of important events gave rise to counter-events that were often destructive.

PART XV

•

THE COMMONS APPROPRIATE
THE HOUSE OF LORDS

44. POST-IMPERIAL GOVERNMENT

44.1. The Life and Death Instincts of Society

Like individuals, all human societies are seen by some as imbued with a life instinct and a death instinct, and when one is in the ascendancy, the other is suppressed. The functioning of the constitution can be as much affected by this as the society that it orders. The life instinct is expressed in social optimism and even euphoria, a notable example being the Imperial Age, which lasted from about 1880 until about 1939; another being what has sometimes been described as 'rampant capitalism', which the United States experienced on a grand scale. The expression of the death instinct, which leads to self-destruction, is more subdued. The one instinct often gives way to the other. Both instincts rose to the surface, one after the other, in National Socialist Germany, for example. Prime examples of a society succumbing to the death instinct, after finding themselves in an impossible situation, are provided by Rhodesia in 1979, which had previously experienced an exuberance of the life instinct, and White South Africa, which in despair committed political suicide in 1990, as also did the Soviet Union, when both countries had found themselves in a seemingly impossible position. The expression of both instincts obviously has profound constitutional implications.

44.2. Reform of the Civil and Criminal Courts (1971)

The distinction between civil and criminal appeals, which had been dealt with by the Courts of Appeal and Criminal Appeal, respectively, was ended in 1966, when the Court of Criminal Appeal was incorporated into the Court of Appeal. Although there was now only the Court of Appeal, it continued to recognise the difference between civil and criminal cases by dividing its work between a Civil Division and a Criminal Division.

The basis of the distinction between criminal and civil cases has long been forgotten and is only partly understood. This is illustrated by the statement of an eminent authority that: 'The Criminal justice system exists to help protect us from crime, and to ensure that criminals are punished. The Civil justice system is there to help people resolve their disputes fairly and peacefully'.[1] The use of the words 'crime' and 'criminals' merely begs the question. Nor is it a distinction between statutory and common law offences, even though this may often be the case. As we concluded earlier, in the context of Anglo-Saxon justice, the distinction between a criminal and a civil offence appears to have continued, from the Middle Ages onwards, recapitulating the Early English distinction between an offence against the King's peace, which poses a threat to the Crown or to public order, and one that does not, such as a private dispute between individuals. The King, with the approval of a Parliament, defines certain offences as posing a threat, in which case the King is deemed to have jurisdiction, exercisable through the Crown courts, which are accordingly defined as 'criminal' courts. Those offences that he does not regard as a threat to his peace, such as breaches of contract and issues of negligence, he leaves to individuals to settle in 'civil' courts. It follows that the distinction between criminal and civil offences is to a large extent arbitrary, and not necessarily fixed.

The rearrangement of the appeal system was followed in 1971, on the criminal side, by the Courts Act, which created the Crown Court. This was a superior court to try criminal cases, which were to be forwarded to it after they had been the subject of a preliminary investigation in the magistrates' courts. The Crown Court was also empowered to pass sentence on those persons who had been convicted by a magistrates' court of a summary offence, that is, one of a less serious nature that did not require the full formalities normally demanded in common law. The Court was also required to hear appeals by persons convicted by the magistrates' courts of a summary offence. The Crown Court was regarded as part of the Supreme Court of Judicature, along with the High Court, with its Divisions of Queen's Bench, Chancery, and Family. All were, of course, Crown or royal courts, presided over as judge by the King or his

1   Lord Irvine of Lairg, Lord Chancellor, *Modernising Justice* (1998).

representative, as opposed to the old traditional courts, so that the title of the new Crown Court was confusing.

Appeals from the Crown Court, and from the Central Criminal Court, which served the Greater London area, were heard by the Criminal Division of the Court of Appeal. Its Civil Division heard appeals from the High Court and the County Courts. Appeals beyond the Court of Appeal to the House of Lords were permitted only where important points of law were seen to be at stake.

By now, appeals to the House of Lords were heard by it in the form of one of two Appellate Committees of the House, presided over by the Lord Chancellor. Their recommendations to the House were still delivered in the full Chamber, since it was the House of Lords that was still the court, but the procedure had degenerated to the point where the House was no longer addressed, the formal judgement of the House being taken for granted, so that it was now simply delivered by the members of the Committee to the parties involved in the case and their legal counsel in the form of a printed document. It was apparently accepted that, so long as the conclusions of the Appellate Committee were delivered to the parties in the Chamber, and nowhere else, the judicial authority of the House of Lords was preserved, which, undoubtedly cannot have been the case in common law. As a symptom of the permanence of the House of Lords (unlike the Commons), its Appellant Committees heard appeals at any time, including during adjournments of the House, and regardless of whether Parliament was prorogued or dissolved. The one important exception to the House's jurisdiction was in respect of Scottish criminal cases.

The division between Scottish and English law was also reflected in the fact that the jurisdiction of the Lord Chancellor did not extend to Scotland. Similarly, whereas the interests of the Crown before the English and Welsh courts were represented by the Attorney General and the Solicitor-General, in Scotland they were represented by the Lord Advocate and the Solicitor-General of Scotland.

44.3. Devolution and Regionalisation

During the height of the Imperial Age, the United Kingdom had been held together by a sense of common purpose and common benefit, engendered by the territorial expansion and economic development of the Empire.

Indeed, the union of England and Scotland may not have occurred, but for the obvious success of the English Empire, which Scotland had failed miserably to emulate. Consequently, when the Empire collapsed, so also did the sense of common benefit and purpose. Having lost her chief reason for the union, Scotland was inclined to turn in on herself once again, and this reawakened Welsh national sentiments. Nationalist movements in Scotland and Wales accordingly demanded a measure of self-government, while some in Scotland sought outright separation. Irish nationalists in Northern Ireland sensed a coming break-up of the United Kingdom and embarked upon a new campaign of terror, in their pursuit of their unification with Southern Ireland.

The other reason for the loosening of the bonds that held the United Kingdom together was its growing political integration with Continental Europe. England now seemed to be little more than an outlying province, ruled from Brussels, and the policy of Brussels was to promote regional devolution, on the principle of divide and rule. Minorities in Western Europe, such as the Bretons, Catalans, Welsh, Cornish and Scots, were given assistance by the European Union (EU) to promote their separate identities. This reviving sense of separateness was both geographical and cultural. The Celts inhabited the western margins – Ireland, Cornwall, Wales and Scotland, with the Scots separated from the English by Solway Firth and the Southern Uplands – making it relatively easy for them to rediscover a separate sense of identity.

In 1979, sensing an electoral opportunity, the Labour Government under Callaghan used local referendums to extend an offer of constitutional devolution to both Wales, which had not asked for it, and Scotland, which had. In Scotland there was only a small majority for home rule, well below the 40 per cent that had been specified for political change, and in Wales the offer was heavily defeated. Devolution was strongly opposed by the Conservatives, among whom the Unionist ideal was still strong, fearing that it would diminish Parliament and lead to a gradual break-up of the United Kingdom. Nearly two decades later, in September 1997, further referendums were held by the Blair Government, and this time there was a substantial majority in favour of devolution in Scotland and a marginal vote in its favour in Wales. In both cases, however, there was a substantial degree of apathy, reflected in the large numbers who failed to vote. In spite of this, the Government proceeded with legislation in the same year to grant a substantial devolution of powers to a Parliament in Scotland, to be established at Edinburgh, and a partial devolution to a similar National Assembly in Wales, for which Cardiff was chosen as the seat, thereby bringing Scotland and Wales into line with Northern Ireland. Devolution included a recognition of the Welsh and Gaelic languages for official purposes, alongside English.

It was notable how little interest the new Scottish and Welsh Assemblies displayed in restoring their countries' ancient traditions. Both opted for ultra-modern legislative buildings, with little in the way of ceremonial pageantry or symbolism beyond what already existed. In Scotland, it is possible that this anxiety to express modernity and egalitarianism was, to some extent, a symbolic rejection of the old order of Scotland's upper classes, which had always been blamed for the union with England in the first place. The only other evidence of an interest in national, as opposed to regional, identity seemed to come from a request for the return of the Scottish – originally Pictish – coronation stone, known as the Stone of Scone, about which it was said that 'wherever the stone should rest, a king of Scots would reign'. Yet there was no interest in a separate Scottish monarchy. This may have been a recognition that the Scottish identity was based on geography, rather than its own kinship and culture.

Meanwhile, Parliament at Westminster, with an estimated 80 per cent of its legislative function lost to the EU, shorn of its Imperial responsibilities, and with much of its remaining jurisdiction delegated to the Assemblies in Scotland, Wales and Northern Ireland, had become a shadow of its former self. Fortunately, it retained some important areas of jurisdiction, notably defence and foreign affairs – although even these were already under threat from the EU – and responsibility for education, health and infrastructure in England. This inevitably caused a reaction in England, based on the anomaly of Scottish, Welsh and Northern Irish governments, but no English government, giving rise to what became known as the 'West Lothian' question. This pointed to the anomaly that, under the new arrangement, Scottish and Welsh members of Parliament in Westminster continued to be involved in deciding domestic English issues, whereas Scottish, Welsh and Northern Irish domestic issues were now decided in their own Parliaments, giving rise to some agitation for the creation of an English Parliament.

This overlooked the historical reality, earlier noted, that the Parliament at Westminster was itself the English Parliament, with its jurisdiction and representation extended to cater for the entire United Kingdom. For the purpose of solely English issues, all that was required, therefore, was the withdrawal of Welsh, Northern Irish and Scottish members when such issues were under consideration. The confusion arose simply from the misunderstanding, self-induced, that, ever since the Union, the Parliament in Westminster had been used as a British Parliament, the only changes required being extensions of jurisdiction and representation. To establish an English Parliament would have provided England with two Parliaments. Rather than destroy the continuity of English constitutional history and long-established traditions, as well as creating a great deal of procedural confusion, it would have been unfortunate now to try to convert Westminster into a purely British assembly.

44.3.1. Intractability of the Irish Problem

The problem of Irish nationalism was not settled by the independence of Southern Ireland, or Éire, because it did not resolve the nationalist claim to all Ireland. Unable to persuade the Protestant majority in Northern Ireland to agree to unification, even though the British Government made clear its willingness to accede to such an arrangement if the majority in the province decided in favour of it, the nationalists embarked on a final effort to achieve union through a campaign of terror and non-cooperation. Faced with a breakdown of civil order, a state of emergency was declared in 1972, the provincial Government was dissolved, and the Conservative Government under Edward Heath imposed direct rule from Westminster. Such was the level of public disorder and violence in Northern Ireland that troops from the British Parachute Regiment, among others, were called in, only to give convincing evidence of the effectiveness of their military training and morale, as might reasonably have been expected, by promptly shooting aggressive individuals in the crowds of assailants who attacked them with gunfire and barrages of stones. The effect was political uproar from the assailants and dismay in the Government.

Meanwhile, Britain's Labour Party and the liberal Establishment generally, in keeping with their antipathy towards all relics or implications of Empire, were largely sympathetic to the Republican cause and barely hid their hostility towards the Protestants. Indeed, following the advent of a Labour Government under Harold Wilson, from 1974, the Protestants found themselves as much vilified by the British Establishment as were the British communities in Africa.

By 1998 it was clear to the Irish nationalists that they were getting nowhere in the struggle and, more importantly, they were losing the support of both the Catholics in Éire and the Catholic Irish in America, who had been their chief source of funding. No less importantly, American sympathy as a whole had swung against them. A partial 'cease-fire' was arranged, but negotiations dragged on until the whole situation was transformed in September 2001, when an Arab terrorist group launched a devastating attack on buildings in New York and Washington. The American reaction was to outlaw all forms of terrorism around the world, leaving the Irish nationalists isolated and confused. By 2005, the leadership had renounced violence, in favour of negotiating for the best concessions possible. The return to normality was slow, however, and the restoration of a devolved Government of Northern Ireland in 2007 soon fell apart, because the nationalists refused to participate in the constitutional process. This was then suspended, and Northern Ireland was again ruled on a temporary basis from Westminster.

44.3.2. The EU Attempts to Undermine the System of National Governments

The European Union, meanwhile, with the aid of the Government, promoted a system of regions and regional governments that ignored traditional boundaries, evidently in the hope that eventually this would replace and erase the existing pattern of national identities, and in so doing undermine the influence of national governments within the Union. One such region, for example, comprised large areas of south-eastern England and northern France, ignoring the disruption caused by the English Channel. The policy met with considerable public opposition and gradually ceased to be promoted. The EU took the view that nationalism had been the basic cause of Europe's wars, and the solution was to oppose and weaken national identities in favour of an alternative scheme that was based on geographical regions and the promotion of older, largely forgotten, ethnic communities.

The partial devolution of legislative and executive authority to Northern Ireland, Scotland and Wales was not unrelated, therefore, to the regional decentralisation of power that Brussels had been promoting, perhaps as a means of undermining the influence of national governments to which the EU Commission in Brussels was subject. While the EU sought a devolution of powers by national governments to such ethnic minorities as the Bretons and Corsicans in France, the Basques and Catalans in Spain, the South Tyroleans in Italy, the Flemings in Belgium, and the Cornish in England, it also favoured a system of regional governments, even where there were no ethnic considerations. By this means, the bureaucracy hoped to by-pass national governments by directly funding regional governments. Thus, England, Scotland and Wales were to be subdivided between regional governments, initially with very limited powers.

Apart from promoting devolution to the member states of the United Kingdom, the Blair government tried to further this idea by establishing regional assemblies, without, at this stage, abolishing the County Councils. The first attempt at implementing this policy ran into opposition. A proposed Council for the North-East was overwhelmingly opposed in a regional referendum, which was swayed by a popular belief that the policy would merely add to the bureaucratic structure and the tax burden, while having little to offer in return. There was simply not the geographical or ethnic basis for such regional authorities in England, and it was clear that the ancient shire basis of local government was more popular than had been realised.

The regionalisation policy was dropped, at least for the time being, but it soon began to be resurrected by means of a different tactic. According to this, the services provided by County Councils would be regionalised, starting with the police. Regional political bodies could then follow, or so it was widely suspected, leaving the County Councils redundant. Thus, a proposal was submitted in 2005 to regionalise the country's police forces, ostensibly to make them more effective through closer coordination and a greater centralisation of specialist facilities. In place of the County

Constabularies, a system of half a dozen or so regional police forces was accordingly promoted, but this also faced public opposition. Few, if any, Chief Constables believed that regionalisation of the police would improve its effectiveness. Indeed, it was alleged by opponents of the scheme that one of the reasons for the high level of crime had been the excessive centralisation already imposed upon the police by the County Constabularies, whereby local policing had been replaced by a more centrally based system of 'fire-brigade' operations.

44.4. Local Government – From Mega-Authorities to Joint Boards

The combined effect of population growth and inter-regional migration within Great Britain, meanwhile, had severely aggravated the problem of administering very large and sprawling urban and semi-urban areas, which no longer bore any relationship to district and county boundaries. The increasing complexity of local government services, and the mounting cost of equipment used to provide them, was also imposing a heavy burden on the highly centralised system of local government finance. Parliament had always been anxious to keep a tight reign over local government by controlling its finances, yet resented the cost to the Treasury. In addition to a parsimonious approach to local government subsidies, a long series of measures had been introduced, in order to reduce the burden by increasing the efficiency of these services. One policy had been to consolidate services into bigger and bigger units. This had called for three different approaches: the transfer of some functions from small local authorities to bigger ones; the integration of larger local authorities into still larger entities; and the transfer of some services from local government altogether to regional or even nationwide statutory bodies. Thus, docks and harbours and hospitals were nationalised in 1946, electrical generation and distribution in 1948, and gasworks in 1949.

The Local Government Boundary Commission Act of 1945 had established a formal, coherent and ongoing basis for the adjustment and amalgamation of local government areas. London had been excluded from its terms of reference, because it was so much larger than the other cities and its rights were entrenched in ancient charters. The stated purpose of the Boundary Commission had been to ensure the maintenance or creation of effective and convenient units of local government administration. Where local government changes were proposed, they were subject to open enquiry, at which the views of all parties concerned, including the financial implications, were to be heard and taken into account.

Later, the Local Government Act of 1972 established six 'metropolitan counties' of Greater Manchester, Merseyside, South Yorkshire, Tyne and Wear, West Midlands, and West Yorkshire. Because these were predominantly urban complexes with economic, social and political identities of their own, they were carved out of the existing counties, and the effect was particularly noticeable where they spread across the county boundaries. Certain lesser, but important, urban centres were established as new 'counties'. Thus, north-eastern Somerset, centred on Bristol, was excised as the new county of Avon. In addition, a number of county boundaries were altered and certain counties were amalgamated, all in the interests of greater administrative efficiency. Meanwhile, the distinction between Urban and Rural Districts disappeared, so that all were now Districts, administered by District Councils. In Scotland, a corresponding Act in the following year referred to 'regions', rather than to districts. The effect of these monolithic structures, subsidised and controlled from Westminster, soon gave rise to a feeling that English local government was suffering from an excess of bureaucracy, which was causing a different type of inefficiency, obscuring responsibility and making the process of decision-making cumbersome. In an attempt to free the system, a further Act of 1985 abolished the Metropolitan County Councils, replacing them with Joint Boards and transferring some of their functions to their constituent districts, with a remnant going to a residuary body for each county. Thus, the local government structure was now based on two tiers of elected authorities: the District Councils formed the lower level, and the County Councils and Metropolitan Joint Boards comprised the upper level.

Thus, the historic shire structure of government in England was increasingly ignored, or was changed to fit the new local government structure. It is difficult to prognosticate on this without detailed study, but the basic principle that national – or traditional shire – boundaries should determine the shape and extent of the local government system would seem to be a fundamental requirement, consistent with the Constitution.

The parishes continued to exist in England as local government entities, but the church parishes had long since been duplicated by civic parishes, with the boundaries of the latter often differing from the boundaries of the church parishes, due to practical considerations. Consequently, each parish either held a parish council or a parish meeting of local government electors to discuss local matters. The latter could still exercise certain limited powers, such as the provision of allotments, recreation grounds, or bus shelters, aligning local boundaries with long-established local sentiments, and removing the administrative muddle that had grown up over the years.

London was excluded from the general process of local government reform, on the grounds of its 'unique problems'. Its separate treatment undoubtedly owed much to its political importance since the Middle Ages as the seat of the great Livery Companies, as a maker and breaker of Kings, and as a source of direct pressure on Parliament. Westminster liked to feel that it could control London, or at least keep it divided and so less likely to be a political nuisance. It may well have been for this reason that the City of London had not been allowed to grow with the city as a whole, but had been overtaken in 1888 by the creation of a separate London County Council. The first major reform of local government in Greater London came in 1963, when the London County Council was abolished and replaced by an enlarged and more centralised body, known as the Greater London Council (GLC), which appropriated yet more of the adjoining counties of Middlesex, Essex, Kent, and Surrey. Intended to increase efficiency and coordination, it suffered from two serious defects. Its sheer size and centralisation made it bureaucratic and inefficient, removing local responsibility and inducing a sharp drop in the morale of professional staff. It also emerged as a political embarrassment to the Labour Governments that had created it, because it fell under the control of radical and often irresponsible groups within the Labour Party, popularly referred to as the 'Loony Left', which tended to set the GLC in direct opposition to Conservative Governments, which, in turn, regarded it as an insufferable provocation. That irresponsible people can take control of a democratic body is normally an indication of popular apathy, implying that the body is not regarded as being appropriate to its purpose. The GLC also used its position to exert pressure on the Government of the day, on matters which lay well outside the competence of the Council, and mostly for a wider propaganda effect that sometimes gave rise to diplomatic embarrassment. Because the GLC proved to be such a political liability, and because it was such an inefficient organisation administratively, the Conservative Government of 1979, under Margaret Thatcher, undertook its further reform in 1986. The Greater London Council was abolished, and its powers returned to its former Metropolitan Boroughs. Only certain planning functions were retained on a common basis. Seven years later, County Hall, the seat of London's administration since 1908, situated by the Thames at Lambeth, significantly and provocatively opposite the Palace of Westminster, was ignominiously sold to a private property company.

Such a dismemberment of the edifice that it had created was unlikely to survive the next Labour Government, whose socialist ideals have typically favoured big, centralised bodies, directly responsible to itself in Parliament. In any case, a centralised London authority was inevitably under the control of Labour voters, whose political power could be used, even when Labour was out of office at Westminster. This apart, there was a need for the more effective coordination of Greater London's development. Blair's Labour Ministry of 1997 accordingly – a year later – set up a new body for Greater London, this time under a directly elected Mayor with wide-ranging powers. This adoption of American practice would, it was hoped, by placing responsibility more clearly on the shoulders of one person, bring about a more responsible and coherent approach to the management of London's affairs.

A basic weakness of local government in Greater London was the lack of any real sense of local identity, leading to low electoral turnouts and persistent rule by local radical minorities. At least part of the explanation is not far to seek. London had two origins, of which the more important initially, was *Lundenwic*, established as a port and centre of trade in the vicinity of the Strand in Anglo-Saxon times. The other was the City of London, which, from the Middle Ages onwards, assumed greater significance because, being opposite London Bridge, it was the centre of the road system for south-east England. In both cases, London was located on the north bank of the lower Thames, in what was east Middlesex, a little west of the confluence of the River Lea with the Thames. It has since expanded into four shires, that is to say, north of the Thames, into much of its native east Middlesex and also, from the Lea, into south-west Essex. South of the Thames, it extends over north-east Surrey and, from and including Deptford, over north-west Kent. Each of these extensions of London have remained constitutionally in their respective shires and would appear, properly, to have retained their representation in their respective shire councils, as well as separate parliamentary representation for each shire within the London conurbation, leaving appropriate scope for a co-ordinating body for the conurbation as a whole.

In spite of the conjunction in 2001 of another Labour Government and a new Labour-controlled Greater London, the two were soon in conflict, particularly over plans for the overhaul of the London underground railway system. Once again, for good or ill, London was proving its capacity to be a thorn in the side of Westminster. Meanwhile, the ancient City of London continued its semi-autonomous existence under its own Lord Mayor, protected by its many royal charters.

44.5. Appropriation of the Work of the Civil Service

At a practical level, the day-to-day government of the realm and the tendering of advice to the appropriate Minister is the function of the Civil Service, which requires a high standard of recruitment at the senior level, in keeping with the reforms adopted from the Indian Civil Service in the nineteenth century, except that the making of policy is the prerogative of Ministers. Unfortunately, standards of selection fell during the twentieth century, in the face of parliamentary policy, which

    a. demanded that the selection of entrants to the senior Civil Service should be guided as much by egalitarian principles as by suitability and competence, and

    b. appropriated more and more of the work of the Civil Service in order to satisfy the growing demand of Parliamentarians for Ministerial office.

Historically, Ministers were drawn from the senior, more able and experienced members of the Second Estate and – prior to the Norman invasion – the more able of the King's thanes. The latter had subsequently been driven to effective extinction by the Conquest, but the lesson was obvious, that all men of standing, who had proved their ability and loyalty in public office, were potential candidates for the Ministry. For centuries, these requirements had been followed, at least, when the Kings themselves had been fit for office. Failures of judgement in the choice of Ministers had once been reduced by the practice of referring such appointments to the advice of the Great Council. Since its confinement, it was the Privy Council that had acted as an alternative source of advice. As the Parties in Parliament had increasingly assumed the functions of the Crown, they had laid claim to Ministerial offices. Consequently, their terms in office were dependent upon the life of Parliament, and usually much less, as inept Ministers came and went.

This was a process, not a revolution, but its beginning can probably be associated with the acceptance, from 1902 onwards, of the principle that all Prime Ministers should be appointed from the House of Commons, making them products of the Party system. It would increasingly lead to a change in the nature of the House of Commons itself, from an assembly elected to represent the interests of the people, to an assembly of aspiring candidates for Ministerial office, decided according to their political orientation, rather than executive ability, of which most had little. The effect was the desire to exercise actual political power, resulting increasingly in the takeover of the direction of the Civil Service, from trained and experienced officials to inexperienced and often quite unsuitable members of Parliament.

44.6. Judicial Review

The task of applying the law falls to the executive arm of government and to the judiciary, both of which are answerable to the King, in his capacity as head of the Executive.[2] It was noted earlier that, under feudal doctrine, the actions of the Executive are covered by two principles, namely, that:

---

2   Much of the following is drawn from various sources, but particularly from A. W. Bradley, and K. D. Ewing, *Constitutional and Administrative Law,*; also, H. Barnett, *Constitutional*

1. the King can do no wrong, therefore he cannot be held liable for any action that would be unlawful if committed by a private individual.
2. the King cannot sue himself, therefore, he cannot be sued in the courts.

The issue lies between the King and God alone.

Although early Kings got away with a great deal, no satisfactory evidence of either principle has been found in the Aryan constitutional tradition, or in common law, which are really the same thing. On the contrary, the common law of the Constitution declares, fairly conclusively, that the King and his officers are equally subject to the law. In the absence of the Great Council, however, there is no legal procedure that would enable the King (or an elected Government) to be called to account. Accordingly, the only remedy available is a petition to the King, seeking redress. Officers who break the law of their own volition are subject to the normal course of the law, as was illustrated by the first known impeachment in 1376. Otherwise, as we now know, the King's officers, in the course of their duty, are answerable, like the King, to the Great Council, sitting in its judicial capacity. This is because the Council is the court of justice for the Second Estate, as well as being the guardian of the Constitution. An offence by the King against the law is a violation of his regal contract, rendering him liable to be deposed. This is unlikely in present circumstances, however, if only because the Great Council is no longer remembered. It is no longer known, in any case, who in the House of Lords are the Councillors, because they have not been elected in modern times. Nevertheless, the authority still resides in the Council in a latent form. Only by the hereditary greater baronage in the Lords, acting in unison, could it be held that a decision of the Council has been made. This leaves the King's officers in a difficult position, bound by their loyalty to the King, but personally liable for breaching the law.

The Crown Proceedings Act of 1947 sought a way around this problem of calling Governments to account, by making a distinction between the King and the Crown, so that the latter could be held liable in matters of both tort and contract.[3] The Act provided that civil proceedings

---

and Administrative Law (London, 2004).

3   By 'tort' is meant those wrongs committed against another, other than breach of contract,

against the Crown should be instituted against the relevant Government department, or, in the absence of a department with clear responsibility, against the Attorney General or, in Scotland, against the Advocate General for Scotland. The Act made it possible for a private person who was offended by an administrative decision by a public authority to seek a ruling by the courts that the decision was *ultra vires*, that is to say, 'beyond the powers' granted to the King by statute. In common law, this would mean that was beyond any powers available to the King (whether through the *imperium* vested in him or by statute). Where the court accepted a plea of *ultra vires*, it could issue an injunction against the decision, or grant compensation for any damages suffered. An exception to the King's liability was in respect of actions by members of the armed forces while on duty or on premises used for the purposes of the armed forces. This immunity of the armed forces was abolished in 1987, but it can be revived in times of war or national emergency,[4] creating a very uncertain and unsatisfactory situation. In 1994, the House of Lords ruled that an injunction could be granted against a Minister personally.

This separation of the King and his Minister for the purposes of legal action is possible because the King has delegated his relevant authority to his Minister, and his Minister is subject to the courts in a way that the King is not. The King cannot be held responsible, in common law, for the decisions of his Minister, unless the latter can be shown to have acted on the express instructions of the King.

Various attempts have been made by the judiciary to define the Crown, particularly for the purpose of contracts. Lord Diplock saw the Crown as personifying the executive government of the country.[5] Lord Woolf concluded, in 1994, that the Crown 'has a legal personality. It can be appropriately described as a corporation sole or a corporation aggregate', comprising many persons and offices, and that 'The Crown can hold property and enter into contracts'.[6] On the other hand, the Crown cannot put itself in a position where it is prevented by the terms of a contract from performing its public duty, and if 'an agreement has

---

such as trespass, negligence, nuisance, or defamation, that entitle the aggrieved party to compensation – G. Rivlin, *Understanding the Law*, 2009.

4   The latter failed to be invoked during the Northern Ireland crisis, or during the Middle Eastern conflicts, placing the members of the armed forces in an almost untenable position.

5   Diplock in *BBC v Johns*, 1965.

6   J. Woolf in *M v Home Office*, 1994.

that consequence, that agreement is of no effect'.[7] A distinction must be made, however, between public authorities created by statute, whose powers are wholly determined by statute, and Government departments, which are created by the King, and which are entitled in common law, like the King himself, and on his behalf, to own property, enter into contracts, employ staff, and so forth.

There seems to be an ill-defined boundary, in common law, between what the King may do administratively in the exercise of his executive function – that is, using the prerogative bequeathed to him in the regal contract at the time of his coronation – and what he must seek the consent of a Parliament to do. The former is known as royal or Crown privilege, which allows the King to act freely, or to ordain royal law (more commonly referred to as prerogative law), to distinguish it from statute law. Where the former conflicts with the latter, it is deemed to be *ultra vires*, that is to say, it is 'beyond the powers' of the King. Irrespective of distinctions and definitions used by statutes and the judiciary, the Crown remains, constitutionally, the face of the King in the performance of his executive duties. The immunity of the Crown, which is normally referred to as 'Crown privilege', derives from the *imperium*, or right to rule. This principle does not find favour with more radical contemporary attitudes, however, and for this reason Crown privilege has latterly been referred to as 'public interest immunity', as part of the policy of divorcing the Crown from the Monarchy.

The right to invoke the principle of *ultra vires* through the courts derives from the common law principles that (a) duties imposed must be performed, and (b) that the powers granted to perform them may not be exceeded, nor may they be misused. The grounds on which the courts may interfere in administrative decisions of the Crown were identified in a ruling by Lord Diplock in 1984. They were: the illegality of a decision, or its irrationality, or its procedural impropriety, that is to say, it does not follow the process prescribed by statute or it is at odds with the rules of common law in ensuring natural justice. He subsequently suggested, in 1985, the possibility that further grounds might gain acceptance, such as proportionality, but this obviously went beyond the interpretation of the law into the equity dimensions of a decision.

---

7   J. Woolf in *R v IRC Ex parte Preston*, 1983, 306.

The process by which an appeal against an administrative decision takes place is known as 'judicial review'. However, the reforms, mainly between 1977 and 1982, which developed the process were based on existing remedies. These remedies were as follow:[8]

  a. A prerogative writ (later re-styled as an 'order') enabled the courts to exercise a supervisory jurisdiction over inferior courts and public authorities. Such writs were thus the principle means by which the Court of King's Bench exercised jurisdiction over local justices and other bodies, being issued on the application of a private person. They were prerogative writs because they were associated with the right of the King (that is, the Crown) to ensure that justice was done by inferior courts. Nevertheless, the Crown plays no part in the proceedings, except where a Government department is itself the applicant.

  b. An injunction is not available against the Crown, but, in all branches of law, public and private, it is available as a remedy to protect an individual's rights against an unlawful infringement by a public authority or official.

  c. A declaratory judgement, or 'declaration', merely declares the legal relationship of the parties concerned in relation to an actual case. It does not contain any sanction or means of enforcement, beyond clarifying the issue, but the authority of the judgement is such that it will normally restrain both the Crown and a public authority from illegal conduct.

It is generally presumed that, where a statute has provided for a specific tribunal to deal with appeals arising from its application, Parliament intends that they should lie through the tribunal, rather than through the courts. Nevertheless, no Act may preclude the right of a complainant to take his case to the courts, making use of the older and more general prerogative writs, as is made clear by the Tribunals and Inquiries Act of 1958. In many cases, there was no option of recourse to a tribunal or an enquiry.

Judicial review of acts of the Crown was expensive, and objectors were hampered by their lack of access to relevant documents. Attention was turned to the Scandinavian practice of appointing an

8   A. W. Bradley, and K. D. Ewing, *Constitutional and Administrative Law*, 803–11.

official investigator, legal representative, or *ombudsman*, with powers to obtain evidence from officials. In 1967 the office of Parliamentary Commissioner for Administration was created, with the intention that he should be accessible to the ordinary citizen on an informal basis, yet with the authority to scrutinise the behaviour of officials. His purpose was to investigate individual complaints about Government action and to remedy any injustice found. His office was regarded as an extension of Parliament, yet it had close links with the executive, but virtually none with the judiciary, even though he discharged an almost judicial function in the dispute between the citizen and the Crown.[9] Because of the origin of the institution and the cumbrous nature of his statutory title, it became common practice for him to be referred to as the 'Parliamentary Ombudsman'. He was appointed by the Crown, following consultation with the chairman of the House of Commons committee on the Ombudsman, and held office on good behaviour. He could be removed by the Crown following addresses by both Houses. The great advantage to the ordinary individual that was provided by the office of Ombudsman was its accessibility, flexibility and informality, but its authority to review the actions of officials did much to maintain acceptable standards of administrative behaviour. Although the role of the Parliamentary Ombudsman was regarded as an innovation, and the office itself certainly was, it was, in principle, a form of exercise of the King's prerogative of equity. Appropriately, therefore, it is by the King, through his Minister, that the Ombudsman is appointed.

Meanwhile, the original remedies – prerogative writs, injunctions and declarations – continued as a residual and very necessary system of procedures, but they suffered from the defect that, as the Law Commission expressed it in 1976, they put a litigant seeking a judicial review in a dilemma. Each could be effective in particular situations, but each had its limitations. Although more than one prerogative order could be sought in the same proceedings, and an injunction and a declaration could be sought together, the two classes of remedy could not be combined, and if the litigant had made the wrong choice, he could not convert from the one procedure to the other. This could be important, because, although damages could be sought with an injunction or a declaration, they could not be sought with a prerogative order. These and other differences led

9   Sir Cecil Clothier, Parliamentary Ombudsman, in his Report for 1983.

to the adoption by the courts in 1978 of a single procedure by which an application for judicial review could be made, and this was given statutory form by the Supreme Court Act of 1981.

From these various changes there followed a considerable growth in the willingness of the courts to review the decisions of public bodies, except where reasons to the contrary could be shown, and this resulted in an increase in the readiness of the public to take their disputes to court. However, there was a limitation in respect of the need to prevent the public authorities from being overwhelmed by judicial interference, and this had to depend on the courts themselves exercising discretion as to whether or not to pursue each application brought before them.

By the late 1980s it had become commonplace for the Home Secretary to be summoned before the courts to account for his executive decisions, taken under powers claimed to be granted to him by statute. This practice of the judiciary interpreting legislation, rather than the Minister to whom the legislation had delegated, the task, came perilously close to passing judgement on the legislation itself, which had already been approved by Parliament. At the same time, it is not possible for the Queen, albeit with the consent of Parliament, to deprive her courts of the right to question the appropriateness of the manner in which an Act of Parliament is applied.

The practice of judicial review has not been confined to statute law. The courts have long assumed the right to determine the extent of a prerogative power, but more recently they have extended this to the regulation of the manner of its exercise.

In a case in 1964, Lord Devlin said that 'The courts will not review the proper exercise of discretionary power (under the royal prerogative) but they will intervene to correct excess or abuse'.[10] It has been pointed out elsewhere that 'Excess means action which exceeds the limits of the prerogative, while "abuse" suggests – though the point was never developed – the unreasonable use of an established power'.[11] In another case in 1967, it was held that the High Court had the power to review the activities of the Criminal Injuries Compensation Board, a body set up under the royal prerogative,[12] while in a judgment of 1977, Lord Denning

---

10   *Chandler v. Director of Public Prosecutions*, 1964.
11   A. W. Bradley, and K. D. Ewing, *Constitutional and Administrative Law*, 282, 283.
12   *Regina v Criminal Injuries Compensation Board, ex p Lain*, 1967.

went further, stating that the use of prerogative power could be examined by the courts, just as any other power that is vested in the executive.[13]

This encroachment by the courts on the Queen's powers continued, with a landmark decision in 1985, when the House of Lords held that the courts could review the manner of exercise of discretionary powers conferred by the royal prerogative, just as they could review the manner of exercise of discretionary powers conferred by statute.[14] Lord Diplock could 'see no reason why, simply because a decision-making power is derived from a common law and not a statutory source, it should for that reason only be immune from judicial review', although there were suggestions in his speech that the scope for such review in respect of the prerogative was limited to matters of illegality and procedural impropriety. Nevertheless, the Lords pointed out that not all prerogative powers would be subject to review in this way, since it depended on the nature of the power whether it was justiciable. For example, the making of treaties, the granting of honours, the disposition of the armed forces, and the dissolution of Parliament are not capable of adjudication in a court of law.[15] The distinction is thus an arbitrary one, which the courts appear to be able to shift at will.

This apparent independence of the courts in their rulings on the royal prerogative arises from the nature and origin of the royal courts themselves as offshoots of Parliament, acting in its judicial capacity. It is only the judiciary, not the courts, that represent the Queen, and then only in her judicial, as opposed to her executive, role.

There are several forms of law in England, Scotland having a slightly different system. It is possible to distinguish between:

- Common law of the Constitution (*mos maiorum*)
  – under the jurisdiction of the Great Council
- Royal prerogative – subject to the Constitution and statute law
- Statute law – subject to *mos maiorum*
- Bye law – subject to statute law, by the
  implied consent of the shire assemblies
- International treaties – terms are subject to popular approval
  in common law, but this has become impracticable,

---

13   *Laker Airways Ltd v Department of Trade and Industry*, 1977.
14   A. W. Bradley, and K. D. Ewing, *Constitutional and Administrative Law*, 283, 284.
15   *Op. cit.*, 284.

because of the number and complexity of such treaties,
and is therefore left to the discretion of the Crown
and Parliament. An international treaty is between the
Queen and the head or heads of state affected.

It has become increasingly commonplace for acts of state to be referred to the courts, on appeal by individuals or groups, where an act of government is believed to conflict with the law. The terms of treaties have no legal effect in Britain, unless approved by statute.

44.7. The Abuse of Democratic Process and Constitutional Principle: The Notion of Human Rights (1998)

The human rights movement was a reaction to the excesses of the Communist system in Russia and National Socialism in Germany, which had resulted in arbitrary arrest, imprisonment, official brutality and worse across Europe. The system of human rights was an early manifestation of the liberalist movement, and took the form of a legal system designed to prevent the emergence of another intolerant form of government. In this it failed, because it proposed nothing to prevent the establishment of another oligarchy, which, arguably, is the worst form of government, because it has an unlimited life and resorts to intolerance in order to avert any possible threat to its continuance. No set of laws can prevent the establishment or perpetuation of a determined oligarchy, and all that the establishment of human rights achieved was to lay the groundwork for a liberalist society, which an oligarchy might easily dispense with.

The British system of government afforded no protection, because it had always been accepted that no Parliament could bind its successors. Thus, a select committee of the House of Lords, appointed to enquire into ways by which a new Bill of Rights could be entrenched, reported in 1978 that there was no way in which such a Bill (or, for that matter, a Bill incorporating the Convention on Human Rights) could protect itself from encroachment by later Acts. The most that it could do, in the opinion of the select committee, would be to include a provision that ensured that the Bill (or the existing Convention) was always taken into account in the construction of later Acts, and that, so far as a later Act could be construed in a way that was compatible with the Bill (or the Convention), such a construction would be preferred to one that was not.

It was on this basis, however, that a Bill to incorporate the European Convention on Human Rights was approved by the Lords in 1979. The Bill provided that the articles of the Convention should prevail over earlier statutes, and that, in the case of conflict between the Convention and any later enactment, the later Act was to be deemed to be subject to the Convention and must be so construed, 'unless such subsequent enactment provides otherwise, or does not admit of any construction compatible with' the Convention. In a reversal of the usual respective attitudes of the two Houses towards innovation, the Bill was rejected by the Commons. A similar Bill met the same fate in 1995, reflecting a widespread concern over its implications for much existing and possible future legislation, and a concern that it would tend to subordinate Parliament to the courts. It was only following the advent of a new Labour Government in 1997, under Tony Blair, that Parliament was finally in a mood to venture into such uncharted legal territory.

Without formally consulting the people on such a radical innovation, Parliament ratified the European Convention on Human Rights, which came into force as a treaty in 1953, although it was not, at that stage, incorporated into British law. The Convention declared certain individual rights, some already implicit in English common law, and others of a more novel or arbitrary nature. The Convention also provided political and judicial procedures by which alleged infringements of these rights might be examined at an international level. In particular, the acts of public authorities might be challenged even though they were in accordance with national law. The Convention thus provided a limitation on the legislative authority of Parliament.[16] When a statute was judged by the courts to conflict with the statute giving effect to the Convention, the courts were required to issue a declaration of incompatibility, and the onus was then on Parliament to honour its treaty commitment by amending or repealing the offending legislation. One notable benefit of human rights lay in the attention that they focussed on unfortunate groups whose interests had hitherto been overlooked, because they had

16   A. W. Bradley, and K. D. Ewing, *Constitutional and Administrative Law*, 466.

little clout with political Parties. This might have been a legitimate area for the concern of the Great Council.

Customary law and its supplement, statutory law, are based on the principle of catering for perceived and acceptable needs. By contrast, human rights law was based on satisfying, in a comprehensive manner, all conceivable needs of the population. It was a system that incorporated many conflicting needs, ranging from the protection of the interests of the individual to ensuring that each individual was well provided for. In so doing, it placed an undefinable financial burden upon society and placed a heavy burden of work upon the courts. Satisfying the needs of this system severely limited the scope of future legislation and gave the courts a considerable control over the policies of Government, greatly widening the scope for judicial review. The functioning of the system was subject, not to the British courts, but to the European Court of Human Rights, sitting in Strasbourg, which looked more to the French legal tradition for guidance. For example, a judgment of the Court in 2011 asserted that prisoners retained their civil right to vote in elections, a principle that conflicted with a basic principle in English common law that imprisonment was a form of banishment, and that readmission to society had to be earned. Also of concern was the tendency of the European court to expand its jurisdiction, on the ground that human rights law was 'a living thing', for example, in that it could overrule decisions of Parliament and overturn the decisions of British courts in matters held to impinge upon the individual's human rights. Undoubtedly, some benefits did accrue from the human rights system, but nothing that could not have been achieved through general elections and referendums, provided they were subject to the advice and guidance of the Great Council.

45. EUROPEAN INTEGRATION

FRANCE HAD BEEN so humiliated by its defeat in the Second World War that it finally accepted that it had no hope of destroying or subjugating a united Germany, and that a policy of pauperizing it, as it had attempted after 1918, was ultimately self-defeating. In any case, France had little or no influence over the peace terms following the war. Luckily, it seems that another option for resolving the Franco-German rivalry had offered itself in the form of Hitler's vision for a united Europe.

In the latter part of 1941, following the collapse of France and the defeat of Britain at Dunkirk, Hitler had faced a dilemma. Anxious to return to his original objective by devoting his attention to the defeat of Russia and its Communist system, he had found himself burdened with most of Western Europe. This now posed a threat to Germany's rear. Unable to withdraw from France and the other occupied countries of Western Europe, because of the threat posed by Great Britain, which, it had become clear by November of that year, had every intention of continuing the war. Hitler's solution had then been a political union of Europe. There had followed a series of meetings with the foreign ministers of Denmark, Finland and Croatia. In these, and in a long and courteous letter to Marshal Pétain of France, Hitler had outlined plans for a united Europe, with a European army. This union was to be led, politically and economically, by Germany, using a single common currency in the form of the German reichsmark. Such a union would be strong enough to match the United States as an economic and political power, and France would be 'an honoured member'. In due course, Great Britain would be admitted.[1] In 1942, a joint report on the proposed 'European Economic Community' by the German finance ministry and the Reichsbank contained a blueprint for the single currency. By this time, such a union could have extended from the Atlantic to the Ukraine, and from Norway to Greece, but there seems to have been no further progress, due undoubtedly to the preoccupations of the Russian campaign. In other ways, however, a degree of unification had occurred. Between 1942 and

1   Rev. Prof. William Frend, *Daily Telegraph*, 29 June 2000.

1945, the iron and steel industries of France, Belgium, Luxemburg and Germany had been harnessed to the war effort, and a crude system of European labour mobility had operated, with the forcible transfer of many workers from the occupied countries to work in German industry.

By the end of the war, the German proposals for a European union seem to have been all but forgotten, but it was not long before new ones appeared. Whether Churchill had been aware of these wartime proposals is not known, but in September of 1946, in a speech in Zürich, he called for the creation of a United States of Europe and the establishment of a Council of Europe, although he did not see Great Britain being involved in these. It was the French who first saw the advantages of this arrangement. In the same year, the French minister, Jean Monnet, introduced a proposal for a restructuring of Western European industry and agriculture. Whereas Churchill seems to have been motivated by a need to build Europe into a political and economic union that was strong enough to stand up to the new super-powers of the United States and the Soviet Union, Monnet was one of a new generation of French policy-makers to whom a European Union, at least, of Western Europe, which France would dominate, would be the means of controlling the new, post-war Germany and preventing any revival of German ambitions. The idea had the support of Belgium, Luxemburg and the Netherlands, which, realising that they were each too small politically to stand up to their giant neighbours, went ahead in the interim with their own economic integration, in 1947, known as the 'Benelux' customs union.

The Monnet Plan was at least as ambitious as that promoted by Hitler, in that it was seen as the first step towards the creation of an ultimate political union under French hegemony, based on the use of French as the common language and the French legal code as its model. The Plan was followed in May 1950, when Robert Schuman, the French foreign minister, outlined his proposals for a single authority to manage the coal, iron and steel industries of France and West Germany, with an option for other countries to join later. East Germany had remained under Russian occupation, and subsequently had been ruled by a separate Communist regime. From an economic point of view, the Schuman Plan was sound. These industries already extended across the border of France and Germany, and into Luxemburg and Belgium, but customs barriers and national policies had prevented them from developing in an efficient manner. From a political point of view, it offered France a degree of control over the much bigger and more efficient German steel industry, but West Germany, now desperate to be rehabilitated politically as part of the community of western democratic nations, greeted the proposal for the setting up of a European Coal and Steel Community. An indication of France's ambitions was to be seen in a proposal that the new Community should be controlled by a High Authority, based in the Saarland, on the Franco-German border, which in turn was to be subject to a deliberative body of member states, known as the European Economic Assembly. The Saarland was a small, industrialised region of Germany, which, to the consternation of a defeated West Germany, France had succeeded in detaching as an autonomous region under French control, with an option for its eventual economic union with France. France's long history of trying to increase its hegemony by annexing German territory as far as the Rhine had clearly not ended. The proposed location of the Authority amounted to an attempt by France to 'internationalise' the region, so as to forestall Germany's claim to it. France's expectation was that, in due course, the Saarlanders could be persuaded to vote to become a part of France, but, after a protracted tug-o'-war between the two countries that lasted for several years, the issue was resolved, to France's consternation, by the Saarlanders voting for reincorporation into Germany.

As the international pariah seeking acceptance back into the comity of nations, West Germany was in no position to question France's leadership. Indeed, Schuman undoubtedly saw economic and political integration with Germany, under France's tutelage, as the first step to asserting France's influence over the whole landscape of Continental European affairs, once it was free of Russian control. This policy would become more assertive under General de Gaulle, from 1958 onwards, and, as a later French foreign minister, Hubert Védrine, was to remark, after a disappointing conference of European leaders at Amsterdam in 1997, in respect of France's hopes, it had been 'frustrating in relation to our ambitions, which remain vast'. Whether the reference was to France's or Europe's ambitions, is not certain, but it may be questioned whether France saw a distinction between the two. In the light of such a glorious future, the shame of the Second World War could easily be eclipsed.

The next important step was the Rome Treaty of 1957, between France, West Germany, Italy and the Benelux countries. Its purpose was to establish a European Economic Community (EEC), better known as the 'Common Market'. It was to come into effect at the beginning of 1958,[2] with a Council of Ministers, in which each Minister representing a member state had one vote, irrespective of the size of the country that he represented, and each had the same right to veto any decision. There was also a permanent Commission, comprising twenty senior political figures, representing the member states, which was responsible for the day-to-day running of the Community. The Council of Ministers, the Commission and the supporting bureaucracy were all based in Brussels. A consultative European Parliament was to sit, however, in Strasbourg, on the Franco-German border, but just inside France. This was a rather ineffectual body, because the delegates came from so many, very different countries, that they had no common outlook or common interests. The Parliament could only submit recommendations to the Council of Ministers.

This impractical geographical division of the European executive and assembly had been insisted upon by France. In order to satisfy French national sentiment that the EEC had its constitutional basis in France, even though practical politics demanded that its actual operations took place in a comparatively neutral country, notably Belgium, where Brussels was French-speaking, thereby underlining the essentially French character of the whole organisation. This was essentially authoritarian, in keeping with the general character of the French administrative tradition, with a Parliament to give legitimacy to its acts, and occasionally to provide a brake. A parallel treaty set up a European Atomic Community, known as Euratom. The Community, with its political ambitions, appeared to mark the concluding chapter in the Franco-German conflict that had begun in 1870. Thus, in spite of losing the War, France had once again, thanks to the wartime successes of Russia, Great Britain and the United States, and now with the willing cooperation of its old adversary, Germany, imposed its hoped-for hegemony over Western Europe.

2   Unknown to the signatories, there was no treaty, only a protocol plus blank pages. According to Pierre Pescatore of Luxemburg, one of the lawyers who helped draft it speaking on its fiftieth anniversary, the French rushed the ceremony, fearing that de Gaulle, then out of office, would return as President and block it. *The Daily Telegraph*, 25 March 2007.

45.1. Britain and the Common Market

For more than a thousand years, England, and more recently Great Britain, had been ruled by the King and the, mostly, hereditary nobility, who held ministerial office, supplemented by the knights and, more recently, the yeomen of the shires, sitting in the House of Commons. This pattern of domestic authority had begun to break down towards the end of the nineteenth century, as new political groups entered Parliament, but its influence had continued into the twentieth century, sustaining Great Britain as the leading world power, until its political and military decline to a secondary role during the Second World War, following the spectacular rise of the United States and Russia. This had been followed during the 1950s and 1960s by the disintegration of the British Empire, reducing Great Britain from a world power to a regional power, and leaving the self-confidence of the Conservative establishment shattered. At a loss to know where she now stood in the world, or which direction to go, and having sacrificed the British Commonwealth of Nations, in favour of a flimsy Commonwealth of former colonies, the new European Common Market had seemed to offer a safe harbour in the storm.

Britain's initial application to join had caused alarm in the former British Commonwealth, and at the Commonwealth Conference in the following year, faced with the prospect of the structure collapsing in acrimony, the Prime Ministers of Australia, New Zealand and Canada, supported by Nigeria and Tanzania,[3] expressed their opposition to the move. Their concern fell on deaf ears, but it was also premature, because Britain's application in 1961 was vetoed by General de Gaulle, who, probably because of his resentment that France was again under the shadow of the 'Anglo-Saxons', had already caused him, in 1959, to withdraw French forces from the command of the North Atlantic Treaty Organization (NATO). In a memorandum to the Prime Minister, Harold Macmillan, dated 14 December 1960, on the constitutional implications of becoming a party to the Treaty of Rome, the Lord Chancellor had stated that 'I must emphasise that in my view the surrenders of sovereignty involved are serious ones ... these objections ought to be brought out into the open'. The concerns over Britain's future may have been premature in any case, because the British economy had adapted sufficiently by the

3   Formerly Tanganyika.

early 1960s to bring a return to prosperity, causing the Prime Minister, Harold Macmillan, to tell the general public that they had 'never had it so good'.

In any case, the price – the surrender of sovereignty – had seemed an excessive price to pay, but Edward Heath, as Conservative Prime Minister from 1970 to 1974, and one of the new wave of post-war members of the commonalty to find advancement in a more liberally inclined Conservative Party, took a different view. As an enthusiastic yachtsman and an individualist, irked by ties and restrictions of any kind, Heath saw the Common Market as a safe port in a storm. Like other outsiders of his generation, he saw Parliament, not as the seat of responsibility (because Brussels and Strasbourg would relieve them of that), but as a place of diversion and opportunity that had the most to offer to the affable and the ambitious. Recognising the widespread unease in Parliament, and in the country at large, Heath promised the electorate during the general election campaign of 1970 that the Government would not take Great Britain into the EEC 'without the full-hearted consent of Parliament and the people'. A British public opinion poll, published on 30 October 1971, showed that the majority were opposed to membership of the Common Market.

It was only on the third attempt, following the death of de Gaulle, that Britain's application to join the EEC was accepted. It required Parliament, in the face of considerable opposition from its members, to approve, automatically, all existing and future Community laws and to permit free trade and labour migration, including the opening up of Britain's fishing-grounds in the North Sea and the Atlantic to Continental operators. As a result of the European Communities Act of 1972, Great Britain, together with Denmark and Éire, and without reference to the people, became party to the Treaty of Rome, with effect from 1 January 1973, and thus a member state of the EEC. The original six members of the Community – France, West Germany, Belgium, the Netherlands, Luxemburg, and Italy – were thereby increased to nine. Éire had little choice but to join the EEC, because her economy was so bound up with the British economy that to have remained outside would have been economically disastrous.

The European Communities Act sought to preserve British sovereignty by declaring that, although Britain had committed itself to apply whatever legislation the EEC chose to approve, regardless of how objectionable it might be to the British people, the sovereignty of Parliament was not affected. Obviously, the sovereignty of Parliament was affected, because it saw itself with no option but to vote laboriously in favour of every decree of the EU handed down to it, regardless of how much, or in what way, it might affect the interests of the people. Viewed in the context of the constitutional procedure of the time, according to which all legislation was proposed by the Sovereign, who then, subject to the consent of Parliament, proclaimed it, membership of the EEC implied that the Queen had surrendered her function to a foreign entity. Viewed from the standpoint of common law, the Act did not have the consent of the people, because they had not been consulted, and consequently, it had no basis in either common or statute law, representing thereby the ultimate abuse of power by Parliament. Fortunately, the abuse was partly ameliorated by a referendum, held a year later, by the succeeding Labour Government under Harold Wilson, in June 1974. By a majority of two-thirds, the referendum approved Britain's membership of the EEC. The change of mood undoubtedly owed much to a new development: the growing popularity of foreign travel, that had first become evident in the 1960s and had been growing rapidly ever since, as freedom from border controls gave rise to a new mood of 'Europhilia'.

The commercial concept of a European Common Market was sound in itself, giving rise for a number of years to a period of exceptional prosperity in Western Europe. This was not without its longer-term side effects, however. One was to draw industry in the EU towards the market's epicentre in the Rhine-Meuse region. Another was to shift the economic balance in Britain to London and the south-east, which had the best access to the centre of the Common Market. This resulted in the relative economic decline of the Midlands and, more particularly, the North of England. In the face of Continental competition in former British territorial waters, the British fishing industry went into a sharp decline. The British farming industry, much more advanced and better run than that in France, was drawn into a new system of controls and subsidies, whose chief purpose was to support French agriculture.

Meanwhile, the new liberal political establishment in West Germany, anxious to escape from the past and to forestall any resurgence of German nationalism, was eager to cement itself into the wider European system. In pursuit of this, Germany led a call by the EEC establishment for a common European currency that would make a full financial integration possible. In so doing, however, the German establishment overruled its own voters, who, while welcoming the idea of a common Europe and a degree of political and economic integration, still saw the retention of Germany's identity as coming first, and the most symbolic element in this identity now was the German currency, the deutschmark. As a transitional stage to a common currency, an Exchange Rate Mechanism was introduced in 1979. Great Britain joined in 1990, but, in a forewarning to itself and others of what was to come, was forced to leave again two years later, because the system of fixed exchange rates had resulted in her industrial economy being crippled by an over-valued pound.

45.1.1. Brussels and the Abuse of Power (2009)

The first step towards the establishment of a European political union had been the formation of the European Coal and Steel Community. This had been followed by the second step, the establishment of a European Common Market, Economic Community, or EEC. While undoubtedly modelled on the United States of America, it had a much more centralised government in Brussels, based on the French system of administration and law, whose antecedents lay with Imperial Rome and had little in common with English common law and its democratic tradition.

By 1990 it was time, in the eyes of the EEC, to take the next step towards a European political union. The move coincided with the implosion of government in the Soviet Union in 1989, followed by the collapse of Communist regimes across Eastern Europe and the breaching of the Iron Curtain in Germany, and with it, a flood of refugees into the West. Germany was re-united, restoring it as a major political and economic powerhouse in Europe, and making it inevitable that the next stage of the European project was jointly led by France and a newly re-united Germany.

The initial step towards a European Union was the Maastricht Treaty of 1991. This expanded the Community's legislative powers, which effectively reduced the member states to little more than autonomous provinces, the intention being to finalise a common European constitution in a treaty to be signed in Lisbon. The terms of this treaty were rejected by some member states, such as Norway, as being too fast, or as a step too far in the prevailing political climate, and this left the European Union in the form that had been agreed at Maastricht. It was formally approved by the Treaty of Lisbon in 2009, to which the United Kingdom, once again, was a signatory. Again, there was no popular consultation, leaving no doubt that the House of Commons now saw itself as representing the Supremacy of Parliament, and therefore the legitimate Government, with no apparent obligation to consult its electors, outside general elections. Even then, the only issues were those which the Parties chose to offer, and these did not include the question of Great Britain's relationship with the EU.

The structure of the EU was a further development of what already existed, but fundamentally different in purpose. Instead of being a common market and integrated economic system, it now progressed to a common currency and banking system, which Britain's Conservative Government under John Major committed Great Britain to joining, except that the introductory fixed exchange rate system precipitated an economic crisis as the value of the pound plummeted. This forced Britain to withdraw from joining the common currency for the time being. Meanwhile, Britain remained within the European Union, with a steadily shrinking scope for its own law-making, as it and other EU states passed increasingly under the administrative control of Brussels. Meanwhile, appeals from the British courts were passed to the European Court of Human rights, whose influence was far more pervasive of British life and justice. The significance of the Government at Westminster became increasingly confined to that of a post-box, as legislation had its origin increasingly in Brussels, and only a few areas, such as defence, remained under the control of Westminster. Even this faced the eventual possibility of being integrated, as the European Union considered the prospect of forming its own army.

Like NATO, meanwhile, the EU had grown with the admission of an increasing number of Eastern European countries, freed from Russian and Communist control, but now facing a resurgence of Russia under a new leader, Vladimir Putin, himself a former Soviet intelligence officer. Putin was more enlightened than his predecessors, in that he presided over the emergence of a market economy, but was a nationalist who pursued the consolidation of Russian influence in Eastern Europe and the Middle East.

Meanwhile, Britain seemed to have learned its lesson, in that it made no new attempt to join the European common currency, the 'euro', whose benefit to those members of the Union who had adopted it was questionable. This resulted from a growing conflict of economic interests between spendthrift member countries of southern Europe and those in northern Europe that applied a greater degree of fiscal discipline.

45.2. Britain and the European Union

At the time of the establishment of the European Union in 2009, Great Britain was ruled by a Labour Government under the Premiership of Gordon Brown, which either assumed that British membership was covered by the referendum of 1974, which it was not, because the terms and conditions were quite different, or simply acted on the assumption that Parliament had the right to manage Britain's affairs as it thought fit. What the majority of the voters appear to have believed themselves to be approving in 1974 had been a free trade agreement and freedom of travel across much of Western Europe. By contrast, membership of the EU in 2009 required the delegation of British sovereignty to the Union Government in Brussels, including legislative and judicial supremacy in most matters of importance, based on an alien judicial system. English common law does not provide for what amounted to rule from a foreign country, by a predominantly foreign government, and such a dramatic extra-legal step required, not a simple majority in a referendum, or in a general election, but a clear consensus of the people, led by the Queen, for the simple reason that such a change amounted to a constitutional revolution. Because this was not obtained, in any form, it undoubtedly followed that Great Britain's membership of the Brussels Union had legally lapsed after 2009, when the terms of the Common Market agreement underwent a significant change.

The view of the Parties in Parliament was rather different. Whether or not they saw the referendum verdict of 1974 as still applying, they had evidently taken the view that they had been elected, not to represent the will of the people, but to assume the royal authority as the Government of the people. Because they had appropriated the royal prerogative, the Parties regarded themselves as having received popular approval to exercise the royal prerogatives in their capacity as Parliament, with the right to exercise its constitutional supremacy. It was the logical outcome of the constitutional revolution that had been taking place since 1689. Indeed, it had been exercised by the Parties through the liberalist movement for the previous sixty years. It had been accompanied by the increasing use of the power to bestow Ministerial offices on members of the ruling Party, evidently to ensure better control by Party leaders and to spread the benefits of political office. It had also been used to decimate the House of Lords, which the Parties had seen as a limitation on the rightful authority of the Commons, and the replacement of the great majority of the Lords by appointees of the Commons, making it an adjunct of the Lower House.

Although denied any part in this process, the people had nevertheless, over the last three hundred years, accepted the revolution as being in their best interests, because, as it had been pointed out to them, it had allowed democracy to triumph over the self-interests of inherited wealth and privilege, represented by the Monarchy and the Lords. In the absence of the Great Council, this had partly released Parliament from its limited role as the representative of the will of the people and allowed, and indeed required, the Parties in Parliament to assume a new role as the Government of the people, through their appropriation of the role and powers of the Crown.

46. THE COMMONS USURP THE HOUSE OF LORDS (1999)

HAVING USURPED THE Crown, it was perhaps inevitable that the Commons would eventually seek to complete their control of Britain's system of government by usurping or abolishing the House of Lords.

It may be remembered that, in common law, the Lords and Commons sat together in Parliament, although in separate groups (the Church having withdrawn), and that the origin of the House of Lords had been the need of the Great Council to meet where the King could not prevent it, and where the lesser lords of the Second Estate had joined them in an act of solidarity. Because the work of the Council was ongoing, the Upper House had functioned as a permanent institution, unlike the Commons. It follows that the only desirable reform now was for members of the Council to renounce its banishment and lodgement in Parliament, and to reassert its position as the highest institution in the land. Unfortunately, its very existence had long ceased to be remembered, making this now very difficult. A further problem arose from the fact that none of its members had been elected for centuries, and could not be certain which of them could lay an historic claim to a seat in the Council.

46.1. Proposals for Basic Reform (1999)

The Commons had usually accepted the leadership of the House of Lords until the mid-nineteenth century, when the Commons had usurped the Crown and taken control of the executive arm of government. Meanwhile, the re-enfranchisement of all those who could be regarded as possessing an historic right to be regarded as free men had begun to make the House of Commons no longer the representative assembly just of the middle class – the presumed freemen of the Middle Ages – but the lawful representatives of the common people as a whole, who were now regarded as freemen entitled to sit or be represented in Parliament. Taking advantage of its newly elevated importance, the Parties in the House of Commons had set their sights on completing their control of the legislative arm of government, either by abolishing the House of Lords or by reducing it to an ancillary role.

Justification for this was based on a new principle: that democracy was incompatible with the continued existence of a wealthy social class that enjoyed the right to veto legislation if it already had the support of the representatives of 'the people'. The Lords were resented particularly for exercising their right of veto over reforms designed to benefit the ordinary people. In any case, the political worth of the individual had long ceased to be measured by his *wergeld* , or even by the amount of land held by him, and was now measured solely by his vote. The new antipathy of the Commons towards the House of Lords owed much, however, to the rise of socialism at the end of the Second World War. This philosophy was opposed to all social distinctions, and, in its more aggressive Communist form, subscribed to the doctrine of revolution.

Not surprisingly, the Lords were usually more conservative in matters of public policy than the Parties in the Commons, not only because they had more to lose, but also because they were able to take a wider view, were suspicious of new social theories and sometimes had a better grasp of the implications of radical changes. They had the benefit of a better education, a wider social and political background since birth and more experience of public policy, which they had imbibed since childhood. What they lacked was a sympathetic insight into the lives and needs of the lower classes. Since the Lords had become restricted merely to reviewing legislation approved by the Commons, which was often ill-considered and poorly drafted, the difference in the standards of policy-making between the two Houses had become evident. Indeed, much of the time of the Lords was now spent on re-drafting legislation approved by the Commons, earning the Lords the reputation of being the world's 'best House of review'.

It had been a convention of Parliament, since the establishment of two Houses, that neither House should interfere in the membership and procedures of the other. Indeed, it was much more than a convention, because the Estates had a right in customary law to decide their own interests. It does much to explain why the King was required he be guided by the advice of each Estates, a requirement that the Parliament Act of 1911 had violated. If, indeed, the Great Council had continued to function as required, the lords and commons would still have been sitting side by side in the Parliament chamber, probably with less scope for friction.[1]

In 1918, the Bryce Commission had submitted proposals for a change in the composition of the Upper House. This had been prompted by the historic decline of the landed Second Estate, in the face of the growth of commerce and manufacturing industry, and with it the size and wealth of the middle and working classes. In 1925, Baldwin's Conservative Government had, in an attempt to satisfy the critics, appointed a Cabinet Committee to consider reform, but its proposals had lacked support, and after 1935 there had been no further serious debate on the issue. The relationship between the House of Lords and the people was largely overlooked. Indeed, with the exception of the radical minority, the House of Lords was widely perceived, not only as an august body, held in awe and respect by the ordinary people, as the writer well remembers, but as a reassuring presence: the ultimate seat of constitutional authority and the guarantor of freedom, whose integrity was held in higher esteem than that of the Parties. It may well be that this reflected a popular, subconscious memory of it as the ancient *Witenagemōt*, or guardian of the rule of law.

There is no procedure whereby the British system of government may reform itself, except in a temporary manner by delegations of authority through 'conventions'. Every institution and practice has its basis, either in common law or in a delegation or a convention. During the constitutional upheavals of the Middle Ages and in more recent times, therefore, changes in powers and procedures have almost invariably taken place through implied delegations. By implication, when they no longer serve their intended purpose, delegations are capable of being withdrawn and conventions broken. By this means, the system of government was changed on various occasions, without any constitutional changes. Since

---

1   If the direction given by the Council to the King had aroused the opposition of the people, the Council members might have been summoned by their electors, who would have been quite entitled to replace them. The general impression created at the time, however, is that the majority of the people did not support the Commons in the matter.

the *de facto* relegation of the Monarchy as the seat of government, its place has been taken by the doctrine of the Supremacy of Parliament.

The issue of the House of Lords had returned with the election of a Labour Government in 1945, this time with a clear majority. The Party had been committed to a heavy programme of reform, particularly the controversial nationalisation of important industries, but the Lords had wisely shown no determined opposition to these policies, much as it disapproved of their wisdom. Nonetheless, the Government had not been prepared to risk obstruction later, particularly over the nationalisation of the iron and steel industry, and in order that this particular item of legislation could be implemented quickly, if the Party were returned to power, a Bill had been introduced in 1947 to weaken further the delaying power of the Lords. Accordingly, the Parliament Act of 1949 had amended the previous Act of 1911 so as to provide that Bills, other than Money Bills, that were rejected or stalled by the Lords might be presented to the King for his assent after a delay of only two sessions, instead of the three years previously required.

It was the Blair Labour Government of 1997 that introduced a Bill for the basic reform of the House of Lords. Blair seems to have had very little idea of what his reform was trying to do, nor was he greatly interested in the outcome. Once he realised the implications of what he had begun, he left the issue very largely to others to solve. Side-stepping the issue of abolition, what he seems to have had in mind was an Upper House for retired members of the House of Commons that would provide them with a continuing influence in affairs, while making way for younger members in the Lower House, and at the same time ensuring a much stronger Labour bias in the Upper Chamber. It would also assert the principle that members of the Upper House should not sit by right of inheritance. This overlooked, of course, the principle that members of the Third Estate also sat in the Commons, or elected its members, by hereditary right.

The purpose of Blair's original Bill, submitted in 1997, was to replace the hereditary Peers with Life Peers, who were to be appointed on the advice of the Prime Minister. Seeing themselves with no real choice in the matter, the members of the Upper House gave way. Effectively, the House of Lords was to be appropriated by the Parties in the Commons.

This brought a clamour from the political Establishment generally, that the policy should go further, causing the House of Lords to be elected by the people, not appointed by the Government, otherwise the House of Commons would be entrenched as an oligarchy. The alternative of popular election found little favour with the Government, perhaps because it hoped that the Bill would enable the Labour Party to achieve a lasting control of the House. Blair took the heat out of the debate by appointing a Royal Commission, headed by Lord Wakeham. This would take time, however, and with the House of Lords obstructing the Bill, an interim compromise was eventually reached with a majority of the hereditary Peers, who had now resigned themselves to accepting a controlled disaster, rather than ending up under a steam-roller. Under the compromise, the hereditary Peers agreed to their expulsion from the House, and with it from Parliament, with the exception of ninety of their number, who were to retain their seats after being chosen by their fellow Peers. In addition, the Earl Marshal and the Lord Great Chamberlain, both hereditary Peers with constitutional functions, were to retain their seats. This compromise was introduced by the House of Lords Act, 1999, which established an interim House, comprising 500 Life Peers, ninety-two Hereditary Peers, twenty-seven Law Lords, and twenty-six Bishops, who, with the exception of the Life Peers, must be assumed still to include the remnants of the dormant Great Council. To achieve this, however, it was necessary for the Prime Minister to advise the Queen to appoint an additional 171 Life Peers. Fortunately, the Act was regarded as no more than the first stage of reform, until the Government could think of a more permanent solution. It hardly needs to be said that the radical reform of one of the great institutions of state, without consulting the people, and without even having an agreed alternative in mind, amounted to the heaping of Ministerial incompetence on top of constitutional abuse. By way of 'compensation', the hereditary Peers who had been evicted were now entitled by the Act to vote with the commonalty in general elections, and to stand for election and sit as commoners, which most undoubtedly saw as an insult. The Act also provided for the Queen to vote in general elections, which was a violation of her impartiality and an insult to her historic position as the summoner of Parliaments to seek their advice – a final act of humiliation. The constitutional and political revolution seemed to be complete, leaving the Queen, already deprived of her Parliaments, now treated in statute law as an ordinary member of the public.

So ended the House of Lords, in a heap, after 611 years as the deliberative seat of the Great Council and the Second Estate. Of great concern was the fact that the opening of the Upper House to professional politicians from the Commons greatly increased the risk of a single political Party in the Commons – or a coalition of Parties – taking effective and lasting control of the whole system of government, making the risk of a permanent oligarchy a real possibility.

The Royal Commission, taking a very different view, reported in January 2000. It expressed its concern that the Lords should not be an institution 'which could threaten the status of the House of Commons and cause constitutional conflict or whose members might challenge those of the House of Commons in fulfilling their constituency representative role'. Nor should it be 'a creature of the political parties'. It went on to favour a chamber that was more representative of the whole of British society (already the purpose of the House of Commons), and able to bring a wider range of expertise and experience to bear on the consideration of public policy questions. It therefore rejected the idea of a wholly, or largely elected House, and proposed a chamber of about 550 members, mostly chosen by an independent Appointments Commission, whose objective should be a composition 'broadly representative of British society and possessed of all the other characteristics mentioned'. In pursuit of its duty to ensure representativeness, the proposed Commission should ensure a proper balance of men and women, a fair representation of ethnic minorities, and a political balance matching that reflected in general elections. If anything, the proposed Upper Chamber would be more representative than the Commons because it would be able to dispense with constituencies. This would appear to make the House of Commons superfluous. On the question of the future of the Lords Spiritual, the Commission proposed that there should be a religious representation in the chamber that was 'broader and deeper than it is today', by including representatives of non-Christian faiths and Christian denominations, in addition to the Church of England.

The Commission's Report was received with a notable lack of enthusiasm, either from the Government itself or from the mass media. It would then be the House of Commons that would become the anomaly, and rivalry between the Houses would be intensified. One important feature of the Report, the establishment of a House of Lords Appointment Commission, was implemented in September 2000, and nominations were invited for what were described as 'independent non-Party-political Peers', so called because those appointed would share the cross-benches with Peers who were non-Party-political. Nominees, had to be over 21 years of age, and therefore were not required to be elders of the land. They also had to be United Kingdom, Commonwealth, or Irish nationals.[2] Because the House had no jurisdiction over the Commonwealth or the Republic of Ireland, the reason for this breadth and range of representation is far from obvious. In any case, it effectively demolished the reason for retaining an Upper House.

In November 2001, the Government published a White Paper setting out the second stage of its proposals for reform. This favoured a House of Lords consisting of 600 members, of whom 120 should be elected, another 120 chosen on their personal merits by an independent cross-Party commission, sixteen bishops and at least a dozen law lords. The remaining 300 or so should be nominated by the political Parties. Whether these nominees were 'fit and proper' individuals (in view of the former standing of the House and its members) should be decided by the Appointments Commission, which should also decide how many members each Party was entitled to appoint, so that the proportion of 'political' members reflected the share of the vote won by the respective Parties in the preceding general election. The existing life Peers should remain, but the existing ninety-two hereditary Peers should lose their seats. Apart from the sheer complexity of the proposed system, the proposals were based on no coherent constitutional principle. The hotchpotch of groups comprising the new House were to be termed 'lords of Parliament', perhaps because of opposition to the wish of some to rename it the 'Senate', following the American example. It was

---

2   This treatment of Irish nationals as British subjects, for constitutional purposes, could be seen in the light of Feudal doctrine as a continued assertion that Southern Ireland was still subject to the Queen.

intended that the current use of the Lords should remain that of a 'House of review'.

The reaction of the general public to the reform was largely one of apathy. There had appeared to be little popular support for the reform in the first place, and, while some applauded the ending of social privilege, others decried what they saw as the sacrifice of such wisdom and experience as the former House had to offer and the desecration of constitutional traditions. There was concern, moreover, that, if the former stabilising influence of the Upper House and the standards that it set were removed or compromised, this would leave the public even more exposed to what they tended to regard as the self-serving interests of the Parties in the Commons. A change of Government in 2010 seems to have reflected a basic opposition within the Conservative Party to Lords reform.

46.2. The Position of the Great Council in the Lords

The effect of the changes to the House of Lords in 1999 completed the overwhelming of what was left of the Great Council, in the face of the continuing influx of life Peers, mainly members of the Third Estate. All that can be said is that the senior members of the hereditary Peerage who had continued to function as the Great Council – although not as lawful members of the Council, because none had been lawfully appointed for centuries – were now separated, some remaining in Parliament and the others evicted. Little did Blair realise that, in his convulsion of the House of Lords, he had come close to dismembering what remained of the most important and vital institution in the land. It would always remain the most crucial part of the Constitution, confined in its capacity as custodian of the *imperium* of the people. Fortunately, the senior members of the hereditary Peerage, whether excluded or not from Parliament, did not cease, collectively and in law, to represent the Council, without which the Constitution had no basis.

It may be added that references to the 'Great Council' had never had a constitutional basis. This is self-evident from the fact that the description implied the existence of a 'Little Council', which can only refer to the King's Council. However, the latter was undoubtedly an offshoot, or 'standing committee', of the former. The earlier name of the Great Council is unknown, but its popular designation in Parliament as the 'House of Lords' may have come from a popular tradition that was much older. It follows that the name 'House of Lords' no longer had any relevance to Parliament, and now referred to the restored and quite separate Great Council.

46.3. The Commons Becomes the Seat of Government (1992)

Now that the House of Commons had appropriated the legislative, executive and judicial functions of the King, whom it now regarded as little more than a figurehead, it was regarded as necessary for the House of Commons itself to become a permanent institution. The House no longer saw it as acceptable that it came into existence only when summoned. That the House of Commons believed in its ability to re-invent itself, and to transform other institutions, had been inspired by Bagehot's conclusion that the English system of government was not fixed, like the American constitution, but evolved over the centuries, and would continue to do so in the face of changing needs. Bagehot's doctrine bore no relationship, either to common law or to feudal doctrine, but, whether from need or self-interest, it had increasingly influenced Parliament since 1867. Bagehot had concluded that the House of Commons was the 'efficient', that is, the effective, part of the Constitution, leaving the Monarchy and the House of Lords as the 'dignified' parts, whose purpose was simply to reassure the people. Armed with this conclusion, the House of Commons now saw its own position as requiring a secure and permanent constitutional existence as a sovereign body.

Hitherto, Parliaments had been provided with a meeting place by the King, who had also provided accommodation against the weather and supplied their needs while they were in session, for example, by employing clerks and general staff, including a Serjeant-at-Arms in the Commons and a Gentleman Usher of the Black Rod in the Lords, for the purpose of maintaining order. These officers and other staff had long been treated by Parliament as its own employees, which was a legal impossibility, because

Parliaments were temporary bodies without assets, and hence there was no means of paying them. In accordance with Bagehot's interpretation, it was now intended by the Conservative Government of John Major, that there should be a single, permanent Parliament of two Houses that was consistent with its new role as the basis of executive government. This required Parliament to appropriate, from the Queen, lawful control of its own arrangements. All revenues accrued, constitutionally, to the Queen, not to Parliament, which had no assets of its own. In order to provide for these changes, therefore, the Parliamentary Corporate Bodies Act of 1992 established 'corporate bodies to hold land and perform other functions for the benefit of the Houses of Parliament', including the making of provision for, and in connection with, the transfer of certain property, rights and liabilities to those corporate bodies'. To this end, the Act established a corporation, to be known as the Corporate Officer of the House of Lords, and another, to be known as the Corporate Officer of the House of Commons. The purpose of these was to ensure that the facilities used by Parliament belonged to the respective Houses, not to the Queen. Because ownership of such facilities could apply only to a permanent body, the whole concept of Parliaments had to be changed.

Care was taken to ensure, however, that the Act did not entrench the position of the House of Lords, and this was achieved by providing that the first of these offices could be abolished by a simple amendment. The new system was accordingly built, not around Parliament, but ultimately around the House of Commons. These arrangements implied a fundamental transfer to Parliament of the remaining constitutional authority and functions of the Sovereign, as head of the executive, legislative and judicial aspects of government, to Parliament. To this end, the Act appointed an officer who was to be employed by, and answerable to Parliament, thereby completing the transition of the Monarchy to the role of a mere figurehead.

The Act was followed by the related Parliament (Joint Departments) Act of 2007, introduced by the Blair Labour Government. This authorised the Corporate Officers, just described, to establish joint departments of the Houses of Parliament, with such functions as the Corporate Officers should allocate to them, including, as with any corporate body, the acquisition and management of land and property, the entering into such contracts as they might deem to be necessary, and the employment of staff. These Officers might, at their discretion, divide, amalgamate or abolish these departments. In all this they must act jointly, but their actions must be approved by the respective Houses of Parliament. Although the Act provided for the interests of each House to be catered for, it is clear, as already noted, that the future of the House of Lords was already in doubt, because the possibility was clearly envisaged of the two corporations being amalgamated into one – presumably as the Corporate Officer of the House of Commons – who would then, doubtless, become the Corporate Officer of Parliament. The new Acts declared Parliament the owner of the Houses of Parliament and any subsidiary property, and the employer of all Parliamentary staff and other officials and workers. Also, Parliament was now a single entity, which remained in legal existence, even when it was not meeting. It was now a permanent institution in its own right.

Because Parliaments have no money, and no means of raising it, they are in no position to pay their members or employ staff and other workers, or meet the cost of maintaining buildings. Taxes are collected by the Inland Revenue, which falls under the direction of the Chancellor of the Exchequer, but the Chancellor is appointed and holds his office from the Sovereign, albeit on the recommendation of his or her Prime Minister, who owes his own position and authority to appointment by the Sovereign, on the advice of Parliament.

Furthermore, if Parliament is correct in its claim that the Sovereign is now a mere figurehead, then he or she has no executive power to bestow upon the Ministry, leaving Parliament without a meaningful function. In practice, following a general election, the newly elected or re-elected members must await a summons from the Sovereign to assemble, rendering it impossible for her to be deemed a private person. Once assembled, elected members, wait to hear from the Sovereign the reasons for their summoning, followed by her declaration that the new Parliament is now open to exercise its constitutional function. By implication, it is still her Parliament, to serve her purposes on behalf of the people, and the Members must then wait for her to summon the leader of the majority Party, whom she then appoints as her First Lord of the Treasury, in which executive capacity he now acts as her Prime Minister. This is only possible because the powers which she delegates are vested in her. Subsequently, she still endows individual members, recommended by the Prime Minister, with various other Ministerial offices, including the executive powers attaching to them. What this confirms is that the Sovereign is still the source of all executive power, held by her from her electors, the people, even though she agrees to be bound by certain rules. For a Bill passed by the Sovereign in Parliament to be given legal validity, the Sovereign must still authorise it by appending his or her signature and royal seal, leaving no doubt that it is the Sovereign who is still the seat of executive power. He or she still appoints judges, through an appropriate Minister appointed by her, on the advice of her Prime Minister, thereby confirming that she is still, also, the source of all judicial authority. If the Monarchy were abolished, or reduced to a nominal role, as some have proposed and even claimed, a new source of legislative, executive and judicial power would need to be found and granted by the people.

Once a Parliament has fulfilled the reasons for its summoning, apart from other issues arising during its life, it is dissolved by the Sovereign, by whose authority it was summoned in the first place. It was pointed out earlier that the cost and inconvenience of general elections have long caused Parliaments to be perceived as remaining in existence continuously, from one election to the next.

Effective government requires a chief executive officer, hitherto and constitutionally the King, to propose policy, and to implement it once it has been approved by a Parliament. He must have the authority to impose and collect taxes, to pay employees of the state and to finance the policies approved, because Parliaments have no money. The executive officer must be answerable to the people, who provide revenues through taxation that enable the system to function. Being answerable to Parliament is not enough, because the executive officer and the Parliament might be perceived as being in league with each other, particularly if the executive officer is appointed by Parliament itself. The executive officer (the Sovereign) and Parliament must therefore be appointed independently of each other by the people, to whom both are separately responsible.

46.4. Attempts to Introduce a Separation of Powers

The doctrine that there should be a rigid separation of powers was first consciously applied to the Constitution of the United States, under the influence of the French writer, Montesquieu. The latter's advocacy had derived from a misunderstanding of the English system of government. In Europe after the Second World War, it was the growth of American power and influence, on the one hand, and the reaction to the excesses of dictatorships in Russia, Italy, and Germany, on the other, that caused the idea of a separation of powers to be widely promoted, in order to lessen the chances of a recurrence.

46.4.1. The Demotion of the Lord Chancellor

In Great Britain, the perceived modernity of the American system resonated with Blair and his Labour Government of 1997–2007, which set out to 'modernise' the British system, in order to make it consistent with the liberalist principle of universal equality and Montesquieu's perception of a division of powers. An obvious problem here was the office of Lord Chancellor. The Chancellor had, for centuries, been appointed as the King's Prime Minister and representative in Parliament, sitting in the House of Lords, until the rise of the Party system. In the process he had accumulated an intolerable burden of duties, most of which he normally delegated. The office of Lord Chancellor had executive, legislative and judicial functions. Thus, he had custody of the Great Seal of England, administered the courts of law, appointed many judges in England and Wales, advised the Sovereign on the appointment of senior judges, was a member of both the Privy Council and the Cabinet (for which reason he was appointed from among the members of the ruling Party). He also determined which barristers should be appointed as Queen's Counsel, sat as a judge in the highest court in the United Kingdom – the Appellate Committee of the House of Lords – and subsequently as President of the newly created Supreme Court. He was also a member of the Judicial Committee of the Privy Council, was consulted on appointments to certain ecclesiastical courts, and was one of the Church Commissioners of the Church of England.

It was King George I who had – probably out of ignorance – appointed a favoured individual, Sir Robert Walpole, the First Lord of the Treasury, to preside in his place at Cabinet meetings, a function that for centuries had belonged to the Lord Chancellor. Such is the glutinousness of English constitutional practice, however, that the innovation became 'traditional' and therefore permanent. It also suited the political Parties in the Commons, because it ended the right of the Lord Chancellor to the function and opened the possibility that they might themselves lay claim to the position. The role of Prime Minister passed accordingly, after 1721, from the Lord Chancellor, in the Upper House, to the leader of the majority Party in the Lower. It was to prove to be a convenient change, as the importance of the House of Commons gradually superseded that of the Lords.

By the time of Blair's reformist Labour Government in 1997 there were certainly good grounds for rationalising the allocation of duties that continued to be borne by the Lord Chancellor, but the attitude of the Government at the time seemed to be that the antiquity of the office was itself an anachronism. The crucial importance of some of his duties, however, made him indispensable. As head of the judiciary, his office was, quite properly, an independent one, and therefore outside the influence of the political Parties. This was evidently too much for the Blair government, however, even though Blair was otherwise a firm supporter of the principle of the division of powers, and the office was effectively modernised and brought to heel. Through the Judicial Appointments Order in Council, of March 2001, the Government gave formality to the principle of judicial separation through the creation of a Commission for Judicial Appointments. This transferred, from the Lord Chancellor to the Commission, the responsibility for recommending all but the most senior judicial appointments in England and Wales. The Prime Minister also changed the title of the Lord Chancellor to that of Secretary of State for Constitutional Affairs, and subsequently changed it again to the Secretary of State for Justice, bringing it more into line with the American predilection for the verbosity and Latinisation of modern titles. Such was the antiquity and standing of the office of the Lord Chancellor in English history, however, that the Government was persuaded to retain his historic title as an alternative to the new one. It was therefore combined in the new and confusing title of 'Lord Chancellor and Secretary of State for Justice', the expectation being probably, and accurately, that the ancient title would disappear through default. The function of the Lord Chancellor was drawn, thereby, into the Party-political system.

The duty of the new Commission was to hold competitions, on the results of which it could submit to the Lord Chancellor (or Secretary of State for Justice) the names of suitable candidates for judicial office for his recommendations, thereby maintaining, through him, as a Cabinet member, Government control of the judiciary, while refraining from doing so in practice. Thus, the office of Lord Chancellor, for centuries the foremost in the land, under the King, was relegated to a fairly obscure role that had no formal protection from political influence. Separate bodies were created for the purpose in Northern Ireland and Scotland. The new arrangement was intended to remove, very largely, any likelihood of appointments being made on an arbitrary basis, yet it did not represent a separation of powers, such as Montesquieu had supposed. All that can be concluded is that the Order in Council greatly reduced the ability of the judiciary to influence Government policy.

Further developments came in 2003, when it was announced that the Blair Government intended to pursue further constitutional reforms in pursuit of the ideal of a full separation of powers. In particular, it sought:

1. The transfer of judicial appointments from the Lord Chancellor to a Judicial Appointments Commission, as a result of which the office of Lord Chancellor was to be abolished.

2. A statutory provision for the House of Lords to appoint its own 'Speaker', like the Commons. The Lords had always had its own official for this purpose, namely, the 'Foreman' of this House. This office was fulfilled as one of the functions of the Lord Chancellor. In pursuit of a policy of standardising titles, by tacit agreement of the Chamber, the Lord Chancellor, in his capacity as the King's deputy in Parliament,[3] a function to which Blair evidently took exception, adopted the title of 'foreman' of the Chamber.

3. The establishment of a Supreme Court, in place of the Appellate Committee of the House of Lords. This also copied

---

3   The Speaker of the House of Commons had no role in Parliament.

the American arrangement, and removed the formal link
between the legislature and the judiciary. In this respect, of
course, it needs to be remembered that the Crown courts
(in contrast to the judicial role of the House of Lords),
were extensions of Parliament in its judicial capacity,
and the new Supreme Court fell into this category.

Blair's reforms were highly selective, because they overlooked the
most glaring confusion of powers by failing to restore the separation
of powers between the executive and the legislature. This required the
separation of the legislative role of Parliament from the executive role of
the Crown.

A more fundamental attempt at securing the separation of the
judiciary was made by the Blair Government in the Constitutional
Reform Act of 2005, a measure that was in accordance also with the
Government's other policy of curtailing the role of the House of Lords,
which was responsible for the hearing of judicial appeals (which in
practice were conducted on its behalf by the Law Lords). The Act was also
directed against the remaining judicial influence of the Lord Chancellor,
who, it may be remembered, was President of the courts of England and
Wales and head of the judiciary under the Queen, who included the
Lord Chief Justice. The remaining role of the Lord Chancellor, in respect
of judicial appointments, was transferred to the Judicial Appointments
Commission. The Act transferred the judicial functions of the Lord
Chancellor to the Lord Chief Justice. Meanwhile, the hearing of judicial
appeals was transferred from the House of Lords to a new court, to be
known as the Supreme Court.

Government antipathy towards the courts has had two main causes.
One has been the seeking of political profit by supporting popular
dissatisfaction with particular court judgments. The other has been
the embarrassing difficulties caused to the courts by the decline in the
standards of legislation, due to the reform of the House of Lords and
the resulting decline in the standard of legislative review that the House
had been able to provide. The greatest difficulties of all, however, were
created by the Human Rights Act of 1998, which introduced a mass of
contradictory laws that were not only impossible to reconcile, except on

an arbitrary basis, but established requirements that were often impossible to fulfil in practice. This not only created huge difficulties for the courts, but resulted in endless judgments that were intensely unpopular. The Government tended to cover itself by blaming the courts. As we have already noted, of course, the House of Lords is a constitutional body quite separate from Parliament, so that interference by the Parliament is not possible in any case.[4]

Little attempt was made to reduce the level of interference of the executive in the judiciary. Perhaps the most direct form of interference was the habit of directing the judiciary on sentencing policy, already laid down in statute law. Whether the judiciary are under any legal obligation to take note of such directions is unclear, but there appear to have been various motives for it. One was financial. A growing shortage of prison space in the early years of the twenty-first century, due to an unwillingness of Government to allocate money for prison construction, together with an unwillingness to accept that crime had reached epidemic proportions, caused the responsible Minister to direct the courts to refrain from imposing prison sentences, except in the most serious cases. This was an interference, not only in the judgement of the courts, but appeared to override the intent of legislation itself. Frequently, also, both Government and Parliament engaged in lambasting the judiciary over sentences passed, or over comments made by individual judges during the conduct of trials. Thus, judges were accused of being 'out of touch with the modern world'. One judge was vehemently attacked for expressing ignorance of a popular entertainer of the day, as if a familiarity with teenage 'pop-idols' had a bearing on justice. If the Prime Minister sought to establish the independence of the judiciary in theory, there seems to have been little intention to observe it in practice.

The purpose of a Supreme Court was to appropriate from the House of Lords[5] the function of resolving difficult questions of law, for which the Court of Appeal was not equipped. Constitutionally, the Supreme Judge is the Sovereign, who, as such, is also the source of equity, and it is from the Sovereign that the judiciary derive their authority. We saw earlier that

---

4   An exception might be if it can be shown that the Lords is not fulfilling its constitutional functions in a proper manner, as we have suggested that it is not, in which case it becomes a matter for the Queen and people (as opposed to an unrepresentative Parliament).

5   In its capacity as the Great Council.

the Sovereign delivers his or her justice to plaintiffs of the Third Estate in her capacity as the Sovereign in Parliament, and to plaintiffs of the Second Estate as the Sovereign in Great Council (the House of Lords). The former has long been delegated to the Sovereign in Privy Council and the Crown courts. For several centuries, the Sovereign has, while sitting, or deemed to be sitting, in the Great Council (or House of Lords), resolving difficult points of law that have been referred to him or her by the Court of Appeal. The Sovereign could alternatively do this while sitting in Privy Council. The Sovereign may not, however, sit in a Crown Court, that is, one that the Sovereign has established by delegation, such as the new Supreme Court. The Sovereign cannot delegate to him/her self.

As earlier noted, the idea of a separation of powers arose from a misunderstanding of the English – and British – Constitution as practised. There was no recognised separation of powers, but, as we noted earlier from the fourteenth century, the Constitution is based, not on separation, but is rather a system of interlocking and counter-balancing powers, in which individuals are not necessarily precluded from holding positions in more than one area of government.[6] Parliaments in the fourteenth century were attended by the King's Counsellors and servants of the Royal Household, in much the same way as the Queen's Ministers attend Parliaments today, not to vote on issues before the chamber, but for purposes of liaison. Judges attended Parliaments and meetings of the King's Council, as well as sitting in the royal courts of law. In this way they were available to help in creating law, as well as applying it. We found, indeed, that an active and valued individual, such as Sir William Shareshull, could be a member of the King's Council, a member of the Commons, and Chief Justice of the Court of King's Bench, the last being a position that he held from 1350 until 1361. He was also active in the development of a new class of local officials, soon to be known as Justices of the Peace, whose purpose was the enforcement of the law. Nevertheless, men such as Shareshull were the exception, rather than the rule, and the different functions of the Constitution – the executive, legislative, and judicial – were much as we would expect to find them, performed by different groups of people, but without a rigid separation. These functions overlook a fourth, that of oversight, provided by the Great Council, but this is normally excluded, because it is not properly a function of government.

6   The constitution as a system of interlocking and counter-balancing powers.

46.5. A Supreme Court of Appeal Displaces the House of Lords

It will be remembered that justice in the shires was conducted by the hundred courts, with the more serious cases referred to the shire assemblies. Juries were drawn from the same Estate as the accused. Following the establishment of the English confederacy in 927, the shire courts were often no longer appropriate, and the problem of disputes between free men of different shires was very likely resolved by the accused being forced to face justice before the shire court of the aggrieved party. Eventually, these and other problems were undoubtedly resolved by the establishment in the Middle Ages of the new circuit courts.

For the few who could afford them, or for cases that were of sufficient importance, trials were increasingly referred to the common English Parliaments, hence the origin of references to the 'High Court of Parliament'. Unfortunately, there is very little surviving evidence to draw upon until the Middle Ages, when Parliaments referred this duty, in all but the most important cases, to the new Crown Courts that they established for the purpose. Meanwhile, disputes between members of the Second Estate were traditionally settled by means of trial by battle, the implication being that the Deity would favour the innocent. Increasingly, however, disputes between members of the Second Estate were referred to the new Crown Courts established by Parliament, with juries provided from fellow members of the same Estate as the accused. Meanwhile, the growing prosperity of the Third Estate increasingly persuaded ordinary litigants to use the Crown Courts, which were more efficiently run, leaving the shire courts to decline in importance. However, Parliament retained its function as the ultimate court of appeal for both Estates, while the Church dealt with its own cases.

Following the relegation of the Great Council to the confines of Parliament in the fourteenth century, in violation of the paramountcy of its Constitutional position,[7] and its subsequent re-establishment there as the House of Lords, it was inevitable that the House was also used as the court of appeal for members of the Second Estate and, much later, in default of the Commons, the ultimate court of appeal for members of the

---

7   Made possible for the King by the Church, which had endowed him as God's appointee.

Third Estate.[8] Ultimate appeals against judgments of the Crown courts had been submitted as petitions to the House of Lords or the House of Commons, according to the Estate of the appellant. This distinction had surely been unnecessary, because appeals were not trials, requiring the presence of juries of peers of the accused, but after 1399 the Commons refused to hear appeals, leaving all final appeals to be heard by the House of Lords (that is to say, not by the Great Council, which was not a court of law, but by the members of the Second Estate in Parliament, sitting in its judicial capacity). Despite its objections, the Commons did not have the option of refusing to hear judicial appeals. Constitutionally, this obligation in respect of appeals from members of the Third Estate was binding. The solution undoubtedly was a legal standing committee of Parliament, sitting as a legal court of appeal for members of the Third Estate. The Second Estate (not the House of Lords), having a lighter task, may have continued to manage. Indeed, there was no reason why separate courts for lords and commons would have been necessary at all, because their function was not to try the appellants, but to consider the verdicts of the lower courts in the light of the law. It follows that Parliament, sitting in its judicial capacity, delegated to a standing committee, like the existing Crown Courts, would have sufficed as an ultimate court of appeal, acting in respect of appellants from both Estates. This is what the Blair Government was really trying to establish.

Meanwhile, the Great Council undoubtedly faced a different problem, in that it is unlikely to have been able to renew itself in a legitimate manner since at least 1066. Faced with the increasing burden of appeals, the House of Lords had struggled, despite initial hearings being referred to the Crown Courts themselves. At the same time, a new problem appeared, in that the growing complexity of statute law had made it increasingly necessary for the Peers to be legally qualified for the work, and very few were. This problem was solved by elevating select members of the judiciary to the Peerage as Life Peers, who were required to submit their verdicts to the whole House for approval, thereby preserving them as verdicts of the House of Lords.

It is against this background that the establishment of a Supreme Court of Appeal, in June of 2003, must be seen. The Blair Labour

---

8   Appeals are not trials, and therefore not subject to the principle of trial by equals. An
     appeal is purely an issue of law, not of guilt versus innocence.

Government may well have seen the issue in political, as much as legal and constitutional, terms, perceiving the Upper House as a bastion of elitist interests. That the House was widely regarded among the general public with deference and even awe, however, on account of its collective but subconscious memory of the institution as the highest and most august in the land, carried no influence with a Government that was dead to such sentiments.

46.6. The Supreme Court and the Constitution

In keeping with Blair's desire to modernise, there seems to be little doubt that, in his proposal for a new court of appeal to replace the House of Lords, he was influenced by the example of the American Supreme Court, but this was based on a very different principle. Whereas, under the American system, a trial is conducted by the people, represented by the Union flag, under the British system, trials are conducted by the people, represented by the King. They cannot be represented by the Union Jack, because its use, in one form or another, preceded the actual Union by nearly a century.

A feature of the British Supreme Court is that its proceedings are conducted on the floor of the chamber, in front of the appellant, implying a negotiation, rather than a plea for justice. The source of the justice being exercised by the court is itself obscure, being represented by a decorative motif of a small garland of flowers, surmounted by an equally small crown, which is hardly reassuring. The royal presence in any Crown Court is indicated by an elevated seat or throne, from which the verdict is issued by the King or his appointed justiciar. This is absent from the Supreme Court, and there is no sign of the presence of the King or his deputy or deputies. The proceedings of the Court are conducted, and the verdict is given, by a number of men in suits and women in dresses, who might have come from anywhere. Indeed, the authority of the court is by no means evident to the plaintiff, and any enquiry in this direction is bound to result in the plaintiff being referred to the relevant Act of Parliament. While Parliament is the source of all the Crown Courts, such courts, like Parliament itself, are presided over by the King or his representative, in his common law capacity as the Supreme Judge.

What Blair had been proposing was the transfer to a new court, to be created for the purpose, of the judicial role of the House of Lords as the final court of appeal. This function had been performed by the members of the Second Estate in Parliament[9] (not in their capacity, where it applied, as members of the Great Council, because the Council was not a court of law).

The description of the new court as the 'Supreme' Court of Appeal raises a constitutional issue. Like other Crown Courts, it was established as a permanent standing committee of Parliament. It cannot be described, however, as the 'Supreme' Court of Appeal, because the highest court of appeal in the land is Parliament itself, sitting in its capacity as the 'High Court' of Parliament, whether it chooses to do so or not. To represent the new court of appeal as 'Supreme' is both an affront to Parliament and a constitutional impossibility. Indeed, the notion of 'supremacy' seems not to exist in English common law. It appears to be a word introduced by the Church, which sees the King as the 'supreme' authority on earth in all temporal matters, and the Church as the 'supreme' authority in spiritual matters.

---

9   Including those who were members of the Great Council. It may be remembered that the Council itself was not a court of law.

PART XVI

•

PARLIAMENT *VERSUS* THE PEOPLE

47. PARLIAMENT *VERSUS* THE PEOPLE

47.1. Parliaments are Subject to Fixed Terms: The Benn Act (2011)

On the advice of the Prime Minister, a Parliament could at any time be dissolved by royal proclamation by the Sovereign, using the royal prerogative, except that a dissolution must take place after five years. This limit left the Prime Minister with considerable flexibility. The actual date of dissolution was left to the Prime Minister, and could occur as much as five years and twenty-two days after the previous summons or longer.

As this could be varied over the years, and in order to mitigate uncertainty, it was decided to set the date of dissolution, including the date of the next election. This led to the Fixed Term Parliaments Act of 2011, usually known as the Benn Act, which was enacted by the Labour-Liberal coalition led by Gordon Brown. Meanwhile, the continued right and duty of the Sovereign, on the Prime Minister's advice, to exercise the royal prerogative in respect of the holding and dissolution of Parliaments, evidently caused offence to the more radical Members of Parliament, and one purpose of the Act was to ensure that the holding and dissolution of Parliaments was subject only to statute law, thereby completing the separation of the Crown from Parliament. This, of course, overlooks the fact that the purpose of a Parliament is to advise the Sovereign.

The Act prescribed that the dissolution be not more than two months later than the five years, creating more certainty for voters (or, more likely, for existing Members). Hence, Parliament could no longer be dissolved by royal prerogative, because it was now determined by statute. The specific date of dissolution was stated to be the first Thursday in May, every five years, following polling day of the previous general election. An early election was possible only if the Commons passed a motion amending the electoral timetable. Meanwhile, the Act provided that there should be a general election on 7 May 2015, and that elections thereafter should be held on the first Thursday in May, in every fifth year, the next election being scheduled for 7 May 2020. Early elections were permissible, however, in the event of a motion agreed by two-thirds of the whole House, or if a motion of no confidence was passed by the House within fourteen days. It provided for a general election on 7 May 2015. Thereafter, it provided that a general election was to take place in every fifth year on the first Thursday in May.

Benefits of the Act have been claimed to be that Governments are no longer able to hold elections when it most suits them, and the Prime Minister is no longer able to threaten his colleagues with an election, as a means of imposing discipline. It is claimed also that the Act reduces the advantage enjoyed by Governments in being able to hold elections when they choose. On the negative side, the Act involves a loss of flexibility, for example, by perpetuating a lame duck Government, because the Prime Minister is not able to seek a fresh mandate mid-term, as in the case of Eden in 1955, and May in 2017–19. The power of dissolution ultimately lies with Members of Parliament, not with the Prime Minister, as Johnson was to discover on 4 September 2019. It may be suggested that the benefits of the Act are more than outweighed by its disadvantages. Indeed, a basic principle is at stake. The purpose of a Parliament in common law, apart from electing or deposing a King, is to advise the King, and therefore his Ministers, on the merit of Bills proposed by him: a principle with which the Act is clearly incompatible. Rather, it seems that a purpose of the Act is to complete the separation of the Sovereign from the function of Parliament, a purpose that is in direct conflict with the constitutional purpose of a Parliament in common law.

47.2. The Parties and the Ship of State

The history of the British system of government over the last three hundred years, since the Bill of Rights of 1689, conveys the impression of ambitious political Parties in the House of Commons accumulating political power by usurping the powers and functions of rival institutions of state – notably the Monarchy and the House of Lords – and using them to assert the doctrine of the Supremacy of Parliament, and more specifically, the House of Commons. There is no evidence, however, of any conscious intent and coherent policy to achieve this end. The more certain reality has been that the ship of state, having lost its rudder in 1339, has drifted at the mercy of the winds, storms, and ocean currents of political crises, narrowly avoiding disaster through the efforts of occasionally competent Kings and, latterly, of leaders in the House of Commons, although none of whom have had the particular competence for the role of ship's captain. This has resulted in the constitutional confusion that exists today. The Parties are not the repository of the law of the Constitution, nor do they hold the *imperium* of the people.

47.3. 'Brexit': Parliament Seeks to Impose its Will on the People (2016–19)

The issue in 1910 had lain between the Commons and the Lords, in which the former deprived the Lords of their right of consent. The constitutional issue now shifted from the Commons versus the Lords to one between the Commons and the People, whom the Commons were elected to represent. In particular, it arose over the question of whether the Commons, once elected, had the right to decide issues of major importance that had fallen within its mandate. The Commons was inclined to the view that, having inherited control over the Executive, it enjoyed much the same prerogative powers as the Monarchy had previously possessed. There was an inherent conflict in this situation however.

The issue in question was Britain's continued membership of the European Union, on which the people had not been consulted in the first place. The Parties appear to have taken the view that the people had been consulted over the issue of membership of the European Common Market, and that further consultation was not needed in this case. However, membership of a European Union was a very different issue from membership of a trading bloc. In particular, it required the surrender of political and constitutional independence. There had continued to be agitation within the ruling Party on the issue, which was now supported by a member of the public, one, Nigel Farage, who had formed a political Party, the United Kingdom Independence Party, or UKIP, to demand a referendum on the issue. The Party obviously had a popular following. Parliament had dealt with such activists in the past by portraying them, rightly or wrongly, as extremists, and legislating against them, or simply allowing other extremist groups to use intimidation to render them ineffective. Farage, however, was obviously an educated man and an elected member of the European Parliament, and his followers were, patently, typical members of the general public. The Conservative Prime Minister of the day, Cameron, was a firm supporter of continued British membership of the EU, as, indeed, were the majority of members of all Parties in the Commons, although they had been elected on entirely different issues. Cameron believed that there was little public support for leaving the EU, and, being anxious to rid himself of the nuisance, agreed to the holding of a referendum on the issue in June 2016. The majority in Parliament, who took the same view, agreed to abide by the result, almost certainly in the belief, like Cameron, that such a referendum would be defeated. Constitutionally, a referendum is a general election on a single-issue, leaving Parliament with no option in common law, but to accept the outcome, leaving the Crown to implement the verdict without any need for further Parliamentary involvement.

To the dismay of Parliament, the referendum produced a small but clear verdict of 52 per cent in favour of leaving the EU. The majority in Parliament left no doubt, however, that they were opposed to implementing the result, implying that Parliament enjoyed, either a royal prerogative in the matter, or an inherent right arising from its proclaimed constitutional supremacy. In either case, members appeared to realise that they were on difficult and untested ground.

The Prime Minister, being unwilling to lead the country out of the EU, resigned, and advised the Queen to appoint Mrs Theresa May, the Home Secretary, in his place. Mrs May was herself opposed to 'Brexit', or 'British exit' from the EU, as it quickly became known, but proceeded to implement it on the basis of what she and the outgoing Prime Minister are reported as referring to, cynically, as a 'damage limitation exercise'.[1] It soon became evident that, by this, she meant, the finding of a compromise

1   Charles Moore, *Daily Telegraph*, 4 March 2019.

solution, according to which Great Britain formally left, but retained important links that would enable it to rejoin with a minimum of readjustment. This proved to be unacceptable to both factions, however. Negotiations between Mrs May and the EU over the withdrawal were delayed by a snap general election in June 2017, in which Mrs May sought to strengthen her own position, only to lose her overwhelming majority, and be left with a hung Parliament. Her Government was able to remain in office because the Conservatives remained the largest Party, albeit with a majority who were still opposed to leaving the EU. The Labour and Liberal Parties in the House also were opposed to leaving.

None of this should have been a problem, because Parliament had already committed itself to accepting the outcome of the referendum, requiring it to withdraw from the European Union without further ado, but it was becoming clear that the majority in Parliament were looking for a formula that provided for effective 'damage limitation'. The conflict between the principle that Parliament represented the will of the people, and the new reality that Parliament was the elected government of the people, had at last come to a head.

In November 2018, Mrs May negotiated a Withdrawal Agreement with the EU, causing the 'Brexit' Secretary to resign over what he saw as fatal flaws in the document, although the 'remainers' who dominated the Cabinet accepted it. Both factions in Parliament rejected the agreement, however, some over its inclusion of the 'Irish backstop provisions', which effectively separated Northern Ireland from Great Britain, in order to avoid customs controls within Ireland.[2] Others objected to a proposed financial compensation for the EU of £39 billion and an alleged requirement to continue following EU regulations in major policy areas. Other obstacles were the continued jurisdiction of the European Court of Justice in respect of appeals from British courts. This implied the continuing application of European law. Otherwise, the Agreement allowed Britain to negotiate its own trade relations with other countries. Meanwhile, the EU undoubtedly saw the Irish backstop issue as giving it a crucial advantage in the negotiations, because if Britain left, it would probably have to leave Northern Ireland in the EU. Parliament refused three times to ratify the Agreement, the 'remainers' being opposed to anything less

---

2   The peace settlement with the Irish nationalists required that the border between North
       and South should remain permanently open.

than the continuation of full membership, while the 'leavers' regarded the Agreement as keeping Britain closely bound to the EU.

Meanwhile, obfuscations by the EU over the negotiation of a trade deal with Great Britain raised the prospect of Britain being forced to leave without one. To opponents of Brexit, this would be catastrophic for the British economy, while supporters asserted that it would pose no more than a major but temporary inconvenience. Thus, the Agreement left the two sides as far apart as ever. It also left the Liberal Democrats, the Scottish Nationalist Party and others in Parliament hoping that a second referendum might now produce a majority against Brexit. A preferred tactic was to force repeated delays to the implementation of the Agreement, evidently in the hope that the issue would eventually die a natural death. Mrs May, tenaciously hoping to obtain support for her Withdrawal Agreement with the EU, herself obtained successive delays in the negotiations until October 2019, with further postponements likely. Unable to gain Parliament's support for the Agreement, Mrs May resigned in July 2019.

She was succeeded as Prime Minister by Boris Johnson, an ardent 'leaver'. In October, he obtained a revised agreement, with new arrangements for Northern Ireland which Parliament approved for further scrutiny, but, as part of its opposition to leaving the EU, refused to pass into law before the deadline of 31 October, drawing upon the requirements of the Benn Act to force the Government to ask for a third delay. Meanwhile, there had long been public demonstrations outside Parliament, in support of both sides, and women Members of Parliament, in particular, were threatened in the streets by irate members of the public, making police escorts necessary, as frustration over Brexit rose to fever pitch. Seeing no alternative to the endless stonewalling of Parliament, Johnson advised the Queen to prorogue it, an action which Parliament ruled was in violation of the Benn Act, causing such outrage in the House that many, mostly women members, gave vent to a near hysteria that caused them desperately to turn to the Speaker – who was widely believed to be an opponent of 'Brexit', in contravention of the impartiality that was expected of his office – clinging to his chair and gown as if a lion had been released into the chamber. The Speaker responded by overruling the Prime Minister's action, but too late, as the Queen followed constitutional precedent in acceding to the Prime Minister's advice by proroguing Parliament. This precipitated a new general election in December 2019.

The outcome of the election was a large majority for the Government, which had wisely precluded opponents of Brexit from standing as Conservative candidates. Johnson now declared that Britain would leave the EU early in 2020, and the Withdrawal Agreement was ratified by the new Parliament (it had already obtained the approval of the EU) in January. Nevertheless, many issues with the EU remained unresolved.

In the meantime, opponents of the prorogation of the previous Parliament, which they had seen as a breach of the Benn Act, and with it their remaining defence against Brexit, won an appeal to the new Supreme Court. This ruled, firstly, that it was competent to hear the appeal against the prorogation of the former Parliament, and secondly, that the prorogation had violated the requirements of the Benn Act, and was therefore in contravention of the law. The Court had no means of enforcing its judgment, however. In any case, in making such a ruling, the Court had violated the principle in common law that, because the royal courts were creations of Parliament, they had no jurisdiction over what Parliament chose to do.

47.3.1. The Antipathy of Parliament Towards Referendums

Parliament has shown a marked antipathy towards referendums, probably because it has seen them as by-passing its own authority. Consequently, some Members regard referendums as having an advisory function only. They are, indeed, symptoms of the failure of Parliament adequately to represent the will of the people. Nevertheless, it is Parliament that provides for them and decides the questions that they are intended to ask. This reluctance to work according to democratic principles overlooks the rule, enunciated long ago by Alcuin, one of the great English ecclesiastical scholars of the eighth century. In a letter to Charlemagne, he had made the remark: *Vox populi, vox dei*, 'The voice of the people is the voice of God', a reference to the expression of the popular will through 'parliaments'. Parliament had come to see itself increasingly, however, not as the expression of the will of the people, but as the Government of the people, which the Brexit crisis had brought into question.

47.4. Significance of the Brexit Crisis

The crisis was significant in two respects. It was the inevitable consequence of nearly three hundred years of constitutional contradiction, manipulation and drift, which had been bound, sooner or later, to lead to an impossible situation, such as that expressed in the Brexit crisis, when the will of Parliament was confronted by the will of the people. The intensity of the crisis, when it came, was due to a conflict with Liberal Egalitarianism, which had guided public policy for nearly half a century, and was committed to the ending of national separatism.

47.5. International 'Law'

Britain's withdrawal from the European Union included a proposal for a revised agreement in respect of Northern Ireland. This would dispense with the requirement that Northern Ireland remain within the European Union in respect of travel and the trade in goods. To this, Mrs May objected in Parliament that it was already the law in respect of her Withdrawal Agreement with the EU, and that it was not possible to break what was, in effect, international law. In the face of this, the Withdrawal Agreement was allowed to remain in place, partitioning the United Kingdom.

The notion of international 'law' has, indeed, become widely accepted. In England, at least, this in itself would seem to be untenable. International relations, including treaties, had, since the Middle Ages at least, been regarded as the subject of 'royal law', or the royal prerogative, as opposed to statute law. In common law, international treaties were seen in many cases as affecting the interests of the people, and thus were subject to popular consent before they could be accepted as law. Exceptions could undoubtedly be made in respect of those agreements that (in the view of the Great Council, had it been functioning) had no adverse effect on the interests of the people. Otherwise, the only exception to the principle that the law was that which was approved by the people was divine law, or *ius divinum*. So-called 'international law' is more properly perceived as international agreements, regulations, precepts, or mandates, otherwise they provide a means by which governments can bind the people. Such agreements only have the force of law, as opposed to commitments of honour, if they have the specific approval of the 'People in Parliament'.

In such circumstances, a newly elected Parliament cannot be held to be committed in law to such an international 'treaty' when it is perceived to be in conflict with the internal interests of the United Kingdom.

47.6. The Parliamentary Expenses Scandal

When the King was extravagant in the use of his revenues for personal purposes, Parliament responded by restricting the Civil List. When the House of Commons appropriated executive power, its members acquired responsibility for the expenditure of public funds and the management of their own affairs, including the determination of their own salaries and expense allowances. To give members credit, a system of allowances was introduced.

In May 2009, however, abuse by Members of Parliament of their expense allowances, including 'systematic misappropriation', was uncovered by the press. The Parliamentary Standards Authority, which Members of the House of Commons had previously set up, tried to suppress publication of the details, on the ground that it would have a 'chilling effect' on its relationship with Members and reduce public confidence in the regulatory system. It even fought legal battles to suppress the publication of details. When the matter eventually reached the High Court, the court ruled that 'public money should be seen to be properly spent', and that the risk of 'embarrassing' Members of Parliament was no reason to keep the information secret. Publication of the details of the abuse led to public outrage. As a result, new rules were introduced by the Authority. Ten years later, in May 2019, the same source[3] revealed that the body set up to ensure greater transparency in the wake of the scandal was trying to prevent further revelations of financial abuse by several hundred Members, including a number of Ministers of the Crown.

There had been a need for Parliament to curb the extravagance of the King, but the transfer of executive power to Parliament had given it a monopoly of its own affairs, which was bound to be abused, sooner or later, not only financially, but also in how Parliament functioned.

3   *The Daily Telegraph*, 8 May 2019.

The public interest is always at risk from the self-interest of privileged individuals and groups. This brings us back to the common law of the Constitution, of which a significant part survived into fairly recent times, not only in respect of the three great institutions of state, but also in respect of certain functions and procedures. Montesquieu was correct in his conclusion that the success of the English system of government owed much to a division of powers between the legislative, executive and judicial functions of government, even though it did not apply in all respects. This division had ensured that no institution could wield absolute power, which it could then abuse. In its reduction of the Monarchy to a nominal role, the Commons had destroyed this division of powers and achieved absolute power for itself, making these abuses possible and creating a constitutional situation with unpredictable consequences, of which the Referendum crisis may only have been the first.

The obvious solution to both crises was to restore the division of powers, which Parliament was now in a position to block. That Britain's system of government had got itself into this disordered state was due to the failure of the Great Council to function during the last 650 years, the reason for which we traced to Edward III, and only a restoration of the common law of the Constitution by the Council offered a solution to this unlawful concentration of political power in the House of Commons. It will be remembered that, in common law, the King (or the Queen regnant) was elected by the people, and could equally be removed by them. It is the King, as head of the Executive, who, on the advice of his Ministers, summons Parliaments, and it is Parliament that, comprising representatives of public opinion, make possible the legislative function of government. Because the Crown needs Parliaments, in order to change the law and raise taxes, it accommodates them and compensates their members for any appropriate expenses and loss of income. It is also responsible for their orderly behaviour and effective functioning through the provision of clerical and security officers. By this division of powers, neither the King nor those attending Parliaments are in a position to exploit their position. We have also seen how the King and his justices preside over the Crown courts of law, in which justice is ensured by the jury system (on the principle that all men are judged by their peers). The proper functioning of the judicial system is ensured by the fact that the royal courts of law are exclaves of Parliament, sitting in its judicial capacity. No system works without problems, however, just as no clock regulates itself without a pendulum, and it was the loss of this constitutional regulator, in the form of the Great Council, that allowed the constitutional disorder that has continued during and since the Middle Ages.

In the event of any disagreement over questions of principle, procedure, or the common law of government itself (the *mos maiorum*), it is the advice of the Great Council that is final. As the members of the Great Council are themselves subject to election by their own shire constituencies, which enjoy the power to recall unsatisfactory members, whose own standards are deemed normally to be underwritten by the code of conduct appropriate to their noble ancestry, there is no reason for errors of judgement to be perpetuated.

47.7. Modern Parliaments and the Estates

In customary law, a Parliament may be defined as an annual assembly, by hereditary right, of all free men of the nation, according to their three Estates. However:

a. The First Estate lost its identity with the spread of the Christian Church, which usurped its function. Nor was the Church hereditary. Furthermore, it has refused to attend Parliament since the Middle Ages, except in respect of taxation of itself, because its teaching precludes its involvement in temporal matters.

b. The Second Estate excludes, since the advent of Norman rule, all except the eldest surviving son of a member of the Estate. This would have resulted over time in the virtual extinction of the Estate, which has survived only because of the arbitrary elevation by the King of members of the common people.

c. The Third Estate was itself greatly reduced in the tenth century by the Viking invasions, but is still identifiable by its adoption, since the thirteenth century, of inherited English surnames.

Although the Estates had become confused by the Early Middle Ages, they were not forgotten. On the contrary, the precedence of the First Estate, which has survived as the Church of England, and has been maintained ever since at all constitutional events; the honour of the Second Estate has remained deeply ingrained in English society until modern times as the preserver of national security and high standards in public life. It is symbolised in the widespread reverence for the former House of Lords and the very principle of nobility, until the Upper House was shattered by the reforms of the Blair government. The Second Estate is maintained only by the frequent elevation, by the King, of members of the Third Estate who are deemed to be distinguished by outstanding achievement, and who have usually won the respect of the majority of Englishmen. Meanwhile, the ideal of the common English freeman is as strong as ever, sustaining the constitutional principles of Parliament and legal rights. Indeed, the retention of the threefold structure of English society as an ideal is still much in evidence. The survival of the Second Estate, however corrupted by political interests, is important because of the support that it lends to the principle of Monarchy and the constitutional idea of 'the Crown'. Indeed, the survival of the Estate structure of English society, reduced though it is to little more than an idea that goes back to antiquity, has allowed England to retain its coherence and strength, which has been dissipated almost everywhere else in Europe, with negative consequences, such as instability and a lack of political coherence. Nowhere, indeed, has this ancient socio-political structure been more in evidence than in England's surviving institutions.

48. THE PREDICAMENT
OF PARLIAMENTS

HE REFERENDUM CRISIS of 2016–19 threw into stark relief the predicament that Parliaments had put themselves into by usurping the Crown. It was the ambition of Parliament to be the Government of the people, while still claiming to represent the people. It could not do both and it was never intended to be the first. Successive dynasties, from the Normans to the Stuarts, had abused the office of the King, and it had been necessary for Parliaments to put an end to this, but instead of being guided by the common law of the Constitution, all memory of which they had lost in any case, they had used their position to usurp the Crown, putting themselves into a contradictory situation. The problem now was that Parliament had long ceased to be a representative institution, as was demonstrated all too clearly by its need to call the referendum of 2016, and its rejection of the result. Yet Parliaments were not designed to rule, and one of the biggest problems faced by a restoration of the Constitution would undoubtedly be the unwillingness of Parliament to return to its proper function of representing the people.

49. THE APPOINTMENT OF MINISTERS

CONSTITUTIONALLY, MINISTERS ARE appointed by the Sovereign, traditionally from the more experienced members of the Second Estate, to enable them to perform their ever-widening range of functions, most of which they will delegate to their Ministers. In practice, this function has been assumed in recent times by the majority Party in Parliament.

A critical requirement of the choice of Ministers is not that they have expertise in the field for which their particular office is responsible, because that is provided by the Civil Service, but that they are individuals who have displayed loyalty, integrity, and competence in affairs of state, in whom the Crown, Parliament and the people can have confidence. Historically, the King made these appointments from the members of the Second Estate, in the light of advice from the Great Council. In the prolonged absence of the latter, however, these appointments left a great deal to be desired. Since the Parties in Parliament usurped the function of the King in the appointment of Ministers, they have followed a practice of appointing their own members, few of whom meet the requirements just mentioned. In spite of the frequent lack of experience and competence that has since followed, the system – particularly in the choice of Prime Minister – has generally enjoyed the confidence of the electors. This is partly because he is known to them, enjoys their confidence, and, more importantly, because he has promised to pursue policies of which they approve. Otherwise, his suitability for high office has often been open to question.

The restoration of the Great Council is likely to be resisted by the Parties, because it would nullify the notion of the Supremacy of Parliament. It would not and could not remove the right of Members of Parliament to hold ministerial office if they met the necessary criteria, but would undoubtedly insist on a higher stand of suitability, as well as restoring the separation of powers by requiring appointees to the Ministry to resign their seats in Parliament. This should not require them to surrender their Party membership, but would require them to surrender their Parliamentary seat, causing a by-election. This separation of powers between the legislative and executive functions of government should, indeed, have been restored long ago. It is important to remember, however, that Ministers of the Crown enjoy a right to sit in Parliament and contribute to the decisions taken. This ensures that the proper contact between the Crown and Parliament is sustained.

50. CONCLUSIONS

THE SAXON, JUTISH and Anglian kingdoms of England were united in the tenth century under a King who undoubtedly ruled with the consent of occasional Parliaments, representative of England as a whole, and with the advice of a Great Council of leading men from the shires. Although no record of these changes appears to have been kept, or, if they were, have not survived, they were undoubtedly in keeping with the requirements of common law, and evidence of them emerged only gradually, during the eleventh and later centuries.

With the onset of the Middle Ages, and particularly the imposition of Norman rule, came the direct influence of the Church of Rome, which replaced the religious teaching of the English Church and redefined the authority of the Crown. Kings, who had previously been elected by the people, now became the appointees of God in temporal matters, which required them to be the eldest surviving sons of their predecessors, dispensing with the election process at the coronation and the duty of the Crown to the people. As a result, many Kings were totally unsuited to their task, indulging in arbitrary rule and financial extravagance. Meanwhile, the existence and function of the Great Council, were lost, admitting another chaotic element into the constitutional process.

At the same time, representative Parliaments were restored. In the face of an often-chaotic state of financial management by successive Kings, the House of Commons used its right to approve taxation of the common people, who were now the main source of revenue to the Treasury, to embark upon a process of usurping the central function of the Monarchy, followed by the effective appropriation of the House of Lords. This allowed the political Parties that controlled the House of Commons to proclaim the 'supremacy' of Parliament. The confederate nature of English government was still reflected in the constituency system, however. This meant that elected delegates to Parliament represented, not England as a whole, but what had once been its member shires, albeit in a thoroughly confused manner.

Although the thirteen American colonies that had asserted their independence from the Crown had ceased to be of relevance to the Constitution, it is of some interest that they had established one of their own that was similarly influenced by their sense of common law, and looked to the surviving system under the Stuart kings for additional guidance. Accordingly, while rejecting the division of society into Estates they had established a confederacy of the member states, like that of the early English kingdoms, and a Congress, or Parliament, of two Houses.[1] As head of the executive function of government, Congress had provided, in lieu of a King, for a President, appointed by popular election. It was a system that faced a particular crisis on 6 January 2021, when the American electorate were bitterly divided, with the majority winning control of both Houses of Congress, while the substantial minority, represented by the outgoing President, Donald Trump, believed mistakenly that the election for a new President had been fraudulent. This had led them to express their frustration in the only manner available to them, by seizing control of the Capitol, or Parliament building in Washington, and indulging in wanton destruction. As in England, this crisis might have been avoided by the restoration of a Council of State (or Great Council), whose constitutional authority and independence of the Party system might have allowed it to intervene with an impartiality that all the other institutions lacked. Its survival in England might, likewise, have enabled the Brexit crisis and other causes of popular dissatisfaction to be avoided. This book reaches no conclusions or recommendations, beyond establishing what is believed to be the common law of the Constitution. Its purpose has been simply to inform. Any conclusions must be for the English people and, by implication, the other peoples of the United Kingdom, whose Continental roots also lie in the common Indo-European tradition.

---

1   In their original intent, the two Houses represented the Second and Third Estates.

PART XVII

•

THE BRITISH CONSTITUTION
IN COMMON LAW

T HE ENGLISH CONSTITUTION had its origin at the founding of a
united England under a common crown. Its features had their
origin in an age when an enterprising leader sought to leave the
main body of his people in order to set out in search of more or better
land. To this end, he would invite other warrior leaders of noble standing
to join the enterprise as his 'companions', each of whom undoubtedly
had his own hopes also of booty, and who brought an army of such free
warriors as they could raise for the purpose. If the enterprise met with
success in finding suitable lands for settlement, to which all members of
the enterprise could bring their families, the leader's companions, in their
capacity as elders of the new, founding nation, would meet in council
to call upon their followers to elect a king. To him, all would renew
their declaration of loyalty, and delegate such of their *imperium* as he
was entitled to, in order to rule. In return, the new king would commit
himself to a regal contract with the people, under which he would give
his protection and service as their common ruler.

Based on traditional practice, this simple procedure surely formed
the basis of the new English confederacy's constitution, comprising the
forty or so member nations, Angle, Jutish and Saxon, with their respective
shires or counties. This included a council of the elders of the people and
a common annual assembly of all free men involved in the enterprise,
summoned from time to time for consultation by the King. Centuries
later, the English were joined by the previously existing indigenous
nations of the British Isles: the Welsh, Scots and Northern Irish, who
had, undoubtedly, inherited similar cultural traditions. Collectively, they
formed the United Kingdom of Great Britain and Northern Ireland,
acknowledging the same Crown and attending the same Parliaments to
consider issues of common concern.

What follows is an attempt to translate the common law of the
Constitution into a form that would be appropriate to the present day.

51. THE LEGAL SOURCE OF POLITICAL POWER: THE *IMPERIUM*

51.1. The Shire (County) Councils

As a confederacy of the forty nations, their respective shires (counties) are the foundation of the English Constitution. It is from the freemen of England, through their respective shires or county Councils, that the Constitution derives its *imperium*, that is to say, its existence and powers. The executive officer of each of these councils is historically the shire reeve, or sheriff, who, although today confined to more humble duties, is properly elected by the free men of the shire. In the early Middle Ages, the confederacy was reduced to thirty-nine nations.

51.1.1 The *Imperium*: Its Source and Nature

The English Constitution derives its authority and, indeed, its very existence, from the *imperium* that was delegated by the free men of the forty or so participating nations, or shires, Saxon, Angle and Jutish, through their respective elders and kings. At the time, they were the over-kings of the West Saxon, Mercian and Northumbrian confederacies, in accordance with the treaty concluded at Eamont Bridge in the year 927, with Æthelstan, of the West Saxon royal house, and his successors, as over-King. The flow of political authority was upwards (the reverse direction to that ordained by the Church), and each nation contributed its own *folcland* (or territorial jurisdiction, better known to us as its 'shire') to the new common kingdom of England. It should be noted that the foregoing has since taken account of the territorial rearrangement, undertaken by some of the communities of western Mercia by Æthelstan's successor, Edward the Elder. To these were added, in 1226, the men of two further shires: Cumberland and, to its south-east, Westmorland, of which the latter belonged to the men of the 'Western Moors'. They were settlers from Northumberland who had migrated westward from the general area of Teesdale. The territory of Cumberland extended from north-western Lancashire, around the western coast, as far north as the Solway Firth, and the admission of these two nations brought the jurisdiction of the common English Constitution to a total of forty-four nations.

Later, the jurisdiction of the men of Lothian was transferred as a gift to the Scottish kings, possibly as a peace offering and because they were beyond the effective jurisdiction of an English King who ruled from Westminster. The effect was to reduce his jurisdiction to forty-two shires. This can only be regarded as a gross abuse of royal authority and obligation, made possible by Church influence in favour of royal autocracy, because there is no evidence of such a request or approval by the men of Lothian.

Excluded from the member shires was Cornwall, which remained Welsh in speech and custom and continued, even after its incorporation under the West Saxon crown, to be governed by its own assembly, known as the Court of Stannary.[1] This incorporation had probably occurred under Egbert in 838, following the battle of Hingston Down. For administrative purposes, however, Cornwall has long been treated on the same basis as an English shire.

Today, the kingdom of England finds itself united under the House of Windsor, having in more recent centuries formed a union, and more recently a confederacy, as it now is in effect, with its neighbours, the Welsh, the Scots, and the people of Northern Ireland, collectively known as Great Britain.[2] The description, 'Great' Britain, has avoided confusion in France and beyond with Brittany, which also is rendered as 'Bretagne' in French, because of the massive immigration from Britain during the time of the Anglo-Saxon-Jutish invasion.

51.1.2. The Constitutional Triangle

The English common law system of government forms a triangle of three separate, but interlocking, institutions: the Great Council, the King,

---

1   'Stannary' appears of Celtic origin, whose antecedent – which could even then have meant assemblies controlling mining and trade – Roman's associated with tin ore, the region's chief export. It seems the Romans coined it from the word *stagnum*, which in Pliny's time referred to an alloy of tin and silver – hence tin becoming *stannum* and Stannary's mistaken association with tin, whose mining continued to be an important activity in Cornwall.
2   Ireland, and hence Northern Ireland, is not geographically a part of Britain.

and Parliament. To these may be added the King's Council (effectively a standing committee of the Great Council, except that its membership has been more widely based and subject to frequent replacement. Later, the King's Council came to be known as the King's Privy Council, which enabled the monarchy to become, administratively, a much more effective institution. It was the relationship in common law between these three main institutions – the King, Council and Assembly – that made possible a strong and stable structure, the most advanced in Western Europe at the time, subject only to the personalities of those who operated it.

51.2. The Great Council

51.2.1. Functions

In so far as the functions of the Great Council of England are properly understood, they are:

1. To meet when summoned by the King, or by its elected leader, or at the request of a quorum of its members;
2. To elect one of its number as caretaker of the Sword of State, whose duties are to precede the King on formal occasions, bearing the Sword, and to ensure the removal of the King from office if he should be so instructed by the Council;
3. To act as custodian of the Constitution;
4. To act as custodian of the *imperium* of the people;
5. To ensure the continuity of the Crown, if necessary, by appointing a regent or regency council;
6. In the absence or default of the King, to summon Parliaments;
7. To advise a Parliament in respect of suitable candidates for succession to the Crown;
8. To arrange for coronations and to endow a King elect with the *imperium*;
9. To endow and uphold the regal contract between the King and the people;
10. To certify that new laws, or amendments to existing laws, for the attention of a Parliament do

not conflict with customary or statute law, except
where they are for the purpose of amendment;

11. At its discretion, to advise the King and, or,
    Parliament, in respect of matters that are, in its view,
    of particular concern to the public interest;

12. To take evidence from such individuals and groups
    as may be of value to the Council in formulating
    its advice to the Crown or to a Parliament;

13. To receive the *imperium* of the people and
    act as custodian of the Constitution;

14. To guide the people in their choice of a new King;

15. To crown the King elect and vest him with
    the royal sceptre, thereby endowing him with
    the *imperium* as ruler of the people;

16. To advise the King on the lawfulness of his proposed acts;

17. To advise the King on any matter believed to be of
    importance to the welfare of the Crown and people;

18. At its discretion, to advise the King and Parliament
    in respect of any matter deemed by it to be of
    particular importance to the national interest;

19. To attend to the interests of any shire deemed by its
    representative in the Council to have just cause;

20. To remove from office any King rejected by the people.

51.2.2. Composition

The Council comprises noble elders of the people, not less than forty years of age, comprising a representative from each of the forty-two shires of England, elected for life by the freemen of each shire, unless and until removed by a clear majority of the same. The freemen of a shire are entitled to recall and replace their representative on the Council. The advice and actions of the Council are liable to affect the interests of England's neighbours, and for this reason the interests of the other members of the Union need to be provided for, not on a county basis, because the counties of Wales, Scotland and Northern Ireland have a different and comparatively recent origin. Protecting the interests of the other members of the Union seems to call for their representation in the Council on a population basis. On this assumption, England's forty-two Councillors would be augmented by two from Wales, four from Scotland, and one from Northern Ireland. The basis of selection in these cases would need to be much the same, that is, respected elders in age and experience, bearing in mind the purposes of the Council.

The English members of the Council are appointed from the highly respected and noble elders of the shires or nations that they represent, in the case of England, at least, companions of the King in the field and learned in the law, each being elected to represent one of the forty-two shires. The only reliable evidence that we have on the size of the original Council comes from one held in 1153, when thirty-six members were recorded as attending. Making allowance for the likelihood that not all were able to attend on that occasion, it suggests that the free men of each of the traditional shires should elect one member of the Council, for life, drawn from among the nobility of the shire, being not less than forty years of age and held in high esteem. On this basis and that described above, a full Council has forty-nine members. Where suitable candidates of noble birth cannot be found within an English shire, they should be sought from outside the shire.

The freemen of a shire are apparently entitled to recall their representative on the Council to explain his actions. Should the later be adjudged by his electors to be unsuitable to remain in office, a new representative may be elected for life in his place. Otherwise, the successor to a Council member is his nearest surviving relative, subject to the confirmation of the freemen of the shire. A member of the Council is deemed to be an elder of the land,[3] of whom one such among the Danes was once said to be the heroic leader, Beowulf.

To enable the Council to carry out its duties, an appropriate chamber, with associated staff and facilities, is required to be provided by the King, as are the Houses of Parliament themselves.[4] The site of the original chamber would have been lost by the end of the fourteenth century, but the constitutional importance of the Council is surely reflected, sub-consciously, in the chamber of the House of Lords, as embellished by

---

3   See *Beowulf*, ed. Alexander, M., line 56, except that 'elder of the people' may be more appropriate then 'elder of the land'.

4   The existing House of Lords, which would now become vacant, was intended for the use of the Council, without its significance being properly recognised. It may be too closely associated with Parliament, however, to be suitable for such an independent body.

Pugin in 1834. The proper location of the Council's chamber and facilities is undoubtedly in or close to Westminster, but not in the Parliament building, whose purpose is rather different. What is currently intended and used as the chamber of the House of Lords properly remains only as the Parliament chamber.

51.2.3. Powers

1. To protect the interests of the nation, where necessary, by advising the King to summon it to arms, or to take other appropriate steps;
2. To meet at the summons of the King, or of a quorum of its members;
3. In the absence of the King, to elect one of its members to preside over its meetings;
4. To ensure the continuity of government by appointing Regents or Regency Councils;
5. To appoint an Accession Council;
6. To assist and advise the people in their choice of a new King;
7. To uphold the regal contract between the King and the people;
8. To render advice to the King and, if appropriate, to an assembled Parliament;
9. To certify, to the best of its ability, that new laws for the attention of a Parliament do not conflict with customary or existing statute law, except where they are for the purpose of amendment;[5]
10. To act as the custodian of customary law;[6]
11. To propound the law when called upon by the King or Parliament;
12. To function as the highest court of law in respect of offences alleged to have been committed by members of the Second Estate;
13. To summon Parliaments in the absence or default of the King;
14. To consider matters of public interest for the purpose, where appropriate, of advising the King or a Parliament;

---

5   See: Schmid, *Gesetze*, 21, and F. Liebermann, *Die Gesetze der Angelsachsen* (1903), i. 12. The assent of Parliament is enacted by the King.
6   With no distinction between law and established custom.

15. To act as custodian of the *imperium* of the people, and to bestow it and the Crown upon the new King;

16. Following the death or abdication of the King, to establish an Accession Council, comprising certain of its members, to be directed to identify one or more likely successors, and to submit his or their names for the decision and approval of a Parliament;

17. In respect of matters of public interest in the conduct of affairs of state, to summon appropriate individuals or groups to render advice;

18. To elect one of its number as caretaker of the Sword of State, to precede the King on state occasions, whose functions are to ensure the removal of the King from office where he is deposed by a Parliament, to which end the Caretaker of the Sword is entitled to summon appropriate assistance;

19. On the request of a Parliament, sitting as a court of law, to summon the attendance of the King to answer charges laid against him, and to ensure the execution of its verdict;

20. On its own initiative, or on the advice of a Parliament, to call for the abdication of the King;

21. Upon the death, abdication or removal of the King from office, to retrieve the *imperium* on behalf of Council.

The financing of the needs of the Council is probably determined by agreement between the Council and the King.

51.3. The King

51.3.1. Succession
Following the death or abdication of the previous King, the usual rules of succession are that the claimant must:

1. Be a male member of the royal house, preferably of close family relationship to the previous king, failing which he may be an individual of great distinction,

proposed by a Parliament summoned for the
purpose, on the advice of the Great Council;
2. Be of age;[7]
3. Be adjudged by the Council, after consultation with the shire
   reeves and others, to be a fit and suitable person to rule;
4. Be approved by a Parliament;
5. At a coronation assembly, (i) render an oath of commitment
   to the people and their leaders, and receive a corresponding
   oath of allegiance from them, (ii) be elected by the people,
   (iii) be granted the *imperium* by the leader of the Great
   Council, through the bestowal of the royal sceptre and
   the sword of state, (iv) be crowned as a sign of his dignity,
   and endowed with his priestly status by the archbishop,
   being also presented with the Sword of State and such
   other sacred insignia of office as is the custom.

51.3.2. Functions
1. In his capacity as the High Priest of the people, the King
   represents them in their relations with the Supreme Deity;
2. In his capacity as the representative and sovereign
   ruler of the people, he appoints intermediaries
   in his relations with foreign powers;
3. In his capacity as the fountain and executor of the
   law, the King acts on the advice of the Great Council,
   subject to the consent of a Parliament, to promote
   the government of the people in their best interests,
   in which capacity he refers to himself as 'we';
4. To act as the Supreme Judge when Parliament is
   sitting as a court of law, and to appoint justices
   to act on his behalf in the lesser courts;
5. To lead the people in times of war, and to
   appoint officers to command in the field.

---

7   Chadwick questions the principle of the election of kings, arguing that English history
    provides no evidence that a vote was taken. See H. Chadwick, *Studies on Anglo-Saxon
    Institutions* (New York, 1905), 357; an election was meant as a collective affirmation,
    gauged according to whether it was convincing or not, not a voting system as perceived
    today. Such affirmations are still used in British coronations, although as a formality.

As the King is elected by the people, and the Council does not over-rule the will of the people, it acts as their agent in ensuring that the King rules in accordance with the law and the popular will. To this end, before their submission to a Parliament, Bills are submitted to the Council for its confirmation that they are consistent with the Constitution and with the law, unless their stated purpose is to amend the law. It is assumed that the purpose of this is to notify the Council as to the intentions of the Crown and to ensure that there is no conflict with the requirements of the Constitution or with existing common or statute law.

To enable him to carry out his duties, the King appoints Ministers and other officers of the Crown, upon such conditions as may be deemed appropriate. He may also, in consultation with the Great Council, appoint members of the King's Council, Ministers of the Crown, and such other officers as are required to enable him to meet his responsibilities. After first obtaining the approval of the Great Council that it is consistent with the requirements of customary law, the King proposes legislation for the consent of a Parliament of the people. Furthermore, where Ministers are appointed from leading members of the majority Party in Parliament, in keeping with current practice, it is appropriate, in order to avoid any conflict of interest, for such members to resign their seats. This gives rise to by-elections. The existing practice, whereby Ministers retain their seats as elected members of Parliament, creates a conflict of interests between the executive and legislative functions of government, in that a single individual sits in Parliament as an officer and representative of the King, and at the same time he continues to sit as the elected representative of the people of his constituency. Many would regard this as an impossible duplication of roles, raising serious doubts about the suitability of any individual to undertake both duties in a satisfactory manner. Thus, one function requires popular appeal and an instinct for political issues, while the other requires administrative competence and a grasp of policy needs, which, in turn, presuppose a long experience of public policy. Also, it is impossible for any individual to give his full attention to both roles. It also raises a practical problem, because the electors have long been used to, and apparently enjoyed, choosing between individual political leaders and pre-selected policy options, which they may be unwilling to forego. Not surprisingly, many members of Parliament enjoy the power and influence that the occupation of both positions offers, and would be unwilling to surrender the opportunity to enjoy the privilege.

51.3.3. Deposition

What the people may give, they may also take away, and a Parliament, in consultation with the Great Council, enjoys the authority to commit the King for trial by the Council if his rule is not regarded as having been conducted in accordance with the law, or for the benefit of the people, or in keeping with the dignity of his office.[8] Such has been the delegation of royal powers, however, that the likelihood of this must be regarded as very low, with the only real exception in today's terms being the risk of a failure to maintain the dignity of the royal office.

51.3.4. The Ministry

Ministers of the Crown are appointed by the King from among the great men of the realm, on the advice of the Great Council, after consultation with the Privy Council. Ministers used to be chosen from among the leading members of the Second Estate, with the Lord Chancellor as the King's chief minister, but, since the rise of the Party System in Parliament in the eighteenth century, it has been the practice for the King to appoint the leader of the majority Party in the House of Commons as his Prime Minister. On the basis of the Prime Minister's advice, other Ministers are appointed from among the leading members of his own Party in Parliament.

This differs from the requirement of common law, according to which the function of a Parliament is to represent the wishes and interests of the people, of all classes, including the approval of Bills which they deem likely to affect them, and the election and depositing of Kings. Since the suppression of the Great Council, however, the members of the Council, who sit and advise by constitutional right, have established themselves as a separate chamber in Parliament. This has come to be known as the House of Lords, because it has attracted all other members of the Second Estate, who originally sat as a separate group in the Parliament chamber, alongside the Commons. This left the original Parliament chamber to the sole use of the Commons, causing it to be known as the House of Commons, adjacent to which sat the new House of Lords.

8   Kemble, *Saxons in England*, ii. 219.

The modern practice, whereby select Members of the House of Commons are appointed to Ministerial office on the advice of the Prime Minister, and collectively form the Government, not only violates the principle of the division of powers, as between the legislative and executive functions of government, as the common law appears to require, but is almost certainly inefficient. This is not only because it is very difficult to fulfil both functions (legislative and executive) effectively, and relies on Ministers with a very limited background who rely heavily upon the advice of the Civil Service, but also because the two functions call for individuals with very different backgrounds and abilities. A good member of today's Parliaments has political intuition, a capacity for effective public speaking and influencing crowds; concern for the welfare of individuals and individual groups; and an instinct for assessing the popular mood. By contrast, a Minister of the Crown is an administrator and effective policy-maker, with a sound background in affairs of state and a capacity, both for compromise and for getting things done in an efficient and effective manner. These two aptitudes, as Members of Parliament and as Ministers of the Crown, are rarely found together, and are best kept separate, as the common law of the Constitution appears to recognise.

Because a Member of Parliament may not assume gainful employment under the Crown, any Member who is offered and accepts such employment should forthwith resign his seat in Parliament, giving rise to the need for a by-election. Nevertheless, a Minister of the Crown may attend a Parliament for the purpose of hearing the views of the House on a matter of interest to him, or in order to address the House in respect of that interest. It is suggested that those seats on the front bench of the Parliament Chamber currently reserved for the use of Ministers continue to be reserved for that purpose.

51.4. The King's Council

Better known as the King's Privy Council, and attached to the Royal Court, its members are appointed by the King at the beginning of his reign, in consultation with the Great Council. Membership includes the King's Ministers. Its purpose is to provide advice to the King on a day-today basis. This Council is effectively a standing committee of the Great Council, except that it includes only a few representatives of the latter, and usually on a temporary basis, while other members of the King's Council, chosen and appointed by the King, are drawn from outstanding men and women of the Second and Third Estates. The Council is available at the King's convenience, often at short notice. It has no powers, other than advisory, with the exception of those members who are appointed by the King as his Ministers.

51.5. Parliaments

The identity and social allegiances of individuals must have begun to break down during the great migrations of the Scandinavian Iron Age, as a result of competition in the search for new lands, because the Saxon, Jutish and Anglian immigrants to Britain were already divided into free men, who took the lead in these migrations, and the unfree, who could do little better than follow, in the hope of improving their own lot in life. The Viking invasions of England in the ninth and tenth centuries resulted in further social breakdown, reducing to a minority those who could still claim an identity as free men, and hence a right to attend and be represented in Parliaments. The Norman occupation of England complicated the situation further, by alleging that the only freemen were those who were still in possession of a smallholding. The situation was reversed only when the right to attend or be represented in a Parliament came to be defined by income. This not only broadened the basis of attendance, but expanded it further, when prosperity increased during the Middle Ages. The rise of political Parties led them to broaden their own bases of popular support, so that it may be said that, today, all men and women who live within the law are once again entitled to attend and speak, or be represented, in Parliaments.

In terms of customary law, an English Parliament may still be defined as an assembly of the Second and Third Estates, summoned each year by the King, where two representatives of the Third Estate are elected from each of the thirty-nine shires of England (which have long since dispensed with their respective under-kings), and additional representatives elected by the larger towns and cities. These are represented on a population basis.

On account of its long association with England, it seems appropriate that representatives of the inhabitants of Cornwall should also attend, even though it is not one of the founding shires. The First Estate has long since withdrawn from Parliamentary proceedings. There are also such representatives of Wales, Scotland and Northern Ireland as have been agreed over the years, making it a British Parliament.[9]

Parliaments are held on hallowed ground, for the purpose of deliberating upon all new laws proposed by the King that are not within his sole prerogative. Parliaments are also convened for the purpose of electing the King. Where it is deemed to be appropriate, in exceptional circumstances, a Parliament may be summoned by the Great Council to deliberate upon such matters as the Council may choose to put before it. These include issues concerning relations between the King and the people, and, following the death of his predecessor, the need to elect a new King.

51.5.1. Attendance

The purpose of a Parliament is to enable the King or, in the absence or default of the King, the Great Council, to consult the people in respect of changes to the law and such other matters as are expected to affect the interests of the realm and its people. It is the right of those attending a Parliament to submit petitions to the King and to raise issues for deliberation.

The accommodation of his Parliaments, and any remuneration deemed to be appropriate to their members, is provided by the King, as also are such clerks and other officers as may be needed for the better order and effectiveness of the proceedings.

It appears that the King, in his judicial capacity, may call upon a Parliament, in its capacity as the highest court of law for appeals in respect of offences committed by members of the Third Estate, to establish permanent standing committees to function as courts of law, under justices appointed by him.

---

9   Based on the medieval requirement that two knights should represent each county in Parliament, which is assumed to derive from earlier practice. The importance attached to local representation is still represented in the current system by the use of constituencies.

A new Parliament must be summoned for the purpose of electing the King. Where the King has lost the confidence of the people, a Parliament may pass a motion of condemnation and, if so inclined, call upon the Great Council to try the King with a view to requiring his abdication.

51.5.2. Issues Particular to Individual Member States of the United Kingdom

One concern, too often overlooked, is that some of the issues that come before the common Parliaments of the United Kingdom are specific only to particular member states. This has largely been dealt with in recent years by the policy of decentralisation, giving Northern Ireland, Scotland and Wales separate governments for regional issues. This has not applied to England, however, and it would seem appropriate that where, in the view of the Speaker of the House of Commons, such an issue comes before Parliament, it is his duty to make an appropriate declaration that will limit voting on that issue to those members who represent English constituencies.

Bibliography

Arnold, Thomas, ed. 1882-1885. Symeonis monachi opera omnia. London: Longman.

Ashley, M. 1999. British Kings and Queens. London: Robinson.

Bede. 1930. The Ecclesiastical History of the English People. Loeb Classical Library. Edited by G.P. Goold. Translated by J.E. King. London: Harvard University Press.

Benveniste, E. 1973. Indo-European Language and Society. London: Faber & Faber.

Blackstone, William. 1893. Commentaries on the Laws of England. Edited by George Sharswood. Philadelphia: J.B. Lippincott Co.

Butler, H. E., ed. 1949. The Chronicle of Jocelin of Brakelond. Thomas Nelson.

Caesar, Julius. 1951. Caesar: The Conquest of Gaul. Translated by S.A. Handford. Harmondsworth: Penguin Books.

Chadwick, H.M. 1963. Studies on Anglo-Saxon Institutions. New York: Russell & Russell, Atheneum Publishers, Inc.

Clark Hall, J.R. 1960. A Concise Anglo-Saxon Dictionary. 2nd. Printed in Canada: Cambridge University Press.

Dicey, A.V. 1923. Introduction to the Study of the Law of the Constitution. 8th. London: Macmillan & Co. Ltd.

Douglas, D. 1953. English Historical Review 526-545.

Edwards, Edward, ed. 1866. Liber monasterii de Hyda : comprising a chronicle of the affairs of England, from the settlement of the Saxons to the reign of King Cnut. London: Longmans, Green, Reader, and Dyer.

Elton, O, trans. 1894. The first Nine Books of the Danish History of Saxo Grammaticus. London: D. Nutt.

Field, J. 2002. The Story of Parliament. London: James & James.

Fitz Nigel, Richard. 1950. De necessariis observantiis Scaccarii dialogus qui vulgo dicitur Dialogus de Scaccario. London: Thomas Nelson & Sons.

Florence. 1848-9. Chronicon ex Chronicis. Edited by B Thorpe. London: Sumptibus Societatis.

Flower, J.W. 1864. "Notices of the Family of Cobham of Sterborough Castle, Lingfield, Surrey." Surrey Archaeological Collections, 115-94.

Fortescue, John. 1885. The Governance of England. 1st. Edited by Charles Plummer. London: Oxford University Press.

Ganshof, F. L. 1952. Feudalism. Translated by Grierson P. London: Longman, Green and Co.

Gimbutas, M. 1991. The Civilization of the Goddess: The World of Old Europe. San Francisco: Harper Collins.

Gimbutas, Marija. 1997. The Kurgan Culture and the Indo-Europeanization of Europe. Edited by M.R. and Jones-Bley, K Dexter. Vols. Journal of Indo-European Studies, Monograph No.18. Washington D.C.: Institute for the Study of Man.

Gneist, Rudolf. 1886. The English Parliament. Translated by R. J. Shee. Boston: Little, Brown, and Co.

Grinnell-Milne, Duncan William. 1968. The Killing of William Rufus. Newton Abbot: David & Charles.

Hearne, T, ed. 1728. Liber Niger Scaccarii. Oxonii: E Theatro Sheldoniano.

Holt, J. 1985. Magna Carta and Medieval Government. London: Hambledon Press.

Joliffe, J.E.A. 1933. Pre-Feudal England: the Jutes. London: Frank Cass & Co. Ltd.

Jumiéges, William. 2003. The Gesta Normannorum Ducum of , Orderic Vitalis, and Robert of Torgni. Edited by E.M.C Van Houts. Vol. II. Oxford: Clarendon Press.

Klindt-Jensen, Ole. 1957. Denmark Before the Vikings. London: Thames and Hudson.

Liebermann, F. 1894. "The Text of Henry I's Coronation Charter." Transactions of the Royal Historical Society (Cambridge University Press) VIII: 21-48.

Liebermann, Felix. 1903. Die Gesetze der Angelsachsen. Halle & S: Niemeyer.

Loyn, H.R. 1962. Anglo-Saxon England and the Norman Conquest. London: Longmans.

Maitland, F.W. 1908. The Constitutional History of England. Cambridge: Cambridge University Press.

Mallory, J.P. 1989. In Search of the Indo-Europeans. London: Thames & Hudson.

Mallory, J.P., and D.Q. Adams. 2006. The Oxford Introduction to Proto-Indo-European and the Indo-European World. Oxford: Oxford University Press.

Mellows, W.T., ed. 1927. Henry of Pytchley's Book of Fees. Kettering: T. Beaty Hart.

Mills, A.D. 2003. Oxford Dictionary of British Place Names. Oxford: Oxford University Press.

Morris, J. 1995. The Age of Arthur. London: Orion Books Ltd.

Müller, E. 1886. Saxonis Grammatici Historia Danica. Strassburg.

Myres, J.N.L. 1998. The English Settlements. Oxford: Oxford University Press.

Newton, Sam. 1993. The Origins of 'Beowulf' and the Pre-Viking Kingdom of East Anglia. Cambridge: Brewer, Athenaeum Press, Ltd.

Northcote Toller, T. 1921. An Anglo-Saxon Dictionary. Oxford: Oxford University Press.

Oleson, T. J. 1957. "Edward the Confessor's Promise of the Throne to Duke William of Normandy." The English Historical Review 72 (283): 221-288.

Oxenstierna, E. 1957. The World of the Norsemen. London: Weidenfeld and Nicolson.

Parris, M. n.d. Historia Anglorum.

Plummer, Charles, and John Earle, . 1892. Two of the Saxon chronicles parallel : with supplementary extracts from the others. Oxford: Clarendon Press.

Powell, J.E. and Wallis, K. 1968. The House of Lords in the Middle Ages. London: Weidenfeld & Nicolson.

Puhvel, J. 1987. Comparative Mythology. Baltimore, Maryland, U.S.A.: Johns Hopkins University Press.

Reed, T. Dayrell. 1947. The Rise of Wessex. London: Methuen & Company.

Richardson, H. G. 1949. "The English Coronation Oath." Speculum XXIV: 44-75.

Ritson, J. 1809. The Jurisdiction of the Court Leet. 2nd. London.

Roger. 1867. Chronica Magistri Rogeri de Houedene. Edited by William Stubbs. London: Longmans, Green, Reader, and Dyer.

Sanders, Ivor John. 1960. English Baronies. A study of their origin and descent, 1086-1327. London: Clarendon Press.

n.d. Saxo Grammaticus: Gesta Danorum.

Schramm, Percy Ernst. 1937. A History of the English Coronation . Oxford: Clarendon Press.

Sedgefield, W.J., ed. 1899. King Alfred's translation of Boethius, with the Metres of Boethius. Oxford: Clarendon Press.

Skeat, W.W., ed. 1871-87. The Anglo-Saxon Gospels (Gospel of St Matthew). Cambridge.

Smith, Albert Hugh. 1964-1965. The place-names of Gloucestershire. Cambridge: Cambridge University Press.

Stenberger, M. 1962. Sweden: Ancient People and Places. London: Thames & Hudson.

Stenton, F.M. 1947. Anglo-Saxon England. 2nd. Oxford: Clarendon Press.

Stubbs, William. 1867. Gesta Regis Henrici Secundi: the chronicle of the reigns of Henry II and Richard I, A.D. 1169-1192. London: Longmans, Green, Reader, and Dyer.

—. 1913. Select Charters: Earliest times to Edward I. 9th. Oxford: Oxford University Press.

Swanton, M.J. 1997. The Anglo-Saxon Chronicle. London: J.M. Dent.

Tacitus, Publius Cornelius. c. AD 98. Germania.

Tait, James, ed. 1920. The Chartulary or Register of the Abbey of St. Werburgh, Chester. Vol. 79: pt 1. Manchester: Chetham Society.

Taylor, H. 1895. The Origin and Growth of the English Constitution. Mass., U.S.A.: Houghton, Mifflin & Co.

Thompson, E.A. 1965. The Early Germans. Oxford: Clarendon Press.

Tolkien, John Ronald Reuel. 1982. Finn and Hengest: The Fragment and the Episode. Edited by A. Bliss. London: Allen & Unwin.

Vinogradoff, Paul. 1892. Villainage in England : essays in English mediaeval history. Oxford: Clarendon Press.

Wakelin, Martyn. 1988. The Archaeology of English. London: Batsford.

Walker, Curtis H. 1924. "The Date of the Conqueror's Ordinance Separating the Ecclesiastical and Lay Courts." The English Historical Review XXXIX: 399-400.

7th century. 'Widsith' in The Exeter Book.

Witney, K.P. 1976. The Jutish Forest, A Study of the Weald of Kent from 450 to 1380 A.D. London: University of London.

—. 1982. The Kingdom of Kent. Chichester: Phillimore.

Zosimus. 1887. Historia Nova. Edited by L Mendelssohn

Index

Volume I, pages i– 955
Volume II, pages 957–1788

A

abbeys 136, 137, 138, 139, 413, 724, 787, 901, 1037
abbots: attendance at Councils 247, 531, 533, 540, 542–543, 549, 626, 634, 635; attendance at Parliament 656, 697, 711, 734, 748, 773, 787–788, 980, 1024, 1037; land ownership 139, 395, 428, 440, 443; mints owned by 348; replaced by Norman clergy 416; taxation 917
Aborigines 1312–1313
absolute monarchy 359, 483, 487, 740, 766, 890, 902, 950–951, 1045, 1417, 1099, 1115, 1128, 1234
Aclea, Battle of 296, 300
acts of Parliament 904, 948, 995, 1002, 1107, 1199–1200; Act Against Tumultuous Petitioning (1661) 1191; Act for the Abolition of Feudal Tenures (1660) 1188; Act for the Advancement of True Religion (1543) 1039; Act for the Dissolution of the Greater Monasteries (1539) 1037; Act for the Union with Ireland (1801) 1391; Act in Restraint of Annates (1532) 977; Act of Accord (1460) 926; Act of Proclamations (1539) 1058–1062, 1199; Act of Six Articles (1539) 1038; Acts of Attainder 1040, 1142; Acts of Oblivion 1161, 1171, 1188; Acts of Repeal 1071; Acts of Settlement 1322, 1336, 1340, 1343, 1364, 1171, 1508, 1235, 1260, 1264–1271, 1612; Acts of Succession 954, 1036, 1067, 1093, 1419–1420, 1214; Acts of Supremacy 943, 1015, 1046, 1074, 1190; Acts of Uniformity 1065–1066, 1075, 1190, 1191; Acts of Union 1064, 1300, 1332–1333, 1615; Administration of Justice Acts 1452; Appellate Jurisdiction Acts 1441, 1442, 1511–1512; Army Regulation Act (1871) 1487; Assessment Act (1660) 1202; Australia Acts 1590; Bishops' Exclusion Act (1642) 1189; British Immigration Act (1971) 1662; British Nationality Act (1948) 1653, 1657; British North America Act (1867) 1589; Church of England Assembly (Powers) Act (1919) 1572; Commonwealth Immigrants Act (1962) 1656; Constitutional Reform Act (2005) 1675, 1745; Coronation Oath Act (1689) 1251, 1265; Corporation Act (1661) 1190; County Courts Act (1846) 1456, 1512–1513; Courts Act (1971) 1696; Crown Proceedings Act (1947) 1635–1636, 1709; Demise of the Crown Act (1901) 1420; East India Act (1785) 1382, 1497; Equal Franchise Act (1928) 1585; European Communities Act (1972) 1724–1725; Government of Ireland Act (1920) 1586; His Majesty's Declaration of Abdication Act (1936) 1613–1614; Home Rule Act (1914) 1556; House of Lords Act (1999) 1734–1735; Human Rights Act (1998) 1745; Ireland Act (1949) 1589; Irish Church Act (1869) 1495; Judicature Acts 1507–1509; Judicial Committee of the Privy Council Act (1833) 1505; Local Government Acts 1448, 1454, 1456, 1459–1460, 1703–1704; Militia Act (1757) 1360; Monopolies Act (1624) 1113; Municipal Corporations Act (1832) 1415, 1421, 1455; Mutiny Act (1689) 1256–1257; Navigation Act (1651) 1282, 1292, 1170; New Zealand Constitution Acts 1591; Parish Councils Act (1894) 1459; Parliament Acts 1524, 1198, 1732, 1733, 1739–1740, 1755–1756, 1760–1761; Peerage Acts 1676, 1678; Place Act (1782) 1400; Poor Law Act (1598) 1089; Public Health Act (1875) 1456; Quaker Act (1664) 1191; Race Relations Acts 1658, 1663; Reform Acts 1408, 1414–1416, 1421, 1431–1435, 1567, 1569; Regency Acts 1336, 1337, 1395–1396, 1614–1615; Representation of the People Acts 1419, 1567, 1569, 1648; Roman Catholic Relief Act (1778) 1378; Royal Marriages Act (1772) 1614; Septennial Act (1715) 1344, 1346; social welfare Acts 1088; spiritual jurisdiction 1032;

Submission of the Clergy Act (1533) 977, 1016; Supreme Court Act (1981) 1714; Test Acts 1399, 1217, 1234, 1236; Toleration Act (1688) 1253–1254; Trade Union Act (1825) 1407; Treasonable and Seditious Practices Act (1795) 1391; Triennial Acts 1344, 1144, 1186, 1190, 1196, 1198, 1209, 1247, 1258; validity of 1027

Aedan, King of Dal Riata 117–118

Ældfrith, King of Northumbria 175–176, 315

Ælfgifu of Northampton, wife of King Cnut 374–375, 376, 381

Ælle, King of Deira 107–108, 169, 177, 270

Ælle, King of the South Saxons 65–68, 69–70, 72–73, 113, 143, 145, 242, 345

Æscwine, King of the East Saxons 80

Æscwine, King of Wessex 156–157, 186

Æthelbald, King of Mercia 176, 189, 191, 193–194, 195, 266, 296–297, 345

Æthelbald, King of Wessex 300

Æthelberht, King of Kent: as *Bretwalda* 85, 172, 345; builds church dedicated to St Paul in London 79; Ceawlin's victories over 100, 101, 144, 147; law codes 86, 158, 209, 221, 253, 277, 284, 285, 314–315, 690, 693; marriage 84–87; succession 263

Æthelberht, King of Wessex 300

Æthelflæd, Lady of the Mercians 317, 318–319, 320–324, 327, 328, 1068

Æthelfrith, King of the Northumbrians 115–117, 120, 165–167, 192

Æthelheard, King of Wessex 164, 193, 296–297

atheling (royal prince) 178, 199, 205, 208, 276

Æthelræd II, King of the English: character 370, 386; conflict with Danes 365–371; coronation 336, 479, 491; Councils 335; law codes 285, 326, 365, 998; marriage 366; protection of Robert I 389; relations with Normandy 364–371; succession 363, 1068

Æthelræd, King of Mercia 174, 187–188, 192, 272

Æthelræd, King of Wessex 300, 301, 302

Æthelræd, Lord of the Mercians 306, 313, 316–318

Æthelric, King of Bernicia 114

Æthelric, King of Deira 115, 120

Æthelstan, King of the English: Battle of Brunanburh 346–347; councils 335,

600; Eamont Bridge 339–340, 1775; election 261; judicial system during reign 288; law codes 285, 286, 333, 396; legacy 347–348; occupation and accession of York 337–339, 347; peace-guild 238–239; popular assembly during reign 240, 272; Scandinavians in courts of 327, 328; succession 351; unification of England 340–346

Æthelwald, King of Deira 171, 182

Æthelwold (*atheling*) 316

Æthelwulf, King of Wessex 199, 271, 295–296, 300, 335

Africa: colonial trade 1283, 1284, 1170; colonisation 1543–1548; decolonisation 1689; federal administration 1681–1682; nationalism 1680; Organization of African Unity (OAU) 1685; regional divisions 1596; slavery 1381, 1487–1488, 1652

agriculture 215, 217, 461, 734, 854, 857, 964, 1367, 1575, 1691, 1725

aid (feudal) 463, 496, 499, 501, 502, 528, 542, 555, 733–734, 856

Albert, Prince Consort 1473–1476, 1498, 1503

Alcuin of York 175–176, 198, 252, 1761

Alemanni 45–46, 103

Alexander III, King of the Scots 621–623, 637

Alfred the Ætheling 382, 386

Alfred the Great, King of the West Saxons and King of the Anglo-Saxons 302–310; Asser on 90; common kingdom 274; coronation 302; Councils 271–272; fortification of boroughs 237; hundred system 233; law codes 238, 250, 285, 314, 688, 693; scholarship of 313–314; thanes 335; translation of Boethius's *Consolation of Philosophy* 203

Alsace-Lorraine 1517, 1564, 1619

Ambrosius Aurelianus, Romano-British leader 52, 55, 63, 71–72, 74, 75

American Civil War 1477, 1589

American Revolution 1290–1296, 1412, 1471

America(s) 965, 1286–1287, 1073, 1088, 1170, 1211 *see also* North America; South America

Anarchy, The 509–512, 544, 844, 1040

Anderida 60–62, 67

Angevin dynasty 485–487; acceptance as English kings 612; alternative names

for 513, 907; Anglo-Saxon influence
492; Church and 593; end of 589, 937,
959, 1555; feudal views of 592; justice
system during rule of 663, 671; nobility
and 600; taxation and 856

Angles: as members of confederacy 143; *ceorls*
210; join confederacy of the English
342; laws 284; noble class 206; North
Angles 103–120; origins of 26, 32–35,
53; return to the Continent 73; royal
line 194, 1289; settlement of Britain 48,
49, 53, 55, 83, 167; South Angles 126–
135, 178, 192; traditions of government
9; West Angles 129, 131–132, 135, 178;
see also East Angles; Middle Angles

Anglicanism 1066, 1125, 1138, 1144, 1160,
1174, 1253

Anglo-Saxon Chronicle: ceases under reign of
Stephen 512; on absence of William
I from England 411; on accession
of Edward the Confessor 385; on
accession of Harold Godwinson 398;
on achievements of Alfred 307, 309; on
assemblies 252; on Battle of Bedcanford
81–83; on Battle of Wibbandun 100;
on Ceolwulf's reign 147; on Cerdic
and Cynric 93–97; on conquest of
Hampshire 87–90; on coronation
of William I 407; on death of Edric
Streona 374; on Edward the Elder 329;
on Hengest and Horsa 55–58; on King
and Council 245, 249; on knighthood
453; on South Saxons 65–66, 75; on
succession of Ecgberht 164; on West
Saxon victories over Britons 145, 152,
161

Anjou 402, 458, 513, 514, 588, 660, 920,
921

Anna, King of East Anglia 149, 182

Anne of Cleves, Queen of England 1039,
1040

Anne, Queen of Great Britain: accession
1271; Cabinet system 1326–1329; claim
to throne 1246, 1256, 1264–1265;
coronation 1333; finances 1345–1346;
Parliaments during reign 1322–1324,
1325–1326; political parties and 1348;
Privy Council during reign 1326–1329,
1333; refusal to assent to Bills 1323,
1326; rule by 'God's grace' 1462;
succession 1340–1341; unification of
England and Scotland 1332–1333

Anselm, Archbishop of Canterbury 477, 482,
489, 492, 516, 536–537, 543

Apulia 406, 639, 640

Aquitaine 513, 524, 526, 588, 617, 725, 735,
740, 743, 804–805, 922

archaeological evidence: absence of 47;
Alemanni in Yorkshire 46; Avon valley
96; Battle of Hastings 403; Dorset 155;
East Yorkshire 104, 107; Hampshire 93;
Isle of Wight 94; Middle Angles 134;
of Richard III's deformity 937; ritual
drowning 931; Saxon 92; Suffolk 122;
Thames valley 73, 74; Warwickshire 188

archbishops: attendance at Councils 626;
attendance at Parliament 622, 656, 711,
773, 809, 978, 979, 981–982, 1025,
1037; judicial function 1117; political
role 565; rivalry 788–789, 790; role in
coronation rite 1530–1532

archery 401, 402, 919

architecture 617, 619, 972, 1368, 1423–
1424, 1427, 1264

Arden (Warwickshire) 129, 132, 134, 188

Argyll 116, 174

aristocracy: English 934; land ownership 413,
433, 467; military 441; Norman 364,
414, 419, 430, 436, 442, 531, 857;
Norse 354; personal honour 278

Aristotle 690, 691, 971, 1337, 1338, 1194,
1268

Arminism 1134, 1135

army 219; Allies of Second World War 1619,
1620, 1624, 1634; Anglian 105; army-
assembly 220; at Battle of Hastings
403; Cardwell reforms 1487; Charles I
1139, 1140, 1142, 1144, 1148, 1153;
Civil War 1158–1159, 1160–1165,
1167–1168, 1170–1171; Danish 300,
301–306, 308–313, 318, 320–325,
327–328; Edward III 805; election of
kings by 91, 221, 404; English 312,
346, 347, 369, 401; French 805, 1390;
German 1618, 1620; identification 506;
immunity of 1710; Irish 117; James
I 1109, 1114, 1124; James II 1234,
1235; Japanese 1621; Jutish 71, 72,
101, 144, 147; Kentish 323; Lancastrian
925, 926–927, 929; mercenary
515–516; Mercian 171, 179, 183,
186, 201, 296, 318, 321; New Model
Army 1160, 1170, 1185; Norman
415, 429, 448, 857; Norse 328–329,
338; Northumbrian 115, 168, 169,

173, 174, 177, 179, 180, 183, 321, 328; parliamentary control over 1486; private 1052; Richard II 888; Saxon 50, 56, 71, 72, 92, 145, 304; Scottish 169, 321, 328; standing armies 1099, 1109, 1114, 1174, 1175, 1234, 1255, 1256–1257; under Protectorate 1176, 1178, 1179–1180; Wars of the Roses 924; Welsh 179, 180; West Saxon 96, 147, 301, 318, 322; William III 1240, 1241; Yorkist 926–927, 930

art 970, 972, 1175, 1182, 1194

Arthur (Artorius) 72, 75

Arthur I, Duke of Brittany 586, 588–589

artillery 929, 934, 949, 953, 963, 964, 967, 1549, 1185, 1563, 1569

Arundel, earldom of 757, 761, 763, 764

Aryans *see* Indo-Europeans

Asquith, H. H. 1520–1523, 1528, 1556, 1567, 1583

assemblies: bearing of arms 625, 650, 659, 837; constitutional role 1183; *gē* assemblies 233, 241; held on sanctified ground 252, 785, 817, 879, 997, 1021–1022; Indo-European 8, 29, 987; *mæthelfrith* 997; national assembly 20, 251–259, 1198; Scandinavia 274; size 334–337, 343; sovereignty and 1097; synods 172, 186, 253, 418, 517, 542, 788–790, 858; warriors 29, 243; West Saxon 99; *see also* popular assembly; hundred assembly; shire assembly

Asser 89, 94, 305, 314

assizes: appropriation of shire assemblies' judicial function 1010, 1512; Assize of Arms 458–459, 471, 515, 853; Assize of Clarendon 546, 548, 549, 581, 582, 585, 610, 664, 668; Assize of Northampton 549, 665, 669; during reign of Henry II 667–669, 688; location 605, 662; origins of term 546, 613; sheriff responsible for assembling juries for 578; tax collection 1086

Athelberht, King of the East Angles 197

Atrebates 76, 93, 97, 98, 100–101, 150

attaint 494, 668, 697, 701

Attlee, Clement 1641, 1657, 1677, 1681

attorneys 579, 622, 630, 631, 855, 983, 1048

Augustine of Canterbury 85–87, 315, 437

Australia: colonisation 1287, 1311–1314, 1506; as Commonwealth realm 1606, 1644; Constitution 1602; federation 1589–1590; First World War 1568; Governor-Generals 1604–1605; immigration 1650; independence 1600; as penal colony 1281–1282, 1283, 1287–1288

Austria: First World War 1557–1559, 1562, 1564, 1570; Franco-Prussian War 1514; Habsburgs 1239; Napoleonic Wars 1387–1389; revolutionary France and 1385–1386; Second World War 1616, 1623; Thirty Years' War 1169; War of the Austrian Succession 1355–1356, 1370; War of the Spanish Succession 1272–1273

Avon (river, Bris) 100, 143, 151, 189, 304, 318

Avon (river, Falk) 168

Avon (river, Hants) 62, 68, 89, 96–99, 100, 154

Avon (river, Warw) 92, 129, 134, 188, 308

Aylesford (Kent) 56, 57, 372

B

Bacon, Francis 1123, 1194, 1214

Badon Hill, Battle of 51, 69–74, 75, 88, 145, 304

Bagehot, Walter 1334, 1351, 1417, 1444, 1460–1464, 1478, 1487, 1581, 1738

Baldred, King of Kent 199

Baldwin, Stanley 1583, 1600, 1605, 1611–1612, 1732

Balkans 9, 11, 970–971, 1558–1559, 1561, 1562, 1617

Balliol, John, King of Scots 732–733, 738, 803

Ball, John 794, 796, 798

Bamburgh (Northumbria) 112, 115, 117, 170, 175, 181, 222, 307, 330, 339, 354, 644

banking 723, 1573, 1261–1263, 1628, 1635, 1727

bannerets 766, 768, 816, 843, 852

Bantu 1303, 1305–1306, 1308, 1627

Barbury Castle (Wiltshire) 97–98, 100, 102

Barnet, Battle of 929, 939, 949

Bar of the House 983, 986, 1019–1022, 1028, 1029, 1424

baronets 845, 1112–1113, 1392, 1400

barons 443–446; attendance at Councils 531–532, 533–536, 539–542, 545, 558, 567, 626, 634, 635; attendance at Parliament 621, 656, 734, 736–737, 748, 809, 834–835, 916, 982, 1024; conflict with Edward II 753–772;

declining status 794, 843, 845; form
of address in Parliament 816; 'greater
baronage' 445, 454, 539, 541, 567, 605,
617, 633, 730, 745, 760, 762, 794,
1671; hostility towards 466; impact of
loss of Normandy on 589–590, 592;
land ownership 449, 514, 773, 843;
Magna Carta and 600–611; opposition
to King 464, 483, 502–503, 595, 599,
607–611, 638, 740–743; origins of
term 439–440; primogeniture and 438,
476–477; private courts 474, 517, 669;
role as sheriffs 580; taxation 739–743,
859; trial by peers 659, 671, 851–852,
881, 943–944; Wars of the Roses 924
barrows 62, 68, 93, 134, 154
Barry, Charles 1423–1424, 1434
Bath (Somerset) 59, 100, 144, 152, 189, 313,
358, 369
Battle of Maldon, poem 207, 280, 365
Bavaria 518, 1341, 1355–1356
Beaufort, Edmund, Duke of Somerset 921,
923–924
Bechuanaland 1541, 1546, 1549–1551
Becket, Thomas 519–526, 534, 541, 545,
548, 593, 1038
Bedcanford, Battle of 82–83
Bede: on Æthelfrith's defeat of Welsh 165; on
Angle migration 126, 127; on Bernicia
112, 113; on *Bretwaldas* 143, 170, 171,
345; on Britons 104; on Cerdic and
Cynric 90; completion of *Ecclesiastical
History* 176; on East Anglian kings 124;
on *Gewisse* defeat of East Saxons 103; on
'Golden Age' of Northumbria 167, 175;
on Hengest and Horsa 54, 55, 56, 58,
64; on hides 192; on laws of Æthelberht
284; on Penda 183; on pre-Christian
beliefs 204; refers to Jutish settlers 63,
94; on Roman withdrawal from Britain
46; site of monastery 112; on succession
of Wihtred 263; on thanes 212
Bedford 82–83, 130, 149, 308, 322–323,
325, 601
Bedford , John, Duke of 910, 912–913,
920–921
Bedfordshire 50, 83, 123, 234, 308, 325, 327,
342
Belgium 1389, 1473, 1515, 1517, 1561,
1618, 1628, 1720–1721, 1722
benevolences 932, 936, 962
Benn, Tony 1678–1679
Beorhford, Battle of 194, 297

Beorhtric, King of Wessex 164, 298
Beorhtwulf, King of Mercia 296
Beornwulf, King of Mercia 199, 277
Beowulf, poem 25, 35, 124–128, 134, 205,
227, 244, 261, 264, 1649, 1779
Berkshire: Battle of Ashdown 302; Cynewulf
regains 297; Danish attacks 309; *Gewisse*
in 257; hundred system 232; inherited
by Ceolwulf 148; Mercian control of
296; not nation state 162; obtained
by Æthelbald 193; part of confederacy
of the English 341; royal estate of
149–151; settled by Men of Surrey 77;
Wulfhere's attack on 185
Berlin 1365, 1388, 1618, 1620, 1623
Bernicia 111–117, 339–340; alliance with
Norse 328, 330; independence from
Deira 106; Middle Angles' settlement of
128; over-kings 270; rivalry with Deira
119, 120, 177, 183; ruling class 175
Berwick-on-Tweed (Northumberland) 222,
238, 744, 766, 767, 803, 1138, 1207,
1253
Bible 974–976, 1039, 1074, 1101, 1304,
1305
bills: Bill of Rights (1689) 1364, 1625–1626,
1716, 1756, 1247, 1252, 1254–1258,
1265; Bills of Attainder 833, 932;
Exclusion Bills 1218; freedom of speech
and 996; Irish Home Rule Bills 1446–
1448, 1555–1556; monarch's approval
of 901, 903–904, 1323, 1326–1327,
1362; money Bills 865–868, 1008,
1011, 1448, 1521, 1202–1203, 1523,
1261, 1673, 1733; origins of term 898;
parliamentary process 954, 984, 989,
1364, 1520–1524; Reform Bills 1319,
1401, 1412–1413, 1431, 1433, 1437,
1443, 1478, 1567; role of House of
Commons 865–868, 1141, 1448; role
of House of Lords 1003, 1008, 1448,
1520–1526, 1671–1673, 1733; royal
assent 798, 1041–1042, 1469, 1481,
1519, 1523; Test Bill (1673) 1217;
Welsh Disestablishment Bill (1914)
1556
Birmingham 1411, 1416
bishoprics 79, 86, 100, 119, 151, 187, 191,
198, 387, 433
bishops: abolition of episcopacy in Scotland
1138; accused of seditious libel 1236;
attendance at Councils 247, 248–249,
334, 416, 533, 534–537, 539–541,

543–544, 626, 634, 635, 638, 1048; attendance at Parliament 621, 656, 697, 711, 748, 773, 788–789, 809, 828, 978, 980–982, 1024, 1030, 1037, 1143, 1225, 1236; Church of England 1101; convocations 641; during Reformation 972, 975–978, 1076; election of 482, 517; exclusion from Parliament 1144, 1157, 1159, 1189, 1556, 1210; guild membership 239; in House of Lords 1734, 1736; judicial responsibilities 271, 1190; land ownership 139, 395, 440, 443, 457; mints owned by 348; Norman 407, 416–417; Puritan attacks on 1125, 1145; role as Chancellor 871, 1347; taxation 917; trial by peers 852; visit England from Gaul in fifth century 48; *wergeld* 206

Bismarck, Otto von 1517, 1557–1558, 1575, 1616

Black Death: decimation of population 791, 855, 1207; economic effects 801, 964, 1105; effect on labour force 728, 796, 800, 854, 953; Hundred Years' War and 806; social class and 792–793, 1189

blackmail 902, 903, 905, 1061, 1345

Blackstone, William 1338, 1339

Blackwater (river) 64–65, 102, 207, 311, 321

Blair, Tony: admiration for American system of government 1669, 1675, 1742–1744; constitutional reforms 1733–1734, 1737, 1739, 1743–1744, 1749–1750, 1766; devolution referendums 1698, 1702; European Convention on Human Rights and 1717; Greater London Council and 1706

Blois, House of 508, 511–513

Bodin, Jean 1097–1098

Bohemia 1340, 1355

Boleyn, Anne, Queen of England 974–975, 1014, 1016, 1035, 1072

bookland 138–139, 229–230

bordars 460–461, 469

borg ('borrow') 280, 291

boroughs 236–240, 653–657; built by Alfred the Great 305; charters granted to 583, 716, 724; Five Boroughs 324, 325–327; independence 1207; political representation 949, 990, 1383, 1410, 1413, 1414–1415, 1431, 1434, 1455–1460, 1187; social class and 725

Bosworth Field, Battle of 937, 959, 960

boundaries 437

Bracton, Henry de 491, 692–693, 893, 950–951, 1118

Bretwaldas 69, 147, 170, 171, 187, 341, 345

Brexit 1757–1761, 1771

bribery 915, 1345, 1052, 1371, 1083, 1123, 1383, 1401, 1433, 1171, 1196

Bristol: British Empire Museum 1652; councils held at 612, 781, 839; as county corporate 580, 1207; duties on goods 500; Edward III elected at 775; merchant adventurers 1278–1279; reform riots 1412; slave trade 1381; Stephen imprisoned at 510

Bristol Channel 71, 144, 152, 165, 171, 310, 321

British Overseas Territories 1690

British South Africa Company (BSAC) 1287, 1546–1550, 1551–1553, 1593–1598, 1684

Britons 44, 51; Angles and 104, 129; Badon Hill 71–76, 75, 88; battles with West Saxons 90–91, 97, 144–145, 157, 161; capture Edinburgh 356; concession of territory 74, 108, 109, 121, 122, 129; control of Hampshire 89; conversion to Christianity 84; defeat by Hengest 106; defeat by Jutes 53, 60, 70; deities 21; kingdom of Elmet 108, 121, 166–167; massacre in *Anderida* 67; Norse invasions 319; in Northumberland 111–112, 114–117; as tenant farmers 228; uprising against Hengest 64; withdrawal from Dorset 155

Brittany: Britons emigrate to 75, 1776; Danish invasions 309, 321; Hundred Years' War 804, 922; independence from France 416, 513; military service in 602; origins of name 771, 1776; petitions from 821; William I's campaigns 391, 402

Bronze Age 9, 10, 23, 25, 36, 415, 441, 858, 970

brooches 50, 56, 64, 70–71, 73, 83, 94, 135

Brough (Yorkshire) 105, 106, 109

Brown, Gordon 1728, 1755

Bruce, Robert 738, 744, 751, 756, 770, 803, 1094

Brunanburh, Battle of 346–347

Buckingham, George Villiers, Duke of 1103, 1104, 1107, 1124, 1126–1127, 1131

Buckingham, Henry Stafford, Duke of 935–936, 959

Buckingham Palace 1369, 1471, 1637

Buckinghamshire 53, 77, 83, 189, 257, 308, 321, 325, 342, 1103
burgesses 653–656; assemblies 580; attendance at Councils 737; attendance at Parliament 455, 735, 835, 864, 990, 1416; as members of *fyrd* 458; origin of term 725; summons 542, 647
Burghal Hidage 233, 313, 317, 320, 448, 585
Burgh, Hubert de, 1st Earl of Kent 565, 607, 612, 614, 615–616
Burgundy 919–920, 928, 929, 1070, 1273
burh (fortification): defence against Danes 235, 312, 409; of Edward the Elder 321; Indo-European origins 317; Norman improvements 414; in place-names 84; Somerset 153; towns built around 236–237, 331, 724; *see also* fortifications
burhgemot (borough assembly) 235, 236, 237, 332
Burhræd, King of Mercia 301, 303
burials: barrows 134; Indo-Europeans 11; Kent 69; kings 264; Northumberland 175; pagan 220; Scandinavian 26–27, 123, 252; as site for popular assembly 228, 234; Sutton Hoo 124; use of churchyards 595
Burke, Edmund 1373, 1375, 1382, 1385, 1400, 1406
Burnel, Robert, Chancellor and Bishop of Bath and Wells 705, 714
Bury St Edmunds (Suffolk) 302, 601, 739, 744, 922
Bute, John Stuart, Earl of 1370–1371
Butler (office) 565, 567, 571
Byrhtnoth, *ealdorman* of Essex 207, 365

C

Cabinet: attendance at meetings 1667; Bagehot on 1461, 1463–1464; Cabinet Committee 1328–1329; and collective responsibility 1432; Commons control of 1349–1350, 1361–1363; crisis of 1679 1219; development of 1212–1215; origins 1055; policy formulation 1473, 1475–1477; role 1322, 1326–1329, 1224, 1267
Cabot, John 1278–1279, 1297
Cade, Jack 922, 931, 938
Cadwallon, King of Gwynedd 168–170, 179–180, 190–191
Cædwalla, King of Wessex 95, 157, 196, 260

Caesar, Julius 28–29, 32, 1385, 1516
Calais: Battle of Agincourt 919; English rule 922, 968; France surrenders sovereignty of 807; lost to France 1072; Siege of Calais 726, 805, 814; Spanish Armada 1080–1081; wool trade 862
Calvinism 1304, 1133–1134, 1137, 1253
Cambridge 123, 303, 323, 325, 327, 585, 692
Cambridgeshire 50, 123, 129, 234, 342, 585
Cameron, David 1758
Campbell-Bannerman, Henry 1519–1520, 1540
Cam (river) 50, 128, 129
Canada 1297–1301; citizenship 1652; as Commonwealth realm 1606, 1644; Constitution 1589, 1602; First World War 1568, 1592; French colonisation 1289, 1293; Governor-Generals 1604–1605; independence 1600–1601; Newfoundland joins as Province 1606; opposition to Geneva Protocol 1599; Pitt's reforms 1382; role in abdication crisis 1613; Treaty of Paris (1783) 1380
canon law 417, 516, 700, 871, 1015, 1034, 1140, 1191
Canterbury (Kent): archbishopric of 176, 187, 197–199, 210, 357, 365, 387, 416, 434, 435, 477, 519, 543, 593, 622, 706, 755, 782, 973, 1017, 1025, 1160, 1530, 1531; Augustine of Canterbury 85, 315; *burh* 237; competition with Churches of Iona and Northumberland 172; Convocation of 1012, 1139, 1140; as county corporate 1207; Danish invasion 296; impact of wool trade on 727; John's dispute with monks of 595; murder of Thomas Becket 522, 1038; Norman castle 644; province of 418, 711, 731, 739, 742, 770, 788, 790, 858, 1074, 1576, 1208; Roman fortification 84; secured by William I 404; site of earliest recorded guild 211; as spiritual seat of England 200
Cantii 84, 86
Cantware 84, 87, 193
capitalism 1427, 1575, 1685, 1695
Carlisle (Cumbria) 113, 115, 165, 478, 510, 518, 746, 747, 783, 835
Carnarvon (Gwynedd) 716, 750
Carteret, John, 2nd Earl Granville 1354
case law 286–287, 692, 694, 696, 1132
Castile 518, 623, 637, 807, 884–885

castles: barons' 503; building materials 450, 512–513; cost 495, 499, 589; custody of 643, 644, 647; of Edward I 711, 716, 717; Norman 453; obsolescence 934, 953; razed by Henry II 514; Scottish 751; of William I 415, 430; of William Rufus 478; *see also* fortifications

Catherine de Valois, Queen of England 910, 911, 920, 959

Catherine of Aragon, Queen of England 966, 973–974, 1011, 1013, 1015, 1035, 1039, 1067, 1069, 1070, 1073

Catholics/Catholicism 1070–1080; Acts 1038–1039, 1378, 1265; banishment of priests 1104; Catholic Emancipation Bill (1829) 1400; Catholic League 1111; and Civil War 1159–1161, 1231–1236; divine right 1152; Ealhfrith's support for 172; Edward VI and 1066; France 1096, 1240; Henry VIII and 1034, 1036–1037, 1040, 1044; hostility towards Catholics 1126, 1229; Ireland 1393, 1399–1400, 1144, 1435, 1168, 1182, 1555, 1588, 1701; Laud and 1133, 1140; Popish Plot 1227–1229; Renaissance and 971; role of Justices of the Peace in law enforcement against 1090; Siege of La Rochelle 1130; Spain 1132–1134; of Stuarts 1100, 1109, 1123–1124, 1152, 1159–1161, 1192, 1214–1223, 1240; Thirty Years' War 1110, 1169–1170

Catterick (Yorkshire) 107, 111, 113, 119, 120

cavalry: at Badon Hill 71–73; Civil War 1158; Estates and 1569; French 805; New Model Army 1185; Norman 402, 403, 414–415, 453, 570; role of Constable 570; role of Marshal 871; Sarmatian 45, 72, 75, 115, 145

Caxton, William 934, 965

Cearl, King of Mercia 166, 178

Ceawlin, King of the West Saxons: as *Bretwalda* 345; campaigns against Britons 77, 82, 100–101, 188; northward advance 96; relations with Kent 84; westward expansion 143–148

Cecil, Robert Arthur Talbot Gascoyne-Cecil, 3rd Marquess of Salisbury 1443, 1450, 1489–1490, 1543

Cecil, William 1074, 1077, 1079

Celtic Church 52, 85–86, 172, 175, 622

Celts 23–24; in Gaul 771; in Germany 31; identity 1698; integration into

Anglian society 110, 111; in Ireland 1555; *Parisii* 103, 104; religion 84; sub-Roman Britain 47, 57; uprising of Deirans against 106; use of Sarmatian cavalry 72–73, 75, 115, 145

cemeteries: Anglian 108, 127, 129; Deiran 106; Jutish 61, 62, 94; Mercian 132; pagan 51; royal 123; Saxon 50–51, 64, 70, 97, 154

Cenred, King of Mercia 187, 191, 193

censorship 1138, 1174, 1259

Centwine, King of Wessex 157, 161

Cenwealh, King of Wessex: accepts Mercian overlordship 185; conquest of Dorset 155; religious conversion 149; succession 156, 260, 264, 267, 1068; takes refuge in East Anglia 150–153, 182

Cenwulf, King of Mercia 142, 197–198, 251, 276, 298

Ceol, King of Wessex 146–148, 151

Ceolred, King of Mercia 187, 193

Ceolwulf, King of Mercia 199, 249, 296

Ceolwulf II, King of Mercia 303, 305

Ceolwulf, King of Northumbria 176

Ceolwulf, King of Wessex 147, 157, 270

ceorls (churls) 209–213; compared to villeins 687; in Kent 214, 254; land allocation 221, 225, 226, 331; membership of guilds 239; post-Conquest 394, 460, 469; *wergeld* 276, 291, 294, 465

Cerdicing dynasty: confederacy of Southumbria 327, 330, 347; debt of Angevins to 890; end of 399, 413, 431; *Gewisse* and 97; Henry II's legitimacy traced to 513; influence on Jutish culture 200; occurrence of Welsh names 157; relations with Church 523; restoration 384–401; succession 260, 375; West Saxon confederacy 162, 163–164, 270, 1649

Cerdic, King of the West Saxons 88–97, 101, 149, 157, 242, 260, 270

Chamberlain, Neville 1617, 1618

Chamberlain (office) 563, 565, 567, 570–572, 621, 815, 980–982, 1734

Chancellor of the Exchequer (office) 1330, 1346–1347, 1361–1362, 1485, 1261, 1740

Chancery: administration 566, 954; appointment of Justices of the Peace 855; Court of 676, 681–685, 699, 700, 820, 823, 827, 872, 1001, 1016,

1051, 1117, 1121, 1122, 1507–1510,
1206; function 571, 574–575, 669,
693, 699–700, 871, 999, 1001, 1005,
1042; location 679; Norman equivalent
569–570; regional 1064
Channel Islands 589, 1392–1393, 1690
Charford (Worcestershire) 89, 90
Charlemagne, King of the Franks: Alcuin
of York and 175, 177, 252, 1761;
annexation of Rhineland 1514; crown
featured in coat of arms of George I
1343; decline of role Count of the
Palace during reign 554; empire 198,
597, 1515; expansion into Frisia 299;
Offa and 197, 201
Charles Edward Stuart (the Young Pretender)
1356
Charles I, King of England: accession 1125;
as 'Lord's anointed' 1462; Cabinet
Council 1212; character 1152; Civil
War 1157–1167; constitutionalism
1125–1127, 1136; coronation oath
1250, 1252; finances 1127, 1131,
1137, 1140; Five Members, arrest of
1147–1148; foreign policy 1132, 1137,
1215; Grand Remonstrance 1145;
granting of monopolies 1136; Great
Council during reign 1140, 1210; Irish
rebellion 1144–1145, 1148; judicial
system during reign 1222; marriage
1123–1124, 1125, 1212; Parliaments
1006, 1125–1134, 1139–1157, 1209;
personal rule 1136–1139; Petition of
Right 1131–1133; Privy Council during
reign 1127, 1132, 1136, 1142, 1145,
1147, 1150, 1211, 1213; proclamations
1147, 1149; relations with France 1127,
1137; relations with Spain 1126, 1127,
1132, 1137, 1140; religious policy
1125–1126, 1133–1140, 1144, 1146,
1154; royal prerogative 1125, 1134,
1143; Scottish crisis 1139–1140, 1142,
1144; taxation during reign 1126, 1127,
1135, 1136, 1138–1139, 1140–1142;
trial and execution 1164–1167, 1180,
1182, 1183–1184, 1185
Charles II, King of England: accession 1185,
1202; adherence to Church-Feudalism
1223; Anglo-Dutch War 1211, 1214,
1216–1218; appropriation of funds
864; army 1256; coronation oath
1250; Declaration of Breda 1180,
1186; finances 1219, 1227, 1230,
1231, 1262; foreign policy 1215–1216,
1219, 1231; Great Council during
reign 1201; Great Fire and Plague of
London 1211, 1214; judicial system
during reign 1222–1223; legacy 1229,
1231; Louis XIV and 1215, 1219,
1227, 1230, 1236; marriage 1192,
1214; Parliaments 1185–1193, 1201,
1205–1206, 1208–1211, 1216–1219,
1227–1230, 1242, 1244; Popish
Plot (1678) 1218–1219, 1227; Privy
Council during reign 1185, 1186,
1207, 1213–1214, 1219–1220, 1224;
proclaimed as King in Scotland 1168;
religion and 1216, 1216–1217, 1231;
Rye House Plot 1230, 1231; scientific
revolution during reign 1194–1195,
1229, 1232; succession 1206, 1216,
1218, 1220, 1227, 1230, 1232–1234;
support for slave trade 1380; taxation
during reign 1186, 1188–1189, 1231;
Treasury during reign 1330; theatrical
patronage 1229
Charles II, King of Spain 1271–1272
Charles III, King of France 348, 364
Charles VI, King of France 910, 911, 919,
921
Charles VII, King of France 911, 912, 920
Charles VIII, King of France 967, 972
Charter Roll 498, 570
charters: Æthelræd 369; Æthelstan 347;
British South Africa Company 1546,
1593, 1594, 1598; *Carta Mercatoria*
859; Charter of Liberties 464, 479–484,
552, 597, 602, 615, 630; Charter of
the Forest 609, 614, 740, 743; cities
and boroughs 583; Cnut 380; Edward
I's confirmation of 740–742, 859; as
evidence of attendance at Parliament
246–247; as evidence of lord's courts
292; Henry I 600; Henry III 1011;
issued by confederacies 269; Kent 335;
King Stephen 498, 509; Master of the
Rolls 684; Mercian 313, 335; Norman
416, 475, 569; origins 688; purpose
546; royal charter 1286; Unknown
Charter of Liberties 601, 603; Wessex
335; witnesses to 254–255; *see
also Magna Carta*
Chartism 1351, 1416, 1428
Cherwell (river) 73, 82, 98, 145, 149, 189
Cheshire 191, 191–192, 320, 329, 342, 410,
990

Chester: abolition of County Palatine 1146;
    Æthelfrith's victory against Welsh at
    165, 167; as county corporate 1207;
    Danish occupation 311, 319; earldom
    of 549–552, 576, 707, 708, 752, 782,
    888; herald 508; Norse occupation 317,
    338; royal March centred around 716;
    writs issued from Great Council at 840
chevaliers 454–455
Chichester (W Sussex) 62, 66, 67–68, 70,
    311
Chief Justice (office): appointment of 643,
    759; attendance at Councils 541;
    attendance at Parliament 782, 983;
    forms of address 829; replaced by
    Chancellor 871; role 564–566, 616,
    662, 675, 703, 1347; under Norman
    rule 571, 572
children 1381, 1406, 1407, 1455
Chilterns 49, 53, 65, 78, 81–83, 129, 130,
    149, 258
China 1621–1622, 1642, 1653, 1661
Chippenham (Wiltshire) 304–305, 307
chivalry 658, 801, 806, 839, 871, 891, 944
Christian Church: appeal to Rome for
    assistance against Picts and Irish 48;
    appointment of members to Council of
    Elders 244; authority of 242; bishopric
    at Hereford 191; civil jurisdiction
    284–285, 291, 333, 516–517, 535;
    constitutional involvement 355,
    434–435, 626–628, 954–955, 1577;
    contact with the Continent ceases 59;
    conversion of pagans 130; convocations
    418, 543, 641, 714, 731, 739, 741,
    770, 788–790, 973, 1012, 1027, 1576–
    1577, 1208; corruption 909, 1009,
    1044, 1046; Counter-Reformation
    1069–1072; diocese of Worcester 189;
    and Estate structure 135–140, 437,
    1525; heresy 909; King becomes 'patron
    paramount' of 792; land ownership
    137–138, 218, 229–230, 428, 1137;
    payment of tithes to 1087; post-
    Conquest 6–7, 416, 420; provision
    of clerical facilities at Winchester
    102; provision of social security 218,
    901, 1034, 1047, 1088, 1493–1494;
    Reformation 799, 801, 910, 973,
    1012–1013, 1015, 1032, 1045–1047,
    1065–1067, 1069–1072, 1074–1077;
    reforms 357–358, 974–978; separation
    of Church and State 414, 416–418,

472, 603, 690, 692; Solemn League and
    Covenant (1643) 1159; succession and
    267, 429–430, 489, 591–593; synods
    172, 186, 253, 418, 517, 543, 788, 858,
    954, 1030, 1572, 1576; under Norman
    rule 414; Wiclif's 'Civil Dominion' 793;
    women and 247; written record and 204
Christianity 84–88; Cædwalla's conversion to
    95, 157; Cenwealh's conversion to 149;
    chivalry and 658; conversion of Danes
    to 364–365; empire and 1286; in Gaul
    52; Guthrum's conversion to 304; Indo-
    Iranian influence 135–140; introduction
    into Northumbria 169, 175, 181;
    Middle Angles' conversion to 183–184
churches: built on ancient sacred sites 136,
    138, 1087; construction financed by
    King 136; dedications 160; destruction
    of art and sculpture during Civil War
    1182; during Reformation 1047, 1066;
    effect of wool trade on construction of
    727; freehold and 139; King's *mund*
    extends to 279; levies on 626, 628;
    parish churches 1021, 1087–1088
Church-Feudalism 424–429, 440–442;
    boundaries and 437; Charles I and
    1154, 1165, 1183; Charles II and
    1223; decline of 961, 1434; Empire
    and 1315; Europe 1109; influence on
    development of British Empire 438;
    king-worship and 505; land ownership
    and 722; Lithuania 824; *Magna Carta*
    and 607; and 'overmighty subject'
    1052; paternalism of 801; and right
    of return 1651; separation of monarch
    from people 817; social status and 465,
    1677; Statute of Winchester and 854;
    succession and 1068, 1528; taxation and
    555, 857; Wars of the Roses and 923
Churchill, Winston 1619–1620, 1623–1624;
    Atlantic Charter 1625; caretaker
    Government 1639; European
    integration 1720; immigration and
    1657; Rhodesia 1681, 1683; visit to
    troops in France 1634
Church of England: Act of Settlement (1701)
    1265; Book of Common Prayer 1065,
    1138, 1190–1191; Charles I and 1125,
    1154; Charles II and 1190–1191;
    disestablishment in Wales 1556;
    division and fragmentation 1133–1140,
    1576–1577; Edward VI and 1066;
    Elizabeth I and 1075–1077; Enabling

Act (1919) 1572; Henry VIII and
1015–1017, 1033–1034, 1038–1039,
1045; involvement in taxation 1576,
1208–1209; Mary I and 1071;
parliamentary control 1208–1209;
Puritans and 1188; ritualism 1478; Test
Acts 1217; Toleration Act (1688) 1254;
Tory support for 1231; union with the
Church of Ireland 1392, 1494–1496;
see also Christian Church
Church of Ireland 1392, 1494–1496
Church of Rome: Church-Feudalism and
424; compared to Celtic Church
172–173; Counter-Reformation 1047,
1069, 1076–1077; eleventh-century
schism 477; Henry VIII and 973, 1033,
1035, 1044; kingship and 472; post-
Conquest influence of 420, 434, 447;
William I and 417
Church of Wales 1495
Cilternsætan 81–83, 342
Cinque Ports 390, 653, 655, 724, 729
Cirencester (Gloucestershire) 71, 144, 179,
188, 305
citizenship 1647–1649; Bodin on 1097;
British Nationality Act (1948) 1657;
common law and 1270; Empire and
1662–1663; free men 655; Green on
1429; *ius soli* 1285, 1288; Rousseau on
1352
civil law 292–293; absolutism 950–952;
barons 672; courts 674, 677, 845, 873,
1083, 1146, 1509, 1695–1696; equity
682; knowledge of 684, 831–832;
replaces canon law in universities 1034;
role of Council of Wales 1064
Civil List 1345, 1354, 1372–1376,
1400–1401, 1467–1469, 1473, 1498,
1262–1263, 1763
Civil Service: control of 1364, 1402;
costs 1374, 1467, 1262; division of
responsibilities 1376; effect of Norman
Conquest on 434, 568; functions 401,
423, 871, 963, 1323–1325, 1327,
1186, 1668–1669, 1768; India 1324,
1707; language of 332; Northcote-
Trevelyan report (1854) 1482–1484;
origins 248; professionalisation 369,
1665; recruitment 1707–1708; South
Africa 1306
Civil War 1063, 1099, 1152, 1157–1167,
1232, 1234, 1248
clans 28, 30, 241

Clarence, George, Duke of 928–929, 931
Clarendon, Edward Hyde, Earl of 1187,
1190, 1201, 1208, 1214–1215
clergy: Act for the Submission of Clergy 977,
1016; anti-clericalism 932, 972–973,
975–977, 1145; attendance at Councils
246–251, 335, 535, 543, 627, 634,
834, 1048; attendance at Parliament
621, 655–656, 734, 735, 773, 786,
787–790, 834–836, 1024; conformity
1101; convocations 418, 543, 714,
731, 739, 741, 770, 788–790, 1577;
effect of Act of Uniformity on 1190;
ejection of secular clergy from Church
357; entitlement to King's *mund* 279;
involvement in temporal matters
414, 604, 637–639, 640, 739, 827;
judgement of 1038; life peerages 1441;
Norman 416, 447, 504; as occupation
437; political representation 858;
privileges removed by Henry VIII
1012–1013; reforms 503, 516; synods
172, 186, 253, 418, 517, 543, 788,
789–791, 1577; taxation 739, 789–790,
797, 865, 917, 1208–1209; withdrawal
from Parliament 713, 811, 814, 823,
865, 867, 978–979, 1765
climate 10, 23, 24, 35, 49, 203, 465
cloth 598, 723–724, 727, 922, 964
cniht 211, 452–454
Cnut, King of Denmark, England
and Norway: accession of 373;
administration under 379–384; alliance
with Normandy 374–377; charters 380;
choice of London for royal residence
394; contact with Rome 375, 377;
coronation 373–378, 392; invasions
370; issue 376; kingship of Norway
376–377; law codes 140–141, 231,
253, 285, 378–379, 662, 687; legacy
404; marriages 374–375; peace treaty
with Edmund Ironside 372; relationship
with Church 373; shire administration
during reign 272, 334; siege of London
371; succession 377
coins/coinage 79, 86, 183, 197, 201, 296,
306, 348, 397, 515, 1105; *see also* money
Coke, Edward 1106, 1114–1123, 1125, 1131
Colchester (Essex) 163, 321, 323, 393
Colonial Office 1546, 1549, 1553, 1598,
1650, 1681, 1684, 1688
colonies and colonisation 1277–1283;
American 1642; Australia 1287–1288,

1290–1300, 1311–1314; Belgian 1682;
Charles II and 1230; decolonisation
1641–1645, 1653–1654, 1680–1688,
1688–1690; Dutch 1289, 1137,
1302–1307, 1211; emigration to
1650; freedom of movement 1651;
French 1289, 1561; German 1570,
1592; Japanese 1623; Kenya 1680;
North America 1136, 1367, 1374,
1377–1381, 1397, 1469, 1502, 1544,
1641; Nyasaland 1283, 1287, 1543,
1681–1682; penal colonies 1281–1282,
1283, 1287, 1312, 1506; Portuguese
1308, 1310, 1311, 1543, 1544, 1545,
1552, 1599, 1682, 1685; Protesantism
of 1232; Rhodesia 1543–1552,
1593–1598, 1681–1687; rise of
imperialism 1450–1451; role in First
World War 1568; role of Privy Council
1212; Scottish 1112; Second World War
1621, 1623; South Africa 1303–1310,
1537–1541; Spanish 1072, 1073, 1079,
1176; trade 1277, 1072, 1073, 1137,
1280–1282, 1292, 1444, 1170, 1652
Columbus, Christopher 1277–1279
commerce: in former Roman empire 441;
growth of 613, 723, 726, 734, 795,
900, 1732; land ownership and 722;
overseas 1287, 1290, 1292, 1379, 1391;
regulation 933; Rhodesia 1596; socialist
policy 1654; taxation and 857, 858;
under Henry VII 964
committees 1110, 1125, 1141, 1144, 1152,
1505–1506, 1212, 1215
Common Council: alternative names 567,
599, 782; attendance at 532–533, 539–
541, 542, 604, 638, 734–737, 774;
co-ordination with other Councils 729;
election to 868; functions 555–557;
granting of aids 537, 610, 616; held at
Westminster 565, 630; judicial decision-
making 624–625; writs 634
common law 285–287, 669–685; absence
or incompetence of King 1149; Acts of
Parliament 1199; adaptation to social
change 795; assemblies 253, 541, 709,
785, 989, 1020; civil law 292–294,
1083; Council of Elders as guarantor of
249; effect of removal of jurisdiction of
Privy Council on 1193; election of kings
267, 486, 941, 1166, 1270; empire
and 1288–1290, 1292; establishment
of confederacies 201; *ius sanguinis* 729,

1288, 1639, 1647; land allocation 221,
229–230, 1313, 1248; origins 673,
674–677, 691; rights and obligations
163, 216, 613, 747, 1032, 1053, 1141,
1436, 1651; royal prerogative 1057,
1113–1116, 1156–1157, 1636–1637,
1711; standardisation of 696; taxation
and 860–861; torture 933
common law Constitution 6–12, 1774–1787;
Act of Proclamations and 1059; Act of
Settlement and 1266; ancient nature
of 1129; Angevins' awareness of 677;
customary law and 490; Edward III and
810; Empire and 1285; Fortescue on
952; Great Council and 1095, 1149;
imperium and 1334; individual rights
and property 1192; judicial review and
1709; jurisdiction of Privy Council
1051; King as legislator 903; memory
of 431, 1114; popular assembly and
142, 1167; restoration of 1764–1765;
role of Council of Elders 243, 244;
shire representation 826; statue law and
1200; undermined by Civil War 1206;
see also mos maiorum
Common Market *see* European Economic
Community (EEC)
common pleas 672–675, 678–681, 684, 697,
701, 820
commonwealth 1289, 1314
Commonwealth of England (1649-1160)
1167–1172, 1173–1174, 1176, 1181,
1182, 1185, 1229, 1231
Commonwealth of Nations 1600–1605,
1643–1644, 1687–1689; citizenship
and 1652, 1653; coronation oath and
1531; European integration and 1723;
immigration and 1656; Irish Free State
and 1615; nationalism and 1681–1682;
representation 1736; Statute of
Westminster (1931) 1393
Communism: Africa 1686; China 1642,
1661; Germany 1608–1609; Indo-
China 1645; Internationals 1584;
origins 1427–1428; Prussia 1557;
Russia 1559, 1564, 1570, 1573–1575,
1575, 1616–1617, 1622–1623, 1716,
1719, 1720, 1726, 1727; Warsaw Pact
1628; xenophobia towards Communists
1568
communitas 634, 642, 652
confederacies 141–202, 268–274; as common
kingdoms 273–274; Deiran 167; East

Anglia 123; English 341–343, 660,
1649, 1774, 1775; Five Boroughs 326;
Germanic 29; *Hwicce* 189; Jutish-
South Saxon 70; land allocation 193;
Mercian 143, 163, 178–200, 269–270,
273–274, 296, 306; Mercia-Wessex
324; Middle Angles 130; Norse 346;
Northumberland 112, 120, 143;
Northumbria 165–178, 186; Roman
Britain 45; Saxon 201; Southumbria
327–332, 340; United States of America
1293, 1296, 1301; West Saxon 99,
143–149, 186, 232, 273–274, 300, 306
conservatism 1422, 1596
Conservative Party: Corn Laws 1474;
as distinct from Tory Party 1437;
European integration 1724, 1727; and
Greater London Council (GLC) 1706;
House of Lords reform 1443–1446,
1519, 1524, 1732, 1737; immigration
policy 1654, 1656; interwar years 1575,
1581, 1583–1584; Ireland 1436, 1489;
leadership 1581; origins 1421–1422,
1431; Second World War 1619;
socialism and 1575; support of Queen
Victoria 1450; Unionism 1698
Constable (office) 570–571, 740, 741, 744,
845, 933, 944, 1360
Constantine II, King of the Scots 321, 330,
346–347
constituencies 1435, 1457, 1162, 1173, 1513,
1196, 1569, 1735, 1770, 1787
Constitution: *Agreement of the People*
1162; American 1294–1297, 1339,
1430, 1742, 1771; ancient origins
764; Aristotle on 1337; Australia
1314–1315, 1590; Bagehot on 1334,
1417, 1460–1464, 1738; Blackstone
on 1339; Canada 1302, 1589, 1601;
constitutional impossibility of Supreme
Court 1751; Constitutional Reform Act
(2005) 1675, 1745; Council of Elders
as repository of 244–245; crisis (1215)
600; crisis (1296-7) 739–745; crisis
(1332-3) 812; crisis (1642) 1144–1157;
crisis of 1908-10 1520–1525, 1673,
1674; customary law and 694–695;
declining respect for 1669; effect
of Civil List Act on 1263; effect of
Glorious Revolution on 1247–1248;
enforcement of 249–251; following
unification of England and Scotland
1334; Fortescue on 951; *Instrument of*

Government, The 1173–1174, 1175–
1176, 1177, 1179; Ireland 1586–1588;
kingship and 480, 483, 1398, 1178,
1220; *Magna Carta* and 600–608;
Montesquieu on 1338–1339, 1461,
1742; New Zealand 1591; overridden
by doctrine of Church 6; overseas
territories and 1288; Parliament and
constitutional change 1031–1041,
1439; personal rule of Charles I and
1136–1139, 1140; policy formulation
565; post-Conquest 419, 483, 488;
provision for consultation between King
and people 532; Pym on 1129–1130;
relationship between King and people
385, 488, 626; represented by charters
742; Rhodesia 1597; right to attend
Parliament 988; royal prerogative and
1123; as separation of functions 875;
South Africa 1541; statutes subject
to requirements of 1419; succession
and 704, 1268–1270; violation of
244; *Voortrekkers* 1305–1306; *see
also* common law Constitution
constitutionalism 1045, 1098, 1125–1127,
1129–1130, 1136, 1472
constitutional monarchy 350, 1580–1581
Constitutions of Clarendon 504, 517, 519,
545, 548
contracts 282, 603, 684, 699, 1429, 1709
Corfe (Dorset) 336, 363, 644
Coritani 109, 128
Corn Laws 1396, 1399, 1438, 1474
Cornwall: boundary 338; *Cornovii* 152,
161, 192; Council of the West 1064;
Cynewulf's campaign in 297; Danish
invasions 300, 321; as dependency
of the Crown 340, 343, 1776, 1787;
Duchy of 1401; earldom of 751, 754,
780; identity 1698; rebellion (1549)
1066; Saxon expansion towards 161–
162; size of assembly hinterland 258;
Stannaries 995; as Welsh state 163
coronation: automatic succession and
704–705, 752, 1613; ceremony 21,
261–262, 707–708, 1333, 1466–1467,
1531–1532; coronation oath 22, 250,
479, 490–493, 592, 603, 1378, 1060,
1392, 1400, 1100, 1494–1496, 1528,
1184, 1530–1533, 1246, 1250–1254,
1265, 1269, 1782; distribution of
Privy Purse monies 1401; rites 939,
1530–1533; role of Lord High Steward

1671; Westminster as location 386, 679, 739, 820, 1467, 1530; West Saxons 80, 1467; of wife of King 928

Cospatric, Earl of Northumbria 409, 410–411

Cotswolds 100, 129, 133, 143, 145, 188, 189, 197, 727

cottars 460–461, 469, 579, 914

cotton 1281, 1284, 1366–1367, 1381, 1652, 1691

Council of Elders 18–20, 29, 91, 106, 141, 220, 242–251, 265, 416, 567

Council of Europe 1627, 1720

Council of State 1167, 1185

Council of the North 1063–1065, 1117, 1129, 1136, 1141, 1146

Council of Wales 1061, 1064–1065, 1117

councils 6–7, 20, 236–240, 334–337, 344, 416–418, 566, 744, 1703–1707, 1737; see also Great Council; King's Council (Curia Regis); Privy Council; Common Council

Counter-Reformation 1069–1072, 1094, 1110–1111, 1152, 1169

counties 442, 577, 1064, 1086, 1433, 1434–1435, 1455–1459, 1207, 1702, 1704, 1775–1776

courts of law: circuit courts 473, 549, 662–667, 672, 674, 680, 1748; commission courts 1038; county courts 578–580, 1455, 1508, 1512–1513; Court of Augmentations 1043; Court of Chancery 676, 681–685, 699, 700, 820, 823, 827, 872, 1001, 1016, 1051, 1117, 1121, 1122, 1507–1510, 1206; Court of Chivalry 845–846, 871, 891, 944; Court of Common Pleas 872, 1121, 1507, 1221; Court of Exchequer 872, 1114, 1138, 1507; Court of High Commission 943, 1038, 1062, 1074, 1117, 1121, 1141, 1190; Court of King's Bench 674–675, 677–680, 684, 784, 820, 872, 1117–1119, 1507, 1712, 1221–1222, 1234, 1747; Court of Requests 1061–1062, 1146, 1392, 1423, 1456; Court of Star Chamber 873, 963, 965, 1042, 1051–1052, 1054, 1055, 1064, 1082–1083, 1103, 1117–1118, 1138, 1141, 1146–1147, 1157, 1186, 1187, 1204, 1207, 1210, 1213, 1221; Court of the Lord High Steward 851; Court of Wards and Liveries 1063, 1146, 1188; courts leet

472–474, 854, 856, 1514; Courts of Appeal 1508–1509, 1510–1512, 1670, 1675, 1695–1697, 1747; Crown Courts 1696, 1745, 1747–1750; ecclesiastical 417–418, 516, 519–522, 535, 690, 701, 706, 972, 1016, 1038, 1074, 1117, 1509, 1234–1235, 1254; European Courts 1718, 1727, 1759; French as language of 695; gē 224; High Court of Justice 1508–1509, 1696; hundred courts 232–235, 236, 255, 288, 333, 397, 472–474, 493, 494, 535, 561, 578–584, 584, 669; husting 238; individual cases 286, 661; Judicial Committee of the Privy Council 1505–1506; Jutish 223; lords' courts 292–294, 661, 663, 666; nineteenth-century reform 1506–1512; and parliamentary privilege 1452–1453; prerogative law 1156–1157, 1221; private courts 397, 474–475, 517, 661, 663, 669, 690, 719; Quarter Sessions 855, 1010, 1089, 1456, 1456, 1458, 1510, 1207; royal courts 557–576, 605, 650, 663, 666–671, 678–681, 696–698, 872, 873, 943, 947, 1051, 1055, 1156, 1328, 1765; Saxon 31; seating arrangements 676; sheriffs' courts 669; Stannaries 995, 1510, 1776; Supreme Court 1675, 1714, 1744, 1746–1750, 1761; tunræd 239; see also shire courts

Covenant/Covenanters 1138, 1140, 1159–1161, 1233

Coventry (Warwickshire) 383, 648, 770, 839, 924

Cranmer, Thomas 976, 1015, 1065–1066, 1071, 1075

Cray (river) 57, 78

Crécy, battle of 696, 800, 805, 814, 874

cremation 104, 128, 129, 132, 154

Creoda, King of Mercia 95, 134, 178

crime 850–853, 1746; on British ships 1508; capital 947; causes 1281, 1493; committed by private armies 1052; effect of centralisation of of policing on 1703; feudal system and 395; genocide 1626; London 1507; naming and definitions 719, 1114; Presentment of Englishry 431, 466; regicide 938

Crimean War 1324, 1449, 1477, 1482

criminal justice 850–855, 1506–1511; barons' rights 444; Bill of Rights (1689) 1255; Bills of Attainder 833; Cape Colony

1309; clerical exemption 978; courts
1695–1697; *habeas corpus* 661, 684,
1386, 1396, 1127, 1186, 1220–1224;
infangentheof 663; jurisdiction of
House of Lords 494, 946–947;
Kentish law 253, 278; kingship and
853, 1220–1224; link to *wergeld* 275;
Magna Carta 604; *mund* 280, 396;
offences 719; peace-guilds 239; peers
of the realm 625, 850–851, 999; penal
colonies 1281–1282, 1283, 1287, 1312;
Rhodesia 1548; role of assemblies 659;
role of Councils 698, 946, 1064; role of
thanes 327; royal proclamations 1059;
Saxon assemblies 31; sentencing 852,
1059, 1746, 1168; in tithings 288, 473–
474; use of torture 933; *see also* courts of
law; jury system; assizes
criminal law 294, 951, 1510, 1674, 1695–
1697
Cromwell, Oliver: death and burial 1178,
1185; dissolution of Parliament 1176,
1178; at Edgehill 1158; on execution of
Charles I 1165; foreign policy 1176–
1177; formation of General Council
1161–1162; Humble Petition 1177–
1178, 1179; *Instrument of Government,
The* 1173–1174, 1175–1176, 1177,
1179; Irish campaign 1167–1169;
legacy 1182, 1187; as Lord Protector
1330, 1174–1176; at Marston Moor
1159–1165; and New Model Army
1160–1161; Nominated Parliament
1172–1173; refuses crown 1178;
religious beliefs 1179; Rump Parliament
1164, 1167–1169, 1171; Scottish
campaign 1164, 1168; split with the
Levellers 1168; succession 1178, 1179,
1181; unpopularity 1181–1182; use of
prerogative 1187
Cromwell, Richard 1179–1180, 1181
Cromwell, Thomas: elevation to peerage 978;
injunctions 1001; parish administration
and 1088; as Principal Secretary 1043–
1044; Privy Council 1054, 1062–1064;
religious reform 1012, 1015, 1035–
1036, 1039–1040, 1066; review of royal
prerogative 976–977, 1057
Crusades: chivalry and 658; costs 478,
500, 501, 555, 575, 639, 640, 656,
710; Edward I 657, 732; Edward III
784, 789; Henry II 593; as impetus
for establishment of English Empire

1277; influence on castle-building 512;
Richard I 525–528, 589
cultivation: agricultural machinery 1367;
commons and wasteland 394, 723,
1066; Kent 210; Lancashire 174;
manors 451; *Parisii* 105; role of Third
Estate 209, 254; Roman Britain 60,
134; tobacco 1554; West Saxon 234
cultural identity 17, 44, 84, 111, 200, 404,
431–432
Cumberland 116, 144, 165, 176, 343, 478,
518, 624–625, 660, 1775
Cumbria: acquisition by Scots 510; becomes
known as Cumberland 176; Edmund
I gains control of 343, 355; eviction of
Strathclyde from 381; incorporated into
Northumbria 170; Norse settlement
330, 330–331; origin of name 144;
reclaimed from Scots by Henry II 514;
under Scottish control 307; William
Rufus reclaims from Strathclyde 478
currency 1574, 1585, 1628, 1719, 1726,
1727
Curtana (ceremonial sword) 549–552, 621,
707–708, 752, 980, 981, 982, 1531,
1777, 1781, 1782
customary law: assemblies 99, 259; Bracton
on 693; *burhs* 317; confederacies 142;
criminal justice 233, 235, 667; as
distinct from edict/statute law 282–287;
Empire and 1315; English constitution
defined by 6; equity 682; folk-memory
689; Indo-European 385, 505, 683,
717, 1270; Jutish 86; kingship 136,
156, 772; land ownership 138, 230,
231, 251, 253; levying of tolls 858;
Magna Carta and 603–604, 607;
national territory 240; obligations and
rights 166, 216; privilege 660, 670;
records of 813; succession of kings 261,
267, 489–490; urban laws 237
Cutha, brother of Ceawlin 82, 145–146
Cuthred, King of Wessex 150–151, 164, 185,
297
Cuthwulf, West Saxon leader 81–83
Cwichelm, King of Wessex 146, 148, 150,
152, 168
cynebōt ('king's compensation') 276, 278
Cynegils, King of the West Saxons 103, 148,
168, 170, 179–180, 182
Cynehof (Royal Court) 557, 567
Cynewulf, King of Wessex 249, 297

Cynric, King of the West Saxons 88–91, 92, 93, 95–100

D

Dafydd ap Gruffydd, Prince of Wales 713–714, 715

Dal Riata 116, 174

Danby, Thomas Osborne, Earl of 1215, 1219, 1223, 1227, 1243, 1266

Danegeld 365, 367, 368, 386, 462, 499, 500, 575, 590, 633

Danelaw 367–371; boundaries 308, 325–327; counting system 288–289; Edgar's relations with 357; Edmund I regains control of 354; Edward the Elder's campaigns 321, 323; influence on jury system 584; land ownership 316; legal system 285, 660; popular assembly 254; trade 308

Danes: attacks on William I 409; Battle of *Aclea* 296, 300; Battle of Maldon 207; conversion to Christianity 305, 364–365; defeat at Edington 304–305; defeat of Mercia 303; defences against 235; effects of invasion on confederacies 270; first invasion (850-975) 298–337; Five Boroughs 324, 325–327, 354, 365; Great Army 309–313, 320; jury system 288–289; land entitlement of Angles 210; London under rule of 238; migration 25; overlordship of Jutes 33–35, 53; permanent settlement in England 307–308; piracy 299; political effects of invasion 233, 293; raids on Southern England 299–313, 364; second invasion (975-1015) 363–384; social and economic effects of invasion 272, 294; St Brice's Day Massacre 367; *wergeld* 226, 309; of York 300–301, 302–303, 308, 311–312, 320, 323, 328

Dartmoor 160, 161, 162

David II, King of Scotland 803, 805

De Laudibus Legum Angliae (Fortescue) 951, 952

De Republica Anglorum (Smith) 1026, 1057

Deben (river) 122, 124

Dee (river) 165, 184, 192, 194, 195

Defenas 160–162, 258

de Gaulle, Charles 1721, 1723

Degsastan, Battle of 117, 118

Deira 106–109; confederacy 269; Danish settlement 301, 309, 316; dynastic feud 176; expansion northward 113,

119–121; independence of 111; kingship 113, 270; overthrow of Mercia's allegiance to 178–188; part of confederacy of the English 115, 166–173; revolt against Danes 303; rivalry with Bernicia 177, 183; size of assembly hinterland 258; suzerainty of Northumberland over 170–172, 178; West Angles' allegiance to 131

deities: divine protection of kings 266; Germanic 25, 27, 29, 252–253, 268; Indo-European 15, 21–22, 946, 1045; influence on place-names 204; Pagan 138, 893, 1087; Parliament held in presence of 785, 1021; Roman 52; Saxon 31, 80; use of sword in sacrificial ceremonies 550–551

democracy: America 1315, 1384; Bagehot on 1461; Bodin on 1097; Civil War and 1099, 1182; class and 1417, 1731; Commonwealth of England 1168; coronation oath and 1252; English local government 952; Hobbes on 1128, 1169; Italy 1428; parliamentary 1480, 1576

Denmark: Angles in 52; in *Beowulf* 124; *ealdormen* 243; kingship 28, 375, 382, 384, 1637; kinship groups 326; *Magna Carta* 610; migration 9; refuge for Englishmen after Conquest 408

depopulation 47, 48, 54, 75

Derby 322, 324, 325, 1357

Derby, Edward George Geoffrey Smith Stanley, 14th Earl of 1431–1432, 1438

Derbyshire 192, 303, 304, 316, 329, 342, 410

Derwent (river) 106, 329, 355

Despenser, Hugh, 1st Baron le Despenser (the Younger) 767, 775

Despenser, Hugh, Earl of Winchester 753, 765

De Valera, Éamon 1556, 1587

Devereux, Robert, Earl of Essex 1152, 1158, 1160

Devil's Dyke 73, 93, 122

Devon 160–162; *Cornovii* 152; Council of the West 1064; Cuthred's campaign in 297; Danish invasions 310; national identity 240; part of confederacy of the English 341; rebellion (1549) 1066; revolts against William I 408, 424; size of assembly hinterland 257, 258;

Stannaries 995; West Saxon conquest of 157

Dicey, A. V. 941, 1060, 1669, 1198–1199

Diplock, Lord 1710, 1711, 1715

Disraeli, Benjamin: Appellate Jurisdiction Act (1876) 1441, 1511; foreign policy 1449; Gladstone and 1490; Reform Bills 1431–1432, 1478; Royal Titles Bill (1876) 1500; second Ministry 1489; Victoria and 1477, 1491, 1502

divine law: Coke on 1116; common law and 1509; comparison with edict law 282–284; customary law and 683, 686; divine protection of First and Second Estates 251, 266–267; *folcriht* 245, 286; free men and 16; international law and 1762; statute law and 689, 1156; St German on 1032; trial by ordeal 290

divine right: authority of kings and 992; Bodin on 1097, 1098; Convocation of Canterbury and 1140; excommunication and 593; feudal doctrine and 626, 813, 1580; Fortescue on 950; freedom of speech and 836; Henry III and 611–612; *Magna Carta* and 606; Parliament and 1323, 1155–1156, 1225, 1246; Stuart dynasty 1113, 1123, 1151, 1152, 1154, 1232, 1248; Tyndale on 975

divorce 974, 976, 1013, 1014, 1016–1017, 1040, 1069, 1073, 1397, 1611–1612

Doctor and Student (St German) 1032

Domesday Book 433–434; burgesses 655; evidence of extinction of English ruling class 412; role of juries 668; Dominions 1589–1603; abdication of Edward VIII 1613–1614; citizenship 1653; coronation oath and 1531; definition 1300; freedom of movement 1651; immigration 1655, 1662; Ireland rejects offer of status of Dominion 1586, 1589; military assistance of 1568; Newfoundland 1302; postwar years 1573, 1623; Southern Rhodesia 1683

Dorchester (Dorset) 100, 151, 153, 156, 1408, 1649

Dornsæte 156, 258

Dorset: Council of the West 1064; as nation state 162; national identity 240; part of confederacy of the English 341; place-names 62; revolts against William I 409; size of assembly hinterland 258; West Saxon expansion into 100

Dover (Kent) 61, 388, 390, 393, 404, 596, 612, 644, 922

Drake, Francis 1079–1081, 1279, 1286

Dublin: Danish raids coordinated from 300; Ivarr the Boneless, king of 302, 320; Norse of 299, 319, 321, 324, 329, 330, 346, 354; support for James II 1253

Dudley, Robert 1077–1078, 1084

Dumnonii 151–152, 159, 161

Dunstan, St. 336, 356–358, 363, 375, 394, 414, 487

Durham 116, 119–121, 320, 342, 367, 805, 1053, 1139, 1508

Durotriges 153

Dyrham (Gloucester) 144, 145, 188

E

Eadred, King of the English 355

Ealdberht, West Saxon rebel 159, 164

ealdormen (aldermen): appointment of 142; attendance at Councils 243, 417, 576; folk-kings replaced by 270, 273, 334; Mercian 173, 192, 367; replaced by earldoms 374; responsibilities 206, 271–272, 580; role in fortification of boroughs 237; South Saxon kings reduced to level of 196; title transferred to magistrates 584

Ealdred (archbishop of York) 404, 406, 407

Ealdred of Bamburgh 320, 328, 330, 339

Ealhfrith, King of Deira 171, 172–173

Ealhmund, King of Kent 200–201, 298

Eamont Bridge treaty 339, 346, 1775

Eanfrith, King of Bernicia 169

Eanred, King of Northumbria 177

Eardwulf, King of Kent 200, 263

earldoms: decline of 576–577; Earl Palatine 549–555, 576, 621, 707–708, 752; Mercia 380; replace Anglo-Saxon aldermanry 374; shift in function 779–781; under Stephen 458; under William I 447

earls: attendance at Councils 533, 635, 736–737; attendance at Parliament 733, 748, 809, 982; conflict with Edward I 740; conflict with Edward II 754–773; conflict with John 740–744; equated with French 'count' 442, 444; land ownership 773; see also eorls

East Angles 121–126, 196–199; alliance with Mercia 185, 194, 197–200, 201, 295; defeated by Penda 170, 180; rebel

against Mercia 199; size of assembly
hinterland 258; as subjects of Danes
302, 305, 307
East Anglia 121–126; Cenwealh seeks refuge
in 182; conceded to Norse 354; Danish
invasions 367; Danish settlement 301,
306, 307, 309–312, 322, 327; during
Civil War 1158, 1159; Edwine seeks
refuge in 166; legal practices 286; peace
treaty with Danes of Northumbria 316;
post-Norman Conquest 407
East India Company 1280–1281, 1282,
1287, 1290, 1311, 1359, 1382, 1483
East Saxons 64–65, 80–81; admission to
West Saxon confederacy 162; alliance
with Mercia 201; defeat by *Gewisse* 103;
fyrd 207; multiple kingships 263; size
of assembly hinterland 258; treaty with
Penda 180; westward expansion 76
ecclesiastical courts 417, 516, 535, 690, 701,
706, 972
ecclesiastical law 519, 1016, 1038
Ecgberht, King of Kent 186, 191
Ecgberht, King of Wessex 164, 177, 199, 201,
276, 295, 298, 300, 345
Ecgfrith, King of Mercia 197
Ecgfrith, King of Northumbria 118,
173–175, 186, 187
economy: advantage of landholding 720;
crash of 1929 1621; depression 1396,
1489, 1573, 1574, 1585, 1610, 1628;
during reign of Edward I 732; during
reign of Henry III 613, 640; effect
of Black Death on 793–800, 801;
European integration 1719–1726;
farming 516, 622; government spending
500; London 392; postwar years 1634,
1641, 1645, 1655–1656, 1659, 1723;
Rhodesia 1681, 1684, 1687; role of
manors 451; significance of royal estates
397; social class and 728–729; under
Protectorate 1176, 1180; villages 460
Edberht, King of Kent 198, 200, 263
Edberht, King of Northumbria 176
Eden, Anthony 1645, 1689, 1756
Edgar *Ætheling* 391, 392, 398, 404–406,
408–409, 411, 477
Edgar, King of the English: accession
355–356; cedes Lothian to Scotland
359; Church reform during reign 137,
357–360, 363; coronation 358, 487,
1530; election 261; law codes 237,
280, 285, 375, 561; ordinances 235;

popular assembly during reign 272, 335;
relations with Danes 356
edict 282–284, 287, 546, 664, 667, 688
Edict of Nantes 1236, 1258
Edinburgh 168, 356, 359, 771, 802, 1094,
1138, 1144, 1154, 1398
Edington, Battle of 304–305, 307
Edmund I, King of the English 285, 343,
354–355
Edmund Ironside, King of the English 261,
370–373, 374, 390, 398
Edmund, King of East Anglia 301–302, 906
Edmund of Langley, 1st Duke of York 889,
892
Edric Streona, *ealdorman* of Mercia 367, 370,
371, 373, 381
Edric the Wild 408, 409, 411
education: effect of disintegration of feudal
system on 795; local government and
1458; Rhodesia 1682; sixteenth century
988, 1066; social class and 1432, 1434,
1521; teaching of English in schools
850; voting rights and 1648; women's
1567; *see also* universities
Edward I, King of England: accession
703–706; appearance of bannerets
during reign 471; appointment of
Admirals 724; castles 711, 716, 717;
Confirmation of the Charters 741–743,
859; confiscation of office of Earl of
the Palace 708–709; coronation 491,
689, 706, 1613; Councils 563, 828;
Crusade 657, 732, 939; establishment
of staples 726; expulsion of Jews 723,
731; in Flanders 739, 740, 741, 743,
744; Gascon campaigns 647, 732–733,
736, 738, 740, 742, 744; judicial system
during reign 665, 669–670, 679, 682,
695; legal reforms 706; ordinances
688–689, 718; Parliaments 621–625,
707, 710, 711–714, 729, 734–737,
983; petitions during reign 573, 709,
783–785; reconstruction of St Stephen's
Chapel 620; relations with Church
706, 737; Scottish campaigns 628,
738–740, 743–744, 746, 748–749;
Second Barons' War 646–649; statutes
during reign 574, 670, 688, 699, 706,
710, 714, 716, 717–718, 720, 721,
722, 900; succession 750–752; taxation
during reign 739–744, 858–860; Welsh
campaign 711, 714–717, 732, 733,
735, 739

Edward II, King of England: attendance of
   clergy at Parliaments 787; baronial
   opposition 753–763; betrothal to
   Queen Margaret of Scotland 732, 738;
   character 750, 760; constitutional
   status of commonalty during reign
   455; coronation 492, 689, 707,
   750–753, 1250, 1252; Councils 558,
   625, 737, 753–772; death 778, 808,
   813; deposition 775–778, 840, 886,
   892, 994; Despenser War 767–771,
   774–776; loans 723; marriage 751–752,
   775; murder 701; ordinances 758–762,
   765–766, 772, 774; as Prince of Wales
   716, 770, 782; regency 741–742,
   758–761; role of Chancellor during
   reign 699; Scottish campaigns 757,
   760, 764–766, 770–771, 783; separate
   consultation between Estates during
   reign 632; statutes during reign 760,
   794; succession 777; taxation during
   reign 859; use of signet 595
Edward III, King of England: accession
   775–776; attendance of clergy at
   Parliaments 787–790; Battle of Crécy
   800, 805, 814; character 801; claim to
   French throne 803, 806, 813; coat of
   arms 779, 909; constitutional status
   of commonalty during reign 455,
   832; construction of Jewel House
   725; coronation 778, 779; Councils
   725, 914, 1200; Crusades 784, 789;
   financial needs 791, 796, 804, 827, 860,
   862–864, 1009; Great Council fettered
   by 625, 807–813, 853, 905, 917, 955,
   1155, 1244, 1320, 1439, 1526, 1531,
   1670, 1764; heralds 508; Hundred
   Years' War 726, 802–808, 810, 813,
   827, 862; John of Gaunt takes control
   during dotage of 879; judicial system
   during reign 680, 681, 682, 699,
   854, 872; laws 695; Parliaments 791,
   807–813, 816, 816–818, 825–827,
   860, 878–882, 988, 992, 1004, 1005,
   1007, 1010; petitions during reign 783,
   899; popularity 801, 805, 810, 813;
   regency 779; Scottish campaigns 792,
   796, 802–805, 810, 814; statutes during
   reign 944, 1016, 1209; succession 489,
   819, 830, 884; suzerainty of Isle of Man
   790, 1392; taxation during reign 808,
   860, 861–862; title 805, 807; use of
   English during reign 850

Edward IV, King of England: accession 926,
   937; alliance with Burgundy 928;
   autocracy of 949; benevolences 932;
   character 928, 931; claim to throne
   923, 925–929, 938; coronation 927;
   Councils 933, 1063; deposition 929;
   elevation of supporters to nobility 928,
   953; execution of Duke of Clarence
   931; illegitimacy 925–926, 929, 930,
   934, 935, 938; judicial system during
   reign 932, 944, 947; marriage 928, 935;
   Parliaments 932, 990; popular support
   927, 929, 938; Privy Council during
   reign 875, 944, 1055; statutes during
   reign 933; succession 934–941
Edward V, King of England 930
Edward VI, King of England: accession
   1065, 1069; coronation 1250, 1252;
   death 1067; Privy Council during reign
   1048; Protectorate 1065; Reformation
   1065–1068, 1075; repeal of Act of
   Proclamations 1059, 1060, 1107, 1199;
   role of lords lieutenant 1085; succession
   1067
Edward VII, King of the United Kingdom:
   accession 1503–1504; constitutional
   crisis 1520–1522; coronation 1504;
   relations with Ministers 1503; scandals
   1498, 1578; succession 1522, 1578
Edward VIII, King of the United Kingdom
   1600, 1605, 1611–1614
Edward of Westminster, Prince of Wales
   929–930, 934–935
Edward the Ætheling 390–392
Edward the Black Prince 805–807, 881, 884
Edward the Confessor, King of the English:
   accession 383, 384–385, 431; appoints
   Tostig as Earl of Northumbria 208;
   asceticism of 386; choice of William
   as successor 392, 413; conflict with
   Godwine 386–390; coronation 1532,
   1251; Councils 531, 532, 1200;
   feudalism 394–396, 397; grants
   immunity for persons attending Church
   synods 253; Great Seal during reign
   1347; inherits advanced system of
   government 5; latter years 391–392;
   laws during reign 423, 432, 480, 481,
   552, 592, 597, 606, 686, 752; legacy
   399, 431–432, 492, 552; as miracle-
   worker 505; relationship with Church
   386–388, 418; Westminster as royal
   residence 394, 617, 619

Edward the Elder, King of the Anglo-Saxons:
administrative reorganisation of Mercia
319–320, 1775; Battle of Tettenhall
318–319; campaign against the Danes
320–324, 327–330; Chancery retained
by William I 569; fortifications 313,
317, 321–322, 323, 327, 329, 330; law
codes 285; opening up of Danelaw to
English settlement 316; overlordship
of the Welsh 328; restoration of the
hundred system 233, 235; succession
315–316, 337, 386–392, 398
Edward the Martyr, King of the English 336,
363–364, 371
Edwig, King of the English 355–356
Edwin, Earl of Mercia 401, 404, 405, 407,
408, 410, 411, 430
Edwine, King of Northumbria 86, 87, 120,
165–169, 172, 178, 179, 180
egalitarianism: Empire and 1656; identity and
1659; Labour Party and 1518, 1657;
liberalism and 1627, 1645, 1660, 1762;
of Lollards 1427; National Socialism
and 1609
Egbert, King of Wessex 99, 332, 1776
Egypt 1287, 1451, 1487–1489, 1543, 1545,
1561, 1566, 1645
Eirik Bloodaxe, Viking leader 347, 348
Elbe (river) 30, 33, 34, 36, 50, 74, 135, 299
Eleanor of Aquitaine 512, 513, 518, 524,
526, 588
Eleanor of Provence, wife of Henry III 549,
568, 707
elections: campaigning 1474; clergy's right
to vote 1208; corruption 855, 1346,
1372, 1384–1385, 1411, 1433;
electoral periods 1197–1198; exclusions
1162, 1174; frequency 1196; general
elections 4, 1323, 1324, 1443, 1470,
1180, 1533–1534, 1662, 1734, 1741,
1756–1757; immigration and 1663;
kingship 6, 249, 260–261, 264–266,
486, 490–492, 555, 591, 611–612,
704, 743, 884, 907, 937, 947, 1323,
1324, 1328, 1340, 1270, 1783–1784,
1788; knights 628, 637, 643; municipal
councils 1455; parliamentary 855,
913, 915–916, 949, 990, 1005–1006,
1009–1011, 1340, 1025, 1103, 1144,
1214, 1255; political representation
824–827, 948–949, 1030; role of press
1449; shires 272, 800, 867; sponsorship

of candidates 1430; under Protectorate
1173, 1176, 1187; validity 1103
electoral reform 1378, 1391, 1396, 1409–
1415, 1431–1435, 1461, 1567, 1569,
1571, 1585
Eliot, John 1126, 1132, 1135–1136
Elizabeth I, Queen of England: affair
with Robert Dudley 1077–1078,
1084; character 996, 1073, 1078,
1082, 1093; claim to throne 1067,
1072, 1093; coronation 1250, 1252;
Court of High Commission 1074;
excommunication 1070; execution of
Mary Stuart 1078, 1080, 1093; finances
1105–1106; foreign policy 1073, 1286;
imprisonment 1071; Irish rebellion
1083, 1112; judicial system during
reign 943, 1038, 1044, 1082–1083;
military service during reign 1086;
Parliaments 725, 986, 987–988, 990,
995–997, 1005, 1007, 1024, 1028,
1029, 1038, 1075, 1081; Privy Council
during reign 1048, 1053, 1054–1055,
1074, 1078, 1081; proclamations 1060,
1061; relations with Spain 1079–1081,
1279; religious policy 943, 1073–1078,
1133; royal prerogative 1057, 1082;
succession 996, 1074, 1078–1079,
1083, 1093–1095; taxation during reign
1088, 1106; titles 1074
Elizabeth II, Queen of the United Kingdom:
accession 1639; claim to throne
1637–1638; coronation 1530; as head
of the Commonwealth 1643; marriage
1637–1638; Rhodesian independence
1686; titles 1642–1643
Elizabeth of York, Queen of England 936,
960, 961, 966
Ellendun, Battle of 199, 295
Elmet 108, 121, 166–167, 258, 339, 342,
768
Eltham Palace 879, 881, 885
Elton, G. R. 1005, 1053
Emma of Normandy 366, 374–375, 382, 413
Empire: anti-imperialism 1652, 1660–1661,
1688, 1691–1692; customary law and
1315; decolonisation and decline 1592,
1640–1656, 1662, 1688–1690, 1723;
development of Civil Service and 1484;
First World War and 1568; freedom of
movement 1650–1651; identity and
1659; and Industrial Revolution 1366–
1368; Japanese 1621–1622; Labour

attitudes to 1588; origins 1277–1281;
and patriotism 1357; rise of imperialism
1450–1451, 1502; Scotland and 1357,
1646; Second World War and 1623;
and slavery 1380–1381; transition to
Commonwealth 1605–1606
employment: colonies 1281, 1312; effect
of enclosure on 1088; free men
654; immigration and 1406–1408;
industrialisation and 1410; payment
793; personal names and 467; retainers
796; social class and 1432; socialism and
1426; wool trade 727
Ems (river) 53, 67, 91
enclosure 723–724, 1280, 1066, 1067, 1085,
1088, 1159, 1519, 1250
England: Hengest as true founder of 53;
hundredmen 31, 232; kingship of 6,
193–196, 264, 434–437; origin of term
'English' 344–345; as premier sea power
1081, 1084; unification of 8, 39, 285,
334, 335, 340–346, 355–356, 400,
735; union with Ireland 1391–1393,
1445, 1175, 1698, 1700–1701; union
with Scotland 3, 732, 1290, 1322,
1331–1334, 1102, 1125, 1343, 1392,
1445, 1175, 1236, 1252, 1646, 1698–
1699; 'West Lothian' question 1699
English Constitution, The (Bagehot) 1334,
1461–1462, 1478
English Channel 48, 61, 299, 309, 806, 1081
English language: of Alfred the Great
304, 305, 314; becomes language of
administration and justice in Wales
1064; corruption of 419, 468, 906;
gradually replaces French in Middle
Ages 691, 744–745, 800, 821, 825,
850, 906; as medium of international
communication 1623; Provisions of
Oxford proclaimed in 651; spoken by
ruling class 613; translation of Bible
into 974; use in courts 414
entails 720–721
eorls 206–207, 239, 242, 272, 275–276, 291,
294 *see also* earls
equity: Court of Chancery 676, 685–686,
699–700, 1507; Court of Requests
1062; role of King 493, 561–562, 660,
662, 664, 666, 680, 682–684, 686, 943,
948, 1063, 1099, 1122, 1509–1511
escheat 426, 445, 497, 663, 720
esquires 868, 916, 945–946, 980, 1048

Essex: admission to West Saxon confederacy
162–164; annexation by Wessex 300;
appropriated by GLC 1705; baronial
uprising 601; Danish raids on 207,
310–311, 321, 322, 365, 372; Danish
settlement 305; Hengest's authority over
53, 57; Mercians take possession of 156;
multiple kingships 263; as nation state
162; part of confederacy of the English
341; place-names 64–65, 222, 234;
rejection of Christianity 87; relations
with Mercia 196, 295; size of assembly
hinterland 258; support for Jack Cade's
rebellion 938
Essex, Earl of *see* Devereux, Robert, Earl of
Essex
Estates 135–140, 204–213, 1202–1204;
decline of First and Second Estates
1274; definition 16, 841; elevation
of members by King 1325; First
Estate displaced by Church 437–464;
Indo-European origins 11, 542, 776;
inheritance and 468, 1325; justice and
251, 672–673, 781, 878, 1747–1750;
loss of functional significance of system
1671; Parliament and 795, 955,
1765–1766, 1786; Royal Family distinct
from 505; separate consultation 536,
546, 631–633, 865; sovereignty and
1097–1098
European Convention on Human Rights
1627, 1663, 1716–1717
European Economic Community (EEC)
1653–1658, 1662, 1664, 1719,
1722–1723, 1757
European Union (EU) 1644, 1653, 1687,
1698, 1699, 1701–1702, 1720,
1726–1728, 1757–1761
Evesham (Worcestershire) 296, 471, 571,
648, 656, 715
Exchequer: accounts of shire not rendered
at 552; backgrounds of officers 581;
declining importance 699, 1330;
Exchequer Pleas 673, 675, 676, 1507;
itinerant justices from 662; location
673, 679, 820, 821, 874; Normandy
drain on 588; origin of 562–563,
673; Parliamentary Rolls kept by 574;
petitions to 699, 709; raising of aids
501; sheriff fee 577, 583; transfer of
revenue to Royal Household 962; under
Henry III 565–566, 642, 643; under
Henry VIII 1043–1044

Exe (river) 160
Exeter (Devon) 152, 160–161, 303, 310, 311,
    313, 338, 644, 1064
exports: cloth 964; colonial 1292; duty on
    858, 1105; Kent 84; manufactured
    goods 1398; postwar reduction in 1657;
    Scandinavia 23; textiles 1367; tin 75,
    152; wool 140, 516, 533, 723–724,
    727, 858, 861

F

Fairfax, Thomas 1160, 1161, 1162, 1164,
    1167, 1168, 1171
Falkland Islands 1689–1690
family 138, 214–215, 216, 226, 229, 230,
    241, 900
famine 27, 410, 766
farming: Angles 114; Australia 1367–1368;
    Britons 228; Cape Colony 1304,
    1308, 1539; Church reform and 357;
    climactic conditions 36; Corn Laws
    1396, 1399, 1438, 1474; decline in face
    of free trade 1444; effect of breakdown
    in feudal structure on 727; enclosure
    of commons and wasteland 723–724,
    1280, 1066, 1085, 1088, 1159, 1519,
    1250; European control and subsidies
    1725; fifteenth-century growth 964;
    Ireland 1587; land clearances 1335,
    1367, 1410; monasteries 516; offences
    concerning 292, 916; on lords'
    demesnes 395, 450–451, 469; Rhodesia
    1554, 1596, 1682; Scandinavia 24;
    villeins 460
Farnham (Hampshire) 50, 102, 310
fascism 1428, 1574–1575, 1609
Faversham (Kent) 69, 223, 224
felony 464, 473, 494, 497, 672, 698, 719,
    722, 851, 854
Fens, the 51, 109, 110, 112, 129, 130, 219,
    609
feorm (tribute in kind) 139, 217, 225, 395,
    856–857
Ferdinand of Aragon 966, 967, 1039
Ferrers, George 999–1000, 1002, 1023
feudalism 424–475; abolition of feudal
    tenures after Restoration 1189–1190;
    aid, levies and reliefs 462–464,
    496–502, 515–516, 537–538, 542,
    547–548, 556, 577, 590, 601, 603,
    604, 633–634, 635–637, 641, 720,
    856–859, 865–867; anomaly of shire

assemblies 578; Constitution and 397–
    398, 694, 1096, 1166; disintegration
    of 468–472, 613, 719–729, 794,
    798, 825; Empire and 1285–1287,
    1290–1291, 1293, 1308, 1313, 1591,
    1592; feudal kingship 484–506, 784,
    894–895, 911, 943, 987, 991, 1008,
    1009, 1057, 1073, 1085, 1094, 1223,
    1244, 1248; France 402, 403–404;
    influence of forms of address 829–830;
    ius soli 1647; Lithuania 876; origins 21,
    394–397, 631–633; Scotland 1335; *see
    also* Church-Feudalism
fiefdom 427–428, 439–446, 495, 513, 587,
    590, 596
fines 498, 604
First World War 1557–1571, 1591, 1595,
    1606, 1640
FitzOsbern, William, 1st Earl of Hereford
    408, 430, 564, 1347
Flanders: Cinque Ports established in response
    to risk of invasion from 390; Dutch
    claim to 1216; Edgar Ætheling seeks
    refuge in 411; Edward I and 739, 740,
    741, 743; French claim to 737, 1273;
    Godwine seeks refuge in 388; merchants
    502, 560; military preparations in 736;
    Second World War 1619; Spanish claim
    to 1239; Tostig seeks refuge in 209,
    398, 401; wool and cloth industry 597,
    723–724, 726, 727, 802, 952
foederati (allies) 45, 51, 54, 57, 107, 108,
    1515
folc (folk) 141, 218, 220, 222, 251, 254, 326
folcgemot (popular assembly): alternative
    names 567; attendance at 251,
    256–259, 538; criminal justice and
    396; function 220, 628, 876, 882;
    judicial role of King 493; location 253;
    origins 5–6, 1027; rehabilitation of 794;
    representation 470
folcriht ('folk-right') 245, 282–284, 286, 663,
    689–690
folkland: colonies 1290; definition 219;
    forests 436; geographical extent
    256–259, 437; replaced by Danelaw
    326; replaced by shires 162, 240–241,
    319, 334, 1775; royal 229–230, 441
folk-peace 216, 218, 291, 292, 293
Foreign Office 1376, 1451, 1476, 1484, 1688
forests: administration 565, 581; Charter of
    the Forest 609, 614, 740, 743; Crown
    income from 1113; forest laws 140,

480, 547–548, 591, 601, 613, 746, 1136; Jutish settlement 62–63; obstacle to West Saxon expansion 100, 151–152, 189

Fortescue, Sir John 493, 947, 950–952, 1120

fortifications: building materials 512; Devon 310–313; of Edward the Elder 317, 321–322, 323, 327, 329, 330; Indo-European 441; lack of use in eleventh century 401; London 305; Mercia 319; Norman 402, 409, 412, 414, 430; role of *ealdormen* 237; Roman 45, 306; Somerset 153, 157; towns built around 236, 331; *see also* castles

France: absolute monarchy 890; Alcuin of York in 175, 177, 252, 1761; alliances 738–739, 807, 961, 966, 968, 1098; American War of Independence 1377, 1379–1380; Angevin claim to throne 909, 932; Black Death 792; Brussels Treaty 1628; Catholicism 1236, 1254, 1272; charters 605; civil law 951; colonies 1280, 1282, 1289, 1297, 1359, 1370, 1380, 1645; costs of defence against 495; Counter-Reformation 1094; coup d'état (1851) 1475; Crimean War 1482; Danish invasions 309, 312, 364; diplomatic marriages 84, 366; Ecgberht seeks asylum in 164; Edict of Nantes 1236, 1258; emigration to 75; Enlightenment 1405; *États Généraux* 841, 1109, 1384; European integration 1719–1725; feudal system 402, 403–404; First World War 1558–1565, 1568, 1570; Franco-Dutch War (1672-1678) 1217; Hundred Years' War 726, 802–808, 909, 910, 918, 919–923; Italian War 1034, 1036, 1072; James II flees to 1242; kingship 389, 403; migration from 36; mints 201; Napoleonic Wars 1387–1390; postwar years 1641; Protestantism 1079, 1096, 1126, 1127, 1133, 1137; Reformation 1096–1098; relations with Charles II 1215; relations with Edward I 737–738; Richard I's travels through 527; royal elections 265; rulers' control of Papacy 594; Second World War 1615–1617, 1618–1623, 1719, 1721; Seven Years' War 1291–1292, 1355–1359, 1370; support for Henry VI 926, 927, 929–930; Third Republic 1570; Thirty Years' War 1170; trade 1311; Treaty of

Troyes 842, 903, 910, 919; War of the League of Augsberg 1257–1258, 1263; Wars of Religion 1096–1097

Franco-Prussian War 1514–1517, 1557, 1561

Franks: Angles return to Continent to join 74; assemblies 29, 252; clergy under William I 503; Danish army joins 309; expansion into Germany 126, 1515–1516; field system 60; fortifications 414; influence of Roman law 628; influence on Normans 403; officers of the court 552, 553, 567; origin of name 472; origin of term 'fee' 439; relations with Kent 200, 201; royal residences 550; Third Estate 841; use of juries 585

freedom: attendance at assemblies 253; citizenship and 1429; effect of Norman rule on 418, 461; freeholders 470–471; *imperium* and 241; kingship and 596; limits of royal proclamations 1059; Montesquieu on 3, 1338; Rousseau on 1351; Universal Declaration of Human Rights 1626

freedom of movement 1649, 1651

freedom of speech: constitutional crisis (1642) 1153; Elizabeth I accused of curbing 1082; legislation curtailing 1658; Lord Chancellor 1028; in Parliament 836, 987–988, 992–999, 1008, 1123–1125, 1155, 1255

freehold and freeholders: allocation 452; attendance at assemblies 533–534; attendance at Councils 567, 868; common law and 470, 1434; deprivation of 614, 833; fiefdom and 440; free status and 465, 604, 631; growth in number 825; held from King in fee 425–429; heritable 496; jurisdiction of manorial courts 474–476, 719; ownership 798, 1115; political importance 647, 650–651, 652, 654–657; possessory assizes 667; post-Conquest 460; representation 827, 855, 913, 948; role in local government 1089; towns 857

free men 16–17, 209–210, 225–231; attendance at Councils 711, 731; attendance at Parliament 774, 914–915, 983, 1432, 1196, 1673; colonists 1295; constitutional rights 657, 747, 1436, 1766; decline in prosperity and status 394–395, 435; *imperium* 241–242; land ownership 221, 333, 425, 429, 434,

439, 449, 460, 465, 470, 631, 795; popular assembly 20, 251, 271, 567, 579, 600, 1027, 1295; representation 795, 825, 827, 948, 1030, 1409–1415, 1421, 1434–1435, 1526, 1567, 1571, 1730, 1786; rights and obligations 216, 253–254, 279–280, 638, 654, 1053, 1649, 1651; right to bear arms 944; as subjects 488; taxation 860

French language: adopted by Danish-speaking Normans 377; coronation of William I conducted in 406; gradually replaced by English 691, 745, 800, 821, 825, 850, 906; Law French 1170; as medium of international communication 1623; as official language 414, 419, 515, 533, 569, 643, 671, 687, 695, 783, 1043, 1720; statutes written in 710

French Revolution 1384–1389; Burke on 1406; causes 1405; cultural vandalism of 1652; effect on German identity 1514; *imperium* and 1470; legacy of 1396, 1412, 1437; nationalism and 1427; trade unionism and 1407

Friesland 33, 35, 54–55, 60, 1389, 1239

Frisians 26, 33, 35, 45, 46, 79, 252, 299, 312, 1239

fyrd (militia): English 402, 462; funded by hides system 234; *fyrd* service 139, 209, 217, 226, 429, 471, 856, 1360; King's rights 547; opposition to Danes 207; in reign of Henry II 458, 515; in reign of William Rufus 478; under command of lieutenants 1085; use against rebellious barons 503

G

Garter rolls 979–980

Gascony: Battle of Castillon 922; Edward I and 574, 623, 635, 637, 647, 723, 732, 736, 738, 744; Edward III and 804–807; English wine trade 589; France invades 775; Henry II becomes Duke of 513; petitions from 821

Gaul: Aëtius evicts Huns from 55; Augustine of Canterbury visits 85; Britons emigrate to 59, 771; Celtic stratum destroyed 1385; Christianity 52; *Chronica Gallica* 48; Germanic settlers 472; Meroving dynasty gains prominence 1515–1517; Migration Age 24; piracy 36; Roman *villae* 52, 450

Gaveston, Piers 707, 750–751, 753–758, 762–764, 767

gē (territory) 78, 192, 221–225, 230, 231, 232–233, 236, 241

Geats/Goths 25, 114, 124, 1649

geneatas (peasant aristocracy) 213, 276, 291, 396, 452–453, 454, 468

Geoffrey of Coutances 430, 474

Geoffrey Plantagenet, Count of Anjou 483, 509, 511, 513

George I, King of Great Britain: Cabinet Council 1329, 1349, 1743; character 1342; claim to throne 1340–1342, 1343–1344; finances 1345–1346; foreign policy 1347; judicial system during reign 700; marriage 1342, 1348; Parliament during reign 1322, 1343–1346, 1362; Privy Council during reign 1347; Protestantism of 1462; succession 1354; taxation during reign 1377; Treasury during reign 1330; Whigs and Tories 1344–1345

George II, King of Great Britain: accession 1354; foreign policy 1355, 1356; Parliaments 1362; Protestantism of 1462; Royal Marriages Act (1772) 1614; Seven Years' War 1354–1357; succession 1369

George III, King of Great Britain: American War of Independence 1377–1381, 1469; assassination attempts 1386; character 1369, 1371; coat of arms 1394; coronation oath 1393–1394; finances 1372–1376; foreign policy 1290, 1293, 1362, 1369; Isle of Man Purchase Act (1765) 791; legacy 1397–1398; marriage 1369; mental health 1394–1395, 1397; ministerial responsibility during incapacity of 1485; Napoleonic Wars 1389, 1397; Parliaments during reign 1002, 1362, 1371–1372, 1375–1377, 1378–1380; popular support for 1462; Private Secretary 1497; slavery during reign 1380–1381; succession 1397; titles 922, 1393; union of Great Britain and Ireland 1392; use of patronage 1371–1372, 1382, 1400, 1469

George IV, King of the United Kingdom: declining health 1398, 1486; economy during reign 1398; House of Commons during reign 1362; marriage 1397;

popularity 1396; Private Secretary 1497; regency 1395–1396; succession 1466
George V, King of the United Kingdom: accession 1522, 1527–1528; changes name of British royal house 1579, 1639; claim to throne 1578; constitutional crisis 1522–1524, 1579; coronation oath 1496, 1557; economic crisis 1584–1585; Irish Free State 1327, 1615; marriage 1578; party politics and 1583–1584; popular support 1579–1580; Privy Council during reign 1527–1528; studies Bagehot 1478; succession 1611–1614; titles 1500, 1600, 1604
George VI, King of the United Kingdom 1589, 1605, 1614, 1637–1639
Germanic peoples: deities 25, 29, 252, 268; dual monarchies 91, 263; Estates 207, 210; Habsburg dynasty 1272; honour 658; land allocation 222–223, 229, 231, 441; legal system 282–283, 554; migration 9, 24–25, 45, 1515–1517; naming of dynasties 961; political confederacies 269; popular assembly 218, 225, 228; priesthood 19, 244; role in Romano-British politics 103; settlement of Britain 43, 46–51, 54, 126, 155, 229, 262
Germany 28–32; abolition of monarchy 1568; assemblies 1109; Catholicism 1137; charters 605; colonial interests 1543, 1546, 1570, 1592; Communism and 1573–1574, 1608–1609; dialects 1239; economic crisis of postwar years 1574, 1608, 1615; Enlightenment 1405; European integration 1719–1721, 1725–1726; feudal system 440; First World War 1557–1563, 1568, 1570–1571, 1588; Franco-Prussian War 1514–1517; Frankish expansion into 126, 1515–1516; heraldry 1343; Hundred Years' War 804; language 450; Lutherism 973, 974, 1044, 1046; nationalism 1557, 1623, 1725; National Socialism 1427, 1608–1609, 1609–1610, 1628, 1645, 1652, 1695, 1716; persecution of Jews 1568, 1609–1611, 1624–1627, 1645, 1660, 1661; political alliance with England 1039; Protestantism 1070, 1079, 1111, 1137, 1265; Queen Victoria and 1500; reunification 1726; Revolution (1918-

19) 1573; revolutionary France and 1387–1389; royal elections 265; rulers' control of Papacy 594; Second World War 1615–1621, 1661; socialism 1564; support for Afrikaners 1539, 1627; support for Irish independence 1556; Thirty Years' War 1111, 1137; title of Earl Palatine 550; unification 1514, 1517, 1557, 1616; War of the League of Augsberg 1258
Gewisse 51–54, 74, 83, 97, 103, 145, 150, 256
Gibraltar 1281, 1283, 1288, 1380, 1450, 1475, 1688, 1689
Gildas 47, 52, 56, 63, 71, 74, 97
Gladstone, William Ewart: electoral reform 1416, 1431, 1433; Home Rule 1436; House of Lords reform 1441, 1443, 1446–1449, 1511; relations with Queen 1477, 1487–1490, 1495–1496, 1502
Glanvil, Ranulf de 497, 690, 692
Glastonbury (Somerset) 157, 161
Glorious Revolution (1688) 1320–1321, 1338, 1383, 1494, 1238–1274
Gloucester: Æthelræd's seat in the west 145, 313, 337; ceded to Penda 179; Councils held at 388, 448, 531, 543, 549, 611, 661; Danish settlement 304; fifth-century destruction of 59; held by supporters of Edward IV 930; impact of wool trade on 727; Norman Castle 644; Parliaments held at 865–867, 882; site of coronation of Henry III 400; Statute of 669–671; West Saxon settlement 144, 165, 188; see also Humphrey, Duke of Gloucester
Gloucester, Duke of (Thomas of Woodstock) 830, 837, 838, 886, 887, 889
Gloucestershire 73, 188–190, 320, 342
gods see deities; divine law
Godwine of Wessex 381–383, 384, 387–389, 398
gold 1279, 1314, 1538, 1545, 1548, 1554, 1574, 1585, 1592, 1659
Gordon, Charles George 1487–1488
Goring Gap 49, 51, 65, 77, 150
grants-in-aid 463, 499–500, 537–538, 555, 609, 756–758, 797, 865–867, 1042
Great Council 1777–1780; alternative to kingship 20; appointment of archbishops 543–544; barons' role 531–532, 538; compared to Privy Council 941; confederacies and 268–270; as

constitutional watchdog 954, 1095, 1151, 1777; co-ordination with other Councils 729–732, 914; *Curtana* sword representative of authority of 551, 1777, 1781; death of a King and 1335–1337, 1259–1261; decline and disappearance 438, 801, 812, 816, 817–820, 849–850, 869, 905, 933, 949, 953–955, 1030, 1151, 1166, 1737, 1184, 1748; during Glorious Revolution 1242; Edward II and 753–772; Edward III and 807–813, 830, 862–864, 905, 992, 1439, 1155, 1244, 1246; Estates and 631–634, 735–736, 830–833; flexibility of attendance at 543–544; following unification of England 336, 340–341; functions 281, 1527–1528, 1777–1778, 1780–1781; granting of aids 537–538, 865; *imperium* and 940, 1336, 1050, 1492, 1527, 1530, 1238, 1737, 1781; influence on American Senate 1295; John and 587–591, 596–598; judicial function 378, 418, 493, 545–546, 625–626, 661, 732–733, 816, 830–833, 853, 882, 895, 946–947, 1320–1321, 1340, 1709; King's absence 768, 1780; King's communication with 745; King subject to judgement of 546–548, 553, 635–636, 1183; life peerages granted to members of 1442; location 394, 620–621, 729, 1779; membership 567, 616, 1440, 1200–1202, 1526, 1765, 1778–1779; origins 5–6, 1737; Parliament and 650, 781–782, 807–813, 888, 1033, 1439; post-Conquest 432, 434, 530–537, 661; promotion of attendance of knights at parliaments 651–652; Provisions of Oxford 640–649; Richard II and 884–885; role in Glorious Revolution (1688) 1237–1238; seating arrangements (1277) 620–623; size 334, 544–545, 1779; statutes and ordinances 718; summoned independently of Parliament 917, 1140; summons to 538–543, 811; timing of meetings 807
Great Seal: custodianship 887, 1336–1337, 1042–1043, 1347, 1214, 1742; Edward II and 762, 775; following unification of England and Scotland 1333; function 759, 1044, 1266; James II drops into Thames 1241, 1244, 1245; origins 594; Privy Seal and 772–773, 872
Great Trek 1304–1307

Greece 441, 932, 1045, 1560, 1617, 1623, 1638
Green, Thomas Hill 1429–1430
Gregory, Pope 85–86, 314, 417, 491, 504
Grey, Charles, 2nd Earl 1412–1413, 1437, 1468
Grey, Lady Catherine 1093
Grey, Lady Jane 968, 1067–1068, 1071, 1077, 1093
guilds 238–239, 453, 583–584, 726, 859
gunpowder 934, 949, 968, 1104
Guotodin 112, 115–116, 118, 120, 170
Guthfrith, Norse leader 338, 340, 346, 347
Guthrum, King of East Anglia 302, 307–308, 324, 688
Gwent 145, 179, 195
Gwynedd 120, 165, 168, 179, 180, 190, 714, 716
Gyrwe 112, 130–131

H

habeas corpus 661, 684, 1386, 1396, 1127, 1186, 1220–1224
Habsburg dynasty 1039, 1070, 1137, 1239, 1240, 1647, 1271
Hadrian's Wall 45, 72, 75, 112
Hæslingas 50, 83
Hæsten, Viking leader 309, 310
Hæstingas 68, 75
Halfdan Ragnarsson, Viking leader 300, 302–303, 306, 320
Hamble (river) 62, 88
Hampden, John 1138–1139, 1140, 1147–1148
Hampshire: Danish invasions 309; identity of Men of 143; inherited by Ceolwulf 148; Jutes of 62–63, 87–95, 99–104, 154, 162, 200, 224, 240, 304; New Forest 436; Offa becomes lord of 75; part of confederacy of the English 341; Saxon occupation 127; size of assembly hinterland 258
Hampton Court 874, 1013, 1100, 1342
Hanover, House of 1340–1343, 1354–1358, 1365, 1369, 1470, 1502, 1503, 1529
Harald Harthrathi, King of Norway 400, 400–402
Harald II, King of Denmark 369–370, 375
Harold Godwinson, King of the English: Battle of Hastings 403–405; campaign against Harald Harthrathi 401–402; claim to throne 391–392; coronation

400; division of estate among Normans
407; expulsion and return of 388–389;
lack of royal ancestry 262; oath to
William of Normandy 391; succession
398–402, 403; Tostig and 208–209
Harold Harefoot, King of the English 376,
382
Harrison, K. 88
Harrow (Middlesex) 77, 204
Harrow Way 49, 50
Harthacnut, King of Denmark and King of
the English 377, 382, 384
Hastings (East Sussex) 68, 75, 223, 305, 341,
390; Battle of 402, 403–405, 411, 420,
453, 1325, 1274
Hatfield Chase, Battle of 169, 180, 184
Haxey case (1397) 835–836, 891, 992–993
health 1368, 1456, 1459, 1493, 1635, 1651
Heath, Edward 1700, 1724
Hegel, Georg 1352, 1660
Hengest and Horsa 53–58, 60, 63–64,
65–66, 67–70, 81, 106, 242, 1343
Henry I, King of England: administrative
achievements 482; Charter of the
Liberties 464, 479–484, 610; claim to
throne 479, 481; coronation 479, 602;
Councils 531, 562, 662; diplomacy
482–483; Exchequer during reign 562–
563; feudal dues 461, 462; invasion
of Normandy 482; issue 509; judicial
system during reign 583, 592, 661,
662, 664; laws during reign 423, 436,
596, 687; marriages 481, 1069; offices
of Chief Justice and Prime Minister
during reign 564; relations with Church
482, 484, 489, 492, 519–524, 543; role
of courts during reign 494, 579–580;
succession 482–483, 508; taxation
during reign 499, 672; title 485
Henry II, King of England: accession
513–514; assizes 546, 548, 549, 688;
building programme at Westminster
523; Church reform 514, 516; civil life
under 516; claim to throne 481, 513;
Constitutions of Clarendon 504, 517,
519, 521; control of Ireland 487, 514,
517–518, 523, 593; coronation 537;
Councils 332, 531, 533–534, 541, 555,
558, 563; dispute with Thomas Becket
519–526; Exchequer during reign 673;
forest law 609, 614; hunting 547–548;
influence through dynastic marriages
518; judicial reforms 470, 563,

664–670, 673–676, 691, 692; offices
of state 563, 571; ordinances 664, 667;
relations with sons 524–525; role of
sheriff during reign 580; succession
489, 511, 518, 522, 524, 703; taxation
during reign 462–463, 515–516, 563,
575; title 610; use of *fyrd* 458
Henry III, King of England: accession 609,
912; baronage as 'realm' but speaking
for all free men 841; character 616;
claim to throne 611; coronation 400,
491, 611; Councils 559, 560–561, 612,
626, 634, 782; function of *Curtana*
sword during reign 550; invasion of
France 615; judicial system during
reign 582, 583, 680, 820, 853, 864;
loss of Poitou 514; *Magna Carta* 610;
offices of state 571, 572; Parliaments
656; Provisions of Oxford 640–649;
recognition of Llewellyn ap Gruffydd as
Prince of Wales 714; regency 612–614,
895; relations with barons 615–616,
641–648; relations with Papacy 616,
623, 626, 640; royal officials during
reign 553, 565, 871; Scotland 519,
623–624, 639; 'Sicilian affair' 639, 640,
641; spending and debt 617, 618, 633,
636–637, 640, 645, 723; succession
623, 648, 657, 703, 939; taxation
during reign 583, 613, 623, 628; title
611; writs of Watch and Ward 702
Henry III, Holy Roman Emperor 390, 445
Henry IV (Bolingbroke), King of England:
accession 842, 893; claim to throne
892, 906–908, 920; coronation 707,
842; Councils 561, 625, 697, 917–919,
1004; Hundred Years' War 909, 918;
inadvertent burial at sea 909; judicial
system during reign 851; Parliament
and 815, 842, 865–867, 870, 875, 903–
905, 907–908, 917–919, 993–994,
1004, 1005, 1008; petitions during
reign 786; relationship with Richard II
891–893; relations with Church 909;
Scottish invasion 909; statutes during
reign 998; succession 908, 947; taxation
during reign 917–919; Welsh rebellion
909, 918
Henry V, King of England: claim to French
throne 910, 919; Councils 697;
Hundred Years' War 919; marriage 910;
Parliaments 797; succession 910, 920

Henry VI, King of England: accession 911, 920; Bills 1327; character 920, 921; claim to French throne 922; coronation 920, 929; deposition 704, 926, 927, 929, 930; electoral system during reign 826–827; Hundred Years' War 920–923; judicial system during reign 933, 942, 993; King's Council during reign 941, 942; marriage 921; mental health 920, 923, 924, 929, 931, 938; murder 930; Privy Council during reign 1055; ranks of peerage during reign 845; regency 911–916, 920–921, 923, 931, 943; statutes during reign 868; succession 923–924; Wars of the Roses 923–927

Henry VII, King of England: accession 960; claim to throne 936, 938, 959–961, 1068; control of revenue 962, 1043; coronation 493, 960, 1250; Council of the North 1063; courts 963; despotism 961, 963, 1060; judicial system during reign 698, 947; King's Council during reign 560; marriage 960, 961; Parliaments 827, 961, 963, 1024; political alliances 965–966; popular support 963; Privy Council during reign 1048, 1050, 1051, 1055–1056, 1062; regency 915; royal prerogative 1057; statutes during reign 948, 961, 1053; succession 966; taxation during reign 961, 963

Henry VIII, King of England: accession 966; administration of revenue during reign 1043; appointment of local government officials 1085; bodyguard 967; character 994, 1044–1045; claim to French throne 968; coronation 966, 1250; defence spending 1034–1035; dissolution of monasteries 953, 1024, 1034–1035, 1037–1038, 1072, 1088; excommunication 1015, 1034, 1036, 1039; foreign policy 967–968; judicial system during reign 1038–1039, 1040, 1052–1053, 1063; legislative powers of King in Council 1060; legitimacy 1068; as Lord/King of Ireland 1040; marriages 966, 974, 976, 1011, 1013, 1015, 1016, 1035–1036, 1039–1041, 1044–1045, 1073; militias 1360; Parliaments 975–987, 990, 994, 1000, 1024, 1025, 1026, 1028, 1031, 1033, 1037; Privy Council during reign

965, 976, 1014, 1023, 1026, 1043, 1044, 1048–1049, 1051, 1054–1056; relations with Church 972–978, 1015–1017, 1018, 1034–1035, 1038–1039, 1044–1048; residences 1013–1015; royal prerogative 943; statutes during reign 1029, 1060, 1106; succession 973–974, 1014, 1016–1017, 1036, 1041, 1044, 1065, 1067–1068, 1072, 1093–1094; taxation during reign 1088; titles 973, 976, 1012, 1074; union with Wales 1064–1065

Henry the Young King 518, 524, 546, 549

heraldry 506–508, 526–529, 658, 779, 909, 1096, 1102, 1343

heralds 846, 980

Hereford 187, 191, 319, 338, 644; earldom of 757, 761, 763, 764, 766, 769–771

Herefordshire 185, 190–191, 197, 296, 320, 342, 388, 408, 409, 926

heregeld 368, 379, 392, 500, 633

heresy 799, 909, 974, 1041, 1065, 1071

Hertford/Hertfordshire 48, 65, 77, 130, 186, 239, 311, 321

Hicce 130, 342

hides 192–193, 210, 213, 214, 231–236, 256, 317

hill-forts 93, 96, 97, 103, 152, 155, 415, 441

Hitler, Adolf 1428–1429, 1609–1610, 1615–1619, 1624, 1627, 1719

Hlothhere, King of Kent 187, 262, 285

Hobbes, Thomas 1351–1352, 1128, 1130, 1169, 1181

Holstein 34, 50, 135, 274

homage 26, 364, 426, 427, 440, 463, 488, 589

Home Office 1376, 1497

Home Secretary (office) 1507, 1714

homicide 278, 285, 290, 291

honour 278–279, 436, 448, 450, 456, 658

Hooker, Richard 1026

horse-riding 10, 256, 312

horses 21, 212, 213, 264, 396, 401, 712

House of Commons 795–799, 814–816, 822–827; antiquity of 5–6; Apology of the Commons (1604) 1104; Bagehot on 1461–1463; bargaining with King 899–905, 1010; Church and 1101, 1577; committees 1110, 1125, 1144, 1152; control of Privy Council 1320–1321; control of taxable resources 859; corruption 1401, 1411; election to 913, 915–916, 990, 1320, 1005–1006, 1325,

1025, 1103, 1383, 1410–1412, 1208, 1214; fiscal policy 865–867, 1105–1106, 1202; freedom of speech 1082; Grand Remonstrance (1641) 1145; Great Protestation (1621) 1123–1125; impeachment of Duke of Suffolk 922; increase in size 990; judicial function 494, 832–833, 946–947, 1002, 1150, 1749, 1192–1193; legislative function 1361–1364, 1166, 1731–1732, 1187, 1209; location 817, 1017–1020, 1030–1031; majorities 1371–1372, 1400, 1633, 1759; membership 567, 1266, 1665–1666, 1267–1268; ministerial responsibility 1479–1486, 1582–1583, 1708; Nineteen Propositions 1150, 1151, 1213; as oligarchy 949, 1005, 1014, 1022, 1321, 1324, 1327, 1518–1519, 1534–1535, 1576, 1734, 1735; opposition to Court of Chancery 699; overtaken by political careerists 1082; parliamentary procedure 983–990; Petition of Right 1131–1133, 1209; privileges 991–1003, 1147–1148, 1204, 1205; Protestantism 1074; publication of speeches 1375; ransacked by mob following lack of response to Act of Oblivion 1162; relations with Lords 1008, 1349, 1436–1448, 1439, 1442–1447, 1478, 1177, 1179, 1200–1207, 1523–1525, 1672–1674, 1730–1736; role in constitutional crisis (1642) 1145–1157; role in Glorious Revolution (1688) 1237; role of Lords Chancellor 1028–1030; Royal Mace 985–986, 994, 999–1002, 1019–1023, 1108, 1110, 1135, 1171, 1172; seating arrangements 1425; size 1104, 1434, 1434, 1247; supremacy of 1449, 1165, 1172, 1182–1183, 1198–1206; voting 989

House of Lords xiii; appellate jurisdiction 1508, 1511–1512, 1670–1671, 1675, 1697–1698, 1744, 1748–1749; appointment of Speaker 1744; Bagehot on 1461–1462; bargaining with King 901–902; bills 898, 1412, 1202–1203, 1671–1673; Civil War and 1157, 1202; constitutional priority 904, 954–955; corruption 1437, 1448; deprives Privy Council of judicial function 1192–1193; during Long Parliament 1144–1146, 1148–1152, 1154; fiscal policy 865–867, 1131–1132; House of Lords Act (1999) 1733–1735; *imperium* and 940; inclusion of women 1676–1677; and Irish Home Rule Bills 1446–1448; judicial function 828, 830–833, 947, 1438–1441, 1670–1671, 1204–1207, 1210, 1745–1747; jurisdiction 494, 1059, 1168, 1203–1205; legislative function 827, 1519–1525, 1579, 1633, 1670–1672, 1731–1732; location 823–824, 1017–1020, 1020, 1030, 1424–1426; membership 567, 876, 953, 1325, 1104, 1392, 1200–1202, 1730, 1736; as moderating factor during Commonwealth and Protectorate 1181; origins 5–6, 814–816, 1730–1731, 1784; partiality 1200; permanence of 1437; political decline 942, 1583; privileges 991–1004, 1444, 1519, 1205, 1674–1675; rejects proposal to create High Court of Justice to try Charles I 1165; relations with Commons 796–797, 1325–1326, 1436–1448, 1439, 1167, 1442–1447, 1478, 1172, 1177, 1179, 1523–1525, 1672–1674, 1730–1736; religious matters 953–954; representativeness 1730, 1735–1736; role in Glorious Revolution (1688) 1237–1238; seating arrangements 840, 852, 1426; secularisation 1023–1025; size 1445, 1448; threatened by socialism 1430, 1518; voting 989

Howard, Katherine, Queen of England 1040

Hudson's Bay Company 1287, 1293, 1298, 1301

hue and cry 287, 853

Huggins, Godfrey 1600, 1606, 1683

Huguenots 1096, 1126, 1127, 1133, 1650

Humber (river) 49, 107–108, 121, 127, 131–132, 181, 368, 393, 401, 402, 409, 410, 840

Humbrenses 108–113, 127–128, 173, 339

Humphrey, Duke of Gloucester 910, 911–913, 920, 921

hundred 61, 101, 193, 230–239, 288–289, 325, 423, 462, 631, 1306

hundred assembly 232, 234, 235, 237, 582, 651

Hundred Years' War: capture of Calais 726; Edward III and 802–808, 813, 827; financial burden 858, 862, 952, 964; Lancastrian period 906, 909, 911, 919–923

Huns 48–49, 55
hunting 47, 78, 140, 226, 432, 436, 547,
        601, 994, 1013, 1422
Huntingdon/Huntingdonshire 129, 322, 323,
        325, 327, 342, 583
Hus, Jan 799, 973
Hwicce 188–190; after fall of Mercia 195;
        allegiance to Mercia 192; Council
        representation 271; creation of bishopric
        at Worcester 187; join confederacy of
        the English 342; kingship 142, 179,
        182, 197, 263, 296, 317; origins 129,
        133; replacement of folkland by shire
        320
Hyde, Edward *see* Clarendon, Edward Hyde,
        Earl of

I

Icel, King of Mercia 134
Iceni 121–122, 122
Icknield Way 49, 50, 73, 81
Icling dynasty: Angles' allegiance to 130, 190;
        control of Northumberland 183; end of
        194, 300; right to *Bretwaldaship* 185;
        South Angles' confederacy under 178;
        succession 135, 168; suzerainty over
        Angle kingdoms 179, 181
Ida, King of Bernicia 108, 112–114, 166, 270
Idle (river) 127, 166
immigration 1406, 1436, 1538, 1555,
        1645–1646, 1649–1658, 1661–1662,
        1662–1663, 1682
impeachment 797, 896, 942, 948, 1150,
        1205; Bill of Rights (1689) 1255;
        bishops 1146; Duke of Buckingham
        1126; Duke of Suffolk 887, 922; Earl
        of Danby 1219; Francis Bacon 1123,
        1214; King's protection 1266; Lords
        Appellant 889; Lyons and Latimer
        494, 880, 895, 1004; origins of term
        946; and prorogation/dissolution of
        Parliament 1210; right of Parliament
        to impeach Ministers 1492; Thomas
        Wentworth 1141, 1142; William Laud
        1141, 1142
Imperial Conferences 1598, 1602–1606,
        1615
imperialism 1450–1451, 1489, 1541–1542,
        1645, 1660–1661, 1691
imperium: delegation upwards 241–242,
        1351, 1354; Dominions and 1604–
        1605; free men 17, 225; Great Council

as custodian of 19, 262, 281, 888,
        1492, 1527, 1202, 1530, 1238, 1737;
        kingship and 358, 485, 534, 897, 969,
        1049, 1334, 1336, 1470, 1480, 1496,
        1532–1533, 1711, 1774; source and
        nature 1775–1776; succession and 264,
        912, 940–941; Sword of State as symbol
        of 577, 708; under Norman rule 423,
        555
Independents (religious groups) 1160, 1161,
        1163, 1164, 1167
India: colonisation 1290; customary law 284;
        immigration 1663; independence 1642,
        1643, 1653; Indian Civil Service 1324,
        1483–1484, 1707; industrialisation
        1657; Mutiny of 1857 1477;
        nationalism 1624, 1641; numbering
        system 971; Pitt's reforms 1382; Queen
        Victoria Empress of 1450, 1500, 1543;
        Second World War 1622; trade 1277,
        1280–1282, 1311; War of the Austrian
        Succession 1357; *see also* East India
        Company
Indo-Europeans: assemblies 8, 29, 987;
        common law 1244; Constitution and
        1098, 1166, 1228; counting system
        289; customary law 385, 505, 603, 683,
        717, 1291, 1270; freedom 992, 1353;
        justice 282–283, 283, 287, 605–606,
        666, 690, 1032, 1056, 1104, 1116,
        1123; kingship 21, 259, 357, 400,
        486, 487–488, 490, 550, 863, 894,
        899, 907, 940, 969, 1016, 1045, 1047,
        1073, 1098, 1128; marriage 1613;
        origins 10; political traditions 269, 465,
        627–628, 709, 824, 841, 876, 952,
        1337, 1029, 1046, 1096, 1354, 1234,
        1626; priesthood 19, 25, 135, 245,
        484; religious practices 1087–1088;
        ritual sacrifice 931; social order 11,
        203, 205, 441, 631–633, 945; tradition
        of government 15–22, 36, 218, 238,
        252, 268, 353, 504, 1008, 1094, 1136,
        1460, 1231
Industrial Revolution 1366–1368; Church
        and 1576; cultural reaction to 1426–
        1427; economic change 1370, 1398,
        1501; electoral reform 1409–1411,
        1435; local government 1454–1456;
        population growth 1383; Prussia 1514;
        Russia 1558, 1559; Scotland 1335; and
        slavery 1284, 1652, 1691; socialism and

1427; social problems created by 1368, 1406, 1519
industry: chemical 968; colonial 1292; during Second World War 1720–1721; immigration and 1653, 1657; iron and steel 1514, 1720, 1725, 1733; Middle Ages 348, 660, 723–727, 795, 964; patriotism and 1357; Rhodesia 1681; state owned 1659; textiles 1366, 1653, 1657
Ine, King of Wessex: abdication 164; Battle of Woden's Barrow 188; campaign against Geraint 161; division of Britain into nation states during reign 162; law codes 158–159, 209, 213, 217, 238, 246, 280, 285–286, 289, 305, 314, 333, 674, 687, 690, 693; relationship with Æthelred 187; succession 260, 296
inheritance: agnatic 282, 446; disputes 878; earldoms 442; Estates 1274; identity and 424; kingship and 429–430, 486, 758, 1398, 1503; knight service 456; land 226–227, 264, 443, 587, 720–721, 843; legitimacy 631; nobility 851, 944, 1325, 1639; peerages 1439, 1733–1734; 'relief' 496–497; social status 213, 275, 471, 944; thanes 213; see also primogeniture
Innocent III, Pope 504, 595
Inns of Court 696–697, 942, 1083, 1148
Inquest of Sheriffs 548, 668
Instrument of Government, The 1173–1174, 1175–1176, 1177, 1179
Iona 169–170, 170, 172, 175
Ireland: Act for the Settlement of Ireland (1652) 1171; alliance with Britons 115; Brexit 1759–1760; British flight to 174–175; Catholics in office 1399; Church of Ireland 1392, 1494–1496; constitutions 1586–1588, 1603; conversion to Christianity 84; customary law 283; Danish raids coordinated from 300; dependency on Great Britain 1382; during Civil War 1159, 1161, 1167–1169, 1182; Easter Rising 1556; European integration 1724; fifth-century invasions 46–49, 54, 111; First World War 1588, 1591; Gaveston exiled to 752, 755–756; Henry II's control of 487, 514, 517–518, 523, 593; Home Rule 1327, 1436, 1446–1448, 1489–1490, 1522, 1523, 1524, 1555–1556; independence 1585–1588, 1601, 1603;

Irish settlement in Wales and Dumnonia 151–152; Jacobitism 1257, 1258; John's control of 596; Kingdom of 1040; national identity 1698; nationalism 1494, 1518, 1522, 1555–1556, 1585–1587, 1698, 1700–1701; Norse settlement 299, 320, 323, 328, 330, 331, 346–347, 624; petitions 574, 821; plantations 1083, 1112, 1588; potato famine 1474; Rebellion of 1641 1144–1145, 1148, 1153; representation 1414–1415, 1432, 1435, 1586, 1736; revival of Royalist cause 1168; revolutionary France and 1386–1387; rule of William and Mary 1253; Statute of Drogheda 965; tuath 141; Tyrone's Rebellion (1594) 1083–1084, 1112; union with England 1391–1393, 1445, 1175, 1698, 1700–1701
Irish Free State 1586–1589, 1601, 1603, 1606, 1615–1616
iron 964, 967, 1366, 1367, 1514, 1559, 1618
Iron Age 11, 26, 203, 841, 1786
Isabella of France, Queen, wife of Edward II 751, 775, 780–781, 803, 994
Isle of Man 343, 838, 1141, 1392, 1690
Isle of Wight: captured from Britons 89, 93–95; Charles I flees to 1163, 1164; Cnut leads expedition to Denmark from 376; cultural identity 200; independence from West Saxon confederacy 99; as Jutish folkland 162; lathe of 224; paganism 157, 185; part of confederacy of the English 341; size of assembly hinterland 257; Victoria withdraws from public life to 1499
Italy: Black Death 792; Charles VIII of France invades 967; classical scholars exiled to 971–972; cloth industry 723; European integration 1722; fascism 1428, 1574–1575; First World War 1562; merchants 502; Protestantism 1079; Richard I's travels through 527; Second World War 1617, 1620; wool trade 516, 726
Itchen (river) 63, 88, 89, 91, 92
Ivarr the Boneless, Viking leader 300, 301, 302, 320

J

Jacobites 1331, 1344, 1356–1357, 1257
James I, King of England: accession 1078, 1095; character 1100; claim to throne

1084, 1093–1095; coat of arms 1096, 1102; constitutional law 1113–1123; coronation 1095, 1100, 1250; feudalism 1095, 1120, 1122, 1136; finances 1105–1106, 1107–1108, 1113; foreign policy 1109–1110, 1123–1125; granting of monopolies 1113; judicial system during reign 1116–1122, 1206, 1222; as King of Scotland 1095–1096, 1604; legacy 1125; on monarchy 1098, 1113; Parliaments 1028, 1102–1108, 1124–1125; Privy Council during reign 1096, 1103, 1124, 1147, 1211; proclamations 1103, 1114, 1119–1120; relations with Church 1100–1101, 1104; relations with Spain 1107, 1109–1110, 1111–1112, 1123–1124; revival of baronetcies 845, 1112–1113, 1200; royal prerogative 1106–1108, 1114–1116, 1119–1121, 1123; rumours of illegitimacy 1094; succession 1125; taxation during reign 1105–1106, 1108, 1114, 1131–1133; Thirty Years' War 1105, 1109, 1110–1111; titles 1095–1096, 1102; and Union Jack flag 1102

James II, King of England: abdication 1242, 1244–1245, 1252, 1255; absolutism 1234; army 1256, 1258; Catholicism 1217, 1232, 1234–1237, 1238, 1240; claim to throne 1207, 1216, 1218–1219, 1220, 1227–1228; coronation 1232, 1250; deposition 1237–1238, 1242, 1244; Glorious Revolution 1241–1242; Irish support for 1253, 1258; judicial system during reign 1234; as Lord Admiral 1217; marriage 1217; Parliaments during reign 1233–1238, 1242, 1322; Popish Plot (1678) 1218; Privy Council during reign 1224, 1235; religious policy 1235; Rye House Plot 1230, 1231; succession 1231, 1236, 1240, 1243, 1244, 1271 1331; support for slave trade 1380

James IV, King of Scotland 966, 968

James Francis Edward Stuart (the Pretender) 1331, 1344, 1356, 1393, 1271

Jameson Raid 1539, 1551–1552, 1560

Japan 1573, 1620–1622, 1641

jarls 207, 272, 324, 380

Jennings, I. 1580–1581, 1585, 1247–1248, 1268, 1669, 1674

Jesuits 1069, 1078, 1101, 1111, 1145, 1244

Jews: blamed for 1918 collapse of Germany 1609–1611; expulsion from England 731; expulsion from Gascony 723; homeland 1566, 1625; immigration 1642, 1650; money-lending 601, 605, 723, 731; persecution 1624–1627, 1645, 1660, 1661; petitions concerning 709; taxation 502, 590, 595, 641; xenophobia towards 1568

John, King of England: baronial conflict 464, 480, 592, 595, 599, 600–606, 607–611; borrowing during reign 502; charters 498; Chief Justices 571; claim to throne 528, 586; control of Ireland 596; coronation 6, 490, 587, 591–592, 596; Councils 559, 587–591, 596–598, 600, 870; dispute with Pope and excommunication 487, 592–594, 595–599, 607; judicial system during reign 665; loss of Normandy 571, 588–591, 592, 595–596, 691, 802; *Magna Carta* 540, 600–603, 607–610; marriages 587; opposition to brother Richard I 527–529, 556, 590; papal support 601, 792, 863; reputation 590–591, 595; succession 609, 703; taxation during reign 500, 501–502, 583, 590, 591, 599, 608–610, 613, 858, 863; title 587; use of Privy Seal 772; Welsh uprising 595

John II, King of France 806

John of Gaunt, Duke of Lancaster 807, 841, 879–880, 883, 885, 892, 936, 992

John of Salisbury 485, 692

Johnson, Boris 1756, 1760–1761

Joliffe, J. E. A. 224

judges 668–670, 671–673, 676–678, 680–682; attendance at Councils 1048; attendance at Parliament 656, 875, 983, 1025, 1512, 1747; conduct 1746, 1266; Court of Appeal 1510; creation of heritable peerages for 1438; dismissal 932, 1510; during Henry III's regency government 612; Guardians of the Peace act as 854; intimidation of 916, 1052–1053; judicial discretion 1222–1223; King as chief judge 685, 1266; peerages 1512; salaries 1374, 1376, 1467, 1509, 1510; seating arrangements 622; seniority 625; social class 1082; under Edward I 695; under Henry II 555

judicial system 472–476, 1505–1515; appeals 1505, 1508–1512, 1205–1206,

1670–1671, 1675, 1695–1697,
1745–1750; assemblies 255;
centralisation of justice in Parliament
659–672; costs 1262; Council of
Elders 251; development of the writ
571; effect of removal of Court of Star
Chamber on 1147, 1186, 1187; equity
493, 561–562, 660, 662, 664, 666,
676, 680, 682–684; European Union
1728; following creation of English
confederacy 660; freedom from arrest
991, 993, 997–1000; independence
1015, 1056; itinerant justices 662–667,
672, 674, 680, 864, 871; judicial review
1708–1714, 1718; Locke on 1338;
London 238; Montesquieu on 4, 1339;
North America 1296; professionalism
of 671; role of House of Lords 828,
947, 1438–1441, 1204–1207, 1210;
role of King 216, 284–286, 291–294,
378–379, 397, 472–475, 493–495,
517, 600–611, 671–687, 698, 872–
875, 985, 1116–1122, 1156–1157,
1220–1224; under Lancastrian Kings
851, 933, 942; under Protectorate 1177;
Wales 716; *see also* courts of law; assizes;
Justices of the Peace
jury system 288–290, 584–585, 667–669,
1764, 1206; assembling jurymen
670–671; attaint 494, 668, 697, 701; in
cases of nobility on trial 946; civil *versus*
criminal cases 951; composition of jury
327, 473, 659, 1675, 1748; exemption
from 445; gross injustice 698–699;
Henry II's reforms 691; intimidation
of 1052, 1062, 1083, 1147; *Magna
Carta* and 604; partisan 1222–1223;
petitions regarding jury 699; Quarter
Sessions 855; refusal to convict 1506;
representation 576, 581, 661; role of
jury 872
justice: Administration of Justice Acts 1452;
centralisation of 660–704; corrupt
practices 1052, 1062; jurisdiction of
Parliaments 676; kingship and 28, 216,
225, 266, 397, 671; as notion 283; shire
assemblies responsible for 272; trial by
jury as feature of 667; *see also* criminal
justice; courts of law
Justices of the Peace: control of ale-houses
1066; independence 1186, 1207;
partiality 1079; responsible to major-
general 1176; role 853–855, 876, 1010,

1086, 1089–1090, 1455–1458, 1512,
1191, 1193, 1747; under control of
King's Council 1084
Justiciar (office) 526, 528, 562, 564, 571,
614, 639, 642, 645
Jutes 33–36; army assists West Saxons
144; *ceorls* 210; customary law 86;
defeat at Badon Hill 88; expansion up
Thames valley 70–75; in Hampshire
89–93, 99–104, 154, 162, 240,
304; identity 194; incorporation
into West Saxon confederacy 202;
jury system 289; in Kent 53–54, 55,
56–58, 59–61, 69, 73, 86–88, 100,
162, 214, 341; kings 84, 91, 100,
1289; land ownership 221, 224; laws
284; as members of confederacy 143;
noble class 206; occupation of Britain
53–64; recognition of Ælle as king
67, 69; return to Continent 84; size of
assembly hinterland 258; traditions of
government 9
Jutland 23–26, 32–33, 35, 50, 104, 194, 274,
289, 298, 307, 366

K

Kenilworth (Warwickshire) 648, 775–776,
778, 994
Kenneth II, King of Scots 359
Kennet (river) 150, 302
Kent: alliance with Northumbria 163, 185;
appropriated by GLC 1705; brought
under rule of Wessex 163, 300; charters
254; as client state 102; concession of
territory to Saxons 74; Council of Elders
246, 248; Danish invasions 300–301,
309; *eorls* 206; Jack Cade's rebellion
922, 938; jurisdiction 76; jury system
288; Jutes of 53–54, 55, 56–58, 59–61,
69, 73, 86–88, 100, 162, 214, 341;
Kentishmen 86–88; land ownership
61, 68, 210, 214, 222–225, 226, 228,
231, 269; law codes 206, 216, 253,
277, 278, 284–285, 998; legal system
200; marauding invasions 47; Mercian
control of 187, 198; Middle Saxon
expansion into 101; multiple kingships
263; place-names 222, 240; political
influence 200–202; political ties with
Isle of Wight 95; revolts against William
I 408, 424; size of assembly hinterland
258; size of freeholdings 452; succession

262; thanes 212; under West Saxons 157; value of *ceorls* 291; West Saxons and 144, 147, 158; William I in 405; Wyatt's rebellion 1071

Kenya 1283, 1680

Kenyon, J. P. 1005, 1130

Kesteven 111, 129, 311

King's Council (*Curia Regis*): alternative names 567, 1737; autonomy of royal courts from 696–698, 697–699; becomes Privy Council 828–829; common pleas 673–677, 684; control over Exchequer 642, 643; co-ordination with other Councils 729–732; Court of King's Bench 674–675, 876; described as 'Sworn Council' 782; establishment of regional councils 1084; Exchequer Pleas 675, 676; functions 557–559, 560–564, 868–874, 914, 1004, 1785; grants of 'bookland' 139, 230; judicial function 378, 561–562, 661, 662–665, 666, 671, 672–678, 689, 871, 916, 943, 1001, 1747; King's communication with 745; location 821, 873–874; members' antagonism with greater baronage 633; membership 558–559, 561, 564, 566, 868, 871–873, 876, 1785; military service and 547; origins 5–6, 530–531, 557, 1777; Provisions of Oxford 644–646; reassembled under Normans 416; remuneration of members 941; role of Chief Justice 564–566, 871; seating arrangements 725; secrecy 559; separation of Chancery from 683–685; Westminster as location of 394

kingship 20–22, 259–267, 1781–1785; abdication 1393, 1468, 1533, 1600, 1605, 1781, 1788; accountability 893–897, 1709–1711; Bagehot on 1462–1463, 1581; blackmail and bribery 902, 903, 905; case law and 286; Church doctrine 356–359, 386, 825; common law and 163, 486, 603, 611, 690, 705, 1149, 1251–1252, 1580, 1253; confederacies and 141–142; Council of Elders and 245–251; death of a King 1419–1421, 1259–1261, 1781, 1787; deposition of kings 249, 251, 893–897, 947, 969, 994, 1323, 1108, 1149, 1154, 1480, 1164, 1165–1167, 1492, 1495, 1223, 1242, 1244, 1784; divine right 1580; dual/multiple 91, 263–264; election of kings 260, 264–266, 486, 490–492, 555, 591, 611–612, 704, 743, 884, 907, 937, 947, 1323, 1324, 1328, 1340, 1270, 1783–1784, 1788; elevation of *dryhten* to 243; empire and 1285–1287; entourage 206, 209, 223, 225, 557; equity 493, 561–562, 660, 662, 664, 666, 680, 682–684, 686, 1099, 1122; expenditure 495–502, 590, 857–864, 1345, 1372–1376, 1400–1401, 1467–1469, 1247, 1262–1263; extended role of king 315, 357; female succession 1068–1069; Germanic 19, 266; *imperium* 281, 940–941, 969, 1049, 1492, 1496, 1532–1533, 1604–1605, 1711, 1774; Indo-European tradition 21, 259, 357, 486, 487–488, 490, 550, 863, 894, 899, 907, 1016, 1098; judicial function 216, 284–286, 291–294, 378–379, 397, 472–475, 493–495, 517, 600–611, 671–687, 698, 872–875, 985, 1116–1122, 1709–1711, 1220, 1746; 'King in Parliament' 977, 1000, 1031, 1032, 1056, 1426, 1108–1110, 1199; King's Peace 216, 218, 292, 293, 378, 489, 494, 662, 671, 870, 1220; King subject to supervision of Council 546–548, 869; king's *wergeld* 276; king-worship 504–505; land ownership 219–236, 331–332, 397–398, 425–429, 433, 440–446, 721–722; *legibus solutus* 1057, 1099, 1113; Mace as symbol of King's presence 969–970, 985–986, 994, 999–1002, 1019–1023, 1424, 1108, 1110, 1135, 1269; and ministerial responsibility 1479–1481; power and 30–33, 359, 483, 487, 535–536, 591–593, 616, 869, 950, 1417–1418, 1464; priestly function 32, 203, 259, 265–266, 486, 1016, 1032, 1033, 1045, 1047, 1065, 1347; regal contract 19, 22, 250, 262, 266, 407, 616, 625, 860, 865, 894, 899, 1288–1289, 1293–1294, 1302, 1050, 1120, 1125, 1130, 1166, 1223, 1231, 1243–1244, 1592, 1602, 1607, 1613, 1686; responsibility for legislation 546, 985, 1327, 1030, 1057–1061, 1106–1108, 1339, 1362, 1469–1470, 1480, 1528, 1237; rights of native African kings 1549–1552; royal seals 594–598, 745, 772–773, 828, 872, 917–919, 1042–1044; rule of King subject to popular will 549–555;

succession 31, 260–264, 429–430; supremacy over Church 1085; Swedes/ Sweden 26–27, 32; symbols of authority 969–970, 1182; Teutonic 56; titles 196, 434–437, 484–486, 489, 694, 963, 968, 1392, 1450; uncrowned King 939–941, 1612–1613; warrior kings 203, 259; *see also* royal prerogative

Kingston-upon-Thames 77, 78–79, 769; coronations 80, 302, 315, 337, 354, 355, 356, 358, 363, 400

kin/kinship 17–18, 138, 192, 214–215, 218–219, 231, 278–279, 290, 293–294

knights: attendance at Councils 531, 533, 534, 540, 599, 634, 731–732, 868, 1048–1049; attendance at Parliament 637, 651–652, 656–657, 711, 735, 736–737, 810, 823, 826, 835, 843, 864, 866, 914–915, 980, 1787; bannerets 766, 768, 816, 843; election 913, 1010; knight's fee 456, 459, 462, 497, 515, 541, 575, 636, 637, 718; land ownership 448, 712, 719; peace-keeping role 853; role in assizes 667; role in local government 578, 581, 582–583, 628–629, 864; social status 453–457, 459, 465, 727, 796, 835, 944; taxation 739–741, 858; *see also cniht*

knight service 456–459; chivalry and 658; compared to tenure by barony 445; contractual relationship 773; due from fiefs 427–428; freeholds subject to 461, 498, 636; King's feudal right to summon to 652; outside England 547; primogeniture and 438; scutage levied *in lieu* of 857

L

labour: Atlantic Charter 1625; colonies 1281; immigration and 1406, 1653, 1655, 1656; impact of Black Death on 854, 964; Industrial Revolution 1367–1368; interwar years 1634; migration 1724; mobility during Second World War 1720; trade unionism and 1407–1408

Labour Party: control of Greater London Council (GLC) 1705; early years 1524; European and 1728; first Labour government 1573, 1579, 1584–1585; and House of Lords 1674, 1733–1734; immigration policy 1656, 1657; interwar years 1575, 1581, 1583–

1584; leadership 1581; origins 1427, 1518–1519; support of Liberal Party 4; sympathy for Irish Republicans 1701; and trade unions 1659

labour service: *ceorls* 395; freeholders 425; labour shortages 461, 793; replaced by liveried retainers 796; tenants 440, 450, 460, 654; transition to paying rent in money 727; *trimoda necessitas* 226, 856; *weorc* 217

laissez faire 1429, 1454

Lambert, John (general) 1173, 1176, 1179

Lancashire 165–167, 173, 181, 329, 330– 331, 339, 342, 624, 906, 1053, 1154

Lancaster: Court of Common Pleas 1508; Duchy of 906, 962, 1043, 1373, 1146, 1401, 1262; earldom of 568, 576, 775–776, 779–780; herald 508

Lancaster, House of 906–923, 923–930; ascendance of Parliament over monarchy 938; Battle of Towton 932–933; claim to throne 934, 959; estates seized by Richard II 892; extinction through male line of descent 937; Hundred Years' War and 919; King's Council during reign 873; Privy Council during reign 875; unites with House of York 960

Lancaster, Thomas, 2nd Earl of 717, 753–754, 757, 761, 762, 764–771, 773, 830, 852

land allocation 60, 61, 192–193, 215, 219–222, 225–231, 1280

land ownership: barons 443–445, 449, 794, 843; Church as landowner 137–141, 218, 363, 375, 706, 1034, 1037, 1071, 1137, 1170, 1188; churls 210, 277; common land 1066, 1085, 1088; in the Danelaw 316; dispossession 1287; entails 720–721; free men 214, 254, 425; function of shire assembly 255; Ireland 1168; kingship and 22, 425–429, 433, 1341, 1373, 1098, 1113, 1189, 1248, 1262; knights 455, 712, 858; legal disputes 665–666, 916; *Magna Carta* 609; Norman 411, 433, 439, 589–590; payment in kind 217; and political influence 1345; private ownership 719–723; related to summons to Parliament 773; Rhodesia 1593–1594, 1597–1598; social hierarchy and 587, 1409, 1250; sub-infeudation 447, 721, 795, 953; and suffrage 1431, 1433–1434, 1444; *terra nullius* 1288, 1312; thanes 212–213; *wergeld* and 276; *see also* feudalism

Lanfranc, Archbishop of Canterbury 416, 435, 477, 504

Langton, Stephen, Archbishop of Canterbury 592, 593, 595–597, 598, 602, 607, 608

Laski, H. 1584

lathes 61, 63, 65, 67, 95, 101, 221, 222–224

Latimer, William, 4th Baron Latimer 494, 838, 880–882, 895, 1004

Latin: adopted by West Franks 1516; diplomatic correspondence 1043; language of legislation 643, 650, 687; literacy under Alfred the Great 305, 314; Parliamentary Rolls 844; preservation in post-Roman Britain 75; proficiency of members of the Council 531; replaces English as language of writs 569; royal proclamations 850; suppression of 1065

Laud, William, Archbishop of Canterbury 1133–1134, 1136, 1137, 1139–1143, 1144, 1160, 1225

law codes 284–285; Æthelberht, King of Kent 86, 158, 209, 221, 253, 277; Æthelstan, King of the English 285, 286, 333, 396; Alfred the Great 250, 305; Cnut, King of England 140, 231, 253, 285, 378–379; Edgar, King of the English 237, 280, 285, 375; Ine, King of Wessex 158, 209, 213, 217, 238, 246, 280, 285, 289, 305, 314, 333; Kent 278; Offa, King of the Mercians 197, 285

law enforcement 215, 216, 230–231, 231–235, 287–294, 423, 853–856, 876, 1747

law-making 282–288, 898–905; assemblies 252–253, 728; coronation oath 1250–1252; Council 245, 248–250; kingship and 1365, 1056, 1098, 1150, 1250–1252; Parliament 701, 1031–1034; in post-feudal age 795; written laws 416

lawyers 516, 563, 581, 666, 672, 685, 696, 710, 1083

League of Augsburg 1236, 1241, 1243, 1257, 1273

League of Nations 1565, 1571, 1573, 1626, 1628

Lea (river) 77, 79, 308, 311

learning 175, 313–315, 691, 970–972

legislation: against Popery 1079; approval of House of Lords 1519–1525, 1633; attaint 701; charters 269; designated

as 'provisions' 613, 643, 649–650; distinction between early English and modern 287; enclosure of land 1067, 1085; House of Commons usurps function of King in proposing 798, 817; impact of Glorious Revolution on 1249–1250; imperial 1602–1605; judicial review 1714; King's Council 561, 870; Montesquieu on 3, 1339; role of King 546, 898–905, 985, 1327, 1030, 1057–1061, 1106–1108, 1339, 1362, 1469–1470, 1480, 1528, 1237; role of Parliament 947, 954, 1324, 1031–1032, 1339, 1187, 1717; role of Privy Council 941, 1050; subject to consent of people 951

Leicester: Danish occupation 308, 319, 321–322, 323, 324, 325; defended by Humbermen 108, 128; earldom of 568, 625, 653, 851; Olaf Gothfrithson besieged at 354; Parliaments held at 766; Roman town 131

Leicestershire 128, 304, 342

Leofric, Earl of Mercia 380–381

Leopold I, Holy Roman Emperor 1272–1273

Levellers 1159, 1162–1163, 1164, 1167–1168, 1174, 1178

Lewes (East Sussex) 68, 646, 652

liberalism 1405–1408, 1660–1662; Burke on 1385; economic 1399; effect on employment 1428–1429; human rights and 1716; immigration and 1645–1646, 1653–1654, 1658; Rhodesia and 1597; South Africa 1304, 1627

Liberal Party 1443–1447; coalition with Labour Party 4, 1573; commitment to Home Rule 1489, 1555; defection of radicals to Labour Party 1518, 1519; first Government 1477; and House of Lords 1447, 1519, 1521, 1524–1525, 1579, 1674; opposition of Queen Victoria 1450, 1489; origins 1421–1422

Lichfield (Staffordshire) 134, 197, 198

lieutenants 1085–1086, 1090, 1360

Lilburne, John 946, 1167–1168

Lincoln: battles fought at 612; bishopric of 457; castle 510; Danish occupation 323, 324, 325, 326, 328; earldom of 757; knights summoned to Parliament 109, 653; Norse invasion 329; Parliaments held at 628, 743, 746, 747, 765, 766, 782, 898; seventh-century revival 110; violence against Jews in 723

Lincolnshire 109–111, 269, 303, 304, 326, 346, 631, 766, 929, 1036

Lindisfarne 115, 169, 172, 175, 177, 299

Lindiswaras 109–111, 129, 131, 258

Lindsey 170, 181–182, 185, 186, 195, 342, 369

literature 414, 419, 618, 934, 970, 972

Lithuania 630, 651, 824, 876–877

liveries 1052–1053

livestock-rearing 11, 24, 36, 105, 209, 226, 254, 276

Llewellyn ap Gruffydd, Prince of Wales 621–622, 714–715, 717

Lloyd George, David 1496, 1520–1521

Lobengula (Matabele king) 1545, 1547–1548, 1549–1550, 1553

local government 577–586; breakdown in traditional system under Cnut 380; *burhgemot* 235, 236–240, 237, 332; Civil War and 1207–1208; county councils 1703–1707; Danish 325; following Glorious Revolution 1250; Guardians of the Peace 853–854; jurisdiction of Privy Council 1193; Justices of the Peace 856, 876, 1089–1090; legislation 1079, 1448, 1456, 1459–1460; office-holders 566, 1085–1086, 1235; parishes 1086–1087, 1088; provision of social welfare 1088; Puritan influence on 1188; reform 529, 1416, 1438, 1454–1459; reorganisation under Æthelræd 365; role of thanes 412; *scirgemōt* 272, 332, 1010; Sussex 68; tithing 230; *tunræd* 215

Locke, John 1291, 1338, 1351–1352, 1405

Loddon Bridge 527–528, 548

Loddon (river) 77, 102

Lollardism 796, 799, 801, 884, 909, 910, 972, 1044, 1046, 1076, 1427

London: allegiance to Count John 527–528, 549, 586; becomes governmental capital 801; bishopric of 387; Blitz 1637; building programmes of Henry II 524; Cade's rebels take control of 922; City of London 1140, 1143; Cnut's siege of 370–371; county status 580, 583, 1459–1460; curfew during reign of Edward IV 932; Danish invasions of 296, 368; depot for Hanseatic League 859; East Saxon control of 81; Edward the Elder gains control of 321; emergence as political centre 392–394, 1459; establishment of diocese 85;

exemption from Domesday survey 449; extension across shire boundaries 1457, 1460, 1706–1707; fifth-century destruction of 59, 60, 71, 77; Great Fire and Plague 1211, 1214; guilds 238; inns of court 696; John II of France prisoner in 806; judicial administration 288; Jutish expansion towards 57; Kentish control of 187; local government 238–240, 584, 1457, 1459–1460, 1703, 1705–1707; Louis VIII captures 608; Margaret of Anjou refused entry to 926; Mercian control of 78–80, 185, 194, 196, 295; mints and exchanges 644; 'Old Bailey' 1508; Ordinances of 759–760, 765–766, 774; petition against Richard III 933, 936; policing 1507; port of 163, 299; Putney Debates 1162; refortification under Alfred 305–307; rioting during Long Parliament 1139, 1143, 1144, 1146, 1148; see of 357; Spa Fields riots 1396; Stock Exchange 1262; submission to William I 405; support for Edward IV 926, 927; support for rebel barons against John 601–602, 607; tax collection 509; violence against Jews in 723; Wyatt's rebellion 1071

Longchamp, William 527–528, 548–549

Lord Chancellor (office): appointment of 639, 643, 645, 759; attendance at Councils 541; attendance at Parliament 621, 725, 782, 981–982, 984, 986, 988, 1028; demotion 1742–1746; duties 865, 868, 999–1002, 1010, 1024–1025, 1348–1349, 1056, 1511–1512, 1214, 1697–1698, 1742–1743; forms of address 829; origins of office 565, 569–570; petitions to 574, 682–684, 699–701, 709; replaces Chief Justiciar as King's prime minister and chief advisor 871; under Norman rule 571–573; Westminster layout and 820; Wolsey replaced by More as 1012

Lord High Steward (office) 572, 625, 1671

lords: attendance at Parliament 1023–1025; forms of address 829–830; land tenure 395–397, 424–429, 450–451, 460–461, 462–463; Marcher lordships 716, 767, 930, 966, 1036, 1063–1064; as 'overmighty subjects' 1052; *see also* House of Lords; peers and peerages

Lords Appellant 830, 835–836, 836–837, 842, 889, 891, 892, 897, 912
Lords Commissioners (office) 1346, 1361, 1485
lords spiritual: attendance at Parliament 834, 978–980, 979–985, 1038; as distinct from lords temporal 883; during Reformation Parliament 975, 1012; first decision made on basis of a majority vote 977; honorary peerages 1441; Irish 1391; loss of independence 955; non-Christian 1735; opposition to Henry VIII's marriage annulment 1013; as tenants-in-chief of the King 438; Trial of the Commissioners 837; use of White Chamber 830
lords temporal: attendance at Parliament 455, 979–985, 1037, 1104, 1146; creation of 838; decide in favour of poll tax 798; as distinct from lords spiritual 883; first decision made on basis of majority vote 977; as tenants-in-chief of the King 438–439; use of White Chamber 830
Lothian 116–117; alliance with Æthelstan 342; British occupation 356; Ecgfrith establishes as kingdom 173; establishment of border 168; *Guotodin* of 169; Men of 118; ruled by Oswulf 355; Scottish jurisdiction 359–360, 381, 393, 1776; size of assembly hinterland 257, 258
Louis VII, King of France 513
Louis VIII, King of France 608, 611–612, 612
Louis XI, King of France 926, 929
Louis XIV, King of France: allows James II court-in-exile 1242; Catholicism 1254; Edict of Nantes 1236; finances 1219, 1227, 1230; James Edward proclaimed King by 1271; Treaty of Dover (1670) 1215; Treaty of Ryswick (1697) 1263; War of Spanish Succession 1240–1241, 1271–1272
Louis XVI, King of France 1384–1385
Ludeca, King of Mercia 262, 277, 295
Luther, Martin 973–975, 1044, 1046
Luxemburg 1628, 1720–1721
Lyons, Richard 494, 880–881, 895

M

MacDonald, Ramsay 1573, 1579, 1583–1584, 1599

Mace 969–970, 985–986, 999–1002, 1019–1023, 1029, 1108, 1110, 1135, 1171, 1172, 1269
Macmillan, Harold 1656, 1676, 1683, 1723
Magna Carta 600–611, 1364; arbitrary arrest 1127; confirmation of 740; distinction between greater and minor barons 445, 538; Edward I's failure to observe 746, 747; freedom of movement 1647, 1649; inheritance payments 456, 464; itinerant justices 672; judicial role of sheriff 582; marriage 498; printed statutes 574; property rights 605, 1430; reissued 612; rights and liberties of Church 954; rights of free men 540, 586, 628, 1674; shire courts 669; taxation 230, 610, 858, 861; trial by jury 681
Magonsæte 182, 185, 187, 190–191, 320, 342, 372
Maine (France) 402, 476, 513, 920, 921
Maitland, F. W. 493, 531, 576, 759, 1060, 1118, 1669
Major, John 1660, 1727, 1739
Malcolm III, King of the Scots 408, 411, 477, 481
Maldon (Essex) 207, 280, 321–323, 365
manors 451, 470, 474–475, 721, 1414
manufacturing 598, 723–724, 727, 1284, 1292, 1366, 1399, 1621
Manwaring, Roger (bishop) 1128–1129
Mare, Peter de la 825, 879–881, 998
Margaret of Anjou, Queen of England 921, 924–925, 926–927, 927, 929–931, 938, 950
markets 236, 256, 331, 461, 654, 726
Marlborough (Wiltshire) 548, 626, 648, 650, 719
marriage 213–214; bride-price 279; diplomatic 110, 149, 181, 890, 928, 1039, 1192, 1218; feudal aid used to pay for 463, 601, 604; held under God's sanction 593; heraldry and 507; Jutes 90; requiring consent of lord 460, 464; Royal Marriages Act (1772) 1614; social status and 471; succession and 1611–1614; voting rights and 1648; wardships 497–498; *wergeld* and 275
Marshal (office) 565, 567, 570, 643, 740, 741, 744, 845, 871, 1734
Marshal, William, 1st Earl of Pembroke 612–613, 615, 635
Marxism 1553, 1574

Marx, Karl 1352, 1427, 1429–1430
Mary I, Queen of England: accession 1069–
    1070; claim to throne 1067–1068,
    1093; foreign policy 1072; marriage
    1070–1071, 1073; Privy Council during
    reign 1048, 1054; proclamations 1060;
    religious policy 1071–1072, 1074;
    reputation 1071; succession 1070, 1072
Mary II, Queen of England: accession
    1245–1246, 1248, 1251; claim to
    throne 1229, 1235, 1238, 1240, 1243;
    coronation 1246, 1251–1254; finances
    1261–1264; marriage 1217, 1240;
    Parliaments during reign 1251–1252;
    religious policy 1253–1254; as ruler of
    Great Britain 1252; succession 1246,
    1256, 1331; taxation during reign
    1262–1263
Mary, Queen of Scots 1073, 1078–1079,
    1080, 1093
Maserfield, Battle of 182, 184
Mashona 1544, 1549, 1552, 1593
Matabele 1544–1552, 1593
Matilda, Empress 481–483, 508–510, 544
Matilda, Queen, wife of William I 407, 412
Maximilian I, Holy Roman Emperor 968,
    1039
mayors 554, 556, 584, 1416, 1455, 1706
May, Theresa 1669, 1756, 1758–1759, 1762
Melbourne, William Lamb, 2nd Viscount
    1421, 1472–1473, 1491
Mendips 100, 148, 151
Meonware 62, 89, 95, 143
mercenaries: Angle 104, 128; Celtic 111;
    Civil War 1160; expulsion of 514;
    French 807; funding 515, 525, 573,
    589; German 47; Norman reliance on
    462, 588, 591, 595, 608; permanent
    fleet composed of 724; Roman Britain
    45; Saxon 48, 51, 59
merchants: Carta Mercatoria 859; lobbying
    1107; Parliamentarianism of 1153;
    rights 729, 1649; staples and 726;
    Statute of Merchants 714, 718;
    summons 744; taxation 734, 797, 858,
    1132; wool seized from 740
Mercia 132–136; administrative
    reorganisation under Edward the Elder
    319–320; aldermanry 173, 206, 367;
    alliance with East Angles 185, 194,
    197, 201, 295; alliance with West
    Saxons 148, 163, 178, 185; Battle of
    Ellendun 199, 295; capitulation to

Danes 369; Cnut's invasion of 370, 372;
    confederacy 163, 178–200, 269–270,
    273–274, 296, 306; confederacy with
    Wessex 324; control of Kent 198,
    200–201; control of Lindiswaras 110;
    Council of Elders 246, 247; Danes in
    303–304, 321–324, 326; earldoms
    under Cnut 380–381; East Saxons fall
    under control of 142; expansion 149,
    150–151, 156, 179, 184, 190, 194,
    195, 317; fortification following Danish
    attacks 313, 319; hides system 234–235;
    intervention in Northumbria 176, 178–
    188, 186, 194; invasions 182, 186, 296;
    legal system 286, 660; origins of name
    132; Penda's withdrawal to 171; political
    control of London 78, 163; popular
    assemblies 251; regains independence
    355; succession 164, 262; Tribal Hidage
    192–193, 256; wergeld 276, 292
Mersey (river) 165, 174, 317, 319, 329, 330,
    331, 342
metalworking 145, 209
Middle Angles 128–131; in Bedford
    area 83, 149; East Saxon suzerainty
    over 81; establishment of 108;
    folklands obliterated by Danes 326;
    size of assembly hinterland 258; in
    Warwickshire 188; within Mercian
    confederacy 178, 181
middle class 963–965; beneficiaries of
    dissolution of monasteries 1037;
    definition 1432–1433; emergence
    of 629, 725, 726, 728, 867;
    enfranchisement 1414–1415;
    freeholding 651; in House of Commons
    1447; immigration and 1655; juries
    drawn from 474, 585; Lithuania 824;
    political influence 942, 953, 965, 1226;
    taxation 864
Middle Saxons 75–79; absorption
    into Mercian jurisdiction 185;
    administration of London 163, 196;
    Cilternsætan and 83; expansion into
    Kent 101–102; expansion into Surrey
    102; size of assembly hinterland 258
Middlesex: admission to West Saxon
    confederacy 162–164; appropriated by
    GLC 1705; British re-conquest of 73,
    75–80; Cnut establishes royal seat in
    393; election dispute 1372; guilds 239;
    Hengest's authority over 57; as nation
    state 162; part of confederacy of the

English 341; size of assembly hinterland 258

Midlands: Angles' settlement of 127, 130, 131; Danish invasions and settlement 303, 324–327, 357, 367; Edwine takes refuge with Cearl in 166; hundreds system 234; local government 1704; Mercian settlement of 134; Parliamentarian army raised in 1158; Penda's control of 168, 190; radknights 452; Saxon access to 49; size of assembly hinterland 258

migration: British imperialism as 1451; of Britons 75; effect on legal profession 284; Industrial Revolution and 1410; legislation 1649–1656, 1662–1664; South Angles 126–136; Treaty of Rome 1664

Migration Age 24–39; British imperialism compared 1786; feudal aid compared to practices of 462; Franco-German rivalry 1515–1516; kingship 259, 263, 265; priesthood 19, 244; Scandinavian 203; social status 945; transition to Middle Ages 396, 876

military leadership 19, 30, 51, 72, 85, 166, 347, 398

military service: *ceorls* 395; Cnut's laws 378; First World War 1566, 1571; free men 11, 209, 256, 712, 1390; *fyrd* service 139, 856; *geneatas* 396; included in *feorm* 228; knights 448, 712; land ownership and 425, 426–427, 440; lieutenants 1086; monastic summonses 787; obligatory 397, 1360, 1391; overseas 547, 601, 1086; representation and 1648; Rhodesia 1596, 1684; Roman Britain 45; scutage in lieu of 498, 590; social class and 401, 945; social obligation 217, 226; tenants-in-chief 652; thanes 212; types 541

militia 870, 1085, 1086, 1148–1149, 1161, 1486, 1176

Mill, John Stuart 1444, 1460, 1463, 1567

mining: Australia 1650; coal 1366, 1634, 1659; Cumberland 518; iron 964; Rhodesia 1545–1546, 1554, 1593, 1596, 1681; rights of workers 1409; silver 1105; South Africa 1537–1538; Stannaries 995, 1776; working conditions 1407, 1493

mints 163, 196, 348, 644

monarchy: abdication 1611–1615; abolition 1165, 1167, 1568, 1608, 1741, 1172, 1178, 1181; absolute 359, 483, 487, 740, 766, 890, 950–951, 1045, 1099, 1115, 1128, 1417; antiquity of 5–6; Bagehot on 1461–1465, 1478, 1738; Bodin on 1097–1098; centre of recurring constitutional crises 649; Church-Feudalism and 438, 939, 1183; constitutional failure 1469–1470; constitutional monarchy 350, 1580–1581; decline in status under Stephen 458; despotism 963, 1084; Dominions 1600–1601; dual monarchy 91–94, 1333; effect of Wars of the Roses on 949; Germany 1608; Hobbes on 1169; Indo-European 21; James I on 1098, 1113–1114; legal standing 1635–1636; origin of term 442; Protectorate as return towards 1175; public attitude towards 385, 1397, 1474–1475, 1498–1502, 1579–1580, 1637; reduction to nominal role 1385, 1518, 1580, 1738–1740, 1764; restoration 1282, 1172, 1181, 1182–1184; ritual of 1500–1501; and secular state 1496; Sovereign as executive officer 1738–1741; uncrowned King 939–941

monasteries: of Bede 112; dissolution of 953–954, 1024, 1034–1035, 1037–1038, 1043, 1088; farming 516; King's *mund* extends to 279; land ownership 137, 433, 1034, 1037; levies on 595, 749; provision of social security 218, 901, 1034, 1047, 1411; restoration under Mary I 1072; as seats of learning 175; under Norman rule 414; Viking raids 299, 357, 363, 365; Winchester 156

Monck, George, 1st Duke of Albemarle 1175, 1180, 1182, 1190

money 276–278, 290, 294, 441, 669, 1088, 1105–1106, 1261–1263; *see also* coins/coinage

Monmouth, James Scott, Duke of 1233–1234

Monnet, Jean 1720

Montesquieu 3, 1338–1340, 1461, 1742, 1744, 1764

Montfort, Simon de, Earl of Leicester 568, 619, 635, 641, 646–649, 651, 715, 719

Morcar, Earl of Northumbria 208, 404, 405, 407, 408, 410, 411, 430

More, Sir Thomas 975, 977, 983, 992, 1011, 1013, 1015

Mortimer, Roger, 1st Earl of March 705, 767, 770, 775, 778, 779–781

mos maiorum 15; Cicero on 18; compared to common law 1200; Great Council and 1715, 1266, 1765; King's Council and 869; kingship and 1033, 1513, 1244, 1270; Parliament and 831, 1116, 1121; statute law and 1525; *see also* common law Constitution

Moslems 970–971, 1303

Mul, King of Kent 95, 158

mund ('protection/guardianship') 278–280, 291, 293–294, 687

murder 187, 291, 364, 431, 466, 662, 695, 984, 1052

Mussolini, Benito 1428, 1574–1575, 1609, 1617

N

Nadder (river) 96, 98

Napoleon I 1365, 1387–1390, 1517

Napoleonic Wars 1281, 1298, 1299, 1387–1390, 1394, 1396, 1397, 1401, 1557

Natal 1307–1308, 1309–1310

nation 218, 220, 240, 250, 424, 437, 505; *see also* folkland

nationalisation 1635, 1654, 1659, 1703, 1733

nationalism: after French Revolution 1427–1428; Bohemia 800; colonialism and 1450; Egypt 1487; English 906; foreign policy of Palmerston 1475; Germany 1517, 1557, 1608–1609, 1726; identity and 1659; imperialism and 1451, 1682–1683; India 1624, 1641; Ireland 1435, 1494, 1518, 1522, 1555–1556, 1585–1587, 1698, 1700–1701; jingoism 1483; religion and 1077, 1082, 1100; Russia 1046; Scotland 1646, 1698; South Africa 1687; Wales 1698; White 1646

National Socialism 1427–1428, 1609–1610, 1628, 1645, 1652, 1695, 1716

nation states 162, 274, 337

Native Americans 1280, 1282, 1286, 1291, 1293, 1298

natural law: equity 683, 685; Estates and 16; Fortescue on 950; Hobbes on 1169; Indo-European origins 1056, 1116; Locke on 1291; rights and obligations 216; sovereignty and 1097; statute law and 286, 689–691, 695, 1032

navy: Anglo-Dutch Wars 1211, 1214, 1217; Battle of Trafalgar 1387; Commonwealth 1170; defeat of Spanish Armada 1079, 1080, 1280; Don Pacifico affair 1475; during Glorious Revolution 1241; funding 1124; Germany 1558, 1560; Hundred Years' War 804, 806, 807, 814, 884; origins 724–725; under Protectorate 1176; use of Union Jack 1102; *see also* Royal Navy

Nene (river) 49, 127, 128, 149, 609

Nennius 56, 66, 72, 104, 115, 126, 131, 180

Netherlands 1239–1241; Anglo-Dutch Wars 1170, 1171, 1175, 1189, 1211, 1214, 1216–1218; Brussels Treaty 1628; colonies 1289, 1302–1305, 1380, 1537–1541, 1621; Danish invasions 364; dynastic alliances 928, 1070, 1175, 1185; Edward IV flees to 929; European integration 1720; Franco-Dutch War (1672-1678) 1217; Protestantism 1070, 1079; revolutionary France and 1386–1387; Thirty Years' War 1169; trade 1280–1281, 1311–1312, 1170; Triple Alliance (1668) 1215; War of the League of Augsberg 1258, 1263; war with Spain 1080, 1111, 1137, 1272–1274

Neville, Richard, Earl of Warwick 928–930

Newcastle-on-Tyne (Northumberland) 408, 510, 644, 762, 1050, 1139

New Forest 62, 63, 479

Newfoundland 1278, 1286, 1293, 1301, 1302, 1600–1601, 1606

New Zealand 1311, 1506, 1568, 1590–1591, 1600, 1602, 1604, 1606, 1644

nobility 205–209; Anglo-Norman 587, 589, 590, 607, 613, 760, 796; decline in status 542, 851, 934, 950, 953, 963, 1037, 1104, 1444, 1766; dispute with John 595; divine protection 999; impact of First World War on 1568; impact of Wars of the Roses on 927, 928, 932, 937, 938, 949, 963, 990, 991; inheritance 1677, 1274; land ownership 227, 434, 720, 1373; personal honour 278–279; position on Councils 242, 243, 245, 265, 335, 1048; receipt of customs 237; Royalism of 1153; titles 424, 944–945; trials 493, 895, 916, 942, 946, 948, 1221; under Norman rule 407, 410, 412, 413, 419–420, 430, 436, 442, 467, 483, 1325

Norfolk 49, 74, 342, 1067, 1383

Norman Conquest 403–420; English boundaries at time of 325, 338; Estate structure and 1526, 1647; land ownership and 1786; position of Church following 6, 503; summary of effects of 952; survival of Constitution 1129, 1130; union with Wales and Ireland as result of 1392

Normandy: as base for Danish raiders 364–373; conquered by Geoffrey of Anjou 511; dukedom of 432; Edward the Confessor educated in 374–377, 386–391; Estates 1274; feudal system 428; Hundred Years' War 804, 806, 919, 922, 923; independence from France 416, 419; John loses control of 571, 588–591, 596, 691, 802; military service in 602; personal names 467; political position 411; primogeniture 476; Second World War 1620; William assembles army in 401

Norse: bride-price 279; of Dublin 317, 319, 323; effects of invasion on confederacies 270; invasions 320–321, 328–331; origins 298–299; settlement of Westmorland 624; of York 319, 320, 337–339, 346, 354–355

North America: Civil War 1477, 1589; origins of federal government 1295–1296; Puritan emigration to 1136, 1289, 1290, 1292, 1293; Revolution 1290–1296, 1412, 1471; Seven Years' War 1291–1292; sovereignty 1281; War of Independence 1374, 1377–1381; *see also* United States of America

Northampton: Assize of 549; Councils held at 442, 446, 520, 545, 587, 628, 711; Danish occupation 308, 321, 322, 325, 326, 327; Norman castle 545, 644; Parliaments held at 712, 751, 797, 811, 815, 818, 883; Tostig's destruction of 209; Yorkist victory at 925

Northamptonshire 53, 129, 133, 188, 189, 325, 326, 471, 601

North Atlantic Treaty Organisation (NATO) 1628, 1723

Northcote-Trevelyan report (1854) 1482–1484

North Downs 60, 61, 76

Northern Ireland 3, 116, 1421, 1555, 1586–1588, 1698–1701, 1759–1760, 1762, 1788

North, Frederick, Lord North 1362, 1377–1379

North Sea 32–33, 35, 37–38, 50, 65, 107, 108–109, 126, 298–299, 1081

Northumberland: acquisition by Scots 510; alliance with Æthelstan 340, 342; claims to succession 260; incorporation of liberty of Tynedale into 1053; independence from Danes 307; legal system 660; Men of 111–118; Norse invasion 328, 354–355; place-names 116; reclaimed from Scots by Henry II 514; religious activities 172; revolt against William I 409; Scottish invasion 367; size of assembly hinterland 257, 258

Northumbria: alliances 148, 163; baronial uprising 601; Celtic Church 86; confederacy 143, 165–178, 186; Danish invasion and settlement 299, 301, 303, 318; deposition of Tostig 208; Edwig's overlordship of 356; *Hymbre* 108; legal practices 286; Mercian strike on 194; nobility 206; peace treaty with Danes of East Anglia 316; place-names 222; reeves 334; refusal to accept election of Harold 400; relations with East Angles 196; size of assembly hinterland 258

Norway 23; claim to English crown 375–376; Edward the Confessor and 384, 398; kingship 347, 381, 400; Olaf Tryggvason returns to 302; origins of name 223; Swein Forkbeard extends rule over 366

Nottingham: Councils held at 549, 765; Danish occupation 301, 322, 323, 324, 325, 328; Mortimer seized at 780; Norman castle 644; Norse invasion 329

Nottinghamshire 127, 131, 304, 342, 470, 732

Nyasaland 1283, 1287, 1543, 1681–1682

O

Odo, Bishop of Bayeux 411, 430, 435, 485, 550, 552, 564, 585, 1347

Oeric, King of Kent 69, 73, 84

Offa, King of the Mercians 195–198, 200–201; as *Bretwalda* 143, 164, 172, 345; charters 138; coinage 183; defeat of *Hæstingas* 75; law codes 285, 314; succession 297–298

Offa's Dyke 195, 317

Oiscinga dynasty 69, 200
Oisc, King of Kent 56–58, 69–70, 72, 73, 76
Olaf Guthfrithson, Norse leader 346,
    354–355
Olaf Tryggvason, King of Norway 302, 365
Old Sarum (Wiltshire) 90, 93, 96–98, 644,
    1383, 1411
oligarchy: Communist Russia 1576; House
    of Commons as 950, 1005, 1022,
    1324, 1327, 1734; and human rights
    1716; political parties and 1518–1519,
    1533–1534, 1735; Whigs 1321
Orange, House of 1175, 1185, 1218, 1240,
    1257
ordinances 1199; Edward I 688–689, 718;
    Edward II 758–762, 765–766, 772,
    774; Edward III 822, 899; Henry II
    664, 667; Militia Ordinance (1642)
    1149–1151; proclamation of 579, 1057;
    recording of 574, 660; relating to clergy
    504, 653; repeal of 837; Richard II 870,
    901; role of Privy Council 941; under
    Protectorate 1174, 1177; William I 417
Osberht, King of Northumbria 177, 307
Osric, King of Deira 169
Oswald, King of Northumbria 169–171,
    180–183, 345
Oswestry (Shropshire) 170, 181, 194
Oswine, King of Deira 171, 182
Oswy, King of Northumbria 170–172, 174,
    181–184, 187, 247, 345
Ottoman Empire 971, 1277, 1558–1559,
    1560, 1565–1566, 1642
Ouse (river) 49, 50, 121, 127, 129, 149, 308,
    321
Oxford: *burhs* 305; Councils held at 375,
    382, 528, 599, 612, 613, 625; Danish
    occupation 321, 370; fortifications 330;
    Norman castle 644; parliaments and
    provisions of 640–649, 651, 759, 850,
    869, 1159, 1211; University of 692,
    1066, 1235, 1238
Oxfordshire 51–54, 98, 145, 189, 257, 447

P

paganism: cemeteries 51, 106; Christian
    churches built on sacred sites 136, 138,
    1087; conversion to Christianity 136,
    138, 220; Germany 1609; location
    of assemblies on pagan sites 234;
    London 79; Middle Angles 131; Native
    Americans 1286; Northumberland 118,

169, 175, 184; priesthood 204–205;
    symbolism of 1076
Paine, Thomas 1626
Pakistan 1642–1643, 1657
Palatinate 1137, 1240, 1258, 1265
Palestine 525, 575, 703, 704, 804
Palmerston, Henry John Temple, 3rd
    Viscount 1438–1439, 1443, 1475–
    1477, 1480, 1486–1487, 1517
Papacy: absolution of England from censures
    1071; Acts of Supremacy 943, 1074;
    annulment of marriage 1011, 1015;
    attempts to establish foothold in
    France 85; Catholic Emancipation Bill
    and 1400; Cenwulf and 198; chain
    of authority 486; dispute with John
    593–599; election 91; eleventh-century
    schism 477; England rejects renewal of
    Papal tribute 792; excommunication
    1015, 1034, 1036, 1039, 1070, 1256;
    Henry III and 616; introduction of
    foreign clergy to England 827; legate
    sent to Northumbria 176; Papal
    bulls 626–627, 706, 739, 742, 1077;
    payments to 857, 858, 863, 977, 979;
    political authority 523–524, 593–594;
    Popery 996, 1076, 1079, 1123, 1133,
    1134–1135, 1140, 1174, 1227;
    praemunire 697, 792, 973, 976, 1012;
    recognition of unification of England
    344; Reformation 973–977; support for
    Wulfred 198; supremacy within Church
    504–505; threat of nationalism 1046;
    trade embargoes 968; under Norman
    rule 536; William I 417
Paris (France): foundation of university
    692; French Revolution 1384; Henry
    II inspired by Sainte Chapelle 619;
    Hundred Years' War 919, 921; kingdom
    of 84; Napoleonic Wars 1389; National
    Convention 1386; *Parlement* 1272;
    Revolution of 1848 1416; Treaties 642
parishes 1086–1087, 1088, 1458–1459,
    1577, 1705
Parisii 103, 104
Paris, Matthew 6, 592, 633, 634, 636
Parliament xiii; absolutism and 1099; Addled
    Parliament (1614) 1107; appointment
    of Ministers 639, 1004, 1005, 1151,
    1350, 1468, 1484–1486, 1581–1582,
    1667–1668, 1669, 1708–1709, 1768; as
    career choice 1664–1666; attendance at
    651–652, 655–656, 697, 711, 734–737,

748, 773, 883, 914–916, 988–989, 1787–1788, 1196–1197; behaviour in 745, 988–989, 992, 1020, 1028, 1666; bills 798, 833, 898, 984, 989, 996, 1003, 1008, 1327, 1041, 1141, 1143–1144, 1148–1150, 1202–1203, 1217–1219; Cavalier Parliament (1661-79) 1188, 1190, 1209, 1214, 1219; Church and 953–954, 997, 1021, 1027, 1032–1035, 1065, 1075, 1494–1496, 1572, 1191, 1208–1209, 1577; clergy and 621, 865, 978–979, 1208–1209; consultation on taxation 626–628, 859–864, 865–867, 1008, 1127, 1131; control of militia 1148–1150, 1161; control of royal finances 1373–1377, 1400–1401; control over King's Council 869; Convention Parliament (1660) 1180, 1185, 1188, 1201, 1210; Convention Parliament (1689) 1242, 1245, 1247; Corporate Officers 1739–1740; death of the King 1335–1337, 1419–1421, 1470; decline from Edward IV onwards 933, 949, 953–955; detailed record (1305) 748–750; detailed record (1332) 784; detailed record (1376) (Good Parliament) 878; detailed record (1510) 980–985; dissolution 1335–1336, 1419–1420, 1139–1140, 1143, 1162, 1715, 1755–1756, 1172, 1186, 1210, 1259–1260; division into two Houses 796, 822–827, 832, 849, 879, 1030, 1519, 1523, 1527; Dominions and 1600–1601; duration 19–20, 783, 1022, 1344, 1346, 1035, 1437, 1139, 1524, 1173, 1196–1198, 1247, 1258–1259, 1678, 1755–1756; election of members 855, 949–950, 1324, 1009–1011, 1340, 1030, 1144, 1180, 1255, 1784–1785; enactment of statutes 718–719, 1061; Exclusion Bill and Parliament (1679-80) 1218, 1220, 1222, 1227; executive function 898–905, 1001, 1320, 1324, 1327, 1337–1339, 1417–1418, 1469, 1480–1486, 1491–1492, 1184, 1528–1529, 1738–1741; expenses scandal 1763–1764, 1785; foreign policy consultation 791; fourteenth-century reform 760–763, 781–782, 787–790, 794–801, 807–827; freedom from arrest 991, 993, 997–1000; freedom of speech 836, 987–988, 992–999, 1008, 1028,

1123–1125, 1155, 1255; frequency 759, 782, 891, 932, 964, 997, 1143, 1173, 1186, 1190, 1196–1198, 1209–1211, 1247, 1255, 1258–1259; Good Parliament (1376) 878, 998; grants 711–714, 718, 727, 730–731, 733–734, 739–743, 797, 865–867, 1010, 1153, 1247; Great Council and 781–782, 807–813, 994, 1004; hours of sittings 1665, 1666; illustrations 677, 707, 817, 981, 983, 1019, 1022, 1028, 1029, 1172; immigration and 1663; judicial function 830–833, 852–853, 873, 878–897, 1748, 1750; 'King in Parliament' 978, 1000, 1349, 1031, 1032, 1056, 1108–1110, 1426, 1199; language of 744–745, 850, 988, 992; legality of decisions outside Parliament 817–820; legislative authority 561, 672–686, 686–687, 947, 954, 1031–1032, 1155–1156, 1166, 1717, 1198, 1764; location 620–621, 712, 785, 879, 1017–1020, 1020–1024, 1029–1030, 1423–1426, 1738, 1787; Long Parliament (1640-1660) 1282, 1006, 1140–1144, 1159, 1161–1165, 1170, 1171, 1180, 1186, 1210, 1225, 1227; ministerial responsibility 1479–1486, 1665–1668; naming 786; Nominated Parliament (1653) 1172–1173; offices 747–748, 785, 825–826, 829–830, 846, 883, 1028–1029; origins of term 634–635, 882; Oxford Parliament (1681) 1229; parliamentary procedure 983–990, 1675, 1195–1198; Parliament of Bats (1425) 913; Parliament of the Devils (1459) 924; Privy Council answerable to 942; prorogation 1336, 1419, 1143–1144, 1760–1761, 1197, 1210, 1260; Protectorate Parliaments 1174–1182; Reformation Parliament (1529-31) 975–987, 1012, 1031–1041, 1035, 1065–1066; Reform Bills 1319, 1401, 1412–1413, 1431, 1433, 1437, 1443, 1478; representation 653–657, 701, 709, 862, 1064, 1383–1384, 1409–1413, 1421–1422; responsibility for statutes 948–952; rights and privileges 947–948, 987–988, 991–1011, 1023, 1104, 1133, 1452–1453; role of Ombudsman 1713; Rump Parliaments 1164, 1167, 1170–1171, 1179–1180, 1210; salaries 1665, 1740,

1763; seating arrangements 620–623,
844, 979–980, 981–984, 1019–1020,
1025–1026, 1425; Short Parliament
(1640) 1139–1142, 1142; Tory control
of 1233; 'West Lothian' question
1699–1700; Wonderful Parliament
(1388) 889; see also House of Commons;
House of Lords; acts of Parliament
Parliamentarians 1157–1160, 1163, 1180,
1227, 1231
Parliamentary Rolls 574–575, 826, 844, 899,
907, 1033
parliamentary sovereignty 1479–1481,
1534–1535, 1198–1199, 1267–1268,
1738–1741; Act of Settlement and
1268; Civil War and 1163, 1183;
European integration and 1725, 1758;
fallacious doctrine of 1325; following
Restoration 1282; Glorious Revolution
and 1338, 1249; political parties and
1757; restoration of Great Council and
1768; South Africa 1603
Parr, Catherine, Queen of England 1041
Parrett (river) 152–153, 159
Party system 1322–1324; corruption 1383;
growth of 1449, 1582; and ministerial
responsibility 1479–1481, 1678;
origins 1361, 1422, 1225–1227, 1229;
popularity 1662; risks of 1232; two-
Party system 1518–1519; see also political
parties
patriotism 1357, 1390, 1475, 1567, 1634
patronage 1371, 1382, 1400
Peada, King of the South Mercians 171, 181,
184, 187
peasantry 162, 467, 468, 503, 512, 724, 796,
824, 1575, 1250
Peasants' Revolt 798, 885
Pecsætan 133, 192
Peel, Robert 1399, 1437, 1472, 1474, 1507
peers and peerages 831–833, 834–835;
creation of 845–846, 1413, 1104, 1437,
1438–1441, 1445, 1447, 1200, 1201,
1521–1524, 1676–1677; Cromwell's
elevation to peerage 978; definitions
773–774; hereditary peerages 1441,
1448, 1733–1734, 1736, 1737;
legitimacy of 1525–1526; life peerages
1438–1442, 1445, 1447–1448, 1522,
1676–1677, 1733–1734, 1736, 1737,
1749; origins 786; privileges 1003,
1023; right to renounce title 1677–

1678; trial of Peers 625, 850–851, 999,
1671, 1675
Pelham, Henry 1355, 1356, 1358
Pembroke, earldom of 757, 761, 763, 766
Pencersætan 133
Penda, King of Mercia 80, 148, 149, 150,
168–171, 178–184, 188, 190–191
Pennines 133, 165, 167, 181, 258, 307, 1366
Peredur and Gwrgi 113, 119
personal names 467–468, 850, 961
Petition of Right 1131–1133, 1209
petitions 573–574, 717–718, 746–749, 783–
785, 835–836, 839–840, 899–904;
Act Against Tumultuous Petitioning
(1661) 1191; addressed to Chancellor
683; administration of 699–702;
compared to bills 898; during reign
of Edward III 783, 899; Haxey case
(1397) 835–836; increase in thirteenth
century 795; rights 1162, 1626, 1255;
role of Parliament 709–710, 947, 984,
997, 1187, 1196, 1519, 1217; role of
Privy Council 1051, 1062; Westminster
location of triers of petitions 821
Pevensey (East Sussex) 60, 61, 63, 66, 67, 68,
402
Philip I, King of France 411
Philip II, King of France 587, 594, 597, 601,
737
Philip II, King of Spain 1070–1072, 1080
Philip III, King of France 737
Philip IV, King of France 738
Philip VI, King of France 802–803
Philip, Prince, Duke of Edinburgh 1637–
1638
Picts: alliance with Northumbria 169, 171,
176; annexation of territory 174;
Caledonii 116–117; civil war 176;
coronation stone 739, 1333; post-
Roman raids 54, 55, 104, 111, 121;
revolt against Northumbria 173; in
Roman Britain 37, 45–48; West Saxons
and 148
Pipe Rolls 482, 498, 501, 524, 563, 570
piracy 33, 36, 48, 49, 299, 381, 1280, 1136,
1283, 1207
Pitt, William, the Elder 605, 1358, 1384
Pitt, William, the Younger 1351, 1400–1401;
approval of Herbert Taylor as Private
Secretary 1497; as Chancellor of
the Exchequer 1379; concessions to
Catholics 1392; fiscal reforms 1376;
foreign affairs 1382–1383; measures

against revolutionary agitation 1386; support of George III 1397; and Whigs 1445

place-names: Celtic 128, 162; Chilterns 82–83; containing the name Icel 134; Cumberland 165; Devon 161, 162; Dorset 62; Essex 222; freeholds 22; Hampshire 88, 94; Jutish 96, 98; Kent 222; kinship groups 215, 223; Lancashire 165; local topography and 215, 223; Northumberland 116, 222; relating to boundaries 844; religious beliefs and 204, 266; Saxon 50; Severn valley 190; Somerset 153, 159, 214, 305; Sussex 67; 'wick' 450; Yorkshire 167

Plague 1211, 1214

Plantagenet, House of 513, 907, 925, 959

Poitou 513, 588, 598, 599, 600, 623, 643, 645

Poland 1559, 1565, 1616–1617, 1623

Pole, Michael de la, 1st Earl of Suffolk 830, 885–887, 888, 889–890

Pole, William de la, Duke of Suffolk 921

policing: County Council provision of 1458, 1702; London 288, 1507; role of Justices of the Peace 1090, 1455; South Africa 1547, 1548–1550, 1551; tithing system 325; watch and ward 854

policy-making 1321, 1326, 1328–1329, 1422, 1480–1481, 1582, 1665, 1667–1669, 1731

political parties xiii–xv; Bagehot and 1463, 1464; Cabinet Council and 1363–1364; caucus 1319–1320; and class division 1445; and electoral reform 1432–1433; expenditure 1433; leadership 1581, 1667; manifestos 4; North America 1296, 1319; payment 1346; relations with monarch 1348; and royal power 1417–1418, 1728; Whips 1361, 1422, 1667; see also Party system

Pontefract (West Yorkshire) 765, 768, 771, 842

Poor Law 1456, 1482

popular assembly 19–20, 218–219, 251–259; arrangement of 240; attendance at 210, 216, 259, 271–272, 533, 538–543, 545, 555, 578, 579, 599–600; colonies 1295; free men's rights 17, 461; Germans 29–32; Indo-Europeans 8, 15; Jutes 91, 223; kingship and 142, 164, 397; location 228, 234, 252, 542, 546, 557;

representation 599–600; Scandinavia 8; South Saxons 225; Swedes 26–27; terminology 781–782; thing 5–6; timing of 268, 1196; under Norman rule 532; Voortrekkers 1306

population: colonies 1294; density 259, 1383; effect of Black Death on 793; effect of Industrial Revolution on 1576; land and 465; Migration Age 24; Poland 1623

population growth 36, 100, 164, 394, 1406, 1457, 1458, 1651, 1703

ports: administration 565; Cinque Ports 390, 653, 655, 724, 729, 777, 818; defence of 408; duty and levies 500, 1136; growth of towns around 237, 332; London 79, 163, 185, 196, 1706; obligation to provide ships 724; Roman 60, 109; sacked by French 807

Portugal: colonies 1308, 1310, 1311, 1543, 1544, 1545, 1552, 1599; exploration and conquest 1277, 1278, 1286; marriage alliances 1473; Napoleonic Wars 1388

postal system 1195, 1203

pottery 25, 45, 50, 56, 65, 70, 106

poverty 1088–1090; effect of Napoleonic Wars on 1396; Industrial Revolution and 1501, 1671; Irish workers 1406; petitions relating to 1062; Poor Law 1455, 1459; reason to cancel contract or obligation 699; Scotland 1331; social support 1047, 1493–1494, 1193; workhouses 1066

Powell, J. E. 763

Powys 120, 165, 180, 185, 195, 199, 296, 301, 716

praemunire 697, 734, 735, 787–790, 792, 973, 976, 979, 993, 1012

precedent 694–695, 1002, 1006, 1104, 1115, 1116, 1127, 1131, 1132, 1507

Presbyterians/Presbyterianism: eviction from Parliament 1164, 1165, 1188; objection to Book of Common Prayer 1190; Puritanism and 1144; Scotland 1331–1332, 1159–1161, 1163–1165, 1228–1229, 1252; under Protectorate 1178

press 1449, 1507, 1259

priesthood: as custodian of knowledge 19; as First Estate 16, 204–205; Germanic society 135, 244; hereditary 11; in Indo-European society 25, 245, 357, 484;

lay appointment 482; ordination 357; punishment of offenders 31

Prime Minister (office) 1347–1350; appointment of 1484–1486, 1489–1490, 1581, 1583–1584, 1708, 1768; Commonwealth and 1605–1606; dismissal by William IV 1321; dissolution of Parliament 1755–1756; as First Lord of the Treasury 1740; function 1361–1362, 1462, 1533, 1667–1670; origins 564; relations with King 1371; religious beliefs 1496–1497

primogeniture: Church doctrine and 267, 489, 1533; election of kings and 907–909, 911; and extinction of English Second State 1526–1527; land ownership and 425, 426, 587; Norman rule and 476, 489, 1325; origins 438, 1639; succession and 359, 432, 488, 592, 649, 704, 920, 930, 1440, 1528–1529, 1260, 1268–1269; uncrowned King 939–941

printing 800, 934, 965

priories 139, 414

prison 661–662, 684, 747, 1281, 1000, 1220–1221, 1746

Private Secretary (office) 1497–1498

Privy Council: Act of Settlement (1701) 1267; calendar 1050; Catholics appointed to 1235; committees 1050, 1212–1213, 1214, 1219, 1224; conservatism of 1044; Cromwell becomes member of 976; death of a King and 1336, 1527–1528; decline under James I 1125, 1212; during regency of Henry VI 913; election of Privy Councillors to Parliament 908, 1026; elevation of members of House of Commons to 1082; enunciation and enforcement of ordinances 1058; functions 1327–1330, 1049, 1147, 1328, 1260; Grand Remonstrance and 1145; House of Commons and 1103, 1321–1322; impeachment of members 797; judicial role 933, 963, 1328, 1051, 1053–1057, 1141, 1505–1506, 1510, 1192–1193, 1213; legislative function 952; location 873, 875, 1014, 1050, 1055; membership 567, 875, 887, 1150, 1211, 1220, 1260, 1265, 1267–1268; offices 1049, 1050, 1054–1055, 1090, 1505, 1211, 1215; origins 5, 493; petitions to 936, 1051, 1062;

political stability of 965; redundancy under Elizabeth I 1074; replaced by Council of State 1167; Rhodesia and 1593–1594; royal prerogative and 941–944, 1048–1059, 1120; Scottish 1333; size 1328–1329, 1054, 1212, 1213, 1214, 1220; as source of advice for Tudor rulers 953, 1125; subject to *coup d'état* 1527–1528; transition from King's Council to 828–829, 916; under Protectorate 1178, 1179; use of Privy Seal 1055; usurped by Cabinet Committee 1327–1330; writs 1005

Privy Seal 594–598, 772–773, 917–919, 1042–1043; forms 745, 828; Keepers 887; used by Court of Requests 1062; used by Privy Council 1055; warrants 1044; writs 872

proclamations 1057–1061; Charles I 1147; in event of invasion 1360; increase in Tudor age 1056; James I 1103, 1114; language of 850; legality of 1106, 1119–1120; power to legislate repealed by Edward VI 1199; reduced to Orders in Council 1365–1366; taxation legislated by 858

property: acts of Parliament 1060, 1434, 1739–1740; bookland 230; Christian Church 909, 1072; common law 694, 1113; criminal justice 292, 922; inheritance 720; *Magna Carta* and 605, 1430; marital rights 214; natural law and 1098; Parliamentary 1739–1740; peerage and 774; role of guilds in protection of 238; Roman law 665; Rousseau on 1352; Royalist 1170; statute law and 1250; and suffrage 1415–1416, 1431, 1567; taxation 575, 590, 734, 1155, 1458

protectorates 1283, 1287

Protectorate, the (1653-1659) 1330, 1173–1184, 1185, 1187

Protestants/Protestantism: Act of Settlement (1701) 1264; colonists 1232; contribution to Industrial Revolution 1366; denominations 1576; effect on religious buildings 1017, 1038–1039; formation of United Church of England and Ireland 1392, 1393; France 1079, 1096, 1126, 1127, 1133, 1236, 1258; Gordon Riots (1780) 1378; Ireland 1436, 1555, 1586, 1588, 1700–1701; and legacy of Civil War 1183;

Lutherism 973, 1110; Monmouth Rebellion 1380, 1233–1234; origins 801, 909; Parliamentarians comprised from Protestant sects 1158–1160; Parliamentary support 1015, 1017, 1125; Popish Plot (1678) 1218; religious freedom 1162, 1235; Scotland 1095, 1101; Thirty Years' War 1110, 1169; under Charles II 1191; under Edward VI 1065–1077; under Elizabeth I 1081; under Henry VIII 1044–1045; under James I 1101; under James II 1232, 1235; under Mary I 1078–1079; under William and Mary 1253–1254, 1264

Provisions of Oxford 640–649, 651, 759, 850, 869

proxy 630–631, 1004

Prussia 1355, 1357–1358, 1370, 1385, 1387–1388, 1405, 1514–1517, 1557, 1565

public administration: Angevin 671; Australia 1314–1315; decline in competence 1583; development of civil service 1324; during regency of Henry III 613; during Wars of the Roses 942; English as language of 1064; Justices of the Peace 1090; Lords Ordainers 772; Norman 415, 661, 671; Provisions and Establishments 650; role of House of Commons 1364; role of King 565–576; role of Privy Council 933, 1050; towns 654

public services 1374, 1582, 1634, 1651, 1658, 1663

Puritans/Puritanism: anti-Royalism 1144–1145, 1148, 1152–1153; attacks on bishops 1125; decline under Elizabeth I 1100; during Civil War 1157–1159, 1171; emigration to North America 1136, 1289, 1290, 1292, 1293; laws against 1090; membership of House of Commons 1006, 1125, 1133, 1141; merchant class 1137; origins 1076; removal from Parliament following Restoration 1188; under Elizabeth I 1081; under Protectorate 1175–1176; under William and Mary 1254

Pybba, King of Mercia 178

Pym, John 1108, 1129, 1130, 1140, 1142, 1145–1148, 1153, 1189

Q

Quebec 1287, 1291, 1293, 1297, 1298, 1302, 1359

R

race 1303–1304, 1592, 1624–1627, 1652, 1657–1658, 1661, 1663

racial discrimination: human rights and 1626; immigration and 1314, 1646; liberalism and 1658–1659; postwar years 1641; Rhodesia 1597, 1643; social class and 1654–1656, 1658; South Africa 1304, 1600, 1643, 1681, 1687

radicalism 1391, 1396, 1422, 1464, 1648

radknights 211, 276, 291, 452, 454

Rædwald, King of East Anglia 123, 166, 345

Rægnald, Norse leader 320–321, 324, 328–330

Ragnar Lothbrok, Viking leader 177, 300, 320

railways 1295, 1301, 1367, 1550, 1554, 1563, 1595, 1634, 1707

ransom 368, 463, 496, 501, 528–529, 589, 604, 725, 806

Reading (Berkshire) and *Readingas* 77, 93, 150, 302

realm 505, 753–754, 769, 773–775, 775–776, 779, 831, 834, 841

record-keeping 285, 530, 532

reeves: election 583; origins 189, 225, 240; role 5, 232, 233, 235–236, 248, 253, 334, 599, 1512

referendum 1302, 1664, 1698, 1725, 1728–1729, 1758–1760, 1764, 1767

Reform Acts 1408, 1414–1416, 1421, 1431–1435, 1463, 1482, 1505, 1567

Reformation 1045–1047, 1065–1068, 1069–1072, 1074–1077; Act of Supremacy (1534) 1015; effect on succession 1257; France 1094, 1096–1098; influence of Lollardism 799, 801, 910; land ownership and 1137; Lutherism and 973; as main cause of Civil War 1152

Reformation Parliament (1529-31) 975–987, 1012, 1031–1041, 1035, 1065–1066

regency/interregnum: age of candidate 261, 940–941; death of a King 1420, 1269; Edward I 703; Edward II 741–742, 751, 758–761; Edward VIII 1613; female 1068; George III 1395; Glappa of Bernicia 114; Henry III 612–614, 895;

Henry VI 911–914, 931, 943; Regency
    Act (1937) 1614–1615; Richard II
    884, 887–888; role of Councils 243,
    248, 250, 267–268, 336, 942, 1335,
    1260, 1777, 1780; Seaxburh 156, 1068;
    William III 1229, 1242
regio/provincia 193, 223, 224
Regni 62, 63, 66
religion *see also* Jews: Enlightenment and
    1405; extremism 1077, 1655; freedom
    of religion 1162, 1174, 1216, 1235;
    India 1642; jurisdiction of Parliament
    1031–1034; Lincolnshire Rising
    1036; Lollardism 796, 799–802,
    884, 909, 910, 972, 1044, 1046,
    1076; Lutherism 973–975; Moslems
    970; Northumberland 172; religious
    devotion 466; Roman Empire 136–141;
    social unrest and 1658; succession of
    kings 264; Swedes 26; Toleration Act
    (1688) 1253–1254; under Norman rule
    414
religious orders 414, 502, 516, 595, 653, 656,
    734, 748, 757, 787
Renaissance 967, 970–972, 1037, 1045–
    1046, 1366, 1405, 1194, 1264
representation: boroughs 990, 1431, 1434;
    distribution of electorate 1434–1435;
    equality of 642, 951, 1006, 1026; free
    men 653–657, 915, 948, 1409–1415,
    1434–1435, 1526, 1730; Lithuania 824;
    London 1707; Reform Acts 1414–1416,
    1421, 1431–1435; Representation of
    the People Acts 1419, 1567, 1569,
    1648; representative government 1371–
    1372, 1383–1384, 1166, 1428, 1463,
    1209, 1248; right of proxy 630–631,
    1004; shires 599–600, 638, 709, 990,
    1457; supplementary writ 744; towns
    and cities 344, 709, 735, 737, 1383,
    1409–1413, 1421, 1431, 1454
Repton (Derbyshire) 295, 296, 303
republicanism: and Civil War 1099, 1182–
    1184, 1186; during reign of George
    III 1397; following Restoration 1231,
    1233; France 1386; Ireland 1556, 1587,
    1701; of Levellers 1160; Protectorate
    and 1175, 1177, 1178–1179, 1230;
    Puritans 1292; Queen Victoria and
    1499; socialism and 1518; Whigs 1229
Restoration 1282, 1185–1238
Retief, Piet 1306, 1307–1308
Rheged 116, 170, 173

Rhineland 60, 84, 1514, 1557, 1568, 1573,
    1608, 1616
Rhine (river) 28, 36, 37, 49, 54, 60, 299,
    1514–1515, 1564
Rhodes, Cecil 1451, 1501, 1538, 1542–1552,
    1596
Rhodesia 1543–1552, 1568, 1592–1597,
    1600, 1604, 1606, 1643, 1681–1687
Rhuddlan (Denbighshire) 711, 713, 714, 716
Richard I, King of England: accession 524;
    adoption of motto *Dieu et mon Droit*
    487–488; baronage as 'realm' 841;
    borrowing during reign 457, 502;
    character 526; coronation 525, 707,
    730; Crusades 525–528, 589; held for
    ransom 496, 501, 528, 556, 589, 725;
    judicial system during reign 571, 581,
    670; legacy 603; regency of William
    Longchamp 527, 548–549; succession
    529, 703; taxation during reign 576;
    visit to England 525
Richard II, King of England: absolutism
    890–891, 902; accession 819, 863;
    claim to throne 881; coronation
    492, 884; Councils 540, 828, 869,
    870, 884–885; deposition 839–842,
    885–887, 906, 947; Estates as 'realm'
    841; Haxey case (1397) 835–836, 891,
    992; Henry Bolingbroke and 891–893;
    heraldic disputes 507; Irish campaign
    835, 839, 892; judicial system during
    reign 725, 830–839, 855; marriages
    835, 890; Parliaments 797, 798, 830,
    835–843, 846, 885–893, 992, 1004;
    ranks of peerage during reign 843–846;
    regency 884, 887–888, 912; relations
    with France 835; relations with Lords
    835; Scottish campaign 885; statutes
    during reign 902, 915; succession 841,
    893, 906; taxation during reign 863;
    trial of the Commissioners 830–831,
    836–839, 842, 887–892, 897
Richard III, King of England: character 935;
    charters 508; claim to throne 925, 934–
    936; coronation 935; Council of the
    North 1063; death 937, 959; judicial
    system during reign 936; London
    submits petition against 933, 936;
    as Lord Protector 935; Princes in the
    Tower 935–938, 938; public opposition
    to 936, 938; reputation 937, 960;
    statutes during reign 936; succession
    937, 959; taxation during reign 936

Richard, Duke of York 921, 922, 923–925
Richard I, Duke of Normandy 364, 366
Richard of Cornwall 614–615
Ridgeway 49, 50, 71, 97, 146
ridings 167, 269, 339, 631
rights and obligations 216–218, 281–283; Act
     of Proclamations (1539) 1058–1059;
     ancient 1053; attendance at assemblies
     253, 259, 578; Bill of Attainder 833;
     civic rights 1436; colonies 1592;
     contractual relationship between King
     and people 593; free men 465, 654,
     834, 1412; Hobbes on 1169; human
     rights 1626–1627, 1627, 1663, 1664,
     1716–1718, 1745; *ius divinum* 1032,
     1353; natural law 287, 1626; of
     Parliament 987, 1452; Rousseau on
     1352; slaves 1315; Tyndale and 975; *see
     also* royal prerogative
Robert, 1st Earl of Gloucester 509–511
Robert Curthose 476–478, 479, 481–483
Robert de Vere, Duke of Ireland 830, 885,
     888, 889–890
Robert of Jumièges 387, 390
Roches, Peter des, Bishop of Winchester 612,
     615–616
Rochester (Kent) 85, 187, 237, 306, 315,
     644, 653, 741
Rodingas 65
Roger, Bishop of Salisbury 482, 509
Roman Britain 36, 45–51, 52, 103, 109,
     393–394
Roman Church *see* Church of Rome
Roman Empire: architecture 1368; charters
     138; legacy 970–972, 1574; legal system
     441; Migration Age 24; plundering war
     bands 37; religion 136; Rhine frontier
     of 28, 49, 1515–1517; Tyne marks
     northern frontier 111; withdrawal from
     Britain 53
Roman institutions 18–19, 20–22, 231, 232,
     238, 268
Roman law: Chancellors' knowledge of 871;
     Church as advocate of 244, 516; clergy
     and 699; *Decemvir* 230; distinction
     between possession and proprietorship
     665; exclusion of 696; *fas and ius* 282;
     Fortescue on 950; France 738; in Gaul
     52; influence on Anglo-Saxon codes
     285; influence on fourteenth-century
     law-making 728; influence on Glanvil
     treatise 692; *ius civile* 663; natural law

683, 685; principle of consultation 627;
     repudiation of 47; revival of 1085
Roman roads 50, 70, 93, 105, 109, 144, 152,
     167, 321, 393
Romanticism 1427, 1572, 1609
Romney Marsh 61, 68, 224, 309
Rouen 527, 528, 588, 922, 925
Rousseau, Jean-Jacques 1351–1352
Royal Council 643, 646–647
Royalists 1157–1160, 1161, 1162, 1163,
     1168, 1170, 1175, 1176, 1178, 1229
Royal Navy: financing of 1137, 1359;
     Franco-German War 1560; George
     V and 1578; Henry VIII's expansion
     of 967; imperialism and 1542–1543;
     Napoleonic Wars 1390, 1396;
     permanence 1257; slavery and 1284;
     William III and 1322, 1330
royal prerogative 1056–1058, 1156–1157;
     bills and 996; Charles I 1125, 1134,
     1144, 1213; in common law 1711–
     1715; creation of peerages and 1437;
     curtailment of 1319; effect of abolition
     of Court of Star Chamber on 1207,
     1213; Elizabeth I 1082; excess of
     1129; Fortescue on 950; High Court
     of Admiralty established under 724;
     immigration and 1649; imposition of
     tolls 861; James I 1099, 1114–1116,
     1119–1121, 1123; James II 1228–1229,
     1234; King's Bench and 678; King's
     Council and 872; legislation by
     1106–1108; limitation of 1249–1250;
     origins 660, 1016; overseas territories
     1286; Parliament and 896, 1031,
     1032, 1099–1102, 1491, 1227; Privy
     Council and 941–947; Restoration and
     1186–1187; Thomas Cromwell initiates
     review of 977
rule of law 281, 405, 414, 434, 1527, 1592,
     1186, 1220, 1626, 1732
Runnymede (Surrey) 602–603, 607, 610, 782
Rupert, Prince 1158, 1159, 1298
Russell, John, 1st Earl 1416, 1437, 1443,
     1475, 1476, 1486
Russia: Communism 1427, 1559, 1570,
     1573, 1575, 1716, 1719, 1720, 1727;
     Crimean War 1482; First World War
     1557–1559, 1561–1562, 1564, 1565,
     1570; Napoleonic Wars 1387–1388;
     relations with South Africa 1685–1686;
     Revolution 1575, 1652; Second World

War 1616–1618, 1620–1621, 1622–
1625; Warsaw Pact 1628
Rutland 129, 326, 342, 868

S

Salisbury, 3rd Marquess of *see* Cecil, Robert
Arthur Talbot Gascoyne-Cecil, 3rd
Marquess of Salisbury
Salisbury Plain 49, 96
Salisbury (Wiltshire) 89, 90, 93, 99, 736,
740, 779, 922
Sandwich (Kent) 390, 401
Sarmatians 45, 46, 72–73, 75, 115, 145
Saxe-Coburg and Gotha, House of 1473,
1503–1504, 1579, 1639
Saxo Grammaticus 28, 33–34, 226
Saxons: confederacies 341, 1289; defeat at
Badon Hill 70–75, 88; defeats by Danes
34–35, 210; deities 80; in East Anglia
121–125; *Gewisse* 51–54, 74, 83, 97,
103, 145, 150, 256; law 284; noble class
206; popular assembly 254; raids on
Britain 35–36, 45, 58–59; in Roman
Britain 30; settlement of Britain 48–56,
60, 76; traditions of government 9, 29;
see also East Saxons; Middle Saxons; West
Saxons
Saxon Shore 36, 46
Saxony 24, 80, 518, 597, 1341, 1343, 1355,
1358, 1265
Scandinavia 23–38; confederacies 274–275;
counting system 255; criminal justice
586; English coinage 140; kingship 261,
263, 488, 1242; knowledge of Britain
155; political traditions 269, 709;
Protestantism 1070; *wergeld* 294
Schleswig 33, 48, 50, 53, 104, 122, 126, 130,
134, 274
science 1405, 1569, 1193–1194, 1229, 1691
scirgemōt (shire assembly) 235, 272–273, 332,
1010, 1421
Scotland: Acts of Union 1332, 1615; alliances
346, 738–739, 805, 961, 966, 968,
1073, 1098, 1109; annexation of
Lothian 359–360; Battle of Brunanburh
346–347; Catholicism 1159, 1378;
Christianity in 169; Church reform
1139, 1159; Cnut receives submission
of king 381; coronation stone 739,
1699; Counter-Reformation 1094;
Covenanters 1138, 1140, 1159–1161,
1233; criminal justice 1456, 1697;

devolution and local government
1698–1699, 1702–1703, 1704, 1788;
Edgar *Ætheling* flees to 408; Edward
III's invasion 792; Edward I ordered
to withdraw from 628; Enlightenment
1335, 1405; heraldry 508; hundreds as
defence against Scots 234; interregnum
738; invasion of Northumberland 367;
Jacobitism 1356–1357, 1257, 1258;
jurisdiction of Council of the North
1063; jurisdiction of Supreme Court
1675; national identity 1398, 1646,
1698–1699; nationalism 1698; Norse
invasions 299, 319, 321, 329–330,
331; Northumbrian raids 177; origins
of Stuart dynasty 1094–1095; petitions
to the King 574; Presbyterianism
1331–1332, 1159–1161, 1163–1165,
1228–1229, 1252; Protestantism
1070, 1095, 1101, 1138, 1159, 1236;
rebellions during reign of Henry IV
909, 918; relations with Wales 117–118;
representation 1414–1415, 1421, 1431;
revival of Royalist cause 1168–1169;
Richard I sells rights and castles 525;
role in Civil War 1159–1160, 1160,
1163–1164; Scots of Dal Riata 116–
117, 174; succession to Strathclyde and
Lothian 356; support for Henry VI 926,
927; taxation 1332–1333, 1335; trade
1331, 1332; Treaty of York 623–624;
union with England 3, 732, 1290,
1331–1334, 1392, 1445, 1175, 1646,
1698–1699; Wars of Independence
743–744, 751, 756, 760, 764–766,
770–772, 802, 805, 814; West Saxons
and 148
scutage 498, 608–610; as alternative to
military service 515, 575, 590, 857;
Charter of Liberties 601, 603–604;
forfeited following military service
748; Henry III's reliance on 641;
obsolescence 861; origins of term 461;
role of Parliament 718; tallage and 500
Seaxburh, queen of Wessex 156–157, 264,
267, 324, 1068
Second World War 1591–1592, 1615–1626,
1641–1642, 1719, 1721
Secretary (office) 566, 595, 976, 1042–1043,
1049, 1376
Secretary of State (office) 1043, 1074, 1354,
1358, 1486

Selwood Forest 53, 100, 151, 152, 155, 162, 189, 304
Senate 18, 20, 29
separation of powers 1337–1339, 1461, 1742–1747, 1756, 1764–1765, 1768, 1785
Serjeant-at-Arms (office) 985–986, 999–1000, 1002, 1022–1023, 1028, 1172, 1738, 1205
serjeants 457, 945–946, 980, 983
Seven Years' War 1354–1359, 1370, 1389
Severn (river) 143, 152, 296, 310, 311, 318
Severn valley 71, 133, 144–145, 148, 162, 179, 184, 188, 321
Seymour, Edward, Duke of Somerset 1065
Seymour, Jane 1035–1036, 1039, 1065
Shaftesbury, Anthony Ashley Cooper, Earl of 1222, 1227–1228
Shaftesbury (Dorset) 100, 153, 364, 868
sheriffs: accounts 482; corruption 856, 868, 1010, 1052, 1083; declining status 845, 856, 1089, 1459; earls replaced by 444, 577–584; freeholders serve under banner of 427; hundred courts 474; Inquest of Sheriffs 548, 668; Norman 386, 1513; oppressive behaviour 668; replaced by lieutenants 1086; role 533, 541, 599, 628–629, 637, 737, 826, 868, 915, 1009, 1360; shire courts conducted by 494; under control of King's Council 1084; under Richard I 525
shire assembly 271–272, 332–334, 576–580; decline and disappearance 855, 1010, 1030, 1413, 1421, 1454, 1457, 1513, 1198; imperium and 225, 423; judicial function 255, 475, 563, 1010, 1513–1514; meeting place 237; representation 599, 638, 1410; tax assessment 864; under Norman rule 462, 475, 576–580, 651
shire courts 576–580, 582–584; appeals heard by King 493; assizes held in 605, 662; cases not settled in hundred courts 255; disputes between men of different shires 1748; election of knights 826; freedom granted to villeins in 471; frequency 475; Guardians of the Peace replace functions of 854–856; interpretation of the law 561; jurisdiction 333; removal of earls from 444; revived as County Courts 1512–1513; royal courts and 494, 669, 671; sheriffs' role 494;

summons to 540; tax assessment 864; trial of members of Third Estate 378
shire-moot 583, 599, 638, 1512
shires: authority of earls 444; decline in significance 1090, 1457; depopulated by Black Death 1207; division of folklands into 158, 231–233, 239–241, 320, 1775–1776; and local government structure 1704; militia 1085; political representation 653, 709, 731, 867, 916, 990, 1409–1413, 1435, 1454, 1457, 1201, 1786; size 256–259, 269–270, 275; under Danish rule 326; under Norman rule 442
Shrewsbury (Shropshire) 713–714, 716, 839, 891
Shropshire 170, 185, 191–192, 296, 320, 342, 410, 780
Sicily 412, 518, 526, 605, 639, 640, 641
Sigeberht, King of East Anglia 124, 180, 249
Sigeberht, King of Wessex 297
Sigered, King of Kent 263
Sigered, King of the East Saxons 142, 163, 198
Signet 595, 1042–1043, 1044
Sigtrygg, King of York 324, 329, 330, 337
Silchester (Hampshire) 71, 93, 98, 101, 102, 393
Sinn Fein 1556, 1585
Siward, Earl of Northumbria 381
Six Livres de la République (Bodin) 1097
slavery: abolition 1304, 1380–1381, 1472, 1542, 1645, 1658; anti-slavery protests 1652; Atlantic slave trade 1079, 1283–1284, 1367, 1650, 1691; emancipation of slaves 460; feudal system and 228, 470; Ireland 299; Monmouth Rebellion and 1233; right to earn freedom 1315; Saxon war bands 37; South Africa 1303; Sudan 1488; Vagrant Act (1547) 1047; wergeld of freed slave 35
Smith, Adam 1335, 1405, 1406
Smith, G. A. 1099
Smith, Sir Thomas 1026–1027, 1054, 1057, 1120
Smuts, Jan 1540, 1596–1597, 1627
Soar (river) 128, 131, 132–133
socage/soke 224–225, 284, 293, 425, 438, 444, 497
social class: Bagehot on 1461; effect of First World War on 1571; and enfranchisement 1409, 1415, 1417, 1429, 1431–1435, 1446, 1521; fifteenth

century 944–946; France 1384–1385;
free men 796; Indo-European tradition
203; knights 211, 455, 629, 712, 727;
membership of House of Commons and
1082; merchant class 658, 726, 1077,
1137; ninth and tenth centuries 394;
North America 1295; *nouveaux riches*
1368, 1433, 1445; postwar years 1634;
religious beliefs 799–800, 1066, 1076,
1080; Settlement Laws and 1193; under
Norman rule 412, 420, 442, 466, 672,
687; yeomanry 800, 868; *see also* middle
class
social contract 1351–1353
socialism: and colonialism 1553; creation of
socialist-oriented Peers 1447; education
and 1434; Estates and 1569; Germany
1564, 1608–1609; interwar years 1572–
1574, 1579, 1584; origins 1352, 1407;
postwar years 1624, 1625, 1627, 1634,
1641, 1645, 1656, 1731; Prussia 1557;
revolutionary aspect 1518; Romantic
movement and 1427–1428
social order 11, 16–17, 275–282, 291, 1077,
1128–1129, 1146, 1405
social security 1411, 1575, 1625, 1634
social status 213, 242, 277, 291, 293, 459,
466–467, 795, 816, 944–946, 1444
social structure 213–219, 427, 447, 587, 732,
794, 796, 1432–1433, 1569
social welfare: acts of Parliament 1088;
kinship and 215; Law of Settlement
(1662) 1193; liberalism and 1408;
responsibility of Crown 1432, 1493–
1494; role of Church 138, 218, 230,
900, 1034, 1047, 1411; Utilitarianism
1507
Soemil, King of Deira 104, 106, 111
Solway Firth 36, 116, 165, 170, 307, 331,
343, 355, 360, 624, 1698
Somaliland 1689
Somerset 151–153; Ceolwulf inherits 148;
Council of the West 1064; county
of Avon 1704; Danish raids 300,
304–305; identity 240; Mercian control
of 194; as nation state 162; part of
confederacy of the English 341; place-
names 214; revolts against William I
409; size of assembly hinterland 257,
258; under-kings 156; West Saxon
expansion into 158, 161; *Wilsæte* in
259; *see also* Beaufort, Edmund, Duke

of Somerset; Seymour, Edward, Duke of
Somerset
Somerton (Somerset) 153, 157
Sophia Dorothea of Celle 1342–1343, 1348
Sophia of Hanover 1340, 1265
South Africa 1302–1309, 1537–1543;
Boer War 1539; Cape Colony 1289,
1304–1305, 1308–1310, 1451, 1539,
1544, 1546, 1550; as Commonwealth
realm 1606, 1644; First World War
1568, 1591; Governor-Generals 1604;
independence 1600–1601, 1603–1604,
1680–1683; Jameson Raid 1538, 1550,
1560; policing 1547, 1548, 1551;
proposed union with Southern Rhodesia
1596, 1596–1597; racial policy 1627,
1643, 1681, 1687; withdrawal from
Commonwealth 1644, 1682; *see
also* British South Africa Company
(BSAC)
South America 1278–1280, 1109, 1216,
1685
Southampton (Hampshire) 63, 88–89, 99,
237, 240, 580
Southampton Water 62–63, 66, 67, 89–90,
91, 94, 99, 102, 304
South Downs 60, 61–62, 65–67, 70
South Saxons 65–71; battles with West
Saxons 159; contact with Men of
Wight 95; conversion to Christianity
185; expansion up the Thames valley
74, 76; in Hampshire 89, 91; Ine
imposes under-king on 158; jewellery
73; land allocation 193; Mercian
control of 196; multiple kingships 263;
popular assembly 225; size of assembly
hinterland 258; support for West Saxons
161
Southumbria 327–332, 340
sovereignty: Atlantic Charter 1625; Bodin on
1097; confederacies and 274; empire
and 1286–1287; European integration
and 1724–1725, 1728; feudalism and
1061; Hobbes on 1128, 1169; kingship
and 487, 1286–1287, 1084, 1108–
1109, 1326, 1234–1235; of Parliament
1282, 1033, 1108, 1120–1121, 1199,
1725; of people 29, 30, 487, 606, 794,
1415, 1444, 1470
Spain: alliances 966–967, 1073–1074; Anglo-
Spanish War (1654-60) 1176; Armada
1079–1081, 1280; Catholicism 1069,
1070, 1109, 1123; colonies 1370,

1380; Cortes 1109; exploration and conquest 1277–1278, 1286; Italian War 1034, 1036, 1072; Netherlands and 1080, 1111, 1137, 1239; revolutionary France and 1388–1389; Third Estate 841; Thirty Years' War 1111, 1169; War of Succession 1321, 1342, 1344, 1240, 1271–1274; War of the Austrian Succession 1355, 1370; War of the League of Augsberg 1258, 1263

Speaker (office) 998–1000; corruption 964; election of 977–978, 1007–1008, 1744; origins 883; residence 1423; role 984, 985–986, 988–989, 996, 1002, 1026, 1029, 1108, 1110, 1760; seating arrangements 983, 1019–1020, 1022, 1172

Spengler, Oswald 1640

Staffordshire 178, 191, 192, 231, 318–319, 320, 342, 409, 780

St Albans (Hertfordshire) 48, 596, 646, 651, 924, 926

Stalin, Joseph 1428, 1575, 1617–1618, 1621

Stamford (Lincolnshire) 323, 324, 325, 326, 327, 601, 614, 756, 929

Stane Street (Roman Road) 60, 70

Stanford, William 1056, 1120

staples 726, 861, 862

statute law xv, xviii: absence of record of English Constitution 5; civic rights 1436; Court of Star Chamber exceeds authority granted by 1146; as distinct from customary law 282; enforcement 1156–1157, 1207; equity and 685; kingship and 951, 1055, 1156, 1492; *mos maiorum* and 1525, 1200; natural law and 286–287; necessity of legal qualifications 1749; origins 688–690; Petition of Right 1131; record-keeping 813; royal prerogative and 1113–1116, 1121; subordinate to canon law 1015

statutes: compared to ordinances 759, 901, 1057; *De Haeretico Comburendo* 799; Edward I 717–718, 720, 721, 722; Edward II 760, 794; Edward III 822, 827; Edward IV 933; enabling legislation 1249; function 701; Henry IV 998; Henry VIII 1029; penal statutes 961; responsibility for 573, 899–904, 948–952; Richard II 901; and royal will 1060–1061; spiritual jurisdiction 1032; Statute of Drogheda 965; Statute of Gloucester 669–671; Statute of

Labourers 793, 796, 922; Statute of Marlborough 719; Statute of Merchants 714, 718; Statute of Proclamations 1058, 1106; Statute of Provisors 1016; Statute of Staples 861; Statute of Treason 944; Statute of Wales 714, 1277; Statute of Winchester 702, 853; Statute Roll 900; Statutes of Liberties 1052; Statutes of Westminster 718, 720, 721, 854, 1590, 1600, 1602, 1604; subject to requirements of Constitution 1419; titles 574

statutory law 282, 287, 423, 689, 695, 753, 943, 1718

Stenton, Frank M. 88, 159, 162, 165, 239, 240, 330, 336, 584

Stephen, King of England: barons' opposition to 502; breakdown of Councils 531; builds chapel at Westminster 478; charters 498, 509, 610; Chief Justice during reign 565; civil war during reign 509–512, 544, 844; claim to throne 508–510; coronation 509; Councils 544; creation of earldoms 458; judicial system during reign 664; legacy 512; relations with Church 516, 544; restoration as King 511; succession 512, 513; taxation during reign 575; use of *fyrd* 462

Steward (office) 541, 565, 567–568, 571–573, 759, 837, 843, 949

St German, Christopher 1032

Stigand, Archbishop of Canterbury 389, 405, 407, 416, 430

stone buildings 415, 420, 430, 512

Stoppingas 133

Stour (river) 61, 62, 92, 154–155, 222

Strafford, Earl of *see* Wentworth, Thomas

Strathclyde: alliance with Northumbria 171, 176; Britons of 117, 170, 174, 356; evicted from Cumbria 381; Norse invasions 329, 331, 354; Treaty of Eamont Bridge 339, 346; *Westmoringas* freed from rule of 623; William Rufus reclaims Cumbria from 478

Stuart, House of 1094–1095; claim to throne 1265; downfall 1357, 1529; dynastic origins 1340; kingship and 1084, 1103, 1123, 1321; origins of political parties and 1319, 1633; relations with House of Orange 1175; restoration under Queen Anne 1271–1273; role in loss of American colonies 1293; role of the Speaker under 1110

Stubbs, W. 480, 533, 555, 599, 629, 638, 735, 740, 742, 895

Stuf and Wihtgar 88, 90, 92, 94–95

succession 260–264, 1781–1782; Acts of Settlement 1336, 1235, 1260, 1264–1271; Acts of Succession 954, 1016, 1036, 1067, 1419–1420, 1214; Church and 592–594; consent of the Dominions 1600; dynastic 1263; female 1068–1069, 1470, 1473, 1638; *imperium* and 264, 912; land ownership and 720–721, 773; law of 488–490, 695, 912; Mercia 200; Northumbria 176; to parliamentary summons 917; religious adherence 1257; role of Council of Elders 250; role of Privy Council 1527–1528; *see also* primogeniture

Suez Canal 1449, 1487, 1558, 1565–1566, 1645, 1653

Suffolk 50, 65, 127, 342

suffrage 913, 915, 1400, 1416, 1431, 1567, 1685

sugar 1281, 1284, 1379, 1381, 1650, 1652

summons 545, 555, 558, 604, 655–657, 711–714, 734–737, 868

Sumorsætan 151–153, 157, 159, 258

Sunningas 77, 223, 258

surety 280, 330

Surrey 75–80, 101–102; appropriated by GLC 1705; brooches and pottery 70; Danish invasions 296, 300; guilds 239; Jutes in 70, 71; Kentish rule 147, 187; Men of Surrey 150; Mercian control of 186; as nation state 162; origin of name 222; part of confederacy of the English 341; place-names 61; Saxon settlement 76; size of assembly hinterland 258; under-kings 182; under West Saxon rule 158

Sussex 61–62, 65–70; concession of territory to Saxons 74; Danish raids 311; decline after Badon Hill 73; development of water-power 964; Hengest's authority over 57; Jack Cade's rebellion 922, 938; land allocation 192, 224, 231; marauding invasions 47; Mercian control of 186, 196; multiple kingships 263; as nation state 162; part of confederacy of the English 341; size of

assembly hinterland 257, 258; under West Saxons 157, 300

Sutton Hoo ship burial 124, 125

Swabes 25, 30, 32

Sweden 23; assemblies 252, 274; Danes driven out of 298; East Anglian kings' connection to 124–125; hundred system 231; migration 24–29, 123; origins of name 223; Swein Forkbeard's rule over 366; Triple Alliance (1668) 1215; War of the League of Augsberg 1258

Swein Estrithson, King of Denmark 409, 410

Swein Forkbeard, King of Denmark 364–365, 366–369, 370, 373

Swein Godwinson 384, 388–389, 659

Swein Knutsson, son of Cnut 374, 376, 381

T

Tacitus 28, 31, 38, 207, 244, 269

tallage 470, 500, 502, 575, 641, 723, 808, 857, 859, 861

Tamar (river) 161, 257, 300, 338, 343

Tamworth (Staffordshire) 178, 192, 195, 319, 323–324, 338, 354

taxation 856–868; Aggregate Fund 1345, 1373, 1375; assessment of taxes 236, 333, 628; boroughs 655; carucage 462, 499, 613, 861; Church and 136, 138, 599, 706, 1519, 1576; clergy 739, 789–790, 797, 858, 1765, 1208–1209; collection of taxes 61, 228, 233, 273, 562, 583, 613, 672, 1086, 1468, 1189; colonies 1292–1293, 1314, 1541, 1590, 1595; Commonwealth 1170; confederation and 344; Councils and 561–563, 1050; customs 500, 653, 725, 772, 801, 858, 861, 866, 936, 1376, 1105, 1189; *Danegeld* 28, 365, 367, 368, 386, 462, 499, 500, 575, 590, 633; goods 857, 860, 1108, 1399, 1657; *heregeld* 368, 379, 392, 462, 500, 633; of House of Lords 1202–1203; hundred system 234, 1086; income tax 1155; levies 500–501, 555, 604, 626, 637, 733, 740, 743, 810, 856–859, 1255; linked to attendance at Councils 737; *Magna Carta* 230, 610, 858, 861; mercantile class 726; monastic and military orders 734; Norman 411, 435, 478; northern counties exempted from 760; parliamentary approval 626–628, 858–861, 1008, 1024, 1492,

1262–1263; 'People's Budget' 1520–
1521, 1555; Petition of Right (1629)
1131–1133; poll taxes 796, 797, 860,
861, 885, 1142, 1660, 1202–1203;
'poor rates' 1089; property 590, 734,
1155, 1458; Protectorate 1174, 1176,
1177; reform under Henry II 575;
representation and 858, 860, 862; role
of Parliament 711–714, 1377; Scotland
1332–1333, 1335; Ship Money
1105–1106, 1136–1137, 1138, 1186;
tallage 470, 500, 502, 575, 641, 723,
808, 857, 859, 861; tariffs 1314, 1332,
1541, 1585, 1587, 1590; tithings 230,
555; tobacco 1354; tolls 858; Treasury's
control of 1330; tunnage and poundage
1373, 1105, 1126–1127, 1131–1132,
1135, 1136, 1141, 1262; Wales 716;
wine 1354; wool 501, 711, 734, 741,
742, 861, 862, 866, 936, 964, 1105; see
also scutage
Tees (river) 113, 119, 120, 167, 269, 285,
303, 307, 360
Temple, William 1213, 1219, 1260, 1261
tenancy-in-chief 439, 443–445, 456, 461,
537, 540, 553, 599, 721–722
terrorism 1586, 1655, 1685, 1698, 1700–
1701
Test (river) 63, 67, 89, 91, 92
Tettenhall, Battle of 318–319, 320, 321
Teutons 24, 57, 138, 141, 238
Tewkesbury (Gloucestershire) 930, 939, 949
Thames (river): boundary between Mercians
and Saxons 149, 179, 185, 295; Danes'
use of 300, 302, 309, 310, 311; division
of Saxon territory 64–65, 78–81,
97; James II drops Great Seal into
1241, 1244, 1245; Saxons' use of 49;
Sunningas settlement 258; as trade route
162, 308, 393; Westminster location
819, 821
Thames valley 50–51, 70–71, 73–80, 83–84,
100–101, 149–151; Atrebates 93, 98;
Britons concede 58, 60, 65; Britons
regain control of 88; Gewisse 256; Saxon
advance up 72
thanes 210–212, 276–278; as distinct from
knights 453–454; membership of
councils 248, 335–337, 1048, 1708;
mund 291; role in local government
238, 239, 412; social status 466; under
Norman rule 443–444, 578
Thanet 55, 58, 85, 223, 300

Thatcher, Margaret 1660, 1689–1690, 1706
theft 232–233, 235, 236, 239, 253, 292, 663,
922
theod (nation) 141, 218–219, 268
thing (assembly) 5, 20, 26, 251, 252, 567
Thirty Years' War 1105, 1109, 1110–1111,
1133, 1169–1170
Thorkell the Tall, Viking leader 368–369,
370, 373, 376
Thorney Island (Westminster) 393–394, 618,
819
tithing 230–231, 236, 239, 288–289, 325,
473–474
Tiwaz, god 25, 29, 252, 268
tobacco 1280–1281, 1284, 1354, 1381,
1554, 1593
Tomsætan 132, 133
Tory Party: adoption of 'Conservative' label
1421–1422; compared to Whigs
1319, 1229; control of Parliament
1321, 1323–1325, 1233, 1264, 1273;
emergence of liberal faction 1399;
opposition to England's involvement
in War of Spanish Succession 1321;
opposition to George I 1341, 1344–
1345; origins of name 1228–1229;
parliamentary reform 1413, 1478;
support for Stuarts 1231, 1253; under
Queen Anne 1326; see also Conservative
Party
Tostig Godwinson, earl of Northumbria 208,
390, 398
towns and cities 236–240, 331–332,
654–658; effect of Black Death on
793; freeholdings 857; guilds 583;
independence 1207; industrial 1368,
1576; Jutish 99; levies 733, 809;
markets 461; political representation
344, 709, 735, 737, 1383, 1409–1413,
1421, 1431, 1454–1455; self-
government 724, 1250; as staples 726
Towton, Battle of 926, 932, 953, 1325, 1274
trade: Brexit and 1759, 1762; Britain and
Baltic 377; Britain and Byzantium
75; colonial 1277, 1072, 1073, 1137,
1280–1282, 1292, 1444, 1170, 1652;
Danelaw 308; disruption by Saxon
piracy 48; during Second World War
1591; embargoes 560, 968, 1365,
1170; Flanders 598, 723, 726, 727,
1239; freedom of 859; free trade 1398,
1408, 1444, 1454, 1653, 1661, 1664,
1724, 1728; Frisians 79, 299; guilds

238; Hampshire 99; Holland 1239; and immigration 1649–1650; increase under Henry VII 964, 966; interwar years 1574; Ireland 1587; Kent 84, 285; legal aspects 294, 660; London 1706; *Magna Carta* 605; officials responsible for 566; regulation 583, 1115; relation to criminal justice 397; Scandinavia 23, 24, 33; Scotland 1331, 1332; spice trade 1280, 1281, 1311; stability of currency 348; staples 726; Thames as chief route 163; tolls 860; in towns 331, 654; under Protectorate 1175; wine 30, 75, 500, 589; with Wales 716; wool 140, 516, 533, 598, 622, 657, 724
trade unions 1407–1408, 1426, 1428, 1429–1430, 1518, 1582, 1654, 1659, 1665
transport 1154, 1295, 1301, 1367, 1634
treason: against Charles I 1126, 1141–1142, 1160; against Charles II 1219; against Edward I 780; against Edward II 624, 768, 771, 830–832; against Henry VIII 1040; against Jane Grey 1069; against John 556; against Mary I 1071; against Richard II 836, 837, 889, 891, 992–993; Charles I tried for 1165–1166; definition of 933, 944; during reign of Edward III 695; during reign of Edward the Confessor 385–392; Earl of Lancaster 767; exception to freedom from arrest 999; fines for 961; jurisdiction of High Constable extended to cases of 933, 944; jurisdiction of House of Lords 946; land forfeit in cases of 722, 890; offence of 397, 473, 878, 896, 1391, 1077, 1166, 1505, 1220; rescinded by Act of Indemnity and Oblivion (1660) 1188; Rhodesia regarded by Britain as guilty of 1687–1688; Treasonable and Seditious Practices Act (1795) 1391; Treasons Act (1649) 1168; trial for 494, 672, 851, 947, 1255; Wolsey accused of 976
Treasurer (office): accounts held in Pipe Rolls 482; appointment of 639, 645, 759; attendance at Councils 541; attendance at Parliament 621, 783, 981, 984, 1024–1025; origins of office 565–566, 568–572; role 1330, 1346–1347, 1485; scrutiny of King 962
Treasury: administration by Board of Commissioners 1330, 1346–1347;

Chancellor of the Exchequer assumes responsibility for 1361, 1485; move to Whitehall 1264; at Winchester 382, 449, 479, 481, 568, 570
treaties: after Badon Hill 74; Bernicians and *Guotodin* 120; Danes 301, 316; Eamont Bridge (927) 339, 346, 1775; England and Normandy 365; international 1715, 1762; Jutes and Saxons 65; Maastricht Treaty (1991) 1726; Mercians and East Saxons 180; Mercians and Welsh 190; Mercians and West Saxons 179, 198; role of King's Council 870; Saxons and *Regnenses* 66; Treaty of Aachen (1748) 1357; Treaty of Amiens (1802) 1387; Treaty of Breda (1667) 1211; Treaty of Brussels (1948) 1628; Treaty of Dover (1670) 1216–1217; Treaty of Edinburgh (1328) 802; Treaty of Limerick (1691) 1258; Treaty of Lisbon (2009) 1727; Treaty of Lunéville (1801) 1387; Treaty of Paris (1783) 1297, 1370, 1379, 1387; Treaty of Paris (1814) 1303; Treaty of Ripon (1640) 1139; Treaty of Rome (1957) 1664, 1722, 1723; Treaty of Ryswick (1697) 1263, 1271; Treaty of Tordesillas (1494) 1278, 1286; Treaty of Troyes (1420) 842, 903, 910, 919; Treaty of Union (1706) 1332; Treaty of Utrecht (1713) 1344, 1273; Treaty of Wedmore (878) 307–308; Treaty of Westminster (1674) 1218
Trent (river) 49, 127–128, 131–135, 174, 319, 329, 368
trial procedure 475, 493, 556, 585–586, 625, 667–669, 701
Tribal Hidage 130, 191, 192–193, 233, 256, 337, 448, 585
Trinovantes 121–123
Trussell, William 777–778
Tudor, House of 960–961; constitutional power of King 1084, 1103; election of King's ministers to Commons 1320; emblem 960, 1014; Great Council and 955; Palace of Westminster 1425; popularity 1069; Privy Council and 941, 953, 1327; reduction of Crown Lands by 1373; relations between Lords and Commons 1436; role of Speaker 1110; Welsh origins 926, 959
Turkey 971, 1482, 1558–1559, 1570
Tweed (river) 112, 118, 257, 307, 360
Tyndale, William 974–975

Tyne (river) 111–112, 113, 116, 119, 165, 257, 303, 328

U

Ukraine 1560, 1575, 1616, 1618, 1626
Ulster 1112, 1447, 1139, 1144, 1555–1556, 1253, 1586, 1588
ultra vires 1421, 1525, 1710, 1711
unemployment 1281, 1396, 1493, 1573, 1574, 1584, 1608–1610, 1634, 1655, 1659
Union Jack flag 1102, 1393, 1547, 1750
Union of Soviet Socialist Republics (USSR) 1575, 1616, 1625, 1695, 1726
United Nations 1626–1628, 1628
United States of America: Bill of Rights 1626; colonies 1641, 1642; confederation 1293, 1314, 1379; Constitution 1294–1297, 1339, 1353, 1430, 1742, 1771; cosmopolitanism 1656; First World War 1563, 1570; House of Representatives 1296; interwar years 1573; judicial system 1745, 1750; political relations with Britain 1653; population displacement following slavery abolition 1658; postwar years 1628–1629, 1641–1642; relations with South Africa 1685; Second World War 1620, 1621–1622; terrorism and 1701; Treaty of Paris (1783) 1297–1301; Trent Affair 1477; *see also* North America
universities: advise in favour of Henry VIII's marriage annulment 1015; book-burning during Reformation 1066; canon law replaced by civil law in 1034; Catholics appointed to positions in 1235; development of 691, 988, 1390; disputes over price of victuals 1147; petitions to King 573; social class and 1082; teaching of Greek 801; voting rights for degree-holders 1567
urban development 219, 237–238, 1454, 1459, 1501, 1635
Urban II, Pope 477, 536
Urien, King of Reged 113, 115–116
Usmere 133

V

Vale of Aylesbury 82, 83, 129, 149
Vale of Pewsey 97–98, 100, 146
Vale of York 105–106, 111, 113, 119

Victoria, Queen of the United Kingdom of Great Britain and Ireland: accession 1471; assassination attempts 1474; Church of England during reign 1577; claim to throne 1466, 1470; coronation 1494–1496, 1502; domestic policy 1478, 1489–1490; Don Pacifico affair 1475; finances 1471, 1473; foreign policy 1476–1477, 1487–1490, 1598; House of Lords during reign 1438, 1671; marriage 1473; moral integrity of reign 1463, 1474, 1498, 1579; Parliament during reign 1450, 1480, 1490; political sympathies 1450, 1471–1472; popular support 1463, 1490, 1498, 1501–1503; Private Secretary 1497–1498; Privy Council during reign 1266; relations with Ministers 1472, 1475–1478, 1476, 1479, 1484–1489, 1495–1497, 1503; succession 1499, 1503; titles 1450, 1500, 1543
Vikings: common law of entry and 1649; confederacies 274; counting system 289; effect of invasions on free men 254, 1786; effect of raids on *eorls* 207; Eirik Bloodaxe 347; *jarls* 272; Jomsvikings 366, 376; legacy of invasions 435; Lindisfarne invasions 177; origin of term 298–299; raids on Kent 202; ridings 167
villages: administration of justice 31, 239; development of 36, 210; effect of Black Death on 793; growing prosperity of 965; land allocation 469; nucleated 214–215, 227; origins of term 396, 450
villeins/villeinage 459–462, 469–472; attendance at Parliament 914; decline and disappearance 1053; definition 425; origins of term 450, 687; precluded from jury service 579; social status 465, 654, 727, 728; *wergeld* 687
Voortrekkers 1305–1309, 1540, 1550
Vortigern 51–52, 55–56, 60, 63, 66, 71, 151
voting rights 1409–1415; of monarch 1734; Representation of the People Acts 1436, 1446, 1567, 1569, 1571, 1648–1649; women 1566–1567, 1585; working class 1429, 1431–1433, 1521

W

wages 728, 793, 854, 922, 1088, 1406, 1407, 1455, 1654, 1655

Wales: alliance with Æthelstan 339; Church
    in Wales 1495, 1496, 1556; Civil
    War violence in 1164; Councils 1061,
    1064–1065, 1117; criminal justice
    1697; Danish invasions 310, 311;
    defeat of Welsh at Dyrham 144; deities
    21; Despenser War 767–771, 775;
    devolution 1698–1699, 1702–1703,
    1788; *Dumnonii* 151–152; Edward
    I's campaigns in 714–717, 735; Latin
    inscriptions 75; Mercian raids 134, 198;
    national identity 1698; Northumbrian
    victory at Chester 165; origins of House
    of Tudor 926, 959; petitions from
    821; Principality of 714–717, 1064;
    Protestantism 1070; rebellions against
    Henry IV 909, 918; relations with
    England under Henry VII 966; relations
    with Mercia 178, 179–181, 184, 191,
    296, 317–319, 328; representation 990,
    1036, 1064, 1414, 1421; settlement of
    English areas 317; Statute of 714, 716,
    1277; unification with England 3, 1036,
    1064, 1392; uprising of 1211 595; war
    with Henry II 514; Welsh language 44,
    53, 1036, 1699; West Saxons and 148,
    152, 158, 159–161
Wallace, Sir William 743–744
Wallis, K. 763
Walpole, Robert 1344, 1348–1349, 1354,
    1361, 1368, 1407, 1743
Walter, Hubert, Archbishop of Canterbury 6,
    528, 590, 591–592, 595
Waltheof, Earl of Northumbria 407, 409,
    410, 430
Wansdyke 146
wapentake 325, 326, 631
war bands 37, 206, 242, 1677
Wardrobe 565, 573, 759, 822
wardship 497, 601, 663, 720, 1106, 1146,
    1188
warfare: Ældfrith 175; Æthelræd 365;
    centralisation of authority and 293; First
    World War 1563–1564, 1569; honour
    and 278; Norman 402; role of heralds
    507; Second World War 1618, 1620;
    use of horses 401; Wulfhere 185
War Office 1394, 1486–1487
warriors 37–38, 211, 227, 231, 242
Wars of the Roses: constitutional effects
    949–950, 953, 955; effect on House
    of Lords 990, 991; First War 923–930,
    964; and 'overmighty subject' 1052;

public administration during 942;
    Second War 934–939; state of anarchy
    following 1055
Warwick 756, 761, 763, 764–765; *see
    also* Neville, Richard, Earl of Warwick
Warwickshire 73, 129, 133, 134, 149,
    188–189, 308, 320, 342
Wash, the 50, 51, 109, 121, 127, 128,
    128–129, 400, 611
watch and ward 702, 853
Watling Street (Roman road) 57, 61, 308,
    322, 323, 325, 393
Wat's Dyke 191, 194, 195
Weald, the 47, 61, 62, 66, 70–71, 76, 219,
    297, 964
weaponry: artillery 929, 949, 963, 964, 1549,
    1563; bronze 10; longbow 800, 805;
    in Parliament 1028; Saxon swords 31;
    social status and 853; stone battle-axes
    26
Wedmore, Treaty of 305, 307–308
Wehha, King of the East Angles 123, 125
Welland (river) 49, 128, 308, 311, 323, 326,
    327
Wellington, Arthur Wellesley, 1st Duke of: on
    appointment of Prime Ministers 1350;
    Battle of Waterloo 1387, 1389; Corn
    Laws 1474; as Prime Minister 1399–
    1400, 1413, 1437, 1467, 1468; Queen
    Victoria and 1472
Welsh Marches 714–716, 769–771, 780,
    1063–1064; barons join royalist army
    648; Council of the Marches 1141;
    courts 1146; defence 478, 509; Marcher
    Lords 716, 767, 930, 966, 1036, 1063;
    origins of term 844, 1649
Wentworth, Paul and Peter 995–997, 1082
Wentworth, Thomas 1129, 1132, 1136,
    1139, 1141, 1142–1143, 1144, 1210,
    1226
weorc (labour service) 217, 425, 856
wergeld ('man-value') 275–279, 687; *ceorls*
    294; Danes 309; definition 204; *eorls*
    206; free men 226; King 208; in *Leges
    Henrici Primi* 687; replaced by political
    worth 1731; value of oath based on
    289–291
Wessex: Alfred's fortification of 312; *Anglo-
    Saxon Chronicle* written in 87; claims
    to succession 260; claim to Isle of
    Wight 94; Cnut's invasion of 370;
    confederacy with Mercia 324; Council
    of Wessex 243, 246; Danish invasions

302, 304–305, 367; dispute with Kent over territory of Middle Saxons 78; earldoms under Cnut 380; land allocation 214, 231, 232–235; legal system 660; Mercian invasion of 199; seat of political power 151; Winchester political capital of 102

Westerne 191–192, 320

West Indies 1280, 1284, 1379–1380, 1381, 1467, 1542, 1653, 1657

Westminster: as seat of government 1392; coronations 587, 752; Councils held at 531, 546, 560, 562, 565, 624, 626, 629, 630, 636, 661, 715, 755, 757, 918; fourteenth-century layout 819–822; Henry II's building programme 523; location of royal courts 678–679, 699, 874; Painted Chamber 620, 758, 774, 783, 811, 814–816, 866, 983, 1029; Palace of Westminster 1423–1426; as seat of government 392–394, 400, 434, 617–620, 801, 1013–1014; site of Exchequer 573, 674, 820, 821; Star Chamber 984; Statutes of 670, 706, 710, 718, 720, 721; St Stephen's Chapel 479, 524, 619, 817, 820, 1013, 1017–1018, 1020, 1030, 1425; White Chamber 814–816, 845, 1018, 1023; White Hall 953, 983, 1020, 1055, 1062–1063, 1392; William II and 478–479

Westminster Abbey: burials 399, 703, 1178; Chapter House 814, 821, 822, 822–823, 830, 879, 985, 1029; construction 386, 394; coronations 400, 406–407, 433, 525, 966, 1467, 1530; location of Councils 620, 636, 640, 754; parliamentary procession to 980; rebuilt by Henry III 618, 657; Scottish coronation stone transferred to 739

Westmorland and *Westmoringas* 339, 343–344, 478, 518, 623–624, 660, 1775

West Saxons: alliances 145, 148, 178, 182, 185, 188, 301; assistance of Jutish army 144; Battle of *Aclea* 296, 300; Battle of Cirencester 179, 188; Battle of Ellendun 199, 295; Battle of *Wibbandun* 100, 102, 144, 147; capitulation to Danes 369; confederacy 143–149, 186, 232, 270–271, 273–274, 300, 306, 1649; conquest of Isle of Wight 90, 95; *ealdormen* 206; emergence of confederacy 99; folkland 240; Great

Council 271; jurisdiction over Kent 201; land allocation 193, 234; law codes 158, 206, 209, 213, 217, 285–286, 289, 291; northward expansion 96–98, 100, 179; shire government 272; site of royal coronations 80, 102; succession of kings 88, 92, 260; victory at Barbury Castle 97; westward expansion 143–162, 188; *Witan* 250

Whig Party 1228–1231; adoption of term 'Liberal' 1421–1422, 1445; Bedchamber Question 1472; Charles II and 1232; compared to Tories 1319; Corn Laws 1474; electoral reform 1412, 1416, 1467; Exclusion Parliament (1679) 1222; Glorious Revolution 1237, 1243; hostility towards George III 1397; James II and 1235; leadership rivalry 1486; Monmouth Rebellion 1233; origins of name 1218, 1228; Scottish membership 1322, 1371; support of George I 1344; William III and 1321–1322, 1326, 1253, 1259; *see also* Liberal Party

Whitby, Synod of 172

Whitehall 1013–1015, 1017–1018, 1045, 1376, 1423, 1146, 1165, 1247, 1264

Wibbandun, Battle of 100, 102, 144, 147

Wiclif, John 793, 798–801, 884, 909, 972–973, 975, 1044, 1046, 1076

Widsith, poem 26, 125, 135, 228

Wiglaf, King of Mercia 177, 295–296

Wihtred, King of Kent 158, 193, 248–249, 262, 285, 674, 693

Wihtware 94–96, 185

Wilhelm II, German Emperor 1502, 1557, 1560, 1608

Wilkes, John 1372, 1373, 1397

William I, Duke of Normandy and King of England: character 412; Chief Justices 564, 585; Church reform 414, 416, 503; claim to throne 386–388, 388–391, 402, 413, 433; comparison with Cnut 404; coronation 406, 491, 1129; Councils 531–532, 660; creation of earldom of Chester 550, 552; fortifications 402; Harrying of the North 409–410, 412; illegitimacy 406, 412; invasion of Scotland 411; judicial system 663, 672; laws 405, 414, 434, 603, 660, 689; marches to London 404; ordinances 417; rejection by English 430–432, 435, 439; relations with Philip I 411; retinue 568, 569;

returns to France after Conquest 408, 411, 432; rivalry with Edgar *Ætheling* 405–406, 408; role of courts during reign 494; secures surrender of Harold at Ponthieu 391; separation of Church and State 414, 416–418, 472, 504, 577, 603; succession 432, 476; as successor to Edward the Confessor 392, 413; title 416, 485; treaty with Scotland 409; use of juries during reign 585; visits England in 1051 388; warfare 402, 403–405

William II, King of England (William Rufus): accession 432; character 476–477, 478; claim to throne 476–477; Councils 564, 626; death 479; extortion of 497; justice system during reign 661, 687; legacy 478–479, 603; origins of term 'knight' and 453; popular support 483, 485; relations with barons 531, 537; relations with Church 477–478, 484, 536; reliefs 464; use of *fyrd* 462

William III, King of England: accession 1245–1246, 1248, 1251; ancestry 1239–1240; claim to throne 1235, 1237–1238, 1240; coronation 1246, 1251–1254; finances 1261–1264; foreign policy 1241, 1257–1258, 1259, 1261, 1263–1264, 1266, 1330; Louis XIV and 1240–1241; marriage 1218, 1240; offices of state during reign 1329–1330; Parliaments during reign 1241–1249, 1251–1252, 1258–1260, 1262–1263, 1264, 1320–1321, 1326, 1462; Privy Council during reign 1266, 1320–1321; as regent 1229, 1242; religious policy 1253–1254; as ruler of Great Britain 1252; succession 1246, 1256, 1264–1271, 1331; taxation during reign 1262–1263; unpopularity 1264

William IV, King of the United Kingdom: accession 1466–1467; coronation 1466; dismissal of Whig administration 1467; finances 1467–1470; Parliament during reign 1491; Private Secretary 1497; succession 1470

William of Malmesbury 146, 159, 188

Wilsæte 98–99, 143, 258, 259

Wilson, Harold 1684, 1687, 1701, 1725

Wiltshire: Alfred's army assembled from Saxons of 304; Battle of Ellendun 199; Ceol's expansion westward from

151; Cynewulf regains 297; earthwork defences 154; inherited by Ceolwulf 148; meetings of Great Council 336, 363; as nation state 162; origins of name 240; part of confederacy of the English 341; seat of Ambrosius's authority 71; size of assembly hinterland 258; *Wilsæte* 143; Woden's Barrow 146

Winchester (Hampshire): Æthelberht defeats Danes at 300; burial site of kings 392; coronation site 384, 385; Councils held at 531, 661, 818; Emma of Normandy resides in 382; exemption from Domesday survey 449; fortification 313; Godwine dies at 390; impact of wool trade on 727; location of councils 335; monastery 156; Parliaments held at 655; as political capital of Wessex 102; Saxon occupation 92; seat of West Saxon diocese 151; Statute of Winchester 702, 853, 854; submission to William I 405; treasury 382, 449, 479, 481, 569, 570; West Saxons capitulate at 369

Windsor Castle 508, 523, 543, 559, 646, 652, 814, 1163–1164, 1395

Windsor, House of 1579, 1639, 1776

wine 30, 75, 500, 589, 861, 1354

Wintra, King of Lindsey 109

Winwæd (river), Battle of 171, 183, 184

Witan (Council of Wise Men): function 19, 220, 876; justice and 239; location 157; membership 91, 337, 1048, 1296, 1442; origins 244, 567; subconscious memory of 1732; ultimate authority of 745; West Saxon 250, 297

Witham (river) 49, 109, 110, 127, 128

Witney, K. P. 88, 90

Wlancingas 67

Woccingas 77, 150

Woden, god 134, 204, 205, 268, 1087

Woden's Barrow, Battle of 146–147, 188

Wolds, the 105, 109

Wolsey, Thomas 973–976, 982, 1011–1012, 1025, 1033, 1043, 1054

women: in Christian Church 247; employment 1406, 1407; enfranchisement 1567–1568, 1569, 1585; in House of Lords 1676–1677, 1735; inheritance 17, 212, 488–489; marriage 17, 213–214, 460, 464, 497; matrilineality 9, 1640; *mund* 279; parliamentary careers 1666; personal names 467; as regents 156, 324; rights

672, 1647; safety 167; succession 1068–
1069; *wergeld* 687; yeowomen 945
Woodstock (Oxfordshire) 547–548, 549
wool 723–727; exports 140, 516, 533, 742,
803, 858, 861; Flanders 598, 802, 952;
manufacturing 1366–1367; prosperity
due to trade in 657, 801, 806, 913, 953,
1066; seized by Edward I 646, 706,
740, 742; taxation 501, 710, 734, 741,
742, 861, 862, 866, 936, 964, 1105;
use of woolsacks in Parliament 622,
983, 1025–1026
Worcester 187, 188–189, 190, 304, 313, 357,
383, 585, 611, 1168
Worcestershire 189–190, 190, 320, 342
working class: First World War 1570;
Immigration and 1654, 1658; political
activity 1428–1429; representation
1408, 1415, 1417, 1429, 1431–1434,
1447, 1521; Second World War 1634;
social welfare 1411, 1426
Wreocensætan 187, 191, 320, 342
writs: authentication of 1042; Bracton on
693; development of legal thinking and
469; *habeas corpus* 661, 1220–1221;
issued by Great Council 1210; language
of 569–570; *praemunientes* 734–737;
prerogative writs 1712; provenance 571,
700, 871; role of sheriff 578, 628; *sub
pœna* 872; summons 538–543, 655;
supplementary 369; titles created by 446
Wuffa, King of East Anglia 124, 125
Wulfhere, King of Mercia 95, 156–157, 163,
173, 184–187, 192, 345
Wulfings dynasty 124–125
Wulfred, Archbishop of Canterbury 198–199
Wyatt, Thomas 1070
Wye (river) 145, 184, 195, 329, 338
Wylye (river) 96, 98

Y

yeomanry 800, 868, 916, 945, 960, 1345,
1089, 1153, 1203
York: alliance with Æthelstan 340;
archbishopric of 87, 176, 653, 755,
1025; bishopric of 86, 172; *burh* 237;
Councils held at 757, 1063, 1140; as
'county corporate' 580, 1207; Danish
occupation of 300–301, 302–303, 308,
311–312, 320, 323, 328; herald 508;
kingship of 111, 113, 119, 324, 331,
337–338, 346, 347; knights summoned

to Parliament 653; Mercian attack on
194; Norse invasion 319, 320–321,
329, 354–355; Northumbrian attack
and possession 120, 208; Parliaments
held at 712, 764, 767, 774, 809; Pictish
raids 105; province of 297, 418, 621,
711, 731, 739, 742, 788, 790, 1074,
1576, 1208; revolts against William
I 409–410; suitability as regional seat
of government 393; under Deiran
administration 106; *see also* Richard,
Duke of York
York, House of 923–926, 934, 937, 938, 939,
944, 960, 961, 1084
Yorkshire 103–108; Alemanni in 46; Angles
in 54, 57, 119, 127; carucage 861;
Danish invasions 329; Harrying of the
North 409; local government 1704;
part of confederacy of the English 342;
Pilgrimage of Grace 1036; ridings 269,
339, 631; Scottish raids 766, 767; size
of assembly hinterland 258; source of
alum 968

Z

Zulus 1305, 1307–1308, 1309–1310, 1538

Ingram Content Group UK Ltd.
Milton Keynes UK
UKHW022210210623
423834UK00005B/164